THE COLLECTED ESSAYS

OF

RALPH ELLISON

THE COLLECTED ESSAYS OF
RALPH ELLISON

EDITED, WITH AN INTRODUCTION BY
JOHN F. CALLAHAN

PREFACE BY
SAUL BELLOW

THE MODERN LIBRARY

NEW YORK

1995 Modern Library Edition

Biographical note copyright © 1994 by Random House, Inc.
Preface © 1995 by Saul Bellow
Introduction © 1995 by John F. Callahan

Portions of this work have been previously published in *Shadow and Act* and
Going to the Territory. Additionally, some of the essays were previously
published in *Saturday Review*, *New Masses*, *The Nation*, *The Atlantic*, *The
Harvard Advocate*, *The New York Times Sunday Magazine*, and *Callaloo*.

Jacket photo by © 1995 Nancy Crampton

Printed on recycled, acid-free paper.

Library of Congress Cataloging-in-Publication Data

Ellison, Ralph.
 [Selections. 1995]
 The collected essays of Ralph Ellison/edited by John F. Callahan;
preface by Saul Bellow.—Modern Library ed.
 p. cm.
 ISBN 0-679-60176-7 (acid-free paper)
 1. Ellison, Ralph—Authorship. 2. Afro–Americans in literature.
3. Afro–Americans—Civilization. I. Callahan, John F. II. Title.
PS3555.L625A6 1995
814'.54—dc20 95-4719

Manufactured in the United States of America

2 4 6 8 9 7 5 3 1

RALPH ELLISON

Ralph Waldo Ellison was born in Oklahoma City, Oklahoma, on March 1, 1914. His father was a construction foreman and later the owner of a small ice-and-coal business who died when his son was three. Ellison and his younger brother, Herbert, were raised by their mother, who worked as a nursemaid, janitress, and domestic, and was active in politics. As a child he was drawn to music, playing trumpet from an early age and studying classical composition at Tuskegee Institute under the instruction of William L. Dawson. Of his musical influences he later said: "The great emphasis in my school was upon classical music, but such great jazz musicians as Hot Lips Page, Jimmy Rushing, and Lester Young were living in Oklahoma City. . . . As it turned out, the perfection, the artistic dedication which helped me as a writer, was not so much in the classical emphasis as in the jazz itself."

In July 1936, after his junior year at Tuskegee, Ellison went to New York to earn money for his senior year and to study sculpture, and stayed. In June 1937 his friendship with Richard Wright began and led him toward becoming a writer. Ellison also made the acquaintance of Langston Hughes and the painter Romare Bearden, among others. From 1938 until World War II he worked on the New York Federal Writers Project of the WPA. Starting in the late 1930s, he contributed reviews, essays, and short fiction to *New Masses, Tomorrow, The Negro Quarterly* (of which he was for a time the editor), *New Republic, Saturday Review, Antioch Review, Reporter,* and other periodicals. During the war he served in the Merchant Marine, and afterward he worked at a variety of jobs, including freelance photography and the building and installation of audio systems.

Over a period of seven years Ellison wrote *Invisible Man*, which was recognized upon its publication in 1952 as one of the most important works of fiction of its time. It was on the bestseller list for sixteen weeks and won the National Book Award. Its critical reputation and popularity have only grown in the more than four decades since its publication. Although an excerpt from a second novel was published in *Noble Savage* in 1960, and seven other selections in various literary magazines between then and 1977, no other long work of fiction has yet appeared under Ellison's name. *Shadow and Act* (1964) and *Going to the Territory* (1986) collect essays and interviews written over more than forty years.

From 1956 to 1958 Ellison was a fellow of the American Academy in Rome. Returning to the United States, he taught and lectured at a wide range of institutions including Bard College, the State University of New York at Stony Brook, the University of Chicago, Rutgers, Harvard, Brown, and Yale. He was awarded the Presidential Medal of Freedom in 1969; the *Chevalier de l'Ordre des Arts et Lettres* in 1970 by the French Minister of Culture, Andre Malraux; and the National Medal of Arts in 1985. He was a charter member of the National Council on the Arts and Humanities, and from 1970 to 1979 was Albert Schweitzer Professor in the Humanities at New York University.

After a brief first marriage Ellison married Fanny McConnell in 1946; for more than forty years, until his passing on April 16, 1994, they lived on Riverside Drive in Harlem.

ACKNOWLEDGMENTS

I wish to acknowledge the generous help of several persons. My research assistant, Adam Francis Bradley, was diligent, dedicated, and efficient gathering Ellison's published articles from various journals and magazines. Nathan A. Scott, Jr., William R. Kenan Professor Emeritus of Religious Studies and Professor Emeritus of English at the University of Virginia, spotted and suggested felicitous corrections to errors in the first editions of *Shadow and Act* and *Going to the Territory*. Leon Forrest, novelist and professor of English and Afro-American studies at Northwestern University, perceptively responded to queries concerning unpublished essays and speeches. Robert G. O'Meally, Zora Neale Hurston Professor of English and Comparative Literature at Columbia University, opened his abundant files, provided a tape and transcription of Ellison's 1971 speech honoring William L. Dawson, and offered helpful suggestions about possible sequences for the essays.

I am more indebted than I can say to Mrs. Fanny Ellison. She endured and aided my perusal of her late husband's files and papers, and, as Ralph Ellison's "best reader," she shared indispensable information and insight about the composition and context of previously uncollected or unpublished writing.

PREFACE

by Saul Bellow

RALPH ELLISON, who died last year at the age of eighty, published only one novel in his lifetime.

In 1953 at a Bard College Symposium dinner attended by foreign celebrities, Georges Simenon, who sat at our table, asked Ellison how many novels he had written, and when he learned that there was only one he said, "To be a novelist one must produce many novels. Ergo, you are not a novelist."

The author of hundreds of books, writing and speaking at high speed, was not in the habit of pausing to weigh his words. Einstein, a much deeper thinker, had said in reply to a "sociable" lady's question about quantum theory (why, under such and such conditions, was there only one quantum?), "But isn't one a lot, madam?"

In Ralph's case it certainly was a lot. Simenon remains readable and enjoyable, but Inspector Maigret is finally like an overly exploited mine. Novels in the suspense genre developed by Simenon can be considered as the chapters of a single fat novel. Maigret belongs to a large family of cops or private eyes, geniuses of detection like Sherlock Holmes or the heroes of Dashiell Hammett, Raymond Chandler, et al. These gifted men worked honorably at the writers' trade. Ellison did no such thing. He had a calling, not a trade and what we witness in *Invisible Man* is the discovery by an artist of his true subject matter. Some fifty years after it was published, this book holds its own among the best novels of the century.

Toward the end of the fifties, the Ellisons and the Bellows lived together in a spooky Dutchess County house with the Catskills on the western horizon and the Hudson River—"the lordly Hudson," as Paul Goodman has described it—in between. Ralph was then teaching at Bard College, two miles down the road. Ralph's wife, Fanny, had a city job; she was, I think, chief fund-raiser for Gordon

C. Grove, the Burma Surgeon. My children spent their holidays with me, and occasionally my Aunt Jennie came up from New York. Fanny arrived regularly on Friday evening and returned on Sunday afternoon. As writers are natural solitaries, Ralph and I did not seek each other out during the day. A nod in passing was enough. We had our daily tasks. When he was not writing, Ralph tended his African violets in the emptiness of the sunny ballroom, watering them with a turkey baster. He tinkered in the driveway with his Chrysler engine. He walked in the woods with the black Labrador retriever he had bought from John Cheever.

Cheever didn't live nearby—he was in Ossining—but we did have literary company in Dutchess County. Richard Rovere lived in Rhinebeck; near him was Fred Dupee; Gore Vidal had bought a fine house on the riverbank just beyond the New York Central tracks. Ralph and I in our slummy mansion could not entertain these far more prosperous literary country squires. The Dupees and the Roveres gave us dinner from time to time, and Gore Vidal viewed us with a certain ironic pity; socially we didn't exist for him. A complex character, Gore, a man of the world in many worlds. "A campy patrician," said Ralph. We were as amused by him as he was by us.

As for me, well, Max Weber described the Jews as aristocratic pariahs. Ralph himself had an aristocratic demeanor. No one in our Dutchess County group was altogether free from pride. Gore had genealogical claims, and money as well. Dupee had his affinities with Henry James and Marcel Proust. The presence of a Jew or a Negro in any group is apt to promote a sense of superiority in those who—whatever else—are neither Jews nor Negroes. The only genuine democrat in our literary set was Dick Rovere.

Ralph had the bearing of a distinguished man. Proper pride, Aristotle might have called it—an appropriate kind of avowal. A man should claim his due.

And why shouldn't he have thought well of himself? A young Negro from Oklahoma City and Tuskegee, he had set his sights high; he had learned from Malraux as well as from Richard Wright, and with *Invisible Man* he had earned the right to be taken seriously. Unlike the majority of his Negro contemporaries he was not limited in his interests to the race problem. He was an artist.

In the Tivoli, New York, mansion, locally known as the Larrabee farm most of the great rooms were empty. We did not seek each other out. We occasionally passed each other in the bare corridors. Our habitual meeting place was the flagstone-paved kitchen at breakfast and again at cocktail time. In the morning Ralph came below in a many-colored dressing gown from North Africa—a Joseph's coat one was not likely to see elsewhere in the Hudson Valley. On his feet were substantial slippers that turned up at the toes, Turkish style. Silent, he brewed coffee in a Chemex (and for the last forty years I have followed the same method). As he waited for the water, carefully measured to work through the grounds, he would occasionally massage his nose so strongly that you could hear the crack of the cartilage. Perhaps the object was to expel the sleep from his face. I never asked him why it was only in the morning that he did it.

There was little or no conversation at breakfast. But late in the afternoon Ralph mixed martinis, and we didn't drink them in silence. During our long conversations I came to know his views, some of which I shall now transmit in his own words.

"We did not develop as a people in isolation," Ralph told James MacPherson in an interview. "We developed within a context of white people. Yes, we have a special awareness, because our experience has in certain ways been different from that of white people, but it was not absolutely different."

"I tell white kids that instead of talking about black men in a white world or black men in a white society, they should ask themselves how black *they* are, because black men have been influencing the values of the society and the art forms of the society. . . ."

"For me," Ralph said, "some effort was necessary . . . before I could identify the areas of life and personality which claimed my mind beyond any limitations apparently imposed by my racial identity."

And again: "This was no matter of sudden insight but of slow and blundering discovery of a struggle to stare down the deadly and hypnotic temptation to interpret the world and all its devices in terms of race."

It took great courage in a time when racial solidarity was demanded, or exacted, from people in public life, to insist as Ralph did on the priority of art and the independence of the artist.

"Fiction," he says, "became the agency of my efforts to answer the questions: Who am I, what am I, how did I come to be? What should I make of the life around me? . . . What does American society mean when regarded out of my *own* eyes, when informed by my *own* sense of the past and viewed by my *own* complex sense of the present? . . . It is quite possible," he adds, "that much potential fiction by Negro Americans fails precisely at this point: through the writers' refusal (often through provincialism or lack of courage or opportunism) to achieve a vision of life and a resourcefulness of craft commensurate with the complexity of their actual situation. Too often they fear to leave the uneasy sanctuary of race to take their chances in the world of art." He himself did no such thing.

I have let Ralph speak for himself, *but* there is one thing more, of a personal nature, that I should like to add in closing. Often when I think of Ralph a line from e. e. cummings comes to me: "Jesus! He was a handsome man," cummings wrote. He was referring to Buffalo Bill. Ralph did not ride a watersmooth stallion, nor was he a famous marksman, but he did have the look of a man from an earlier epoch, one more sane, more serious and more courageous than our own.

CONTENTS

GOING TO THE TERRITORY

INTRODUCTION

In his 1988 eulogy for the painter Romare Bearden, Ralph Ellison made the collage a metaphor for America. Paying tribute to the artist as "a great master of collage," Ellison told his mourners that "we are a *collage of a nation*, a nation that is ever shifting about and grousing as we seek to achieve the promised design of democracy." He considered the country and the culture to be compositions forged out of the experimental attitude and improvisatory impulse so unsuppressible in American experience. As discrete compositions and an unfolding oeuvre, Ellison's essays, too, are literary variations on the form and materials of collage. In shape, he wrote, "my essays tend to be somewhat 'mammy-made' or eclectic," meaning that they have the fluid, familiar yet arresting texture of jazz improvisations on a well-known theme. Grounding his riffs and variations on the bass line of American identity, Ellison pursues the copious, contradictory manifestations of this country's "promised design of democracy."

Whether writing autobiographical essays about his life and times in Oklahoma, Tuskegee, or New York City; or literary essays in which he reminds us that the American ideal is equality, the American theory pragmatism, and the American style the vernacular; or music criticism in which he articulates how "in improvised jazz, performance and creation can consist of a single complex act"; or cultural criticism reminiscent of Henry James's "conscientious consciousness," Ellison interprets the American scene. Equality, improvisation, pragmatism as enacted by the American "thinker-tinker," the vernacular, consciousness, and that unity born of true complexity: these outcroppings of American identity mark the terrain of everything Ellison wrote, fiction and nonfiction alike. The territory he explores as an essayist becomes a slowly settled, open country of the imagination through which he pursues the meaning and mystery, the promise and betrayals, and above all the complex past and present possibilities of American democracy.

For Ellison writing is a password to freedom. His writer's middle passage is a liberating examination of the fluid democratic experience wherein "the values, ideals, assumptions and memories of unique individuals and groups reach out across the divisions wrought by our national diversity and touch us all." Keeping in mind the "very stern discipline" of artist and citizen, Ellison observes of our shared American traditions and ideals that "again and again they must be given further extension." In essay after essay, from his 1940 "A Congress Jim Crow Didn't Attend" to the 1992 Address at the Whiting Foundation, he writes simultaneously of the ideal, actual, and aspired-to condition of the American collage.

"Geography is fate," Ellison wrote, and he invoked Heraclitus's axiom on more than one occasion. Who we are is bound up with where we are, he believed, and, unsurprisingly, Oklahoma, where he was born, has a special provenance in his essays. Despite its prominence as a haven for escaped slaves, its history as the bitter destination of the five great Indian nations compelled to walk the Trail of Tears, and as a freewheeling "Indian territory" opened for white settlement in the late 1880s, Oklahoma did not become a state until 1907, a mere seven years before Ellison's birth. Its fluid, vigorous Southwestern character (maintained in the face of Governor Alfalfa Bill Murray's odiously effective efforts to give it the jim crow texture and laws of a Southern state), encouraged Ellison to dream, along with several other young black companions, of becoming a unifying Renaissance man in a society he hoped he would move closer to fulfilling its democratic ideal of equality and opportunity. Even in his boyhood sense of geography Ellison realized that Oklahoma was the territory (the "Indian nation") lit out for by Huck Finn, that prototypical potential vernacular American Renaissance man. (Later, conscious of his literary descent from Mark Twain, Ellison would write that "the territory is an ideal place—ever to be sought, ever to be missed, but always there.")

As a young man pursuing his dream, Ellison aspired to become a symphonic composer, and to equal Wagner by completing his first symphony by the time he was twenty-six. From an early age he read widely and voraciously, listening to and beginning to master the improvisational techniques of jazz and the complex forms of classical music. Asked much later if his "desire to be a symphony composer rather than a jazz instrumentalist [stood] for a sort of denial of [his] own cultural situation," he changed the questioner's frequency without hesitation: "No, no. You see, what is often misunderstood nowadays is that there wasn't always this division between the ambitions of jazz musicians and the standards of classical music; the idea was to master both traditions."

Perhaps, too, Ellison's sense of himself as an Oklahoman became a strong force mediating between North and South in his adult imagination. Frequently in his writing he declares allegiance to ideals embraced fitfully before, during, and after the Civil War by Northerners, though, as he notes in his "Commencement Address at the College of William and Mary," these ideas were first enunciated by Virginians in the eighteenth century. At the same time he is loyal to the human ties and sensuous feel of things associated with the South—what, at Ellison's funeral, novelist William Styron recalled as "Southern matters" cherished by his friend: the love of dogs, whiskey, and hunting that was part of both men's quest for identity and that longing for kinship with the land and the fathers immortalized in Faulkner's "The Bear."

As many of his essays attest, Oklahoma offered Ellison a synthesizing principle for his life and art. His background and experience there with music, religion, politics, sports, and sundry odd jobs and occupations made it easier for him to keep to the high ground in that lower-case civil war of literature, culture, art, and politics carried on by many of his contemporaries into the 1950s, 1960s, and beyond. His "cold Oklahoma Negro eye" provided him perspective on Alabama, where he had lived during three years at Tuskegee, and New York—Harlem where he made his home and the other diverse circles of "social hierarchy" in the city where he resided for some fifty-five years.

"Just before the terrible [Tulsa] riot of 1921," Ellison moved to Gary, Indiana, where his mother's brother lived. Soon after, however, "a depression in steel" aborted the move, and together with his mother and younger brother Herbert, he returned to Oklahoma City. There he stayed until 1933 when, hoboing on the freights of half a dozen railroads, he zigzagged his way to Alabama. In July 1936, after three years at Tuskegee, he made what he thought would be a temporary move to New York to earn money for his senior year. The plan didn't work out; besides, New York was a seductive artistic, intellectual, and social milieu for the aspiring composer, so he stayed. His early New York years were interrupted by some six months in Dayton, Ohio, occasioned by his mother's unexpected fatal illness and death in October 1937.

Soon after returning in 1938 to work on the Federal Writers Project, Ellison became a quintessential New Yorker—an Oklahoman who adopted and was adopted by the city. There he met many who, like him, brought vivid memories to New York and were sustained by a continuing inner experience of their places of origin. As a black American staking his claim to the society's "unknown territory" of art and imagination, Ellison strove to make the invisible visible, the unheard heard. Asked by the *Paris Review* in 1955 if "the search for identity is primarily an American theme," he dropped his right hand, paused, and followed with a mock uppercut to the interviewer's chin before replying: "It is *the* American theme."

Ellison sought a formal center of gravity for his essays, knowing that there is little which is static or simple about the country's *e pluribus unum* creed. He "was aware that when one attempts to mix literary modes in the interest of making disparate materials into rhetorical wholes one runs the risk of leaving structural holes— YET." In the name of complexity Ellison accepts "structural holes" as a fair price for embracing the "disparate materials" of his culture. Nevertheless, as his musician's ear caught the bottled-up quality of idiom and cadence, he broke up his sentence with "YET." Ellison's "YET" is characteristic of his resilient, syncopated style. Sounding a jazzman's note in the midst of a somewhat stuffy and formal étude, a note as "irreverent" as what he called, describing Invisible Man's intrusion into his writer's consciousness in the summer of 1945, "a honky-tonk trumpet blasting through a performance, say, of Britten's *War Requiem*," Ellison bends the essay into a vernacular as well as a classical form—in short, into a collage. In this spirit he brews his essays out of "disparate materials" from every facet of American life. Low and high and in the middle; it makes no difference, he might have said of these diverse vernacular ingredients: "It all good."

The vernacular Ellison inhaled from the music and speech riding the air in Oklahoma City was more than what he called "our most characteristic American style." For him, vernacular became "a dynamic process in which the most refined styles from the past are continually merged with the play-it-by-eye-and-by-ear improvisations which we invent in our efforts to control our environment and entertain ourselves." To bridge classical and vernacular idioms and techniques, he remembered and relied on the black church as a nourishing, inspirational, sometimes underground national institution, "wherein you heard the lingering accents of nineteenth-century rhetoric with its emphasis upon freedom and individual responsibility, a rhetorical style which gave us Lincoln, Harriet Tubman, Harriet Beecher Stowe and the other abolition-preaching Beechers. Which gave us Frederick Douglass, John Jasper and many other eloquent and heroic Negroes whose spirit still moves among us through the contributions they made to the flexibility, music and idealism of the American language." In the rhythms and periods of this passage from "Remembering Richard Wright" (1971), Ellison's prose moves across nineteenth-century waters to a twentieth-century territory where he puts modern literary craft in touch with the techniques of oratorical eloquence. He chose for ancestors those rhetoricians who assumed a responsibility for the American language consciously bound up with their responsibility for the nation's and their own moral identity.

. . .

"Either I'm nobody or I'm a nation," declares one of poet Derek Walcott's characters. This memorable line calls up Ellison's dangerous whole-souled commitment to American identity—what Invisible Man called the "beautiful absurdity of [our] American identity"—and his embrace of citizenship as a necessary affirmation of what Invisible Man identified as "the principle." Yet there was nothing easy or unexamined about Ellison's allegiance. As he wrote in response to the claim that he was a patriotic writer: "It ain't the theory which bothers me, it's the practice. My problem is to affirm while resisting." And his complex individual passion about American identity and "the moral imperatives of American life" only intensified his allegiance to his people, his group. "We need as many individuals developing their individual talents as possible," he told James Alan McPherson, "*but* dedicating some part of their energies to the group." About his own efforts as a conscious and conscientious member of the tribe, Ellison is positively fierce: "And damnit, I've *done* that. I've always written out of a sense of the group experience as filtered through my individual experiences, talent, and vision."

Not for nothing did Ellison follow Richard Wright's suggestion that he study Henry James's prefaces. Introspection about the meaning and sensibility of black American identity is an imperative for Ellison. "We do too little of this," he once said of the need to "evaluate Negro experience from the inside." He went on to bear witness to the fact that "over and over again when we find bunches of Negroes enjoying themselves, when they're feeling good and in a mood of communion, they sit around and marvel at what a damnably marvelous human being, what a confounding human type the Negro American really is." Here, on Ellison's ground, is the case for his conviction that "the way home we seek is that condition of man's being at home in the world, which is called love, and which we term democracy." According to his paradox, the type of individual who evolved into the black American did so within the American crucible despite and, perforce, because of terrific obstacles. More than that,

Ellison's essays revisit Invisible Man's speculation that "they had exhausted in us some—not much, but some—of the human greed and smallness, yes, and the fear and superstition that had kept them running."

Ellison's compassionate, exacting focus on Lincoln and other figures from the American past prefigures Reverend Hickman's brooding testimony in the novel-in-progress that "[Lincoln] joined us in what we have been forced to learn about living." Like Lincoln and Lincoln's friend and sometime moral adversary Frederick Douglass, Ellison would sustain and enhance the self's union as well as the nation's. In Ellison's case, the union in question was the union of musician with writer, jazzman with classicist, black man with American, and the man of form with the respecter of chaos.

In terms of race, self, and nation much has been made of the way Invisible Man's last words—"Who knows but that, on the lower frequencies, I speak for you?"—generalize the predicament of invisibility from its specific location in African-American experience. Without the rich, vivid, various explicitness of the black American experience, including the protest, which the author put into *Invisible Man*, the novel would have lacked universal appeal. The book's power to compel others to see *their* reality through the prism of African-American experience rests on Ellison's fidelity to the particulars of that experience. Clothed in the discursive prose and Burkean "representative anecdotes" of his essays, Ellison's theme remains the complexity of the African-American experience. Convinced of its indivisibility from American experience, he offers his readers lessons in how to see and hear "around corners"—"whatever else the true American is, he is also somehow black."

None of this implies that Ellison minimizes the racial injustice perpetrated by Americans, often in the name of America. (" 'If It's Optic White, It's the Right White' goes the motto of Liberty Paints in *Invisible Man* [1952].) Threaded through Ellison's essays like a

watermark is one taut acknowledgment after another of racial oppression in America. The physical, psychological, and emotional
cruelties of slavery are here, and so are the legal, illegal, and habitual
violent betrayals of Reconstruction. So are lynching and its rippling
effects of fear and terror. So are painful incidents of discrimination
from Ellison's youth and adulthood.

Far from ignoring the attempts to brutalize black Americans into
permanent social, political, economic, cultural, and psychological inequality and inferiority, Ellison makes his people's condition and
status the testing ground for the ideals and the experiment of the
nation. For him the Civil War, Reconstruction, and its tragic aftermath were the crux of American history and the most dramatic
instances of the country's struggle with the potentially fatal contradiction between its democratic theory and practice. Notwithstanding the victories and advances of the civil rights movement, which
Ellison noted and rejoiced in, he observed that the American Civil
War had "continued on as *civil war*, lower case, in which that war of
arms was replaced by a war of politics, racial and ethnic violence,
ritual sacrifice based on race and color, and by economic and judicial
repression." Asking "if indeed the outcome of that war has yet been
decided," he told a group of Harvard alumni in a 1974 address that
"quite frankly it is my opinion that it is still in the balance, and only
our enchantment by the spell of the possible, our endless optimism,
has led us to assume that it ever really ended." Therefore the challenge to national moral identity revolves around a "play-it-by-eye-
and-ear" pursuit of the ideal reminiscent of the vernacular style in
music, literature, and, for that matter, every facet of what we call
American culture.

To complement the vernacular and counterpoint his sense of
nemesis in the wake of American hubris, Ralph Waldo Ellison falls
back "upon the teaching of that earlier Ralph Waldo." He calls for
"conscience and consciousness, more consciousness and more conscientiousness!" Ellison also riffs upon that "spirit of public happiness" with which John Adams and his fellow revolutionaries,

including slaves like James Armistead Lafayette, pledged their "lives, their fortunes, and their sacred honor" to the "principle" in the Declaration.

From 1937 when, at Richard Wright's urging, Ellison published his first piece, a review of Waters Edward Turpin's novel, *These Low Grounds* (even here he called for "greater development in technique" and "closer examination of consciousness"), until his passing in 1994, he wrote more than seventy-five essays, addresses, reviews, and conference talks. Almost half of these, along with a few of his numerous interviews, were collected in *Shadow and Act* (1964) and *Going to the Territory* (1986). Most of the essays, he noted in his introduction to *Shadow and Act*, "are occasional pieces, written for magazines whose editors provided opportunities for me to reduce my thinking—indeed, often to discover what I *did* think—to publishable form." His observations about the occasional and improvisational nature of *Shadow and Act* hold true for the work in *Going to the Territory* and for the uncollected and the unpublished pieces included here. *Occasion* is truly the given of his essays.

The Modern Library *Collected Essays* includes complete texts of the first editions of *Shadow and Act* and *Going to the Territory*, to which I have made silent minor corrections. I have also included eleven previously published but uncollected essays: "February" (1955), "Flamenco" (1954), "A Congress Jim Crow Didn't Attend" (1940), "Tell It Like It Is, Baby" (1965), "A Special Message to Subscribers" (1980), "Alain Locke" (1974), "Presentation to Bernard Malamud of the Gold Medal for Fiction" (1983), "Introduction to the Thirtieth Anniversary Edition of *Invisible Man*" (1982), "On Being the Target of Discrimination" (1989), "Bearden" (1988), and Ellison's Foreword to the 1988 reissue of John Kouwenhoven's *The Beer Can by the Highway*—again with minor silent corrections. Of these, "A Congress Jim Crow Didn't Attend" was written earliest, in 1940. I selected it for its intrinsic merit and as an intriguing example of the more than thirty articles and reviews Ellison wrote for *New Masses* and other publications on the left in the late 1930s and early 1940s.* From Ellison's interviews I chose James Alan McPherson's "Indivisible Man" and "A Completion of Personality" conducted by the late John Hersey. Both of these emerged from conversations over many months and, in the case of the Hersey piece, years. In each, departing from his usual silence, Ellison engages in extended discussion of what he had done and what he aspired to do on his novel in progress.

Finally, the *Collected Essays* includes nine pieces that appear in print for the first time. For one of these, Ellison's lyrical homage to William L. Dawson at a 1971 Tuskegee Club banquet in Philadelphia, I am indebted to Professor Robert G. O'Meally of Columbia University, who generously provided a tape and transcript which I edited into the present text. Like the writer's other essays and addresses, these nine are occasional and are instances of his continuing fascination with the complexities of leadership and identity for black Americans. The essays on James Armistead Lafayette (1974), William L. Dawson (1971), Roscoe Dunjee (1972), and, in powerful generalized fashion, Ellison's "Haverford Statement" (1969) and "Working Notes for *Invisible Man*" (undated) celebrate the special contributions of the African-American to the originality of American life. Along with the "Commencement Address at the College of William and Mary" (1972), the "Address to the Harvard College Alumni, Class of 1949" (1974), "Notes for Class Day Talk at Columbia University" (1990), and "Address at the Whiting Foundation" (1992), they show the continuity of Ellison's preoccupation with American identity, the cultural and social metamorphoses around him, and the democratic flux of American life in the late twentieth century.

---

*See Robert G. O'Meally's bibliography, "The Writings of Ralph Ellison," in *Speaking for You: The Vision of Ralph Ellison*, ed. Kimberly Benston (Washington, D.C.: Howard University Press, 1987), pp. 411–19.

As he grew older, Ellison gave himself more and more to making sense of the American experience "through the wry perspective of sanity-saving comedy." In his last essays, especially "Bearden", "Notes for Class Day Talk at Columbia University", and his "Address at the Whiting Foundation," his sensibility approaches serenity. His mind continues to defy shallow simplicities and easy categories of perception and experience—whether from right, left, or center. And his prose grows luminous with an ever-stronger faith in the possibilities—not the achievement, but the possibilities—of the American ideal. The wisdom of the last essays is all the more moving because of Ellison's spirit of playfulness. For example, he closes his "Class Day" notes with a witty, admonishing paraphrase of Francis Thompson's "The Hound of Heaven" in which he transforms God's hound into the "ideal of social equality"—recall Invisible Man's slip of "social equality" for "social responsibility." Pursued by our outraged ideal even as we flee it, in Ellison's conceit Americans hear the voice of our sacred democratic muse: "All things betray thee, who betrayest Me."

The sequences Ellison chose for *Shadow and Act* and *Going to the Territory* respected continuities of form, idea, and theme more than they did chronology. In similar fashion, the opening sequence of the *Collected Essays* calls attention to his different guises as essayist: the lyricism of "February," his union of narrative and analytical styles in "Flamenco," the sense of participation as well as reportage in his stance toward the black voices quoted in "A Congress Jim Crow Didn't Attend," and, finally, in "Tell It Like It Is, Baby," his mingling of dream (nightmare, really) with keenly remembered and realized historical details in the flow of the writer's waking consciousness.

The sequence following *Shadow and Act* is framed by essays that reconstruct the origins of *Invisible Man*, its genesis and, in the "Working Notes," Ellison's early projection of Invisible Man's evolution as a representative type of the black American. In between are essays and addresses which elaborate his sense of the mythic importance of ritual to American history and delineate the achievements of several black Americans, as well as the special responsibilities of black intellectuals and every American artist. "A Completion of Personality" follows *Going to the Territory* because of its "aura of a summing up."

I concluded the volume with five late essays in which Ellison keeps up the good fight to make "rhetorical wholes" out of the "disparate materials" of his writer's mind and experience. These last pieces resonate with his old determination to be true to his American theme and, if he is lucky (you almost hear him chuckle), to inch along toward "helping this country discover a fuller sense of itself as it goes about making its founders' dream a reality." To the end Ellison is true to the writer's mystery—the pain and pleasure of "pouring into that thing which is being created all of what he cannot understand, cannot say, cannot even admit in any other way." As these last essays come into the reader's mind and life from the page, Ellison's word is made flesh, and, in fulfillment of his writer's dream, "the artifact is a completion of personality."

Through the essays flows Ellison's defiant personal responsibility for democracy and for the parallel vernacular experiment of an American culture indivisible from the nation's theory and practice. His "eclectic" and "mammy-made" prose projects two artistic possibilities and realities that he cared about passionately enough to risk the sometimes perilous, self-targeting act of the occasional essay. The first is the American language, the second the mystery, absurdity, and complexity of American identity. The language, Ellison felt, was as supple, fluid, and varied as a jazzman's horn in the range of frequencies it offered to writers. In his 1953 address, "Brave Words for a Startling Occasion," he sees, hears, and feels the language "swirling with over three hundred years of American living, a mixture of the folk, the Biblical, the scientific and the political. Slangy in one stance, academic in another, loaded poetically with imagery at one moment, mathematically bare of imagery in the next," his essays mingle the quirks of idiom and experience he found from Oklahoma to Alabama to New York, and felt as a mysterious complex unity on his travels throughout the American territory. It is this sense of a living American language seething with change, with new accents, expressions, and voices that Ellison keeps faith with through his fluid blend of vernacular and classical.

He also keeps faith with what he observes and embraces as "mysterious and uncertain" in American reality and personality. "What's inside you, brother?" he asked in "A Very Stern Discipline" (1967). "What's your heart like?" As Ellison keeps faith with the theme and language of America, we feel, to paraphrase Woodridge, Invisible Man's literature professor, that essay by essay he has composed his own heart's collage and thereby helped create a culture. Over and over again Ellison improvises variations on Invisible Man's brooding question about the potential and the fate of the American experiment: "And could politics ever be an expression of love?" Ellison would have it so, for there appear in this collage of a collection states of mind and being which compose a union of self, people, and nation. Always a vigilant kinsman aware of "the chaos which lives within the pattern of [our] certainties," Ralph Waldo Ellison writes with a generosity of spirit and perception that, if heeded, might lead to a true end to the civil war still waged in the personal, political, and cultural provinces of America.

JOHN F. CALLAHAN

FEBRUARY

Ellison wrote this lyrical reminiscence long after the desolate winter of 1937–38 when, after his mother's unexpected death in October "in that strange city [Cincinnati, he] had survived three months off the fields and woods by [his] gun; through ice and snow and homelessness." "February" was published in Saturday Review, January 1, 1955.

FEBRUARY is a brook, birds, an apple tree—a day spent alone in the country. Unemployed, tired of reading, and weary of grieving the loss of my mother, I'd gone into the woods to forget. So that now all Februarys have the aura of that early morning coldness, the ghost of quail tracks on the snow-powdered brook which I brushed aside as I broke the brook to drink: and how the little quail tracks went up the ice, precise and delicate, into the darker places of the bank-ledge undisturbed. February is climbing up a hill into the full glare of the early sun, alone in all that immensity of snowscape with distant Dayton drowsing wavery to my eyes like the sound of distant horns. It's walking through a parklike grove, the tall trees stark, the knee-high snow windblown and pathless, to a decaying shed sheltering a fine old horsedrawn sleigh, carved and scrolled with traces of goldleaf clinging to its flaking wood.

And the birds: I descended into a little valley in the windless quiet and the smell of apples and saw the air erupt with red tracer-bullet streaks of flight—across the snows, a carnival of cardinals. The red birds zoomed, the flickers flew, pheasants roared up like gaudy Chinese kimono rags. My heart beat hard and I saw the single tree, black-limbed against the sky, here and there the miracle of a dark red apple still hanging after months of ice and snow. I bent forward and knelt within the circle of the fruit-fall, searching out an apple missed by the birds. Sweet and mellow to the taste, it had been preserved by the leaves and grasses, protected by the snows. And I recalled the valley of two months before: *At the sound of my gun the birds came up along the hill in pairs and swooped with a circling down into the thicket on the other side, and I had gone down into the valley, soft, then, with the glow of sunset, and found the cock quail dead upon the snow, its plumage undisturbed, the vapor rising slowly from its sinking blood. . . . And now in this* place of hidden fruit and bird-tracked snow, I was seized with a kind of exhilaration. For I was in my early twenties then, and I had lived through my mother's death in that strange city, had survived three months off the fields and woods by my gun; through ice and snow and homelessness. And now in this windless February instant I had crossed over into a new phase of living. Shall I say it was in those February snows that I first became a man?

FLAMENCO

Ellison had a long-standing passion for flamenco. Invisible Man hears "an old woman singing a spiritual as full of Weltschmerz as flamenco." In 1954 after lecturing at the Harvard seminars in Salzburg, Ellison heard flamenco in Madrid and Paris. This essay describes the old masters Vicente Escudero and Pepe el del Matrona, and the connections Ellison finds between Spanish folklore and music and American vernacular, especially the blues. "Flamenco" was published in Saturday Review, *December 11, 1954.*

RECENTLY in Paris in Leroy Haynes's restaurant in the Rue de Martyrs, where American Negro fliers and jazz musicians bend over their barbecue and red beans and rice in an attitude as pious as that of any worshiper in Sacre Coeur, which dominates Montmartre above, a gypsy woman entered and told my fortune. She was a handsome woman, dressed in the mysterious, many-skirted costume of the gypsies, and she said that I was soon to take a journey, and that I was to find good fortune. I said jokingly that I had had good fortune, for after dreaming of it for many years I had been to Madrid.

"You went when you should have gone," she said, peering at my hand. "Had you gone earlier you might have found death. But that is of the past. I speak of good fortune in the future."

"There I heard real flamenco," I said, "and that is a good fortune I shall never forget."

"Flamenco," she said. "You understand flamenco? Then you must go see Escudero. You must hear Pepe el del Matrona and Rafael Romero."

"I've heard of Escudero," I said, "but who are these others?"

"You will see," she said. "You will see and hear also."

"This is real good fortune," I said. "I thought Escudero was dead."

"Not dead," she said, holding my hand over a damp spot on the tablecloth, "only old. But to see *him* is a little more than to take a walk. The fortune of your hand comes after a journey over water."

She then offered, for a further consideration, to tell me other things, but this was enough. I was amused (for sure enough we were flying home two days hence), my wife and friends were laughing that I had submitted to having my palm read, and the knowledge that the legendary Vicente Escudero was dancing again after so many years of retirement was enough good fortune for any one day.

7

So that evening we saw the old master in the full glory of his resurrection. Dry, now, and birdlike in his grace, Escudero is no longer capable of floor-resounding vigor, but conveys even the stamping fury of the Spanish dance with the gentlest, most delicate, precise, and potent of gestures and movement—reasserting in terms of his own medium a truth which Schumann-Heink, Roland Hayes, and Povla Frijsh have demonstrated in terms of the art of song: that with the great performer it is his style, so tortuously achieved, so carefully cultivated, which is the last to go down before age. And so with the singer Pepe el del Matrona, who at seventy-four is able to dominate the space of even the largest theatre with his most pianissimo arabesques of sound.

But more important here than the inspiring triumph of artistic style over Time was the triumph, in this most sophisticated of Western cities, of Cante Flamenco, a folk art which has retained its integrity and vitality through two centuries during which the West assumed that it had, through enlightenment, science, and progress, dispensed with those tragic, metaphysical elements of human life which the art of flamenco celebrates. Certainly Escudero and Matrona draw a great deal of their vitality from this tradition that contains many elements which the West has dismissed as "primitive," that epithet so facile for demolishing all things cultural which Westerners do not understand or wish to contemplate. Perhaps Spain (which is neither Europe nor Africa but a blend of both) was once more challenging our Western optimism. If so, it was not with pessimism but with an affirmative art which draws its strength and endurance from a willingness to deal with the whole man (Unamuno's man of flesh and blood who must die) in a world which is viewed as basically impersonal and violent; if so, through her singers and dancers and her flamenco music she was making the West a most useful and needed gift.

I haven't yet discovered the specific nature of the gift of fortune which my gypsy promised me, but until something better appears I'll accept Westminster's new three-volume "Anthology of Cante Flamenco," which has just won the Grand Prix de Disque, as the answer. Escudero isn't in it, but members of his entourage are: Pepe el del Matrona, Rafael Romero, and the great flamenco guitarist Perico el del Lunar, who along with eight other artists presents thirty-three excellently recorded examples of flamenco song style.

Cante Flamenco is the very ancient folk music of the Andalusian gypsies of southern Spain. Its origins are as mysterious as that of those of the gypsies themselves, but in it are heard Byzantine, Arabic, Hebraic, and Moorish elements fused and given the violent, rhythmical expressiveness of the gypsies. Cante Flamenco, or *cante hondo* (deep song, as the purer, less florid form is called), is a unique blending of Eastern and Western modes and as such it often baffles when it most intrigues the Western ear. In our own culture the closest music to it in feeling is the Negro blues, early jazz, and the slave songs (now euphemistically termed "spirituals"). Even a casual acquaintance with Westminster's anthology reveals certain parallels, and jazz fans will receive here a pleasant shock of recognition. Soon to be released free to those who purchase the "Anthology" is a forty-page booklet containing the text of the songs and a historical survey of flamenco literature written by Professor Tomas Andrade de Silva of the Royal Conservatory at Madrid.

Like Negro folk music, Cante Flamenco (which recognizes no complete separation between dance and song, the basic mood, the guitar and castanets, hold all together) is a communal art. In the small rooms in which it is performed there are no "squares" sitting around just to be entertained, everyone participates very much as during a non-commercial jam session or a Southern jazz dance. It can be just as noisy and sweaty and drunken as a Birmingham "breakdown"; while one singer "riffs" (improvises) or the dancers "go to town" the others assist by clapping their hands in the intricate percussive manner called *palmada* and by stamping out the rhythms with their feet. When a singer, guitarist, or dancer has negotiated a particularly subtle passage (and this is an art of great refinements) the shouts of *Ole!* arise to express appreciation of his art, to agree with the sentiments expressed, and to encourage him on to even greater eloquence. Very often the "Anthology" side containing the *cantes con baile* (dance songs) sounds like a revivalists' congregation saying "Amen!" to the preacher.

Flamenco, while traditional in theme and choreography, allows a maximum of individual expression, and a democratic rivalry such as is typical of a jam session; for, like the blues and jazz, it is an art of improvisation, and like them it can be quite graphic. Even one who doesn't understand the lyrics will note the uncanny ability of the singers presented here to produce pictorial effects with their voices. Great space, echoes, rolling slopes, the charging of bulls, and the prancing and galloping of horses flow in this sound much as animal cries, train whistles, and the loneliness of night sound through the blues.

The nasal, harsh, anguished tones heard on these sides are not the results of ineptitude or "primitivism"; like the "dirty tone" of the jazz instrumentalist, they are the result of an esthetic which rejects the beautiful sound sought by classical Western music.

Not that flamenco is simply a music of despair; this is true mainly of the seguidillas, the soleares, and the saetas (arrows of song) which are sung when the holy images are paraded during Holy Week, and which Rafael Romero sings with a pitch of religious fervor that reminds one of the great Pastora Pavon (*La Niña de los Peines*). But along with these darker songs the "Anthology" offers all the contrasts, the gay alegrías, bulerías, sevillanas, the passionate peteneras, lullabies (nana), prison songs, mountain songs, and laments. Love, loneliness, disappointment, pride—all these are themes for Cante Flamenco. Perhaps what attracts us most to flamenco, as it does to the blues, is the note of unillusioned affirmation of humanity which it embodies. The gypsies, like the slaves, are an outcast though undefeated people who have never lost their awareness of the physical source of man's most spiritual moments; even their Christ is a man of flesh and bone who suffered and bled before his apotheosis. In its more worldly phases flamenco voice resembles the blues voice, which mocks the despair stated explicitly in the lyric, and it expresses the great human joke directed against the universe, that joke which is the secret of all folklore and myth: that though we be dismembered daily we shall always rise up again. Americans have long found in Spanish culture a clarifying perspective on their own. Now in this anthology of Spanish folklore we have a most inviting challenge to listen more attentively to the deeper voice of our own.

A CONGRESS JIM CROW
DIDN'T ATTEND

Between 1938 and 1942 Ellison contributed numerous articles and reviews, signed and unsigned, and two short stories to New Masses. *"A Congress Jim Crow Didn't Attend" is a narrative essay with personal and public overtones. In it Ellison uses the Third National Negro Congress as an early occasion for speculation on "the ambiguity of Negro leadership." As he soon would do in pieces like "The Way It Is," Ellison celebrates the courageous lives and voices of ordinary Negroes, even declaring that "the age of the Negro hero had returned to American life." It was published in* New Masses, *May 14, 1940.*

WE drove all night to beat the crowd. We were going to Washington to attend the Third National Negro Congress. Fog hung over the Delaware roads, over the fields and creeks, so that we could not tell water from grass, except in spots where the fog had lifted. Our headlights brought no answering reflection from the red glass disks on the road signs. Coming out of some town the driver failed to see a road marker and almost wrecked the car. It shook us awake and we talked to keep the driver alert.

Then two things happened to give the trip to the Congress a sharp meaning. It was the sun that started it. It appeared beyond the fog like a flame, as though a distant farmhouse was afire. One of the boys remembered Natchez, Mississippi,* and began talking about it. I felt depressed. A friend of mine was from Natchez and some of the victims had his family name and I wondered if any had been his relatives. We talked about conditions down south and I hoped someone from Natchez would attend the Congress, so I could hear about the fire firsthand.

Outside of Baltimore we began passing troops of cavalry. They were stretched along the highway for a mile: Young fellows in khaki with campaign hats strapped beneath their chins, jogging stiffly in their saddles. I asked one of my companions where they were going and was told that there was an army camp nearby. Someone said that I would find out "soon enough" and I laughed and said that I was a black Yank and was not coming. But already the troops of cavalry

---

*Ellison refers to the Rhythm Club fire of April 1940 in Natchez, Mississippi. Exits inside the Negro nightclub became blocked while decorations of Spanish moss fueled the flames, and before help arrived over two hundred Negroes burned to death in the crowded club.

were becoming linked in my mind with the Natchez fire. Where *were* the troops going? We in the car were going to the Third National Negro Congress—but what did *that* mean? Then I was aware that all five of us in the car were of army age and that just as suddenly as the troops had appeared atop the hill, we might be called to war. Here we were, young Negroes, bitter about the conditions responsible for Natchez and faced with the danger of war, heading for Washington, D.C.

I thought about the Congress. I remembered that some of the Negro papers had been carrying glowing accounts of army life and of the joys of the black French soldiers. Would there be many at the Congress who had succumbed to these stories? John L. Lewis had asked the support of the Congress in forming a new political movement—possibly a third party—to continue the New Deal measures forsaken by Roosevelt; what would be the response of the Congress? There were rumors that one of the Congress leaders had sold out; how would the rank and file react? Would *I* find in Washington an affirmation of the Negroes' will to unity and freedom that would remove the deep sense of the danger of war which had made the sudden appearance of the troops of cavalry seem like a revelation of our fate?

For years Negroes have struggled for that unity, seeking to find their allies; sometimes gaining, and sometimes losing ground. And in all Negroes at some period of their lives there is that yearning for a sense of group unity that is the yearning of men for a flag: for a unity that cannot be compromised, that cannot be bought; that is conscious of itself, of its strength, that is militant. I had come to realize that such a unity is unity of a nation, and of a class. I had thought vaguely of the Congress in such terms, but it was more like a hope to be realized. I had not thought to seek this sense of affirmation in it. Now I realized that this was the need it must fill for myself and for others.

Negroes from the North, South, East, and West were heading for Washington, seeking affirmation of their will to freedom. They were coming with their doubts and with their convictions. It was more than just another trip to another congress. When we entered the suburbs of Washington I noticed that the car moved much more slowly than before and started to ask why. But I remembered: there is always that fear among Negroes going from the North into the South of running afoul of Southern custom and Jim Crow laws. The driver knew that we were driving into the capital of the United States—and of legal Jim Crow. The car nosed its way cautiously.

Once in Washington, the first thing to do was to go to convention headquarters and make arrangements for rooms. We drove to the Department of Labor building. It is a new building and we were relieved to see so many Negro faces, to find them in charge. Delegates were already grouped about the big lobby; it hummed with conversation. They looked up expectantly as we came through the high portals. We made our way to the tables arranged about the lobby where a number of girls were busy registering delegates. They were pretty girls and we were surprised; usually the pretty girls avoided that part of conventions. We were registered and given credentials: a delegate's card, a badge, a list of instructions, which, among other things, told us to buy a meal ticket. Under Section 2 it told about housing:

> After your meal ticket the next important thing is a place to stay. We have done our best. But Washington is a Jim Crow town. We have not broken down Jim Crowism . . . in large hotels. But we have made history in the matter of housing accommodations for Negroes. First: for 119 delegates we have accommodations in the modern up-to-date Washington Tourist Camp—four blocks away from our place. . . . Second: for 250 delegates we have arranged for the building of an entire village a few yards away from the Washington Monument and two blocks away from the convention meeting place. You will be housed in waterproof tents with wooden floors—clean linen—individual cots—warm blankets. There will be ample facilities for showers. . . .

Also listed were rooms in private homes. I asked why the village had been built and was told that it was a protest against the miserable housing conditions for Negroes in the capital city. So stretched out beneath the long shadow of Washington's monument, we found lying a village of tents like those discovered by Steinbeck's Joads. Not far away is where the annual Cherry Blossom Festival is held.

Returning to convention headquarters, we find the delegates pouring in. There is a steady roar of voices. We look about for acquaintances.

"Look! What's that guy's name?" I look up; a short man with a high forehead and glasses squeezes past.

"That's John P. Davis."

"*Davis*, the national secretary?"

"Sure."

"But I've seen his pictures. I thought he was a big guy."

"He's big, all right," someone says. "He told off Dies."

"Thought that was *Ben* Davis."

"Yeah, but this one told him too."

A tall man in a cattleman's hat has been listening: "Now wasn't that something?" he says, "*Both* of 'em got him told. All my life I been wanting to see some of our Negro leaders go down there to Congress and let them know how we felt about things. Didn't think I would live to see it, but it happened. And that's why I'm here this morning!"

The lobby is still filling. There are young people and old people, both from the farms, the small towns, and the cities. I can tell the New Yorkers by their manner, their confidence. But there are also many faces that I learned to know in the South. And I know that someone has sacrificed to get them here. Some are farmers, others sharecroppers. They look stiff in their "Sunday" clothes. There are many whites also. And on the lapels of both whites and blacks are to be seen the maroon and white "Stop Lynching" buttons. I walk about the lobby, from group to group, trying to see if I can pick out those from down where being militant, being a man, carries a penalty of dispossession, of flogging, of rape charges, of lynching death. They too are here; one, James McMillian, a preacher–coal miner from Kentucky, has felt the sting of a lynch rope around his neck and lived to tell about it. His first question is, "What's being done about the Anti-Lynching Bill?"

I talk with a steelworker from Gary, Indiana. He speaks about the war and ties it up to the convention. He is well informed. Passing another group I hear:

"I come over three hundred miles to this congress."

"Where you come from?"

"I come from Zenia, Ohio."

"Hell, you ain't come nowhere. I come all the way from Texas!" the other said proudly.

Behind me now, someone is saying: "They tell me John L. Lewis is going to be here."

"That's right, it's here in the program."

"You know, I been wanting to see that guy. I want to get up close, so's I can see what he looks like."

"He sure is talking my way these days. Because from what I know about the Triple A and the FSA out there in Arkansas where I come from, he's talking sense!"

"He sounds all right to me, too, but I want to see what he looks like."

"Well, he'll be here."

I walk inside the auditorium where the convention is to be held. The carpet is thick and deep blue, the ceiling high and soothing to the eyes. In front, on both sides of the speakers' platform, there are gigantic columns that seem to pull you upward, out of yourself, as your eyes follow them aloft.

The auditorium had that overwhelming air usually associated with huge churches, and I remembered what André Malraux once said about the factory becoming for the workers what the cathedral formerly was, and that they must come to see in it not ideal gods but human power struggling against the earth. The building is dedicated to labor. I hoped that what was to happen there during the Congress would help bring nearer that transformation of which Malraux wrote. When I walked outside the building I learned that it *was*, for the three days of the convention, sacred ground. I suggested to one of my companions that we go uptown for a bite to eat in a cafeteria. He reminded me simply that we were in Washington.

The Congress began that evening, called to order by the rapping of a gavel made from timber from the last slave ship to touch American shores. There on the platform were the speakers. John L. Lewis appeared with his daughter, Kathryn, and there was a burst of applause from the audience. Lewis spoke plainly and with force, and was frequently interrupted by applause. The audience was with him. He spoke like a man who knew how to speak to ordinary folks, and they understood him and agreed with him. Lewis said:

> No group in the population feels more heavily the burden of unemployment and insecurity than the Negro citizens. . . . The denials of civil liberties lie with heavy discrimination upon Negroes. Only when these economic and political evils are wiped out will the Negro people be free of them.
>
> I therefore call upon you to join in common cause with labor that we may seek out as American citizens together those political means and instruments by which the common welfare may be promoted. . . .

Then as his final word was spoken and applause roared up, they saw John P. Davis step forward and halt Lewis before he could return to his seat. He spoke into the microphone. "I am going to ask Mr. Lewis to come forward with two Negro coal miners who know better than any other group of Negro people of the character, of the leadership of the president of the Congress of Industrial Organizations." There was a burst of applause and the flashing of press cameras as Davis presented Lewis with a plaque for his "distinguished service to the Negro people." In his acceptance Lewis stated what

his offer to the Congress seems to prove and what Negroes throughout the country are beginning to believe:

> You know, I am one American who believes in equality of
> opportunity for the Negro people. And I do not try to conceal
> the fact; in fact, I am rather anxious that a great many people
> find out about our views in this country and I am doing what I
> can to educate them on that particular point.

From the applause I was quite sure there was not a single person in the
auditorium who did not see in the ceremony a historical importance.

Following John L. Lewis came A. Philip Randolph. He brought
into play that deep, resonant voice which had helped him to the presidency of the largest Negro union and of the National Negro Congress itself. The audience was quiet, waiting for him to reveal
himself. Several of his recent actions had been strange; his name had
appeared in places where the members had not expected to see it,
and they were waiting for him to confirm the faith that had led them
to make him their president. He spoke of the world crisis, of the split
in the ranks of labor, of unemployment. But his voice droned out
abstract phrases; statistics rolled forth; the speech became involved,
and through it sounded unmistakable notes of Red-baiting. From
time to time he said things which the people felt strongly and they
applauded. But soon they became restless; they had heard these arguments before, arguments that sounded strange in the mouth of
one who was supposed to be their leader. The speech continued and,
before its end, delegates were leaving the auditorium. I had sat
through the address with a feeling of betrayal. I did not realize it, but
I had witnessed a leader in the act of killing his leadership.

In his report next morning the national secretary, John P. Davis,
voiced the things the delegates felt. He spoke out for the program
that they wished to support, and, judging from the reception of the
speech, the delegates were assured that theirs was a common will.

We want peace for ourselves and America [Davis said].

We want peace and freedom for the peoples of India, of China, of Africa. . . . The administration is taking sides in this imperialist conflict. Its actions menace our neutrality and our peace. We must join with labor, we must join with youth to insist upon an end to this disastrous policy. . . . The American Negro people will refuse to follow American imperialism in an attack upon the Soviet Union, will refuse to fall victim to anti-Soviet adventures. . . . I have witnessed the real and genuine equal rights of its [the Soviet Union's] many nations and people busy and working in amity, collaboration, and peace. I know of their deep friendship and aid to all oppressed people.

The whole spirit of the convention rose and enthusiasm mounted.

That afternoon the delegates divided into several panels. The discussions on economic security were led by Louis Burnham, a young man from Harlem. Goldie Ervin of Pennsylvania, an intense young woman, spoke on the problems of the Negro woman. David Lasser of the Workers Alliance was greeted by the audience as a friend. He spoke on unemployment. Other panels were in progress and the delegates discussed their problems with Congressman Marcantonio of New York, with Joseph Gelders of Alabama, and other leaders from urban centers.

But I am looking for those whose very presence here means a danger faced and a fear conquered, and danger to be faced again. She is a tall black woman from Arkansas. She has asked to address the panel on economic security. She walks slowly to the microphone, and when she raises her head there are strands of gray hair beneath her flopping black straw hat. She is not accustomed to speaking through a microphone and has to be instructed to stand before it. She speaks slowly:

Ladies and gentlemen, I'm here to tell youall that we in Arkansas is having a tight time. Folks down there is working for 60 and 75 cents a day. Folks with kids, I mean. Now youall know that ain' nothing fo' no folks with children to be gitting.

I come up here to tell youall about it; and to ask youall if there's *anything* youall can do fo' us down in Arkansas, please to do it.

I was proud to come. I mean I was proud to come to this Congress. I was proud my people sent me. You know, we got other people down there who wants to see the hard tasks done. But they's shaky. They's scared they'd be moved off the land. Well, I tell 'em that they moving every day anyhow! I told them if they put me off the land I'll go. I'll do like them folks out there in Missouri done: let 'em put me out on the highway. They got to do something for me. They bet' not harm me. An' if they was to kill me, they'd have to *bury* me. So I'm just on they hands. *I'm* looking for better conditions for my people.

Well, I want to thank youall for letting me tell you 'bout Arkansas. It ain't all I got to tell you, but it's all for right now. Later on I'm going to tell you some more.

She searches in her bag, brings forth what appears to be a roll of bills.

Oh, yes, I forgot to tell youall about this. Now there's lots of other people down there what wants to come up here. But they ain't got no money. They works all day for 60 and 75 cents and when they through they gits paid off in this stuff.

She holds the bills so the audience may see.

I forgits what they calls it—oh, yes, that's right, it's scrip. Scrip. This is what they pay you with. They even got they own money; them planters I mean. You git this and you have to take it to what they call the commissary store to spend it. You cain't spend it nowhere else. So you see, they's other people who would be up here today, but they ain't got no money. That's the way things is down where I come from. I got lots more to tell youall, but I ain't going to take up any more of youall's time right now. An' I want' thank youall agin for letting me speak.

After the session I found her in the crowd. The city people were shaking her hand. I asked her to tell me more of conditions in Arkansas. She told me that the men were being thrown out of work by mechanical plows, that the children had no fuel for their schoolhouse—how could they learn? She told me that a merchant, upon hearing that the people were trying to send her to the Congress, had given the cannery and agricultural union a contribution. She is the president of her local union, an affiliate of the CIO with 260 members. There is a calm dignity about this woman. Where did she get it? I asked her about religion. "Well, son," she told me, "we used to go to the graveyard and preach to folks 'bout heaven. But I done found that the way to serve Christ is by helping folks here on earth."

What I found among the delegates was a temper of militant indignation. They were people sure of their strength. I listened to Owen Whitfield, the hero of the convention. In many of the speeches I had heard the names Gabriel, Denmark Vesey, Harriet Tubman, Frederick Douglass. And in these mouths the names had a new meaning. And I suddenly realized that the age of the Negro hero had returned to American life.

Whitfield led the Missouri highway demonstration of last year. He is the father of twelve children, a farmer for thirty-five years. He speaks with the skill of the Negro folk-preacher, in terms and images the people understand. The people from the farm country shout "Amen!" and "It's the truth!" Whitfield is of the earth and his speech is of the earth, and I said "Amen!" with the farmers. His is not a speech from above, like Randolph's. He speaks with pride of his Missouri people, and the audience is with him when he lashes out at leaders who avoid positive action out of fear of their "status." Whitfield sacrificed his home and farm and led his wife and family out with two thousand white and black families to face the January weather and the Missouri Highway Patrol. His is the pride of one who knows what it means to fight and win. He made the nation listen to the voices of his people.

Hank Johnson is an urban hero. He is a powerful brown-skinned man over six feet tall. His face is round and in it there is the humor of a small boy. Hank entered the building trades when he was twelve. He and his father were made to pay a Texas local of the AFL a fee for work permits higher than the regular union dues and were not allowed to attend union meetings. He is now a CIO organizer from the Chicago region and led in organizing the packing-house workers. "How can I defend America right or wrong?" he asks. "I am as good an American as *anybody*, but what would I do if I went down round my home in Austin, Texas, and reported some spies, but got myself lynched?" What Hank Johnson did to me is hard to convey. I have seen many of my friends frustrated in their effort to create themselves. They are boys full of protest and indignation who have no social outlet. They are unhappy working at jobs they hate, living under restrictions they hate. Hank Johnson was like one of them *transformed*. He is full of indignation, but indignation that has found a direction. When he spoke, all the violence that America has made our Negro heritage was flowing from him transformed into a will to change a civilization. The people said of him: "That Hank Johnson, he's *my* kinda Negro."

Whitfield and Johnson and the people behind them are the answer to those who wonder why there is such a scramble to raise the Booker T. Washington symbol anew in Negro life; why a bad documentary film of Tuskegee's Carver found distribution through RKO. A new pole of leadership has developed among the Negro people, and the National Negro Congress is their organization. It came suddenly out of the betrayal of the New Deal. First there was the highway demonstration of Missouri; then the defiance of the Klan in Florida, and later Ben Davis "got Dies told." All these things I felt in the process of crystallization at the Third National Negro Congress. I heard the resolution to join with the CIO and I listened, after Randolph had protested that such an agreement would make for controversy, to a delegate shout out from the floor: "Peonage, Anti-Lynch Bill, poll tax, these are our issues. They are the most controversial issues in American life, and some of us will have to die for them! Yes, we want to join with the CIO! We cannot stop for controversy!" And there in the faces of my people I saw strength. There with the whites in the audience I saw the positive forces of civilization and the best guarantee of America's future.

"TELL IT LIKE IT IS, BABY"

*M*ostly written in Rome in 1956 in response to a letter from Virgil Branam, Ellison's friend since boyhood in Oklahoma City, this essay was not finished until 1965. Angry at the "Southern Congressmen's defiance of the Supreme Court," Ellison struggles to articulate the connections he feels and dreams between the loss of his father and the Civil War, Abraham Lincoln, the Gettysburg Address, and his pursuit of eloquence as a writer. It was published in the hundredth-anniversary issue of The Nation, September 20, 1965.

Dear Uncle Raf:

. . . What are you doing over there in Rome with all those Italians? What do you think about over there? Are you keeping up with what's happening here at home? Have you read about those cracker senators cussing out the Supreme Court and all that mess? Let me hear what a home-boy done gone intellectual thinks when he's away from the Apple and all the righteous studs. . . . How's the writing going? Do you find it makes a difference being over there? Tell a man how it is. . . .

Virgil B., who wrote the above excerpt in 1956 after the Southern Congressmen had drawn up their manifesto against the Supreme Court, is a childhood friend who is now a cook and baker on merchant ships. Inevitably his letters contain a trace of mockery, directed at my odd metamorphosis into a writer, which is meant to remind me whence I come. Nor is he merely amused; he seriously expects insight and eloquence and a certain quality of attention to the reality experienced by our group—demands which, since that experience is often bafflingly complex, I am not always able to meet. After answering his letter, however, I was led to make an attempt at an essay which, perhaps because too many things were happening to me at the time, I was unable to complete. My wife and I were living the dormitory life of the American Academy in Rome and I was much preoccupied: with writing a novel, with literary concepts, with reviewing my own life's resources for literary creation; with the experience of discovering a foreign culture in which the old structures and guides that sustained my thoughts, emotions and conduct at home were so relaxed, whether awake or sleeping, that it was as though I was living in a barely controlled chaos.

So the essay failed. I simply could not organize the various elements—literary, political, psychological, personal—into the complex, meaningful whole which my sense of reality and my concern with fiction demanded. But I could not forget the essay, or at least not the dream which was its core; for in its way it seemed to symbolize my state of diffusion, my concerns, conscious and unconscious. Therefore the following attempt at salvage (made at the suggestion of the late David Boroff) represents, if nothing more, a further episode in my discovery that for me it was by no means a simple task to "tell it like it is"—even when the subject was desegregation and the Southern Congressmen's defiance of the Supreme Court. I was outraged and angered by the event, but the anger was not isolated or shallowly focused, rather it suffused my most non-political preoccupations. More unsettling, I discovered that there lay deeply within me a great deal of the horror generated by the Civil War and the tragic incident which marked the reversal of the North's "victory," and which foreshadowed the tenor of the ninety years to follow.

Since I attempted the essay, some nine years ago now, the power of the Southern Congressmen has been broken and the reconstruction of the South is once more under way. Nevertheless, the hooded horrors parading, murdering and shouting defiance in the South today suggest that the psychic forces with which I tried to deal (in both dream and essay) are still there to be dispersed or humanized; the individual white Southerner's task of reconciling himself to the new political reality remains. In retrospect, then, it was perhaps not too naïve after all to have tried to approach the problem consciously through the insights made available by the wisdom of tragedy. One thing is certain, the mind in sleep will have its way, and I *had* fallen asleep while reading Gilbert Murray's *The Classical Tradition in Poetry*, puzzling over how its insights might possibly be useful to a writer who is American, a Negro, and most eager to discover a more artful, more broadly significant approach to those centers of stress within our national life wherein he finds his task and being.

—*New York, June 1965*

Let me begin with a personal dream—for with what are we concerned, the moment we try to think about the problem of desegregation, but the clash between the American dream and everyday American reality; between the ideal of equality and the actuality of our society in which social, educational, and economic inequalities are enforced explicitly on the irremediable ground of race? And even in so practical and (until recently) so far removed an area as that of foreign policy, does not this clash, especially when we regard Asia and Africa, make for an atmosphere of dream-like irrationality?

Perhaps more to the point, when a Negro American novelist tries to write about desegregation he must regard, in all its tortuous ambiguity, the South. And here immediately he confronts three clusters of conflicting images: the myth-image propagated by orthodox White Southern spokesmen, by costume movies and popular novels of the Civil War; the image, almost completely negative, held by self-righteous white Northerners—and not a few Negroes—who have never known the South; and the more heavily qualified image (far more than a simple synthesis of the others) held by his black Southern relatives and their fellow Negroes. Among these images (none absolutely true or false) there is a great clashing, with the exponents of each set making scapegoats of the others: Northerners for Southerners, the South for the North, the black for the white and the white for the black, and when we try to find stable points of reality in this whirling nightmare of terms and attitudes, they change constantly into their opposites.

If we honestly say "Southerner," then we must, since most Negroes are *also* Southerners, immediately add *white* Southerner. If we say "white South" our recognition that the "white South" is far from solid compels us to specify *which* white South we mean. And so on for the North and for the Negro until even the word "democracy"—the ground-term of our concept of justice, the basis of our scheme of social rationality, the rock upon which our society was built—changes into its opposite, depending upon who is using it, upon his color, racial identity, the section of the country in which he happened to have been born, or where and with whom he happens to be at the moment of utterance. These circumstances have, for me at least, all of the elements of a social nightmare, a state of *civil* war, an impersonal and dreamlike chaos. To what then, and in his own terms, does a Negro writer turn when confronting such chaos—to politics, history, sociology, anthropology, art? War, it has been said, is a hellish state; so, too, is equivocation, that state (born of the Hayes-Tilden Compromise of 1877 and faintly illumined by the candle of liberty) in which we live. It is the candle alone which guides us through our chaos and when the candle flickers we're in the dark. And so in the Roman dark I dreamed.

It was a bright spring morning and I was walking along Classen Boulevard in Oklahoma City. Birds sang high in the trees that lined the walk and I could see the flash of wings and the quick, downward swoop ending in a nervous run along the walk, where, with alerted heads and flipping tails, they busily harvested a horde of catalpa worms. The worms were everywhere, the walk smeared green and white with their pulp and skin. But they were relentless. They kept dropping from the trees to the walk and moving over the curb and into the street in a steady wave, providing an ambulatory feast for the birds. Trying to avoid both worms and smears, I moved past the well-trimmed walks that led through handsome lawns to the distant houses, showing bright and gay with awnings. There were flowers too, and a clarinet running arpeggios in middle register, and the call of a huckster sounding hoarse-voiced in the limpid distance. I was filled with the expectation of some pleasantness, some long looked-for reward. Then it came over me that I was going to see my father.

I hurried now and almost immediately I saw in the distance under the high archway of worm-damaged leaves a tall, familiar man coming toward me. We were approaching an intersection, which he reached ahead of me, and stood looking steadily toward me and I felt a certain joy.

But then, as I drew closer, he was no longer familiar, but a stranger wearing a dull black and gray diamond-checked suit, his face narrow as he watched me out of small, staring eyes. I didn't know him at all, was even uncertain of his race. Standing quite still now, feeling a cold sensation along the ridge of my spine, I looked across the empty street, trying to interpret his accusatory look. We stared for a breathless time, then he turned away, retreating quickly beyond a privet hedge and out of sight, just as a mirror or window pane nearby sent the sun glaring into my eyes. It was odd.

I moved again, feeling now as though I had lost something precious. Who was this man, and what was the meaning of his staring accusation? What had I done—what had I failed to do? Had I been mistaken for someone else? But who?

The weather had changed and the city become strange. I was walking through an arcade lined with shops and on into an old street-car terminal covered with dirty glass through which the light filtered gloomily down. Passengers stood about in little groups, silently waiting for the long, yellow cars that came and went with a groaning and grinding, the motormen retracting and shifting the trolley poles with a great showering of sparks. An old man in a white apron and yellow paper cap was selling popcorn and peanuts from a stand topped by a whistle which sent forth a thin plume of steam each time a little mechanical clown, wearing a white, polka-dotted suit and peaked hat with a red pompon, turned the crank of a glass drum containing unshelled peanuts. The man smiled, holding out a paper cone of popcorn, gleaming with butter, as I moved past and out into a great public square, in the center of which I saw a tall, equestrian statue standing level with the second story of the surrounding buildings. The rider, poised in full gallop, stood high in the stirrups flourishing a broad military hat with plume. An expression of victory showed on his bronze face, despite the fact that his saber had lost three-fourths of its blade. Gazing upward past his head, I saw on the balcony of a building across the square the man who had stared; now, accompanied by a mysterious woman, he was looking toward me. They leaned forward, gripping the rail, staring at me intensely. Then a clock struck three with a mournful sound, followed by the creaking of cogs and pendulum—an ancient, dirty, cobwebbed sound. Then a flock of pigeons flew up, casting a shadow between us as they rustled the light with their wings and a voice spoke from a hidden loudspeaker.

"Is he the one?" it said.

"He's the one," a woman's voice answered, "truly."

"Is he the one? I say is he the *one!*"

"He's young, too young; he's not the one. It's been too long."

"Then he's the one," the male voice said. "Strength is not a requirement."

Then I became aware of a crowd standing behind me, before a building decorated with flags and bunting. It was quite hostile and I had the hot feeling that it was capable of almost anything. I moved away, aware that the crowd was following and feeling that somehow I had fallen from a high place, from a cliff or high protecting wall; and now I was running down a hill on which the tracks of a trolley line gleamed, and the air, suddenly breathless, was portentous.

I ran desperately, until, somehow, I was in a dark, colonial alley in Washington. And as I emerged into a crowded thoroughfare it was as though a book of nineteenth-century photographs had erupted into vivid life. The street was full of rubber-tired carriages—broughams, phaetons, landaus—and I could hear the creak-snap-jangle and thud of wall-eyed pacing horses. Gas lamps flickered the shadows with a chill white light, revealing a relentless crowd moving with sweating excitement, and as I moved out into the crush I became aware of the strangely sinister, high-frequency swishing of women's skirts. All around me people were rushing swiftly past to gather before a building from which, looking past their bobbing heads, I could see a sheet-covered form being removed on a litter.

It was a man, I could see now, his body having lost its covering as his litter-bearers jolted him roughly about. It was a tall man who seemed familiar: there was something about the way the disarranged sheet draped the toes of his shoes. Then it was now and yet another time, and I moved forward with a feeling of dread, thinking, "It's happening again."

We had said good-by and he had made me a present of the tiny pink and yellow wild flowers that had stood in the vase on the window sill, had put a blue cornflower in my lapel. Then a nurse and two attendants had wheeled in the table and put him on it. He was quite tall and I could see the pain in his face as they moved him. But when they got him covered his feet made little tents of the sheet and he made me a joke about it, just as he had many times before. He smiled then and said good-by once more, and I had watched, holding on to the cold white metal of the hospital bed as they wheeled him away. The white door closed quietly and I just stood there, looking at nothing at all. Nearby I could hear my mother talking quietly with the physician. He was explaining and she was asking questions. They didn't talk long, and when they finished we went out of the room for the last time. Holding on to my wrist as I clutched my flowers in my fist, my mother led me down the silent corridor heavy with the fumes of chloroform. She hurried me along. Ahead of us I saw a door swing ajar and watched it, but no one came out, then as we passed I looked inside to see him, lying in a great tub-like basin, waiting to be prepared for his last surgery. I could see his long legs, his knees propped up and his toes flexing as he rested there with his arms folded over his chest, looking at me quite calmly, like a kindly king in his bath. I had only a glimpse, then we were past. We had taken the elevator then and the nurse had allowed me to hold the control and she had laughed and talked with me as we went down to the street. Outside, as we moved along the winding drive into the blazing sun, I had told my mother but she wouldn't believe that I had seen him. I had though, and he had looked at me and smiled. It was the last time I saw my father alive. Years later, while telling me who he was and what he had been and what it meant to be his fatherless child, my mother had said that difficulties with money and the weather caused his body to be withheld from burial until it stank in the dark back room of the funeral parlor. Such was her respect for the naked reality of the human condition. . . . But what quality of love sustains us in our orphan's loneliness; and how much is thus required of fatherly love to give us strength for all our life thereafter? And what statistics, what lines on whose graphs can ever convince me that by his death I was fatally flawed and doomed—afraid of women, derelict of duty, sad in the sack, cold in the crotch, a rolling stone in social space, a spiritual delinquent, a hater of self— me in whose face his image shows? My mother loved him through all the years, cherished his memory until she died, apotheosized his vital years. For in effect he only perished, he did not pass away. His strength became my mother's strength and my brother and I the confused, sometimes bitter, but most often proud, recipients of their values and their love. . . .

But as I moved closer now it was Washington again and I could see the man's head snap suddenly back to reveal a short, carefully trimmed beard and I was confused, thinking: *But he didn't wear a beard.* As I pressed forward to get a better look, the crowd came between and I thought: *He's either drunk or sick—but why aren't they more careful?* Some were even laughing.

"What are they laughing at?" I asked a man going past.

"At our American cousin, fool."

"What? Whose—"

Then there came over me an inexpressible anguish, like a great weight suspended on a blunt hook driven through that part of my throat, the region of the thyroid gland, where grief and anguish collect, bearing down like doom.

For now, looking at the balustraded steps I recognized the building, and recognizing the building I knew the man; and knowing the man I wanted to cry, but could not cry. I wanted to scream, but could not scream. And suddenly the air resounded with the obscene melodramatics of the assassin's *"Sic semper tyrannis!"* and the night was filled with a great weeping and a great laughter.

And yet I was still unsure.

"What are they laughing at?" I said.

"Are you kidding, boy?" came the reply. "Face the facts!"

I knew now, even in the dream, that I had fallen out of time into chaos, and although the sight of the body filled me with horror, there was still room for personal embarrassment. And an embarrassment over the embarrassment—a chattering, degenerating echo of vanity before sad public events. For suddenly I discovered that I, whose grandparents were quite young at the time of Emancipation, had become a child again and was dressed in the one-piece garment of a young slave. I had no pants, nor shoes nor underwear; and when I tried in my dual shame to leave the street I was swept forward by the crowd, forced to follow after the litter which was now being moved along the street in what had suddenly become a funeral cortege. And now, though barefoot and quite young, I discovered that nevertheless I was literate, a slave who could read.

For as I was swept along, history-book descriptions of the event flickered through my mind in visual counterpoint and I kept trying to anticipate the route which the crowd would take through the dim and shadowed streets. But nothing was going as it was written. Instead of an escort of grieving high dignitaries, military men and weeping gentlewomen following a flag-draped camion, and with a crowd of weeping, recently freed slaves forming an anguished second line (perhaps the archetype of all such lines, joyful or sad, associated today with their descendants), the slain man, lanky and not yet cold, the complexion darker than I'd ever imagined, and with an ironic yet benign expression on the transcendent features, was being conveyed by a mob.

In a flash it became a carnival, an *Oktoberfest*, a Mardi Gras, with the corpse become the butt of obscene jokes. In the light of the hissing street lamps I saw a burly, bald-headed man waving his arms about, announcing in stentorian tones, "We've caught the old coon at last! Haven't we now!" Then as he broke into a fit of wheezing laughter the others responded, "COON! COON! COON! Hep-hep- Hep-john-step COON-COON!" And it quickly became a wild marching chant that filled me with a special terror. For hearing this epithet applied to the slain leader warned me that something terrible was about to occur, that some further support was to be torn from the foundation of that which I had thought was reality, from that which I held most sacred.

And how can I be me, if Old Abe be a "coon," I thought. *Yes, and how can I be a slave or even human?* And I looked down at my hands, fully prepared to see them turn into hairy paws.

Just then I saw a squat man with a toothbrush mustache shoot out of the crowd flashing a knife in the lamplight, yelling, "Make way! Make way!"

Please, not that, please not that! I thought, striking out about me as he bent low over the litter, the knife poised. Then I was spun around and when I looked again, he held a black piece of cloth, a wedge-shaped lapel, its lining gutted, yelling, "Hey! For my grandbaby boy, a souvenir for little Joey!" And this triggered the mob to a frenzy.

They rushed in to rip at the black coat with their fingers, they hacked it with pieces of broken bottle. One elegant man produced a straight-edged razor from the folds of his rich purple cravat and went to work distributing delicate bits of cloth among those unable to share directly in the dismemberment. Bits of cloth flittered down like blackened snow. And the coat swiftly disappearing, they went to work on his trousers.

Someone tugged off a homely gaiter. I saw several men and women, squawking like carrion crows, close in, fighting to take it away. A bent little old woman wearing a poke bonnet like that of the "Old Dutch Cleanser" woman grabbed the gaiter's mate and disappeared. Two small boys snatched off the socks, slashing them to shreds between them with nails astonishingly sharp.

They were insatiable. They ripped up the slain Lincoln's tie. His collar was seized, his white shirt ripped away, his vest torn to surreal tatters.

"Peace, Peace," a thin voice cried. "Remember the old buzzard's advice to its young: Hit a deadhead-horse in the eye and move straight up through his vastness. I say: Remember, Find the place, Strike!"

This enthusiastic *elegante* in Edwardian suit and with suave Eliotonian stoop was knocked aside by a rough-looking man who produced the President's stovepipe hat, and I saw him sail it curving through the air and into a second-story window—in which a wrathful woman promptly appeared and sailed it down again, dusting her hands indignantly as the high hat hovered above us like a battered Saturn with its radiant rings turned gray. A man grabbed it as it fell and, turning on his toes like a ballet dancer, jammed it on the head of a floozy, cotton-topped blonde, who wiggling wobbly a few steps, shook her head of cotton-candy hair to the crowd's applause. She wore a feather boa and a skin-tight satin dress, and flouncing about on unsteady legs she showed off a pair of monstrous, heavily powdered breasts which, as she stumbled and lurched on shoes with vicious heels, kept flipping out of her low-cut bodice and tossing about like two bloated, moon-mad, oxygen-starved flounders. For a fitful moment she caught the crowd's attention by cutting a clumsy cakewalk as she waved the hat and weaved, singing in a tinny little-lost-girl voice,

> *Come on boys*
> *And name your play*
> *We put the last clean shirt*
> *On Abe today . . . ,*

punctuated with a suggestion of bump and grind.

We moved again, the crowd growing with every step, the heat oppressive, the noise expanding in hysterical volume. Suddenly I noticed that the body was now being carried by four ragged Negro men who, kicked and pummeled as they stumbled along, held grimly to their burden, their stolid black faces disapproving.

"Get on. Get on!" the crowd cried. But hardly had they gone a dozen feet than they were beaten to a halt and rested the litter high on their shoulders while the crowd jeered at the slain President. He lay now in his underwear, his bony railsplitter's wrists hanging awkward and bare, his thin ankles sticking from the bottom of his underdrawers much as the rapidly growing Uncle Sam of the nineteenth-century cartoons had stuck from his outgrown heel-strapped britches.

"Stars, stripes and nigger minstrels!" someone called. "Now he's

Happy Hooligan!" At which, to the crowd's wild delight, a short, fat man wearing a long, gray coat, and who resembled Edmund Wilson, turned from drinking beer from a tin bucket and shook his head as with sudden revelation. Taking a final sip, he dashed the remains into the street and with an inspired, slow-mushrooming belch, jammed the "growler" on the Great Emancipator's head, clamping the wire handle beneath the bearded chin.

"Beautiful," someone said. "Beautiful!"

The applause was like the shattering of great sheets of glass. Whereupon the inspired fat man completed the Happy Hooligan transformation by pushing the stem of a corncob pipe between the once so eloquent lips, twisting the bowl so that its contents spilled upon the shrunken chest. Then a group of men labored up with a railway baggage wagon and the Negroes were forced to put the body upon it and then made to pull it through the cursing, flailing crowd.

"Push dat barge, boys!" a joker commanded in a thick foreign accent. "Push dat dar ole cotton-picking barge!"

I wanted to kill him along with all the callous crowd, but was too powerless *and* too fascinated, too held by horror and the anguished need to see it ended.

We were rushing through wide streets now, with broad lawns and stately buildings on either side. The ragged Negroes strained away, conveying now, beside the President, a number of women in tacky Sunday dresses, whose high-laced shoes dangled contentedly as they fluttered beside the body, joking and laughing and plying their little lace, mother-of-pearl-embellished fans. Then straight ahead I saw the Washington Monument, seeming to break through the floor of a barren plain like a periscope from the sea, rushing to meet us. Then we were there, at the base of the austere shaft, where the four Negroes were again beaten to a halt and made to lay their burden on the grass, then sent fleeing into the darkness. I tried to follow them, but was quickly restrained.

But why not me, I thought. *Why not me as well?* For I wished to join them in their forced detachment, I envied them their anonymity, their freedom to *not* participate. But my brown skin and slave's garment notwithstanding, I was held and forced to the front of the crowd.

I found myself standing near a tall, thin grandame who was laughing hysterically, screaming like a great tropical bird. Then she stopped and sniffed solemnly at a bottle of smelling salts, an expression of utmost complacency settling over her thin, aristocratic face, while the others joked, cursed, and made obscene remarks about the President until abruptly the composure of her face broke apart like the shattering of rock, and she laughed to put my teeth on edge. She bent double, then back, her stiff black garments snapping visibly with the motion and enveloping me in the rank fumes of female senility laced with threat and mystery.

Squeezing around her, and against an invisible hand that now seemed to hold me, I looked down at the lanky figure sprawled at the base of the marble shaft, thinking, *Now it's all over, they'll leave him alone, it's over.*

But not yet. I looked up to see a man wearing a voluminous opera cape, and who looked oddly like Mr. Justice Holmes, skipping slowly forward, decorous and tall, and with the toe of his elegant high-button shoe, flipping the corpse into a grotesque attitude. Then, throwing open his cape, he shouted, "Look at these! I say, *look at these!*" sticking a long finger through a series of bullet holes.

"Poor noble man!" they cried. "Poor betrayed innocent!"

"That dirty coon!"

"He did him wrong, the clod! He swindled him!"

"He wasted his land! He spoiled the cream! Get him!" This initiated a contest. Now they pushed one another about as they tried to see who could kick the corpse into the most fantastic positions, standing it on its head, doubling it over, twisting it in the cordwood postures of Dachau, shouting and cursing all the while.

"He's all to blame!"

"Give it to him good. There, there, how about that!"

"Yeah, but now you just watch this."

"That was a good one!"

"Look at ole Abe, he's dead but he won't lie down!"

"Watch it there, McDuffy, turn him over easy—but turn him!" I wanted to cry, my throat feeling as though it would burst apart, but no tears would flow to bring relief.

I closed my eyes as they knocked me about. And I now realized an odd thing. Up to this point, such is the contradiction of the dream, that I had not felt the President was actually dead. He isn't dead: I wouldn't have it so. It was a pitiful denial born of horror, a wish born of an anguished need to deny the hegemony of terrible fact—an attitude with which I had been familiar since childhood, when I had been bemused by a recurring fantasy in which, on my way to school of a late winter day I would emerge from a cold side street into the warm spring sun and there see my father, dead since I was three, rushing toward me with a smile of recognition and outstretched arms. And I would run proudly to greet him, his son grown tall. And then I could awake at last from the tortuous and extended dream that was my childhood with my father gone. So urgent had been my need for a sense of familial completeness, to have our family whole and happy as it had been until shortly before I saw him placed at last into the earth, that this thin fantasy had been made to serve for the man of flesh and blood, the man of the tales, the ghost stories, the gifts and strength and love. From the age of three to thirteen, the processes of time and the cold facts of death alike were—in this special area of my mind, for I *understood* death and was eager for change and for my own manhood's attainment—held off by this recurring daydream.

So I could not believe Mr. Lincoln dead. Thus, in the dislocated, is-and-isn't world of dream, I felt that the President bore his indignities out of a temporary weakness incurred by his wound or out of war weariness—even out of a saint-like patience, out of a hero's grace before the mob's wild human need. It was as though the noisy desecration of his body was being accepted as he had accepted the tragic duty of keeping the country unified even through an act of fratricidal war. Or as later it had been his task to seek reconciliation of the sundered parts. Yes, it was no less an act of duty than that of receiving the assassin's bullet in his brain. He is not dead, I told myself in the dream; he is not tolerating the mob's outrages out of the insensitivity of death, but submitting willingly to them out of the most sublime and tragic awareness of the requirements of his fated role. For we must take our heroes where we find them, and in all their wisdom and their guile, and in all their frustrating enigmas as in their bright lucidities.

For in him at least, there was a man who, having taken the oath, would do, and did, all that it was necessary for him to do, even before his own foreboding dream of obliteration.

But now in the suddenly accelerated tempo of the dream the corpse rebelled. I saw it grow rigid, then swell, transformed before my eyes into an advanced state of putrefaction. So inflated was the corpse becoming that soon the underwear resembled the series of inner tubes that form the body of the figure in the Michelin trademark. Death undeniable looked out at me, the sublime mocking its earthly shell.

"Now it is over," I thought. "At last they can see what they've done and I'll awaken."

But not even the ultimate protest of decomposing flesh could halt them. A man reached down and grasped the inflated underwear, trying to tear it away—and it was then that a sound like a fusillade of shots ripped the air and a dense cloud of gray, slime-drenched birds burst up from the earth on swift metallic wings and attacked the onlookers with feet of fire.

Screaming with pain, they burst apart like an exploding grenade, turning to claw at one another as they milled wildly about. And in the confusion I was pinned against the monument, burned by the flying slime. The four Negroes had returned now, and they stood silently, looking first at me and then down at Mr. Lincoln. They grasped with one hand the handles of a black box; in their free hands they carried gleaming spades. There was some cryptic exchange among them, then they looked at me, and now I was no longer a child. The scene became a scene on a movie screen, which I was watching from a distance and with a feeling of utmost clarity, as though I grasped the mystery of all experience. Then, just as suddenly, I was in the scene again, only now the mysterious Negroes were resting on their spades around a great hole. They motioned for me to look over the edge. Approaching fearfully, I looked down, seeing the crowd transported there, a multitude, some black faces among them, sitting at table making a ghoulish meal of some frightful thing that a white sheet hid from view. Then as I saw something stirring and expanding beneath the sheet, the earth seemed to crumble, plunging me screaming into a terrible wakefulness. . . .

I lay there in the hushed Roman night, aware of a nightingale singing somewhere beyond the venetian blinds, the lonely play of the fountain in the gravel-strewn *cortile* below. The air was breathlessly hot, yet I lay in a cold sweat, trying now, by way of exorcizing the dream, to recall some of Mr. Lincoln's eloquent words—grasping desperately for the Gettysburg Address. I had known it most of my life, had been moved by it even before its implications had become meaningful; had memorized its stately lines as a class assignment back in an old high school named Frederick Douglass; had studied it on my own in Sherwin Cody's little booklet on composition and rhetoric, where it was grouped with passages from Ecclesiastes and Benjamin Franklin; had pondered its themes of sectional reconciliation and national rebirth many times long since, as the awareness grew that there was little about it that was simple and that it was profoundly implicated both in my life and in the failure of my promised freedom.

But now, although I could feel the mood of its noble rhythms as physically as the pounding of my heart, the words had hidden themselves, become mute before the vivid mist of nightmare. I sat up abruptly, seeing the dim bars of moonlight seeping through the blinds as the rhythms called forth a swirl of imagery. Then scenes of

Charles Laughton performing the title role of the movie *Ruggles of Red Gap* suddenly reeled through my mind. Once more he was the much put-upon immigrant English butler, enduring the jibes and abuses of his *nouveau riche* American employers, whose vulgar "Gilded Age" materialism mocked all that is ideal in the American tradition. And once more, at the high point, he drew himself up proudly to recite the compassionate words uttered by Lincoln at Gettysburg, becoming in their measured flow transformed into a most resonant image of the American's post–Civil War imperative of conscience and consciousness achieved.

So here at last, in remembered art, the words of hope and recon-ciliation born of war and bloodshed rejoined the hallowed rhythms to dispel the nightmare images of the great man defiled. I was, though badly shaken, at last awakened.

Thank God it was only a dream! But as I became more fully awake it struck me that more dismaying than having such events erupt in one's dream life was that no living hero or surrogate had appeared to play Anthony to Lincoln's Caesar. Even the villains were less than individualized, the figure who looked like Mr. Justice Holmes only resembling him and the man in the long gray coat only *looking* like Mr. Edmund Wilson (but with no aura of scholarly eminence). And so the women. None struck me as mother-figures, neither the rump-sprung blonde, the poke-bonneted granny, nor the tall boom-and-bust figure in the stiff black dress—though I'm sure that some critic expert in the interior life of writers could write a fascinating essay on these ladies as three phases of the same personage—say: "The Woman as Earth-Mother, as Matron, and as Scold." Seriously, I could not ignore the fact that no one tried to stop the mob, nor that I myself was but a trapped and impotent observer—in fact, most in-fantile, my mind become an incongruous scene for historical horrors horribly personalized.

But enough, let me not pretend objectivity; my dream, being a dream, was absurd. For how else describe its mixture of obscene, his-torical and mythical elements? During the bright Roman day I had read my friend's questioning letter, and at night had fallen asleep reading Gilbert Murray's chapter on "Hamlet and Orestes," which here would seem to shed no light at all. Yet this immediately suggests, whatever its Freudian implications, a possible relationship between my dream and a pattern of classical tragedy: the hero-father murdered (for Lincoln *is* a kind of father of twentieth-century America), his life evilly sacrificed and the fruits of his neglected labors withering some ninety years in the fields; the state fallen into corruption, and the citizens into moral anarchy, with no hero come to set things right. Perhaps this is too far-fetched, but when living abroad one is compelled to look homeward through one's own inner eyes and through the objectives that lie at hand. Perhaps, therefore—any lens being better than no lens at all—the present optics provided by Murray's essay on tragedy will serve without too much distortion when we consider the possibility that the last true note of tragedy was sounded (and quickly muffled) in our land when the North buried Lincoln and the South buried Lee, and between them cast the better part, both of our tragic sense—except perhaps the Negroes'— and our capacity for tragic heroism into the grave. On the national scale, at least, this seems true. The sheet-covered figure in my dream might well have been General Robert E. Lee.

So I confess defeat; it is too complex for me to "tell it like it is." I can only suggest that here at least is how the Southern Congressmen's defiance of the Supreme Court joined with matters which bemused my writer's waking mind in Rome; this is how the incident "dreamed." For a writer who depends upon the imagination for his insights and his judgments, perhaps this is usually the way. Current events and events from the past, both personal and historical, ever collide within his interior life—either to be jumbled in the chaos of dream, or brought to ordered significance through the forms and techniques of his art. Following my defeat with the essay, I returned to my novel—which, by the way, has as its central incident the assassination of a Senator.

Rome, 1956
New York, 1965

SHADOW AND ACT

Published in 1964, Ellison's first book of essays contains an eclectic selection of essays, addresses, reviews, and interviews written from 1942 to 1964. Oklahoma, music and the vernacular, the mysterious inheritance of his name, his discovery of literature and emergence as a writer, the complexities of Negro identity, the contradictions of democracy: Ellison essays these themes in Shadow and Act as, with the continuing impact of Invisible Man, he becomes more and more consciously an American man of letters.

Introduction

WHEN the first of these essays was published I regarded myself—in my most secret heart at least—a musician. This was the result, in part, of a complicated, semiconscious strategy of self-deception, a refusal by my right hand to recognize where my left hand was headed. Actually I had been devoting as much time and energy to reading and writing as to music, and was passionately engaged, night and noon, in acquiring the basic knowledge and skills of the novelist. Thus the earliest, most agonizingly written pieces presented here (none has been retouched) were the results of a crucial conflict raging deep within me, the products of an activity, dreamlike yet intense, which was waxing on the dark side of my mind and assuming even then a major importance in shaping my life. In this sense, writing was an acting out, symbolically, of a choice which I dared not acknowledge. Indeed, I repressed it beneath my old concern with music and my current involvement in the intense social and political activity which claimed so many of us who came of age during the thirties.

One might say that with these thin essays for wings I was launched full flight into the dark.

At stake here, beyond the veil of consciousness, was the question of what seemed possible for me in terms of self-achievement, and linked to this was the question of what was the most desirable agency for defining myself. Writing provided me a growing satisfaction and required, unlike music, no formal study—but the designation "writer" seemed to me most unreal. Not only this, for despite the naïveté of my involvement with literature—and ignoring the crucial question of talent—my standards were impossibly high. Therefore, the chances of my producing anything of quality seemed nonexistent. Besides, I still believed that my real self was destined to be fulfilled in music, that art which had focused my ambitions from the age of eight and the only art, given my background, that seemed to offer some possibility for self-definition. Obviously I was still quite young and, fortunately, still given to play and adventure.

For in the beginning writing was far from a serious matter; it was playing with the secret lore of a fascinating but less glorious art to which I owed, I believed, no prior dedication. (It would be many years before I was to learn of my father's hope that I would become a poet.) Nor had I invested in writing any long hours of practice and study. Rather it was a reflex of reading, an extension of a source of pleasure, escape and instruction. In fact, I had become curious about writing by way of seeking to understand the aesthetic nature of literary power, the devices through which literature could command my mind and emotions. It was not, then, the *process* of writing which initially claimed my attention, but the finished creations, the artifacts—poems, plays, novels. The act of learning writing technique was, therefore, an amusing investigation of what seemed at best a secondary talent, an exploration, like dabbling in sculpture, of one's potentialities as a "Renaissance man." This, surely, would seem a most unlikely and even comic concept to introduce here, and yet it is precisely because I come from where I do (the Oklahoma of the years between World War I and the Great Depression) that I must introduce it, and with a straight face.

Anything and everything was to be found in the chaos of Oklahoma; thus the concept of the Renaissance man has lurked long within the shadow of my past, and I shared it with at least a half dozen of my Negro friends. How we actually acquired it I have never learned, and since there is no true sociology of the dispersion of ideas within the American democracy, I doubt if I ever shall. Perhaps we breathed it in with the air of the Negro community of Oklahoma City, the capital of that state whose Negroes were often charged by exasperated white Texans with "not knowing their place." Perhaps we took it defiantly from one of them. Or perhaps I myself picked it up from some transplanted New Englander whose shoes I had shined of a Saturday afternoon. After all, the most meaningful tips do not always come in the form of money, nor are they intentionally extended. Most likely, however, my friends and I acquired the idea from some book or from some idealistic Negro teacher, some dreamer seeking to function responsibly in an environment which at its most normal took on some of the mixed character of nightmare and of dream.

One thing is certain; ours was a chaotic community, still characterized by frontier attitudes and by that strange mixture of the naïve and sophisticated, the benign and malignant, which makes the American past so puzzling and its present so confusing; that mixture which often affords the minds of the young who grow up in the far provinces such wide and unstructured latitude, and which encourages the individual's imagination—up to the moment "reality" closes in upon him—to range widely and sometimes even to soar.

We hear the effects of this in the southwestern jazz of the thirties, that joint creation of artistically free and exuberantly creative adventurers, of artists who had stumbled upon the freedom lying within the restrictions of their musical tradition as within the limitations of their social background, and who in their own unconscious way have set an example for any Americans, Negro or white, who would find themselves in the arts. They accepted themselves and the complexity of life as they knew it; they loved their art and through it they celebrated American experience definitively in sound. Whatever others thought or felt, this was their own powerful statement, and only nonmusical assaults upon their artistic integrity—mainly economically inspired changes of fashion—were able to compromise their vision.

Several of the essays deal with jazz, and it is perhaps pardonable if I recall that much of so-called Kansas City jazz was actually brought to perfection in Oklahoma by Oklahomans. It is an important circumstance for me as a writer to remember, because while these musicians and their fellows were busy creating out of tradition, imagination and the sounds and emotions around them a freer, more complex and driving form of jazz, my friends and I were exploring an idea of human versatility and possibility which went against the barbs or over the palings of almost every fence which those who controlled social and political power had erected to restrict our roles in the life of the country. Looking back, one might say that the jazzmen, some of whom we idolized, were in their own way better examples for youth to follow than were most judges and ministers, legislators and governors (we were stuck with the notorious Alfalfa Bill Murray). For as we viewed these pillars of society from the confines of our segregated community we almost always saw crooks, clowns or hypocrites. Even the best were revealed by their attitudes toward us as lacking the respectable qualities to which they pretended and for which they were accepted outside by others, while despite the outlaw nature of their art, the jazzmen were less torn and damaged by the moral compromises and insincerities which have so sickened the life of our country.

Be that as it may, our youthful sense of life, like that of many Negro children (though no one bothers to note it—especially the specialists and "friends of the Negro" who view our Negro American life as essentially nonhuman) was very much like that of Huckleberry Finn, who is universally so praised and enjoyed for the clarity and courage of his moral vision. Like Huck, we observed, we judged, we imitated and evaded as we could the dullness, corruption and blindness of "civilization." We were undoubtedly comic because, as the saying goes, we weren't supposed to know what it was all about. But to ourselves we were "boys," members of a wild, free, outlaw tribe which transcended the category of race. Rather we were Americans born into the forty-sixth state, and thus, into the context of Negro-American post–Civil War history, "frontiersmen." And isn't one of the implicit functions of the American frontier to encourage the individual to a kind of dreamy wakefulness, a state in which he makes—in all ignorance of the accepted limitations of the possible—rash efforts, quixotic gestures, hopeful testings of the complexity of the known and the given?

Spurring us on in our controlled and benign madness was the voracious reading of which most of us were guilty, and the vicarious identification and empathic adventuring which it encouraged. This was due, in part, perhaps to the fact that some of us were fatherless— my own father had died when I was three—but most likely it was because boys are natural romantics. We were seeking examples, patterns to live by, out of a freedom which for all its neglect by the sociologists and subtle thinkers was implicit in the Negro situation. Father and mother substitutes also have a role to play in aiding the child to help create himself. Thus we fabricated our own heroes and ideals catch-as-catch-can, and with an outrageous and irreverent sense of freedom. Yes, and in complete disregard for ideas of respectability or the surreal incongruity of some of our projections. Gamblers and scholars, jazz musicians and scientists, Negro cowboys and soldiers from the Spanish-American and first world wars, movie stars and stunt men, figures from the Italian Renaissance and literature, both classical and popular, were combined with the special virtues of some local bootlegger, the eloquence of some Negro preacher, the strength and grace of some local athlete, the ruthlessness of some businessman-physician, the elegance in dress and manners of some headwaiter or hotel doorman.

Looking back through the shadows upon this absurd activity, I realize now that we were projecting archetypes, re-creating folk figures, legendary heroes, monsters even, most of which violated all ideas of social hierarchy and order and all accepted conceptions of the hero handed down by cultural, religious and racist tradition. But we, remember, were under the intense spell of the early movies, the silents as well as the talkies, and in our community, life was not so tightly structured as it would have been in the traditional South—or even in deceptively "free" Harlem. And our imaginations processed reality and dream, natural man and traditional hero, literature and folklore, like maniacal editors turned loose in some frantic film-cutting room. Remember, too, that being boys, yet in the play stage of our development, we were dream-serious in our efforts. But serious, nevertheless, for *culturally* play is a preparation, and we felt that somehow the human ideal lay in the vague and constantly shifting figures—sometimes comic but always versatile, picaresque and self-effacingly heroic—which evolved from our wildly improvisionary projections, figures neither white nor black, Christian nor Jewish, but representative of certain desirable essences, of skills and powers physical, aesthetic and moral.

The proper response to these figures was, we felt, to develop ourselves for the performance of many and diverse roles, and the fact that certain definite limitations had been imposed upon our freedom did not lessen our sense of obligation. Not only were we to prepare but we were to perform—not with mere competence but with an almost reckless verve, with, may we say (without evoking the quaint and questionable notion of *negritude*), Negro American style? Behind each artist there stands a traditional sense of style, a sense of the felt tension indicative of expressive completeness, a mode of humanizing reality and of evoking a feeling of being at home in the world. It is something which the artist shares with the group, and part of our boyish activity expressed a yearning to make any- and everything of quality *Negro American*—to appropriate it, possess it, re-create it in our own group and individual images.

And we recognized and were proud of our group's own style wherever we discerned it—in jazzmen and prize fighters, ballplayers and tap dancers; in gesture, inflection, intonation, timbre and phrasing. Indeed, in all those nuances of expression and attitude which reveal a culture. We did not fully understand the cost of that style but we recognized within it an affirmation of life beyond all question of our difficulties as Negroes.

Contrary to the notion currently projected by certain specialists in the "Negro problem" which characterizes the Negro American as self-hating and defensive, we did not so regard ourselves. We felt, among ourselves at least, that we were supposed to be whoever we would and could be, and do anything and everything which other boys did, and do it better. Not defensively, because we were ordered to do so, nor because it was held in the society at large that we were naturally, as Negroes, limited—but because we demanded it of ourselves. Because to measure up to our own standards was the only way of affirming our notion of manhood.

Hence it was no more incongruous, as seen from our own particular perspective in this land of incongruities, for young Negro Oklahomans to project themselves as Renaissance men than for white Mississippians to see themselves as ancient Greeks or noblemen out of Sir Walter Scott. Surely our fantasies have caused far less damage to the nation's sense of reality, if for no other reason than that ours were expressive of a more democratic ideal. Remember, too, as William Faulkner made us so vividly aware, that the slaves often took the essence of the aristocratic ideal (as they took Christianity) with far more seriousness than their masters, and that we, thanks to the tight telescoping of American history, were but two generations from that previous condition. Renaissance men, indeed!

I managed, by keeping quiet about it, to cling to our boyish ideal during three years in Alabama, and I brought it with me to New York, where it not only gave silent support to my explorations of what was then an unknown territory, but served to mock and caution me when I became interested in the Communist ideal. And when it was suggested that I try my hand at writing, it was still with me; thus I went about writing rashly unaware that my ambitions as a composer had been fatally diverted.

Once involved, however, I soon became consciously concerned with craft, with technique. And through my discipline of consciousness acquired from the study of music theory I was gradually led, often reluctantly, to become consciously concerned with the nature of the culture and the society out of which American fiction is fabricated. The pieces collected here are one of the results, and their basic significance, whatever their value as information or speculation, is autobiographical.

They are concerned with three general themes: with literature and folklore, with Negro musical expression—especially jazz and the blues—and with the complex relationship between the Negro American subculture and North American culture as a whole. Most are occasional pieces, written for magazines whose editors provided opportunities for me to reduce my thinking—indeed, often to discover what I *did* think—to publishable form. Nevertheless, they are a byproduct of that effort, basic to the fiction-writer's confrontation of the world, of converting experience into symbolic action. Good fiction is made of that which is real, and reality is difficult to come by. So much of it depends upon the individual's willingness to discover his true self, upon his defining himself—for the time being at least—against his background.

Thus these essays represent, in all their modesty, some of the necessary effort which a writer of my background must make in order to possess the meaning of his experience. They are an attempt to transform some of the themes, the problems, the enigmas, the contradictions of character and culture native to my predicament, into what André Malraux has described as "conscious thought." For me some such effort was necessary before I could discover the true subject matter of my fiction, before I could identify the areas of life and personality which claimed my mind beyond any limitations *apparently* imposed by my racial identity.

The act of writing requires a constant plunging back into the shadow of the past where time hovers ghostlike. When I began writing in earnest I was forced to relate myself consciously and imaginatively to my mixed background as American, as Negro American, and as a Negro from what in its own belated way was a pioneer background. More important, and inseparable from this particular effort, was the necessity of determining my true relationship to that body of American literature to which I was most attracted and through which, aided by what I could learn from the literatures of Europe, I would find my own voice, and to which I was challenged, by way of achieving myself, to make some small contribution, and to whose composite picture of reality I was obligated to offer some necessary modifications.

This was no matter of sudden insight, but of slow and blundering discovery, of a struggle to stare down the deadly and hypnotic temptation to interpret the world and all its devices in terms of race. To avoid this was very important to me, and in light of my background far from simple. Indeed, it was quite complex, involving as it does a ceaseless questioning of those formulas through which historians, politicians, sociologists, and an older generation of Negro leaders and writers—those of the so-called "Negro Renaissance"—had evolved to describe my group's identity, its predicament, its fate and its relation to the larger society and the culture which we share.

Here the questions of reality and personal identity merge. Yes, and the question of the nature of the reality which underlies American fiction and thus the human truth which gives fiction viability. In this quest, for such it soon became, I learned that nothing could go unchallenged, especially that feverish industry dedicated to telling Negroes who and what they are, and which can usually be counted upon to deprive both humanity and culture of their complexity. I had undergone, not too many months before taking the path which led to writing, the humiliation of being taught in a class in sociology at a Negro college (from Park and Burgess, the leading textbook in the field) that Negroes represented the "lady of the races." This contention the Negro instructor passed blandly along to us without even bothering to wash his hands, much less his teeth. Well, I had no intention of being bound by any such humiliating definition of my relationship to American literature. Not even to those works which depicted Negroes negatively. Negro Americans have a highly developed ability to abstract desirable qualities from those around them, even from their enemies, and my sense of reality could reject bias while appreciating the truth revealed by achieved art. The pleasure which I derived from reading had long been a necessity, and in the *act* of reading, that marvelous collaboration between the writer's artful vision and the reader's sense of life, I had become acquainted with other possible selves—freer, more courageous and ingenuous and, during the course of the narrative, at least, even wise.

At the time I was under the influence of Ernest Hemingway, and his description, in *Death in the Afternoon*, of his thinking when he first went to Spain became very important as translated in my own naïve fashion. He was trying to write, he tells us . . .

> and found the greatest difficulty aside from knowing truly what you really felt, rather than what you were supposed to feel, and had been taught to feel, was to put down what really happened in action; what the actual things were which produced the emotion that you experienced . . .

His statement of moral and aesthetic purpose which followed focused my own search to relate myself to American life through literature. For I found the greatest difficulty for a Negro writer was the problem of revealing what he truly felt, rather than serving up what Negroes were supposed to feel, and were encouraged to feel. And linked to this was the difficulty, based upon our long habit of deception and evasion, of depicting what really happened within our areas of American life, and putting down with honesty and without bowing to ideological expediencies the attitudes and values which give Negro American life its sense of wholeness, and which render it bearable and human and, when measured by our own terms, desirable.

I was forced to this awareness through my struggles with the craft of fiction; yes, and by my attraction (soon rejected) to Marxist political theory, which was my response to the inferior status which society sought to impose upon me (I did not then, now, or ever *consider* myself inferior). I did not know my true relationship to America—what citizen of the United States really does?—but I did know and accept how I felt inside. And I also knew, thanks to the old Renaissance man, what I expected of myself in the matter of personal discipline and creative quality. Since, by the grace of the past and the examples of manhood picked willy-nilly from the continuing-present of my background, I rejected all negative definitions imposed upon me by others, there was nothing to do but search for those relationships which were fundamental.

In this sense fiction became the agency of my efforts to answer the questions: Who am I, what am I, how did I come to be? What shall I make of the life around me, what celebrate, what reject, how confront the snarl of good and evil which is inevitable? What does American society *mean* when regarded out of my *own* eyes, when informed by my *own* sense of the past and viewed by my *own* complex sense of the present? How, in other words, should I think of myself and my pluralistic sense of the world, how express my vision of the human predicament, without reducing it to a point which would render it sterile before that necessary and tragic—though enhancing—reduction which must occur before the fictive vision can come alive? It is quite possible that much potential fiction by Negro Americans fails precisely at this point: through the writers' refusal (often through provincialism or lack of courage or opportunism) to achieve a vision of life and a resourcefulness of craft commensurate with the complexity of their actual situation. Too often they fear to leave the uneasy sanctuary of race to take their chances in the world of art.

Be that as it may, these essays are a witness of that which I have known and that which I have tried and am still trying to confront. They mark a change of role, a course, and a slow precarious growth of consciousness. They were written in New York and in Rome, and the last were composed during my time as Writer-in-Residence at Rutgers University. The very least I can say about their value is that they performed the grateful function of making it unnecessary to clutter up my fiction with half-formed or outrageously wrongheaded ideas. At best they are an embodiment of a conscious attempt to confront, to peer into, the shadow of my past and to remind myself of the complex resources for imaginative creation which are my heritage. Consciousness and conscience are burdens imposed upon us by the American experiment. They are the American's agony, but when he tries to live up to their stern demands they become his justification. What more is there to say? What more need be said? Beyond expressing my thanks to those publishers, editors and magazines which granted me an audience.

. . .

Over the years many people have encouraged me in my writing, by example, by confidence in my talent, and by helpful criticism. Indeed, there are far too many, considering that the essays collected here go back almost to the beginning of my writing, to be mentioned. Nevertheless, I wish to acknowledge my special indebtedness to Stanley Edgar Hyman, with whom I've shared a community of ideas and critical standards for two decades, and to Kenneth Burke, the stimulating source of many of these; to Albert L. Murray, who has insisted upon the importance of the overall point of view developed here since we were students at Tuskegee Institute, and whose memory, files and criticism have been invaluable; to Jimmy Rushing, who through his friendship and through our many hour-long telephone conversations has helped to keep my sense of my Oklahoma background—especially the jazz—so vividly alive; to Irving Kolodin, at whose requests most of the essays on music came to be written; and to Albert R. Erskine and James H. Silberman of Random House, without whom this book would be most formless indeed. Finally, there has been the help of my beloved wife, Fanny McConnell, who has shown, again and again, through her sacrifices, encouragement and love, more faith in the writer and his talent than the writer has shown in himself.

May, 1964

I

THE SEER AND THE SEEN

That Same Pain,
That Same Pleasure:

An Interview

RICHARD G. STERN: Last night we were talking about the way in which your literary situation has been special, the way in which you as a Negro writer have vaulted the parochial limitations of most Negro fiction. Accepting this, not debating it, would you want to talk a bit about the sources of the strength by which you escaped them?

RALPH ELLISON: Well, to the extent that one cannot ever escape what is given, I suppose it had less to do with writing per se than with my desire, beginning at a very early age, to be more fully a part of that larger world which surrounded the Negro world into which I was born. It was a matter of attitude. Then there were the accidents through which so much of that world beyond the Negro community became available to me. Ironically, I would have to start with some of the features of American life which it has become quite fashionable to criticize in a most unthinking way: the mass media. Like so many kids of the twenties, I played around with radio—building crystal sets and circuits consisting of a few tubes, which I found published in the radio magazines. At the time we were living in a white middle-class neighborhood, where my mother was custodian for some apartments, and it was while searching the trash for cylindrical ice-cream cartons which were used by amateurs for winding tuning coils that I met a white boy who was looking for the same thing. I gave him some of those I'd found and we became friends. Oddly enough, I don't remember his family name even though his father was pastor

From *December*, Winter 1961.

of the leading Episcopal church in Oklahoma City at that time, but his nickname was Hoolie, and for kids of eight or nine that was enough.* Due to a rheumatic heart Hoolie was tutored at home and spent a great deal of time playing by himself and in taking his parents' elaborate radio apart and putting it back together again, and in building circuits of his own. For all of his delicate health, he was a very intelligent and very alive boy. It didn't take much encouragement from his mother, who was glad to have someone around to keep him company, for me to spend much of my free time helping with his experiments. By the time I left the community, he had become interested in short-wave communication and was applying for a ham license. I moved back into the Negro community and began to concentrate on music, and was never to see him again, but knowing this white boy was a very meaningful experience. It had little to do with the race question as such, but with our mutual loneliness (I had no other playmates in that community) and a great curiosity about the growing science of radio. It was important for me to know a boy who could approach the intricacies of electronics with such daring and whose mind was intellectually aggressive. Knowing him led me to expect much more of myself and of the world.

The other accident from that period lay in my mother's bringing home copies of such magazines as *Vanity Fair* and of opera recordings which had been discarded by a family for whom she worked. You might say that my environment was extended by these slender threads into the worlds of white families whom personally I knew not at all. These magazines and recordings and the discarded books my mother brought home to my brother and me spoke to me of a life

---

*Thanks to the Reverend Kenneth R. Coleman, Chaplain of the Episcopal Church at Yale University, to whom (in 1963) I related the circumstances of this old friendship, I was put in touch with the Reverend R. A. Laud Humphreys, Historiographer of the Episcopal Diocese of Oklahoma, who in turn kindly interested himself in the mystery of my childhood friend. Thus I now know not only that "Hoolie" is the son of the Reverend Franklin Davis and Mrs. Davis, but that his real name is Henry Bowman Otto Davis. He is now an electronics expert connected with the Air Force.

which was broader and more interesting, and although it was not really a part of my own life, I never thought they were not for me simply because I happened to be a Negro. They were things which spoke of a world which I could some day make my own.

STERN: Were you conscious at this time of peculiar limitations upon your freedom of action, perhaps even your freedom of feeling?

ELLISON: Well, now, remember that this was in Oklahoma, which is a border state, and as the forty-sixth state was one of the last of our territories to achieve statehood. Although opened to American settlers in 1889, at the time of my birth it had been a state only seven years. Thus it had no tradition of slavery, and while it was segregated, relationships between the races were more fluid and thus more human than in the old slave states. My parents, like most of the other Negroes, had come to the new state looking for a broader freedom and had never stopped pushing against the barriers. Having arrived at the same time that most of the whites had, they felt that the restriction of Negro freedom was imposed unjustly through the force of numbers and that they had the right and obligation to fight against it. This was all to the good. It made for a tradition of aggressiveness and it gave us a group social goal which was not as limited as that imposed by the old slave states. I recognized limitations, yes, but I thought these limitations were unjust and I felt no innate sense of inferiority which would keep me from getting those things I desired out of life. There were those who stood in the way but you just had to keep moving toward whatever you wanted.

As a kid I remember working it out this way: there was a world in which you wore your everyday clothes on Sunday, and there was a world in which you wore your Sunday clothes every day. I wanted the world in which you wore your Sunday clothes every day. I wanted it because it represented something better, a more exciting and civilized and human way of living, a world which came to me through certain scenes of felicity which I encountered in fiction, in the movies, and which I glimpsed sometimes through the windows of great houses on Sunday afternoons when my mother took my brother and me for walks through the wealthy white sections of the city. I know it now for a boy's vague dream of possibility. Hoolie was part of it, and shop-window displays of elegant clothing, furniture, automobiles—those Lincolns and Marmons!—and of course music and books. And for me none of this was hopelessly beyond the reach of my Negro world, really, because if you worked and you fought for your rights, and so on, you could finally achieve it. This involved our American Negro faith in education, of course, and the idea of self-cultivation, although I couldn't have put it that way back during the days when the idea first seized me. Interestingly enough, by early adolescence the idea of Renaissance man had drifted down to about six of us, and we discussed mastering ourselves and everything in sight as though no such thing as racial discrimination existed. As you can see, quite a lot of our living was done in the imagination.

STERN: At one part of your life you became conscious that there was something precious in being a Negro in this country at this time. Can you remember when you discovered this?

ELLISON: Well, part of it came from the affirmation of those things in the Negro environment which I found warm and meaningful. For instance, I had none of the agricultural experience of my mother, who had grown up on a farm in Georgia, and although in twenty minutes you could move from Oklahoma City into deep farm country, I shared none of the agricultural experience of many of my class-mates. I was of the city, you see. But during the fall cotton-picking season certain kids left school and went with their parents to work in the cotton fields. Now, most parents wished their children to have no contact with the cotton patch; it was part of an experience which they wanted to put behind them. It was part of the Old South which they had come west to forget. Just the same, those trips to the cotton patch seemed to me an enviable experience because the kids came back with such wonderful stories. And it wasn't the hard work which they stressed, but the communion, the playing, the eating, the dancing and the singing. And they brought back jokes, *our* Negro jokes—not those told about Negroes by whites—and they always returned with Negro folk stories which I'd never heard before and which couldn't be found in any books I knew about. This was something to affirm and I felt there was a richness in it. I didn't think too much about it, but what my schoolmates shared in the country and what I felt in their accounts of it, seemed much more real than the Negro middle-class values which were taught in school.

Or again: I grew up in a school in which music was emphasized and where we were taught harmony from the ninth through the twelfth grades, and where much time was given to music appreciation and the study of the shorter classical forms, but where jazz was considered disreputable. Of course, this is part of the story of jazz even today. So much of the modern experimentation in jazz springs—as far as Negro jazz modernists are concerned—from a misplaced shame over the so-called low-class origins of jazz. These are usually men of Negro middle-class background who have some formal training in music and who would like for jazz to be a "respectable" form of expression tied up with other forms of revolt. They'd like to dry up the deep, rowdy stream of jazz until it becomes a very thin trickle of respectable sound indeed. Be that as it may, despite my teachers, the preachers and other leaders of the community, I was with those who found jazz attractive, an important part of life. I hung around the old Blue Devils Orchestra out of which the famous Basie band was formed. I knew these people and admired them. I knew Jimmy Rushing, the blues singer, who then was not quite the hero of the middle-class people whom I knew that he is today after years of popular success. But for us, even when he was a very young man, a singer who came home to the city once in a while, Jimmy represented, gave voice to, something which was very affirming of Negro life, feelings which you couldn't really put into words. Of course, beyond jazz there was all the boasting, the bragging that went on when no one but ourselves was supposed to be listening, when you weren't really being judged by the white world. At least when you *thought* you weren't being judged and didn't care if you were. For instance, there is no place like a Negro barbershop for hearing what Negroes really think. There is more unselfconscious affirmation to be found there on a Saturday than you can find in a Negro college in a month, or so it seems to me.

Getting back to your question, I suppose my attitude toward these elements of Negro life became a discipline toward affirming that which felt desirable to me over and beyond anything which we were taught in school. It was more a matter of the heart than of the mind.

STERN: You found something precious, special, and associated it with jazz. Now, between finding that jazz was a vehicle for special qualities which you admired in Negroes and finding that literature was a vehicle, you yourself wanted to employ—

ELLISON: I wanted to be a composer but not a jazz composer, interestingly enough. I wanted to be a symphonist.

STERN: How about that, then?

ELLISON: Well, I had always listened to music, and as far back as I can remember I had the desire to create. I can't remember when I first wanted to play jazz or to create classical music. I can't remember a time when I didn't want to make something, whether it was a small one-tube radio or a crystal set, or my own toys. This was a part of the neighborhood where I spent most of my childhood. There were a number of us who were that way.

STERN: Did your desire to be a symphony composer rather than a jazz instrumentalist stand for a sort of denial of your own cultural situation as a Negro?

ELLISON: No, no. You see, what is often misunderstood nowadays is that there wasn't always this division between the ambitions of jazz musicians and the standards of classical music; the idea was to master both traditions. In school the classics were pushed at us on all sides, and if you danced, if you shared any of the social life of the young people, jazz was inescapable; it was all around you. And if you were a *musician* you were challenged by its sounds and by the techniques required to produce them. In fact, we admired such jazzmen as the late bassist Walter Page and the trumpeter Icky Lawrence over all other local musicians because although they usually played in jazz bands, they could go into any theater pit and play the scores placed before them. They played the arrangements for the silent movies at sight, and we found this very impressive. Such men as Lawrence and Page—and there were several others—had conservatory training as well as a rich jazz experience and thus felt no need to draw a line between the two traditions. Following them, our ideal was to master both. It wasn't a matter of wanting to do the classics because they denied or were felt to deny jazz, and I suppose my own desire to write symphonies grew out of an attraction to the bigger forms and my awareness that they moved many people as they did me in a different way. The range of mood was much broader.

STERN: Can you describe the difference in your own feelings about the two forms?

ELLISON: I can try, but since I shall be trying to recall emotions having to do with the non-verbal medium of music, and at a time when I was a very young and inarticulate boy, I can only give you vague impressions. You see, jazz was so much a part of our total way of life that it got not only into our attempts at playing classical music but into forms of activities usually not associated with it: into marching and into football games, where it has since become a familiar fixture. A lot has been written about the role of jazz in a certain type of Negro funeral marching, but in Oklahoma City it got into military drill. There were many Negro veterans from the Spanish-American War who delighted in teaching the younger boys complicated drill patterns, and on hot summer evenings we spent hours on the Bryant School grounds (now covered with oil wells) learning to execute the commands barked at us by our enthusiastic drillmasters. And as we mastered the patterns, the jazz feeling would come into it and no one was satisfied until we were swinging. These men who taught us had raised a military discipline to the level of a low art form, almost a dance, and its spirit was jazz.

On the other hand, I became a member of the school band while in the eighth grade, and we played military music, the classical marches, arrangements of symphonic music, overtures, snatches of opera, and so on, and we sang classical sacred music and the Negro spirituals. So all this was a part of it, and not only did we have classes in music appreciation right through school, but on May Day we filled the Western League Ball Park, wrapping maypoles and dancing European folk dances. You really should see a field of little Negro kids dancing an Irish jig or a Scottish fling. There must have been something incongruous about it for the few whites who came to see us, but there we were, and for us the dance was the thing. Culturally everything was mixed, you see, and beyond all question of conscious choices there was a level where you were claimed by emotion and movement and moods which you couldn't put into words. Often we wanted to share both: the classics and jazz, the Charleston and the Irish reel, spirituals and the blues, the sacred and the profane. I remember the breakfast dances, the matinée dances along with the tent meetings, and the more formal Afro-Methodist Episcopal Christmas services which took place in our church; they all had their special quality. During adolescence I remember attending sunrise services, which took place before Christmas morning. It was a very sacred service, but I remember my mother permitting me to leave after the services were over to attend a breakfast dance. She didn't attend dances herself and was quite pious by that time, but there was no necessary clash between these quite different celebrations of Christmas, and for me the two forms added quite a bit to my sense of the unity of the life I lived. Just the same, there were certain yearnings which I felt, certain emotions, certain needs for other forms of transcendence and identification which I could only associate with classical music. I heard it in Beethoven, I heard it in Schumann. I used to hear it in Wagner—he is really a young man's composer;

especially a young bandsman with plenty of brass. I was always a trumpeter, so I was always listening for those composers who made the most use, the loudest use, of the brass choir. Seriously, though, you got glimpses, very vague glimpses, of a far different world than that assigned by segregation laws, and I was taken very early with a passion to link together all I loved within the Negro community and all those things I felt in the world which lay beyond.

STERN: So pretty early you had a sense of being part of a larger social or cultural complex?

ELLISON: Put it this way: I learned very early that in the realm of the imagination all people and their ambitions and interests could meet. This was inescapable, given my reading and my daydreaming. But this notion, this vague awareness, was helped along by the people I came to know. On the level of race relations, my father had many white friends who came to the house when I was quite small, so that any feelings of distrust I was to develop toward whites later on were modified by those with whom I had warm relations. Oklahoma offered many opportunities for such friendships. I remember also an English actress named Emma Bunting—I wonder what happened to her? Anyway, when I was a child, Emma Bunting used to bring over a repertory company each summer, and when she performed in Oklahoma City, her maid, a very handsome Negro woman named Miss Clark, used to stay with us. There was no segregation in the downtown theatres during that period—although it came later—and my mother went frequently to plays and was very proud of a lace bag which Emma Bunting had given her. You see, there is always some connection. Miss Clark brought not only the theater into our house but England as well. I guess it's the breaks in the pattern of segregation which count, the accidents. When I reached high school I knew Dr. Ludwig Hebestreit, a conductor who formed the nucleus of what became the Oklahoma Symphony—a German for whom I used to cut the grass in exchange for trumpet lessons. But these lessons were about everything else. He'd talk to me about all that lay behind music, and after I'd performed my trumpet lesson and been corrected he'd say, "You like such and such a composition, don't you?" And I'd say, "Yes," and he'd sit down at the piano with a piece of scoring paper and in a few minutes he would have written out passages of the orchestration and show me, bar by bar, how the sounds were blended.

"The strings are doing this," he'd say, "and the trumpets are playing this figure against the woodwinds," and so on.

Most of it was over my head, but he made it all so logical and, better still, he taught me how to attack those things I desired so that I could pierce the mystery and possess them. I came to feel, yes, that if you want these things and master the technique, you could get with it. You could make it yours. I came to understand, in other words, that all that stood between me and writing symphonies was not simply a matter of civil rights, even though the civil rights struggle was all too real. At that time my mother was being thrown into jail every other day for violating a zoning ordinance by moving into a building in a section where Governor Alfalfa Bill Murray had decided Negroes shouldn't live.

STERN: You went on then to Tuskegee, and you studied music seriously, and came up to New York more or less intending to—

ELLISON: To go back to Tuskegee. I came up during my junior year hoping to work and learn a little about sculpture. And although I did study a bit, I didn't get the job through which I hoped to earn enough money for my school expenses, so I remained in New York, where I soon realized that although I had a certain facility with three-dimensional form I wasn't really interested in sculpture. So after a while I blundered into writing.

STERN: The music you had given up by this time?

ELLISON: No, no, I was still trying to be a musician. I was doing some exercises in composition under Wallingford Riegger, and although I was much behind his advanced students I stayed there and studied with him until I had to have a tonsillectomy. It turned out to be a pretty chronic case and caused a lot of trouble, and by the time I tried to go back to my classes my mother died out in Ohio and I left New York for a good while. It was during the period in Dayton I started trying seriously to write and that was the breaking point.

STERN: Can you remember why you started to write or how?

ELLISON: I can remember very vividly. Richard Wright had just come to New York and was editing a little magazine. I had read a poem of his which I liked, and when we were introduced by a mutual friend he suggested that I try to review a novel for his magazine. My review was accepted and published and so I was hooked.

STERN: You were launched . . .

ELLISON: Oh, no, not really launched.

STERN: You were conscious that such a thing was possible. Was Wright famous at that time?

ELLISON: No, Wright hadn't written *Native Son*. He had published *Uncle Tom's Children*, which was the real beginning of his fame, and he was already working on *Native Son*. I remember the first scene that he showed me was the poolroom scene; it isn't the first scene but it was one of the first written and I was to read the rest of the book as it came out of the typewriter.

STERN: At that time were you dissatisfied with the sort of work Wright was doing?

ELLISON: Dissatisfied? I was too amazed with watching the process of creation. I didn't understand quite what was going on, but by this time I had talked with Wright a lot and he was very conscious of technique. He talked about it not in terms of mystification but as writing know-how. "You must read so-and-so," he'd say. "You have to go about learning to write *consciously*. People have talked about such and such a problem and have written about it. You must learn how Conrad, Joyce, Dostoevsky get their effects . . ." He guided me to Henry James and to Conrad's prefaces, that type of thing. Of course, I knew that my own feelings about the world, about life, were different, but this was not even a matter to question. Wright knew what he was about, what he wanted to do, while I hadn't even discovered myself. I knew only that what I would want to express would not be an imitation of his kind of thing.

STERN: So what sort of thing did you feel Wright was not doing that you wanted to do?

ELLISON: Well, I don't suppose I judged. I am certain I did not judge in quite so conscious a way, but I think I felt more complexity in life, and my background made me aware of a larger area of possibility. Knowing Wright himself and something of what he was doing increased that sense of the possible. Also, I think I was less interested in an ideological interpretation of Negro experience. For all my interest in music, I had been in love with literature for years and years—if a writer may make such a confession. I read everything. I must have read fairy tales until I was thirteen, and I was always taken with the magical quality of writing, with the poetry of it. When I came to discover a little more about what I wanted to express I felt that Wright was overcommitted to ideology—even though I, too, wanted many of the same things for our people. You might say that I was much less a social determinist. But I suppose that basically it comes down to a difference in our concepts of the individual. I, for instance, found it disturbing that Bigger Thomas had none of the finer qualities of Richard Wright, none of the imagination, none of the sense of poetry, none of the gaiety. And I preferred Richard Wright to Bigger Thomas. Do you see? Which gets you in on the . . . directs you back to the difference between what Wright was himself and how he conceived of the individual—back to his conception of the quality of Negro humanity.

STERN: Did you think you might write stories in which Negroes did not appear?

ELLISON: No, there was never a time when I thought of writing fiction in which only Negroes appeared, or in which only whites appeared. And yet, from the very beginning I wanted to write about American Negro experience, and I suspected that what was important, what made the difference, lay in the perspective from which it was viewed. When I learned more and started thinking about this consciously, I realized that it was a source of creative strength as well as a source of wonder. It's also a relatively unexplored area of American experience simply because our knowledge of it has been distorted through the overemphasis of the sociological approach. Unfortunately many Negroes have been trying to define their own predicament in exclusively sociological terms, a situation I consider quite shortsighted. Too many of us have accepted a statistical interpretation of our lives, and thus much of that which makes us a source of moral strength to America goes unappreciated and undefined. Now, when you try to trace American values as they find expression in the Negro community, where do you begin? To what books do you go? How do you account for Little Rock and the sit-ins? How do you account for the strength of those kids? You can find sociological descriptions of the conditions under which they live but few indications of their morale.

STERN: You felt as you were starting to get serious about writing that you had a special subject to write about?

ELLISON: Yes, I think so. Well, let's put it this way: Sometimes you get a sense of mission even before you are aware of it. An act is demanded of you but you're like a sleepwalker searching for some important object, and when you find it you wake up to discover that it is the agency through which that mission, assigned you long ago, at a time you barely understood the command, could be accomplished. Thus while there appeared to be no connection between my wanting to write fiction and my mother's insistence, from the time I was a small boy, that the hope of our group depended not upon the older Negroes but upon the young—upon me, as it were—this sense of obligation got into my work immediately. Of course these are very complicated matters, because I have no desire to write propaganda. Instead I felt it important to explore the full range of American Negro humanity and to affirm those qualities which are of value beyond any question of segregation, economics or previous condition of servitude. The obligation was always there and there is much to affirm. In fact, all Negroes affirm certain feelings of identity— certain foods, certain types of dancing, music, religious experiences, certain tragic attitudes toward experience and toward our situation as Americans. You see, we do this all within the community, but when it is questioned from without—that's when things start going apart. Like most Americans, we are not yet fully conscious of our identity either as Negroes or Americans. This affirmation of which I speak, this insistence upon achieving our social goal, has been our great strength and also our great weakness because the terms with which we have tried to define ourselves have been inadequate. We know we're not the creatures which our enemies in the white South would have us be, and we know too that neither color nor our civil predicament explain us adequately. Our strength is that with the total society saying to us, *"No, No, No, No,"* we continue to move toward our goal. So when I came to write I felt moved to affirm and to explore all this—not as a social mission but as the stuff of literature and as an expression of the better part of my own sense of life.

STERN: Somebody has described a literary situation as one which commemorates what a man feels is passing or threatened. Did you feel that your work might be a commemoration of values which were disappearing as you wrote about them?

ELLISON: How shall I say? Yes, I do feel this. Now, just how consciously I was concerned with it at the time I wrote I don't know. When I started writing *Invisible Man* I was reading Lord Raglan's *The Hero*, in which he goes into figures of history and myth to account for the features which make for the mythic hero, and at the same time I got to thinking about the ambiguity of Negro leadership during that period. This was the late forties, and I kept trying to account for the fact that when the chips were down, Negro leaders did not represent the Negro community.

Beyond their own special interests they represented white philanthropy, white politicians, business interests, and so on. This was an unfair way of looking at it, perhaps, but there was something missing, something which is only now being corrected. It seemed to me that they acknowledged no final responsibility to the Negro community for their acts, and implicit in their roles were constant acts of betrayal. This made for a sad, chronic division between their values and the values of those they were supposed to represent. And the fairest thing to say about it is that the predicament of Negroes in the United States rendered these leaders automatically impotent until they recognized their true source of power—which lies, as Martin Luther King perceived, in the Negro's ability to suffer even death for the attainment of our beliefs. Back in the forties only preachers had real power through which to effect their wills, but most of these operated strictly within the Negro community. Only Adam Powell was using the power of the Negro church to assert the Negro's political will. So at that time a thick fog of unreality separated the Negro group from its leaders.

But let me tell you a story: At Tuskegee during graduation week countless high-powered word artists, black and white, descended upon us and gathered in the gym and the chapel to tell us in highflown words what the Negro thought, what our lives were and what our goals should be. The buildings would be packed with visitors and relatives and many guardians of race relations—Northern and Southern. Well, the Negro farm people from the surrounding countryside would also come to the campus at the same time. Graduation week was a festive time for the surrounding Negro community, and very often these people would have children and relatives taking part in the ceremonies in progress in the chapel and the gym. But do you know that while the big-shot word artists were making their most impressive speeches, the farm people would be out on the old athletic field dancing square dances, having picnics, playing baseball and visiting among themselves as though the ceremonies across the wide lawns did not exist—or at best had no connection with the lives they led. Well, I found their celebrations much more attractive than the official ceremonies, and I would leave my seat in the orchestra and sneak out to watch them, and while my city background had cut me off from the lives they led and I had no desire to live the life of a sharecropper, I found their unrhetorical activities on the old football field the more meaningful.

STERN: The familiar liberal hope is that any specialized form of social life which makes for invidious distinctions should disappear. Your view seems to be that anything that counts is the result of such specialization.

ELLISON: Yes.

STERN: Now, a good many people, millions, are damaged permanently, viciously, unfairly by such distinctions. At the same time, they contribute, as you more than perhaps any writer in the world have seen, to something marvelous. Some sort of decision probably has to be made by an individual who is sensitive to this paradox. I wonder what yours is. Do you want the preservation of that which results in both the marvelous and the terrible, or do you feel that the marvelous should not endure while the terrible endures along with it?

ELLISON: I am going to say something very odd. In the first place, I think that the mixture of the marvelous and the terrible is a basic condition of human life, and that the persistence of human ideals represents the marvelous pulling itself up out of the chaos of the universe. In the fairy tale, beauty must be awakened by the beast; the beastly man can only regain his humanity through love. There are other terms for this but they come to much the same thing. Here the terrible represents all that hinders, all that opposes human aspiration, and the marvelous represents the triumph of the human spirit over chaos. While the terms and the conditions are different and often change, our triumphs are few and thus must be recognized for what they are and preserved. Besides, I would be hard put to say where the terrible could be localized in our national experience, for I see in so much of American life which lies beyond the Negro community the very essence of the terrible.

STERN: Yes, but in the last few days we have been talking about some of the particular meannesses which are characteristic of the Negro situation . . . Just the fact that there are four Negro congressmen, when adequate representation would mean that there'd be twenty . . .

ELLISON: Yes.

STERN: And hundreds of things of this sort, many of which result in crippling injustices and meannesses. Now, can this go on? And if it doesn't go on, will this mean the elimination of that which you have commemorated in fiction?

ELLISON: Well, what I have tried to commemorate in fiction is that which I believe to be enduring and abiding in our situation, especially those human qualities which the American Negro has developed despite, and in rejection of, the obstacles and meannesses imposed upon us. If the writer exists for any social good, his role is that of preserving in art those human values which can endure by confronting change. Our Negro situation is changing rapidly, but so much which we've gleaned through the harsh discipline of Negro American life is simply too precious to be lost. I speak of the faith, the patience, the humor, the sense of timing, the rugged sense of life and the manner of expressing it which all go to define the American Negro. These are some of the things through which we've confronted the obstacles and meannesses of which you speak, and which we dare not fail to adapt to changed conditions lest we destroy ourselves. Times change, but these possessions must endure forever—not simply because they define us as a group, but because they represent a further instance of man's triumph over chaos. You know, the skins of those thin-legged little girls who faced the mob in Little Rock marked them as Negro, but the spirit which directed their feet is the old universal urge toward freedom. For better or worse, whatever there is of value in Negro life is an American heritage, and as such it must be preserved. Besides, I am unwilling to see those values which I would celebrate in fiction as existing sheerly through terror; they are a result of a tragicomic confrontation with life.

I think that art is a celebration of life even when life extends into death, and that the sociological conditions which have made for so much misery in Negro life are not necessarily the only factors which make for the values which I feel should endure and shall endure. I see a period when Negroes are going to be wandering around because, you see, we have had this thing thrown at us for so long that we haven't had a chance to discover what in our own background is really worth preserving. For the first time we are given a choice, we are making a choice. And this is where the real trouble is going to start. The South could help. If it had a sense of humor, you know, the South could say, "All right, we will set aside six months and there will be complete integration—all right, you don't have to integrate the women—but there will be complete integration as far as anything else is concerned. Negroes may go anywhere, they may see how we entertain, how we spend our leisure, how we worship, and so on," and that would be the end of the whole problem. Because most Negroes could not be nourished by the life white Southerners live. It is too hag-ridden, it is too obsessed, it is too concerned with attitudes which could change everything that Negroes have been conditioned to expect of life. No, I believe in diversity, and I think that the real death of the United States will come when everyone is just alike.

As for my writer's necessity of cashing in on the pain undergone by my people (and remember I write of the humor as well), writing is my way of confronting, often for the hundredth time, that same pain and that same pleasure. It is my way of seeing that it be not in vain.

Twentieth-Century Fiction and
the Black Mask of Humanity

When this essay was published in 1953, it was prefaced with the following note:

When I started rewriting this essay it occurred to me that its value might be somewhat increased if it remained very much as I wrote it during 1946. For in that form it is what a young member of a minority felt about much of our writing. Thus I've left in much of the bias and shortsightedness, for it says perhaps as much about me as a member of a minority as it does about literature. I hope you still find the essay useful, and I'd like to see an editorial note stating that this is an unpublished piece written not long after the Second World War.

PERHAPS the most insidious and least understood form of segregation is that of the word. And by this I mean the word in all its complex formulations, from the proverb to the novel and stage play, the word with all its subtle power to suggest and foreshadow overt action while magically disguising the moral consequences of that action and providing it with symbolic and psychological justification. For if the word has the potency to revive and make us free, it has also the power to blind, imprison and destroy.

The essence of the word is its ambivalence, and in fiction it is never so effective and revealing as when both potentials are operating simultaneously, as when it mirrors both good and bad, as when it blows both hot and cold in the same breath. Thus it is unfortunate for the Negro that the most powerful formulations of modern American fictional words have been so slanted against him that when he

---

Written in 1946. Published in *Confluence*, December 1953.

approaches for a glimpse of himself he discovers an image drained of humanity.

Obviously the experiences of Negroes—slavery, the grueling and continuing fight for full citizenship since Emancipation, the stigma of color, the enforced alienation which constantly knifes into our natural identification with our country—have not been those of white Americans. And though as passionate believers in democracy Negroes identify themselves with the broader American ideals, their sense of reality springs, in part, from an American experience which most white men not only have not had, but one with which they are reluctant to identify themselves even when presented in forms of the imagination. Thus, when the white American, holding up most twentieth-century fiction, says, "This is American reality," the Negro tends to answer (not at all concerned that Americans tend generally to fight against any but the most flattering imaginative depictions of their lives), "Perhaps, but you've left out this, and this, and this. But most of all, what you'd have the world accept as *me* isn't even human."

Nor does he refer only to second-rate works but to those of our most representative authors. Either like Hemingway and Steinbeck (in whose joint works I recall not more than five American Negroes), they tend to ignore them, or like the early Faulkner, who distorted Negro humanity to fit his personal versions of Southern myth, they seldom conceive Negro characters possessing the full, complex ambiguity of the human. Too often what is presented as the American Negro (a most complex example of Western man) emerges an oversimplified clown, a beast or an angel. Seldom is he drawn as that sensitively focused process of opposites, of good and evil, of instinct and intellect, of passion and spirituality, which great literary art has projected as the image of man. Naturally the attitude of Negroes toward this writing is one of great reservation. Which, indeed, bears out Richard Wright's remark that there is in progress between black and white Americans a struggle over the nature of reality.

Historically this is but a part of that larger conflict between older, dominant groups of white Americans, especially the Anglo-Saxons, on the one hand, and the newer white and non-white groups on the other, over the major group's attempt to impose its ideals upon the rest, insisting that its exclusive image be accepted as *the* image of the American. This conflict should not, however, be misunderstood. For despite the impact of the American idea upon the world, the "American" himself has not (fortunately for the United States, its minorities, and perhaps for the world) been finally defined. So that far from being socially undesirable this struggle between Americans as to what the American is to be is part of that democratic process through which the nation works to achieve itself. Out of this conflict the ideal American character—a type truly great enough to possess the greatness of the land, a delicately poised unity of divergencies—is slowly being born.

But we are concerned here with fiction, not history. How is it then that our naturalistic prose—one of the most vital bodies of twentieth-century fiction, perhaps the brightest instrument for recording sociological fact, physical action, the nuance of speech, yet achieved—becomes suddenly dull when confronting the Negro?

Obviously there is more in this than the mere verbal counterpart of lynching or segregation. Indeed, it represents a projection of processes lying at the very root of American culture, and certainly at the central core of its twentieth-century literary forms, a matter having less to do with the mere "reflection" of white racial theories than with processes molding the attitudes, the habits of mind, the cultural atmosphere and the artistic and intellectual traditions that condition men dedicated to democracy to practice, accept and, most crucial of all, often blind themselves to the essentially undemocratic treatment of their fellow citizens.

It should be noted here that the moment criticism approaches Negro-white relationships it is plunged into problems of psychology and symbolic ritual. Psychology, because the distance between Americans, Negroes and whites, is not so much spatial as psychological; while they might dress and often look alike, seldom on deeper levels do they think alike. Ritual, because the Negroes of fiction are so consistently false to human life that we must question just what they truly represent, both in the literary work and in the inner world of the white American.*

Despite their billings as images of reality, these Negroes of fiction are counterfeits. They are projected aspects of an internal symbolic process through which, like a primitive tribesman dancing himself into the group frenzy necessary for battle, the white American prepares himself emotionally to perform a social role. These fictive Negroes are not, as sometimes interpreted, simple racial clichés introduced into society by a ruling class to control political and economic realities. For although they are manipulated to that end, such an externally one-sided interpretation relieves the individual of personal responsibility for the health of democracy. Not only does it forget that a democracy is a collectivity of *individuals*, but it never suspects that the tenacity of the stereotype springs exactly from the fact that its function is no less personal than political. Color prejudice springs not from the stereotype alone, but from an internal psychological state; not from misinformation alone, but from an inner need to believe. It thrives not only on the obscene witch-doctoring of men like Jimmy Byrnes and Malan, but upon an inner craving for symbolic magic. The prejudiced individual creates his own stereo-

---

*Perhaps the ideal approach to the work of literature would be one allowing for insight into the deepest psychological motives of the writer at the same time that it examined all external sociological factors operating within a given milieu. For while objectively a social reality, the work of art is, in its genesis, a projection of a deeply personal process, and any approach that ignores the personal at the expense of the social is necessarily incomplete. Thus, when we approach contemporary writing from the perspective of segregation, as is commonly done by sociologically minded thinkers, we automatically limit ourselves to one external aspect of a complex whole, which leaves us little to say concerning its personal, internal elements. On the other hand, American writing has been one of the most important twentieth-century literatures, and though negative as a social force it is technically brilliant and emotionally powerful. Hence were we to examine it for its embodiment of these positive values, there would be other more admiring things to be said.

types, very often unconsciously, by reading into situations involving Negroes those stock meanings which justify his emotional and economic needs.

Hence whatever else the Negro stereotype might be as a social instrumentality, it is also a key figure in a magic rite by which the white American seeks to resolve the dilemma arising between his democratic beliefs and certain antidemocratic practices, between his acceptance of the sacred democratic belief that all men are created equal and his treatment of every tenth man as though he were not.

Thus on the moral level I propose that we view the whole of American life as a drama acted out upon the body of a Negro giant, who, lying trussed up like Gulliver, forms the stage and the scene upon which and within which the action unfolds. If we examine the beginning of the Colonies, the application of this view is not, in its economic connotations at least, too far-fetched or too difficult to see. For then the Negro's body was exploited as amorally as the soil and climate. It was later, when white men drew up a plan for a democratic way of life, that the Negro began slowly to exert an influence upon America's moral consciousness. Gradually he was recognized as the human factor placed outside the democratic master plan, a human "natural" resource who, so that white men could become more human, was elected to undergo a process of institutionalized dehumanization.

Until the Korean War this moral role had become obscured within the staggering growth of contemporary science and industry, but during the nineteenth century it flared nakedly in the American consciousness, only to be repressed after the Reconstruction. During periods of national crises, when the United States rounds a sudden curve on the pitch-black road of history, this moral awareness surges in the white American's conscience like a raging river revealed at his feet by a lightning flash. Only then is the veil of anti-Negro myths, symbols, stereotypes and taboos drawn somewhat aside. And when we look closely at our literature it is to be seen operating even when the Negro seems most patently the little man who isn't there.

· · ·

I see no value either in presenting a catalogue of Negro characters appearing in twentieth-century fiction or in charting the racial attitudes of white writers. We are interested not in quantities but in qualities. And since it is impossible here to discuss the entire body of this writing, the next best thing is to select a framework in which the relationships with which we are concerned may be clearly seen. For brevity let us take three representative writers: Mark Twain, Hemingway and Faulkner. Twain for historical perspective and as an example of how a great nineteenth-century writer handled the Negro; Hemingway as the prime example of the artist who ignored the dramatic and symbolic possibilities presented by this theme; and Faulkner as an example of a writer who has confronted Negroes with such mixed motives that he has presented them in terms of both the "good nigger" and the "bad nigger" stereotypes, and who yet has explored perhaps more successfully than anyone else, either white or black, certain forms of Negro humanity.

For perspective let us begin with Mark Twain's great classic, *Huckleberry Finn.* Recall that Huckleberry has run away from his father, Miss Watson and the Widow Douglas (indeed the whole community, in relation to which he is a young outcast), and has with him as companion on the raft upon which they are sailing down the Mississippi Miss Watson's runaway Negro slave, Jim. Recall, too, that Jim, during the critical moment of the novel, is stolen by two scoundrels and sold to another master, presenting Huck with the problem of freeing Jim once more. Two ways are open: he can rely upon his own ingenuity and "steal" Jim into freedom, or he might write Miss Watson and request reward money to have Jim returned to her. But there is a danger in this course, remember, since the angry woman might sell the slave down the river into a harsher slavery. It is this course which Huck starts to take, but as he composes the letter he wavers.

> It was a close place. I took it up, and held it in my hand. I
> was a trembling, because I'd got to decide, forever, betwixt

two things, and I knowed it. I studied a minute, sort of holding my breath, and then says to myself:

"All right, then, I'll *go* to hell"—and tore it up.

It was awful thoughts, and awful words, but they was said. And I let them stay said; and never thought no more about reforming. I shoved the whole thing out of my head; and said I would take up wickedness again, which was in my line, being brung up to it, and the other warn't. And for a starter I would go to work and steal Jim out of slavery again. . . .

And a little later, in defending his decision to Tom Sawyer, Huck comments, "I know you'll say it's dirty, low-down business but *I'm* low-down. And I'm going to steal him . . ."

We have arrived at a key point of the novel and, by an ironic reversal, of American fiction, a pivotal moment announcing a change of direction in the plot, a reversal as well as a recognition scene (like that in which Oedipus discovers his true identity), wherein a new definition of necessity is being formulated. Huck Finn has struggled with the problem posed by the clash between property rights and human rights, between what the community considered to be the proper attitude toward an escaped slave and his knowledge of Jim's humanity, gained through their adventures as fugitives together. He has made his decision on the side of humanity. In this passage Twain has stated the basic moral issue centering around Negroes and the white American's democratic ethics. It dramatizes as well the highest point of tension generated by the clash between the direct, human relationships of the frontier and the abstract, inhuman, market-dominated relationships fostered by the rising middle class—which in Twain's day was already compromising dangerously with the most inhuman aspects of the defeated slave system. And just as politically these forces reached their sharpest tension in the outbreak of the Civil War, in *Huckleberry Finn* (both the boy and the novel) their human implications come to sharpest focus around the figure of the Negro.

Huckleberry Finn knew, as did Mark Twain, that Jim was not only a slave but a human being, a man who in some ways was to be envied, and who expressed his essential humanity in his desire for freedom, his will to possess his own labor, in his loyalty and capacity for friendship, and in his love for his wife and child. Yet Twain, though guilty of the sentimentality common to humorists, does not idealize the slave. Jim is drawn in all his ignorance and superstition, with his good traits and his bad. He, like all men, is ambiguous, limited in circumstance but not in possibility. And it will be noted that when Huck makes his decision he identifies himself with Jim and accepts the judgment of his superego—that internalized representative of the community—that his action is evil. Like Prometheus, who for mankind stole fire from the gods, he embraces the evil implicit in his act in order to affirm his belief in humanity. Jim, therefore, is not simply a slave, he is a symbol of humanity, and in freeing Jim, Huck makes a bid to free himself of the conventionalized evil taken for civilization by the town.

This conception of the Negro as a symbol of Man—the reversal of what he represents in most contemporary thought—was organic to nineteenth-century literature. It occurs not only in Twain but in Emerson, Thoreau, Whitman and Melville (whose symbol of evil, incidentally, was white), all of whom were men publicly involved in various forms of deeply personal rebellion. And while the Negro and the color black were associated with the concept of evil and ugliness far back in the Christian era, the Negro's emergence as a symbol of value came, I believe, with Rationalism and the rise of the romantic individual of the eighteenth century. This romantic was in revolt against the old moral authority, and if he suffered a sense of guilt, his passion for personal freedom was such that he was willing to accept evil (a tragic attitude), even to identifying himself with the "noble slave"—who symbolized the darker, unknown potential side of his personality, that underground side, turgid with possibility, which might, if given a chance, toss a fistful of mud into the sky and create a "shining star."

Even that prototype of the bourgeois, Robinson Crusoe, stopped to speculate as to his slave's humanity. And the rising American industrialists of the late nineteenth century were to rediscover what their European counterparts had learned a century before: that the good man Friday was as sound an investment for Crusoe morally as he was economically, for not only did Friday allow Crusoe to achieve himself by working for him, but by functioning as a living scapegoat to contain Crusoe's guilt over breaking with the institutions and authority of the past, he made it possible to exploit even his guilt economically. The man was one of the first missionaries.

Mark Twain was alive to this irony and refused such an easy (and dangerous) way out. Huck Finn's acceptance of the evil implicit in his "emancipation" of Jim represents Twain's acceptance of his personal responsibility for the condition of society. This was the tragic face behind his comic mask.

But by the twentieth century this attitude of tragic responsibility had disappeared from our literature along with that broad conception of democracy which vitalized the work of our greatest writers. After Twain's compelling image of black and white fraternity the Negro generally disappears from fiction as a rounded human being. And if already in Twain's time a novel which was optimistic concerning a democracy which would include all men could not escape being banned from public libraries, by our day his great drama of interracial fraternity had become, for most Americans at least, an amusing boy's story and nothing more. But while a boy, Huck Finn has become by the somersault motion of what William Empson terms "pastoral," an embodiment of the heroic, and an exponent of humanism. Indeed, the historical justification for his adolescence lies in the fact that Twain was depicting a transitional period of American life; its artistic justification is that adolescence is the time of the "great confusion," during which both individuals and nations flounder between accepting and rejecting the responsibilities of adulthood. Accordingly, Huck's relationship to Jim, the river and all they symbolize, is that of a humanist; in his relation to the community he is an individualist. He embodies the two major conflicting drives operating in nineteenth-century America. And if humanism is man's basic attitude toward a social order which he accepts, and individualism his basic attitude toward one he rejects, one might say that Twain, by allowing these two attitudes to argue dialectically in his work of art, was as highly moral an artist as he was a believer in democracy, and vice versa.

History, however, was to bring an ironic reversal to the direction which Huckleberry Finn chose, and by our day the divided ethic of the community had won out. In contrast with Twain's humanism, individualism was thought to be the only tenable attitude for the artist.

Thus we come to Ernest Hemingway, one of the two writers whose art is based most solidly upon Mark Twain's language, and one who perhaps has done most to extend Twain's technical influence upon our fiction. It was Hemingway who pointed out that all modern American writing springs from *Huckleberry Finn*. (One might add here that equally as much of it derives from Hemingway himself.) But by the twenties the element of rejection implicit in Twain had become so dominant an attitude of the American writer that Hemingway goes on to warn us to "stop where the Nigger Jim is stolen from the boys. That is the real end. The rest is just cheating."

So thoroughly had the Negro, both as man and as a symbol of man, been pushed into the underground of the American conscience that Hemingway missed completely the structural, symbolic and moral necessity for that part of the plot in which the boys rescue Jim. Yet it is precisely this part which gives the novel its significance. Without it, except as a boy's tale, the novel is meaningless. Yet Hemingway, a great artist in his own right, speaks as a victim of that culture of which he is himself so critical, for by his time that growing rift in the ethical fabric pointed out by Twain had become completely sundered—snagged upon the irrepressible moral reality of the Negro. Instead of the single democratic ethic for every man, there now existed two: one, the idealized ethic of the Constitution and the Declaration of Independence, reserved for white men, and the other, the pragmatic ethic designed for Negroes and other minorities, which took the form of discrimination. Twain had dramatized the conflict leading to this division in its earlier historical form, but what was new here was that such a moral division, always a threat to the sensitive man, was ignored by the artist in the most general terms, as when Hemingway rails against the rhetoric of the First World War.

Hemingway's blindness to the moral values of *Huckleberry Finn* despite his sensitivity to its technical aspects duplicated the one-sided vision of the twenties. Where Twain, seeking for what Melville called "the common continent of man," drew upon the rich folklore of the frontier (not omitting the Negro's) in order to "Americanize" his idiom, thus broadening his stylistic appeal, Hemingway was alert only to Twain's technical discoveries—the flexible colloquial language, the sharp naturalism, the thematic potentialities of adolescence. Thus what for Twain was a means to a moral end became for Hemingway an end in itself. And just as the trend toward technique for the sake of technique and production for the sake of the market lead to the neglect of the human need out of which they spring, so do they lead in literature to a marvelous technical virtuosity won at the expense of a gross insensitivity to fraternal values.

It is not accidental that the disappearance of the human Negro from our fiction coincides with the disappearance of deep-probing doubt and a sense of evil. Not that doubt in some form was not always present, as the works of the lost generation, the muckrakers and the proletarian writers make very clear. But it is a shallow doubt, which seldom turns inward upon the writer's own values; almost always it focuses outward, upon some scapegoat with which he is seldom able to identify himself as Huck Finn identified himself with the scoundrels who stole Jim, and with Jim himself. This particular naturalism explored everything except the nature of man.

And when the artist would no longer conjure with the major moral problem in American life, he was defeated as a manipulator of profound social passions. In the United States, as in Europe, the triumph of industrialism had repelled the artist with the blatant hypocrisy between its ideals and its acts. But while in Europe the writer became the most profound critic of these matters, in our country he either turned away or was at best half-hearted in his opposition—perhaps because any profound probing of human values, both within himself and within society, would have brought him face to face with the rigidly tabooed subject of the Negro. And now the tradition of avoiding the moral struggle had led not only to the artistic segregation of the Negro but to the segregation of real fraternal, i.e., democratic, values.

The hard-boiled school represented by Hemingway, for instance, is usually spoken of as a product of World War I disillusionment; yet it was as much the product of a tradition which arose even before the Civil War—that tradition of intellectual evasion for which Thoreau criticized Emerson in regard to the Fugitive Slave Law, and which had been growing swiftly since the failure of the ideals in whose name the Civil War was fought. The failure to resolve the problem symbolized by the Negro has contributed indirectly to the dispossession of the artist in several ways. By excluding our largest minority from the democratic process, the United States weakened all national symbols and rendered sweeping public rituals which would dramatize the American dream impossible; it robbed the artist of a body of unassailable public beliefs upon which he could base his art; it deprived him of a personal faith in the ideals upon which society supposedly rested; and it provided him with no tragic mood indigenous to his society upon which he could erect a tragic art. The result was that he responded with an attitude of rejection, which he expressed as artistic individualism. But too often both his rejection and individualism were narrow; seldom was he able to transcend the limitations of pragmatic reality, and the quality of moral imagination—the fountainhead of great art—was atrophied within him.

Malraux has observed that contemporary American writing is the only important literature not created by intellectuals, and that the creators possess "neither the relative historical culture, nor the love of ideas (a prerogative of professors in the United States)" of comparable Europeans. And is there not a connection between the non-intellectual aspects of this writing (though many of the writers are far more intellectual than they admit or than Malraux would suspect) and its creators' rejection of broad social responsibility, between its non-concern with ideas and its failure to project characters who grasp the broad sweep of American life, or who even attempt to state its fundamental problems? And has not this affected the types of heroes of this fiction? Is it not a partial explanation of why it has created no characters possessing broad insight into their situations or the emotional, psychological and intellectual complexity which would allow them to possess and articulate a truly democratic world view?

It is instructive that Hemingway, born into a civilization characterized by violence, should seize upon the ritualized violence of the culturally distant Spanish bullfight as a laboratory for developing his style. For it was, for Americans (though not for the Spaniards), an amoral violence which he was seeking. Otherwise he might have studied that ritual of violence closer to home, that ritual in which the sacrifice is that of a human scapegoat, the lynching bee. Certainly this rite is not confined to the rope as agency, nor to the South as scene, nor even to the Negro as victim.

But let us not confuse the conscious goals of twentieth-century fiction with those of the nineteenth century; let us take it on its own terms. Artists such as Hemingway were seeking a technical perfection rather than moral insight. (Or should we say that theirs was a morality of technique?) They desired a style stripped of unessentials, one that would appeal without resorting to what was considered worn-out rhetoric, or best of all without any rhetoric whatsoever. It was felt that through the default of the powers that ruled society the artist had as his major task the "pictorial presentation of the evolution of a personal problem." Instead of re-creating and extending the national myth as he did this, the writer now restricted himself to elaborating his personal myth. And although naturalist in his general style, he was not interested, like Balzac, in depicting a society, or even, like Mark Twain, in portraying the moral situation of a nation. Rather he was engaged in working out a personal problem through the evocative, emotion-charged images and ritual therapy available through the manipulation of art forms. And while art was still an instrument of freedom, it was now mainly the instrument of a questionable personal freedom for the artist, which too often served to enforce the "unfreedom" of the reader.

This because it is not within the province of the artist to determine whether his work is social or not. Art by its nature *is* social. And while the artist can determine within a certain narrow scope the type of social effect he wishes his art to create, here his will is definitely limited. Once introduced into society, the work of art begins to pulsate with those meanings, emotions, ideas brought to it by its audience, and over which the artist has but limited control. The irony of the "lost generation" writers is that while disavowing a social role it was the fate of their works to perform a social function which reenforced those very social values which they most violently opposed. How could this be? Because in its genesis the work of art, like the stereotype, is personal; psychologically it represents the socialization of some profoundly personal problem involving guilt (often symbolic murder—parricide, fratricide, incest, homosexuality—all problems at the base of personality) from which by expressing them along with other elements (images, memories, emotions, ideas) he seeks transcendence. To be effective as personal fulfillment, if it is to be more than dream, the work of art must simultaneously evoke images of reality and give them formal organization. And it must, since the individual's emotions are formed in society, shape them into socially meaningful patterns (even Surrealism and Dadaism depended upon their initiates). Nor, as we can see by comparing literature with reportage, is this all. The work of literature differs basically from reportage not merely in its presentation of a pattern of events, nor in its concern with emotion (for a report might well be an account of highly emotional events), but in the deep personal necessity which cries full-throated in the work of art and which seeks transcendence in the form of ritual.

Malcolm Cowley, on the basis of the rites which he believes to be the secret dynamic of Hemingway's work, has identified him with Poe, Hawthorne and Melville, "the haunted and nocturnal writers," he calls them, "the men who dealt with images that were symbols of an inner world." In Hemingway's work, he writes, "we can recognize rites of animal sacrifice . . . of sexual union . . . of conversion . . . and of symbolic death and rebirth." I do not believe, however, that the presence of these rites in writers like Hemingway is as important as the fact that here, beneath the deadpan prose, the cadences of understatement, the anti-intellectualism, the concern with every "fundamental" of man except that which distinguishes him from the animal—that here is the twentieth-century form of that magical rite which during periods of great art has been to a large extent public and explicit. Here is the literary form by which the personal guilt of the pulverized individual of our rugged era is expatiated: not through his identification with the guilty acts of an Oedipus, a Macbeth or a Medea, by suffering their agony and loading his sins upon their "strong and passionate shoulders," but by being gored with a bull, hooked with a fish, impaled with a grasshopper on a fishhook; not by identifying himself with human heroes, but with those who are indeed defeated.

On the social level this writing performs a function similar to that of the stereotype: it conditions the reader to accept the less worthy values of society, and it serves to justify and absolve our sins of social irresponsibility. With unconscious irony it advises stoic acceptance of those conditions of life which it so accurately describes and which it pretends to reject. And when I read the early Hemingway I seem to be in the presence of a Huckleberry Finn who, instead of identifying himself with humanity and attempting to steal Jim free, chose to write the letter which sent him back into slavery. So that now he is a

Huck full of regret and nostalgia, suffering a sense of guilt that fills even his noondays with nightmares, and against which, like a terrified child avoiding the cracks in the sidewalk, he seeks protection through the compulsive minor rituals of his prose.

The major difference between nineteenth- and twentieth-century writers is not in the latter's lack of personal rituals—a property of all fiction worthy of being termed literature—but in the social effect aroused within their respective readers. Melville's ritual (and his rhetoric) was based upon materials that were more easily available, say, than Hemingway's. They represented a blending of his personal myth with universal myths as traditional as any used by Shakespeare or the Bible, while until *For Whom the Bell Tolls* Hemingway's myth was weighted on the personal side. The difference in perspective is that Melville's belief could still find a public object. Whatever else his works were "about," they also managed to be about democracy. But by our day the democratic dream had become too shaky a structure to support the furious pressures of the artist's doubt. And as always when the belief which nurtures a great social myth declines, large sections of society become prey to superstition. For man without myth is Othello with Desdemona gone: chaos descends, faith vanishes and superstitions prowl in the mind.

Hard-boiled writing is said to appeal through its presentation of sheer fact, rather than through rhetoric. The writer puts nothing down but what he pragmatically "knows." But actually one "fact" itself—which in literature must be presented simultaneously as image and as event—became a rhetorical unit. And the symbolic ritual which has set off the "fact"—that is, the fact unorganized by vital social myths (which might incorporate the findings of science and still contain elements of mystery)—is the rite of superstition. The superstitious individual responds to the capricious event, the fact that seems to explode in his face through blind fatality. For it is the creative function of myth to protect the individual from the irrational, and since it is here in the realm of the irrational that, impervious to science, the stereotype grows, we see that the Negro stereotype is really an image of the unorganized, irrational forces of American life, forces through which, by projecting them in forms of images of an easily dominated minority, the white individual seeks to be at home in the vast unknown world of America. Perhaps the object of the stereotype is not so much to crush the Negro as to console the white man.

Certainly there is justification for this view when we consider the work of William Faulkner. In Faulkner most of the relationships which we have pointed out between the Negro and contemporary writing come to focus: the social and the personal, the moral and the technical, the nineteenth-century emphasis upon morality and the modern accent upon personal myth. And on the strictly literary level Faulkner is prolific and complex enough to speak for those Southern writers who are aggressively anti-Negro and for those younger writers who appear most sincerely interested in depicting the Negro as a rounded human being. What is more, he is the greatest artist the South has produced. While too complex to be given more than a glance in these notes, even a glance is more revealing of what lies back of the distortion of the Negro in modern writing than any attempt at a group survey might be.

Faulkner's attitude is mixed. Taking his cue from the Southern mentality in which the Negro is often dissociated into a malignant stereotype (the bad nigger) on the one hand and a benign stereotype (the good nigger) on the other, most often Faulkner presents characters embodying both. The dual function of this dissociation seems to be that of avoiding moral pain and thus to justify the South's racial code. But since such a social order harms whites no less than blacks, the sensitive Southerner, the artist, is apt to feel its effects acutely— and within the deepest levels of his personality. For not only is the social division forced upon the Negro by the ritualized ethic of discrimination, but upon the white man by the strictly enforced set of anti-Negro taboos. The conflict is always with him. Indeed, so rigidly has the recognition of Negro humanity been tabooed that the white Southerner is apt to associate any form of personal rebellion with the Negro. So that for the Southern artist the Negro becomes a symbol of his personal rebellion, his guilt and his repression of it. The Negro is thus a compelling object of fascination, and this we see very clearly in Faulkner.

Sometimes in Faulkner the Negro is simply a villain, but by an unconsciously ironic transvaluation his villainy consists, as with Loosh in *The Unvanquished*, of desiring his freedom. Or again the Negro appears benign, as with Ringo, of the same novel, who uses his talent not to seek personal freedom but to remain the loyal and resourceful retainer. Not that I criticize loyalty in itself, but that loyalty given where one's humanity is unrecognized seems a bit obscene. And yet in Faulkner's story "The Bear," he brings us as close to the moral implication of the Negro as Twain or Melville. In the famous "difficult" fourth section, which Malcolm Cowley advises us to skip very much as Hemingway would have us skip the end of *Huckleberry Finn*, we find an argument in progress in which one voice (that of a Southern abolitionist) seeks to define Negro humanity against the other's enumeration of those stereotypes which many Southerners believe to be the Negro's basic traits. Significantly, the mentor of the young hero of this story, a man of great moral stature, is socially a Negro.

Indeed, through his many novels and short stories Faulkner fights out the moral problem which was repressed after the nineteenth century, and it was shocking for some to discover that for all his concern with the South, Faulkner was actually seeking out the nature of man. Thus we must turn to him for that continuity of moral purpose which made for the greatness of our classics. As for the Negro minority, he has been more willing perhaps than any other artist to start with the stereotype, accept it as true, and then seek out the human truth which it hides. Perhaps his is the example for our writers to follow, for in his work technique has been put once more to the task of creating value.

Which leaves these final things to be said. First, that this is meant as no plea for white writers to define Negro humanity, but to recognize the broader aspects of their own. Secondly, Negro writers and those of the other minorities have their own task of contributing to the total image of the American by depicting the experience of their own groups. Certainly theirs is the task of defining Negro humanity, as this can no more be accomplished by others than freedom, which must be won again and again each day, can be conferred upon another. A people must define itself, and minorities have the responsibility of having their ideals and images recognized as part of the composite image which is that of the still-forming American people.

The other thing to be said is that while it is unlikely that American writing will ever retrace the way to the nineteenth century, it might be worthwhile to point out that for all its technical experimentation it is nevertheless an ethical instrument, and as such might well exercise some choice in the kind of ethic it prefers to support. The artist is no freer than the society in which he lives, and in the United States the writers who stereotype or ignore the Negro and other minorities in the final analysis stereotype and distort their own humanity. Mark Twain knew that in *his* America humanity masked its face with blackness.

Change the Joke and
Slip the Yoke

This essay originated in the form of a letter in which, from Rome, I expressed my reactions to a lecture which Stanley Edgar Hyman, an old friend and intellectual sparring partner, was preparing for what was to be the first of the Ludwig Lewisohn lectures at Brandeis University. Hyman wrote back suggesting that I work up my ideas as part of a publishable debate, and the two essays were presented in Partisan Review, Spring 1958. *They were titled "The Negro Writer in America: An Exchange," and they are apt to yield their maximum return when read together. Hyman's part of the exchange, which is a most useful discussion of the Negro American's relation to the folk tradition, appears in his book of essays and reviews,* The Promised End, *published by The World Publishing Company, 1963.*

STANLEY Edgar Hyman's essay on the relationship between Negro American literature and Negro American folklore concerns matters in which my own interest is such that the very news of his piece aroused my enthusiasm. Yet after reading it I find that our conceptions of the way in which folk tradition gets into literature—and especially into the novel; our conceptions of just what is *Negro* and what is *American* in Negro American folklore, and our conceptions of a Negro American writer's environment—are at such odds that I must disagree with him all along the way. And since much of his essay is given over so generously to aspects of my own meager writings, I am put in the ungrateful—and embarrassing—position of not only evaluating some of his statements from that highly dubious (but

From *Partisan Review*, Spring 1958.

privileged) sanctuary provided by one's intimate knowledge of one's personal history, but of questioning some of his readings of my own novel by consulting the text.

Archetypes, like taxes, seem doomed to be with us always, and so with literature, one hopes; but between the two there must needs be the living human being in a specific texture of time, place and circumstance who must respond, make choices, achieve eloquence and create specific works of art. Thus I feel that Hyman's fascination with folk tradition and the pleasure of archetype-hunting leads to a critical game that ignores the specificity of literary works. And it also causes him to blur the distinction between various archetypes and different currents of American folklore, and generally to oversimplify the American tradition.

Hyman's favorite archetypical figure is the trickster, but I see a danger here. From a proper distance *all* archetypes would appear to be tricksters and confidence men: part God, part man, no one seems to know his, her, its true name, because he-she-it is protean with changes of pace, location and identity. Further, the trickster is everywhere and anywhere at one and the same time, and, like the parts of some dismembered god, is likely to be found on stony as well as on fertile ground. Folklore is somewhat more stable, in its identity if not in its genealogy, but even here, if we are to discuss *Negro* American folklore let us not be led astray by interlopers.

Certainly we should not approach Negro folklore through the figure Hyman calls the " 'darky' entertainer." For even though such performers as he mentions appear to be convenient guides, they lead us elsewhere, into a Cthonic labyrinth. The role with which they are identified is not, despite its "blackness," *Negro* American (indeed, Negroes are repelled by it); it does not find its popularity among Negroes but among whites; and although it resembles the role of the clown familiar to Negro variety-house audiences, it derives not from the Negro but from the Anglo-Saxon branch of American folklore. In other words, this " 'darky' entertainer" is white. Nevertheless, it might be worthwhile to follow the trail for a while, even though we seem more interested in interracial warfare than the question of literature.

These entertainers are, as Hyman explains, professionals, who in order to enact a symbolic role basic to the underlying drama of American society assume a ritual mask—the identical mask and role taken on by white minstrel men when *they* depicted comic Negroes. Social changes occurring since the 1930s have made for certain modifications (Rochester operates in a different climate of rhetoric, say, than did Stepin Fetchit), but the mask, stylized and iconic, was once required of anyone who would act the role—even those Negroes whose natural coloration should, for any less ritualistic purposes at least, have made it unnecessary.

Nor does the role, which makes use of Negro idiom, songs, dance motifs and wordplay, grow out of the Negro American sense of the comic (although we too have our comedy of blackness), but out of the white American's Manichean fascination with the symbolism of blackness and whiteness expressed in such contradictions as the conflict between the white American's Judeo-Christian morality, his democratic political ideals and his daily conduct—indeed in his general anti-tragic approach to experience.

Being "highly pigmented," as the sociologists say, it was our Negro "misfortune" to be caught up associatively in the negative side of this basic dualism of the white folk mind, and to be shackled to almost everything it would repress from conscience and consciousness. The physical hardships and indignities of slavery were benign compared with this continuing debasement of our image. Because these things are bound up with their notion of chaos, it is almost impossible for many whites to consider questions of sex, women, economic opportunity, the national identity, historic change, social justice—even the "criminality" implicit in the broadening of freedom itself—without summoning malignant images of black men into consciousness.

In the Anglo-Saxon branch of American folklore and in the entertainment industry (which thrives on the exploitation and debasement of all folk materials), the Negro is reduced to a negative sign that usually appears in a comedy of the grotesque and the unacceptable. As Constance Rourke has made us aware, the action of the early minstrel show—with its Negro-derived choreography, its ringing of banjos and rattling of bones, its voices cackling jokes in pseudo-Negro dialect, with its nonsense songs, its bright costumes and sweating performers—constituted a ritual of exorcism. Other white cultures had their gollywogs and blackamoors, but the fact of Negro slavery went to the moral heart of the American social drama, and here the Negro was too real for easy fantasy, too serious to be dealt with in anything less than a national art. The mask was an inseparable part of the national iconography. Thus even when a Negro acted in an abstract role, the national implications were unchanged. His costume made use of the "sacred" symbolism of the American flag—with red and white striped pants and coat, and with stars set in a field of blue for a collar—but he could appear only with his hands gloved in white and his face blackened with burnt cork or greasepaint.

This mask, this willful stylization and modification of the natural face and hands, was imperative for the evocation of that atmosphere in which the fascination of blackness could be enjoyed, the comic catharsis achieved. The racial identity of the performer was unimportant, the mask was the thing (the "thing" in more ways than one), and its function was to veil the humanity of Negroes thus reduced to a sign, and to repress the white audience's awareness of its moral identification with its own acts and with the human ambiguities pushed behind the mask.

Hyman sees the comic point of the contemporary Negro's performance of the role as arising from the circumstance that a skilled man of intelligence is parodying a subhuman grotesque; this is all very kind, but when we move in from the wide-ranging spaces of the archetype for a closer inspection we see that the specific rhetorical situation involves the self-humiliation of the "sacrificial" figure, and that a psychological dissociation from this symbolic self-maiming is one of the powerful motives at work in the audience. Motives of race, status, economics and guilt are always clustered here. The comic point is inseparable from the racial identity of the performer—as is clear in Hyman's example from Wright's *Black Boy*—who by assuming the group-debasing role for gain not only substantiates the audience's belief in the "blackness" of things black, but relieves it, with dreamlike efficiency, of its guilt by accepting the very profit motive that was involved in the designation of the Negro as national scapegoat in the first place. There are all kinds of comedy: here one is reminded of the tribesman in *Green Hills of Africa* who hid his laughing face in shame at the sight of a gut-shot hyena jerking out its own intestines and eating them, in Hemingway's words, "with relish."

Down at the deep dark bottom of the melting pot, where the private is public and the public private, where black is white and white black, where the immoral becomes moral and the moral is anything that makes one feel good (or that one has the power to sustain), the white man's relish is apt to be the black man's gall.

It is not at all odd that this black-faced figure of white fun is for Negroes a symbol of everything they rejected in the white man's thinking about race, in themselves and in their own group. When he appears, for example, in the guise of Nigger Jim, the Negro is made uncomfortable. Writing at a time when the blackface minstrel was still popular, and shortly after a war which left even the abolitionists weary of those problems associated with the Negro, Twain fitted Jim into the outlines of the minstrel tradition, and it is from behind this stereotype mask that we see Jim's dignity and human capacity—and Twain's complexity—emerge. Yet it is his source in this same tradition which creates that ambivalence between his identification as an adult and parent and his "boyish" naïveté, and which by contrast makes Huck, with his street-sparrow sophistication, seem more adult. Certainly it upsets a Negro reader, and it offers a less psychoanalytical explanation of the discomfort which lay behind Leslie Fiedler's thesis concerning the relation of Jim and Huck in his essay "Come Back to the Raft Ag'in, Huck Honey!"

A glance at a more recent fictional encounter between a Negro adult and a white boy, that of Lucas Beauchamp and Chick Mallison in Faulkner's *Intruder in the Dust*, will reinforce my point. For all the racial and caste differences between them, Lucas holds the ascendency in his mature dignity over the youthful Mallison and refuses to lower himself in the comic duel of status forced on him by the white boy whose life he has saved. Faulkner was free to reject the confusion between manhood and the Negro's caste status which is sanctioned by white Southern tradition, but Twain, standing closer to the Reconstruction and to the oral tradition, was not so free of the white dictum that Negro males must be treated either as boys or "uncles"—never as men. Jim's friendship for Huck comes across as that of a boy for another boy rather than as the friendship of an adult for a junior; thus there is implicit in it not only a violation of the manners sanctioned by society for relations between Negroes and whites but also a violation of our conception of adult maleness.

In Jim the extremes of the private and the public come into focus, and before our eyes an "archetypal" figure gives way before the realism implicit in the form of the novel. Here we have, I believe, an explanation in the novel's own terms of that ambiguity which bothered Fiedler. Fiedler was accused of mere sensationalism when he named the friendship homosexual, yet I believe him so profoundly disturbed by the manner in which the deep dichotomies symbolized by blackness and whiteness are resolved that, forgetting to look at the specific form of the novel, he leaped squarely into the middle of that tangle of symbolism which he is dedicated to unsnarling, and yelled out his most terrifying name for chaos. Other things being equal, he might have called it "rape," "incest," "parricide" or "miscegenation." It is ironic that what to a Negro appears to be a lost fall in Twain's otherwise successful wrestle with the ambiguous figure in blackface, is viewed by a critic as a symbolic loss of sexual identity. Surely for literature there is some rare richness here.

Although the figure in blackface looks suspiciously homegrown, Western and Calvinist to me, Hyman identifies it as being related to an archetypical trickster figure originating in Africa. Without arguing the point I shall say only that if it *is* a trickster, its adjustment to the contours of "white" symbolic needs is far more intriguing than its alleged origins, for it tells us something of the operation of American values as modulated by folklore and literature. We are back once more to questions of order and chaos, illusion and reality, nonentity and identity.

The trickster, according to Karl Kerenyi (in a commentary included in Paul Radin's study, *The Trickster*), represents a personification of the body

> which is . . . never wholly subdued, ruled by lust and hunger, forever running into pain and injury, cunning and stupid in action. Disorder belonging to the totality of life . . . the spirit of this disorder is the trickster. His function in an archaic society, or rather the function of his mythology, of the tales told about him, is to add disorder to order and to make a whole, to render possible, within the fixed bounds of what is permitted, an experience of what is not permitted. . . .

But ours is no archaic society (although its archaic elements exert far more influence in our lives than we care to admit), and it is an ironic reversal that in what is regarded as the most "open" society in the world, the license of the black trickster figure is limited by the rigidities of racial attitudes, by political expediencies and by the guilt bound up with the white compulsion to identify with the ever-present man of flesh and blood whose irremediable features have been expropriated for "immoral" purposes. Hyman, incidentally, would have found in Louis Armstrong a much better example of the trickster, his medium being music rather than words and pantomime. Armstrong's clownish license and intoxicating powers are almost Elizabethan; he takes liberties with kings, queens and presidents; he emphasizes the physicality of his music with sweat, spittle and facial contortions; he performs the magical feat of making romantic melody issue from a throat of gravel; and some few years ago was recommending to all and sundry his personal physic, "Pluto Water," as a purging way to health, happiness and international peace.

When the white man steps behind the mask of the trickster his freedom is circumscribed by the fear that he is not simply miming a personification of his disorder and chaos, but that he will become in fact that which he intends only to symbolize; that he will be trapped somewhere in the mystery of hell (for there is a mystery in the whiteness of blackness, the innocence of evil and the evil of innocence, though, being initiates, Negroes express the joke of it in the blues), and thus lose that freedom which, in the fluid, "traditionless," "classless" and rapidly changing society, he would recognize as the white man's alone.

Here another ironic facet of the old American problem of identity crops up. For out of the counterfeiting of the black American's identity there arises a profound doubt in the white man's mind as to the authenticity of his own image of himself. He, after all, went into the business when he refused the king's shilling and revolted. He had put on a mask of his own, as it were, and when we regard our concern with identity in the light of what Robert Penn Warren has termed the "intentional" character of our national beginnings, a quotation from W. B. Yeats proves highly meaningful:

> There is a relation between discipline and the theatrical sense. If we cannot imagine ourselves as different from what we are and assume the second self, we cannot impose a discipline upon ourselves, though we may accept one from others. Active virtue, as distinct from the passive acceptance of a current code, is the wearing of a mask. It is the condition of an arduous full life.

For the ex-colonials, the declaration of an American identity meant the assumption of a mask, and it imposed not only the discipline of national self-consciousness, but gave Americans an ironic awareness of the joke that always lies between appearance and reality, between the discontinuity of social tradition and that sense of the past which clings to the mind. And perhaps even an awareness of the joke that society is man's creation, not God's. Americans began their revolt from the English fatherland when they dumped the tea into the Boston Harbor masked as Indians, and the mobility of the society created in this limitless space has encouraged the use of the mask for good and evil ever since. As the advertising industry, which is dedicated to the creation of masks, makes clear, that which cannot gain authority from tradition may borrow it with a mask. Masking is a play upon possibility and ours is a society in which possibilities are many. When American life is most American it is apt to be most theatrical.

And it is this which makes me question Hyman's designation of the "smart man playing dumb" role as primarily Negro, if he means by "conflict situations" those in which racial pressure is uppermost. Actually it is a role which Negroes share with other Americans, and it might be more "Yankee" than anything else. It is a strategy common to the culture, and it is reinforced by our anti-intellectualism, by our tendency toward conformity and by the related desire of the individual to be left alone; often simply by the desire to put more money in the bank. But basically the strategy grows out of our awareness of the joke at the center of the American identity. Said a very dark Southern friend of mine in laughing reply to a white businessman who complained of his recalcitrance in a bargaining situation, "I know, you thought I was colored, didn't you." It is across this joke that Negro and white Americans regard one another. The white American has charged the Negro American with being without past or tradition (something which strikes the white man with a nameless horror), just as he himself has been so charged by European and American critics with a nostalgia for the stability once typical of European cultures, and the Negro knows that both were "mammy-made" right here at home. What's more, each secretly believes that he alone knows what is valid in the American experience, and that the other knows he knows but will not admit it, and each suspects the other of being at bottom a phony.

The white man's half-conscious awareness that his image of the Negro is false makes him suspect the Negro of always seeking to take him in, and assume his motives are anger and fear—which very often they are. On his side of the joke the Negro looks at the white man and finds it difficult to believe that the "grays"—a Negro term for white people—can be so absurdly self-deluded over the true inter-relatedness of blackness and whiteness. To him the white man seems a hypocrite who boasts of a pure identity while standing with his humanity exposed to the world.

Very often, however, the Negro's masking is motivated not so much by fear as by a profound rejection of the image created to usurp his identity. Sometimes it is for the sheer joy of the joke; some-times to challenge those who presume, across the psychological dis-tance created by race manners, to know his identity. Nonetheless it is in the American grain. Benjamin Franklin, the practical scientist, skilled statesman and sophisticated lover, allowed the French to mis-take him for Rousseau's Natural Man. Hemingway poses as a non-literary sportsman, Faulkner as a farmer; Abe Lincoln allowed himself to be taken for a simple country lawyer—until the chips were down. Here the "darky" act makes brothers of us all. America is a land of masking jokers. We wear the mask for purposes of aggression as well as for defense, when we are projecting the future and preserv-ing the past. In short, the motives hidden behind the mask are as numerous as the ambiguities the mask conceals.

My basic quarrel with Hyman is not over his belief in the impor-tance of the folk tradition, nor over his interest in archetypes, but over his tendency, when he turns to specific works of literature, to distort their content to fit his theory. Since he refers so generously to my own novel, let us take it as a case in point. So intense is Hyman's search for archetypical forms that he doesn't see that the narrator's grandfather in *Invisible Man* is no more involved in a "darky" act than was Ulysses in Polyphemus' cave. Nor is he so much a "smart-man-playing-dumb" as a weak man who knows the nature of his oppressor's weakness. There is a good deal of spite in the old man, as there comes to be in his grandson, and the strategy he advises is a kind of jiujitsu of the spirit, a denial and rejection through agreement. Samson, eyeless in Gaza, pulls the building down when his strength returns; politically weak, the grandfather has learned that conformity leads to a similar end, and so advises his children. Thus his mask of meekness conceals the wisdom of one who has learned the secret of saying the "yes" which accomplishes the expressive "no." Here, too, is a rejection of a current code and a denial become metaphysical. More important to the novel is the fact that he represents the ambiguity of the past for the hero, for whom his sphinxlike deathbed advice poses a riddle which points the plot in the dual direction which the hero will follow throughout the novel.

Certainly B. P. Rhinehart (the P. is for "Proteus," the B. for "Bliss") would seem the perfect example of Hyman's trickster figure. He is a cunning man who wins the admiration of those who admire skulduggery and know-how, an American virtuoso of identity who thrives on chaos and swift change; he is greedy, in that his masquerade is motivated by money as well as by the sheer bliss of impersonation; he is godlike, in that he brings new techniques—electric guitars, etc.—to the service of God, and in that there are many men in his image while he is himself unseen; he is phallic in his role of "lover"; as a numbers runner he is a bringer of manna and a worker of miracles, in that he transforms (for winners, of course) pennies into dollars, and thus he feeds (and feeds on) the poor. Indeed, one could extend this list in the manner of much myth-mongering criticism until the fiction dissolved into anthropology, but Rhinehart's role in the formal structure of the narrative is to suggest to the hero a mode of escape from Ras, and a means of applying, in yet another form, his grandfather's cryptic advice to his own situation. One could throw Rhinehart among his literary betters and link him with Mann's Felix Krull, the Baron Clappique of Malraux's *Man's Fate* and many others, but that would be to make a game of criticism and really say nothing.

The identity of fictional characters is determined by the implicit realism of the form, not by their relation to tradition; they are what they do or do not do. Archetypes are timeless, novels are time-haunted. Novels achieve timelessness through time. If the symbols appearing in a novel link up with those of universal myth they do so by virtue of their emergence from the specific texture of a specific form of social reality. The final act of *Invisible Man* is not that of a concealment in darkness in the Anglo-Saxon connotation of the word, but that of a voice issuing its little wisdom out of the substance of its own inwardness—after having undergone a transformation from ranter to writer. If, by the way, the hero is pulling a "darky act" in this, he certainly is not a smart man playing dumb. For the novel, his memoir, is one long, loud rant, howl and laugh. Confession, not concealment, is his mode. His mobility is dual: geographical, as Hyman points out, but, more importantly, it is intellectual. And in keeping with the reverse English of the plot, and with the Negro American conception of blackness, his movement vertically downward (not into a "sewer," Freud notwithstanding, but into a coal cellar, a source of heat, light, power and, through association with the character's motivation, self-perception) is a process of *rising* to an understanding of his human condition. He gets his restless mobility not so much from the blues or from sociology but because he appears in a literary form which has time and social change as its special province. Besides, restlessness of the spirit is an American condition that transcends geography, sociology and past condition of servitude.

Discussions of folk tradition and literature which slight the specific literary forms involved seem to me questionable. Most of the writers whom Hyman mentions are novelists, workers in a form which has absorbed folk tradition into its thematic structures, its plots, symbolism and rhetoric, and which has its special way with folklore as it has with manners, history, sociology and psychology. Besides, novelists in our time are more likely to be inspired by reading novels than by their acquaintance with any folk tradition.

I use folklore in my work not because I am Negro, but because writers like Eliot and Joyce made me conscious of the literary value of my folk inheritance. My cultural background, like that of most Americans, is dual (my middle name, sadly enough, is Waldo).

I knew the trickster Ulysses just as early as I knew the wily rabbit of Negro American lore, and I could easily imagine myself a pint-sized Ulysses but hardly a rabbit, no matter how human and resourceful or Negro. And a little later I could imagine myself as Huck Finn (I so nicknamed my brother), but not, though I racially identified with him, as Nigger Jim, who struck me as a white man's inadequate portrait of a slave.

My point is that the Negro American writer is also an heir of the human experience which is literature, and this might well be more important to him than his living folk tradition. For me, at least, in the discontinuous, swiftly changing and diverse American culture, the stability of the Negro American folk tradition became precious as a result of an act of literary discovery. Taken as a whole, its spirituals along with its blues, jazz and folk tales, it has, as Hyman suggests, much to tell us of the faith, humor and adaptability to reality necessary to live in a world which has taken on much of the insecurity and blues-like absurdity known to those who brought it into being. For those who are able to translate its meanings into wider, more precise vocabularies it has much to offer indeed. Hyman performs a service when he makes us aware that Negro American folk tradition constitutes a valuable source for literature, but for the novelist of any cultural or racial identity, his form is his greatest freedom, and his insights are where he finds them.

Stephen Crane and the
Mainstream of American Fiction

OF all our nineteenth-century masters of fiction—Hawthorne, Melville, Henry James, Mark Twain and Stephen Crane—it was Crane, the youngest, arrived most distantly from the Civil War in point of time, who was the most war-haunted. Born in Newark, New Jersey, six years after the firing ceased, Crane was the youngest of fourteen offspring of parents whose marriage marked the union of two lines of hard-preaching, fundamentalist Methodist ministers. The time and place of his birth and his parents' concern with conduct, morality and eloquence were, when joined with his self-dedication to precise feeling and writing, perhaps as portentous and as difficult a gift to bear as any seer's obligation to peer through walls and into the secret places of the heart, or around windy corners and into the enigmatic future. Indeed, such words as "clairvoyant," "occult" and "uncanny" have been used to describe his style, and while these tell us little, there was nonetheless an inescapable aura of the marvelous about Stephen Crane. For although there is no record of his eyes having been covered at birth with that caul which is said to grant one second sight, he revealed a unique vision of the human condition and an unusual talent for projecting it. His was a costly vision, won through personal suffering, hard living and harsh artistic discipline, and by the time of his death, at twenty-nine, he was recognized as one of the important innovators of American fictional prose and master of a powerful and original style.

Fortunately it was the style and not the myth which was important. Thus today, after sixty years during which there was little interest in the meaning and sources of Crane's art, the best of the work

Introduction to *The Red Badge of Courage*, 1960.

remains not only alive but capable of speaking to us with a new resonance of meaning. While recent criticism holds that the pioneer style, which leads directly to Ernest Hemingway, sprang from a dedication to the moral and aesthetic possibilities of literary form similar to that of Henry James, Crane's dedication to art was no less disciplined or deadly serious than that which characterized his preaching forefathers' concern with religion. Indeed, John Berryman and Robert Wooster Stallman, the most perceptive of Crane's recent critics, see much of the tension in the work as arising from his desperate struggle with the rejected angel of his parents' Methodism—an insight which we find highly suggestive.

Surely if fundamentalist Christianity could get so authoritatively into national politics (especially in the Bible Belt), so ambiguously into our system of education (as in the Scopes trial issue), into our style of crime (through Prohibition's spawn of bootleggers, gangsters, jellybeans and flappers), and so powerfully into jazz, it is about time we recognized its deeper relationship to the art of our twentieth-century literature. And not simply as subject matter, but as a major source of its technique, its form and rhetoric. For while much has been made of the role of the high church in the development of modern poetry, and with Kierkegaard become a household god for many contemporary novelists, Crane's example suggests that for the writer a youthful contact with the emotional intensity and harsh authority of American fundamentalism can be as important an experience as contact with those churches which possess a ritual containing elements of high art and a theology spun subtle and fine through intellectualization. Undoubtedly the Methodist Church provided Crane an early schooling in the seriousness of spiritual questions—of the individual's ultimate relationship to his fellow men, to the universe and to God—and was one source of the youthful revolt which taught him to look upon life with his own eyes. Just as important, perhaps, is the discipline which the church provided him in keeping great emotion under the control of the intellect, as during the exciting services (which the boy learned to question quite early), along with an awareness of the disparity between the individual's public testimony (a rite common to evangelical churches) and his private deeds—a matter intensified by the fact that the celebrant of this rite of public confession was his own father. In brief, Crane was concerned very early with private emotions publicly displayed as an act of purification and self-definition, an excellent beginning for a writer interested in the ordeals of the private individual struggling to define himself as against the claims of society. Crane, who might well have become a minister, turned from religion but transferred its forms to his art.

For his contemporaries much of the meaning of Crane's art was obscured by a personal myth compounded of elements ever fascinating to the American mind: his youth and his early mastery of a difficult and highly technical skill (like a precocious juvenile delinquent possessed of an uncanny knowledge not of pocket pool, craps or tap dancing, but of advanced literary technique), coupled with that highly individual way of feeling and thinking which is the basis of all significant innovation in art; his wild bohemian way of life; his maverick attitude toward respectability; his gallantry toward prostitutes no less than toward their respectable sisters; his friendship with Bowery outcasts ("What Must I Do to Be Saved?" was the title of a tract by his mother's uncle, the Methodist Bishop of Syracuse and a founder of the university there); his gambler's prodigality with fame and money; his search for wars to observe and report; and finally the fatality of "genius" which followed the fair, slight, gifted youth from obscurity to association with the wealthy and gifted in England (Joseph Conrad, H. G. Wells, Ford Madox Ford and Henry James were among his friends), to his death from tuberculosis, one of the period's most feared and romanticized scourges, in the far Black Forest of Germany.

Blind to the cost of his knowledge, many of his contemporaries regarded Crane's adventures as undertaken merely to provide them with entertainment: Crane chasing bandits in Mexico; Crane shipwrecked while running guns to Cuba; Crane reporting the Greco-

Turkish War; Crane taking on the New York police force and being obliged to abandon the city; Crane marrying a woman said to have been an ex-madam; Crane on a spree. And there was, in fact, some truth to their assumption. Crane was as gifted at acting out good newspaper copy as Hemingway or F. Scott Fitzgerald were to be, and no less a delight to the reporters.

Yet despite the headlines and malicious gossip concerning his wife's past (which motivated their taking up residence in England), the fiction presented here testifies that whatever else Crane might have been seeking, the playboy author was engaged in a most desperate moral struggle. At a time when the capacity for moral seriousness appeared to have disappeared from American society, Crane was attempting to live his own life as cleanly, as imaginatively, and with as much immediacy and realistic poetry as he aspired to convey in his writing. If there was something of the entertainer in his public role (and this was still the time of that great popular entertainer, Mark Twain), there was also an element of the self-sacrificial, and the sensational features of the public adventures hint at the cost of the art. There was in Crane something of Emerson and Thoreau as well as the fundamentalist moralist-designate, and the quiet, desperate, unthinking life was to be avoided at the cost of life itself.

At the center of Crane's myth there lay, of course, the mystery of the creative talent with which a youth of twenty-one was able to write what is considered one of the world's foremost war novels when he had neither observed nor participated in combat. And, indeed, with this second book, *The Red Badge of Courage*, Crane burst upon the American public with the effect of a Civil War projectile lain dormant beneath a city square for thirty years. Two years before he had appeared with *Maggie: A Girl of the Streets*, a stripped little novel of social protest written in a strange new idiom. But although Hamlin Garland and William Dean Howells had recognized the work's importance, the reading public was prepared neither for such a close look at the devastating effect of the Bowery upon the individual's sense of life, nor for the narrow choice between the sweatshop and prostitution which Crane saw as the fate of such girls as Maggie. Besides, with its ear attuned to the languid accents of genteel fiction, it was unprepared for the harsh, although offbeat, poetic realism of Crane's idiom.

In a famous inscription in which he exhorted a reader to have the "courage" to read his book to the end, Crane explained that he had tried to show that

> environment is a tremendous thing in the world, and fre-
> quently shapes lives regardless. If one proves that theory, one
> makes room in heaven for all sorts of souls, notably an occa-
> sional street girl, who are not confidently expected to be there
> by many excellent people. . . .

Crane's statement reveals that the young author knew the mood of his prospective audience much better than it was prepared to know him. For although Crane published *Maggie* at his own expense (significantly, under a pseudonym) and paid four men to read it conspicuously while traveling up and down Manhattan on the El, it failed.

This was for American literature a most significant failure; indeed; afterward, following *Maggie*, Crane developed the strategy of understatement and the technique of impressionism which was to point the way for Hemingway and our fiction of the twenties. Crane was not to return to an explicit projection of his social criticism until "The Monster," a work written much later in his career; he turned, instead, to exploring the psychology of the individual under extreme pressure. *Maggie*, which is omitted here in favor of the neglected and more mature "The Monster," stands with *The Adventures of Huckleberry Finn* as one of the parents of the modern American novel, but it is *The Red Badge of Courage* which claims our attention with all the authority of a masterpiece.

One cannot help but feel, however, that the romantic mystery made of the fact that Crane had no direct experience of war before

writing *The Red Badge* has served to obscure much of its true importance. For even while rejecting the assumption that the creative act is
completely accountable, it is evident that Crane was the type of
writer upon whom, to use Henry James's phrase, "nothing was lost,"
and the possessor of an imagination for which minor experiences
ever revealed their more universal implications. It is not necessary
for even the most unimaginative of us to be consumed by flame in
order to envision hellfire—the hot head of a match against the fin-
gernail suffices—and the embers of the Civil War, let us recall, had
far from ceased their burning in the American mind.

We know that one of Crane's brothers was an expert on the Civil
War; that while attending the Hudson River Institute at Claverack,
N.Y., Crane had listened to the exciting war experiences of Lieutenant John Van Petten, a hero of the old 34th New York, then teaching
elocution and drill at the little military academy; that he possessed an
excellent memory for detail and a marvelous ear for speech accents,
rhythms and idioms; and that as a college athlete he had gained some
notion of the psychology of men engaged in mass action while on the
football field. As for his concern with the ambiguities of fear and of
courage, cowardice and heroism, and the problem of the relation of
the individual to the group and to God, these were a part of his religious and family background, while the deeper insights were available to him (as they are to each of us) through a ruthless plunging into
the dark depths of his own heart and mind. More than this, we know
truly that although the fighting had ceased six years before Crane's
birth, the moral climate which it created formed the only climate
Crane was ever to know. Having been born in the world which the
war had brought into being, much of his activity was a search for
ways of living within it with meaningful intensity. Historically wars
and revolutions form the background for the high periods of the
novel, and civil wars, Hemingway has written, are the best wars for
the writer. To which we would add, yes, because they have a way of
continuing long after wars between nations are resolved; because,
with the combatants being the same people, civil wars are never re-

ally won; and because their most devastating engagements are fought within the individual human heart.

For all our efforts to forget it, the Civil War was the great shaping event not only of our political and economic life, but following Crane, of our twentieth-century fiction. It was the agency through which many of the conflicting elements within the old republic were brought to maximum tension, leaving us a nation fully aware of the continental character of our destiny, preparing the emergence of our predominantly industrial economy and our increasingly urban way of life, and transforming us from a nation consisting of two major regions which could pretend to a unity of values despite their basic split over fundamental issues, to one which was now consciously divided. To put it drastically, if war, as Clausewitz insisted, is the continuation of politics by other means, it requires little imagination to see American life since the abandonment of the Reconstruction as an abrupt reversal of that formula: the continuation of the Civil War by means other than arms. In this sense the conflict has not only gone unresolved, but the line between civil war and civil peace has become so blurred as to require of the sensitive man a questioning attitude toward every aspect of the nation's self-image. Stephen Crane, in his time, was such a man.

The America into which Crane was born was one of mirrorlike reversals in which the victors were the defeated and the defeated the victors; with the South, its memory frozen at the fixed moment of its surrender, carrying its aggression to the North in the form of guerrilla politics, and with the North, compromising as it went, retreating swiftly into the vast expanse of its new industrial development, eager to lose any memory traces of those values for which it had gone to war. Mark Twain had attacked this postwar society, infamous for its carpetbaggers, its Hayes-Tilden Compromise, its looting of the nation's resources during the Grant administrations, in "The Man That Corrupted Hadleyburg," and Henry James depicted the inversion of its moral values in *The Bostonians* and was stimulated by it to those subtleties of moral perception which inform his major fiction.

For all of this, however, Twain's bitter satire was taken for comedy and the best of James was left unread. Despite the prosperity and apparent openness and freedom of the society, it was as though a rigid national censorship had been imposed—and not by an apparatus set up in Washington, but within the center of the American mind. Now there was much of which Americans were morally aware but little which they wished to confront in literature, and the compelling of such confrontation was the challenge flung down to Crane by history.

Let us not forget, then, that while the setting of *The Red Badge* is the Civil War, its issues are drawn from the lax society of the eighteen-eighties and nineties, a society which Crane viewed as hostile to those who would achieve manhood and moral identity, whose tendency toward moral evasion he set out to overcome with his technique of understatement, and whose capacity for reality and moral responsibility he sought to ensnare through the realistic poetry of his diction.

Thus, in *The Red Badge* social reality is filtered through the sensibility of a young Northern soldier who is only vaguely aware of the larger issues of the war, and we note that for all the complex use of the symbolic connotations of blackness, only one Negro, a dancing teamster, appears throughout the novel. The reader is left to fill in the understated background, to re-create those matters of which the hero, Henry Fleming, is too young, too self-centered and too concerned with the more immediate problems of courage, honor and self-preservation to be aware. This leaves the real test of moral courage as much a challenge to the reader as to the hero; he must decide for himself whether or not to confront the public issues evoked by Henry's private ordeal. *The Red Badge* is a novel about a lonely individual's struggle for self-definition, written for lonely individualists, and its style, which no longer speaks in terms of the traditional American rhetoric, implies a deep skepticism as to the possibility of the old American ideals being revived by a people who had failed to live up to them after having paid so much to defend them in hardship and blood. Here in place of the conventional plot—which implies the public validity of private experiences—we find a series of vividly impressionistic episodes that convey the discontinuity of feeling and perception of one caught up in a vast impersonal action, and a concentration upon the psychology of one who seeks first to secede from society and then to live in it with honor and courage.

Indeed, for a novel supposedly about the war, *The Red Badge* is intensely concerned with invasion of the private life, a theme announced when the men encounter the body of their first dead soldier, whose shoe soles, "worn to the thinness of writing paper," strike Henry as evidence of a betrayal by fate which in death had exposed to the dead Confederate's enemies "that poverty which in life he had perhaps concealed from his friends." But war is nothing if not an invasion of privacy, and so is death (the "invulnerable" dead man forces his way between the men as they open ranks to avoid him), and society more so. For society, even when reduced to a few companions, invades personality and demands of the individual an almost impossible consistency while guaranteeing the individual hardly anything. Or so it seems to the naïve Henry, much of whose anguish springs from the fear that his friends will discover that the wound which he received from the rifle butt of another frightened soldier is not the red badge of courage they assume but a badge of shame. Thus the Tattered Soldier's questions as to the circumstance of his injury (really questions as to his moral identity) fill Henry with fear and hostility, and he regards them as

> the assertion of a society that probed pitilessly at secrets until all is apparent. . . . His late companion's chance persistency made him feel that he could not keep his crime [of malingering] concealed in his bosom. It was sure to be brought plain by one of those arrows which cloud the air and are constantly pricking, discovering, proclaiming those things which are willed to be forever hidden. He admitted that he could not defend himself against this agency. It was not within the power of vigilance. . . .

In time Henry learns to act with honor and courage and to perceive something of what it means to be a man, but this perception
depends upon the individual fates of those who make up his immediate group, upon the death of Jim Conklin, the most mature and responsible of the men, and upon the Loud Soldier's attainment of
maturity and inner self-confidence. But the cost of perception is primarily personal, and for Henry it depends upon the experience of
the moral discomfort which follows the crimes of malingering and
assuming a phony identity, and the further crime of allowing the
voice of conscience, here symbolized by the Tattered Soldier, to
wander off and die. Later he acquits himself bravely and comes to
feel that he has attained

> a quiet manhood, non-assertive but of sturdy and strong
> blood. He knew that he would no more quail before his guides
> wherever they should point. He had been to touch the great
> death, and found that, after all, it was but the great death. He
> was a man.

Obviously although Henry has been initiated into the battle of life,
he has by no means finished with illusion—but that, too, is part of
the human condition.

That *The Red Badge* was widely read during Crane's own time was
a triumph of his art, but the real mystery lay not in his re-creation of
the simpler aspects of battle: the corpses, the wounds, the sound of
rifle fire, the panic and high elation of combat; the real mystery lay in
the courage out of which one so young could face up to the truth
which so many Americans were resisting with a noisy clamor of optimism and with frantic gestures of materialistic denial. War, the jungle and hostile Nature became Crane's underlying metaphors for the
human drama and the basic situations in which the individual's capacity for moral and physical courage were put to their most meaningful testing.

And so with "The Open Boat." In January 1897, Crane was one of four men who spent thirty hours in a ten-foot dinghy after their ship, bound on a gun-running expedition to Cuba, developed a leak and sank. It was from this experience that Crane shaped what is considered his most perfect short story. When "The Open Boat" is compared with the report which Crane wrote for the New York *Press*, we can see that it keeps to the order of events as they actually occurred, but such is the power of Crane's shaping vision that the reader is made to *experience* the events as a complete, dynamic, symbolic action. We become one with the men in the boat, who pit their skill and courage against the raging sea, living in their hope and despair and sharing the companionship won within the capricious hand of fate. Under the shaping grace of Crane's imagination the actual event is reduced to significant form, with each wave and gust of wind, each intonation of voice and gesture of limb combining toward a single effect of meaning.

And as with most of Crane's fiction, the point at issue is the cost of moral perception, of achieving an informed sense of life, in a universe which is essentially hostile to man and in which skill and courage and loyalty are virtues which help in the struggle but by no means exempt us from the necessary plunge into the storm-sea-war of experience. For it is thus and thus only that humanity is won, and often the best are destroyed in the trial—as with Higgins, the oiler, whose skill and generosity have helped save the men from the sea but who in the end lies dead upon the shore. Through their immersion into the raging sea of life, and through Higgins's sacrificial death, the survivors are initiated into a personal knowledge of the human condition—and "when the wind brought the sound of the great sea's voice to the men on the shore . . . they felt that they could be interpreters."

In his essay on storytelling, Mark Twain informs us that the humorous story is especially American and that

> it depends for its effect upon the manner of its telling . . . [it] is told gravely; the teller doing his best to conceal the fact that he even dimly suspects that there is anything funny about it. . . .

It is this same noncommittal manner which Stephen Crane brings to the depiction of events which are far from humorous, and while he is seldom comic in the manner of Twain, the method gives his fiction an endless complexity of meaning, and among those matters of which his style pretends unawareness are the social and historical references of his stories. Here, too, the effect depends upon a collaboration between the teller, who conceals the range of his intention, and the listener, who must pit his sense of reality against the enigmatic order of the narrated events—as in "The Bride Comes to Yellow Sky," a story which dances over its apparent terrain with such a tight choreography of ironic reversals that the reader must be extremely light-footed lest he fall out of the pattern of the dance.

Scratchy Wilson, the drunken badman of deadly marksmanship, terrorizes the town and appears to have Jack Potter at his mercy—until the unarmed marshal's announcement of his marriage unnerves him. For Scratchy, who is the last of a local gang, the news is like a "glimpse of another world," and he sees the bride as foreshadowing the end of his way of life. The point, it would seem, is that history has played a joke on Scratchy; the man with the gun is defeated by the unarmed man who has embraced those civilized values symbolized by marriage. But is this all? Doesn't the story pivot at this point and return to the westward-moving train of its beginning?

When the marshal faces the badman's pistol it is clear that despite being unarmed he reacts out of an old habit of courage; he has fought Scratchy many times and even shot him once—in the leg (the red-topped boots with gilded imprints "of the kind beloved in winter by little sledding boys on the hillsides of New England" rob Scratchy of much of his menace for the contemporary reader). But the marshall is also sustained by a vision of the Pullman car from which he and his bride have just departed. He sees in its sea-green velvet, its glass and its gleaming surfaces of silver, brass and darkly brilliant wood "all the glory of marriage, the environment of [his] new estate," and it is this vision, when conveyed to Scratchy, which defeats the badman.

But here we have a double reversal. Because for all of Scratchy's simplemindedness, his moment of defeat is also one of perception; he has learned where he is. While in his moment of unarmed triumph the marshal is even more unarmed than he knows, for he is unaware that his new estate has its own complications—even though he has already been subjected to them. In the actual Pullman car the Negro porter has played with him and his bride much as the gunman has played with the town (and as Crane plays with the reader's susceptibilities), and they have been bullied

> with skill in ways that did not make it exactly plain to them that they were bullied. He [the porter] subtly used all the manners of the most unconquerable kinds of snobbery. He oppressed them; but of his oppression they had small knowledge, and they speedily forgot that infrequently a number of travelers covered them with stares of derisive enjoyment.

And again, in the dining car the waiter's patronage had been so entwined with deference that when they returned to their coach their faces revealed "a sense of escape."

"Historically," we are told, "there was supposed to be something infinitely humorous in their situation . . ." And there is indeed something humorous in their situation which is limited neither to the circumstances of their middle-aged wedlock nor to their provincial discomfort in the Pullman car; there is the humor arising from their *historical* situation. For in face of the complexities of American civilization represented by the bullying yet patronizing Negro servants, the marshal is no less a "child of the earlier plains" than Scratchy Wilson. The Stephen Crane who wrote "The Bride" was essentially the same moral man who wrote the social protest of *Maggie*, only he has learned to hide his perceptions behind a sardonic smile. Still, the form of the story is at one with its meaning: the necessity for vigilance in confronting historical change is unending, and living with American change is much like Crane's description of keeping a small boat afloat in an angry sea, where "after successfully surmounting one wave you discover that there is another behind it just as important and just as nervously anxious to do something effective in the way of swamping boats." A similar vigilance is required when reading his fiction.

Perhaps at the root of our American fascination with the humorous story lies the awareness that if we don't know *where* we are, we have little chance of knowing *who* we are, that if we confuse the *time* we confuse the *place*; and that when we confuse these we endanger our humanity, both physically and morally. "Any room," writes Crane in "The Blue Hotel," "can present a tragic front; any room be comic." Thus men determine their own social weather, and human fate is a creation of human confusion.

The background of "The Blue Hotel" is that same confusion of time and place underlying "The Bride," and the Swede's failure to understand the rapidity of American historical change and its effect upon social relationships and personality is his undoing. Frightened and believing himself to be in a West that has long since passed, he evokes the violence which he associates with it out of the very intensity of his illusion. Arriving at a place where he believes he is to be killed, he forces a fight from men who are usually peaceful, wins it, then goes, full of his victory, to a peaceful barroom and there, confused perhaps by his ten years of hiding the reality of the human form (he is a tailor), as well as by drinking, he picks on the man who appears least likely to defend himself and is killed. No other Crane fiction—except, perhaps, "The Monster"—expresses such a violence of disgust with man and his condition, and one feels behind the noncommittal mask of the prose a conviction that man exists in the universe ever at the mercy of a capricious fate, a hostile nature, an indifferent and unjust god—*and* his own misconceptions.

And yet, for all the self-destructive actions of the Swede, the Easterner sees his death as the corporate sin of society. Society is responsible to itself *for* itself; the death is thus a failure of social charity. It is the same failure of social charity which characterizes "The Monster." Here Crane presents the cost of two acts of human loyalty and courage when they occur in a small, smug Northern town. Henry Johnson's self-sacrificial act, which destroys his face and his mind, is repaid first with applause and then with demands for his death or banishment. Dr. Trescott's loyalty to his oath as physician and to the man who has saved his son's life costs him his practice, his friends and ultimately his social identity. In short, "The Monster" places us in an atmosphere like that of post–Civil War America, and there is no question as to the Negro's part in it, nor to the fact that the issues go much deeper than the question of race. Indeed, the work is so fresh that the daily papers tell us all we need to know of its background and the timeliness of its implications.

As for Crane, the conscious artist, "The Monster" reminds us that he not only anticipated many of the techniques and themes of Hemingway, but that he also stands as the link between the Twain of *Pudd'nhead Wilson* and *Huckleberry Finn* and the Faulkner of *The Sound and the Fury*. The point is not simply that in *The Sound and the Fury*, as in Crane's work, a young boy is warned against "projecking" with flowers, or that Benjy is as much a "monster" as Henry Johnson, or Henry as much an idiot as Benjy, or that their communities are more monstrous than either, or that to touch either is considered a test of courage by the small fry, or even that both suffer when young white girls are frightened by them. The important point is that between Twain and the emergence of the driving honesty and social responsibility of Faulkner, no artist of Crane's caliber looked so steadily at the wholeness of American life and discovered such far-reaching symbolic equivalents for its unceasing state of civil war. Crane's work remains fresh today because he was a great artist, but perhaps he became a great artist because under conditions of pressure and panic he stuck to his guns.

Richard Wright's Blues

> If anybody ask you
> who sing this song,
> Say it was ole [Black Boy]
> done been here and gone.*

As a writer, Richard Wright has outlined for himself a dual role: to discover and depict the meaning of Negro experience, and to reveal to both Negroes and whites those problems of a psychological and emotional nature which arise between them when they strive for mutual understanding.

Now, in *Black Boy*, he has used his own life to probe what qualities of will, imagination and intellect are required of a Southern Negro in order to possess the meaning of his life in the United States. Wright is an important writer, perhaps the most articulate Negro American, and what he has to say is highly perceptive. Imagine Bigger Thomas projecting his own life in lucid prose guided, say, by the insights of Marx and Freud, and you have an idea of this autobiography.

Published at a time when any sharply critical approach to Negro life has been dropped as a wartime expendable, it should do much to redefine the problem of the Negro and American democracy. Its power can be observed in the shrill manner with which some professional "friends of the Negro people" have attempted to strangle the work in a noose of newsprint.

What in the tradition of literary autobiography is it like, this work described as a "great American autobiography"? As a non-white intellectual's statement of his relationship to Western culture, *Black*

---

*Signature formula used by blues singers at conclusion of song.

From *The Antioch Review*, Summer 1945.

Boy recalls the conflicting pattern of identification and rejection found in Nehru's *Toward Freedom*. In its use of fictional techniques, its concern with criminality (sin) and the artistic sensibility, and in its author's judgment and rejection of the narrow world of his origin, it recalls Joyce's rejection of Dublin in *A Portrait of the Artist*. And as a psychological document of life under oppressive conditions, it recalls *The House of the Dead*, Dostoevsky's profound study of the humanity of Russian criminals.

Such works were perhaps Wright's literary guides, aiding him to endow his life's incidents with communicable significance, providing him with ways of seeing, feeling and describing his environment. These influences, however, were encountered only after these first years of Wright's life were past, and were not part of the immediate folk culture into which he was born. In that culture the specific folk-art form which helped shape the writer's attitude toward his life and which embodied the impulse that contributes much to the quality and tone of his autobiography was the Negro blues.

This would bear a word of explanation. The blues is an impulse to keep the painful details and episodes of a brutal experience alive in one's aching consciousness, to finger its jagged grain, and to transcend it, not by the consolation of philosophy but by squeezing from it a near-tragic, near-comic lyricism. As a form, the blues is an autobiographical chronicle of personal catastrophe expressed lyrically. And certainly Wright's early childhood was crammed with catastrophic incidents. In a few short years his father deserted his mother, he knew intense hunger, he became a drunkard begging drinks from black stevedores in Memphis saloons; he had to flee Arkansas, where an uncle was lynched; he was forced to live with a fanatically religious grandmother in an atmosphere of constant bickering; he was lodged in an orphan asylum; he observed the suffering of his mother, who became a permanent invalid, while fighting off the blows of the poverty-stricken relatives with whom he had to live; he was cheated, beaten and kicked off jobs by white employees who disliked his eagerness to learn a trade; and to these objective circumstances must be added the subjective fact that Wright, with his sensitivity, extreme shyness and intelligence, was a problem child who rejected his family and was by them rejected.

Thus, along with the themes, equivalent descriptions of milieu and the perspectives to be found in Joyce, Nehru, Dostoevsky, George Moore and Rousseau, *Black Boy* is filled with blues-tempered echoes of railroad trains, the names of Southern towns and cities, estrangements, fights and flights, deaths and disappointments, charged with physical and spiritual hungers and pain. And like a blues sung by such an artist as Bessie Smith, its lyrical prose evokes the paradoxical, almost surreal image of a black boy singing lustily as he probes his own grievous wound.

In *Black Boy* two worlds have fused, two cultures merged, two impulses of Western man become coalesced. By discussing some of its cultural sources I hope to answer those critics who would make of the book a miracle and of its author a mystery. And while making no attempt to probe the mystery of the artist (who Hemingway says is "forged in injustice as a sword is forged"), I do hold that basically the prerequisites to the writing of *Black Boy* were, on the one hand, the microscopic degree of cultural freedom which Wright found in the South's stony injustice, and, on the other, the existence of a personality agitated to a state of almost manic restlessness. There were, of course, other factors, chiefly ideological, but these came later.

Wright speaks of his journey north as

> . . . taking a part of the South to transplant in alien soil, to see if it could grow differently, if it could drink of new and cool rains, bend in strange winds, respond to the warmth of other suns, and perhaps, to bloom. . . .

And just as Wright, the man, represents the blooming of the delinquent child of the autobiography, just so does *Black Boy* represent the flowering—cross-fertilized by pollen blown by the winds of strange cultures—of the humble blues lyric. There is, as in all acts of creation, a world of mystery in this, but there is also enough that is comprehensible for Americans to create the social atmosphere in which other black boys might freely bloom.

For certainly in the historical sense Wright is no exception. Born on a Mississippi plantation, he was subjected to all those blasting pressures which in a scant eighty years have sent the Negro people hurtling, without clearly defined trajectory, from slavery to emancipation, from log cabin to city tenement, from the white folks' fields and kitchens to factory assembly lines, and which, between two wars, have shattered the wholeness of its folk consciousness into a thousand writhing pieces.

Black Boy describes this process in the personal terms of *one* Negro childhood. Nevertheless, several critics have complained that it does not "explain" Richard Wright. Which, aside from the notion of art involved, serves to remind us that the prevailing mood of American criticism has so thoroughly excluded the Negro that it fails to recognize some of the most basic tenets of Western democratic thought when encountering them in a black skin. They forget that human life possesses an innate dignity and mankind an innate sense of nobility; that all men possess the tendency to dream and the compulsion to make their dreams reality; that the need to be ever dissatisfied and the urge ever to seek satisfaction is implicit in the human organism; and that all men are the victims and the beneficiaries of the goading, tormenting, commanding and informing activity of that imperious process known as the Mind—the Mind, as Valéry describes it, "armed with its inexhaustible questions."

Perhaps all this (in which lies the very essence of the human, and which Wright takes for granted) has been forgotten because the critics recognize neither Negro humanity nor the full extent to which the Southern community renders the fulfillment of human destiny impossible. And while it is true that *Black Boy* presents an almost unrelieved picture of a personality corrupted by brutal environment, it also presents those fresh, human responses brought to its world by the sensitive child:

> There was the *wonder* I felt when I first saw a brace of mountainlike, spotted, black-and-white horses clopping down a dusty road . . . the *delight* I caught in seeing long straight rows of red and green vegetables stretching away in the sun . . . the faint, cool kiss of *sensuality* when dew came on to my cheeks . . . the vague *sense of the infinite* as I looked down upon the yellow, dreaming waters of the Mississippi . . . the echoes of *nostalgia* I heard in the crying strings of wild geese . . . the *love* I had for the mute regality of tall, moss-clad oaks . . . the hint of *cosmic cruelty* that I *felt* when I saw the curved timbers of a wooden shack that had been warped in the summer sun . . . and there was the *quiet terror* that suffused my senses when vast hazes of gold washed earthward from star-heavy skies on silent nights. . . . [italics mine]

And a bit later, his reactions to religion:

> Many of the religious symbols appealed to my sensibilities and I responded to the dramatic vision of life held by the church, feeling that to live day by day with death as one's sole thought was to be so compassionately sensitive toward all life as to view all men as slowly dying, and the trembling sense of fate that welled up, sweet and melancholy, from the hymns blended with the sense of fate that I had already caught from life.

There was also the influence of his mother—so closely linked to his hysteria and sense of suffering—who (though he only implies it here) taught him, in the words of the dedication prefacing *Native Son*, "to revere the fanciful and the imaginative." There were also those white men—the one who allowed Wright to use his library privileges and the other who advised him to leave the South, and still others whose offers of friendship he was too frightened to accept.

Wright assumed that the nucleus of plastic sensibility is a human heritage: the right and the opportunity to dilate, deepen and enrich sensibility—democracy. Thus the drama of *Black Boy* lies in its depiction of what occurs when Negro sensibility attempts to fulfill itself in the undemocratic South. Here it is not the individual that is the immediate focus, as in Joyce's *Stephen Hero*, but that upon which his sensibility was nourished.

Those critics who complain that Wright has omitted the development of his own sensibility hold that the work thus fails as art. Others, because it presents too little of what they consider attractive in Negro life, charge that it distorts reality. Both groups miss a very obvious point: that whatever else the environment contained, it had as little chance of prevailing against the overwhelming weight of the child's unpleasant experiences as Beethoven's quartets would have of destroying the stench of a Nazi prison.

We come, then, to the question of art. The function, the psychology, of artistic selectivity is to eliminate from an art form all those elements of experience which contain no compelling significance. Life is as the sea, art a ship in which man conquers life's crushing formlessness, reducing it to a course, a series of swells, tides and wind currents inscribed on a chart. Though drawn from the world, "the organized significance of art," writes Malraux, "is stronger than all the multiplicity of the world; . . . that significance alone enables man to conquer chaos and to master destiny."

Wright saw his destiny—that combination of forces before which man feels powerless—in terms of a quick and casual violence inflicted upon him by both family and community. His response was likewise violent, and it has been his need to give that violence significance which has shaped his writings.

What were the ways by which other Negroes confronted their destiny?

In the South of Wright's childhood there were three general ways: they could accept the role created for them by the whites and perpetually resolve the resulting conflicts through the hope and emotional cartharsis of Negro religion; they could repress their dis-like of Jim Crow social relations while striving for a middle way of respectability, becoming—consciously or unconsciously—the ac-complices of the whites in oppressing their brothers; or they could reject the situation, adopt a criminal attitude, and carry on an un-ceasing psychological scrimmage with the whites, which often flared forth into physical violence.

Wright's attitude was nearest the last. Yet in it there was an all-important qualitative difference: it represented a groping for *individ-ual* values, in a black community whose values were what the young Negro critic Edward Bland has defined as "pre-individual." And herein lay the setting for the extreme conflict set off, both within his family and in the community, by Wright's assertion of individuality. The clash was sharpest on the psychological level, for, to quote Bland,

> In the pre-individualistic thinking of the Negro the stress is on the group. Instead of seeing in terms of the individual, the Negro sees in terms of "races," masses of peoples separated from other masses according to color. Hence, an act rarely bears intent against him as a Negro individual. He is singled out not as a person but as a specimen of an ostracized group. He knows that he never exists in his own right but only to the extent that others hope to make the race suffer vicariously through him.

This pre-individual state is induced artificially, like the regression to primitive states noted among cultured inmates of Nazi prisons. The primary technique in its enforcement is to impress the Negro child with the omniscience and omnipotence of the whites to the point that whites appear as ahuman as Jehovah, and as relentless as a Mississippi flood. Socially it is effected through an elaborate scheme of taboos supported by a ruthless physical violence, which strikes not only the offender but the entire black community. To wander from the paths of behavior laid down for the group is to become the agent of communal disaster.

In such a society the development of individuality depends upon a series of accidents, which often arise, as in Wright's case, from conditions within the Negro family. In Wright's life there was the accident that as a small child he could not distinguish between his fair-skinned grandmother and the white women of the town, thus developing skepticism as to their special status. To this was linked the accident of his having no close contacts with whites until after the child's normal formative period.

But these objective accidents not only link forward to these qualities of rebellion, criminality and intellectual questioning expressed in Wright's work today. They also link backward into the shadow of infancy where environment and consciousness are so darkly intertwined as to require the skill of a psychoanalyst to define their point of juncture. Nevertheless, at the age of four, Wright set the house afire and was beaten near to death by his frightened mother. This beating, followed soon by his father's desertion of the family, seems to be the initial psychological motivation of his quest for a new identification. While delirious from this beating, Wright was haunted "by huge wobbly white bags like the full udders of a cow, suspended from the ceiling above me [and] I was gripped by the fear that they were going to fall and drench me with some horrible liquid . . ."

It was as though the mother's milk had turned acid, and with it the whole pattern of life that had produced the ignorance, cruelty and fear that had fused with mother love and exploded in the beating. It is significant that the bags were of the hostile color white, and the female symbol that of the cow, the most stupid (and, to the small child, the most frightening) of domestic animals. Here in dream symbolism is expressed an attitude worthy of an Orestes. And the significance of the crisis is increased by virtue of the historical fact that the lower-class Negro family is matriarchal; the child turns not to the father to compensate if he feels mother-rejection, but to the grandmother, or to an aunt—and Wright rejected both of these.

Such rejection leaves the child open to psychological insecurity, distrust and all of those hostile environmental forces from which the family functions to protect it.

One of the Southern Negro family's methods of protecting the child is the severe beating—a homeopathic dose of the violence generated by black and white relationships. Such beatings as Wright's were administered for the child's own good—a good which the child resisted, thus giving family relationships an undercurrent of fear and hostility, which differs qualitatively from that found in patriarchal middle-class families, because here the severe beating is administered by the mother, leaving the child no parental sanctuary. He must ever embrace violence along with maternal tenderness, or else reject in his helpless way the mother.

The division between the Negro parents of Wright's mother's generation, whose sensibilities were often bound by their proximity to the slave experience, and their children, who historically and through the rapidity of American change stand emotionally and psychologically much farther away, is quite deep. Indeed, sometimes as deep as the cultural distance between Yeats's *Autobiographies* and a Bessie Smith blues. This is the historical background to those incidents of family strife in *Black Boy* which have caused reviewers to question Wright's judgment of Negro emotional relationships.

We have here a problem in the sociology of sensibility that is obscured by certain psychological attitudes brought to Negro life by whites. The first is the attitude which compels whites to impute to Negroes sentiments, attitudes and insights which, as a group living under certain definite social conditions, Negroes could not humanly possess. It is the identical mechanism which William Empson identifies in literature as "pastoral." It implies that since Negroes possess the richly human virtues credited to them, then their social position is advantageous and should not be bettered, and, continuing syllogistically, the white individual need feel no guilt over his participation in Negro oppression.

The second attitude leads whites to misjudge Negro passion,

looking upon it as they do out of the turgidity of their own frustrated yearning for emotional warmth, their capacity for sensation having been constricted by the impersonal mechanized relationships typical of bourgeois society. The Negro is idealized into a symbol of sensation, of unhampered social and sexual relationships. And when *Black Boy* questions whites' illusion, they are thwarted much in the manner of the Occidental who, after observing the erotic character of a primitive dance, "shacks up" with a native woman, only to discover that far from possessing the hair-trigger sexual responses of a Stork Club "babe," she is relatively phlegmatic.

The point is not that American Negroes are primitives, but that as a group their social situation does not provide for the type of emotional relationships attributed to them. For how could the South, recognized as a major part of the backward third of the nation, nurture in the black, most brutalized section of its population, those forms of human relationships achievable only in the most highly developed areas of civilization?

Champions of this "Aren't-Negroes-Wonderful?" school of thinking often bring Paul Robeson and Marian Anderson forward as examples of highly developed sensibility, but actually they are only its *promise*. Both received their development from an extensive personal contact with European culture, free from the influences which shape Southern Negro personality. In the United States, Wright, who is the only Negro literary artist of equal caliber, had to wait years, and escape to another environment before discovering the moral and ideological equivalents of his childhood attitudes.

Man cannot express that which does not exist—either in the form of dreams, ideas or realities—in his environment. Neither his thoughts nor his feelings, his sensibility nor his intellect are fixed, innate qualities. They are processes which arise out of the interpenetration of human instinct with environment, through the process called experience, each changing and being changed by the other. Negroes cannot possess many of the sentiments attributed to them because the same changes in environment which, through experience, enlarge man's intellect (and thus his capacity for still greater change) also modify his feelings—which in turn increase his sensibility, i.e., his sensitivity to refinements of impression and subtleties of emotion. The extent of these changes depends upon the quality of political and cultural freedom in the environment.

Intelligence tests have measured the quick rise in intellect which takes place in Southern Negroes after moving north, but little attention has been paid to the mutations effected in their sensibilities. However, the two go hand in hand. Intellectual complexity is accompanied by emotional complexity, refinement of thought, and refinement of feeling. The movement north affects more than the Negro's wage scale; it affects his entire psychosomatic structure.

The rapidity of Negro intellectual growth in the North is due partially to objective factors present in the environment, to influences of the industrial city and to a greater political freedom. But there are also changes within the "inner world." In the North energies are released and given *intellectual* channelization—energies which in most Negroes in the South have been forced to take either a *physical* form or, as with potentially intellectual types like Wright, to be expressed as nervous tension, anxiety and hysteria. Which is nothing mysterious. The human organism responds to environmental stimuli by converting them into either physical and/or intellectual energy. And what is called hysteria is suppressed intellectual energy expressed physically.

The "physical" character of their expression makes for much of the difficulty in understanding American Negroes. Negro music and dances are frenziedly erotic, Negro religious ceremonies violently ecstatic, Negro speech strongly rhythmical and weighted with image and gesture. But there is more in this sensuousness than the unrestraint and insensitivity found in primitive cultures; nor is it simply the relatively spontaneous and undifferentiated responses of a people living in close contact with the soil. For despite Jim Crow, Negro life does not exist in a vacuum, but in the seething vortex of those tensions generated by the most highly industrialized of Western nations. The welfare of the most humble black Mississippi sharecropper is affected less by the flow of the seasons and the rhythm of natural events than by the fluctuations of the stock market, even though, as Wright states of his father, the sharecropper's memories, actions and emotions are shaped by his immediate contact with nature and the crude social relations of the South.

All of this makes the American Negro far different from the "simple" specimen for which he is taken. And the "physical" quality offered as evidence of his primitive simplicity is actually the form of his complexity. The American Negro is a Western type whose social condition creates a state which is almost the reverse of the cataleptic trance: instead of his consciousness being lucid to the reality around it while the body is rigid, here it is the body which is alert, reacting to pressures which the constricting forces of Jim Crow block off from the transforming, concept-creating activity of the brain. The "eroticism" of Negro expression springs from much the same conflict as that displayed in the violent gesturing of a man who attempts to express a complicated concept with a limited vocabulary; thwarted ideational energy is converted into unsatisfactory pantomime, and his words are burdened with meanings they cannot convey. Here lies the source of the basic ambiguity of *Native Son*, wherein in order to translate Bigger's complicated feelings into universal ideas, Wright had to force into Bigger's consciousness concepts and ideas which his intellect could not formulate. Between Wright's skill and knowledge and the potentials of Bigger's mute feelings lay a thousand years of conscious culture.

In the South the sensibilities of both blacks and whites are inhibited by the rigidly defined environment. For the Negro there is relative safety as long as the impulse toward individuality is suppressed. (Lynchings have occurred because Negroes painted their homes.) And it is the task of the Negro family to adjust the child to the Southern milieu; through it the currents, tensions and impulses generated within the human organism by the flux and flow of events are given their distribution. This also gives the group its distinctive character, which, because of Negroes' suppressed minority position, is very much in the nature of an elaborate but limited defense mechanism. Its function is dual: to protect the Negro from whirling away from the undifferentiated mass of his people into the unknown, symbolized in its most abstract form by insanity, and most concretely by lynching; and to protect him from those unknown forces *within himself* which might urge him to reach out for that social and human equality which the white South says he cannot have. Rather than throw himself against the charged wires of his prison, he annihilates the impulses within him.

The pre-individualistic black community discourages individuality out of self-defense. Having learned through experience that the whole group is punished for the actions of the single member, it has worked out efficient techniques of behavior control. For in many Southern communities everyone knows everyone else and is vulnerable to his opinions. In some communities everyone is "related," regardless of blood ties. The regard shown by the group for its members, its general communal character and its cohesion are often mentioned, for by comparison with the coldly impersonal relationships of the urban industrial community, its relationships are personal and warm.

Black Boy, however, illustrates that this personal quality, shaped by outer violence and inner fear, is ambivalent. Personal warmth is accompanied by an equally personal coldness, kindliness by cruelty, regard by malice. And these opposites are as quickly set off against the member who gestures toward individuality as a lynch mob forms at the cry of rape. Negro leaders have often been exasperated by this phenomenon, and Booker T. Washington (who demanded far less of Negro humanity than Richard Wright) described the Negro community as a basket of crabs, wherein should one attempt to climb out, the others immediately pull him back.

The member who breaks away is apt to be more impressed by its negative than by its positive character. He becomes a stranger even to his relatives and he interprets gestures of protection as blows of oppression—from which there is no hiding place, because every area of Negro life is affected. Even parental love is given a qualitative balance akin to "sadism," and the extent of beatings and psychological maimings meted out by Southern Negro parents rivals those described by the nineteenth-century Russian writers as characteristic of peasant life under the Czars. The horrible thing is that the cruelty is also an expression of concern, of love.

In discussing the inadequacies for democratic living typical of the education provided Negroes by the South, a Negro educator has coined the term *mis-education*. Within the ambit of the black family this takes the form of training the child away from curiosity and adventure, against reaching out for those activities lying beyond the borders of the black community. And when the child resists, the parent discourages him, first with the formula, "That there's for white folks. Colored can't have it," and finally with a beating.

It is not, then, the family and communal violence described by *Black Boy* that is unusual, but that Wright *recognized* and made no peace with its essential cruelty—even when, like a babe freshly emerged from the womb, he could not discern where his own personality ended and it began. Ordinarily both parent and child are protected against this cruelty, seeing it as love and finding subjective sanction for it in the spiritual authority of the Fifth Commandment, and on the secular level in the legal and extralegal structure of the Jim Crow system. The child who did not rebel, or who was unsuccessful in his rebellion, learned a masochistic submissiveness and a denial of the impulse toward Western culture when it stirred within him.

Why then have Southern whites, who claim to "know" the Negro, missed all this? Simply because they, too, are armored against the horror and the cruelty. Either they deny the Negro's humanity and feel no cause to measure his actions against civilized norms; or they protect themselves from their guilt in the Negro's condition—and from their fear that their cooks might poison them, or that their nursemaids might strangle their infant charges, or that their field hands might do them violence—by attributing to them a superhuman capacity for love, kindliness and forgiveness. Nor does this in any way contradict their stereotyped conviction that all Negroes (meaning those with whom they have no contact) are given to the most animal behavior.

It is only when the individual, whether white or black, *rejects* the pattern that he awakens to the nightmare of his life. Perhaps much of the South's regressive character springs from the fact that many, jarred by some casual crisis into wakefulness, flee hysterically into the sleep of violence or the coma of apathy again. For the penalty of wakefulness is to encounter ever more violence and horror than the sensibilities can sustain unless translated into some form of social action. Perhaps the impassioned character so noticeable among those white Southern liberals so active in the Negro's cause is due to their sense of accumulated horror; their passion, like the violence in Faulkner's novels, is evidence of a profound spiritual vomiting.

This compulsion is even more active in Wright and the increasing number of Negroes who have said an irrevocable "no" to the Southern pattern. Wright learned that it is not enough merely to reject the white South, but that he had also to reject that part of the South which lay within him. As a rebel he formulated that rejection negatively, because it was the negative face of the Negro community upon which he looked most often as a child. It is this he is contemplating when he writes:

> Whenever I thought of the essential bleakness of black life in America, I knew that Negroes had never been allowed to catch the full spirit of Western civilization, that they lived somehow in it but not of it. And when I brooded upon the cultural barrenness of black life, I wondered if clean, positive tenderness, love, honor, loyalty and the capacity to remember were native to man. I asked myself if these human qualities were not fostered, won, struggled and suffered for, preserved in ritual from one generation to another.

But far from implying that Negroes have no capacity for culture, as one critic interprets it, this is the strongest affirmation that they have. Wright is pointing out what should be obvious (especially to his Marxist critics): that Negro sensibility is socially and historically conditioned; that Western culture must be won, confronted like the animal in a Spanish bullfight, dominated by the red shawl of codified experience and brought heaving to its knees.

Wright knows perfectly well that Negro life is a by-product of Western civilization, and that in it, if only one possesses the humanity and humility to see, are to be discovered all those impulses, tendencies, life and cultural forms to be found elsewhere in Western society.

The problem arises because the special condition of Negroes in the United States, including the defensive character of Negro life itself (the "will toward organization" noted in the Western capitalist appears in the Negro as a will to camouflage, to dissimulate), so distorts these forms as to render their recognition as difficult as finding a wounded quail against the brown and yellow leaves of a Mississippi thicket; even the spilled blood blends with the background. Having himself been in the position of the quail—to expand the metaphor—Wright's wounds have told him both the question and the answer which every successful hunter must discover for himself: "Where would I hide if *I* were a wounded quail?" But perhaps that requires more sympathy with one's quarry than most hunters possess. Certainly it requires such a sensitivity to the shifting guises of humanity under pressure as to allow them to identify themselves with the human content, whatever its outer form, and even with those Southern Negroes to whom Paul Robeson's name is only a rolling sound in the fear-charged air.

Let us close with one final word about the blues: their attraction lies in this, that they at once express both the agony of life and the possibility of conquering it through sheer toughness of spirit. They fall short of tragedy only in that they provide no solution, offer no scapegoat but the self. Nowhere in America today is there social or political action based upon the solid realities of Negro life depicted in *Black Boy;* perhaps that is why, with its refusal to offer solutions, it is like the blues. Yet in it thousands of Negroes will for the first time see their destiny in public print. Freed here of fear and the threat of violence, their lives have at last been organized, scaled down to possessable proportions. And in this lies Wright's most important achievement: he has converted the American Negro impulse toward self-annihilation and "going-under-ground" into a will to confront the world, to evaluate his experience honestly and throw his findings unashamedly into the guilty conscience of America.

Beating That Boy

DURING these post-military-phase-of-the-war days when a Negro is asked what occurs when he visits with white friends, he is likely to chuckle and drily reply, "Oh, we beat that boy," meaning to belabor in polite conversation what is commonly called the "Negro problem." Though Negroes laugh when the phrase is used, beneath its folksy surface there lies—like a booby trap in a music box of folk tunes—a disillusionment that only its attitude of detached participation saves from exploding into violent cynicism, its counterpart among those Negroes who know no whites as friends.

For the racial situation has become like an irrational sea in which Americans flounder like convoyed ships in a gale. The phrase rotates like a gyroscope of irony of which the Negro maintains a hazardous stability as the sea-tossed ship of his emotions whirls him willy-nilly along: lunging him toward the shoals of bitter rejection (of the ideology that makes him the sole sacrifice of America's tragedy); now away toward the mine-strewn shores of hopelessness (that despite the war, democracy is still discussed on an infantile level and himself in pre-adult terms); now smashing him flush against waves of anger that threaten to burst his seams in revolt (that his condition is so outrageously flagrant); now teetering him clear on a brief, calm, sun-lit swell of self-amusement (that he must cling to the convoy though he doubts its direction); now knocking him erect, like a whale on its tail, before plunging again into the still dark night of the one lone "rational" thing, the pounding irrational sea.

This is a nightmarishly "absurd" situation, and perhaps no major problem affecting the destiny of a nation has ever received such superficial discussion. As Bucklin Moon knew when he conceived *Primer for White Folks*, a great deal of the superficiality comes from

From *The New Republic*, October 22, 1945.

the general ignorance prevailing in our society of the historical and social condition of the black tenth of the population. He might have subtitled his anthology, *A Short Course on the American Negro for Those Who "Beat That Boy."*

Primer for White Folks comes as a result of the long fight which Negroes have made to make their story known, and the aroused efforts of liberal whites, many of them Southerners, to chart more accurately that heart-lashing sea of irrationality called the "Negro problem." The fair-minded but uninformed should read the book to learn how much they have been humiliated, insulted and injured by the Rankins and Bilbos who speak in their name to the world.

Primer for White Folks is something new in its genre. Unlike similar anthologies, it does not consist solely of Negro contributions, but of writings on the racial situation as seen by both white and Negro authors. The book, which presents such writers as Will W. Alexander, Kay Boyle, Sterling Brown, Henrietta Buckmaster, Fanny Kemble, Langston Hughes, Wendell Wilkie, Lillian Smith, Dorothy Parker, James T. Farrell and Richard Wright, divides into three major sections. The first, "Heritage," covers slavery, the Civil War and the end of Reconstruction in Negro disfranchisement, and presents unfamiliar information on Negro slave revolts and heroism; the second consists of short stories about the mores of our society and the relationships, "sometimes ludicrous, sometimes tragic, between Negroes and whites"; and the third, "Today and Tomorrow," presents the thoughts of contemporary white and Negro writers on the "Negro question" and their recommendations for its solution. This section is especially valuable and will bear repeated reference as the tense period we have just entered unfolds. Here are the most democratically informed discussions of the racial situation to appear in print since Pearl Harbor.

But if you believe you have read many of these pieces before, then you're mistaken; even if you *have*, you haven't. For here, under Bucklin Moon's creative editing, they have been placed in a fresh context of meaning where, like the subtle relationships of forms in a great painting, they ever reveal something new. Encountering some of them here, one wonders whether Moon's conception was not superior to even the best images which he found to give it articulation. What an astounding book this could have been had every piece been on a par with its conception! Since hardly any aspect of our culture escapes the blight of hypocrisy implicit in our social institutions, it is not surprising that many of the pieces mix appeal for fair play with double-talk; or that most are much too fearful of that absolute concept "democracy," circling above it like planes being forced to earth in a fog. They seemed concerned most often with patching up the merry-go-round-that-broke-down than with the projection of that oh-so-urgently-needed new American humanism. Here, too, the boy comes in for a bit of a beating.

These negative criticisms of its parts do not, however, apply to the anthology as a whole. For the negative when piled up quantitatively often assumes a positive value; and certainly it is valuable to detect the cracks in the tones of our most Liberty Bell voices. Then, too, such studies inevitably reveal as much about the white American as about the American Negro—which lends them a value that is generally ignored. When viewed from a perspective which takes this circumstance into account, *Primer for White Folks* will be prized for the oblique light it throws upon an aspect of American writing which was not its immediate concern.

One notices, for instance, that most of the fiction presented here, with the exception of stories by Dorothy Parker, Kay Boyle, Erskine Caldwell and William March, is by writers who have appeared since the Depression, and that most of the widely read authors of the between-wars period are, with the exceptions of James T. Farrell and Richard Wright, conspicuously missing. We are reminded that from 1776 to 1876 there was a conception of democracy current in this country that allowed the writer to identify himself with the Negro, and that had such an anthology been conceivable during the nineteenth century, it could have included such writers as Whitman, Emerson, Thoreau, Hawthorne, Melville and Mark Twain. For slavery (it was not termed a "Negro problem" then) was a vital issue in the American consciousness, symbolic of the condition of Man, and a valid aspect of the writer's reality. Only after the Emancipation and the return of the Southern ruling class to power in the counter-revolution of 1876, was the Negro issue pushed into the underground of the American conscience and ignored.

To ignore, however, is not to nullify, and the fact that so many of our important writers are missing from *Primer for White Folks* raises the question whether the existence of the race problem in our culture has not had an insidiously powerful effect upon twentieth-century writing that has not been generally suspected. Perhaps here, too, lies a partial explanation of why we have come to regard certain faults of this writing as excellences.

But first let me hasten to say that I do not mean to imply that whites had any obligation to write of Negroes, nor that in the depiction of the racial situation lies any blueprint for a supreme fiction (if so, all Negro writers would rate with Tolstoy and Balzac, Shakespeare and Dostoevsky). Unfortunately, the connection between literature and society is seldom so naïvely direct. There is, nevertheless, an inescapable connection between the writer and the beliefs and attitudes current in his culture, and it is here exactly that the "Negro problem" begins to exert a powerful, uncalculated influence.

For since 1876 the race issue has been like a stave driven into the American system of values, a stave so deeply imbedded in the American *ethos* as to render America a nation of ethical schizophrenics. Believing truly in democracy on one side of their minds, they act on the other in violation of its most sacred principles; holding that all men are created equal, they treat thirteen million Americans as though they were not.

There are, as always, political and economic motives for this rending of values, but in terms of the ethical and psychological, what was opportunistically labeled the "Negro problem" is actually a guilt problem charged with pain. Just how painful might be judged from the ceaseless effort expended to dull its throbbings with the anesthesia of legend, myth, hypnotic ritual and narcotic modes of thinking. And not only have our popular culture, our newspapers, radio and cinema been devoted to justifying the Negro's condition and the conflict created thereby, but even our social sciences and serious literature have been conscripted—all in the effort to drown out the persistent voice of outraged conscience.

This unwillingness to resolve the conflict in keeping with his democratic ideals has compelled the white American, figuratively, to force the Negro down into the deeper level of his consciousness, into the inner world, where reason and madness mingle with hope and memory and endlessly give birth to nightmare and to dream; down into the province of the psychiatrist and the artist, from whence spring the lunatic's fancy and the work of art. It is a dangerous region even for the artist, and his tragedy lies in the fact that in order to tap the fluid fire of inspiration, he must perpetually descend and re-encounter not only the ghosts of his former selves, but all of the unconquered anguish of his living.

Obviously this position need not be absolutely disadvantageous for the Negro. It might, in a different culture, be highly strategic, enlisting in his cause the freedom-creating powers of art. For imprisoned in the deepest drives in human society, it is practically impossible for the white American to think of sex, of economics, his children or womenfolk, or of sweeping socio-political changes, without summoning into consciousness fear-flecked images of black men. Indeed, it seems that the Negro has become identified with those unpleasant aspects of conscience and consciousness which it is part of the American's character to avoid. Thus, when the literary artist attempts to tap the charged springs issuing from his inner world, up float his misshapen and bloated images of the Negro, like the fetid bodies of the drowned, and he turns away, discarding an ambiguous substance which the artists of other cultures would confront boldly and humanize into the stuff of a tragic art. It is as though we were to discard the beneficial properties of the x-ray simply because when used without the protection of a leaden screen it might burn us or produce sterility.

Indeed, the racial situation has exerted an influence upon the writer similar to that of an x-ray concealed in a radio. Moving about, perhaps ignoring, perhaps enjoying Jack Benny and Rochester or a hot jazz band, he is unaware of his exposure to a force that shrivels his vital sperm. Not that it has rendered him completely sterile, but that it has caused him to produce deformed progeny—literary offspring without hearts, without brains, viscera or vision, and some even without genitalia.

Thus it has not been its failure to depict racial matters that has determined the quality of American writing, but that the writer has formed the habit of living and thinking in a culture that is opposed to the deep thought and feeling necessary to profound art; hence its avoidance of emotion, its fear of ideas, its obsession with mere physical violence and pain, its overemphasis of understatement, its precise and complex verbal constructions for converting goatsong into carefully modulated squeaks.

Nor are the stories and articles included in *Primer for White Folks* free of these faults. But if they bear the mark of the culture out of which they spring, they are also appeals for a superior society and a more vital literature. As arranged here, they offer a vivid statement of the strengths and weaknesses of the new mood born in the hearts of Americans during the war, a mood more precise in its fears (of racial bloodshed) than definite in its hopes (symbolized most concretely in the frantic efforts of interracial organizations and mayors' committees to discover a foolproof technique of riot control). But more significant than their obvious fears and vacillations, they are valuable for something practically missing from American writing since *Huckleberry Finn:* a search for images of black and white fraternity.

Brave Words for a
Startling Occasion

FIRST, as I express my gratitude for this honor which you have bestowed on me, let me say that I take it that you are rewarding my efforts rather than my not quite fully achieved attempt at a major novel. Indeed, if I were asked in all seriousness just what I considered to be the chief significance of *Invisible Man* as a fiction, I would reply: its experimental attitude, and its attempt to return to the mood of personal moral responsibility for democracy which typified the best of our nineteenth-century fiction. That my first novel should win this most coveted prize must certainly indicate that there is a crisis in the American novel. You as critics have told us so, and current fiction sales would indicate that the reading public agrees. Certainly the younger novelists concur. The explosive nature of events mocks our brightest efforts. And the very "facts" which the naturalists assumed would make us free have lost the power to protect us from despair. Controversy now rages over just what aspects of American experience are suitable for novelistic treatment. The prestige of the theorists of the so-called novel of manners has been challenged. Thus, after a long period of stability we find our assumptions concerning the novel being called into question. And though I was only vaguely aware of it, it was this growing crisis which shaped the writing of *Invisible Man*.

After the usual apprenticeship of imitation and seeking with delight to examine my experience through the discipline of the novel, I became gradually aware that the forms of so many of the works which impressed me were too restricted to contain the experience which I knew. The diversity of American life with its extreme fluidity

Address for Presentation Ceremony, National Book Award, January 27, 1953.

and openness seemed too vital and alive to be caught for more than the briefest instant in the tight, well-made Jamesian novel, which was, for all its artistic perfection, too concerned with "good taste" and stable areas. Nor could I safely use the forms of the "hard-boiled" novel, with its dedication to physical violence, social cynicism and understatement. Understatement depends, after all, upon commonly held assumptions, and my minority status rendered all such assumptions questionable. There was also a problem of language, and even dialogue, which, with its hard-boiled stance and its monosyllabic utterance, is one of the shining achievements of twentieth-century American writing. For despite the notion that its rhythms were those of everyday speech, I found that when compared with the rich babel of idiomatic expression around me, a language full of imagery and gesture and rhetorical canniness, it was embarrassingly austere. Our speech I found resounding with an alive language swirling with over three hundred years of American living, a mixture of the folk, the Biblical, the scientific and the political. Slangy in one stance, academic in another, loaded poetically with imagery at one moment, mathematically bare of imagery in the next. As for the rather rigid concepts of reality which informed a number of the works which impressed me and to which I owe a great deal, I was forced to conclude that reality was far more mysterious and uncertain, and more exciting, and still, despite its raw violence and capriciousness, more promising. To attempt to express that American experience which has carried one back and forth and up and down the land and across, and across again the great river, from freight train to Pullman car, from contact with slavery to contact with a world of advanced scholarship, art and science, is simply to burst such neatly understated forms of the novel asunder.

A novel whose range was both broader and deeper was needed. And in my search I found myself turning to our classical nineteenth-century novelists. I felt that except for the work of William Faulkner something vital had gone out of American prose after Mark Twain. I came to believe that the writers of that period took a much greater responsibility for the condition of democracy and, indeed, their works were imaginative projections of the conflicts within the human heart which arose when the sacred principles of the Constitution and the Bill of Rights clashed with the practical exigencies of human greed and fear, hate and love. Naturally I was attracted to these writers as a Negro. Whatever they thought of my people per se, in their imaginative economy the Negro symbolized both the man lowest down and the mysterious, underground aspect of human personality. In a sense the Negro was the gauge of the human condition as it waxed and waned in our democracy. These writers were willing to confront the broad complexities of American life, and we are the richer for their having done so.

Thus to see America with an awareness of its rich diversity and its almost magical fluidity and freedom, I was forced to conceive of a novel unburdened by the narrow naturalism which has led, after so many triumphs, to the final and unrelieved despair which marks so much of our current fiction. I was to dream of a prose which was flexible, and swift as American change is swift, confronting the inequalities and brutalities of our society forthrightly, yet thrusting forth its images of hope, human fraternity and individual self-realization. It would use the richness of our speech, the idiomatic expression and the rhetorical flourishes from past periods which are still alive among us. And despite my personal failures, there must be possible a fiction which, leaving sociology to the scientists, can arrive at the truth about the human condition, here and now, with all the bright magic of a fairy tale.

What has been missing from so much experimental writing has been the passionate will to dominate reality as well as the laws of art. This will is the true source of the experimental attitude. We who struggle with form and with America should remember Eidothea's advice to Menelaus when in the *Odyssey* he and his friends are seeking their way home. She tells him to seize her father, Proteus, and to hold him fast "however he may struggle and fight. He will turn into all sorts of shapes to try you," she says, "into all the creatures that live and move upon the earth, into water, into blazing fire; but you must hold him fast and press him all the harder. When he is himself, and questions you in the same shape that he was when you saw him in his bed, let the old man go; and then, sir, ask which god it is who is angry, and how you shall make your way homewards over the fish-giving sea."

For the novelist, Proteus stands for both America and the inheritance of illusion through which all men must fight to achieve reality; the offended god stands for our sins against those principles we all hold sacred. The way home we seek is that condition of man's being at home in the world, which is called love, and which we term democracy. Our task then is always to challenge the apparent forms of reality—that is, the fixed manners and values of the few—and to struggle with it until it reveals its mad, vari-implicated chaos, its false faces, and on until it surrenders its insight, its truth. We are fortunate as American writers in that with our variety of racial and national traditions, idioms and manners, we are yet one. On its profoundest level American experience is of a whole. Its truth lies in its diversity and swiftness of change. Through forging forms of the novel worthy of it, we achieve not only the promise of our lives, but we anticipate the resolution of those world problems of humanity which for a moment seem to those who are in awe of statistics completely insoluble.

Whenever we as Americans have faced serious crises we have returned to fundamentals; this, in brief, is what I have tried to do.

The World and the Jug

"The World and the Jug" is actually a combination of two separate pieces. The first, bearing the original title, was written at the suggestion of Myron Kolatch of The New Leader, *who was interested in my reactions, via telephone, to an essay by Irving Howe titled "Black Boys and Native Sons," which appeared in the Autumn 1963 issue of Howe's magazine,* Dissent.

Usually such a reply would have appeared in the same magazine in which the original essay was published, but in this instance, and since it hadn't occurred to me to commit my reactions to paper, they went to the editor who asked for them. The second section of the essay, originally entitled, "A Rejoinder," was written after Irving Howe had consented to reply, in The New Leader, *of February 3, 1964, to my attack. There is, unfortunately, too little space here to do justice to Howe's arguments, and it is recommended that the interested reader consult Mr. Howe's book of essays,* A World More Attractive—*a book worthy of his attention far beyond the limits of our exchange—published by Horizon Press in 1963.*

> What runs counter to the revolutionary convention is, in revolutionary histories, suppressed more imperiously than embarrassing episodes in private memoirs, and by the same obscure forces. . . .
>
> —*André Malraux*

I

FIRST, three questions: Why is it so often true that when critics confront the American as *Negro* they suddenly drop their advanced critical armament and revert with an air of confident superiority to quite primitive modes of analysis? Why is it that sociology-oriented

From *The New Leader*, December 9, 1963, and February 3, 1964.

critics seem to rate literature so far below politics and ideology that they would rather kill a novel than modify their presumptions concerning a given reality which it seeks in its own terms to project? Finally, why is it that so many of those who would tell us the meaning of Negro life never bother to learn how varied it really is?

These questions are aroused by "Black Boys and Native Sons," an essay by Irving Howe, the well-known critic and editor of *Dissent*, in the Autumn 1963 issue of that magazine. It is a lively piece, written with something of the Olympian authority that characterized Hannah Arendt's "Reflections on Little Rock" in the Winter 1959 *Dissent* (a dark foreshadowing of the Eichmann blowup). And in addition to a hero, Richard Wright, it has two villians, James Baldwin and Ralph Ellison, who are seen as "black boys" masquerading as false, self-deceived "native sons." Wright himself is given a diversity of roles (all conceived by Howe): he is not only the archetypal and true-blue black boy—the "honesty" of his famous autobiography established this for Howe—but the spiritual father of Ellison, Baldwin and all other Negroes of literary bent to come. Further, in the platonic sense he is his own father and the cultural hero who freed Ellison and Baldwin to write more "modulated" prose.

Howe admires Wright's accomplishments, and is frankly annoyed by the more favorable evaluation currently placed upon the works of the younger men. His claims for *Native Son* are quite broad:

> The day [it] appeared, American culture was changed forever . . . it made impossible a repetition of the old lies . . . it brought into the open . . . the fear and violence that have crippled and may yet destroy our culture. . . . A blow at the white man, the novel forced him to recognize himself as an oppressor. A blow at the black man, the novel forced him to recognize the cost of his submission. *Native Son* assaulted the most cherished of American vanities: the hope that the accumulated injustices of the past would bring with it no lasting penalties, the fantasy that in his humiliation the Negro somehow retained a sexual potency . . . that made it necessary to envy and

still more to suppress him. Speaking from the black wrath of retribution, Wright insisted that history can be a punishment. He told us the one thing even the most liberal whites preferred not to hear: that Negroes were far from patient or forgiving, that they were scarred by fear, that they hated every moment of their suppression even when seeming most acquiescent, and that often enough they hated *us*, the decent and cultivated white men who from complicity or neglect shared in the responsibility of their plight. . . .

There are also negative criticisms: that the book is "crude," "melodramatic" and marred by "claustrophobia" of vision, that its characters are "cartoons," etc. But these defects Howe forgives because of the book's "clenched militancy." One wishes he had stopped there. For in his zeal to champion Wright, it is as though he felt it necessary to stage a modern version of the Biblical myth of Noah, Ham, Shem and Japheth (based originally, I'm told, on a castration ritual), with first Baldwin and then Ellison acting out the impious role of Ham: Baldwin by calling attention to Noah—Wright's artistic nakedness in his famous essays, "Everybody's Protest Novel" (1949) and "Many Thousands Gone" (1951); Ellison by rejecting "narrow naturalism" as a fictional method, and by alluding to the "diversity, fluidity and magical freedom of American life" on that (for him at least) rather magical occasion when he was awarded the National Book Award. Ellison also offends by having the narrator of *Invisible Man* speak of his life (Howe either missing the irony or assuming that *I* did) as one of "infinite possibilities" while living in a hole in the ground.

Howe begins by attacking Baldwin's rejection in "Everybody's Protest Novel" of the type of literature he labeled "protest fiction" (*Uncle Tom's Cabin* and *Native Son* being prime examples), and which he considered incapable of dealing adequately with the complexity of Negro experience. Howe, noting that this was the beginning of Baldwin's career, sees the essay's underlying motive as a declaration of Baldwin's intention to transcend "the sterile categories of 'Negroness,' whether those enforced by the white world or those defensively erected by the Negroes themselves. No longer mere victim or rebel, the Negro would stand free in a self-achieved humanity. As Baldwin put it some years later, he hoped to 'prevent himself from becoming merely a Negro; or even, merely, a Negro writer.'" Baldwin's elected agency for self-achievement would be the novel—as it turns out, it was the essay *and* the novel—but the novel, states Howe, "is an inherently ambiguous genre: it strains toward formal autonomy and can seldom avoid being public gesture."

I would have said that it is *always* a public gesture, though not necessarily a political one. I would also have pointed out that the American Negro novelist is himself "inherently ambiguous." As he strains toward self-achievement as artist (and here he can only "integrate" and free himself), he moves toward fulfilling his dual potentialities as Negro and American. While Howe agrees with Baldwin that "literature and sociology are not one and the same," he notes nevertheless that "it is equally true that such statements hardly begin to cope with the problem of how a writer's own experience affects his desire to represent human affairs in a work of fiction." Thus Baldwin's formula evades "through rhetorical sweep, the genuinely difficult issue of the relationship between social experience and literature." And to Baldwin's statement that one writes "out of one thing only—one's own experience" (I would have added, for the novelist, this qualification: one's own experience as understood and ordered through one's knowledge of self, culture and literature), Howe, appearing suddenly in blackface, replies with a rhetorical sweep of his own:

> What, then, was the experience of a man with a black skin, what *could* it be here in this country? How could a Negro put pen to paper, how could he so much as think or breathe, without some impulsion to protest, be it harsh or mild, political or private, released or buried? . . . The "sociology" of his exis-

tence forms a constant pressure on his literary work, and not merely in the way this might be true of any writer, but with a pain and ferocity that nothing could remove.

I must say that this brought a shock of recognition. Some twelve years ago, a friend argued with me for hours that I could not possibly write a novel because my experience as a Negro had been too excruciating to allow me to achieve that psychological and emotional distance necessary to artistic creation. Since he "knew" Negro experience better than I, I could not convince him that he might be wrong. Evidently Howe feels that unrelieved suffering is the only "real" Negro experience, and that the true Negro writer must be ferocious.

But there is also an American Negro tradition which teaches one to deflect racial provocation and to master and contain pain. It is a tradition which abhors as obscene any trading on one's own anguish for gain or sympathy; which springs not from a desire to deny the harshness of existence but from a will to deal with it as men at their best have always done. It takes fortitude to be a man, and no less to be an artist. Perhaps it takes even more if the black man would be an artist. If so, there are no exemptions. It would seem to me, therefore, that the question of how the "sociology of his existence" presses upon a Negro writer's work depends upon how much of his life the individual writer is able to transform into art. What moves a writer to eloquence is less meaningful than what he makes of it. How much, by the way, do we know of Sophocles' wounds?

One unfamiliar with what Howe stands for would get the impression that when he looks at a Negro he sees not a human being but an abstract embodiment of living hell. He seems never to have considered that American Negro life (and here he is encouraged by certain Negro "spokesmen") is, for the Negro who must live it, not only a burden (and not always that) but also a *discipline*—just as any human life which has endured so long is a discipline teaching its own insights into the human condition, its own strategies of survival. There is a fullness, even a richness here—and here *despite* the realities of politics, perhaps, but nevertheless here and real. Because it is *human* life. And Wright, for all of his indictments, was no less its product than that other talented Mississippian, Leontyne Price. To deny in the interest of revolutionary posture that such possibilities of human richness exist for others, even in Mississippi, is not only to deny us our humanity but to betray the critic's commitment to social reality. Critics who do so should abandon literature for politics.

For even as his life toughens the Negro, even as it brutalizes him, sensitizes him, dulls him, goads him to anger, moves him to irony, sometimes fracturing and sometimes affirming his hopes; even as it shapes his attitudes toward family, sex, love, religion; even as it modulates his humor, tempers his joy—it *conditions* him to deal with his life and with himself. Because it is *his* life and no mere abstraction in someone's head. He must live it and try consciously to grasp its complexity until he can change it; must live it *as* he changes it. He is no mere product of his socio-political predicament. He is a product of the interaction between his racial predicament, his individual will, and the broader American cultural freedom in which he finds his ambiguous existence. Thus he, too, in a limited way, is his own creation.

In his loyalty to Richard Wright, Howe considers Ellison and Baldwin guilty of filial betrayal because, in their own work, they have rejected the path laid down by *Native Son*, phonies because, while actually "black boys," they pretend to be mere American writers trying to react to something of the pluralism of their predicament.

In his myth Howe takes the roles of both Shem and Japheth, trying mightily (his face turned backward so as not to see what it is he's veiling) to cover the old man's bare belly, and then becoming Wright's voice from beyond the grave by uttering the curses which Wright was too ironic or too proud to have uttered himself, at least in print:

In response to Baldwin and Ellison, Wright would have said (I virtually quote the words he used in talking to me during the summer of 1958) that only through struggle could men with black skins, and for that matter, all the oppressed of the world, achieve their humility. It was a lesson, said Wright, with a touch of bitterness yet not without kindness, that the younger writers would have to learn in their own way and their own time. All that has happened since bears him out.

What, coming eighteen years after *Native Son* and thirteen years after World War II, does this rather limp cliché mean? Nor is it clear what is meant by the last sentence—or is it that today Baldwin has come to out-Wrighting Richard? The real questions seem to be: How does the Negro writer participate *as a writer* in the struggle for human freedom? To whom does he address his work? What values emerging from Negro experience does he try to affirm?

I started with the primary assumption that men with black skins, having retained their humanity before all of the conscious efforts made to dehumanize them, especially following the Reconstruction, are unquestionably human. Thus they have the obligation of freeing themselves—whoever their allies might be—by depending upon the validity of their own experience for an accurate picture of the reality which they seek to change, and for a gauge of the values they would see made manifest. Crucial to this view is the belief that their resistance to provocation, their coolness under pressure, their sense of timing and their tenacious hold on the ideal of their ultimate freedom are indispensable values in the struggle, and are at least as characteristic of American Negroes as the hatred, fear and vindictiveness which Wright chose to emphasize.

Wright believed in the much abused idea that novels are "weapons"—the counterpart of the dreary notion, common among most minority groups, that novels are instruments of good public relations. But I believe that true novels, even when most pessimistic and bitter, arise out of an impulse to celebrate human life and therefore

are ritualistic and ceremonial at their core. Thus they would preserve as they destroy, affirm as they reject.

In *Native Son* Wright began with the ideological proposition that
what whites think of the Negro's reality is more important than what
Negroes themselves know it to be. Hence Bigger Thomas was presented as a near-subhuman indictment of white oppression. He was
designed to shock whites out of their apathy and end the circumstances out of which Wright insisted Bigger emerged. Here environment is all—and interestingly enough, environment conceived solely
in terms of the physical, the non-conscious. Well, cut off my legs and
call me Shorty! Kill my parents and throw me on the mercy of the
court as an orphan! Wright could imagine Bigger, but Bigger could
not possibly imagine Richard Wright. Wright saw to that.

But without arguing Wright's right to his personal vision, I would
say that he was himself a better argument for my approach than Bigger was for his. And so, to be fair and as inclusive as Howe, is James
Baldwin. Both are true Negro Americans, and both affirm the broad
possibility of personal realization which I see as a saving aspect of
American life. Surely, this much can be admitted without denying
the injustice which all three of us have protested.

Howe is impressed by Wright's pioneering role and by the
". . . enormous courage, the discipline of self-conquest required to
conceive Bigger Thomas. . . ." And earlier: "If such younger novelists as Baldwin and Ralph Ellison were able to move beyond
Wright's harsh naturalism toward more supple modes of fiction, that
was only possible because Wright had been there first, courageous
enough to release the full weight of his anger."

It is not for me to judge Wright's courage, but I must ask just why
it was possible for me to write as I write "only" because Wright released his anger? Can't I be allowed to release my own? What does
Howe know of my acquaintance with violence, or the shape of my
courage or the intensity of my anger? I suggest that my credentials
are at least as valid as Wright's, even though he began writing long
before I did, and it is possible that I have lived through and commit-

ted even more violence than he. Howe must wait for an autobiography before he can be responsibly certain. Everybody wants to tell us what a Negro is, yet few wish, even in a joke, to be one. But if you would tell me who I am, at least take the trouble to discover what I have been.

Which brings me to the most distressing aspect of Howe's thinking: his Northern white liberal version of the white Southern myth of absolute separation of the races. He implies that Negroes can only aspire to contest other Negroes (this at a time when Baldwin has been taking on just about everyone, including Hemingway, Faulkner and the United States Attorney General!), and must wait for the appearance of a Black Hope before they have the courage to move. Howe is so committed to a sociological vision of society that he apparently cannot see (perhaps because he is dealing with Negroes—although not because he would suppress us socially or politically, for in fact he is anxious to end such suppression) that whatever the efficiency of segregation as a sociopolitical arrangement, it has been far from absolute on the level of *culture*. Southern whites cannot walk, talk, sing, conceive of laws or justice, think of sex, love, the family or freedom without responding to the presence of Negroes.

Similarly, no matter how strictly Negroes are segregated socially and politically, on the level of the imagination their ability to achieve freedom is limited only by their individual aspiration, insight, energy and will. Wright was able to free himself in Mississippi because he had the imagination and the will to do so. He was as much a product of his reading as of his painful experiences, and he made himself a writer by subjecting himself to the writer's discipline—as he understood it. The same is true of James Baldwin, who is not the product of a Negro store-front church but of the library, and the same is true of me.

Howe seems to see segregation as an opaque steel jug with the Negroes inside waiting for some black messiah to come along and blow the cork. Wright is his hero and he sticks with him loyally. But if we are in a jug it is transparent, not opaque, and one is allowed not only to see outside but to read what is going on out there, and to make identifications as to values and human quality. So in Macon County, Alabama, I read Marx, Freud, T. S. Eliot, Pound, Gertrude Stein and Hemingway. Books which seldom, if ever, mentioned Negroes were to release me from whatever "segregated" idea I might have had of my human possibilities. I was freed not by propagandists or by the example of Wright (I did not know him at the time and was earnestly trying to learn enough to write a symphony and have it performed by the time I was twenty-six, because Wagner had done so and I admired his music), but by composers, novelists, and poets who spoke to me of more interesting and freer ways of life.

These were works which, by fulfilling themselves as works of art, by being satisfied to deal with life in terms of their own sources of power, were able to give me a broader sense of life and possibility. Indeed, I understand a bit more about myself as a Negro because literature has taught me something of my identity as a Western man, as a political being. It has also taught me something of the cost of being an individual who aspires to conscious eloquence. It requires real poverty of the imagination to think that this can come to a Negro *only* through the example of *other Negroes*, especially after the performance of the slaves in re-creating themselves, in good part, out of the images and myths of the Old Testament Jews.

No, Wright was no spiritual father of mine, certainly in no sense I recognize—nor did he pretend to be, since he felt that I had started writing too late. It was Baldwin's career, not mine, that Wright proudly advanced by helping him attain the Eugene Saxton Fellowship, and it was Baldwin who found Wright a lion in his path. Being older and familiar with quite different lions in quite different paths, I simply stepped around him.

But Wright was a friend for whose magazine I wrote my first book review and short story, and a personal hero in the same way Hot Lips Paige and Jimmy Rushing were friends and heroes. I felt no need to attack what I considered the limitations of his vision because I was quite impressed by what he had achieved. And in this, although I saw with the black vision of Ham, I was, I suppose, as pious as Shem and Japheth. Still I would write my own books and they would be in themselves, implicitly, criticisms of Wright's; just as all novels of a given historical moment form an argument over the nature of reality and are, to an extent, criticisms each of the other.

While I rejected Bigger Thomas as any *final* image of Negro personality, I recognized *Native Son* as an achievement, as one man's essay in defining the human condition as seen from a specific Negro perspective at a given time in a given place. And I was proud to have known Wright and happy for the impact he had made upon our apathy. But Howe's ideas notwithstanding, history is history, cultural contacts ever mysterious, and taste exasperatingly personal. Two days after arriving in New York I was to read Malraux's *Man's Fate* and *The Days of Wrath*, and after these how could I be impressed by Wright as an ideological novelist? Need my skin blind me to all other values? Yet Howe writes:

> When Negro liberals write that despite the prevalence of bias there has been an improvement in the life of their people, such statements are reasonable and necessary. But what have these to do with the way Negroes feel, with the power of the memories they must surely retain? About this we know very little and would be well advised not to nourish preconceptions, for their feelings may well be closer to Wright's rasping outbursts than to the more modulated tones of the younger Negro novelists. *Wright remembered*, and what he remembered other Negroes must also have remembered. And in that way he kept faith with the experience of the boy who had fought his way out of the depths, to speak for those who remained there.

Wright, for Howe, is the genuine article, the authentic Negro writer, and his tone the only authentic tone. But why strip Wright of his individuality in order to criticize other writers? He had his memories and I have mine, just as I suppose Irving Howe has his—or has

Marx spoken the final word for him? Indeed, very early in *Black Boy*, Wright's memory and his contact with literature come together in a way revealing, at least to the eye concerned with Wright the literary man, that his manner of keeping faith with the Negroes who remained in the depths is quite interesting:

> (After I had outlived the shocks of childhood, after the habit of reflection had been born in me, I used to mull over the strange absence of real kindness in Negroes, how unstable was our tenderness, how lacking in genuine passion we were, how void of great hope, how timid our joy, how bare our traditions, how hollow our memories, how lacking we were in those intangible sentiments that bind man to man and how shallow was even our despair. After I had learned other ways of life I used to brood upon the unconscious irony of those who felt that Negroes led so passional an existence! I saw that what had been taken for our emotional strength was our negative confusions, our flights, our fears, our frenzy under pressure.
>
> (Whenever I thought of the essential bleakness of black life in America, I knew that Negroes had never been allowed to catch the full spirit of Western civilization, that they lived somehow in it but not of it. And when I brooded upon the cultural barrenness of black life, I wondered if clean, positive tenderness, love, honor, loyalty and the capacity to remember were native with man. I asked myself if these human qualities were not fostered, won, struggled and suffered for, preserved in ritual from one generation to another.)

Must I be condemned because my sense of Negro life was quite different? Or because for me keeping faith would never allow me to even raise such a question about any segment of humanity? *Black Boy* is not a sociological case history but an autobiography, and therefore a work of art shaped by a writer bent upon making an ideological point. Doubtless, this was the beginning of Wright's exile, the making of a decision which was to shape his life and writing thereafter.

And it is precisely at this point that Wright is being what I would call, in Howe's words, "literary to a fault."

For just as *How Bigger Was Born* is Wright's Jamesian preface to *Native Son*, the passage quoted above is his paraphrase of Henry James's catalogue of those items of a high civilization which were absent from American life during Hawthorne's day, and which seemed so necessary in order for the novelist to function. This, then, was Wright's list of those items of high humanity which he found missing among Negroes. Thank God, I have never been quite that literary.

How awful that Wright found the facile answers of Marxism before he learned to use literature as a means for discovering the forms of American Negro humanity. I could not and cannot question their existence; I can only seek again and again to project that humanity as I see it and feel it. To me Wright as *writer* was less interesting than the enigma he personified: that he could so dissociate himself from the complexity of his background while trying so hard to improve the condition of black men everywhere; that he could be so wonderful an example of human possibility but could not for ideological reasons depict a Negro as intelligent, as creative or as dedicated as himself.

In his effort to resuscitate Wright, Irving Howe would designate the role which Negro writers are to play more rigidly than any Southern politician—and for the best of reasons. We must express "black" anger and "clenched militancy"; most of all we should not become too interested in the problems of the art of literature, even though it is through these that we seek our individual identities. And between writing well and being ideologically militant, we must choose militancy.

Well, it all sounds quite familiar, and I fear the social order which it forecasts more than I do that of Mississippi. Ironically, during the 1940s it was one of the main sources of Wright's rage and frustration.

II

I am sorry Irving Howe got the impression that I was throwing bean-balls when I only meant to pitch him a hyperbole. It would seem, however, that he approves of angry Negro writers only until one questions his ideas; then he reaches for his honor, cries "misrepresentation" and "distortion," and charges the writer with being both out of control of himself and with fashioning a "strategy calculated to appeal, ready-made, to the preconceptions of the liberal audience." Howe implies that there are differences between us which I disguised in my essay; yet whatever the validity of this attempt at long-distance psychoanalysis, it was not his honor which I questioned but his thinking, not his good faith but his critical method.

And the major differences which these raised between us I tried to describe. They are to be seen by anyone who reads Howe's "Black Boys and Native Sons" not as a collection of thematically related fragments but as the literary exposition of a considered point of view. I tried to interpret this essay in the light of the impact it made upon my sense of life and literature, and I judged it through its total form—just as I would have Howe base his judgments of writers and their circumstances on as much of what we know about the actual complexity of men living in a highly pluralistic society as is possible. I realize that the *un*common sense of a critic, his special genius, is a gift to be thankful for whenever we find it. The very least I expected of Howe, though, was that he would remember his *common* sense, that he would not be carried away by that intellectual abandon, that lack of restraint, which seizes those who regard blackness as an absolute, and who see in it a release from the complications of the real world.

Howe is interested in militant confrontation and suffering; yet evidently he recognizes neither when they involve some act of his own. He *really* did not know the subject was loaded. Very well, but I was brought into the booby-trapped field of his assumptions, and finding myself in pain, I did not choose to "hold back from the suffering" inflicted upon me there. Out of an old habit I yelled—without seeking Howe's permission, it is true—where it hurt the most. For oddly enough, I found it far less painful to have to move to the back of a Southern bus, or climb to the peanut gallery of a movie house—matters about which I could do nothing except walk, read, hunt, dance, sculpt, cultivate ideas, or seek other uses for my time—than to tolerate concepts which distorted the actual reality of my situation or my reactions to it.

I could escape the reduction imposed by unjust laws and customs, but not that imposed by ideas which defined me as no more than the *sum* of those laws and customs. I learned to outmaneuver those who interpreted my silence as submission, my efforts at self-control as fear, my contempt as awe before superior status, my dreams of far-away places and room at the top of the heap as defeat before the barriers of their stifling, provincial world. And my struggle became a desperate battle which was usually fought, though not always, in silence; a guerrilla action in a larger war in which I found some of the most treacherous assaults against me committed by those who regarded themselves either as neutrals, as sympathizers, or as disinterested military advisers.

I recall this not in complaint, for thus was I disciplined to endure the absurdities of both conscious and unconscious prejudice, to resist racial provocation and, before the ready violence of brutal policemen, railroad "bulls," and casual white citizens, to hold my peace and bide my time. Thus was I forced to evaluate my own self-worth, and the narrow freedom in which it existed, against the power of those who would destroy me. In time I was to leave the South, although it has never left me, and the interests which I discovered there became my life.

But having left the South I did not leave the battle—for how could I leave Howe? He is a man of words and ideas, and since I, too, find my identity in the world of ideas and words, where would I flee? I still endure the nonsense of fools with a certain patience, but when a respected critic distorts my situation in order to feel comfortable in the abstractions he would impose upon American reality, then it is indeed "in accordance with my nature" to protest. Ideas are important in themselves, perhaps, but when they are interposed between me and my sense of reality I feel threatened; they are too elusive, they move with missile speed and are too often fired from altitudes rising high above the cluttered terrain upon which I struggle. And too often those with a facility for ideas find themselves in the councils of power representing me at the double distance of racial alienation and inexperience.

Taking leave of Howe for a moment—for his lapse is merely symptomatic—let me speak generally. Many of those who write of Negro life today seem to assume that as long as their hearts are in the right place they can be as arbitrary as they wish in their formulations. Others seem to feel that they can air with impunity their most private Freudian fantasies as long as they are given the slightest camouflage of intellectuality and projected as "Negro." They have made of the no-man's land created by segregation a territory for infantile self-expression and intellectual anarchy. They write as though Negro life exists only in light of their belated regard, and they publish interpretations of Negro experience which would not hold true for their own or for any other form of human life.

Here the basic unity of human experience that assures us of some possibility of empathic and symbolic identification with those of other backgrounds is blasted in the interest of specious political and philosophical conceits. Prefabricated Negroes are sketched on sheets of paper and superimposed upon the Negro community; then when someone thrusts his head through the page and yells, "Watch out there, Jack, there're people living under here," they are shocked and indignant. I am afraid, however, that we shall hear much more of such protest as these interpositions continue. And I predict this not out of any easy gesture of militancy (and what an easy con-game for ambitious, publicity-hungry Negroes this stance of "militancy" has become!), but because as Negroes express increasingly their irritation in this critical area, many of those who deal so lightly with our image shall find their own subjected to a most devastating scrutiny.

One of the most insidious crimes occurring in this democracy is that of designating another, politically weaker, less socially acceptable, people as the receptacle for one's own self-disgust, for one's own infantile rebellions, for one's own fears of, and retreats from, reality. It is the crime of reducing the humanity of others to that of a mere convenience, a counter in a banal game which involves no apparent risk to ourselves. With us Negroes it started with the appropriation of our freedom and our labor; then it was our music, our speech, our dance and the comic distortion of our image by burnt-corked, cotton-gloved cornballs yelling, "Mammy!" And while it would be futile, non-tragic, and un-Negro American to complain over the processes through which we have become who and what we are, it is perhaps permissible to say that the time for such misappropriations ran out long ago.

For one thing, Negro American consciousness is not a product (as so often seems true of so many American groups) of a will to historical forgetfulness. It is a product of our memory, sustained and constantly reinforced by events, by our watchful waiting, and by our hopeful suspension of final judgment as to the meaning of our grievances. For another, most Negroes recognize themselves as themselves despite what others might believe them to be. Thus, although the sociologists tell us that thousands of light-skinned Negroes become white each year undetected, most Negroes can spot a paper-thin "white Negro" every time simply because those who masquerade missed what others were forced to pick up along the way: discipline—a discipline which these heavy thinkers would not undergo even if guaranteed that combined with their own heritage it would make of them the freest of spirits, the wisest of men and the most sublime of heroes.

•   •   •

The rhetorical strategy of my original reply was not meant, as Howe interprets it, to strike the stance of a "free artist" against the "ideological critic," although I *do* recognize that I can be free only to the extent that I detect error and grasp the complex reality of my circumstances and work to dominate it through the techniques which are my means of confronting the world. Perhaps I am only free enough to recognize those tendencies of thought which, actualized, would render me even less free.

Even so, I did not intend to take the stance of the "knowing Negro writer" against the "presuming white intellectual." While I am without doubt a Negro and a writer, I am also an *American* writer, and while I am more knowing than Howe where my own life and its influences are concerned, I took the time to question his presumptions as one responsible for contributing as much as he is capable to the clear perception of American social reality. For to think unclearly about that segment of reality in which I find my existence is to do myself violence. To allow others to go unchallenged when they distort that reality is to participate not only in that distortion but to accept, as in this instance, a violence inflicted upon the art of criticism. And if I am to recognize those aspects of my role as writer which do not depend primarily upon my racial identity, if I am to fulfill the writer's basic responsibilities to his craft, then surely I must insist upon the maintenance of a certain level of precision in language, a maximum correspondence between the form of a piece of writing and its content, and between words and ideas and the things and processes of his world.

Whatever my role as "race man" (and it knocks me out whenever anyone, black or white, tries to tell me—and the white Southerners have no monopoly here—how to become their conception of a "good Negro"), I am as writer no less a custodian of the American language than is Irving Howe. Indeed, to the extent that I am a writer—I lay no claims to being a thinker—the American language, including the Negro idiom, is all that I have. So let me emphasize that my reply to Howe was neither motivated by racial defensiveness nor addressed to his own racial identity.

It is fortunate that it was not, for considering how Howe identifies himself in this instance, I would have missed the target, which would have been embarrassing. Yet it would have been an innocent mistake, because in situations such as this many Negroes, like myself, make a positive distinction between "whites" and "Jews." Not to do so could be either offensive, embarrassing, unjust or even dangerous. If I would know who I am and preserve who I am, then I must see others distinctly whether they see me so or not. Thus I feel uncomfortable whenever I discover Jewish intellectuals writing as though *they* were guilty of enslaving my grandparents, or as though the *Jews* were responsible for the system of segregation. Not only do they have enough troubles of their own, as the saying goes, but Negroes know this only too well.

The real guilt of such Jewish intellectuals lies in their facile, perhaps unconscious, but certainly unrealistic, identification with what is called the "power structure." Negroes call that "passing for white." Speaking personally, both as writer and as Negro American, I would like to see the more positive distinctions between whites and Jewish Americans maintained. Not only does it make for a necessary bit of historical and social clarity, at least where Negroes are concerned, but I consider the United States freer politically and richer culturally because there are Jewish Americans to bring it the benefit of their special forms of dissent, their humor and their gift for ideas which are based upon the uniqueness of their experience. The diversity of American life is often painful, frequently burdensome and always a source of conflict, but in it lies our fate and our hope.

To Howe's charge that I found his exaggerated claims for Richard Wright's influence upon my own work presumptuous, I plead guilty. Was it necessary to impose a line of succession upon Negro writers simply because Howe identified with Wright's cause? And why, since he grasps so readily the intentional absurdity of my question regarding his relationship to Marx, couldn't he see that the notion of an intellectual or artistic succession based upon color or racial background is no less absurd than one based upon a common religious background? (*Of course, Irving, I know that you haven't believed in final*

words for twenty years—not even your own—and I know, too, that the line
from Marx to Howe is as complex and as dialectical as that from Wright to
Ellison. My point was to try to see to it that certain laspes in your thinking
did not become final.) In fact, this whole exchange would never have
started had I not been dragged into the discussion. Still, if Howe
could take on the role of man with a "black skin," why shouldn't I
assume the role of critic-of-critic?

But how surprising are Howe's ideas concerning the ways of controversy. Why, unless of course he holds no respect for his opponent, should a polemicist be expected to make things *hard* for
himself? As for the "preconceptions of the liberal audience," I had
not considered them, actually, except as they appear in Howe's own
thinking. Beyond this I wrote for anyone who might hesitate to
question his formulations, especially very young Negro writers who
might be bewildered by the incongruity of such ideas coming from
such an authority. Howe himself rendered complicated rhetorical
strategies unnecessary by lunging into questionable territory with
his flanks left so unprotected that any schoolboy sniper could have
routed him with a bird gun. Indeed, his reaction to my reply reminds
me of an incident which occurred during the 1937 Recession when a
companion and I were hunting in the country outside Dayton, Ohio.

There had been a heavy snowfall and we had just put up a covey of
quail from a thicket which edged a field when, through the rising
whirr of the rocketing, snow-shattering birds, we saw, emerging
from a clump of trees across the field, a large, red-faced, mackinawed
farmer, who came running toward us shouting and brandishing a
rifle. I could see strands of moisture tearing from his working mouth
as he came on, running like a bear across the whiteness, the brown
birds veering and scattering before him; and standing there against
the snow, a white hill behind me and with no tree nor foxhole for
cover I felt as exposed as a Black Muslim caught at a meeting of the
K.K.K.

He had appeared as suddenly as the quail, and although the rifle
was not yet to his shoulder, I was transfixed, watching him zooming

up to become the largest, loudest, most aggressive-sounding white man I'd seen in my life, and I was, quite frankly, afraid. Then I was measuring his approach to the crunching tempo of his running and praying silently that he'd come within range of my shotgun before he fired; that I would be able to do what seemed necessary for me to do; that, shooting from the hip with an old twelve-gauge shotgun, I could stop him before he could shoot either me or my companion; and that, though stopped effectively, he would be neither killed nor blinded nor maimed.

It was a mixed-up prayer in an icy interval which ended in a smoking fury of cursing, when, at a warning from my companion, the farmer suddenly halted. Then we learned that this reckless man had meant only to warn us off of land which was not even his but that of a neighbor, my companion's foster father. He stood there between the two shotguns pointing short-ranged at his middle, his face quite drained of color now by the realization of how close to death he'd come, sputtering indignantly that we'd interpreted his rifle, which wasn't loaded, in a manner other than he'd intended. He truly did not realize that situations can be more loaded than guns and gestures more eloquent than words.

Fortunately, words are not rifles, but perhaps Howe is just as innocent of the rhetorical eloquence of situations as the farmer. He does not see that the meaning which emerges from his essay is not determined by isolated statements, but by the juxtaposition of those statements in a context which creates a larger statement. Or that contributing to the judgment rendered by that larger statement is the one in which it is uttered. When Howe pits Baldwin and Ellison against Wright and then gives Wright the better of the argument by using such emotionally weighted terms as "remembered" and "kept faith," the implication to me is that Baldwin and Ellison did *not* remember or keep faith with those who remained behind. If this be true, then I think that in this instance "villain" is not too strong a term.

Howe is not the first writer given to sociological categories who has had unconscious value judgments slip into his "analytical" or "scientific" descriptions. Thus I can believe that his approach was meant to be "analytic, not exhortatory; descriptive, not prescriptive." The results, however, are something else again. And are we to believe that he simply does not recognize rhetoric when he practices it? That when he asks, "what *could* [his italics] the experience of a man with a black skin be . . ." etc., he thinks he is describing a situation as viewed by each and every Negro writer rather than expressing, yes, and in the mode of "exhortation," the views of Irving Howe? Doesn't he recognize that just as the anti-Negro stereotype is a command to Negroes to mold themselves in its image, there sounds through his descriptive "thus it is" the command "thus you become"? And doesn't he realize that in this emotion-charged area definitive description is, in effect, prescription? If he does not, how then can we depend upon his "analysis" of politics or his reading of fiction?

Perhaps Howe could relax his views concerning the situation of the writers with a "black skin" if he examined some of the meanings which he gives to the word "Negro." He contends that I "cannot help being caught up with *the idea* of the Negro," but I have never said that I could or wished to do so—only Howe makes a problem for me here. When he uses the term "Negro" he speaks of it as a "stigma," and again he speaks of "Negroness" as a "sterile category." He sees the Negro writer as experiencing a "constant pressure upon his literary work" from the "sociology of his existence . . . not merely in the way this might be true of any writer, but with a *pain* and *ferocity* that nothing could remove." (Italics mine.)

Note that this is a condition arising from a *collective* experience which leaves no room for the individual writer's unique existence. It leaves no room for that intensity of personal anguish which compels the artist to seek relief by projecting it into the world in conjunction with other things; that anguish which might take the form of an acute sense of inferiority for one, homosexuality for another, an overwhelming sense of the absurdity of human life for still another.

Nor does it leave room for the experience that might be caused by humiliation, by a harelip, by a stutter, by epilepsy—indeed, by any and everything in this life which plunges the talented individual into solitude while leaving him the will to transcend his condition through art. The individual Negro writer must create out of his own special needs and through his own sensibilities, and by these alone. Otherwise all those who suffer in anonymity would be creators.

Howe makes of "Negroness" a metaphysical condition, one that is a state of irremediable agony which all but engulfs the mind. Happily, the view from inside the skin is not so dark as it appears to be from Howe's remote position, and therefore my view of "Negroness" is neither his nor that of the exponents of *negritude*. It is not skin color which makes a Negro American but cultural heritage as shaped by the American experience, the social and political predicament, a sharing of that "concord of sensibilities" which the group expresses through historical circumstance and through which it has come to constitute a subdivision of the larger American culture. Being a Negro American has to do with the memory of slavery and the hope of emancipation and the betrayal by allies and the revenge and contempt inflicted by our former masters after the Reconstruction, and by the myths, both Northern and Southern, which are propagated in justification of that betrayal. It involves, too, a special attitude toward the waves of immigrants who have come later and passed us by.

It has to do with a special perspective on the national ideals and the national conduct, and with a tragicomic attitude toward the universe. It has to do with special emotions evoked by the details of cities and countrysides, with forms of labor and with forms of pleasure, with sex and with love, with food and with drink, with machines and with animals, with climates and with dwellings, with places of worship and places of entertainment, with garments and dreams and idioms of speech, with manners and customs, with religion and art, with life styles and hoping, and with that special sense of predicament and fate which gives direction and resonance to the Freedom

Movement. It involves a rugged initiation into the mysteries and rites of color which makes it possible for Negro Americans to suffer the injustice in which race and color are used to excuse without losing sight of either the humanity of those who inflict that injustice or the motives, rational or irrational, out of which they act. It imposes the uneasy burden and occasional joy of a complex double vision, a fluid, ambivalent response to men and events which represents, at its finest, a profoundly civilized adjustment to the cost of being human in this modern world.

More important, perhaps, being a Negro American involves a *willed* (who wills to be a Negro? *I* do!) affirmation of self as against all outside pressures—an identification with the group as extended through the individual self which rejects all possibilities of escape that do not involve a basic resuscitation of the original American ideals of social and political justice. And those white Negroes (and I do not mean Norman Mailer's dream creatures) are Negroes too—if they wish to be.

Howe's defense against my charge that he sees unrelieved suffering as the basic reality of Negro life is to quote favorable comments from his review of *Invisible Man*. But this does not cancel out the restricted meaning which he gives to "Negroness," or his statement that "the sociology of [the Negro writer's] existence forms a constant pressure with a *pain* and *ferocity* that nothing could remove." He charges me with unfairness for writing that he believes ideological militancy is more important than writing well; yet he tells us that "there may of course be times when one's obligation as a human being supersedes one's obligation as a writer. . . ." I think that the writer's obligation in a struggle as broad and abiding as the one we are engaged in, which involves not merely Negroes but all Americans, is best carried out through his role as writer. And if he chooses to stop writing and take to the platform, then it should be out of personal choice and not under pressure from would-be managers of society.

Howe plays a game of pitty-pat with Baldwin and Ellison. First he throws them into the pit for lacking Wright's "pain," "ferocity," "memory," "faithfulness" and "clenched militance"; then he pats them on the head for the quality of their writing. If he would see evidence of this statement, let him observe how these terms come up in his original essay when he traces Baldwin's move toward Wright's position. Howe's rhetoric is weighted against "more modulated tones" in favor of "rasping outbursts"; the Baldwin of *Another Country* becomes "a voice of anger, rasping and thrusting," and he is no longer "held back" by the "proprieties of literature." The character of Rufus in that novel displays a "ferocity" quite new in Baldwin's fiction, and Baldwin's essays gain resonance from "the tone of unrelenting protest . . . from [their] very anger, even the violence," etc. I am afraid that these are "good" terms in Howe's essay and they led to part of my judgment.

In defense of Wright's novel *The Long Dream*, Howe can write:

> . . . This book has been attacked for presenting Negro life in the South through "old-fashioned" images of violence, but [and now we have "prescription"] one ought to hesitate before denying the relevance of such images or joining in the criticism of their use. *For Wright was perhaps justified* in not paying attention to the changes that have occurred in the South these past few decades. [Italics mine.]

If this isn't a defense (if not of bad writing at least of an irresponsible attitude toward good writing), I simply do not understand the language. I find it astonishing advice, since novels exist, since the fictional spell comes into existence precisely through the care which the novelist gives to selecting the details, images, tonalities, specific social and psychological processes of specific characters in specific milieus at specific points in time. Indeed, it is one of the main tenets of the novelist's morality that he should write of that which he knows, and this is especially crucial for novelists who deal with a society as mobile and rapidly changing as ours. To justify ignoring this basic obligation is to encourage the downgrading of literature in favor of other values—in this instance "anger," "protest" and "clenched militancy." Novelists create not simply out of "memory" but out of memory modified, extended, transformed by social change. For a novelist to heed such advice as Howe's is to commit an act of artistic immorality. Amplify this back through society and the writer's failure could produce not order but chaos.

Yet Howe proceeds on the very next page of his essay to state, with no sense of contradiction, that Wright failed in some of the stories which comprise *Eight Men* ("The Man Who Lived Underground" was first published, by the way, in 1944) because he needed the "accumulated material of circumstance." If a novelist ignores social change, how can he come by the "accumulated material of circumstance"? Perhaps if Howe could grasp the full meaning of that phrase he would understand that Wright did not report in *Black Boy* much of his life in Mississippi, and he would also see that Ross Barnett is not the whole state, that there is also a Negro Mississippi which is much more varied than that which Wright depicted.

For the critic there simply exists no substitute for the knowledge of history and literary tradition. Howe stresses Wright's comment that when he went into rooms where there were naked white women he felt like a "non-man . . . doubly cast out." But had Howe thought about it he might have questioned this reaction, since most young men would have been delighted with the opportunity to study, at first hand, women usually cloaked in an armor of taboos. I wonder how Wright felt when he saw Negro women acting just as shamelessly? Clearly this was an ideological point, not a factual report. And anyone aware of the folk sources of Wright's efforts to create literature would recognize that the situation is identical with that of the countless stories which Negro men tell of the male slave called in to wash the mistress' back in the bath, of the Pullman porter invited in to share the beautiful white passenger's favors in the berth, of the bellhop seduced by the wealthy blond guest.

It is interesting that Howe should interpret my statement about

Mississippi as evidence of a loss of self-control. So allow me to repeat it coldly: I fear the implications of Howe's ideas concerning the Negro writer's role as actionist more than I do the State of Mississippi. Which is not to deny the viciousness which exists there, but to recognize the degree of freedom which also exists there precisely because the repression is relatively crude, or at least it was during Wright's time, and it left the world of literature alone. William Faulkner lived neither in Jefferson nor Frenchman's Bend but in Oxford. He, too, was a Mississippian, just as the boys who helped Wright leave Jackson were the sons of a Negro college president. Both Faulkner and these boys must be recognized as part of the social reality of Mississippi. I said nothing about Ross Barnett, and I certainly did not say that Howe was a "cultural authoritarian," so he should not spread his honor so thin. Rather, let him look to the implications of his thinking.

Yes, and let him learn more about the South and about Negro Americans if he would speak with authority. When he points out that "the young Ralph Ellison, even while reading these great writers, could not in Macon County attend the white man's school or movie house," he certainly appears to have me cornered. But here again he does not know the facts and he underplays choice and will. I rode freight trains to Macon County, Alabama, during the Scottsboro trial because I desired to study with the Negro conductor-composer William L. Dawson, who was, and probably still is, the greatest classical musician in that part of the country. I had no need to attend a white university when the master I wished to study with was available at Tuskegee. Besides, why should I have wished to attend the white state-controlled university where the works of the great writers might not have been so easily available?

As for the movie-going, it is ironic but nonetheless true that one of the few instances where "separate but equal" was truly separate and equal was in a double movie house in the town of Tuskegee, where Negroes and whites were accommodated in parallel theaters, entering from the same street level through separate entrances, and with the Negro side viewing the same pictures shortly after the showing for whites had begun. It was a product of social absurdity and, of course, no real relief from our resentment over the restriction of our freedom, but the movies were just as enjoyable or boring. And yet, is not knowing the facts more interesting, even as an isolated instance, and more stimulating to real thought than making abstract assumptions? I went to the movies to see pictures, not to be with whites. I attended a certain college because what I wanted was there. What is more, I *never* attended a white school from kindergarten through my three years of college, and yet, like Howe, I have taught and lectured for some years now at Northern, predominantly white, colleges and universities.

Perhaps this counts for little, changes little of the general condition of society, but it *is* factual and it does form a part of my sense of reality because, though it was not a part of Wright's life, it is my own. And if Howe thinks mine is an isolated instance, let him do a bit of research.

I do not really think that Howe can make a case for himself by bringing up the complimentary remarks which he made about *Invisible Man*. I did not quarrel with them in 1952, when they were first published, and I did not quarrel with them in my reply. His is the right of any critic to make judgment of a novel, and I do not see the point of arguing that I achieved an aesthetic goal if it did not work for him. I can only ask that my fiction be judged as art; if it fails, it fails aesthetically, not because I did or did not fight some ideological battle. I repeat, however, that Howe's strategy of bringing me into the public quarrel between Baldwin and Wright was inept. I simply did not belong in the conflict, since I knew, even then, that protest is *not* the source of the inadequacy characteristic of most novels by Negroes, but the simple failure of craft, bad writing; the desire to have protest perform the difficult tasks of art, the belief that racial suffering, social injustice or ideologies of whatever mammy-made variety, is enough. I know, also, that when the work of Negro writers has been rejected they have all too often protected their egos by blaming racial discrimination, while turning away from the fairly obvious fact that good art—and Negro musicians are ever present to demonstrate this—commands attention of itself, whatever the writer's politics or point of view. And they forget that publishers will publish almost anything which is written with even a minimum of competency, and that skill is developed by hard work, study and a conscious assault upon one's own fear and provincialism.

I agree with Howe that protest is an element of all art, though it does not necessarily take the form of speaking for a political or social program. It might appear in a novel as a technical assault against the styles which have gone before, or as a protest against the human condition. If *Invisible Man* is even "apparently" free from "the ideological and emotional penalties suffered by Negroes in this country," it is because I tried to the best of my ability to transform these elements into art. My goal was not to escape or hold back, but to work through; to transcend, as the blues transcend the painful conditions with which they deal. The protest is there not because I was helpless before my racial condition, but because I *put* it there. If there is anything "miraculous" about the book it is the result of hard work undertaken in the belief that the work of art is important in itself, that it is a social action in itself.

I cannot hope to persuade Irving Howe to this view, for it seems quite obvious that he believes there are matters more important than artistic scrupulousness. I will point out, though, that the laws of literary form exert their validity upon all those who write, and that it is his slighting of the formal necessities of his essay which makes for some of our misunderstanding. After reading his reply, I gave in to my ear's suggestion that I had read certain of his phrases somewhere before, and I went to the library, where I discovered that much of his essay was taken verbatim from a review in the *Nation* of May 10, 1952, and that another section was published verbatim in the *New Republic* of February 13, 1962—the latter, by the way, being in its original context a balanced appraisal and warm farewell to Richard Wright.

But when Howe spliced these materials together with phrases from an old speech of mine, swipes at the critics of the *Sewanee* and *Kenyon* reviews (journals in which I have never published), and the Baldwin-Wright quarrel, the effect was something other than he must have intended. A dialectical transformation into a new quality took place, and despite the intention of Howe's content, the form made its own statement. If he would find the absurdities he wants me to reduce to a quotation, he will really have to read his essay whole. One gets the impression that he did a paste-and-scissors job and, knowing what he intended, knowing how the separated pieces had operated by themselves, did not bother to read very carefully their combined effect. It could happen to anyone; nevertheless, I'm glad he is not a scientist or a social engineer.

I do not understand why Howe thinks I said anything on the subject of writing about "Negro experience" in a manner which excludes what he calls "plight and protest"; he must have gotten his Negroes mixed. But as to answering his question concerning the "ways a Negro writer can achieve personal realization apart from the common effort of his people to win their full freedom," I suggest that he ask himself in what way a Negro writer will achieve personal realization (as writer) *after* his people shall have won their full freedom. The answer appears to be the same in both instances: he will have to go it alone! He must suffer alone even as he shares the suffering of his group, and he must write alone and pit his talents against the standards set by the best practitioners of the craft, both past and present, in any case. For the writer's real way of sharing the experience of his group is to convert its mutual suffering into lasting value. Is Howe suggesting, incidentally, that Heinrich Heine did not exist?

His question is silly, really, for there is no such thing as "full freedom" (Oh, how Howe thirsts and hungers for the absolute for *Negroes!*), just as the notion of an equality of talent is silly. I am a Negro who once played trumpet with a certain skill, but alas, I am no Louis Armstrong or Clark Terry. Willie Mays has realized himself quite handsomely as an individual despite coming from an impoverished Negro background in oppressive Alabama, and Negro Americans, like most Americans who know the value of baseball, exult in his success. I am, after all, only a minor member, not the whole damned tribe; in fact, most Negroes have never heard of me. I could shake the nation for a while with a crime or with indecent disclosures, but my pride lies in earning the right to call myself quite simply "writer." Perhaps if I write well enough the children of today's Negroes will be proud that I did, and so, perhaps, will Irving Howe's.

Let me end with a personal note: Dear Irving, I have no objections to being placed beside Richard Wright in any estimation which is based not upon the irremediable ground of our common racial identity, but upon the quality of our achievements as writers. I respected Wright's work and I knew him, but this is not to say that he "influenced" me as significantly as you assume. Consult the text! I *sought out* Wright because I had read Eliot, Pound, Gertrude Stein and Hemingway, and as early as 1940 Wright viewed me as a potential rival—partially, it is true, because he feared I would allow myself to be used against him by political manipulators who were not Negro and who envied and hated him. But perhaps you will understand when I say he did not influence me if I point out that while one can do nothing about choosing one's relatives, one can, as artist, choose one's "ancestors." Wright was, in this sense, a "relative", Hemingway an "ancestor." Langston Hughes, whose work I knew in grade school and whom I knew before I knew Wright, was a "relative"; Eliot, whom I was to meet only many years later, and Malraux and Dostoevsky and Faulkner, were "ancestors"—if you please or don't please!

Do you still ask why Hemingway was more important to me than Wright? Not because he was white, or more "accepted." But because he appreciated the things of this earth which I love and which Wright was too driven or deprived or inexperienced to know: weather, guns, dogs, horses, love *and* hate and impossible circumstances which to the courageous and dedicated could be turned into benefits and victories. Because he wrote with such precision about the processes and techniques of daily living that I could keep myself and my brother alive during the 1937 Recession by following his descriptions of wing-shooting; because he knew the difference between politics and art and something of their true relationship for the writer. Because all that he wrote—and this is very important—was imbued with a spirit beyond the tragic with which I could feel at home, for it was very close to the feeling of the blues, which are, perhaps, as close as Americans can come to expressing the spirit of tragedy. (And if you think Wright knew anything about the blues, listen to a "blues" he composed with Paul Robeson singing, a *most* unfortunate collaboration!; and read his introduction to Paul Oliver's *Blues Fell This Morning*.) But most important, because Hemingway was a greater artist than Wright, who although a Negro like myself, and perhaps a great man, understood little if anything of these (at least to me) important things. Because Hemingway loved the American language and the joy of writing, making the flight of birds, the loping of lions across an African plain, the mysteries of drink and moonlight, the unique styles of diverse peoples and individuals come alive on the page. Because he was in many ways the true father-as-artist of so many of us who came to writing during the late thirties.

I will not dwell upon Hemingway's activities in Spain or during the liberation in Paris, for you know all of that. I will remind you, however, that any writer takes what he needs to get his own work done from wherever he finds it. I did not need Wright to tell me how to be a Negro, or how to be angry or to express anger—Joe Louis was doing that very well—or even to teach me about socialism; my mother had canvassed for the socialists, not the Communists, the year I was born. No, I had been a Negro for twenty-two or twenty-three years when I met Wright, and in more places and under a greater variety of circumstances than he had then known. He was generously helpful in sharing his ideas and information, but I needed instruction in other values and I found them in the works of other writers—Hemingway was one of them, and T. S. Eliot initiated the search.

I like your part about Chekhov arising from his sickbed to visit the penal colony at Sakhalin Island. It was, as you say, a noble act. But shouldn't we remember that it was significant only because Chekhov was *Chekhov*, the great writer? You compliment me truly, but I have not written so much or so well, even though I *have* served a certain apprenticeship in the streets and even touch events in the Freedom Movement in a modest way. But I can also recall the story of a certain writer who succeeded with a great fanfare of publicity in having a talented murderer released from prison. It made for another very short story which ended quite tragically—though not for the writer: A few months after his release the man killed the mother of two young children. I also know of another really quite brilliant writer who, under the advice of certain wise men who were then managing the consciences of artists, abandoned the prison of his writing to go to Spain, where he was allowed to throw away his life defending a worthless hill. I have not heard his name in years but I remember it vividly; it was Christopher Cauldwell, *né* Christopher St. John Sprigg. There are many such stories, Irving. It's heads you win, tails you lose, and you are quite right about my not following Baldwin, who is urged on by a nobility—or is it a demon—quite different from my own. It has cost me quite a pretty penny, indeed, but then I was always poor and not (and I know this is a sin in our America) too uncomfortable.

Dear Irving, I am still yakking on and there's many a thousand gone, but I assure you that no Negroes are beating down my door, putting pressure on me to join the Negro Freedom Movement, for the simple reason that they realize that I am enlisted for the duration. Such pressure is coming only from a few disinterested "military advisers," since Negroes want no more fairly articulate would-be Negro leaders cluttering up the airways. For, you see, my Negro friends recognize a certain division of labor among the members of the tribe. Their demands, like that of many whites, are that I publish more novels—and here I am remiss and vulnerable, perhaps. You will recall what the Talmud has to say about the trees of the forest and the making of books, etc. But then, Irving, they recognize what you have not allowed yourself to see: namely, that my reply to your essay is in itself a small though necessary action in the Negro struggle for freedom. You should not feel unhappy about this or think that I regard you either as dishonorable or an enemy. I hope, rather, that you will come to view this exchange as an act of, shall we say, "antagonistic co-operation"?

Hidden Name and Complex Fate

A Writer's Experience in the United States

In *Green Hills of Africa*, Ernest Hemingway reminds us that both Tolstoy and Stendhal had seen war, that Flaubert had seen a revolution and the Commune, that Dostoevsky had been sent to Siberia, and that such experiences were important in shaping the art of these great masters. And he goes on to observe that "writers are forged in injustice as a sword is forged." He declined to describe the many personal forms which injustice may take in this chaotic world—who would be so mad as to try?—nor does he go into the personal wounds which each of these writers sustained. Now, however, thanks to his brother and sister, we do know something of the injustice in which he himself was forged, and this knowledge has been added to what we have long known of Hemingway's artistic temper.

In the end, however, it is the quality of his art which is primary. It is the art which allows the wars and revolutions which he knew, and the personal and social injustice which he suffered, to lay claims upon our attention, for it was through his art that they achieved their most enduring meaning. It is a matter of outrageous irony, perhaps, but in literature the great social clashes of history, no less than the painful experience of the individual, are secondary to the meaning which they take on through the skill, talent, imagination and personal vision of the writer who transforms them into art. Here they are reduced to more manageable proportions; here they are imbued with humane values; here injustice and catastrophe become less important in themselves than what the writer makes of them. This is *not* true, however, of the writer's struggle with that recalcitrant angel

Address sponsored by the Gertrude Clarke Whittall Foundation, Library of Congress, January 6, 1964.

called Art, and it was through *this* specific struggle that Ernest Hemingway became *Hemingway* (now refined to a total body of transcendent work, after forty years of being endlessly dismembered and resurrected, as it continues to be, in the styles, themes, sense of life and literature of countless other writers). And it was through this struggle with form that he became the master, the culture hero, whom we have come to know and admire.

It was suggested that it might be of interest if I discussed here this evening some of my notions of the writer's experience in the United States; hence I have invoked the name of Hemingway, not by way of inviting far-fetched comparisons but in order to establish a perspective, a set of assumptions from which I may speak, and in an attempt to avoid boring you by emphasizing those details of racial hardship which for some forty years now have been evoked whenever writers of my own cultural background have essayed their experience in public.

I do this *not* by way of denying totally the validity of these by now stylized recitals, for I have shared and still share many of their detailed injustices—what Negro can escape them?—but by way of suggesting that they are, at least in a discussion of a writer's experience, as *writer*, as artist, somewhat beside the point.

For we select neither our parents, our race nor our nation; these occur to us out of the love, the hate, the circumstances, the fate, of others. But we *do* become writers out of an act of will, out of an act of choice: a dim, confused and ofttimes regrettable choice, perhaps, but choice nevertheless. And what happens thereafter causes all those experiences which occurred before we began to function as writers to take on a special quality of uniqueness. If this does not happen then as far as writing goes, the experiences have been misused. If we do not make of them a value, if we do not transform them into forms and images of meaning which they did not possess before, then we have failed as artists.

Thus for a writer to insist that his personal suffering is of special interest in itself, or simply because he belongs to a particular racial or religious group, is to advance a claim for special privileges which members of his group who are not writers would be ashamed to demand. The kindest judgment one can make of this point of view is that it reveals a sad misunderstanding of the relationship between suffering and art. Thomas Mann and André Gide have told us much of this, and there are critics, like Edmund Wilson, who have told of the connection between the wound and the bow.

As I see it, it is through the process of making artistic forms—plays, poems, novels—out of one's experience that one becomes a writer, and it is through this process, this struggle, that the writer helps give meaning to the experience of the group. And it is the process of mastering the discipline, the techniques, the fortitude, the culture, through which this is made possible that constitutes the writer's real experience as *writer*, as artist. If this sounds like an argument for the artist's withdrawal from social struggles, I would recall to you W. H. Auden's comment:

> In our age, the mere making of a work of art is itself a political act. So long as artists exist, making what they please, and think they ought to make, even if it is not terribly good, even if it appeals to only a handful of people, they remind the Management of something managers need to be reminded of, namely, that the managed are people with faces, not anonymous members, that *Homo Laborans* is also *Homo Ludens*. . . .

Without doubt, even the most *engagé* writer—and I refer to true artists, not to artists *manqués*—begins his career in play and puzzlement, in dreaming over the details of the world in which he becomes conscious of himself.

Let Tar Baby, that enigmatic figure from Negro folklore, stand for the world. He leans, black and gleaming, against the wall of life utterly noncommittal under our scrutiny, our questioning, starkly unmoving before our naïve attempts at intimidation. Then we touch him playfully and before we can say *Sonny Liston!* we find ourselves stuck. Our playful investigations become a labor, a fearful struggle, an *agon*. Slowly we perceive that our task is to learn the proper way of freeing ourselves to develop technique.

Sensing this, we give him our sharpest attention, we question him carefully, we struggle with more subtlety; while he, in his silent way, holds on, demanding that we perceive the necessity of calling him by his true name as the price of our freedom. It is unfortunate that he has so many "true names"—all spelling chaos, and in order to discover even one of these we must first come into possession of our own names. For it is through our names that we first place ourselves in the world. Our names, being the gift of others, must be made our own.

Once, while listening to the play of a two-year-old girl who did not know she was under observation, I heard her saying over and over again, at first with questioning and then with sounds of growing satisfaction, "I am Mimi Livisay? . . . *I* am Mimi Livisay. I *am* Mimi Livisay . . . I am *Mimi* Li-vi-say! I am Mimi . . ."

And in deed and in fact she was—or became so soon thereafter, by working playfully to establish the unity between herself and her name.

For many of us this is far from easy. We must learn to wear our names within all the noise and confusion of the environment in which we find ourselves, make them the center of all of our associations with the world, with man and with nature. We must charge them with all our emotions, our hopes, hates, loves, aspirations. They must become our masks and our shields and the containers of all those values and traditions which we learn and/or imagine as being the meaning of our familial past.

And when we are reminded so constantly that we bear, as Negroes, names originally possessed by those who owned our enslaved grandparents, we are apt, especially if we are potential writers, to be more than ordinarily concerned with the veiled and mysterious events, the fusions of blood, the furtive couplings, the business transactions, the violations of faith and loyalty, the assaults; yes, and the unrecognized and unrecognizable loves through which our names were handed down unto us.

So charged with emotion does this concern become for some of us, that we have, earlier, the example of the followers of Father Divine and, now, the Black Muslims, discarding their original names in rejection of the bloodstained, the brutal, the sinful images of the past. Thus they would declare new identities, would clarify a new program of intention and destroy the verbal evidence of a willed and ritualized discontinuity of blood and human intercourse.

Not all of us, actually only a few, seek to deal with our names in this manner. We take what we have and make of them what we can. And there are even those who know where the old broken connections lie, who recognize their relatives across the chasm of historical denial and the artificial barriers of society, and who see themselves as bearers of many of the qualities which were admirable in the original sources of their common line (Faulkner has made much of this); and I speak here not of mere forgiveness, nor of obsequious insensitivity to the outrages symbolized by the denial and the division, but of the conscious acceptance of the harsh realities of the human condition, of the ambiguities and hypocrisies of human history as they have played themselves out in the United States.

Perhaps, taken in aggregate, these European names (sometimes with irony, sometimes with pride, but always with personal investment) represent a certain triumph of the spirit, speaking to us of those who rallied, reassembled and transformed themselves, and who under dismembering pressures refused to die. "Brothers and sisters," I once heard a Negro preacher exhort, "let us make up our faces before the world, and our names shall sound throughout the land with honor! For we ourselves are our *true* names, not their epithets! So let us, I say, Make Up Our Faces and Our Minds!"

Perhaps my preacher had read T. S. Eliot, although I doubt it. And in actuality, it was unnecessary that he do so, for a concern with names and naming was very much a part of that special area of American culture from which I come, and it is precisely for this reason that this example should come to mind in a discussion of my own experience as a writer.

Undoubtedly writers begin their *conditioning* as manipulators of words long before they become aware of literature—certain Freudians would even say at the breast. Perhaps, but if so, that is far too early to be of use at this moment. Of this, though, I am certain: that despite the misconceptions of those educators who trace the reading difficulties experienced by large numbers of Negro children in Northern schools to their Southern background, these children are, in *their* familiar South, facile manipulators of words. I know, too, that the Negro community is deadly in its ability to create nicknames and to spot all that is ludicrous in an unlikely name or that which is incongruous in conduct. Names are not qualities; nor are words, in this particular sense, actions. To assume that they are could cost one his life many times a day. Language skills depend to a large extent upon a knowledge of the details, manners, objects, folkways and psychological patterns of a given environment. Humor and wit depend upon much the same awareness, and so does the suggestive power of names.

"A small brown bowlegged Negro with the name 'Franklin D. Roosevelt Jones' might sound like a clown to someone who looks at him from the outside," said my friend Albert Murray, "but on the other hand he just might turn out to be a hell of a fireside operator. He might just lie back in all of that comic juxtaposition of names and manipulate you deaf, dumb and blind—and you not even suspecting it, because you're thrown out of stance by his name! There you are, so dazzled by the F.D.R. image—which you *know* you can't see—and so delighted with your own superior position that you don't realize that it is *Jones* who must be confronted."

Well, as you must suspect, all of this speculation on the matter of names has a purpose, and now, because it is tied up so ironically with my own experience as a writer, I must turn to my own name.

For in the dim beginnings, before I ever thought consciously of writing, there was my own name, and there was, doubtless, a certain magic in it. From the start I was uncomfortable with it, and in my earliest years it caused me much puzzlement. Neither could I understand what a poet was, nor why, exactly, my father had chosen to name me after one. Perhaps I could have understood it perfectly well had he named me after his own father, but that name had been given to an older brother who died and thus was out of the question. But why hadn't he named me after a hero, such as Jack Johnson, or a soldier like Colonel Charles Young, or a great seaman like Admiral Dewey, or an educator like Booker T. Washington, or a great orator and abolitionist like Frederick Douglass? Or again, why hadn't he named me (as so many Negro parents had done) after President Teddy Roosevelt?

Instead, he named me after someone called Ralph Waldo Emerson, and then, when I was three, he died. It was too early for me to have understood his choice, although I'm sure he must have explained it many times, and it was also too soon for me to have made the connection between my name and my father's love for reading. Much later, after I began to write and work with words, I came to suspect that he was aware of the suggestive powers of names and of the magic involved in naming.

I recall an odd conversation with my mother during my early teens in which she mentioned their interest in, of all things, prenatal culture! But for a long time I actually knew only that my father read a lot, and that he admired this remote Mr. Emerson, who was something called a "poet and philosopher" so much that he named his second son after him.

I knew, also, that whatever his motives, the combination of names he'd given me caused me no end of trouble from the moment when I could talk well enough to respond to the ritualized question which grownups put to very young children. Emerson's name was quite familiar to Negroes in Oklahoma during those days when World War I was brewing, and adults, eager to show off their knowledge of literary figures, and obviously amused by the joke implicit in such a small brown nubbin of a boy carrying around such a heavy moniker, would invariably repeat my first two names and then, to my great annoyance, they'd add "Emerson."

And I, in my confusion, would reply, "No, *no*, *I'm* not Emerson; he's the little boy who lives next door." Which only made them laugh all the louder. "Oh, no," they'd say, "*you're* Ralph Waldo Emerson," while I had fantasies of blue murder.

For a while the presence next door of my little friend Emerson made it unnecessary for me to puzzle too often over this peculiar adult confusion. And since there were other Negro boys named Ralph in the city, I came to suspect that there was something about the combination of names which produced their laughter. Even today I know of only one other Ralph who had as much comedy made out of his name, a campus politician and deep-voiced orator whom I knew at Tuskegee, who was called, in friendly ribbing, *Ralph Waldo Emerson Edgar Allan Poe*, spelled Powe. This must have been quite a trial for him, but I had been initiated much earlier.

During my early school years the name continued to puzzle me, for it constantly evoked in the faces of others some secret. It was as though I possessed some treasure or some defect which was invisible to my own eyes and ears; something which I had but did not *possess*, like a piece of property in South Carolina, which was mine but which I could not have until some future time.

I recall finding, at about this time, while seeking adventure in back alleys—which possess for boys a superiority over playgrounds like that which kitchen utensils possess over toys designed for infants—a large photographic lens. I remember nothing of its optical qualities, of its speed or color correction, but it gleamed with crystal mystery and it was beautiful. Mounted handsomely in a tube of shiny brass, it spoke to me of distant worlds of possibility. I played with it, looking through it with squinted eyes, holding it in shafts of sunlight, and tried to use it for a magic lantern. But most of this was as unrewarding as my attempts to make the music come from a phonograph record by holding the needle in my fingers. I could burn holes through newspapers with it, or I could pretend that it was a telescope, the barrel of a cannon, or the third eye of a monster—*I* being the monster—but I could do nothing at all about its proper function of making images, nothing to make it yield its secret. Still, I could not discard it. Older boys sought to get it away from me by offering knives or tops, agate marbles or whole zoos of grass snakes and horned toads in trade, but I held on to it. No one, not even the white boys I knew, had such a lens, and it was my own good luck to have found it. Thus I would hold on to it until such time as I could acquire the parts needed to make it function. Finally I put it aside and it remained buried in my box of treasures, dusty and dull, to be lost and forgotten as I grew older and became interested in music.

By now I had reached the grades where it was necessary to learn something about Mr. Emerson and what he had written, such as the "Concord Hymn" and the essay "Self-Reliance," and in following his advice I reduced the "Waldo" to a simple and, I hoped, mysterious "W," and in my own reading I avoided his works like the plague. I could no more deal with my name—I shall never really master it—than I could find a creative use for my lens. Fortunately there were other problems to occupy my mind. Not that I forgot my fascination with names, but more about that later.

Negro Oklahoma City was starkly lacking in writers. In fact, there was only Roscoe Dunjee, the editor of the local Negro newspaper and a very fine editorialist in that valuable tradition of personal journalism which is now rapidly disappearing, a writer who in his emphasis upon the possibilities for justice offered by the Constitution anticipated the anti-segregation struggle by decades. There were also a few reporters who drifted in and out, but these were about all. On the level of *conscious* culture the Negro community was biased in the direction of music.

These were the middle and late twenties, remember, and the state was still a new frontier state. The capital city was one of the great centers for southwestern jazz, along with Dallas and Kansas City. Orchestras which were to become famous within a few years were constantly coming and going. As were the blues singers Ma Rainey and Ida Cox, and the old bands like that of King Oliver. But best of all, thanks to Mrs. Zelia N. Breaux, there was an active and enthusiastic school music program through which any child who had the interest and talent could learn to play an instrument and take part in the band, the orchestra, the brass quartet. And there was a yearly operetta and a chorus and a glee club. Harmony was taught for four years and the music appreciation program was imperative. European folk dances were taught throughout the Negro school system, and we were also taught complicated patterns of military drill.

I tell you this to point out that although there were no incentives to write, there was ample opportunity to receive an artistic discipline. Indeed, once one picked up an instrument it was difficult to escape. If you chafed at the many rehearsals of the school band or orchestra and were drawn to the many small jazz groups, you were likely to discover that the jazzmen were apt to rehearse far more than the school band; it was only that they seemed to enjoy themselves more, and to possess a freedom of imagination which we were denied at school. And one soon learned that the wild, transcendent moments which occurred at dances or "battles of music," moments in which memorable improvisations were ignited, depended upon dedication to a discipline observed even when rehearsals had to take place in the crowded quarters of Halley Richardson's shoeshine parlor. It was not the place which counted, although a large hall with good acoustics was preferred, but what one did to perfect one's performance.

If this talk of musical discipline gives the impression that there were no forces working to nourish one who would one day blunder, after many a twist and turn, into writing, I am misleading you. And here I might give you a longish lecture on the ironies and uses of segregation. When I was a small child there was no library for Negroes in our city, and not until a Negro minister invaded the main library did we get one. For it was discovered that there was no law, only custom, which held that we could not use these public facilities. The results were the quick renting of two large rooms in a Negro office building (the recent site of a pool hall), the hiring of a young

Negro librarian, the installation of shelves and a hurried stocking of the walls with any and every book possible. It was, in those first days, something of a literary chaos.

But how fortunate for a boy who loved to read! I started with the fairy tales and quickly went through the junior fiction, then through the Westerns and the detective novels, and very soon I was reading the classics—only I didn't know it. There were also the Haldeman Julius Blue Books, which seem to have floated on the air down from Girard, Kansas, the syndicated columns of O. O. McIntyre, and the copies of *Vanity Fair* and the *Literary Digest* which my mother brought home from work; how could I ever join uncritically in the heavy-handed attacks on the so-called Big Media which have become so common today?

There were also the pulp magazines and, more important, that other library which I visited when I went to help my adopted grandfather, J. D. Randolph (my parents had been living in his rooming house when I was born), at his work as custodian of the law library of the Oklahoma State Capitol. Mr. Randolph had been one of the first teachers in what became Oklahoma City, and he'd also been one of the leaders of a group who walked from Gallatin, Tennessee, to the Oklahoma Territory. He was a tall man, as brown as smoked leather, who looked like the Indians with whom he'd herded horses in the early days.

And while his status was merely as the custodian of the law library, I was to see the white legislators come down on many occasions to question him on points of law, and often I was to hear him answer without recourse to the uniform rows of books on the shelves. This was a thing to marvel at in itself, and the white lawmakers did so, but even more marvelous, ironic, intriguing, haunting—call it what you will—is the fact that the Negro who knew the answers was named after Jefferson Davis. What Tennessee lost, Oklahoma was to gain, and after gaining it (a gift of courage, intelligence, fortitude and grace), used it only in concealment and, one hopes, with embarrassment.

So, let us, I say, make up our faces and our minds!

• • •

In the loosely structured community of that time, knowledge, news of other ways of living, ancient wisdom, the latest literary fads, hate literature—for years I kept a card warning Negroes away from the polls, which had been dropped by the thousands from a plane which circled over the Negro community—information of all kinds found its level, catch-as-catch-can, in the minds of those who were receptive to it. Not that there was no conscious structuring—I read my first Shaw and Maupassant, my first Harvard Classics in the home of a friend whose parents were products of that stream of New England education which had been brought to Negroes by the young and enthusiastic white teachers who staffed the schools set up for the freedmen after the Civil War. These parents were both teachers, and there were others like them in our town.

But the places where a rich oral literature was truly functional were the churches, the schoolyards, the barbershops, the cotton-picking camps—places where folklore and gossip thrived. The drug store where I worked was such a place, where on days of bad weather the older men would sit with their pipes and tell tall tales, hunting yarns and homely versions of the classics. It was here that I heard stories of searching for buried treasure and of headless horsemen, which I was told were my own father's versions told long before. There were even recitals of popular verse, "The Shooting of Dan McGrew," and, along with these, stories of Jesse James, of Negro outlaws and black United States marshals, of slaves who became the chiefs of Indian tribes, and of the exploits of Negro cowboys. There was both truth and fantasy in this, intermingled in the mysterious fashion of literature.

In their formative period, writers absorb into their consciousness much that has no special value until much later, and often much which is of no special value even then, perhaps, beyond the fact that it throbs with affect and mystery and in it "time and pain and royalty in the blood" are suspended in imagery. So, long before I thought of writing, I was claimed by weather, by speech rhythms, by Negro voices and their different idioms, by husky male voices and by the high shrill singing voices of certain Negro women, by music, by tight spaces and by wide spaces in which the eyes could wander, by death, by newly born babies, by manners of various kinds, company manners and street manners, the manners of white society and those of our own high society, and by interracial manners, by street fights, circuses and minstrel shows, by vaudeville and moving pictures, by prize fights and foot races, baseball games and football matches. By spring floods and blizzards, catalpa worms and jack rabbits, honeysuckle and snapdragons (which smelled like old cigar butts), by sunflowers and hollyhocks, raw sugar cane and baked yams, pigs' feet, chili and blue haw ice cream. By parades, public dances and jam sessions, Easter sunrise ceremonies and large funerals. By contests between fire-and-brimstone preachers and by presiding elders who got "laughing-happy" when moved by the spirit of God.

I was impressed by expert players of the "dozens" and certain notorious bootleggers of corn whiskey. By jazz musicians and fortunetellers and by men who did anything well, by strange sicknesses and by interesting brick or razor scars, by expert cursing vocabularies as well as by exalted praying and terrifying shouting, and by transcendent playing or singing of the blues. I was fascinated by old ladies, those who had seen slavery and those who were defiant of white folk and black alike, by the enticing walks of prostitutes and by the limping walks affected by Negro hustlers, especially those who wore Stetson hats, expensive shoes with well-starched overalls, usually with a diamond stickpin (when not in hock) in their tireless collars as their gambling uniforms.

And there were the blind men who preached on corners, and the blind men who sang the blues to the accompaniment of washboard and guitar, and the white junkmen who sang mountain music and the famous hucksters of fruit and vegetables.

And there was the Indian-Negro confusion. There were Negroes who were part Indian and who lived on reservations, and Indians who had children who lived in towns as Negroes, and Negroes who were Indians and traveled back and forth between the groups with no trouble. And Indians who were as wild as wild Negroes, and others who were as solid and as steady as bankers. There were the teachers, too: inspiring teachers and villainous teachers who chased after the girl students, and certain female teachers who one wished would chase after young male students. And a handsome old principal of military bearing who had been blemished by his classmates at West Point when they discovered on the eve of graduation that he was a Negro. There were certain Jews, Mexicans, Chinese cooks, a German orchestra conductor and an English grocer who owned a Franklin touring car. And certain Negro mechanics—"Cadillac Slim," "Sticks" Walker, Buddy Bunn and Oscar Pitman—who had so assimilated the automobile that they seemed to be behind a steering wheel even as they walked the streets or danced with girls. And there were the whites who despised us and the others who shared our hardships and our joys.

There is much more, but this is sufficient to indicate some of what was present even in a segregated community to form the background of my work and my sense of life.

And now comes the next step. I went to Tuskegee to study music, hoping to become a composer of symphonies, and there, during my second year, I read *The Waste Land* and that, although I was then unaware of it, was the real transition to writing.

Mrs. L. C. McFarland had taught us much of Negro history in grade school, and from her I'd learned of the New Negro Movement of the twenties, of Langston Hughes, Countee Cullen, Claude McKay, James Weldon Johnson and the others. They had inspired pride and had given me a closer identification with poetry (by now, oddly enough, I seldom thought of my hidden name), but with music so much on my mind it never occurred to me to try to imitate them. Still, I read their work and was excited by the glamour of the Harlem which emerged from their poems, and it was good to know that there were Negro writers. Then came *The Waste Land*.

I was much more under the spell of literature than I realized at the time. *Wuthering Heights* had caused me an agony of unexpressible emotion, and the same was true of *Jude the Obscure*, but *The Waste Land* seized my mind. I was intrigued by its power to move me while eluding my understanding. Somehow its rhythms were often closer to those of jazz than were those of the Negro poets, and even though I could not understand then, its range of allusion was as mixed and as varied as that of Louis Armstrong. Yet there were its discontinuities, its changes of pace and its hidden system of organization which escaped me.

There was nothing to do but look up the references in the footnotes to the poem, and thus began my conscious education in literature. For this, the library at Tuskegee was quite adequate and I used it. Soon I was reading a whole range of subjects drawn upon by the poet, and this led, in turn, to criticism and to Pound, Ford Madox Ford, Sherwood Anderson, Gertrude Stein, Hemingway and Fitzgerald and "round about 'til I was come" back to Melville and Twain—the writers who are taught and doubtless overtaught today. Perhaps it was my good luck that they were not taught at Tuskegee; I wouldn't know. But at the time I was playing, having an intellectually interesting good time.

Having given so much attention to the techniques of music, the process of learning something of the craft and intention of modern poetry and fiction seemed quite familiar. Besides, it was absolutely painless because it involved no deadlines or credits. Even then, however, a process which I described earlier had begun to operate. The more I learned of literature in this conscious way, the more the details of my background became transformed. I heard undertones in remembered conversations which had escaped me before, local customs took on a more universal meaning, values which I hadn't understood were revealed, some of the people whom I had known were diminished, while others were elevated in stature. More important, I began to see my own possibilities with more objective and in some ways more hopeful eyes.

The summer of 1936 I went to New York seeking work, which I

did not find, and remained there, but the personal transformation continued. Reading had become a conscious process of growth and discovery, a method of reordering the world. And that world had widened considerably.

At Tuskegee I had handled manuscripts which Prokofiev had given to Hazel Harrison, a Negro concert pianist who taught there and who had known him in Europe, and through Miss Harrison I had become aware of Prokofiev's symphonies. I had also become aware of the radical movement in politics and art, and in New York had begun reading the work of André Malraux, not only the fiction but chapters published from his *Psychology of Art.* And in my search for an expression of modern sensibility in the works of Negro writers I discovered Richard Wright. Shortly thereafter I was to meet Wright, and it was at his suggestion that I wrote both my first book review and my first short story.

These were fateful suggestions. For although I had tried my hand at poetry while at Tuskegee, it hadn't occurred to me that I might write fiction, but once he suggested it, it seemed the most natural thing to try. Fortunately for me, Wright, then on the verge of his first success, was eager to talk with a beginner, and I was able to save valuable time in searching out those works in which writing was discussed as a craft. He guided me to Henry James's prefaces, to Conrad, to Joseph Warren Beach and to the letters of Dostoevsky. There were other advisers and other books involved, of course, but what is important here is that I was consciously concerned with the art of fiction, and that almost from the beginning I was grappling quite consciously with the art through which I wished to realize myself. But this was not done in isolation; the Spanish Civil War was now in progress and the Depression was still on. The world was being shaken up, and through one of those odd instances which occur to young provincials in New York, I was to hear Malraux make an appeal for the Spanish Loyalists at the same party where I first heard the folk singer Leadbelly perform. Wright and I were there seeking money for the magazine which he had come to New York to edit.

Art and politics: a great French novelist and a Negro folk singer, a young writer who was soon to publish *Uncle Tom's Children*, and I who had barely begun to study his craft. It is such accidents, such fortuitous meetings, which count for so much in our lives. I had never dreamed that I would be in the presence of Malraux, of whose work I became aware on my second day in Harlem when Langston Hughes suggested that I read *Man's Fate* and *Days of Wrath* before returning them to a friend of his. And it is this fortuitous circumstance which led to my selecting Malraux as a literary "ancestor," whom, unlike a relative, the artist is permitted to choose. There was in progress at the time all the agitation over the Scottsboro boys and the Herndon Case, and I was aware of both. I had to be; I myself had been taken off a freight train at Decatur, Alabama, only three years before while on my way to Tuskegee. But while I joined in the agitation for their release, my main energies went into learning to write.

I began to publish enough, and not too slowly, to justify my hopes for success, and as I continued, I made a most perplexing discovery— namely, that for all his conscious concern with technique, a writer did not so much create the novel as he was created *by* the novel. That is, one did not make an arbitrary gesture when one sought to write. And when I say that the novelist is created by the novel, I mean to remind you that fictional techniques are not a mere set of objective tools, but something much more intimate: a way of feeling, of seeing and of expressing one's sense of life. And the process of *acquiring* technique is a process of modifying one's responses, of learning to see and feel, to hear and observe, to evoke and evaluate the images of memory and of summoning up and directing the imagination, of learning to conceive of human values in the ways which have been established by the great writers who have developed and extended the art. And perhaps the writer's greatest freedom, as artist, lies precisely in his possession of technique, for it is through technique that he comes to possess and express the meaning of his life.

Perhaps at this point it would be useful to recapitulate the route— perhaps as mazelike as that of *Finnegans Wake*—which I have been

trying to describe: that which leads from the writer's discovery of a
sense of purpose, which is that of becoming a writer, and then the
involvement in the passionate struggle required to master a bit of
technique, and then, as this begins to take shape, the disconcerting
discovery that it is *technique* which transforms the individual before
he is able in turn to transform it. And in that personal transformation
he discovers something else; he discovers that he has taken on certain obligations, that he must not embarrass his chosen form, and
that in order to avoid this he must develop taste. He learns—and this
is most discouraging—that he is involved with values which turn in
their *own* way, and not in the ways of politics, upon the central issues
affecting his nation and his time. He learns that the American novel,
from its first consciousness of itself as a literary form, has grappled
with the meaning of the American experience, that it has been aware
and has sought to define the nature of that experience by addressing
itself to the specific details, the moods, the landscapes, the city-
scapes, the tempo of American change. And that it has borne, at its
best, the full weight of that burden of conscience and consciousness
which Americans inherit as one of the results of the revolutionary
circumstances of our national beginnings.

We began as a nation not through the accidents of race or religion
or geography (Robert Penn Warren has dwelled on these circumstances), but when a group of men, *some* of them political philosophers, put down, upon what we now recognize as sacred papers, their
conception of the nation they intended to establish on these shores.
They described, as we know, the obligations of the state to the citizen, of the citizen to the state; they committed themselves to certain
ideas of justice, just as they committed us to a system which would
guarantee all of its citizens equality of opportunity.

I need not describe the problems which have arisen from these
beginnings. I need only remind you that the contradiction between
these noble ideals and the actualities of our conduct generated a
guilt, an unease of spirit, from the very beginning, and that the
American novel at its best has always been concerned with this basic

moral predicament. During Melville's time and Twain's, it was an implicit aspect of their major themes; by the twentieth century and after the discouraging and traumatic effect of the Civil War and the Reconstruction it had gone underground, had become *understated.* Nevertheless it did not disappear completely, and it is to be found operating in the work of Henry James as well as that of Hemingway and Fitzgerald. And as one who believes in the impelling moral function of the novel and who believes in the moral seriousness of the form, it pleases me no end that it then comes into explicit statement again in the works of Richard Wright and William Faulkner, writers who lived close to moral and political problems which would not stay put underground.

I go into these details not to recapitulate the history of the American novel but to indicate the trend of thought which was set into motion when I began to discover the nature of that process with which I was actually involved. Whatever the opinions and decisions of critics, a novelist must arrive at his own conclusions as to the meaning and function of the form with which he is engaged, and these are, in all modesty, some of mine.

In order to orient myself I also began to learn that the American novel had long concerned itself with the puzzle of the one-and-the-many; the mystery of how each of us, despite his origin in diverse regions, with our diverse racial, cultural, religious backgrounds, speaking his own diverse idiom of the American in his own accent, is, nevertheless, American. And with this concern with the implicit pluralism of the country and with the composite nature of the ideal character called "the American," there goes a concern with gauging the health of the American promise, with depicting the extent to which it was being achieved and made manifest in our daily conduct.

And with all of this there still remained the specific concerns of literature. Among these is the need to keep literary standards high, the necessity of exploring new possibilities of language which would allow it to retain that flexibility and fidelity to the common speech which has been its glory since Mark Twain. For me this meant learning to add the wonderful resources of Negro American speech and idiom, and to bring into range as fully and eloquently as possible the complex reality of the American experience as it shaped and was shaped by the lives of my own people.

Notice that I stress as "fully as possible," because I would no more strive to write great novels by leaving out the complexity of circumstances which go to make up the Negro experience, and which alone go to make the obvious injustice bearable, than I would think of preparing myself to become President of the United States simply by studying Negro American history or confining myself to studying those laws affecting civil rights.

For it seems to me that one of the obligations I took on when I committed myself to the art and form of the novel was that of striving for the broadest range, the discovery and articulation of the most exalted values. And I must squeeze these from the life which I know best. (A highly truncated impression of that life I attempted to convey to you earlier.)

If all this sounds a bit heady, remember that I did not destroy that troublesome middle name of mine; I only suppressed it. Sometimes it reminds me of my obligations to the man who named me.

It is our fate as human beings always to give up some good things for other good things, to throw off certain bad circumstances only to create others. Thus there is a value for the writer in trying to give as thorough a report of social reality as possible. Only by doing so may we grasp and convey the cost of change. Only by considering the broadest accumulation of data may we make choices that are based upon our own hard-earned sense of reality. Speaking from my own special area of American culture, I feel that to embrace uncritically values which are extended to us by others is to reject the validity, even the sacredness, of our own experience. It is also to forget that the small share of reality which each of our diverse groups is able to snatch from the whirling chaos of history belongs not to the group alone, but to all of us. It is a property and a witness which can be ignored only to the danger of the entire nation.

I could suppress the name of my namesake out of respect for the achievements of its original bearer, but I cannot escape the obligation of attempting to achieve some of the things which he asked of the American writer. As Henry James suggested, being an American is an arduous task, and for most of us, I suspect, the difficulty begins with the name.

The Art of Fiction:
An Interview

RALPH ELLISON: Let me say right now that my book [*Invisible Man*] is not an autobiographical work.

INTERVIEWERS (ALFRED CHESTER, VILMA HOWARD): You weren't thrown out of school like the boy in your novel?

ELLISON: No, though, like him, I went from one job to another.

INTERVIEWERS: Why did you give up music and begin writing?

ELLISON: I didn't give up music, but I became interested in writing through incessant reading. In 1935 I discovered Eliot's *The Waste Land*, which moved and intrigued me but defied my powers of analysis—such as they were—and I wondered why I had never read anything of equal intensity and sensibility by an American Negro writer. Later on, in New York, I read a poem by Richard Wright, who, as luck would have it, came to town the next week. He was editing a magazine called *New Challenge* and asked me to try a book review of E. Waters Turpin's *These Low Grounds*. On the basis of this review Wright suggested that I try a short story, which I did. I tried to use my knowledge of riding freight trains. He liked the story well enough to accept it, and it got as far as the galley proofs when it was bumped from the issue because there was too much material. Just after that the magazine failed.

INTERVIEWERS: But you went on writing—

ELLISON: With difficulty, because this was the Recession of 1937. I went to Dayton, Ohio, where my brother and I hunted and sold

---

From *The Paris Review*, Spring 1955.

game to earn a living. At night I practiced writing and studied Joyce, Dostoevsky, Stein and Hemingway. Especially Hemingway; I read him to learn his sentence structure and how to organize a story. I guess many young writers were doing this, but I also used his description of hunting when I went into the fields the next day. I had been hunting since I was eleven, but no one had broken down the process of wing-shooting for me, and it was from reading Hemingway that I learned to lead a bird. When he describes something in print, believe him; believe him even when he describes the process of art in terms of baseball or boxing; he's been there.

INTERVIEWERS: Were you affected by the social realism of the period?

ELLISON: I was seeking to learn, and social realism was a highly regarded theory, though I didn't think too much of the so-called proletarian fiction even when I was most impressed by Marxism. I was intrigued by Malraux, who at that time was being claimed by the Communists. I noticed, however, that whenever the heroes of *Man's Fate** regarded their condition during moments of heightened self-consciousness, their thinking was something other than Marxist. Actually they were more profoundly intellectual than their real-life counterparts. Of course Malraux was more of a humanist than most of the Marxist writers of that period—and also much more of an artist. He was the artist-revolutionary rather than a politician when he wrote *Man's Fate,* and the book lives not because of a political position embraced at the time, but because of its larger concern with the tragic struggle of humanity. Most of the social realists of the period were concerned less with tragedy than with injustice. I wasn't, and am not, primarily concerned with injustice, but with art.

INTERVIEWERS: Then you consider your novel a purely literary work as opposed to one in the tradition of social protest.

---

*La Condition Humaine.

ELLISON: Now mind! I recognize no dichotomy between art and protest. Dostoevsky's *Notes from Underground* is, among other things, a protest against the limitations of nineteenth-century rationalism; *Don Quixote, Man's Fate, Œdipus Rex, The Trial*—all these embody protest, even against the limitation of human life itself. If social protest is antithetical to art, what then shall we make of Goya, Dickens and Twain? One hears a lot of complaints about the so-called "protest novel," especially when written by Negroes, but it seems to me that the critics could more accurately complain about their lack of craftsmanship and their provincialism.

INTERVIEWERS: But isn't it going to be difficult for the Negro writer to escape provincialism when his literature is concerned with a minority?

ELLISON: All novels are about certain minorities: the individual is a minority. The universal in the novel—and isn't that what we're all clamoring for these days?—is reached only through the depiction of the specific man in a specific circumstance.

INTERVIEWERS: But still, how is the Negro writer, in terms of what is expected of him by critics and readers, going to escape his particular need for social protest and reach the "universal" you speak of?

ELLISON: If the Negro, or any other writer, is going to do what is expected of him, he's lost the battle before he takes the field. I suspect that all the agony that goes into writing is borne precisely because the writer longs for acceptance—but it must be acceptance on his own terms. Perhaps, though, this thing cuts both ways: the Negro novelist draws his blackness too tightly around him when he sits down to write—that's what the anti-protest critics believe—but perhaps the white reader draws his whiteness around himself when he sits down to read. He doesn't want to identify himself with Negro characters in terms of our immediate racial and social situation, though on the deeper human level, identification can become compelling when the situation is revealed artistically. The white reader doesn't want to get too close, not even in an imaginary re-creation of society. Negro writers have felt this and it has led to much of our failure.

Too many books by Negro writers are addressed to a white audience. By doing this the authors run the risk of limiting themselves to the audience's presumptions of what a Negro is or should be; the tendency is to become involved in polemics, to plead the Negro's humanity. You know, many white people question that humanity, but I don't think that Negroes can afford to indulge in such a false issue. For us the question should be, What are the specific *forms* of that humanity, and what in our background is worth preserving or abandoning? The clue to this can be found in folklore, which offers the first drawings of any group's character. It preserves mainly those situations which have repeated themselves again and again in the history of any given group. It describes those rites, manners, customs, and so forth, which insure the good life or destroy it, and it describes those boundaries of feeling, thought and action which that particular group has found to be the limitation of the human condition. It projects this wisdom in symbols which express the group's will to survive; it embodies those values by which the group lives and dies. These drawings may be crude, but they are nonetheless profound in that they represent the group's attempt to humanize the world. It's no accident that great literature, the products of individual artists, is erected upon this humble base. The hero of Dostoevsky's *Notes from Underground* and the hero of Gogol's *The Overcoat* appear in their rudimentary forms far back in Russian folklore. French literature has never ceased exploring the nature of the Frenchman . . . Or take Picasso—

INTERVIEWERS: How does Picasso fit into all this?

ELLISON: Why, he's the greatest wrestler with forms and techniques of them all. Just the same, he's never abandoned the old symbolic forms of Spanish art: the guitar, the bull, daggers, women, shawls, veils, mirrors. Such symbols serve a dual function: they allow the artist to speak of complex experiences and to annihilate time with simple lines and curves, and they allow the viewer an orientation, both emotional and associative, which goes so deep that a total culture may resound in a simple rhythm, an image. It has been said that Escudero could recapitulate the history and spirit of the Spanish dance with a simple arabesque of his fingers.

INTERVIEWERS: But these are examples from homogeneous cultures. How representative of the American nation would you say Negro folklore is?

ELLISON: The history of the American Negro is a most intimate part of American history. Through the very process of slavery came the building of the United States. Negro folklore, evolving within a larger culture which regarded it as inferior, was an especially courageous expression. It announced the Negro's willingness to trust his own experience, his own sensibilities as to the definition of reality, rather than allow his masters to define these crucial matters for him. His experience is that of America and the West, and is as rich a body of experience as one would find anywhere. We can view it narrowly as something exotic, folksy or "low-down," or we may identify ourselves with it and recognize it as an important segment of the larger American experience—not lying at the bottom of it, but intertwined, diffused in its very texture. I can't take this lightly or be impressed by those who cannot see its importance; it is important to *me*. One ironic witness to the beauty and the universality of this art is the fact that the descendants of the very men who enslaved us can now sing the spirituals and find in the singing an exaltation of their own humanity. Just take a look at some of the slave songs, blues, folk ballads; their possibilities for the writer are infinitely suggestive. Some of them have named human situations so well that a whole corps of writers could not exhaust their universality. For instance, here's an old slave verse:

> *Ole Aunt Dinah, she's just like me*
> *She work so hard she want to be free*

But old Aunt Dinah's gittin' kinda ole
She's afraid to go to Canada on account of the cold.

Ole Uncle Jack, now he's a mighty "good nigger"
You tell him that you want to be free for a fac'
Next thing you know they done stripped the skin
    off your back.

Now old Uncle Ned, he want to be free
He found his way north by the moss on the tree
He cross that river floating in a tub
The patateroller* give him a mighty close rub.

It's crude, but in it you have three universal attitudes toward the problem of freedom. You can refine it and sketch in the psychological subtleties and historical and philosophical allusions, action and what not, but I don't think its basic definition can be exhausted. Perhaps some genius could do as much with it as Mann has done with the Joseph story.

INTERVIEWERS: Can you give us an example of the use of folklore in your own novel?

ELLISON: Well, there are certain themes, symbols and images which are based on folk material. For example, there is the old saying amongst Negroes: If you're black, stay back; if you're brown, stick around; if you're white, you're right. And there is the joke Negroes tell on themselves about their being so black they can't be seen in the dark. In my book this sort of thing was merged with the meanings which blackness and light have long had in Western mythology: evil and goodness, ignorance and knowledge, and so on. In my novel the narrator's development is one through blackness to light; that is, from ignorance to enlightenment: invisibility to visibility. He leaves the South and goes North; this, as you will notice in reading Negro folktales, is always the road to freedom, the movement upward. You

---

*Patroller.

have the same thing again when he leaves his underground cave for the open.

It took me a long time to learn how to adapt such examples of myth into my work—also ritual. The use of ritual is equally a vital part of the creative process. I learned a few things from Eliot, Joyce and Hemingway, but not how to adapt them. When I started writing, I knew that in both *The Waste Land* and *Ulysses* ancient myth and ritual were used to give form and significance to the material, but it took me a few years to realize that the myths and rites which we find functioning in our everyday lives could be used in the same way. In my first attempt at a novel—which I was unable to complete—I began by trying to manipulate the simple structural unities of *beginning, middle* and *end,* but when I attempted to deal with the psychological strata—the images, symbols and emotional configurations—of the experience at hand, I discovered that the unities were simply cool points of stability on which one could suspend the narrative line, but beneath the surface of apparently rational human relationships there seethed a chaos before which I was helpless. People rationalize what they shun or are incapable of dealing with; these superstitions and their rationalizations become ritual as they govern behavior. The rituals become social forms, and it is one of the functions of the artist to recognize them and raise them to the level of art.

I don't know whether I'm getting this over or not. Let's put it this way: take the "Battle Royal" passage in my novel, where the boys are blindfolded and forced to fight each other for the amusement of the white observers. This is a vital part of behavior pattern in the South, which both Negroes and whites thoughtlessly accept. It is a ritual in preservation of caste lines, a keeping of taboo to appease the gods and ward off bad luck. It is also the initiation ritual to which all greenhorns are subjected. This passage which states what Negroes will see I did not have to invent; the patterns were already there in society, so that all I had to do was present them in a broader context of meaning. In any society there are many rituals of situation which, for the most part, go unquestioned. They can be simple or elaborate, but they are the connective tissue between the work of art and the audience.

INTERVIEWERS: Do you think a reader unacquainted with this folklore can properly understand your work?

ELLISON: Yes, I think so. It's like jazz; there's no inherent problem which prohibits understanding but the assumptions brought to it. We don't all dig Shakespeare uniformly, or even Little Red Riding Hood. The understanding of art depends finally upon one's willingness to extend one's humanity and one's knowledge of human life. I noticed, incidentally, that the Germans, having no special caste assumptions concerning American Negroes, dealt with my work simply as a novel. I think the Americans will come to view it that way in twenty years—if it's around that long.

INTERVIEWERS: Don't you think it will be?

ELLISON: I doubt it. It's not an important novel. I failed of eloquence, and many of the immediate issues are rapidly fading away. If it does last, it will be simply because there are things going on in its depth that are of more permanent interest than on its surface. I hope so, anyway.

INTERVIEWERS: Have the critics given you any constructive help in your writing, or changed in any way your aims in fiction?

ELLISON: No, except that I have a better idea of how the critics react, of what they see and fail to see, of how their sense of life differs with mine and mine with theirs. In some instances they were nice for the wrong reasons. In the United States—and I don't want this to sound like an apology for my own failures—some reviewers did not see what was before them because of this nonsense about protest.

INTERVIEWERS: Did the critics change your view of yourself as a writer?

ELLISON: I can't say that they did. I've been seeing by my own candle too long for that. The critics did give me a sharper sense of a larger audience, yes, and some convinced me that they were willing to judge me in terms of my writing rather than in terms of my racial identity. But there is one widely syndicated critical bankrupt who made liberal noises during the thirties and has been frightened ever since. He attacked my book as a "literary race riot." By and large, the critics and readers gave me an affirmed sense of my identity as a writer. You might know this within yourself, but to have it affirmed by others is of utmost importance. Writing is, after all, a form of communication.

INTERVIEWER: When did you begin *Invisible Man*?

ELLISON: In the summer of 1945. I had returned from the sea, ill, with advice to get some rest. Part of my illness was due, no doubt, to the fact that I had not been able to write a novel for which I'd received a Rosenwald Fellowship the previous winter. So on a farm in Vermont where I was reading *The Hero* by Lord Raglan and speculating on the nature of Negro leadership in the United States, I wrote the first paragraph of *Invisible Man*, and was soon involved in the struggle of creating the novel.

INTERVIEWERS: How long did it take you to write it?

ELLISON: Five years, with one year out for a short novel which was unsatisfactory, ill-conceived and never submitted for publication.

INTERVIEWERS: Did you have everything thought out before you began to write *Invisible Man*?

ELLISON: The symbols and their connections were known to me. I began it with a chart of the three-part division. It was a conceptual frame with most of the ideas and some incidents indicated. The three parts represent the narrator's movement from, using Kenneth Burke's terms, purpose to passion to perception. These three major sections are built up of smaller units of three which mark the course of the action and which depend for their development upon what I hoped was a consistent and developing motivation. However, you'll note that the maximum insight on the hero's part isn't reached until the final section. After all, it's a novel about innocence and human error, a struggle through illusion to reality. Each section begins with a sheet of paper; each piece of paper is exchanged for another and contains a definition of his identity, or the social role he is to play as defined for him by others. But all say essentially the same thing: "Keep this nigger boy running." Before he could have some voice in his own destiny he had to discard these old identities and illusions; his enlightenment couldn't come until then. Once he recognizes the hole of darkness into which these papers put him, he has to burn them. That's the plan and the intention; whether I achieved this is something else.

INTERVIEWERS: Would you say that the search for identity is primarily an American theme?

ELLISON: It is *the* American theme. The nature of our society is such that we are prevented from knowing who we are. It is still a young society, and this is an integral part of its development.

INTERVIEWERS: A common criticism of "first novels" is that the central incident is either omitted or weak. *Invisible Man* seems to suffer here; shouldn't we have been present at the scenes which are the dividing lines in the book—namely, when the Brotherhood organization moves the narrator downtown, then back uptown?

ELLISON: I think you missed the point. The major flaw in the hero's character is his unquestioning willingness to do what is required of him by others as a way to success, and this was the specific form of his "innocence." He goes where he is told to go; he does what he is told to do; he does not even choose his Brotherhood name. It is chosen for him and he accepts it. He has accepted party discipline and thus cannot be present at the scene since it is not the will of the Brotherhood leaders. What is important is not the scene but his failure to question their decision. There is also the fact that no single person can be everywhere at once, nor can a single consciousness be aware of all the nuances of a large social action. What happens up-town while he is downtown is part of his darkness, both symbolic and actual. No, I don't feel that any vital scenes have been left out.

INTERVIEWERS: Why did you find it necessary to shift styles throughout the book, particularly in the prologue and epilogue?

ELLISON: The prologue was written afterwards, really—in terms of a shift in the hero's point of view. I wanted to throw the reader off balance, to make him accept certain non-naturalistic effects. It was really a memoir written underground, and I wanted a foreshadowing through which I hoped the reader would view the actions which took place in the main body of the book. For another thing, the styles of life presented are different. In the South, where he was trying to fit into a traditional pattern and where his sense of certainty had not yet been challenged, I felt a more naturalistic treatment was adequate. The college trustee's speech to the students is really an echo of a certain kind of Southern rhetoric, and I enjoyed trying to re-create it. As the hero passes from the South to the North, from the rela-tively stable to the swiftly changing, his sense of certainty is lost and the style becomes expressionistic. Later on, during his fall from grace in the Brotherhood, it becomes somewhat surrealistic. The styles try to express both his state of consciousness and the state of society. The epilogue was necessary to complete the action begun when he set out to write his memoirs.

INTERVIEWERS: After four hundred pages you still felt the epilogue was necessary?

ELLISON: Yes. Look at it this way. The book is a series of reversals. It is the portrait of the artist as a rabble-rouser, thus the various mediums of expression. In the epilogue the hero discovers what he had not discovered throughout the book: you have to make your own decisions; you have to think for yourself. The hero comes up from underground because the act of writing and thinking necessitated it. He could not stay down there.

INTERVIEWERS: You say that the book is "a series of reversals." It seemed to us that this was a weakness, that it was built on a series of provocative situations which were canceled by the calling up of conventional emotions—

ELLISON: I don't quite see what you mean.

INTERVIEWERS: Well, for one thing, you begin with a provocative situation of the American Negro's status in society. The responsibility for this is that of the white American citizen; that's where the guilt lies. Then you cancel it by introducing the Communist Party, or the Brotherhood, so that the reader tends to say to himself: "Ah, they're the guilty ones. They're the ones who mistreat him, not us."

ELLISON: I think that's a case of misreading. And I didn't identify the Brotherhood as the C.P., but since you do I'll remind you that they, too, are white. The hero's invisibility is not a matter of being seen, but a refusal to run the risk of his own humanity, which involves guilt. This is not an attack upon white society. It is what the hero refuses to do in each section which leads to further action. He must assert and achieve his own humanity; he cannot run with the pack and do this, and this is the reason for all the reversals. The epilogue is the most final reversal of all; therefore it is a necessary statement.

INTERVIEWERS: And the love affairs—or almost love affairs?

ELLISON: *(Laughing)* I'm glad you put it that way. The point is that when thrown into a situation which he thinks he wants, the hero is sometimes thrown at a loss; he doesn't know how to act. After he had made this speech about the Place of the Woman in Our Society, for example, and was approached by one of the women in the audience, he thought she wanted to talk about the Brotherhood and found that she wanted to talk about brother-*and-sisterhood*. Look, didn't you find the book at all *funny*? I felt that such a man as this character would have been incapable of a love affair; it would have been inconsistent with his personality.

INTERVIEWERS: Do you have any difficulty controlling your characters? E. M. Forster says that he sometimes finds a character running away with him.

ELLISON: No, because I find that a sense of the ritual understructure of the fiction helps to guide the creation of characters. Action is the thing. We are what we do and do not do. The problem for me is to get from A to B to C. My anxiety about transitions greatly prolonged the writing of my book. The naturalists stick to case histories and sociology and are willing to compete with the camera and the tape recorder. I despise concreteness in writing, but when reality is deranged in fiction, one must worry about the seams.

INTERVIEWERS: Do you have difficulty turning real characters into fiction?

ELLISON: Real characters are just a limitation. It's like turning your own life into fiction: you have to be hindered by chronology and fact. A number of the characters just jumped out, like Rinehart and Ras.

INTERVIEWERS: Isn't Ras based on Marcus Garvey?*

ELLISON: No. In 1950 my wife and I were staying at a vacation spot where we met some white liberals who thought the best way to be friendly was to tell us what it was like to be Negro. I got mad at hearing this from people who otherwise seemed very intelligent. I had already sketched Ras, but the passion of his statement came out after I went upstairs that night feeling that we needed to have this thing out once and for all and get it done with; then we could go on living like people and individuals. No conscious reference to Garvey is intended.

INTERVIEWERS: What about Rinehart? Is he related to Rinehart in the blues tradition, or Django Rheinhardt, the jazz musician?

---

*Marcus Garvey, Negro nationalist and founder of a "Back to Africa" movement in the U.S. during the early 1900s.

ELLISON: There is a peculiar set of circumstances connected with my choice of that name. My old Oklahoma friend, Jimmy Rushing, the blues singer, used to sing one with a refrain that went:

> *Rinehart, Rinehart,*
> *It's so lonesome up here*
> *On Beacon Hill . . .*

which haunted me, and as I was thinking of a character who was a master of disguise, of coincidence, this name with its suggestion of inner and outer came to my mind. Later I learned that it was a call used by Harvard students when they prepared to riot, a call to chaos. Which is interesting, because it is not long after Rinehart appears in my novel that the riot breaks out in Harlem. Rinehart is my name for the personification of chaos. He is also intended to represent America and change. He has lived so long with chaos that he knows how to manipulate it. It is the old theme of *The Confidence Man*. He is a figure in a country with no solid past or stable class lines; therefore he is able to move about easily from one to the other.

You know, I'm still thinking of your question about the use of Negro experience as material for fiction. One function of serious literature is to deal with the moral core of a given society. Well, in the United States the Negro and his status have always stood for that moral concern. He symbolizes among other things the human and social possibility of equality. This is the moral question raised in our two great nineteenth-century novels, *Moby-Dick* and *Huckleberry Finn*. The very center of Twain's book revolves finally around the boy's relations with Nigger Jim and the question of what Huck should do about getting Jim free after the two scoundrels have sold him. There is a magic here worth conjuring, and that reaches to the very nerve of the American consciousness, so why should I abandon it? Our so-called race problem has now lined up with the world problems of colonialism and the struggle of the West to gain the allegiance of the remaining non-white people who have thus far remained outside the

Communist sphere; thus its possibilities for art have increased rather than lessened. Looking at the novelist as manipulator and depictor of moral problems, I ask myself how much of the achievement of democratic ideals in the United States has been affected by the steady pressure of Negroes and those whites who were sensitive to the implications of our condition, and I know that without that pressure the position of our country before the world would be much more serious even than it is now. Here is part of the social dynamics of a great society. Perhaps the discomfort about protest in books by Negro authors comes because since the nineteenth century American literature has avoided profound moral searching. It was too painful, and besides, there were specific problems of language and form to which the writers could address themselves. They did wonderful things, but perhaps they left the real problems untouched. There are exceptions, of course, like Faulkner, who has been working the great moral theme all along, taking it up where Mark Twain put it down.

I feel that with my decision to devote myself to the novel I took on one of the responsibilities inherited by those who practice the craft in the United States: that of describing for all that fragment of the huge diverse American experience which I know best, and which offers me the possibility of contributing not only to the growth of the literature but to the shaping of the culture as I should like it to be. The American novel is in this sense a conquest of the frontier; as it describes our experience, it creates it.

II

SOUND AND THE
MAINSTREAM

Living with Music

In those days it was either live with music or die with noise, and we chose rather desperately to live. In the process our apartment—what with its booby-trappings of audio equipment, wires, discs and tapes—came to resemble the Collier mansion, but that was later. First there was the neighborhood, assorted drunks and a singer.

We were living at the time in a tiny ground-floor-rear apartment in which I was trying to write. I say "trying" advisedly. To our right, separated by a thin wall, was a small restaurant with a juke box the size of the Roxy. To our left, a night-employed swing enthusiast who took his lullaby music so loud that every morning promptly at nine Basie's brasses started blasting my typewriter off its stand. Our living room looked out across a small backyard to a rough stone wall to an apartment building which, towering above, caught every passing thoroughfare sound and rifled it straight down to me. There were also howling cats and barking dogs, none capable of music worth living with, so we'll pass them by.

But the court behind the wall, which on the far side came knee-high to a short Iroquois, was a forum for various singing and/or preaching drunks who wandered back from the corner bar. From these you sometimes heard a fair barbershop style "Bill Bailey," free-wheeling versions of "The Bastard King of England," the saga of Uncle Bud, or a deeply felt rendition of Leroy Carr's "How Long Blues." The preaching drunks took on any topic that came to mind: current events, the fate of the long-sunk *Titanic*, or the relative merits of the Giants and the Dodgers. Naturally there was great argument and occasional fighting—none of it fatal but all of it loud.

I shouldn't complain, however, for these were rather entertaining drunks, who, like the birds, appeared in the spring and left

From *High Fidelity*, December 1955.

with the first fall cold. A more dedicated fellow was there all the time, day and night, come rain, come shine. Up on the corner lived a drunk of legend, a true phenomenon, who could surely have qualified as the king of all the world's winos, not excluding the French. He was neither poetic like the others nor ambitious like the singer (to whom we'll presently come), but his drinking bouts were truly awe-inspiring and he was not without his sensitivity. In the throes of his passion he would shout to the whole wide world one concise command, "Shut up!" Which was disconcerting enough to all who heard (except, perhaps, the singer), but such were the labyrinthine acoustics of courtyards and areaways that he seemed to direct his command at me. The writer's block which this produced is indescribable. On one heroic occasion he yelled his obsessive command without one interruption longer than necessary to take another drink (and with no appreciable loss of volume, penetration or authority) for three long summer days and nights, and shortly afterwards he died. Just how many lines of agitated prose he cost me I'll never know, but in all that chaos of sound I sympathized with his obsession, for I, too, hungered and thirsted for quiet. Nor did he inspire me to a painful identification, and for that I was thankful. Identification, after all, involves feelings of guilt and responsibility, and since I could hardly hear my own typewriter keys I felt in no way accountable for his condition. We were simply fellow victims of the madding crowd. May he rest in peace.

No, these more involved feelings were aroused by a more intimate source of noise, one that got beneath the skin and worked into the very structure of one's consciousness—like the "fate" motif in Beethoven's Fifth or the knocking-at-the-gates scene in *Macbeth*. For at the top of our pyramid of noise there was a singer who lived directly above us; you might say we had a singer on our ceiling.

Now, I had learned from the jazz musicians I had known as a boy in Oklahoma City something of the discipline and devotion to his art required of the artist. Hence I knew something of what the singer faced. These jazzmen, many of them now world-famous, lived for and with music intensely. Their driving motivation was neither money nor fame, but the will to achieve the most eloquent expression of idea-emotions through the technical mastery of their instruments (which, incidentally, some of them wore as a priest wears the cross) and the give and take, the subtle rhythmical shaping and blending of idea, tone and imagination demanded of group improvisation. The delicate balance struck between strong individual personality and the group during those early jam sessions was a marvel of social organization. I had learned too that the end of all this discipline and technical mastery was the desire to express an affirmative way of life through its musical tradition, and that this tradition insisted that each artist achieve his creativity within its frame. He must learn the best of the past, and add to it his personal vision. Life could be harsh, loud and wrong if it wished, but they lived it fully, and when they expressed their attitude toward the world it was with a fluid style that reduced the chaos of living to form.

The objectives of these jazzmen were not at all those of the singer on our ceiling, but though a purist committed to the mastery of the *bel canto* style, German *lieder*, modern French art songs and a few American slave songs sung as if *bel canto*, she was intensely devoted to her art. From morning to night she vocalized, regardless of the condition of her voice, the weather or my screaming nerves. There were times when her notes, sifting through her floor and my ceiling, bouncing down the walls and ricocheting off the building in the rear, whistled like tenpenny nails, buzzed like a saw, wheezed like the asthma of a Hercules, trumpeted like an enraged African elephant, and the squeaky pedal of her piano rested plumb center above my typing chair. After a year of non-co-operation from the neighbor on my left I became desperate enough to cool down the hot blast of his phonograph by calling the cops, but the singer presented a serious ethical problem: could I, an aspiring artist, complain against the hard work and devotion to craft of another aspiring artist?

. . .

Then there was my sense of guilt. Each time I prepared to shatter the ceiling in protest I was restrained by the knowledge that I, too, during my boyhood, had tried to master a musical instrument and to the great distress of my neighbors—perhaps even greater than that which I now suffered. For while our singer was concerned basically with a single tradition and style, I had been caught actively between two: that of Negro folk music, both sacred and profane, slave song and jazz, and that of Western classical music. It was most confusing; the folk tradition demanded that I play what I heard and felt around me, while those who were seeking to teach the classical tradition in the schools insisted that I play strictly according to the book and express that which I was *supposed* to feel. This sometimes led to heated clashes of wills. Once during a third-grade music appreciation class a friend of mine insisted that it was a large green snake he saw swimming down a quiet brook instead of the snowy bird the teacher felt that Saint-Saëns's *Carnival of the Animals* should evoke. The rest of us sat there and lied like little black, brown and yellow Trojans about that swan, but our stalwart classmate held firm to his snake. In the end he got himself spanked and reduced the teacher to tears, but truth, reality and our environment were redeemed. For we were all familiar with snakes, while a swan was simply something the Ugly Duckling of the story grew up to be. Fortunately some of us grew up with a genuine appreciation of classical music *despite* such teaching methods. But as an aspiring trumpeter I was to wallow in sin for years before being awakened to guilt by our singer.

Caught mid-range between my two traditions, where one attitude often clashed with the other and one technique of playing was by the other opposed, I caused whole blocks of people to suffer.

Indeed, I terrorized a good part of an entire city section. During summer vacation I blew sustained tones out of the window for hours, usually starting—especially on Sunday mornings—before breakfast. I sputtered whole days through M. Arban's (he's the great authority on the instrument) double- and triple-tonguing exercises, with an effect like that of a jackass hiccupping off a big meal of briars. During school-term mornings I practiced a truly exhibitionist "Reveille" before leaving for school, and in the evening I generously gave the ever-listening world a long, slow version of "Taps," ineptly played but throbbing with what I in my adolescent vagueness felt was a romantic sadness. For it was farewell to day and a love song to life and a peace-be-with-you to all the dead and dying.

On hot summer afternoons I tormented the ears of all not blessedly deaf with imitations of the latest hot solos of Hot Lips Paige (then a local hero), the leaping right hand of Earl "Fatha" Hines, or the rowdy poetic flights of Louis Armstrong. Naturally I rehearsed also such school-band standbys as the *Light Cavalry* Overture, Sousa's "Stars and Stripes Forever," the *William Tell* Overture, and "Tiger Rag." (Not even an after-school job as office boy to a dentist could stop my efforts. Frequently, by way of encouraging my development in the proper cultural direction, the dentist asked me proudly to render Schubert's *Serenade* for some poor devil with his jaw propped open in the dental chair. When the drill got going, or the forceps bit deep, I blew real strong.)

Sometimes, inspired by the even then considerable virtuosity of the late Charlie Christian (who during our school days played marvelous riffs on a cigar-box banjo), I'd give whole summer afternoons and the evening hours after heavy suppers of black-eyed peas and turnip greens, cracklin' bread and buttermilk, lemonade and sweet potato cobbler, to practicing hard-driving blues. Such food oversupplied me with bursting energy, and from listening to Ma Rainey, Ida Cox and Clara Smith, who made regular appearances in our town, I knew exactly how I wanted my horn to sound. But in the effort to make it do so (I was no embryo Joe Smith or Tricky Sam Nanton), I sustained the curses of both Christian and infidel—along with the encouragement of those more sympathetic citizens who understood the profound satisfaction to be found in expressing oneself in the blues.

Despite those who complained and cried to heaven for Gabriel to blow a chorus so heavenly sweet and so hellishly hot that I'd forever

put down my horn, there were more tolerant ones who were willing
to pay in present pain for future pride.

For who knew what skinny kid with his chops wrapped around a
trumpet mouthpiece and a faraway look in his eyes might become
the next Armstrong? Yes, and send you, at some big dance a few
years hence, into an ecstasy of rhythm and memory and brassy affirmation of the goodness of being alive and part of the community?
Someone had to, for it was part of the group tradition, though that
was not how they said it.

"Let that boy blow," they'd say to the protesting ones. "He's got
to talk baby talk on that thing before he can preach on it. Next thing
you know he's liable to be up there with Duke Ellington. Sure,
plenty Oklahoma boys are up there with the big bands. Son, let's
hear you try those 'Trouble in Mind Blues.' Now try and make it
sound like ole Ida Cox sings it."

And I'd draw in my breath and do Miss Cox great violence.

Thus the crimes and aspirations of my youth. It had been years since
I had played the trumpet or irritated a single ear with other than the
spoken or written word, but as far as my singing neighbor was concerned I had to hold my peace. I was forced to listen, and in listening
I soon became involved to the point of identification. If she sang
badly I'd hear my own futility in the windy sound; if well, I'd stare at
my typewriter and despair that I would ever make my prose so sing.
She left me neither night nor day, this singer on our ceiling, and as
my writing languished I became more and more upset. Thus one
desperate morning I decided that since I seemed doomed to live
within a shrieking chaos I might as well contribute my share; perhaps
if I fought noise with noise I'd attain some small peace. Then a miracle: I turned on my radio (an old Philco AM set connected to a small
Pilot FM tuner) and heard the words

> *Art thou troubled?*
> *Music will calm thee . . .*

I stopped as though struck by the voice of an angel. It was Kathleen Ferrier, that loveliest of singers, giving voice to the aria from Handel's *Rodelinda*. The voice was so completely expressive of words and music that I accepted it without question; what lover of the vocal art could resist her?

Yet it was ironic, for after giving up my trumpet for the typewriter I had avoided too close a contact with the very art which she recommended as balm. For I had started music early and lived with it daily, and when I broke I tried to break clean. Now in this magical moment all the old love, the old fascination with music superbly rendered, flooded back. When she finished I realized that with such music in my own apartment, the chaotic sounds from without and above had sunk, if not into silence, then well below the level where they mattered. Here was a way out. If I was to live and write in that apartment, it would be only through the grace of music. I had tuned in a Ferrier recital, and when it ended I rushed out for several of her records, certain that now deliverance was mine.

But not yet. Between the hi-fi record and the ear, I learned, there was a new electronic world. In that realization our apartment was well on its way toward becoming an audio booby trap. It was 1949, and I rushed to the Audio Fair. I have, I confess, as much gadget resistance as the next American of my age, weight and slight income, but little did I dream of the test to which it would be put. I had hardly entered the fair before I heard David Sarser's and Mel Sprinkle's Musician's Amplifier, took a look at its schematic and, recalling a boyhood acquaintance with such matters, decided that I could build one. I did—several times—before it measured within specifications. And still our system was lacking. Fortunately my wife shared my passion for music, so we went on to buy, piece by piece, a fine speaker system, a first-rate AM-FM tuner, a transcription turntable and a speaker cabinet. I built half a dozen or more preamplifiers and record compensators before finding a commercial one that satisfied my ear, and finally we acquired an arm, a magnetic cartridge and— glory of the house—a tape recorder. All this plunge into electronics, mind you, had as its simple end the enjoyment of recorded music as it was intended to be heard. I was obsessed with the idea of reproducing sound with such fidelity that even when using music as a defense behind which I could write, it would reach the unconscious levels of the mind with the least distortion. But it didn't come easily. There were wires and pieces of equipment all over the tiny apartment (I became a compulsive experimenter), and it was worth your life to move about without first taking careful bearings. Once we were almost crushed in our sleep by the tape machine, for which there was space only on a shelf at the head of our bed.

But it was worth it. For now when we played a recording on our system even the drunks on the wall could recognize its quality. I'm ashamed to admit, however, that I did not always restrict its use to the demands of pleasure or defense. Indeed, with such marvels of science at my control I lost my humility. My ethical consideration for the singer up above shriveled like a plant in too much sunlight. For instead of soothing, music seemed to release the beast in me. Now when jarred from my writer's reveries by some especially enthusiastic flourish of our singer, I'd rush to my music system with blood in my eyes and burst a few decibels in her direction. If she defied me with a few more pounds of pressure against her diaphragm, then a war of decibels was declared.

If, let us say, she were singing "*Depuis le Jour*" from *Louise*, I'd put on a tape of Bidu Sayão performing the same aria, and let the rafters ring. If it was some song by Mahler, I'd match her spitefully with Marian Anderson or Kathleen Ferrier; if she offended with something from *Der Rosenkavalier*, I'd attack her flank with Lotte Lehmann. If she brought me up from my desk with art songs by Ravel or Rachmaninoff, I'd defend myself with Maggie Teyte or Jennie Tourel. If she polished a spiritual to a meaningless artiness I'd play Bessie Smith to remind her of the earth out of which we came. Once in a while I'd forget completely that I was supposed to be a gentleman and blast her with Strauss's *Zarathustra*, Bartók's *Concerto for Orchestra*, Ellington's "Flaming Sword," the famous crescendo from *The Pines of Rome*, or Satchmo scatting "I'll be Glad When You're Dead" (you rascal you!). Oh, I was living with music with a sweet vengeance.

One might think that all this would have made me her most hated enemy, but not at all. When I met her on the stoop a few weeks after my rebellion, expecting her fully to slap my face, she astonished me by complimenting our music system. She even questioned me concerning the artists I had used against her. After that, on days when the acoustics were right, she'd stop singing until the piece was finished and then applaud—not always, I guessed, without a justifiable touch of sarcasm. And although I was now getting on with my writing, the unfairness of this business bore in upon me. Aware that I could not have withstood a similar comparison with literary artists of like caliber, I grew remorseful. I also came to admire the singer's courage and control, for she was neither intimidated into silence nor goaded into undisciplined screaming; she persevered, she marked the phrasing of the great singers I sent her way, she improved her style.

Better still, she vocalized more softly, and I, in turn, used music less and less as a weapon and more for its magic with mood and memory. After a while a simple twirl of the volume control up a few decibels and down again would bring a live-and-let-live reduction of her volume.

We have long since moved from that apartment and that most interesting neighborhood, and now the floors and walls of our present apartment are adequately thick, and there is even a closet large enough to house the audio system; the only wire visible is that leading from the closet to the corner speaker system. Still, we are indebted to the singer and the old environment for forcing us to discover one of the most deeply satisfying aspects of our living. Perhaps the enjoyment of music is always suffused with past experience; for me, at least, this is true.

It seems a long way and a long time from the glorious days of Oklahoma jazz dances, the jam sessions at Halley Richardson's place on Deep Second, from the phonographs shouting the blues in the back alleys I knew as a delivery boy, and from the days when watermelon men with voices like mellow bugles shouted their wares in time with the rhythm of their horses' hoofs, and farther still from the washerwomen singing slave songs as they stirred sooty tubs in sunny yards; and a long time, too, from those intense, conflicting days when the school music program of Oklahoma City was tuning our earthy young ears to classical accents, with music appreciation classes and free musical instruments and basic instruction for any child who cared to learn, and uniforms for all who made the band. There was a mistaken notion on the part of some of the teachers that classical music had nothing to do with the rhythms, relaxed or hectic, of daily living, and that one should crook the little finger when listening to such refined strains. And the blues, the spirituals and jazz? They would have destroyed them and scattered the pieces. Nevertheless, we learned some of it all, for in the United States when traditions are juxtaposed they tend, regardless of what we do to prevent it, irresistibly to merge. Thus, musically at least, each child in our town was an heir of all the ages. One learns by moving from the familiar to the unfamiliar, and while it might sound incongruous at first, the step from the spirituality of the spirituals to that of the Beethoven of the symphonies or the Bach of the chorales is not as vast as it seems. Nor is the romanticism of a Brahms or Chopin completely unrelated to that of Louis Armstrong. Those who know their native culture and love it unchauvinistically are never lost when encountering the unfamiliar.

Living with music today we find Mozart and Ellington, Kirsten Flagstad and Chippie Hill, William L. Dawson and Carl Orff all forming part of our regular fare. For all exalt life in rhythm and melody; all add to its significance. Perhaps in the swift change of American society in which the meanings of one's origin are so quickly lost, one of the chief values of living with music lies in its power to give us an orientation in time. In doing so, it gives significance to all those indefinable aspects of experience which nevertheless help to make us what we are. In the swift whirl of time music is a constant, reminding us of what we were and of that toward which we aspire. Art thou troubled? Music will not only calm, it will ennoble thee.

The Golden Age, Time Past

That which we do is what we are. That which we remember is,
more often than not, that which we would like to have been, or that
which we hope to be. Thus our memory and our identity are ever at
odds, our history ever a tall tale told by inattentive idealists.

It has been a long time now, and not many remember how it was in
the old days, not really. Not even those who were there to see and
hear as it happened, who were pressed in the crowds beneath the dim
rosy lights of the bar in the smoke-veiled room, and who shared,
night after night, the mysterious spell created by the talk, the laughter, grease paint, powder, perfume, sweat, alcohol and food—all
blended and simmering, like a stew on the restaurant range, and
brought to a sustained moment of elusive meaning by the timbres
and accents of musical instruments locked in passionate recitative. It
has been too long now, some seventeen years.

Above the bandstand there later appeared a mural depicting a
group of jazzmen holding a jam session in a narrow Harlem bedroom. While an exhausted girl with shapely legs sleeps on her stomach in a big brass bed, they bend to their music in a quiet
concatenation of unheard sound: a trumpeter, a guitarist, a clarinetist, a drummer, their only audience a small, cock-eared dog. The
clarinetist is white. The guitarist strums with an enigmatic smile.
The trumpet is muted. The barefooted drummer, beating a folded
newspaper with whisk-brooms in lieu of a drum, stirs the eye's ear
like a blast of brasses in a midnight street. A bottle of port rests on a
dresser, but like the girl it is ignored. The artist, Charles Graham,
adds mystery to, as well as illumination within, the scene by having
them play by the light of a kerosene lamp. The painting, executed in

From *Esquire*, January 1959.

a harsh documentary style reminiscent of W.P.A. art, conveys a feeling of musical effort caught in timeless and unrhetorical suspension, the sad remoteness of a scene observed through a wall of crystal.

Except for the lamp, the room might well have been one in the Hotel Cecil, the building on 118th Street in which Minton's Playhouse is located, and although painted in 1946, some time after the revolutionary doings there had begun, the mural should help recall the old days vividly. But the décor of the place has been changed, and now it is covered most of the time by draperies. These require a tricky skill of those who would draw them aside. And even then there will still only be the girl who must sleep forever unhearing, and the men who must forever gesture the same soundless tune. Besides, the time it celebrates is dead and gone, and perhaps not even those who came when it was still fresh and new remember those days as they were.

Neither do those remember who knew Henry Minton, who gave the place his name. Nor those who shared in the noisy lostness of New York the rediscovered community of the feasts, evocative of home, of South, of good times, the best and most unself-conscious of times, created by the generous portions of Negro American cuisine—the hash, grits, fried chicken, the ham-seasoned vegetables, the hot biscuits and rolls and the free whiskey—with which, each Monday night, Teddy Hill honored the entire cast of current Apollo Theatre shows. They were gathered here from all parts of America, and they broke bread together, and there was a sense of good feeling and promise, but what shape the fulfilled promise would take they did not know, and few except the more restless of the younger musicians even questioned. Yet it was an exceptional moment and the world was swinging with change.

Most of them, black and white alike, were hardly aware of where they were or what time it was; nor did they wish to be. They thought of Minton's as a sanctuary, where in an atmosphere blended of nostalgia and a music-and-drink-lulled suspension of time they could retreat from the wartime tensions of the town. The meaning of time-present was not their concern; thus when they try to tell it now the meaning escapes them. For they were caught up in events which made that time exceptionally and uniquely *then*, and which brought, among the other changes which have reshaped the world, a momentous modulation into a new key of musical sensibility—in brief, a revolution in culture.

So how *can* they remember? Even in swiftly changing America there are few such moments, and at best Americans give but a limited attention to history. Too much happens too rapidly, and before we can evaluate it, or exhaust its meaning or pleasure, there is something new to concern us. Ours is the tempo of the motion picture, not that of the still camera, and we waste experience as we wasted the forest. During the time it was happening the sociologists were concerned with the riots, unemployment and industrial tensions of the time, the historians with the onsweep of the war, and the critics and most serious students of culture found this area of our national life of little interest. So it was left to those who came to Minton's out of the needs of feeling, and when the moment was past no one retained more than a fragment of its happening. Afterward the very effort to put the fragments together transformed them, so that in place of true memory they now summon to mind pieces of legend. They retell the stories as they have been told and written, glamorized, inflated, made neat and smooth, with all incomprehensible details vanished along with most of the wonder—not how it was as they themselves knew it.

When asked how it was back then, back in the forties, they will smile; then, frowning with the puzzlement of one attempting to recall the details of a pleasant but elusive dream, they'll say: "Oh, man, it was a hell of a time! A wailing time! Things were jumping, you couldn't get in here for the people. The place was packed with celebrities. Park Avenue, man! Big people in show business, college professors along with the pimps and their women. And college boys and girls. Everybody came. You know how the old words to the 'Basin Street Blues' used to go before Sinatra got hold of it? *Basin Street is the street where the dark and the light folks meet*—that's what I'm talking about. That was Minton's, man. It was a place where everybody could come to be entertained because it was a place that was jumping with good times."

Or some will tell you that it was here that Dizzy Gillespie found his own trumpet voice; that here Kenny Clarke worked out the patterns of his drumming style; where Charlie Christian played out the last creative and truly satisfying moments of his brief life, his New York home; where Charlie Parker built the monument of his art; where Thelonius Monk formulated his contribution to the chordal progressions and the hide-and-seek melodic methods of modern jazz. And they'll call such famous names as Lester Young, Ben Webster and Coleman Hawkins; or Fats Waller, who came here in the after-hours stillness of the early morning to compose. They'll tell you that Benny Goodman, Art Tatum, Count Basie and Lena Horne would drop in to join in the fun; that it was here that George Shearing played on his first night in the United States; or of Tony Scott's great love of the place; and they'll repeat all the stories of how, when and by whom the word "bebop" was coined here—but, withal, few actually remember, and these leave much unresolved.

Usually music gives resonance to memory (and Minton's was a hotbed of jazz), but not the music then in the making here. It was itself a texture of fragments, repetitive, nervous, not fully formed; its melodic lines underground, secret and taunting; its riffs jeering— "Salt peanuts! Salt peanuts!"—its timbres flat or shrill, with a minimum of thrilling vibrato. Its rhythms were out of stride and seemingly arbitrary, its drummers frozen-faced introverts dedicated to chaos. And in it the steady flow of memory, desire and defined experience summed up by the traditional jazz beat and blues mood seemed swept like a great river from its old, deep bed. We know better now, and recognize the old moods in the new sounds, but what we know is that which was then becoming. For most of those who gathered here, the enduring meaning of the great moment at Minton's took place off to the side, beyond the range of attention, like a death blow glimpsed from the corner of the eye, the revolutionary rumpus sounding like a series of flubbed notes blasting the talk with discord. So that the events which made Minton's *Minton's* arrived in conflict and ran their course; then the heat was gone and all that is left to mark its passage is the controlled fury of the music itself, sealed pure and irrevocable, banalities and excellencies alike, in the early recordings, or swept along by our restless quest for the new, to be diluted in more recent styles, the best of it absorbed like drops of fully distilled technique, mood and emotions into the great stream of jazz.

Left also to confuse our sense of what happened is the word "bop," hardly more than a nonsense syllable, by which the music synthesized at Minton's came to be known. A most inadequate word which does little, really, to help us remember. A word which throws up its hands in clownish self-deprecation before all the complexity of sound and rhythm and self-assertive passion which it pretends to name, a mask-word for the charged ambiguities of the new sound, hiding the serious face of art.

Nor does it help that so much has come to pass in the meantime. There have been two hot wars and that which continues, called "cold." And the unknown young men who brought a new edge to the sound of jazz and who scrambled the rhythms of those who used the small clear space at Minton's for dancing are no longer so young or unknown; indeed, they are referred to now by nickname in even the remotest of places. And in Paris and Munich and Tokyo they'll tell you the details of how, after years of trying, "Dizzy" (meaning John Birks Gillespie) vanquished "Roy" (meaning Roy Eldridge) during a jam session at Minton's, to become thereby the new king of trumpeters. Or how, later, while jetting over the world on the blasts of his special tilt-belled horn, he jammed with a snake charmer in Pakistan. "Sent the bloody cobra, man," they'll tell you in London's Soho. So their subsequent fame has blurred the sharp, ugly lines of their rebellion even in the memories of those who found them most strange and distasteful.

What's more, our memory of some of the more brilliant young men has been touched by the aura of death, and we feel guilt that the fury of their passing was the price paid for the art they left us to enjoy unscathed: Charlie Christian, burned out by tuberculosis like a guitar consumed in a tenement fire; Fats Navarro, wrecked by the tensions and needling temptations of his orgiastic trade, a big man physically as well as musically, shrunken to nothingness; and, most notably of all, Charlie Parker, called "Bird," now deified, worshiped and studied and, like any fertility god, mangled by his admirers and imitators, who coughed up his life and died—as incredibly as the leopard which Hemingway tells us was found "dried and frozen" near the summit of Mount Kilimanjaro—in the hotel suite of a Baroness. (Nor has anyone explained what a "yardbird" was seeking at that social altitude, though we know that ideally anything is possible within a democracy, and we know quite well that upper-class Europeans were seriously interested in jazz long before Newport became hospitable.) All this is too much for memory; the dry facts are too easily lost in legend and glamour. (With jazz we are yet not in the age of history, but linger in that of folklore.) We know for certain only that the strange sounds which they and their fellows threw against the hum and buzz of vague signification that seethed in the drinking crowd at Minton's, and which, like disgruntled conspirators meeting fatefully to assemble the random parts of a bomb, they joined here and beat and blew into a new jazz style these sounds we know now to have become the clichés, the technical exercises and the standard of achievement not only for fledgling musicians all over the United States, but for Dutchmen and Swedes, Italians and Frenchmen, Germans and Belgians, and even Japanese. All these, in places which came to mind during the Minton days only as points where the war was in progress and where one might soon be sent to fight and die, are now spotted with young men who study the discs on which the revolution hatched in Minton's is preserved with all the intensity that young American painters bring to the works, say, of Kandinsky, Picasso and Klee. Surely this is an odd swing of the cultural tide. Yet Stravinsky, Webern and Berg notwithstanding, or, more recently, Boulez or Stockhausen, such young men (many of them excellent musicians in the highest European tradition) find in the music made articulate at Minton's some key to a fuller freedom of self-realization. Indeed, for many young Europeans the developments which took place here and the careers of those who brought it about have become the latest episodes in the great American epic. They collect the recordings and thrive on the legends as eagerly, perhaps, as young Americans.

Today the bartenders at Minton's will tell you how they come fresh off the ships or planes, bringing their brightly expectant and—in this Harlem atmosphere—startlingly innocent European faces, to buy drinks and stand looking about for the source of the mystery. They try to reconcile the quiet reality of the place with the events which fired, at such long range, their imaginations. They come as to a shrine—as we to the Louvre, Notre Dame or St. Peter's; as young Americans hurry to the Café Flore, the Deux Magots, the Rotonde or the Café du Dôme in Paris. For some years now they have been coming to ask, with all the solemnity of pilgrims inquiring of a sacred relic, to see the nicotine-stained amplifier which Teddy Hill provided for Charlie Christian's guitar. And this is quite proper, for every shrine should have its relic.

Perhaps Minton's has more meaning for European jazz fans than for Americans, even for those who regularly went there. Certainly it has a *different* meaning. For them it is associated with those continental cafés in which great changes, political and artistic, have been plotted; it is to modern jazz what the Café Voltaire in Zurich is to the Dadaist phase of modern literature and painting. Few of those who visited Harlem during the forties would associate it so, but there is a context of meaning in which Minton's and the musical activities which took place there can be meaningfully placed.

Jazz, for all the insistence of the legends, has been far more closely associated with cabarets and dance halls than with brothels, and it was these which provided both the employment for the musicians and an audience initiated and aware of the overtones of the music; which knew the language of riffs, the unstated meanings of the blues idiom, and the dance steps developed from, and complementary to, its rhythms. And in the beginning it was in the Negro dance hall and night club that jazz was most completely a part of a total cultural expression, and in which it was freest and most satisfying, both for the musicians and for those in whose lives it played a major role. As a night club in a Negro community, then, Minton's was part of a national pattern.

But in the old days Minton's was far more than this; it was also a rendezvous for musicians. As such, and although it was not formally organized, it goes back historically to the first New York center of Negro musicians, the Clef Club. Organized in 1910, during the start of the great migration of Negroes northward, by James Reese Europe, the director whom Irene Castle credits with having invented the fox trot, the Clef Club was set up on West 53rd Street to serve as a meeting place and booking office for Negro musicians and entertainers. Here wage scales were regulated, musical styles and techniques worked out, and entertainment was supplied for such establishments as Rector's and Delmonico's, and for such producers as Florenz Ziegfeld and Oscar Hammerstein. Later, when Harlem evolved into a Negro section, a similar function was served by the Rhythm Club, located then in the old Lafayette Theatre building on 132nd Street and Seventh Avenue. Henry Minton, a former saxophonist and officer of the Rhythm Club, became the first Negro delegate to Local 802 of the American Federation of Musicians, and was thus doubly aware of the needs, artistic as well as economic, of jazzmen. He was generous with loans, was fond of food himself and, as an old acquaintance recalled, "loved to put a pot on the range" to share with unemployed friends. Naturally when he opened Minton's Playhouse many musicians made it their own.

Henry Minton also provided, as did the Clef and Rhythm clubs, a necessity more important to jazz musicians than food: a place in which to hold their interminable jam sessions. And it is here that

Minton's becomes most important to the development of modern jazz. It is here, too, that it joins up with all the countless rooms, private and public, in which jazzmen have worked out the secrets of their craft. Today jam sessions are offered as entertainment by night clubs and on radio and television, and some are quite exciting, but what is seen and heard is only one aspect of the true jam session: the "cutting session," or contest of improvisational skill and physical endurance between two or more musicians. But the jam session is far more than this, and when carried out by musicians in the privacy of small rooms (as in the mural at Minton's), or in such places as Halley Richardson's shoeshine parlor in Oklahoma City (where I first heard Lester Young jamming in a shine chair, his head thrown back, his horn even then outthrust, his feet working on the footrests, as he played with and against Lem Johnson, Ben Webster—(this was 1929—and other members of the old Blue Devils Orchestra) or during the after hours in Piney Brown's old Sunset Club in Kansas City; in such places as these, with only musicians and jazzmen present, then the jam session is revealed as the jazzman's true academy.

It is here that he learns tradition, group techniques and style. For although since the twenties many jazzmen have had conservatory training and are well grounded in formal theory and instrumental technique, when we approach jazz we are entering quite a different sphere of training. Here it is more meaningful to speak not of courses of study, of grades and degrees, but of apprenticeship, ordeals, initiation ceremonies, of rebirth. For after the jazzman has learned the fundamentals of his instrument and the traditional techniques of jazz—the intonations, the mute work, manipulation of timbre, the body of traditional styles—he must then "find himself," must be reborn, must find, as it were, his soul. All this through achieving that subtle identification between his instrument and his deepest drives which will allow him to express his own unique ideas and his own unique voice. He must achieve, in short, his self-determined identity.

In this his instructors are his fellow musicians, especially the acknowledged masters, and his recognition of manhood depends upon their acceptance of his ability as having reached a standard which is all the more difficult for not having been rigidly codified. This does not depend upon his ability to simply hold a job, but upon his power to express an individuality in tone. Nor is his status ever unquestioned, for the health of jazz and the unceasing attraction which it holds for the musicians themselves lies in the ceaseless warfare for mastery and recognition—not among the general public, though commercial success is not spurned, but among their artistic peers. And even the greatest can never rest on past accomplishments, for, as with the fast guns of the Old West, there is always someone waiting in a jam session to blow him literally, not only down, but into shame and discouragement.

By making his club hospitable to jam sessions even to the point that customers who were not musicians were crowded out, Henry Minton provided a retreat, a homogeneous community where a collectivity of common experience could find continuity and meaningful expression. Thus the stage was set for the birth of bop.

In 1941 Mr. Minton handed over his management to Teddy Hill, the saxophonist and former band leader, and Hill turned the Playhouse into a musical dueling ground. Not only did he continue Minton's policies, he expanded them. It was Hill who established the Monday Celebrity Nights, the house band which included such members from his own disbanded orchestra as Kenny Clarke, Dizzy Gillespie, Thelonius Monk, sometimes Joe Guy, and later Charlie Christian and Charlie Parker, and it was Hill who allowed the musicians free rein to play whatever they liked. Perhaps no other club except Clarke Monroe's Uptown House was so permissive, and with the hospitality extended to musicians of all schools the news spread swiftly. Minton's became the focal point for musicians all over the country.

Herman Pritchard, who presided over the bar in the old days, tells us that every time they came, "Lester Young and Ben Webster used to tie up in battle like dogs in the road. They'd fight on those saxophones until they were tired out; then they'd put in long-distance calls to their mothers, both of whom lived in Kansas City, and tell them about it."

And most of the masters of jazz came either to observe or to participate and be influenced and listen to their own discoveries transformed, and the aspiring stars sought to win their approval, as the younger tenor men tried to win the esteem of Coleman Hawkins. Or they tried to vanquish them in jamming contests as Gillespie is said to have outblown his idol, Roy Eldridge. It was during this period that Eddie "Lockjaw" Davis underwent an ordeal of jeering rejection until finally he came through as an admired tenor man.

In the perspective of time we now see that what was happening at Minton's was a continuing symposium of jazz, a summation of all the styles, personal and traditional, of jazz. Here it was possible to hear its resources of technique, ideas, harmonic structure, melodic phrasing and rhythmical possibilities explored more thoroughly than was ever possible before. It was also possible to hear the first attempts toward a conscious statement of the sensibility of the younger generation of musicians as they worked out the techniques, structures and rhythmical patterns with which to express themselves. Part of this was arbitrary, a revolt of the younger against the established stylists; part of it was inevitable. For jazz had reached a crisis, and new paths were certain to be searched for and found. An increasing number of the younger men were formally trained, and the post-Depression developments in the country had made for quite a break between their experience and that of the older men. Many were even of a different physical build. Often they were quiet and of a reserve which contrasted sharply with the exuberant and outgoing lyricism of the older men, and they were intensely concerned that their identity as Negroes place no restriction upon the music they played or the manner in which they used their talent. They were concerned, they said, with art, not entertainment. Especially were they resentful of Louis Armstrong, whom (confusing the spirit of his music with his clowning) they considered an Uncle Tom.

But they too, some of them, had their own myths and misconceptions: that theirs was the only generation of Negro musicians who listened to or enjoyed the classics; that to be truly free they must act exactly the opposite of what white people might believe, rightly or wrongly, a Negro to be; that the performing artist can be completely and absolutely free of the obligations of the entertainer, and that they could play jazz with dignity only by frowning and treating the audience with aggressive contempt; and that to be in control, artistically and personally, one must be so cool as to quench one's own human fire.

Nor should we overlook the despair which must have swept Minton's before the technical mastery, the tonal authenticity, the authority and the fecundity of imagination of such men as Hawkins, Young, Goodman, Tatum, Teagarden, Ellington and Waller. Despair, after all, is ever an important force in revolutions.

They were also responding to the nonmusical pressures affecting jazz. It was a time of big bands, and the greatest prestige and economic returns were falling outside the Negro community—often to leaders whose popularity grew from the compositions and arrangements of Negroes—to white instrumentalists whose only originality lay in the enterprise with which they rushed to market with some Negro musician's hard-won style. Still there was no policy of racial discrimination at Minton's. Indeed, it was very much like those Negro cabarets of the twenties and thirties in which a megaphone was placed on the piano so that anyone with the urge could sing a blues. Nevertheless, the inside-dopesters will tell you that the "changes" or chord progressions and melodic inversions worked out by the creators of bop sprang partially from their desire to create a jazz which could not be so easily imitated and exploited by white musicians to whom the market was more open simply *because* of their whiteness. They wished to receive credit for what they created; besides, it was easier to "get rid of the trash" who crowded the bandstand with inept playing and thus make room for the real musicians, whether white or black. Nevertheless, white musicians like Tony Scott, Remo Palmieri and Al Haig who were part of the development at Minton's became so by passing a test of musicianship, sincerity and temperament. Later, it is said, the boppers became engrossed in solving the musical problems which they set themselves. Except for a few sympathetic older musicians, it was they who best knew the promise of the Minton moment, and it was they, caught like the rest in all the complex forces of American life which comes to focus in jazz, who made the most of it. Now the tall tales told as history must feed on the results of their efforts.

As the Spirit Moves Mahalia

THERE are certain women singers who possess, beyond all the boundaries of our admiration for their art, an uncanny power to evoke our love. We warm with pleasure at mere mention of their names; their simplest songs sing in our hearts like the remembered voices of old dear friends, and when we are lost within the listening anonymity of darkened concert halls, they seem to seek us out unerringly. Standing regal within the bright isolation of the stage, their subtlest effects seem meant for us and us alone: privately, as across the intimate space of our own living rooms. And when we encounter the simple dignity of their immediate presence, we suddenly ponder the mystery of human greatness.

Perhaps this power springs from their dedication, their having subjected themselves successfully to the demanding discipline necessary to the mastery of their chosen art. Or perhaps it is a quality with which they are born, as some are born with bright orange hair. Perhaps, though we think not, it is acquired, a technique of "presence." But whatever its source, it touches us as a rich abundance of human warmth and sympathy. Indeed, we feel that if the idea of aristocracy is more than mere class conceit, then these surely are our natural queens. For they enchant the eye as they caress the ear, and in their presence we sense the full, moony glory of womanhood in all its mystery—maid, matron and matriarch. They are the sincere ones whose humanity dominates the artifices of the art with which they stir us, and when they sing we have some notion of our better selves.

Lotte Lehmann is one of these, and Marian Anderson. Both Madame Ernestine Schumann-Heink and Kathleen Ferrier possessed it. Nor is it limited to these mistresses of high art. Pastoria Pavon, "La Niña de Los Peines," the great flamenco singer, is another, and

From *Saturday Review*, September 27, 1958.

so is Mahalia Jackson, the subject of this piece, who reminds us that while not all great singers possess this quality, those who do, no matter how obscure their origin, are soon claimed by the world as its own.

Mahalia Jackson, a large, handsome brown-skinned woman in her middle forties, who began singing in her father's church at the age of five, is a Negro of the *American* Negroes, and is, as the Spanish say, a woman of much quality. Her early experience was typical of Negro women of a certain class in the South. Born in New Orleans, she left school in the eighth grade and went to work as a nursemaid. Later she worked in the cotton fields of Louisiana and as a domestic. Her main social life was centered in the Baptist church. She grew up with the sound of jazz in her ears, and, being an admirer of Bessie Smith, was aware of the prizes and acclaim awaiting any mistress of the blues, but in her religious views the blues and jazz are profane forms and a temptation to be resisted. She also knew something of the painful experiences which go into the forging of a true singer of the blues.

In 1927, following the classical pattern of Negro migration, Mahalia went to Chicago, where she worked as a laundress and studied beauty culture. Here, too, her social and artistic life was in the Negro community, centered in the Greater Salem Baptist Church. Here she became a member of the choir and a soloist with a quintet which toured the churches affiliated with the National Baptist Convention. Up until the forties she operated within a world of music which was confined, for the most part, to Negro communities, and it was by her ability to move such audiences as are found here that her reputation grew. It was also such audiences which, by purchasing over two million copies of her famous "Move On Up a Little Higher," brought her to national attention.

When listening to such recordings as *Sweet Little Jesus Boy, Bless This House, Mahalia Jackson,* or *In the Upper Room,* it is impossible to escape the fact that Mahalia Jackson is possessed of a profound religious conviction. Nor can we escape the awareness that no singer living has a greater ability to move us, regardless of our own religious attitudes, with the projected emotion of a song. Perhaps with the interpretive artist the distinction so often made between popular and serious art is not so great as it seems. Perhaps what counts is the personal quality of the individual artist, the depth of his experience and his sense of life. Certainly Miss Jackson possesses a quality of dignity and the ability to project a sincerity of purpose which is characteristic of only the greatest of interpretive artists.

Nor should it be assumed that her singing is simply the expression of the Negro's "natural" ability as is held by the stereotype (would that it were only true!). For although its techniques are not taught formally, Miss Jackson is the master of an art of singing which is as complex and of an even older origin than that of jazz.

It is an art which was acquired during those years when she sang in the comparative obscurity of the Negro community, and which, with the inevitable dilutions, comes into our national song style usually through the singers of jazz and the blues. It is an art which depends upon the employment of the full expressive resources of the human voice—from the rough growls employed by blues singers, the intermediate sounds, half-cry, half-recitative, which are common to Eastern music, the shouts and hollers of American Negro folk cries, the rough-edged tones and broad vibratos, the high, shrill and grating tones which rasp one's ears like the agonized flourishes of flamenco, to the gut tones, which remind us of where the jazz trombone found its human source. It is an art which employs a broad rhythmic freedom and accents the lyric line to reinforce the emotional impact. It utilizes half-tones, glissandi, blue notes, humming and moaning. Or again, it calls upon the most lyrical, floating tones of which the voice is capable. Its diction ranges from the most precise to the near liquidation of word-meaning in the sound: a pronunciation which is almost of the academy one instant and of the broadest cotton-field dialect the next. And it is most eclectic in its use of other musical idiom; indeed, it borrows any effect which will aid in the arousing and control of emotion. Especially is it free in its use of the effects of jazz; its tempos (with the characteristic economy of Negro expression, it shares a common rhythmic and harmonic base with jazz) are taken along with its intonations, and, in ensemble singing, its orchestral voicing. In Mahalia's own "Move On Up a Little Higher" there is a riff straight out of early Ellington. Most of all it is an art which swings, and in the South there are many crudely trained groups who use it naturally for the expression of religious feeling who could teach the jazz modernists quite a bit about polyrhythmics and polytonality.

Since the forties this type of vocal music, known loosely as "gospel singing," has become a big business, both within the Negro community and without. Negro producers have found it highly profitable to hold contests in which groups of gospel singers are pitted against one another, and the radio stations which cater to the Negro market give many hours of their air time to this music. Today there are groups who follow regular circuits just as the old Negro jazzmen, blues singers and vaudeville acts followed the old T.O.B.A. circuit through the Negro communities of the nation. Some form the troupes of traveling evangelists and move about the country with their organs, tambourines, bones and drums. Some are led by ex-jazzmen who have put on the cloth, either sincerely or in response to the steady employment and growing market. So popular has the music become that there is a growing tendency to exploit its generic relationship to jazz and so-called rock-and-roll.

Indeed, many who come upon it outside the context of the Negro community tend to think of it as just another form of jazz, and the same confusion is carried over to the art of Mahalia Jackson. There is a widely held belief that she is really a blues singer who refuses, out of religious superstitions, perhaps, to sing the blues, a jazz singer who coyly rejects her rightful place before a swinging band. And it *is* ironically true that just as a visitor who comes to Harlem seeking out many of the theaters and movie houses of the twenties will find them converted into churches, those who seek today for a living idea of the rich and moving art of Bessie Smith must go not to the night clubs and variety houses where those who call themselves blues singers find their existence, but must seek out Mahalia Jackson in a Negro church. And I insist upon the church and not the concert hall, because for all her concert appearances about the world she is not primarily a concert singer but a high priestess in the religious ceremony of her church. As such she is as far from the secular existentialism of the blues as Sartre is from St. John of the Cross. And it is in the setting of the church that the full timbre of her sincerity sounds most distinctly.

Certainly there was good evidence of this last July at the Newport Jazz Festival, where one of the most widely anticipated events was Miss Jackson's appearance with the Ellington Orchestra. Ellington had supplied the "Come Sunday" movement of his *Black, Brown and Beige Suite* (which with its organ-like close had contained one of Johnny Hodges's most serenely moving solos, a superb evocation of Sunday peace) with lyrics for Mahalia to sing. To make way for her, three of the original movements were abandoned, along with the Hodges solo, but in their place she was given words of such banality that for all the fervor of her singing and the band's excellent performance, that Sunday sun simply would not arise. Nor does the recorded version change our opinion that this was a most unfortunate marriage and an error of taste, and the rather unformed setting of the Twenty-third Psalm which completes the side does nothing to improve things. In fact, only the sound and certain of the transitions between movements are an improvement over the old version of the suite. Originally "Come Sunday" was Ellington's moving *impression* of Sunday peace and religious quiet, but he got little of this into the words. So little, in fact, that it was impossible for Mahalia to release that vast fund of emotion with which Southern Negroes have charged the scenes and symbols of the Gospels.

Only the fortunate few who braved the Sunday-morning rain to attend the Afro-American Episcopal Church services heard Mahalia at her best at Newport. Many had doubtless been absent from church or synagogue for years, but here they saw her in her proper setting and the venture into the strangeness of the Negro church was worth the visit. Here they could see, to the extent we can visualize such a thing, the world which Mahalia summons up with her voice, the spiritual reality which infuses her song. Here it could be seen that the true function of her singing is not simply to entertain, but to prepare the congregation for the minister's message, to make it receptive to the spirit, and with effects of voice and rhythm to evoke a shared community of experience.

As she herself put it while complaining of the length of the time allowed her during a recording session, "I'm used to singing in church, where they don't stop me until the Lord comes." By which she meant, not until she had created the spiritual and emotional climate in which the Word is made manifest; not until, and as the spirit moves her, the song of Mahalia the high priestess sings within the heart of the congregation as its own voice of faith.

When in possession of the words which embody her religious convictions, Mahalia can dominate even the strongest jazz beat and instill it with her own fervor. *Bless This House* contains songs set to rumba, waltz and two-step, but what she does to them provides a triumphal blending of popular dance movements with religious passion. In *Sweet Little Jesus Boy*, the song "The Holy Babe" is a Negro version of an old English count-rhyme, and while enumerating the gifts of the Christian God to man, Mahalia and Mildred Falls, her pianist, create a rhythmical drive such as is expected of the entire Basie band. It is all joy and exultation and swing, but it is nonetheless religious music. Many who are moved by Mahalia and her spirit have been so impressed by the emotional release of her music that they fail to see the frame within which she moves. But even *In the Upper Room* and *Mahalia Jackson*—in which she reminds us most poignantly of Bessie Smith, and in which the common singing techniques of the spirituals and the blues are most clearly to be heard—are directed toward the afterlife and thus are intensely religious. For those who cannot, or will not, visit Mahalia in her proper setting, these records are the next best thing.

On Bird, Bird-Watching and Jazz

BIRD: The Legend of Charlie Parker, a collection of anecdotes, testimonies and descriptions of the life of the famous jazz saxophonist, may be described as an attempt to define just what species of bird Bird really was. Introduced by Robert Reisner's description of his own turbulent friendship and business relations with Parker, it presents contributions by some eighty-three fellow Bird watchers, including a wife and his mother, Mrs. Addie Parker. There are also poems, photographs, descriptions of his funeral, memorial and estate, a chronology of his life, and an extensive discography by Erik Wiedemann.

One of the founders of postwar jazz, Parker had, as an improviser, as marked an influence upon jazz as Louis Armstrong, Coleman Hawkins or Johnny Hodges. He was also famous for his riotous living, which, heightened by alcohol and drugs, led many of his admirers to consider him a latter-day François Villon. Between the beginning of his fame in about 1945 and his death in 1955, he became the central figure of a cult which glorified in his escapades no less than in his music. The present volume is mainly concerned with the escapades, the circumstances behind them and their effect upon Bird's friends and family.

Oddly enough, while several explanations are advanced as to how Charles Parker, Jr., became known as "Bird" ("Yardbird," in an earlier metamorphosis), none is conclusive. There is, however, overpowering internal evidence that whatever the true circumstance of his ornithological designation, it had little to do with the chicken yard. Randy roosters and operatic hens are familiars to fans of the animated cartoons, but for all the pathetic comedy of his living—and despite the crabbed and constricted character of his style—Parker

From *Saturday Review,* July 28, 1962.

was a most inventive melodist, in bird-watcher's terminology, a true songster.

This failure in the exposition of Bird's legend is intriguing, for nicknames are indicative of a change from a given to an achieved identity, whether by rise or fall, and they tell us something of the nicknamed individual's interaction with his fellows. Thus, since we suspect that more of legend is involved in his renaming than Mr. Reisner's title indicates, let us at least consult Roger Tory Peterson's *Field Guide to the Birds* for a hint as to why, during a period when most jazzmen were labeled "cats," someone hung the bird on Charlie. Let us note too that "legend" originally meant "the story of a saint," and that saints were often identified with symbolic animals.

Two species won our immediate attention, the goldfinch and the mockingbird—the goldfinch because the beatnik phrase "Bird lives," which, following Parker's death, has been chalked endlessly on Village buildings and subway walls, reminds us that during the thirteenth and fourteenth centuries a symbolic goldfinch frequently appeared in European devotional paintings. An apocryphal story has it that upon being given a clay bird for a toy, the infant Jesus brought it miraculously to life as a goldfinch. Thus the small, tawny-brown bird with a bright red patch about the base of its bill and a broad yellow band across its wings became a representative of the soul, the Passion and the Sacrifice. In more worldly late-Renaissance art, the little bird became the ambiguous symbol of death and the soul's immortality. For our own purposes, however, its song poses a major problem: it is like that of a canary—which, soul or no soul, rules the goldfinch out.

The mockingbird, *Mimus polyglottos*, is more promising. Peterson informs us that its song consists of "long successions of notes and phrases of great variety, with each phrase repeated a half-dozen times before going on to the next," that mockingbirds are "excellent mimics" who "adeptly imitate a score or more species found in the neighborhood," and that they frequently sing at night—a description which not only comes close to Parker's way with a saxophone but even hints at a trait of his character. For although he *usually* sang at night, his playing was characterized by velocity, by long-continued successions of notes and phrases, by swoops, bleats, echoes, rapidly repeated bebops—I mean rebopped bebops—by mocking mimicry of other jazzmen's styles, and by interpolations of motifs from extraneous melodies, all of which added up to a dazzling display of wit, satire, burlesque and pathos. Further, he was as expert at issuing his improvisations from the dense brush as from the extreme treetops of the harmonic landscape, and there was, without doubt, as irrepressible a mockery in his personal conduct as in his music.

Mimic thrushes, which include the catbird and brown thrasher, along with the mockingbird, are not only great virtuosi, they are the tricksters and con men of the bird world. Like Parker, who is described as a confidence man and a practical joker by several of the commentators, they take off on the songs of other birds, inflating, inverting and turning them wrong side out, and are capable of driving a prowling ("square") cat wild. Utterly irreverent and romantic, they are not beyond bugging human beings. Indeed, on summer nights in the South, when the moon hangs low, mockingbirds sing as though determined to heat every drop of romance in the sleeping adolescent's heart to fever pitch. Their song thrills and swings the entire moon-struck night to arouse one's sense of the mystery, promise and frustration of being human, alive and hot in the blood. They are as delightful to eye as to ear, but sometimes a similarity of voice and appearance makes for a confusion with the shrike, a species given to impaling insects and smaller songbirds on the points of thorns, and they are destroyed. They are fond of fruit, especially mulberries, and if there is a tree in your yard, there will be, along with the wonderful music, much chalky, blue-tinted evidence of their presence. Under such conditions, be careful and heed Parker's warning to his friends—who sometimes were subjected to a shrike-like treatment—"you must pay your dues to Bird."

Though notes of bitterness sound through Mr. Reisner's book, he and his friends paid willingly for the delight and frustration which Parker brought into their lives. Thus their comments—which are quite unreliable as history—constitute less a collective biography than a celebration of his living and a lamentation of his dying, and are, in the ritual sense, his apotheosis or epiphany into the glory of those who have been reborn in legend.

Symbolic birds, myth and ritual—what strange metaphors to arise during the discussion of a book about a jazz musician! And yet who knows very much of what jazz is really about? Or how shall we ever know until we are willing to confront anything and everything which it sweeps across our path? Consider that at least as early as T. S. Eliot's creation of a new aesthetic for poetry through the artful juxta-positioning of earlier styles, Louis Armstrong, way down the river in New Orleans, was working out a similar technique for jazz. This is not a matter of giving the music fine airs—it doesn't need them—but of saying that whatever touches our highly conscious creators of culture is apt to be reflected here.

The thrust toward respectability exhibited by the Negro jazzmen of Parker's generation drew much of its immediate fire from their understandable rejection of the traditional entertainer's role—a heritage from the minstrel tradition—exemplified by such an outstanding creative musician as Louis Armstrong. But when they fastened the epithet "Uncle Tom" upon Armstrong's music they confused artistic quality with questions of personal conduct, a confusion which would ultimately reduce their own music to the mere matter of race. By rejecting Armstrong they thought to rid themselves of the entertainer's role. And by way of getting rid of the role, they demanded, in the name of their racial identity, a purity of status which by definition is impossible for the performing artist.

The result was a grim comedy of racial manners, with the musicians employing a calculated surliness and rudeness, treating the audience very much as many white merchants in poor Negro neighborhoods treat their customers, and the white audiences were shocked at first but learned quickly to accept such treatment as evidence of "artistic" temperament. Then comes a comic reversal. Today the white audience expects the rudeness as part of the entertainment. If it fails to appear, the audience is disappointed. For the jazzmen it has become a proposition of the more you win, the more you lose. Certain older jazzmen possessed a clearer idea of the division between their identities as performers and as private individuals. Offstage and while playing in ensemble, they carried themselves like college professors or high church deacons; when soloing they donned the comic mask and went into frenzied pantomimes of hotness—even when playing "cool"—and when done, dropped the mask and returned to their chairs with dignity. Perhaps they realized that whatever his style, the performing artist remains an entertainer, even as Heifetz, Rubinstein or young Glenn Gould.

For all the revolutionary ardor of his style, Dizzy Gillespie, a co-founder with Parker of modern jazz and a man with a savage eye for the incongruous, is no less a clown than Louis, and his wide reputation rests as much upon his entertaining personality as upon his gifted musicianship. There is even a morbid entertainment value in watching the funereal posturing of the Modern Jazz Quartet, and doubtless part of the tension created in their listeners arises from the anticipation that during some unguarded moment, the grinning visage of the traditional delight-maker (inferior because performing at the audience's command, superior because he can perform effectively through the magic of his art) will emerge from behind those bearded masks. In the United States, where each of us is a member of some minority group and where political power and entertainment alike are derived from viewing and manipulating the human predicaments of others, the maintenance of dignity is never a simple matter, even for those with highest credentials. Gossip is one of our largest industries, the President is fair game for caricaturists, and there is always someone around to set a symbolic midget upon J. P. Morgan's unwilling knee.

No jazzman, not even Miles Davis, struggled harder to escape the entertainer's role than Charlie Parker. The pathos of his life lies in the ironic reversal through which his struggles to escape what in Armstrong is basically a *make-believe* role of clown—which the irreverent poetry and triumphant sound of his trumpet makes even the squarest of squares aware of—resulted in Parker's becoming something far more "primitive": a sacrificial figure whose struggles against personal chaos, onstage and off, served as entertainment for a ravenous, sensation-starved, culturally disoriented public which had only the slightest notion of its real significance. While he slowly died (like a man dismembering himself with a dull razor on a spotlighted stage) from the ceaseless conflict from which issued both his art and his destruction, his public reacted as though he were doing much the same thing as those saxophonists who hoot and honk and roll on the floor. In the end he had no private life and his most tragic moments were drained of human significance.

Here, perhaps, is an explanation, beyond all questions of reason, drugs or whiskey, of the violent contradictions detailed in Mr. Reisner's book of Parker's public conduct. In attempting to escape the role, at once sub- and super-human, in which he found himself, he sought to outrage his public into an awareness of his most human pain. Instead, he made himself notorious, and in the end became unsure whether his fans came to enjoy his art or to be entertained by the "world's greatest junky," the "supreme hipster." Sensitive and thoroughly aware of the terrifying cost of his art and his public image, he had to bear not only the dismemberment occasioned by rival musicians who imitated every nuance of his style—often with far greater financial return—but the imitation of his every self-destructive excess of personal conduct by those who had in no sense earned the right of such license. Worse, it was these who formed his cult.

Parker operated in the underworld of American culture, on that turbulent level where human instincts conflict with social institutions, where contemporary civilized values and hypocrisies are challenged by the Dionysian urges of a between-wars youth born to prosperity, conditioned by the threat of world destruction, and inspired—when not seeking total anarchy—by a need to bring social reality and our social pretensions into a more meaningful balance. Significantly enough, race is an active factor here, though not in the usual sense. When the jazz drummer Art Blakey was asked about Parker's meaning for Negroes, he replied, "They never heard of him." Parker's artistic success and highly publicized death have changed all that today, but interestingly enough, Bird was indeed a "white" hero. His greatest significance was for the educated white middle-class youth whose reactions to the inconsistencies of American life was the stance of casting off its education, language, dress, manners and moral standards: a revolt, apolitical in nature, which finds its most dramatic instance in the figure of the so-called white hipster. And whatever its justification, it was, and is, a reaction to the chaos which many youth sense at the center of our society.

For the postwar jazznik, Parker was Bird, a suffering, psychically wounded, law-breaking, life-affirming hero. For them he possessed something of the aura of that figure common to certain contemporary novels which R.W.B. Lewis describes as the "picaresque saint." He was an obsessed outsider—and Bird was thrice alienated: as Negro, as addict, as exponent of a new and disturbing development in jazz—whose tortured and in many ways criminal striving for personal and moral integration invokes a sense of tragic fellowship in those who saw in his agony a ritualization of their own fears, rebellions and hunger for creativity. One of the most significant features of Reisner's book lies, then, in his subtitle, even though he prefers to participate in the recreation of Bird's legend rather than perform the critical function of analyzing it.

Reisner, a former art historian who chooses to write in the barely articulate jargon of the hipster, no more than hints at this (though Ted Joans spins it out in a wild surrealist poem). But when we read through the gossip of the accounts we recognize the presence of a modern American version of the ancient myth of the birth and death of the hero. We are told of his birth, his early discovery of his vocation, his dedication to his art, of his wanderings and early defeats; we are told of his initiation into the mysteries revealed by his drug and the regions of terror to which it conveyed him; we are told of his obsessive identification with his art and his moment of revelation and metamorphosis. Here is Parker's own version:

> I remember one night I was jamming in a chili house (Dan Wall's) on Seventh Avenue between 139th and 140th. It was December, 1939 . . . I'd been getting bored with the stereotyped changes that were being used all the time, all the time, and I kept thinking there's bound to be something else. I could hear it sometimes but I couldn't play it. Well, that night, I was working over "Cherokee," and, as I did, I found that by using the higher intervals of a chord as a melody line and backing them with appropriately related changes, I could play the thing I'd been hearing. I came alive.

From then on he reigns as a recognized master, creating, recording, inspiring others, finding fame, beginning a family. Then comes his waning, suffering, disintegration and death.

Many of the bare facts of Parker's life are presented in the useful chronology, but it is the individual commentator's embellishments on the facts which create the mythic dimension. Bird was a most gifted innovator and evidently a most ingratiating and difficult man—one whose friends had no need for an enemy, and whose enemies had no difficulty in justifying their hate. According to his witnesses, he stretched the limits of human contradiction beyond belief. He was lovable and hateful, considerate and callous; he stole from friends and benefactors and borrowed without conscience, often without repaying, and yet was generous to absurdity. He could be most kind to younger musicians or utterly crushing in his contempt for their ineptitude. He was passive and yet quick to pull a knife and pick a fight. He knew the difficulties which are often the lot of jazz musicians, but as a leader he tried to con his sidemen out of their wages. He evidently loved the idea of having a family and being a good father and provider, but found it as difficult as being a good son to his devoted mother. He was given to extremes of sadism and mas-

ochism, capable of the most staggering excesses and the most exacting physical discipline and assertion of will. Indeed, one gets the
image of such a character as Stavrogin in Dostoevsky's *The Possessed*,
who while many things to many people seemed essentially devoid of
a human center—except, and an important exception indeed, Parker
was an artist who found his moments of sustained and meaningful
integration through the reed and keys of the alto saxophone. It is the
recordings of his flights of music which remain, and it is these which
form the true substance of his myth.

Which brings us, finally, to a few words about Parker's style. For
all its velocity, brilliance and imagination there is in it a great deal of
loneliness, self-depreciation and self-pity. With this there is a quality
which seems to issue from its vibratoless tone: a sound of amateurish
ineffectuality, as though he could never quite make it. It is this ama-
teurish-sounding aspect which promises so much to the members of
a do-it-yourself culture; it sounds with an assurance that you too can
create your own do-it-yourself jazz. Dream stuff, of course, but there
is a relationship between the Parker *sound* and the impossible genre
of teen-age music which has developed since his death. Nevertheless
he captured something of the discordancies, the yearning, romance
and cunning of the age and ordered it into a haunting art. He was not
the god they see in him, but for once the beatniks are correct: Bird
lives, perhaps because his tradition and his art blew him to the meaningful center of things.

But what kind of bird was Parker? Back during the thirties members of the old Blue Devils Orchestra celebrated a certain robin by
playing a lugubrious little tune called "They Picked Poor Robin." It
was a jazz-community joke, musically an extended "signifying riff"
or melodic naming of a recurring human situation, and was played to
satirize some betrayal of faith or loss of love observed from the bandstand. Sometimes it was played as the purple-fezzed musicians returned from the burial of an Elk, whereupon reaching the Negro
business and entertainment district the late Walter Page would announce the melody dolefully on his tuba; then poor robin would

transport the mourners from their somber mood to the spirit-lifting beat of "Oh, didn't he ramble" or some other happy tune. Parker, who studied with Buster Smith and jammed with other members of the disbanded Devils in Kansas City, might well have known the verse which Walter Page supplied to the tune:

> *Oh, they picked poor robin clean*
> *(repeat)*
> *They tied poor robin to a stump*
> *Lord, they picked all the feathers*
> *Round from robin's rump*
> *Oh, they picked poor robin clean.*

Poor robin was picked again and again, and his pluckers were ever unnamed and mysterious. Yet the tune was inevitably productive of laughter even when we ourselves were its object. For each of us recognized that his fate was somehow our own. Our defeats and failures, even our final defeat by death, were loaded upon his back and given ironic significance and thus made more bearable. Perhaps Charlie was poor robin come to New York and here to be sacrificed to the need for entertainment and for the creation of a new jazz style, and awaits even now in death a meaning-making plucking by perceptive critics. The effectiveness of any sacrifice depends upon our identification with the agony of the hero-victim; to those who would still insist that Charlie was a mere yardbird, our reply can only be, "Aint nobody *here* but us chickens, boss!"

The Charlie Christian Story

JAZZ, like the country which gave it birth, is fecund in its inventiveness, swift and traumatic in its developments and terribly wasteful of its resources. It is an orgiastic art which demands great physical stamina of its practitioners, and many of its most talented creators die young. More often than not (and this is especially true of its Negro exponents) its heroes remain local figures known only to small-town dance halls, and whose reputations are limited to the radius of a few hundred miles.

A case in point, and a compelling argument for closer study of roots and causes, is a recording devoted to the art of Charlie Christian, probably the greatest of jazz guitarists. He died in 1942 after a brief, spectacular career with the Benny Goodman Sextet. Had he not come from Oklahoma City in 1939 at the instigation of John Hammond, he might have shared the fate of many we knew in the period when Christian was growing up (and I doubt that it has changed very much today).

Some of the most brilliant of jazzmen made no records; their names appeared in print only in announcements of some local dance or remote "battles of music" against equally uncelebrated bands. Being devoted to an art which traditionally thrives on improvisation, these unrecorded artists very often have their most original ideas enter the public domain almost as rapidly as they are conceived, to be quickly absorbed into the thought and technique of their fellows. Thus the riffs which swung the dancers and the band on some transcendent evening, and which inspired others to competitive flights of invention, become all too swiftly a part of the general style, leaving the originator as anonymous as the creators of the architecture called Gothic.

From *Saturday Review*, May 17, 1958.

There is in this a cruel contradiction implicit in the art form itself, for true jazz is an art of individual assertion within and against the group. Each true jazz moment (as distinct from the uninspired commercial performance) springs from a contest in which each artist challenges all the rest; each solo flight, or improvisation, represents (like the successive canvases of a painter) a definition of his identity as individual, as member of the collectivity and as a link in the chain of tradition. Thus, because jazz finds its very life in an endless improvisation upon traditional materials, the jazzman must lose his identity even as he finds it; how often do we see even the most famous of jazz artists being devoured alive by their imitators, and, shamelessly, in the public spotlight?

So at best the musical contributions of these local, unrecorded heroes of jazz are enjoyed by a few fellow musicians and by a few dancers who admire them and afford them the meager economic return which allows them to keep playing. But often they live beyond the period of youthful dedication, hoping in vain that some visiting big-band leader will provide the opportunity to break through to the wider spheres of jazz. Indeed, to escape these fates the artists must be very talented, very individual, as restlessly inventive as Picasso, and very lucky.

Charles Christian, when Hammond brought him to the attention of Goodman, had been for most of his life just such a local jazz hero. Nor do I use the term loosely, for having known him since 1923, when he and my younger brother were members of the same first-grade class, I can recall no time when he was not admired for his skillful playing of stringed instruments. Indeed, a great part of his time in the manual-training department of Douglass School was spent constructing guitars from cigar boxes, instruments upon which both he and his older brother, Clarence, were dazzlingly adept. Incidentally, in their excellent notes to the album Al Avakian and Bob Prince are mistaken when they assume that Christian was innocent of contact with musical forms more sophisticated than the blues, and it would be well that here I offer a correction. Before Charlie was big enough to handle a guitar himself he served as a guide for his father, a blind guitarist and singer. Later he joined with his father, his brothers Clarence and Edward (an arranger, pianist, violinist and performer on the string bass and tuba), and made his contribution to the family income by strolling with them through the white middle-class sections of Oklahoma City, where they played serenades on request. Their repertory included the light classics as well as the blues, and there was no doubt in the minds of those who heard them that the musical value they gave was worth far more than the money they received. Later on Edward, who took leading roles in the standard operettas performed by members of the high-school chorus, led his own band and played gigs from time to time with such musicians as "Hot Lips" Paige, Walter Page, Sammy Price and Lem C. Johnson (to mention a few), all members at some point of the Blue Devils Orchestra, which later merged with the Benny Moten group to become the famous Count Basie Band. I need only mention that Oklahoma City was a regular stopping point for Kansas City–based orchestras, or that a number of the local musicians were conservatory-trained and were capable of sight-reading the hodgepodge scores which during the "million-dollar production" stage of the silent movies were furnished to the stands of pit orchestras.

The facts in these matters are always more intriguing than the legends. In the school which we attended, harmony was taught from the ninth through the twelfth grades; there was an extensive and compulsory music-appreciation program, and, though Charles was never a member, a concert band and orchestra and several vocal organizations. In brief, both in his home and in the community Charles Christian was subjected to many diverse musical influences. It was the era of radio, and for a while a local newspaper gave away cheap plastic recordings of such orchestras as Jean Goldkette's, along with subscriptions. The big media of communication were active for better or worse even then, and the Negro community was never completely isolated from their influence.

However, perhaps the most stimulating influence upon Christian, and one with whom he was later to be identified, was that of a tall, intense young musician who arrived in Oklahoma City sometime in 1929 and who, with his heavy white sweater, blue stocking cap and up-and-outthrust silver saxophone, left absolutely no reed player and few young players of any instrument unstirred by the wild, excitingly original flights of his imagination. Who else but Lester Young, who with his battered horn upset the entire Negro section of the town? One of our friends gave up his valved instrument for the tenor saxophone and soon ran away from home to carry the new message to Baltimore, while a good part of the efforts of the rest was spent trying to absorb and transform the Youngian style. Indeed, only one other young musician created anything like the excitement attending Young's stay in the town. This was Carlton George, who had played with Earl Hines and whose trumpet style was shaped after the excursions of Hines's right hand. He, however, was a minor influence, having arrived during the national ascendancy of Louis Armstrong and during the local reign of Oran ("Hot Lips") Paige.

When we consider the stylistic development of Charles Christian we are reminded how little we actually know of the origins of even the most recent of jazz styles, or of when and where they actually started, or of the tensions, personal, sociological or technical, out of which such an original artist achieves his stylistic identity. For while there is now a rather extensive history of discography and recording sessions, there is but the bare beginnings of a historiography of jazz. We know much of jazz as entertainment, but a mere handful of clichés constitutes our knowledge of jazz as experience. Worse, it is this which is frequently taken for all there is, and we get the impression that jazz styles are created in some club on some particular occasion, and there and then codified according to the preconceptions of the jazz publicists in an atmosphere as grave and traditional, say, as that attending the deliberations of the Académie Française. It is this which leads to the notion that jazz was invented in a particular house of ill fame by "Jelly Roll" Morton, who admitted the crime himself; that swing was invented by Goodman in about 1935; and that

T. Monk, K. Clarke and J. B. "D" Gillespie invented "progressive" jazz at Minton's Playhouse in Harlem about 1941.

This is, of course, convenient but only relatively true, and the effort to let the history of jazz as entertainment stand for the whole of jazz ignores the most fundamental knowledge of the dynamics of stylistic growth which has been acquired from studies in other branches of music and from our knowledge of the growth of other art forms. The jazz artist who becomes nationally known is written about as though he came into existence only upon his arrival in New York. His career in the big cities, where jazz is more of a commercial entertainment than part of a total way of life, is stressed at the expense of his life in the South, the Southwest and the Midwest, where most Negro musicians found their early development. Thus we are left with an impression of mysterious rootlessness, and the true and often annoying complexity of American cultural experience is over-simplified.

With jazz this has made for the phenomena of an art form existing in a curious state of history and pre-history simultaneously. Not that it isn't recognized that it is an art with deep roots in the past, but that the nature of its deep connection with social conditions here and now is slighted. Charlie Christian is a case in point. He flowered from a background with roots not only in a tradition of music, but in a deep division in the Negro community as well. He spent much of his life in a slum in which all the forms of disintegration attending the urbanization of rural Negroes ran riot. Although he himself was from a respectable family, the wooden tenement in which he grew up was full of poverty, crime and sickness. It was also alive and exciting, and I enjoyed visiting there, for the people both lived and sang the blues. Nonetheless, it was doubtless here that he developed the tuberculosis from which he died.

More important, jazz was regarded by most of the respectable Negroes of the town as a backward, low-class form of expression, and there was a marked difference between those who accepted and lived close to their folk experience and those whose status strivings led them to reject and deny it. Charlie rejected this attitude in turn, along with those who held it, even to the point of not participating in the musical activities of the school. Like Jimmy Rushing, whose father was a businessman and whose mother was active in church affairs, he had heard the voice of jazz and would hear no other. Ironically, what was perhaps his greatest social triumph came in death, when the respectable Negro middle class not only joined in the public mourning, but acclaimed him as a hero and took credit for his development. The attention which the sheer quality of his music should have secured him was won only by his big-town success.

Fortunately for us, Charles concentrated on the guitar and left the school band to his brother Edward, and his decision was a major part of his luck. For although it is seldom recognized, there is a conflict between what the Negro American musician feels in the community around him and the given (or classical) techniques of his instrument. He feels a tension between his desire to master the classical style of playing and his compulsion to express those sounds which form a musical definition of Negro American experience. In early jazz these sounds found their fullest expression in the timbre of the blues voice, and the use of mutes, water glasses and derbies on the bells of their horns arose out of an attempt to imitate this sound. Among the younger musicians of the thirties, especially those who contributed to the growth of bop, this desire to master the classical technique was linked with the struggle for recognition in the larger society, and with a desire to throw off those nonmusical features which came into jazz from the minstrel tradition. Actually, it was for this reason that Louis Armstrong (who is not only a great performing artist but a clown in the Elizabethan sense of the word) became their scapegoat. What was not always understood was that there were actually two separate bodies of instrumental technique: the one classic, widely recognized and "correct"; and the other eclectic, partly unconscious and "jazzy." And it was the tension between these two bodies of technique which led to many of the technical discoveries of jazz. Further, we are now aware of the existence of a fully developed and endlessly flexible technique of jazz expression, which has become quite independent of the social environment in which it developed, if not of its spirit.

Interestingly enough, the guitar (long regarded as a traditional instrument of Southern Negroes) was subjected to little of this conflict between techniques and ways of experiencing the world. Its role in the jazz orchestra was important but unobtrusive, and before Christian little had been done to explore its full potentialities for jazz. Thus Christian was able to experiment with the least influence from either traditional or contemporary sources. Starting long before he was aware of his mission—as would seem to be the way with important innovators in the arts—he taught himself to voice the guitar as a solo instrument, a development made possible through the perfecting of the electronically amplified instrument, and the rest is history.

With Christian the guitar found its jazz voice. With his entry into jazz circles his musical intelligence was able to exert its influence upon his peers and to affect the course of the future development of jazz. This album of his work—so irresistible and danceable in its swing, so intellectually stimulating in its ideas—is important not only for its contribution to our knowledge of the evolution of contemporary jazz style; it also offers one of the best arguments for bringing more serious critical intelligence to this branch of our national culture.

Remembering Jimmy

In the old days the voice was high and clear and poignantly lyrical. Steel-bright in its upper range and, at its best, silky smooth, it was possessed of a purity somehow impervious to both the stress of singing above a twelve-piece band and the urgency of Rushing's own blazing fervor. On dance nights, when you stood on the rise of the school grounds two blocks to the east, you could hear it jetting from the dance hall like a blue flame in the dark, now soaring high above the trumpets and trombones, now skimming the froth of reeds and rhythm as it called some woman's anguished name—or demanded in a high, thin, passionately lyrical line, "Baaaaay-bay, Bay-aaaay-bay! Tell me what's the matter now!"—above the shouting of the swinging band.

Nor was there need for the by now famous signature line: "If anybody asks you who sang this song / Tell 'em / it was little Jimmy Rushing / he's been here and gone," for everyone on Oklahoma City's "East Side" knew that sweet, high-floating sound. "Deep Second" was our fond nickname for the block in which Rushing worked and lived, and where most Negro business and entertainment were found, and before he went on to cheer a wider world his voice evoked the festive spirit of the place. Indeed, he was the natural herald of its blues-romance, his song the singing essence of its joy. For Jimmy Rushing was not simply a local entertainer; he expressed a value, an attitude about the world for which our lives afforded no other definition. We had a Negro church and a segregated school, a few lodges and fraternal organizations, and beyond these there was all the great white world. We were pushed off to what seemed to be the least desirable side of the city (but which some years later was found to contain one of the state's richest pools of oil), and our system of jus-

From *Saturday Review*, July 12, 1958.

tice was based upon Texas law; yet there was an optimism within the Negro community and a sense of possibility which, despite our awareness of limitation (dramatized so brutally in the Tulsa riot of 1921), transcended all of this, and it was this rock-bottom sense of reality, coupled with our sense of the possibility of rising above it, which sounded in Rushing's voice.

And how it carried! In those days I lived near the Rock Island roundhouse, where, with a steady clanging of bells and a great groaning of wheels along the rails, switch engines made up trains of freight unceasingly. Yet often in the late-spring night I could hear Rushing as I lay four blocks away in bed, carrying to me as clear as a full-bored riff on "Hot Lips" Paige's horn. Heard thus, across the dark blocks lined with locust trees, through the night throbbing with the natural aural imagery of the blues, with high-balling trains, departing bells, lonesome guitar chords simmering up from a shack in the alley, it was easy to imagine the voice as setting the pattern to which the instruments of the Blue Devils Orchestra and all the random sounds of night arose, affirming, as it were, some ideal native to the time and to the land. When we were still too young to attend night dances, but yet old enough to gather beneath the corner street-lamp on summer evenings, anyone might halt the conversation to exclaim, "Listen, they're raising hell down at Slaughter's Hall," and we'd turn our heads westward to hear Jimmy's voice soar up the hill and down, as pure and as miraculously unhindered by distance and earthbound things as is the body in youthful dreams of flying.

"Now, that's the Right Reverend Jimmy Rushing preaching now, man," someone would say. And rising to the cue another would answer, "Yeah, and that's old Elder 'Hot Lips' signifying along with him, urging him on, man." And, keeping it building, "Huh, but though you can't hear him out this far, Ole Deacon Big-un [the late Walter Page] is up there patting his foot and slapping on his big belly [the bass viol] to keep those fools in line." And we might go on to name all the members of the band as though they were the Biblical four-and-twenty elders, while laughing at the impious wit of applying church titles to a form of music which all the preachers assured us was the devil's potent tool.

Our wit was true, for Jimmy Rushing, along with the other jazz musicians whom we knew, had made a choice, had dedicated himself to a mode of expression and a way of life no less "righteously" than others dedicated themselves to the church. Jazz and the blues did not fit into the scheme of things as spelled out by our two main institutions, the church and the school, but they gave expression to attitudes which found no place in these and helped to give our lives some semblance of wholeness. Jazz and the public jazz dance was a third institution in our lives, and a vital one, and though Jimmy was far from being a preacher, he was, as official floor manager or master-of-the-dance at Slaughter's Hall, the leader of a public rite.

He was no Mr. Five-by-five in those days, but a compact, debonair young man who dressed with an easy elegance. Much later, during theater appearances with Basie's famous band, he sometimes cut an old step from slavery days called "falling off the log" for the sheer humor provided by the rapid and apparently precarious shifting of his great bulk, but in the Oklahoma days he was capable of an amazing grace of movement. A nineteenth-century formality still clung to public dances at the time, and there was quite a variety of steps. Jimmy danced them all, gliding before the crowd over the polished floor, sometimes with a girl, sometimes with a huge megaphone held chest-high before him as he swayed. The evenings began with the more formal steps, to popular and semi-classical music, and proceeded to become more expressive as the spirit of jazz and the blues became dominant. It was when Jimmy's voice began to soar with the spirit of the blues that the dancers—and the musicians—achieved that feeling of communion which was the true meaning of the public jazz dance. The blues, the singer, the band and the dancers formed the vital whole of jazz as an institutional form, and even today neither part is quite complete without the rest. The thinness of much of so-called "modern jazz" is especially reflective of this loss of wholeness, and it is quite possible that Rushing retains his vitality simply because he has kept close to the small Negro public dance.

The occasion for this shamelessly nostalgic outburst is provided by a series of Rushing recordings issued over the past few years: Vanguard's *Jazz Showcase*; Columbia's *Goin' to Chicago, Listen to the Blues with Jimmy Rushing, If This Ain't the Blues, The Jazz Odyssey of James Rushing, Esq.*, and *Little Jimmy Rushing and the Big Brass*. An older recording, Decca's *Kansas City Jazz*, contains Rushing's best version of his classic "Good Morning, Blues," and offers a vivid idea of the styles and combinations of musicians which made up the milieu in which Rushing found his early development. These discs form a valuable introduction to the art of Jimmy Rushing in all its fervor and variety.

Rushing is known today primarily as a blues singer, but not so in those days. He began as a singer of ballads, bringing to them a sincerity and a feeling for dramatizing the lyrics in the musical phrase which charged the banal lines with the mysterious potentiality of meaning which haunts the blues. And it was, perhaps, Rushing's beginning as a ballad singer which gives his blues interpretations their special quality. For one of the significant aspects of his art is the imposition of a romantic lyricism upon the blues tradition (compare his version of "See See Rider" with that of Ma Rainey), a lyricism which is not of the Deep South, but of the Southwest: a romanticism native to the frontier, imposed upon the violent rawness of a part of the nation which only thirteen years before Rushing's birth was still Indian territory. Thus there is an optimism in it which echoes the spirit of those Negroes who, like Rushing's father, had come to Oklahoma in search of a more human way of life.

Rushing is one of the first singers to sing the blues before a big band, and even today he seldom comes across as a blues "shouter," but maintains the lyricism which has always been his way with the blues. Indeed, when we listen to his handling of lyrics we become aware of that quality which makes for the mysteriousness of the blues: their ability to imply far more than they state outright, and their capacity to make the details of sex convey meanings which touch upon the metaphysical. For, indeed, they always find poetry in the limits of the Negro vocabulary. Perhaps because he is more educated and came from a family already well on its rise into what is called the "Negro middle class," Jimmy has always shown a concern for the correctness of language, and out of the tension between the traditional folk pronunciation and his training in school, he has worked out a flexibility of enunciation and a rhythmical agility with words which make us constantly aware of the meanings which shimmer just beyond the limits of the lyrics. The blues is an art of ambiguity, an assertion of the irrepressibly human over all circumstance, whether created by others or by one's own human failings. They are the only consistent art in the United States which constantly remind us of our limitations while encouraging us to see how far we can actually go. When understood in their more profound implication, they are a corrective, an attempt to draw a line upon man's own limitless assertion.

Significantly, Jimmy Rushing was able to spread the appeal of the blues to a wider American audience after the Depression had made us a bit more circumspect about the human cost of living of our "American way of life." It seems especially fitting now, when circumstance and its own position of leadership has forced the nation once more to examine its actions and its intentions, that the blues are once more becoming popular. There is great demand for Rushing in Europe, from which he has just returned with the Goodman band. And I think we need him more here at home. Certainly this collection of discs will make us aware that there is emotional continuity in American life, and that the abiding moods expressed in our most vital popular art form are not simply a matter of entertainment; they also tell us who and where we are.

Blues People

In his introduction to *Blues People* LeRoi Jones advises us to approach the work as

> . . . a strictly theoretical endeavor. Theoretical, in that none of the questions it poses can be said to have been answered definitely or for all time (sic!), etc. In fact, the whole book proposes more questions than it will answer. The only questions it will properly move to answer have, I think, been answered already within the patterns of American life. We need only give these patterns serious scrutiny and draw certain permissible conclusions.

It is a useful warning and one hopes that it will be regarded by those jazz publicists who have the quite irresponsible habit of sweeping up any novel pronouncement written about jazz and slapping it upon the first available record liner as the latest insight into the mysteries of American Negro expression.

Jones would take his subject seriously—as the best of jazz critics have always done—and he himself should be so taken. He has attempted to place the blues within the context of a total culture and to see this native art form through the disciplines of sociology, anthropology and (though he seriously underrates its importance in the creating of a viable theory) history, and he spells out explicitly his assumptions concerning the relation between the blues, the people who created them and the larger American culture. Although I find several of his assumptions questionable, this is valuable in itself. It would be well if all jazz critics did likewise; not only would it expose those who have no business in the field, but it would sharpen the thinking of the few who have something enlightening to contribute.

From *The New York Review*, February 6, 1964.

Blues People, like much that is written by Negro Americans at the present moment, takes on an inevitable resonance from the Freedom Movement, but it is in itself characterized by a straining for a note of militancy which is, to say the least, distracting. Its introductory mood of scholarly analysis frequently shatters into a dissonance of accusation, and one gets the impression that while Jones wants to perform a crucial task which he feels *someone* should take on—as indeed someone should—he is frustrated by the restraint demanded of the critical pen and would like to pick up a club.

Perhaps this explains why Jones, who is also a poet and editor of a poetry magazine, gives little attention to the blues as lyric, as a form of poetry. He appears to be attracted to the blues for what he believes they tell us of the sociology of Negro American identity and attitude. Thus, after beginning with the circumstances in which he sees their origin, he considers the ultimate values of American society:

> The Negro as slave is one thing. The Negro as American is quite another. But the *path* the slave took to "citizenship" is what I want to look at. And I make my analogy through the slave citizen's music—through the music that is most closely associated with him: blues and a later, but parallel, development, jazz. And it seems to me that if the Negro represents, or is symbolic of, something in and about the nature of American culture, this certainly should be revealed by his characteristic music. . . . I am saying that if the music of the Negro in America, in all its permutations, is subjected to a socio-anthropological as well as musical scrutiny, something about the essential nature of the Negro's existence in this country ought to be revealed, as well as something about the essential nature of this country, i.e., society as a whole. . . .

The tremendous burden of sociology which Jones would place upon this body of music is enough to give even the blues the blues. At one point he tells us that "the one peculiar reference to the drastic

change in the Negro from slavery to 'citizenship' is in his music."
And later with more precision, he states:

> . . . The point I want to make most evident here is that I cite
> the beginning of the blues as one beginning of American
> Negroes. Or, let me say, the reaction and subsequent relation
> of the Negro's experience in this country in *his* English is one
> beginning of the Negro's conscious appearance on the Ameri-
> can scene.

No one could quarrel with Mr. Jones's stress upon beginnings. In
1833, two hundred and fourteen years after the first Africans were
brought to these shores as slaves, a certain Mrs. Lydia Maria Child, a
leading member of the American Anti-Slavery Society, published a
paper entitled: *An Appeal in Favor of that Class of Americans Called
Africans*. I am uncertain to what extent it actually reveals Mrs.
Child's ideas concerning the complex relationship between time,
place, cultural and/or national identity and race, but her title sounds
like a fine bit of contemporary ironic *signifying*—"signifying" here
meaning, in the unwritten dictionary of American Negro usage,
"rhetorical understatements." It tells us much of the thinking of her
opposition, and it reminds us that as late as the 1890s, a time when
Negro composers, singers, dancers and comedians dominated the
American musical stage, popular Negro songs (including James
Weldon Johnson's "Under the Bamboo Tree," now immortalized
by T. S. Eliot) were commonly referred to as "Ethiopian Airs."

Perhaps more than any other people, Americans have been locked
in a deadly struggle with time, with history. We've fled the past and
trained ourselves to suppress, if not forget, troublesome details of
the national memory, and a great part of our optimism, like our
progress, has been bought at the cost of ignoring the processes
through which we've arrived at any given moment in our national
existence. We've fought continuously with one another over who
and what we are, and, with the exception of the Negro, over who and

what is American. Jones is aware of this and, although he embarrasses his own argument, his emphasis is to the point.

For it would seem that while Negroes have been undergoing a process of "Americanization" from a time preceding the birth of this nation—including the fusing of their bloodlines with other non-African strains—there has persisted a stubborn confusion as to their American identity. Somehow it was assumed that the Negroes, of all the diverse American peoples, would remain unaffected by the climate, the weather, the political circumstances—from which not even slaves were exempt—the social structures, the national manners, the modes of production and the tides of the market, the national ideals, the conflicts of values, the rising and falling of national morale, or the complex give and take of acculturalization which was undergone by all others who found their existence within American democracy. This confusion still persists, and it is Mr. Jones's concern with it which gives *Blues People* a claim upon our attention.

Mr. Jones sees the American Negro as the product of a series of transformations, starting with the enslaved African, who became Afro-American slave, who became the American slave, who became, in turn, the highly qualified "citizen" whom we know today. The slave began by regarding himself as enslaved African during the time when he still spoke his native language or remembered it, practiced such aspects of his native religion as were possible and expressed himself musically in modes which were essentially African. These cultural traits became transmuted as the African lost consciousness of his African background, and his music, religion, language and speech gradually became that of the American Negro. His sacred music became the spirituals, his work songs and dance music became the blues and primitive jazz, and his religion became a form of Afro-American Christianity. With the end of slavery Jones sees the development of jazz and the blues as results of the more varied forms of experience made available to the freedman. By the twentieth century the blues divided and became, on the one hand, a professionalized form of entertainment, while remaining, on the other, a form of folklore.

By which I suppose he means that some Negroes remained in the country and sang a crude form of the blues, while others went to the city, became more sophisticated, and paid to hear Ma Rainey, Bessie or some of the other Smith girls sing them in night clubs or theaters. Jones gets this mixed up with ideas of social class—middle-class Negroes, whatever that term actually means, and light-skinned Negroes, or those Negroes corrupted by what Jones calls "White" culture—preferring the "classic" blues, and black, uncorrupted, country Negroes preferring "country blues."

For as with his music, so with the Negro. As Negroes became "middle class" they rejected their tradition and themselves; ". . . they wanted any self which the mainstream dictated, and the mainstream *always* dictated. And this black middle class, in turn, tried always to dictate that self, or this image of a whiter Negro, to the poorer, blacker Negroes."

One would get the impression that there was a rigid correlation between color, education, income and the Negro's preference in music. But what are we to say of a white-skinned Negro with brown freckles who owns sixteen oil wells sunk in a piece of Texas land once farmed by his ex-slave parents who were a blue-eyed, white-skinned, redheaded (kinky) Negro woman from Virginia and a blue-gummed, black-skinned, curly-haired Negro male from Mississippi, and who not only sang bass in a Holy Roller church, played the market and voted Republican, but collected blues recordings and was a walking depository of blues tradition? Jones's theory no more allows for the existence of such a Negro than it allows for himself, but that "concord of sensibilities" which has been defined as the meaning of culture allows for much more variety than Jones would admit.

Much the same could be said of Jones's treatment of the jazz during the thirties, when he claims its broader acceptance (i.e., its economic success as entertainment) led to a dilution, to the loss of much of its "black" character which caused a certain group of rebellious Negro musicians to create the "anti-mainstream" jazz style called bebop.

Jones sees bop as a conscious gesture of separatism, ignoring the fact that the creators of the style were seeking, whatever their musical intentions—and they were the least political of men—a fresh form of entertainment which would allow them their fair share of the entertainment market, which had been dominated by whites during the swing era. And although the boppers were reacting, at least in part, to the high artistic achievement of Armstrong, Hawkins, Basie and Ellington (all Negroes, all masters of the blues-jazz tradition), Jones sees their music as a recognition of his contention "that when you are black in a society where black is an extreme liability [it] is one thing, but to understand that it is the society which is lacking and is impossibly deformed because of this lack, and not *yourself*, isolates you even more from that society."

Perhaps. But today nothing succeeds like rebellion (which Jones as a "beat" poet should know), and while a few boppers went to Europe to escape, or became Muslims, others took the usual tours for the State Department. Whether this makes *them* "middle class" in Jones's eyes I can't say, but his assertions—which are fine as personal statement—are not in keeping with the facts; his theory flounders before that complex of human motives which makes human history, and which is so characteristic of the American Negro.

Read as a record of an earnest young man's attempt to come to grips with his predicament as Negro American during a most turbulent period of our history, *Blues People* may be worth the reader's time. Taken as a theory of American Negro culture, it can only contribute more confusion than clarity. For Jones has stumbled over that ironic obstacle which lies in the path of any who would fashion a theory of American Negro culture while ignoring the intricate network of connections which binds Negroes to the larger society. To do so is to attempt delicate brain surgery with a switchblade. And it is possible that any viable theory of Negro American culture obligates us to fashion a more adequate theory of American culture as a whole. The heel bone is, after all, connected through its various linkages to the head bone. Attempt a serious evaluation of our national morality, and up jumps the so-called Negro problem. Attempt to discuss jazz as a hermetic expression of Negro sensibility, and immediately we must consider what the "mainstream" of American music really is.

Here political categories are apt to confuse, for while Negro slaves were socially, politically and economically separate (but only in a special sense even here), they were, in a cultural sense, much closer than Jones's theory allows him to admit.

"A slave," writes Jones, "cannot be a man." But what, one might ask, of those moments when he feels his metabolism aroused by the rising of the sap in spring? What of his identity among other slaves? With his wife? And isn't it closer to the truth that far from considering themselves only in terms of that abstraction, "a slave," the enslaved really thought of themselves as *men* who had been unjustly enslaved? And isn't the true answer to Mr. Jones's question, "What are you going to be when you grow up?" not, as he gives it, "a slave" but most probably a coachman, a teamster, a cook, the best damned steward on the Mississippi, the best jockey in Kentucky, a butler, a farmer, a stud, or, hopefully, a free man! Slavery was a most vicious system, and those who endured and survived it a tough people, but it was *not* (and this is important for Negroes to remember for the sake of their own sense of who and what their grandparents were) a state of absolute repression.

A slave was, to the extent that he was a *musician*, one who expressed himself in music, a man who realized himself in the world of sound. Thus, while he might stand in awe before the superior technical ability of a white musician, and while he was forced to recognize a superior social status, he would never feel awed before the music which the technique of the white musician made available. His attitude as "musician" would lead him to seek to possess the music expressed through the technique, but until he could do so he would hum, whistle, sing or play the tunes to the best of his ability on any available instrument. And it was, indeed, out of the tension between desire and ability that the techniques of jazz emerged. This was likewise true of American Negro choral singing. For this, no literary explanation, no cultural analyses, no political slogans—indeed, not even a high degree of social or political freedom—was required. For the art—the blues, the spirituals, the jazz, the dance—was what we had in place of freedom.

Technique was then, as today, the key to creative freedom, but before this came a will toward expression. Thus, Jones's theory to the contrary, Negro musicians have never, as a group, felt alienated from any music sounded within their hearing, and it is my theory that it would be impossible to pinpoint the time when they were not shaping what Jones calls the mainstream of American music. Indeed, what group of musicians has made more of the sound of the American experience? Nor am I confining my statement to the sound of the slave experience, but am saying that the most authoritative rendering of America in music is that of American Negroes.

For as I see it, from the days of their introduction into the colonies, Negroes have taken, with the ruthlessness of those without articulate investments in cultural styles, whatever they could of European music, making of it that which would, when blended with the cultural tendencies inherited from Africa, express their own sense of life, while rejecting the rest. Perhaps this is only another way of saying that whatever the degree of injustice and inequality sustained by the slaves, American culture was, even before the official founding of the nation, pluralistic, and it was the African's origin in cultures in which art was highly functional which gave him an edge in shaping the music and dance of this nation.

The question of social and cultural snobbery is important here. The effectiveness of Negro music and dance is first recorded in the journals and letters of travelers but it is important to remember that they saw and understood only that which they were prepared to accept. Thus a Negro dancing a courtly dance appeared comic from the outside simply because the dancer was a slave. But to the Negro dancing it—and there is ample evidence that he danced it well—burlesque or satire might have been the point, which might have been difficult for a white observer to even imagine. During the 1870s Laf-

cadio Hearn reports that the best singers of Irish songs, in Irish dialect, were Negro dockworkers in Cincinnati, and advertisements
from slavery days described escaped slaves who spoke in Scottish dialect. The master artisans of the South were slaves, and white Americans have been walking Negro walks, talking Negro-flavored talk
(and prizing it when spoken by Southern belles), dancing Negro
dances and singing Negro melodies far too long to talk of a "mainstream" of American culture to which they're alien.

Jones attempts to impose an ideology upon this cultural complexity, and this might be useful if he knew enough of the related subjects
to make it interesting. But his version of the blues lacks a sense of the
excitement and surprise of men living in the world—of enslaved and
politically weak men successfully imposing their values upon a powerful society through song and dance.

The blues speak to us simultaneously of the tragic and comic aspects of the human condition, and they express a profound sense of
life shared by many Negro Americans precisely because their lives
have combined these modes. This has been the heritage of a people
who for hundreds of years could not celebrate birth or dignify death,
and whose need to live despite the dehumanizing pressures of slavery
developed an endless capacity for laughing at their painful experiences. This is a group experience shared by many Negroes, and any
effective study of the blues would treat them first as poetry and as
ritual. Jones makes a distinction between classic and country blues,
the one being entertainment and the other folklore. But the distinction is false. Classic blues were both entertainment *and* a form of
folklore. When they were sung professionally in theaters, they were
entertainment; when danced to in the form of recordings or used as a
means of transmitting the traditional verses and their wisdom, they
were folklore. There are levels of time and function involved here,
and the blues which might be used in one place as entertainment (as
gospel music is now being used in night clubs and on theater stages)
might be put to a ritual use in another. Bessie Smith might have been
a "blues queen" to society at large, but within the tighter Negro

community where the blues were part of a total way of life, and a major expression of an attitude toward life, she was a priestess, a celebrant who affirmed the values of the group and man's ability to deal with chaos.

It is unfortunate that Jones thought it necessary to ignore the aesthetic nature of the blues in order to make his ideological point, for he might have come much closer had he considered the blues not as politics but as art. This would have still required the disciplines of anthropology and sociology, but as practiced by Constance Rourke, who was well aware of how much of American cultural expression is Negro. And he could learn much from the Cambridge School's discoveries of the connection between poetry, drama and ritual as a means of analyzing how the blues function in their proper environment. Simple taste should have led Jones to Stanley Edgar Hyman's work on the blues instead of Paul Oliver's sadly misdirected effort.

For the blues are not primarily concerned with civil rights or obvious political protest; they are an art form and thus a transcendence of those conditions created within the Negro community by the denial of social justice. As such they are one of the techniques through which Negroes have survived and kept their courage during that long period when many whites assumed, as some still assume, that they were afraid.

Much has been made of the fact that *Blues People* is one of the few books by a Negro to treat the subject. Unfortunately for those who expect that Negroes would have a special insight into this mysterious art, this is not enough. Here, too, the critical intelligence must perform the difficult task which only it can perform.

III

THE SHADOW AND THE ACT

Some Questions and
Some Answers

What do you understand today *by "Negro culture"?*

What I understand by the term "Negro culture" is so vague as to be meaningless. Indeed, I find the term "Negro" vague even in its racial connotations, for in Africa there are several non-white racial strains, and one suspects that the term came into usage as a means of obliterating cultural differences between the various African peoples. In this way the ruthless disruption of highly developed cultures raised no troubling moral questions. The term, used mainly by whites, represented a "trained incapacity" to make or feel moral distinctions where black men were concerned.

As for the term "culture," used in this connection, I know of no valid demonstration that culture is transmitted through the genes.

In Africa the blacks identify themselves by their tribal names; thus it is significant that it is only in the United States that the term "Negro" has acquired specific cultural content. Spelled with a capital "N" by most publications (one of the important early victories of my own people in their fight for self-definition), the term describes a people whose origin began with the introduction of African slaves to the American colonies in 1619, and which today represents the fusing with the original African strains of many racial bloodlines—among them English, Irish, Scotch, French, Spanish and American Indian. Although the American Civil War brought an end to the importation of African peoples into the United States, this mixture of bloods has by no means ceased, not even in the South where the whites are obsessed with racial purity, so that today anthropologists tell us that very few American Negroes are of pure African blood. It

From *Preuves*, May 1958.

occurs to me that in light of this, even if culture were transmitted through the bloodstream we would encounter quite a problem in explaining just how the genes bearing "Negro" culture could so overpower those bearing French or English culture, which in all other ways are assumed to be superior.

But to continue, the American Negro people are North American in origin and have evolved under specifically American conditions: climatic, nutritional, historical, political and social. They take their character from the experience of American slavery and the struggle for, and the achievement of, emancipation; from the dynamics of American race and caste discrimination; and from living in a highly industrialized and highly mobile society possessing a relatively high standard of living and an explicitly stated equalitarian concept of freedom. Its spiritual outlook is basically Protestant, its system of kinship is Western, its time and historical sense are American (United States), and its secular values are those professed, ideally at least, by all of the people of the United States.

Culturally this people represents one of the many subcultures which make up that great amalgam of European and native American cultures which is the culture of the United States. This "American Negro culture" is expressed in a body of folklore, in the musical forms of the spirituals, blues and jazz; an idiomatic version of American speech (especially in the southern United States); a cuisine; a body of dance forms; and even a dramaturgy which is generally unrecognized as such because it is still tied to the more folkish Negro churches. Some Negro preachers are great showmen.

It must, however, be pointed out that due to the close links which Negro Americans have with the rest of the nation, these cultural expressions are constantly influencing the larger body of American culture and are in turn influenced by them. Nor should the existence of a specifically "Negro" idiom in any way be confused with the vague, racist terms "white culture" or "black culture"; rather, it is a matter of diversity within unity. One could indeed go further and say that in this sense there is no other "Negro" culture. Haitians, for instance, are an "American" people and predominantly dark, but their culture is an expression of Haitian conditions; it reflects the influence of French culture and the fusion of Catholic and native Haitian religious outlooks. Thus, since most so-called "Negro cultures" outside Africa are necessarily amalgams, it would seem more profitable to stress the term "culture" and leave the term "Negro" out of the discussion. It is not culture which binds the peoples who are of partially African origin now scattered throughout the world, but an identity of passions. We share a hatred for the alienation forced upon us by Europeans during the process of colonization and empire, and we are bound by our common suffering more than by our pigmentation. But even this identification is shared by most non-white peoples, and while it has political value of great potency, its cultural value is almost nil.

In your opinion was there before the arrival of Europeans a single Negro culture that all Negroes shared, or was it the case, as among the whites, that there had been many different cultures, such as Judeo-Christianity, Brahmanism, etc.?

Before the arrival of Europeans there were many African cultures.

What is the role of modern industrial evolution in the spiritual crisis of the Negro people of our times? Does industrial progress (capitalist or socialist) endanger the future of a genuine Negro culture?

The role of modern industrial evolution in the spiritual crisis of those whom you refer to as "Negro" peoples seems to me to be as ambiguous as its role in the lives of peoples of any racial identity: it depends upon how much human suffering must go into the achievement of industrialization, upon who operates the industries, upon how the products and profits are shared, and upon the wisdom used in imposing technology upon the institutions and traditions of each particular society. Ironically, black men with the status of slaves contributed much of the brute labor which helped get the Industrial Revolution under way; in this process they were exploited, their natural resources were ravaged, their institutions and their cultures were devastated, and in most instances they were denied anything like participation in the European cultures which flowered as a result of the transformation of civilization under the growth of technology. But now it is precisely technology which promises them release from the brutalizing effects of over three hundred years of racism and European domination. Men cannot unmake history: thus it is not a question of reincarnating those cultural traditions which were destroyed, but a matter of using industrialization, modern medicine, modern science generally, to work in the interest of these peoples rather than against them. Nor is the disruption of continuity with the past necessarily a totally negative phenomenon; sometimes it makes possible a modulation of a people's way of life which allows for a more creative use of its energies. The United States is ample proof of this, and though we suffer much from the rupture of tradition, great good has come to the world through those achievements which were made possible. One thing seems clear: certain possibilities of culture are achievable only through the presence of industrial techniques.

It is not industrial progress per se which damages peoples or cultures; it is the exploitation of peoples in order to keep the machines fed with raw materials. It seems to me that the whole world is moving toward some new cultural synthesis, and partially through the discipline imposed by technology. There is, I believe, a threat when industrialism is linked to a political doctrine which has as its goal the subjugation of the world.

Is the birth of various religions in present Negro societies progressive or regressive as far as culture is concerned?

I am unacquainted with the religious movements in the societies to which you refer. If the Mau Mau is one of these, then I must say that for all my disgust for those who provoked the natives to such obscene extremes, I feel it to be regressive indeed.

Several Negro poets from Africa explain that they write in French or English because the ancient languages are not adequate to express their feeling any longer. What do you think about this?

When it comes to poetry the vagueness of the term "Negro" becomes truly appalling, for if there is a "Negro" language I am unacquainted with it. Are these people Bantu, Sudanese, Nigerian, Watusi or what? As for the poets in question, it seems to me that in a general way they are faced by the problem confronted by the Irish, who for all their efforts to keep their language vital have had nevertheless their greatest poets expressing themselves in English, as in the case of Shaw, Yeats, Joyce and O'Casey. Perhaps the poet's true language is that in which he dreams. At any rate, it is true that for some time now poets throughout the world have drawn freely from all the world's tongues in order to create their vocabularies. One uses whatever one needs to best express one's vision of the human predicament.

Another way of approaching the matter is to view the poem as a medium of communication; to whom do these poets wish to speak? Each poet creates his own language from that which he finds around him. Thus if these poets find the language of Shakespeare or Racine inadequate to reach their own peoples, then the other choice is to re-create their original language to the point where they may express their complex emotions. This is the manner in which the poet makes his contribution to literature, and the greatest literary creation of any culture is its language. Further, language is most alive when it is capable of dealing with the realities in which it operates. In the myth, God gave man the task of naming the objects of the world; thus one of the functions of the poet is to insist upon a correspondence between words and ever-changing reality, between ideals and actualities. The domain of the unstated, the undefined is his to conquer.

In my own case, having inherited the language of Shakespeare and Melville, Mark Twain and Lincoln and no other, I try to do my part in keeping the American language alive and rich by using in my work the music and idiom of American Negro speech, and by insisting that the words of this language correspond with the reality of American life as seen by my own people. Perhaps if I were a member of a bilingual society I would approach my task differently, but my work is addressed primarily to those who have my immediate group experience, for I am not protesting nor pleading my humanity; I am trying to communicate, to articulate and define a group experience.

What do you think of the present level of Negro sculpture? What future do you see for it?

I know little of current work in sculpture by Africans, but that which I have seen appears to possess little of that high artistic excellence characteristic of ancient African art. American Negro sculpture is, of course, simply American sculpture done by Negroes. Some is good, some bad. I don't see any possibility of work by these artists being created in a vacuum outside of those influences, national and international, individual and abstract, which influence any other American artist. When African sculpture is one influence, it comes to them through the Cubists, just as it did to most contemporary artists. That phenomenon which Malraux calls the "Imaginary Museum" draws no color line.

As for the future of African sculpture, it depends upon the future role which art will play in African societies which are now struggling into being. I doubt, however, that sculpture will ever play the same role that the so-called primitive art played, because the tribal societies which called this art into being have either been shattered or are being rapidly transformed. And if the influence of the primitive sculptures is to be seen in European art wherever one turns, so have the influences of modern Western art found their way to Africa. This process is more likely to increase rather than lessen. To the extent that art is an expression of transcendent values, the role of sculpture in these societies will depend upon the values of those societies.

What do you think of the future of "Negro music"?

I know only American Negro music, in this sense of the term. This music consists of jazz and the spirituals, but as with all things cultural in the United States these forms have been and are still being subjected to a constant process of assimilation. Thus, although it was the specific experience of Negroes which gave rise to these forms, they expressed and gave significance to feelings and sounds so characteristically American that both spirituals and jazz have been absorbed into the musical language of the culture as a whole. On the other hand, American Negro music was never created in a vacuum; it was the shaping of musical elements found in the culture—European, American Indian, the Afro-American rhythmical sense, the sound of the Negro voice—to the needs of a particular group. Today jazz is a national art form, but for me personally the source of the purist stream of this music is the Negro community, wherein the commercial motive in popular music is weaker, and where jazz remains vital because it is still linked with the Saturday night or Sunday morning breakfast dance, which are still among the living social forms functioning within the Negro community.

Nor does this in any way contradict the fact that some of the leaders in the modern jazz movement are Negroes; we still move from the folk community to a highly conscious acquaintance with twelve-tone composers and their methods in less time than it takes to complete a course in counterpoint, and these modern methods are quickly absorbed into the body of classical jazz. A man like Duke Ellington remains a vital and imaginative composer precisely because he has never severed his tie with the Negro dance, and because his approach to the world's musical speech is eclectic.

Nevertheless there is the danger that the rapid absorption of

Negro American musical forms by commercial interests and their rapid vulgarization and dissemination through the mass media will corrupt the Negro's own taste, just as in Mexico the demand for modern designs in silver jewelry for export is leading to a dying away of native design. Thus I say that much of the future depends upon the self-acceptance of the Negro composer and his integrity toward his musical tradition. Nor do I exclude the so-called serious composer; all are faced with the humanist American necessity of finding the balance between progress and continuity, between tradition and experimentation. For the jazz artist there is some insurance in continuing to play for dance audiences, for here the criticism is unspoiled by status-directed theories; Negroes simply won't accept shoddy dance music, so the artist has a vital criticism danced out in the ritual of the dance.

Since the spirituals are religious music, it would seem that their future is assured by the revitalization of Negro American churches, as is demonstrated in the leadership which these churches are giving in the struggle for civil rights. The old songs play quite a part in this, and they in turn throb with new emotion flowing from the black American's revaluation of his experience. Negroes are no longer ashamed of their slave past but see in it sources of strength, and it is now generally recognized that the spirituals bespoke their birth as a people and asserted and defined their humanity. The desegregation struggle is only the socio-political manifestation of this process. Commercial rock-and-roll music is a brutalization of one stream of contemporary Negro church music, but I do not believe that even this obscene looting of a cultural expression can permanently damage the vital source—not for racial reasons but because for some time to come Negroes will live close to their traditional cultural patterns. Nor do I believe that as we win our struggle for full participation in American life we will abandon our group expression. Too much living and aspiration have gone into it, so that, drained of its elements of defensiveness and alienation, it will become even more precious to us, for we will see it ever clearer as a transcendent value.

What we have counterpoised against the necessary rage for progress in American life (and which we share with other Americans) will have been proved to be at least as valuable as all our triumphs of technology. In spilling out his heart's blood in his contest with the machine, John Henry was asserting a national value as well as a Negro value.

What do you think of the attempt of Brazilian and American Negroes to adopt "white values" in place of "Negro values"? Is this only an illusion on their part, or will it be a source of creative development?

I am unqualified to speak of Brazil, but in the United States, the values of my own people are neither "white" nor "black"; they are American. Nor can I see how they could be anything else, since we are a people who are involved in the texture of the American experience. And indeed, today the most dramatic fight for American ideals is being sparked by black Americans. Significantly, we are the only black peoples who are not fighting for separation from the "whites," but for a fuller participation in the society which we share with "whites." And it is of further significance that we pursue our goals precisely in terms of American constitutionalism. If there is anything in this which points to "black values" it must lie in the circumstance that we really believe that all men are created equal and that they should be given a chance to achieve their highest potentialities, regardless of race, creed, color or past condition of servitude.

The terms in which the question is couched serve to obscure the cultural fact that the dynamism of American life is as much a part of the Negro American's personality as it is of the white American's. We differ from certain white Americans in that we have no reason to assume that race has a positive value, and in that we reject race thinking wherever we find it. And even this attitude is shared by millions of whites. Nor are we interested in being anything other than *Negro* Americans. One's racial identity is, after all, accidental, but the United States is an international country, and its conscious character makes it possible for us to abandon the mistakes of the past. The point of our struggle is to be both Negro and American and to bring about that condition in American society in which this would be possible. In brief, there is an American Negro idiom, a style and a way of life, but none of this is inseparable from the conditions of American society, nor from its general modes or culture—mass distribution, race and intra-national conflicts, the radio, television, its system of education, its politics. If general American values influence us; we in turn influence them—in speech, concept of liberty, justice, economic distribution, international outlook, our current attitude toward colonialism, our national image of ourselves as a nation. And this despite the fact that nothing which black Americans have won as a people has been won without struggle. For *no* group within the United States achieves anything without asserting its claims against the counterclaims of other groups. Thus, as Americans we have accepted this conscious and ceaseless struggle as a condition of our freedom, and we are aware that each of our victories increases the area of freedom for all Americans, regardless of color. When we finally achieve the right of full participation in American life, what we make of it will depend upon our sense of cultural values and our creative use of freedom, not upon our racial identification. I see no reason why the heritage of world culture, which represents a continuum, should be confused with the notion of race. Japan erected a highly efficient modern technology upon a religious culture which viewed the Emperor as a god. The Germany which produced Beethoven and Hegel and Mann turned its science and technology to the monstrous task of genocide; one hopes that when what are known as "Negro" societies are in full possession of the world's knowledge and in control of their destinies, they will bring to an end all those savageries which for centuries have been committed in the name of race. From what we are witnessing in certain parts of the world today, however, there is no guarantee that simply being nonwhite offers any guarantee of this. The demands of state policy are apt to be more influential than morality. I would like to see a qualified Negro as President of the United States, but I suspect that even if this were today possible, the necessities of the office would shape his actions far more than his racial identity.

Would that we could but put the correct questions in these matters, perhaps then great worlds of human energy could be saved, especially by those of us who would be free.

The Shadow and the Act

FAULKNER has given us a metaphor. When, in the film *Intruder in the Dust*, the young Mississipian Chick Mallison falls into an ice-coated creek on a Negro's farm, he finds that he has plunged into the depth of a reality which constantly reveals itself as the reverse of what it had appeared before his plunge. Here the ice—white, brittle and eggshell-thin—symbolizes Chick's inherited views of the world, especially his Southern conception of Negroes. Emerging more shocked by the air than by the water, he finds himself locked in a moral struggle with the owner of the land, Lucas Beauchamp, the son of a slave who, while aiding the boy, angers him by refusing to act toward him as Southern Negroes are expected to act.

To Lucas, Chick is not only a child but his guest. Thus he not only dries the boy's clothes, but insists that he eat the only food in the house, Lucas's own dinner. When Chick (whose white standards won't allow him to accept the hospitality of a Negro) attempts to pay him, Lucas refuses to accept the money. What follows is one of the most sharply amusing studies of Southern racial ethics to be seen anywhere. Asserting his whiteness, Chick throws the money on the floor, ordering Lucas to pick it up; Lucas, disdaining to quarrel with a child, has Chick's young Negro companion, Aleck Sander, return the coins.

Defeated but still determined, Chick later seeks to discharge his debt by sending Lucas and his wife a gift. Lucas replies by sending Chick a gallon of molasses by—outrage of all Southern Negro outrages!—a white boy on a mule. This is too much, and from that moment it becomes Chick's passion to repay his debt and to see Lucas for once "act like a nigger." The opportunity has come, he thinks, when Lucas is charged with shooting a white man in the back. But

From *The Reporter*, December 6, 1949.

instead of humbling himself, Lucas (from his cell) tells, almost orders, Chick to prove him innocent by violating the white man's grave.

In the end we see Chick recognizing Lucas as the representative of those virtues of courage, pride, independence and patience that are usually attributed only to white men—and, in his uncle's words, accepting the Negro as "the keeper of our [the whites'] consciences." This bit of dialogue, coming after the real murderer is revealed as the slain man's own brother, is, when viewed historically, about the most remarkable concerning a Negro ever to come out of Hollywood.

With this conversation, the falling into creeks, the digging up of corpses and the confronting of lynch mobs that mark the plot, all take on a new significance: not only have we been watching the consciousness of a young Southerner grow through the stages of a superb mystery drama, but we have participated in a process by which the role of Negroes in American life has been given what, for the movies, is a startling new definition.

To appreciate fully the significance of *Intruder in the Dust* in the history of Hollywood we must go back to the film that is regarded as the archetype of the modern American motion picture, *The Birth of a Nation*.

Originally entitled *The Clansman*, the film was inspired by another Southern novel, the Reverend Thomas Dixon's work of that title, which also inspired Joseph Simmons to found the Knights of the Ku Klux Klan. (What a role these malignant clergymen have played in our lives!) Retitled *The Birth of a Nation* as an afterthought, it was this film that forged the twin screen image of the Negro as bestial rapist and grinning, eye-rolling clown—stereotypes that are still with us today. Released during 1915, it resulted in controversy, riots, heavy profits and the growth of the Klan. Of it Terry Ramsaye, a historian of the American motion-picture industry writes: "The picture . . . and the K.K.K. secret society, which was the afterbirth of a nation, were sprouted from the same root. In subsequent years they reacted upon each other to the large profit of both. The film presented predigested dramatic experience and thrills. The society made the customers all actors in costume."

Usually *The Birth of a Nation* is discussed in terms of its contributions to cinema technique, but as with every other technical advance since the oceanic sailing ship, it became a further instrument in the dehumanization of the Negro. And while few films have gone so far in projecting Negroes in a malignant light, few before the 1940s showed any concern with depicting their humanity. Just the opposite. In the struggle against Negro freedom, motion pictures have been one of the strongest instruments for justifying some white Americans' anti-Negro attitudes and practices. Thus the South, through D. W. Griffith's genius, captured the enormous myth-making potential of the film form almost from the beginning. While the Negro stereotypes by no means made all white men Klansmen, the cinema did, to the extent that audiences accepted its image of Negroes, make them participants in the South's racial ritual of keeping the Negro "in his place."

After Reconstruction the political question of what was to be done with Negroes, "solved" by the Hayes-Tilden deal of 1876, came down to the psychological question: "How can the Negro's humanity be evaded?" The problem, arising in a democracy that holds all men as created equal, was a highly moral one; democratic ideals had to be squared with anti-Negro practices. One answer was to *deny* the Negro's humanity, a pattern set long before 1915. But with the release of *The Birth of a Nation* the propagation of subhuman images of Negroes became financially and dramatically profitable. The Negro as scapegoat could be sold as entertainment; it could even be exported. If the film became the main manipulator of the American dream, for Negroes that dream contained a strong dose of such stuff as nightmares are made of.

We are recalling all this not so much as a means of indicting Hollywood as by way of placing *Intruder in the Dust*, and such recent films as *Home of the Brave*, *Lost Boundaries* and *Pinky*, in perspective. To direct an attack upon Hollywood would indeed be to confuse portrayal with action, image with reality. In the beginning was not the shadow but the act, and the province of Hollywood is not action, but illusion. Actually, the anti-Negro images of the films were (and are) acceptable because of the existence throughout the United States of an audience obsessed with an inner psychological need to view Negroes as less than men. Thus, psychologically and ethically, these negative images constitute justifications for all those acts, legal, emotional, economic and political, which we label Jim Crow. The anti-Negro image is a ritual object of which Hollywood is not the creator, but the manipulator. Its role has been that of justifying the widely held myth of Negro unhumanness and inferiority by offering entertaining rituals through which that myth could be reaffirmed.

The great significance of the definition of Lucas Beauchamp's role in *Intruder in the Dust* is that it makes explicit the nature of Hollywood's changed attitude toward Negroes. Form being, in the words of Kenneth Burke, "the psychology of the audience," what is taking place in the American movie patron's mind? Why these new attempts to redefine the Negro's role? What has happened to the audience's mode of thinking?

For one thing, there was the war; for another, there is the fact that the United States' position as a leader in world affairs is shaken by its treatment of Negroes. Thus the thinking of white Americans is undergoing a process of change, and reflecting that change, we find that each of the films mentioned above deals with some basic and unusually negative assumption about Negroes: are Negroes cowardly soldiers? (*Home of the Brave*); are Negroes the real polluters of the South? (*Intruder in the Dust*); have mulatto Negroes the right to pass as white, at the risk of having black babies, or if they have white-skinned children, of having to kill off their "white" identities by revealing to them that they are, alas, Negroes? (*Lost Boundaries*); and, finally, should Negro girls marry white men or—wonderful non sequitur—should they help their race? (*Pinky*).

Obviously these films are not *about* Negroes at all; they are about what whites think and feel about Negroes. And if they are taken as accurate reflectors of that thinking, it becomes apparent that there is much confusion. To make use of Faulkner's metaphor again, the film makers fell upon the eggshell ice but, unlike the child, weren't heavy enough to break it. And being unable to break it, they were unable to discover the real direction of their film narratives. In varying degree, they were unwilling to dig into the grave to expose the culprit, and thus we find them using ingenious devices for evading the full human rights of their Negroes. The result represents a defeat not only of drama, but of purpose.

In *Home of the Brave*, for instance, a psychiatrist tells the Negro soldier that his hysterical paralysis is like that of any other soldier who has lived when his friends have died, and we hear the soldier pronounced cured; indeed, we see him walk away prepared to open a bar and restaurant with a white veteran. But here there is an evasion (and by *evasion* I refer to the manipulation of the audience's attention away from reality to focus it upon false issues), because the guilt from which the Negro is supposed to suffer springs from an incident in which, immediately after his friend has called him a "yellowbelly nigger," he has wished the friend dead—only to see the wish granted by a sniper's bullet.

What happens to this racial element in the motivation of his guilt? The psychiatrist ignores it and becomes a sleight-of-hand artist who makes it vanish by repeating again that the Negro is like everybody else. Nor, I believe, is this accidental, for it is here exactly that we come to the question of whether Negroes can rightfully be expected to risk their lives in an army in which they are slandered and discriminated against. Psychiatry is not, I'm afraid, the answer. The soldier suffers from concrete acts, not hallucinations.

And so with the others. In *Lost Boundaries* the question evaded is whether a mulatto Negro has the right to practice the old American pragmatic philosophy of capitalizing upon one's assets. For after all, whiteness *has* been given an economic and social value in our culture, and for the doctor upon whose life the film is based, "passing" was the quickest and most certain means to success.

Yet Hollywood is uncertain about his right to do this. The film does not render the true circumstances. In real life Dr. Albert Johnson, the Negro doctor who "passed" as white, purchased the thriving practice of a deceased physician in Gorham, New Hampshire, for a thousand dollars. Instead, a fiction is introduced in the film wherein Dr. Carter's initial motivation for "passing" arises after he is refused an internship by dark Negroes in an Atlanta hospital because of his color! It just isn't real, since there are thousands of mulattoes living as Negroes in the South, many of them Negro leaders. The only functional purpose served by this fiction is to gain sympathy for Carter by placing part of the blame for his predicament upon black Negroes. Nor should the irony be missed that part of the sentiment evoked when the Carters are welcomed back into the community is gained by painting Negro life as horrible, a fate worse than a living death. It would seem that in the eyes of Hollywood it is only "white" Negroes who ever suffer—or is it merely the "white" corpuscles of their blood?

Pinky, for instance, is the story of another suffering mulatto, and the suffering grows out of a confusion between race and love. If we attempt to reduce the heroine's problem to sentence form we'd get something like this: "Should white-skinned Negro girls marry white men, or should they inherit the plantations of old white aristocrats (provided they can find any old aristocrats to will them their plantations), or should they live in the South and open nursery schools for black Negroes?" It doesn't follow, but neither does the action. After sitting through a film concerned with interracial marriage, we see it suddenly become a courtroom battle over whether Negroes have the right to inherit property.

Pinky wins the plantation, and her lover, who has read of the fight in the Negro press, arrives and still loves her, race be hanged. But now Pinky decides that to marry him would "violate the race" and that she had better remain a Negro. Ironically, nothing is said about the fact that her racial integrity, whatever that is, was violated before she was born. Her parents are never mentioned in the film. Following the will of the white aristocrat, who, before dying, advises her to "be true to herself," she opens a school for darker Negroes.

But in real life the choice is not between loving or denying one's race. Many couples manage to intermarry without violating their integrity, and indeed their marriage becomes the concrete expression of their integrity. In the film Jeanne Crain floats about like a sleepwalker, which seems to me to be exactly the way a girl so full of unreality would act. One thing is certain: no one is apt to mistake her for a Negro, not even a white one.

And yet despite the absurdities with which these films are laden, they are all worth seeing, and if seen, capable of involving us emotionally. That they do is testimony to the deep centers of American emotion that they touch. Dealing with matters which, over the years, have been slowly charging up with guilt, they all display a vitality which escapes their slickest devices. And naturally enough, one of the most interesting experiences connected with viewing them in predominantly white audiences is the profuse flow of tears and sighs of profound emotional catharsis heard on all sides. It is as though there were some deep relief to be gained merely from seeing these subjects projected upon the screen.

It is here precisely that a danger lies. For the temptation toward self-congratulation which comes from seeing these films and sharing in their emotional release is apt to blind us to the true nature of what is unfolding—or failing to unfold—before our eyes. As an antidote to the sentimentality of these films, I suggest that they be seen in predominantly Negro audiences, for here, when the action goes phony, one will hear derisive laughter, not sobs. (Perhaps this is what Faulkner means about Negroes keeping the white man's conscience.) Seriously, *Intruder in the Dust* is the only film that could be shown in Harlem without arousing unintended laughter, for it is the only one of the four in which Negroes can make complete identification with their screen image. Interestingly, the factors that make this identification possible lie in its depiction not of racial but of human qualities.

Yet in the end, turning from art to life, we must even break with the definition of the Negro's role given us by Faulkner. For when it comes to conscience, we know that in this world each of us, black and white alike, must become the keeper of his own. This, in the deepest sense, is what these four films, taken as a group, should help us realize.

Faulkner himself seems to realize it. In the book *Intruder in the Dust*, Lucas attempts not so much to be the keeper of anyone else's conscience as to preserve his own life. Chick, in aiding Lucas, achieves that view of truth on which his own conscience depends.

The Way It Is

THE boy looked at me through the cracked door and stood staring with his large eyes until his mother came and invited me in. It was an average Harlem apartment, cool now with the shift in the fall weather. The room was clean and furnished with the old-fashioned furniture found so often up our way: two old upholstered chairs and a divan upon a faded blue and red rug. It was painfully clean, and the furniture crowded the narrow room.

"Sit right there, sir," the woman said. "It's where Wilbur use to sit before he went to camp; it's pretty comfortable."

I watched her ease herself tiredly upon the divan, the light from the large red lamp reflected upon her face from the top of a mirrored side table.

She must have been fifty, her hair slightly graying. The portrait of a young soldier smiled back from the top of a radio cabinet beside her.

She pointed. "That's my boy Wilbur right there," she said proudly. "He's a sergeant."

"Wilbur's got a medal for shooting so good," the boy said.

"You just be quiet and go eat your supper," she said. "All you can think about is guns and shooting." She spoke with the harsh tenderness so often used by Negro mothers.

The boy went, reluctantly opening the door. The odor of peas and rice and pork chops drifted through.

"Who was it, Tommy?" shrilled a voice on the other side.

"You two be quiet in there and eat your supper now," Mrs. Jackson called. "Them two just keeps my hands full. They just get into something *all* the time. I was coming up the street the other day and like to got the fright of my life. There was Tommy hanging on the

From *New Masses*, October 20, 1942.

back of a streetcar! But didn't I tan his bottom! I bet he won't even *look* at a streetcar for a long, long time. It ain't really that he's a *bad* child; it's just that he tries to do what he sees the other boys do. I wanted to send both him and his sister away to camp for the summer, but things was so tight this year that I couldn't do it. Raising kids in Harlem nowadays is more than a notion."

As is true so often in Negro American life, Mrs. Jackson, the mother, is the head of her family. Her husband had died several years ago; the smaller children were babies. She had kept going by doing domestic work, and had kept the family together with the help of the older boy.

There is a quiet courage about Mrs. Jackson, and yet now and then the clenching and unclenching of her work-hardened fingers betray an anxiety that does not register in her face. I offer to wait until after she has eaten, but she says no, that she is too tired right now and would rather talk than eat.

"You finding the writing business any better since the war?" she asked.

"I'm afraid not," I said.

"Is that so? Well, I don't know nothing about the writing business. I just know that don't many colored go in for it. But I guess like everything else, some folks is doing good while others ain't. The other day I was over on 126th Street and saw them dispossessing a lawyer! Yes, sir, it was like back in the thirties. Things piled all over the sidewalk, the Negroes a-hanging out of the windows, and the poor man rushing around trying to get his stuff off the streets before it got dark and everything."

I remembered the incident myself, having passed through the street that afternoon. Files, chest of drawers, bedsteads, tables and barrels had been piled along the sidewalk with pink, blue and white mattresses and bundles of table linen and bedclothing piled on top. And the crowd had been as she described: some indignant, some curious, and all talking in subdued tones so as not to offend the evicted family. Law books had been piled upon the sidewalk near where a black and white kitten—and these are no writer's details—played games with itself in the coils of an upright bedspring. I told her I had seen the incident.

"Lord," she said. "And did you see all those law books he had? Looks like to me that anybody with all those books of law oughtn't to never get dispossessed.

"I was dispossessed, myself, back in thirty-seven, when we were all out of work. And they threatened me once since Wilbur's been in the Army. But I stood up for my rights, and when the government sent the check we pulled through. Anybody's liable to get dispossessed, though." She said it defensively.

"Just how do you find it otherwise?" I asked.

"Things is mighty tight, son . . . You'll have to excuse me for calling you 'son,' because I suspect you must be just about Wilbur's age." She sat back abruptly. "How come you not in the Army?" she asked.

"I've a wife and dependents," I said.

"I see." She pondered. "Wilbur would have got married too, but he was helping me with the kids."

"That's the way it goes," I said.

"Things is tight," she said again. "With food so high and everything, I sometimes don't know what's going to happen. Then, too, with Wilbur in the Army we naturally misses the money he use to bring in." She regarded me shrewdly. "So you want to know about how we're doing? Don't you live in Harlem?"

"Oh, yes, but I want to know what *you* think about it."

"So's you can write it up?"

"Some of it, sure, but I won't use your name."

"Oh, I don't care 'bout that. I *want* them to know how I feel."

She became silent. Then, "You didn't tell me where you live, you know," she said cagily. I had to laugh and she laughed too.

"I live up near Amsterdam Avenue," I said.

"You telling me the truth?"

"Honest."

"And is your place a nice one?"

"Just average. You know how they go," I said.

"I bet you live up there on Sugar Hill."

"Not me," I said.

"And you're sure you're not one of these investigators?"

"Of course not."

"I bet you are too." She smiled.

I shook my head and she laughed.

"They always starting something new," she said. "You can't keep up with them."

But now she seemed reassured and settled down to talk, her hands clasped loosely in her lap against the checkered design of her dress.

"Well, we're carrying on somehow. I'm still working and I manage to keep the young uns in school, and I pays the rent too. I guess maybe it would be a little better if the government would send the checks on time . . ."

She paused and pointed across the room to the picture of a young woman. "And it would be even better if Mary, that's my next oldest after Wilbur—if she could get some of that defense training so she could get a job what pays decent money. But it don't look like she's going to get anything. She was out to the Western Electric plant in Kearney, New Jersey, the other day and they give her some kind of test, but that was the end of that."

"Did she pass the test?" I asked.

"Sure she passed. But they just put her name down on a card and told her they would keep her in mind. They always do that. They ask her a lot of questions; then they want to know if she ever had any experience in running machines, and when she says she ain't, they just take down her name. Now where is a colored girl going to get any experience in running all these kinds of machines they never even seen before?"

When I could not answer she threw up her hands.

"Well, there you have it, they got you any which way you turn. A few gets jobs, but most don't."

"Things are much better outside of New York," I said.

"So I hear," she said. "Guess if I was younger I'd take the kids and move to Jersey or up to Connecticut, where I hear there's some jobs for colored. Or even down South. Only I keep hearing about the trouble they're having down there, and I don't want the kids to grow up down there nohow. Had enough of that when I was a kid . . ."

"Have any of your friends gotten work through the F.E.P.C.?"

She thought for a moment.

"No, son. It seems to me that that committee is doing something everywhere but here in New York. Maybe that's why it's so bad for us—and you know it's bad 'cause you're colored yourself."

As I heard the clatter of dishes coming from the kitchen, her face suddenly assumed an outraged expression.

"Now you take my sister's boy, William. God bless his poor soul. William went to the trade schools and learned all about machines. He got so he could take any kind of machine apart and fix it and put it together again. He was machine-crazy! But he was a smart boy and a good boy. He got good marks in school too. But when he went to get a job in one of those factories where they make war machines of some kind, they wouldn't take him 'cause he was colored—*and they told him so!*"

She paused for breath, a red flush dyeing her skin. The tinted portrait of a brown mother holding a brown, shiny-haired baby posed madonna-like from a calendar above her head.

"Well, when they wouldn't take him some of the folks over to the church told him to take his case to the F.E.P.C., and he did. But they had so many cases and it took so long that William got discouraged and joined up in the Merchant Marine. That poor boy was just so disgusted that he said that he would have enlisted in the Army, only that his mamma's got two little ones like I have. So he went out on that boat 'cause it paid good money and a good bonus. It was real good money and he helped his mamma a heap. But it didn't last long before one of those submarines sunk the boat."

Her eyes strayed to the window, where a line of potted plants crowded the sill, a profusion of green things slowly becoming silhouettes in the fading light. Snake plants, English ivy, and others, a potato plant in a glass jar, its vines twining around a cross of wood and its thousand thread-fine roots pushing hungrily against the wall of glass. A single red bloom pushed above the rest, and in one corner a corn plant threatened to touch the ceiling from the floor with its blade-like leaves.

The light was fading and her voice had slipped into the intense detachment of recent grief. "It was just about four months yesterday," she said. "He was such a fine boy. Everybody liked William."

She shook her head silently, her fingers gripping her folded arms as she swallowed tensely.

"It hurts to think about it," she said, getting up and snapping on another light, revealing a child's airplane model beneath the table. "Well, the folks from his union is being very nice to my sister, the whites as well as the colored. And you know," she added, leaning toward me, "it really makes you feel a little better when they come round—the white ones, I mean—and really tries to help. Like some of these ole relief investigators who come in wanting to run your life for you, but really like they interested in you. Something like colored folks, in a way. We used to get after William for being with white folks so much, but these sure have shown themselves to be real friends."

She stared at me as though it was a fact which she deeply feared to accept.

"Some of them is going to try and see that my sister gets some sort of defense work. But what I'm trying to tell you is that it's a sin and a shame that a fine boy like William had to go fooling round on them ships when ever since he was a little ole boy he'd been crazy about machines."

"But don't you think that the Merchant Marine is helping to win the war?" I said. "It takes brave men to go out there, and they've done a lot."

"Sure they have," she said. "Sure they have. But I'm not talking about that. Anybody could do what they had him doing on that boat. Anybody can wait tables who's got sense enough to keep his fingernails clean! Waiting tables, when he could *make* things on a machine!

"You see that radio there? Well, William made that radio. It ain't no store set, no, sir, even though it looks like one. William made it for the kids. Made everything but the cabinet, and you can hear way down to Cuba and Mexico with it. And to think of that boy! Oh, it makes me so mad I don't know what to do! He ought to be here right now helping his mamma and lil brother and sister. But what can you do? You educated, son, you one of our educated Negroes that's been to college and everything. Now you tell me, *what can we do?*" She paused. "I'm a colored woman, and colored women can take it. I can hit the chillies to the subway every morning and stand in the white folks' kitchen all day long, but so much is happening in the world that I don't know which way to turn. First it's my sister's boy, and then they sends my own boy down to Fort Bragg. I tells you I'm even afraid to open Wilbur's letters, some of the things he tells is so awful. I'm even afraid to open letters that the *government* sends sometimes about his insurance or something like that 'cause I'm afraid it might be a message that Wilbur's been beaten up or killed by some of those white folks down there. Then I gets so mad I don't know what to do. I use to pray, but praying don't do no good. And too, like the union folks was telling us when we was so broken up about William, we got to fight the big Hitler over yonder even with all the little Hitlers over here. I wish they'd hurry up and send Wilbur on out of the country 'cause then maybe my mind would know some ease. Lord!" she sighed. "If it wasn't so serious I'd break down and laugh at my own-self."

She smiled now and the tension eased from her face and she leaned back against the divan and laughed. Then she became serious again.

"But son, you really can't laugh about it. Not honestly laugh like you can about some things. It reminds me of that crazy man what's always running up and down the streets up here. You know, the one who's always hollering at the cars and making out like he's throwing bombs?"

"Of course, I've seen him often," I said.

"Sure you have. Well, I use to laugh at that poor man when he'd start acting the fool—you know how it is, you feel sorry for him but you can't help but laugh. They say he got that way in the last war. Well, I can understand him better now. 'Course I ain't had no bombs bursting in my ears like he had. But yet and still, with things pulling me thisaway and thataway, I sometimes feel that I'm going to go screaming up and down the streets just like that poor fellow does."

"He's shell-shocked," I said. "Sometimes I've seen him talking and acting just as normal as anyone."

"Is that so?" she said. "I always thought it was funny he never got hit by a car. I've seen them almost hit him, but he goes right back. One day I heard a man say, 'Lord, if that crazy fellow really had some bombs he'd get rid of every car in Harlem!' "

We laughed and I prepared to go.

"Sorry you found me so gloomy today, son. But you know, things have a way of just piling up these days and I just had to talk about them. Anyway, you asked for me to tell you what I thought."

She walked with me to the door. Streetlamps glowed on the avenue, lighting the early dark. The after-school cries of children drifted dimly in from the sidewalk.

She shivered close beside me. "It's getting chilly already," she said. "I'm wondering what's going to happen this winter about the oil and coal situation. These ole holes we have to live in can get mighty cold. Now can't they though?"

I agreed.

"A friend of mine that moved up on Amsterdam Avenue about a month ago wanted to know why I don't move out of Harlem. So I told her it wouldn't do no good to move 'cause anywhere they let us go gets to be Harlem right on. I done moved round too much not to know that. Oh yes!"

She shook her head knowingly.

"Harlem's like that old song says:

> *It's so high you can't get over it*
> *So low, you can't get under it,*
> *And so wide, you can't get round it . . .*

"That's the way it really is," she said. "Well, good-bye, son."

And as I went down the dimmed-out street the verse completed itself in my mind, *You must come through by the living gate . . .*

So there you have Mrs. Jackson. And that's the way "it really is" for her and many like her who are searching for that gate of freedom. In the very texture of their lives there is confusion, war-made confusion, and the problem is to get around, over, under and through this confusion. They do not ask for a lighter share of necessary war sacrifices than other Americans have to bear. But they do ask for equal reasons to believe that their sacrifices are worthwhile, and they *do* want to be rid of the heavy resentment and bitterness which has been theirs for long before the war.

Forced in normal times to live at standards much lower than those the war has brought to the United States generally, they find it emotionally difficult to give their attention to the war. The struggle for existence constitutes a war in itself. The Mrs. Jacksons of Harlem offer one of the best arguments for the stabilization of prices and the freezing of rents. Twenty-five percent of those still on relief come from our five percent of New York's population. Mrs. Jackson finds it increasingly difficult to feed her children. She must pay six cents more on the dollar for food than do the mothers of similar-income sections elsewhere in the city. With the prospect of a heatless winter, Harlem, with its poor housing and high tuberculosis death rate, will know an increase of hardship.

It is an old story. Touch any phase of urban living in our democracy, and its worst aspects are to be found in Harlem. Our housing is the poorest, and our rents the highest. Our people are the sickest, and Harlem Hospital the most overcrowded and understaffed. Our unemployment is the greatest, and our cost of food the most exorbitant. Our crime is the most understandable and easily corrected, but the policemen sent among us are the most brutal. Our desire to rid the world of fascism is the most burning, and the obstacles placed in our way are the most frustrating. Our need to see the war as a struggle between democracy and fascism is the most intense, and our temptation to interpret it as a "color" war is the most compelling. Our need to believe in the age of the "common man" is the most hope-inspiring, and our reasons to doubt that it will include us are the most disheartening. (This is no Whitmanesque catalogue of democratic exultations, while more than anything else we wish that it could be.) And that's the way it is.

Many of Mrs. Jackson's neighbors are joining in the fight to freeze rents and for the broadening of the F.E.C.P. for Negroes and all other Americans. Their very lives demand that they back the President's stabilization program. That they must be victorious is one of the necessities upon which our democratic freedom rests. The Mrs. Jacksons cannot make the sacrifices necessary to participate in a total war if the conditions under which they live, the very ground on which they must fight, continues its offensive against them. Nor is this something to be solved by propaganda. Morale grows out of realities, not out of words alone. Only concrete action will be effective, lest irritation and confusion turn into exasperation, and exasperation change to disgust and finally into anti-war sentiment (and there is such a danger). Mrs. Jackson's reality must be democratized so that she may clarify her thinking and her emotions. And that's the way it really is.

Harlem Is Nowhere

ONE must descend to the basement and move along a confusing mazelike hall to reach it. Twice the passage seems to lead to a blank wall; then at last one enters the brightly lighted auditorium. And here, finally, are the social workers at the reception desks, and there, waiting upon the benches in rows beneath the pipes carrying warmth and water to the floors above, are the patients. One sees white-jacketed psychiatrists carrying charts appear and vanish behind screens that form the improvised interviewing cubicles. All is an atmosphere of hurried efficiency, and the concerned faces of the patients are brightened by the friendly smiles and low-pitched voices of the expert workers. One has entered the Lafargue Psychiatric Clinic.

This clinic (whose staff receives no salary and whose fee is only twenty-five cents—to those who can afford it) is perhaps the most successful attempt in the nation to provide psychotherapy for the underprivileged. Certainly it has become in two years one of Harlem's most important institutions. Not only is it the sole mental clinic in the section; it is the only center in the city wherein both Negroes and whites may receive extended psychiatric care. Thus its importance transcends even its great value as a center for psychotherapy; it represents an underground extension of democracy.

As one of the few institutions dedicated to recognizing the total implication of Negro life in the United States, the Lafargue Clinic rejects all stereotypes, and may be said to concern itself with any possible variations between the three basic social factors shaping an American Negro's personality: he is viewed as a member of a racial and cultural minority, as an American citizen caught in certain political and economic relationships, and as a modern man living in a revolutionary world. Accordingly, each patient, whether white or

Unpublished. Written for *Magazine of the Year*, 1948.

black, is approached dynamically as a being possessing a cultural and biological past who seeks to make his way toward the future in a world wherein each discovery about himself must be made in the here and now at the expense of hope, pain and fear—a being who in responding to the complex forces of America has become confused.

Leaving the Lafargue Clinic for a while, what are some of the forces which generate this confusion? Who is this total Negro whom the clinic seeks to know; what is the psychological character of the scene in which he dwells; how describe the past which he drags into this scene; and what is the future toward which he stumbles and becomes confused? Let us begin with the scene: Harlem.

To live in Harlem is to dwell in the very bowels of the city; it is to pass a labyrinthine existence among streets that explode monotonously skyward with the spires and crosses of churches and clutter underfoot with garbage and decay. Harlem is a ruin; many of its ordinary aspects (its crimes, casual violence, crumbling buildings with littered area-ways, ill-smelling halls and vermin-invaded rooms) are indistinguishable from the distorted images that appear in dreams, and which, like muggers haunting a lonely hall, quiver in the waking mind with hidden and threatening significance. Yet this is no dream, but the reality of well over four hundred thousand Americans, a reality which for many defines and colors the world. Overcrowded and exploited politically and economically, Harlem is the scene and symbol of the Negro's perpetual alienation in the land of his birth.

But much has been written about the social and economic aspects of Harlem; we are here interested in its psychological character, a character that arises from the impact between urban slum conditions and folk sensibilities. Historically, American Negroes are caught in a vast process of change that has swept them from slavery to the condition of industrial man in a space of time so telescoped (a bare eighty-five years) that it is literally possible for them to step from feudalism into the vortex of industrialism simply by moving across the Mason-Dixon line.

This abruptness of change and the resulting clash of cultural factors within Negro personality account for some of the extreme contrasts found in Harlem, for both its negative and its positive characteristics. For if Harlem is the scene of the folk-Negro's death agony, it is also the setting of his transcendence. Here it is possible for talented youths to leap through the development of decades in a brief twenty years, while beside them white-haired adults crawl in the feudal darkness of their childhood. Here a former cotton picker develops the sensitive hands of a surgeon, and men whose grandparents still believe in magic prepare optimistically to become atomic scientists. Here the grandchildren of those who possessed no written literature examine their lives through the eyes of Freud and Marx, Kierkegaard and Kafka, Malraux and Sartre. It explains the nature of a world so fluid and shifting that often within the mind the real and the unreal merge, and the marvelous beckons from behind the same sordid reality that denies its existence.

Hence the most surreal fantasies are acted out upon the streets of Harlem; a man ducks in and out of traffic shouting and throwing imaginary grenades that actually exploded during World War I; a boy participates in the rape-robbery of his mother; a man beating his wife in a park uses boxing "science" and observes Marquis of Queensberry rules (no rabbit punching, no blows beneath the belt); two men hold a third while a lesbian slashes him to death with a razor blade; boy gangsters wielding homemade pistols (which in the South of their origin are but toy symbols of adolescent yearning for manhood) shoot down their young rivals. Life becomes a masquerade; exotic costumes are worn every day. Those who cannot afford to hire a horse wear riding habits; others who could not afford a hunting trip or who seldom attend sporting events carry shooting sticks.

For this is a world in which the major energy of the imagination goes not into creating works of art, but to overcome the frustrations of social discrimination. Not quite citizens and yet Americans, full of the tensions of modern man but regarded as primitives, Negro Americans are in desperate search for an identity. Rejecting the second-class status assigned them, they feel alienated and their whole lives have become a search for answers to the questions: Who am I, What am I, Why am I, and Where? Significantly, in Harlem the reply to the greeting, "How are you?" is often, "Oh, man, I'm *nowhere*"—a phrase revealing an attitude so common that it has been reduced to a gesture, a seemingly trivial word. Indeed, Negroes are not unaware that the conditions of their lives demand new definitions of terms like *primitive* and *modern*, *ethical* and *unethical*, *moral* and *immoral*, *patriotism* and *treason*, *tragedy* and *comedy*, *sanity* and *insanity*.

But for a long time now—despite songs like the "Blow Top Blues" and the eruption of expressions like *frantic*, *buggy* and *mad* into Harlem's popular speech, doubtless a word-magic against the states they name—calm in the face of the unreality of Negro life has become increasingly difficult. And while some seek relief in strange hysterical forms of religion, in alcohol and drugs, and others learn to analyze the causes for their predicament and join with others to correct them, an increasing number have found their way to the Lafargue Psychiatric Clinic.

In relation to their Southern background, the cultural history of Negroes in the North reads like the legend of some tragic people out of mythology, a people who aspired to escape from its own unhappy homeland to the apparent peace of a distant mountain, but who, in migrating, made some fatal error of judgment and fell into a great chasm of mazelike passages that promise ever to lead to the mountain but ever end against a wall. Not that a Negro is worse off in the North than in the South, but that in the North he surrenders and does not replace certain important supports to his personality. He leaves a relatively static social order in which, having experienced its brutality for hundreds of years—indeed, having been formed within it and by it—he has developed those techniques of survival which Faulkner refers to as "endurance," and an ease of movement within explosive situations which makes Hemingway's definition of courage, "grace under pressure," appear mere swagger. He surrenders the protection of his peasant cynicism—his refusal to hope for the fulfillment of hopeless hopes—and his sense of being "at home in the world" gained from confronting and accepting (for day-to-day living, at least) the obscene absurdity of his predicament. Further, he leaves a still authoritative religion which gives his life a semblance of metaphysical wholeness, a family structure which is relatively stable, and a body of folklore—tested in life-and-death terms against his daily experience with nature and the Southern white man—that serves him as a guide to action.

These are the supports of Southern Negro rationality (and, to an extent, of the internal peace of the United States); humble, but of inestimable psychological value,* they allow Southern Negroes to maintain their almost mystical hope for a future of full democracy, a hope accompanied by an irrepressible belief in some Mecca of equality located in the North and identified by the magic place names New York, Chicago, Detroit. A belief sustained (as all myth is sustained by ritual) by identifying themselves ritually with the successes of Negro celebrities, by reciting their exploits and enumerating their dollars, and by recounting the swiftness with which they spiral from humble birth to headline fame. And doubtless the blasting of this dream is as damaging to Negro personality as the slum scenes of filth, disorder and crumbling masonry in which it flies apart.

When Negroes are barred from participating in the main institutional life of society, they lose far more than economic privileges or the satisfaction of saluting the flag with unmixed emotions. They lose one of the bulwarks which men place between themselves and the constant threat of chaos. For whatever the assigned function of social institutions, their psychological function is to protect the citizen against the irrational, incalculable forces that hover about the edges of human life like cosmic destruction lurking within an atomic stockpile. And it is precisely the denial of this support through segre-

---

*Its political and economic value is the measure of both the positive and negative characteristics of American democracy.

gation and discrimination that leaves the most balanced Negro open to anxiety.

Though caught not only in the tensions arising from his own swift history, but in those conflicts created in modern man by a revolutionary world, the Negro cannot participate fully in the therapy which the white American achieves through patriotic ceremonies and by identifying himself with American wealth and power. Instead, he is thrown back upon his own "slum-shocked" institutions.

But these, like his folk personality, are caught in a process of chaotic change. His family disintegrates, his church splinters, his folk wisdom is discarded in the mistaken notion that it in no way applies to urban living, and his formal education (never really his own) provides him with neither scientific description nor rounded philosophical interpretation of the profound forces that are transforming his total being. Yet even his art is transformed; the lyrical ritual elements of folk jazz—that artistic projection of the only real individuality possible for him in the South, that embodiment of a superior democracy in which each individual cultivated his uniqueness and yet did not clash with his neighbors—have given way to the near-themeless technical virtuosity of bebop, a further triumph of technology over humanism. His speech hardens, his movements are geared to the time clock, his diet changes, his sensibilities quicken and his intelligence expands. But without institutions to give him direction, and lacking a clear explanation of his predicament—the religious ones being inadequate, and those offered by political and labor leaders obviously incomplete and opportunistic—the individual feels that his world and his personality are out of key. The phrase "I'm nowhere" expresses the feeling borne in upon many Negroes that they have no stable, recognized place in society. One's identity drifts in a capricious reality in which even the most commonly held assumptions are questionable. One "is" literally, but one is nowhere; one wanders dazed in a ghetto maze, a "displaced person" of American democracy.

And as though all this were not enough of a strain on a people's sense of the rational, the conditions under which they live are seized upon as proof of their inferiority. Thus the frustrations of Negro life (many of them the frustrations of *all* life during this historical moment) permeate the atmosphere of Harlem with what Dr. Frederick Wertham, Director of the Lafargue Clinic, terms "free-floating hostility," a hostility that bombards the individual from so many directions that he is often unable to identify it with any specific object. Some feel it the punishment of some racial or personal guilt and pray to God; others (called "evil Negroes" in Harlem) become enraged with the world. Sometimes it provokes dramatic mass responses, and the results are the spontaneous outbreaks called the "Harlem riots" of 1935 and 1943.

And why have these explosive matters, which are now a problem of our foreign policy, been ignored? Because there is an argument in progress between black men and white men as to the true nature of American reality. Following their own interests, whites impose interpretations upon Negro experience that are not only false but, in effect, a denial of Negro humanity (witness the shock when A. Philip Randolph questions, on the basis of Negro experience, the meaning of *treason*). Too weak to shout down these interpretations, Negroes live nevertheless as they have to live, and the concrete conditions of their lives are more real than white men's arguments.

And it is here exactly that lies the importance of the Lafargue Psychiatric Clinic, both as a scientific laboratory and as an expression of forthright democratic action in its scientific willingness to dispense with preconceived notions and accept the realities of Negro—i.e., *American*—life. It recognizes that the personality damage that brought it into being represents not the disintegration of a people's fiber, but the failure of a way of life. For not only is it an antidote to this failure, but it represents a victory over another of its aspects.

For ten years, while heading various psychiatric institutions, Dr. Wertham had fought for a psychiatric center in which Negroes could receive treatment. But whether he approached politicians, city agencies or philanthropists, all gave excuses for not acting. The agencies were complacent; the politicians accused him of harboring political rather than humanitarian motives; certain liberal middle-men, who stand between Negroes and philanthropic dollars, accused him of trying to establish a segregated institution. Finally it was de-cided to establish the clinic without money or official recognition. The results were electric. When his fellow psychiatrists were asked to contribute their services, Dr. Wertham was overwhelmed with offers. These physicians, all of whom hold jobs in institutions which discriminate against Negroes, were eager to overcome this frustra-tion to their science, and like some Southern Negroes who consider that part of themselves best which they hide beneath their servility, they consider their most important work that which is carried out in a Harlem basement.

Here, in the basement, a frustrated science goes to find its true object: the confused of mind who seek reality. Both find the source of their frustrations in the sickness of the social order. As such, and in spite of the very fine work it is doing, a thousand Lafargue clinics could not dispel the sense of unreality that haunts Harlem. Knowing this, Dr. Wertham and his interracial staff seek a modest achieve-ment: to give each bewildered patient an insight into the relation between his problems and his environment, and out of this under-standing to reforge the will to endure in a hostile world.

An American Dilemma:
A Review

GUNNAR MYRDAL's *An American Dilemma* is not an easy book for an American Negro to review. Not because he might be overawed by its broad comprehensiveness; nor because of the sense of alienation and embarrassment that the book might arouse by reminding him that it is necessary in our democracy for a European scientist to affirm the American Negro's humanity; not even because it is an implied criticism of his own Negro social scientists' failure to define the problem as clearly. Instead, it is difficult because the book, as a study of a social ambiguity, is itself so nearly ambiguous that in order to appreciate it fully and yet protect his own humanity, the Negro must, while joining in the chorus of "Yeas" which the book has so deservedly evoked, utter a lusty and simultaneous "Nay."

In our society it is not unusual for a Negro to experience a sensation that he does not exist in the real world at all. He seems, rather, to exist in the nightmarish fantasy of the white American mind as a phantom that the white mind seeks unceasingly, by means both crude and subtle, to lay to rest. Myrdal proves this no idle Negro fancy. He locates the Negro problem "in the heart of the [white] American . . . the conflict between his moral valuations on various levels of consciousness and generality." Indeed, the main virtue of *An American Dilemma* lies in its demonstration of how the mechanism of prejudice operates to disguise the moral conflict in the minds of whites produced by the clash on the social level between the American Creed and anti-Negro practices. There is, however, a danger in this very virtue.

For the solution of the problem of the American Negro and de-

Unpublished. Written in 1944 for *The Antioch Review*.

mocracy lies only partially in the white man's free will. Its full solution will lie in the creation of a democracy in which the Negro will be free to define himself for what he is and, within the large framework of that democracy, for what he desires to be. Let this not be misunderstood. For one is apt, in welcoming *An American Dilemma*'s democratic contribution, to forget that all great democratic documents—and there is a certain greatness here—contain a strong charge of anti-democratic elements. Perhaps the wisest attitude for democrats is not to deplore the ambiguous element of democratic writings, but to seek to understand them. For it is by making use of the positive contributions of such documents and rejecting their negative elements that democracy can be kept dynamic.

Since its inception, American social science has been closely bound with American Negro destiny. Even before the Civil War the Southern ruling class had inspired a pseudoscientific literature attempting to prove the Negro inhuman and thus beyond any moral objections to human slavery. Sociology did not become closely concerned with the Negro, however, until after Emancipation gave the slaves the status—on paper at least—of nominal citizens. And if the end of the slave system created for this science the pragmatic problem of adjusting our society to include the new citizens, the compromise between the Northern and Southern ruling classes created the moral problem which Myrdal terms the American Dilemma.

This was a period, the 1870s, wherein scientific method, with its supposed objectivity and neutrality to values, was thought to be the answer to all problems. There is no better example of the confusion and opportunism springing from this false assumption than the relation of American social science to the Negro problem. And let us make no easy distinctions here between Northern and Southern social scientists; both groups used their graphs, charts and other paraphernalia to prove the Negro's biological, psychological, intellectual and moral inferiority, one group to justify the South's exploitation of Negroes, and the other to justify the North's refusal to do anything basic about it. Here was a science whose role, beneath its illusionary non-concern with values, was to reconcile the practical morality of American capitalism with the ideal morality of the American Creed.

Now, the task of reconciling moralities is usually the function of religion and philosophy, of art and psychoanalysis—all of which find myth-making indispensable. And in this, American sociological literature rivals all three, its myth-making consisting of its "scientific" justification of anti-democratic and unscientific racial attitudes and practices. If Myrdal has done nothing else, he has used his science to discredit all of the vicious non-scientific nonsense that has cluttered our sociological literature. He has, in short, shorn it of its mythology.

It is rewarding to trace the connection between social science and the Negro a bit further. Usually when the condition of Negroes is discussed we get a morality-play explanation in which the North is given the role of good and the South that of evil. This oversimplifies a complex matter. For at the end of the Civil War, the North lost interest in the Negro. The conditions for the growth of industrial capitalism had been won and, according to Myrdal, the Negro "stood in the way of a return to national solidarity and a development of trade relations" between the North and the South. This problem was not easy to solve. Groups of Negroes had discovered the effectiveness of protest and what Myrdal shows to be the Negro's strongest weapon in pressing his claims: his hold upon the moral consciousness of Northern whites.

In order to deal with this problem the North did four things: it promoted Negro education in the South; it controlled his economic and political destiny, or allowed the South to do so; it built Booker T. Washington into a national spokesman of Negroes with Tuskegee Institute as his seat of power; and it organized social science as an instrumentality to sanction its methods.

It might be said that this explanation sounds too cynical, that much of the North's interest in Negro education grew out of a philanthropic impulse, and that it ignores the real contribution to the understanding of Negroes made by social science. But philanthropy on the psychological level is often guilt-motivated, even when most unconscious. And here, again, we have the moral conflict. When we look at the connection between Tuskegee and our most influential school of sociology, the University of Chicago, we are inclined to see more than an unconscious connection between economic interests and philanthropy, Negroes and social science.

But if on the black side of the color line Washington's "Tuskegee Machine" served to deflect Negro energy away from direct political action, on the white side of the line the moral problem nevertheless remained. It does not, therefore, seem quite accidental that the man responsible for inflating Tuskegee into a national symbol, and who is sometimes spoken of as the "power behind Washington's throne," was none other than Dr. Robert E. Park, co-founder of the University of Chicago School of Sociology.

The positive contributions of Dr. Park and those men connected with him are well established. American Negroes have benefited greatly from their research, and some of the most brilliant of Negro scholars have been connected with them. Perhaps the most just charge to be made against them is that of timidity. They have been, in the negative sense, victims of the imposed limitations of bourgeois science. Because certainly their recent works have moved closer and closer toward the conclusions made by Myrdal. Indeed, without their active participation, *An American Dilemma* would have been far less effective. Nevertheless, it was Myrdal who made the most of their findings. Perhaps it took the rise of fascism to free American social science of its timidity. Certainly it was necessary to clear it of some of the anti-Negro assumptions with which it started.

Dr. Robert E. Park was both a greater scientist and, in his attitude toward Negroes, a greater democrat than William Graham Sumner. (It will perhaps pain many to see these names in juxtaposition.) In our world, however, extremes quickly meet. Sumner believed it "the greatest folly of which man can be capable to sit down with a slate and pencil and plan out a new social world," a point of view containing little hope for the underdog. But for all his good works, some of Park's assumptions were little better. The Negro, he felt, "has always been interested rather in expression than in action; interested in life itself rather than in its reconstruction or reformation. The Negro is, by natural disposition, neither an intellectual nor an idealist, like the Jew; nor a brooding introspective, like the East Indian; nor a pioneer and frontiersman, like the Anglo-Saxon. He is primarily an artist, loving life for its own sake. His *métier* is expression rather than action. He is, so to speak, the lady among the races."

Park's descriptive metaphor is so pregnant with mixed motives as to birth a thousand compromises and indecisions. Imagine the effect such teachings have had upon Negro students alone! Thus what started as part of a democratic attitude, ends not only uncomfortably close to the preachings of Sumner, but to those of Dr. Goebbels as well.

One becomes impatient with those critics who accuse American capitalism of neglecting social planning. Actually its planning lay in having the loosest plan possible, and when it was economically expedient to change plans it has been able to do so. During the Abolitionist period the moral nature of the Negro problem was generally recognized, but with the passing of the Reconstruction the moral aspect was forced out of consciousness. Significantly, Booker T. Washington wrote a biography in which he deliberately gave the *coup de grâce* to the memory of Frederick Douglass, the Negro leader who, in his aggressive career, united the moral and political factions for the anti-slavery struggle.

Following World War I, under the war-stimulated revival of democracy, there was a brief moment when the moral nature of the problem threatened to come alive in the minds of white Americans. This time it was rationalized by projecting into popular fiction the stereotype of the Negro as an exotic primitive, while social science, under the pressure of war production needs, was devoted to proving that Negroes were not so inferior as a few decades before. It was during this period that some of the most scientifically valid concepts for understanding the Negro were advanced. But social science did not have the courage of its own research. Following its vital Jamesian influence it began to discover the questionable values it supported and, until Myrdal arrived, timidly held its breath. Why, then, should Myrdal be brought into the country in 1937 by the Carnegie Foundation to prepare this study and not before? Why this sudden junking of ideological fixtures?

According to F. P. Keppel, who writes the foreword for the trustees of the Carnegie Corporation: "The underlying purpose of these studies is to contribute to the general advancement and diffusion of knowledge and understanding." There was, Mr. Keppel admits, another reason, namely "the need of the foundation itself for fuller light in the formulation and development of its own program." Former Secretary of War Newton D. Baker, target of much Negro discontent over the treatment of Negro soldiers during the last war, suggested the study, and the board agreed with him that "more knowledge and better organized and interrelated knowledge [of the Negro problem] were essential before the Corporation could intelligently distribute its own funds," and that "the gathering and digestion of the material might well have a usefulness far beyond our own needs."

These, we must admit, are all good reasons, although a bit vague. One thing, however, is clear: a need was felt for a new ideological approach to the Negro problem. This need was general, and if we look for a moment at those two groups—the left-wing parties and the New Deal—that showed the greatest concern with the Negro problem during the period between the Depression and the outbreak of the war, we are able to see how the need expressed itself.

Both the Left and the New Deal showed a far less restrained approach to the Negro than any groups since the Abolitionists. The Left brought the world view of Marxism into the Negro community, introduced new techniques of organization and struggle, and included the Negro in its program on a basis of equality. Within its far more rigid framework the New Deal moved in the same democratic direction. Nevertheless, for all their activity, both groups neglected sharp ideological planning where the Negro was concerned. Both, it might be said, went about solving the Negro problem without defining the nature of the problem beyond its economic and narrowly political aspects. Which is not unusual for politicians, only here both groups consistently professed and demonstrated far more social vision than the average political party.

The most striking example of this failure is to be seen in the New Deal administration's perpetuation of a Jim Crow army, and the shamefaced support of it given by the Communists. It would be easy—on the basis of some of the slogans attributed to Negro people by the Communists from time to time, and the New Deal's frequent retreats on Negro issues—to question the sincerity of these two groups. Or, in the case of the New Deal, to attribute its failure to its desire to hold power in a concrete political situation, while the failure of the Communists could be laid to "Red perfidy." But this would be silly. Sincerity is not a quality that one expects of political parties, not even revolutionary ones. To question their sincerity makes room for the old idea of paternalism, and the corny notion that these groups have an obligation to "do something *for* the Negro."

The only sincerity to be expected of political parties is that flexible variety whereby they are enabled to put their own programs into effect. Regardless of their long-range intentions, on the practical level they are guided not by humanism as much as by expediencies of power. Thus if there is any insincerity here, it lies in the failure of these groups to make the best of their own interests by basing their alliances with Negroes upon a more scientific knowledge of the subtleties of Negro-white relations.

Dismissing the New Deal point of view as the eclectic creation of a capitalism in momentary retreat, what was influencing the Communists, who emphasized the unity of theory and practice? This, we believe, sprang from their inheritance of the American Dilemma (which, incidentally disproves the Red-baiters' charge that left-wingers are alien). Despite its projection of a morality based upon Marxist internationalism, it had inherited the moral problem centering upon the Negro which Myrdal finds in the very tissue of American thinking. And while we disagree with Myrdal's assumption that the psychological barrier between black and white workers is relatively rigid—their co-operation in unions and war plants disproves this—he has done the Left a service in pointing out that there *is* a psychological problem which in this country requires special attention.

For in our culture the problem of the irrational, that blind spot in our knowledge of society where Marx cries out for Freud and Freud for Marx, but where approaching, both grow wary and shout insults lest they actually meet, has taken the form of the Negro problem.

In Europe it was the fascists who made the manipulation of myth and symbol a vital part of their political technology. But here at home, it was only the Southern ruling class that showed a similar skill for psychology and ideological manipulation. By contrast, the planning of the Northern ruling groups in relation to the South and the Negro has always presented itself as non-planning and philanthropy on the surface, and as sociological theory underneath. Until the Depression the industrial and social isolationism of the South was felt to offer the broadest possibility for business exploitation. But attempts at national economic recovery proved this idea outdated; Northern capital could no longer turn its head while the Southern ruling group went its regressive way. Hence the New Deal's assault upon the ignorance and backwardness of the Southern "one-third of a nation." There was a vague recognition that the economic base of American capitalism had become dislocated from its ideological superstructure. However, the nation, so technologically advanced and scientifically alert, showed itself amazingly backward in creating or borrowing techniques to bring these two aspects of social reality into focus. Not that the nature of the problem was not understood. Writers ranging from Earl Browder, to Max Lerner, to the New Deal braintrusters had a lot to say about it. Lerner especially emphasized the technological and psychological nature of the problem, stressed the neutrality of techniques, and suggested learning even from the Nazis, if necessary. But for the most part, both New Deal and the official Left concentrated more upon the economic aspects of the problem, important though they were, than upon those points where economic and psychological pressures conflicted.

There is a certain ironic fittingness about the fact that these volumes, prepared with the streamlined thoroughness of a *Fortune* magazine survey, and offering the most detailed documentation of the American Negro's humanity yet to appear, should come sponsored by a leading capitalist group. I say this grudgingly, for here the profit motive of the Right—clothed, it is true, in the guilt-dress of philanthropy—has proven more resourceful, imaginative and aware of its own best interests than the overcautious socialism of the Left. Not that we expect the Left to have at its disposal the funds—some $300,000—that went into the preparation of this elaborate study. But it has failed even to *state* the problem in such broadly human terms, or with that cultural sophistication and social insight springing from Marxist theory, which, backed by passion and courage, has allowed the Left in other countries to deal more creatively with reality than the Right, and to overcome the Right's advantages of institutionalized power and erudition.

The reviewers have made much of Dr. Myrdal's being a foreigner, imported to do the study as one who had no emotional stake in the American Dilemma. And while this had undoubtedly aided his objectivity, the extent of it is apt to be overplayed.

The whole setting is dramatic. A young scholar-scientist of international reputation, a banker, economic adviser to the Swedish government and a member of the Swedish senate, is invited by one of the wealthiest groups in the United States to come in and publicly air its soiled democratic linen. Bearing this set of circumstances in mind while we consider the writing problem faced by Myrdal, we can see how the various social and economic factors which we have discussed come to bear upon his book.

First, Myrdal had to delve into those areas of the American mind most charged with emotion; he had to question his hosts' motivation and present his findings in such a way that his hosts would not be too offended. He had also to tell the South some unpleasant things about itself; he had to present facts unacceptable to certain reactionary sections of the capitalist class, and, in the words of Mr. Keppel, he had, "since the emotional factor affects Negroes no less than whites," to present his material in such a manner as not to "lessen the confidence of the Negroes in the United States."

And when we consider the great ideological struggle raging since the Depression, between the Left and the Right, we see an even further problem for the author: a problem of style, which fades over into a problem of interpretation. It also points to the real motivation for the work: An American Dilemma *is the blueprint for a more effective exploitation of the South's natural, industrial and human resources.* We use the term "exploitation" in both the positive and negative sense. In the positive sense it is the key to a more democratic and fruitful usage of the South's natural and human resources; in the negative, it is the plan for a more efficient and subtle manipulation of black and white relations, especially in the South.

In interpreting the results of this five-year study, Myrdal found that it confirmed many of the social and economic assumptions of the Left, and throughout the book he has felt it necessary to carry on a running battle with Marxism. Especially irritating to him has been the concept of class struggle and the economic motivation of anti-Negro prejudice which to an increasing number of Negro intellectuals correctly analyzes their situation:

> As we look upon the problem of dynamic social causation, this approach is unrealistic and narrow. We do not, of course,

deny that the conditions under which Negroes are allowed to earn a living are tremendously important for their welfare. But these conditions are closely interrelated to all other conditions of Negro life. When studying the variegated causes of discrimination in the labor market, it is, indeed, difficult to perceive what precisely is meant by "the economic factor. . . ." In an interdependent system of dynamic causation there is no "primary cause" but everything is cause *to* everything else.

To which one might answer, "Only if you throw out the class struggle." All this, of course, avoids the question of power *and* the question of who manipulates that power. Which to us seems more of a stylistic maneuver than a scientific judgment. For those concepts Myrdal substitutes what he terms a "cumulative principle" or "vicious circle." And like Ezekiel's wheels in the Negro spiritual, one of which ran "by faith" and the other "by the grace of God," this vicious circle has no earthly prime mover. It "just turns."

L. D. Reddick has pointed out that Myrdal tends to use history simply as background and not as a functioning force in current society. And we see this as one with Myrdal's refusal to locate the American *ethos* in terms of its material manifestations, or to point out how it is manipulated, although he makes it the basis of his stylistic appeal. It is unlikely in this mechanist-minded culture that such a powerful force would go "unused."

Myrdal's stylistic method is admirable. In presenting his findings he uses the American *ethos* brilliantly to disarm all American social groupings by appealing to their stake in the American Creed, and to locate the psychological barriers between them. But he also uses it to deny the existence of an American class struggle, and with facile economy it allows him to avoid admitting that actually there exist *two* American moralities, kept in balance by social science.

The limitations of Myrdal's vision of American democracy do not lie vague and misty beyond the horizon of history. They can be easily discerned through the Negro perspective.

Myrdal's study of the Negro is, in comparison with others, micro-scopic. Here, to name only a few aspects, we find analyses of Negro institutions, class groupings, family organization, economic prob-lems, race theories and prejudices, the Negro press, church and lead-ership. Some of the insights are brilliant, especially those through which he demonstrates how many Negro personality traits, said to be "innate," are socially conditioned, even to types of Negro laugh-ter and vocal intonation. But with all this he can only conclude that "the Negro's entire life and, consequently, also his opinions on the Negro problem are, in the main, to be considered as secondary reac-tions to more primary pressures from the side of the dominant white majority."

But can a people (its faith in an idealized American Creed not-withstanding) live and develop for over three hundred years simply by *reacting*? Are American Negroes simply the creation of white men, or have they at least helped to create themselves out of what they found around them? Men have made a way of life in caves and upon cliffs; why cannot Negroes have made a life upon the horns of the white man's dilemma?

Myrdal sees Negro culture and personality simply as the product of a "social pathology." Thus he assumes that "it is to the advantage of American Negroes as individuals and as a group to become assimi-lated into American culture, to acquire the traits held in esteem by the dominant white Americans." This, he admits, contains the value premise that "*here in America*, American culture is 'highest' in the pragmatic sense. . . ." Which, aside from implying that Negro cul-ture is not also American, assumes that Negroes should desire noth-ing better than what whites consider highest. But in the "pragmatic sense" lynching and Hollywood, fadism and radio advertising are products of the "higher" culture, and the Negro might ask, "Why, if my culture is pathological, must I exchange it for these?"

It does not occur to Myrdal that many of the Negro cultural man-ifestations which he considers merely reflective might also embody a *rejection* of what he considers "higher values." There is a dualism at work here. It is only partially true that Negroes turn away from white patterns because they are refused participation. There is nothing like distance to create objectivity, and exclusion gives rise to counter values. Men, as Dostoevsky observed, cannot live in revolt. Nor can they live in a state of "reacting." It will take a deeper science than Myrdal's, deep as that might be, to analyze what is happening among the masses of Negroes. Much of it is inarticulate, and Negro scholars have for the most part ignored it through clinging, as does Myrdal, to the sterile concept of "race."

Much of Negro culture might be negative, but there is also much of great value and richness, which, because it has been secreted by living and has made their lives more meaningful, Negroes will not willingly disregard.

What is needed in our country is not an exchange of pathologies, but a change of the basis of society. This is a job which both Negroes and whites must perform together. In Negro culture there is much of value for America as a whole. What is needed are Negroes to take it and create of it "the uncreated consciousness of their race." In doing so they will do far more; they will help create a more human American.

Certainly it would be unfair to expect Dr. Myrdal to see what Negro scholars and most American social scientists have failed to see. After all, like most of its predecessors, *An American Dilemma* has a special social role. And while we do not quarrel with it on these grounds necessarily, let us see it clearly for what it is. Its positive contribution is certainly greater at this time than those negative elements—hence its uncritical reception. The time element is important. For this period of democratic resurgence created by the war, *An American Dilemma* justifies the desire of many groups to see a more democratic approach to the Negro. The military phase of the war will not, however, last forever. It is then that this study might be used for less democratic purposes. Fortunately its facts are to an extent neutral. This is a cue for liberal intellectuals to get busy to see that *An American Dilemma* does not become an instrument of an American tragedy.

WORKING NOTES FOR
INVISIBLE MAN

*S*ometime *after beginning* Invisible Man *in 1945, Elli-son composed these undated notes. They show him ground-ing his metaphor of invisibility in the American Negro experience—"out of this conflict personalities of extreme complexity emerge." The notes point toward the deepening evolution of* Invisible Man's *personality in the finished novel. Found in his papers, this selection from the "Work-ing Notes" appears in print here for the first time.*

First a couple of underlying assumptions: "Invisibility," as our rather strange character comes in the end to conceive it, springs from two basic facts of American life: from the racial conditioning which often makes the white American interpret cultural, physical, or psychological differences as signs of racial inferiority; and, on the other hand, it springs from a great formlessness of Negro life wherein all values are in flux, and where those institutions and patterns of life which mold the white American's personality are missing or not so immediate in their effect. Except for its upper levels, where it tends to merge with the American whole, Negro life is a world psychologically apart. Its tempo of development from the feudal-folk forms of the South to the industrial urban forms of the North is so rapid that it throws up personalities as fluid and changeable as molten metal rendered iridescent from the effect of cooling air. Its class lines are fluid, its values unstable, and it is in conflict with the white world to which it is bound. Out of this conflict personalities of extreme complexity emerge, personalities which in a short span of years move from the level of the folk to that of the sophisticate, who combine enough potential forms of Western personality to fill many lives, and who are "broad" in the sense of which Ivan Karamazov spoke. Sometimes in responding to the conflict between their place in life as Negroes and the opportunities of America which are denied them, these personalities act out their wildest fantasies; they assume many guises without too much social opposition (Father Divine becomes God) first because within the Negro world the necessities of existence, those compromises men must make in order to survive, are such that they do not allow for a too rigid defining of value or personality (only the lower-class Negroes create their own values, the middle class seeks to live up to those of the whites);

second, because whites tend to regard Negroes in the spirit of the old song "All Coons Look Alike to Me," seldom looking past the abstraction "Negro" to the specific "man." Thus a Negro is rendered invisible—and to an extent invincible when he, as our hero comes to do, attempts to take advantage of the white man's psychological blind spot. And even this involves a sacrifice of personality and manhood on the Negro's part, and many of his actions are motivated by spite and an effort to revenge himself against this scheme of things.

The other thing to be said about our character specifically is that he is a man born into a tragic national situation who attempts to respond to it as though it were completely logical. He has accepted the definition of himself handed down by the white South and the paternalism of northern philanthropy. He sets out with the purpose of succeeding within the tight framework granted him by jim crow, and he blinds himself to all those factors of reality which reveal the essential inadequacy of such a scheme for the full development of personality.

Ironically, he also represents the Negro individualist, the personality that breaks away from the pre-individual community of southern Negro life to win its way in the jim crow world by guile, uncletomming, or ruthlessness. In order to do this he must act within the absurd predicament in which Negroes find themselves upon the assumption that all is completely logical. Against the tragic-comic attitude adopted by folk Negroes (best expressed by the blues and in our scheme by Trueblood) he is strictly, during the first phase of his life, of the nineteenth century. Thus neither he nor Mr. Norton, whose abolitionist father's creation he is, can respond to Trueblood's stoicism, or to the Vet's need to get close to the naked essence of the world as he has come to see it. Life is either tragic or absurd, but Norton and the boy have no capacity to deal with such ambivalence. The boy would appease the gods; it costs him much pain to discover that he can satisfy the gods only by rebelling against them. Invisible Man has dedicated himself to a false dream but one that has been presented couched in the form of the great rituals of human hope, such as Barbee with a semi-folk evocation of the Founder—mocked by time and reality in the very process—attempts to manipulate in his address to the student body. It is this hope which gives Invisible Man's quest any semblance of dignity.

A SPECIAL MESSAGE TO SUBSCRIBERS

Ellison wrote this account of the transition from his "prison camp novel" to the first stirrings of Invisible Man *in 1979 for the Franklin Library edition. It was published in 1980 as the preface to this limited special edition.*

In the winter of 1944, during the Battle of the Bulge, I served on a ship which was too busy keeping war materiel flowing across the North Atlantic to take time out for the routine flushing of its water tanks. As a result, two months of drinking water so supersaturated with rust that it trickled from the taps as red as tomato soup had given me a kidney infection. This, fortunately, was a gradual development and had allowed me to continue functioning. But once we had reached the decimated harbor area of Le Havre, the condition was suddenly precipitated.

During most of that voyage I had managed to give my off-duty hours over to writing, but writers—like athletes—are more or less dependent upon their physical and mental condition. Thus it was, ailing in kidney and in art, that I had returned to New York, taken sick leave, and gone with my wife to Vermont for recuperation. The abrupt transition from war to peace, however, made for a wry sense of discontinuity. I kept grappling in the depths of my subconscious to pump the air of inspiration into the depths where it was needed, and complete the novel I had just begun prior to my entering the merchant service. It was a prison-camp novel of imagination that hinged on a combustible alignment of national and racial antagonism.

As I sat at my typewriter in the open doorway of a spacious old barn in the green Vermont shade, creatures from Afro-American fables—Jack-the-Rabbit and Jack-the-Bear—blended in my mind with figures of myth and history about whom I'd been reading: those tracings of the sinister ties which bind the generations in that basic parade of human vision whereby the sighted are often blind and the sightless most perceptive, the son his own father-in-law, and the dedicated and self-righteous detective his own elusive criminal. Images of incest and murder, dissolution and rebirth whirled in my head.

As though such a weird gush of flotsam wasn't enough to plunge me into despair, it all became mixed with memories of such inter-connected events as the Moscow Trials, the Spanish Civil War, the Russo-German Pact; agitation for equal employment in the war in-dustries, protests against segregation in the armed forces and for the assignment of the 99th Fighter Squadron to combat; A. Phillip Ran-dolph's threat to lead Negroes in a march on Washington and F.D.R.'s positive response; and the struggle to prevent Harlem's ab-sentee landlords from evicting their indigent tenants. It was as though I had entered a haunted wood wherein every detail of scene, each thought and incipient action, sprang together and became en-dowed with a surreal and sinister significance. Almost everything about me seemed bent upon contributing to my growing sense of the irrational disorder of life and the utter futility of my desperate pro-ject.

But then, one afternoon, when my mind was still bent on its nutty wanderings, my fingers took over and typed what was to become the very first sentence of the present novel, "I am an invisible man"—an assertion so outrageous and unrelated to anything I was trying to write that I snatched it from the machine and was about to destroy it. But then, rereading it, I became intrigued. And as I sat musing, the words began to sound with a familiar timbre of voice. Who, I asked myself, would make such a statement—and out of what kind of expe-rience? And suddenly I could hear in my head a blackface comedian bragging on the stage of Harlem's Apollo Theatre to the effect that each generation of his family was becoming so progressively black of complexion that no one, not even its own mother, had ever been able to see the two-year-old baby. The audience had roared with laugh-ter, and I recognized something of the same joking, in-group Negro American irony sounding from my rumpled page. Slowly, like an image surfacing from the layers of an exposed Polaroid exposure, a shadow of the speaker arose in my mind and I grasped at his range of implication.

He had described himself as "invisible" which, given his Afro-American linguistic style, suggested a play on words inspired by a then popular sociological formulation which held that black Americans saw dark days because of their "high visibility." Translated into the ironic mode of Negro American idiom this meant that God had done it all with his creative tar brush back when He had said, "Let there be light," and that Negroes suffered discrimination and were penalized not because of their individual infractions of the rules which give order to American society, but because they, like flies in the milk, were just naturally more visible than white folk. In other words, this was a condition more damning than the original misconduct of Adam and Eve. And if this were true, there was no God-given or man-made ritual through which blacks could achieve social redemption. In this dark light "high visibility" and "in-visibility" were, in effect, one and the same. And, since black folk did not look at themselves out of the same eyes with which they were viewed by whites, their condition and fate rested within the eye of the beholder. If this were true, the obligation of making oneself seen and heard was an imperative of American democratic individualism. It even raised the possibility that whites didn't always regard one another with the same focus of vision—but that was another matter.

INDIVISIBLE MAN

Crafted from observation, correspondence, and conversation, this essay is a collaboration between Ellison and James Alan McPherson, author of Hue and Cry *and* Elbow Room. *Throughout Ellison casts his "cold Oklahoma Negro eye" upon literature, race, culture, and craft, confessing that for him "craft is an aspect of morality." It was published in* The Atlantic, *December 1970.*

> The Individual stands in opposition to society, but he is nourished
> by it. And it is far less important to know what differentiates him
> than what nourishes him.
>
> —*André Malraux*

July, 1969

RALPH Ellison, a pair of high-powered binoculars close to his eyes, sits by the window of his eighth-floor Riverside Drive apartment, looking down. Across the street, in the long strip of green park which parallels the Hudson River, two black boys are playing basketball. "I watch them every afternoon," he says, and offers the binoculars to me. I look down and recognize the hope of at least two major teams, ten years hence, developing. Perhaps future sociologists will say that they possess superior athletic abilities because of biological advantages peculiar to blacks; but perhaps by then each of these black boys will have gained enough of a sense of who he is to reply, "I'm good at what I do because I practiced it all my life." The encouragement of this sort of self-definition has become almost a crusade with Ellison. But I also recognize that if I ran down and waved my arms and shouted to them, "Did you know that Ralph Ellison watches you playing every afternoon?" they would continue to shoot at the basket and answer, "Who is Ralph Ellison?"

"He spoke at Tougaloo last year," a black exchange student at Santa Cruz told me. "I can't stand the man."

"Why?"

"I couldn't understand what he was saying. He wasn't talking to *us.*"

"Did you read his book?"

"No. And I don't think I will, either. I can't stand the man."

If you ask him about the Tougaloo experience, Ellison will laugh and then tell an anecdote about the stuttering black student who said: "Mr. E-i-li-s-s-s-*on*, I r-r-*ead* your b-b-o*ok The* Inv-v-v-si-b-b-*ble* M-m-*man*. B-b-but after he-e-e-ar*ing* you tonight I f-f-*feel* like I j-j-ju-*ust* hear-r-*rd* J-j-je-*sus* C-c-ch-r-r-*rist* d-d-d-runk on *Thunder-bird Wine!*" And if you laugh along with him, and if you watch Ellison's eyes as you laugh, you will realize that he is only testing a deep scar to see if it has healed.

Ellison's difficulty, one cause of all the cuts, is that matter of self-definition. At a time when many blacks, especially the young, are denying all influences of American culture, Ellison, as always, doggedly affirms his identity as a Negro-American, a product of the blending of both cultures. But more than this, he attempts to explore most of the complex implications of this burden in his fiction, his essays, his speeches, and his private life. He is nothing as simple as a "brown-skinned aristocrat" (as Richard Kostelanetz characterized him in a *Shenandoah* essay-portrait last summer); rather, he is a thinking black man who has integrated his homework into the fabric of his private life. "I don't recognize any white culture," he says. "I recognize no American culture which is not the partial creation of black people. I recognize no American style in literature, in dance, in music, even in assembly-line processes, which does not bear the mark of the American Negro." And he means it. For this reason he has difficulty reconciling some of the ideas of black nationalists, who would view black culture as separate from the broader American culture. To these people he says, "I don't recognize any black culture the way many people use the expression." And Ellison is one of the few black intellectuals who have struggled to assess the influence of the black on American culture and the relationships between the two. But, until fairly recently, not many blacks—perhaps even college-educated blacks—knew that he existed.

In 1952 Ellison published his first novel, *Invisible Man*, which won a National Book Award; and this at a time when the white critical Establishment was less eager to recognize literary achievement by black Americans. Now, almost nineteen years later, he is still the only black American who has received this honor. The novel has gone through twenty paperback printings and was judged, in a 1965 *Book Week* poll of two hundred authors, critics, and editors, "the most distinguished single work published in the last twenty years." A second book, a collection of essays and interviews called *Shadow and Act*, was published in 1964, and is essential reading for any attempt at understanding Ellison, the man or the artist. While *Invisible Man* is a story of one man's attempt to understand his society and himself, the essays outline Ellison's own successful struggle to master the craft of the writer and to understand, and then affirm, the complexities of his own rich cultural experience.

Ellison likes to call himself a college dropout because he completed only three years of a music major at Tuskegee Institute before coming to New York in 1936. Before that he was a shoeshine boy, a jazz musician, a janitor, a free-lance photographer, and a man who hunted game during the Depression to keep himself alive.

Today he is a member, and a former vice president, of the National Institute of Arts and Letters, a member of New York's Century club and the American Academy of Arts and Sciences, and a trustee of the John F. Kennedy Center for the Performing Arts. He is a former teacher at Bard, Rutgers, and Chicago, and presently is Albert Schweitzer Professor in the Humanities at New York University. He has an interest in noncommercial television which began with his work on the Carnegie Commission on Educational Television, and continues with his trusteeships in the Educational Broadcasting Corporation, and the National Citizens' Committee for Broadcasting. Among his awards are listed the Russwurm Award, the Medal of Freedom (awarded by President Johnson), five honorary Ph.D.'s, and one of the highest honors which France can bestow on a foreign writer: Chevalier de l'Ordre des Arts et Lettres, awarded to him in 1970 by the French Minister of Cultural Affairs, André Malraux. But all these experiences seem to have equal weight in his mind; all seem to have given equal access to information, equal opportunity for observation of the culture. And he is as likely to begin a discussion with some observation made when he was a shoeshine boy as he is to mention the first names of some of America's most respected writers and critics.

Ellison's success does not prove, as one writer says, that "a fatherless American Negro really does have the opportunity to become the author of one of America's greatest novels, as well as an aristocratic presence and an all but universally respected literary figure." His achievements are too enormous to be reduced to a sociological cliché, a rhetorical formulation. If anything, his success proves that intelligence, perseverance, discipline, and love for one's work are together too great a combination to be contained, or even defined, in terms of race.

Although he lives in New York and has access to literary and intellectual areas, Ellison seems to have very limited contact with the black writers who also live there. Yet his shadow lies over all their writers' conferences, and his name is likely to be invoked, and defamed, by any number of the participants at any conference. One man has said that he would like to shoot Ellison. Another, whom Ellison has never met, has for almost ten years blamed Ellison for his not receiving the last Prix de Rome Award, given by the American Academy of Arts and Letters. On the other hand, a growing number of young black writers, among them Ernest J. Gaines, Cecil Brown, Michael Harper, Ishmael Reed, and Al Young, are quick to admit their respect for him.

He reads the work of black writers, dismisses some of it, and is always willing to give an endorsement. And although he is very protective of his time, his telephone number is listed in the Manhattan directory, and he will usually grant an interview or a few hours of conversation in the afternoon (his working day usually ends at 4:00 P.M.) to anyone who is insistent.

"A fellow called me one morning," Ellison chuckles, lighting up a cigar, "said he just had to see me. So I consented. I went to the door, and there was a brown-skinned fellow from the Village. He brought a bottle of wine, several records, and four attempts at short stories. I looked at these things, and they weren't really stories, so I asked, 'What do you want me to tell you?' He said, 'Well, what I want you to do is to tell me, should I just write, or should I tell the truth?' " Ellison pauses to laugh deep in his chest. "I said, 'Tell the truth.' "

"He came to Oberlin in April of 1969," a black girl in Seattle recalled. "His speech was about how American black culture had blended into American white culture. But at the meeting with the black caucus after the speech, the black students said, 'You don't have anything to tell us.' "

"What did he say?"

"He just accepted it very calmly. One girl said to him, 'Your book doesn't mean anything because in it you're shooting down Ras the Destroyer, a rebel leader of black people.' "

"What was his answer?"

"He said, 'Remember now, this book was written a long time ago. This is just one man's view of what he saw, how he interpreted what he saw. I don't make any apologies for it.' Well, she went on to tell him, 'That just proves that you're an Uncle Tom.' "

Another of Ellison's problems, one peculiar to any black who attempts to assert his own individuality in his own terms, is that he challenges the defense mechanisms of the black community. Because of a history of enforced cohesiveness, some blacks have come to believe in a common denominator of understanding, even a set number of roles and ideas which are assumed to be useful to the community. Doctors, lawyers, teachers, social workers, some orthodox thinkers, some orthodox writers are accepted—as long as they do not insist on ideas which are foreign to the community's own sense of itself. But when a black man attempts to think beyond what has been thought before, or when he asserts a vision of reality which conflicts with or challenges the community's conception, there is a movement, some-times unconscious, to bring him back into line or, failing that, to ostracize him. The "mass man" of sociological terminology is the "right-on man" of black slang, gliding smoothly and simplistically, and perhaps more comfortably, over questionable assumptions, and reducing himself to a cliché in the process. For a black thinker such as Ellison, this assertion of individual vision is especially painful be-cause the resultant ostracism carries with it the charge of "selling out" or "trying to be white." Yet a white thinker who challenges assumptions held by whites about themselves is not charged with "trying to be black." The underlying assumption is that whites have a monopoly on individuality and intelligence, and in order for a black man to lay claim to his own, he must necessarily change color.

In response to charges by attackers that he is a "token Negro" because he is very often the only black serving on cultural commis-sions, Ellison says, "All right, if you don't want me on, I'll resign. But you had better put a *cardboard Negro* in my place because when deci-sions are made which will affect black people you had better make sure that those people who make the decisions remember that you exist and are forced to make sure that some of your interests are being met."

This impulse toward leveling, however, is not confined to the black community. It is a minority-group reaction. And while Ellison remembers a black professor at Tuskegee who tore up a leather-bound volume of Shakespeare's plays to discourage his interest in literature, he also remembers a white professor friend who said, "Ah, here's Ralph again, talking about America. There's no goddamn America out there."

"At Oberlin," the Seattle girl said, "one of the ideas they couldn't accept was Ellison's statement that black styles had historically been incorporated into American life. He went on to say that in the future, don't be surprised if white people begin to wear Afros because that's now a part of American popular culture. Well, the kids went out screaming, 'Who is he to insult what we wear? No honky could wear an Afro. They're stealing what is ours.' "

One year later, disenchanted white youth, on both coasts and in between, are sporting their versions of the Afro.

Iowa City, Iowa
June, 1969

Dear Mr. Ellison:
    I would like to come and talk with you. . . .

New York, New York
June, 1969

Dear Mr. McPherson:
    Will you be in the East on July 7? I can see you at 3:00 P.M.

Ellison is as practiced a listener as he is a speaker, and gives even the most naïvely put question thorough consideration before responding. He is a bit guarded at first, perhaps unwinding from a day at his desk, perhaps adjusting to the intellectual level of his guest. Then he begins talking, occasionally pausing to light a cigar, occasionally glancing out the window at the street, the park, the river beyond. After a while you both are trading stories and laughing while Mrs. Ellison makes noises in the kitchen, just off the living room. A parakeet flutters into the room. Ellison calls it, imitating its chirps, and the bird comes and hovers near his hand. "Have you ever heard a dog talk?" he asks.

"No."

We go into his study, and he plays a tape of a dog clearly imitating the rhythm and pitch of a human voice saying "hello." We listen again, and laugh again. Mrs. Ellison calls us to dinner. It is difficult to enjoy the food and digest his conversation at the same time.

"Ralph, stop talking and let him eat," Mrs. Ellison says.

After dinner we move back into the living room and continue the conversation. Finally Ellison's dog, Tucka Tarby, comes into the room and walks back and forth between us. Then you realize that it is well after midnight and that you have put a serious dent in the essential personal rhythm of a writer's day. Tucka has been patient, waiting for his evening walk. Ellison puts on an army jacket and we go down in the elevator. This is an old building, just on the edge of Harlem, and most of the tenants are black. The lobby has colored tiles, a high ceiling, and live flowers protected by glass. "I've lived here for eighteen years," he says. "But it wasn't until 1964 that some of the people found out I was a writer." Tucka pulls us up 150th Street toward Broadway. We shake hands, and he and the dog walk off into the Harlem night.

"I think that what made it hard for him," the Seattle girl said, "was that LeRoi Jones was coming to Oberlin that next day. The kids figured that Jones the Master is coming, so let's get rid of this cat. But I think he's very gutsy, in a day like today with all these so-called militants trying to run him into the ground, coming to Oberlin saying to the kids, 'You are American, not African.' "

"Did anyone come to his defense?"

"One of the teachers stopped the meeting at one point and said, 'Would you please listen to what the man has to say? You're sitting here criticizing, and some of you haven't even read the damn book.' "

Among his peers Ellison's presence or even the mention of his name causes the immediate arming of intellectual equipment. There can be no soft-pedaling, no relaxation of intellect where he is involved. At Brown University in November of 1969, novelists and critics gathered at the annual Wetmore Lecture to discuss form, the future of the novel, and each other. Critic Robert Scholes opened one discussion on form by reading from Ellison's acceptance speech before the National Book Award Committee. "Ah, Ellison," Leslie Fiedler said, throwing his arm out in a gesture of dismissal. "He's a black Jew."

Ellison chuckles. "Leslie's been trying to make me a Jew for years," he says. "I have to look at these things with a Cold Oklahoma Negro Eye. But someone should have said that *all* us old-fashioned Negroes are Jews."

Iowa City, Iowa
August, 1969

Dear Mr. Ellison:

From what I have read of recent American fiction, I sense a shift in interest on the part of the reading public, and consequently in the focus of those who write the books which become popular. The trend seems to be a movement away from traditional forms (the naturalism, for example, which has always been so convenient for black writers), and a change in content as well. Science fiction, mythological experiences, journalistic accounts and pornography, for example, are very popular now. Do you see this as a passing trend, or is something more revolutionary at work? And if these present interests are only temporary, do you think that the more serious areas of the black cultural experience will still be of sufficient interest to sustain an audience for serious black writers?

ELLISON: "I think that we are always going to have periods in which we will shift toward an interest in the pornographic. But this country has a tendency to get fed up with any novelty very quickly, and then we tend to put things back into perspective. We like novelty. It's pretty shocking to have a book which has a theme about masturbation. That's interesting, but not unexpected; we are always interested in revealing that which is supposed to be unrevealable. That's part of the American thing. But I don't think that this indicates that our interest in form has changed.

"I think that our sense of formal completeness is a psychological thing that is rooted in our sense of the seasons, in our sense of lightness and darkness. I think the tendency now is to feel that an interest in form is beside the point. But I also note that those people who tell you this and who write in a supposed disregard of form are always trying to get a group of people who will accept their form. There is no art without form. The form becomes a convention. And once you get enough people to accept that as a proper way of doing a novel or of writing a play, then you have imposed a new convention of form. So you can say that form is conventional on the one hand, but at the same time our sense of a beginning, middle, and end is built into human biology. And that isn't going to go away.

"One plays around with form, extends form, contracts form—depending on the convention popular at the time, but I don't think you ever get completely away from it. And I think that writers who tell themselves that they don't *have* to learn form are deluding themselves, because it is in form itself that a great part of the psychology of the character, the reader, and the writer, is involved. . . .

"I just don't think that we can escape from form, because when you write a piece of fiction, you write it to be read. I'm reminded that when Joyce was writing *Finnegans Wake* he was spending as much time writing to critics and friends as to how those sections which were being published over a period of years were supposed to be read. He was setting them up for a formal reception of a new form.

"As for the future popularity of black writers, I'm hesitant to make a prediction because so many of them seem to be still caught up at the point of emphasizing *inwardness* without emphasizing the inward-outwardness. There is a rhetoric of fiction, and in order to master the rhetoric of the form, you have to be aware of the people who are outside your immediate community. And the rhetoric depends upon not only a knowledge of human passion, but the specific situations in which that passion is expressed: the manners, the formal patterns, and so on, as well as the political issues around which they are clustered. So that if our black writers are going to become more influential in the broader community, they will do it in terms of style: by imposing a style upon a sufficient area of American life to give other readers a sense that this is true, that here is a revelation of reality. I think that this is the way it works. And this is going to depend upon writers who get a clear sense of what they're doing.

"Black writers could sustain a place for themselves in American literature. It's possible, but I couldn't predict it because I don't know what's going on. It's just hard for me to tell. There is a lot of activity, and very often the people who make the breakthroughs are not the people who are doing a lot of talking and getting the attention. They are quietly trying to make something new out of their experience and out of their experience of literature. I can just say that I hope that as we learn to translate and to interpret the intricacies of our experience as a group of people, we can do it with enough art and with an impact which will raise it from the specific to the universal."

Ellison is not only interested in the fiction written by young black writers; he is concerned about young black people in general: what they are thinking, what they are doing, what their ambitions are. But his knowledge of them is limited to sessions during speaking engagements, letters, and what he hears from the media. "A hell of a lot of them are reading my book," he observes with obvious pleasure. "I have a way of checking this. And for a long time they didn't read much of anything."

Yet Ellison worries that despite the increased educational opportunities available to them, young black people are becoming too involved in, and almost symbolic of, the campus reactions against intellectual discipline, the life of the mind. "It's too damn bad," he says. "You see that men are now analyzing the song of the whales, the talk of dolphins, planning to go to the moon; computer technology is becoming more and more humanized and miniaturized; great efforts are being made to predetermine sex, to analyze cells, to control the life process in the human animal. And all of this is done with the *mind*. Indeed," he goes on, "the irony is that we've never really gotten away from that old *body* business, the Negro as symbolic of *instinctual* man. Part of my pride in being what I am is that as a dancer, as a physical man . . ." and again that distant chuckle comes from deep within his chest, "I bet you I can outdance, outriff most of these intellectuals who're supposed to have come back." Now he is serious again. *"But that isn't the problem, damnit!* I was *born* doing *this*! It's a glorious thing to know the uses of the body and not to be afraid of it, but *that has to be linked to the mind.* I don't see any solution for literary art. If you're a dancer, fine. If you're a musician, fine. But what are you going to do as a writer, or what are you going to do as a critic?" He sighs as if he were weighed down by these considerations.

"I find this very interesting," he continues, "but not new. When I think about Tuskegee and people with whom I went to school, I know that over and over again they really did not extend themselves because they didn't have the imagination to look thirty years ahead to a point where there would be a place for them in the broader American society if they had been prepared."

He says: "I understand ambition; I understand the rejection of goals because they're not self-fulfilling. I've turned down too many things, starting as a youngster."

Ellison looks out the window toward the Hudson, then continues in a lower tone. "I was married once before, and one reason that marriage came to an end was that my in-laws were disgusted with me, thought I had no ambition, because I didn't want a job in the Post Office. And here I was with a dream of myself writing the symphony at twenty-six which would equal anything Wagner had done at twenty-six. This is where my ambitions were. So I can understand people getting turned off on that level. But what I can't understand is people who do not master a technique or discipline which will get them to a point where they can actually see that it's not what they want or that something else is demanded. But over and over again I see black kids who are dropping out or rejecting intellectual discipline as though what exists now will always exist, and as though they don't have the possibility of changing it by using these disciplines as techniques to affirm *their* sense of what a human life should be. It's there where I get upset."

Ellison has a habit of pausing whenever the discussion begins to touch areas pregnant with emotion, as if careful of remaining within a certain context. But on some subjects he is likely to continue. "I also get upset when I see announcements of prizes and medical discoveries, and scientific advances, and I don't see any black names or black faces. I believe that we are *capable*," he says. "I believe that there are enough unique features in our background to suggest solutions to problems which seem very far removed from our social situation."

The duality of cultural experience which Ellison insists on in his writing is acted out in his professional and personal life. He is just as much at home, just as comfortable, in a Harlem barbershop as he is as a panelist before the Southern Historical Association exchanging arguments with C. Vann Woodward, Robert Penn Warren, and William Styron. He is a novelist well respected by his peers (when his name is mentioned in almost any literary circle, there will invariably be an inquiry about his current project), and he brings to bear the same respect for craft in an introduction to the stories of Stephen Crane as he uses to evaluate the work of the black artist Romare Bearden. Yet precisely because of his racial identity, he is also the leading black writer in American letters. And while he disclaims this position as "an accident, part luck and part a product of the confusion over what a black writer is and what an American writer is," the reality is there, nevertheless, and has to be coped with.

MCPHERSON: "It seems to me that much of our writing has been, and continues to be, sociological because black writers have been concerned with protesting black humanity and racial injustice to the larger society in those terms most easily understood by nonblack people. It also seems to me that we can correct this limitation either by defining and affirming the values and cultural institutions of our people for their education, or by employing our own sense of reality and our own conception of what human life should be to explore, and perhaps help define, the cultural realities of contemporary

American life. In either case, do you think that naturalism is sufficient to deal adequately with the subtle complexities of contemporary black cultural experience?"

ELLISON: "I don't think that naturalism is enough for us because so much that is negative has been made of our naturalistic or our physical variations from other Americans. Besides, the implicit mode of Negro-American culture is abstract, and this comes from the very nature of our relationship to this country.

"First, we came from Africa. We had to learn English. We had, in other words, to create ourselves as a people—and this I take right down to the racial, the bloodlines, the mingling of African blood with bloodlines indigenous to the New World. A few people can trace their connections back to a given African tribe, but most of us can't. We can't even trace our blood back only to Africa because most of us are part Indian, Spanish, Irish, part any and every damn thing. But *culturally* we represent a synthesis of any number of these elements, and that's a problem of abstraction in itself; it's abstraction and recombining.

"When we began to build up a sense of ourselves, we did it by abstracting from the Bible, abstracting the myths of the ancient Jews, the early Christians, modifying them as we identified with these people and projecting ourselves. This was an abstract process. We knew that we were not white; we knew that we were not Hebrews; but we also knew something else: we knew that we didn't *have* to be in order to make these abstractions and recombinations. This was a creative process, one of the most wonderful things which ever happened on the face of the earth. This is one of the great strengths which now people seem to want to deny. But this was the *reunification* of a shattered group of people.

"Now, American Negro music was not simply the product of remembered African rhythms. It took Western melodic forms and modified them, took Western rhythmical forms and combined them, and produced a music. American Negro dance is a result of abstracting the courtly dances which were danced in the manor houses. The jigs and flings which the Irish and Scotch had brought over from the British Isles were appropriated by the slaves and combined with African dance patterns. And out of this abstraction and recombination you got the basis of the American choreography.

"Our experience in the acculturative process differed from the European's because he didn't have the necessity. This can be said about American culture in general: it *was* an extension of European culture. What is new about it is the presence of the African influence as projected by black Americans. Irish folklore, English folklore, Scottish folklore, the music and so on all found a place in colonial America. Not only was there a conscious effort to preserve the forms of high European culture, but at the same time there was a vernacular style—the speech which people spoke on the streets as they came to grips with the nature of the New World—the plants, the rivers, the climate, and so on. There was a modification of language necessary to communicate with the slaves and with people who came from other parts of Europe. All of these created a tension which in turn created what we call the vernacular style. Our technology was vernacular. And it grew so fast precisely because they had to throw off the assumptions of European technology and create one which was in keeping with conditions in the New World: the availability of materials, the wide distances, the need to build things which could be quickly assembled and abandoned without much waste. Nevertheless, on the level of the educated classes, there was an effort to preserve the European heritage which did not stop when we made a revolutionary break with England.

"But *we* didn't have that. We had some of the same pressures to assert identity in another place at another time—which the Irish and the Germans had. But *they* could do it. And you had this fact too: these people came in waves, but many of them still spoke the brogue. Other people from other European countries, the first generation at least, didn't speak English. But we happen to be a people who can't remember when we didn't speak English. So we had that to help us, and the Bible, the language of the King James version, to shape whatever literary or religious efforts we made. And nothing else. We couldn't fall back on African language. Thus we see immediately that there was a vast difference between our options and the options of Americans of European background."

Before he accepted the professorship at New York University, Ellison earned a good part of his income from college speaking engagements. He accepted around twenty each year. He tends to favor the East Coast or Midwest and avoids the West Coast, partially because of the great distance and partially because of the political nature of the West. He is much in demand, although his fee is usually $1500 to $2000. In the past year he has spoken at such colleges as Millsaps, East Texas State, Rockland, Illinois, West Point, and Iowa State University at Ames.

Ellison takes pride in being able to deliver a ninety-minute speech without the aid of notes. He will make some few digressions to illuminate his points, but will always pick up the major thread and carry it through to its preconceived end.

March, 1970

Ralph Ellison stands on a stage broad enough to seat a full symphony orchestra. Before him, packed into a massive new auditorium of gray concrete and glass and deep red carpets, 2700 Ames students strain to hear the words of the man billed as "Ralph Ellison: Writer." Ames is almost an agricultural school, and its students still have fraternity rows, beer parties, frat pins and ties, white shirts and jackets. Most of them are the beardless sons of farmers and girls whose ambitions extend only as far as engagement by the senior year. The American Dream still lingers here, the simple living, the snow, the hamburgers and milk shakes, the country music and crickets and corn. This is the breadbasket of the country, the middle of Middle America. And yet, ninety miles away in Iowa City, students torn from these same roots are about to burn buildings. "When the pioneers got to your part of the country," Ellison tells them, speaking again of the vernacular, the functional level of the American language, "there was no word for 'prairie' in the *Oxford English Dictionary*." His speech is on "The Concept of Race in American Literature." And he delivers just that. But it is abstract, perhaps over the heads of many of the students there (even though parts of it later appeared as a *Time* essay in the issue on "Black America"). Still, the students are quiet, respectful, attempting to digest. Speaking of the ethnic blending which began with the formation of the country, he says, "And, to make it brief, there was a whole bunch of people from Africa who were not introduced by the British, but quite some time before were introduced into what later became South Carolina by the Spanish. Whereupon they immediately began to revolt—" Here loud applause floats down to the lower audience from black students in the second balcony. Ellison pauses, then continues: "—and went wild, and started passing for Indians. I hear a lot about black people passing for white, but remember, they first started passing for Indians." There is some giggling and laughter at this, but behind me I notice a black student cringing.

During the question-and-answer session afterwards, the students ask the usual things: the conflict between Richard Wright and James Baldwin, the order of symbols in *Invisible Man*. One girl wants to know if racial miscegenation is a necessary ingredient of racial integration. He laughs, "Where'd you get that word?" he says, and answers, "I don't think that any of us Americans wants to lose his ethnic identity. This is another thing which has been used to manipulate the society in terms of race. Some few people might want to lose their identities; this has happened. But I would think that the very existence of such strong Negro-American influences in the society, the style, the way things are done, would indicate that there's never been the desire to lose that. There's just too much self-congratulation in so much of Negro-American expression. They wouldn't want to give that up." He says, "The thing that black people have been fighting for for so long was the opportunity to decide whether they *wanted* to give it up or not. And the proof is that in this period when there is absolutely more racial freedom than has ever existed before, you have the most militant rejection of integration. These are individual decisions which will be made by a few people. But if I know anything about the human being, what *attracts* a man to a woman has usually been picked up very early from the first woman he's had contact with. There is enough of a hold of tradition, of ways of cooking, of ways of just relaxing, which comes right out of the family circle, to keep us in certain groups."

At the reception after the speech, the whites dominate all three rooms; the few black students cluster together in one. Ellison moves between the two, sometimes almost tearing himself away from the whites. He talks to the black students about books, LeRoi Jones, Malcolm X, color, their personal interests. They do not say much. A white woman brings a book for his autograph; a professor gives a nervous explanation of the source of the miscegenation question: the girl has been reading Norman Podhoretz's essay, "My Negro Problem and Ours" in his course. Ellison smiles and shifts back and forth on his feet like a boxer. Everyone is pleasantly high. The black students, still in a corner, are drinking Coke. I am leaving, eager to be out in the Iowa snow. We shake hands. "This is awkward," he says. "Call me Ralph and I'll call you Jim."

Santa Cruz, California
April, 1970

Dear Ralph:

In 1961 you predicted that a period would come "when Negroes are going to be wandering around because we've had this thing (assumed restrictions imposed by sociological conditions) thrown at us so long that we haven't had a chance to discover what in our own background is really worth preserving." Despite the present movement toward "black awareness," and despite the attempts of blacks to assert their own values and attitudes over those of the white group, do you think that we are any further along in discovering or defining whatever there is in our cultural traditions, beyond reactions to externally imposed restrictions, which has contributed to our strength as a people?

ELLISON: "I think that too many of our assertions continue to be in response to whites. I think that we're polarized by the very fact that we keep talking about 'black awareness' when we really should be talking about black American awareness, an awareness of where we fit into the total American scheme, where our influence is. I tell white kids that instead of talking about black men in a white world or black men in white society, they should ask themselves how black *they* are because black men have been influencing the values of the society and the art forms of the society. How many of their parents fell in love listening to Nat King Cole?

"We did not develop as a people in isolation. We developed within a context of white people. Yes, we have a special awareness because our experience has, in certain ways, been uniquely different from that of white people, but it was not absolutely different. A poor man is a poor man whether he's black or white. A white man might rationalize and get a sense of satisfaction out of his whiteness, but as far as meat on the table and clothes on the back are concerned, he's still a poor man. And if he isn't in the position to *get* more clothes, then he's in no better position than the black person. And that's one of the things that various groups are now beginning to emphasize: the unity between black and white on an economic level, a unity of interest between poor people, black, white, Indians, Mexican-Americans. To move into some sort of black awareness which is narcissistic is a mistake because it's false. For me to try to look at American literature written by whites—say Melville, for example—and not know that I'm there, my people are there, not just in terms of character but in terms of symbols, in terms of vision, in terms of speech, in terms of mythology . . . The stuff is there. If you go back and look at photographs or paintings,

Early American or nineteenth-century, you'll always see *us*. We're there. We are part of the scene. Constance Rourke [American cultural historian (1885–1941), author of *The Roots of American Culture*] is right when she points out the role we have played as archetypal figures. So the movement backwards to get a fuller sense of ourselves, to get a sense of the community and its needs, of the traditions and so on, is good. There's an assumption that every black person knows the traditions. Many don't, but many do. And those who don't should talk to those who do.

"That's one of the advantages of a Southern upbringing: a lot of things which got lost up here were not lost back there. I mean just things you took for granted, things I assumed everybody knew. I had friends who grew up in New Jersey telling me that Southern Negroes didn't know how to box. I said, 'Where the hell do you think Jack Johnson came from?' But they had built up that notion of Northern Black Superiority. I remember serving on a ship during the war where one of the messmen referred to Southern Negroes as 'boogies.' I said, 'Well, *I'm* from the South.' And he said, 'But you're not one of *them.*' He was just as prejudiced against Southern blacks as whites were. But you got that sense of a loss of continuity which has to be regained. Part of the tragedy—one of the pathetic and ironic things—about Stokely Carmichael's activities is that he went down South and condescended. No one has pointed this out, but there was a hell of a lot of condenscension from this West Indian boy toward blacks. And he did a lot of damage.

"You can look at Booker T. Washington, for example—and I'm very critical of the man, but any objective view which isn't hung up on the black-white issue as such, and which tries to look at the man in terms of the distribution of power, would make you realize that Washington was one of the most powerful politicians the South had ever known. That was reality. You don't have to like the circumstances which *allowed* him to assume that kind of power—and I'm talking about his relationship with government and great economic powers. We have to come to grips with this. It has to be a part of our awareness of who we are. And simply by moving back and saying, 'Well, this was slavery, and this man said that we should get education and not worry about political rights' is not enough. We have to learn *why* DuBois never became the same kind of power figure, no matter what we think of DuBois. We have to know what happened to those linkages with power after Washington left. We've got to quit imposing second-class standards on ourselves. When you tell me that a man is a great sociologist, and you tell me he was a student for a while of Max Weber's, then I am compelled, out of my own sense of Negro humanity, to compare his achievements with those of Weber. My wish, my hope, my dream is that he achieve more than Weber, but if he didn't, damn it, he just didn't. And the next man who comes along will have to go beyond not only him but beyond Max Weber. And our relationship to reality is such that, given the mind and the energy and industry, our social thinkers *will* go beyond. But they won't go beyond by simply receiving the ideas handed down to them and just making it by simply repeating these ideas. They have to be more creative.

"We need to get a human perspective, and if we could get this we could put things into a more fruitful, creative perspective. So many of our kids who are most militant really believe that whites are superior to them. That's why they keep asserting 'Blackness! Blackness! Blackness!' The thing to do, I would think, would be to recognize that there have been certain advantages. There's no doubt that many of these whites have had better educational opportunities, and it's going to be difficult competing with them *for a while*. But it seems to me that if you recognize that they've had the advantage and that you are going to have to work harder, once your brain is programmed with the proper amount of information you're going to catch up. I've seen this happen. But I see some of these kids at universities all clustered together, and they look a little bit pathetic. I want to say to them, 'Look, it just isn't so. It just isn't so! Just drop this and take some chances. You're as good as anybody here.'

"As for those charges of white paternalism, part of this business is a way of relating, which becomes offensive because it's presumptuous. My experience with that kind of conversation came from the left, from the Communist Party. They had their theories straight from wherever they came from, and they interpreted everything. That was one of the problems with Wright; they were always trying to tell Wright that he wasn't following the line. This was so because they thought they had the complexity of his experience down on paper. I guess that's inevitable in this country, and our kids are going to have to learn what their forefathers learned; that there is a certain forbearance, and a certain acceptance of our own maturity, our own human maturity. And in some ways Negroes are much more mature; we damn well should be because we've had a harder time. But we keep getting this mixed up with obsequiousness or with fear, which is the way the *white* man interprets it. When blacks come right along they say, 'You've been brainwashed.' Well, they don't realize that *they* are the ones who have been programmed.

"I remember my mother talking to me about a friend of my family's who kind of went off her rocker. Her father was very, very fond of me, and she began to say that she thought maybe he *was* my father, which just upset me because I was an adolescent. I went to my mother telling her how offended I was, and my mother didn't get angry. She simply said, 'Now, look. You're old enough to know that this woman is kind of crazy. You keep that in your mind.' And that was that.

"Some years ago when I was making certain statements, there were critics who in conversation would say, 'Ah, you don't know what you're talking about.' But what I couldn't get across a few years ago has become more and more clear to people who are really thinking about it. You see, the one thing that happened in this country after the Hayes-Tilden Compromise was that the whole focus upon the relationship of black people and their culture to the broader culture was sort of shut down. Not much light could come through. Historians wrote histories of the Civil War, and social critics wrote interpretations of American culture and society which did not give us very much of a role. We were pushed to the back of the head, to the underside of the mind, so to speak. And it wasn't until the agitations started in the South and began to spread that they began to look back. Now I don't mean to imply that we were the sole force which made for the re-evaluation of the culture, because there has been revisionism going on across the board. But the agitations made it a little bit more impossible to ignore our presence. They made it a little bit more impossible not to ask the questions: who are they? what are they doing? what have they done? what is their influence? After all, there are millions of them and they're always present. How have they been affecting us other than in terms of music and dance?

"In 1942 when I was on the *Negro Quarterly* I sent around a lot of letters to critics asking, What is it you would like to see discussed as to the relationship between the Negro cultural background and the larger American culture? Only a few responded. They had never thought about it. But I knew that the relationship was there because if I, in order to make something out of the folklore which I knew, had to go often to white writers because we didn't write about it much, I knew that there had to be some reciprocal action on *their* part because they could live with the assumption that we were not important, while *I* never could. And I think that political developments and the sheer pressure of time—the role in the world which the nation achieved after the Second World War—made all these questions come to the fore. So that now when I make a statement which previously would have sounded wild, it isn't wild anymore. We've had enough people studying the music, collecting the folklore; just a simple thing like traveling in the South and seeing black people in our natural habitat—seeing some of the contrasts—has done a lot. There are questions about American society which need to be answered, and if a black critic can answer them, these answers will be accepted. If an American sociologist can take the theories of E. Franklin Frazier and use them partially against us in all good faith, and these theories can find their way into legislative programs, there's no reason why literary interpretations—interpretations of the culture coming from us—can't be just as effective. Because the kids want to know."

There are thousands and thousands of books in the rooms of Ellison's apartment, and besides the pieces of sculpture, paintings, African violets, self-designed furniture, and other symbols of a highly cultivated sensibility, are deep drawers and file cabinets which, if opened, reveal thick sheaves of notes and manuscripts. Ellison's huge desk, which sits in a study just off the living room, is covered with books, a red electric typewriter, well-thumbed manuscripts, and tape equipment. In conversation he always sits away from it, in the leather-strap chair by the window, looking out on the Hudson and the street below.

He is a very direct and open man, even though there are silent levels of intimidating intelligence and unexpressed feeling beneath much of what he says. And he tends to approach even the most abstract idea from a personal point of view, usually including in any observation some supportive incident drawn from his own experience.

He talks freely of his mother, who died when he was in his early twenties, his relatives in Oklahoma, his professional relationships with other writers and critics, conversations with people on the subway or in the streets of Harlem, a recent chance meeting with Kurt Vonnegut in the streets of Manhattan, his respect for Saul Bellow as an extremely well read novelist. There is not an unkind, unprofessional, or imperceptive word for anyone, not even his most rabid critics. But he does become irritated if you question too closely his sense of identity as an American writer as opposed to a black writer, and is likely to react when he senses a too containing category being projected onto him. "Let's put it this way, Jim," he says, irritation in his voice. "You see, I *work* out of American literature. In order to write the kind of fiction that I write I would *have* to be in touch with a broader literary culture than our own particular culture." He pauses, and then says, "This is not to denigrate what we have done, but in all *candor* we haven't begun to do what we can do or what we should have done. I think one reason why we haven't is that we've looked at our relationship to American literature in a rather negative way. That is, we've looked at it in terms of our trying to break into it. Well, damn it"—and his voice rises, and his hand hits the arm of the chair—"*that literature is built off our folklore, to a large extent!*" Then he laughs that deep honest chuckle, and says, "I ain't conceding that to *nobody!*"

Santa Cruz, California
April, 1970

Dear Amelia:

I was very pleased to have met you during my stay in Ames. Now, before the spring holidays begin, I wish you would tell me your impressions of Ellison as an artist, as a black man in touch with young black people as a man of ideas. . . .

Ames, Iowa
April, 1970

Dear James:

As an artist the man is beautiful. I think that is what was so captivating about his book. The symbolism that he uses and the combination of literary mechanics that he employs will probably make his work much more lasting than that of his black contemporaries. *Invisible Man* is a classic, and to say any more or less about it would be an understatement.

As for being in touch with the ideas of young people today, I think that he is quite aware, but he doesn't have the charisma that one would expect after hearing his reputation as a speaker and taking into account the acclaim his book has received. Part of my feeling is due to the disappointment of hearing him explain the figure in *Invisible Man*. So many concerned blacks had read the plight of the Afro-American into this figure with no face and no name. So many people saw the author riding to champion the cause of the black man. Those same people heard him say that the symbol was representative of a universal man. I found that most disheartening.

We are unfortunate at Ames, as well as at many other places across this nation, to have a group of young people who have been introduced to new ideologies and a new rhetoric, and are attempting to adopt both when they do not understand either. Therefore when they see or hear anyone who does not speak in their rhetoric they cannot, do not, and will not try to communicate with him. This was very true of Ellison.

He has a lot to say to a people who will listen to him. Today's youth are angry, and many times this anger closes their ears to a different rationale. Ellison's language and approach, I fear, attach to him the stigma of black bourgeois and conservatism. This figure does not communicate well with the vocal black youth. . . .

Santa Cruz, California
April, 1970

Dear Ralph:

There is a popular phrase, widely circulated now by militants, to the effect that the present "movement" cannot afford any individuals, that if you "are not part of the solution, you are part of the problem."

For the black writer, I assume this means that he cannot deal analytically with the complexities of black experience in fiction unless he asserts the current ideological thoughts of the group as construed by its "spokesmen." This, of course, is an ancient argument (food, usually, for those abortive black writers' conferences), and I know that your position has always been that the writer, whether or not he is black, must assert his special vision above all other considerations, go it alone, even at the risk of eliciting criticisms from the community and from "friends of the Negro." But do you find that maintaining this position has alienated you and your work from the masses of the black community and has made you a symbol, a point of convenient attack for certain members of the white critical Establishment whose simplistic conceptions of black people and black life are threatened by your constant assertions of the complexities? Have you altered in any way the views you expressed in the essay "The World and the Jug"?*

ELLISON: "I'm a little tougher than that. In the first place, I suppose I was disciplined for the predicament which I find myself in now—if it is a predicament—by all of my life. I've always had the strange role of being before the public and yet not quite part of the crowd. As a kid, I was always in the plays and programs; as a trumpeter in the school band I, in a couple of years, was student conductor. I played varsity football, I was part of the popular set, and yet I was always a loner. That was temperamental, and it made for certain difficulties. I guess I lived far too much in books, or took books far too seriously, to allow some of my schoolmates to feel comfortable. But my own role was inside and outside. And it continued to be that way. I was never really shy, but I was never one of those individuals who had absolute approval; nor did I want it.

"Now I've studied enough of the lives of writers and other artists to know that it costs you something to function in this field with any sort of individuality. I know that the pressures toward conformity are not just imposed by whites; they are part of the defense mechanism of the black community itself. Years ago, when I was in the Federal Writers' Project and was just beginning to write, there were friends of mine, some of whom were also in the Project, who happened to be at a party. It was reported to me afterwards that my name came up, and they decided, then and there, that I would never write anything. Now it isn't just that these people were not in the position to judge, because I can say quite frankly that not too many of them knew much about writing. But somehow they made the decision that I was never going to produce anything. This friend came and told me about it, and we had a big laugh. But I was hurt, I won't deny that, because

---

*In the "The World and the Jug" Ellison defends his right to an individual vision against critic Irving Howe, who, in his essay "Black Boys and Native Sons," assessed the merits of Wright, Baldwin, and Ellison as "black writers." The essay appears on page 155.

they weren't giving me a goddamn chance! And yet already I was publishing in the *New Masses* and the *New Republic* and slowly trying to find where I was going. Later I realized that this activity was a way of protecting them from being too ambitious. What they were saying was, 'He's too damn ambitious.' Well, maybe I was. But I think that we should be more generous.

"I also know this: whether you really have achieved anything or not, in this country we are so under the spell of publicity that if your name appears a little bit too frequently you're going to become a target.

"I responded to Irving Howe in that way because these issues go beyond *me*. They become important for young black writers who are trying to orient themselves. I'm just saying to them that there is something about their experience which other people might tend to overlook because they're outside it. I'm saying that I'm in a better position to see certain things about American literature or American culture precisely *because* I'm a black man, but I'm not restricted by those frames which have been imposed upon us. I think that one has to keep this constantly in mind; otherwise, somebody else is going to be interpreting your experience for you, and you're going to be repeating it. And they might be in error."

Presently, as part of the increased public and academic interest in literature written by blacks, there is a movement under way to reevaluate the position of Richard Wright. And, because of the double standard of criticism, Wright's work is not measured against the works of his peers (*Native Son* was published in 1940, along with John Steinbeck's *Grapes of Wrath* and Ernest Hemingway's *For Whom the Bell Tolls*), but against the works of James Baldwin and Ralph Ellison. So in order for Wright's legend to rise on the black scale, the esteem of Baldwin and Ellison must be lowered. Consequently, a review in the May 8, 1970, issue of *Life* magazine, called, honestly enough, "Black Fiction: A Second Look," suggested that "Ellison himself, and James Baldwin after him, both helped to create the image of Wright as a novelist too much given to social protest, too preoccupied with one level of black society and too constrained by the limitations of his brutish protagonist really to qualify as a master." The author, a mysterious critic named Clifford Mason, notes that much of the "grandiloquent praise" of Wright's accomplishments by black writers issues from a "strong reaction to the obsequious bleatings of white appeasement that has characterized Ellison's politics."

Ellison admits that this sort of thing annoys him. "But here," he says, "I was just as annoyed by the fact that this man calls himself a teacher and a critic, and he hasn't done his homework. I never wrote a review of *Native Son*, nor did I ever call Bigger Thomas a brute. Nor did I lead the attack on *Native Son*. I was Wright's best man," he says, nostalgia clearly in his voice, his head turned toward the Hudson. "I led to the reconciliation between Wright and his wife. I think my essay on *Black Boy* is a tribute to Wright, and I've praised his achievements in any number of places." Now his tone is severe; his head shifts back to the room. "But somehow this man wanted to set up something. And what he knows about my politics, I don't know. I've been criticized because I was *not* political. Privately," he says, his voice steady but rising, *"my politics are my own!* I'm *not* a spokesman. I'm *not* a politician. And I've very, very carefully tried to avoid pretending to be what I am not. But that kind of thing is cheap. Whatever the quarrel between Wright and Baldwin was, I don't think that it should be generalized into a principle. People meet, people exchange ideas, and hopefully the exchange is creative. Sometimes it isn't; but why kill off someone? I wrote a review of Langston Hughes's *The Big Sea* and was very critical of it. I think that it hurt him a little, but it was not a vicious review. It was a considered review, written as well as I could at the time. But I never felt the need to attack Langston Hughes to raise up Ralph Ellison. *I* could never *be* a Langston Hughes, no matter how good he became or how poor he became as an artist. I can only be myself. So that I don't have to envy other people. It seems to me a waste of time and a discredit to oneself."

MCPHERSON: "In the novel *The Outsider*, Richard Wright seems to have attempted a sort of projection of the possibilities which would become available to American black writers as our people gained greater participation in the society. In the novel a white district attorney says to Cross Damon, 'Negroes, as they enter our culture, are going to inherit the problems we have, but with a difference. They are outsiders and they are going to *know* that they have these problems. They are going to be self-conscious; they are going to be gifted with a double vision, for, being Negroes, they are going to be both *inside* and *outside* of our culture at the same time. Every emotional and cultural convulsion that ever shook the heart and soul of Western man will shake them. Negroes will develop unique and specially defined psychological types. They will become psychological men, like the Jews. They will not only be Americans or Negroes; they will be centers of *knowing*, so to speak. The political, social and psychological consequences of this will be enormous.' Considering the quality of the fiction presently being produced by black writers, do you think that Wright's prediction was accurate?"

ELLISON: "This is one of the greatest advantages of being black; you have a perspective which is fairly uncluttered if you will use it. By being in it and outside you can evaluate. Housekeepers, bellhops, domestics, have done this for *years*. You can listen to women talk about what happens in the white family. They're not always malicious in their discussions, but they have a standard, and they can see. And they're wise in certain ways; they're wise in the ways of human folly and aspiration. This isn't limited by color. But in terms of their position in the social hierarchy, they were outside but right in the *bedroom*. So what better position can you have? A *psychiatrist* doesn't have that advantage of observation.

"Wright was right. We have that, and have always had it. American writers have not yet learned to use what has been available to us: that listening post, that point of observation, which puts one in the position of making judgments, of seeing, or of exercising sympathy.

And the suspicion of this haunted whites in the South. That's why they're just as obsessed with what Negroes are doing. That's what's not talked about. But, they have as much curiosity about how the maid is faring and what Negroes do.

"But this is an opportunity to make judgments and to use the imagination. One problem that I've always felt as a writer was the restriction placed on me by my racial status to be in those areas where important decisions are arrived at. And what I find most ironic about the separatist positions taken by black students is that they are removing themselves from those areas where they can observe and even participate in the formation of values on the part of their white fellow students.

"When we study the lives of the great writers by social class, or by function, we find that they were in the position to observe from the very top of the society to the very bottom. Dickens moved among the very top people of England while he was studying the abuses of child labor. Cervantes was in prison most of his life, and when he was not, he moved in the circle of clericals. Stendhal had that same advantage. I don't know of any European writer who didn't manage to do some of this. And in our own country the Hemingways certainly had access to the top intellectual and artistic circles and, when they wanted it, to political circles. This was true of Faulkner, and right down the line. Well, this isn't just for fun. These are positions of observation, positions where values can be studied in action. And *we* have to do *more* of that. We have to project the imagination.

"One reason why I tell black kids to read novels is that we've been choked off from knowing how society operates. And often American novels, even those we don't think so highly of, do tell us something about the dilemmas of people and institutions, of areas of American life from which we are restricted because of our race. So that one of the main objectives of black writers certainly should be to *use* that gift in disguise which has been given us through the history of segregation.

"You see, what happens in this country is that many of us come from the South or the Southwest or the Midwest. And we come to New York or we go to the West Coast, and we're sort of processed; we're kind of stylized, blacks and whites alike. Much of what gets into American literature gets there because so much is left out. I think the problems of the writings of a man like Wright Morris come precisely because he has written so extensively about a little-known part of the United States in a very understated way. He's a very good writer, but people don't really know enough about the reality out of which he writes to make them fully appreciate what he's doing. I think that this happens over and over again and builds a need in the minds of writers, even those who become successful, to have *more* information, to have imaginative projections of the great variety of the country. That's a central problem of American literature. Always has been. Under the great emphasis on the novel of manners what do you get? You get Jewish boys whose parents were peasants often assuming the values of Boston mandarins. I've always found this ironic, and yet I can't overlook the fact that some of them did this very well. America is a country in which these strange transformations occur, and can be made to occur consciously, even though often we end up like Gatsby, following the wrong green light under the wrong name."

Ellison is still a first novelist, despite his reputation. And that one novel was published over eighteen years ago. He contributes a steady flow of articles to intellectual journals and periodicals, and scholars and critics are rapidly making a permanent place for him in the archives of American literary criticism. But while students continue to read and his critics continue to write, there is the expectation of his long-awaited second novel. So far he has read from it in universities and on public television, published sections of it in intellectual journals, allowed a few close friends to read some of it, and has remained strangely silent about publication of the rest. Inestimable numbers of people, black and white, in and out of universities, friends and enemies, await the publication of the complete novel. Whenever his name is mentioned among a group of writers or literati, the immediate response is, "When is his novel coming out?" One man has heard that he has pulled it back from his publisher again for more revisions; another says that Ellison worries about its being dated; a third says he has heard that Ellison cannot finish it.

Concerning that novel there are many other stories. Perhaps the best one is that which some friends of the Ellisons supposedly heard from the writer's wife. "She says she hears him in his study at night, turning pages and laughing to himself. He enjoys the book so much that he isn't in a hurry to share it with the public."

Whether or not this is true, Ellison is extremely reluctant, at first, to discuss the book. A fire in his summer home in Plainfield, Massachusetts, destroyed a year's worth of revisions, he says, and he is presently in the process of revising it again. "I want what I do to be good," he says.

"Are you worried about the quality of it?"

"No," he says. "But you want to be sure when you write so slowly, because if it's not good, if it's just passable, they'll be terribly disappointed."

He has enough typed manuscripts to publish three novels, but is worried over how the work will hold up as a total structure. He does not want to publish three separate books, but then he does not want to compromise on anything essential. "If I find that it is better to make it a three-section book, to issue it in three volumes, I would do that as long as I thought that each volume had a compelling interest in itself. But it seems to me that one of the decisions one has to make about long fiction is whether the effect of *reading* it is lengthy. If you don't get the impression that you're reading a long thing, then you've licked the problem of the battle of time."

The setting of the novel, he says, is roughly around 1955. The form of it, he says, chuckling to himself, is in the direction of a "realism extended beyond realism." There are several time schemes operating within it, and the sections already published heavily suggest that it is complexly involved with the Negro church and its ritual. In fact, three of its major characters, Bliss, Eatmore, and Hickman, are ministers.

On an afternoon, after a martini and before dinner, if the flow of conversation has been relaxing, and if the mood is right, Ellison might read a few sections from the book. It may take him a while to thumb through several huge black-bound manuscripts, perhaps numbering thousands of pages, to find an appropriate section. But when he does begin to read there is the impression, from the way the rhythms rise and fall and blend and flow out of him, that he is proud of every word. He chuckles as he reads, stops to explain certain references, certain connections, certain subtle jokes about the minister whose sermon he is reading. And in those sermons his voice becomes that of a highly sophisticated black minister, merging sharp biblical images with the deep music of his voice, playing with your ears, evoking latent memories of heated Southern churches and foot-stomping and fanning ladies in long white dresses and sweating elders swaying in the front rows. And suddenly the sermons are no longer comic, and there is no writer reading from his work. You see a minister, and you feel the depth of his religion, and you are only one soul in a huge congregation of wandering souls hearing him ask, over and over, *"Oh Yes, Yes, Yes, Yes, Yes. DO You Love, Ah DO You Love?"*

Berkeley, California
June, 1970

Dear Ralph:

You once stated in an interview that American Negro culture is expressed in a certain dramaturgy which is generally unrecognized as such because it is still tied to the more folkish Negro churches ("Some Negro Preachers are great show-men"). It is my belief that since the church plays a major part in his life, the Southern black is closer to his cultural institutions, his evolved values and way of life than his Northern brother. His relationships are far more organic and whole than the fragmented relationships found among blacks in the North. But since the church as this kind of institution is largely restricted to the South, what other areas are available for Northern black writers to study the values of our people? Also, do you think that a Southern background gives a black writer, who is concerned with the Southern black aspects of American culture, pronounced advantages over his fellow black writer who was raised in the North?

ELLISON: "I would think that people working in the theater would be experimenting with anything and everything which is available in an attempt to forge useful dramatic forms. One way would be to take the theatrical activities of the Nationalist Movement in Irish letters, Sean O'Casey and Yeats, and see what we can learn from them as a way of utilizing the dramatic forms implicit in the black community. We know that we have the church; we know that the ritual is Episcopalian, modified by the Negro idiom. We know that in lodge ceremonies or other secret and public ceremonies there are rituals which have been put together from many places. It would seem to me that we could abstract from these if we studied them and looked at them as ritual, as theater, and not just as a bunch of Negroes having a good time or burying their dead.

"There are certain forms which have been repeated and proved valid, if only through the fact that they have existed for so many years. That is a place to study. Anywhere you get our people gathered together for ceremonial purposes has something to tell us about drama, about what we could use as drama. For example, I see certain of these fellows getting into the life of bars where people gather. I know that there is a sort of ritual pattern: certain things are discussed at certain times; certain people come at certain times; certain things are not discussed when one group of people is there. A certain atmosphere will prevail after football games or after someone has made a big numbers hit. You have many of these patterns which no one has done anything with.

"Now, in terms of capturing the idiom, we are not restricted to the stage. When you're dealing with oral tonalities you need bodies and you need the stage. But when you start translating this kind of thing into speech, you do what Joyce did, I think that he has a lot to teach us, especially in *Finnegans Wake*. It's annoying at first, but when you get into it you begin to see how he plays with rhythms, how he will extrapolate from popular songs and everything else. The problem is that you're not going to put the actual sound on paper, but you can evoke it. Or you can study the verbal play of Negro children, who can do a hell of a lot with words and sounds. So much of this is highly rhythmical precisely because the intellectual content is not too great, and you have models for translating this into prose forms. When I was on the Writers' Project I worked on a subproject collecting folklore. I went into hundreds of apartments and talked to people about folklore and took some of the stuff down. Often I was able to get it on paper by using a kind of Hemingway typography, by using the repetitions. I couldn't quite get the tone of the sounds in, but I could get some of the patterns and get an idea of what it was like. One of the things said over and over again by people who have read *Invisible Man* is that they can hear the difference in talk, in the speech patterns between Ras and Tarp. And this is a matter of playing with the rhythms, indicating pronunciation without falling into an attempt at the transcription of dialect.

"As for the possibility of a deeper understanding of cultural values and institutions on the part of Southern blacks, I will just say that it's dangerous to generalize in this area. One man brought up in the North who has done his homework as far as reading is concerned and who has that *respect* for the mysteries of black cultural experiences in the South—to which he is not necessarily superior because he enjoyed a broader social freedom in the North—might well make *more* of that Southern experience than a writer who is so caught up in it that he doesn't achieve objectivity. On the other hand, I believe that a black Southern writer who does know his traditions has some of the advantages which William Faulkner or other white Southern writers have had: the advantage of contact with a long accumulation of history in a given place; an experience which has been projected in other forms of artistic expression, which has traditional values and variants, and which has been refined by being *defined* by generations of people who have told what it seemed to be. *'This is the life of black men here. These are the variations. This type of character turns up over and over again.'* For example, you get many guys who nickname themselves *Jack the Bear* or *Peter Wheatstraw*.

"What we have in the South is an oral tradition which extends right back into slavery and which has been projected in terms of archetypal characters: John the Slave, John Henry, Stagolee, a whole group of them, and they're real-life versions of local characters. People know them by word of mouth rather than their having been written about. For example, a man like Kingsberry who shot up a whole bunch of Texas Rangers in Oklahoma City when Jimmy Rushing was a little boy. People still talk about Kingsberry. And fabulous fishermen, fabulous hunters, fabulous bootleggers, fabulous cooks, fabulous headwaiters, fabulous hustling bellhops, fabulous evangelists. I can go south now and mention an evangelist named McDuffy whom I knew when I was about five years old, and there'll be people who know about McDuffy.

"This is one of the advantages of the South. In the stories you get the texture of an experience and the projection of values, and the distillation of a kind of wisdom. And this must never be laughed at or rejected, because this was precisely what Shakespeare was doing when he wrote his historical plays; it is what Aeschylus and others were doing when they wrote their plays, because these things go back to myth. This is one of our great heritages, but we haven't learned how to get the most out of it. One way of getting the most out of it is to recognize that these figures are universal; they are our versions of universal figures who repeat the broader patterns of human life on this earth. And we can see the human implications of them when we put them side by side with some of these great characters. In some essay I point out that if you put John Henry beside Hercules, they're the same figure given the differences between the cultures out of which they come; they're both men with clubs, they're both heroes capable of fabulous feats of strength, and they're both sacrificial heroes because they die to affirm something about human life."

"Stephen's [Daedalus] problem," Ellison wrote in *Invisible Man*, "like ours, was not actually one of creating the uncreated conscience of his race, but of creating the *uncreated features of his face.*" Ellison is fifty-six. His face does not show very much of it, but enough is visible. He has a receding hairline, a broad forehead, and deep curved lines on either side of his nose running down to the corners of his mouth. It is a handsome brown face, from either point of view, and there is a healthy stubbornness, besides all else inside that forehead, which helps him to protect it. The face can be cold, severe, analytical, pensive, even smiling. But it is not going to change.

Berkeley, California
June, 1970

Dear Ralph:

Some of the bravest words ever written by an artist are these: "But there is also an American Negro tradition which teaches one to deflect racial provocation and to master and contain pain. It is a tradition which abhors as obscene any trading on one's own anguish for gain or sympathy, which springs not from a desire to deny the harshness of existence but from a will to deal with it as men at their best have always done. It takes fortitude to be a man, and no less to be an artist. Perhaps it takes even more if the black man would be an artist. If so, there are no exemptions." Considering this pain, and considering what it has done to certain of your fellow black writers, what have you done that they did not do which has helped you to survive as an artist? Have you ever revised your *credo* in the eighteen years since publication of *Invisible Man?* How have you been able to maintain that double discipline as artist and Negro?

ELLISON: "No, I haven't revised my feelings about those words. Maybe I've gone on to generalize them. I think that at our best we've contained our pain. We didn't like to have white folks see us crying.

I was in Jackson, Mississippi, recently, and one thing a fellow kept saying was, "My father had his own home, and he didn't let any *goddamn* white insurance man come *around!*' He was also saying that what was in his home was his own private business, and it was to be kept there.

"I don't think that I'm in a position to discuss the pain of other writers. Individuals deal with it as they can. But I *do* say that sometimes you can get so *uptight* about your *dis*advantages that you ignore your advantages. And sometimes we are encouraged to talk about how bad we've been treated, and this becomes a sort of perverse titillation for white people. It has this negative effect: a man who is a very elegant and eloquent man, a very gifted man, begins to overemphasize his disadvantages as a *black man* and finally sets up a reaction. Someone will say, 'Well, goddamnit, what's he complaining about? This was *good* for him. I'm out here slugging in the rat race, and he's a celebrity. What the hell *is* this?' It happens that way. But you'd better be objective about what you're doing if you want to have some sort of psychic peace.

"I notice that over and over again some of our black writers treat whites as though they were *omniscient*, requiring a perfection of them which we don't have ourselves and which, in the South, whites have tried to pretend they have. That's insanity. I want to say, 'Look damnit! Don't you know who that *is*? His father was a small-time groceryman who struggled to send him to school. And he's learned a few things. It didn't transform him into any great humanist or into any great sophisticated intellectual. This is only a *relative* matter. You're dealing with a man who still doesn't know what to do when he goes to the opera or a football game, and who would be completely lost if he had to go to a dice game, so don't overrate him.'

"A writer writes out of his own family background, out of his own immediate community, during his formative period. And he writes out of his own talent and his own individual vision. Now if he doesn't, if he tries to get away from that by bending it to some ideological line, then he is depriving the group of his uniqueness. What we need is individuals. If the white society has tried to do anything to us, it has tried to keep us from being individuals. There's no reason why the individual can't be a member of the group. And, incidentally, the people who make the greatest cry against individuals are themselves trying to be leaders. You can't miss *this* irony. They're doing all they can to suppress all individuality except their own. This is *nonsense*. This we do not need. We need as many individuals developing their individual talents as possible, *but* dedicating some part of their energies to the experience of the group. And damnit, I've *done* that. I've always written out of a sense of the group experience as filtered through my individual experiences, talent, and vision. And I think this kind of accommodation has to be made. In fact, it's inexcusable. We can be proud of Duke Ellington and Johnny Hodges, we can be proud of any number of people, but we're proud of them not because they were anonymous bumps within the crowd, but because they were themselves.

"I think that now a very articulate group of young writers doesn't quite know what to make of me. I'm standing up there—speaking in terms of metaphor now—like a black militant leader with his bodyguard. I don't have a bodyguard, but there's nothing like that to compel people to see if they can't knock you off. I think that since I have not embraced some of their literary theories, they feel that I am the enemy. My position has always been that ideology is one thing. Show me what you make of it. If you make art out of it, I will praise the art even while I argue with the ideology. But I haven't seen enough of the art. I suspect that I have annoyed a few people by insisting upon the mastery of craft. Craft to me is an aspect of morality. I don't mean that I've mastered it. I think that this irritates some writers and makes them think, 'That guy, he thinks he's so good.' Well, that's not what I'm talking about. Everytime I walk into my study or into another room of books down the hall I see the great masters. *They're* the ones I have to measure myself against, not because I want to but because that's what is stuck up there. Those are the standards. *I* didn't create them; they were there. Lord knows it would be much easier if you didn't have to work out of a knowledge of what had gone before.

"These arguments over theory will continue. It bothers me to see this generation repeating so many of the mistakes which were around during the 1930s and 1940s. Sometimes these people can be as aggressive in their attacks on writers as the Communists were.

"Well, so what? I've been a Negro-American—a black American if you will—for a hell of a long time, and I know one thing to be true: we haven't changed that much."

JAMES ARMISTEAD LAFAYETTE

Ellison wrote this essay about a slave and little-known hero of the American Revolution in 1974 for the U.S. Bicentennial Society's Profile of Patriots. *For reasons of space, this text—what he called "the longer and more meaningful version"—was not included in the volume. It appears in print here for the first time.*

At Lafayette College in Easton, Pennsylvania, there hangs a portrait in which the Marquis de Lafayette is attended by a black man. Rendered by John-Baptiste Paon, the painting commemorates the victorious Siege of Yorktown. In the center of its canvas, attired in the uniform of a general of the Continental Army, the young French aristocrat points with enigmatic expression to the site of that climactic struggle in the War of Independence. He is hatless, his powdered wig showing white against a cloudy sky in which a slight rift promises sunny days ahead.

To his left, gripping the bridle of a spirited horse in black-gloved hands, stands his devoted body-servant and orderly, James Armistead. Following a convention of such portraiture, Paon has intensified the hierarchical, master-servant symbolism of his composition by rendering the black orderly's features so abstract, stylized, and shadowy that the viewer's attention is drawn not to the individuality of Armistead's features but to the theatrical splendor of his costume.

Dark-skinned and muscular, Armistead is dressed in skintight breeches and handsome boots. He is armed with a fine sword and wears a silken sash and neckerchief. His jacket's cuffs and borders are trimmed with satin. A wide-brimmed hat, plumed with ostrich feathers, covers his massive head, and in the lobe of his left ear the gleam of a golden earring evokes European fantasies of exotic blackamoors. Truly, the Florentine splendor of his garb adds glamour and mystery even to Lafayette, who is at once a wealthy French aristocrat, an American patriot, and a triumphant general. Indeed, Armistead is clothed so exotically and his delineation is so stylized that it is as though, possessing no tradition that would allow him to visualize realistically (much less project) a black American of such incongruous status—socially a slave, and yet a fighter for American independence—the artist has sought guidance from the theater or from the *Arabian Nights.* Thus, while Lafayette and his horse are drawn realistically, the shadowy Armistead appears a figure of fable, perhaps a lesser noble who has strayed to the New World after accompanying the blacker of the Three Wise Men to Bethlehem.

In reality James Armistead was far from a figure of fantasy. An Afro-American slave, he was the property of William Armistead of Virginia, and whether the artist intended it or not, the theatrical note introduced into the scene by James's costume was justified symbolically by the role of make-believe that the slave had played at Yorktown. James Armistead was an important American spy and a fighter in the struggle for freedom within a struggle for freedom that was the American Negro's view of that revolution.

In July 1775, when George Washington took command of the Continental armies, he banned the further enlistment of Negroes. Ignoring the fact that black Americans, both slave and free, had fought against the British from the beginning of the rebellion, Washington's policy enacted an increasing concern over the implications of Negroes bearing arms and risking their lives under the banner and slogans of the Revolution. So perplexing did the issue become that on September 26, 1775, Edward Rutledge of South Carolina moved in the Continental Congress for the discharging of all Negroes then serving in the army, and on October 8 a council of war, headed by Washington, agreed to reject all Negroes from military service, whether slave or free. The contradiction of struggling for democracy while maintaining the institution of slavery had caught fire as a political issue, and this policy was an ill-considered effort at a solution. Denying Afro-Americans the right to continue fighting for the new nation's independence was designed to avoid the possibility of having to deal with a Negro population that could justify its demand for citizenship on the ground of military service. Nor was it comfortable to contemplate the possibility of living with large numbers of disgruntled Negroes who were familiar with weapons and trained in military tactics.

In light of the struggling nation's military predicament, however, this policy turned out to reflect not only a flawed moral position and political naïveté, but a poverty of military imagination. For in the Americans' exclusion of Negroes the British saw, and quickly seized, a political opportunity with important military consequences. Thus, on November 7, 1775, Lord Dunmore, the governor of Virginia, issued a proclamation offering freedom to all "indentured servants or others . . . that are able and willing to bear arms," a move that proved so alarmingly effective that by December 26, 1775, General Washington was complaining in a letter to Richard Henry Lee that Dunmore's strength was increasing "as a snowball, by rolling," and that "if some expedient [was not] hit upon to convince the slaves and servants of the impotency of [Dunmore's] design" he would become the Revolution's most formidable enemy. Reacting to the loss of thousands of fighting men, Washington reversed his policy to the extent of enlisting *free* Negroes, while urgent efforts were made to win the support of slaves with promises of better treatment, and by offering pardons to all Negroes then serving the enemy. Fortunately the appeal of democracy was broader than Washington's foresight; most Negroes were either loyal or neutral, and it was after this reversal of American policy that James Armistead made the move that won him a place, no matter how shadowy, in Paon's portrait of Lafayette.

The time was March 1781. In Virginia General Lafayette was commanding forces pitted against the British under General Cornwallis, to whose victory over General Gates in South Carolina black enlistees had contributed. Trying desperately to raise four hundred laborers, teamsters, and cavalry mounts, Lafayette advised Washington that "nothing but a treaty of alliance with the Negroes can find us dragoon horses [because] it is by this means the enemy have so formidable a Cavalry." It was during this period, with Cornwallis still formidable, and the Americans' seeking intelligence about his strength and strategy, that James Armistead sought his master's permission to join Lafayette. His owner willing, Armistead enlisted and served the future hero of the French Revolution so effectively that after the war the general was to state that his spying activities were "industriously collected and more faithfully delivered. He perfectly acquitted himself with . . . important commissions . . . [and was] entitled to every reward his situation [his owner and the American government willing] could admit of."

The brevity of Lafayette's testimonial understated his orderly-spy's resourcefulness. Taking advantage of the British eagerness for Negro aid, Armistead risked his life by pretending to supply Cornwallis with information damaging to the Americans—a bit of playacting that proved so effective that not until the defeated Cornwallis encountered him in Lafayette's headquarters was the black man's true loyalty and identity revealed.

The rest is irony. In 1786, Armistead, who by now expressed continuing admiration for the marquis by calling himself "James Armistead Lafayette," was rewarded for his services to the Revolution by being emancipated at the expense of the General Assembly of Virginia. In 1818, still free but little changed in circumstances, the old ex-spy successfully petitioned the state for relief, acquiring after thirty years a veteran's pension. The incongruity of his position, however, was unchanged. He was a recognized veteran of the Revolution and a free man, but not a citizen. Nevertheless, he had emerged somewhat from the symbolic shadow in which he stands in the Paon portrait, and in 1824, during Lafayette's visit to Virginia following the French Revolution, Armistead's now aging features were to share a bit more of the general's sun. For once again James Armistead Lafayette's image was committed to canvas, this time by John B. Martin, an artist as skilled in delineating a revolutionary veteran who was a former slave and spy as one who, like John Marshall, would become Secretary of State and Chief Justice of the Supreme Court. In Martin's portrait, Armistead, the former spy, is no longer clothed in fantasy. Proud and dignified, he appears with his highly individualized features forcefully drawn, a dark, ruggedly handsome man looking out at the viewer with quizzical expression. Armistead wears a white neck cloth, and his blue military coat is adorned with bright buttons embossed with the American eagle. Asserting an individual identity earned at the repeated risk of his life and offering an unshakable faith in the ideal of democracy, James Armistead Lafayette's portrait now hangs in the Valentine Museum at Richmond.

COMMENCEMENT ADDRESS
AT THE COLLEGE OF
WILLIAM AND MARY

During the sixties and seventies Ellison delivered a number of commencement addresses. This one, given at the College of William and Mary in 1972, explores the peculiar continuities of ritual, race and change in American experience. It appears in print here for the first time.

MR. President, members of the Board of Visitors, honored guests, members of the faculty, and the William and Mary class of 1972. If there are those among the members of the graduating class who feel uncomfortable out there in the sun, let me assure you that you are not alone. Nor should you be surprised by the fact. For you have been undergoing an initiation, a rite of passage. Here in a setting and atmosphere which resounds and echoes with tradition, new identities have been conferred upon you. With us here is a member of the highest court of the land and the governor of the state of Virginia. Here are representatives of the sciences, and of course illustrious members of the academic community. Here we have heard stirring patriotic music and the sweet music of young voices raised in song. Here we are surrounded by banners and flags, by friends and family. Present here, in fact, is everything necessary to make this a high and transcendent moment.

None of this, of course, is unusual in such a place as Colonial Williamsburg, because these very stones make us abundantly aware of tradition. If, however, we were to go back a few years into the history of mankind, instead of my standing here with my own face exposed, I would be wearing a ritual mask; my role in this ceremony of initiation would require it. And the mask itself would contain frightening features designed to remind you of serious things: of the past and of those terrors which are an inevitable part of human existence. Indeed, perhaps it is one of the most interesting achievements of American culture to have made it unnecessary for me to wear, on such a hot day, a ritual mask. Because, you see, it is an established part of all such rites of passage that the initiate be made aware that his moment of transcendent glory, his moment of joy, is also one which involves the most serious values of the tribe. It is the function of such masks to remind us that the spirits, the ghosts of the honored dead, are present on the scene. And in the presence of such terrifying images as are symbolized by the mask, the initiate is tested as to his ability to endure pain and his suitability for fulfilling the new role which he is about to assume. In our culture, during this moment of history, it is not required that I wear such a mask, but a painful testing is still required and I, I'm afraid you are aware, have been given the role of inflicting the pain.

Yet it is a symbolic pain, and if my maskless presence evokes values and difficulties which such ritual masks are intended to evoke, then you must understand that as a writer I feel the pain and difficulties which you feel even more painfully. Because, you see, it was here several hundred years ago that certain ideas were first enunciated by those honored men who preceded you as graduates of William and Mary. These were men who forged, or helped to forge, what I speak of as the "sacred documents" of this nation—the Declaration of Independence, the Constitution, and the Bill of Rights. So that if there is a relationship between a historical scene and the words uttered and documented there, then certainly for one who is an American writer this is a sacred place. I say "sacred" because no matter what his ideology, no matter what his racial or religious background happens to be, the writer recognizes that the underlying motives of American literature were first expressed here by those rash and dissenting young men who bore such illustrious names as Washington and Jefferson and Madison. You know this better than I do; if not, it is one of the purposes of this transcendent moment to remind you of your ties to these honored predecessors and to their ideals.

In such a sacred place, on such a ceremonial occasion as this, an American writer cannot but realize that he is stuck with the ideals which were proclaimed before the world in these sacred documents. And as in the case of the original utterers of those words, those daring forgers of our sacred documents of state, they cause him a great deal of discomfort. Because, you see, those predecessors of yours did more than create beautiful rhetoric. They made magic. With their words and deeds they laid upon all of us an obligation to conscious-ness and conscience. By which I mean an obligation to be con-sciously aware of the ideals to which they had committed us, and conscientiously concerned with making their ideas manifest in the quality of this nation's life. In the very severing of their ritual ties with England through acts of war, through the severing of their ties of kinship with the English and their negating of all that had been considered sacred in their traditional ties, they thrust upon those of us who were to come upon this scene the obligation of carrying out and fulfilling that vision of democratic freedom which they had con-ceived, fought for, and made sacred through acts of courage, sacri-fice, and bloodshed.

Here was an elite of intellectuals—educated men whose vision of freedom was not confined to the interests of their own class, but who saw the need for universal education as an agency in the fulfillment of their social vision. These were men who by way of making certain that Americans could understand one another in carrying out the imperative of the democratic vision insisted that the new nation adopt a uniform method of spelling. This, in order that New En-glanders and Southerners could at least understand one another on the printed page. The Founding Fathers spoke the same language, but even then with regional accents. Nor should you forget that in this section of the new nation there were a lot of *my* ancestors who were lending their particular music to the English language. So in the new nation universal education and spelling bees were instituted. What a country! What a marvelously unformed country, wherein the social ritual of the spelling bee could be used as an agency for achieving social and political cohesion. Yes, and wherein the spelling of words in a uniform way could be used to instill and revitalize the sacred principles of the democratic faith. What a marvelously open, challenging and hopeful world of new possibilities!

Ah, but there was a flaw in their hopeful project of nation build-ing—and we all know it. We know it because it has shaped the pres-ent. It is a flaw which shapes the drama that underlies your drama of initiation, giving it an undercurrent of uncertainty and threat. It is that flaw which renders my presence here today meaningful in terms other than my role as writer. And it is that flaw which makes my role resonantly symbolic despite the absence of a fright-inspiring ritual mask.

For we know that in the very discussions out of which our sacred documents were drawn up, a war of words broke out. There was contention between the Founding Fathers over the distribution of authority and property. But more important, there was a contention over the very concept of freedom, over its breadth and limits, and over who was to share and not share its promises. Indeed, over the nature of human identity itself. The war of words continued for some eighty years; it grew hot, and from a mere war of words it erupted into a war of arms. That costly and disillusioning war formed a chastening moment of our history and cast a shadow upon the lives of millions yet unborn. It formed that fateful moment wherein we glimpsed the tragic implications of our democratic faith. It was a moment during which tens of thousands of young men from both sides of the Mason-Dixon line were killed (in which they were joined by many of my own people), and it marked the nation's awakening to what lay ahead for all of us. It was a fateful moment during which the future was formed.

In dealing with this new awareness we improvised, just as Americans, having forsaken tradition, have always done. We "made do" as we could, and soon the war that was settled in military terms flowed back to become a contention of words again. And with this came the development of elaborate rituals of exclusion enforced by violence, a reversal of that bright hopefulness concerning the possibility of mankind, really a reduction of it—and you know that story (which is the story of the post-Reconstruction). What is important to remember here today is that in that moment of disenchantment the country was so blessed by natural resources, so blessed by inventive and fertile imaginations, so blessed by that great stretch of land which lay to the west, that we could temporize our new sense of democratic ideals by developing techniques of avoidance.

Americans are known as a people without memory. Americans are known as a people who take things lightly, just as we tend to take such ceremonies as this in which we are engaged as one of reward. It is assumed that you are being paid off for having completed certain necessary work, and some of you have completed that work with great brilliance and verve. But this ceremony is not simply one of reward. I'm sorry, but my role here is to inform you that rewards notwithstanding, this is indeed a rite of preparation. Because the world into which you go now is a world which came into being as a result of what the Founding Fathers were unable to bring themselves to do, and of what those who made peace after the Civil War, or the War Between the States, were unable to do. And the state of the world into which you are about to enter isn't just a matter of laws. It is also a matter of the spiritual quality of our American principles and the manner in which they infuse not only our words and our laws, but the arrangements of our cities, the quality of our education and the disposition of our neighborhoods.

No, the moral conflict which marks the world into which you go was present even in our sacred documents of state, even in the clerical forms which made it possible for our bureaucracies to get on with their work. So you see, even though we could look away from certain unpleasant moral realities, they did not go away. They were woven into the texture of our society. They remained to color even our most sublime gestures. And as surely as the values stated in our sacred documents were compelling and all-pervasive, and as surely as they were being made a living reality in the social structure, such people as were excluded from the rewards and promises of that social structure would rise up and insist on being included. Such people as were brutalized and designated a role beneath the social hierarchy were sure to rise up, and with the same rhetoric and in the name of the same sacred principles, accuse the nation and insist upon a rectification.

I would like to think that we have come to grips with that problem, and the indications here are that we have. Our forefathers created a civilization of quantity—of such quantity that much of the mystery has gone out of life. Perhaps because ours is such a mobile society, one in which change comes rapidly, one in which there is such a multiplicity of events that in order to protect ourselves we take on a stance, a posture of cynicism. Yes, but the old sacred words still work within us. Morality still claims us, because these words in whose name we act were made luminous by human sacrifice, with the shedding of blood. We are not so sophisticated that we are able to throw that off. So now, as I say, we have a society, a civilization, of quantity in which all may be well fed and clothed, and given the opportunity to achieve their own best possibilities. The world into which you are about to enter is such a world, and I can think of no generation of graduates of the College of William and Mary in Virginia which is better able to deal with the problems of such a world.

For you know something of your opposite numbers. You do not have to ask yourselves, "Is the black man an American?"

You do not have to ask yourselves whether the melting pot melts—because it has indeed melted. We are united by the principles enunciated by those young men who preceded you here as graduates so long ago.

We are united in the language we speak.

We are united in the national cultural style and in all of its manifestations.

We are united, certainly, on the field of athletics.

But best of all, we are better able to think together about the cost of the daring and heroic dream which made this country. We know—you know—that no man lives simply his own life. He lives in great part the lives of his ancestors, of his parents. He lives the lives of his children and the lives of those who are to follow them. He lives but a small part of his life for himself. What you are able to do today, what Virginia and the College of William and Mary have been making it possible for you to do, is to live your *own* life. That is not to be irreverent to the ties of the past, but to understand its tragic dimensions and to take on that conscious awareness as you try to make *your* way and as you try to deal with the difficulties which are common to all men and women.

We do not bury the past, because it is within us. But we *do* modify the past as we live our own lives. And because of this we are now able to resuscitate in all its boldness, and with great sophistication, that conscious and conscientious concern for others which is the essence of the American ideal. I would remind you, however, that we are a nation that plays it by ear. We are inventive both in creating sublime visions and in copping out on them. These too are a part of the human response.

Now, in completing my unusual role, I want to thank you for having invited me here. I want to thank you for giving an American writer a renewed sense of the complexity of change, the resurrection of hope, the continuing presence of courage, and that old American desire to move on and to make things a little better.

ADDRESS TO THE
HARVARD COLLEGE ALUMNI,
CLASS OF 1949

In this address Ellison uses his namesake, Ralph Waldo Emerson, and the mystery and sacrifice of the Civil War to ground his meditation on the unfolding fate of American ideals and American innocence. He delivered the address at the annual meeting of the Associated Harvard Alumni on June 12, 1974. It appears in print here for the first time.

MESSRS. Presidents, members of the illustrious class of 1949, honored guests, fellow students, ladies and gentlemen:

I must confess to having accepted your invitation with certain apprehensions. Not only was I aware that words uttered here in the past have launched lofty visionary programs that helped to reshape the world, but I also recalled having read that some one hundred and thirty-six years ago, another writer, whose first and middle names I happen to share, gave a talk here at Harvard that was so rankling and ill-received that it got him banished from this campus for close to thirty years! Indeed, before he was allowed to return, the Civil War had been fought and terminated by an uneasy peace, Abraham Lincoln had been assassinated, and American society had been so utterly transformed that my paternal grandfather, a recently freed slave, had become actively involved in South Carolina politics.*

Therefore, my first impulse was to thank you for considering me worthy of such an honor and then to excuse myself in the name of that discretion which is prudence. But then I began to view your request as a call to adventure and experience. I was nudged even closer to acceptance by a question of personal consistency. "How," I asked myself, "could you who have protested against policies of social exclusion and denials of opportunity now refuse one of the rarest opportunities of all?" To this I had no easy answer; for as I see it, protest is not an end in itself, but an effort in the direction of respon-

---

*In July 1838 Ralph Waldo Emerson delivered his "Divinity School Address" at the Harvard Divinity School. The ensuing outcry among the faculty and Boston clergy over "infidelity," "pantheism," and "atheism" led to a ban on speaking engagements for Emerson at Harvard which lasted nearly thirty years.

sible and creative participation. And although I was still a bit uneasy and perhaps overly mindful of the glamour of the occasion and the mystique with which words spoken here have inspirited this platform, I reassured myself that such uneasiness was only normal, and that like any young black freshman entering an Ivy League college for the first time, I was reacting to the presence of a mystery. Please! Not of race, but of social hierarchy, that mystery which arises from strangeness and from the differences in experience between individuals and groups occupying different regions, neighborhoods, and levels of the social pyramid. Such mysteries arise out of the difficulty of communicating across the hierarchical divisions of American society, and a great deal of our misunderstanding springs from our failures of communication. Such mystery is a product of psychological distance and our ignorance of one another, and it is so persistent that even our great improvements in communications technology make it easier for Americans to misunderstand one another.

Should a writer be balked by such a mystery? Surely not if he has the curiosity characteristic of novelists, and certainly not when he realizes that he has not only been asked to communicate, but also to break bread and take part in nothing less than a Cantabrigian pageant rite of spring! Therefore, like any young initiate, I could do nothing less than confront whatever mystery might lurk within this symbolic occasion, take my chances, and hope that at the least I wouldn't be banished. Then something happened that almost changed my mind: I received a letter from Harvard addressed to Ralph Waldo Emerson!

Lord, but what tenacious memories you Harvards have!

And now that I stand before you, how fortunate for me that my unmistakable pigmentation shines forth no less as sign than as symbol. I assure you that even though I've insisted for years that our American obsession with practical joking was originally not intentional, but arose out of the incongruities abounding in a man-and-mammy-made society set up within an unexplored and alien land, it was still somewhat shocking to find, under the most decorous of circumstances, the image of a Negro American novelist made to show forth through the ghostly (and I hope benign) lineaments of a white philosopher and poet.

But then, this was not the first time that my contact with Harvard was productive of shock. During the summer of 1953, a few short years after you gentlemen set forth upon the journey which you celebrate here today, I found myself in Memorial Hall taking part in a conference on the contemporary novel. There had been an impassioned exchange of ideas, and after the session ended I was approached by a lady who complimented me on some of the remarks I had made—and then without pause or transition informed me that she was in communication with intelligent beings on the planet Mars.

Now at the time man hadn't even set foot on the moon, so I needn't tell you how surprised I was. But this was obviously a genteel and learned lady, and she spoke quietly but with an impressive ring of conviction. So much so that I stood fascinated, hearing her out, and only when she had excused herself to exchange ideas with others of the participants did I stumble out into the hall with my head awhirl as I tried to tie what I'd been saying about the relationship between the novel and American experience together with what *she* had said about communicating with Marsmen.

And it was then that it happened.

As I stumbled along, my attention was drawn upward and I was aware of the marble walls, somber and carved with names. Then came a moment in which perception leaped dizzily ahead of the processes of normal thought. Up to that time no history book that I had read had told me anything of what I stood before, but I knew its significance almost without knowing, and the shock of recognition filled me with a kind of anguish. Something within me cried out "No!" against that painful knowledge, for I knew that I stood within the presence of Harvard men who had given their young lives to set me free. But no, not for me personally, because I didn't exist, nor perhaps for any slave they'd ever seen. They had sacrificed their lives, had paid what Abraham Lincoln termed "the last full measure of devotion," for an ideal of freedom. And what filled me with anguish was that I had been ignorant of their sacrifice, had been unaware of my indebtedness. Standing there I was ashamed of my ignorance and of the circumstance that had assigned these young men to the shadows of our historical knowledge. Upon them a discontinuity had been imposed by the living, and their heroic gestures had been repressed along with the details of the shameful abandonment of those goals for which they had given up their lives. Without question, the consequences of that imposed discontinuity, that betrayal of ideal and memory, are still with us today.

That shock of recognition, that epiphany, occurred back in 1953. A few weeks ago I had occasion to observe to the graduating class of a great state university that they were among the first American generations to have grown up under the full impact of the malignant forces generated by the suppression of such heroic details, no less than by the more shameful details of our national conduct. The result of this, I suggested, was to deny them an easy access to that convenient posture of "American innocence" that had been the concern of American writers from Emerson to Faulkner, and which engaged much of the artistic energy of Henry James.

Here "innocence" refers to our tendency to ignore the evil which can spring from our good intentions, as well as to the consternation with which Americans react upon discovering the negative, often appalling, results that can erupt from actions conceived as totally positive. In the terminology of tragic drama such "innocence" is viewed as an aspect of human character, and when operative in the psychology of the Hero it is termed a *tragic flaw*. The Greeks termed this flaw in character and perception *hubris*, and to the force which springs up from the enactment of such tragic flaws, and which clings to tragic action like the clicks of erasure to magnetic recording tape, the Greeks gave the name of *nemesis*.

I find it interesting that such American failures of perception were termed "innocence," because *hubris* is usually accompanied by some form of arrogance and insolence, by some form of overbearing pride. Perhaps this is because in the drama of American society one of the most damaging forms of insolence and pride is racism. Now lest I appear about to take off on a tirade of indictment—of which we've had quite enough—let me hasten to add that neither tragic arrogance nor insolence is limited to Americans; these flaws arise from the nature of the human animal and from the limitations encountered by human consciousness when asserting itself against the vast multiplicity of the universe.

As for *nemesis*, well, here I think it best to reject the definitions of literary critics as perhaps too moralistic in favor of that offered by a mathematician and philosopher who once taught here at Harvard—namely, Scott Buchanan. Buchanan defines *nemesis* as "the eventual consequence of that blindness and arrogance produced by *hubris*, and as the vengeance that the ignored factor in a situation takes on man and his virtues." Note that he speaks of man's pride as an aspect of his virtues, for I'd not have you miss the fact that *I* see Americans as motivated, even in their failures, by the virtues embodied in the American creed. I'd even go so far as to give the pride of racism its due by reminding you that when Faust asked Mephistopheles what he was, the reply was, "A part of that force which always seeks evil and always does good."

It is a tough answer to accept, but it suggests that we look carefully into our own motives. At any rate, pride of race is not an evil in itself—even black men possess such pride. The evil lies in the brutalities committed in its name. The same goes for our pride in production, in the size of our gross national product, in sheer bigness, in our inventiveness, in our ability to create and fulfill needs both false and real, and in our ingenuity in exploiting the natural resources of this great land. Yes, but in all of these areas we have recently begun to suffer startling reversals. Our most seriously considered enterprises have taken on the character of maliciously motivated practical jokes. Even our ability to govern ourselves appears to have gotten out of hand. So if I speak here at length of *nemesis*, it is because I suspect that whatever else the times in which we live turn out to be, they are *our* days of *nemesis*.

Hence my suggestion to those students that the society which they were about to enter as adults would be quite unlike the society of their parents. Nor could they ignore its tragic realities by adopting a posture of innocence. Since 1954, say, events both negative and positive have rendered such innocence impossible. American society and the world alike have changed more drastically than at any time during our relatively short history, and this generation of students has observed and been a part of that change. Fundamental to that change has been the broadening of our dispensing of justice, an action that has solved many crucial problems and created still others. But with the legal supports of racism giving way, there has come a broadening of access to our institutions. The individuality and talent, the potential, of those once assigned to the anonymity of the racial stereotype are now being recognized, and a wavering struggle toward an equalizing of opportunity is under way. Further, the patterns of political alliances have been changing, bringing new chaos and indecision as well as a rectification of past inequities. Regional antagonisms have receded, along with the smug hypocrisies used to justify them. In brief, chaos has come with order, and some good things have been exchanged for other good things, some bad things for other bad things, and some, thank God, for good.

Yes, but before such experience, such knowledge, what innocence? This generation of students has, like ourselves, observed vast changes in the direction of the American social drama and felt the shock and trauma of acts that have deprived us of a president, a senator, and a great spiritual leader. We have witnessed startling reversals of attitudes and alliances in the field of politics. Following the lead of a native Texan whom many despised for his liberalism, Southern politicians at first grudgingly and then with that bewildering mixture of motives and shift of position characteristic of politicians, show a growing willingness to obey the law and share the common power with their black fellow Southerners. One could almost believe that racial discrimination and disenfranchisement were nothing more than a tactic, a symbolic gesture. One could, that is, if he could forget either the recent past or the names engraved on the wall of Memorial Hall.

But accompanying these reversals in attitudes and customs is yet another, wherein Northern whites have reacted to the pressures of black Northerners for more equality as vehemently and in some cases as violently and irrationally as their Southern counterparts. And this resistance is accompanied by reams of pseudoscientific justification, double-talk, and diversionary tactics. So the tensions and contentions continue, but for the first time in our history the social drama that is American society is beginning to proceed according to the original script—by which I mean the Constitution and Bill of Rights. Virtue and *nemesis* exert their tensions, yes. But for the first time we appear to be facing up to the reality of the Americanness of American diversity, and to the past which made us what we are. For the first time we are facing up to the tragic cost paid by some for the achievements of our form of government without recognition or recompense.

T. S. Eliot's reminder that *What we have inherited from the fortunate / We have taken from the defeated* must not be forgotten, for such forgetfulness leaves us vulnerable to *nemesis*. Because today *nemesis* exerts its force in forms and places we least expect: in areas of society thought safe from chaos; in the form of criminal acts, including murder, proclaimed as being committed in the name of human freedom; in the corruption of art and the perversion of fashion; in drug cults and Satan worship; in superstition and false science; and in the distortion of the communicative function of language. None of this is new, I know, only its extent and the malignity which it embodies. And what is the antidote? Here I can only fall back upon the teaching of that earlier Ralph Waldo and suggest, conscience and consciousness, more consciousness and more conscientiousness! This achieved, and it will take time, perhaps we can then say truly of the 1960s what Henry James had to say mistakenly of the late 1860s, that they mark "an era in the history of the American mind [in which there was] introduced into the national consciousness a certain sense of proportion and relation, of the world being a more complicated place than it had hitherto seemed, the future more treacherous, success more difficult. At the rate at which things are going, it is obvious that good Americans will be more numerous than ever; but the good American, in days to come, will be a more critical person than his complacent and confident grandfather. He will have eaten of the tree of knowledge. He will not, I think, be a skeptic, and still less, of course, a cynic; but he will be, without discredit to his well-known capacity for action, an observer. He will remember that the ways of the Lord are inscrutable, and that this is a world in which everything happens; and eventualities, as the late Emperor of the French used to say, 'will not find him intellectually unprepared.' "

What a glorious exhortation! For exhortation it was, yes, but when taken at short range, what a flawed act of prophecy! But then, if I may say so, James's imagination was always ahead of his times. Besides, his experience, class identity, and refinement of taste placed him at a distance which made knowledge of the recalcitrant complexity of much of the humanity for which he had such bright hopes difficult to come by. What is more, he had no idea of the great potential for chaos and order that was embodied in those who had been liberated by the forces that made for and decided the outcome of the Civil War—if indeed the outcome of that war has yet been decided. Quite frankly, it is my opinion that it is still in the balance, and only our enchantment by the spell of the possible, our endless optimism, has led us to assume that it ever really ended. Instead, it would seem that while the military phase of that war ended in 1865, there actually occurred a reversal of Clausewitz's famous formula through which the Civil War, upper case, continued on as *civil* war, lower case, in which that war of arms was replaced by a war of politics, racial and ethnic violence, ritual sacrifice based on race and color, and by economic and judicial repression.

American awareness of this metamorphosis of that ongoing conflict was obscured for all but its victims by the burgeoning growth of our industrial capacity and technological potential—all made possible by the defeat of a rival, slavery-based economic system. Yes, and by the assertion of that American innocence of which I spoke earlier. Yes, I know, viewed in this light that "innocence" took the basic form of a flaunting disregard for the principles upon which this nation was founded.

So I think by now my meaning is clear: All of the signs, both positive and negative, seem to indicate that the nation has been pushed toward an awareness of the tragic nature of the American experience; the dark underside of our history has taken on the form of a many-headed *nemesis*. But if all this seems too pessimistic, remember that the antidote to *hubris*, to overweening pride, is irony, that capacity to discover and systemize clear ideas. Or, as Emerson insisted, the development of consciousness, consciousness, *consciousness*. And with consciousness, a more refined conscientiousness, and most of all, that tolerance which takes the form of humor, for when Americans can no longer laugh at each other, they have to fight one another.

Gentlemen of the Class of 1949, you have been termed fortune's darlings by no less an authority than *Fortune* magazine. This alone suggests that the many forms of *nemesis* that threaten the nation haven't completely overwhelmed us. We admire your achievements and are well aware that many of the rectifications of past failures are the results of your willingness to deal with change. If I have sounded pessimistic, your involvement with the complexities of American society allows you to know where to say amen and where to say nay. All American society since 1954 has undergone a profound change. Let us not be dismayed, let us not lose faith, simply because the correctives which we have set in motion, and you have set in motion, took a long time. It took strong stomachs, it took strong arms, it took our capacity for violence and for humor to get us to this point. I say this to you, as one who believes that the difficulties which we face today are indeed minor. What seems to be called for is an honest confrontation with our mistakes, as any scientist or scholar would say, and a willingness to confront the chaos, the *nemesis*, which is about us. After all, *nemesis* is only another word for peril.

HAVERFORD STATEMENT

Ellison made this statement using his "situation as a Negro American" to explain his "personal affirmation of integration without the surrender of our unique identity as a people" and his belief that "the only way to be an effective Negro intellectual is by being a most perceptive and responsible American intellectual." His comment followed discussions in Haverford, Pennsylvania, May 30–31, 1969. It appears in print here for the first time.

In spite of all the writing I do, and for all of the lectures I give each year, there are many matters which I won't write about, nor, except with my wife and a few intimate friends, do I discuss them. Perhaps this is because they have to do with ideas, emotions, and attitudes which grow out of my situation as a Negro American, and with those undefined and uncodified aspects of our lives which require the sympathy and insight usually found only among those who have been conditioned and disciplined by our specific group experience. Today such in-group discussion is no mere luxury; it is a necessity both for ourselves, for our restless youth, and for the American intellectual community as a whole. There is no question but that my own participation in our discussions at Haverford had something of the effect of a catharsis. I was cleansed of some of my doubts and confusions, and thankfully I was stimulated not by the sound of my own all-too-familiar voice, but by your ideas and by your passion. If this is to any extent true of the other participants, I believe our enterprise was well worth the effort and should be continued on a permanent basis. Certainly it points to the necessity of our no longer working in isolation from one another, and it is clear that we have much to offer that has been missing from discussions in the larger American intellectual community. There is simply no avoiding the fact that there are many aspects of American life which can only be described, analyzed, and defined by black intellectuals, for no other group possesses an adequate perspective or so urgent a need.

In summing up what I tried to say in our discussions, I would emphasize my personal affirmation of integration without the surrender of our unique identity as a people to be a viable and, indeed, inescapable goal for black Americans. As a writer who tries to reduce the flux and flow of life to meaningful artistic forms, I am stuck with integration, because the very process of the imagination as it goes about bringing together a multiplicity of scenes, images, characters, and emotions and reducing them to significance is nothing if not integrative. Further, the object of my fictional imagination is American society and the American experience as experienced fundamentally by Negroes, and I find it impossible to deal with either in isolation, for they are intricately united in their diversity. The judgments implied by the fictional products of my imagination might well repudiate many accepted American values and definitions of reality, but this by no means infers that the integrative role of the imagination—and of the intellect—is invalid. It does imply that the larger American ideals of freedom are the ultimate ground upon which any literary evaluations of the cost, pain, joy, and triumph of being human are tested.

The American people are united in all their regional, class, ethnic, and religious diversity by a bond of language. There are many idioms of that language, and it is partially the creation of a voice which found its origin in Africa. Indeed, the language began to be influenced by this voice long before the American nation was formed. In the beginning was the word, and our voice sounded in the language with which the word was spoken. The American language owes something of its directness, flexibility, music, imagery, mythology, and folklore to the Negro presence. It is not, therefore, a product of "white" culture as against "black" culture; rather it is the product of cultural integration. And the realities of discrimination and racism notwithstanding, it is a fact that *culturally* the melting pot has indeed melted, and that one of the strongest forces shaping the general American culture has been what I call the Negro American idiom.

I am calling attention to the cultural pluralism of American life because until the present college generation this pluralism as expressed in art, folkways, and style was an important source of Negro American optimism—just as that optimism was a support of the general faith in the workability of the American system. Our elders recognized their presence and influence in areas of American life from which they were physically barred, and while the American house was of many mansions, they knew that despite racial discrimination there was something of themselves dwelling in most of them, and not merely as servants. Sometimes they made hue and cry over the theft of their substance and their style, and sometimes they were silent, but they saw themselves in all the movements of American life no matter how confused the scene. For them the problem was not that of identifying with the scene, but of having others give public recognition to their contributions. Certainly there was no question of trying to withdraw in a pique or of surrendering their investment in the experiment.

Today that sense of having shared creatively in the common American experiment is under assault by passionate young blacks who have lost their mooring in tradition. They are romantic, earnest, and ignorant, a state for which I believe that we as intellectuals are responsible because in pursuing our specialties we have failed to interpret the past and define the present and project the future in ways that are available to the young. Far too frequently black youth have been forced to depend upon intellectuals of other groups for interpretations of their relationship to the larger society. In fact other groups of intellectuals have given more time to the task than we ourselves. Often they appear so obsessively concerned with defining our lifestyles, character, traditions, and values as to reduce us to silence and pliable inaction. Frequently they seem motivated by a desire to manipulate our image for political and economic purposes of their own, and some have taken the concepts of Negro sociologists and turned them against us, creating thereby much confusion and great resentment. But whatever their motives, the fact is that they are functioning as intellectuals, and it is their legitimate task, as it is ours, to explore the wholeness of American life and the interrelationships between the various groups which compose it.

That they have co-opted our role is a criticism of ourselves, for we have failed to address ourselves effectively to many of the broader problems of American life, and we have failed to follow up our often creative analysis of specifically Negro American problems into the broader areas where they inevitably lead. In other words, we often forget that the only way to be an effective Negro intellectual is by being a most perceptive and responsible *American* intellectual. I believe that the state of black youth points to our failure, and if we have failed them, then we have failed American youth generally. For all their talk of black separatism—really another version of secessionism, an old American illusion which arises whenever groups reach an explosive point of frustration—and for all their stance of alienation, they are really acting out a state of despair. They are frightened by the existence of opportunities for competing with their white peers on a basis of equality which did not exist for us. They suffer traumatically from the shock of sudden opportunity. The shackles have been struck from at least one of their ankles, and their skin is sensitive to the turbulent air and the illusory possibility of unrestrained movement. Actually they are in the position of pioneers who must enter an unknown territory armed only with the knowledge and skills which they have brought with them from the past, but instead of plunging in and testing themselves against the unknown, they choose rather to argue with the deficiencies of the past and to direct accusations against their parents. They accuse us of lacking manhood and courage, and they have declared themselves a new breed—which perhaps they are. One thing is certain: they have thrown us a challenge, and I believe that we should meet them head on. I don't think that we should be put in a position of apologizing for our backgrounds, values, or goals, but I do think we must provide a forum wherein the unwritten wisdom of the group can be intellectualized and passed on to those who are sincerely seeking for answers and orientation.

HOMAGE TO
WILLIAM L. DAWSON

Although Ellison left Tuskegee in 1936 after his junior year, what he learned and experienced there resonated in his mind and work for the rest of his life. Ellison gave this talk honoring the conductor, composer, and teacher William L. Dawson, whom he considered to be "the greatest classical musician in that section of the country," to the Philadelphia Tuskegee Club in 1971. It appears in print here for the first time.

FELLOW Tuskegeeans: I hope it isn't lost on you that something natural is happening which is at the same time a little unexpected if we consider the reputation of Tuskegee. Here a very great composer, a master of choral music, is being honored by a fellow who studied under him, who went to Tuskegee because there was a man named Dawson there, who—since this seems to be a part of the tradition, and it actually happens—rode freight trains (it was too far to walk) to get to a place where there was musical excellence and a tradition of musical creativity. Most people didn't think about it in these terms, and yet it was there. It was there, I suspect, before Mr. Dawson graduated and returned to work his wonders on the scene. But it was also there as a deep tradition, one which bathed each and every thing that was done at Tuskegee with the overtones and undertones of a sense of life which perhaps could not have been expressed except through art. It was there perhaps out of the sheer desperate need to assert our hopes and dreams against the complications of living in the South—or for that matter of living in America. For we were up against definitions of our humanity which we could not accept, and we were too busy trying to go where *we* wanted to go, and to become what *we* wanted to become, to stop and spend much time arguing about it. It was an assertion of our own sense of life, the insistent drive to define human hope in the United States, not through avoiding those aspects of reality, and especially of our condition, which were brutal and dehumanizing, but taking that too as part of the given scene, and then determining to go beyond it. Not to ignore it, not to pretend that it didn't exist, but to humanize it, to take it in, to make it connect with other aspects of living—with the dream, with the sounds of the future and the sounds of hope. We did this through music. It was the tradition far back in the slave past which enhances the activities of Tuskegee. Underneath the desire for education or the possession of more technology, underneath the drive for intellectual competency is that other thing which can only be expressed through art.

As I said, it is rather odd that a fellow who didn't make it as a musician should be here trying to say something about William L. Dawson. But I think just as he reached out through his choir, through his ability to make people who were not really musicians give voice to sublime music, he was doing something else: acting as a cultural hero, acting as a living symbol of what was possible. So we came to Tuskegee, so we played in the band and in the orchestra, so we studied. (He once threw a piece of crayon at me!) You learned that even here life was real, life was honest, life was ambiguous. But you got certain messages which you weren't quite aware that you were getting.

When Mr. Dawson stood before a choir or the band or the orchestra, you had the sense that you were dealing with realities beyond yourself—that you were being asked to give yourself to meanings which were undefinable except in terms of music and musical style. But you also had the sense that with his elegance and severity, with his grasp of the meaning of verse, the value that he could draw out of a word and make you *draw* out of it, the way he could make you phrase, could teach you to grasp the meaning of a line of verse which sometimes he had set to music—sometimes Handel—all this gave you a sense that through this activity and dedication to the arts, you were going beyond and were getting insight into your other activities.

As I have said, Tuskegee has been a place of music, and it is ironic that through all of the years of its identity as a place of agriculture and industry, it has had this other dimension, that dimension of art which went beyond the simple matter of our singing and playing instruments. During the thirties Tuskegee was one of the major musical centers of the South. It was to Tuskegee that the Metropolitan

Opera groups came; it was to Tuskegee that the great string quartets and the Philharmonic came. It was not to the University of Alabama; it was not to white schools in this area, but to Tuskegee. It was here that the tradition was. I will tell you something else: it wasn't a new thing when the Tuskegee choir opened Radio City during the thirties. It was only the event through which the broader America, the broader United States became aware of what had been going on there for many, many years. We live in ourselves; we grow from what went before. What comes after us depends on what we do in preserving that which we share, and which has been handed over into our keeping.

I think it important during the fiftieth anniversary of the Philadelphia Tuskegee Club that you honor Mr. Dawson and impress upon the nation at large that something very crucial to the cultural life of the United States—and perhaps to the political life of the United States—will be lost if we allow the tradition of Tuskegee to go down. I'm not talking now about politics. I'm talking about living examples; I'm talking about musical traditions. Because what is frequently overlooked—usually overlooked—in these days when we talk of discovering our identities, is that there was an identity here all along. And when you see a choir like this—two choirs: one improvised, I understand, and one which has been together—when you hear the articulation, when you hear the blending of the voices that grew out of an *identity*, you are aware of an identity based upon struggle with basic realities. A tradition which has been extended, broadened, and enriched by William L. Dawson, a tradition which is made up of music which our forefathers heard and created out of what was around them and what they brought with them from Africa. But the magical thing about it is that it is not simply an in-group music. This tradition is an artistic definition of what the American experience *is* when faced with grace and a willingness to give oneself to the tragic dimensions of the American experience. It is very precious, and the entire nation depends upon it because there is not enough of it.

We are very lucky that an artist of Mr. Dawson's stature found his way to Tuskegee at the age of thirteen. (He must have been a little criminal, because he ran away from home.) But he spent many years there, and received the basis of his musical training at Tuskegee. Some years ago, in speaking with a group of my white colleagues along with another Tuskegeean, we were talking about the writings of Joyce and Eliot and Pound, and all of a sudden Albert Murray said, "Well, Ralph, aren't you glad that we discovered these people at Tuskegee for ourselves?" And yes, I was glad, because now I can never read the poetry of those poets without associating it with Tuskegee; without seeing the magenta skies at dusk and sunup; without seeing the clock in White Hall. I must say that I was the fellow who used to wake Dr. Bryce up when I was there, because I was a trumpeter. I used to stand out there early in the morning and blow first call, and most of the time I put you to bed too.

Through tradition, the place, the association, the sense of discovering that which is ever new in the old and the continuing, the abiding—in this way the artist fulfills his role. If you can't spell it out—and some of these things cannot be spelled out in words—they can be felt, can be grasped, can enter you, can animate your body and thus animate your mind. This is a great gift. We are very fortunte that such a man as Mr. Dawson has touched so many of our lives. Through his dedication to art he has made it possible for me, for instance, to be as dedicated and disciplined about literature. I'm sure that the same is true for most of you who have been taught by him and touched by him. This is a secret of education which goes beyond grades, which goes beyond even brilliance of mind. This is a secret of the place, the people, the times, and that deep art of music which is far more important to us than such poor critics as I have been able to spell out.

If there were a choir here, I would say let us sing "Let Us Break Bread Together." I am not particularly religious, but I am claimed by music, and I was claimed by William L. Dawson.

ALAIN LOCKE

On December 1, 1973, Ellison participated with Albert Murray, Nathan Huggins, and Harold Cruse in the Alain L. Locke Symposium at Harvard University. Ellison's autobiographical tribute to Locke's "conscious approach to American *culture" was published in the* Harvard Advocate, *Spring 1974.*

I'LL start by recalling my brief acquaintance with Alain Locke. He came to the Tuskegee campus in 1935 to visit Hazel Harrison. Most of you won't know that name, but Hazel Harrison was a pianist of such a quality that had she come along in this generation, you would be as familiar with her name as you are with those of Shirley Verrett or Leontyne Price. Hazel Harrison was an artist, a teacher, a great person—one of those people at Tuskegee who sponsored and encouraged all sorts of artistic and intellectual activities both within her classroom and outside it. Dr. Locke came down to visit his friend Hazel Harrison, and she, in her generosity and sense of dedication, saw to it that a whole group of us were able to meet him.

I met Dr. Locke again not much later when I went to Harlem. The morning after I arrived, as I was walking on 125th Street I met two people who were heroic figures for me at the time, Alain Locke and Langston Hughes. It was a brief meeting, no more than Locke introducing me to Hughes, and some small talk. I was to see Locke only once or twice again over the next twenty years, but, as with Albert Murray, I knew of his work, I had read his book thanks to a teacher in the city school of Oklahoma City, and I was to reread it many times.

I mention this because I was reading everything I could get my hands on which tried to make sense out of the mysteries of art and music. You see, I thought I was a musician in those days, and spent most of my time with books and music. What Locke did for me, as he did for Al Murray, was to act as a guide. He stood for a conscious approach to *American* culture—and I stress American culture because I think we are in a great deal of confusion over our role in the creation of American culture. It is so easy to become unconsciously racist by simply stressing one part of our heritage, thus reducing the complexity of our cultural heritage to a genetic reality which is only partially dealt with.

Al Murray has said that all blacks are part white, and all whites part black. If we can deal with that dilemma—and it is a dilemma—then we can begin to deal with the problem of defining the American experience as we create it. You cannot have an American experience without having a black experience. Nor can you have the technology of jazz, as original as many of those techniques are, without having had long centuries of European musical technology, not to mention the technologies of various African musical traditions. Locke thought about these matters. I didn't always agree with him, and I don't today, but he did point a direction, he did act as a role model, he did move in the direction of some sort of conscious assessment of the pluralistic condition of the United States. I think it was sometime in the 1830s that Lowelessa Hoy and Walt Whitman suggested that there would be an American grand opera and that the language of that opera would be found in Afro-American speech, "the speech of the slaves," as Whitman put it. Locke felt very much the same way. Thus it seems amazing to me that we have moved away from that complex, mysterious, perplexing sense of our role in this country to something which is much too simplistic.

I can remember having first heard the name Richard B. Harrison, when he was performing in something called *Green Pastures*. I don't know whether *Green Pastures* has been done in recent years so that the younger students in the audience would be aware of it. But it was a play, done after a piece of fiction written by a white Southerner called *Old Man Adam's Children*. This slightly burlesque work was stereotyped, but Mr. Harrison, in acting out the role of the Lord, somehow transformed the original tenor of the play and made it something transcendent. Perhaps it is time for it to be revived. But what finally struck me about Richard B. Harrison was what I discovered after I went back home and began to reminisce about the early days in Oklahoma City. I was born in the rooming house where he used to stop. I asked what he was doing there, and was told he was giving Shakespeare readings all over the place, giving one-man recitals, reading the soliloquies and so on, evidently with a great deal of effect. This was years after he had gone on and become known as an actor.

What I am suggesting is that when you go back you do not find a pure stream; after all, Louis Armstrong, growing up in New Orleans, was taught to play a rather strict type of military music before he found his jazz and blues voice. Talk about cultural pluralism! It's the air we breathe; it's the ground we stand on. It's what we have to come to grips with as we discover who we are and what we want to add to the ongoing definition of the American experience. I think in his effort to define what was different about that group of Negroes of the 1920s, Locke was trying to resolve those questions, and to bring to bear all that he knew about the complexities of culture. It is very difficult in this country to find a pure situation. Usually when you find some assertion of purity, you are dealing with historical, if not cultural ignorance.

Al Murray mentioned Mr. Brown and the imperatives which were to be found in his particular school. I can remember another figure whom I held in as much esteem as Alain Locke when as I was growing up, and this was a man by the name of Melvin Tolson. Many of you might know his poetry, but I first knew Tolson as a teacher at Wiley College in Texas. Tolson was training a drama group, but his special pride and joy was a debating society through which he had inherited all the techniques of debate and rhetoric from the nineteenth century as they had been filtered down through those young New Englanders who went South during the Reconstruction to teach the freedmen. Tolson extended these traditions and techniques to such an extent that more than once the debating team of Oxford used to come out there and get clobbered. Now, this isn't the kind of knowledge of American education or American cultural history that you find easily available, but I assure you I am not creating fantasies. I am speaking of what actually happened. How confusing it was to find that what was considered so excellent that it could defeat the members of a great university was not honored throughout the larger society.

Well, be that as it may, what we had to do—and there were a few along with me—was to decide where the action was. This was one way of dealing with that imposed sense of alienation: by taking what you had, learning to look at it through what was available, looking at and listening to those people who spoke in that pluralistic idiom—men like Bingham Page, the great Count Basie (who was conservatory trained!)—people who in their own way defined what the American experience was, who defined that which was affirmative beyond all contradictions of social hierarchy and racism.

Those people and many others projected in artistic, rhetorical, and other forms the essence of the American experience as members of a minority group, and as individuals who responded, as best they could, to what was there to be expressed. They affirmed and defined not only the black experience, but what was basically an American experience, and, when it was most transcended, the experience of human beings living in a world of turbulent transition. This, it seems to me, was something Alain Locke sensed. It led him to deal with Afro-American folklore and music from a background that included his studies with James and Royce. This is all one can really ask of any individual: that he not deny where he comes from, and that he plumb this background with all of the conscious thought that he possibly can. To do less than this is to be a second-rate human being. That we cannot afford.

Locke did something else in projecting his idea of cultural pluralism; he moved, it seems to me, toward that sense of freedom which lies with the complex "unfreedom" we as a people experience in the United States. The slaves first sensed it when they looked at the people in the big house dancing their American versions of European social dances. First the slaves mocked them, and then decided, coming from dancing cultures, that they could do them better—so they went on to define what is surely the beginnings of an American choreography. Most of the time these dances were done in rags, which to the people in the big house looking out at the activity in the yard appeared hilariously comic. Well, the new frequently does appear so, the new frequently appears strange—it has to. But when Americans, all Americans, began to dance on the popular stage or whatever, one place they could look and be sure that they were Americans was back there in those slave yards, and later the Negro dance halls and juke joints where that original American choreography had found its direction. I don't like racial bragging, so I'm not talking about our African genes so much as what our people have made of the chaos of America as they tried to find new forms of expression. They had the freedom to do so because, being at the bottom of the social hierarchy, there was no one to take them too seriously. They had the freedom of experimentation, of trying out things no matter how ridiculous they might seem, and in doing so they found ways of making the human body "move," as Flip Wilson might say, in stylized ways which were different. Inevitably these forms came together; there is always integration of artistic styles whether it is done out of admiration, out of need, or out of a motive of economic exploitation. It finds its way to the larger American public, and as such, everyone who is touched by it becomes a little bit Afro-American. Sometimes they become Afro-American Episcopal Zion; sometimes they become Black Baptist (as most rock singers are now); sometimes they become a little bit Southern in their talk and a little colored in their walk.

Speaking of language, whenever anyone tells you that you're outside the framework of American culture, and when they deflect you into something called "black English," remember that the American version of the English language was born in rebellion against proper English usage, and that the music of the African voice and the imagery coming from the people who lived close to the soil and under the conditions of slavery added greatly to that language. And when you look for the spiritual context of that language, you can be sure that some of the passion for the unfulfilled ideals of democracy comes from the voices of those black and unknown bards, as well as from my mama and papa and your mama and papa crying in church, protesting in pool halls, cussing in shine parlors, and celebrating Juneteenth (that's what we call emancipation). The language of the United States is partly black people's creation; Locke understood that. There is no imagery of the great nineteenth-century writers which ignores our existence as metaphor of the human condition. There is no specifically American vernacular and language which has not been touched by us and our style. Locke sensed this.

Some of us have tried—not as disciples; certainly I'm no disciple of Locke—to think consciously of what it meant to be an American and a Negro. The true meaning, perhaps, will be found by those who come after us, because this is a changing situation; about the only thing which is unchanged about it is the confusion. We still do not know who we are. I had hoped that by the 1960s people like you would be telling me who I am, and maybe you tell me sometimes, but what I have found is that during the decade these strains of continuity, these linkages between people on the basis of ideas and experience were automatically, arbitrarily thrown overboard. That is disastrous for writers; it is disastrous for any sort of human enterprise because we live one upon the other; we follow, we climb upon the shoulders of those who have gone before.

When Locke was at Tuskegee, he had much to say about what was happening among the artists and intellectuals in Paris. In the studio where I met Dr. Locke, Hazel Harrison, who had been one of Busoni's prize pupils, had manuscripts of Prokofiev which I had the privilege of listening to her play as she rehearsed her repertoire. It struck me later that here I was at what some would have called a "cow college," and I was in touch with the living work of Prokofiev. This was no accident. Miss Harrison had dedicated herself to music. She had lived in Busoni's home in Berlin. She knew Petrie and Prokofiev. She knew many of the great musicians of the time, and it was not incongruous that she could be a black woman whose possibilities of being recognized as a great star were strictly limited, while at the same time she was fulfilling her obligation as a teacher and musician.

That she did so was very important to me. That Dr. Locke saw the importance of trying to define us in that sophisticated moment, in that moment of great transition, in that moment wherein jazz was being felt (if not understood as being more than a primitive folk music), in that moment when we were far enough away from the traumas of Reconstruction to begin to think of leadership on a very broad scale, in that moment when we realized whatever the new leadership, there would not be another Frederick Douglass, or Williams and Walker, or Scott Joplin. There would be a metamorphosis of their ideas and styles. There would be an incarnation of young people still unknown who would have some sense of what lay back there, some sense of the unspoken meaning, and who would try to translate into articulate forms that feeling about life, that assertion of identity which always made our particular contributions to the arts in this country immediately recognized as what America has instead of a sacred past.

We provided the past; we provided the suggestions. It didn't come from across the water; it came from the land. It came from beneath the social hierarchy. I don't make mystification, but I speak of that sense of individualism and group consciousness, which in conflict and travail seek to define the country and the various pluralistic styles of American life—define it and define that which is new in human possibility. Back when Al Murray and I were at Tuskegee, we sometimes talked about Dr. Kittredge. I wanted to study with Dr. Kittredge, but though I could ride a freight train to Tuskegee, I don't believe I could have gotten this far, and I had great doubts about what would have happened had I gotten here. Now it seems to me a certain faith has been fulfilled, because at this moment we can stand here on this campus and discuss an important American figure who for so many years has been thought of as simply a spokesman for a minor aesthetic position mainly of interest to minority people.

Don't kid yourself: he was talking about all of us.

ROSCOE DUNJEE AND THE AMERICAN LANGUAGE

Roscoe Dunjee, editor of The Black Dispatch *in Oklahoma City, was a personal and public force in Ellison's early life—"a writer who in his emphasis upon the possibilities for justice offered by the Constitution anticipated the antisegregation struggle by decades." During subsequent years in New York, Ellison continued to rely on the newspaper and on Dunjee's editorials. Here he discusses the impact of Dunjee's acting out of American ideals through the American language on his own writer's vocation. First delivered as a talk to the Black Perspective Conference in New York City on May 14, 1972, the revised essay appears in print here for the first time.*

I confess my debt to a great newspaperman who influenced me long before I realized that I would ever be anything but a musician. That man's name is Roscoe Dunjee. He was editor of *The Black Dispatch* in Oklahoma City. It is still in existence, and still an important paper. I sold it when I was fresh out of diapers. There's a pun in that, but I mean to imply only that I sold it when I could barely talk, and continued to sell it up into my teens. Of course there were other black newspapers as well as the *Dispatch—The Afro-American, The Pittsburgh Courier, The Kansas City Call*—and my early childhood and adolescence were tied up with reading and selling them. I sold them in Oklahoma City, sometimes from a bicycle, but more often walking and peddling them. In McAlester, Oklahoma, where I spent my eleventh year, I would get up at 4:00 A.M. and a friend and I would load our wagons with the local papers—the white papers and those we called Negro papers—and deliver them. We shouted their headlines through the black community for hours until we had either lost our voices or had all the money we could make on those Sunday mornings.

Better still, I am of an age to have been present as a very young child in Tulsa, Oklahoma, just before the terrible riot of 1921. My mother hoped to bring up my brother and me in the North, so she took us to Gary, Indiana, where she had a brother. On our way North we stopped in Tulsa to see an older cousin who had a fine brick home in the prosperous Negro community of Greenwood. But shortly after we arrived in Gary, as luck would have it—and luck is always ambiguous and ambivalent—there was a depression in steel, so it was my fate to have been brought back through Tulsa and see that Greenwood had been devastated and all but destroyed by bomb and fire in that riot of 1921.

I don't bring this up to bore you with how hard life has been for us in the United States, but to emphasize the courage of Roscoe Dunjee. Dunjee was a fighter, but he was more than that. His family was originally from Virginia, and had come to Oklahoma City out of Minnesota, where his father had been minister of a church. He got to Oklahoma in 1907, which was the beginning of statehood, and established his paper with little or no money but with a great sense of adventure, much courage, and a strong faith in his people. He also had faith in something which is not always held in such respect today. Roscoe Dunjee understood what it has taken me many years to understand. He understood that not only were the American people a revolutionary people, but that in the shedding of blood, sacrifice, agony, and anguish of establishing this nation, all Americans became bound in a covenant. Roscoe Dunjee understood, at a time when hardly anybody else did, that there was an irrational element in the American Constitution, a mysterious binding force which was the secret to moving people. Perhaps you couldn't move them too far. Perhaps you couldn't move them to the point where they would actually live up to their commitment to the American covenant. But in his time and his place Roscoe Dunjee was a constitutionalist, a great Negro American newspaperman who, starting from the betrayal of the Emancipation in the 1870s, somehow understood how to carve a chicken. (Those of you who have any acquaintance with Marxism realize that I am paraphrasing Lenin's comment that if you want to change history you have to know where the chicken bones are articulated.) Anyway, Roscoe Dunjee, coming out of the South by way of Minnesota to the soon-to-be new state, the Indian territory of Oklahoma, started a newspaper on hardly anything. In a very American way he focused on that awareness of what newspapers were supposed to do, and what every good newspaper in this country has focused on.

One of the major problems of American civilization has been a struggle with the English language and its proper usage. For Americans to become themselves they had to revamp their concept and use of the English language. They had to understand and, when necessary, reinterpret the overtones and undertones of a language forged in a world they had never made, with a king at the top and God above him, a language which had given birth to great poetry, philosophical writings, and drama. Here in this new land these English immigrants were involved in bloodshed, slaughter, and sacrifice in the process of seizing the land from its indigenous peoples, the Indians. These colonials imported our black forefathers, an act which subsequently involved them in a terrific struggle to save the American reality, to come to grips with a New World reality through a fog of English terminology.

So one of the first problems of the United States was to master the language, to convert it, to squeeze the assumptions out of it and adapt it into a flexible instrumentality which would tell people what was new here. The birds, the climate, the waters, the weather, and the terrain were all different. There was no word in the English language to describe those long, flat stretches of land which had few trees and a great abundance of grass, so we took the word *prairie* from the French. There was no precise way of expressing in the King's English the groping spirit which men were exhibiting in this country, where they were no longer held in the bounds of a class structure supposedly handed down from God through kingship, so the term "individualism" came into being.

I suspect that in the effort to adapt the American language, to make it tell the truth about processes and relationships between people in this country, there somehow lay the beginnings of the American Revolution. I suspect that its seeds came from the impact of the American experience upon life as we were living it. When I say "we," I am quite conscious that we black people were already here causing all sorts of turbulence in the king's town—in religion, music, science, and so on. Somehow in the struggle to articulate words to fit with reality and reality to fit with words, we had the beginnings of the American Revolution. As we fought this revolution in fire and blood and sacrifice, a covenant was made, and that covenant, to use the biblical terminology, was the Constitution, the Declaration of Independence, and the Bill of Rights. These are the grounds upon which we stand today.

"In the beginning was the word." The founders of this country understood very well that one of the problems was how to make a unity of diversity. How do you make a society in which for the first time you have to face the fact of race? Black people were already here. We were here as slaves; everyone tells us that. We all know it, and I am sick of hearing about it. Yes, we were slaves, but we were living persons. We were chattel, but speaking chattel, chattel with a moral sense, chattel with an artistic sense and with a great capacity for creation. So a social hierarchy was set up, open at both ends, it was said, wherein equality ruled, wherein man was no longer bound to the status of his forefathers, where the injustices of the past no longer obtained, where men and women could amplify their talents and go where they wished to go. Yet at the same time, in the name of God we black folk were put below the threshold, placed outside the bounds of humanity.

This conflict between profession and practice set up a certain turbulence within the language which affected poets as well as reporters and other writers. The standard against which the ideal and the reality were tested was always the Constitution, the Bill of Rights and the Declaration of Independence. In those documents is a great moral force, and Roscoe Dunjee understood this when it seemed least believable and most undeserving of attention. Somehow this little bandy-legged, hawk-nosed, brilliant, luminous man understood that the American covenant was not to be thrown away; that here, with intelligence and passion, was the secret, the play within the play which would catch the conscience of kings.

Wanting to be a composer, I grew up selling Dunjee's paper, reading it, and talking with my peers and friends about what appeared in it. And I found myself learning, questioning, being transformed, even though I didn't quite realize it, by Roscoe Dunjee's editorials in *The Black Dispatch*. Not only did they bear on the Constitution, but they were written by a man who understood that he was in the great tradition of American journalism. From the beginning he understood intuitively and consciously that the English language had to be made our own before we could unlock the secret of other Americans, before we could understand how we were different from Englishmen or Europeans, before we could come to grips with the new possibilities of individualism in those sermons preached by Thoreau, Emerson, and, yes, by Melville and Hawthorne. Somehow, with his courage, this man understood that the American newspaper was a force for cohesion, just as Benjamin Franklin and others understood that Americans would speak the English language in a different way, with a unity that was impossible in Mother England, and that in speaking, describing, and bringing together the diversity of the experience that was occurring throughout this vast nation, we would discover ourselves and perhaps create new hope for mankind.

What Dunjee understood—and here as a newspaperman, reporter, and editorialist he was kin to the Hawthornes, Melvilles and Twains—was that there was evil in the notion of racial superiority, and that it involved the idea of color. He understood that what undercut the bright dream of America both then and now was the unwillingness to come to grips with a problem with which we had asserted we would come to grips. I mean the promise to make a unity out of the diversity of all mankind, the promise to surrender the past and pay the price of coming close to the unfamiliar so that we could discover ourselves and our opposite forms.

As a constitutionalist, Dunjee understood the possibility of words made sacred, so it is no surprise to me that many of the gains which have transformed this country came through efforts he led as an official of the NAACP in Oklahoma. The first real inroads for desegregated education on the university level came out of Oklahoma City. Some of the first battles won against lynching—the Jess Hollins case and others—originated in Oklahoma. These battles were fought by a newspaperman who had the courage to meet his obligations as a reporter and editorialist. In these efforts the word was made flesh by a man who understood what America was about better than most of his colleagues on the other side of the color line. He was in the great tradition of American journalism. Fortunately there were dedicated people, some of them white, who kept him going, just as a black sailmaker, a successful businessman in Philadelphia, kept William Lloyd Garrison's paper, *The Liberator*, going in the name of Abolition. Sometimes there are people who sacrifice for their ideal and for morality. In this instance you have it both ways: whites kept Frederick Douglass going and blacks kept Garrison going.

The point is that a black newspaper set out to instill democratic ideals, and to make cohesive the widely diversified experience of black people. Someone had to know how the brothers and sisters were doing beyond the state and the plantation. Someone had to know what was being taught and what was being suffered. We all wanted to know. This curiosity is very American because it is from comparing notes that we define who we are. Whether black or white, we are all Americans. We are all subjected to that condition which came about through throwing Africans and Europeans together upon this continent, and through the unstructured nature of the societies everywhere we spread.

Being black, we sometimes forget that our experience is diversified. Our forefathers didn't; they understood that slavery in North Carolina was a bit different from slavery in Alabama or Georgia or Mississippi. They understood that slavery on rocky ground was different from slavery near watercourses. They understood that slavery in the Delta was different from slavery in the Tidewater country. They understood because through understanding they got some conception of who they were and how diversified they were. In the same way the American newspaper tried to tell the American white who he was as he moved westward from the eastern seaboard and confronted the different geographical characteristics of the country. As he went west, he evolved different social processes: processes of government, newspapers, universal education, the uniformity of spelling which was imposed upon the English language for the first time in this country. All were processes of unification and self-discovery.

Frederick Douglass understood this when he talked, wrote, and reported the life of "the brother," as you now say. He was helping us to come together, to identify our interests and where we were. But at the same time he was defining the American reality, adding a fourth dimension to the American experience because you could not know who the white American was without knowing something about who the black American was. Neither lived in a vacuum. There was a unity of place and of purpose, although the purpose led to contentions, even to murder. But a unity, a basic interest, and a unified mystery existed about what had been wrought in this country. Somehow this spurred black newspapers, and by Emancipation something new came into the picture. We were no longer identified with the interests of our masters; we had a future which may not have been absolutely separate, but it certainly was far more mysterious.

One of the first Negro newspapers was called *The Alienated American.* You may think that term is new; it isn't. Even then some brother in Cleveland or Cincinnati realized that we were alienated. Another newspaper name was *The Disenfranchised American.* That is from about 1859. Others are *The Colored American, The Afro-American* and—hold on to your hats—*The Anglo-American.* Great numbers of these papers came into being at a time when they were most needed, when we were thrown more upon our own resources as freedmen. So, if anyone thinks that a newspaper is an arbitrary enterprise, realize that our ancestors were responding to a very American situation in which we were exhorted to faith, to hope, and to militancy. We had to be reminded that the way white Americans defined us was not what we were, and that the way we were described in the white press was not an adequate description of the breadth of our humanity.

Our need was to feel out the land, to test the people, to project the possible, and to inspirit the ideals of the Constitution, the Bill of Rights, and the Declaration of Independence into our own reality.

Thus the black newspaper started out as a voice of moral accusation documenting the failure of American ideals. From the very beginning, at its best the black press was also a rectifier of news reporting from the other side. Its purpose was to tell what was underneath what was being said, to penetrate and affirm the moral ideals of the country, and to describe the failure and breakdown of a society where easy optimism and equivocation were the mode. Who could so describe if not a people who are the creators of comic style in this country, and that mixture of comedy and tragedy which we know as the blues? And describe vividly, at least for ourselves, the tragic aspects of American experience—not only describing the darker side, but making it available to anyone who had the fortitude to face up to the realities without losing our basic optimism.

Editorially and in its spirit, the American Negro press has always belonged to the entire American experience. That it has not been read and still isn't read by most whites today is to their disadvantage and to our detriment. This country cannot be run without adequate reporting from all levels, directions, and frontiers. Anyone who thinks that it can, anyone who thinks that he has all the answers, is foolish because the questions change rapidly. There is no sociology of ideas in this country. You cannot tell who is thinking what or where he gets the ideas. This was vaguely understood back during the Haitian Revolution early in the nineteenth century, when Southern governors and politicians became distraught because the ideas of the French Revolution had surfaced among the slaves. This tells you something about the availability of ideas beyond the levels of literacy. In our society, modes of conduct, styles, ideas, and even the most esoteric intellectual concepts find their ways into strange places, and even the most unfree or illiterate American is aware of ideas and will act on them.

The Oklahoma *Black Dispatch* launched sit-ins before they occurred in North Carolina. They started with grade-school children in Oklahoma City. I don't know whether it was reported accurately, but that is what happened. The whole concept of changing segregation through appeals to the Supreme Court was present in Oklahoma City when I was a boy, and was propagated through the columns of a weekly newspaper. We never complained about the issue of black history because Dunjee was always printing black history for us to read. From the very beginnings of statehood in Oklahoma, Negroes went among the Indians as interpreters, and they were the founders of towns and cities, some of which still exist, even though most people living in them do not realize that they were founded by black men. But we knew it, we knew it.

Somehow Roscoe Dunjee understood that America moves through myth—and by myth I don't mean lies. He understood that heroic efforts and sacrifice are repeated by the nature of things. The problem is to keep up with the metamorphosis and find out who Frederick Douglass is today, who Nat Turner is today, who Louis Armstrong and Bessie Smith are today, who Sojourner Truth is. Men change, die, suffer, and express themselves, but the patterns of society demand again and again repetition of that same heroism with a new body and new face—even with a new hairstyle, perhaps. Patterns repeat themselves as long as human circumstances endure.

We need great myths; we need to understand, translate, and interpret for ourselves the meaning of our experience. We have been too glib about this. We have come a long way. We look back and say, "That was slavery" or "He was an Uncle Tom," while in our hearts we understand that we are by the nature of our circumstances a complex people, torn in many ways. Men and women define themselves in action, not verbally, and here I am speaking this way, even though I must confess that I am a writer. That is when I make my decisions, but I know that the decisions I make in reaching some description of human action come from examples of people who have not expressed themselves on a page, but who somehow understood that in variation of "Jack be nimble, Jack be quick," you better have the cunning of Brer Rabbit in the briar patch. You better understand that we are Americans and we have our demagogues and that a man's actions are the true test of his faith. This is the obligation of the Negro press, and I would hope you understand that its obligation is to the broader complexity.

If a jazz musician or the slaves, those unknown bards, could take all the complexity of music and refine it, redesign it, restructure it to make it their own statement, then certainly as reporters it is our responsibility not to wait for others to initiate issues but to use our training, vision, and passion to find paths for the entire nation. There are no second-class standards, certainly not in music, in literature, in medicine, or in science.

We are the descendants of courageous, insightful people, people who had the tragic sense of life and who could spend themselves preciously. If we can't look out upon this nation and foresee where problems are going to surface, no one can. And if we think that we can walk away from problems or substitute easy rhetoric for analysis, description, and eloquence, we're kidding ourselves. I'm not talking about political solutions; I'm talking about that much maligned, misused phrase, "telling it like it is." If you tell it like it is, everyone has to look and listen, because you will cut right down to the bark.

What do I ask of the Negro press? Nothing. But I will be glad when I see you making use of the years of brutalization and of the insights into reality which have forced us to change the basic ground on which we stand. The black press belongs to the American nation, but first it belongs to us.

We don't have to have anyone else tell us about the complexity of American experience. But no one else in this country can tell it as well as we can if we ever have the will to tell it in its fullness and complexity, with all of its comic overtones and tragedy. Remember that Americans have run from understanding the cost of this great country. We have paid much of that cost. Having paid it, we have the obligation to accuse, to prescribe, and to rectify.

I would always write as though the governor of Mississippi was looking over my shoulder.

PRESENTATION TO
BERNARD MALAMUD
OF THE GOLD MEDAL
FOR FICTION

Ellison was elected to the National Institute of Arts and Letters in 1964, and to the American Academy of Arts and Letters in 1975; he was secretary of the Institute from 1977 to 1980. In 1983 he used the Academy-Institute's awarding of the Gold Medal for Fiction to Bernard Malamud to deliver these remarks on American fiction and the democratic ideal, on "the mystery of how, in a nation of minorities, the last becomes first and outstanding among equals." The address was published in the Proceedings of the American Academy and Institute of Arts and Letters *in 1983.*

IT is unnecessary for me to acquaint you with the name of Bernard Malamud, or even to explain his having been selected to receive the Academy-Institute's Gold Medal for Fiction. You know him well as the prize-winning author of numerous short stories and novels, and as a highly respected teacher.

Indeed, Malamud's reputation ranges far beyond those who are concerned with literary values. In the popular mind he is readily identified as one of a quartet of novelists whose very names—Bellow, Mailer, Malamud and Roth—convey an aura of authorial glamour. But because it ignores crucial distinctions of style, theme and vision, these authors would probably dismiss this grouping as pointless. I would agree; as an attempt to impose an easy unity upon such a prickly diversity of talent it is superficial. Yet it *does* focus upon two basic facts: Malamud shares with the others a background of the American Jewish experience, and like them he is highly successful in a difficult art.

For the uninitiated, this is enough to evoke the image of four literary musketeers shouting "All for one and one for all!" while pounding the keys of their typewriters—an amusing notion even though their implied opposition is left to one's imagination. But when literary personalities engage the popular imagination almost anything can happen, from their being associated with figures of nineteenth-century romance to an identification with heroes of ancient myth and ritual. Here, I think, it is a matter of two modes of the imagination coinciding, for while interrogating social reality is a function of serious fiction, adding glamour to the "American Dream" is a function of popular myth-making. Malamud has drawn creatively upon folklore, so now in a turnabout the popular mind would convert his career into the stuff of dreams. Thus while fiction feeds upon social fact, myth-making would feed upon a fabulist. Thus Malamud is transformed into a latter-day incarnation of Horatio Alger!

Not that Malamud has sprung exactly from rags to riches, but in enriching American literature he is viewed as having struck the mother lode from which success and glamour flow. Usually we dismiss such popular myth-making for the dream stuff it is, but it continues to perform certain useful, if covert, functions: it delights and encourages by celebrating feats of self-achievement; it reminds us of those negative circumstances that render success both difficult and risky; and in its riddling fashion it allows us to approach American experience with an unthreatening sense of wonder. In its fanciful way it poses the old abiding questions of who and what is "American," and asks, "By what dint of effort or turn of fate is 'Americanness' achieved?"

Usually we are far too busy just *being* American to give these questions much conscious thought, but they keep popping up to haunt us, in this instance, when Malamud's accomplishments raise the issue of how it is that a member of a minority group can win recognition as a representative American writer. How, in other words, has Malamud been able to speak to the wholeness of American experience when the diversity of the whole is so much greater and more unavailable than its parts?

These questions issue from the interaction between our culture, politics, and the fluid character of American social hierarchy. Although held in a volatile synthesis by intricate structures and processes of law and politics, our people spring from such a diversity of backgrounds and traditions that American culture constitutes a "culture of cultures"—and these are always in conflict as they repel and attract and blend, each with the other. Related to this is our plurality of social classes, the discrete divisions among both our rich and our poor, as among and within our ethnic and religious groupings. Thus our conflicting social and economic interests make for a rock-and-roll shifting of political alignments. Here private lives are invaded by public disrelationships, and our national morality has unchartered consequences in private fates.

As Malamud knows all too well, it is one thing to embrace the ideal of democracy, but quite another to live peacefully with the responsibilities and sacrifices that flow therefrom. Hence we live in a symbolic state of civil war, and are bedeviled by a built-in conundrum which constantly questions our moral identity by measuring our assertions of democratic faith against the undemocratic contents of our attitudes and actions.

Bonded by the democratic ideal, we identify with each other as members of a single nation, but we also share the guilt which arises from our endless contentions. If in a general sense we are brothers, in specific relationships we can be so uncertain that the slightest disagreement can transform us into hostile strangers. Worse, the inescapable fact that our communal bond fails so often to provide communication across our divisions of race, creed, background and tradition makes for a state of free-floating embarrassment. Fortunately ours is a prosperous country, and along with its self-evident opportunities for social advancement our national morale is sustained by optimism, by our belief in "progress," and by our famous "American humor." These allow us to deal pragmatically with our inconsistencies, and we laugh at one another even though it is often in order to keep from crying.

Still, on a deeper, more tragic level of our minds, we realize that our "national unity" is actually less fact than political fiction, a future condition to which we were committed by the Founding Fathers. Thus democratic equality is sometimes a goal toward which we advance with Old Glory flying, and again a combat zone from which we retreat in dereliction of our most sacred commitments. From this perspective we are all at some point or another secessionists.

For any novelist, the contradictions arising from our unity-within-diversity pose both a mystery and a challenge, especially for one of minority background. Because for him our complaints born of social inequity join up with his fiction-writer's compulsion to re-create the real-life drama of American social hierarchy. When he confronts its baffling mixture of order and chaos he discovers that he has committed himself to the task of disentangling the pathologies of democracy from its failures, its attempts at melioration, and its assertions of a transcendent ideal. As fictionist he seeks to reduce the complexity of experience to eloquent form, but in doing so he risks the embarrassment of not only violating the self-protective pieties of other groups, but of exposing the self-serving maneuvering of his own. Naturally this makes him no less a target for censure than for praise. But whether he chooses the modes of tragedy or comedy or a combination of both, he descends imaginatively into the underworld of democracy and a realm of fear and hatred, stereotypes and bias, code words and epithets, and these must be depicted in the context of his characters' efforts to achieve their better selves.

Not that it is the novelist's role to "create the uncreated conscience" of his group or nation, for that was in motion long ago; rather it is to sensitize the nation's ever-floundering conscience by making us conscious of the strengths in our weaknesses and the triumphs in our failures. Thus, even when concerned mainly with the perfection of his art, the novelist finds himself compelled to consider the moral and political consequences of his fiction. His raw material consists of a society caught in the process of being improvised out of the democractic ideal as pragmatically as any tall tale is spun out of the recurring adventures of hunter, fisherman, beggarman or trickster. In order to achieve the maximum resonance from his symbolic actions he must hang loose and try to be as receptive, resourceful and encompassing in capturing truth as his larger subject is in evading it.

For whatever else a novelist of minority background happens to be, he too shares the American dream and its compulsions. So while remaining true to his own group's unique perception of experience, he is also goaded to add his individual voice to the futuristic effort of fulfilling the democratic ideal. He too acts to describe the nation to itself, and sometimes in making his own segment of experience available to all he manages to reduce our social confusion to forms of lucid insight. When this occurs he is able to dispel some of the hier-archal embarrassment and generalized "anxiety of diversity" en-demic to American society.

Malamud demonstrates that in this effort a minority background is far from a hindrance. Indeed, such artists are indispensable in ren-dering crucial aspects of our common reality. For we are in fact a nation of minorities, and if the reality of one is neglected, the com-mon truth of experience is done incalculable violence. Thus when a writer of Malamud's gifts confronts the mystery of our unity-within-diversity and clings faithfully to his own perception of truth, he tran-scends the given in the interest of the ideal. By following the artistic standards and moral dictates of the novel, he not only reinvigorates the American language, but clarifies our perception of reality. By speaking resonantly for himself he speaks the truth in different ac-cents. This is his answer to the mystery of how, in a nation of minorities, the last becomes first and outstanding among equals.

Therein lies the magic in Malamud's barrel of fiction, and the se-cret of its power to assault the fictions and hypocrisies of politics. Yes, and therein lie the possibilities for writers of minority back-ground to render the complex wholeness of American experience. Malamud has performed such feats of fictional magic again and again. He is an artist who entertains us as he instructs us, and if he upsets our complacency as he ranges from comedy to tragedy, that is the price we must pay for being transported into his world of possi-bility.

Bern, this marvelous object is no fiction; it is all true gold and loaded with magical affect that far out-gleams its material substance. It is my pleasure to extend it to you as a symbolic expression of the high regard and deep admiration with which you and your work are held by our friends and colleagues, all of whom recognize all too well how difficult a feat it is to contribute a new and resonant note to that diverse unity of fictional expression which is American literature.

INTRODUCTION TO THE
THIRTIETH-ANNIVERSARY
EDITION OF
INVISIBLE MAN

In 1981 Ellison wrote this extended introduction—part memoir, part meditation, part vernacular and mythic tall tale, perhaps—about the birth of Invisible Man. *It was published in the thirtieth-anniversary edition in 1982.*

WHAT, if anything, is there that a novelist can say about his work that wouldn't be better left to the critics? They at least have the advantage of dealing with the words on the page, while for him the task of accounting for the process involved in putting them there is similar to that of commanding a smoky genie to make an orderly retreat—not simply back into the traditional bottle, but into the ribbon and keys of a by now defunct typewriter. And in this particular instance all the more so, because from the moment of its unexpected inception this has been a most self-willed and self-generating piece of fiction. For at a time when I was struggling with a quite different narrative, it announced itself in what were to become the opening words of its prologue, moved in, and proceeded to challenge my imagination for some seven years. What is more, despite its peacetime scenery it erupted out of what had been conceived as a war novel.

It all began during the summer of 1945, in a barn in Waitsfield, Vermont, where I was on sick leave from service in the merchant marine, and with the war's end it continued to preoccupy me in various parts of New York City, including its crowded subways, in a converted 141st Street stable, in a one-room ground floor apartment on St. Nicholas Avenue, and, most unexpectedly, in a suite otherwise occupied by jewelers located on the eighth floor of 608 Fifth Avenue. It was there, thanks to the generosity of Beatrice and Francis Steegmuller, then spending a year abroad, that I discovered that writing could be just as difficult in a fellow writer's elegant office as in a crowded Harlem apartment. There were, however, important differences, some of which worked wonders for my shaky self-confidence and served, perhaps, as a catalyst for the wild mixture of elements that went into the evolving fiction.

The proprietors of the suite, Sam and Augusta Mann, saw to it that I worked undisturbed, took time off for lunch (often at their own expense), and were most encouraging of my efforts. Thanks to them I found myself keeping a businessman's respectable hours, and the suite's constant flow of beautiful objects and its occupants' expert evaluations of pearls, diamonds, platinum and gold gave me a sense of living far above my means. Thus actually and symbolically the eighth floor was the highest elevation upon which the novel unfolded, but it was a long, far cry from our below-street-level apartment and might well have proved disorientating had I not been consciously concerned with a fictional character who was bent upon finding his way in areas of society whose manners, motives and rituals were baffling.

Interestingly enough, it was only the elevator operators who questioned my presence in such an affluent building, but this, after all, was during a period when the doormen of buildings located in middle- and upper-class neighborhoods routinely directed such as myself to their service elevators. I hasten to add, however, that nothing of the kind ever happened at 608, for once the elevator men became accustomed to my presence they were quite friendly. And this was true even of the well-read immigrant among them who found the idea of my being a writer amusing.

By contrast, certain of my St. Nicholas Avenue neighbors considered me of questionable character. This ostensibly was because Fanny, my wife, came and went with the regularity of one who held a conventional job, while I was often at home and could be seen at odd hours walking our Scottish terriers. But basically it was because I fit none of the roles, legal or illegal, with which my neighbors were familiar. I was neither a thug, numbers runner, pusher, postal worker, doctor, dentist, lawyer, tailor, undertaker, barber, bartender nor preacher. And while my speech revealed a degree of higher education, it was also clear that I was not of the group of professionals who lived or worked in the neighborhood. My indefinite status was therefore a subject of speculation and a source of unease, especially among those whose attitudes and modes of conduct were at odds with the dictates of law and order. This made for a nodding relationship in which my neighbors kept their distance and I kept mine. But I remained suspect, and one snowy afternoon as I walked down a shady street into the winter sunshine a wino lady let me know exactly how I rated on her checklist of sundry types and characters. Leaning blearily against the façade of a corner bar as I approached, and directing her remarks at me through her woozy companions, she said, "Now that nigger *there* must be some kinda sweetback, 'cause while his wife has her some kinda little 'slave,' all I ever see *him* do is walk them damn dogs and shoot some damn pictures!"

I was startled by such a low rating, for by "sweetback" she meant a man who lived off the earnings of a woman, a type usually identified by his leisure, flashy clothes, flamboyant personal style and the ruthless business enterprise of an out-and-out pimp—all qualities which I was so conspicuously lacking that she had to laugh at her own provocative sally. However, the ploy was intended to elicit a response, whether angry or conciliatory she was too drunk or reckless to care as long as it threw some light into the shadows of my existence. Therefore I was less annoyed than amused, and since I was returning home with fifty legally earned dollars from a photographic assignment, I could well afford to smile while remaining silently concealed in my mystery.

Even so, the wino lady had come close to one of the economic arrangements which made my writing a possibility, and that too is part of the story behind this novel. My wife did indeed provide the more dependable contributions to our income, while mine came catch-as-catch-can. During the time the novel was in progress she worked as a secretary for several organizations and was to crown her working career as the executive director of the American Medical Center for Burma, a group that supported the work of Dr. Gordon S. Seagrave, the famous "Burma Surgeon." As for myself, I reviewed a few books, sold a few articles and short stories, did freelance photography (including book-jacket portraits of Francis Steegmuller and Mary McCarthy), built audio amplifiers and installed high-fidelity sound systems. There were also a few savings from my work on ships, a Rosenwald grant and its renewal, a small publisher's advance, and for a while a monthly stipend from our friend and patron of the arts, the late Mrs. J. Caesar Guggenheimer.

Naturally our neighbors knew nothing of this, and neither did our landlord, who considered writing to be such a questionable occupation for a healthy young man that during our absence he was not above entering our apartment and prowling through my papers. Still, such annoyances were to be endured as a part of the desperate gamble involved in my becoming a novelist. Fortunately my wife had faith in my talent, a fine sense of humor and a capacity for neighborly charity. Nor was I unappreciative of the hilarious inversion of what is usually a racially restricted social mobility that took me on daily journeys from a Negro neighborhood, wherein strangers questioned my moral character on nothing more substantial than our common color and my vague deviation from accepted norms, to find sanctuary in a predominantly white environment wherein that same color and vagueness of role rendered me anonymous, and hence beyond public concern. In retrospect it was as though writing about invisibility had rendered me either transparent or opaque and set me bouncing back and forth between the benighted provincialism of a small village and the benign disinterestedness of a great metropolis. Which, given the difficulty of gaining an authorial knowledge of this diverse society, was not a bad discipline for an American writer.

But the Fifth Avenue interval aside, most of the novel still managed to get itself written in Harlem, where it drew much of its substance from the voices, idioms, folklore, traditions and political concerns of those whose racial and cultural origins I share. So much, then, for the economics, geography and sociology of the struggle sustained in writing the novel, and back to the circumstances in which it began.

The narrative that was upstaged by the voice which spoke so knowingly of invisibility (pertinent here because it turned out to have been a blundering step toward the present novel) focused upon the experiences of a captured American pilot who found himself in a Nazi prisoner-of-war camp in which he was the officer of highest rank, and thus by a convention of war the designated spokesman for his fellow prisoners. Predictably, the dramatic conflict arose from the fact that he was the only Negro among the Americans, and the resulting racial tension was exploited by the German camp commander for his own amusement. Having to choose between his passionate rejection of both native and foreign racisms while upholding those democratic values which he held in common with his white countrymen, my pilot was forced to find support for his morale in his sense of individual dignity and in his newly awakened awareness of human loneliness. For him that war-born vision of virile fraternity of which Malraux wrote so eloquently was not forthcoming, and much to his surprise he found his only justification for attempting to deal with his countrymen as comrades-in-arms lay precisely in those old betrayed promises proclaimed in such national slogans and turns-of-phrase as those the hero of Hemingway's *A Farewell to Arms* had found so obscene during the chaotic retreat from Caporetto. But while Hemingway's hero managed to put the war behind him and opt for love, for my pilot there was neither escape nor a loved one waiting. Therefore he had either to affirm the transcendent ideals of democracy and his own dignity by aiding those who despised him, or accept his situation as hopelessly devoid of meaning, a choice tantamount to rejecting his own humanity. The crowning irony of all this lay in the fact that neither of his adversaries was aware of his inner struggle.

Undramatized, all this might sound a bit extreme, yet historically most of this nation's conflicts of arms have been—at least for Afro-Americans—wars within wars. Such was true of the Civil War, the last of the Indian Wars, of the Spanish-American War, and of World Wars I and II. And in order for the Negro to fulfill his duty as a citizen it was often necessary that he fight for his self-affirmed right to fight. Accordingly, my pilot was prepared to make the ultimate wartime sacrifice that most governments demand of their able-bodied citizens, but his was one that regarded his life as of lesser value than the lives of whites making the same sacrifice. This reality made for an existential torture, which was given a further twist of the screw by his awareness that once the peace was signed, the German camp commander could immigrate to the United States and immediately take advantage of freedoms that were denied the most heroic of Negro servicemen. Thus, democratic ideals and military valor alike were rendered absurd by the prevailing mystique of race and color.

I myself had chosen the merchant marine as a more democratic mode of service (as had a former colleague, a poet, who was lost off Murmansk on his first trip to sea), and as a seaman ashore in Europe I had been encountering numerous Negro soldiers who gave me vivid accounts of the less-than-democratic conditions under which they fought and labored. But having had a father who fought on San Juan Hill, in the Philippines and in China, I knew that such complaints grew out of what was by then an archetypical American dilemma: how could you treat a Negro as equal in war and then deny him equality during times of peace? I also knew something of the trials of Negro airmen, who after being trained in segregated units and undergoing the abuse of white officers and civilians alike were prevented from flying combat missions.

Indeed, I had published a short story which dealt with such a situation, and it was in this attempt to convert experience into fiction that I discovered that its implicit drama was far more complex than I had assumed. For while I had conceived of it in terms of a black-white, majority-minority conflict, with white officers refusing to recognize the humanity of a Negro who saw mastering the highly technical skills of a pilot as a dignified way of serving his country while improving his economic status, I came to realize that my pilot was also experiencing difficulty in seeing *himself.* This had to do with his ambivalence before his own group's divisions of class and diversities of culture—an ambivalence which was brought into focus after he crash-landed on a Southern plantation and found himself being aided by a Negro tenant farmer whose outlook and folkways were a painful reminder of his own tenuous military status and their common origin in slavery. A man of two worlds, my pilot felt himself to be misperceived in both, and thus was at ease in neither. In brief, the story depicted his conscious struggle for self-definition and for an invulnerable support for his individual dignity. I by no means was aware of this relationship to the invisible man, but clearly he possessed some of the symptoms.

During the same period I had published yet another story in which a young Afro-American seaman, ashore in Swansea, South Wales, was forced to grapple with the troublesome "American" aspects of his identity after white Americans had blacked his eye during a wartime blackout on the Swansea street called Straight (no, his name was *not* Saul, nor did he become a Paul!). But here the pressure toward self-scrutiny came from a group of Welshmen who rescued him and surprised him by greeting him as a "Black Yank" and inviting him to a private club, and then sang the American national anthem in his honor. Both stories were published in 1944, but now in 1945 on a Vermont farm, the theme of a young Negro's quest for identity was reasserting itself in a far more bewildering form.

For while I had structured my short stories out of familiar experiences and possessed concrete images of my characters and their backgrounds, now I was confronted by nothing more substantial than a taunting, disembodied voice. And while I was in the process of plotting a novel based on the war then in progress, the conflict which that voice was imposing upon my attention was one that had been ongoing since the Civil War. Given the experiences of the past, I had felt on safe historical grounds even though the literary problem of conveying the complex human emotions and philosophical decisions faced by a unique individual remained. It was, I thought, an intriguing idea for an American novel, but a difficult task for a fledgling novelist. Therefore I was most annoyed to have my efforts interrupted by an ironic, down-home voice that struck me as being as irreverent as a honky-tonk trumpet blasting through a performance, say, of Britten's *War Requiem*.

And all the more so because the voice seemed well aware that a piece of science fiction was the last thing I aspired to write. In fact, it seemed to tease me with allusions to that pseudoscientific sociological concept which held that most Afro-American difficulties sprang from our "high visibility"; a phrase as double-dealing and insidious as its more recent oxymoronic cousins, "benign neglect" and "reverse discrimination," both of which translate as "Keep those Negroes running—but in their same old place." My friends had made wry jokes out of the term for many years, suggesting that while the darker brother was clearly "checked and balanced"—and kept far more checked than balanced—on the basis of his darkness he glowed nevertheless within the American conscience with such intensity that most whites feigned moral blindness toward his predicament; these included the waves of late arrivals who refused to recognize the vast extent to which they too benefited from his second-class status while placing all of the blame on white Southerners.

Thus, despite the bland assertions of sociologists, "high visibility" actually rendered one *un*-visible—whether at high noon in Macy's window or illuminated by flaming torches and flashbulbs while undergoing the ritual sacrifice that was dedicated to the ideal of white supremacy. After such knowledge, and given the persistence of racial violence and the unavailability of legal protection, I asked myself, what else *was* there to sustain our will to persevere but laughter? And could it be that there was a subtle triumph hidden in such laughter that I had missed, but one which still was more affirmative than raw anger? A secret, hard-earned wisdom that might, perhaps, offer a more effective strategy through which a floundering Afro-American novelist could convey his vision?

It was a startling idea, yet the voice was so persuasive with echoes of blues-toned laughter that I found myself being nudged toward a frame of mind in which suddenly current events, memories and artifacts began combining to form a vague but intriguing new perspective.

Shortly before the spokesman for invisibility intruded, I had seen in a nearby Vermont village a poster announcing the performance of a "Tom Show," that forgotten term for blackface minstrel versions of Mrs. Stowe's *Uncle Tom's Cabin.* I had thought such entertainment a thing of the past, but there in a quiet northern village it was alive and kicking, with Eliza, frantically slipping and sliding on the ice, still trying—and this during World War II!—to escape the slavering hounds. . . . *Oh, I went to the hills / To hide my face / The hills cried out, No hiding place / There's no hiding place / Up here!*

No, because what is commonly assumed to be past history is actually as much a part of the living present as William Faulkner insisted. Furtive, implacable and tricky, it inspirits both the observer and the scene observed, artifacts, manners and atmosphere, and it speaks even when no one wills to listen.

So as I listened, things once obscure began falling into place. Odd things, unexpected things. Such as the poster that reminded me of the tenacity which a nation's moral evasions can take on when given the trappings of racial stereotypes, and the ease with which its deepest experience of tragedy could be converted into blackface farce. Even information picked up about the backgrounds of friends and acquaintances fell into the slowly emerging pattern of implication. The wife of the racially mixed couple who were our hosts was the granddaughter of a Vermonter who had been a general in the Civil War, adding a new dimension to the poster's presence. Details of old photographs, rhymes, riddles, children's games, church services, college ceremonies, practical jokes and political activities observed during my prewar days in Harlem—all fell into place. I had reported the riot of 1943 for the *New York Post,* had agitated earlier for the release of Angelo Herndon and the Scottsboro Boys, had marched behind Adam Clayton Powell, Jr., in his effort to desegregate the stores along 125th Street, and had been part of a throng which blocked off Fifth Avenue in protest of the role being played by Germany and

Italy in the Spanish Civil War. Everything and anything appeared as grist for my fictional mill, some speaking up clearly, saying, "Use me right here," while others were disturbingly mysterious.

Like my sudden recall of an incident from my college days when, opening a vat of Plasticine donated to an invalid sculptor friend by some Northern studio, I found enfolded within the oily mass a frieze of figures modeled after those depicted on Saint-Gaudens's monument to Colonel Robert Gould Shaw and his 54th Massachusetts Negro Regiment, a memorial which stands on the Boston Common. I had no idea why it should surface, but perhaps it was to remind me that since I was writing fiction and seeking vaguely for images of black and white fraternity I would do well to recall that Henry James's brother Wilky had fought as an officer with those Negro soldiers, and that Colonel Shaw's body had been thrown into a ditch with those of his men. Perhaps it was also to remind me that war could, with art, be transformed into something deeper and more meaningful than its surface violence.

At any rate, it now appeared that the voice of invisibility issued from deep within our complex American underground. So how crazy-logical that I should finally locate its owner living—and oh, so garrulously—in an abandoned cellar. Of course the process was far more disjointed than I make it sound, but such was the inner-outer, subjective-objective process of the developing fiction, its pied rind and surreal heart.

Even so, I was still inclined to close my ears and get on with my interrupted novel, but like many writers atoss in what Conrad described as the "destructive element," I had floundered into a state of hyper-receptivity, a desperate condition in which a fiction writer finds it difficult to ignore even the most nebulous idea-emotion that might arise in the process of creation. For he soon learns that such amorphous projections might well be unexpected gifts from his day-dreaming muse that might, when properly perceived, provide exactly the materials needed to keep afloat in the turbulent tides of composition. On the other hand, they might wreck him, drown him in the quicksands of indecision. I was already having enough difficulty trying to avoid writing what might turn out to be nothing more than another novel of racial protest instead of the dramatic study in comparative humanity which I felt any worthwhile novel should be, and the voice appeared to be leading me precisely in that direction. But then as I listened to its taunting laughter and speculated on what kind of individual would speak in such accents, I decided that it would be one who had been forged in the underground of American experience and yet managed to emerge less angry than ironic. That he would be a blues-toned laughter-at-wounds who included himself in his indictment of the human condition. I liked the idea, and as I tried to visualize the speaker I came to relate him to those ongoing conflicts, tragic and comic, that had claimed my group's energies since the abandonment of the Reconstruction. And after coaxing him into revealing a bit more about himself, I concluded that he was without question a "character," and this in the dual meaning of the term. I saw that he was young, powerless (reflecting the difficulties of Negro leaders of the period) and ambitious for a role of leadership—a role at which he was doomed to fail. Having nothing to lose, and by way of providing myself with the widest field for success or failure, I associated him, ever so distantly, with the narrator of Dostoevsky's *Notes from Underground*. With that *I* began to structure the movement of my plot, while *he* began to merge with my more specialized concerns with fictional form and with certain problems arising out of the pluralistic literary tradition from which I spring.

Among these was the question of why most protagonists of Afro-American fiction (not to mention the black characters in fiction written by whites) were without intellectual depth. Too often they were figures caught up in the most intense forms of social struggle, subject to the most extreme forms of the human predicament, yet seldom able to articulate the issues which tortured them. Not that many worthy individuals aren't in fact inarticulate, but that there were, and are, enough exceptions in real life to provide the perceptive novelist with models. And even if they did not exist it would be necessary, both in the interest of fictional expressiveness and as examples of human possibility, to invent them. Henry James had taught us much with his hyperconscious, "Super subtle fry," characters who embodied in their own cultured, upper-class way the American virtues of conscience and consciousness. Such ideal creatures were unlikely to turn up in the world I inhabited, but one never knew because so much in this society is unnoticed and unrecorded. On the other hand, I felt that one of the ever-present challenges facing the American novelist was that of endowing his inarticulate characters, scenes and social processes with eloquence. For it is by such attempts that he fulfills his social responsibility as an American artist.

Here it would seem that the interests of art and democracy converge, with the development of conscious, articulate citizens an established goal of this democratic society, and the creation of conscious, articulate characters indispensable to the creation of resonant compositional centers through which an organic consistency can be achieved in the fashioning of fictional forms. By way of imposing meaning upon our disparate American experience the novelist seeks to create forms in which acts, scenes and characters speak for more than their immediate selves, and in this enterprise the very nature of language is on his side. For by a trick of fate (our racial problems notwithstanding) the human imagination is integrative—and the same is true of the centrifugal force that inspirits the democratic process. And while fiction is but a form of symbolic action, a mere game of "as if," therein lies its true function and its potential for effecting change. For at its most serious, just as is true of politics at its best, it is a thrust toward a human ideal. And it approaches that ideal by a subtle process of negating the world of things as given in favor of a complex of man-made positives.

So if the ideal of achieving a true political equality eludes us in reality—as it continues to do—there is still available that fictional *vision* of an ideal democracy in which the actual combines with the ideal and gives us representations of a state of things in which the highly placed and the lowly, the black and the white, the Northerner and the Southerner, the native-born and the immigrant combine to tell us of transcendent truths and possibilities such as those discovered when Mark Twain set Huck and Jim afloat on the raft.

Which suggested to me that a novel could be fashioned as a raft of hope, perception and entertainment that might help keep us afloat as we tried to negotiate the snags and whirlpools that mark our nation's vascillating course toward and away from the democratic ideal.

There are, of course, other goals for fiction. Yet I recalled that during the early, more optimistic days of this republic it was assumed that each individual citizen could become (and should prepare to become) President. For democracy was considered not only a collectivity of individuals, as was defined by W. H. Auden, but a collectivity of politically astute citizens who, by virtue of our vaunted system of universal education and our freedom of opportunity, would be prepared to govern. As things turned out it was an unlikely possibility—but not entirely, as attested by the recent examples of the peanut farmer and the motion-picture actor.

Even for Afro-Americans there was the brief hope that had been encouraged by the presence of black congressmen in Washington during the Reconstruction. Nor could I see any reason for allowing our more chastened view of political possibility (not long before I began this novel A. Phillip Randolph had to threaten our beloved F.D.R. with a march on Washington before our war industries were opened to Negroes) to impose undue restrictions upon my novelist's freedom to manipulate imaginatively those possibilities that existed both in Afro-American personality and in the restricted structure of American society. My task was to transcend those restrictions. As an example, Mark Twain had demonstrated that the novel *could* serve as a comic antidote to the ailments of politics, and since in 1945, as well as now, Afro-Americans were usually defeated in their bouts with circumstance, there was no reason why they, like Brer Rabbit and his more literary cousins, the great heroes of tragedy and comedy, shouldn't be allowed to snatch the victory of conscious perception from the forces that overwhelmed them. Therefore I would have to create a narrator who could think as well as act, and I saw a capacity for conscious self-assertion as basic to his blundering quest for freedom.

So my task was one of revealing the human universals hidden within the plight of one who was both black and American, and not only as a means of conveying my personal vision of possibility, but as a way of dealing with the sheer rhetorical challenge involved in communicating across our barriers of race and religion, class, color and region—barriers which consist of the many strategies of division that were designed, and still function, to prevent what would otherwise have been a more or less natural recognition of the reality of black and white fraternity. And to defeat this national tendency to deny the common humanity shared by my character and those who might happen to read of his experience, I would have to provide him with something of a world view, give him a consciousness in which serious philosophical questions could be raised, provide him with a range of diction that could play upon the richness of our readily shared vernacular speech, and construct a plot that would bring him in contact with a variety of American types as they operated on various levels of society. Most of all, I would have to approach racial stereotypes as a given fact of the social process and proceed, while gambling with the reader's capacity for fictional truth, to reveal the human complexity which stereotypes are intended to conceal.

It would be misleading, however, to leave the impression that all the process of writing this book was so solemn, for in fact there was a great deal of fun along the way. I knew that I was composing a work of fiction, a work of literary art and one that would allow me to take advantage of the novel's capacity for telling the truth while actually telling a "lie," which is the Afro-American folk term for an improvised story. Having worked in barbershops where that form of oral art flourished, I knew that I could draw upon the rich culture of the folk tale as well as that of the novel, and that uncertain of my skill, I would have to improvise upon my materials in the manner of a jazz musician putting a musical theme through a wild star-burst of metamorphosis. By the time I realized that the words of the Prologue contained the germ of the ending as well as that of the beginning, I was free to enjoy the surprises of incident and character as they popped into view.

And there were surprises. Five years before the book was completed, Frank Taylor, who had given me my first book contract, showed a section to Cyril Connolly, the editor of the English magazine *Horizon*, and it was published in an issue devoted to art in America. This marked the initial publication of the first chapter, which appeared in America shortly afterward in the 1948 volume of the now defunct *Magazine of the Year*—a circumstance which accounts for the 1947 and 1948 copyright dates that have caused confusion for scholars. The actual publication date of the complete volume was 1952.

These surprises were both encouraging and intimidating because after savoring that bit of success I became afraid that this single section, which contained the "Battle Royal" scene, might well be the novel's only incident of interest. But I persisted and finally arrived at the moment when it became meaningful to work with my editor, Albert Erskine. The rest, as the saying goes, is history. My highest hope for the novel was that it would sell enough copies to prevent my publishers from losing their investment and my editor from having wasted his time. But as I said in the beginning, this has always been a most willful, most self-generating novel, and the proof of this statement is witnessed by the fact that here, thirty astounding years later, it has me writing about it again.

—November 10, 1981

GOING TO THE TERRITORY

Ellison's second book of essays was published in 1986. Except for "Society, Morality and the Novel" (1957), the selections were written or published between 1963 and 1986. The collection's mix of prose forms, like that of Shadow and Act, reflects Ellison's fascination with "making disparate materials into rhetorical wholes." Here, even more than in Shadow and Act, Ellison enacts the American journey to the territory, believing "that the territory is an ideal place—ever to be sought, ever to be missed, but always there."

The Little Man at Chehaw Station

The American Artist and His Audience

I T was at Tuskegee Institute during the mid-1930s that I was made aware of the little man behind the stove. At the time I was a trumpeter majoring in music, and had aspirations of becoming a classical composer. As such, shortly before the little man came to my attention, I had outraged the faculty members who judged my monthly student's recital by substituting a certain skill of lips and fingers for the intelligent and artistic structuring of emotion that was demanded in performing the music assigned to me. Afterward, still dressed in my hired tuxedo, my ears burning from the harsh negatives of their criticism, I had sought solace in the basement studio of Hazel Harrison, a highly respected concert pianist and teacher. Miss Harrison had been one of Ferruccio Busoni's prize pupils, had lived (until the rise of Hitler had driven her back to a U.S.A. that was not yet ready to recognize her talents) in Busoni's home in Berlin, and was a friend of such masters as Egon Petri, Percy Grainger and Sergei Prokofiev. It was not the first time that I had appealed to Miss Harrison's generosity of spirit, but today her reaction to my rather adolescent complaint was less than sympathetic.

"But, baby," she said, "in this country you must always prepare yourself to play your very best wherever you are, and on all occasions."

"But everybody tells you that," I said.

"Yes," she said, "but there's more to it than you're usually told. Of course you've always been taught to *do* your best, *look* your best, *be* your best. You've been told such things all your life. But now you're becoming a musician, an artist, and when it comes to per-

From *The American Scholar*, Winter 1977/78.

forming the classics in this country, there's something more involved."

Watching me closely, she paused. "Are you ready to listen?"

"Yes, ma'am."

"All right," she said, "you must *always* play your best, even if it's only in the waiting room at Chehaw Station, because in this country there'll always be a little man hidden behind the stove."

"A *what*?"

She nodded. "That's right," she said. "There'll always be the little man whom you don't expect, and he'll know the *music*, and the *tradition*, and the standards of *musicianship* required for whatever you set out to perform!"

Speechless, I stared at her. After the working-over I'd just received from the faculty, I was in no mood for joking. But no, Miss Harrison's face was quite serious. So what did she mean? Chehaw Station was a lonely whistle-stop where swift north- or southbound trains paused with haughty impatience to drop off or take on passengers; the point where, on homecoming weekends, special coaches crowded with festive visitors were cut loose, coupled to a waiting switch engine, and hauled to Tuskegee's railroad siding. I knew it well, and as I stood beside Miss Harrison's piano, visualizing the station, I told myself, *She has* got *to be kidding!*

For in my view, the atmosphere of Chehaw's claustrophobic little waiting room was enough to discourage even a blind street musician from picking out blues on his guitar, no matter how tedious his wait for a train. Biased toward disaster by bruised feelings, my imagination pictured the vibrations set in motion by the winding of a trumpet within that drab, utilitarian structure: first shattering, then bringing its walls "a-tumbling down"—like Jericho's at the sounding of Joshua's priest-blown ram horns.

True, Tuskegee possessed a rich musical tradition, both classical and folk, and many music lovers and musicians lived or moved through its environs, but—and my regard for Miss Harrison notwithstanding—Chehaw Station was the last place in the area where I would expect to encounter a connoisseur lying in wait to pounce upon some rash, unsuspecting musician. Sure, a connoisseur might hear the haunting, blues-echoing, train-whistle rhapsodies blared by fast express trains as they thundered past, but the classics? Not a chance!

So as Miss Harrison watched to see the effect of her words, I said with a shrug, "Yes, ma'am."

She smiled, her prominent eyes a-twinkle. "I hope so," she said. "But if you don't just now, you will by the time you become an artist. So remember the little man behind the stove."

With that, seating herself at her piano, she began thumbing through a sheaf of scores, a signal that our discussion was ended.

So, I thought, *you ask for sympathy and you get a riddle*. I would have felt better if she had said, "Sorry, baby, I know how you feel, but after all, I was *there*, I *heard* you, and you treated your audience as though you were some kind of confidence man with a horn. So forget it, because I will not violate my own standards by condoning sterile musicianship." Some such reply, by reaffirming the "sacred principles" of art to which we were both committed, would have done much to supply the emotional catharsis for which I was appealing. By refusing, she forced me to accept full responsibility and thus learn from my offense. The condition of artistic communication is, as the saying goes, hard but fair.

But although disappointed and puzzled by Miss Harrison's sibylline response, I respected her artistry and experience too highly to dismiss it. Besides, something about her warning of a cultivated taste that asserted its authority out of obscurity sounded faintly familiar. Hadn't I once worked for an eccentric millionaire who prowled the halls and ballrooms of his fine hotel looking like a derelict who had wandered in off the street? Yes! And woe unto the busboy or waiter, hallman or maid—or anyone else—caught debasing the standards of that old man's house. For then, lashing out with the abruptness of reality shattering the contrived façade of a practical joke, the apparent beggar revealed himself as an extremely irate and exacting host of taste.

Thus, as I leaned into the curve of Miss Harrison's Steinway and listened to an interpretation of a Liszt rhapsody (during which she carried on an enthusiastic, stylistic analysis of passages that Busoni himself had marked for expressional subtlety), the little man of Chehaw Station fixed himself in my memory. And so vividly that today he not only continues to engage my mind, but often materializes when I least expect him.

As, for instance, when I'm brooding over some problem of literary criticism—like, say, the rhetoric of American fiction. Indeed, the little stove warmer has come to symbolize nothing less than the enigma of aesthetic communication in American democracy. I especially associate him with the metamorphic character of the general American audience, and with the unrecognized and unassimilated elements of its taste. For me he represents that unknown quality which renders the American audience far more than a receptive instrument that may be dominated through a skillful exercise of the sheerly "rhetorical" elements—the flash and filigree—of the artist's craft. While that audience is eager to be transported, astounded, thrilled, it counters the artist's manipulation of forms with an attitude of antagonistic cooperation, acting, for better or worse, as both collaborator and judge. Like a strange orchestra upon which a guest conductor would impose his artistic vision, it must be exhorted, persuaded, even wooed, as the price of its applause. It must be appealed to on the basis of what it assumes to be truth as a means of inducting it into new dimensions of artistic truth. By playing artfully upon the audience's sense of experience and form, the artist seeks to shape its emotions and perceptions to his vision, while it, in turn, simultaneously cooperates and resists, says yes and says no in an it-takes-two-to-tango binary response to his effort. As representative of the American audience writ small, the little man draws upon the uncodified *Americanness* of his experience, whether of life or of art, as he engages in a silent dialogue with the artist's exposition of forms, offering or rejecting the work of art on the basis of what he feels to be its affirmation or distortion of American experience.

Perhaps if they were fully aware of his incongruous existence, the little man's neighbors would reject him as a source of confusion, a threat to social order, and a reminder of the unfinished details of this powerful nation. But out of a stubborn individualism born of his democratic origins, he insists upon the cultural necessity of his role, and argues that if he didn't exist, he would have to be invented. If he were not already manifest in the flesh, he would still exist and function as an idea and ideal because—like such character traits as individualism, restlessness, self-reliance, love of the new, and so on—he is a linguistic product of the American scene and language, and a manifestation of the idealistic action of the American word as it goads its users toward a perfection of our revolutionary ideals.

For the artist, a lightning rod attracting unexpected insights and a warning against stale preconceptions, the man behind Chehaw's stove also serves as a metaphor for those individuals we sometimes meet whose refinement of sensibility is inadequately explained by family background, formal education or social status. These individuals seem to have been sensitized by some obscure force that issues undetected from the chromatic scale of American social hierarchy: a force that throws off strange, ultrasonic ultrasemi-semitones that create within those attuned to its vibrations a mysterious enrichment of personality. In this, heredity doubtless plays an important role, but whatever that role may be, it would appear that culturally and environmentally such individuals are products of errant but sympathetic vibrations set up by the tension between America's social mobility, its universal education, and its relative freedom of cultural information. Characterized by a much broader "random accessibility" than class and economic restrictions would appear to allow, this cultural information includes many of the finest products of the arts and intellect—products that are so abundantly available in the form of books, graphics, recordings, and pictorial reproductions as to escape sustained attempts at critical evaluation. Just how these characteristics operate in concert involves the mysterious interaction between environment and personality, instinct and culture. But the frequency and wide dispersal of individuals who reveal the effects of this mysterious configuration of forces endows each American audience, whether of musician, poet, or plastic artist, with a special mystery of its own.

I say "mystery," but perhaps the phenomenon is simply a product of our neglect of serious cultural introspection, our failure to conceive of our fractured, vernacular-weighted culture as an intricate whole. And since there is no reliable sociology of the dispersal of ideas, styles, or tastes in this turbulent American society, it is possible that, personal origins aside, the cultural circumstances here described offer the intellectually adventurous individual what might be termed a broad "social mobility of intellect and taste"—plus an incalculable scale of possibilities for self-creation. While the force that seems to have sensitized those who share the little man of Chehaw Station's unaccountable knowingness—call it a climate of free-floating sensibility—appears to be a random effect generated by a society in which certain assertions of personality, formerly the prerogative of high social rank, have become the privilege of the anonymous and the lowly.

If this be true, the matter of the artist's ability to identify the mixed background and general character of his audience can be more problematical than might be assumed. In the field of literature it presents a problem of rhetoric, a question of how to fashion strategies of communication that will bridge the many divisions of background and taste which any representative American audience embodies. To the extent that American literature is both an art of discovery and an artistic agency for creating a consciousness of cultural identity, it is of such crucial importance as to demand of the artist not only an eclectic resourcefulness of skill, but an act of democratic faith. In this light, the American artist will do his best not only because of his dedication to his form and craft, but because he realizes that despite an inevitable unevenness of composition, the chances are that any American audience will conceal at least *one* individual whose knowledge and taste will complement or surpass his own. This (to paraphrase Miss Harrison) is because even the most homogeneous

audiences are culturally mixed and embody, in their relative anonymity, the mystery of American cultural identity.

This identity—tentative, controversial, constantly changing—is
confusing to artist and audience alike. To the audience, because it is
itself of mixed background, and seldom fully conscious of the cultural
(or even political) implications of its own wide democratic range. To
the artist, because in the broadest thrust of his effort he directs his
finest effects to an abstract (and thus ideal) refinement of sensibility
which, because it is not the exclusive property of a highly visible elite,
is difficult to pinpoint. As one who operates within the historical
frame of his given art, the artist may direct himself to those who are
conscious of the most advanced state of his art: his artistic peers. But if
his work has social impact, which is one gauge of its success as symbolic communication, it will reach into unpredictable areas. Many of
us, by the way, read our first Hemingway, Fitzgerald, Mann in barbershops, and heard our first opera on phonographs. Thus, the ideal
level of sensibility to which the American artist would address himself
tends to transcend the lines of class, religion, region, and race—floating, as it were, free in the crowd. There, like the memory registers of
certain computer systems, it is simultaneously accessible at any point
in American society. Such are the circumstances that render the little
man at Chehaw Station not only possible but inevitable.

But who, then, *is* this little man of Miss Harrison's riddle? From behind what unlikely mask does he render his judgments? And by what
magic of art can his most receptive attention, his grudging admiration, be excited? No idle questions these; like Shakespeare's Hamlet,
the little man has his pride and complexity. He values his personal
uniqueness, cherishes his privacy, and clings to that tricky democratic anonymity which makes locating him an unending challenge.
Hamlet masked himself with madness; the little man plays mute.
Drawn to the brightness of bright lights, he cloaks himself in invisibility—perhaps because in the shadow of his anonymity he can be
both the vernacular cat who looks at (and listens to) the tradition-

bound or fad-struck king *and* the little boy who sees clearly the artist-emperor's pretentious nakedness. García Lorca writes of a singer who presented an audience of *cante hondo* lovers with a voice and restraint of passion better suited to a recital of *bel canto*. "Hurray," responded a deadpan Spanish cousin of the ghost of Chehaw Station, "for the school of Paris!"

Which is to say that having been randomly exposed to diverse artistic conventions, the little man has learned to detect the true transcendent ambience created by successful art from chic shinola. "Form should fit function," says he, "and style theme. Just as punishment should fit crime—which it seldom does nowadays—or as a well-made shoe the foot." Something of an autodidact, he has his own hierarchal ranking of human values, both native American and universal. And along with these, his own range of pieties—filial, sacred, racial—which constitute, in effect, the rhetorical "stops" through which his sensibilities are made responsive to artistic structurings of symbolic form.

Connoisseur, critic, trickster, the little man is also a day-coach, cabin-class traveler, but the timing of his arrivals and departures is uncertain. Sometimes he's there, sometimes he's here. Being quintessentially American, he enjoys the joke, the confounding of hierarchal expectations fostered by his mask: that cultural incongruity through which he, like Brer Rabbit, is able to convert even the most decorous of audiences into his own brier patch and temper the chilliest of classics to his own vernacular taste. Hence, as a practitioner of art, a form of symbolic communication that depends upon a calculated refinement of statement and affect, the American artist must also know the special qualities of that second instrument: his native audience; an audience upon which—arousing, frustrating, and fulfilling its expectations to the conventionalized contours of symbolic action—he is called upon to play as a pianist upon a piano. But here a special, most American problem arises. Thanks to the presence of the little man, this second instrument can be most unstable in its tuning, and downright ornery in its responses. In approaching it, the artist may, if he will, play fast and loose with modes and traditions, techniques and styles, but only at his peril does he treat an American audience as though it were as easily manipulated as a jukebox.

Reject the little man in the name of purity or as one who aspires beyond his social station or cultural capacity—fine! But it is worth remembering that one of the implicitly creative functions of art in the U.S.A. (and certainly of narrative art) is the defining and correlating of diverse American experiences by bringing previously unknown patterns, details and emotions into view along with those that are generally recognized. Here one of the highest awards of art is the achievement of that electrifying and creative collaboration between the work of art and its audience that occurs when, through the unifying force of its vision and its power to give meaningful focus to apparently unrelated emotions and experiences, art becomes simultaneously definitive of specific and universal truths.

In this country, the artist is free to choose, but cannot limit, his audience. He may ignore the unknown or unplaced sector of the public, but the mystifications of snobbery are of no avail against the little man's art hunger. Having arrived at his interest in art through familiar but uncharted channels, he disdains its use either as a form of social climbing or of social exclusion. Democratically innocent of hierarchal striving, he takes his classics as he takes his tall tales or jazz: without frills. But while self-effacing, he is nevertheless given to a democratic touchiness, and is suspicious of all easy assumptions of superiority based upon appearances. When fretted by an obtuse artistic hand, he can be quite irritable, and what frets him utterly is any attitude that offends his quite human pieties by ignorance or disregard for his existence.

And yet the little man feels no urge to impose censorship upon the artist. Possessing an American-vernacular receptivity to change, a healthy delight in creative attempts at formalizing irreverence, and a Yankee trader's respect for the experimental, he is repelled by works of art that would strip human experience, especially American experience, of its wonder and stubborn complexity. Not that he demands that his own shadowy image be dragged into each and every artistic effort; that would make a shambles of art's necessary illusion by violating the social reality in which he finds his being. It is enough that the artist (above all, the novelist, dramatist, poet) forge images of American experience that resonate symbolically with his own ubiquitous presence. In *The Great Gatsby*, Nick Carraway tells us, by way of outlining his background's influence upon his moral judgments, that his family fortune was started by an Irish uncle who immigrated during the Civil War, paid a substitute to fight in his stead, and went on to become wealthy from war profiteering. Enough said! This takes hardly a paragraph, but the themes of history, wealth and immigration are struck like so many notes on a chime. Assuming his Afro-American identity, costume and mask, the little man behind the stove would make the subtle symbolic connections among Gatsby's ill-fated social climbing, the wealthy wastrels whose manners and morals are the focus of the action, the tragic ironies echoing so faintly from the Civil War (that seedbed of so many Northern fortunes), and his own social condition; among the principles of democracy that form the ground upon which the novel's drama of manners and social hierarchy is enacted, and the cost to Gatsby of confusing the promises of democracy with the terms governing their attainment. In so doing, the little underground-outsider would incorporate the inside-outsider Gatz-Gatsby's experience into his own, and his own into Gatsby's—a transposition that Gatsby would probably have abhorred but one that might have saved his life.

Or again, the little man, by imposing collaboratively his own vision of American experience upon that of the author, would extend the novel's truth to levels below the threshold of that frustrating and illusory social mobility which forms the core of Gatsby's anguish. Responding out of a knowledge of the manner in which the mystique of wealth is intertwined with the American mysteries of class and color, he would aid the author in achieving the more complex vision of American experience that was implicit in his material. As a citizen, the little man endures with a certain grace the social restrictions that limit his own social mobility, but *as a reader* he demands that the relationship between his own condition and that of those more highly placed be recognized. He senses that American experience is of a whole, and he wants the interconnections revealed. This not out of a penchant for protest, nor out of petulant vanity, but because he sees his own condition as an inseparable part of a larger truth in which the high and the lowly, the known and the unrecognized, the comic and the tragic are woven into the American skein. Having been attuned at Chehaw Station to the clangor of diverse bell sounds, he asks not for *whom* the bell tolls, only that it be struck artfully and with that fullness of resonance which warns all men of man's fate. At his best he does not ask for scapegoats, but for the hero as witness. How ironic it was that in the world of *The Great Gatsby* the witness who could have identified the driver of the death car that led to Gatsby's murder was a black man whose ability to communicate (and communication implies moral judgment) was of no more consequence to the action than that of an ox that might have observed Icarus's sad plunge into the sea. (This, by the way, is not intended as a criticism of Fitzgerald, but only to suggest some of the problems and possibilities of artistic communication in the U.S.A.) In this light, the little man is a cautionary figure who challenges the artist to reach out for new heights of expressiveness. If we ignore his possible presence, violence might well be done to that ideal of cultivated democratic sensibility which was the goal of the likes of Emerson and Whitman, and for which the man at Chehaw Station is a metaphor. Respect his presence and even the most avant-garde art may become an agency for raising the general level of artistic taste. The work of art is, after all, an act of faith in our ability to communicate symbolically.

But why would Hazel Harrison associate her humble metaphor for the diffusion of democratic sensibility with a mere whistle-stop? Today I would guess that it was because Chehaw Station functioned as a point of arrival and departure for people representing a wide diversity of tastes and styles of living. Philanthropists, businessmen, sharecroppers, students and artistic types passed through its doors. But the same, in a more exalted fashion, is true of Carnegie Hall and the Metropolitan Museum; all three structures are meeting places for motley mixtures of people. So while it might require a Melvillean imagination to reduce American society to the dimensions of either concert hall or railroad station, their common feature as gathering places, as juncture points for random assemblies of sensibilities, reminds us again that in this particular country even the most homogeneous gatherings of people are mixed and pluralistic. Perhaps the mystery of American cultural identity contained in such motley mixtures arises out of our persistent attempts to reduce our cultural diversity to an easily recognizable unity.

On the other hand, Americans tend to focus on the diverse parts of their culture (with which they can more easily identify), rather than on its complex and pluralistic wholeness. But perhaps they identify with the parts because the whole is greater, if not of a different quality, than its parts. This difference, that new and problematic quality—call it our "Americanness"—creates out of its incongruity an uneasiness within us, because it is a constant reminder that American democracy is not only a political collectivity of individuals, but culturally a collectivity of styles, tastes and traditions.

In this lies the source of many of our problems, especially those centering upon American identity. In relationship to the cultural whole, we are, all of us—white or black, native-born or immigrant—members of minority groups. Beset by feelings of isolation because of the fluid, pluralistic turbulence of the democratic process, we cling desperately to our own familiar fragment of the democratic rock, and from such fragments we confront our fellow Americans in that combat of civility, piety and tradition which is the drama of American social hierarchy. Holding desperately to our familiar turf, we engage in that ceaseless contention whose uneasily accepted but unrejectable purpose is the projection of an ever more encompassing and acceptable definition of our corporate identity as Americans.

Usually this contest (our improvised moral equivalent for armed warfare) proceeds as a war of words, a clash of styles, or as rites of symbolic sacrifice in which cabalistic code words are used to designate victims consumed with an Aztec voracity for scapegoats. Indeed, so frequently does this conflict erupt into physical violence that one sometimes wonders if there is any other viable possibility for co-existing in so abstract and futuristic a nation as this.

The rock, the terrain upon which we struggle, is itself abstract, a terrain of ideas that, although man-made, exerts the compelling force of the ideal, of the sublime: ideas that draw their power from the Declaration of Independence, the Constitution, and the Bill of Rights. We stand, as we say, united in the name of these sacred principles. But indeed it is in the name of these same principles that we ceaselessly contend, affirming our ideals even as we do them violence.

For while we are but human and thus given to the fears and temptations of the flesh, we are dedicated to principles that are abstract, ideal, spiritual: principles that were conceived linguistically and committed to paper during that contention over political ideals and economic interests which was released and given focus during the period of our revolutionary break with traditional forms of society, principles that were enshrined—again linguistically—in the documents of state upon which this nation was founded. Actuated by passionate feats of revolutionary will which released that dynamic power for moralizing both man and nature, instinct and society, which is a property of linguistic forms of symbolic action, these principles—democracy, equality, individual freedom and universal justice—now move us as articles of faith. Holding them sacred, we act (or *fail* to act) in their names. And in the freewheeling fashion of words that are summoned up to name the ideal, they prod us ceaselessly toward the refinement and perfection of those formulations of policy and configurations of social forms of which they are the signs and symbols. As we strive to conduct social action in accordance with the ideals they evoke, they in turn insist upon being made flesh. Inspiriting our minds and bodies, they dance around in our bones, spurring us to make them ever more manifest in the structures and processes of ourselves and our society. As a nation, we exist in the communication of our principles, and we argue over their application and interpretation as over the rights of property or the exercise and sharing of authority. As elsewhere, they influence our expositions in the area of artistic form and are involved in our search for a system of aesthetics capable of projecting our corporate, pluralistic identity. They interrogate us endlessly as to who and what we are; they demand that we keep the democratic faith.

Words that evoke our principles are, according to Kenneth Burke, charismatic terms for transcendent order, for perfection. Being forms of symbolic action, they tend, through their nature as language, to sweep us in tow as they move by a process of linguistic negation toward the ideal. As a form of *symbolic* action, they operate by negating nature as a given and amoral condition, creating endless series of man-made or man-imagined positives. By so doing, they nudge us toward that state of human rectitude for which, ideally, we strive. In this way, Burke contends, man uses language to moralize both nature and himself. Thus, in this nation the word democracy possesses the aura of what Burke calls a "god-term," and all that we are and do exists in the magnitude of its intricate symbolism. It is the rock upon which we toil, and we thrive or wane in the communication of those symbols and processes set in motion in its name.

In our national beginnings, all redolent with Edenic promises, was the word *democratic*, and since we vowed in a war rite of blood and sacrifice to keep its commandments, we act in the name of a word made sacred. Yes, but since we are, as Burke holds, language-using, language-misusing animals—beings who are by nature vulnerable to both the negative *and* the positive promptings of language as symbolic action—we Americans are given to eating, regurgitating, and, alas, re-eating even our most sacred words. It is as though they contain a substance that is crucial to our national existence but that, except in minute and infrequently ingested doses, we find extremely indigestible. Some would call this national habit of word-eating an exercise in the art of the impossible; others attribute it to the limitations imposed by the human condition. Still others would describe it as springing from the pathology of social hierarchy, a reaction to certain built-in conditions of our democracy that are capable of amelioration but impossible to cure. Whatever the case may be, it would seem that for many our cultural diversity is as indigestible as the concept of democracy in which it is grounded. For one thing, principles in action are enactments of ideals grounded in a vision of perfection that transcends the limitations of death and dying. By arousing in the believer a sense of the disrelation between the ideal and the actual, between the perfect word and the errant flesh, they partake of mystery. Here the most agonizing mystery sponsored by the democratic ideal is that of our unity-in-diversity, our oneness-in-manyness. Pragmatically we cooperate and communicate across this mystery, but the problem of identity that it poses often goads us to symbolic acts of disaffiliation. So we seek psychic security from within our inherited divisions of the corporate American culture while gazing out upon our fellows with a mixed attitude of fear, suspicion and yearning. We repress an underlying anxiety aroused by the awareness that we are representative not only of one but of several overlapping and constantly shifting social categories, and we stress our affiliation with that segment of the corporate culture which has emerged out of our parents' past—racial, cultural, religious—and which we assume, on the basis of such magical talismans as our mother's milk or father's beard, that we "know." Grounding our sense of identity in such primary and affect-charged symbols, we seek to avoid the mysteries and pathologies of the democratic process. But that process was designed to overcome the dominance of tradition by promoting an open society in which the individual could achieve his potential unhindered by his ties to the past. Here, theoretically, social categories are open, and the individual is not only considered capable of transforming himself, but is encouraged to do so. However, in undertaking such transformations he opts for that psychic uncertainty which is a condition of his achieving his potential, a state he yearns to avoid. So despite any self-assurance he might achieve in dealing with his familiars, he is nevertheless (and by the nature of his indefinite relationship to the fluid social hierarchy) a lonely individual who must find his own way within a crowd of other lonely individuals. Here the security offered by his familiar symbols of identity is equivocal. And an overdependence upon them as points of orientation leads him to become bemused, gazing backward at a swiftly receding—if not quasi-mythical—past, while stumbling headlong into a predescribed but unknown future.

So perhaps we shy from confronting our cultural wholeness because it offers no easily recognizable points of rest, no facile certainties as to who, what or where (culturally or historically) we are. Instead, the whole is always in cacophonic motion. Constantly changing its mode, it appears as a vortex of discordant ways of living and tastes, values and traditions, a whirlpool of odds and ends in which the past courses in uneasy juxtaposition with those bright, futuristic principles and promises to which we, as a nation, are politically committed. In our vaguely perceived here and now, even the sounds and symbols spun off by the clashing of group against group appear not only alarmingly off-key, but threatening to our inherited eyes, ears, and appetites. Thus in our intergroup familiarity there is a brooding strangeness, and in our underlying sense of alienation a poignant, although distrusted, sense of fraternity. Deep down, the American condition is a state of unease.

During the nineteenth century an attempt was made to impose a loose conceptual order upon the chaos of American society by viewing it as a melting pot. Today that metaphor is noisily rejected, vehemently disavowed. In fact, it has come under attack in the name of the newly fashionable code word "ethnicity," reminding us that in this country code words are linguistic agencies for the designation of sacrificial victims, and are circulated to sanction the abandonment of policies and the degrading of ideas. So today, before the glaring inequities, unfulfilled promises and rich possibilities of democracy, we hear heady evocations of European, African and Asian backgrounds accompanied by chants proclaiming the inviolability of ancestral blood. Today blood magic and blood thinking, never really dormant in American society, are rampant among us, often leading to brutal racial assaults in areas where these seldom occurred before. And while this goes on, the challenge of arriving at an adequate definition of American cultural identity goes unanswered. (What, by the way, is one to make of a white youngster who, with a transistor radio screaming a Stevie Wonder tune glued to his ear, shouts racial epithets at black youngsters trying to swim at a public beach—and this in the name of the ethnic sanctity of what has been declared a neighborhood turf?)

The proponents of ethnicity—ill concealing an underlying anxiety, and given a bizarre bebopish stridency by the obviously American vernacular inspiration of the costumes and rituals ragged out to dramatize their claims to ethnic (and genetic) insularity—have helped give our streets and campuses a rowdy, All Fool's Day carnival atmosphere. In many ways, then, the call for a new social order based upon the glorification of ancestral blood and ethnic background acts as a call to cultural and aesthetic chaos. Yet while this latest farcical phase in the drama of American social hierarchy unfolds, the irrepressible movement of American culture toward the integration of its diverse elements continues, confounding the circumlocutions of its staunchest opponents.

In this regard I am reminded of a light-skinned, blue-eyed, Afro-American-featured individual who could have been taken for anything from a sun-tinged white Anglo-Saxon, an Egyptian, or a mixed-breed American Indian to a strayed member of certain tribes of Jews. This young man appeared one sunny Sunday afternoon on New York's Riverside Drive near 151st Street, where he disrupted the visual peace of the promenading throng by racing up in a shiny new blue Volkswagen Beetle decked out with a gleaming Rolls-Royce radiator. As the flow of strollers came to an abrupt halt, this man of parts emerged from his carriage with something of that magical cornucopian combustion by which a dozen circus clowns are exploded from an even more miniaturized automobile. Looming as tall as a professional basketball center, he unfolded himself and stretched to his full imposing height.

Clad in handsome black riding boots and fawn-colored riding breeches of English tailoring, he took the curb wielding, with an ultra-pukka-sahib haughtiness, a leather riding crop. A dashy dashiki (as bright and as many-colored as the coat that initiated poor Joseph's troubles in biblical times) flowed from his broad shoulders down to the arrogant, military flare of his breeches-tops, while six feet six inches or so above his heels, a black homburg hat tilted at a jaunty angle floated majestically on the crest of his huge Afro-coiffed head.

As though all this were not enough to amaze, delight, or discombobulate his observers—or precipitate an international incident involving charges of a crass invasion of stylistic boundaries—this apparition proceeded to unlimber an expensive Japanese single-lens reflex camera, position it atop the ornamental masonry balustrade which girds Riverside Park in that area, and activate its self-timer. Then, with a ballet leap across the walk, he assumed a position beside his car. There he rested his elbow upon its top, smiled, and gave himself sharp movie director's commands as to desired poses, then began taking a series of self-portraits. This done, he placed the camera upon the hood of his Volkswagen and took another series of self-shots in which, manipulating a lengthy ebony cigarette holder, he posed himself in various fanciful attitudes against the not-too-distant background of the George Washington Bridge. All in all, he made a scene to haunt one's midnight dreams and one's noon repose.

Now, I can only speculate about what was going on in the elegant gentleman's mind, who he was, or what visual statement he intended to communicate. I only know that his carefully stylized movements (especially his "pimp-limp" walk) marked him as a native of the U.S.A., a home-boy bent upon projecting and recording with native verve something of his complex sense of cultural identity. Clearly he had his own style, but if—as has been repeatedly argued—the style is the man, who on earth was this fellow? Viewed from a rigid ethno-cultural perspective, neither his features nor his car nor his dress was of a whole. Yet he conducted himself with an obvious pride of person and of property, inviting all and sundry to admire and wonder in response to himself as his own sign and symbol, his own work of art. He had gotten himself, as the Harlem saying goes, "together," and whatever sheerly ethnic identity was communicated by his costume depended upon the observer's ability to see order in an apparent cultural chaos. The man himself was hidden somewhere within, his complex identity concealed by his aesthetic gesturing. And his essence lay not in the somewhat comic clashing of styles, but in the mixture, the improvised form, the willful juxtaposition of modes.

Perhaps to the jaundiced eyes of an adversary of the melting-pot concept, the man would have appeared to be a militant black nationalist bent upon dramatizing his feelings of alienation—and he may have been. But most surely he was not an African or an Englishman. His Volks-Rolls-Royce might well have been loaded with Marxist tracts and Molotov cocktails, but his clashing of styles nevertheless sounded an integrative, vernacular note, an American compulsion to improvise upon the given. His garments were, literally and figuratively, of many colors and cultures, his racial identity interwoven of many strands. Whatever his politics, sources of income, hierarchal status and such, he revealed his essential "Americanness" in his free-wheeling assault upon traditional forms of the Western aesthetic. Whatever the identity he presumed to project, he was exercising an American freedom and was a product of the melting pot and the conscious or unconscious comedy it brews. Culturally he was an American joker. If his Afro and dashiki symbolized protest, his boots, camera, Volkswagen and homburg imposed certain qualifications upon that protest. In doing so, they played irreverently upon the symbolism of status, property and authority, and suggested new possibilities of perfection. More than expressing protest, these symbols ask the old, abiding American questions: Who am I? What about me?

Still, ignoring such questions (as they would ignore the little man of Chehaw Station), the opponents of the melting-pot concept utter their disavowals with an old-fashioned, camp-meeting fervor—solemnly, and with an air of divine revelation. Most amazingly, these attacks upon the melting pot are led by the descendants of peasants or slaves or inhabitants of European ghettos, people whose status as spokesmen is a product of that very melting of hierarchal barriers they now deny. With such an attitude, it is fortunate that they, too, are caught up in the society's built-in, democracy-prodded movement toward a perfection of self-definition. Hence such disavowals, despite their negative posture, have their positive content. And to the extent that they are negatives uttered in an attempt to create certain attitudes and conditions that their exponents conceive as positives, these disavowals are, in part, affirmations of the diverse and unique pasts out of which have emerged the many groups that this nation comprises. As such they might well contribute to a clarification of our pluralistic cultural identity, and are thus a step in the direction of creating a much-needed cultural introspection.

As of now, however, I see the denial of that goal of cultural integration for which the melting pot was an accented metaphor as the current form of an abiding American self-distrust. I see it as an effort to dismiss the mystery of American identity (our unity-within-diversity) with a gesture of democracy-weary resignation, as an attempt to dispel by sociological word-magic the turbulence of the present, and as a self-satisfied vote against that hope which is so crucial to our cultural and political fulfillment. For if such disavowals be viable, what about the little man behind the stove?

Ironically, the attacks on the melting-pot idea issue from those who have "made it." Having been reborn into a higher hierarchal status, they now view those who have *not* made it as threats to their newly achieved status, and therefore would change both the rules and the game plan. Thus they demonstrate anew the built-in opportunism of their characteristically American shortness of memory. But lest we ourselves forget, the melting-pot concept was never so simplistic or abstract as current arguments would have it. Americans of an earlier day, despite their booster extravagances, recognized the difference between the ideal and the practical, even as they clung desperately to, and sought to default upon, the responsibilities that went with achieving their democratic ideal. Their outlook was pragmatic, their way with culture vernacular, an eclectic mixing of modes. Having rejected the hierarchal ordering of traditional societies, they improvised their culture as they did their politics and institutions—touch and go, by ear and by eye—fitting new form to new function, new function to old form. Deep down they sensed that in the process of nation-building their *culture*, like their institutions, was always more "American" (that futuristic concept) than they could perceive—or even fully accept—it to be. Even the slaves, although thrust below the threshold of social hierarchy, were given a prominent place in our national iconography; their music, poetic imagery and choreography were grudgingly recognized as seminal sources of American art. In the process of creating (and re-creating or diverting) themselves, the melting-pot Americans brazenly violated their ideals. They kept slaves or battened on the products of slave labor. They exploited and abused those who arrived later than themselves, kinsmen and aliens alike. While paying lip service to their vaunted forms of justice, they betrayed, brutalized and scapegoated one another in the name of the Constitution, the Bill of Rights, and the Ten Commandments. But because of their fidelity to their parents' customs and their respect for the pieties of their traditions, if not for those of their fellows, none of the groups that made up the total culture ever really desired to lose its sense of its unique past, not even when that past lay clouded in slavery.

Instead, they wished to use the techniques, ways of life, and values developed within their respective backgrounds as sources of morale in that continuing process of antagonistic cooperation, and of adjusting the past to the present in the interest of the future, which was so necessary in building what they imagined as a more humane society. Indeed, during their most candid, self-accepting moments they saw themselves as living embodiments of the ancestral past, people who had seized the democracy-sponsored opportunity to have a second chance. As such, they saw themselves as the best guarantee that whatever was most desirable and salvageable from that past would be retained and brought to flower, free of hierarchal hindrances. The little man behind the stove would know from his own condition that the melting-pot concept was a conceit, but his forced awareness of American cultural pluralism would assure him that it was by no means the product of a con game contrived by the powerful. Here not even the powerful were so perceptive.

So our current disavowals are not only misdirected; they are productive of more social disorder, more crises of cultural and personal identity than they could possibly resolve. It is here, on the level of culture, that the diverse elements of our various backgrounds, our heterogeneous pasts, have indeed come together, "melted" and undergone metamorphosis. It is here, if we would but recognize it, that elements of the many available tastes, traditions, ways of life, and values that make up the total culture have been ceaselessly appropriated and made their own—consciously, unselfconsciously, or imperialistically—by groups and individuals to whose own backgrounds and traditions they are historically alien. Indeed, it was through this process of cultural appropriation (and misappropriation) that Englishmen, Europeans, Africans, and Asians *became* Americans.

The Pilgrims began by appropriating the agricultural, military, and meteorological lore of the Indians, including much of their terminology. The Africans, thrown together from numerous ravaged tribes, took up the English language and the biblical legends of the ancient Hebrews and were "Americanizing" themselves long before the American Revolution. They also had imposed upon them a goodly portion of European chromosomes, and thereby "inherited" both an immunity to certain European diseases and a complexity of bloodlines and physical characteristics that have much to do with the white American's reluctance to differentiate between race and culture, African and American, and are a major source of our general confusion over American identity. One of the many questions posed by the man on Riverside Drive is how one so "white" could be simply "black" without being impossibly simpleminded. Especially when his skin and facial bone structure ask, "Where went the blood of yesteryear?" There is no point in answering the question as did Villon, because the man's face was as Anglo and his hairstyle as Afro as his car's radiator and body were English and German.

Everyone played the appropriation game. The whites took over any elements of Afro-American culture that seemed useful: the imagery of folklore, ways of speaking, endurance of what appeared to be hopeless hardship, and singing and dancing—including the combination of Afro-American art forms that produced the first musical theater of national appeal: the minstrel show. And in improvising their rather tawdry and opportunistic version of a national mythology, the moviemakers—Christian and Jewish, Northerners and Southerners—ransacked and distorted for their own purposes the backgrounds and images of everyone, including the American Indians.

So, melting-pot disclaimers notwithstanding, Americans seem to have sensed intuitively that the possibility of enriching the individual self by such pragmatic and opportunitistic appropriations has constituted one of the most precious of their many freedoms. Having opted for the new, and being unable to create it out of thin air or from words inscribed on documents of state, they did what came naturally: they pressured the elements of the past and present into new amalgams. In lieu of a usable cultural tradition, there were always the cultural improvisations of the Afro-Americans, the immigrants, or design-gifted religious groups like the Shakers—all so close to eye and ear, hand and imagination. Considering that the newness achieved by Americans has often been a matter of adapting to function and a matter of naming, of designation, we are reminded of how greatly the "Americanness" of American culture has been a matter of Adamic wordplay—of trying, in the interest of a futuristic dream, to impose unity upon an experience that changes too rapidly for lin-

guistic or political exactitude. In this effort we are often less interested in what we are than in projecting what we will be. But in our
freewheeling appropriations of culture we appear to act on the assumption that as members of a "nation of nations," we are, by definition and by the processes of democratic cultural integration, the
inheritors, creators and creations of a culture of cultures.

So perhaps the complex actuality of our cultural pluralism is perplexing because the diverse interacting elements that surround us,
traditional and vernacular, not only elude accepted formulations, but
take on a character that is something other than their various parts.
Our old familiar pasts become, in juxtaposition with elements appropriated from other backgrounds, incongruously transformed, exerting an energy (or synergy) of a different order than that generated by
their separate parts—and this with incalculable results. Nor should
we forget the role played by objects and technology in the integration of our cultural styles, and in the regional and political unification of the nation. If we put the blues, bluegrass music, English folk
songs, et cetera, together with Afro-American rhythms and gospel
shouts, we have, God help us, first rock and now "funk," that most
odoriferous of musical(?) styles. Still, such mixtures of cultural elements are capable of igniting exciting transformations of culture.
Even more mysteriously (and here, perhaps, we have a further source
of the little man of Chehaw Station's rich sensibility), they provide
for exciting and most unexpected metamorphoses within the self-
creating personality.

Frankly, many of the foregoing speculations have been arrived at
over the years since I left Tuskegee. If I had been more mature or
perceptive back when I first heard of the little man behind the stove,
an object that lay atop Miss Harrison's piano would have been most
enlightening. It was a signed Prokofiev manuscript that had been
presented to her by the composer. Except for the signature, it looked
like countless other manuscripts. Yet I suspect that to anyone who
possessed a conventional notion of cultural and hierarchal order, its
presence in such a setting would have been as incongruous as a

Gutenberg Bible on the altar of a black sharecropper's church or a dashiki worn with a homburg hat. Still, there it was, an artifact of contemporary music, a folio whose signs and symbols resonated in that setting with the intricate harmonies of friendship, admiration and shared ideals through which it had found its way from Berlin to Tuskegee. Once there, and the arrangement of society beyond the campus notwithstanding, it spoke eloquently of the unstructured possibilities of culture in this pluralistic democracy. Yet despite its meticulous artistic form, in certain conventional minds its presence could arouse intimations of the irrational—of cultural, if not social, chaos.

Given the logic of a society ordered along racial lines, Miss Harrison's studio (or even the library) was simply off limits for such an artifact, certainly in its original form. But there it was, lying in wait to play havoc with conventional ideas of order, lending a wry reality to Malraux's observation that art is an assault upon logic. Through its presence, the manuscript had become an agency of cultural transformation and synthesis. By charging Miss Harrison's basement studio with the spirit of living personages, ideals and purposes from afar, it had transformed that modest room from a mere spot on a segregated Negro campus into an advanced outpost on the frontiers of contemporary music, thus adding an unexpected, if undetected, dimension to Alabama's cultural atmosphere. In my innocence I viewed the manuscript as a property of Miss Harrison's, a sign of her connection with gifted artists across the ocean. It spoke to me of possibility. But that it also endowed the scene—place, studio, campus—with a complex cultural ambiguity escaped my conscious mind. Though aware of certain details of the total scene, I was unattuned to the context in which they sounded, the cultural unity-within-diversity that the combination of details made manifest. Perhaps we are able to see only that which we are prepared to see, and in our culture the cost of insight is an uncertainty that threatens our already unstable sense of order and requires a constant questioning of accepted assumptions.

Had I questioned Miss Harrison as to how the racial identity of her little Chehaw man squared with the culture she credited to him, she might well have replied:

"Look, baby, the society beyond this campus is constantly trying to confuse you about the relationship between culture and race. Well, if you ask me, artistic talent might have something to do with race, but you do *not* inherit culture and artistic skill through your genes. No, sir. These come as a result of personal conquest, of the individual's applying himself to that art, that music—whether jazz, classical, or folk—which helps him to realize and complete himself. And that's true *wherever* the music or art of his choice originates."

Or in the words of André Malraux (whom I was to discover a year or two later), she might have told me that music is important as an artistic form of symbolic action "because its function is to let men escape from their human condition, not by means of an evasion, but through a possession, [for] art is a way of possessing destiny." And that therefore, even at racially segregated Tuskegee (as witnessed by, among countless other details, the library and Miss Harrison's Prokofiev manuscript), one's "cultural heritage is the totality, not of works that men must respect [or that are used to enhance the mystifications that support an elite], but those that can help them live." Entering into a dialogue with Malraux, she might have added on a more specifically American note: "Yes, and most important, you must remember that in this country things are always all shook up, so that people are constantly moving around and rubbing off on one another culturally. Nor should you forget that here all things—institutions, individuals and roles—offer more than the function assigned them, because beyond their intended function they provide forms of education and criticism. They challenge, they ask questions, they offer suggestive answers to those who would pause and probe their mystery. Most of all, remember that it is not only the images of art or the sound of music that pass through walls to give pleasure and inspiration; it is in the very *spirit* of art to be defiant of categories and obstacles. They are, as transcendent forms of symbolic expression, agencies of human freedom."

. . .

Three years later, having abandoned my hope of becoming a musician, I had just about forgotten Miss Harrison's mythical little man behind the stove. Then, in faraway New York, concrete evidence of his actual existence arose and blasted me like the heat from an internally combusted ton of coal.

As a member of the Federal Writers' Project, I was spending a clammy late-fall afternoon of freedom circulating a petition in support of some now long-forgotten social issue that I regarded as indispensable to the public good. I found myself inside a tenement building in San Juan Hill, a Negro district that disappeared with the coming of Lincoln Center. Starting on the top floor of the building, I had collected an acceptable number of signatures, and having descended from the ground floor to the basement level, was moving along the dimly lit hallway toward a door through which I could hear loud voices. They were male Afro-American voices, raised in violent argument. The language was profane, the style of speech a Southern idiomatic vernacular such as was spoken by formally uneducated Afro-American workingmen. Reaching the door, I paused, sounding out the lay of the land before knocking to present my petition.

But my delay led to indecision. Not, however, because of the loud, unmistakable anger sounding within; being myself a slum dweller, I knew that voices in slums are often raised in anger, but that the *rhetoric* of anger, itself cathartic, is not necessarily a prelude to physical violence. Rather, it is frequently a form of symbolic action, a verbal equivalent of fisticuffs. No, I hesitated because I realized that behind the door a mystery was unfolding. A mystery so incongruous, outrageous, and surreal that it struck me as a threat to my sense of rational order. It was as though a bizarre practical joke had been staged and its perpetrators were waiting for me, its designated but unknowing scapegoat, to arrive: a joke designed to assault my knowledge of American culture and its hierarchal dispersal. At the very least, it appeared that my pride in my knowledge of my own people was under attack.

For the angry voices behind the door were proclaiming an inti-

mate familiarity with a subject of which, by all the logic of their linguistically projected social status, they should have been oblivious.
The subject of their contention confounded all my assumptions regarding the correlation between educational levels, class, race and
the possession of conscious culture. Impossible as it seemed, these
foul-mouthed black workingmen were locked in verbal combat over
which of two celebrated Metropolitan Opera divas was the superior
soprano!

I myself attended the opera only when I could raise the funds, and
I knew full well that opera-going was far from the usual cultural pursuit of men identified with the linguistic style of such voices. Yet,
confounding such facile logic, they were voicing (and loudly) a familiarity with the Met far greater than my own. In their graphic, irreverent, and vehement criticism they were describing not only the two
sopranos' acting abilities, but were ridiculing the gestures with
which each gave animation to her roles, and they shouted strong
opinions as to the ranges of the divas' vocal equipment. Thus, with
such a distortion of perspective being imposed upon me, I was challenged either to solve the mystery of their knowledge by entering
into their midst or to leave the building with my sense of logic reduced forever to a level of college-trained absurdity.

So challenged, I knocked. I knocked out of curiosity, I knocked
out of outrage. I knocked in fear and trembling. I knocked in anticipation of whatever insights—malicious or transcendent, I no longer
cared which—I would discover beyond the door.

For a moment there was an abrupt and portentous silence; then
came the sound of chair legs thumping dully upon the floor, followed by further silence. I knocked again, loudly, with an authority
fired by an impatient and anxious urgency.

Again silence, until a gravel voice boomed an annoyed "Come
in!"

Opening the door with an unsteady hand, I looked inside, and was
even less prepared for the scene that met my eyes than for the content of their loudmouthed contention.

In a small, rank-smelling, lamplit room, four huge black men sat sprawled around a circular dining-room table, looking toward me with undisguised hostility. The sooty-chimneyed lamp glowed in the center of the bare oak table, casting its yellow light upon four water tumblers and a half-empty pint of whiskey. As the men straightened in their chairs I became aware of a fireplace with a coal fire glowing in its grate, and leaning against the ornate marble facing of its mantelpiece, I saw four enormous coal scoops.

"All right," one of the men said, rising to his feet. "What the hell can we do for *you*?"

"And we ain't buying nothing, buddy," one of the seated men added, his palm slapping the table.

Closing the door, I moved forward, holding my petition like a flag of truce before me, noting that the men wore faded blue overalls and jumper jackets, and becoming aware that while all were of dark complexion, their blackness was accentuated in the dim lamplight by the dust and grime of their profession.

"Come on, man, speak up," the man who had arisen said. "We ain't got all day."

"I'm sorry to interrupt," I said, "but I thought you might be interested in supporting my petition," and began hurriedly to explain.

"Say," one of the men said, "you look like one of them relief investigators. You're not out to jive us, are you?"

"Oh, no, sir," I said. "I happen to work on the Writers' Project . . ."

The standing man leaned toward me. "You on the Writers' Project?" he said, looking me up and down.

"That's right," I said. "I'm a writer."

"Now is that right?" he said. "How long you been writing?"

I hesitated. "About a year," I said.

He grinned, looking at the others. "Y'all hear that? Ol' Homeboy here has done up and jumped on the *gravy* train! Now that's pretty good. Pretty damn good! So what did you do before that?" he said.

"I studied music," I said, "at Tuskegee."

"Hey, now!" the standing man said. "They got a damn good choir down there. Y'all remember back when they opened Radio City? They had that fellow William L. Dawson for a director. Son, let's see that paper."

Relieved, I handed him the petition, watching him stretch it between his hardened hands. After a moment of soundlessly mouthing the words of its appeal, he gave me a skeptical look and turned to the others.

"What the hell," he said, "signing this piece of paper won't do no good, but since Home here's a musician, it won't do us no harm to help him out. Let's go along with him."

Fishing a blunt-pointed pencil from the bib of his overalls, he wrote his name and passed the petition to his friends, who followed suit.

This took some time, and as I watched the petition move from hand to hand, I could barely contain myself or control my need to unravel the mystery that had now become far more important than just getting their signatures on my petition.

"There you go," the last one said, extending the petition toward me. "Having our names on there don't mean a thing, but you got 'em."

"Thank you," I said. "Thank you very much."

They watched me with amused eyes, expecting me to leave, but, clearing my throat nervously, I stood in my tracks, too intrigued to leave and suddenly too embarrassed to ask my question.

"So what're you waiting for?" one of them said. "You got what you came for. What else do you want?"

And then I blurted it out. "I'd like to ask you just one question," I said.

"Like what?" the standing one said.

"Like where on earth did you gentlemen learn so much about grand opera?"

For a moment he stared at me with parted lips; then, pounding the mantelpiece with his palm, he collapsed with a roar of laughter.

As the laughter of the others erupted like a string of giant firecrackers, I looked on with growing feelings of embarrassment and insult, trying to grasp the handle of what appeared to be an unfriendly joke. Finally, wiping coal-dust-stained tears from his cheeks, he interrupted his laughter long enough to initiate me into the mystery.

"Hell, son," he laughed, "we learn it down at the Met, that's where . . ."

"You learned it *where*?"

"At the Metropolitan Opera, just like I told you. Strip us fellows down and give us some costumes and we make about the finest damn bunch of Egyptians you ever seen. Hell, we been down there wearing leopard skins and carrying spears or waving things like palm leafs and ostrich-tail fans for *years*!"

Now, purged by the revelation, and with Hazel Harrison's voice echoing in my ears, it was my turn to roar with laughter. With a shock of recognition I joined them in appreciation of the hilarious American joke that centered on the incongruities of race, economic status and culture. My sense of order restored, my appreciation of the arcane ways of American cultural possibility was vastly extended. The men were products of both past *and* present; were both coal heavers *and* Met extras; were both workingmen *and* opera buffs. Seen in the clear, pluralistic, melting-pot light of American cultural possibility, there was no contradiction. The joke, the apparent contradiction, sprang from my attempting to see them by the light of social concepts that cast less illumination than an inert lump of coal. I was delighted, because during a moment when I least expected to encounter the little man behind the stove (Miss Harrison's vernacular music critic, as it were), I had stumbled upon four such men. Not behind the stove, it is true, but even more wondrously, they had materialized at an even more unexpected location: at the depth of the American social hierarchy and, of all possible hiding places, behind a coal pile. Where there's a melting pot there's smoke, and where there's smoke it is not simply optimistic to expect fire, it's imperative to watch for the phoenix's vernacular, but transcendent, rising.

On Initiation Rites and Power:
A Lecture at West Point

I hardly know where to start. It should be with an apology, I suppose, because as I recall how annoyed I was that I had been assigned certain novels as a student, I find it extremely ironic that now my own is being passed along to you, and that I'm responsible.

I suppose the best way to get into this is to just be autobiographical, since you are concerned with my novel, because the novel isn't autobiographical in an immediate sense, and it'll be necessary to enlarge upon what Colonel Capps had to say about my background in order to spell out to you just why, and in what way, it is *not* autobiographical. I was, as he said, a music major at Tuskegee, but I was also one who read a lot, who lived in books as well as in the sound of music. At Tuskegee I found myself reading *The Waste Land*, and for the first time I was caught up in a piece of poetry which moved me but which I couldn't reduce to a logical system. I didn't know quite why it was working on me, but being close to the jazz experience— that is, the culture of jazz—I had a sense that some of the same sensibility was being expressed in poetry.

Now, the jazz musician, the jazz soloist, is anything if not eclectic. He knows his rhythms; he knows the tradition of his form, so to speak, and he can draw upon an endless pattern of sounds which he recombines on the spur of the moment into a meaningful musical experience, if he's successful. I had a sense that all of these references of Eliot's, all of this snatching of phrases from the German, French, Sanskrit, and so on, were attuned to that type of American cultural expressiveness which one got in jazz and which one still gets in good jazz. But between feeling intuitively that this

From *Contemporary Literature*, Spring 1974; transcript of an address given on March 26, 1969.

was what was going on and being able to confirm it, there was quite a gap. Fortunately Mr. Eliot appended to the original edition of *The Waste Land* a long body of footnotes, and I began to get the books out of the library and read them. That really was a beginning of my literary education, and actually it was the beginning of my transformation (or shall we say, metamorphosis) from a would-be composer into some sort of novelist.

The thing about reading these footnotes, and about reading criticism generally, was that they made me as conscious of the elements and traditions which went into the creation of literature as I had long been taught to be conscious of the various elements which went into musical styles and traditions. One had to be conscious; there was no question about this. And for me there was another powerful motive for being conscious, and that was because I came out of my particular Southwestern background (as an Oklahoma native), with parents who were from Georgia and South Carolina, and my racial background, which naturally at that moment seemed to separate me from the conscious intentions of American literature. Because in far too many instances, I seemed to appear, or my *people* seemed to appear, only in the less meaningful writing. I felt that I would have to make some sort of closer identification with the tradition of American literature, if only by way of finding out why I was *not* there—or better, by way of finding how I could use that very powerful literary tradition by way of making literature my own, and by way of using literature as a means of clarifying the peculiar and particular experience out of which I came.

Well, to jump ahead. During the war, I was a sea cook in the Merchant Marine. During the winter of 1944, I had received a fellowship from the Rosenwald Foundation in order to write a novel. It was about $1,500, as I recall, and I had an interesting story to tell. Some of my friends were in the Air Force. That is, friends from college, friends from Tuskegee, had become pilots, combat pilots, and so on, and during that moment of the war, they were very active. But preceding that activity, there had been a lot of political agitation on the part of Negro Americans because we were not being allowed to fight, and those young men, those friends of mine, those pilots, were being withheld from duty, and that concerned me very much. So I thought that my first novel would have such a plot as this (you can see that I was very naïve at the time), and I set my story in Nazi Germany in a prisoner-of-war camp. (This is where it becomes complicated.) The ranking officer of the camp was to have been a black pilot who had beneath him in rank a whole slew of white pilots. The devil of the piece was to have been a Machiavellian Nazi prison-camp official who spent his time pitting the black American against the white Americans. I was trying to write this, by the way, as our ship traveled in convoys of some eighty ships and flattops, and so on, taking supplies over during what was actually the Battle of the Bulge. Well, we got into Le Havre during the night, and it was so "hot" around there that that novel went up in sweat, and it's very good that it did.

However, one good effect of that experience was that I not only forgot the novel, but I experienced such tension under these conditions of combat that when I got back to stateside the physicians told me that I should take a rest. I took that rest by going up to Waitsfield, Vermont, where a friend had an old farmhouse on which a few years before I'd helped make some repairs. While there, I tried to write, not knowing quite what I would write but quite aware that my original idea would not work. One afternoon I wrote some words while sitting in an old barn looking out on the mountain, and these words were "I am an invisible man." I didn't know quite what they meant, and I didn't know where the idea came from, but the moment I started to abandon them, I thought: "Well, maybe I should try to discover exactly what it was that lay behind the statement. What type of man would make that type of statement, would conceive of himself in such terms? What lay behind him?" After that, it was a process of trying to make a meaningful story out of what seemed to be a rather wild notion.

Now, having said that, let me say something else. By this time I was very much aware of the elements which went into fiction. I wanted to tell a story. I felt that there was a great deal about the nature of American experience which was not understood by most Americans. I felt also that the diversity of the total experience rendered much of it mysterious. And I felt that because so much of it which appeared unrelated was actually most intimately intertwined, it needed exploring. In fact, I believed that unless we continually explored the network of complex relationships which bind us together, we would continue being the victims of various inadequate conceptions of ourselves, both as individuals and as citizens of a nation of diverse peoples.

For after all, American diversity is not simply a matter of race, region or religion. It is a product of the complex of intermixing of all these categories. For even our racial experience is diverse within itself, and rendered more complex by the special relationships existing between my own group and the various regions in which Negro Americans find their existence—and by reason of the varied relationships shared by blacks and whites of various social backgrounds. These, in turn, are shaped by the politics, social history, and climatic conditions existing within the country's various political and geographical regions. Nor is this all, for there is also the abiding condition of mystery generated by the diversity of cultural and political experience within the Negro American group itself. For despite the overall unity of black experience in the United States, the experience of Southern blacks differs in certain important aspects, both cultural and political, from that of Northern blacks; that of Southwestern blacks differs from that of *Southeastern* blacks, while the experience of those who grew up in Nevada, California, and Washington State differs in many ways from all of these, if only for having developed during a later period of historical time. Such factors make for important variations in experience, and make necessary the exercise of conscious thought even on the part of those black Americans who would "know the Negro." So that was one part of it.

The other part of it was the fact that I was reading certain books. I was reading Lord Raglan's *The Hero,* which has to do with tradition, myth and drama. As you will recall, Lord Raglan was concerned with the manner in which myth became involved with the histories of living persons, became incorporated into their personal legends. I seem to recall that he noted about twenty-two aspects of character and experience that were attributed to most heroes, and he discovered that historical figures—figures from religion, military heroes, and so on—all tended to embody clusterings of these same mythological aspects, and this whether they were figures of fact or fantasy. Thus it would seem that the human imagination finds it necessary to take exemplary people—charismatic personalities, cultural heroes—and enlarge upon them. The mythmaking tendency of the human imagination enlarges such figures by adding to their specific histories and characters accomplishments and characteristics attributed to heroes in the past. So that it isn't unusual in the mythology of mankind to find figures said to have been conceived (that's the proper term, any way you see it) through virgins. Nor is it unusual to find leaders who were exposed to death as infants only to have their lives saved by humble people, and who then through various accidents attending the mysterious process of life, and through their own heroic assertions in the drama of social intercourse, became great leaders. According to various accounts, a number of them married their mothers and killed their fathers, but if that still happens today, we no longer talk about it.

Anyway, I was concerned with such findings of Lord Raglan's as a literary matter, but at the same time I was concerned with the nature of leadership, and thus with the nature of the hero, precisely because during the historical moment when I was working out the concept of *Invisible Man* my people were involved in a terrific quarrel with the federal government over our not being allowed to participate in the war as combat personnel in the armed forces on an equal basis, and because we were not even being allowed to work in the war industries on an equal basis with other Americans. This quarrel led to my concern with the nature of Negro leadership, from a different and nonliterary direction. I was very much involved with the question of just why our Negro leadership was never able to enforce its will. Just what was there about the structure of American society that prevented Negroes from throwing up effective leaders? Thus it was no accident that the young man in my book turned out to be hungry and thirsty to prove to himself that he could be an effective leader.

On the other hand, as I began working seriously on the novel, I had to become aware of something else. I had to learn that in such a large and diverse country, with such a complex social structure, a writer was called upon to conceive some sort of model which would represent that great diversity, to account for all these people and for the various types of social manners found within various levels of the social hierarchy, a structure of symbolic actions which could depict the various relationships between groups and classes of people. He was called upon to conceive some way of getting that complexity into his work in the form of symbolic action and metaphor. In other words, I discovered, for myself at least, that it was necessary to work out some imaginative integration of the total American experience and discover through the work of the imagination some way of moving a young black boy from a particular area and level of the society as close as he could be "realistically" moved to sources of political power. This was not only necessary in order to structure a meaningful story, but also necessary if I were to relate myself to certain important and abiding themes which were present—or which I *thought* were present—in the best of American literature.

So now I was working in the exalted form of the novel, or trying to work in that literary form, and as I read back in American literature and tried very seriously to identify myself with the concerns of the classical American novelists, it began to seem to me that American fiction had played a special role in the development of the American nation. It had had to play that role, had had to concern itself with certain uniquely American tasks even in those instances in which it was not read (or not widely read, and I think here of *Moby-Dick*). This was for a number of reasons. One, as a literary form the novel has been primarily concerned with charting changes within society and with changes in personality as affected by society. Two, the novel developed during a period which marked the breakup of traditional societies, of kingship, and so on, and by the 1850s, the great masters of the nineteenth century had fashioned it into a most sensitive and brilliant form for revealing new possibilities of human freedom, for depicting the effects of new technologies upon personality, and for charting the effects wrought by new horizons of expectation upon the total society.

Of course this type of change (and its consequences) has been an enduring part of the American experience, and it has always concerned our great American novelists. But even if we concern ourselves with those American writers who were *not* novelists, we see that the makers of American literature were also concerned with spelling out that which was peculiarly *American* about the American experience—this, because we did not start here. We started in Europe. We made a formulation here of what we were and who we were, and what we expected to be, and we wrote it down in the documents of the Bill of Rights, the Constitution, the Declaration of Independence. I mean that we put ourselves on the books as to what we were and would become, and we were stuck with it. And we were stuck with it partially through a process of deification which came through the spilling of blood and through the sacrifices which were endured by those people who set up this great institution here on this particular point of the Hudson River.

By the 1830s, or the late 1820s, several things were being demanded. One, that we have a literature which would be specifically American, which would tell us who we were and how we varied, and how we had grown, and where we were going—and most importantly, how the ideals for which we had sacrificed so many young men were being made manifest within the society. There's no point in spelling this out too much. I think the very walls around here speak to you about such matters. But for novelists, for poets, for men of literature, something else obtains. You find that American artists are stuck with two major problems which come upon them through the very tradition itself, through the very history of this society. One is the necessity of being conscious of how one section of the country differs from the others, of how one section of the society differs from the others. And, two, we have upon our shoulders the burden of conscientiousness. I think in your motto you say "duty," a sense of duty, a sense of responsibility, for the health of the society. You might not like the society; invariably we Americans (as Henry James pointed out, and as others have pointed out) have an on-going quarrel with our lives, with the condition that we live in. At our best moments we have a quarrel with how we treat or fail to treat and extend the better part, the better aspects, the better values, the good things of the society, to all levels of the society.

So I found, as I worked with my little book—trying to build my fiction, trying to structure my "lie" in such a way as would reveal a certain amount of truth—that I, too, had to be aware of how we were faring and where we were going. I realized, fighting for a certain orientation (as a Negro writer who was taking on the burden of the American literary tradition), that I would have to master, or at least make myself familiar with, the major motives of American literature, *even when written by people who philosophically would reject me as a member of the American community.* How would I do that without being, in my own eyes, something of a slave, something less than a man?

It occurred to me that what some of my "teachers" were calling "white literature" was not really *white* at all. Because as I began to grasp the background of the American experience in literature, I began to realize that even before we were a nation, people of African background had been influencing the nature of the American language, that amalgam of English English, of French and German and Dutch and American Indian dialects, and so on. All of this, long before we were a nation, had already begun to form; American culture began to evolve before we were a nation. And some of the people contributing to it were my own people. This was very necessary for my sense of morale and for my sense of the complexity of the society, or at least of the *culture* of the society, because there's no doubt that we were slaves; both of my grandparents on both sides were slaves. (It hasn't been that long ago.) Nevertheless, part of the music of the language, part of the folklore which informed our conscious American literature, came through the interaction of the slave and the white man, and particularly so in the South. Mr. Faulkner, who has lectured here, had no doubt about that, and some of our most meaningful insights into the experience of the South have come through his understanding of that complex relationship. And because he did understand, he has been responsible for some of the real glories of our literature.

But here again I had to find out where *I* stood. In reading, I came across Whitman, who was writing very early (I think 1848 or so), finding in the American Negro dialect—the dialect of the slaves, as he put it—the possibility of an American grand opera, the possibility of a new music in speech. Of course this possibility was there. As I looked around the South, and as I looked around New York, and as I noticed the white crewmen on my ships at sea, I began to say, "Well, now, something here that you are saying, a certain rhythm in your speech, I first heard in my particular community. A certain way that you swing your shoulders, or your legs when you walk (especially Southern boys), you've gotten a lot of that from us." Maybe we got it from them, too. The point, of course, was to be relieved of the burden of interpreting all of life and its works in racial terms. Therefore, for me personally it was a matter of saying, "I am going to learn how to write a novel; I will not ignore the racial dimensions at all, but I will try to put them into a human perspective."

So my little book starts out by taking a young man who has an infinite capacity for making mistakes (and being a fool, I think), and who—in his *passion* for leadership, in his *passion* to prove himself within the limitations of a segregated society—blunders from one point to another until he finally realizes that American society cannot define the role of the individual, or at least not that of the *responsible* individual. For it is our fate as Americans to achieve that sense of self-consciousness through our own efforts.

The story itself, after all this pretentious-sounding talk, was a rather simple story: about how a young man grew up, and about the conditions which it was necessary for him to confront as he grew up. Because our society was divided, at that time, into one region which was primarily agricultural, and another which was primarily industrial (or more dominated by technological considerations than by the seasons), the narrator of the story goes through a number of rites of passage, rites of initiation. And as I tried to tell my story, I began looking at the meaning of certain rituals. No one had ever told me that the "battle royal" was a rite, but I came to see that it was. It was a rite which could be used to project certain racial divisions into the society and reinforce the idea of white racial superiority. On the other hand, as a literary person trying to make up stories out of recognizable experience, and as one who was reading a lot about myth and the function of myth and ritual in literature, it was necessary that I see the "battle royal" situation as something more than a group of white men having sadistic fun with a group of Negro boys. Indeed, I would have to see it for what it was beyond the question of the racial identities of the actors involved: a ritual through which important social values were projected and reinforced.

To use it artistically, I would have to step away from it a bit so that I could see it even more objectively and identify it as one of those rites of initiation called "fool's errands." When I played hooky for the first time and went to water the elephants of the Ringling Brothers Circus in Oklahoma City, I was sent on such an errand. The circus workers told me to go to a certain man and bring back the "tent wrench." Well, after I had exhausted myself traveling around the circus grounds I learned that there was no such thing as a "tent wrench." But I also discovered that this practical joke was not necessarily a racial device, because I observed it being used on other people as well. In hotels new workers ("squares") are also sent on such errands. In fact, many of the rites of passage, those rituals of growing up, found in our society are in the form of such comic, practical-joking affairs which we ignore in the belief that they possess no deeper significance. Yet it is precisely in their being regarded as unimportant that they take on importance. For in them we ritualize and dramatize attitudes which contradict and often embarrass the sacred values which we proclaim through our solemn ceremonies and rituals of nationhood.

Because while great institutions glamorize themselves through rituals, Americans tend to require supplementary rites that are more modest, more down-to-earth, and often it is these which serve to give dramatic form to our warmest emotions.

But in our democratic society, which is relatively unstructured as societies go (and unstructured precisely because we had to play it by ear as we got it going), such patterns are not widely recognized for what they are, or at least they are not codified, and thus are not institutionalized. Primitive societies are much more efficient and consistent; they are much more concerned with guiding the young through each stage of their social development, while we leave much of this to chance, perhaps as part of the responsibility of freedom. Today we are having great trouble with young people of educated, sheltered and financially well-heeled backgrounds who despite their social advantages have not been taught that they shouldn't play with heroin. I suppose that in a tightly structured and well-run society we would develop a special rite of initiation for dealing with the availability of drugs. Or at least we would teach such individuals how to take heroin without destroying themselves. Now that, of course, is a joke, meant to demonstrate that it is indeed possible to make comedy of such serious matters.

But not only have we failed to provide rites of passage adequate to the wide variety and broad freedom of experience available to the young, we also have failed to find ways of keeping up with much of what happens in our society. Therefore one of the things I wanted to do was to provide the reader with—or discover for myself—some sense of how *ideas* moved from one level of society to another. This was important for me to understand because, after all, when I was at Tuskegee, I couldn't go to a theater without being discriminated against, and in Birmingham, I couldn't move around the streets without worrying about Bull Conner (oh yes, Bull Conner was there even then); yet under such conditions of social deprivation, I was reading T. S. Eliot. I was concerned with the nature of power; I was trying to find a way of relating myself to the major concerns of our society.

So I felt that if we had a real sociology of ideas in this country, we would have a means of judging the impact of ideas as they came to rest within the diverse groups which make up American society. We would have a way of predicting, of saying, "Well, now, out there in such and such a section there are persons whose background, experience and temperament have made them receptive to certain notions, concepts and ideas. Therefore we can expect one or two such people to go about making something out of them, or at least making a try." But our failure to deal with the mystery of our diversity makes such generalized predictions impossible. Relying upon race, class and religion as guides, we underestimate the impact of ideas and the power of lifestyles and fashion to upset custom and tradition. Some of our intellectuals even forget that Negroes are not just influenced by ideas that are within the public domain, and that such is the nature of freedom in our democracy that even shoeshine boys may criticize the lifestyles and tastes of great entrepreneurs, which shoeshine boys are given to doing, and that they can also go to the library and read books which entrepreneurs *should* be reading but usually don't. So that our failure to grasp the mysterious possibilities generated by our unity within diversity and our freedom within unfreedom can lead to great confusion. It also leads to the loss of potential talent, just as our failure to recognize the social implications of cultural developments taking place on the lower levels of the social hierarchy can lead to social confrontations which can rock society to its very summit.

But however we choose to look at it, there exist pressures which compel the individual American (and the individual black American) to respond to the intellectual, emotional, political currents and pressures which affect the entire society—just as the stock market or fads in clothing or automobiles affect the lives of sharecroppers, whether or not the sharecropper knows that the stock market exists. Thus I tried as best I could to weave a tale which would at least be cognizant of these many interconnecting possibilities of relationships.

About the story, there is little I can say, unless you ask me questions. Because I haven't read it in a good while and I don't think I'll ever read it again in its entirety. It was too difficult for me to get rid of, and not because I didn't write fast and wasn't inventive. But there was something else. There was a sense of isolation, a feeling that for all my concern to make it so, it couldn't possibly have much value to others. I thought that I would be lucky if I sold between five hundred and a thousand copies. I was very much concerned with the link between the scenes and the actions—that is, the problem of continuity—because I realized even then that it was not enough for me simply to be angry, or simply to present horrendous events or ironic events. I would have to do what every novelist does: tell my tale and make it believable, at least for as long as it engaged the attention of the reader. I could not violate the reader's sense of reality, his sense of the way things were done, at least on the surface. My task would be to give him the surface and then try to take him into the internalities, take him below the level of racial structuring and down into those areas where we are simply men and women, human beings living on this blue orb, and not always living so well. This is what I tried to do.

The rest became a confrontation with technical problems: How do you "tell" it, how do you put it together? How do you foreshadow events, how do you handle irony? How do you fabricate that artifact which we call a novel? How, in other words, do you tell a story that will not embarrass the great literature which has gone before you? How do you join the club? How do you justify the assertion of arrogance that is necessary to a man who would take a society which everyone "knows" and abstract certain of its elements in an effort to reduce it to a symbolic form which will simultaneously involve the reader's sense of life while giving expression to his, the writer's, own most deeply held values? I refer to the arrogance of the artist, and a very necessary arrogance it is. For I think it is one reason why the novel is important. I think its presence aids the novelist in attacking the enormity of his task, which is that of reducing a society, through the agency of mere words, to manageable proportions—to proportions which will reflect *one* man's vision, *one* man's sense of the human condition, and in such volatile and eloquent ways that each rhythm, each nuance of character and mood, indeed each punctuation mark, becomes expressive of *his* sense of life and, by extension, that of the reader.

Related to this is a discovery which I think most American writers must make before they are through: it is that each writer has a triple responsibility: to himself, to his immediate group, and to his region. He must convey each of these aspects of his own experience as he knows them. And he must convey them not only in such a manner that members of his own particular group can become aware of what has been happening in the flux and flow, the thunder and lightning of daily living, but in such a way that individuals belonging to groups and regions of the society other than his own can have his report on what was happening in his particular area of the society, to his particular type of people, and at that particular point in time. All this so that readers may become more conscious of themselves and more aware of the complex unity and diversity not only of Americans but of all human life. Here the movement is from the specifically imagined individuals to the group, to the nation and, it is hoped, to the universal.

This becomes a function of creating and broadening our consciousness of American character, of creating and re-creating the American experience. It is a serious function because it is our good-and-bad fortune that we Americans exist at our best only when we are conscious of who we are and where we are going. In this process our traditions and national ideals move and function like a firm ground bass, like the deep tones of your marvelous organ there in the chapel, repeating themselves continually while new melodies and obbligatos sound high above. In literature this is the process by which the values, ideals, assumptions and memories of unique individuals and groups reach out across the divisions wrought by our national diversity and touch us all. It is one of the important social functions of literature because our traditions and values must be constantly revivified; again and again they must be given further extension.

Having said all that, I'll now say this, and then I'm finished. My first principal in grade school was a Professor Whittaker. He was a man of erect military bearing, although he must have been fairly old when I knew him. He had white hair, clear, piercing blue eyes, and a goatee. Professor Whittaker was a West Point man. Somehow he did not graduate; he must have been here during the Reconstruction. Nevertheless he was a marvelous man who managed to get something of West Point into those little Negro grade and high schools in which he taught when I was growing up. I suppose I mention him because I never thought I would ever come to West Point. But I also mention him by way of suggesting that even here there are extensions and dimensions of which we are not aware and of which we *should* be aware. Because in these United States the crucial question is not one of having a perfect society, or even of having at any given moment a viable society. Rather, it is to keep struggling, to keep trying to reduce to consciousness all of the complex experience which ceaselessly unfolds within this great nation. Certainly that was all I was trying to do with my book, and if I managed even a little of that, then I think the effort worthwhile.

I'm pleased to have been here, and if you have questions, I would be very pleased to answer them, or to try.

Mr. Ellison, I have a question about the whole point of the novel, the purpose of the novel: whether you considered it to be just about the Negro relationship with the white man, or, as your last statement indicates, perhaps to everyone. Part of the class thought it was merely the Negro–white man relationship, and then that perhaps toward the end as an afterthought you sort of put in the everyone idea, because it didn't seem to tie in. And the other part of the class thought you tried to show the relationship between all minority groups and majority groups.

Yes, thank you. Well, I conceived of the novel as an account, on the specific level, of a young Negro American's experience. But I hoped at the same time to write so well that anyone who shared everything except his racial identity could identify with it, because there was never any question in my mind that Negroes were human, and thus being human, their experience became metaphors for the experiences of other people. I thought, further, that if literature has any general function within any society and throughout the world, it must serve at its best as a study in comparative humanity. The role of the writer, from that point of view, is to structure fiction which will allow a universal identification, while at the same time not violating the specificity of the particular experience and the particular character.

Mr. Ellison, concerning your novel, I'd like to know exactly to what extent some of the scenes in it happened to you.

Well, let's put it this way, they all happened to me—in my head. Now, remember that you're dealing with the imagination and not with sociology. For instance, one summer when I was still in high school, I was looking for a job (and it gets to be 105 to 110 in the shade in Oklahoma City; it used to, anyway). I met a friend and he said, "If you go up to Broadway between Ninth and Tenth, there's a car lot there, and the man wants someone to help him around the car lot." He said, "I couldn't take it because I got another job, but you better hurry up there." So I turned on the fan, as they say, and by the time I arrived, I was pretty moist. There was this white man sitting out under a tree; and I said, "Sir, I understand you need someone to work here"; and he said, "Yes, sit over here on this box." (He had a crate with a cushion on it.) He said, "Sit over here and tell me about yourself." He began to ask me about my grades, about my parents, and so on, and I began to feel that I was getting the job. Then, at the moment when I was most certain that the job was mine, I felt a charge of electricity in my tail, and I went up into the air and I came down.

The whole thing, again, was a ritual of initiation—a practical joke—wherein a Ford coil, a coil from the old Model T Ford, had been hooked up to a battery. That was the whole point. Of course there was no job, but what my imagination has made of that is the scene in the battle royal where the boys struggle for money on the rug. Am I giving away secrets, do you believe that? But that's how the imagination worked and conjured up the scene.

Sir, your novel has been called "episodic," with the theme of white domi- nation over the Negro with the express purpose of keeping the Negro in his primitive state; however, in your lecture here I've gotten a different idea, that it was merely a thematic representation of the American Negro and his drive to excel. The question I have is, was it your purpose to show this white domination over the Negro and of keeping the Negro in his primitive state, or was it merely to show in an episodic manner this drive to excel?

Certainly I didn't start . . . Do you want to repeat that? The answer is *No*.

Mr. Ellison, would you consider yourself a pioneer in writing about the Negro relationship to white groups; if not, who else besides Eliot influenced your writing?

Well, in the first place, I don't think that it's a function of writing to tell the reader what it feels like to be a Negro, as critics say over and over again about plays and novels and poems by black writers. I think the function of literature, all literature that's worthy of the name, is to remind us of our common humanity and the cost of that humanity. This is the abiding theme of great literature, and all serious writers find themselves drawn to spelling it out in all its detail and multiplicity. As for people who influenced me, the first two novels that I read when I arrived in New York were given to me by Langston Hughes (whom I had just met), who wanted me to deliver them to a friend of his, but he told me that I could keep them long enough to read them. Those two novels were André Malraux's *Man's Fate* and *The Days of Wrath*. I have certainly been influenced by Dostoevsky. The first words of *Invisible Man*, the rhythm of the Prologue, go right back to *Notes from Underground*. I have been influenced by Malraux, by Melville, by Faulkner, by almost all of the good ones.

Sir, in your story it seems as if the narrator was struggling with disillusionment, and then toward the end of the story, when you cut it off, you don't explain simply whether he found himself or not. Was it your intention to start the narrator off being disillusioned and follow him throughout this complete cycle to where he did find himself, or were we simply supposed to draw our own conclusion?

Well, as I recall the book . . . the narrator managed to avoid a basic confrontation through most of the story, and when he finally makes that confrontation, he's freed. Part of his problem was not that of being dominated by white society. Part of his problem was a refusal to demand that people see him for what he wanted to be. Always he was accommodating. If you notice, he was being told who he was, he was given several names throughout the novel, and always he accepted them till the very last. As to the last part of your question, I would say that yes, he comes out of the ground, and this can be seen when you realize that although *Invisible Man* is *my* novel, it is really *his* memoir. I'm a little prejudiced here, because I do feel that books represent socially useful acts—so we can say that. I left it at this point because I assumed that by finally taking the initial step of trying to sum up the meaning of his experience, he had moved to another stage of his development.

Mr. Ellison, the Brotherhood has the characteristics of a socialistic society; I was wondering what this had to do with the Communist tradition that in such an organization the depressed can find a way out of their condition.

Here again is a fabrication, just as the machines in the paint factory are fabrications. They never existed. They're images there for certain literary reasons. I did not want to describe an existing Socialist or Communist or Marxist political group, primarily because it would have allowed the reader to escape confronting certain political patterns, patterns which still exist and of which our two major political parties are guilty in their relationships to Negro Americans. But what I wanted to do at the same time was to touch upon certain techniques of struggle, of political struggle, certain concepts of equality and political possibility which were very much present in our society. I think we have absorbed them into the larger parties in many ways.

I also wanted to draw upon the tinge of subversion which some of these parties tend to represent. So the Brotherhood was this, but at the same time, in the life of the narrator it was one more obstacle that he had to confront in order to arrive at some viable assessment of his own possibilities as a political leader. Remember, Tod Clifton is killed, and there's a funeral, an improvisation, an improvised funeral, that he (the narrator) leads, which polarizes feelings around what the narrator thought would have been to the Brotherhood's best interest. But they were no longer interested because they were not concerned basically with Negro freedom, but with effecting their own ends. It was very important for this young man, this would-be leader, to understand that all political parties are basically concerned with power and with maintaining power, not with humanitarian issues in the raw and abstract state.

Mr. Ellison, could you tell us the significance of the scene near the end of Invisible Man *when the narrator falls down the open manhole? Two white men are chasing him, and after he falls in the manhole he tells them, "I still have you in this brief case."*

Well, I'll try. What I wanted him to be saying was that these men who were hurling racial epithets down at him were not aware that *their* fate was in this bag that he carried—this bag that he had hauled around with his various identifications, his diploma, with Clifton's doll, with Tarp's slavery chainlink, and so on—and that this contained a very important part of their history and of their lives. I was also trying to say that you will have to become aware of the connection between what is in this bag (which is his fate, that is, the fate of the Negro narrator) and the racist whites who look upon him mainly as a buffoon and a victim.

Sir, there seem to be a few comparisons between your novel and Native Son *in that both protagonists seem to be fighting a losing cause through the entire novel, and the fact that they both have ties with the Communist party and confront white women. Was this by coincidence or were you influenced by Mr. Wright as you wrote the novel?*

I knew Mr. Wright from about the second day he arrived in New York in 1937; I guess it was June. I wrote my first book review for him, a published book review, and I wrote my first short story for a magazine which he was in New York to edit. It was a Harlem-based magazine, a literary magazine, and not a Communist organ. But he accepted my story, and then the magazine failed. But by 1940 I was not showing Mr. Wright any of my writing because by that time I understood that our sensibilities were quite different, and what I was hoping to achieve in fiction was something quite different from what he wanted to achieve.

As to what you call Communism and the white women, I would say that anyone writing from the Negro American point of view with any sort of thoroughness would certainly have had to write about the potential meaning and effects of the relationship between black women and white men and black men and white women, because this became an essence, and a great part of the society was controlled by the taboos built around the fear of the white woman and the black man getting together. Great political power and, to some extent, great military ardor were brewed from this socio-sexual polarization. Hence any novelist who is going to write from the Negro background would certainly have to deal with these particular aspects of our society. They're unpleasant, and yet it is in the unpleasant, in that which is charged with emotion, with fears, with irrationality, that we find great potential for transforming attitudes. So I tried to face them with a certain forthrightness, to treat them ironically, because they are really destructive in a kind of comic and absurd way—except when we consider the old rite of lynching. But you'll notice that I did not drag in that particular aspect of the sociology of interracial relationships.

Sir, was it your intention to include any protest in the novel?

Protest in the novel?

Yes, sir, would you call it a protest novel?

I would think that implicitly the novel protests. It protests the agonies of growing up. It protests the problem of trying to find a way into a complex, intricately structured society in a way which would allow this particular man to behave in a manly way, and which would allow him to seize some instrumentalities of political power. That is where the protest is on one level. On another level, the protest lies in my trying to make a story out of these elements without falling into the clichés which have marked and marred most fiction about American Negroes—that is, to write literature instead of political protest. Beyond this, I would say simply that in the very act of trying to create something, there is implicit a protest against the way things are, a protest against man's vulnerability before the larger forces of society and the universe. We make fiction out of that kind of protest, which is similar to the kind of protest that is involved in your mastering your bodies; your mastering the physical, intellectual, military and legal disciplines which you are here for. All of this is a protest, a human protest against that which *is*, against the raw and unformed way that we come into the world. I don't think you have to demand any more protest than that. I think, on the other hand, if the novelist tells the truth, if he writes eloquently and depicts believable human beings and believable human situations, then he has done more than simply protest. I think that his task is to present the human, to make it eloquent, and to provide some sense of transcendence over the given—that is, to make his protest meaningful, significant and eloquent of human value.

What These Children Are Like

I assume you all know that I really have no business attending this sort of conference. I have no technical terminology and no knowledge of an academic discipline. This isn't boasting, nor is it an apology; it is just a means of reminding myself of what my reality has been and of what I am. At this point it might be useful for us to ask ourselves a few questions: what is this act, what is this scene in which the action is taking place, what is this agency and what is its purpose?

The act is to discuss "these children," the difficult thirty percent. We know this very well; it has been hammered out again and again. But the matter of *scene* seems to get us into trouble.

The American scene is a diversified one, and the society which gives it its character is a pluralistic society—or at least it is supposed to be. Ideally it is, but we seem to insist, on the other hand, that this society is *not* pluralistic. We have been speaking as though it were *not* made up of diversified cultures but was in fact one monolithic culture. And one which is perfect, the best of all possible cultures, with the best of all people affirming its perfection.

Well, if this were true there would be no point in our being here. But we are here, and since we are, let us try to see American society in all of its diversity. One of the things that has been left out in our discussion is imagination. But imagination exists even in the backwoods of Alabama, and here too is to be found a forthright attitude toward what it is possible to achieve and to become in this country.

The education which goes on outside the classroom, which goes on as they walk within the mixed environment of Alabama, teaches children that they should not reach out for certain things. Much of the education that I received at Tuskegee (this isn't quite true of Oklahoma City) was an education *away* from the uses of the imagi-

---

Lecture given at seminar on "Education for Culturally Different Youth," conducted by Bank Street College of Education at Dedham, Mass., September 3–15, 1963.

nation, *away* from the attitudes of aggression and courage. This is not an attack. This is descriptive, this is autobiographic. You did not do certain things because you might be destroyed. You didn't do certain things because you were going to be frustrated. There were things you didn't do because the world outside was not about to accommodate you.

But we're still talking about scene, and thus we're talking about environment. A discussion of scene in terms of culture and diversity serves to remind us that there is no absolutely segregated part of this country. There is no such thing as a culturally deprived kid. That kid down in Alabama whose parents have no food, where the mill owner has dismantled the mills and moved out west and left them to forage in the garbage cans of Tuskegee, has nevertheless some awareness that he is part of a larger American scene, and he is being influenced by this scene. But how *does* the fluctuation of the stock market get down there to him? How does the electronic manipulation of music get into his musical language? How do the literary theories of the "Fugitives," which have so much prestige in the North, influence his destiny? How is his badly trained teacher going to view him and his possibilities as a future American adult? What I'm trying to say is that the problem seems to me to be one of really scrutinizing the goals of American education.

It does me no good to be told that I'm down on the bottom of the pile and that I have nothing with which to get out. I know better. It does me no good to be told that I have no heroes, that I have no respect for the father principle because my father is a drunk. I would simply say to you that there are good drunks and bad drunks. The Eskimos have sixteen or more words to describe snow because they live with snow. I have about twenty-five different words to describe Negroes because I live principally with Negroes. "Language is equipment for living," to quote Kenneth Burke. One uses the language which helps to preserve one's life, which helps to make one feel at peace in the world, and which screens out the greatest amount of chaos. *All* human beings do this.

When you have one body of people who have been sewn together by a common experience—I won't even talk about the cultural heritage from Africa—and you plant this people in a highly pressurized situation and they survive, they're surviving with all of those motivations and with all of the basic ingenuity which any group develops in order to remain alive. Let's not play these kids cheap; let's find out what they have. What do they have that is a strength? What do they have that you can approach and build a bridge upon? Education is all a matter of building bridges, it seems to me. Environment is bouncing everything off everybody in this country. It is wide open; television is around. You see antennas on shacks, electric iceboxes on back porches, with the electricity brought in from a neighbor's pole, cars are flying around, jazz musicians are invading the backwoods with modifications of language, verbal as well as musical, new styles of dress are being introduced. The things which come at you in a Negro grade school are just as diverse as those which come at you in an upper-class white school. The question is how can you relate the environment to yourself? How can one discover, for instance, that well-cooked chitterlings are part of a cuisine? It took me a lot of living and going to France to realize this obvious fact. I said to myself, "What on earth are these Frenchmen doing? This is peasant food; chitterlings are peasant food. There are some great masters of Negro cooking. Chitterlings must be part of a high low-class cuisine!"

Some of us look at the Negro community in the South and say that these kids have no capacity to manipulate language. Well, these are not the Negroes I know. Because I know that the wordplay of Negro kids in the South would make the experimental poets, the modern poets, green with envy. I don't mean that these kids possess broad dictionary knowledge, but within the bounds of their familiar environment and within the bounds of their rich oral culture, they possess a great virtuosity with the music and poetry of words. The question is how can you get this skill into the mainstream of the language, because it is without doubt there. And much of it finds its way into the broader language. Now *I* know this just as William Faulkner knew it. This does not require a lot of testing; all you have to do is to walk into a Negro church.

What filters out this richness when the children come North? It is, in part, a reflection of their sense of being dispossessed of the reality to which their vocabulary referred. Where they once possessed the keys to a traditional environment—the South—they now confront an environment that appears strange and hostile. An environment cluttered with objects and processes for which they have no words and which too often they are prevented from approaching by poverty, custom and race. They are being educated in the streets.

Sanity suggests that the street child learns that which prepares him to live in a world that is immediate and real. To fail to recognize this is to expect far too much of a human being while crediting him with far too little humanity.

Thus we must recognize that the children in question are not so much "culturally deprived" as products of a different cultural complex. I'm talking about how people deal with their environment, about what they make of what is abiding in it, about what helps them to find their way, and about that which helps them to be at home in the world. All this seems to me to constitute a culture. If you can abstract their manners, their codes, their customs and attitudes into forms of expression, if you can convert them into forms of art, if you can stylize them and give them many and subtle ranges of reference, then you are dealing with a culture. People have learned this culture; it has been transferred to them from generation to generation, and in its forms they have projected their most transcendent images of themselves and of the world.

Therefore one of the problems is to get the so-called "culturally deprived" to realize that if they take what we would give them, they don't have to give up all of that which gives them their own sense of identity. Indeed, the nation needs some of the very traits which they bring with them: the group discipline, the patience, the ability to withstand ceaseless provocation without breaking down or losing sight of their ultimate objective. We need aggressiveness. We need daring. We even need the little guy who, in order to prove himself, goes out to conquer the world. Psychologically Napoleon was not different from the slum kid who tries to take over the block; he just had big armies through which to amplify his aggression.

But how can we keep the daring and resourcefulness which we often find among the dropouts? I ask this as one whose work depends upon the freshness of language. How can we keep the discord flowing into the mainstream of the language without destroying it? One of the characteristics of a healthy society is its ability to rationalize and contain social chaos. It is the steady filtering of diverse types and cultural influences that keeps us a healthy and growing nation. The American language is a great instrument for poets and novelists precisely because it could absorb the contributions of those Negroes back there saying "dese" and "dose" and forcing the language to sound and bend under the pressure of their need to express their sense of the real. The damage done to formal grammar is frightful, but it isn't absolutely bad, for here is one of the streams of verbal richness.

As we approach the dropouts, let us identify who *we* are and where we are. Let us also have a little bit of respect for what we were and from whence we came. There is a bit of the phony built into every American. This is inevitable in a conscious society that has developed as swiftly as ours has. We are faced with endless possibilities for change, for metamorphosis. We change our environment, our speech, our styles of living, our dress, and often our values. So, in effect, we become somebody else—or so we are tempted to believe—and often we act as though we have no connection with our past. We are all tempted to become actors, and when we forget who we are and where we are from, our phony selves take command.

When the phony me appears, there is a favor I would ask of anyone: nudge me and say, "Look, you, you're really just *you*!" Because the great mystery of identity in this country, really on the level of a religious mystery, and one of our greatest challenges is that everybody here is an American and yet is a member of some unique minority. Everyone knows this when he starts out into the world, but often we forget it. The best teacher, it seems to me, for those Negro youngsters who have been so harmed, so maimed by the sudden confrontation of a world that is more complex than any that they are prepared to deal with, is the teacher who can convey to them an awareness that they do indeed come from somewhere, some place of human value, and that what they've learned there does count in the larger society.

Let us remind ourselves that it is not merely the lower-class Negro child who has difficulties in dealing with our society. After teaching three years in a progressive school where I had only two or three Negro students, I am aware that we here should also be concerned with people who come from sections of the society lying far distant from Negro slums. Therefore I do not believe that the basic problem is a Negro problem, no matter what the statistics tell us. I do believe that there has to be some effort made to bring our system of education into line with what we say we are, and into line with those ideals which we celebrate in ritual and ceremony on patriotic occasions. If you have a society in which all men are declared equal (I am not speaking racially now), then it seems to me that you must act out of an assumption that any people which has not been destroyed after three hundred years of our history, and which is still here among us, is a people possessing great human potentialities and strengths which its members have derived from their background. And it follows that those potentialities are to be respected.

One of the worst things for a teacher to do to a Negro child is to treat him as though he were completely emasculated of potentiality. But this, I'm sorry to say, is also true of some Negro teachers. Not all, fortunately, but far too many. At Tuskegee during the thirties, most of the teachers would not speak to a student outside the classroom. The students resented it, *I* resented it, and I could never take them very seriously as teachers. Something was in the way. A fatal noise had been introduced into the communication.

As you can see, I am not making this a racial matter. I insist, in fact, that the harm can be done by anyone from any background. To speak topically, there are a lot of distortions getting into the picture of the Negro situation now as we Negroes become more publicly agitated over our condition. Our enemies are being sharply desig- nated, and this is a good thing. Nevertheless, the first people to do Negroes damage are usually other Negroes. If it were otherwise, we wouldn't be human; we'd be somehow immune to the shaping force of our parents and relatives and to the presence of our immediate community. Much of the damage sustained by Negroes begins in the Negro family, and much of it occurs in the Negro nursery school, kindergarten, and the first few grades. Worse, the people who do the harm are not always vicious, but often they dislike themselves, and often they have utter contempt for us little "burr-heads."

Consider this: one of the most influential musicians to come out of Oklahoma was a gifted boy who never took part in school musical activities (and ours was a musically oriented Negro community) be- cause he was considered "lower class" in his attitudes. I refer to Charlie Christian, the jazz guitarist, who accomplished that rare feat of discovering the jazz idiom, the jazz voice, of a classical instrument. Yet here was a child who lived in a hotbed of everything that middle- class people fear: the tuberculosis rate was sky-high, crime, prostitu- tion, bootlegging, illness. There was all of the disintegration which you find among rural Negroes who are pounding themselves to death against the sharp edges of an urban environment. Yet Okla- homa City at that time was one of the most wonderful places I've ever known. Imagination was freely exercised by the kids. They made toys. They made and taught themselves to play musical instru- ments. They lived near the city dump, and they converted the trea- sures they found there to their own uses. This was an alive community in which the harshness of slum life was inescapable, but in which the strength and imagination of these people was much in evidence. Yet you would have to say that it was indeed lower class, and lower-lower class and, according to the sociologists, utterly hopeless. Certainly it was no place to search for good minds or fine talent.

But how many geniuses do you get *anywhere*? And where *do* you find a first-class imagination? Who really knows? Imagination is where you find it; thus we must search the whole scene. But how many pretentious little kids have we been able to develop through progressive education! We can turn out a hell of a lot of these. I once taught at Bard College, where the students were highly articulate, some of them highly imaginative and creative. But many were utterly unprepared by their education to live in this world without extensive aid. What I'm trying to say is that it is *not* that we are all estranged from our backgrounds and given skills that don't apply to the real world, but that something basically wrong is happening to our educational system. We are missing the target, and *all* of our children are suffering as a result. To be ill-clothed, ill-housed and ill-fed is not the only way to suffer deprivation. Frank Reissman, who taught at Bard, has much to say about the "culturally deprived child," but does he recognize that many there were also culturally deprived kids? When a child has no sense of how he should fit into the society around him, he is culturally deprived, no matter how high his parents' income. When a child has no fruitful way of relating the cultural traditions and values of his parents to the diversity of cultural forces with which he must live in a pluralistic society, he is culturally deprived. When he has to spend a great part of his time in the care of a psychoanalyst, he is, again, culturally deprived. Thus I would broaden the definition.

Now, what is the source of this trouble? Obviously this is not a Negro problem. Obviously it is not only the result of great cultural deprivation or family dislocation, because the students there were for the most part middle class, and in fact eighty percent were Jewish. When compared with the Negro slum family, their backgrounds were quite stable indeed. Therefore it seems to me that there has been some more basic dislocation between that which an education is supposed to guarantee the child and the nature of the world in which he has to live. For one thing, many American children have not been trained to reject enough of the negative values which our society presses upon them. Nor have they been trained sufficiently to preserve those values which sustained their forefathers and which constitute an important part of their heritage. Frequently they are not trained to identify those aspects of the environment to which it is to their best interest—and to the best interest of the nation—to say "No." Too often they have not been taught that there are situations, processes, experiences that are not only to be avoided, but feared. Think of how many of our youths from the best middle-class families have taken to drugs.

Which brings me back to the education the child gets in the street. There is a conflict between the child's own knowledge, his own intuitive feeling, and the sense of security he gets through the gang that leads him to *reject* many of the values which are offered him by the schools. He has found a counter-scheme for living. Museums are rejected because they make him think of going places and doing things that are ultimately frustrating. The New York theaters have been open to Negroes for years and years. How many attend them? How many of us do you see in downtown audiences? More than ever before, true, but certainly not in proportion to the Negro population. Let us not discuss the irrelevance of the plays presented there. The point is that this represents a world beyond reach. Indeed, do I dare turn my imagination, even as a writer, upon the possibility of living in that world from which I'm partially barred? I could do so only as an act of faith or recklessness. The schools weren't the least bit encouraging, but I was always interested in writing, and finally I became interested in how writing was written. And then I realized that I couldn't afford *not* to become a writer; I had to become a writer because I had gotten the spirit of literature and had become aware of the possibilities offered by literature—not to make money, but to feel at home in the world, to feel that I could come into the possession of a certain part of reality.

I'm fascinated by this whole question of language because when you get people who come from a Southern background, where language is manipulated with great skill and verve, and who upon coming north become inarticulate, then you *know* that the proper function of language is being frustrated.

The great body of Negro slang—that unorthodox language—exists precisely because Negroes need words which will communicate, which will designate the objects, processes, manners and subtleties of their urban experience with the least amount of distortion from the outside. So the problem is, once again, what do we choose and what do we reject of that which the greater society makes available? These kids with whom we're concerned, these dropouts, are living critics of their environment, of our society and our educational system, and they are quite savage critics of some of their teachers.

I don't know what intelligence is. But this I do know, both from life and from literature: whenever you reduce human life to two plus two equals four, the human element within the human animal says, "I don't give a damn." *You* can work on that basis, but the kids cannot. If you can show me how I can cling to that which is real to me, while teaching me a way into the larger society, then I will not only drop my defenses and my hostility, but I will sing your praises and help you to make the desert bear fruit.

The Myth of the
Flawed White Southerner

THE question of how I regarded the President's statement that "Art is not a political weapon" was put to me by a group of young Negro writers during 1965, following President Johnson's sponsoring of a National Festival for the Arts at the White House. The Festival had been attacked by certain well-known writers, and these young men were seriously concerned with the proper relationship between the artist and government. I replied to their question by reading aloud from the President's address to the artists attending the Festival:

> Your art is not a political weapon, yet much of what you do is profoundly political, for you seek out the common pleasures and visions, the terrors and cruelties of man's day on this planet. And I would hope you would help dissolve the barriers of hatred and ignorance which are the source of so much of our pain and danger . . .

a statement to which I was sympathetic, both as a foreshortened description and as the expression of a hope.

The young men then asked my opinion of the President's grasp of political reality, and I replied that I thought him far ahead of most of the intellectuals who were critical of him, "especially those Northern liberals who have become, in the name of the highest motives, the new apologists for segregation." I went on to say that "President Johnson's speech at Howard University spelled out the meaning of full integration for Negroes in a way that no one, no President, not Abraham Lincoln nor Franklin Roosevelt, no matter how much we loved and respected them, has ever done before. There was no hedging in it, no escape clauses."

From *To Heal and to Build*, McGraw-Hill, Inc., 1968.

My reference to the segregationist tendencies of certain intellectuals and Northern liberals caused a few of my white colleagues to charge that I had "changed" or sold out to the "establishment," and I lost a few friends. The incident forced me to realize once again that for all the values that I shared, and still share, with my fellow intellectuals, there are nevertheless certain basic perspectives and attitudes toward art and politics, cultural affairs and politicians, which we are far from sharing. I had to accept the fact that if I tried to adapt to their point of view, I would not only be dishonest but would violate disastrously that sense of complexity, historical and cultural, political and personal, out of which it is my fate and privilege to write. My colleagues spoke out of their own interests, and properly so, but I found it irritating that they seemed to assume that *their* interests were automatically mine, and that supposedly I and those of my background possess no interest that they, my friends and colleagues, had any need to understand or respect.

Later, in thinking of this disagreement, I found myself recalling that during 1963 I was among those present at the White House for a celebration of the First Centennial of the Emancipation Proclamation given by President John F. Kennedy, an occasion of special significance for me, both as the grandson of slaves and as a writer and former student of Tuskegee Institute. For I was aware of the fact that in 1901, during the first month of his administration, Theodore Roosevelt had provoked a national scandal by inviting Booker T. Washington, Tuskegee's founder, to a White House dinner, a gesture taken by some as more menacing to the national security than an armed attack from a foreign nation. The invitation changed political alignments in the South, upset the structure of the Republican party, and caused President Roosevelt to advise Negro Americans to avoid careers in the professions and to subjugate their own political and social interests to those of antagonistic white Southerners.

As a novelist interested in that area of the national life where political power is institutionalized and translated into democratic ritual and national style, I was impressed by the vividness with which a

White House invitation had illuminated the emotional complexities and political dynamite underlying American social manners, and I welcomed the opportunity for closer observation that the occasion afforded. It seemed to me that one of the advantages that a novelist such as Henry James had over those of my generation was his familiarity with the movers and shakers of the nation, an advantage springing from his upper-class background and the easy availability of those who exercised political and social power. Artists who came later were likely to view such figures from a distance, and thus have little opportunity to know at firsthand the personalities who shape the nation's affairs. It is fortunate that with the Kennedy and Johnson administrations this was no longer true.

At the celebration of the Emancipation Proclamation, some sixty-two years after the Washington incident, the majority of the four hundred or more White House guests were Negroes, and I was struck by how a cordial gesture once considered threatening to the national stability had with the passing of time become an accepted routine. Where Theodore Roosevelt had been put on the defensive and bowed before anti-Negro taboos, President Kennedy was free to celebrate the freeing of the slaves as an important step toward achieving a truer American democracy. So as I brooded over the Festival controversy I asked myself if my memory of the Booker T. Washington incident had influenced the stand I took, and whether I had been so influenced by historical and racial considerations that I underevaluated the issues which so concerned my fellow intellectuals.

I concluded that perhaps I had. Nor was it simply that as a charter member of the National Council on the Arts, I felt that governmental aid to the American arts and artists was of a more abiding importance than my hopes that the Vietnam war would be brought to a swift conclusion. My response to the President's critics was shaped, in fact, by that personal and group history which had shaped my background and guided my consciousness, a history and background that marked a basic divergence between my own experience and that of the dissenting intellectuals. So for me the Festival was charged with meanings that went deeper than the issue of the government's role in the arts or the issue of Vietnam; it had also to do with the President's own background, his accent of speech and his values. And when I put the two social occasions into juxtaposition, the Emancipation celebration and the Festival for the Arts, I found it symbolic that my disagreement with my fellow intellectuals had been brought into focus around the figure of a President of Southern origin.

I say symbolic because, historically speaking, my presence at the Festival for the Arts was the long-range result of an act, in 1863, of an even more controversial holder of the presidency, Abraham Lincoln. For it was Lincoln who, after a struggle involving much vacillation, procrastination and rescissions, finally issued the Proclamation that allowed me to be born a relatively free American. Obviously this was not as important a factor in my friends' conception of the nation's history; therefore it has not become a functioning factor in shaping their social and political awareness. Hence, while we may agree as to the importance of art in shaping the values of American society, we are apt to disagree about the priorities in attacking social and political issues.

Some of the intellectuals in question spring from impoverished backgrounds, but for historical reasons none has ever been poor in the special ways that Negro Americans are poor. Some began to write, as did I, during the 1930s, but here again none came to writing careers from a background so barren of writers as mine. To these racial and historical differences is added the fact that we spring from different regions of the land. I had come from a different part of the country and had been born of parents who were of this land far longer than many of theirs had been, and I had grown up under conditions far more explicitly difficult than they. Which outlines another important difference: I had come from a region adjacent to that from which the President emerged, and where the American language was spoken—by whites, at least—with an accent much like that with which he speaks. It is a region that has grown faster and in a more unplanned way than the East has grown, and it is a place where one must listen beneath the surface of what a man has to say, and where rhetorical style is far less important than the relationship between a man's statements and his conduct.

When I was growing up, a Negro Oklahoman always listened for a threat in the accent of a white Texan, but one learned to listen to the individual intonation, to *what* was said as well as to *how* it was said, to content and implication as well as to style. Black provincials cannot afford the luxury of being either snobbish or provincial. Nor can they ignore the evidence of concrete acts.

President Johnson's style and accent are said to be an important factor in his difficulties with many intellectuals, especially those of the literary camp. But perhaps what one listens for in the utterance of any President is very similar to what one listens for in a novel: the degree to which it contains what Henry James termed "felt life," which can here be translated to mean that quality conveyed by the speaker's knowledge and feeling for the regional, racial, religious, and class unities and differences within the land, and his awareness of the hopes and values of a diverse people struggling to achieve the American promise in their own time, in their own place, and with the means at hand.

It would seem that a few literary intellectuals would impose a different style and accent upon the President, but they forget that all individual American styles reflect a regional background, and this holds true for national leaders no less than others. Thus, while a President's style and way with language are of national importance, he cannot violate the integrity between his inherited idiom and his office without doing violence to his initial source of strength. For in fact his style and idiom form a connective linkage between his identity as representative of a particular group and region of people and his identity as President of *all* the people.

It is possible that much of the intellectuals' distrust of President Johnson springs from a false knowledge drawn from the shabby myths purveyed by Western movies. Perhaps they feel that a Texan intoning the values of humanism in an unreconstructed Texas accent is to be regarded as suspiciously as a Greek bearing gifts; thus they can listen to what he says with provincial ears and can ignore the President's concrete achievements here at home while staring blindly at the fires of a distant war.

Well, I too am concerned with the war in Vietnam and would like to see it ended, but the fact remains that I am also familiar with other costly wars of much longer duration right here at home—the war against poverty and the war for racial equality—and therefore I cannot so easily ignore the changes that the President has made in the condition of my people and still consider myself a responsible intellectual. My sense of priorities is of necessity different.

One thing is certain. I must look at the figure of the President from a slightly different angle, and although I try to approach people and events with something of that special alertness granted to those who give themselves over to the perceptive powers of the novel, I must dismiss any temptation to see President Johnson, or any living President, strictly in terms of his possibilities as a fictional character—which, I believe, is an impulse of many literary intellectuals when confronting the presidential role.

For example, when the image of President Lincoln is evoked by the resemblance between the 1960s and the 1860s—war, racial unrest, technological change, the inadequacies of established institutions and processes before the demand for broader economic and social freedom—the Lincoln who emerges is that figure released by the bullets fired at Ford's Theatre. It is not the backwoods politician who fought throughout the tragic years of the Civil War to keep the nation whole, not the troubled man who rode the whirlwind of national chaos until released by death while watching the comedy *Our American Cousin*.

Yet it was that unpopular, controversial Lincoln whose deeds, whose manipulation of power—political, rhetorical, and moral— made possible the figure we create for ourselves whenever we think of the personification of democratic grandeur and political saint-hood.

Lyndon B. Johnson is credited even by his enemies as being a political genius, but the phenomenon of a great politician becoming President confronts us with a dual figure, for even while entangled in the difficulties of his office, he is identified by role with the achievements of the proven great who preceded him there. In our minds he is locked in a struggle with the illustrious dead even though he must be a man who manipulates power and involves himself in the muck and mire out of which great political parties are composed. He must be a man who initiates uneasy compromises and deals, who blends ideals and expediencies, who achieves what he can in order to give reality to his vision. He is a figure who knows better than most of us that politics is the art of the possible, but *only* of the possible, and that it is only by fighting against the limits of the politically possible that he can demonstrate his mastery and his worth.

But when such a figure is elevated to the presidency an element of doubt soon enters the picture. Political action, his native mode, is tied to techniques—persuasion, eloquence, social pressure, compromises, and deals—all techniques that during our troubled times are increasingly confounded by the press and by the apparent clairvoyance of electronic data media which, as they seek to convert events into drama, work to undermine the mysteries of presidential power. The question of credibility is raised, and we approach the presidency with demands for a minute-to-minute knowledge of intricate events that is impossible even between the most devoted husband and wife. Little allowance is made for secrecy, indecision, interpersonal or international process. He is expected to be master not only of the present but of the future as well, and able to make decisions with the omniscience of a god. Most of all, he is expected to be an incarnation of Justice.

Part of the difficulty springs from the notion that great personalities are the results not of technical mastery but of some mysterious leap out of the past of race, class and family onto a plateau from which an inherent mastery may be exercised with a superhuman facility. To this view great deeds are assumed to be the attributes of great personality. President Lincoln is taken to be the author of great deeds not because he was a great and persistent politician, but because he possessed a great personality, very much as great poets are assumed to be great men because they composed great poems. And in the case of great Presidents now dead, the arrogance, the blind spots, the failures of will and vision are forgotten before the great transforming deeds that their deaths delineated as having marked their administrations.

Literary intellectuals make this mistake because they owe the formation of their functional personalities and their dreams to literature. Thus, for them a great President is first of all a master of "style," a mythical figure born of all the great (and preferably eloquent) Presidents who preceded him. But having attained the presidency, he is paradoxically expected to have no further function as a politician. Indeed, he is expected to be above politics in a way virtually impossible if he is to exercise the powers and responsibilities of office.

But to my mind, in these perpetually troubled United States a great President is one through whom the essential conflicts of democracy—the struggle between past and present, class and class, race and race, region and region—are brought into the most intense and creative focus. He is one who releases chaos as he creates order. He arouses hopes and expectations, even as he strives to modify the structures that have supported an unjust stability in the interest of securing a broader social freedom. He is not necessarily a man possessing a new style of action or eloquence, but rather one who recognizes that the American is one whose basic problem is that of accepting the difficult demands of his essential newness in a world grown increasingly turbulent. He is one who knows instinctively, in the words of W. H. Auden, that for the American "it is not a question of the Old Man transforming himself into the New, but of the

New Man becoming alive to the fact that he is new, that he has been transformed [by the land, by technology, by the break with the past, by the diversity of a pluralistic society] without his having realized it."

The great President is also a man possessed by his role, and one who becomes, to a painful extent, a prisoner of his role, and there is evidence that President Johnson is aware of this. "Every day," he has said,

> there come to this office new problems and new crises and new difficulties demanding discussion and consultation and decision. I must deal with them, possessing no gift of prophecy, no special insight into history. Instead, I must depend, as my thirty-five predecessors depended, on the best wisdom and judgment that can be summoned to the service of the nation. This counsel must come from people who represent the diversity of America.

Nor is he unaware of the limitations of his power:

> A President must have a vision of the America and the world he wants to see. But the President does not put his purely personal stamp upon the future. His vision is compounded of the hopes and anxieties and values of the people he serves. The President can help guide them toward the highest and most noble of their desires. He cannot take them where they do not want to go. Nor can he hope to move ahead without the help of all those who share a common purpose. I believe the presidency was conceived as an office of persuasion more than of sheer power. That is how I have tried to use the office since it was thrust upon me.

One of the most persistent criticisms of President Johnson is that he is arrogant, but few who echo the charge bother to question its source or the sinister irony it expresses. Although it is too early for final judgments, it is possible that what has been called the President's arrogance is actually an expression of a profound and dedicated humility before the demands and responsibilities of his office. Perhaps he is becoming possessed by the office in much the manner that Abraham Lincoln was possessed, and is being consumed before our television-focused eyes by the role that he might well have expected, as politician, to have dominated.

As I see it, there is anguish here: an anguish born of strenuous efforts which turn endlessly into their opposites, of efforts to communicate which fail to get through, an anguish born of measures passed and projects set up only to be blocked, stalled, deprived of funds, and kept from functioning often by those who should in the nation's broader interest render all assistance. His most successful measures have produced impatience and released forces and energies which obscure the full extent of his accomplishments. And they are great accomplishments. No one has initiated more legislation for education, for health, for racial justice, for the arts, for urban reform than he. Currently it is the fashion of many intellectuals to ignore these accomplishments and promises of a broader freedom to come, but if those of other backgrounds and interests can afford to be blind to their existence, my own interests and background compel me to bear witness.

For I must be true to the hopes, dreams and myths of my people. So perhaps I am motivated here by an old slave-born myth of Negroes—not the myth of the "good white man," nor that of the "great white father," but the myth, secret and questioning, of the flawed white Southerner who while true to his Southern roots has confronted the injustices of the past and been redeemed. Such a man, the myth holds, will do the right thing however great the cost, whether he likes Negroes or not, and will move with tragic vulnerability toward the broader ideals of American democracy. The figure evoked by this myth is one who will grapple with complex situations that have evolved through history, and is a man who has so identified with his task that personal considerations have become secondary.

Judge Waties J. Waring of South Carolina was such a man, and so—one hopes and suspects—is Lyndon Baines Johnson. If this seems optimistic, it is perhaps because I am of a hopeful people. Considering that he has changed inescapably the iconography of federal power, from his military aides to the Cabinet, from the Federal Reserve Board to the Supreme Court, there appears to be ample reason for hope.

When all of the returns are in, perhaps President Johnson will have to settle for being recognized as the greatest American President for the poor and for Negroes, but this, as I see it, is a very great honor indeed.

If the Twain Shall Meet

HOWARD Zinn's *The Southern Mystique* is yet another reminder that American history is caught again in the excruciating process of executing a spiral—that is, in returning at a later point in time to an earlier point in historical space—and the point of maximum tortuosity is once again the South.

It would seem that the basic themes of our history may be repressed in the public mind, but like corpses in mystery dramas, they always turn up again—and are frequently more troublesome. Yes, and with an added element of mystery. "To hit," as hunters say, "is history, to miss is mystery." For while our history is characterized by a swift and tightly telescoped continuity, our *consciousness* of history is typically discontinuous. Like quiescent organisms in the blood, our unresolved issues persist, but with our attention turned to other concerns we come to regard the eruption of boils and chancres that mark their presence with our well-known "American innocence." Naturally, this leaves us vulnerable to superstition, rumor, and the manipulation of political medicine men.

Nevertheless, so imperative are our national commitments that while one group in our historical drama inevitably becomes inactive once the issues that aroused it are repressed, a resuscitation of the old themes will find a quite similar group taking its place on the redecorated stage. Frequently unaware of the earlier performers of its roles—because flawed, as are most Americans, by an ignorance of history—the new group dresses in quite different costumes but speaks in its own accents the old vital lines of freedom.

Thus the first Reconstruction saw a wave of young whites hurrying south to staff the schools the Freedmen's Bureau was establishing for emancipated slaves. Enthusiastic, energetic, self-sacrificial,

---

Review in *Book Week* (New York *Herald Tribune*), November 8, 1964.

these young teachers are long forgotten, yet they were the true predecessors of the young white Northerners now participating in the sit-ins and voter-registration drives that mark the second—or resumption of—Reconstruction. Today's young crusaders are predominantly students, but here too, acting in the ranks and as advisers, are teachers like the author of *The Southern Mystique*.

Currently an associate professor of government at Boston University, Mr. Zinn has been chairman of the history department at Spelman College, a school for Negro women located in Atlanta, Georgia. His book is an account of his experiences as a member of an integrated faculty, as a resident in a predominantly Negro university community, and as an adviser to the Student Non-Violent Coordinating Committee. It attempts to confront the problems arising from the Negro's quest for civil rights—and the white Southerner's agony in accepting change—not with slogans nor with that smug attitude of moral superiority typical of many Northerners' approach to the South, but with a passion to discover a rationale for hope and a theoretical basis for constructive action. Significantly, Mr. Zinn places the burden of insight and sympathy upon the outsider, and thus upon himself.

With such works as *The Southern Mystique*, Calvin Trillin's *An Education in Georgia*, and Bernard Taper's *Gomillion vs. Lightfoot*, the second Reconstruction is receiving its on-the-spot documentation, as once again young Northerners are bent upon trying to reduce the chaos and mystery of the South, and our involvement in it, to some semblance of human order. Mr. Zinn would give us a human perspective on the present struggle, and in this sense his book belongs with such works of the first Reconstruction as *The Journal of Charlotte L. Forten* and Thomas Wentworth Higginson's *Army Life in a Black Regiment*. Like these, in reporting a social action it reveals a state of mind.

In achieving change Mr. Zinn would base his actions upon sound thinking. He would not only reexamine our major assumptions concerning man and society, but would also appropriate any new concepts developed by social psychology, Neo-Freudian analysis, and the findings of such specialists in Southern history as C. Vann Woodward. Philosophically he has tried to forge, for himself at least, a fresh concept of man. In the areas of race relations this is a most necessary endeavor, and while I disagree with some of his procedures and conclusions, I am sympathetic with his attempt to do pragmatically what our best critical minds have failed even to recognize as important.

Mr. Zinn's example reminds us that one of the most exciting intellectual phenomenons of recent years has been the stir created among Northern intellectuals by the French Existentialists' theory of *engagement.* How frequently has the word turned up in their writings! How often have I been asked to sign—and have signed—their petitions decrying injustices in Europe, Asia and the Middle East! Yes, and how sensitive have they been to those who have struggled in the Soviet Union, in Hungary, in Algeria—and well they might, for injustice always wears the same harsh face wherever it shows itself. Yet today one of the most startling disjunctures in our national life has been the failure of many of these intellectuals to involve themselves either by their writings or their activities (except, perhaps, for wearing CORE's equality buttons in their lapels) in our own great national struggle.

One wouldn't suspect that the South has been the center of our national dilemma, both political and moral, for most intellectuals have never seriously confronted the South or its people, few have visited there, and most have drawn their notions about Southerners from novels or from political theorists and sociologists who themselves have never been there. And while in all probability most of these intellectuals reject the values or debasement of values for which the South has stood (even though they admire and often imitate the poets, novelists and critics whom the South has produced), few feel any obligation to obtain firsthand knowledge—not even those who write so confidently (and there are Negroes among these) about the "meaning" of Negro experience. The events set in motion by the Supreme Court decision of 1954 and accelerated by the Civil Rights Act of 1964, and which are now transforming not only the South but the entire nation—events that are creating a revolution not only in our race relations but in our political morality—have found them ominously silent.

My complaint isn't simply that they don't know the South or the Negro, but that their failures to learn about the country leave them at the mercy of politicians, unreliable reporters and rumormongers. Nor does it help their posture of intellectual authority. Indeed, many confuse the "Negro revolution" with the so-called "sexual revolution" (really a *homo*-sexual revolution), and this has led them to praise unbelievably bad art in the mistaken notion that they are helping to extend Negro freedom. No wonder that when the civil rights struggle moves into their own neighborhoods, many of them have nothing to fall back upon except the same tired clichés about sexual rivalry, miscegenation and Negro self-hate that have clouded the human realities of the South.

Well, Howard Zinn is no Zen Buddhist; he is a passionate reformer, and his passion lends his book the overtones of symbolic action. In this sense it involves a dual journey, one leg of which took him and his family to live in what, in his own words, "is often thought to be the womb of the South's mystery, the Negro community of the Deep South," and the other of which led him into that violent and mysterious region evoked in the mind by the work of Margaret Mitchell, Wilbur J. Cash and William Faulkner—a region cloaked by an "invisible mist" which not only blurred perspective but distorted justice and defied reason. Here *The Southern Mystique* relates a journey into the unknown, involving an *agon* of dangerous action, a reversal of purpose leading to a "revolution in perception," and a return to the North with what Mr. Zinn offers as a life-preserving message—i.e., his book.

From his base in the Negro community—this "womb," this sanctuary, this place of growth, rebirth, and vision, resting in the "tranquil eye" of the South's hurricane of racial tensions—Mr. Zinn was to discover "those tiny circles of shadow out of sight, where people of several colors meet and touch as human beings . . ." And now he believes that contact between the races is a key to understanding and change, because contact—"intimate, massive and more than momentary—reshuffles all sensory memories and dissolves the mystique built upon the physical characteristics of the Negro." One gathers that, for him, contact, in a context of ameliorative action, produces a catharsis that is not only sensory and psychological, but intellectual and moral. Fear is exorcised, the errors springing from prejudice are corrected, and a redefinition of purpose, both personal and social, becomes possible. The assumption here is that social change is sparked by the concern of responsible individuals, and an overtone of individual salvation sounds throughout Mr. Zinn's book. He specifies, however, that interracial contact must be *equal*, which excludes most of the usual contacts between Negroes and whites, whether North or South. Thus the coming together of whites and Negroes in the interest of change is change in itself, and therefore threatening to those who fear the widening of American democracy.

In the "womb" of the Negro community, Mr. Zinn was moved to the passionate purpose of dispelling the mystique which he found cloaking the human realities of the South. After living there for seven intense years, he believes that he has discovered the reality underlying the Southern mystique: racial fear is its core. He sees the white Southerner not as a figure of horror but as an American who exhibits certain national characteristics in an exaggerated form. The South, he writes, "is still the most terrible place in America [but] because it is, it is filled with heroes." Yet I must say that his perception (and he is conscious of this) has by no means been completely purified. Not when he can write that "every cliché uttered about the South, every stereotype attached to its people, white and Negro, is true," even though he adds the qualification that "a thousand other characteristics, complex and subtle, are also true . . ."

Surely this is to concede too much to rhetorical strategy. The clichés and stereotypes attached to the South are no more "true" than those attached to any other region or people. What Zinn means, perhaps, is that they contain an *element* of truth. Stereotypes are fabricated from fragments of reality, and it is these fragments that give them life, continuity and availability for manipulation. Even this depends upon the psychological predisposition of those who accept them. Here, in fact, is the secret of the stereotypes' tenaciousness. Some people must feel superior on any ground whatsoever, and I'm afraid that for far too many, "whiteness" is the last desperate possibility. Unfortunately this need has become contagious, and now, as should be expected, certain Negroes, who for years have been satisfied to be merely human and stake their chances upon individual attainment, are succumbing to *blackness* as a value.

As would be expected of a book involved with race and color in the United States, *The Southern Mystique* is concerned with seeing and non-seeing, with illusion and reality, but also with intellectual clarity. His own efforts to see clearly and act effectively lead Mr. Zinn to believe that certain key concepts influencing our view of personality tend to inhibit action in the field of civil rights. He is critical of Freudian psychology, for instance, because he feels that a concern with its categories leads to a "pervasive pessimism" about men in society. Agreeing with Sartre's "man is condemned at every instance to invent man," he suggests that in achieving change in the South, the point of departure is not a philosophical investigation of cause, because "once you acknowledge *cause* as the core of a problem, you have built something into it that not only baffles people, but, worse, immobilizes them." (Evidently he really believes that the devil appears only at man's bidding.)

Mr. Zinn would therefore leave cause to the philosophers and, as an activist, concentrate on results. After all, he argues, "A physicist may . . . not know what *really* lies behind the transformation of matter into energy, but if he has figured out how to release this energy, his achievement is stupendous." It is true that in many tightly controlled experiments the scientist must still play it by ear, and true again that civilizations have produced great art while leaving unsolved the problem of where babies come from, yet Zinn's argument makes me uneasy if for no other reason than that it evokes the myth of the sorcerer's apprentice. Not only does it blithely put aside the intractable fact that human beings are creatures of memory and spirit, as well as of conscious motivation, but it makes too much mystery of what, in its political aspects, is really a struggle for power, as white and Negro Southerners understand very well.

Nevertheless, Mr. Zinn's rejection of the gradualists' assumption that a change in thinking must precede changes in behavior seems justified by the actual dynamics of recent social changes in the South. Thus his observation that "first you change the way people behave by legal or extralegal pressures of various kinds, in order to transform the environment which is the ultimate determinant of the way they think" seems valid not only on the basis of current events, but also because it describes what actually happened to Negroes following the betrayal of Reconstruction. Indeed, Mr. Zinn draws upon the researches of C. Vann Woodward to demonstrate how comparatively recent segregation has been a support of the "Southern way of life."

In answer to the fear that white Southerners will accept change and then retaliate violently, he considers this no reason to slow the pace of action. Today, he holds, neither change nor its approval depends upon the white Southerner's will, but only upon his "quiescence." For now, he writes, what is called "intelligent white leadership . . . is really the exercise of influence by some whites to get other whites to follow, however grumblingly, the leadership of Negroes . . . whose decisions on tactics are the parents of those decisions on law that are made in the courts and announced in the headlines."

In other words, we've spiraled back to a situation similar to the one that followed the Hayes-Tilden Compromises; where the violence of sheriff's deputies and nightriders formed the force by which the white leadership then achieved its will. Today Negroes have converted their grievously acquired discipline in absorbing violence nonviolently into a force for changing their condition. Perhaps we have made too much of the "moral" nature of Negroes' struggle because their demands for freedom have *always* been moral; what is new is that their efforts now have sanction in national law. Thus they can, if only in extreme instances, call upon the ultimate force of federal troops, a protection denied them since the end of Reconstruction.

Mr. Zinn points out, however, that except in rare instances change is being achieved in the South through a "mammoth internal convulsion," and that "in almost all cases where desegregation has occurred, the white South has made its own decision for acceptance." He explains this by noting a human fact long obscured by the Southern mystique (though not for Southern Negroes who have had to know better): the white Southerner has a "hierarchy of values, in which some things are more important than others, and segregation, while desirable, does not mean as much to him as certain other values [which] he has come to cherish." Thus he makes choices "with the guidance of some subconscious order of priorities, in a field of limited possibilities."

To his awareness of the relationship between the individual's hierarchy of values and Southern change, Mr. Zinn adds Kurt Lewin's dictum, derived from the "field theory" of theoretical physics, that "behavior depends neither upon the past nor the future, but on the present field"—a view which, if true, is true only in a highly qualified sense. Nevertheless it allows Zinn a certain optimism in approaching Southern white behavior "not as the inevitable results of a fixed set of psychological traits, but as the response to a group atmosphere which is susceptible of manipulation."

Whatever the validity of applying "field theory" to human psychology, one of the strategies of the Negro freedom movement is to exert pressures in the social field that will move whites to make choices favorable to Negroes' goals. This actually is a very old maneuver of Negro strategy, characterized by careful timing and flexibility within what, since the 1870s, has been a fairly rigid field. But theory is theory and practice is what we make it, while the past asserts itself regardless.

If Southern whites (who seem as unfamiliar with "field theory" as with Edmund Wilson's "sea slug" theory of the Civil War) respond to change as they have in the past—that is, often violently—then Negroes have usually reacted as they did most frequently in their own past—namely, nonviolently. Today, however, the absorbing of blows has become a political technique, and thus a value. A prime source of Negro morale is their knowledge that their forefathers survived so much violence (one of the major supports of the "American way of life," by the way) during times when the highest court in the land was against them. How, by the way, does one say "Negro American" without at once implying "slave" and, one hopes, "free man and equal and responsible citizen"?

But do not let me quibble here, for I am aware that theory has no necessary correspondence in action, nor means with results. Social change, nevertheless, involves the use of words, and words, even Mr. Zinn's words, are rooted deep in the realities of the past.

Zinn bolsters his argument with Harry Stack Sullivan's observation on the importance of the "significant other" in interpersonal relationships. He also suggests that intellectuals, scholars and especially policy makers should be aware that in confronting (or failing to confront) problems of social change, they are no mere neutral observers but participants who modify the situation by affecting the field of social forces. In this sense, then, there is no escape; one acts even by not acting—a useful reminder for those who trouble over how to apply the concept of *engagement* to the current struggle; one wishes to shout "Hear, Hear!" But his suggestion that an administration that recognizes its own activity as a force affecting white behavior might "map much bolder policies than one basing its moves on the passive situation represented by public opinion polls" seems far too charitable toward politicians' motives.

For while the myths and mysteries that form the Southern mystique are *irrational* and even *primitive*, they are nevertheless real, even as works of the imagination are "real." Like all mysteries and their attendant myths, they imply—as Jane Harrison teaches us in *Themis*, her study of ancient Greek religion—a rite. And rites are *actions*, the goal of which is the manipulation of power—in primitive religions magical power, in the South (and in the North) political power.

Further, in our own representative form of government the representatives of the white South (few of whom represent Negroes) are all too often the most dedicated, most magic-befouled manipulators of the mystique that surrounds American race prejudice. Neither Strom Thurmond nor Governors Johnson and Wallace have any intention of surrendering the power issuing from the Southern mystique out of the goodness of their hearts. They will give way only before the manifestation within the South of the broader, more human American myth of equality and freedom for all. Not even the presence in the White House of an even more significant Southern "other" has inhibited the celebrants of the rites of Southern prejudice, and now they have been joined by Senator Goldwater. Race remains an active political force because they make it so, and their techniques of manipulation are traditional.

"The most vicious thing about segregation—more deadly than its immediate denials of certain goods and services—is," in Mr. Zinn's opinion, "its perpetuation of the mystery of racial differences." I would have thought that the impact of segregation and discrimination upon individual and group alike would be more important. Most Negroes ignore the mystique of race differences, even as they comply with Southern law and custom. For they know through their own experience the superficiality of the evidence upon which the myth of white superiority rests. They also know that they haven't lived all these years as servants to a race of gods. The folk verse—"These white folk think / That they so fine, / But their dirty linen stinks / Just like mine!"—while irreverent and a bit bawdy, is a sharp-nosed, clear-eyed observation of reality. No, it is less the mystique that harms us than the denial of basic freedom. It is not the myth that places dynamite in a Sunday school but terrorists carrying out a ritual of intimidation; while the word slanders, the practice inflicts death. If whites can accept change without surrendering their prejudices—and here Mr. Zinn sees quite clearly—so have Negroes existed under that prejudice without accepting its contentions.

I must leave it to more qualified critics to assess the broader implications of Mr. Zinn's theoretical approach, but I believe that his effort to see freshly and act constructively is, despite all objections, overwhelmingly important. His speculations have followed courageous action, and he is aware of how urgently the activities of the Negro Freedom Movement demand clarification in theoretical structuring. One source of the problem is our lack of any adequate definition of Negro life and experience, which is far from being as simple as many thinkers assume.

But here Mr. Zinn's own urgency blurs his perception. He believes that man has in his power the means to bring himself and society closer to a more human ideal, and his key term is *action*. His assault upon the viciousness committed in the name of instinct, race and history makes him prefer theories that underplay the influence of the past—ironically, a tendency that reformers share with reactionaries and conservatives, who would repress all details of the past that would unmask their mythologies. Thus Gordon Allport's hypothesis that "motives are contemporary . . . not bound functionally to historical origins or to early goals, but to present goals only" affords Zinn optimism in the field of action. But action does not imply insight, because the past is clearly present in the motivation of the Negroes with whom Zinn worked in the South. Perhaps in shrugging off the encumbrances of the past, he failed to observe them (or even to identify with them) in sufficient depth.

Zinn suggests that half a generation ago the Southern Negro personality was essentially that of the archstereotype of "Sambo" (that craven creation of nineteenth-century white Southern pseudosociology, recently reintroduced into what passes for intellectual discussion by Stanley M. Elkins), but was suddenly transformed by the

Supreme Court Decision of 1954 into the "proud Negro demonstra-
tor who appears in exactly those little towns and hamlets . . . that
produced silence and compliance a half generation ago."

But here he is being taken in—both by Elkins and by his own need
to re-create man, or at least Negro man, in terms of the expediencies
of the historical moment. Didn't he notice that some of the older
sharecroppers who are sheltering and advising the young Northern
crusaders would seem to look, talk and, when the occasion requires
it, *act* like this alleged "Sambo"? He is perceptive when he notes that
the terrible aspects of Southern life have made for many heroes, but
he might also have noted that Southern life is the most dramatic
form of life in the United States, and because of this is full of actors.
In fact, the Southern mystique has assigned roles to whites as well as
to Negroes—except that for Negroes the outcome of abandoning
the role is frequently tragic, for it leads to terror, pitiful suffering and
death.

In concentrating on the mystery of race, Mr. Zinn overlooks the
more intriguing mystery of culture (it is interesting how often, for an
activist, *culture* means *politics*!). Still, the Southern Negroes who have
revealed themselves since 1954 are not products of some act of legal
magic; they are the products of a culture, a culture of the Southern
states, and of a tradition that ironically they share with white Southerners. But with Negroes it developed out of slavery and through
their experiences since the Civil War and the first Reconstruction.
Thus when Zinn writes, "There are two things that make a person a
'Negro': a physical fact and a social artifice," he misses the wonderful
(and fortunate) circumstance that the Negro American is something
more. He is the product of the synthesis of his blood mixture, his
social experience, and what he has made of his predicament, i.e., his
culture. His quality of wonder and his heroism alike spring no less
from his brutalization than from that culture.

Indeed, those Negroes whom Mr. Zinn has joined in action risk
their lives out of a sense of life that has been expressed movingly in
the blues but seldom on a more intellectually available level—even

though, I believe, it is one of the keys to the meaning of American experience. For if Americans are by no means a *tragic* people, we might well be a people whose fundamental attitude toward life is best expressed in the blues. Certainly the Negro American's sense of life has forced *him* to go beyond the boundaries of the tragic attitude in order to survive. That, too, is the result of his past.

One needn't agree with Mr. Zinn that the initiative in the South is now in Negro hands (there is the matter of antagonistic cooperation to be considered), but many clues to action are to be found in their own dramatic experience. They have known for a long time, for instance, that you can change the white Southerner's environment without changing his beliefs because such changes have marked the fluctuations of Negro freedom. Negroes also know the counterpart of this fact: namely, that you prepare yourself for desegregation and the opportunities to be released thereby *before* this freedom actually exists. Indeed, it is in the process of preparation for an elected role that the techniques of freedom are discovered and that freedom itself is released.

The Negro Freedom Party of Mississippi, for instance, arose out of a mock political action, and as a mockery of the fraudulent democracy of the Democratic party of Mississippi. Its mockery took the form of developing techniques for teaching Negroes denied the right to vote how to form a political party and participate in the elective process. In the beginning it possessed all of the "artificiality" of a ritual, but the events, the "drama" acted out in Atlantic City, saw the transformation of their mockery and playacting into a significant political gesture that plunged them into the realms of conscious history. Here the old slave proverb "Change the joke and slip the yoke" proved a lasting bit of wisdom. For Negroes the Supreme Court Decision of 1954 and the Civil Rights Act of 1964 induced no sudden transformation of character; it provided the stage upon which they could reveal themselves for what their experiences have made them, and for what they have made of their experiences. Here past and present come together, making possible a collaboration across the years between the old abolitionists and such contemporary activists as Howard Zinn. Nor should we forget that today Negroes are freeing themselves.

If I seem overly critical of *The Southern Mystique*, it is by no means out of a lack of respect for its author and what he has attempted to do. His is an act of intellectual responsibility in an area that has been cast outside the range of intellectual scrutiny through our timidity of mind in the face of American cultural diversity. Mr. Zinn has not only plunged boldly into the chaos of Southern change, but has entered that mazelike and barely charted area wherein twenty million Negro Americans impinge upon American society socially, politically, morally, and therefore culturally. One needn't agree with Zinn, but one cannot afford not to hear him out. And once we read him—and we must read him with our best attention—we can no longer be careless in our thinking about the Negro revolution, for he makes it clear that it involves us all.

What America Would Be Like
Without Blacks

THE fantasy of an America free of blacks is at least as old as the dream of creating a truly democratic society. While we are aware that there is something inescapably tragic about the cost of achieving our democratic ideals, we keep such tragic awareness segregated in the rear of our minds. We allow it to come to the fore only during moments of great national crisis.

On the other hand, there is something so embarrassingly absurd about the notion of purging the nation of blacks that it seems hardly a product of thought at all. It is more like a primitive reflex, a throwback to the dim past of tribal experience, which we rationalize and try to make respectable by dressing it up in the gaudy and highly questionable trappings of what we call the "concept of race." Yet despite its absurdity, the fantasy of a blackless America continues to turn up. It is a fantasy born not merely of racism but of petulance, exasperation and moral fatigue. It is like a boil bursting forth from impurities in the bloodstream of democracy.

In its benign manifestations, it can be outrageously comic, as in the picaresque adventures of Percival Brownlee, who appears in William Faulkner's story "The Bear." Exasperating to his white masters because his aspirations and talents are for preaching and conducting choirs rather than for farming, Brownlee is "freed" after much resistance and ends up as the prosperous proprietor of a New Orleans brothel. In Faulkner's hands the uncomprehending drive of Brownlee's owners to "get shut" of him is comically instructive. Indeed, the story resonates certain abiding, tragic themes of American history with which it is interwoven, and which are causing great turbulence

From *Time*, April 6, 1970.

in the social atmosphere today. I refer to the exasperation and bemusement of the white American with the black, the black American's ceaseless (and swiftly accelerating) struggle to escape the misconceptions of whites, and the continual confusing of the black American's racial background with his individual culture. Most of all, I refer to the recurring fantasy of solving one basic problem of American democracy by "getting shut" of the blacks through various wishful schemes that would banish them from the nation's bloodstream, from its social structure, and from its conscience and historical consciousness.

This fantastic vision of a lily-white America appeared as early as 1713, with the suggestion of a white "native American," thought to be from New Jersey, that all the Negroes be given their freedom and returned to Africa. In 1777, Thomas Jefferson, while serving in the Virginia legislature, began drafting a plan for the gradual emancipation and exportation of the slaves. Nor were Negroes themselves immune to the fantasy. In 1815 Paul Cuffe, a wealthy merchant, shipbuilder and landowner from the New Bedford area, shipped and settled at his own expense thirty-eight of his fellow Negroes in Africa. It was perhaps his example that led in the following year to the creation of the American Colonization Society, which was to establish in 1821 the colony of Liberia. Great amounts of cash and a perplexing mixture of motives went into the venture. The slaveowners and many Border-state politicians wanted to use it as a scheme to rid the country not of slaves but of the militant free Negroes who were agitating against the "peculiar institution." The abolitionists, until they took a lead from free Negro leaders and began attacking the scheme, also participated as a means of righting a great historical injustice. Many blacks went along with it simply because they were sick of the black-and-white American mess and hoped to prosper in the quiet peace of the old ancestral home.

Such conflicting motives doomed the Colonization Society to failure, but what amazes one even more than the notion that anyone could have believed in its success is the fact that it was attempted during a period when blacks, slave and free, made up eighteen percent of the total population. When we consider how long blacks had been in the New World and had been transforming it and being Americanized by it, the scheme appears not only fantastic, but the product of a free-floating irrationality—indeed, a national pathology.

Nevertheless, some of the noblest of Americans were bemused. Not only Jefferson but later Abraham Lincoln was to give the scheme credence. According to historian John Hope Franklin, Negro colonization seemed as important to Lincoln as emancipation. In 1862, Franklin notes, Lincoln called a group of prominent free Negroes to the White House and urged them to support colonization, telling them. "Your race suffers greatly, many of them by living among us, while ours suffers from your presence. If this is admitted, it affords a reason why we should be separated."

In spite of his unquestioned greatness, Abraham Lincoln was a man of his times and limited by some of the less worthy thinking of his times. This is demonstrated both by his reliance upon the concept of race in his analysis of the American dilemma and by his involvement in a plan of purging the nation of blacks as a means of healing the badly shattered ideals of democratic federalism. Although benign, his motive was no less a product of fantasy. It envisaged an attempt to relieve an inevitable suffering that marked the growing pains of the youthful body politic by an operation which would have amounted to the severing of a healthy and indispensable member.

Yet like its twin, the illusion of secession, the fantasy of a benign amputation that would rid the country of black men to the benefit of a nation's health not only persists; today, in the form of neo-Garveyism, it fascinates black men no less than it once hypnotized whites. Both fantasies become operative whenever the nation grows weary of the struggle toward the ideal of American democratic equality. Both would use the black man as a scapegoat to achieve a national catharsis, and both would, by way of curing the patient, destroy him.

What is ultimately intriguing about the fantasy of "getting shut" of the Negro American is the fact that no one who entertains it seems ever to have considered what the nation would have become had Africans *not* been brought to the New World, and had their descendants not played such a complex and confounding role in the creation of American history and culture. Nor do they appear to have considered with any seriousness the effect upon the nation of having any of the schemes for exporting blacks succeed beyond settling some fifteen thousand or so in Liberia.

We are reminded that Daniel Patrick Moynihan, who has recently aggravated our social confusion over the racial issue while allegedly attempting to clarify it, is co-author of a work which insists that the American melting pot didn't melt because our white ethnic groups have resisted all assimilative forces that appear to threaten their identities. The problem here is that few Americans know who and what they really are. That is why few of these groups—or at least few of the children of these groups—have been able to resist the movies, television, baseball, jazz, football, drum-majoretting, rock, comic strips, radio commercials, soap operas, book clubs, slang, or any of a thousand other expressions and carriers of our pluralistic and easily available popular culture. It is here precisely that ethnic resistance is least effective. On this level the melting pot did indeed melt, creating such deceptive metamorphoses and blending of identities, values and lifestyles that most American whites are culturally part Negro American without even realizing it.

If we can resist for a moment the temptation to view everything having to do with Negro Americans in terms of their racially imposed status, we become aware of the fact that for all the harsh reality of the social and economic injustices visited upon them, these injustices have failed to keep Negroes clear of the cultural mainstream; Negro Americans are, in fact, one of its major tributaries. If we can cease approaching American social reality in terms of such false concepts as white and nonwhite, black culture and white culture, and think of these apparently unthinkable matters in the realistic manner of Western pioneers confronting the unknown prairie, perhaps we can begin to imagine what the United States would have been, or not been, had there been no blacks to give it—if I may be so bold as to say—color.

For one thing, the American nation is in a sense the product of the American language, a colloquial speech that began emerging long before the British colonials and Africans were transformed into Americans. It is a language that evolved from the King's English but, basing itself upon the realities of the American land and colonial institutions—or lack of institutions—began quite early as a vernacular revolt against the signs, symbols, manners and authority of the mother country. It is a language that began by merging the sounds of many tongues, brought together in the struggle of diverse regions. And whether it is admitted or not, much of the sound of that language is derived from the timbre of the African voice and the listening habits of the African ear. So there is a *de'z* and *do'z* of slave speech sounding beneath our most polished Harvard accents, and if there is such a thing as a Yale accent, there is a Negro wail in it—doubtless introduced there by Old Yalie John C. Calhoun, who probably got it from his mammy.

Whitman viewed the spoken idiom of Negro Americans as a source for a native grand opera. Its flexibility, its musicality, its rhythms, freewheeling diction and metaphors, as projected in Negro American folklore, were absorbed by the creators of our great nineteenth-century literature even when the majority of blacks were still enslaved. Mark Twain celebrated it in the prose of *Huckleberry Finn;* without the presence of blacks, the book could not have been written. No Huck and Jim, no American novel as we know it. For not only is the black man a co-creator of the language that Mark Twain raised to the level of literary eloquence, but Jim's condition as American and Huck's commitment to freedom are at the moral center of the novel.

In other words, had there been no blacks, certain creative tensions arising from the cross-purposes of whites and blacks would also not have existed. Not only would there have been no Faulkner; there would have been no Stephen Crane, who found certain basic themes of his writing in the Civil War. Thus also there would have been no Hemingway, who took Crane as a source and guide. Without the presence of Negro American style, our jokes, tall tales, even our sports would be lacking in the sudden turns, shocks and swift changes of pace (all jazz-shaped) that serve to remind us that the world is ever unexplored, and that while a complete mastery of life is mere illusion, the real secret of the game is to make life swing. It is its ability to articulate this tragic-comic attitude toward life that explains much of the mysterious power and attractiveness of that quality of Negro American style known as "soul." An expression of American diversity within unity, of blackness with whiteness, soul announces the presence of a creative struggle against the realities of existence.

Without the presence of blacks, our political history would have been otherwise. No slave economy, no Civil War, no violent destruction of the Reconstruction, no K.K.K. and no Jim Crow system. And without the disenfranchisement of black Americans and the manipulation of racial fears and prejudices, the disproportionate impact of white Southern politicians upon our domestic and foreign policies would have been impossible. Indeed, it is almost impossible to conceive of what our political system would have become without the snarl of forces—cultural, racial, religious—that make our nation what it is today.

Absent, too, would be the need for that tragic knowledge which we try ceaselessly to evade: that the true subject of democracy is not simply material well-being, but the extension of the democratic process in the direction of perfecting itself. The most obvious test and clue to that perfection is the inclusion, *not* assimilation, of the black man.

Since the beginning of the nation, white Americans have suffered from a deep inner uncertainty as to who they really are. One of the ways that has been used to simplify the answer has been to seize upon the presence of black Americans and use them as a marker, a symbol of limits, a metaphor for the "outsider." Many whites could look at the social position of blacks and feel that color formed an easy and reliable gauge for determining to what extent one was or was not American. Perhaps that is why one of the first epithets that many European immigrants learned when they got off the boat was the term "nigger"; it made them feel instantly American. But this is tricky magic. Despite his racial difference and social status, something indisputably American about Negroes not only raised doubts about the white man's value system, but aroused the troubling suspicion that whatever else the true American is, he is also somehow black.

Materially, psychologically and culturally, part of the nation's heritage is Negro American, and whatever it becomes will be shaped in part by the Negro's presence. Which is fortunate, for today it is the black American who puts pressure upon the nation to live up to its ideals. It is he who gives creative tension to our struggle for justice and for the elimination of those factors, social and psychological, which make for slums and shaky suburban communities. It is he who insists that we purify the American language by demanding that there be a closer correlation between the meaning of words and reality, between ideal and conduct, between our assertions and our actions. Without the black American, something irrepressibly hopeful and creative would go out of the American spirit, and the nation might well succumb to the moral slobbism that has always threatened its existence from within.

When we look objectively at how the dry bones of the nation were hung together, it seems obvious that some one of the many groups that compose the United States had to suffer the fate of being allowed no easy escape from experiencing the harsh realities of the human condition as they were to exist under even so fortunate a democracy as ours. It would seem that some one group had to be stripped of the possibility of escaping such tragic knowledge by taking sanctuary in moral equivocation, racial chauvinism or the advantage of superior social status. There is no point in complaining over the past or apologizing for one's fate. But for blacks there are no hiding places down here, not in suburbia or in penthouse, neither in country nor in city. They are an American people who are geared to what *is*, and who yet are driven by a sense of what it is possible for human life to be in this society. The nation could not survive being deprived of their presence because, by the irony implicit in the dynamics of American democracy, they symbolize both its most stringent testing and the possibility of its greatest human freedom.

Portrait of Inman Page:
A Dedication Speech

WHEN confronted by such an unexpected situation as this, what does one say? It's not that I haven't been aware of Dr. Page's influence upon my life, for after all these years he is apt to be conjured up by a wide variety of contacts and situations. And he was so dominant a figure during my school days that his voice and image are still evoked by certain passages of the Bible. I remember him in a context of ceremonies, in most of which he acted as the celebrant, but never in my wildest fantasies would I have anticipated my being called upon to play a role in a ceremony dedicated to his memory. Such a development would have seemed impossible because in my mind my relationship with Dr. Page has remained what it was back in the 1930s, which was that of a boy to a grand, dignified elder. In my scheme of things there remained between us a fixed hierarchal distance that had been dictated by age, accomplishment and authority. So while I would have had no problem in imagining myself witnessing such a ceremony as this, the idea of my having an active role in it would have been in the realm of the impossible. And now that I find myself standing here, it is as though a preordained relationship has been violated, and as a result my sense of time has begun leaping back and forth over the years in a way which assaults the logic of clock and calendar, and I am haunted by a sense of the uncanny.

All the more so as I look at these portraits in which Richard Yarde depicted Dr. Page as he appeared when a student here at Brown. He was a much older man when I came to know him, but the dignified educator with whom I was familiar is prefigured in the portraits, especially in the cast of the eyes. This makes for a pleasant surprise,

From *The Carleton Miscellany*, Winter 1980; address given September 19, 1979, at the Ralph Ellison Festival at Brown University.

because during my school days it never occurred to me that Inman Page had *ever* been a young man. To me he was always lofty and enigmatic, a figure of authority and penetrating vision. Perhaps that is why I am haunted by a feeling that somehow Dr. Page must have prearranged today's proceedings years ago, with the foreknowledge that at some predestined time and place they would culminate, at least for me, in a moment of astonishment and instruction.

Now, I don't know whether Dr. Page ever indulged in the old American pastime of practical joking when he was a student here, but I *do* know that practical jokes can be used as agencies of instruction, and that they can indeed be calculated to challenge one's wits and test one's alertness. I also know that they can be staged in such a way that a narrowing of the hierarchal distance between those of lowly status and their superiors is brought about. Not necessarily by effecting a ritual deflation of those who are glamorous and exalted (as happens in the celebration of Mardi Gras), but by way of elevating the lowly for a brief moment to the level of their superiors, and thus initiating them into the mysterious processes of time and authority. Because they sponsor a sense of equality, such symbolic elevations have an important function in our democracy, and are likely to be operating when we least expect. I say this because if there is such a joke at play in these proceedings, doubtless it is asserting its presence by forcing me to respond to the implication of this ceremony in spontaneous words. Perhaps this is why it is as though I am once again undergoing an examination, which this time Dr. Page is conducting from a point beyond time and space.

But such speculations aside, how could such an occasion as this come about? Through the medium of time, of course, and through the interplay, both intentional and accidental, between certain American ideals and institutions and their human agents. More specifically, it has come about through the efforts exerted by the members of one generation of Americans in the interest of the generations which were to follow. Such occasions are a product of the living continuity of earlier historical contacts and relationships which were initiated during the turbulent days of our nineteenth century, and which have persisted even when their origins have been forgotten or ignored. Such occasions are made possible because ideas and ideals retain their vitality by being communicated from concerned individuals to other (sometimes resistant) individuals. But when these ideas and ideals succeed in finding embodiment in receptive personalities, they become linkages which have the power to shape obscure destinies in unexpected ways. Sometimes they manage to affirm our faith by reversing our expectations. Thus we are gathered here today as the result of such linkages between ideals and personalities which were forged and began forming a chain of cause and effect more than a hundred years ago.

Which is to suggest that from the period of the Emancipation there has been transmitted throughout the Afro-American areas of this country a continuing influence that sprang from the early New England tradition of education. This tradition, which has contributed so much to this nation's vitality, was introduced into the areas of the South from which I spring by young graduates of New England colleges who went south to teach newly freed slaves. I am, incidently, the grandson of a freedman, which would appear to be something of an irony of history. But despite the rapid acceleration of historical change in the United States, the period of slavery isn't so far in the past as it might seem. Inman Page, who was himself a slave and who left this campus at a time when the dismantling of the Reconstruction was well under way, was a bearer of that same tradition of New England education of which I speak, and through him its standards were imparted to many ex-slaves and their descendants. Since that transmitted tradition is still alive, I think it a good idea to keep this historical circumstance in mind when we hear glib talk of a "white culture" and a "black culture" in the United States. Because the truth of the matter is that between the two racial groups there has always been a constant exchange of cultural and stylistic elements. Whether in the arts, education, athletics, or in certain conceptions and misconceptions of democratic justice, interchange, appropriation and integration (not segregation) have been the constants of our developing nation. So at this particular moment of our history I think it important that we keep in mind that the culture of the United States is a composite, pluralistic culture-of-cultures, and that all of its diverse elements have been to some extent inspirited by those ideals which were enshrined during the founding of this nation. In our embrace of these ideals we are one and yet many, and never more so than after they led to the Civil War, the Emancipation and the Reconstruction. It was these ideals which inspired the many examples of personal courage such as can be seen in the life of Inman E. Page. Certainly his act of implanting the ideals of New England education out in the "Territory," that then wild young state of Oklahoma, called for both courage and a dedication to education. Because by the time he graduated from Brown, Reconstruction, which had promised full citizenship to the freedmen, was, as I have said, well on the way toward betrayal. It was a most pessimistic period for his people, but he did his best, and therefore, thanks to Inman Page, no matter how incongruously, I am here.

I must confess, however, that as a student I always found the man forbidding. I realize now that much of my intimidation was due to his sheer personal style, his quality of command. At Brown he was chosen the orator of his class, and during my school days he was indeed eloquent. I can still hear him reading from Saint Paul's Letters to the Corinthians, as he did so often during our daily chapel exercises. Just listening to him taught one the joy and magic of words. He made one believe in his message because he expressed authority in the smallest gesture. I don't mean that he was pompous; indeed, he was quite fatherly. But for me at least he possessed an aura of the untouchable. In his presence one was careful of one's manners, and since it was his role to punish those guilty of serious misconduct with a strapping, personal contact with him was to be avoided. Usually I managed to keep out of his way, but one memorable day I failed.

It was at a time when the student body was gathering in the

school's auditorium for chapel services. During these exercises the junior and senior high school boys were seated on the platform behind the lectern from which Dr. Page conducted the religious services. This platform was actually a stage that was used for concerts and theatricals, and was equipped with a curtain that could be raised and lowered by ropes that were lashed to the floor on either side. We took our places on stage left and right by marching up short flights of stairs, which were favorite sites for horseplay. This involved much pushing and shoving, not to mention other attacks upon one's anatomy. Sometimes these could be both painful and degrading; therefore, being on this occasion somewhat out of sorts, I told myself that if some guy pushed me, I was going to swing on him and start punching.

Well, I got pushed and went into action; unfortunately for me, it wasn't a student who took my punch, but Dr. Page. Before I realized what was happening, Dr. Page had grabbed me, I had grabbed the ropes of the stage curtain, and the two of us went swinging in a tight circle that carried us around and around over the platform and steps until I lost my grip and caused the two of us to fall, with me landing on top of Dr. Page.

Well, Dr. Page was probably as shocked by this sudden eruption of chaos as I was, but he was still in command.

"What do you think you're doing, boy," he roared. "What do you think you're doing!"

Even today I'm unsure of my reply, but for years afterward a good friend used to remind me of the incident by suddenly breaking out with high-pitched cries of "We fell, Mister Page! Mister Page, we *fell!*"

I'm still unsure of what I said, because I was too excited. But as Dr. Page pushed me off and snatched me to my feet a most amazing thing occurred: in spite of my fear and excitement and the teeth-rattling shaking he was giving me, I could hear Dr. Page chuckling under his breath. Then he was chasing me, literally, straight up the aisle and out of the auditorium, and as I headed up a flight of stairs to the walk, with him right behind me, I could hear him thundering, "And don't come back! Don't you *dare* come back!"

It was a rough moment for me, a fall into chaos and disgrace, with the student body roaring its delight. All the more so because of that mysterious chuckle, a chuckle which was so incongruous that I could not be certain I had heard it. But I had, because the next day Dr. Page relented and got word to me that I hadn't been permanently expelled. In fact, I returned and managed to keep out of serious trouble from that day until I graduated. That one chaotic contact with authority was enough for me.

Now I'll bring these remarks to a close by suggesting that if Dr. Page is present with us in spirit, and I'm sure he is, no doubt he is still chuckling as he did on the day he chased me from school. Because here, once again, he finds himself a participant in another most incongruous juxtaposition, a juxtaposition in which his old student Ralph Ellison is linked unexpectedly to the exaltation of *his* principal.

Going to the Territory

ONCE again I must wonder at the sheer unexpectedness of life in these United States. Even the most celebrated of writers would find this scene exhilarating, but for me—well, it is simply overwhelming. It's as though I am being rebuked, even if ever so gently, for every instance in which I doubted the possibility of communicating my peculiar vision to my fellow Americans. Now I realize how fortunate I am to have held on to literature as a medium for transcending the divisions of our society, for your presence affirms that faith most generously.

But Lord knows I had no idea that such emotional turmoil would be the price for becoming the focus of such a scene. It reminds me of how often I've been told that extremes will meet, and it proves the correctness of those who advised me that in this country it is always wise to expect the unexpected. I say this because your campus has become the scene in which certain lines of interpersonal, institutional, and even historical relationships have not only come together but have collided in a way which I find most confounding. And it all began yesterday with the ceremony in Rockefeller Library, during which I was presented with one of Richard Yarde's portraits of Dr. Inman E. Page. Now, here in Sayles Hall, the shock wave set off by that collision appears on its way toward a rousing Wagnerian crescendo of the unexpected.

Since Inman Page was the first Afro-American to graduate from Brown University, the honor paid him here last September wasn't surprising, but that it should be *my* fate to be honored a year later with the presentation of his portrait is an example of the unexpected outdoing itself in demonstrating its power to surprise. Because in

---

From *The Carleton Miscellany*, Winter 1980; address given September 20, 1979, at the Ralph Ellison Festival at Brown University.

yesterday's ceremony two lines of destiny, which had touched during
the early 1920s and then diverged rather abruptly during the Great
Depression, were brought together again under circumstances
which in those days would have been unimaginable. It is true that
their divergence began with an educational ceremony, but no one
would have been so rash as to predict that a recapitulation would
occur, not even at a point in what was then the far distant future. In
other words, yesterday's ceremony would have been unthinkable—
even as a comic, practical-joking inflation of the original. Yet all of
the elements were already in motion.

One of Dr. Page's many roles after his graduation from Brown
was that of supervisor of education for Negroes and principal of the
old Douglass High School in Oklahoma City. I attended old Douglass (which was named in honor of Frederick Douglass, the ex-slave
abolitionist) from the first grade through the twelfth, and at my
graduation Dr. Page presented me with my diploma. Thus ended—
or appeared to end—our years of relationship. I went south to college, and except for the summer vacation of my sophomore year, I
was not to return home again for some seventeen years. On my return I was to see Dr. Page for the last time, and with my attention
turned elsewhere, I thought his influence upon my life had concluded.

But for me as for most members of our community, students and
adults alike, Dr. Page served as a representative figure. As such he
inspired the extremes of ambivalent emotion: love and hate, admiration and envy, fear and respect. He moved many of his students to
secret yearnings to possess some of his implicit authority, some of his
wisdom and eloquence, and in fact quite a number became teachers
and community leaders. Today his influence is such that although he
passed away some forty years ago, one has only to bring a group of
his old students together and immediately he lives again in apotheosis. This has been happening out in the Southwest for many years,
but I have no doubt that much of the turmoil which I feel this evening springs from the unexpectedness of finding his personality such

a powerful presence in a place so far from where I knew him. So perhaps that which we term the "unexpected" is really a product of that which we do not know or fail to take into account. Learn enough about a given phenomenon and the unexpected becomes fairly predictable.

Which suggests that although Dr. Page spent his life working in segregated institutions and thus was overlooked by those who record the history of American education, he was nonetheless a figure of national importance, and one who influenced history despite having been forced to work outside its rather arbitrarily drawn framework. If so, the honor paid him here last year celebrated not only his relationship with Brown, but marked the recognition of his national significance as an educator. At any rate, once in a while the veil which shrouds the details of our unwritten history is thrown back, and not only do the deserving find belated recognition, but sometimes marvelous interconnections between the past and the present spring to light.

So, thanks to the administrators of Brown University, thanks to Michael Harper and his assistants, and thanks to the intricate relationship which obtains between Brown and American history generally, an attempt was made to rediscover some of the more obscure connections through which the past has become a part of the living present. Somehow in that process of retrieval, an Oklahoma boy was found whose life was profoundly influenced by Inman E. Page, and so I stand before you.

Yet considering the ironic fact that Americans continue to find themselves stumbling into (as well as over) details of their history, tonight's is a most *American* occasion. For it is one in which by seeking to move forward, we find ourselves looking back and discovering with some surprise from whence we've come. Perhaps this is how it has to be. Given the circumstances of our national origins, our vast geopolitical space and the improvised character of our society, and given the mind-boggling rapidity of our national growth, perhaps it is understandably difficult for Americans to keep in touch with what has happened to them. At any rate, in the two hundred years of our national existence a great deal has been overlooked or forgotten. Some developments become obscure because of the sheer rush and density of incidents which occur in any given period of time; others fade through conscious design, either because of an unwillingness to solve national dilemmas or because we possess such a short attention span and are given to a facile waning of our commitments. Moreover, having had no adequate model to guide us in establishing what we told ourselves was to be a classless society, it has often been difficult for us to place people and events in a proper perspective of national importance. So it is well that we keep in mind the fact that not all of American history is recorded. In some ways we are fortunate that it isn't, for if it were, we might become so chagrined by the discrepancies which exist between our democratic ideals and our social reality that we would soon lose heart. Perhaps this is why we possess two basic versions of American history: one which is written and as neatly stylized as ancient myth, and the other unwritten and as chaotic and full of contradictions, changes of pace and surprises as life itself. Perhaps this is to overstate a bit, but there is no denying the fact that Americans can be notoriously selective in the exercise of historical memory.

Surely there must be some self-deceptive magic in this, for in spite of what is left out of our recorded history, our unwritten history looms as its obscure alter ego, and although repressed from our general knowledge of ourselves, it is always active in the shaping of events. It is always with us, questioning even when not accusing its acclaimed double, and with the two locked in mute argument which is likely to shock us when it becomes visible during periods of national stress. Meanwhile, yearning and thirsting for a rational social order, and being forced as human beings to live in what we like to identify as the "present," we go on struggling against the built-in conditions which comprise the pathology of American democracy. Perhaps it is our need to avoid the discouraging facts of our experience that accounts for the contradiction between those details of our history which we choose to remember and those which we ignore or leave unstated.

But no matter how we choose to view ourselves in the abstract, in the world of work and politics Americans live in a constant state of debate and contention. We do so no matter what kinds of narrative, oral or written, are made in the reconstruction of our common experience. American democracy is a most dramatic form of social organization, and in that drama each of us enacts his role by asserting his own and his group's values and traditions against those of his fellow citizens. Indeed, a battle-royal conflict of interests appears to be basic to our conception of freedom, and the drama of democracy proceeds through a warfare of words and symbolic actions by which we seek to advance our private interests while resolving our political differences. Since the Civil War this form of symbolic action has served as a moral substitute for armed warfare, and we have managed to restrain ourselves to a debate which we carry on in the not always justified faith that the outcome will serve the larger interests of democracy. Unfortunately this doesn't always work out, and when it doesn't, the winners of a given contention are likely to concern themselves with only the fruits of victory, while leaving it to the losers to grapple with the issues that are left unresolved.

Something like this was taking place at the time Inman Page was graduating from Brown, and it set the tone of the scene in which he was to act. Having won its victory, the North could be selective in its memory, as well as in its priorities, while leaving it to the South to struggle with the national problems which developed following the end of Reconstruction. And even the South became selective in its memory of the incidents that led to its rebellion and defeat. Of course a defenseless scapegoat was easily at hand, but my point here is that by pushing significant details of our experience into the underground of unwritten history, we not only overlook much which is positive, but we blur our conceptions of where and who we are. Not only do we confuse our moral identity, but by ignoring such matters as the sharing of bloodlines and cultural traditions by groups of widely differing ethnic origins, and by overlooking the blending and metamorphosis of cultural forms which are so characteristic of our society, we misconceive our cultural identity. It is as though we dread to acknowledge the complex, pluralistic nature of our society, and as a result find ourselves stumbling upon our true national identity under circumstances in which we least expect to do so. This is because some of our brightest achievements have been like lights hidden under a basket of myths. Who would have expected that through one of the members of the class of 1877, Brown University would play a role in the fate of a writer from Oklahoma? More important, who would have thought that Brown's standards of education would affect the outlook of so many thousands who would never see it?

Thus in the underground of our unwritten history, much of that which is ignored defies our inattention by continuing to grow and have consequences. This happens through a process of apparently random synthesis, a process which I see as the unconscious logic of the democratic process. Set in motion over two hundred years ago with the founding of this nation, it is an irrepressible force which draws its power from those fateful promises that were made in Philadelphia, and it moves all too slowly, but steadily, against and around those forces which would thwart our progress toward the fulfillment of the democratic ideal. An aspect of the democratic principles which inspirit our institutions and social processes, it expresses itself in the unremarked contacts between individuals of differing status and background, and through the impact, accidental or intended, which significant individuals exert upon our institutions. Ever at work in our lives, it reveals itself in those gestures and elements of style through which we find our definition as Americans. This includes the way we walk, talk and move, but ironically it is likely to become our conscious possession during those moments when events force us to measure that which we have been taught formally and abstractly, against that which we have learned through hard experience. Sometimes when this happens we discover that we are a bit worse than we have been taught, but then again, much better than we would dare believe.

Sometimes we become aware of the underground logic of the democratic process quite consciously, but are likely to perceive the rightness of its products with a feeling of unease. Our perception of justice attained doesn't always square with our conception of that which is best for our own interests. Sometimes it works its transformations of society so quietly (as during periods of war or economic depression) that we fail to realize that in such interruptions of normal order, injustices that have been long accepted have been resolved. Let's face it, no matter what motives are ascribed as leading to the Civil War, it took that conflict for Inman Page to be able to come to Brown. So it is often on this unrecognized level that our democratic ideals are most successful in nudging us toward our goal.

And so it is that we go on striving. We take chances—and are taken by the random working of the democratic impulse—and we continue to assert the old received values, modifying them as seems necessary, but seeking to affirm them nevertheless. This we do out of our individual yearnings, out of our individual passions, and out of our often halfhearted hopes that some day we will achieve the transcendent dream which was projected by the Founding Fathers when they committed their conception of an ideal society to paper.

That conception was arrived at, remember, through strenuous debate, and we have been arguing with one another ever since. Still, ours is a debate, a contention, in which we seek to make our conception of democracy manifest in every detail of our living. Not only in flags and emblems, or in words and rituals, but even in such details as the architecture of your magnificent buildings, which are among the glories of your campus, and in such minor artifacts as the blue jeans which parade the names of heiresses on the hip pocket. There has to be a powerful democratic magic in the latter, because for Inman Page's generation education was seen as a way of *not* having to live in blue jeans. But as I say, extremes meet—and this in more ways than one. For in this country we seem to go to any extreme in promoting our notions of excellence, and this can lead to incongruous juxtapositions. There is also the fact that any way one takes it, democracy is a leveling process which moves in any direction along the scale of taste. There is also the fact that in order for democratic principles and ideals to remain vital, they must be communicated not only across the built-in divisions of class, race and religion, but across the divisions of aesthetic styles and tastes as well. When this is achieved, not only do we find communication and communion, but we learn a bit more about how to live within the mystery which haunts American experience, and that is the mystery of how we are many and yet one. I suppose that when used as costume, blue jeans are a way of dramatizing our basic unity.

Which reminds me that since arriving on campus I've had the pleasure of listening to a number of discussions of my fiction, and I've been amazed to discover how much of what I conceived to be a basic pattern of American experience appears to have been communicated to readers who originate on opposite sides of the color line. To me this is most important, not only because I wish to be understood, but because race and color have been basic determinants in structuring what is one of the most aggravating barriers to free communication in this society. Approach the reality of racial differences, and our dictionary of democratic terminology can be thrown into confusion, with such common terms as "equality" and "freedom" turning into their opposites. But when I was listening to these discussions this didn't happen. It was as though my novel had become a lens through which readers of widely differing backgrounds were able to see elements of their own experience brought to a unifying focus. In some instances I found this a bit bewildering, even though I am aware that a novel can come alive only through the collaboration of its readers' imaginations, and it was quite evident that the students who participated with the panelists had been taught to read. But something more was taking place, for it was as though a group of sophisticated minds were functioning like a group of jazz musicians and were working in a spirit of antagonistic cooperation to explore the novel's hidden possibilities. In a jam session this process works in such a way that not only is the original theme enhanced, but the listener is compelled to experience a feeling of catharsis.

Let me hasten to say that I don't mean to flatter myself by implying that those involved in these discussions were *themselves* undergoing a catharsis. But *I* certainly did, and it left me not only intellectually gratified but physically weak. Perhaps this was because when one works with words and situations that are commonly charged with divisive emotions, it is gratifying to discover that despite this, you have been able to communicate. And all the more when you know that in this country effective artistic communication requires a symbolic sharing of emotions and situations which have usually blocked communication in the world of work and politics. What is important in all this lies in the fact that the terms which allow for communication are the same which we use to spell out our democratic ideals. They are the same terms which inspired Inman Page to take his chances here at Brown, and thus my being here tonight is not only an occasion in which certain details of our common history have come together, but it is also one in which there is revealed something of the fate of those principles in whose name we struggle and in whose spirit we have often died. I say *struggle* because for all our many achievements as a nation, we have never been able to make our principles adequately manifest in either our conduct or in our social structure. Yet once in a while we have been capable of enormous efforts. Today many agree that the ideals of the Great Society, which were a restatement of the ideals of Reconstruction, have proved to be dross. I would say that this depends upon where one looks. For here in an area that is somewhat buffered against the contentions of politics, there is evidence that at least some of our efforts have found a measure of success, even as did certain efforts that were launched during the period when Inman Page came to Brown.

Inman Page arrived at Brown University at a time when the optimism which was released among the former slaves by their emancipation was still buoyed by the promises of the already fading

Reconstruction. For the first time Afro-Americans were participating as a group in political affairs, and their right to do so was being protected by federal troops. Thus the nation's tragic drama of sectional warfare appeared to have ended their subjugation. We know now, however, that the freedmen were actors within a play-within-a-play, and that theirs was a tragic action within a larger drama in which events would convert tragedy into farce. And if the larger drama was resolved in the ambiguous victory of the North, theirs would proceed through an abrupt reversal of their group expectations to social and political defeat, because after the Hayes-Tilden Compromise they were forced to live under a system which was close to, and in some ways worse than, slavery. Here, surely, is an example of the rapidity of historical change of which I have spoken. Within thirteen years Afro-Americans were swept from slavery to a brief period of freedom, to a condition of second-class citizenship. And from a condition of faint hope, through a period of euphoric optimism, to a condition of despair. The familiar world of slavery was gone, but now they faced a world of ambiguity in which their access to even the most fundamental of life's necessities was regulated strictly on the basis of race and color.

Such was the general picture, but in spite of these dismal developments, there were still reasons for cautious optimism. This lay in the physical fact that they were now the owners of their own bodies and had the freedom to express something of their aspirations as individuals. As slaves they had long been aware that for themselves, as for most of their countrymen, geography was fate. Not only had they observed the transformation of individual fortune made possible by the westward movement along the frontier, but the Mason-Dixon line had taught them the relationship between geography and freedom. They knew that to be sold down the Mississippi River usually meant that they would suffer a harsher form of slavery, and they knew that to escape across the Mason-Dixon line northward was to move in the direction of a greater freedom. But freedom was also to be found in the West of the old Indian Territory. Bessie Smith gave voice to this knowledge when she sang of "Goin' to the Nation, Going to the Terr'tor'," and it is no accident that much of the symbolism of our folklore is rooted in the imagery of geography. The slaves had learned through the repetition of group experience that freedom was to be attained through geographical movement, and that freedom required one to risk his life against the unknown. Geography as a symbol of the unknown included not only places, but conditions relating to their racially defined status and the complex mystery of a society from which they had been excluded. Emancipation had intensified their awareness of the mystery which cloaked the larger society, and they realized that education, the freeing of the mind, was necessary if they were to make the most of their change in legal status. It was out of such circumstances that Inman Page chose to enhance his freedom by coming to Brown, and it was here that he was able to establish his individual worth and prepare himself for his liberating role as an educator. This much of his story I have known since I was a child, but I am still amazed by the extent to which his willingness to take his chances in unknown territories has affected my own life. The theme of this festival is "Goin' to the Territory"; well, I met Dr. Page in what was first known as the Indian Territory, and then the Oklahoma Territory. Long before it became the State of Oklahoma the Territory had been a sanctuary for runaway slaves who sought there the protection of the Five Great Indian Nations. Dr. Page went to the Territory in 1898 to become president of what is now Langston University, and by the time he became the principal of my old school he was a man in his seventies. At that time the state of Oklahoma had attracted many of the descendants of the freed slaves, who considered it a territory of hope, and a place where they could create their own opportunities. It was a magnet for many individuals who had found disappointment in the older area of the country, white as well as black, but for Negroes it had a traditional association with freedom which had entered their folklore. Thus the uneducated and educated alike saw Oklahoma as a land of opportunity. In fact, as principal of Douglass High School, Dr. Page was to succeed a former West Point cadet, Professor Johnson Chestnut Whittaker, whose experiences as a cadet led to a cause célèbre that brought about the dismissal of West Point's superintendent.

Professor Whittaker was a *white* black man. Which is to say that visually he was whiter than almost anyone here in Sayles Hall. But by birth and native background he was a South Carolina slave who had been born the property of the family of U.S. Senator James Chestnut, Jr. His mother was the personal servant of Mary Boykin Chestnut, the author of *A Diary From Dixie*, a famous work of the Civil War period in which the Whittaker family is mentioned. A year before Inman Page graduated from Brown, Johnson C. Whittaker was appointed to West Point, which is an example of the type of transformations that were made possible by Emancipation. But it was also an example of the reversal of expectations wrought by the betrayal of Reconstruction. Whittaker's career ended in a racial attack during which he was seized by other cadets, who tied him to his cot and notched his ear. My mother, who knew Professor Whittaker in South Carolina, told me that this was done so that he could not measure up to a West Point tradition which held that its graduates had to be physically perfect. This incident caused much indignation in the North, but Cadet Whittaker had to leave the Point, and thus the Army's loss was to become the Territory's gain. After taking a law degree and practicing in South Carolina, Professor Whittaker became the principal of Douglass High School, where he was to introduce elements of West Point discipline and military style to young Oklahoma Negroes. Thus once again we have an example of the unnoticed logic of the democratic process.

I hope you will understand that I haven't mentioned this unpleasant incident just to shock you. I do so to suggest that our unknown history doesn't stop having consequences even though we ignore them, and I *am* trying to give you some idea of the scene and the political and social climate which led such people as Dr. Page and my parents from the southeastern part of the country to make a life out in the Old Territory. Geography is fate, and in moving west they were repeating a pattern begun by runaway slaves and by the Negroes who accompanied the Indian tribes along the death march which took so many lives that it became known as "The Trail of Tears," a march initiated by Andrew Jackson in fulfillment of the treaty of Dancing Rabbit.

Thus it was that Dr. Page first became a representative figure in the Territory and later in the new state, where we were very much aware that he was a graduate of Brown. It is understandable that this university occupies a warm place in our hearts, since we felt a tie to you through our principal. So it was that certain ideals which Dr. Page gained here, and certain testings of his manhood and faith which were affirmed here became a part of my own heritage as an Oklahoman. This came about through his role as educator, but there was a more important link between us, and this had to do with my introduction to the arts, and ultimately with my becoming a writer.

Dr. and Mrs. Page were the parents of a wonderful daughter whose name was Zelia N. Breaux, and her impact upon our community was in some ways as profound as that of her father. We are now in the area of culture where we may see how the generation which came between Dr. Page's and my own functioned in structuring the cultural life of the then wild territory of Oklahoma—and I assure you that it was wild! Yes, but wild mainly in the sense of its being a relatively unformed frontier state. I have stressed that in this country geography has performed the role of fate, but it is important to remember that it is not geography alone which determines the quality of life and culture. These depend upon the courage and personal culture of the individuals who make their homes in any given locality.

In *The Oregon Trail*, Francis Parkman writes of his surprise at coming upon a snug little cottage, far on the other side of the great prairie, wherein he discovered vintage French wines and the latest French novels. Well, those cultural artifacts didn't get there by magic; they were transported there to supply the cultural tastes of the cottage's owner. Thus they formed a cultural synthesis between the culture of France and that of the prairie. But of course such apparently incongruous juxtapositions are a norm on the frontiers of American society. Today most of the geographical frontier is gone, but the process of cultural integration continues along the lines that mark the hierarchal divisions of the United States.

Be that as it may, Mrs. Breaux was a musician and a teacher of music. By the time I entered the primary grades she was supervisor of music for Oklahoma City's Negro schools, and the connection between Mrs. Breaux and my presence here began in a second-grade classroom. At the time we were dancing and singing to a little nursery tune which went, "Oh, busy squirrel with bushy tail and shiny eyes so round / Why do you gather all the nuts that fall upon the ground." There were quite a number of us hopping about, but she must have been struck by the way this particular little nut was doing his squirrel act, because she gathered me up for special attention. So began one of the most important relationships in my life. For more than ten years Mrs. Breaux was a sort of second mother. Naturally, I had my own mother and I loved her very much, but between us there arose the usual conflicts which affect the relationships between parent and child, and when this happened Mrs. Breaux was always there to be turned to. Better still, she was an agent of music, which soon became the main focus of my attempts to achieve my own identity.

This was during the 1920s, the period in which what was known as the Public School Music Program was sweeping the nation. Mrs. Breaux was a leader in this movement which did so much to broaden and enrich the nation's musical culture. She did so by teaching musical theory and by training what became famous marching bands. She organized school orchestras and choral groups, she staged and directed operettas, and she was responsible for the high quality of our music-appreciation program. Thanks to her, ours became a music-centered culture which involved as many of the other arts as was possible in a system that was limited in budget and facilities. On May Day children from all of the Negro schools were assembled on the playing field of the old Western League baseball stadium, the girls in their white dresses and the boys in blue serge knickers and white shirts, and there, to the music of the Douglass High School Band, we competed in wrapping dozens of maypoles and engaged in mass dancing of a variety of European folk dances. As was to be expected, there were those who found the sight of young Negroes dancing European folk dances absurd, if not comic, but their prejudiced eyes missed the point of this exercise in democratic education. In learning such dances, we were gaining an appreciation of the backgrounds and cultures of our fellow Americans whose backgrounds lay in Europe. Not only did it narrow the psychological distance between them and ourselves, but we saw learning their dances as an *artistic* challenge. While there were those who thought that we were stepping out of the role assigned Negroes and were expressing a desire to become white, we ignored them. For we knew that dancing such dances would no more alter our racial identity or social status than would our singing of Bach chorales. Our interest lay in competing to master the steps, and our reward came in the form of a painless absorption of information which we might otherwise have found uninteresting. Thanks to Mrs. Breaux, we were being introduced to one of the most precious of American freedoms, which is our freedom to broaden our personal culture by absorbing the cultures of others. Even more important was the fact that we were being taught to discover and exercise those elements of freedom which existed unobserved (at least by outsiders), within our state of social and political unfreedom. This gift, this important bit of equipment for living, came through the efforts of a woman educator who by acting as agent of the broader American culture was able to widen our sense of possibility and raise our aspirations.

Nor was this all, for while I was to become a writer instead of a musician, it was Mrs. Breaux who introduced me to the basic discipline required of the artist. It was she who made it possible for me to grasp the basic compatibility of the mixture of the classical and vernacular styles which were part of our musical culture. She was one of the owners of what for many years was the only Negro theater in Oklahoma City, and it was here that she made valuable contributions to the popular arts. While she discouraged her students from playing jazz, she also saw to it that our community was provided the best of Negro entertainers. In her Aldridge Theater one could see and hear the great blues singers, dancers and comedians, the famous jazz orchestras and such repertory drama groups as the Lafayette Players. In other words, just as she taught Negro spirituals along with Bach and Handel, she provided a cultural nexus in which the vernacular art forms could be encountered along with the classical. Just as her father transmitted the ideals which he had gained at Brown University across the color line and down the annals of our unwritten history, so did his daughter bring together and make possible an interaction of art forms, styles and traditions. Interesting enough, it wasn't until years later that I learned how unusual this was, or the extent to which it cleared away the insidious confusion between race and culture which haunts this society.

Today we hear much discussion of what is termed "Black English," a concept unheard of during my school days. Yet we were all the grandchildren of slaves, and most of us spoke in the idioms that were native to the regions from which our families had migrated. Still, no one, much less our teachers, suggested that standard American English was beyond us; how could they, with such examples as Dr. Page before us? He could make the language of Shakespeare and the King James version of the Bible resound within us in such ways that its majesty and beauty seemed as natural and as normal coming from one of our own as an inspired jazz improvisation or an eloquently sung spiritual. By daily examples he made us aware that great poetry and fluent English were a part of our heritage; thus we developed an ear for a variety of linguistic idioms. And with so many other masters of America's nineteenth-century oratorical style—many of them preachers—living among us, we had no difficulty in grasping how elevated styles of speech related to the spoken vernacular. For example, as a boy I heard the debate team of Wiley College, which was coached by the late Afro-American poet Melvin Tolson, defeat the team of England's Oxford University, who did not disdain to debate with Negroes. Tolson's team was made up of young men whose backgrounds were similar to our own, and they appeared to have no difficulty in mastering the King's English.

No, being of a people whose backgrounds were in slavery, we were taught that it was necessary to acquire the skills needed for communicating in a mixed society, and we knew from experience that this required a melting and blending of vernacular and standard speech and a grasp of the occasions in which each, or both, were called for. Hence instead of clinging defensively to our native idiom, we sought consciously to extend its range. Actually, language was our most easily available toy, and we played with its capacity to create the unexpected and to blunt its capacity to surprise. The ever-present conflict of American linguistic styles was a source of comedy which sharpened our eye for the incongruous—a matter encouraged both by our condition as boys and as members of a group whose social situation was most ambiguous. Verbal comedy was a way of confronting social ambiguity. Being familiar with racial violence— we were living in the aftermath of the race riots that followed World War I, remember—we learned quite early that laughter made the difficulties of our condition a bit more bearable. We hadn't read Henry James at that time, but we realized nevertheless that American society contained a built-in joke, and we were aware, even if James wasn't (or did not choose to admit), that this joke was in many ways centered in our condition. So we welcomed any play on words or nuance of gesture which gave expression to our secret sense of the way things really were. Usually this took the comic mode, and it is quite possible that one reason the popular arts take on an added dimension in our democracy lies in an unspoken, though no less binding, agreement that popular culture is not to be taken seriously. Thus the popular arts have become an agency through which Americans can contemplate those aspects of our experience that are deemed unspeakable.

Perhaps that is why it was left to such comedians as Redd Foxx to notify us that since the 1950s a major change has occurred in our attitudes toward racial minorities. Thus when he, a black comedian, makes remarks about ugly white women which once were reserved only for black women, he allows us to bring attitudes and emotions that were once tabooed into the realm of the rational, where, protected by the comic mode, we may confront our guilt and prejudices and perhaps resolve them.

Today I have heard some interesting discussions of the American vernacular style in literature, and found them most informative. It seems to me that our most characteristic American style *is* that of the vernacular. But by "vernacular" I mean far more than popular or indigenous language. I see the vernacular as a dynamic *process* in which the most refined styles from the past are continually merged with the play-it-by-eye-and-by-ear improvisations which we invent in our efforts to control our environment and entertain ourselves. This is not only in language and literature, but in architecture and cuisine, in music, costume, dance, tools and technology. In it the styles and techniques of the past are adjusted to the needs of the present, and in its integrative action the high styles of the past are democratized. From this perspective the vernacular is, no less than the styles associated with aristocracy, a gesture toward perfection.

Which is to suggest that although the perfection toward which it moves is democratic rather than aristocratic, there is no necessary contradiction between our vernacular style and the pursuit of excellence. After all, "democracy" is our term for social perfection (or a perfect society), while "excellence" is a general term for perfect quality. And while the vernacular is shy of abstract standards, it still seeks perfection in the form of functional felicity. That is why considerations of function and performance figure so prominently in the scale of vernacular aesthetics. Perfection is arrived at through a process of refinement, elimination and integration in which form and function become aesthetically one.

Today there is much discussion of a supposedly unresolvable conflict between elitist and populist values. But this assumes that the vernacular process destroys the so-called elitist styles, when in truth past standards of excellence remain to be used again and again, and indeed often undergo metamorphosis as they contribute to the needs of the present. In a sense jazz, which is an amalgam of past musical styles, may be seen as a rejection of a music which expressed the values of a social elite, but although jazz musicians are practitioners of a vernacular style, they are also unreconstructed elitists when it comes to maintaining the highest standards of the music which expresses their sense of the American experience. So was Mark Twain, who transformed elements of regional vernacular speech into a medium of uniquely American literary expression and thus taught us how to capture that which is essentially American in our folkways and manners. Indeed, the vernacular process is a way of establishing and discovering our national identity.

But wherever we find the vernacular process operating, we also find individuals who act as transmitters between it and earlier styles, tastes and techniques. In the United States all social barriers are vulnerable to cultural styles. Therefore Dr. Page and Mrs. Breaux—and there were many others, both white and black—worked to maintain high standards wherever they originated. They also tried to give their students a sense of the fact that as Americans, they too were heirs to the culture of all the ages. Their type of teaching was both an act of individual idealism and a fulfillment of their faith in democracy. It was also a great, if unrecognized, service to this nation; while preparing us for the next stage in our education, they were conditioning us to take advantage of such opportunities as the built-in logic of the democratic process would throw our way.

There was a time when a Negro singer of classical music was viewed as a mere exotic, so if you are surprised that there are now so many Afro-American opera and concert singers, I would remind you that it didn't happen accidentally. God didn't reach down and say, "All right, Leontyne Price, Shirley Verrett, Betty Allen, Jessye Norman, Simon Estes, you may now sing opera as well as your native Negro spirituals." No, this came about because there were agents of culture among us who embraced the ideals of art and found ways of imparting them to their students.

I am saying that within an area of our society which has been treated as though it were beyond the concerns of history, the democratic process has been made to operate by dedicated individuals—at least on the level of culture—and that it has thus helped to define and shape the quality of the general American experience. Which is something that those who were charged with making our ideals manifest on the political level were not doing. But fortunately, American culture is of a whole, for that which is essentially "American" in it springs from the synthesis of our diverse elements of cultural style. It is the product of a process which was in motion even before the founding of this nation, and it began with the interaction between Englishmen, Europeans, and Africans and American geography. When our society was established, this "natural" process of Americanization continued in its own unobserved fashion, defying the social, aesthetic and political assumptions of our political leaders and tastemakers alike. This, as I say, was the vernacular process, and in the days when our leaders still looked to England and the Continent for their standards of taste, the vernacular stream of our culture was creating itself out of whatever elements it found useful, including the Americanized culture of the slaves. In this sense the culture of the United States has always been more "democratic" and "American" than the social and political institutions in which it was emerging. Ironically, it was the vernacular which gave expression to that very newness of spirit and outlook of which the leaders of the nation liked to boast. Such Founding Fathers as Franklin and Webster feared the linguistic vernacular as a disruptive influence and sought to discourage it, but fortunately they failed, for otherwise there would have been no Mark Twain.

They failed because thanks to the pluralistic character of our society, there is no way for any one group to discover by itself the intrinsic forms of our democratic culture. This has to be a cooperative effort, and it is achieved through contact and communication across our divisions of race, class, religion and region. In the past the cultural contributions of those who were confined beneath the threshold of social hierarchy—which is to say outside the realm of history—were simply appropriated without credit by those who used them to their own advantage. But today we have reached a stage of general freedom in which it is no longer possible to take the products of a slave or an illiterate artist without legal consequence. Today the vernacular artist knows his own value, and thanks to our increased knowledge of our cultural pluralism, such artists are identified less by their race or social status than by the excellence of their art. Our awareness of what we are culturally is still inadequate, but the process of synthesis through which the slaves took the music and religious lore of others and combined them with their African heritage in such ways as to create their own cultural idiom continues. Through the democratizing action of the vernacular, almost any style of expression may be appropriated, and today such appropriation continues at an accelerating pace. I must confess, however, that I find some of its products incongruous, if not unexpected. As when I hear a group of middle-class white kids doing their best to sound like members of an old-fashioned black Baptist congregation. They would probably find the churches in which such sounds are a form of religious exaltation bizarre, but I recognize that by appropriating the style—and profaning it, as it were—they are simply trying to attain some vague ideal of perfection. In this country it is in the nature of cultural styles to become detached from their places of origin, so it is possible that in their frenzy the kids don't even realize that they are sounding like black Baptists. As Americans who are influenced by the vernacular, it is natural for them to seek out those styles which provide them with a feeling of being most in harmony with the undefined aspects of American experience. In other words, they're seeking the homeness of home.

In closing, let me say that our pluralistic democracy is a difficult system under which to live, our guarantees of freedom notwithstanding. Socially and politically we have yet to feel at ease with our principles, and on the level of culture no one group has managed to create the definitive American style. Hence the importance of the vernacular in the ongoing task of naming, defining and creating a consciousness of who and what we have come to be. Each American group has dominated some aspect of our corporate experience by reducing it to form; thus we might well make a conscious effort to seek out and explore such instances of domination and make them our conscious possession. I say "conscious" because in pursuing our democratic promises, we do this even when we are unaware. What is more, our unwritten history is always at work in the background to provide us with clues as to how this process of self-definition has worked in the past. Perhaps if we learn more of what has happened and *why* it happened, we will learn more of who we really are, and perhaps if we learn more about our unwritten history, we won't be so vulnerable to the capriciousness of events as we are today. In the process of becoming more aware of ourselves we will recognize that one of the functions of our vernacular culture is that of preparing for the emergence of the unexpected, whether it takes the form of the disastrous or the marvelous. Such individuals as Dr. Page and his daughter worked, it seems to me, to such an end. Ultimately theirs was an act of faith: faith in themselves, faith in the potentialities of their own people, and despite their social status as Negroes, faith in the potentialities of the democratic ideal. Coming so soon after the betrayal of the Reconstruction, theirs was a heroic effort. It is my good fortune that their heroism became my heritage, and thanks to Inman Page and Brown University it is also now a part of the heritage of all Americans who would become conscious of who they are.

An Extravagance of Laughter

In December 1983 the good news that Erskine Caldwell had reached his eightieth birthday reminded me that although I have had the pleasure of seeing him on and off for some twenty years, I have never been able to offer him an apology for an offense of which I was guilty back in the 1930s. Perhaps I failed because my offense took the form of laughter—or, to be more precise, of a particular quality and an *extravagance* of laughter, which, since it came at the expense of Caldwell's most famous work of comedy, may explain both my confusion and my reluctance. Since the work in question was *designed* and intended to evoke laughter, any account of why I should term my particular laughter "offensive" will require a bit of autobiographical exploration which may well enable me both to understand my failure to apologize and to clarify the role which that troublesome moment of laughter was to play in my emotional and intellectual development.

Charles Baudelaire observed, "The wise man never laughs but that he trembles." Therefore, for the moment let it suffice to say that being both far from wise and totally unaware of Baudelaire's warning, I not only laughed extravagantly but trembled even *as* I laughed, and thus I found myself utterly unprepared for the Caldwell-inspired wisdom which erupted from that incongruous juxtaposition of mirth and quaking. This is no excuse, however, because Aesop and Uncle Remus have taught us that comedy is a disguised form of philosophical instruction, and especially when it allows us to glimpse the animal instincts operating beneath the surface of our civilized affectations. For by allowing us to laugh at that which is normally *un*laughable, comedy provides an otherwise unavailable clarification of vision that calms the clammy trembling which ensues whenever

Written in 1985, especially for first publication of *Going to the Territory*.

we pierce the veil of conventions that guard us from the basic absurdity of the human condition. During such moments the world of appearances is turned upside down, and in my case Caldwell's comedy plunged me quite unexpectedly into the deepest levels of a most American realm of the absurd while providing me with the magical wings with which to ascend back to a world which, for all his having knocked it quite out of kilter, I then found more rational. Caldwell had no way of knowing what I was experiencing, but even though I caused unforeseen trouble, he was a wise and skillful guide, and thus it is that I offer him both my apologies and, for reasons to be made clear a bit later, my heartfelt thanks.

It all began in 1936, a few weeks after my arrival in New York, when I was lucky enough to be invited by an old hero and new-found friend, Langston Hughes, to be his guest at what would be my introduction to Broadway theater. I was so delighted and grateful for the invitation that I failed to ask my host the title of the play, and it was not until we arrived at the theater that I learned that it would be Jack Kirkland's dramatization of Erskine Caldwell's famous novel *Tobacco Road*. No less successful than in its original form, the play was well on its way to a record-breaking seven-year run in the theater, and that alone was enough to increase my expectations. So much so that I failed to note the irony of circumstance that would have as my introduction to New York theater a play with a Southern setting and characters that were based upon a type and class of whites whom I had spent the last three years trying to avoid. Had I been more alert, it might have occurred to me that somehow a group of white Alabama farm folk had learned of my presence in New York, thrown together a theatrical troupe, and flown north to haunt me. But being dazzled by the lights, the theatrical atmosphere, the babble of the playgoing crowd, it didn't. Yet that irony arose precisely from the mixture of motives—practical, educational, and romantic—that had brought me to the North in the first place.

Among these was my desire to enjoy a summer free of the South and its problems while meeting the challenge of being on my own for the first time in a great Northern city. Fresh out of Alabama, with my junior year at Tuskegee Institute behind me, I was also in New York seeking funds with which to complete my final year as a music major—a goal at which I was having less success than I had hoped. However, there had been compensations. Between working in the Harlem YMCA cafeteria as a substitute for vacationing waiters and countermen and searching for a more profitable job, I had used my free time exploring the city's many cultural possibilities, making new acquaintances, and enjoying the many forms of social freedom that were unavailable to me in Alabama. The very idea of being in New York was dreamlike, for like many young Negroes of the time, I thought of it as the freest of American cities, and considered Harlem as the site and symbol of Afro-American progress and hope. Indeed, I was both young and bookish enough to think of Manhattan as my substitute for Paris, and of Harlem as a place of Left Bank excitement. So now that I was there in its glamorous scene, I meant to make the most of its opportunities.

Yes, but I had discovered, much to my chagrin, that while I was physically out of the South, I was restrained—sometimes consciously, sometimes not—by certain internalized thou-shalt-nots that had structured my public conduct in Alabama. It was as though I had come to the Eden of American culture and found myself indecisive about which of its fruits were free for my picking. Thus, for all my bright expectations, my explorations had taken on certain aspects of an unanticipated and amorphous rite of initiation in which the celebrant—if indeed one existed—remained mute and beyond my range of ear and vision. Therefore I found myself forced to act as my own guide and instructor, and had to enact, touch-and-go, the archetypical American role of pioneer in what was our most sophisticated and densely populated city. In the process I found myself being compelled, as it were, to improvise a makeshift map of the city's racially determined do's-and-don'ts, and impose it upon the objective scene by dealing consciously with such complications of character and custom as might materialize in the course of my explorations.

I missed, in brief, a sense of certainty which the South imposed in the forms of signs and symbols that marked the dividing lines of racial segregation. This was an embarrassing discovery, so given what I assumed would be the shortness of my visit, I tried to deal with it and remained eager to take the risks necessary to achieve New York's promises. After certain disappointments, however, I had been going about it in the manner of one learning to walk again upon a recently mended leg that still felt strange without the protective restraint of a plaster cast now left happily behind. So there were moments when I reminded myself of the hero of the old Negro folktale who, after arriving mistakenly in heaven and being issued a pair of wings, was surprised to learn that there were certain earth-like restrictions which required people of his complexion to fly with one wing strapped to their sides. But while surprised, the new arrival came to the philosophical conclusion that even in heaven, that place of unearthly perfection, there had to be rules and regulations. And since rules were usually intended to make one think, no less than to provide guidance, he decided to forgo complaint and get on with the task of mastering the challenge of one-wing flying. As a result, he soon became so proficient at the art that by the time he was cast out of heaven for violating its traffic regulations, he could declare (and so truthfully that not even Saint Peter could say him nay) that he was the most skillful one-winged flyer ever to have been grounded by heavenly decision.

So, following the example of my legendary ancestor, I determined to master my own equivalent of one-winged flying in such a manner as to do the least violence to myself or to such arcane rules of New York's racial arrangements that I might encounter. Which meant that I would have to mask myself and confront its mysteries with a combination of uncertainty and daring. Thus it was that by the time I stumbled onto *Tobacco Road*, I had been nibbling steadily at the "Big Apple" (which even in those days was the Harlemite's fond name for the city), and in the process had discovered more than an ambiguous worm or two. Nevertheless it should be remembered that worms teach small earthly truths even as serpents teach theology.

Beyond the borders of Harlem's brier patch—which seemed familiar because of my racial and cultural identification with the majority of its people and the lingering spell that had been cast nationwide by the music, dance and literature of the so-called Harlem Renaissance—I viewed New Yorkers through the overlay of my Alabama experience. Contrasting the whites I encountered with those I had observed in the South, I weighed class against class and compared Southern styles with their Northern counterparts. I listened to diction and noted dress, and searched for attitudes in inflections, carriage and manners.

In pursuing this aspect of my extracurricular education, I explored the landscape. I crossed Manhattan back and forth from river to river and up, down and around again, from Spuyten Duyvil Creek to the Battery, looking, listening and gadding about, rode streetcar, el, subway and bus, took a hint from Edna Millay and spent an evening riding back and forth on the Staten Island Ferry. For given my Oklahoma-Alabama perspective, even New York's forms of transportation were unexpected sources of education. From the elevated trains I saw my first penthouses with green trees growing atop tall buildings, caught remote glimpses of homes, businesses and factories while moving above the teeming streets, and felt a sense of quiet tranquillity despite the bang and clatter.

Yes, but the subways were something else again. In fact, the subways were utterly confusing to my Southern-bred idea of good manners, and especially the absence of a certain gallantry that men were expected to extend toward women. Subway cars appeared to be underground arenas in which Northern social equality took the form of an endless shoving match in which the usual rules of etiquette were turned upside down—or so I concluded after watching a five-o'clock foot race in a crowded car.

The contest was between a huge white woman who carried an

armful of bundles, and a small Negro man who lugged a large suitcase. At the time I was standing against the track-side door, and
when the train stopped at a downtown station I saw the two come
charging through the opening doors like race horses leaving the
starting gate at Belmont. As they spied and dashed for the single
empty seat, the outcome appeared up for grabs, but it was the
woman, thanks to a bustling, more ruthless stride (and more subway
know-how) who won—though only by a hip and a hair. Just as they
reached the seat she swung a well-padded hip and knocked the man
off stride, thus causing him to lose his balance as she turned, slipped
beneath his reeling body, and plopped into the seat. It was a maneuver which produced a startling effect, at least on me, for as she
banged into the seat it caused the man to spin and land smack-dab in
her lap—in which massive and heaving center of gravity he froze,
stared into her face nose tip to nose, and then performed a springlike
leap to his feet as from a red-hot stove. It was but the briefest conjunction, and then, as he reached down and fumbled for his suitcase,
the woman began adjusting her bundles, and with an elegant toss of
her head looked up into his face with the most ladylike and triumphant of smiles.

I had no idea of what to expect next, but to her sign of good
sportswomanship the man let out an exasperated "Hell, you can have
it, I don't want it!" A response which evoked a phrase from an old
forgotten ditty to which my startled mind added the unstated line—
"Sleeping in the bed with your hand right on it"—and shook me
with visions of the train screeching to a stop and a race riot beginning.

But not at all. While the defeated man pushed his way to another
part of the car the crowd of passengers simply looked on and
laughed. The interracial aspects of the incident, with its evocation of
the naughty lyric, left me shaken, but I was learning something of
the truth of what Henry James meant by the arduousness of being an
American. This went double for a Tuskegee student who was trying
to adjust to the New York underground. I never knew what to ex-

pect, because there appeared to be no agreed-upon rules of conduct. Indeed, in the subways the operating slogan appeared to be "Every Man and Woman for Themselves." Or perhaps it was "Hurray for Me and Phoo-phoo on You!" But *whatever* its operating principle, whenever I rode the subway trains something I had never seen before seemed fated to happen.

As during a trip in another crowded car when I found myself standing beside a Negro man who stood just in front of a seat that was about to be vacated—when suddenly from his other side a woman decided to challenge him for its possession. This time, however, it was the man who won, for in a flash he folded his arms, dropped into the posture of a Cossack dancer, and was in the seat before the woman could make her move. Then, as she grabbed a handhold and glared down into his face, he restored something of my sense of reality by saying, "Madam, all you had to do was risk the slight possibility that I just *might* be a gentleman. Because if you had, I would have been *compelled* to step aside." Then, opening a copy of *The Wall Street Journal*, he proceeded to read.

But for all their noise and tension, it was not the subways that most intrigued me. Although a pleasant way to explore the city, my rides in New York buses soon aroused questions about matters that I had hoped to leave behind. Yet the very fact that I encountered little on Northern buses that was distressing allowed me to face up to a problem which had puzzled me down South: the relationship between Southern buses and racial status. In the South you occupied the back of the bus, and nowhere *but* the back, or so help you God. So being in the North and encouraged by my anonymity, I experimented by riding all *over* New York buses, excluding only the driver's seat— front end, back end, right side, left side, sitting or standing as the route and flow of passengers demanded. *And*, since those were the glorious days of double-deckers, both enclosed and open, I even rode *top*side.

Thus having convinced myself that no questions of racial status would be raised by where I chose to ride, I asked myself whether a seat in the back of the bus wasn't actually more desirable than one in the front. Not only did it provide more legroom, but it offered a more inclusive perspective on both the interior and exterior scenes. I found the answer obvious and quite amusing, but then, as though to raise to consciousness more serious questions that I had too long ignored, the buses forced a more troubling contradiction upon my attention. Now that I was no longer forced by law and compelled by custom to ride in the back and to surrender my seat to any white who demanded it, what was more desirable: the possibility of exercising what was routinely accepted in the North as an abstract, highly symbolic (even trivial) form of democratic freedom, or the creature comfort which was to be had by occupying a spot from which more of the passing scene could be observed? In my own personal terms, what was more important, my own individual comfort, or the exercise of the democratic right to be squeezed and jostled by strangers? The highly questionable privilege of being touched by anonymous whites—not to mention reds, browns, blacks, and yellows—or the minor pleasure afforded by having a maximum of breathing space? Such questions were akin to that of whether you lived in a Negro neighborhood because you were forced to do so, or because you preferred living among those of your own background. Which was easy to answer, because having experienced life in mixed neighborhoods as a child, I preferred to live where people spoke my own version of the American language, and where misreadings of tone or gesture were less likely to ignite lethal conflict. Segregation laws aside, this was a matter of personal choice, for even though class and cultural differences existed among Negroes, it was far easier to deal with hostilities arising between yourself and your own people than with, say, Jeeter Lester or, more realistically, Lester Maddox. And this even though I would have found it far better to be Lestered by Jeeter than mattock-handled by Maddox, that most improbable governor of a state that I had often visited!

But my interrogation by the New York scene (for that is what it had become) was not to stop there, for once my mind got rolling on buses, it was difficult to stop and get off. So I became preoccupied with defining the difference between Northern and Southern buses. Of the two, New York buses were simpler, if only for being earth-bound. They were merely a form of transportation, an inflated version of a taxicab or passenger car which one took to get from one locality to another. As far as one's destination and motives were concerned, they were neutral. But this was far from true of Southern buses; when compared with its New York counterparts, even the most dilapidated of Southern buses seemed (from my New York perspective) to be a haunted form of transportation.

A Southern bus was a contraption contrived by laying the South's social pyramid on its side, knocking out a few strategic holes, and rendering it vehicular through the addition of engine, windows and wheels. Thus converted, with the sharp apex of the pyramid blunted and equipped with fare box and steering gear, and its sprawling base curtailed severely and narrowly aligned (and arrayed with jim crow signs), a ride in such a vehicle became, at least for Negroes, as unpredictable as a trip in a spaceship doomed to be caught in the time warp of history, that man-made "fourth dimension" which always confounds our American grasp of "real" or *actual* time or duration.

For blacks and whites alike, Southern buses were places of hallucination, but especially for Negroes, because once inside, their journey ended even before the engine fired and the wheels got rolling. Then, as with a "painted ship upon a painted ocean," the engine chugged, the tires scuffed, and the scenery outside flashed and flickered, but they themselves remained, like Zeno's arrow, forever in the same old place. Thus the motorized mobility of the social pyramid did little to advance the Negroes' effort toward equality. Although they were allowed to enter the section that had been (in its vertical configuration) its top, any semblance of upward mobility ended at the fare box—from whence, once their fares were deposited, they were sent forthwith straight to the rear, or horizontalized bottom. Along the way almost anything could happen, from push to shove, assaults on hats, heads or aching corns, to unprovoked tongue-lashings from the driver or from any white passenger, drunk or sober, who took exception to their looks, attitude or mere existence. Nor did the perils of this haunted, gauntletlike passage end at the back of the bus. Often it was so crowded that there was little breathing space, and since the segregated passengers were culturally as "Southern" as the whites, the newcomer might well encounter a few contentious Negroes who would join in the assault—if only because he appeared uneasy in his command of the life-preserving "cool" which protected not only the individual Negro but each member of the group in his defenseless, nonindividualized status. In brief, all were faceless nobodies caught up in an endless trip to nowhere—or so it seemed to me in my Northern sanctuary.

For even as the phantomized bus went lurching and fuming along its treadmill of a trajectory, the struggle within scuffled and raged in fitful retrograde. Thus, as it moved without moving, those trapped inside played out their roles like figures in dreams, with one group ever forcing the other to the backmost part, and the other ever watching and waiting as they bowed to force and clung to sanity. Indeed, the time would come when such bus en-scened pantomime would erupt in a sound and fury of action that would engulf the South and change American society. Most surprising and yet most fittingly, it would begin when a single tired Negro woman refused to go on with what had now become an unbearable farce. Then would come fire and gunshot, cattle prods and attack dogs, but the enchantment would end, and at last the haunted bus would shift gears and move on to the road of reality and toward the future.

But of this I had no way of knowing at the time. I only knew that Southern bus rides had the power to haunt and confuse my New York passage. Moreover, they were raising an even more troublesome question: to what extent had I failed to grasp a certain degree of freedom that had always existed in my group's state of unfreedom? Of what had I neglected to avail myself through fear or lack of interest while sitting silently behind jim crow signs? After all, a broad freedom of expression within restrictions could be heard in jazz and seen in sports, and this freedom was made movingly manifest in religious worship. There was an Afro-American dimension in Southern culture, and the lives of many black Southerners possessed a certain verve and self-possessed fullness, so to what extent had I overlooked similar opportunities for self-discovery while accepting a definition of possibility laid down by those who would deny me freedom?

Thus, while I enjoyed my summer, such New York–provoked questions made for a certain unease which I tried to ignore. Nevertheless they made me aware that whatever its true shape turned out to be, Northern freedom could be grasped only by my running the risk of the unknown and by acting in the face of uncertainty. Which meant that I would have to keep moving into racially uncharted areas. Otherwise I would remain physically in Harlem and psychologically in Alabama—neither of which was acceptable. Harlem was "Harlem," a dream place of glamour and excitement—what with its music, its dance, its style. But it was all of this because it was a part of (and apart *from*) the larger city. Harlem, I came to feel, was the shining transcendence of a national negative, and it took its fullest meaning from that which it was not, and without which I would have regarded it as less interesting than, say, Kansas City, Missouri or South Side Chicago. Harlem, whose ironic inhabitants described it a thousand times a day as being "nowhere," took much of its meaning from the larger metropolis, so I could only achieve the fullest measure of its attractions by experiencing that which it was not. Which meant, in the broadest sense, that I would have to use Harlem as a base and standard of measurement from which to pursue, in all its plenitude, that which was denied me in the South. In brief, if I were to grasp American freedom, I was compelled to continue my explorations of downtown Manhattan.

Yes, but as I say, my explorations of the city were rendered uncertain by the ongoing conflict between the past and the present as they existed within me: between the dream in my head and the murky, seek-

and-find-it shiftings of the New York scene; between the confounding complexity of America's racial arrangements as they coincided
and differed according to the customs, laws, and values fostered by
both North and South. I still clung to the Southern Negro's conception of New York as the freest of American cities, but although now
far removed from the geographical region where old-time things are
defiantly not forgotten, I was learning that even here, where memories of the past were deliberately repressed, if not forgotten, the past
itself continued to shape perceptions and attitudes. It appeared that
for some New Yorkers, I *myself* constituted a living symbol of that
complexity of American experience which they had never known,
and a disquieting reminder of their involvement in certain unsavory
aspects of America's social reality that they preferred to ignore.

Yet given my persistent questioning, how could they? For I, who
was an unwilling and not always conscious embodiment of that historical complexity, and a symbol of the Civil War's sacrificial bloodshed, kept showing up in areas of culture where few of my people
were to be seen. Thus in my dark singularity I often appeared to be
perceived more as a symbol than as an individual, more as a threatening sign (a dark cloud no larger than a human hand, but somehow
threatening) than as a disinterested seeker after culture. This made
for problems because I had no way of anticipating the response to my
presence.

Prior to stumbling onto *Tobacco Road* (at which I shall presently
arrive), I had already encountered some of the complexity evoked by
my probings. As the guest of a white female friend who reported
musical events for a magazine, I had occupied a seat in the orchestra
section of Carnegie Hall without inciting protest. But shortly thereafter I had been denied admission to a West Side cinema house that
featured European movies. Then I had learned that while one mid-
town restaurant would make you welcome, in another (located in
Greenwich Village, Harlem's twin symbol of Manhattan's freedom),
the waiters would go through the polite motions of seating you but
then fill your food with salt. Then, to make certain that you got the
message, they would enact a rite of exorcism in which the glasses and

crockery, now considered hopelessly contaminated by your touch, were enfolded in the tablecloth and smithereened in the fireplace.

Or again, upon arriving at a Central Park West apartment building to deliver a music manuscript for the Tuskegee composer William L. Dawson, you encountered a doorman with a European accent who was so rude that you were tempted to break his nose. Fortunately you didn't, for after you refused to use the servant's elevator he rang up the tenant into whose hands alone you were instructed to make the delivery, Jacques Gordon of the Gordon String Quartet, who hurried down and invited you up to his apartment. Where, to your surprise and delight, he talked with you without condescension about his recordings, questioned you sympathetically about your musical background, and encouraged you in your ambitions to become a composer. So if you weren't always welcome to break bread in public places, an interest in the arts *could* break down social distance and allow for communication that was uninhibited by questions of race—or so it seemed.

As on a Madison Avenue bus when an enthusiastic, bright-eyed little old Jewish lady, fresh from an art exhibition with color catalogue in hand, would engage you in conversation and describe knowingly the styles and intentions of French painters of whom you'd never heard.

"Then you must go to galleries," she insisted.

"Stir yourself and go to museums," she demanded.

"This is one of the world's great centers of art, so learn about them! Why are you waiting? Enough already!" she exhorted.

And eventually, God bless her, I did.

But then, on another bus ride, a beautifully groomed and expensively dressed woman would become offended when I retrieved and attempted to return the section of a newspaper that she had dropped when preparing to depart, apparently mistaking what was intended as an act of politeness for a reprimand from a social inferior. Hence it appeared that in New York one had to choose the time, place and person even when exercising one's Southern good manners.

On the other hand, it soon became clear that one could learn the subtleties of New York's racial manners only by being vulnerable and undiscriminating oneself, an attitude which the vast anonymity of the great metropolis encouraged. Here the claustrophobic provincialism which marked, say, Montgomery, Alabama, of that period, was absent, but one had to be on guard because reminders of the South could spring up from behind the most unlikely façades.

Shopping for a work of T. S. Eliot's in a 59th Street bookstore, I struck up a conversation with a young City College student who turned out to share my literary interests, and in recounting an incident of minor embarrassment having to do with my misinterpretation of a poetic trope, I used the old cliché "And was my face red"—whereupon, between the utterance and the reality, the idea I intended to convey and my stereotype phrase, there fell the shadow of things I sought to forget.

"What do you mean by 'red'?" he said, impaling me upon the points of his smirking stare. "What you *really* mean is 'ashes of roses'!"

Suddenly I was slapped into a conscious awareness of certain details of his presence that my eyes had registered, but to which, in the context of our exchange, my brain had attached no special significance. Intent upon sharing his ideas of Eliot, I had seen only that which I wished to see, but now, out of the eyes of my past, I saw that our differences of background and religion were imprinted upon his face no less indelibly than mine upon my own. To my Southern-trained ear the echo of his trace of accent became amplified, the slight kink in his hair sprang into focus, and his nose evoked superimposed images of the Holy Land and Cyrano.

I didn't like it, but there it was—I had been hit in midflight—so, brought down to earth, I joined in his laughter. But while he laughed in bright major chords I responded darkly in minor-sevenths and flatted-fifths, and I doubted that he was attuned to the deeper source of our inharmonic harmony. How could he know that when a child in Oklahoma, I had played with members of his far-flung tribe and thus learned in friendly games of mutual insult the hoary formulae with which to make him squirm? But why bother? Out of some obscure need a stranger had chosen to define to his own advantage that which was at best a fleeting relationship, perhaps because I had left an opening that was irresistible. Or perhaps he saw my interest in poetry as an invasion of his special turf, which had to be repelled with a reminder of my racial status. What right had *I* to be interested in Eliot, even though the great poet had written of himself as having been "a small boy with a nigger drawl"?

Or was he implying that I was trying verbally to pass for white? If so, wasn't that to confuse words with reality, and a metaphor with the thing or condition it named? Didn't he realize that there might be as much of irony in one of his background embracing Eliot as he seemed to find in my doing so? And how take poetry seriously if he himself would limit the range of metaphor, that indispensable linguistic device for making unities of diversities?

This chance encounter left me a bit disenchanted, but also consciously aware of certain vague assumptions which I held concerning racial relations that I would find in the North. I had hoped that in New York there would exist generally a type of understanding which obtained in the South between certain individual whites and Negroes. This was a type of Southern honor that did little to alter the general system of inequity, but it allowed individual whites to make exceptions in exerting the usual gestures of white supremacy. Such individuals refused to use racial epithets and tried, within the limitations of the system, to treat Negroes fairly. This was a saving grace and a balm to the aches and pains of the South's endless racial contention.

Thus I had assumed that in the North there would exist a general understanding between outsiders of whatever color or background, and that all would observe a truce or convention through which they would shun insults that focused on race, religion or physical appearance, entities that were inherited, and about which all were powerless to modify or change. (At that time I was unaware that there were whites who passed themselves off as being of other backgrounds.)

Yet I realized that except for those rare Southern examples, there was no firm base for my expectations. I knew from the days of the minstrel shows to the musicals and movies then current, that many non-Negro outsiders had reaped fame and fortune by assuming the stereotyped mask of blackness. I also knew that our forms of popular culture, from movies to comic strips, were a source of a national mythology in which Negroes were the chief scapegoats, and that the function of this mythology was to allow whites a more secure place (if only symbolically) in American society. Only years later would I learn that during periods of intense social unrest, even sensitive intellectuals who had themselves been victims of discrimination would find it irresistible to use their well-deserved elevation to the upper levels of their professions as platforms from which, in the name of the most abstract and fashionable philosophical ideas, to reduce Negroes to stereotypes that were no less reductive and demeaning than those employed by the most ignorant and bigoted white Southerners. Fortunately this knowledge was still in the future, and so, doing unto another as I would have had him do unto me, I dismissed my chance acquaintance as an insecure individual, and not the representative of a group or general attitude. But he did serve as a warning that if I wished to communicate with New Yorkers, I must watch my metaphors, for here one man's cliché was another man's facile opportunity for victimage.

So I was learning that exploring New York was a journey without a map, Baedeker or Henry James, and that how one was received by the natives depended more upon how one presented oneself than upon any ironclad rule of exclusion. Here the portals to many places of interest were guarded by hired help, and if you approached with uncertain mien, you were likely to be turned away by anyone from doormen to waiters to ticket agents. However, if you acted as though you were in fact a New Yorker exercising a routine freedom, chances were that you would be accepted. Which is to say that in many instances I found that my air and attitude could offset the inescapable fact of my color. It seemed that in the hustle and bustle of that most theatrical of American cities, one was accepted on the basis of what one *appeared* to be. This involved risks to one's self-esteem, not to mention the discipline demanded by a constant state of wariness.

But W. B. Yeats reminded us that "There is a relation between personal discipline and the theatrical sense, [and that] if we cannot imagine ourselves as different from what we are and assume the second self, we cannot impose a discipline upon ourselves, though we may accept one from others." He also advised us that "Active virtue, as distinct from the passive acceptance of a current code, is the wearing of a mask."

At the time I was unaware of Yeats's observation, but if I had been so fortunate, I would have applied it to my own situation by changing his "we" to "an Afro-American," his "what we are" to "what many whites assume an American Negro to be," and his "current code" to "prevailing racial attitudes." But with his contention that the assertion of a second self is to assume a mask, and that to do so is "the condition of an arduous full life," I would have agreed wholeheartedly. In effect, I was attempting to act out a self-elected role and to improvise into being a "second self" that I strongly felt but vaguely visualized. Although I was finding life far from full, I was certainly finding it arduous.

In Yeats's sense, "masking" is more than the adoption of a disguise. Rather it is a playing upon possibility, a strategy through which the individual projects a self-elected identity and makes of himself a "work of art." In my case it was a means of discovering the dimensions and cost of Northern freedom. In his critical biography *Yeats: The Man & the Masks*, Richard Ellman notes that the great Irish poet was writing about himself, but his theory nevertheless applies to the problematic nature of American identity. While all human societies are "dramatic"—at least to the extent that, as Kenneth Burke points out, the members of all societies "enact roles . . . change roles . . . participate . . . [and] develop modes of social appeal"—the semi-open structure of American society, with its many opportunities for individual self-transformation, intensifies the dramatic element by increasing the possibilities for both cooperation and conflict. It is a swiftly changing society in which traditional values are ever under attack, even as they are exploited by individuals and group alike. And with its upward—yes, and *downward*—mobility and its great geographical space, masking (which includes speech and costume as well as pose and posture) serves the individual as a means of projecting that aspect of his social self which seems useful in a given situation.

Such a state of affairs encourages hope and confidence in those who are not assigned and restricted to predesignated roles in the hierarchal drama of American society. Melville has great fun with the comic aspects of this situation in *The Confidence Man*. To an extent, and for an endless variety of motives—benign or malignant, competitive or cooperative, creative and/or destructive—the "American" is a self-confident man or woman who is engaged in projecting a second self and dealing with the second selves of others. The American creed of democratic equality encourages the belief in a second chance that is to be achieved by being born again—and not simply in the afterlife, but here and now, on earth. Change your name and increase your chances. Create by an act of immaculate self-conception an autobiography like that which transformed James Gatz into "Jay Gatsby." Alter the shape of your nose, tint of skin, or texture of hair. Change your sexual identity by dress or by surgery. "Get thee to boutique and barbershop and *Unisex* thyself," the ads exhort us, for anything is possible in pursuit of the second self. It sounds fantastic, but the second self's hope for a second chance has now been extended even beyond the limits of physical death, thanks to the ability of medical science to transplant hearts, lungs and kidneys. Are you dissatisfied with your inherited self? Your social status? Then have a change of heart and associate with those of a different kidney!

> *College boy, thy courage muster,*
> *Shave off that Fuzzy*
> *Cookie duster—*
> *Use Burma Shave!*

So to enjoy the wonders of New York, I assumed a mask which I conceived as that of a "New Yorker," and decided to leave it to those whites who might object to seek out the questioning Tuskegeian who was hidden behind the mask.

But a famous poet had invited me to see *Tobacco Road*, and suddenly, there in the darkness of a Broadway theater, I was snatched back to rural Alabama and, before I realized what was happening, I had blown my cover.

Not that the likes of Jeeter Lester and his family were new to me. As a Tuskegee student I had often seen them in Macon County, Alabama, but in that setting their capacity for racial violence would have been far more overwhelming than their comical wrong-headedness. Indeed, in look, gesture and deed they had crowded me so continuously that I had been tempted to armor myself against their threat by denying them *their* humanity as they sought to deny me mine. Hence in my mind I assigned them to a limbo beneath the threshold of basic humanity.

Which was one of the Southern Negroes' strategies for dealing with poor whites, and an attitude given expression in the child's jingle:

> *My name is Ran,*
> *I work in the sand, but*
> *I'd rather be a* nigger
> *Than a poor white man . . .*

But while such boasting brags—and there were others (*These white folks think they so fine / But their raggedy drawers / Stink just like mine* is another)—provided a release of steam, they were not only childish but ultimately frustrating. For if such sentiments were addressed directly, their intended targets could prove dangerous. Thus the necessity for keeping one's negative opinions of whites within one's own group became a life-preserving discipline. One countered racial provocation by cloaking one's feelings in that psychologically inadequate equivalent of a plaster cast—or bulletproof vest—known as "cool." I had read Hemingway's definition, but for Negroes, "grace under pressure" was far less a gauge of courage than of good common sense. The provocative words of whites were intended to goad one *beyond* words and into the area of physical violence. But while sticks and stones broke bones, mere words could be dismissed by considering their source and keeping a cool eye on the odds arrayed against one. So when racial epithets flew, we reminded ourselves that our mission was not that of proving our courage to any mouthy white who sought to provoke us, but to stay alive and pursue our education. Coolness helped to keep our values warm, and racial hostility stoked our fires of inspiration. But even for students protected by a famous campus, this was an arduous discipline, and one which obviated any superstitious overevaluation of whiteness.

Nevertheless I tried, as I say, to avoid the class of whites from which Erskine Caldwell drew the characters of *Tobacco Road*. During the summer of 1933, while hoboing to Tuskegee, I had been hustled off a freight train by railroad detectives in the rail yards of Decatur, Alabama. This was at a time when the town and surrounding countryside were undergoing a siege of lynch fever stirred up by the famous trial in which the Scottsboro boys were charged with the rape of two white girls on a freight train. I escaped unharmed, but the incident returned to mind whenever I went traveling. Therefore I gave Jeeter Lester types a wide berth, but found it impossible to avoid them entirely because many were law-enforcement officers who served on the highway patrols with a violent zeal like that which Negro slave narratives ascribed to the "paterollers" who had guarded the roads during slavery. (As I say, Southern buses were haunted, and so in a sense were Southern roads and highways.) This was especially true of a section of the route between Tuskegee and Columbus, Georgia. I traveled it frequently, both as a member of a jazz orchestra and when on pleasure trips to Columbus.

It was on such travels that I was apt to relive my Decatur experience. By a fateful circumstance of geography the forty-mile route passed through Phenix City, Alabama, then a brawling speed-trap of a town through which it was impossible to drive either slow enough or fast enough to satisfy the demands of its traffic policemen. No one, black or white, escaped their scrutiny, but since Tuskegee students were regarded as on their way to becoming "uppity educated nigras," we were especially vulnerable. The police lay in wait for us, clocked our speed by a standard known only to themselves, and used any excuse to delay and harass us. Usually they limited themselves to fines and verbal abuse, but I was told that the year before I arrived the police had committed an act that had caused great indignation on campus and become the inspiration of much bull-session yarn-spinning. On that occasion, I was told, two Phenix City policemen had stopped a carload of Tuskegee students and learned during the course of routine questioning that one of the group, a very black-skinned young man, bore the surname of "Whyte"—and then, as one of my informants said, "It was shame on him!"

When Whyte uttered his name the cops stared, exchanged looks of mock disbelief, and became red-faced with manic inspiration.

"Damn, boy," one of them said, "y'all been drinking?"

"No, sir," Whyte said.

"Well, now, I don't know about that," the cop said, " 'cause you sho sound drunk to *me*."

"No, sir," Whyte said. "Because I don't drink."

"You sho?"

"Yes, sir!"

Then the cop turns to his buddy and says, "What you think, Lonzo? Is he drunk, or am I mistaken?"

"Well, now, if you want my opinion," the other cop said, "he's either drunk or something very serious is wrong with him. Yes, suh, something *seerious* is wrong with this boy."

"Why is that, Lonzo?" the first cop said.

" 'Cause it stands to reason that there's no way in the *world* for a nigra as black as that to pretend that his name is 'White.' Not unless he's blind-staggers drunk or else plum out of his nappy-headed, cotton-pickin' mind!"

"That's *my* exact opinion," the first cop said. "But lets us give 'im another chance. So now once agin, boy, what is your last name?"

"Officer, it's Whyte," Whyte said. "That's the truth and I'll swear to it."

That's when the other cop takes over. He frowns at Whyte and shakes his head like he's dealing with a *very* sad case. Naturally he's a big potbellied mother who chews Brown Mule tobacco.

"Damn, boy," he says (in what proved to be a long-range prediction of then unimaginable things to come), "if we let you git away with a damn lie like that, next thing we know that ol' Ramblin' Wreck over at Georgia Tech'll have a goddamn nigra *engineer*! Now, you think about that and let's have that name agin!"

"But, Officer," Whyte said, "Whyte's the only last name I have."

Then my informant, a sergeant in the ROTC and student of veterinary medicine, said, "The battle was *on*!" He described how with simulated indignation the policemen forced Whyte to pronounce his name again and again while insisting that they simply couldn't believe that such a gross misnaming was possible, especially in the South, and gave a detailed account of the policemen's reactions.

"Man," he said, "they went after Whyte like he had insulted their mammas! And when he still wouldn't deny his name, they came down on him like he was responsible for all the fuckup [meaning the genetic untidiness and confusion of black and white nomenclature] of Southern history!"

"Then, man," another informant broke in, "those crackers got so damn disgusted with ol' Whyte that every time he said his name, the ignorant bastards tried to dot where they thought an 'i' should have been by pounding his head with their blackjacks. They did everything but shoot that cat!"

"That's right, cousin," someone else said, "they made him whisper his name and they made him shout it. They made him write it down on a pad and then they made him spell it out—and I mean out *loud*! And when he spelled it with a 'y' instead of an 'i' they swore he was lying and trying to be smart, and really went up side his head!"

"Yeah, man," my original informant said, "and when Whyte still wouldn't change his statement, they made him give the names of his mother and father, his granddaddys and grandmammas on both sides and their origins in slavery, present whereabouts, police records, and occupations—"

"That's right, cousin, and since ol' Whyte came from a very large family and the cops were putting all that pressure on him, the poor cat sounded like a country preacher scatting out the 'begats' from the Book of Genesis!"

Then it was back to Whyte's offensive surname, and the head-whipping sounded, in the words of another informant, a music major and notorious prevaricator, "like somebody beating out the *Anvil Chorus* on a coconut!"

"Yeah, cousin, but what really made the bastards mad was that ol' Whyte wouldn't let some crackers beat him out of his name!"

"Oh, yes, and you have to give it to him. That Whyte was a damn good man!"

Finally, tired of the hazing and defeated in their effort to make Whyte deny his heritage, the cops knocked him senseless and ordered his friends to place him in the car and get out of town.

Although obviously exaggerated in the telling, it was a nasty incident. However, my point is not its violence, but the contradiction between its ineffectiveness as intimidation while serving as a theme for a tall-tale improvisation. Thus was violence transcended with cruel but homeopathic laughter, and racial cruelty transformed by a traditional form of folk art. It did nothing to change the Phenix City police, and probably wouldn't have even if they had heard the recitation. They continued to make life so uncertain that each time we reached Columbus and returned safely to Tuskegee, it was as though we had passed through fire and emerged, like the mythical phoenix bird (after which, presumably, the town was named), from the flames. Still, we continued to risk the danger, for such was our eagerness for the social life of Columbus—the pleasure of parties, dances and picnics in the company of pretty girls—that we continued to run the gauntlet.

But it didn't cancel out the unpleasantness or humiliation. Thus, back on campus we were compelled to buffer the pain and negate the humiliation by making grotesque comedy out of the extremes to which whites would go to keep us in what they considered to be our "place." Once safe at Tuskegee, we would become almost hysterical as we recounted our adventures and laughed as much at ourselves as at the cops. We mocked their modes of speech and styles of intimidation, and teased one another as we parodied our various modes of feigning fear when telling them who we were and where we were headed. It was a wild, he-man, schoolboy silliness, but the only way we knew for dealing with the inescapable conjunction of laughter and pain. My problem was that I couldn't completely dismiss such experiences with laughter. I brooded and tried to make sense of it beyond that provided by our ancestral wisdom. That a head with a few knots on it was preferable to a heart with bullets through it was obviously true. If the philosopher's observation that absolute power corrupts absolutely was also true, then an absolute power based on mere whiteness made for a deification of madness. Depending on the circumstance, whiteness might well be a sign of evil, of a "motiveless malignancy" which was to be avoided as much as strange dogs in rabid weather.

But you were surrounded by whiteness, and it was far from secure in its power. It thrived on violence and sought endlessly for victims, and in its hunger to enforce racial discrimination it was indiscriminating about its victims. It didn't care whether its victims were guilty or innocent, for guilt lay not in individual acts of wrongdoing but in non-whiteness, in Negro-ness. Whiteness was a form of manifest destiny which designated Negroes as its territory and challenge. Whiteness struck at signs, at coloration, hair texture and speech idiom, and thus denied you individuality. How then avoid it, when history and geography brought it always in juxtaposition with blackness? How escape it when it asserted itself in law, in the layout of towns, the inflections of voices, the nuances of manners, the quality of mercy, justice, and charity? When it raged at interracial sex, but then violated its own values in the manner of Senator Bilbo (the name means "shackle"), who was said to find sexual satisfaction only with Negro prostitutes? How escape it when it violated its own most sacred principles, both in spirit and in law, while converting the principles of democracy by which we sought to live into their opposites?

Considered soberly and without the consolation of laughter, it was mad, surreal, and further complicated by the fact that not all whites abhorred Negroes. The evil expressed itself most virulently in the mass and appeared to be regional, a condition of place and climate, since most whites who supported the school were Northerners who appeared for a few days in spring and then departed. Moreover, since not even all white Southerners were hostile, you always had to make fine distinctions between individuals, just as you had to distinguish between the scenes and circumstances in which you encountered them. Your safety demanded a careful attention to detail and mood of social scene, because you had to avoid even friendly whites when they were in the company of their fellows, because it was in crowds that the hate, fear, and blood madness took over. When it did, it could transform otherwise friendly whites into mindless members of mobs. Most of all, you must avoid them when women of their group were present. When a Negro male came into view, the homeliest white woman became a goddess, a cult figure deified in the mystique of whiteness, a being from whom a shout or cry or expression of hand or eye could unleash a rage for human sacrifice. When the ignorant, torch-bearing armies assembled by night, black men burned in the fire of white men's passions.

If all of this seems long ago and far away, it is worth remembering that the past, as William Faulkner warned, is never past. Nor are its social and political consequences guaranteed to be limited to a single geographical area. The past emerges no less in the themes and techniques of art than in the contentions of politics, and since art (and especially the art of the Depression period) is apt to be influenced by politics, it is necessary at this point to take a backward glance at my Tuskegee student's perception, admittedly immature and subjective, of Southern society as it influenced my reaction to *Tobacco Road*.

• • •

In the South of that day the bottom rung of the social ladder was reserved for that class of whites who were looked down upon as "poor white trash," and the area immediately beneath them and below the threshold of upward social mobility was assigned to Negroes, whether educated or ignorant, prosperous or poor. But although they were barely below the poor whites in economic status (and were sometimes better off), it was the Negroes who were designated the South's untouchable caste. As such, they were perceived as barely controllable creatures of untamed instincts, and a group against whom all whites were obligated to join in the effort required for keeping them within their assigned place. This mindless but widely held perception was given doctrinal credibility through oppressive laws and an endless rhetorical reiteration of anti-Negro stereotypes. Negroes were seen as ignorant, cowardly, thieving, lying, hypocritical and superstitious in their religious beliefs and practices, morally loose, drunken, filthy of personal habit, sexually animalistic, rude, crude and disgusting in their public conduct, and aesthetically just plain unpleasant. If a few were not, it was due to the presence of "white" blood, a violation of the Southern racial code which rendered mixed-bloods especially dangerous and repugnant.

In brief, Negroes were considered guilty of all the seven deadly sins except the sin of pride, and were seen as a sometimes comic but nevertheless threatening negative to the whites' idealized image of themselves. Most Negroes were characterized, in the jargon of sociology, by a "high visibility" of pigmentation which made the group easily distinguishable from other citizens, and therefore easy to keep in line and politically powerless. This powerlessness was justified and reinforced by the stereotypes, which denied blacks individuality and allowed any Negro to be interchangeable with any other. Thus, as far as many whites were concerned, not only were blacks faceless, but this facelessness made the idea of mistaken identity meaningless, and the democratic assumption that Negro citizens should share the individual's recognized responsibility for the welfare of society was regarded as subversive.

In this denial of personality (sponsored by both law and custom), anti-Negro stereotypes served as an efficient and easily manipulated instrument of governance. Moreover, they prepared Negroes for the role of sacrificial scapegoat in the ritual drama of Southern society, and helped bind the poor whites to the middle and upper classes with whom they shared ethnic identity. Being uncomfortably close to Negroes in economic status, the poor whites clung to the stereotypes as to a life raft in turbulent waters, and politicians were able to use their fear and antipathy toward blacks as a surefire source of power. Because not only were the stability of social order and the health of business seen as depending upon white dominance, but the sanctity of the *moral* order as well. Whether denied or admitted, in this area religion was in the service of politics.

Thus, by pitting the interests of the poor whites against those of the Negroes, Southern congressmen countered the South's Civil War defeat by using its carefully nurtured racial conflict as a means for amassing great political power in Washington. Being representatives of what were, in effect, one-party states, enabled them to advance to the chairmanship of powerful governmental committees, and through the political horse-trading which keeps the national government functioning, this power was used to foil the progress of Negroes in areas far from the geopolitical center of white supremacy. Here, however, it should be noted that Negroes owe much of their progress since the Second World War to presidents who were of Southern background and heritage. People change, but as Faulkner has pointed out, "was" is never "was"; it is "now," and in the South a concern with preserving the "wasness" of slavocracy was an obsession which found facile expression in word and deed. Their memories of the War Between the States, of Reconstruction, and the difficult times that followed the Hayes-Tilden Compromise had long been mythologized both as a means for keeping Negroes powerless, and for ensuring the loyalty of poor whites in keeping them so. Thus it is ironic that even though the condition of blacks became a national standard by which many whites, both North and South, measured their social advancement, Negroes themselves remained at the bottom of society and the most anti-Negro of whites remained with them. It was Booker T. Washington who had warned that it is impossible to keep another man in a ditch without remaining there with him; unfortunately this advice came from a powerful Southern leader who was also an ex-slave.

More and more, through depression and war, America lived up to its claim of being the land of opportunity whose rewards were available to the individual through the assertion of a second self. But for many poor and unambitious Southern whites the challenge of such an assertion was far less inviting than clinging to the conviction that they, by the mere fact of race, color, and tradition alone, were superior to the black masses below them. Yet in their own way they were proud idealists to whom the South's racial arrangement was sacred beyond most benefits made possible by social change. Therefore they continued to wrestle with the stereotype of Negro inferiority much as Brer Rabbit kept clinging to Tar Baby's stickiness. They were so eager to maintain their grip on the status quo and to ignore its costs and contradictions that they willingly used anything, including physical violence, to do so. In rationalizing their condition, they required victims, real or symbolic, and in the daily rituals which gave support to their cherished myth of white supremacy, anti-Negro stereotypes and epithets served as symbolic substitutes for that primitive blood rite of human sacrifice to which they resorted in times of racial tension—but which, for a complexity of reasons, political, economic and humane, were rejected by their more responsible leaders. So it was fortunate, both for Afro-Americans and for the nation as a whole, that the Southern rituals of race were usually confined to the realm of the symbolic. Anti-Negro stereotypes were the currency through which the myth of white supremacy was kept alive, while the awe-inspiring enactment of the myth took the form of a rite in which a human victim was sacrificed. It then became a ritual drama that was usually enacted in a preselected scene (such as a clearing in the woods or in the courthouse square) in an atmosphere of high excitement and led by a masked celebrant dressed in a garish costume who manipulated the numinous objects (lynch ropes, the American flag, shotgun, gasoline and whiskey jugs) associated with the rite as he inspired and instructed the actors in their gory task. This was the anthropological meaning of lynching, a blood rite that ended in the death of a scapegoat whose obliteration was seen as necessary to the restoration of social order. Thus it served to affirm white goals and was enacted to terrorize Negroes.

Normally, the individual dies his own death, but because lynch mobs are driven by a passionate need to destroy the distinction between the actual and the symbolic, its victim is forced to undergo death for all his group. Nor is he sacrificed to ensure its fertility or save its soul, but to fill its members with an unreasoning fear of whiteness.

For the lynch mob, blackness is a sign of satanic evil given human form. It is the dark consubstantial shadow which symbolizes all that its opponents reject in social change and in democracy. Thus it does not matter if its sacrificial victim is guilty or innocent, because the lynch mob's object is to propitiate its insatiable god of whiteness, that myth-figure worshipped as the true source of all things bright and beautiful, by destroying the human attributes of its god's antagonist which they perceive as the power of blackness. In action, racial discrimination is as nondiscriminating as a car bomb detonated in a crowded public square, because both car bomb and lynch rope are savagely efficient ways of destroying distinctions between the members of a hated group while rendering quite meaningless any moral questioning that might arise regarding the method used. The ultimate goal of lynchers is that of achieving ritual purification through destroying the lynchers' identification with the basic *humanity* of their victims. Hence their deafness to cries of pain, their stoniness before the sight and stench of burning flesh, their exhilarated and grotesque self-righteousness. And hence our horror at the idea of supposedly civilized men destroying, in the name of their ideal conception of the human, an aspect of their own humanity. But for the group thus victimized, such sacrifices are the source of emotions that move far beyond the tragic conception of pity and terror and down into the abysmal levels of conflict and folly from which arises our famous American humor. Brother, the blackness of *Afro-American* "black humor" is not black; it is tragically human and finds its source and object in the notion of "whiteness."

But let me not overstate beyond the point necessary for conveying an idea of my state of mind prior to my unanticipated stumble into *Tobacco Road*. The threat, real or imagined, of being the subject of such victimization was offset by that hopeful attitude that is typical of youth and necessary for dealing with life everywhere. While racial danger was always with me, I lived with it as with threats of natural disaster or acts of God. Just as Henry James felt it prudent to warn Americans against a "superstitious evaluation of Europe," Negro folklore with its array of survival strategies warned me against an overevaluation of white pretensions. Despite their dominance and low opinion of Negro intelligence, whites suspected the presence of profound reservations even when Negroes were far less assertive than they are today. This made for a constant struggle over the nature of reality, in which each group probed and sparred as it tried to determine the other's true motives and opinions. A poignant instance of such a struggle appears in Faulkner's *The Sound and the Fury* when Quentin Compson gives Deacon, a raffish Negro mythomaniac who does odd jobs around Harvard, an important letter to be delivered to Quentin's roommate the following afternoon. But when Deacon notes that the envelope is sealed, he suspects that he is being sent on a fool's errand such as whites delighted in sending Negroes down South. This causes him to drop his Northern mask for that of an old inarticulate "darkey," a pose which reminds Quentin of a Negro retainer whom he had known as a child. Deacon then asks if a joke is being played on him, which Quentin denies. But then, appealing for that flattering reassurance that Southern whites were accustomed to exacting from Negroes, he asks Deacon if any Southerner had ever played a joke on him.

Deacon's reply, as was often true of such exchanges, is ambiguous. "You're right," he says, "they're fine folks. But you cant live with them."

Then, looking through Deacon into his own hopeless despair, Quentin asks, "Did you ever try?"

The answer is not forthcoming, for in a flash the transplanted black Southerner had retired behind one of the many trickster's masks which his second self had assumed upon coming north and agrees briskly to deliver the letter. Ironically, however, there *is* a fool's errand involved, but it isn't Deacon's; the letter conveys Quentin's intention to drown himself. Thus Deacon, who has rejected the role assigned him by his native South, ends up playing not the traditional black fool but, all unknowingly, the death-messenger for a pathetic Southern aristocrat who is driven to self-destruction by the same prideful confusion of values from which, as Southerners, both suffer. Having tried to live in the South, both had come north dragging the past behind them, but while Deacon used his Southern craftiness to play upon life's possibilities, the past-haunted Quentin destroyed himself because he was unable to reconcile the mythical South he loved with that which had sent Deacon packing.

As Deacon said, many white Southerners were "fine folks," and that was the problem. Whites both hostile and friendly were part of my college scene, and thus a good part of my extracurricular education consisted in learning to live with them while retaining my self-esteem. Negro folklore taught the preservation of one's humanity by masking one's motives and emotions, just as it prepared one to be unsurprised at anything that whites might do, because a concern with race could negate all human bonds, including those of shared blood and experience.

So I tried to observe such ancestral wisdom as I awaited the day when I could leave the South. The catch here was that even the roads that led *away* from the South were also haunted, a circumstance which I should have learned, but did not, from numerous lyrics that were sung to the blues. Full of great expectations, I went north, and where uneducated Deacon assumed the mask of a former Harvard divinity student, I took on that of a sophisticated New Yorker.

In *Tobacco Road*, Erskine Caldwell appears to have taken a carefully screened assemblage of anti-Negro stereotypes and turned them against the very class in which they found their most fervent proponents, and what he did with them was outrageous. Indeed, he turned things around in such a manner that it was as though Whyte, the Tuskegee victim of the Phenix City hazing, had read Mark Twain, George Washington Harris, Rabelais, Groucho Marx and Voltaire, learned to write, and then, passing for "white" in order to achieve a more intimate knowledge of his characters, had proceeded to embody the most outrageous stereotypes in the Jeeter Lester family, in-laws and friends. (Caldwell, I hasten to add, is a Georgia-born Anglo-Saxon.)

Nevertheless, Caldwell presents Jeeter Lester as an ignorant, impoverished, Depression-ruined poor white who urges Ellie May, his sixteen-year-old younger daughter, to seduce her older sister's husband so that he, Lester, may steal the equally impoverished young man's only food, a bag of turnips. The father of other mature children who now live in the city, he is a slothful farmer whose run-down farm is in such neglect that even the rats have abandoned the corncrib, and a criminally negligent son whose aged mother must forage for food in the woods, where, by the play's end, she dies alone and neglected. Yet Caldwell keeps Jeeter within the range of the human by having him be so utterly himself. He makes him a poor-white version of the "great sinner" on the order of Dostoevsky's elder Karamazov, and with a similar vitality and willfulness. He is a lecher who has fathered children by his neighbor's wife, and has incestuous inclinations toward one of his married daughters. But it is his stubborn refusal to bow before the economic and ecological developments that have rendered his type of farming no longer possible which gives the play its movement. Jeeter is a symbol of human willfulness reduced to its illogical essence.

Ada, Mrs. Lester, is an ineffectual wife and mother who has no control over either her husband or their children. Half-starved and worn-out from childbearing, she exerts what physical and moral strength she has in trying to save Pearl, her pride and joy through a casual affair with a stranger, from the decay of Tobacco Road.

Pearl, whom Jeeter married off at the age of twelve, is the wife of Lov, a struggling young workman with whom she refuses either to sleep or talk—a situation utterly baffling for Lov, and annoying to Jeeter because it has become a subject for local Negro laughter.

Ellie May, the younger daughter, is harelipped, and so helplessly frustrated sexually that Jeeter tries to persuade Lov to exchange her for Pearl and take her away from Tobacco Road before, as he says, the Negroes get her. But if in Ellie May the Lester sex drive has gotten quite out of hand, in her brother Dude it is unawakened.

Dude, the adolescent son (who opens the play with a mindless bouncing of a ball against the house), is sadistic, disdainful of parental authority, and utterly disrespectful of life and death. If Jeeter is a comic embodiment of selfish wrongheadedness, Dude (who takes more than his share of Jeeter's stolen turnips by physical force) is the embodiment of his father's character gone to violence. He is also the agent of his mother's death.

In brief, the Lester family is as seedy as the house in which they live. They have plunged through the fragile floor of civilized humanity, and even the religion which had once given a semblance of order to their lives has become as superstitious as that which the stereotypes attribute to Negroes.

This superstition is exploited by Sister Bessie Rice, a dowdy itinerant preacher of no known denomination who sees sin in even the most innocent of human actions, and uses prayer as a magical incantation through which to manipulate her listener's residue of religious belief to her own advantage. She is a confidence woman who promises for small contributions to cure all ills through the magic of prayer.

Homely and gregarious in manner, Sister Bessie is a widow in search of a mate, both as husband and as a preaching partner with whom she can be more efficient in spreading her version of religion. Her unlikely choice for this goal is teen-age Dude, but while Jeeter is quite agreeable to such a union of April and December, Dude is uninterested—until, that is, Sister Bessie promises to use the money left by her deceased husband to purchase a new automobile. This does the trick. With Dude in tow, Sister Bessie buys first a marriage license and then the car, whereupon they speed back to the Lester farm. There Sister Bessie loses no time in performing her own marriage ceremony. This accomplished, she rushes Dude to their wedding chamber, outside of which Jeeter stands on a chair in an effort to watch her initiate Dude into the sexual mysteries of wedlock.

As it turns out, however, Dude is less interested in connubial pleasure than in driving the new car—which, blowing its horn idiotically and speeding, he does so recklessly that he runs into a loaded wagon and wrecks the car. Later he backs the car over his mother and kills her. Thus, not even the wedding of modern technology with sex and religion can restore Tobacco Road to a state of fertility. The sex instinct remains out of control, religious values are corrupted, the laws guiding the relations between parents and children are destroyed, and the words and rituals that once imposed religious and political ideals upon human conduct are used to justify greed, incest, sloth and theft. In brief, the economic Depression, abetted by Jeeter's sloth and wrongheadedness, has deprived the family not only of its livelihood but denuded them of civilized humanity. Ultimately it is Ada's efforts to save Pearl from further humiliation and Jeeter's dogged will to survive the imbalance of nature and the bank's foreclosure on his farm that redeems the family from a total fall into bestiality.

Yet Caldwell's handling of such material does not produce a response of disgust and hopelessness in the audience. Instead it is swept by a wave of cathartic laughter which leaves it optimistic. Perhaps, as has been noted in Cleanth Brooks, R.W.B. Lewis, and Robert Penn Warren's *American Literature: The Makers and the Making,* the Lesters' "lack of any burden of guilt and their ability to dispense with most of the contrivances of civilization gave a sense of release to a great many people."

I would add that during the Depression days of the play's great success, there was such great need for relief, both economic and spiritual, that the grotesque nature of its comedy was fully justified. Perhaps its viewers laughed, and then in retrospect grasped the interplay of social and economic forces upon which the play is focused, and trembled. Which, given Caldwell's anger over the despoliation of the South, must have been his intention.

According to Kenneth Burke, "Comedy should enable us to be observers of ourselves while acting. Its ultimate end would not be passiveness but maximum consciousness. [It should allow] one to 'transcend' himself by noting his own foibles . . . [and should] provide a rationale for locating the irrational and the non-rational."

To follow the action of a comedy is to react through its actors, and to identify either with them or with the values with which they struggle. As David Daziel Duncan has written, "the difference between symbolic and social drama is the difference between imaginary and real obstacles, but to produce effects on audiences, symbolic drama must reflect the real obstacles of social drama. Conflict must be resolved in the symbolic realm by the expression of attitudes which make conformity possible. All such expression, like prayer, is an exhortation to the self and to others. It is a preparation for social action, an investment of the self with confidence and strength." Duncan is speaking of the drama of everyday life in which all successful stage plays are rooted, and when we consider the popularity of *Tobacco Road*, it suggests that during the Great Depression it was most successful in providing its viewers with a rationale for locating the irrational both in themselves and in their society.

The greater the stress within society the stronger the comic antidote required. In this instance the stress imposed by the extreme dislocations of American society was so strong and chaotic that it called for a comedy of the grotesque. Jeeter Lester, the poor white as fool, was made to act the clown in order to save his audience's sanity. Here it is instructive to use Southern Negroes' handling of stress for comparison. Since such stress was an enforced norm of their lives, Negroes struggled with the role assigned them for the same ends that Shakespeare juxtaposed the Fool with Lear, which was to maintain a measure of common sense before the extreme assertions of Lear's kingly pride. In the Lear-like drama of white supremacy, Negroes were designated both clowns and fools, but they "fooled" by way of maintaining their own sense of rational order, no matter how they were perceived by whites. It was far better to be looked down upon as "niggers" than to lose themselves in a world rendered surreal through an excess of racial pride. Their challenge was to endure while imposing their claims upon America's conscience and consciousness, just as they had imposed their style upon its culture. Forced to be wary observers, they recognized that American life is of a whole, and that what happens to blacks will accrue eventually, one way or another, to the nation as a whole. This is their dark-visioned version of the broader "American Joke." Like Faulkner, Caldwell appears to have recognized its existence, for in responding to the imbalance which was shaking American social hierarchy from its apex to its base, he placed the yokelike anti-Negro stereotypes upon the necks of whites, and his audience reacted with a shock of recognition. Caldwell was answering a deeply felt need, and it is interesting that it was during the period of *Tobacco Road*'s record-breaking run that the Museum of Modern Art's presentation of its famous exhibit of Dadaist art was widely successful.

For me the shock of Caldwell's art began when Ellie May and Lov were swept up by a forbidden sexual attraction so strong that, uttering sounds of animal passion, they went floundering and skittering back-to-back across the stage in the startling action which father Jeeter, that randy Adam in an Eden gone to weed, named "horsing." When the two went into their bizarre choreography of sexual "frustrabation" I was reduced to such helpless laughter that I distracted the entire balcony and embarrassed both myself and my host. It was a terrible moment, for before I could regain control, more attention was being directed toward me than at the action unfolding on the stage.

Then it was as though I had been stripped naked, kicked out of a low-flying plane onto an Alabama road, and ordered to laugh for my life. I laughed and laughed, bending and straightening in a virtual uncontrollable cloud-and-dam-burst of laughter, a self-immolation of laughter over which I had no control. Yet I was hypersensitive to what was happening around me, a fact which left me all the more embarrassed.

Seeing an expression of shocked disbelief on the face of my host, I imagined him saying, "Damn, if I'd known this would be his reaction I would have picked a theater with laughing barrels!"

Suddenly, in addition to my soul-wracking agony of embarrassment, I was being devastated by an old in-group joke which played upon the themes of racial conflict, social freedom and the blackness of Negro laughter, a joke whose setting was some small Southern town in which Negro freedom of expression was so restricted that its public square was marked by a series of huge whitewashed barrels labeled FOR COLORED, and into which any Negro who felt a laugh coming on was forced, *pro bono publico*, to thrust his boisterous head.

The joke was used by Tuskegee students, who considered themselves more sophisticated, to kid freshmen from small Southern towns, but although I had heard it many times, it now flashed in my mind with implications that had hitherto escaped me. As it played a counterpoint between my agony of laughter and the action taking place on the stage set of *Tobacco Road* below, it was as though Erskine Caldwell had snared me as an offstage instrument for extending the range of his outrageous plotting—and I mean with a cacophony of minor thirds and flatted-fifths voiced fortissimo by braying gut-bucket brasses!

For now, in my hypersubjective state, viewers around me in the balcony were no longer following the action unfolding on the stage; they were getting to their feet to gawk at me. It was as though I had plunged into a nightmare in which my personality was split in twain, with the lucid side looking on in wonder while the manic side convulsed my body as though a drunken accordionist was using it to belt out the "Beer Barrel Polka." While I wheezed and choked with laughter, my disgusted lucid self dramatized its cool detachment by noting that things were getting so out of control that Northern white folk in balcony and loge were now catching fire and beginning to howl and cheer the disgraceful loss of self-control being exhibited by a young Negro who had become deranged by the shock wave of comedy set in motion by a troupe of professional actors who were doing nothing more extraordinary than portraying the outrageous antics of a group of Southern whites who were totally imaginary—a young man who was so gross as to demonstrate his social unacceptability by violating a whole *encyclopedia* of codes that regulated proper conduct no less in the theater than in society at large.

In my distorted consciousness the theater was rapidly becoming the scene of a virtual orgy of disgraceful conduct, with everyone getting into the scene-stealing action. So much so, that now the lucid side of me noted with despair that Jeeter Lester (played by Will Geer) and the other Lesters were now shading their eyes and peering open-mouthed toward the balcony as if to say, "What the hell's happening? Who's upstaging the stage and turning *Tobacco Road* upside down?" Or perhaps, in shock and dismay, they too were thinking of laughing barrels.

In the joke the barrels were considered a civic necessity and had been improvised as a means of protecting the sensibilities of whites from a pecular form of insanity suffered exclusively by Negroes, who in light of their social status and past condition of servitude were regarded as having absolutely *nothing* in their daily experience which could possibly inspire *rational* laughter. Yet Negroes continued, much as one side of me was doing, to laugh.

They laughed even when overcome by mirth while negotiating the public square, an area graced by its proud military statue, its Civil War cannon and pyramid of cannon balls, which was especially off-limits to all forms of Negro profanation. Thus, since any but the most inaudible Negro laughter was forbidden in public, Negroes who were wise, or at least fast on their feet, took off *posthaste* for a laughing barrel. (Just as I, in my present predicament, would gladly have done.) Despite their eccentric risibility, the local Negroes bowed to public pressure and cooperated, at least to the extent that they were physically able.

But now as I continued to roar at the weird play-without-a-play in which part of me was involved, my sober self marked the fact that the entire audience was being torn in twain. Most of the audience was white, but now many who occupied seats down in the orchestra section were beginning to protest the unscheduled disruption taking place above them. Leaping to their feet, they were shaking their fists at those in the balcony, and they in turn were shouting their disdain for those so lacking in an appreciation for the impromptu broadening of the expected comedy. As they raged at one another in what was rapidly becoming a Grangerford-Shepherdson feud of expletives, I recalled a similar conflict which took place in the laughing barrel town and cracked up again.

There, too, certain citizens had assumed their democratic right of dissent to oppose the barrels as an *ipso jure* form of reverse discrimination. Why not, they argued, force Negroes to control themselves at their *own* expense, as did everyone else. It was an argument which fell on deaf ears, because it ignored the self-evident fact that Negro self-control was the very *last* thing in the world that they really wanted, whether in this or in any other area of Negro lives. Therefore, these passionate quodlibetarians and their objections to quotas were ignored because the great majority of the citizenry regarded their unique form of public accommodation as bestowing a dual blessing upon their town. To an extent, this blessing included Negroes, for not only did the laughing barrels save many a black a sore behind (and the understaffed police force energy sorely needed in other areas), they performed the far more important function of providing whites a means of saving face before the confounding, persistent and embarrassing mystery of black laughter.

Unfortunately it was generally agreed that the barrels were by no means an *elegant* solution of what whites regarded as a most grievous and inelegant problem. After all, having to observe the posture of a Negro stuck halfway into a laughing barrel (or rising and falling helplessly in a theater balcony) was far from an aesthetic experience. Nor was that all, for often when seen laughing with their heads stuck in a barrel and standing, as it were, upside down upon the turbulent air, Negroes appeared to be taken over by a form of schizophrenia which left them even more psychically frazzled than whites regarded them as being by nature.

But while the phenomenon was widely discussed, not even the wisest of whites could come up with a satisfactory explanation. All they knew was that when such an incident occurred, instead of sobering up, as any white man in a similar situation would have done, a Negro might well take off and laugh all the harder (as I in my barrel-less state was doing). It appeared that in addition to reacting to whatever ignorant, harebrained notion had set him off in the first place, the Negro was apt to double up with a second gale of laughter, triggered, apparently, by his own mental image of himself laughing at himself laughing upside down. It was, all whites agreed, another of the many Negro mysteries with which it was their lot to contend, but *whatever* its true cause, it was most disturbing to a white observer.

And especially on Market Day, a time when the public square teemed with whites and blacks seeking in their separate-but-equal fashions to combine business with pleasure while taking advantage of the square's holiday atmosphere. On Market Days, thanks to the great influx of Negroes, the uproar from laughing barrels could become so loud and raucous that it not only disturbed the serenity of the entire square, but shook up the whites' fierce faith in the stability of their most cherished traditions. On such occasions the uproar from the laughing barrels could become so contagious and irresistible that any whites who were so unfortunate as to be caught near the explosions of laughter would find themselves compelled to join in— and this included even such important figures as the mayor, lawyer, cotton broker, Baptist minister and brewers of prime "white-lightning" whiskey. It was an appalling state of affairs, for despite their sternest resistance, even such distinguished whites literally cracked up and roared. Although it was recognized that it sprang from the *unnatural* and corrupting blackness of Negro laughter, it was a fact of Southern life, and thus it was that from time to time even the most dignified and tradition-bound whites found themselves joining in (as, much to the discomfort of my somber, balcony-trapped self, the whites around me were doing).

Nor did it help that many of the town's whites suspected that when a Negro had his head thrust into a laughing barrel he became endowed with a strange form of extrasensory perception—or second sight—which allowed him to respond uproariously to their unwilling participation. It was clear that given a black laugher's own uncouth uproar, he could not possibly *hear* its infectious damage to them. When such reversals occurred, the whites assumed that in some mysterious fashion the Negro involved was not only laughing at *himself* laughing, but was also laughing at *them* laughing at his laughing against their own most determined wills. If such was the truth, it suggested that somehow a Negro (and this meant *any* Negro) could become with a single hoot-and-cackle both the source and master of an outrageous and untenable situation. Hence it was viewed as a most aggravating problem, indeed the most vicious of vicious circles ever to be imposed upon the long-suffering South by the white man's burden.

Since it was an undisputed fact that whites and blacks were of different species, it followed that they could by no means be expected to laugh at the same things. Therefore, when whites found themselves joining in with the coarse merriment issuing from the laughing barrels, they suffered the double embarrassment of laughing against their own God-given nature while being unsure of exactly why, or at what specifically, they were laughing. Which meant that somehow the Negro in the barrel had them *over* a barrel.

This, then, was the crux of the town's dilemma: efforts to control Negro laughter with laughing barrels were as futile as attaining

Christian grace by returning to the womb, because a Negro laughing in a laughing barrel simply turned the world upside down and inside out. In so doing, he *in*-verted (and thus *sub*-verted) tradition, and thus the preordained and cherished scheme of Southern racial relationships was blasted asunder. Therefore, it was feared that if such unhappy instances of interracial laughter occurred with any frequency, it would create a crisis in which social order would be fatally undermined by something as unpolitical as a bunch of Negroes with their laughing heads stuck into the interiors of a batch of old whitewashed whiskey barrels.

The outrageous absurdity of this state of affairs was as vexing to the town as that in which I found myself while the old joke banged and shuddered through my memory. Despite the fact that the whites had done everything they could think of to control the blackness of Negro laughter, Negroes continued to laugh. The disapproval of the general public notwithstanding, they were even *bursting* barrels all over the public square, and thus adding to the high cost of maintaining public order. Since this was (in more ways than one) at white expense, the whites were faced with a Hobson's choice between getting rid of Negroes and suffering the economic loss of their labor, or living with the commotion in the laughing barrels. (Yes, but they had at least a ghost of a choice, while by now it was as though I had been taken over by embattled Siamese twins who couldn't agree for disagreeing, and neither of whom could exit the scene, thanks to the detachment of one and the mirth-wracked state of the other.)

In the town, however, great argument raged on both sides of the question. All agreed that the laughing barrels were an economic burden, but the proponents of the "Barrel Act," as it was known, justified their position with philosophical arguments to the effect that while it was true that these unique public facilities were costly, they served not only as a form of noise-pollution control, but the higher—and more spiritual—purpose of making it unnecessary for white folks to suffer the indignity of having to observe the confounding and degrading spectacle of a bunch of uncultivated Negroes knocking themselves out with a form of laughter that had no apparent motivation or discernible target.

What a terrible time and place to be ambushed by such an irreverent joke! By now my eyes were so full of tears that I could no longer see Hughes or anyone else, but at least the moisture had the effect of calming me down. Then, as the unruly world of *Tobacco Road* finally returned, my divided selves were made one again by a sense of catharsis. Yes, but at the expense of undergoing a humiliating, body-wracking conflict of emotions! Embarrassment, self-anger, ethnic scorn, and at last a feeling of comic relief—all because Erskine Caldwell compelled me to laugh at his symbolic and therefore nonthreatening Southern whites. Thus he shocked me into recognizing certain absurd aspects of our common humanity. Kenneth Burke would probably have said that I had been hit with a "perspective by incongruity," leading to a reversal of expectations in which the juxtaposition of past and present, comic Southland and quasi-illusory New York, had set up vibrations that routed my self-composure. It was as though I had plunged through the wacky mirrors of a fun house to discover on the other side a weird distortion of perspective which made for a painful but redeeming rectification of vision. In a flash, time was telescoped and the imaginary assumed the lineaments of past experiences through which Jeeter Lester's comic essence became a recognizable property of characters and events that I had known in the past.

After all, thanks to Governor "Alfalfa Bill" Murray's Jeeter Lesterish appeal to the bias of Oklahoma's farm vote, hadn't I seen the state capitol's grounds a-wave with grain "as high as an elephant's eye" (which proved to be a foreshadowing of events which led, years later, to the adoption of Rodgers and Hammerstein's "Oklahoma" as the state's official song)? A bit later, hadn't I seen those same graciously landscaped grounds splattered with far more oil rigs than there were holes dug by Ty Ty in his futile search for gold in Caldwell's *God's Little Acre*? I had indeed, and the main difference was that the oil rigs produced oil; otherwise, Alfalfa Bill might have stepped out of a Caldwell novel. Thus I now recognized that there was much more of Jeeter Lester's outrageousness in my past than I had ever imagined, and quite a bit of it showed up on my side of the color line.

There were uneducated men whose attitudes and bearing ripped through the usual stereotypes like a Brahma bull goring the paper image displayed on Bull Durham Tobacco Company billboards. Their violence was usually directed against their own kind, but they were known to go after whites as well, and were no more respectful of what most people considered civilized conduct than Jeeter Lester. I had known the type in Oklahoma and admired a few for insisting upon being themselves. Often they were of vernacular folk culture but with active minds and were absolutely unrestrained in attacking any subject that caught their attention. Once, while working as a barbershop shoeshine boy, I had heard such a group engage in a long discussion of Mr. John D. Rockefeller Senior's relations with the women whom they assumed it natural for such a powerful man to have. They took it for granted that he had no less than a "stable full," speculated on how much he paid for their favors, and concluded that he rewarded them with trunks full of brand-new dimes. Then they discussed the brands of brandy and whiskey which they assumed Mr. Rockefeller drank, argued over the designs and costs of the silk underwear worn by his favorite fancy women, and then almost came to blows when estimating the number of "yard chillun" he had scattered around the country and abroad.

Poor old John D. didn't know it, but they put him through the windmill of their fantasies with gusto. What's more, he emerged enhanced in their sight as an even more exceptional man among such exceptional men as themselves, thanks to their having endowed him with a sexual potency and an utter disregard for genteel conduct that would have blown that gentleman's mind. Before they were done they had the founder of Standard Oil shooting pool, playing strip poker, and engaging in a barbecue-eating contest with J. P. Morgan and Henry Ford—from which, naturally, he emerged the winner.

Only when they put him through a Charleston contest with "Tickle-toes from Tulsa," a famous Negro dancer, did he fall below their exacting standards. Nevertheless he remained the mighty Rockefeller, though so magnified that he was far more "John Henry" than John Davidson. In working him over, they created such an uproar of laughter that the owner had to ask them to leave the barbershop. But by that time, both to my bewilderment and delight, they had touched one of the most powerful men of the nation with the tar-brush of their comic imaginations, Afro-Americanized him, and claimed him as one of their very own. It was amazing how consistently they sought (like Jeeter Lester) to make the world conform to the narrow compass of their own hopes and dreams.

There were still others who in pursuing their self-reliant wrong-headedness had given me a glimpse of the "tragic." Had not I seen a good part of my community, including teen-age boys, reduced to despair over the terrible death of a self-taught genius of an automobile mechanic, who after burning his fingers while working with the electrical system of a Model T Ford had cut out the offending flesh with his pocketknife, an act of ignorant pride which resulted in his death by lockjaw? In those days any boy who could lay hands on a coil from a Model T and the hand-cranked magneto from a discontinued telephone would rig it as a device for shocking his unsuspecting friends, but now, to our dismay, death was revealed to be lurking within our rare electrical toys.

Even closer to my immediate experience, wasn't Ellie May's and Lov's "horsing" all over the stage of *Tobacco Road* embarrassingly symbolic of my own frustration as a healthy young man whose sexual outlet was limited, for the most part, to "belly-rubbing" with girls met casually at public dances? It was and it wasn't, depending upon my willingness to make or withhold a human identification. Actually, I had no choice but to identify, for Caldwell's art had seen to that.

Thus, for all its intentional outrageousness, the comedy of *Tobacco Road* was deeply rooted in the crazy-quilt life I knew. Caldwell had me both coming and going, black side, white side, and straight down my improvised American middle. On one side of my mind I had thought of my life as being of a whole, segregated but in many ways superior to that of the Lesters. On the other side, I thought of the Lester type as being, in the Negro folk phrase, "a heap of whiteness gone to waste," and therefore a gross caricature of anything that was viable in the idea of white superiority. But now Caldwell had highlighted the warp and woof of my own ragtag American pattern. So, laughing hysterically, I felt like the fat man whom I'd seen slip and fall on the icy sidewalk and who lay there laughing while passersby looked on in bewilderment, until he got to his feet still laughing and punched the one man who had joined in his laughter square in the mouth. In my case, however, there was no one to punch, because I embodied both fat man and the passerby who was so rash as to ignore Baudelaire's warning. Therefore I laughed and I trembled, and gained thereby a certain wisdom.

I could not have put it into words at the time, but by forcing me to see the comedy in Jeeter Lester's condition and allowing me to react to it in an interracial situation without the threat of physical violence, Caldwell told me something important about who I was. By easing the conflict that I was having with my Southern experience (yes, and with my South-Southwestern identity), he helped initiate me into becoming, if not a "New Yorker," at least a more tolerant American. I suppose such preposterous comedy is an indispensable agency for dealing with American experience precisely because it allows for redeeming perspectives on our rampant incongruities. Given my background and yearnings, there was no doubt that I needed such redemption, and for that I am eternally grateful to Erskine Caldwell: Southerner, American humorist, and mighty destroyer of laughing barrels.

Remembering Richard Wright

EARLIER today while considering my relationship with Richard Wright, I recalled Heraclitus' axiom "Geography is fate," and was struck by the ironic fact that in this country, where Frederick Jackson Turner's theory of the frontier has been so influential in shaping our conception of American history, very little attention has been given to the role played by geography in shaping the fate of Afro-Americans.

For example, Wright was a Mississippian who migrated to Chicago and then to New York. I, by contrast, am an Oklahoman, and by geographical origin a Southwesterner. Wright grew up in a part of what was the old Confederacy, while I grew up in a state which possesses no indigenous tradition of chattel slavery. Thus, while we both grew up in segregated societies, mine lacked many of the intensities of custom, tradition and manners which "colored" the institutions of the Old South, and which were important in shaping Wright's point of view. Both of us were descendants of slaves, but since my civic, geographical and political circumstances were different from those of Mississippi, Wright and I were united by our connection with a past condition of servitude, and divided by geography and a difference of experience based thereupon. Yet it was this very difference of experience and background which had much to do with Wright's important impact upon my sensibilities.

Then there was New York. I met Wright there in 1937, and it was no accidental encounter. It came about because through my reading and working in the library at Tuskegee Institute, I had become fascinated by the exciting developments that were taking place in modern literature. Somehow in my uninstructed reading of Eliot and

---

Lecture presented at the Institute for Afro-American Culture, University of Iowa, July 18, 1971.

Pound, I had recognized a relationship between modern poetry and jazz music, and this led me to wonder why I was not encountering similar devices in the work of Afro-American writers. Indeed, such reading and wondering prepared me not simply to *meet* Wright, but to seek him out. It led, in other words, to a personal quest. I insist upon the "seeking out" because, you see, I too have an ego, and it is important to me that our meeting came about through my own initiative. Not only is this historically true, but it has something to do with my being privileged to be here on what I consider to be a very important moment in the history of our literature. Perhaps Richard Wright would have dismissed such a moment as impossible even as late as 1957, but still, here we are, gathered in the hot summertime to pay him honor. *I* would not have been surprised, since it was my reading of one of Wright's poems in the *New Masses* which gave me a sense of his importance. I had arrived in New York on July 5, 1936—a date of no broad symbolic importance, but one highly significant to me because it made a meeting with Wright a possibility. Although the *New Masses* poem was not a masterpiece, I found in it traces of the modern poetic sensibility and technique that I had been seeking.

The morning after my arrival in New York, I encountered standing in the entrance of the Harlem YMCA two fateful figures. They were Langston Hughes, the poet, and Dr. Alain Locke, the then head of the philosophy department at Howard University. I had never seen Langston Hughes before, but regardless of what is said about the quality of education provided by the old Negro schools (ours was named for Frederick Douglass), we were taught what is now termed "Black History" and were kept abreast of current events pertaining to our people. Thus, as early as the sixth grade we were made aware of the poetry of Langston Hughes, along with the work of the other Negro Renaissance writers, so I recognized Hughes from his photographs. But I recognized Dr. Locke because he had been at Tuskegee only a few weeks prior to my arrival in New York, having gone there to visit Hazel Harrison, a teacher in the music department, and a very fine pianist who had been one of Ferruccio Busoni's prize pupils. Here I'm trying to provide a bit of historical background to give you an idea of the diverse cultural forces at play in the lives of Afro-Americans from the early 1920s to 1936.

Miss Harrison was a friend of Prokofiev, and possessed some of his scores at a time when few would have imagined that a Russian master's music was being made a part of the musical consciousness of an Afro-American college. And certainly not in such a college as Tuskegee—even though Tuskegee's musical tradition was actually rich and quite varied. This is but another example of the contradictions of American culture which escape our attention because they are obscured by racism. Yet thanks to Miss Harrison, I could, like any eager, young, celebrity-fascinated college junior, walk straight up to Dr. Locke and say, "Dr. Locke, do you remember me?" To my delight he said, "Why, of course I do." He then introduced me to Langston Hughes and told Hughes of my interest in poetry.

Langston Hughes had with him copies of Malraux's *Man's Fate* and *The Days of Wrath*, and after a few moments' conversation he said, "Since you like to read so much, maybe you'd like to read these novels and then return them to their owner," and so I did. The returns were tremendous. This incident and this meeting later made it possible for me to ask Langston Hughes if he knew Richard Wright. "Yes," he said, "and it so happens that he's coming here from Chicago next week." Then, with his great generosity, and without telling me, Hughes wrote Richard Wright that there was a young Negro something-or-the-other in New York who wanted to meet him. The next thing I knew I received a postcard—which I still have—that said, "Dear Ralph Ellison, Langston Hughes tells me that you're interested in meeting me. I will be in New York . . ." on such and such a date in July . . . signed Richard Wright. Thus I was to meet Wright on the day after his arrival in New York in July of 1937.

At the time I still thought that I would return to Tuskegee to take my degree in music, but I was not to make it. I had come to New

York to earn expenses for my senior year, but it was during the Depression and I was unable to make enough money. Then, in talking with Wright, my plans and goals were altered—were, in fact, fatefully modified by Wright's.

Wright had come to New York for two purposes, one which was talked about openly, and the other quietly underplayed. The first was to become the editor of the magazine *New Challenge*. The other was to work in the Harlem bureau of the Communist newspaper *The Daily Worker*. With Wright's presence in the *Worker*'s 135th Street office, my introduction to the craft of writing leaped ahead, for it was there that I read many of his unpublished stories and discussed his ideas about literature and culture.

Wright was quiet concerning his assignment to the *Worker*'s staff because he had left Chicago under a cloud. In 1936 he had been thrown out of the May Day parade, sacred to all Communists, for refusing to carry out some assignment. The fact that he had been publicly humiliated by both white *and* black Communists had left him quite bitter. However, someone higher up in the hierarchy recognized his value and was able to persuade him to go to New York, which proved to be to my good fortune.

Being unemployed much of the time, I began to hang around the Harlem bureau, not so much for the ideology being purveyed there—although I found it fascinating—but because of Wright and the manuscripts of a sheaf of novelettes (later published as *Uncle Tom's Children*) that lay in an open desk drawer. Of all those who visited the office, I was the only one who bothered to read these now famous stories. Perhaps this was because his comrades looked upon Wright as an intruder. He was distrusted not only as an "intellectual" and thus a potential traitor, but as a possible "dark horse" in the race for the Harlem party leadership, a "ringer" who had been sent from Chicago to cause them trouble. Wright had little sense of humor about their undisguised hostility, and this led, as would be expected, to touchy relationships. Despite his obvious organizational and journalistic abilities—the *Worker* featured his reportage—the members of the Communist rank and file sneered at his intellectuality, ridiculed his writings, and dismissed his concern with literature and culture as an affectation. In brief, they thought him too ambitious, and therefore a threat to their own ambitions as possible party functionaries.

A true outsider, I was amused by this comedy of misperception, for Wright seemed anything but a threat to their petty ambitions. Besides, I was absolutely intrigued by his talent and felt privileged to read his writings. I had never met anyone who, lacking the fanfare of public recognition, could move me with the unpublished products of his fictional imagination. Of course I read Wright's work uncritically, but there was no doubt in my mind that he was an exceptional writer. Even better, he was delighted to discuss the techniques, the ideological and philosophical implications of his writings, and this with someone who had never attempted to write anything beyond classroom assignments and a few poems. Evidently Wright wished to exchange ideas with someone of his own general background, and I was fortunate in being able to contribute more than curiosity to our discussion. I had studied with creative musicians, both classical and jazz, and had been taught to approach the arts analytically. I had also read fairly widely on my own. But to encounter the possessor of such literary talent and have him make me his friend and confidant was indeed an exciting and inspiring experience.

Nor did it end with mere talk. As editor of *New Challenge*, Wright asked me to contribute a book review in its first issue. To one who had never attempted to write anything, this was the wildest of ideas. Still, pressed by his editorial needs, and sustained by his belief that an untapped supply of free-floating literary talent existed in the Negro community, Wright kept after me, and I wrote a review and he published it. Then he went even further by suggesting that I write a short story!

I said, "But I've never even tried to write a story . . ."

He said, "Look, you talk about these things, you've read a lot, and you've been around. Just put something down and let me see it . . ."

So I wrote a story, titled "Hymie's Bull," that was based upon experiences that I'd had a few years before when riding freight trains from Oklahoma to Alabama. I was dubious over the outcome, but to my delight Wright accepted the story and sent it to the printer.

Ah, but fate, as they say, was in the wings, and *New Challenge* was not to appear again. I hasten to add that this was not a disaster created by my first attempt at fiction. Rather, it had to do with an aspect of Afro-American cultural history and involved certain lingering echoes of the Negro Renaissance, a movement which ran out of gas with the Crash of 1929. As the period ended, a number of figures important to the movement had died, and with the Great Depression upon them, those members of the white community who had sponsored the Renaissance were unable to continue. The money was no longer available, and so the movement languished. However, with the deepening of the Depression there came a significant development in the form of the federal projects for the arts that were organized by the Works Progress Administration. These projects were important to the continuing development of Afro-American artists. Although a reaction to a national disaster, they provided, as have most national disasters, the possibility for a broader Afro-American freedom. This is a shocking thing to say, but it is also a very *blues*, or tragicomic, thing to say, and a fairly accurate description of the manner in which, for Negroes, a gift of freedom arrived wrapped in the guise of disaster. It is ironic, but no less true, that the most tragic incident of our history, the Civil War, was a disaster which ended American slavery.

Wright himself worked on both the Chicago and the New York Federal Writers' Project, and I could not have become a writer at the time I began had I not been able to earn my board and keep by doing research for the New York project. Through Wright's encouragement, I had become serious about writing, but before going on the project I sometimes slept in the public park below City College because I had neither job nor money. But my personal affairs aside, the WPA provided an important surge to Afro-American cultural activity. The result was not a "renaissance," but there was a resuscitation and transformation of that very vital artistic impulse that is abiding among Afro-Americans. Remember that our African forefathers originated in cultures wherein even the simple routines of daily living were highly ritualized, and that even their cooking utensils were fashioned with forms of symbolism which resonated with overtones of godhead. Though modified, if not suppressed, by the experience of American slavery, this tradition of artistic expressiveness has infused the larger American culture. Afro-American cultural style is an abiding aspect of our culture, and the economic disaster which produced the WPA gave it an accelerated release and allowed many Negroes to achieve their identities as artists.

But back to Wright and *New Challenge*. That magazine was organized by people active in the Negro Renaissance, whose outlook was in many ways at odds with Wright's. Thus, according to Wright, *New Challenge* ended publication because the two young women who were in charge before he came on the scene were afraid that his connection with the Communist party would lead to its being taken over. Rather than lose control, they got rid of Wright.

History has no vacuum. There are transformations, there are lesions, there are metamorphoses, and there are mysteries that cloak the clashing of individual wills and private interests. *New Challenge* faded, but Wright went on to publish *Uncle Tom's Children*, and shortly afterward *Native Son*. When Wright came to New York his talents as a writer were, to a large extent, already formed. Indeed, even before 1927, when he migrated to Chicago, he had published fiction in Robert S. Abbott's magazine *The Bronzeman*. So it isn't true, as has been said, that the Communist party "discovered" his talent. Wright was literary in an informed way even in Jackson, Mississippi. But what happened to him in Chicago resulted from his coming into contact with an organized political group which possessed a concept of social hierarchy that was a conscious negation of our racially biased social system. Thus, through his political affiliation, Wright was able to identify his artistic ambitions with what was, for him, a totally new conception of social justice. In the discussions that took place in the Chicago John Reed Club he sharpened his conception of literary form and the relationship between fictional techniques and the world view of Marxism. He came to see art and society in terms of an ideology that was concerned with power, and willing to forgo racial differences in order to take over the world. I realize that this is all rather abstract, but I am trying to suggest the tenor of our discussions. Fortunately Wright's interest in literary theory was not limited to areas prescribed by the party line.

For instance, I was very curious about how one could put Marx and Freud together. No real problem now, I suppose, but coming from where I did, it was puzzling. I was to discover that it was also a problem for Communist intellectuals and for many of their opponents. Either Marx was raised up and Freud put down, or Freud raised up and Marx put down. For me all of this was pretty strange, but at least I could discuss such matters with Richard Wright. This was important for a young writer (and of course I became a young writer, for I soon realized that I wasn't going back to Tuskegee and to music). Since Wright had assured me that I possessed a certain talent, I decided that writing was the direction I would take. I don't know whether he was satisfied with my talent or not; I suspect not. This was interesting, for while I possessed more formal education, it was he who encouraged me and gave me a sense of direction. I'd like you to appreciate the irony of this development: here was a young Afro-American who had gone only to grade school, but who had arrived in Chicago possessing a certain articulateness and an undeveloped talent for writing. He had no further formal education—although he was aware of the University of Chicago and came to associate with a number of its intellectuals—but he gave himself over to the complex reality of late 1927 Chicago and made it his own. Chicago, the city where after years of Southern Negro migration great jazz was being played and reinvented, where the stockyards and railroads, and the steel mills of Gary, Indiana, were transforming a group of rural, agricultural Americans into city people and into a *lumpenproletariat,* a class over whom we now despair.

Wright found the scene challenging. He learned that wherever one wanders in this country, one must pay his dues to change and take advantage of possibility by asserting oneself. You'll recall my saying earlier that "geography is fate"; now let me say that one's fate is also determined by what one does and by what one does *not* do. Wright set out to come into a conscious possession of his experience as Negro, as political revolutionary, as writer, and as citizen of Chicago.

Somehow, getting into the John Reed Club, Wright had learned the techniques of agitprop art—which he came later to despise—and before he went to Harlem he had been a contributing editor of the original *Partisan Review,* and a founder of such magazines as *Anvil.* He had been poor in accepting discipline, and had had his political troubles in the Communist party, but when I knew him he was not shrinking from the challenges of his existence. Nor complaining that he'd been " 'buked and scorned." Nor did he feel that he had handicaps that could not be overcome because of his identity as a Negro writer. Instead he was striving to live consciously—at least artistically and intellectually—at the top of his times. Wright's spirit was such, and his sense of possibility was such, that even during the time when he was writing *Native Son* he was concerned with learning the stylistic and dialectical fine points found in the work of Steinbeck, Hemingway, Malraux, and Thomas Mann; it was these he viewed as his competitors. I warn you that this is only *my* interpretation, but it was as though Wright was thinking, "I have a finer sense, a more basic knowledge of American reality than Hemingway or Steinbeck or anybody else who is writing." He had the kind of confidence that jazzmen have, although I assure you that he knew very little about jazz and didn't even know how to dance. Which is to say that he didn't possess the full range of Afro-American culture. But having the confidence of his talent, having the sense (which he gained from Marxism) that he was living in a world in which he did not have to be

confused by the mystifications of racism, Wright harnessed his revolutionary tendencies to a political program which he hoped would
transform American society. Through his cultural and political activities in Chicago he made a dialectical leap into a sense of his
broadest possibilities as man and as artist. He was well aware of the
forces ranked against him, but in his quiet way he was as arrogant in
facing up to them as was Louis Armstrong in a fine blaring way.

To a young Oklahoman this attitude of Wright's was affirmative,
and again, "geography is fate." For in that state our people fought
back. We seldom won more than moral victories, but we fought
back, as can be seen from the many civil rights victories that were
initiated there. And as can be heard in the Southwestern jazz and the
performances of the Jimmy Rushings, the Hot Lips Pages, the
Count Basies, the Benny Motens and Charlie Christians, we were an
assertive people, and our mode of social assertion was artistic, mainly
musical, as well as political. But there was also the Negro church,
wherein you heard the lingering accents of nineteenth-century rhetoric with its emphasis upon freedom and individual responsibility, a
rhetorical style which gave us Lincoln, Harriet Tubman, Harriet
Beecher Stowe and the other abolition-preaching Beechers. Which
gave us Frederick Douglass, John Jasper and many other eloquent
and heroic Negroes whose spirit still moves among us through the
contributions they made to the flexibility, music and idealism of the
American language. Richard Wright was a possessor of that tradition. It is resonant in his fiction and it was a factor in his eager acceptance of social responsibility.

But now I should add that as far as Negroes in New York were
concerned, Wright was for the most part friendless. Part of this was
due to the fact that he kept to Communist circles and was intensely
involved with writing and political activities. But as far as his rapid
development as a writer is concerned, it would not have been possible but for the Chicago John Reed Club. This required an intellectual environment, and in Negro communities such were few and far
between. Thus, given his talent and driving ambition, it was fortunate that he found the necessary associations among other young

writers, many of whom were not Communists. Within such integrated groups he could question ideas, programs, theories. He could argue over philosophical interpretations of reality and say, if he chose, "Well, dammit, I'm black, and this concept of this program doesn't seem valid to me." This was important for Wright, and since he affirmed many impulses which I felt and understood in my own way, it proved important to me. No less important was his willingness to discuss problems encountered within the Communist party, and especially his difficulty in pursuing independent thought.

Because there, too, he was encountering a form of intellectual racism. It was not couched in the rhetoric of Negro inferiority *à l'américain*, but in the form of an insistence upon blind discipline and a constant pressure to follow unthinkingly a political line. It was dramatized in the servile attitudes of certain black Communist functionaries who regarded Wright, with his eloquence and his tendency toward an independence of thought, as a dangerous figure who had to be kept under rigid control.

Of course Wright's personality would not allow him to shun a battle. He fought back and was into all kinds of trouble. He had no interest in keeping silent as the price of his freedom of expression. Nor was he so dazzled by his freedom to participate in the councils of newspapers and magazines as to keep his mouth shut. Instead he felt that his experience, insight and talent were important to the party's correct assessment of American reality. Thus he fought to make his comrades understand that they didn't know a damn thing about the complexities of the South, whether black or white, and insisted that they could not possibly understand America's racial situation by approaching it through such facile slogans as "Black and White Unite and Fight." Not when the white workingman was doing us the greatest face-to-face damage, and when the unions were practicing policies of racial exclusion. In trying to get this across, in saying, as it were, "Your approach is too simple," Wright met all kinds of resistance, both ideological and personal, but at least he made the fight.

I bring this up here by way of offering you something of the background of emotional and intellectual conflict out of which *Native Son* was written. I read most of *Native Son* as it came off the typewriter, and I didn't know what to think of it except that it was wonderful. I was not responding critically. After all, how many of you have had the unexpected privilege of reading a powerful novel as it was literally ripped off the typewriter? Such opportunities are rare, and being young, I was impressed beyond all critical words. I am still impressed. I feel that *Native Son* is one of the major literary events in the history of American literature. I can say this even though at this point I have certain reservations about its view of reality. Yet it continues to have a powerful effect, and it seems to me a mistake to say, as was said not long ago in *Life* magazine, that *Native Son* is a "neglected" novel. Here I should remind those of you who are too young to remember, that *Native Son* was such a popular work that the dust jacket of the Book-of-the-Month Club edition could consist of a collage made of accolades written by critics and reviewers throughout the country. It was a financial as well as a critical success, and with its publication Wright became a famous man.

But its success by no means stilled his burning passion—not simply for justice, but to become the author of other compelling works of literature. His response to the reception of *12 Million Black Voices*, which is, I think, his most lyrical work, is an example. He was bemused by the fact that this work could move his white readers to tears, and saw this as an evasion of the intended impact of his vision. Thus he began to talk over and over again of forging such hard, mechanical images and actions that no white reading them could afford the luxury of tears.

But here I must turn critic. For in *my* terms, Wright failed to grasp the function of artistically induced catharsis, which suggests that he failed also to understand the Afro-American custom of shouting in church (a form of ritual cartharsis), or its power to cleanse the mind and redeem and rededicate the individual to forms of ideal action. Perhaps he failed to understand, or else rejected, those moments of exultation wherein man's vision is quickened by the eloquence of an orchestra, an actor, orator or dancer, or by anyone using the arts of music, speech or symbolic gesture to create within us moments of high consciousness—moments wherein we grasp, in the instant, a knowledge of how transcendent, abysmal and yet affirmative it can be to be human. Yet it is for such moments of inspired communication that the artist lives. The irony here is that Wright could evoke them, but felt, for ideological reasons, that tears were a betrayal of the struggle for freedom.

I disagreed with his analysis, for tears can induce as well as deter action. Nevertheless it is imperative that I say that through his writings Richard Wright achieved, here in the social and racial chaos of the United States, a position of artistic equality. He insisted upon it—and not only in his own political party, with which he eventually broke, but internationally. He was never at peace. He was never at rest. The restlessness which sent our forefathers hurtling toward the West Coast, and which now has us climbing up all sorts of walls, was very much within him. In 1956, in Paris, when we were leaving the headquarters of the magazine *Présence Africaine* (this is the first time I've revealed this, and I hope he won't mind, since it might be meaningful to some scholar), he said to me, "Really, Ralph, after I broke with the Communist party I had nowhere else to go . . ." This was said in resigned explanation of his continued presence in Europe. I think he was telling me that his dedication to Communism had been so complete and his struggle so endless that he had had to change his scene, that he had had to find a new ground upon which to struggle. Because as long as he stayed within the framework of his political party, he had to struggle on two fronts, asserting on one the principles of equality and possibility (which the Communists stood for, or *pretended* to stand for), and on the other, insisting upon the fact *not* that it took a Negro to tell the truth about the Afro-American experience, but that you had to at least get down into the mud and live with its basic realities to do so. You could not deal with its complexities simply from a theoretical perspective.

Black Boy was an attempt to depict some of those complexities. So much of this autobiography (originally entitled *American Hunger*) is exaggerated, I think, precisely because Wright was trying to dramatize—indeed, because of its many fictional techniques he could with justice have called it a "nonfiction" novel—the complexity of Negro American experience as he knew it and had lived it. The fictional techniques were not there in order to con anyone, but to drive home to Americans, black and white, something of the complexity and cost in human terms, in terms of the loss to literature and to art, and to the cause of freedom itself, imposed by racial discrimination—the cost, that is, of growing up in a society which operated on one side of its mind by the principle of equality while qualifying that principle severely according to the dictates of racism. Wright was thinking and fighting over these issues at close quarters, fighting with the Communists especially because he had thought that they offered a viable solution. Instead he discovered that they were blind.

But now to more delightful relationships with Wright. He had as much curiosity about how writing is written as I had about how music is composed, and our curiosity concerning artistic creation became the basis of our friendship. Having studied music from the age of eight, and having studied harmony and symphonic form in our segregated school, I was also interested in how music related to the other arts. This, combined with my growing interest in literary creation, made my contact with Wright's enthusiasm an educational and spirit-freeing experience. Having read Pound, Eliot, Shaw and the criticism of Harriet Monroe and I. A. Richards—all available in Tuskegee's excellent little library—it was important that in Wright I had discovered a Negro American writer who possessed a working knowledge of modern literature, its techniques and theories. My approach to literature was by no means racial, but Wright was not only available, he was eager to share his interests, and it gave me something of that sense of self-discovery and exaltation which is implicit in the Negro church and in good jazz. Indeed, I had found it in baseball and football games, and it turns up in almost any group activity of Afro-Americans when we're not really thinking about white folks and are simply being our own American selves.

I am reminded of a discussion that another Tuskegeian and I were having with a group of white friends. The discussion had to do with our discovery of Hemingway (whom I discovered in a Negro barbershop) and Conrad (another writer I often discussed with Wright), and suddenly the Tuskegee graduate said to me, "Aren't you glad that we found those guys on our own at Tuskegee?"

Now, that was not Negro chauvinism, but a meaningful observation about the relationship between social scene and experience, and I concurred. I had had the same reaction when I first talked with Wright about fictional technique, and we had gone on to discuss some of the complications and interconnections between culture and society that claimed our conscious attention despite the fact that we were segregated. The question reminded me of how wonderful it was to have read T. S. Eliot in the context of Tuskegee. The question was not raised to celebrate a then segregated college in a violently segregated state, but to inform our white friends that racism aside, there are other important relationships between scenes, ideas and experience. Scene and circumstance combined to give ideas resonance, and to compel a consciousness of perspective. What one reads becomes part of what one sees and feels. Thus it is impossible for me to reread certain passages from Joyce or Eliot or Sir Thomas Browne without seeing once again the deep magenta skies that descend upon the Tuskegee campus at dusk in summer. The scene, then, is always a part of personality, and scene and personality combine to give viability to ideas. Scene is thus always a part, the ground, of action—and especially of *conscious* action. Its associations and implicit conflicts provide the extra dimension which anchors poetry in reality and structures our efforts toward freedom.

Richard Wright was trying to add to our consciousness the dimension of being a black boy who grew up in Jackson, Mississippi (a scene that was not always so rugged, even for him, as he pictured it artistically), but a boy who grew up and who achieved through his reading a sense of what was possible out there in the wider world. A boy who grew up and achieved and accepted his own *individual* responsibility for seeing to it that America become conscious of itself. He insisted that this country recognize the interconnections between its places and its personalities, its act and its ideals. This was the burden of Richard Wright, and, as I see it, the driving passion of Richard Wright. It led to his triumphs as it led, inevitably, to some of his defeats. But one thing must be said of Richard Wright: in him we had for the first time a Negro American writer as randy, as courageous and as irrepressible as Jack Johnson. And if you don't know who Jack Johnson was, I'll tell you that when I was a little boy this early heavyweight boxing champion was one of the most admired underground heroes. He was rejected by most whites and by many respectable Negroes, but he was nevertheless a hero among veterans of the Spanish-American War who rejoiced in the skill and élan with which Johnson set off the now-outrageous search for a "White Hope."

This suggests that we literary people should always keep a sharp eye on what is happening in the unintellectualized areas of our experience. Our peripheral vision had better be damned good, because while baseball, basketball and football players cannot really tell us how to write our books, they *do* demonstrate where much of the significant action is taking place. Often they are themselves cultural heroes who are responsible for a powerful modification in American social attitudes. They tell us in nonliterary terms much about the nature of possibility. They tell us about the cost of success, and much about the nonpolitical aspects of racial and national identity, about the changing nature of social hierarchy, and about the role which individual skill and excellence can play in creating social change.

In this country there were good Negro writers before Wright arrived on the scene—and my respects to all of them—but it seems to me that Richard Wright wanted more and dared more. I think now as I offer you the memories of a middle-aged man, he was sometimes too passionate, but at least he wanted and demanded as much as any novelist, any artist should want: He wanted to be tested in terms of his talent, not in terms of his race or Mississippi upbringing. Rather he had the feeling that his vision of American life, and his ability to project it eloquently, justified his being considered among the best of American writers. And in this crazy, mixed-up country, as is witnessed by this conference dedicated to his works and to his memory, it turns out that he was right.

Homage to Duke Ellington
on His Birthday

It is to marvel: the ageless and irrepressible Duke Ellington is seventy, and another piano player of note, President Richard M. Nixon, has ordered in his honor a state dinner to be served in the house where, years ago, Duke's father, then a butler, once instructed white guests from the provinces in the gentle art and manners proper to such places of elegance and power. It is good news in these times of general social upheaval that traces of the old American success story remain valid, for now where the parent labored, the son is to be honored for his achievements. Perhaps it is inevitable that Duke Ellington should be shown the highest hospitality of the nation's First Family in its greatest house, and that through the courtesy of the chief of state all Americans may pay, symbolically, their respects to our greatest composer.

Perhaps it is also inevitable (and if not inevitable, certainly proper) that that which a Pulitzer Prize jury of a few years ago was too insecure or shortsighted to do, and that which our institutions dedicated to the recognition of artistic achievement have been too prejudiced, negligent or concerned with European models and styles to do, is finally being done by presidents. For it would seem that Ellington's greatness has been recognized by everyone except those charged with recognizing musical excellence at the highest levels, and even some of these have praised him privately while failing to grant him public honor.

Nevertheless, he is far from being a stranger to the White House, for during the occupancy of President and Mrs. Lyndon B. Johnson, Ellington became something of a regular guest there; indeed, it was

From *The Sunday Star* (Washington, D.C.), April 27, 1969.

President Johnson who appointed him to the National Council on the Arts, thereby giving recognition to our most important indigenous art form in the person of its most outstanding creator. Certainly there is no better indication that those on the highest levels of governmental power have at last begun to recognize our arts and their creators as national treasures. Perhaps in Ellington's special case this is a proper and most fitting path to official national recognition, since for more than forty years his music has been not only superb entertainment but an important function of national morale. During the Depression whenever his theme song "East St. Louis Toodle-oo" came on the air, our morale was lifted by something inescapably hopeful in the sound. Its style was so triumphant and the moody melody so successful in capturing the times, yet so expressive of the faith which would see us through them. And when the "Black and Tan Fantasy" was played we were reminded not only of how fleeting all human life must be, but in its blues-based tension between content and manner, it warned us not only to look at the darker side of life, but also to remember the enduring necessity for humor, technical mastery and creative excellence. It was immensely danceable and listenable music, and ever so evocative of other troubled times and other triumphs over disaster. It was also most Negro American in its mocking interpolations from Chopin's B-flat minor piano concerto, to which, as Barry Ulanov has reminded us, it was once popular to sing the gallows-humored words: "Where shall we all / Be / A hundred years / From now?"

How many generations of Americans, white and black, wooed their wives and had the ceremonial moments of their high school and college days memorialized by Ellington's tunes? And to how many thousands has he defined what it should mean to be young and alive and American? Yes, and to how many has he given a sense of personal elegance and style? A sense of possibility? And who, seeing and hearing Ellington and his marvelous band, hasn't been moved to wonder at the mysterious, unanalyzed character of the Negro American, and at the white American's inescapable Negro-ness?

Even though few recognized it, such artists as Ellington and Louis Armstrong were the stewards of our vaunted American optimism, and guardians against the creeping irrationality which ever plagues our form of society. They created great entertainment, but for them (ironically) and for us (unconsciously), their music was a rejection of that chaos and license which characterized the so-called Jazz Age associated with F. Scott Fitzgerald, and which has returned once more to haunt the nation. Place Ellington with Hemingway; they are both larger than life, both masters of that which is most enduring in the human enterprise: the power of man to define himself against the ravages of time through artistic style.

I remember Ellington from my high school days in Oklahoma City, first as a strangely familiar timbre of orchestral sounds issuing from phonograph records and radio. Familiar because beneath the stylized jungle sounds (the like of which no African jungle had ever heard), there sounded the blues, and strange because the mutes, toilet plungers and derby hats with which I was acquainted as a musician had been given a stylized elegance and extension of effect unheard of even in the music of Louis Armstrong. It was as though Ellington had taken the traditional instruments of Negro American music and modified them, extended their range and enriched their tonal possibilities. We were studying the classics then, working at harmony and the forms of symphonic music. While we affirmed the voice of jazz and the blues despite all criticism from our teachers because they spoke to a large extent of what we felt about the life we lived most intimately, it was not until the discovery of Ellington that we had any hint that jazz possessed possibilities of a range of expressiveness comparable to that of classical European music.

Then Ellington and his great orchestra came to town—came with their uniforms, their sophistication, their skills; their golden horns, their flights of controlled and disciplined fantasy; came with their art, their special sound; came with Ivy Anderson and Ethel Waters singing and dazzling the eye with their high-brown beauty and with the richness and bright feminine flair of their costumes and promising manners. They were news from the great wide world, an example and a goal, and I wish that all those who write so knowledgeably about Negro boys having no masculine figures with whom to identify would consider the long national and international career of Ellington and his band, and the thousands of one-night stands played in the black communities of this nation. Where in the white community, in *any* white community, could there have been found examples such as these? Who were so worldly, who so elegant, who so mockingly creative? Who were so skilled at their given trade and who treated the social limitations placed in their paths with greater disdain?

Friends of mine were already collecting Ellington records, and the more mature jazzmen were studying, without benefit of formal institutions of learning, his enigmatic style. Indeed, during the thirties and forties, when most aspiring writers of fiction were learning from the style and example of Hemingway, many jazz composers, orchestrators and arrangers were following the example of Ellington, attempting to make something new and uniquely their own out of the traditional elements of the blues and jazz. For us Duke was a culture hero, a musical magician who worked his powers through his mastery of form, nuance and style, a charismatic figure whose personality influenced even those who had no immediate concern with the art of jazz.

My mother, an Afro-American Methodist Episcopalian who shouted in church but who allowed me nevertheless to leave sunrise Christmas services to attend breakfast dances, once expressed the hope that when I had completed my musical studies I would have a band like Ellington's. I was pleased and puzzled at the time, but now I suspect that she recognized a certain religious element in Ellington's music, an element which has now blossomed forth in compositions of his own form of liturgical music. Either that, or she accepted the sound of dedication wherever she heard it, and thus was willing to see Duke as an example of the mysterious way in which God showed His face in music.

I did not meet Ellington at the time. I was only a young boy in the crowd who stood entranced around the bandstand at Slaughter's Hall. But a few years later, when I was a student in the music department at Tuskegee, I shook his hand and talked briefly with him of my studies and my dreams. He was kind and generous even though harassed (there had been some trouble in travel, and the band had arrived hours late, with the instruments misplaced and the musicians evil as only tired, black, Northern-based musicians could be in the absurdly segregated South of the 1930s), and those of us who talked with him were renewed in our determination to make our names in music.

A few years later, a stranger in Harlem, I lived at the YMCA and spent many a homesick afternoon playing Duke's records on the jukebox in Small's Paradise Bar, asking myself why I was in New York and finding reassurance in the music. Although the way seemed cloudy (I had little money and would soon find it necessary to sleep in the park below City College), I decided I should remain there and take my chances.

Later I met Langston Hughes, who took me up to Sugar Hill to visit the Duke in his apartment. Much to my delight, the great musician remembered me, was still apologetic because of the lateness of the band's arrival at Tuskegee, and asked me what he could do to aid the music department. I said that we were sadly deficient in our library of classical scores and recordings, and he offered to make the school a gift of as extensive a library of recordings as was needed. It was an offer which I passed on to Tuskegee with great enthusiasm, but which, for some reason, perhaps because it had not come directly from Ellington himself, or perhaps because several people in the department regarded jazz as an inferior form of music, was rejected. That his was a genuine gesture I had no doubt, for at the time I was to see a further example of his generosity when Jimmie Lunceford's orchestra, then considered an Ellington rival, came on the radio. The other musicians present kidded Ellington about the challenge of Lunceford's group, to which he responded by listening intently until the number was finished and then commenting, "Those boys are interesting. They are trying, they are really trying," without a trace of condescension but with that enigmatic Ellington smile. The brief comment and the smile were enough; the kidding stopped, for we had all been listening, and not for the first time, and we knew that Duke had little to fear from the challenge of Lunceford or anyone else.

Somewhere during his childhood a friend had nicknamed Edward Kennedy Ellington "Duke," and he had proceeded to create for himself a kingdom of sound and rhythm that has remained impregnable to the fluctuations of fad and novelty, even to the death of key members of his band. Jazz styles have come and gone, and other composer-conductors have been given the title "King of Jazz." Duke knew the reason why, as did the world, just as he knew the value of his own creation, but he never complained; he simply smiled and made music. Now the other kings have departed, while his work endures and his creativity continues.

When the Pulitzer Prize committee refused to give him a special award for music (a decision which led certain members of the committee to resign), Ellington remarked, "Fate is being kind to me. Fate doesn't want me to be too famous too young," a quip as mocking of our double standards, hypocrisies, and pretensions as the dancing of those slaves who, looking through the windows of a plantation manor house from the yard, imitated the steps so gravely performed by the masters within and then added to them their own special flair, burlesquing the white folks and then going on to force the steps into a choreography uniquely their own. The whites, looking out at the activity in the yard, thought that they were being flattered by imitation, and were amused by the incongruity of tattered blacks dancing courtly steps, while missing completely the fact that before their eyes a European cultural form was becoming Americanized, undergoing a metamorphosis through the mocking activity of a people partially sprung from Africa. So, blissfully unaware, the whites laughed while the blacks danced out their mocking reply.

In a country which began demanding the projection of its own unique experience in literature as early as the 1820s, it was ironic that American composers were expected to master the traditions, conventions and subtleties of European music, and to force their own American musical sense of life into the forms created by Europe's greatest composers. Thus the history of American classical music has been marked by a struggle to force American experience into European forms.

In other words, our most highly regarded musical standards remained those of the Europe from which the majority of Americans derived. Fortunately, however, not all Americans spring from Europe (or not only from Europe), and while these standards obtained, Negro American composers were not really held to them, since it seemed obvious that blacks had nothing to do with Europe— even though during slavery Negroes had made up comic verses about a dance to which "Miss Rose come in her mistress's clothes / But how she got them nobody knows / And long before the ball did meet / She was dancing Taglioni at the corner of the street," Taglioni being a dancer who was the rage of Europe during the 1850s.

Be that as it may, the dominance of European standards did work a hardship on the Negro American composer because it meant that no matter how inventive he might become, his music would not be considered important, or even American (1) because of his race and (2) because of the form, if he was a jazzman, in which he worked. Therefore a composer such as Ellington was at odds with European music and its American representatives, just as he was at odds with the racial attitudes of the majority of the American population, and while primarily a creative composer, he was seen mainly in his role as entertainer. Doubtless this explains the withholding from Ellington of the nation's highest honors.

It isn't a matter of being protected, as Duke suggests, from being too famous too young—he is one of the world's most famous composers and is recognized by the likes of Stravinsky, Stokowski and Milhaud as one of the greatest moderns—but the fact that his creations are far too *American*. There is also the fact of Ellington's aura of mockery. Mockery speaks through his work and bearing. He is one of the most handsome of men, and to many his stage manners are so suave and gracious that they appear a put-on—which quite often they are. His manner, like his work, serves to remind us of the inadequacies of our myths, legends, conduct and standards. However, Ellington's is a creative mockery in that it rises above itself to offer us something better, more creative and hopeful, than we've attained while seeking other standards.

During a period when groups of young English entertainers who based their creations on the Negro American musical tradition have effected a questionable revolution of manners among American youths, perhaps it is time we paid our respects to a man who has spent his life reducing the violence and chaos of American life to artistic order. I have no idea where we will all be a hundred years from now, but if there is a classical music in which the American experience has finally discovered the voice of its own complexity, it will owe much of its direction to the achievements of Edward Kennedy Ellington. For many years he has been telling us how marvelous, mad, violent, hopeful, nostalgic and (perhaps) decent we are. He is one of the musical fathers of our country, and throughout all these years he has, as he tells us so mockingly, loved us madly. We are privileged to have lived during his time and to have known so great a man, so great a musician.

The Art of Romare Bearden

I regard the weakening of the importance given to objects as the
capital transformation of Western art. In painting, it is clear that a
painting of Picasso's is less and less a "canvas," and more and more
the mark of some discovery, a stake left to indicate the place
through which a restless genius has passed . . .

—*André Malraux*

THIS series of collages and projections by Romare Bearden represents a triumph of a special order. Springing from a dedicated
painter's unending efforts to master the techniques of illusion and
revelation which are so important to the craft of painting, they are
also the result of Bearden's search for fresh methods to explore the
plastic possibilities of Negro American experience. What is special
about Bearden's achievement is, it seems to me, the manner in which
he has made his dual explorations serve one another, the way in
which his technique has been used to discover and transfigure its
object. In keeping with the special nature of his search, and by the
self-imposed "rules of the game," it was necessary that the methods
arrived at be such as would allow him to express the tragic predicament of his people without violating his passionate dedication to art
as a fundamental and transcendent agency for confronting and revealing the world.

To have done this successfully is not only to have added a dimension to the technical resourcefulness of art, but to have modified our
way of experiencing reality. It is also to have had a most successful
encounter with a troublesome social anachronism which, while find-

The introduction in the catalogue *Romare Bearden: Paintings and Projections* for an
exhibition held at the Art Gallery of the State University of New York at Albany,
November 25–December 22, 1968. Reprinted in *The Massachusetts Review*, Winter
1977.

ing its existence in areas lying beyond the special province of the artist, has nevertheless caused great confusion among many painters of Bearden's social background. I say *social*, for although Bearden is by self-affirmation no less than by public identification a Negro American, the quality of his *artistic* culture can by no means be conveyed by that term. Nor does it help to apply the designation "black" (even more amorphous for conveying a sense of cultural complexity), and since such terms tell us little about the unique individuality of the artist or anyone else, it is well to have them out in the open where they can cause the least confusion.

What, then, do I mean by anachronism? I refer to that imbalance in American society which leads to a distorted perception of social reality, to a stubborn blindness to the creative possibilities of cultural diversity, to the prevalence of negative myths, racial stereotypes and dangerous illusions about art, humanity and society. Arising from an initial failure of social justice, this anachronism divides social groups along lines that are no longer tenable, while fostering hostility, anxiety and fear, and in the area to which we now address ourselves it has had the damaging effect of alienating many Negro artists from the traditions, techniques and theories indigenous to the arts through which they aspire to achieve themselves.

Thus in the field of culture, where their freedom of self-definition is at a maximum, and where the techniques of artistic self-expression are most abundantly available, such artists are so fascinated by the power of their anachronistic social imbalance as to limit their efforts to describing its manifold dimensions and its apparent invincibility against change. Indeed, they take it as a major theme and focus for their attention, and they allow it to dominate their thinking about themselves, their people, their country and their art. But while many are convinced that simply to recognize social imbalance is enough to put it to riot, few achieve anything like artistic mastery, and most fail miserably through a single-minded effort to "tell it like it is."

Sadly, however, the problem for the plastic artist is not one of "telling" at all, but of *revealing* that which has been concealed by time, custom and our trained incapacity to perceive the truth. Thus it is a matter of destroying moribund images of reality and creating the new. Further, for the true artist, working from the top of his times and out of a conscious concern with the most challenging possibilities of his form, the unassimilated and anachronistic—whether in the shape of motif, technique or image—is abhorrent evidence of conceptual and/or technical failure, of challenges unmet. Although he may ignore the anachronistic through a preoccupation with other pressing details, he can never be satisfied simply by placing it within a frame. For once there, it becomes the symbol of all that is not art and a mockery of his powers of creation. So at his best he struggles to banish the anachronistic element from his canvas by converting it into an element of style, a device of his personal vision.

As Bearden demonstrated here so powerfully, it is of the true artist's nature and mode of action to dominate all the world and time through technique and vision. His mission is to bring a new visual order into the world, and through his art he seeks to reset society's clock by imposing upon it his own method of defining the times. The urge to do this determines the form and character of his social responsibility, spurs his restless exploration for plastic possibilities, and accounts to a large extent for his creative aggressiveness.

But it is here precisely that the aspiring Negro painter so often falters. Trained by the circumstances of his social predicament to a habit (no matter how reluctant) of accommodation, such an attitude toward the world seems quixotic. He is, he feels, only one man, and the conditions which thwart his freedom are of such enormous dimensions as to appear unconquerable by purely plastic means, even at the hands of the most highly trained, gifted and arrogant artist. "Turn Picasso into a Negro and *then* let me see how far he can go," he will tell you, because he feels an irremediable conflict between his identity as a member of an embattled social minority and his freedom as an artist. He cannot avoid, nor should he wish to avoid, his group identity, but he flounders before the question of how his group's experience might be given statement through the categories of a nonverbal form of art which has been consciously exploring its own unique possibilities for many decades before he appeared on the scene. It is a self-assertive and irreverent art which abandoned long ago the task of mere representation to photography and the role of storytelling to the masters of the comic strip and the cinema. Nor can he draw upon his folk tradition for a simple answer. Beginning with the Bible and proceeding all the way through the spirituals, blues, novels, poems and the dance, Negro Americans have depended upon the element of narrative for both entertainment and group identification. Further, it has been those who have offered an answer to the question, always crucial in the lives of a repressed minority, of who and what they are in the most simplified and graphic terms who have won their highest praise and admiration. Unfortunately there seems to be (the African past notwithstanding) no specifically Negro American tradition of plastic design to offer him support.

How then, he asks himself, does even an artist steeped in the most advanced lore of his craft and most passionately concerned with solving the more advanced problems of painting as *painting* address himself to the perplexing question of bringing his art to bear upon the task (never so urgent as now) of defining Negro American identity, and of pressing its claims for recognition and for justice? He feels, in brief, a near-unresolvable conflict between his urge to leave his mark upon the world through art and his ties to his group and its claims upon him.

Fortunately for them and for us, Romare Bearden has faced these questions for himself, and since he is an artist whose social consciousness is no less intense than his dedication to art, his example is of utmost importance for all who are concerned with grasping something of the complex interrelations between race, culture and the individual artist as they exist in the United States. Bearden is aware that for Negro Americans these are times of eloquent protest and intense struggle, times of rejection and redefinition, but he also knows that all this does little to make the question of the relation of

the Negro artist to painting any less difficult. If the cries in the street
are to find effective statement on canvas, they must undergo a metamorphosis. In painting, Bearden has recently observed, there is little
room for the lachrymose, for self-pity or raw complaint, and if they
are to find a place in painting, this can only be accomplished by in-
fusing them with the freshest sensibility of the times as it finds existence in the elements of painting.

During the late thirties when I first became aware of Bearden's
work, he was painting scenes of the Depression in a style strongly
influenced by the Mexican muralists. This work was powerful, the
scenes grim and brooding, and through his depiction of unemployed
workingmen in Harlem he was able, while evoking the Southern
past, to move beyond the usual protest painting of this period to reveal something of the universal elements of an abiding human condition. By striving to depict the times, by reducing scene, character
and atmosphere to a style, he caught something of both the universality of Harlem life and the "harlemness" of the national human
predicament.

I recall that later, under the dual influences of Hemingway and
the poetic tragedy of Federico García Lorca, Bearden created a voluminous series of drawings and paintings inspired by Lorca's *Lament
for Ignacio Sánchez Mejías.* He had become interested in myth and
ritual as potent forms for ordering human experience, and it would
seem that by stepping back from the immediacy of the Harlem experience, which he knew both from boyhood and as a social worker, he
was freed to give expression to the essentially poetic side of his vision. The products of this period were marked by a palette which, in
contrast with the somber colors of the earlier work and despite the
tragic theme with its underlying allusions to Christian rite and mystery, was brightly sensual. But despite their having been consciously
influenced by the compositional patterns of the Italian primitives
and Dutch masters, these works were also resolutely abstract.

It was as though Bearden had decided that in order to possess his
world artistically, he had to confront it not through propaganda or

sentimentality, but through the finest techniques and traditions of painting. He sought to re-create his Harlem in the light of his painter's vision, and thus avoided the defeats suffered by many of the aspiring painters of this period who seemed to have felt that they had only to reproduce, out of a mood of protest and despair, the scenes and surfaces of Harlem in order to win artistic mastery and accomplish social transfiguration.

It would seem that for many Negro painters even the *possibility* of translating Negro American experience into the modes and conventions of modern painting went unrecognized. This was, in part, the result of an agonizing fixation upon the racial mysteries and social realities dramatized by color, facial structure and the texture of Negro skin and hair. Again, many aspiring artists clung with protective compulsiveness to the myth of the Negro American's total alienation from the larger American culture—a culture which he helped to create in the areas of music and literature, and where in the area of painting he has appeared from the earliest days of the nation as a symbolic figure—and allowed the realities of their social and political situation to determine their conception of their role and freedom as artists.

To accept this form of the myth was to accept its twin variants, one of which holds that there is a pure mainstream of American culture which is "unpolluted" by any trace of Negro American style or idiom, and the other (propagated currently by the exponents of *Negritude*) which holds that Western art is basically racist, and thus anything more than a cursory knowledge of its techniques and history is irrelevant to the Negro artist. In other words, the Negro American who aspired to the title "artist" was too often restricted by sociological notions of racial separatism, and these appear not only to have restricted his use of artistic freedom, but to have limited his curiosity about the abundant resources made available to him by those restless and assertive agencies of the artistic imagination which we call technique and conscious culture.

Indeed, it has been said that these disturbing works of Bearden's (which literally erupted during a tranquil period of abstract painting) began quite innocently as a demonstration to a group of Negro painters. He was suggesting some of the possibilities through which commonplace materials could be forced to undergo a creative metamorphosis when manipulated by some of the nonrepresentational techniques available to the resourceful craftsman. The step from collage to projection followed naturally, since Bearden had used it during the early forties as a means of studying the works of such early masters as Giotto and de Hooch. That he went on to become fascinated with the possibilities lying in such "found" materials is both an important illustrative instance for younger painters and a source for our delight and wonder.

Bearden knows that regardless of the individual painter's personal history, taste or point of view, he must nevertheless pay his materials the respect of approaching them through a highly conscious awareness of the resources and limitations of the form to which he has dedicated his creative energies. One suspects also that as an artist possessing a marked gift for pedagogy, Bearden has sought here to reveal a world long hidden by the clichés of sociology and rendered cloudy by the distortions of newsprint and the false continuity imposed upon our conception of Negro life by television and much documentary photography. Therefore, as he delights us with the magic of design and teaches us the ambiguity of vision, Bearden insists that we see in depth and by the fresh light of his creative vision. He knows that the true complexity of the slum dweller and the tenant farmer requires a release from the prison of our media-dulled perception and a reassembling in forms which would convey something of the depth and wonder of the Negro American's stubborn humanity.

Being aware that the true artist destroys the accepted world by way of revealing the unseen, and creating that which is new and uniquely his own, Bearden has used Cubist techniques to his own ingenious effect. His mask-faced Harlemites and tenant farmers set in their mysteriously familiar but emphatically abstract scenes are nevertheless resonant of artistic and social history. Without compromising their integrity as elements in plastic compositions, his figures are expressive of a complex reality lying beyond their frames. While functioning as integral elements of design, they serve simultaneously as signs and symbols of a humanity that has struggled to survive the decimating and fragmentizing effects of American social processes. Here faces which draw upon the abstract character of African sculpture for their composition are made to focus our attention upon the far from abstract reality of a people. Here abstract interiors are presented in which concrete life is acted out under repressive conditions. Here too the poetry of the blues is projected through synthetic forms which visually are in themselves tragicomic and eloquently poetic. A harsh poetry this, but poetry nevertheless, with the nostalgic imagery of the blues conceived as visual form, image, pattern and symbol—including the familiar trains (evoking partings and reconciliations) and the conjure women (who appear in these works with the ubiquity of the witches who haunt the drawing of Goya) who evoke the abiding mystery of the enigmatic women who people the blues. Here too are renderings of those rituals of rebirth and dying, of baptism and sorcery which give ceremonial continuity to the Negro American community.

By imposing his vision upon scenes familiar to us all, Bearden reveals much of the universally human which they conceal. Through his creative assemblage he makes complex comments upon history, society and the nature of art. Indeed, his Harlem becomes a place inhabited by people who have in fact been *resurrected*, re-created by art, a place composed of visual puns and artistic allusions where the sacred and profane, reality and dream are ambiguously mingled. Resurrected with them in the guise of fragmented ancestral figures and forgotten gods (really masks of the instincts, hopes, emotions, aspirations and dreams) are those powers that now surge in our land with a potentially destructive force which springs from the very fact of their having for so long gone unrecognized and unseen.

Bearden doesn't impose these powers upon us by explicit comment, but his ability to make the unseen manifest allows us some insight into the forces which now clash and rage as Negro Americans seek self-definition in the slums of our cities. There is beauty here, a harsh beauty that asserts itself out of the horrible fragmentation which Bearden's subjects and their environment have undergone. But, as I have said, there is no preaching; these forces have been brought to eye by formal art. These works take us from Harlem through the South of tenant farms and northward-bound trains to tribal Africa; our mode of conveyance consists of every device which has claimed Bearden's artistic attention, from the oversimplified and scanty images of Negroes that appear in our ads and photojournalism, to the discoveries of the School of Paris and the Bauhaus. He has used the discoveries of Giotto and Pieter de Hooch no less than those of Juan Gris, Picasso, Schwitters and Mondrian (who was no less fascinated by the visual possibilities of jazz than by the compositional rhythms of the early Dutch masters), and he has discovered his own uses for the metaphysical richness of African sculptural forms. In brief, Bearden has used—and most playfully—all of his artistic knowledge and skill to create a curve of plastic vision which reveals to us something of the mysterious complexity of those who dwell in our urban slums. But his is the eye of a painter, not a sociologist, and here the elegant architectural details which exist in a setting of gracious but neglected streets, and the buildings in which the hopeful and the hopeless live cheek by jowl, where failed human wrecks and the confidently expectant explorers of the frontiers of human possibility are crowded together as incongruously as the explosive details in a Bearden canvas—all this comes across plastically and with a freshness of impact that employs neither sociological cliché nor raw protest.

Where any number of painters have tried to project the "prose" of Harlem, a task performed more successfully by photographers, Bearden has concentrated upon releasing its poetry, abiding rituals and ceremonies of affirmation, creating a surreal poetry compounded of vitality and powerlessness, destructive impulse and the all-pervading and enduring faith in their own style of American humanity. Through his faith in the powers of art to reveal the unseen through the seen, his collages have transcended their immaculateness as plastic constructions. Or to put it another way, Bearden's meaning is identical with his method. His combination of technique is in itself eloquent of the sharp breaks, leaps in consciousness, distortions, paradoxes, reversals, telescoping of time and surreal blending of styles, values, hopes and dreams which characterize much of Negro American history. Through an act of creative will, he has blended strange visual harmonies out of the shrill, indigenous dichotomies of American life, and in doing so has reflected the irrepressible thrust of a people to endure and keep its intimate sense of its own identity.

Bearden seems to have told himself that in order to possess the meaning of his Southern childhood and Northern upbringing, and to keep his memories, dreams and values whole, he would have to re-create and humanize them by reducing them to artistic style. Thus in the poetic sense these works give plastic expression to a vision in which the socially grotesque conceals a tragic beauty, and they embody Bearden's interrogation of the empirical values of a society that mocks its own ideals through a blindness induced by its myth of race. All this, ironically, by a man who visually, at least (he is light-skinned and perhaps more Russian than "black" in appearance), need never have been restricted to the social limitations imposed upon easily identified Negroes. Bearden's art is therefore not only an affirmation of his own freedom and responsibility as an individual and artist, but is an affirmation of the irrelevance of the notion of race as a limiting force in the arts. These are works of a man possessing a rare lucidity of vision.

Society, Morality and the Novel

SURELY it would be of more value for a novelist to write novels than to spend his energies discussing The Novel, for by carrying out his chosen task there he has the possibility of moving beyond the given level of either his talent or his cold perception of life's meaning—of "playing beyond his game," as it were, and thus achieving for himself and for his readers some new insight into the human predicament, some new facet of human possibility. By risking the unknown which appears whenever he follows the lead of his imagination as driven by his hopes and his fears, he has the chance of achieving the significantly new and thus becoming himself a part of that which he achieves. While on the other hand, theorizing about the form, function, and *raison d'être* of the novel leads him straightway into the fields of social and aesthetic criticism, the domain of specialists. Here he is circumscribed by rules which are alien to his obsessive need to play with the fires of chaos and to rearrange reality to the patterns of his imagination. While it is the drive of the critic to create systems of thought, it is that of the novelist to re-create reality in the forms which his personal vision assumes as it plays and struggles with the vividly illusory "eidetic-like" imagery left in the mind's eye by the process of social change. Life for the novelist is a game of hide-and-seek in which he is eternally the sometimes delighted but more often frustrated "it."

Critics are, on the whole, more "adult" types. They share a liking for order, and have little patience with dashing about trying to pin down the multiple illusions projected by life with arbitrary ones of one's arrogant own; it is their function to dispense with that annoying characteristic of life with the bright pure light of their methods. The novelist must take chances or die, while the critic would make it

---

From *The Living Novel*, Macmillan Inc., 1957.

unnecessary to do so. Critics would give you the formula that would make the achievement of a major fiction as certain as making a pre-mixed apple pie. They analyze, they classify, they man the lines of continuity linking present developments with past achievements of the form, and with their specialized knowledge they compose the novelists' most sensitively aware audience—or so we have long been accustomed to regarding them. Presently we shall take a closer look at just how contemporary fiction criticism mediates between the American novelist and the American reader, but here let us simply observe that novelists have, for the most part, been content to keep out of the critics' domain. They either confine those critical formu-lations necessary to the clarification of their own artistic purposes to their notebooks, or they have used them to give substance to occa-sional book reviews. Most often they have merely played them by ear as they went about composing specific works of fiction. And for good reason.

Actually, the best way for a novelist to discuss the problem of The Novel is in the form of *a specific novel*, for whenever fictional tech-nique makes conjunction with an image of reality, each is mutually transformed. Every serious novel is, beyond its immediate thematic preoccupations, a discussion of the craft, a conquest of the form, a conflict with its difficulties and a pursuit of its felicities and beauty. To engage in this by way of getting at specific aspects of experience is difficult enough to do to keep the novelists busy, but today, with some of our more important critics handing down the death sen-tence of the form (though in their solemn "The novel is dead," there sounds a Platonist "*Let* it be dead"), or when they boast left-hand-edly in print of their loss of interest in contemporary novels, the novelist is feinted into a position of defending his craft. If he is to pay the critics the serious attention which certainly a few of them de-serve, and if he is at all interested in winning those readers who would listen to the critics, he is moved to attempt some broad public formulation of his personal approach to his craft. One writes because one wishes to be read on one's own terms; thus, since the critics dismiss the novel as moribund, a bit of explicit communication between the novelist and his prospective readers is in order. He must prepare to play Antony to the novel's Caesar, for truly an act of assassination has been commissioned. Nor is this all, for a question of personal dignity and rationality is raised. If the critics are correct—and some are so persuaded—how then does the novelist justify, even to himself, his passionate involvement with a literary form which is dead? Why does he pour his energies into a form that dooms his best efforts to dust even before the effort of the imagination takes place, and upon what does he base his faith?

But first an attempt at definition, which inasmuch as such definition represents the general assumptions out of which I personally approach the abstract form, it will make up for what it lacks in precision with its validity as autobiography.

Let us begin by mentioning a characteristic of the novel which seems so obvious that it is seldom mentioned, and which as a consequence tends to make most discussions of the form irritatingly abstract: by its nature the novel seeks to communicate a vision of experience. Therefore, whatever else it achieves artistically, it is basically a form of communication. When successful in communicating its vision of experience, that magic thing occurs between the world of the novel and the reader—indeed, between reader and reader in their mutual solitude—which we know as communion. As with all the fictive arts, the novel's medium of communication consists in a familiar experience occurring among a particular people, within a particular society or nation (the novel is bound up with the notion of nationhood), and it achieves its universality, if at all, through accumulating images of reality and arranging them in patterns of universal significance. It is not, like poetry, concerned primarily with words, but with action depicted in words, and it operates by amplifying and giving resonance to a specific complex of experience until, through the eloquence of its statement, that specific part of life speaks metaphorically for the whole.

The novel can communicate with us only by appealing to that

which we know, through actual experience or through literature, to be the way things occur. "Yes, this is how it is," we tell ourselves when the fictive illusion works its spell—or we say, "Yes, but such and such is left out." Thus, between the novelist and his most receptive reader (really a most necessary collaborator who must participate in bringing the fiction into life), there must exist a body of shared assumptions concerning reality and necessity, possibility and freedom, personality and value, along with a body of feelings, both rational and irrational, which arise from the particular circumstances of their mutual society. Even the technical means through which this collaboration is brought about depends upon the reader's acceptance of a set of artistic conventions, those "once upon a time" devices which announce the telling of a tale and which introduce a mood of receptiveness in the reader, and through which alone the novelist is able to bring his fiction alive. Even surrealism depended for its effects upon those who were initiated into its conventions and who shared its assumptions concerning art and value. It is by appealing to our sense of experience and playing upon our shared assumptions that the novelist is able to reveal to us that which we do not know— that is, the unfamiliar within the familiar—and affirm that which we assume to be truth, and to reveal to us his own hard-won vision of truth.

In this sense the novel is rhetorical. Whatever else it tries to do, it must do so by persuading us to accept the novelist's projection of an experience which, on some level or mixtures of levels, we have shared with him, and through which we become empathetically involved in the illusory and plotted depiction of life which we identify as fictional art. We repay the novelist in terms of our admiration to the extent that he intensifies our sense of the real—or, conversely, *to the extent that he justifies our desire to evade certain aspects of reality which we find unpleasant beyond the point of confrontation.*

In the beginning was not only the word but the contradiction of the word; sometimes we approach life out of a tragic sense of necessity, and again out of its denial. In this lies the novel's flexibility and its ability to transcend the bounds of class and nation, its endless possibilities of mutation. It is rooted in man's most permanent feelings, and it brings into full vision the processes of his current social forms. This is almost enough in itself to keep the novelist at his task, for in it lies the possibility of affirmation and personal definition.

As an art form the novel is obsessed by the relationship between illusion and reality as revealed in duration and process. "All poetry," writes Malraux, "implies the destruction of the relationship between things that seems obvious to us in favor of particular relationships imposed by the poet." Thus the novel seeks to take the surface "facts" of experience and arrange them in such ways that for a magic moment reality comes into sharp and significant focus. I believe that the primary social function of the novel (the function from which it takes its form and which brought it into being) is that of seizing from the flux and flow of our daily lives those abiding patterns of experience which, through their repetition and consequences in our affairs, help to form our sense of reality, and from which emerge our sense of humanity and our conception of human value.

More than any other literary form, the novel is obsessed with the impact of change upon personality. It was no mere historical accident that the novel came into prominence during the eighteenth century, or that it became fully conscious of itself as an art form during the nineteenth. Its appearance marked the fulfillment of a social need that arose out of the accelerated process of historical change. Before the eighteenth century, when man was relatively at home in what seemed to be a stable and well-ordered world (and if not well ordered, stable nevertheless), there was little need for this change-obsessed literary form. Nor was there literacy enough, nor was the individual, tied as he was to an order imposed by religion and kingship, isolated enough. Nor was individual self-consciousness sufficiently widespread. Human beings were agreed both about what constituted reality and about what the limits of human possibility were, and social change—one of our key words to the understanding of the novel—was by no means the problem it became during the nineteenth and twentieth centuries. Nor is it accidental that it was during the nineteenth century that the novel revealed itself as the most flexible art form for dealing with social change. When the middle class broke the bounds of the feudal synthesis and took its fustian stance, such a literary form was needed, and the novel was the answer. It is here that the novel assumed the role which makes it so useful today: it thrives on change and social turbulence.

Vaguely at first, an awareness had grown in men's minds that social reality had cut loose from its traditional base, and that new possibilities of experience and new forms of personality had been born into the awfully expanded world. Old class lines were being liquidated, and new lines were being formed and broken and re-formed; new types of men were arising mysteriously out of a whirling social reality which revealed itself protean in its ability to change its appearance and its alignments rapidly, ruthless in its impiety toward old images of order, toward traditional modes of behavior. This is of course to telescope many things; there were several phases of the novel and many variations on the form, from the picaresque to the more stable and refined novel of manners, from the sociology-obsessed novel to the Flaubertian "art" novel. Nevertheless, the form attempted to deal with the disparate experiences which society now threw up, and it tried to synthesize these disparate elements. Often quite consciously, and by way of being sheer narrative entertainment, it created new values, affirmed those values which endured specific social changes, and rejected those acts and ideals which threatened middle-class society.

Perhaps the novel evolved in order to deal with man's growing awareness that behind the façade of social organization, manners, customs, myths, rituals and religions of the post-Christian era lies chaos. Man knows, despite the certainties which it is the psychological function of his social institutions to give him, that he did not create the universe, and that the universe is not at all concerned with human values. Man knows even in this day of marvelous technology and the tenuous subjugation of the atom, that nature can crush him,

and that at the boundaries of human order the arts and the instruments of technology are hardly more than magic objects which serve
to aid us in our ceaseless quest for certainty. We cannot live, as
someone has said, in the contemplation of chaos, but neither can we
live without an awareness of chaos, and the means through which we
achieve that awareness, and through which we assert our humanity
most significantly against it, is in great art. In our time the most articulate art form for defining ourselves and for asserting our humanity is the novel. Certainly it is our most rational art form for dealing
with the irrational.

In the nineteenth century, during the moment of greatest middle-
class stability—a stability found actually only at the center, and there
only relatively, in England and not in the colonies, in Paris rather
than in Africa, for there the baser instincts, the violence and greed
could destroy and exploit non-European societies in the name of humanism and culture, beauty and liberty, fraternity and equality while
protecting the humanity of those at home—the novel reached its
first high point of formal self-consciousness. Appropriated by the
middle class (for such art forms are the creation of total civilizations,
not of a single class), it was characterized by an expansiveness which
reflected a class of people who had learned to live with the tempo of
change and to absorb the effects of change into its frame of existence.
It also marked the course of its development and charted the health
of its ideals. Perhaps we admire the nineteenth-century European
novel today, in our time of frantic uncertainty, because we find it
vibrant and alive and confidently able to confront good and evil in all
their contradictory entanglement. In it was implicit the tragic realization that the treasure of possibility is always to be found in the
cave of chaos, guarded by the demons of destruction.

It is Abel Magwitch, the jailbird, who makes Pip's dream of a gentleman's life a reality in *Great Expectations*, just as it was the existence
of human slavery and colonial exploitation which made possible
many of the brighter achievements of modern civilization. Likewise,
the muted insincerities and snobberies of Jane Austen's characters

are only highly refined versions of those major insincerities and snobberies, connected with the exercise of power, which have led in our time to the steady crumbling of the empire upon which genteel English society has rested. In that moment of genteel stability, however, those who were most willfully aware of their destiny viewed freedom not simply in terms of necessity, but in terms of possibility, and they were willing to take the risks necessary to attain their goals. It was the novel which could communicate people's awareness of this sense of possibility along with its cost, and it was the novel which could, on the other hand, reconstruct an image of experience which would make it unnecessary for one to be aware of the true reality upon which society rested. Men, it is said, can stand reality in small doses only, and the novel, sometimes consciously, sometimes not, has measured out that dosage.

This was the dark side of the novel's ability to forge images which would strengthen man's will to say no to chaos and affirm him in his task of humanizing himself and the world. It would, even while entertaining him, help create that fragile state of human certainty and stability (or the illusion of it at least, for perhaps illusion is all we ever have) and communion which is sometimes called love, brotherhood, democracy, or sometimes simply the good life. It could limit those who would share that life and justify our rejection of their humanity, and while condemning snobbery, could yet condone it, for society was admittedly hieratic and closed to pressure from below.

Enough of general definition: if the novel had not existed at the time the United States started becoming conscious of itself as a nation—a process still, fortunately, for ourselves and the world, unachieved—it would have been necessary for Americans to invent it. For in no other country was change such a given factor of existence; in no other country were the class lines so fluid and change so swift and continuous *and intentional.* In no other country were men so conscious of having defined their social aims, or so committed to working toward making that definition a reality. Indeed, a conscious awareness of values describes the condition of the American experiment, and often much of our energy goes into finding ways of losing that consciousness. In the beginning was not only the word, but its contradiction.

I would be on dangerous ground if I tried to trace too closely a connection between documents of state and literature, since in literature universality is an accepted aim; yet the novel is an art of the specific, and for my own working orientation this connection exists in the United States beyond all questions of cultural chauvinism. Certainly this is evident in our great nineteenth-century novels. The moral imperatives of American life that are implicit in the Declaration of Independence, the Constitution and the Bill of Rights were a part of both the individual consciousness and the conscience of those writers who created what we consider our classic novels—Hawthorne, Melville, James and Twain—and for all the hooky-playing attitude of the twenties or the political rebelliousness of the thirties, and the reluctance of contemporary writers to deal explicitly with politics, they still are. They are in fact the baffle against which Lionel Trilling's "hum and buzz of implication" (his understandably vague definition of manners in the novel) sound. These documents form the ground of assumptions upon which our social values rest; they inform our language and our conduct with public meaning, and they provide the broadest frame of reference for our most private dramas. One might deliberately overemphasize and say that most prose fiction in the United States—even the most banal bedroom farce or the most rarefied, stylized and understated comedy of manners—is basically "about" the values and cost of living in a democracy. Being an American, wrote Henry James, is a complex fate, but perhaps far more troublesome than the necessity of guarding against superstitious overevaluation of Europe is the problem of dealing with the explicitness of the omnipresent American ideal. Out of the consciously experimental and revolutionary origins of the country has grown the obsession with defining the American experience—first in order to distinguish it from that of Europe, and now to determine our uniqueness as a civilization and our proper historical role among nations. The impetus was twofold: the need to achieve national self-consciousness being, from the beginning, a political goal springing from our rejection of European social forms, and along with this the pressure of our broad cultural diversification brought about by the open character of the society, the waves of immigration and the rapid expansion, horizontally along the frontier and then vertically through the processes of urbanization and industrialization.

Out of this came our most urgent problem of identity, and who and what is American are still perplexing questions even today. Many definitions are offered—in naturalistic art, in *Life* picture portfolios of the American woman, in government photographs of American workers (in which one seldom sees a Negro), in the racial and aesthetic types of movie queens, in works of sociology, in attempts to depict aspects of the American experience in novels—but few are acceptable without qualification, not even during wartime. All Americans are in this sense members of minority groups, even Anglo-Saxons, whose image has from the beginning dominated all the rest, and one meaning of the social friction in American life is the struggle of each racial, cultural and religious group to have its own contribution to the national image recognized and accepted. The novelist can bemoan this pressure, for it can be oppressive, but he cannot escape it; indeed, in our time it might be his road to a meaningful relationship to the community. "Who," asks Constance Rourke in her *American Humor*, "ever heard of a significant English novel called *The Englishman*, or an excellent French novel called *Le Français*? The simple aggressive stress belonged to an imagination perennially engaged by the problem of the national type. . . ."

Moreover, this national need gives us a clue to one of the enduring functions of the American novel, which is that of defining the national type as it evolves in the turbulence of change, and of giving the American experience, as it unfolds in its diverse parts and regions, imaginative integration and moral continuity. Thus it is bound up with our problem of nationhood. During the nineteenth century it was clearly recognized by those writers who speak meaningfully to us today, and it comes through novels which in their own times went, like *Moby-Dick*, unread. *Moby-Dick, The Adventures of Huckleberry Finn* and *The Bostonians* are all "regional" novels; each simultaneously projects an image of a specific phase of American life, and each is concerned with the moral predicament of the nation. For all the optimism of the early years, there was in this literature no easy affirmation, and for all its involvement with a common set of political and social assumptions, there was, as the list makes plain, no lack of variety of theme. It has been observed that modern American fiction is the only body of literature which is not the work of intellectuals; yet from the beginning our novelists have been consciously concerned with the form, technique, and content of the novel, not excluding ideas. What the observer (a Frenchman) missed was that the major ideas of our society were so alive in the minds of every reader that they could be stated implicitly in the contours of the form. For it is grounded in a body of the most abstract and explicitly stated conceptions of human society, and one which in the form of the great documents of state constitutes a body of assumptions about human possibility which is shared by all Americans, even those who resist violently any attempt to embody them in social action.

Indeed, these assumptions have been questioned and resisted from the very beginning, for man cannot simply say, "Let us have liberty, justice and equality for all," and have it. More than any other system, a democracy is always pregnant with its contradiction. This contradiction was to erupt in the Civil War, an event which has had a profound effect upon the direction of our fiction and which continues to influence our thinking about the novel far more than we bother to recognize. It marked an interruption of our moral continuity, and the form of our novels changed as a result.

As Henry James wrote in his study of Hawthorne:

> The subsidence of that great convulsion has left a different tone from the tone it found, and one may say that the Civil

War marks an era in the history of the American mind. It introduced into the national consciousness a certain sense of proportion and relation, of the world being a more complicated place than it had hitherto seemed, the future more treacherous, success more difficult. At the rate at which things are going, it is obvious that good Americans will be more numerous than ever; but the good American, in days to come, will be a more critical person than his complacent and confident grandfather. He has eaten of the tree of knowledge. He will not, I think, be a sceptic, and still less, of course, a cynic; but he will be, without discredit to his well-known capacity for action, an observer. He will remember that the ways of the Lord are inscrutable, and that this is a world in which everything happens; and eventualities, as the late Emperor of the French used to say, will not find him intellectually unprepared.

Actually, the good American fell quite a bit short of James's prediction, and he made far less of his traumatic fraternal conflict than might have been expected. If it did not make him skeptical (and how could he have been really, with all the material progress released after the war with which to affirm his optimism?), it did make him evasive and given to compromise on basic principles. As a result, we have the interruption of moral continuity symbolized in the failure of Reconstruction and the Hayes-Tilden Compromise, and now in the 1950s, at a time when our world leadership has become an indisputable and perplexing fact, we have been forced to return to problems, in the form of the current desegregation issue, which should have been faced up to years ago. What is more, the event of World War I found the good American hardly less innocent than he had been fifty-three years before—only now, instead of such critical and morally affirmative novels as *Huckleberry Finn*, *The Gilded Age*, *The Bostonians* (in which James depicts the decay of moral values among those who had been leaders in the struggle for abolition), *Moby-Dick* or *The Confidence-Man*, we had literature which came out of the individual writer's private need to express a national mood of glamorized social irresponsibility. Certainly the attitude of moral evasion expressed in the failure of Reconstruction and the materialism of the Gilded Age prepared for the mood of glamorized social irresponsibility voiced in the fiction of the twenties, and it created a special problem between the American novelist and his audience.

Being committed to optimism, serious novels have always been troublesome to Americans precisely because of their involvement with our problem of identity. If they depict too much of reality, they frighten us by giving us a picture of society frozen at a point so far from our optimistic ideal (for in depiction there is a freezing as well as a discovery and release of possibility) that we feel compelled to deny it. Yet if they leave out too much, we cannot take them seriously for very long, even though we might buy them in hundreds of thousands of copies. As readers we wait for definition, and even now in this so-called age of conformity we wish to discover some transcendent meaning in at least some of the turbulence which whirls through our lives, and which during a period of highest prosperity makes it necessary for all the media of communication to set up an incessant "hard sell" incantation to reassure us that all is well, all meaningful, the very best state of affairs, that things confer happiness, beauty, and grace, and that fertility is a smiling face in a magazine ad.

Another way of putting it is that we are a people who, while desiring identity, have been reluctant to pay the cost of its achievement. We have been reluctant since we first suspected that we are fated to live up to our sacred commitments or die, and the Civil War was the form of that fateful knowledge. Thus we approach serious novels with distrust until the moment comes when the passage of time makes it possible for us to ignore their moral cutting edge. In the nineteenth century serious fiction was fairly easily disposed of; it was given to children, especially to boys, and then only after being purged of those matters that were less likely to disturb the juvenile than his parents. *Huckleberry Finn* was banned from libraries, *Moby-Dick* went unread, and those who understood James were few. It was as though the older generation was saying, "These are problems which you are likely to encounter when you come of age; we are too busy making progress to give them our attention," but when the younger generation grew up, so much had happened in the swift change, and they had been joined by so many new arrivals, that they forgot both the nature of the problem and its historical source. By the twenties the relationship between the serious novel and themselves as readers had undergone a remarkable change, and if they had lost little of the simplicity of James's earlier good American, they were now full of doubts about the possibility of the ideal, and had begun to resent it, much as they resented the necessity of participating in the war.

And so with the novel; where before it had affirmed the sacred assumptions, now, as in the Caporetto scene in *A Farewell to Arms*, it denied the very words in which the ideals were set down. The nineteenth-century novelist had stood within society even as he criticized its behavior, and now the novelist thought of himself as alienated. Yet ironically, men like Fitzgerald and Hemingway were actually more celebrated than any American writer since Mark Twain. For all her shocks and traumas, America has been an extremely lucky country, and Time, as with the little boy in Dylan Thomas's poem, has let her be "golden in the mercy of his means," allowing her a generosity of mistakes, laxities and a childlike ability to forget her falls from grace, allowing her wealth, movement, a ruddy strength of people, national resources and a ceaseless stream of wonderful toys with which to excite her imagination and to keep her unaware of Time's ambiguousness.

Her luck was extended to her writers of the twenties. After the clangor and pain of the war and its booming echo in the expansion and hysterical faddism of the twenties, the moral irresponsibility had become so chronic that one would have expected writers either to depict it critically or to become silent; instead they had the luck to give at least part of their attention to the so-called revolution of the word, which was offered as a literary equivalent of that distraction

from the realities of the moral situation provided by the material
prosperity of the boom. Nor was it simply a matter of luck. For all
their pose of alienation, the writers of the twenties worked hard, and
found images that were simple enough to project those feelings of
impotence and moral irresponsibility that were typical of the times,
and make them romantically attractive. The brave lonely man, broken by war and betrayed by politicians—who had lost faith in everything except the basic processes of existence and his own physical
strength; who could no longer believe in the old American creed;
who traveled to Pamplona and Paris; who drank too much, who
made love compulsively and was romantically unhappy (but who yet
had the money to indulge in his escape)—became the dominant
image of the American. So gripping was this image that some critics
look back today and actually confuse the image with the reality of the
times.

By the twenties, in other words, the novel, which in the hands of
our greatest writers had been a superb moral instrument, became
morally diffident, and much of its energy was turned upon itself in
the form of technical experimentation. Which is not to deny that a
writer like Hemingway has profound moral seriousness, or to imply
that technique is ever void of moral implications; rather it is to say
that here the personal despair which gave the technique its resonance became a means of helping other Americans to avoid those
aspects of reality which they no longer had the will to face. This is
the tragedy implicit in Hemingway's morality of craftsmanship: the
attempt to make a highly personal morality the informing motive of
an art form which by its very nature is extremely social and, despite
its pose, deeply rooted in the assumption it denied. As I read Hemingway today I find that he affirms the old American values by the
eloquence of his denial, makes his moral point by stating explicitly
that he does not believe in morality, achieves his eloquence through
denying eloquence, and is most moral when he denies the validity of
a national morality which the nation has not bothered to live up to
since the Civil War. The confusion, both for Hemingway's imitators

and his readers, lay in the understatement, and here the basic American assumptions exerted their power. Although it is seldom mentioned, Hemingway is as obsessed with the Civil War and its aftermath as any Southern writer, and this fact turns up constantly in his work. The children of the good Americans of the 1880s had forgotten the historical problems which made Hemingway's understatement fully meaningful, even though it was here exactly that the ideas which were said to be absent were most present and powerful. But many readers, unhappy with the compact we had made with history, took the novelist's point of view as authority to go on a binge of hooky-playing, as an assurance that there were no new lessons to learn—and anyway the old ones were invalid. And this with the Depression only a few years away.

Yet so fascinating were the images of the twenties, and so deep and irrational the feelings which they made articulate, that thirty years later critics who readily admit the superficiality of most novels written during the thirties (for they tried to be responsible by avoiding complexity), and who reject most contemporary fiction even when written to their formulas, insist that we measure ourselves by the triumphs of the twenties. They tell us again and again of the Lost Generation novelists, and their names (with Faulkner's recently added) clang in our ears like gongs in evidence of our failure and doom. They, we are told, did that which we cannot hope to do, and if this fails to discourage us, the nineteenth-century novel of manners is held before us as final evidence of our futility and the novel's point of highest glory and swift decline.

Not that we disagree absolutely with any of this, but we must reply to these charges. Thank God that we can't do what the Lost Generation novelists did, because as good as it was, it was not good enough or broad enough to speak for today. And thank God again that the nineteenth-century European novel of manners is dead, for it has little value in dealing with our world of chaos and catastrophe. We have lived a different life and have seen it with different eyes. Nor are we innocent of the world's new complexity or given to false pieties, easy hopes or facile rejections; nor are we unaware of the weakness implicit in our tremendous strength, or of the possibilities of strength in our apparent weaknesses, for the iron-weight of tragic awareness has descended upon us. Ours is a task which, whether recognized or not, was defined for us to a large extent by that which the novels of the twenties failed to confront, and implicit in their triumphs and follies are our complexity and our travail.

Indeed, so much has been written about the triumphs of the twenties that we either forget its failures or forgive them—which would be fine if the critics would only leave it at that. But the contemporary novelist cannot afford to forget the failures, even if he makes no accusations, and the intentions of such a novelist as Saul Bellow can be properly understood only in light of this failure. After two well-written, neatly constructed novels which paid their respects to the standards of the twenties, Bellow's major work to date is *The Adventures of Augie March*, which at first glance looks like the work of a completely different man. It is characterized by a big conception of human possibility and a quality of wonder arising out of the mysteriousness of a reality which keeps its secret despite the documentation of the social scientists, and it is informed by a knowledge of chaos which would have left the novelists of the twenties discouraged. Certainly it confronts large areas of American reality which simply didn't get into the novels of the twenties.

I would go further here and say that neither the American fiction of the twenties nor that of the fifties can be understood outside the perspective provided by the nineteenth century. Edmund Wilson seems to suggest this by his current re-examination of the Civil War and post-Reconstruction periods, and certainly the younger writers who came through the Depression and who shared the social and political preoccupations of the thirties feel this, even though they have little bothered to write about it. Yet it is one of the goals of the current serious novel to create precisely this moral perspective. Here perhaps is one of our most serious failures, for not only has the drift of our internal social affairs brought this period and its unsolved moral problems back into the national consciousness, but world events have revealed their broad relevance to areas far beyond our national borders. In other words, the events which wracked the United States during the Civil War period and again during the twenties were the archetype of events which are now sweeping all societies, and our failure to confront them when they arose (for perhaps they could not have been *solved*) has proved not only an impediment to our leadership among the nations but a hindrance to our achievement of national identity.

Perhaps the attitude of those novelists who matured during the forties has been too quietly aloof, our absorption in craft problems too concentrated, and our dependence upon the perceptiveness of critics too trusting. Perhaps we who disdain the easy pose are far more alienated than the writers of the Lost Generation, for we have assumed an understanding on the part of both reader and critic which is at best rare, and we fail to say much that is explicit about our intentions or points of view.

By contrast the writers of the twenties did a brilliant job publicizing their own efforts. During the time when *Ulysses* and *Finnegans Wake* were being written, both were eagerly discussed in several languages and several countries. Because Joyce (no member of the Lost Generation but the most "difficult" novelist of the period) was not only writing his books; he was, with the help of magazine editors, friends and critics, just as busily establishing the convention by which he wished his novels read. Whatever his success in absenting himself from his novels as omniscient author—a technical problem already solved by Conrad and James—in his correspondence he did anything but pare his nails; he was far too busy telling those who tell readers how to read just what the godlike author was about. Clearly it is no accident that more people have read about how his books should be read than have read them. And for all of the legend of Hemingway's nonintellectuality, and the aesthetic ideas spun in metaphors from sports, he has nevertheless written so much and so significantly about writing that two younger writers are busy making a volume of his observations. One needs only mention the examples of Eliot, Gertrude Stein, Ezra Pound and Henry James before them.

Looked at coldly, the notion of a Lost Generation was a literary conceit of such major proportions that today it seems like a swindle. The alienation of these writers had something of the character of putting on a mask in Macy's window at high noon and pretending that no one knows who you are. They had not only the comfort of being in the well-advertised advance guard; they were widely read and their characters' way of life was imitated to the extent that several generations of young people stylized their speech and attitudes to the pattern of Fitzgerald's and Hemingway's fiction. "Papa" Hemingway (who *is* the father of many writers who today sneer at him) was so alienated that a song, "Pul-eeze, Mr. Hemingway," could find popularity. With *Esquire* carrying their work to readers in most of the barbershops throughout the country, these writers were lost in a crowd of admirers, of whom I was one.

For all the personal despair which informed it and the hard work which brought it into being, the emphasis on technique gave something of a crossword-puzzle-fad aspect to the literature of the twenties, and often the question of the Sphinx was lost in the conundrums. Without doubt major questions went unanswered. Yet, happily, its concentration upon the problems of craft made it impossible for us to ignore the fact that literature, to the extent that it is art, is artificial. Each of us must learn to read and understand the devices through which fiction achieves its illusion of reality. Thanks to their popularizers and the generations of critics who followed, we know how to read their books extremely well, especially in terms of those matters which preoccupied them, and the level of craft consciousness is so high in the United States that today by keeping to formula and the neat theme (neat because smoothed down and polished since Flaubert's time) the writer may turn out readable, smoothly fashioned novels which evoke a response much like that we extend those miniaturists who work in ivory. The phrases are neatly done, there is a great economy of means (because there is so little of substance), tightness of structure, great texture and facile sensibility.

Anyone who has had a course in modern literature or who has read a little criticism has the satisfaction of knowing just how each image and metaphor operates, who the hero's literary ancestors were, just how Joyce, James, Freud, Marx, Sartre, Camus, Unamuno, Kierkegaard, Fitzgerald, Hemingway and Lionel Trilling came into it. There is, in this writing, no excess of emotion (if any at all) or shrillness of tone, no vulgarity or uncertainties of taste; nor are there any patterns of action that would violate the assumptions concerning life or art that are held by the most timid middle-class reader. The writer may, if he likes, play the turns of the whole corpus of genteel nineteenth- and twentieth-century fiction, especially the European, and never exhaust himself in the process of translating these well-polished themes and situations into American backgrounds, utilizing along the way all the latest verbal techniques approved by the critics.

Despite their skill, however, these novels are not widely read, and the reader who looks here for some acknowledgment of the turbulence he feels around him would be better satisfied by a set of comic books. He thus turns to "fact" books for "scientific" consolation because the orientation in reality which the novel should afford him is not forthcoming, and the critics, appalled by the stillborn children which they have called forth, look backward to those highly dubious Edens of the nineteenth century and of the Lost Generation, and pronounce the novel dead. If so, perhaps they have helped to dig its grave.

If the nineteenth-century way with troublesome novels was to turn them over to children, we in our time, being more sophisticated and literate, turn them over to critics, who proceed to reduce the annoying elements to a minimum. Even more deplorable is the fact that once the critics have spoken, the story is likely to appear in subsequent editions with the troublesome, difficult material edited out, as happened to one of the most sublime stories in the language, really an extremely foreshortened novel—Faulkner's "The Bear." Perhaps the test of a work's becoming a classic in the United States depends upon the extent to which it can withstand this process of conscious reduction. Perhaps what I am saying is that since the novel is a moral instrument possessing for us an integrative function, our typical American reaction to it is to evade as much of its moral truth as possible, perhaps out of an effort to postpone completing that identity which we are compelled nonetheless to seek. But as to the critics' role in this process, I am struck that while their reductions are made on aesthetic grounds, it turns out that what they consider expendable is usually the heart of the fiction. Here, out of fairness, I must include novelists like James and Hemingway, who, by way of defining their own aesthetic positions, have contributed to some of the current confusion.

Let us take Henry James on Hawthorne, Hemingway on *The Adventures of Huckleberry Finn*, and Malcolm Cowley on Faulkner's "The Bear"—these three because each has been influential in shaping our ideas of American fiction and how it should be read, and because at least two have been offered as guides for the younger novelists who have come upon the scene since the thirties. Each of the texts constitutes a definition of American fiction; each has been helpful in giving us orientation; and today all three have become mischievous in adding to the current confusion over the role, character and condition of the contemporary novel. Indeed, it is as though a set of familiar, useful touchstones had become inflated and transformed into a set of wandering rocks which threaten to crush us.

Each of the texts I shall quote is so familiar that there would be no need to cite them except for the fact that each has achieved its importance by virtue of its being a statement by reduction of either a perceptive critical observation or the meaning of an important novel. Hence in order to determine where we are and how we arrived at some of our current convictions concerning the novel, it is useful to take a look at exactly what was discarded from the originals.

Almost alone Mr. Trilling has been responsible for making a single statement of Henry James more prominent in our thinking than all the complex aesthetic ideas spelled out in the prefaces and essays. In developing his theory of the novel of manners, he paraphrases James's catalogue of those items of civilization which were missing from Hawthorne's America, itself an extension of a list which Hawthorne had himself made in the preface to his novel *Transformation (The Marble Faun):*

> No author, without a trial, can conceive of the difficulty of writing a romance about a country where there is no shadow, no antiquity, no mystery, no picturesque and gloomy wrong, nor anything but a commonplace prosperity, in broad and simple daylight, as is happily the case with my dear native land.

This is Mr. Hawthorne, and while admiring what he made of his position one must observe that in this world one finds that which one has the eyes to see. Certainly there was gloomy wrong enough both in the crime against the Indians and in the Peculiar Institution which was shortly to throw the country into conflict, there was enough mystery in Abraham Lincoln's emergence, then in process, still to excite us with wonder, and in that prosperity and "broad and simple daylight" enough evil was brewing to confound us even today. But let us see what James made of this quote, for it is upon James that Mr. Trilling bases much of his argument:

> The perusal of Hawthorne's American Note-Books operates as a practical commentary upon this somewhat ominous text. It does so at least to my own mind; it would be too much perhaps to say that the effect would be the same for the usual English reader. An American reads between the lines—he completes the suggestions—he constructs a picture. I think I am not guilty of any gross injustice in saying that the picture he constructs from Hawthorne's American diaries, though by no means without charms of its own, is not, on the whole, an interesting one. It is characterized by an extraordinary blank-

ness—a curious paleness of colour and paucity of detail. Hawthorne, as I have said, has a large and healthy appetite for detail, and one is therefore the more struck with the lightness of
the diet to which his observation was condemned. For myself,
as I turn the pages of his journals, I seem to see the image of
the crude and simple society in which he lived. I use these epithets, of course, not invidiously, but descriptively; if one
desires to enter as closely as possible into Hawthorne's situation, one must endeavour to reproduce his circumstances. We
are struck with the large number of elements that were absent
from them, and the coldness, the thinness, the blankness, to
repeat my epithet, present themselves so vividly that our foremost feeling is that of compassion for a romancer looking for
subjects in such a field. It takes so many things, as Hawthorne
must have felt later in life, when he made the acquaintance of
the denser, richer, warmer European spectacle—it takes such
an accumulation of history and custom, such a complexity of
manners and types, to form a fund of suggestion for a novelist.
If Hawthorne had been a young Englishman, or a young
Frenchman of the same degree of genius, the same cast of
mind, the same habits, his consciousness of the world around
him would have been a very different affair; however obscure,
however reserved, his own personal life, his sense of the life of
his fellow-mortals would have been almost infinitely more
various. The negative side of the spectacle on which Hawthorne looked out, in his contemplative saunterings and reveries, might, indeed [And it is here that Mr. Trilling's much
repeated paraphrase begins], with a little ingenuity, be made
almost ludicrous; one might enumerate the items of high civilization, as it exists in other countries, which are absent from
the texture of American life, until it should become a wonder
to know what was left. No State, in the European sense of the
word, and indeed barely a specific national name. No sovereign, no court, no personal loyalty, no aristocracy, no church,
no clergy, no army, no diplomatic service, no country gentlemen, no palaces, nor castles, nor manors, nor old country-
houses, nor parsonages, nor thatched cottages, nor ivied ruins;
no cathedrals, nor abbeys, nor little Norman churches; no
great Universities nor public schools—no Oxford, nor Eton,

nor Harrow; no literature, no novels, no museums, no pictures, no political society, no sporting class—no Epsom nor Ascot! Some such list as that might be drawn up of the absent things in American life—especially in the American life of forty years ago, the effect of which, upon an English or a French imagination, would probably as a general thing be appalling. The natural remark, in the almost lurid light of such an indictment, would be that if these things are left out, everything is left out. [And it is here that Mr. Trilling leaves us.] The American knows that a good deal remains; what it is that remains—that is his secret, his joke, as one may say. It would be cruel, in this terrible denudation, to deny him the consolation of his natural gift, that "American humour" of which of late years we have heard so much.

"That is," says Mr. Trilling, "no sufficiency of means for the display of a variety of manners, no opportunity for the novelist to do his job of searching out reality, not enough complication of appearance to make the job interesting." Mr. Trilling states in the same essay that while we have had great novels in America, they "diverge from [the novel's] classic intention . . . the investigation of the problem of reality beginning in the social field."

All this is admittedly a damaging list of reasons why American novelists cannot write French or English novels of manners. But when I read the much quoted passage in context (one of Mr. Trilling's disciples has deduced from it that personality exists in the United States only in New England and in the South), it struck me as amusing that Mr. Trilling missed the point that these lacks were seen as appalling for the French or English imagination—for it seems obvious that in that time neither Frenchmen nor Englishmen were going to try to write American novels (though things are different today), that James was addressing his remarks to Europeans, and that all the energy that has been wasted in bemoaning the fact that American society is not English or French society could have stopped right there.

James's remarks on Hawthorne are justified to the extent that the perspective he was creating helped him to establish his own point of departure; it is to the insistence that his observations be binding upon other writers that I object. Nor can I overlook the fact that James was basing his remarks on the thinness of Hawthorne's note-books—which, compared with James's, were indeed thin. Yet just when, one might ask without too much irreverence, did a writer's quality—James's prolific notebooks notwithstanding—depend upon the kind of notebooks he kept? Did anyone ever see Shakespeare's notebooks? And would anyone who read Dostoevsky's *A Writer's Diary* without an acquaintance with the novels suspect that it was the journal of one of the greatest novelists of all time?

For me the most surprising aspect of Mr. Trilling's paraphrase is that he says nothing at all about what James calls the "American joke"—a matter which, as a novelist, intrigues me no end. I take it that James's reference to American humor was nothing more than condescension, and that he did not mean it in the sense that it was used by Miss Constance Rourke, who saw American humor as hav-ing the function of defining and consolidating the diverse ele-ments—racial, cultural and otherwise—which go into the American character, a business to which James made a profound contribution, even when irritated by what he considered the thinness of American experience. One wonders what the state of novel criticism would be today if Mr. Trilling had turned his critical talent to an examination of the American joke. Perhaps *this* has been the objective of the American novel all along, even the Jamesian novel, and perhaps this is its road to health even today.

But now another touchstone: "All modern American literature comes from one book by Mark Twain called *Huckleberry Finn* . . . it's the best book we've had. All American writing comes from that." So wrote Ernest Hemingway in *Green Hills of Africa* in a much-quoted statement. It is significant that here again we have a statement by reduction which, although it helped Hemingway to create his own position, has helped us to ignore what seems to me to be the very heart of *Huckleberry Finn*. He tells us in the same context that we should stop reading at the point where Jim is stolen from Huck and Tom Sawyer because from that point on it is cheating. Here we have something different from the first example, and perhaps, in light of Hemingway's great influence upon American fiction, more important. In order to define his own position (or perhaps to justify it, since the statement comes some ten years after he caught the public's imagination), Hemingway found it necessary to reduce the meaning of *Huckleberry Finn* to the proportions of his own philosophical position. Far more meaningful to him than the moral vision and sense of language which summoned them into being were the techniques through which Twain gave it expression. So too with the critics who usually quote Hemingway's remarks, with the most important phrase in his statement omitted. For when he goes on to advise us that we should stop reading *Huckleberry Finn* at the point where Jim is stolen from Huck and Tom Sawyer, he reveals either a blindness to the moral point of the novel or his own inability to believe in the moral necessity which makes Huck know that he must at least make the attempt to get Jim free—to "steal" him free is the term by which Twain reveals Huck's full awareness of the ambiguousness of his position, and through which he roots the problem in American social reality and draws upon the contradiction between democratic idealism and the existence of slavery. Nevertheless, it is exactly this part of the action which represents the formal externalization of Huck-Twain's moral position, and if one may speak of ritual here, it is in this part of the action that the fundamental American commitment, the myth, is made manifest. Without this attempt *Huckleberry Finn* becomes the simple boy's book that many would rather it be, a fantasy born of pure delight and not really serious at all.

Yet Hemingway is a serious author, and in this statement he not only tells us more about himself than about Twain or American fiction, but he expresses the basic difference in points of view between nineteenth- and twentieth-century writers. Thus not only did *Huckleberry Finn* lose some of its meaning; many of those whom it might have helped to some sense of the moral and historical continuity of

American life were advised, in effect, that such continuity was non-existent. But it is useless to quarrel with history, and as one who is committed to the craft I can even admit that Hemingway's art justifies what he made of Twain's. But what are we to say of the critics who circulate his statement as though it were the word of God? What of their responsibility to the reader?

One can easily agree with Hemingway about the importance of *Huckleberry Finn* in the continuity of the American novel while rejecting his dismissal of its ethical intention, for we have in William Faulkner a twentieth-century writer who not only continues in his own way the technical direction outlined by Mark Twain, but also, despite Lionel Trilling's dismissal of him as "being limited to a provincial scene," continues the moral commitment which was at the heart of Twain's fiction.

Just as experimental and technically "difficult" as Hemingway, and perhaps as Joyce, Faulkner missed the broad publicity accorded their experimentation, not only because his more important works were published somewhat later, but because there is no doubt that he is involved both as a Southerner and as an artist with those issues which most white Americans have evaded since the Civil War. It was not until about 1946 that Faulkner began to win the attention of Americans generally, and a great aid in this was the Viking Portable, edited by Malcolm Cowley. By this time several of the most important novels were out of print, and one cannot overstress the service rendered by Cowley and the publisher in issuing their collection with Cowley's introduction and commentary. Through it many Americans not only made their first contact with a great writer, but were introduced to a superb imaginative account of what so much of the conflict in American life is all about. Thus my reason for mentioning Cowley's reduction of the meaning of Faulkner's "The Bear" is not to detract from the importance of the Portable, but to illustrate further the reduction of the moral intention of American prose fiction by way of making it easier for the reader.

"The Bear" [writes Mr. Cowley] is the longest of Faulkner's stories and in many ways the best. It is divided into five parts. If you want to read simply a hunting story, and one of the greatest in the language, you should confine yourself to the first three parts and the last, which are written in Faulkner's simplest style. The long fourth part is harder to read and deals with more complicated matters. In it Faulkner carries to an extreme his effort toward putting the whole world into one sentence, between one capital letter and one period. . . . In all this section of "The Bear" the reader may have difficulty in fitting the subjects to the predicates and in disentangling the subordinate clauses; and yet, if he perseveres, he will discover one of Faulkner's most impressive themes: the belief in Isaac McCaslin's heart that the land itself had been cursed by slavery, and that the only way for him to escape the curse was to relinquish the land.

But not only does this fourth section (which takes up thirty-four of the 136 pages) contain this theme; it is in fact the dislocated beginning of the story and the time-present in which the bear hunt is evoked out of the memory of the hero, who at the age of twenty-one confronts his cousin with his decision to give up the land. Although it has recently been included in a volume of hunting stories with the fourth section missing, "The Bear" is not about a bear hunt at all, but about a young American's hunt for moral identity. Significantly, it is the centerpiece of a volume which takes its title from the Negro spiritual "Go Down, Moses," and its main concern is with the problem of American freedom as faced by a specific white Southerner in relation to his individual heritage. Here, in *Go Down, Moses,* Faulkner comes most passionately to grips with the moral implications of slavery, the American land, progress and materialism, tradition and moral identity—all major themes of the American novel. It is in the fourth section—not really difficult once it is grasped that it is a remembered dialogue with the "he saids" left out—where Isaac and his cousin McCaslin argue out the issues between them (McCaslin basing his arguments on tradition and history and Isaac on a form of Christian humanism) that Faulkner makes his most extended effort to define the specific form of the American Negro's humanity and to get at the human values which were lost by both North and South during the Civil War. Even more important, it is here that Isaac McCaslin demonstrates one way in which the individual American can assert his freedom from the bonds of history, tradition and things, and thus achieve moral identity. Whether we accept Isaac McCaslin's solution or not, the problem is nevertheless basic to democratic man, as it was to Ahab and to Huck Finn.

Nor do I wish to oversimplify Mr. Cowley's problem; if serious fiction is to be made available to those to whom it is addressed—those who, as Ike McCaslin puts it, "have nothing else to read with but the heart"—the critic must interpret for them, and in the process of making literature available to all the levels of a democratic society, some loss of quality, some blunting of impact, seems inevitable. Nevertheless the critic has some responsibility in seeing that the reader does not evade the crucial part of a fiction simply because of its difficulty. Sometimes the difficulty is the mark of the writer's deepest commitment to life and to his art. To water down his work is not only to mock the agony and the joy which go into his creation, but to rob the reader of that transcendence which, despite his tendency to evade the tragic aspects of reality, he seeks in literature. The intent of criticism is frustrated, the fiction reduced to mere entertainment, and the reader is encouraged to evade self-scrutiny. In the leveling process to which all things are subjected in a democracy, one must depend always upon the *individual's* ability to rise out of the mass and achieve the possibility implicit in the society. One must depend upon his ability, whoever he is and from whatever class and racial group, to attain the finest perception of human value, to become as consciously aware of life, say, as any of Henry James's "super-subtle fry." Certainly the novelist must make some such assumption if he is to allow himself range in which to work toward the finest possibilities of his talent and his form without a frustrating sense of alienation.

Which tells us something of why the novelists keep writing despite the current attempts to legislate the novel a quiet death. It also gives us a hint about why a number of younger novelists are not at all hindered by the attempt to reduce the novel to only one of its possible forms; yes, and why the picaresque, many-leveled novel, swarming with characters, and with varied types and levels of experience, has appeared among us. Though we love the classics, some of us have little interest in what Mr. Trilling calls the "novel of manners," and I don't believe that a society hot in the process of defining itself can for long find its image in so limited a form. Surely the novel is more than he would have it be, and if it isn't, then we must make it so.

One of the comic aspects of the current controversy over what a novel should be is the implicit assumption, held by Cooper, James and Hawthorne, as well as by several contemporary critics, that society was created mainly so that novelists could write about it. It is felt that society should be of such shape that the novelist can settle it neatly into prefabricated molds with the least spilling of rude life over the sides. This notion started when the forest was still being cleared, and it is understandable that a certain type of writer would have liked to deal with fine cabinetry instead of crude logs. Still, minds that were philosophically and politically most advanced and sophisticated conceived this society, but even they had nonetheless to deal with raw and rapidly moving materials. So in the beginning did the American novel, and so today. We are not so crude now as during James's time, but we have even less stability and there is no longer a stable England to which to withdraw for perspective. World War I, the Depression, World War II and Korea, the Cold War, the threat of the atom, our discovery of the reality of treason, and now Egypt and Hungary make us aware that reality, which during Dickens's time seemed fairly stable, has broken loose from its old historical base, and the Age of Anxiety is truly more than a poetic conceit. Closed societies are now the flimsiest of illusions, for all the outsiders are demanding in.

In fact there is no stability anywhere, there will not be for many years to come, and progress now insistently asserts its tragic side; the evil now stares out of bright sunlight. New groups will ceaselessly emerge, class lines will continue to waver, break and re-form; great wealth there will be, and a broader distribution of that wealth, and a broader distribution of ideas along with it. But the problem of what to do with the increased leisure which wealth makes possible will continue to plague us, as will the problem of deciding just what constitutes a truly human way of life. The fundamental problems of the American situation will repeat themselves again and again, and will be faced more or less by peoples throughout the world: where shall we draw the line upon our own freedom in a world in which culture, tradition and even history have been shaken up? At how fast a pace should we move toward social ideals? What is worth having and what worth holding? Where and in what pattern of conduct does true value lie at a given moment? These questions will continue to press upon us even if the dream of world peace is achieved, for they are questions built into the core of modern experience.

For the novelist the existence of these questions creates a basic problem of rhetoric. How does one in the novel (the novel which is a work of art and not a disguised piece of sociology) persuade the American reader to identify that which is basic in man, beyond all differences of class, race, wealth or formal education? How does one not only make the illiterate and inarticulate eloquent enough so that the educated and more favorably situated will recognize wisdom and honor and charity, heroism and capacity for love when found in humble speech and dress? Conversely, how does one persuade readers with the least knowledge of literature to recognize the broader values implicit in their lives? How, in a word, do we affirm that which *is* stable in human life, beyond and despite all processes of social change? How give the reader that which we do have in abundance, all the countless untold and wonderful variations on the themes of identity, freedom and necessity, love and death, and with all the mystery of personality undergoing its endless metamorphosis?

Here are questions which cannot be answered by criticism; they call for the novel, many novels, and as long as there are writers willing to accept the challenge of reducing the reality in which they exist to living form, there will be readers interested in their answers, and we need have no fear that the novel is moribund.

"A Very Stern Discipline"

Interviewers: Do you think that one of the faults of the Negro writer is that he is unable to come to terms with the human condition, particularly that of the Negro in America?

Ellison: Here I don't like to speak generally. The conception of the human condition varies for every writer just as it does for every individual. Each must live within the isolation of his own senses, dreams and memories; each must die his own death. For the writer the problem is to project his own conception eloquently and artistically. Like all good artists, he stakes his talent against the world. But if a Negro writer is going to listen to sociologists—as too many of us do—who tell us that Negro life is thus and so in keeping with certain sociological theories, he is in trouble because he will have abandoned his task before he begins. If he accepts the clichés to the effect that the Negro family is usually a broken family, that it is matriarchal in form and that the mother dominates and castrates the males, if he believes that Negro males are having all of these alleged troubles with their sexuality, or that Harlem is a "Negro ghetto"—which means, to paraphrase one of our writers, "piss in the halls and blood on the stairs"—he'll never see the people of whom he wishes to write. He'll never learn to use his own eyes and heart, and he'll never master the art of fiction.

I don't deny that these sociological formulas are drawn from life, but I do deny that they define the complexity of Harlem. They only abstract it and reduce it to proportions which the sociologists can manage. I simply don't recognize Harlem in them, and I certainly don't recognize the people of Harlem whom I know. Which is not to

---

This interview (given in 1965), which the author has revised from the original tapes, was conducted by three young Negro writers: James Thompson, Lennox Raphael and Steve Cannon. It appeared in *Harper's Magazine* in March 1967.

deny the ruggedness of life there, nor the hardship, the poverty, the sordidness, the filth. But there is something else in Harlem, something subjective, willful and complexly and compellingly human. It is that "something else" that challenges the sociologists who ignore it, and the society which would deny its existence. It is that "something else" which makes for our strength, endurance and promise. This is the proper subject for the Negro American writer. Hell, he doesn't have to spend all the tedious time required to write novels simply to repeat what sociologists and certain white intellectuals are broadcasting like a zoo full of parrots—*and* getting much more money for it than most Negro writers will ever see. If he does this, he'll not only go begging, but worse, he'll lie to his people, discourage their interest in literature and emasculate his own talent.

This is tricky terrain, because today sociologists are up to their necks in politics and have access to millions of governmental dollars, which, I'm afraid, have been secured at the cost of propagating an image of the Negro condition that is apt to destroy our human conception of ourselves just at the moment when we are becoming politically free. Those who buy this image are surely in trouble, no matter what money it brings.

One of the saddest sights currently to be seen is that provided by one of our most "angry" Negro writers, who has allowed himself to be enslaved by his acceptance of negative sociological data. He rants and raves against society, but he's actually one of the safest Negroes on the scene. Because he challenges nothing, he can only shout " 'taint" to some abstract white " 'tis," countering lies with lies. The human condition? He thinks that white folks have ruled Negroes out of it.

A few years ago there was a drunk who collected newspapers from the shops along Broadway between 145th and 153rd streets. He was a Negro who had fought the wine for a long time, and who when drunk was capable of a metaphysical defiance. His favorite pastime was to take a stand near a stoplight and accost white people who stopped for the traffic signal with shouts of "Why don't you go back downtown! I want all you white motherfuckers—mens *and* womens—to go on back downtown!" Our hate-mongering fellow writer reminds me very much of this man, for he is about as effective and no less obscene. Yes, we do have a terrible time in dealing with the human condition.

One critic has said that the Jewish writer went through a similar period. I think he was trying to say that the Negro writer would very soon get over this and become the major strength in American literature.

I hope he's right, but I wouldn't want to make a prediction. I think, however, that the parallel is much too facile. Jewish writers are more familiar with literature as a medium of expression. Their history provides for a close identification with writers who were, and are, Jewish even when they wrote or write in languages other than Yiddish or Hebrew—and this even when that identification rests simply on a shared religious tradition and hardly on any other cultural ground whatsoever. It reminds me of our attempts to claim Pushkin and Dumas as Negroes.

By contrast, neither Negro American expression nor religion has been primarily literary. We are by no means, as is said of the Jews, "people of the Book." Not that I see this as a matter for regret, for we have a wider freedom of selection. We took much from the ancient Hebrews and we do share, through Christianity, the values embodied in the literature of much of the world. But our expression has been oral as against "literary." When it comes to the question of identifying those writers who have shaped American literature—the framers of the Declaration, the Constitution and Lincoln excepted—we tend to project racial categories into the areas of artistic technique, form and insight, areas where race has no proper place. We seem to forget that one can identify with what a writer has written, with its form, manner and techniques, while rejecting the writer's beliefs, prejudices, philosophy and values.

Jewish American writers have, on the other hand, identified with

Eliot, Pound, Hemingway and Joyce *as writers*, while questioning and even rejecting their various attitudes toward Jews, religion, politics and many other matters. They have taken possession of that which they could use from such writers and converted it to express their own personal and group sense of reality; they have used it to express their own definitions of the American experience. But we Negro writers seem seldom to have grasped this process of acculturation. Too often we've been in such haste to express our anger and our pain as to allow the single tree of race to obscure our view of the magic forest of art.

If Negro writers ever become the mainstay of American literature, it will be because they have learned their craft and used the intensity, emotional and political, of their group experience to express a greater area of American experience than writers of other groups. What the Jewish American writer had to learn before he could find his place was the American-ness of his experience. He had to see himself as American and project his Jewish experience as an experience unfolding within this pluralistic society. When this was done, it was possible to project this variant of the American experience as a metaphor for the whole.

However, I don't believe that any one group can speak for the whole experience—and it isn't, perhaps, even desirable. They can only reduce it to metaphor, and no one has yet forged a metaphor rich enough to reduce American diversity to form. Certainly the current group of Jewish writers, among whom there are several I admire, do not speak adequately for me or for Negroes generally. But during the thirties Jewish writing, although more skillful, was as provincial as most Negro American writing is today. That's the way it was, and we don't solve problems of history by running away from them. What I mean by provincial is an inability to see beyond the confines and constrictions placed upon Jewish life by its religious and cultural differences with the larger society, by its being basically the experience of an immigrant people who were, by and large, far less cultured than their more representative members.

It took long years of living in this country, long years of being a unique part of American society and discovering that they were not *forced* to live on the Lower East Side, of discovering that there *was* a place for the Jews in this society which did not depend upon their losing their group identity. They discovered that they possessed something precious to bring to the broader American culture, on the lowest as well as on the highest levels of human activity, and that it would have a creative impact far beyond the Jewish community. Many had not only to learn the language, but, more wonderful, had to discover that the Jewish American idiom would lend a whole new dimension to the American language.

How do the situations of the Negro and Jewish writers differ?

I think that Negro Americans as *writers* run into certain problems which the Jews don't have. One is that our lives since slavery have been described mainly in terms of our political, economic and social conditions as measured by outside norms, seldom in terms of our *own* sense of life or our *own* unique American experience. Nobody bothered to ask Negroes how they felt about their own lives. Southern whites used to tell the joke about the white employer who said to a Negro worker, "You're a good hand and I appreciate you. You make my business go much better. But although you work well every day, I can never get you to work on Saturday night, even if I offer to pay you overtime. Why is this?" Of course, you know the answer: "If you could just be a Negro one Saturday night, you'd never want to be a white man again." This is a rather facile joke, and a white Southern joke on Negroes; nevertheless, it does indicate an awareness that there is an internality to Negro American life, that it possesses its own attractions and its own mystery.

Now, the pathetic element in the history of Negro American writing is that it started out by reflecting the styles popular at the time, styles uninterested in the human complexity of Negroes. These were the styles of dialect humor transfused into literature from the *white* stereotype of the Negro minstrel tradition. This was Paul Laurence Dunbar and Charles Waddell Chestnutt. It helped them get published, but it got in the way of their subject matter and their goal of depicting Negro personality. Let's face it, those were times when white publishers and the white reading public wished to encounter only certain types of Negroes in poetry and fiction.

Even so, it was not a Negro writer who created the most memorable character in this tradition, but Mark Twain, whose "Nigger Jim" is, I think, one of the important characters in our literature. Nevertheless, Jim is flawed by his relationship to the minstrel tradition. Twain's portrait of Jim reflected the popular culture of the 1880s, just as the Negro characters you get in much of current fiction are influenced by the stereotypes presented by the movies and by sociology, those even more powerful media of popular culture.

The Negro writers who appeared during the 1920s wished to protest discrimination; some wished to show off their high regard for respectability; they wished to express their new awareness of their African background; and as Americans trying to win a place as writers, they were drawn to the going style of literary decadence represented by Carl Van Vechten's work. This was an extremely ironic development for a group whose written literature was still in its infancy—as incongruous as the notion of a decadent baby. Even more ironic, this was a time when Eliot, Pound, Hemingway and Stein were really tearing American literature apart and reshaping its values and its styles in the "revolution of the word." We always picked the moribund style. We took to dialect at a time when *Benito Cereno*, *Moby-Dick* and *Leaves of Grass* were at hand to point a more viable direction for a people whose demands were revolutionary, and whose humanity had been badly distorted by the accepted styles.

For more understandable reasons, during the 1930s we were drawn to the theories of proletarian literature. During the twenties we had wanted to be fashionable, and this ensured, even more effectively than the approaching Depression, the failure of the "New Negro" movement. We fell into that old trap by which the segregated segregate themselves by trying to turn whatever the whites said against us into its opposite. If they said Negroes love fried chicken (and why shouldn't we?), we replied, "We *hate* fried chicken." If they said Negroes have no normal family life, we replied, "We have a staider, more refined, more puritanical family life than you." If they said that Negroes love pork chops, we replied, "We despise them!" With few exceptions, our energies as writers have too often been focused upon outside definitions of reality, and we have used literature for racial polemics rather than as an agency through which we might define experience as we ourselves have seen and felt it. These are negative charges, I know, but they seem true to me.

Indeed, it is very difficult, even today, for younger Negro writers to overcome these negative tendencies. Far too often they have been taught to think in Jim Crow terms: "I can do thus and so—not because human beings express themselves in these ways, but because such and such a *Negro* dared to do so." But if no other Negro has involved himself in the activity in question, then we tend to draw back and doubt that we might do well even as pioneers. Hence the younger writer tries to write on the models of other Negro writers rather than on the best writers regardless of race, class or what have you, completely ignoring the fact that all other writers try to pattern themselves on the achievements of the greatest writers, regardless of who the hell they were.

This is how the Jim Crow experience has gotten into our attitudes and set us back. We have been exiled in our own land, and as for our efforts at writing, we have been little better than silent because we have not been cunning. I find this astounding, because I feel that Negro American folklore is powerful, wonderful and universal. It became so by expressing a people who were assertive, eclectic and irreverent before all the oral and written literature that came within its grasp. It took what it needed to express its sense of life and rejected what it couldn't use.

But what we have achieved in folklore has seldom been achieved in the novel, the short story or poetry. In folklore we tell what Negro experience really is. We back away from the chaos of experience and from ourselves, and we depict the humor as well as the horror of our living. We project Negro life in a metaphysical perspective, and we have seen it with a complexity of vision that seldom gets into our writing. One reason for this lies in the poor teaching common to our schools and colleges, but the main failure lies, I think, in our simpleminded attempt to reduce fiction to a mere protest.

I notice that you mentioned, some time ago, that you learned a lot of skill under Richard Wright. Do you find that he gauged his craft to the great writers of the world?

He certainly tried to do so. He was constantly reading the great masters, just as he read the philosophers, the political theorists, the social and literary critics. He did not limit himself in the manner that many Negro writers currently limit themselves. He also encouraged other writers, who usually rebuffed him, to become conscious craftsmen, to plunge into the world of conscious literature and take their chances unafraid. He felt this to be one of the few areas in which Negroes could be as free and as equal as their minds and talents would allow. Like a good Negro athlete, he believed in his ability to compete. In 1940 he was well aware that *Native Son* was being published at a time when *The Grapes of Wrath* and *For Whom the Bell Tolls* would be his main competition. Nevertheless, he looked toward publication day nervously but eagerly. He wished to be among the most advanced artists and was willing to run the risk required.

Earlier you referred to the minstrel as a stereotype. Is it possible to treat such stereotypes as Sambo, or even Stepin Fetchit, as archetypes or motives instead of using them in the usual format?

Well, in fiction stereotypes partake of archetypes, and to the extent that stereotypes point to something basically human, they overlap.

Yes, in literary form stereotypes function, as do other forms of characterization, as motives. But the point is that they act as *imposed* motives which treat reality and character arbitrarily. Thus, to redeem them as you suggest, the writer is challenged to reveal the archetypical truth hidden within the stereotype. Here archetypes are embodiments of abiding patterns of human existence which underlie racial, cultural and religious differences. In their basic humanity, they are timeless and raceless, while stereotypes are malicious reductions of human complexity which seize upon such characteristics as color, the shape of a nose, an accent or hair texture, and convert them into emblems which render it unnecessary for the prejudiced individual to confront the humanity of those upon whom the stereotype has been imposed.

In answer to your question as to whether it is possible to use such stereotypes as Sambo and Stepin Fetchit, I'd say that it depends upon the writer's vision. If I used such stereotypes in fiction, I'd have to reveal their archetypical aspects because my own awareness *of*, and identification *with*, the human complexity which they deny would compel me to transform them into something more recognizably human. To do less would be to reveal a brutalization of my own sense of human personality.

On the other hand, let's take Faulkner. When Lucas Beauchamp first appears in Faulkner's work, he appears as a stereotype, but as he was developed throughout the successive novels, he became one of Faulkner's highest representatives of human quality. Or again, when Ned in the last book, *The Reivers*, is seen superficially, he appears to be the usual head-scratching, eye-rolling Negro stereotype. But beneath this mask Ned is a version of John, the archetypical Negro slave of Negro folklore, who always outwits and outtalks his master. Ned masterminds the action of the novel, and in so doing he is revealed as Faulkner's own persona. He is the artist disguised as Negro rogue and schemer.

This suggests that attempts to approach stereotypes strictly in racial terms are, for the Negro writer, very, very dangerous. We must first question what they conceal; otherwise we place ourselves in the position of rejecting the basic truth concealed in the stereotype along with its obvious falsehood. Truth is much too precious for that.

On the stage of Town Hall a few days before the 1964 Democratic Convention, a group from the Mississippi Freedom Democratic party talked of their experiences. To the facile eye one of the men who talked there might well have been mistaken for the Sambo stereotype. He was Southern and rural; his speech was heavily idiomatic, his tempo slow. A number of his surface characteristics seemed to support the stereotype. But had you accepted him as an incarnation of Sambo, you would have missed a very courageous man, a man who understood only too well that his activities in aiding and protecting the young Northern students working in the Freedom Movement placed his life in constant contact with death, but who continued to act. Now, I'm not going to reject that man because some misinformed person, some prejudiced person sees him as the embodiment of Uncle Tom or Sambo. What's inside you, brother; what's your heart like? What are your real values? What human qualities are hidden beneath your idiom?

Do you think the reason for this is that Negroes in the U.S. are caught, if they allow themselves to be, in a bind? Do you think that the Negro writer then is forced, sometimes, to go away to gain a perspective? Or can he transcend his situation by remaining in it?

Well, again I would say that the individual must do that which is necessary for him individually. However, I would also say that it is not objectively necessary to go away. He might solve his problem by leaving the Village or by leaving Harlem. Harlem has always been a difficult place for Negroes to gain perspective on the national experience, because it has sponsored a false sense of freedom. It has also sponsored a false sense of superiority toward Negroes who live elsewhere. I remember getting into an argument during World War II with a fellow who insisted that Southern Negroes had no knowledge of boxing or baseball. This came from refusing to use his eyes around New York.

As a writer, one frees oneself by actually going in and trying to get the shape of experience *from the writer's perspective*. I see no other way. But unfortunately this requires a writer's type of memory, which is strongly emotional and associative, and a certain amount of technique. You must pay the Negro community the respect of trying to see it through the enrichening perspectives provided by great literature, using your own intelligence to make up for the differences in economy, class background, education, conscious culture, manners and attitude toward values. Human beings are basically the same and differ mainly in lifestyle. Here revelation is called for, not argument.

How do you mean "argument"?

I mean that it is futile to argue our humanity with those who willfully refuse to recognize it, when art can reveal on its own terms more truth while providing pleasure, insight and, for Negro readers at least, affirmation and a sense of direction. We must assert our own sense of values, beginning with the given and the irrevocable, with the question of heroism and slavery.

Contrary to some, I feel that our experience as a people involves a great deal of heroism. From one perspective, slavery was horrible and brutalizing. It is said that "Those Africans were enslaved, they died in the 'middle passage,' they were abused, their families were separated, they were whipped, they were raped, ravaged, and emasculated." And the Negro writer is tempted to agree. "Yes! God damn it, wasn't that a horrible thing!" But he sometimes agrees to the next step, which holds that slaves had very little humanity because slavery destroyed it for them and their descendants. That's what the Stanley M. Elkins "Sambo" argument implies. But despite the historical past and the injustices of the present, from *my* perspective there is something further to say. I have to *affirm* my forefathers and I *must* affirm my parents or be reduced in my own mind to a white man's inadequate—even if unprejudiced—conception of human complexity. Yes, and I must affirm those unknown people who sacrificed for me. I'm speaking of those Negro Americans who never knew that a Ralph Ellison might exist, but who by living their own lives and refusing to be destroyed by social injustice and white supremacy, real or illusory, made it possible for me to live my own life with meaning. I am forced to look at these people and upon the history of life in the United States and conclude that there is another reality behind the appearance of reality which they would force upon us as truth.

Any people who could endure all of that brutalization and keep together, who could undergo such dismemberment, resuscitate itself, and endure until it could take the initiative in achieving its own freedom is obviously more than the sum of its brutalization. Seen in this perspective, theirs has been one of the great human experiences and one of the great triumphs of the human spirit in modern times—in fact in the history of the world.

Some might say to your argument that you are expressing your own hopes and aspirations for Negroes, rather than reporting historical reality.

But hope and aspiration are indeed important aspects of the reality of Negro American history, no less than that of others. Besides, it's one of our roles as writers to remind ourselves of such matters, just as it is to make assertions tempered by the things of the spirit. It might sound arrogant to say so, but writers and poets help create or reveal hidden realities by asserting their existence. Otherwise they might as well become social scientists.

I do not find it a strain to point to the heroic component of our experience, for these seem to me truths which we have long lived by but which we must now recognize consciously. I am not denying the negative things which have happened to us and which continue to happen, but I am compelled to reject all condescending, narrowly paternalistic interpretations of Negro American life and personality from whatever quarters they come, whether white or Negro. Such interpretations would take the negative details of our existence and make them the whole of our life and personality. But literature teaches us that mankind has always defined itself *against* the negatives thrown it by both society and the universe. It is human will, human hope and human effort which make the difference. Let's not forget that the great tragedies not only treat of negative matters, of violence, brutalities, defeats, but treat them within a context of man's will to act, to challenge reality and to snatch triumph from the teeth of destruction.

You said it's unnecessary for one to leave the country to get a perspective. We notice in some of your older writings that after having come back from Rome, you sat up in New Hampshire and wrote Invisible Man.

No, I started *Invisible Man*—that novel about a man characterized by what the sociologists term "high visibility"—in Vermont, during the few months before the war came to an end. I was cooking on merchant ships at the time and had been given shore leave, so I accepted the invitation of a friend and went up there. I had no idea that I was going to start a book. But maybe I should add this: it isn't *where* you are that's important, but what you seek to depict, and most important of all is perspective. The main perspective through which a writer looks at experience is that provided by literature—just as the perspective through which a physician looks at the human body is the discipline of medicine, an accumulation of techniques, insights, instruments and processes which have been slowly developed over long periods of time. So when I look at my material I'm not looking at it simply through the concepts of sociology—and I do know something about sociology. I look at it through literature; English, French, Spanish, Russian—especially nineteenth-century Russian literature. And Irish literature, Joyce and Yeats, and the international literature of the twenties, and through the perspective of folklore. When I listen to a folk story I'm looking for what it conceals as well as what it states. I read it with the same fullness of attention I bring to *Finnegans Wake* or *The Sound and the Fury* because I'm eager to discover what it has to say to me personally.

Living abroad is necessary for those Negro writers who feel that they've been too cramped here and who wish to discover how it feels to live free of racial restrictions. This is valid. I should also say this: I came to New York from Tuskegee with the intention of going back to finish college. I came up to work. I didn't earn the money, so I stayed. But though I lived at the Harlem YMCA, I did *not* come to New York to live in Harlem, even though I thought of Harlem as a very romantic place. I'm pointing to an attitude of mind; I was not exchanging Southern segregation for Northern segregation, but seeking a wider world of opportunity and, most of all, the excitement and impersonality of a great city. I wanted room in which to discover who I was.

One of the first things I had to do was to enter places from which I was afraid I might be rejected. I had to confront my own fears of the unknown. I told myself, "Well, I might be hurt, but I won't dodge until they throw a punch." Over and over again I found that it was just this attitude (which finally became unselfconsciously nondefensive) which made the difference between my being accepted or rejected—and this during a time when many places practiced discrimination.

This requires submitting oneself to personal ordeals, especially if one grew up in the South and Southwest. Nor is this because you are afraid of white people so much as a matter of not wishing to be rebuffed. You don't wish to be upset when you're going to see a play by having a racial hassle on your hands. This distaste is very human. I've had a white Mississippian stop me on the streets of Rome asking if he would be admitted to a certain place which had caught his eye. I said, with a certain pleasurable irony, "Sure, go ahead; just tell them you're a friend of mine."

*What do you consider the Negro writer's responsibility to American litera-
ture as a whole?*

Any American writer becomes basically responsible for the health of
American literature the moment he starts writing seriously—and
this regardless of his race or religious background. This is no arbitrary matter. Just as there is implicit in the act of voting the responsibility of helping to govern, there is implicit in the act of writing a
responsibility for the quality of the American language—its accuracy, its vividness, its simplicity, its expressiveness—and responsibility for preserving and extending the quality of the literature.

*How do you regard President Johnson's statement that "art is not a political
weapon"? He made it at the White House in 1965.*

I don't think you've got it complete; let's read it. He said, "Your art
is not a political weapon, yet much of what you do is profoundly
political, for you seek out the common pleasures and visions, the terrors and cruelties of man's day on this planet. And I would hope you
would help dissolve the barriers of hatred and ignorance which are
the source of so much of our pain and danger."

You think that he is far ahead of many people?

He is far ahead of most of the intellectuals, especially those Northern liberals who have become, in the name of the highest motives,
the new apologists for segregation. Some of the *Commentary* writers,
for instance. Let's put it this way. President Johnson's speech at
Howard University spelled out the meaning of full integration for
Negroes in a way that no one, no President, not Lincoln nor Roosevelt, no matter how much we love and respect them, has ever done
before. There was no hedging in it, no escape clauses.

*About Robert Lowell's refusal in 1965 to participate in the White House
Art Festival, was this justly done, or do you think that he was engaged too
much in politics? Do you think it was necessary?*

I do not think it was necessary. When Lowell wrote to the President, and it was a skillfully written letter, he stated his motives of conscience, his fear that his presence would commit him to the President's foreign policy. In other words, he feared the potency of his own presence in such a setting, a potency which would seem to rest in his person rather than in the poetry for which we praise him and consider him great. But he didn't stop there; the letter got to the press, and once this happened it became a political act, a political gesture.

I think this was unfortunate. The President wasn't telling Lowell how to write his poetry, and I don't think he was in any position to tell the President how to run the government. Had I been running the Festival, I would simply have had an actor read from Lowell's poetry—with his permission, of course—for then not only would we have had the best of Lowell, but the question of his feelings about foreign policy wouldn't have come up.

Actually, no one was questioned about his attitudes, political or otherwise except by Dwight Macdonald. It wasn't that kind of occasion. Any and every opinion was represented there. Millard Lampell, who had been picketing the White House, had part of his play presented, and his background is no secret. So it was not in itself a political occasion, and all of the hullabaloo was beside the point. I was amazed, having gone through the political madness that marked the intellectual experience of the thirties, to see so many of our leading American intellectuals, poets and novelists—free creative minds— once again running in a herd. One may take a personal position about a public issue that is much broader than his personal morality, and the others make a herd of free creative minds! Some of my best friends are mixed up in it, which leaves me all the more amazed.

Speaking of herd activity, do you think that writers generally band together for the added stimulation or appreciation that they need? Or do you think that it is a lack on their part of a certain kind of intelligence?

It depends upon their reason for coming together. I think it important for writers to come together during the early stages of their careers, especially during the stage when they are learning their techniques, when they are struggling for that initial fund of knowledge on which they form their tastes and on which artistic choices are made. It's good for artists to get together to eat and drink, but when they get together in some sort of political effort, it usually turns out that they are being manipulated by a person or a group who are not particularly interested in art.

In other words, are you denying what happened to you in the thirties, during the New Masses *experience?*

No, I don't deny that at all; indeed, I speak out of that experience. But what happened to me during the thirties was part of a great swell of events which I plunged into when I came to town as an undergraduate musician, and through which I gradually transformed myself into a writer. The stimulus that existed in New York during the thirties was by no means limited to art; it was also connected with politics and was part of the *esprit de corps* developed in the country after we had endured the Depression for a few years. It had to do with my discovering New York and the unfamiliar areas of the society newly available to me. It had to do with working on the New York Writers Project, getting to know white friends, and being around Richard Wright, and around the *New Masses* and the League of American Writers crowd.

But if you'll note—and the record is public—I never wrote the official type of fiction. I wrote what might be called propaganda having to do with the Negro struggle, but my fiction was always trying to be something else, something different even from Wright's fiction. I never accepted the ideology which the *New Masses* attempted to impose on writers. They hated Dostoevsky, but I was studying Dostoevsky. They felt that Henry James was a decadent snob who had nothing to teach a writer from the lower classes, and I was studying James. I was also reading Marx, Gorki, Sholokhov and Isaac Babel. I was reading everything, including the Bible. Most of all, I was reading Malraux. I thought so much of that little Modern Library edition of *Man's Fate* that I had it bound in leather. This is where I was really living at the time, so perhaps it is the writers whose work has most impact upon us that are important, not those with whom we congregate publicly. Anyway, I think style is more important than political ideologies.

Do you see, then, a parallel between the thirties and the sixties, with this new resurgence of young Negro writers, with this turning toward Africa and, shall we say again, the resurgence of a particular kind of provincialism in New Negro writing?

I think that we should be careful in drawing parallels. This is a period of affluence as against the poverty of the Depression. True, during that period a lot of Negroes had the opportunity to work in the WPA at clerical jobs and so on, so that for us the Depression represented in many ways a lunge forward. We were beneficiaries of the government's efforts toward national recovery. Thanks to the national chaos, we found new places for ourselves. Today our lunges forward are facilitated by laws designed precisely to correct our condition as a group—by laws which start at the very top and which have the Supreme Court, the Executive branch and Congress behind them. This is quite different from the thirties.

As to Africa, I think it is probably true that more of the present crop of writers are concerned with Africa than was true then. In fact, quite a number who were concerned with Communism are now fervid black nationalists. Oddly enough, however, their way of writing hasn't changed significantly. Of course I may not know what I'm talking about, but there seem to be fewer Negro writers around who seem publishable at the moment. Surely there are fewer than the more favorable circumstances of today warrant.

Some people think that you should play a larger part in civil rights. This is similar to Sartre's rebuttal to Camus in Situations, *this idea of* engagement.

Well, I'm no Camus and they're no Sartres. But literature draws upon much deeper and much more slowly changing centers of the human personality than does politics. It draws mainly from literature itself, and upon the human experience which has abided long enough to have become organized and given significance through literature. I think that revolutionary political movements move much too rapidly to be treated as subjects for literature in themselves. When Malraux drew upon revolution as the settings for his novels, he drew for his real themes upon much deeper levels of his characters' consciousness than their concern with Marxism; it was to these deeper concerns, to the realm of tragedy, that they turned when facing death. Besides, political movements arise and extend themselves, achieve themselves, through fostering myths which interpret their actions and goals. If you tell the truth about a politician, you're always going to encounter contradiction and barefaced lies, especially when you're dealing with left-wing politicians.

If I were to write an account of the swings and twitches of the U.S. Communist line during the thirties and forties, it would be a revealing account, but I wouldn't attempt to do it in terms of fiction. It would have to be done in terms of political science and reportage. You would have to look up their positions, chart their moves, look at the directives handed down by the Communist International, or whatever the overall body was called. You would be in a muck and a mire of dead and futile activity, much of which had little to do with their ultimate goals or with American reality. They fostered the myth that Communism was twentieth-century Americanism, but to be a twentieth-century American meant, in their thinking, that you had to be more Russian than American and less Negro than either. That's how they lost the Negroes. The Communists recognized no plurality of interests and were really responding to the necessities of Soviet foreign policy, and when the war came, Negroes got caught and were made expedient in the shifting of policy, just as Negroes who fool around with them today are going to get caught in the next turn of the screw.

Do you think there is too much pressure on the Negro writer to play the role of politician instead of mastering his craft and acting as a professional writer?

Yes, and if he doesn't resist such pressure, he's in a bad way. Someone is always going to tell you that you can't write, and then they tell you *what* to write.

Among the first things the Negro writer has to resist is being told that he'll find it difficult to make a buck. I waded through tons of that. But I decided that I would make sacrifices, go without clothing and other necessities, in order to buy books, to be in New York where I could talk to certain creative people, and where I could observe this or that phenomenon. Resisting these warnings is most important. But if you deflect this particular pressure, there will always be people who will tell you that you have no talent. We understand the psychological dynamics of it; Booker T. Washington gave it the "crabs in a basket" metaphor: if a Negro threatens to succeed in a field outside the usual areas of Negro professionals, others feel challenged. It's a protective reaction, a heritage from slavery. We feel "Well, my God, he has the nerve to do that and I don't; what does he think he's doing, endangering the whole group?" Nevertheless, the writer must endure the agony imposed by this group pessimism.

Why do you think this exists?

Because our sense of security and our sense of who we are depends upon our feeling that we can account for each and every member of the group. To this way of thinking, any assertion of individuality is dangerous. I'm reminded of a woman whom I met at a party. We were discussing Negro life and I uttered opinions indicating an approach unfamiliar to her. Her indignant response was "How do you come talking like that? I've never even heard of you!" In her opinion I had no right to express ideas which hadn't been certified by her particular social group. Naturally she thought of herself as a member of a Negro elite, and in the position to know what each and every Negro thought and should think. This is a minority-group phenomenon, and I won't nail it to Negroes because it happens in the Jewish community as well.

In the interview that you had in Robert Penn Warren's Who Speaks for the Negro? *he addressed a question to you that has something to do with Negroes being culturally deprived, and you answered that many of the white students whom you'd taught were also culturally deprived. They were culturally deprived, you said, because while they might have understood many things intellectually, they were emotionally unprepared to deal with them. But the Negro was being prepared emotionally, whether intellectually or not, from the moment he was placed in the crib. Would you expand on that a bit?*

I think you've touched *the* important area that gets lost when we hold such discussions. I get damn tired of critics writing of me as though I don't know how hard it is to be a Negro American. My point is that it isn't *only* hard, but that there are many good things about it.

But they don't want you to say that. This is especially true of some of our Jewish critics. They get quite upset when I say: *I like this particular aspect of Negro life and would not surrender it. What I want is something else to go along with it.* And when I get the other things, I'm not going to try to invade the group life of anybody else. Of course they don't like the idea that I reject many of the aspects of life which they regard highly. But you know, white people can get terribly disturbed at the idea that Negroes are not simply being restricted from many areas of our national life, but that they are also judging certain aspects of our culture and rejecting their values. That's where assumptions of white superiority, conscious or unconscious, make for blindness and naïveté. In fact we've rejected many of their values from the days before there were Jim Crow laws.

Only a narrowly sociological explanation of society could lead to the belief that we Negroes are what we are simply because whites have refused us the right of choice through racial discrimination. Frequently Negroes are able to pay for commodities available in stores, but we reject them as a matter of taste, not economics. There is no *de facto* Jim Crow in many areas of New York, but we don't frequent them, not because we think we won't be welcome—indeed, many Negroes go to places precisely because they are unfairly and illegally rejected—but because they simply don't interest us. All this *we* know to be true.

Negro Americans had to learn to live under pressure; otherwise we'd have been wiped out, or in the position of the Indians, set on a reservation and rendered powerless by opposing forces. Fortunately our fate was different. We were forced into segregation, but within that situation we were able to live close to the larger society and to abstract from it enough combinations of values, including religion and hope and art, which allowed us to endure and impose our own idea of what the world should be, of what man should be, and of what American society should be. I'm not speaking of power here, but of vision, of values and dreams. Yes, and of will.

What is missing today is a corps of artists and intellectuals who can evaluate Negro American experience from the inside, and out of a broad knowledge of how people of other cultures live, deal with experience and give significance to their experience. We do too little of this. Rather, we depend upon outsiders—mainly sociologists—to interpret our lives for us. It doesn't seem to occur to us that our interpreters might well be not so much prejudiced as ignorant, insensitive and arrogant. It doesn't occur to us that they might be of shallow personal culture, or innocent of the complexities of actual living.

It is ironic that we act this way, because over and over again when we find bunches of Negroes enjoying themselves, when they're feeling good and in a mood of communion, they sit around and marvel at what a damnably marvelous human being, what a confounding human type the Negro American really is. This is the underlying significance of so many of our bull sessions. We exchange accounts of what happened to someone whom the group once knew. "You know what that so-and-so did," we say, and then his story is told. His crimes, his loves, his outrages, his adventures, his transformations, his moments of courage, his heroism, buffooneries, defeats and triumphs are recited, with each participant joining in. This catalogue soon becomes a brag, an exciting chant celebrating the metamorphosis which this individual in question underwent within the limited circumstances available to us.

This is wonderful stuff; in the process the individual is enlarged. It's as though a transparent overlay of archetypal myth is being placed over the life of an individual, and through him we see ourselves. Of course, this is what literature does with life; these verbal jam sessions are indeed a form of folk literature and they help us to define our own experience.

But when we Negro Americans start *"writing,"* we lose this wonderful capacity for abstracting and enlarging life. Instead we ask, "How do we fit into the sociological terminology? Gunnar Myrdal said this experience means thus and so. And Dr. Kenneth Clark or Dr. E. Franklin Frazier says the same thing . . ." We try to fit our experience into their concepts. Well, whenever I hear a Negro intellectual describing Negro life and personality with a catalogue of negative definitions, my first question is: how did you escape? Is it that you were born exceptional and superior? If I cannot look at the most brutalized Negro on the street, even when he irritates me and makes me want to bash his head in because he's goofing off, I must still say within myself, "Well, that's you too, Ellison." I'm not talking about guilt, but of an identification which goes beyond race.

You have said that Hemingway tells us much more about how Negroes feel than all the writings done by those people mixed up in the Negro Renaissance.

What I meant was this: Hemingway's writing of the twenties and the thirties, even of the forties, evoked certain basic, deeply felt moods and attitudes within his characters which closely approximated certain basic attitudes held by many Negroes about their position in American society, and about their sense of the human predicament. He did this not only because he was a greater writer than the participants in the Negro Renaissance, but because he possessed a truer sense of what the valid areas of perplexity were and a more accurate sense of how to get life into literature. He recognized that the so-called "Jazz Age" was a phony, while most Negro writers jumped on that illusory bandwagon when they, of all people, should have known better.

I was also referring to Hemingway's characters' attitude toward society, to their morality, their code of technical excellence, to their stoicism, their courage or "grace under pressure," to their skepticism about the validity of political rhetoric and all those abstractions in the name of which our society was supposed to be governed, but which Hemingway found highly questionable when measured against our actual conduct. Theirs was an attitude springing from an awareness that they lived outside the values of the larger society, and I feel that their attitudes came close to the way Negroes felt about the way the Constitution and the Bill of Rights were applied to us.

Further, I believe that in depicting the attitudes of athletes, expatriates, bullfighters, traumatized soldiers and impotent idealists, Hemingway told us quite a lot about what was happening to that most representative group of Negro Americans, jazz musicians—who also lived by an extreme code of withdrawal, technical and artistic excellence, and rejection of the values of respectable society. They replaced the abstract and much-betrayed ideals of that society with the more physical values of eating, drinking, copulating, loyalty to friends and dedication to the discipline and values of their art.

I say all this while fully aware that Hemingway seldom depicted Negroes, and that when he did they were seldom the types we prefer to encounter in fiction. But to see what I mean, one has only to look upon the world of Hemingway's fiction as offering a valid metaphor not only for the predicament of young whites, but as a metaphor for the post–World War I period generally. Seen in this inclusive light, he tells us a hell of a lot about the way Negroes were feeling and acting.

At any rate, this is how I use literature to come to an understanding of our situation. It doesn't have to be, thank God, *about* Negroes in order to give us insights into our own predicament. You do not, to my way of thinking, assume that a writer can treat of his times, if he writes well, without revealing a larger segment of life than that of the specific milieu which engages his attention; if it is to be valid it must go beyond and touch the reality of other groups and individuals. Faulkner tells us a great deal about many different groups who were not his immediate concern because he wrote so truthfully. If you would find the imaginative equivalents of certain civil rights figures in American writing—Rosa Parks and James Meredith, say—you don't go to most fiction by Negroes, but to Faulkner. ʾ

You have said that you don't accept any theory which implies that culture is transmitted through the genes. What, then, is your reaction to the concept of "negritude"?

To me it represents the reverse of that racism with which prejudiced whites approach Negroes. As a theory of art it implies precisely that culture is transmitted through the genes. It is a blood theory.

There are members of my family who are very black, and there are some who are very white—which means that I am very much Negro, very much Negro American, and quite representative of that racial type with its mixture of African, European and indigenous American blood. This is a biological fact, but recognizing this, loving my family, and recognizing that I'm bound to them by blood and family tradition is by no means to agree with the proponents of negritude. Because even while I affirm our common bloodline, I recognize that we are bound less by blood than by our cultural and political circumstances.

Further, I don't believe that my form of expression springs from Africa, although it might be easier for me as an artist if it did, because then, perhaps, a massive transfusion of pure Nigerian blood would transform me into a great sculptor. I've been reading the classics of European and American literature since childhood, and was born to the American tongue, the language of the Bible and the Constitution; these, for better or worse, shaped my thought and attitudes and pointed the direction of my talent long before I became a conscious writer. I also inherited a group style originated by a "black" people, but it is Negro American, not African; it was taught to me by Negroes, or copied by me from those among whom I lived most intimately.

All this is similar to the notion that Negroes have a corner on soul. *Well, we don't.*

You're right, and anyone who listens to a Beethoven quartet or symphony and can't hear *soul* is in trouble. Maybe they can hear the sound of blackness, but they're deaf to *soul*.

Richard Wright was called a white man.

I've had something like that happen. When I was teaching at Bard College a young Negro girl approached one of my white colleagues and said, "Is this Mr. Ellison a Negro?" I can't understand that; it sounds as if she was putting him on, because there I was facing classes with my big African nose, teaching American literature and highlighting the frame so that they could become aware of the Negro experience in it, and she wants to know whether I'm Negro! I suppose the social patterns are changing faster than we can grasp.

Recently we had a woman from the South who helped my wife around the house but who goofed off so frequently that she was fired. We liked her and really wanted her to stay, but she simply wouldn't do her work. My friend Albert Murray told me I shouldn't be puzzled over the outcome. "You know how we can be sometimes," Al said. "She saw the books and furniture and paintings, so she knew you were some kind of white man. You couldn't possibly be a Negro, so she figured she could get away with a little boondoggling on general principles, because she'd probably been getting away with a lot of stuff with Northern whites. But what she didn't stop to notice was that you're a *Southern* white man . . ."

You see, here culture and race and a preconception of how Negroes are supposed to live—a question of taste—had come together and caused a comic confusion. Jokes like Al Murray's are meaningful because in America culture is always cutting across racial characteristics and social designations. Therefore if a Negro doesn't exhibit certain attitudes, or if he reveals a familiarity with aspects of the culture, or possesses qualities of personal taste which the observer has failed to note among Negroes, such confusions in perception are apt to occur.

But the basic cause is, I think, that we are all members of a highly pluralistic society. We possess two cultures—both American—and many aspects of the broader American culture are available to Negroes who possess the curiosity and taste, if not the money, to cultivate them. It is often overlooked, especially in our current state of accelerated mobility, that it is becoming increasingly necessary for Negroes themselves to learn who they are *as Negroes*. Cultural influences have always outflanked racial discrimination wherever and whenever there were Negroes receptive to them, even in slavery times. I read the books which were to free me for my work as a writer while studying at Tuskegee Institute, Macon County, Alabama, during a time when most of the books weren't even taught. Back in 1937, I knew a Negro who swept the floors at Wright Field in Dayton, Ohio, who was nevertheless designing planes and entering his designs in contests. He was working as a porter, but his mind, his ambitions and his attitudes were those of an engineer. He wasn't waiting for society to change; he was changing it by himself.

What advice would you give to a young person of eighteen who was setting out to be a writer?

My first advice would be to make up his mind to the possibility that he might have to go through a period of depriving himself in order to write. I'd remind him that he was entering into a very stern discipline, and that he should be quite certain that he really wanted to do this to the extent of arranging his whole life so that he could get it done. He should regard writing the way a young physician is required to regard his period of training. Next, I'd advise him to read everything, all the good books he could manage, especially those in the literary form in which he desires to become creative. Because books contain the culture of the chosen form, and because one learns from the achievements of other writers. Here is contained the knowledge which he must have at his fingertips as he projects his own vision. Without it, no matter how sensitive, intelligent or passionate he is, he will be incomplete.

Beyond that, he shouldn't take the easy escape of involving himself exclusively in *talking* about writing, or carrying picket signs, or sitting-in as a substitute activity. While he might become the best picket in the world, or the best sitter-inner, his writing will remain where he left it.

Finally, he should avoid the notion that writers require no education. Often Hemingway and Faulkner are summoned up to support this argument, because they didn't finish college. What is overlooked is that these were gifted, brilliant men, and very well-read men of great intellectual capacity. No matter how you acquire an education, you must have it. You must know your society, and know it beyond your own neighborhood or region. You must know its manners, ideals and conduct. You should also know something of what's happening in the sciences, religion, government, and the other arts.

I suppose what I'm saying is that this young writer should have a working model of society and of our national characteristics present within his mind. The problem of enriching that model and keeping it up-to-date is one of the greatest challenges to the Negro writer, who is, by definition, cut off from firsthand contact with large areas of that society—especially from those centers where power is translated into ideas, manners and values. Nevertheless, this can be an advantage, because in this country no writer should take anything for granted, but must use his imagination to question and penetrate the façade of things. Indeed, the integration of American society on the level of the imagination is one of this young writer's basic tasks. It is one way in which he is able to possess his world, and in his writings help shape the values of large segments of a society which otherwise would not admit his existence, much less his right to participate or to judge.

The Novel as a Function of
American Democracy

I am a writer who writes very slowly; because of this, I am often tempted to convince myself that I should spend a lot of time theorizing about what the novel is. One fact I am sure about: the writing of novels is the damnedest thing that I ever got into, and I've been into some damnable things. Nevertheless, there is a certain sincerity in my choice of the title for this address; you will note, however, that I do not say that all novels have a nonartistic function or that they owe something to American democracy. But I do happen to feel that in this country the novel, a particular art form to which I am giving my life, found a function which it did not have in any of the nations where it was developed by artists who made it resound so effectively with their eloquence.

As you know, the emergence of the novel occurred at a time when the stability of social class lines was being shaken. (Please don't let my use of the term "class lines" upset you.) Although the conception of freedom existed before the eighteenth century, it was revitalized during that century of many wars and revolutions; societies began to change, new classes to emerge; new values were established. Traditional forms were modified; the conception of kingship gave way to the conception of democracy and individualism. Change was everywhere.

One of the aesthetic results of this change was the emergence of a literary form which could project the shiftings of society with a facility and an intimacy that had not existed before, either in the theater or in romantic poetry. This form was much concerned with the emergence of new personality types, with what was happening to

From *Wilson Library Bulletin*, June 1967; based on a lecture sponsored by the Philadelphia City Institute, delivered March 23, 1967, at the Free Library of Philadelphia.

tradition, as individuals began to explore the nature of possibility which had been brought about for them through the crack-ups of the old society. The writers themselves were challenged into taking all the traditional forms—oral storytelling, the ballad, poetry, drama— and exploiting them in this new medium of the novel. All of this was necessary, because people no longer knew exactly who they were. They knew that they were doing things; they knew that there were changes; they knew that they were connected to the old values and sometimes wore the old clothing. But inside they felt different; they felt the need to test themselves against the new possibilities because it was *possible* to test themselves. If Robinson Crusoe wanted to go to a desert isle, he took with him certain techniques, certain values, from whence he came; these he adapted to the new environment and to the people whom he found on his isle. Such a plot proved exciting, and it projected for the reader a sense of reality, a sense of what was immanent, a sense of what was possible for himself.

By the middle of the nineteenth century the novel had become a recognized art form which had absorbed all the unstructured techniques of narrative, whether oral or literary, that had preceded it. In the hands of such novelists as Dostoevsky, Flaubert and Melville it had become a literary form which, along with its powers to entertain, was capable of deadly serious psychological and philosophical explorations of the human predicament.

As I see it, the novel has always been bound up with the idea of nationhood. What are we? Who are we? What has the experience of the particular group been? How did it become this way? What is it that stopped us from attaining the ideal? In Russian literature, particularly, we can see this clearly as we follow the work of Pushkin, who wrote knowingly of the superfluous individual, the dilettante, the man of great sensitivity and great possibilities who could not find his way in a society that had been unable to break away from the stagnation of life inherent to that period of Russian history.

In reading Pushkin, Gogol, Dostoevsky and Tolstoy, one can see the drawing out, the investigation, of what the idea of the superfluous individual amid the stagnated society had to suggest to men who came later and who chose the novel as a means of exploring reality. It is the very nature of this exploration which attracts me to the novel, and which causes me to take it very seriously. I can say this without any reference to my personal abilities, which are limited. The novel is a form which deals with change in human personality and human society, bringing to the surface those values, patterns of conduct and dilemmas, psychological and technological, which abide within the human predicament. It can abstract, from the flow and fury of existence, these patterns, which are abiding, and re-create them in the forms of artistic models that can be controlled and imbued with the personal values of the writer, down even to the last punctuation mark. In other words, the novel is a way of possessing life, slowing it down, and giving it the writer's own sense of values in a delicately and subtly structured way. All this, of course, is not simply a matter of entertaining, but is a way of confronting reality, the nature of the soul and the nature of society. As a form, the novel permits a writer to survive the consequences of encountering the chaos he must reckon with when he attempts to deal with the basic truths of human existence.

In turning now to the American novel, I wish to emphasize that the American nation is based upon revolution, dedicated to change through basic concepts stated in the Bill of Rights and the Constitution. It is dedicated also to the ideal of an *open* society, a society in which a great landmass allowed peoples to move about, to change their identities if they would, to advance themselves, to achieve results based on their own talents and techniques. With such a society, it seems only natural that the novel existed to be exploited by certain personality types who found their existence within the United States. What I am trying to describe is the relationship between the form in which I work and the society as I see it. Of course the first writers of any stature in the United States were not novelists; they were essayists, preachers, philosophers and poets. When I think of the meaning of the essays of Ralph Waldo Emerson, now dismissed as being a little too much on the optimistic side, I remind myself that there was a need for his optimism. Some voice had to be raised to remind Americans that they were not Europeans. Emerson's essays fulfilled a need precisely because Americans existed in a society and a country which was not very tightly structured and in which no one, at that time especially, could set a limit upon individual possibility, certainly not at the level of the imagination.

Such limits might have been set on the slaves; even so, there was always some slave who confounded the general conception. So the Emersons, Whitmans and Thoreaus reminded us that the stance of secession had its own value. They told us that this stance was an obligation for us, not only as Americans but as members of a civilization, actors in a long, continued action which started before history and which, through some miracle, produced on this land, after bloody assaults, the condition in which, we hoped, human society could make a leap forward. Someone had to tell us that the price we pay for progress is terrible, but that we cannot afford to close our eyes and stop.

These early writers enjoined us to experience nature and society to the hilt. They asked us to interrogate ourselves, nature and the universe by way of realizing ourselves, by way of paying our debt to history. The Whitmans were necessary to point out to us that this was a lyrical as well as a rugged experience. There is nothing like having a harsh reality nudging you along to make you feel that there is some virtue in song. I am not suggesting, by the way, that life is best for the poet or novelist when it is harshest. What I am saying is that when we are closest to the tragic realities of human existence, we have a deeper appreciation for song and for the lyric mode. Be that as it may, let me remind you that almost as early as the great European nations produced great novelists, this country also produced a few great novelists and some great poets. But as remarkable as this is, it must be remembered that we are a continuation of a European civilization, not an entity in ourselves, although our variations upon the theme and our amplification of the themes are unique.

The Melvilles and Hawthornes, however, were a part of our early nineteenth century; by midcentury this country had reached a certain crisis, implicit in our approach to the new possibility of freedom, a crisis so profound that we fought a civil war, one of the bloodiest in history. It was then that America produced Henry James, Mark Twain and Stephen Crane. By the time I began to write, Henry James was considered a snob, an upper-class expatriate who in New York and around Boston had fallen into some sort of decadent hothouse in which his head became much too large for his body. His sensibility was considered too delicate to interest anyone who was a real man concerned with the things of this world as they existed. It was forgotten, however, that James came on the scene at a time when abolitionists were coming in and out of his father's house, and that he was part of a period in which there was great intellectual, religious and civil rights ferment. Few critics recalled that in that war James lost one of his older brothers, who had been a member of Colonel Shaw's Massachusetts regiment of free slaves. It was also forgotten that James's second published story, "The Story of a Year," was based on an incident which occurred in the Civil War. But what does all of this have to do with Henry James? He was, at first glance, a novelist highly conscious of the form of the novel as an artistic unity, one of the first writers, European or American, to rationalize, or to attempt to rationalize, an aesthetic of the novel. He was a writer with a great and subtle awareness of how the novel differed from all other forms of narrative and drama and other forms of storytelling, one who knew how characters function and relate to each other, who knew that they had to function as an organic form.

Thematically James knew much more. He recognized—as demonstrated in his novel *The Bostonians*—that in his time the United States had reached a moment of crisis, and in fact that he was writing during a new period in the life of the nation, when the lyrical belief in the possibilities of the Constitution and the broadness of the land was no longer so meaningful. Mindful that hundreds of thousands of men had died in the Civil War, James knew for his own time what Emerson knew for his. Emerson constantly reminded Americans that they had to discover the new possibilities of the new land. What James realized was that the old enduring evil of the human predicament had raised its face, revealing itself within this land. This evil could no longer be confronted in the name of religion, kingship or aristocracy, although James was himself an aristocrat. James recognized that each and every individual who lived within the society had to possess, and to be concerned with, the most subtle type of moral consciousness. He was as aware of the labyrinth in which Americans walk as was Emerson. Yet neither man liked the other, perhaps because they approached the same reality from different positions and through different disciplines. Today not many people read James, although he is by no means an ignored writer. For me one minor test of this is the fact that I don't know of many Negro youngsters who are named Henry James Jones. There were, and are, a number who are named Waldo, and I happen to be one of them. Amusing as this is, it reveals something of how the insight and values of literature get past the usual barriers in society and seep below the expected levels. I shall speak more of this later.

Another major writer of this midcentury period was Stephen Crane. Younger than James, Crane nonetheless lived during his lifetime, a young man from upstate New York, born into a Methodist family well known for its preachers. At twenty-nine this young man, who had never experienced warfare, wrote one of our classics, *The Red Badge of Courage*, a unique book about the Civil War, one which was praised at first precisely because the writer was too young to have experienced warfare. Indeed, it is a unique book about *any* war. What was missed, of course, was the fact that Crane used the Civil War as a metaphor for the human condition in the United States. Here is a book about a war in which you see no close-ups of generals. Whenever officers come on the scene, we feel that the camera in the motion picture has been withdrawn about the length of a football field. You can never quite get up to the brass, but you get very close to the dead, even to seeing the ants crawling out of their eye sockets, and you get the fury and panic of deadly action. Most important, you penetrate deeply into the mind of an uninstructed American who had no idea what the war was about, an American for whom the encounter was almost totally personal until he broke and ran and found himself in the false position of pretending that he was a hero when he knew within his soul that he was a coward. Having no conception of the overall strategy of battle, he was the dismembered little man, caught up in a great social action.

Here was the other side, you see, of the early American conception that every man was a king, a philosopher, every American the possessor of insight into the complexity of things, standing right at the tip point of history. No. For Crane the American was a man who tested himself in terms of his personal courage, his moral courage, his ability and willingness to tell himself the truth about himself. *The Red Badge of Courage* offered its readers a metaphor for their own feelings about their relationship to their society. Its significance lay not in the fact that the young man who wrote it had never seen war, but in its articulation for its readers of a sense of loss, a loss of faith and direction, after the great crisis of the Civil War. It is this same sense of loss which James celebrates in his novel *The Bostonians*, a portrait not of courageous people who had fought for abolition while living their lives with quivering nerves and searching intellect, but instead a portrait of a people who had lost their sense of direction and who were floundering in many ways. Even the theme of homosexuality—in this instance, female homosexuality—was introduced, not to shock the reader but to indicate how profound the disintegration of moral tone was in the Boston of that day.

Another book which states the moral predicament of its times, metaphorically, is *Huckleberry Finn*. Written by a white Southerner who had been freed of certain narrow prejudices, the novel dramatizes in a poignant and amusing way the social aspect of the civil rights problem. No great philosopher, Twain was nevertheless a great moralist and storyteller. Like Uncle Remus, he was a great entertainer, a man who looked sharply at reality and made distinctions between what we said we were (our ideals) and how we acted (our conduct). *Huckleberry Finn* projected the truth about slavery, and it will be many years in this country before there will ever again be a novelist so popular, so loved, so understood by people who simply were unable to confront the real moral predicament of their nation in any way other than in the pages of a story.

In the works of all of these men—James, Crane and Twain—the novel was never used merely as a medium of entertainment. These writers suggested possibilities, courses of action, stances against chaos. In their work, as in those who followed them—Hemingway and Fitzgerald, for example—the novel functioned beyond entertainment in helping create the American conception of America.

When Twain wrote *Huckleberry Finn*, some people of my background were already writing, but there were few people indeed who were close to the complexity of this particular aspect of American experience. I don't say this to inflate the experience, but to point to the fact that in this country there is no absolute separation of groups. The American language, this rich, marvelous, relatively unexplored organ, is the creation of many people, and it began with the Indians. As we walk through the streets of our cities their names sing in our heads; great poetry has been made of them, but we do not realize that they are Indian names. We forget, conveniently sometimes, that the language which we speak is not English, although it is based on English. We forget that our language is such a flexible instrument because it has had so many dissonances thrown into it—from Africa, Mexico, Spain, from, God knows, everywhere. Yet it has been reduced to a working, flexible, highly poetic language. I note this in order to say that what is happening in what you now like to call the ghettos, or what was once called the plantations, didn't simply stay there. These milieux influenced how you pronounced your name, how you walked, the things you ate, the tunes you whistled; these things frequently found their way into larger cultures, something we now call the mainstream. When Jewish immigrants arrived in great waves from Europe and settled on the Lower East Side, cultural variations occurred there but found their way into other areas. In this sense, our national style is a product of these elusive variations of styles, manners and customs which emerged from our many sub-communities.

Even today America remains an undiscovered country. Recall, for instance, the shock experienced by the nation when Adam Powell was thrown out of Congress, and people in the Eighteenth District of New York were heard to say: "Put him back, dammit." There is a mystery in this country because we live where we are, wear the same clothing, listen to the same television programs, worship the same God, read the same textbooks, have the same heroes in sports, politics and music. We are at once very unified, and at the same time diversified. On many levels we don't know who we are, and there are always moments of confrontation where we meet as absolute strangers. Race is by no means the only thing which divides us in this still-undiscovered country. We're only a partially achieved nation, and I think this is good because it gives the writer of novels a role beyond that of entertainer. The novel's function permits him a maximum freedom to express his own vision of reality. It allows him to write out of his own group background and his own individual background. But the novel also places upon him a responsibility of reporting—imaginatively of course—what is going on in his particular area of the American experience. How does the individual take the strains of his past and use them to illuminate his own sense of life? How are the great American ideals made manifest in his own particular environment? What is his sense of the good life? What is his sense of high style? What is his sense of the moral dilemma of the nation? These questions and their answers are the novelist's responsibilities. If we do not know as much about ourselves now, if we find that we read sociology and history more than we read novels, it is not our fault as readers. It is the fault of the novelist because he has failed his obligation to tell the truth, to describe with eloquence and imagination life as it appears from wherever he finds his being. It is easy to say this but it's very difficult to do, because in this country there is a tradition of forgetfulness, of moving on, of denying the past, of converting the tragic realities of ourselves but most often of others—even if those others are of our own group—into comedy.

Today we are an affluent society and yet we're unhappy. We no longer know what truth is. We no longer recognize heroism when it is demonstrated to us. We do not understand the nature of forbearance. Far too often we do not take advantage of the wonderful opportunity which we have to project ourselves into the lives of other people—not to modify those lives but to understand them, to add dimensions to our own sense of wonder and sense of the possibility of living in a society like this. We don't know what to do with our money—even poor people. Apparently we have no defenses before the great cacophony of styles poured upon us through the marvelous medium of television. Our streets look like circuses. Our sense of taste seems to have been lost. We don't seem to know where we are. Some responsibility for this must rest with our novelists, for once they attain their fame they begin to forget where they came from; they begin to doubt where they can go.

The state of our novel is not healthy at the moment. Instead of aspiring to project a vision of the complexity and diversity of the total experience, the novelist loses faith and falls back upon something which is called "black comedy"—which is neither black nor comic, but is a cry of despair. Talent, technique and artistic competence are there, but a certain necessary faith in human possibility before the next unknown is not there. I speak from my own sense of the dilemma and of what people who work in my form owe to those who would read us seriously, and who are willing to pay us the respect of lending their imaginations to ours.

The novel was not invented by an American, nor even for Americans, but we are a people who have perhaps most need of it—a form which can produce imaginative models of the total society if the individual writer has the imagination, and can endow each character, scene and punctuation mark with his own sense of value. If there had been more novelists with the courage of Mark Twain, James or

Hemingway, we would not be in the moral confusion in which we find ourselves today. If we do not know good from bad, cowardice from heroism, the marvelous from the mundane and banal, then we don't know who we are. It is a terrible thing to sit in a room with a typewriter and dream, and to tell the truth by telling effective lies, but this seems to be what many novelists opt for. Certainly this society will read books, and we as writers have the responsibility of not disappointing it. It is an old cliché that to have great writers you must have great readers. Yet I suspect that American readers have been irresponsible, too, because they have not said precisely why they find the works of modern novelists wanting.

Perspective of Literature

WHEN I was a young boy I often went out to the Oklahoma State Capitol, where I assisted Mr. J. D. Randolph with his duties as custodian of the State Law Library. I was about eleven years old at the time, quite impressionable, and very curious about the mysterious legal goings-on of the legislators. All the more so because while I was never able to observe the legislature in session, it was not at all unusual for me to look up from pushing a broom or dusting a desk to see one of the legislators dash into the library to ask Jeff—Mr. Randolph was always addressed by his first name—his opinion regarding some point of law. In fact, I soon came to look forward to such moments because I was amazed by the frequency with which Mr. Randolph managed to come up with satisfactory answers, even without consulting the heavy volumes which ranged the walls.

I wasn't surprised that Mr. Randolph was a janitor instead of a lawyer or legislator; Oklahoma was segregated at the time, and Afro-Americans were strictly limited in their freedom to participate in the process of government. We could obey or break laws, but not make or interpret them. In view of this, I was amazed that Mr. Randolph had come to know so much about the subject. This was a tantalizing mystery, but the fact that white men of power would show no shame in exploiting the knowledge of one far beneath them in status aroused my sense of irony. That after all was simply another example of white folks taking advantage of black folks.

I was more impressed with the fact that Mr. Randolph could carry so many of the mysterious details of the laws which governed the state of Oklahoma within his own head. I knew he had been one of the first schoolteachers in the city and the state, and that he read and owned a large collection of books. But just how he had come to learn the law was part of an experience about which I was never to hear

From *American Law: The Third Century*, Fred B. Rothman & Co., 1976.

him talk. I did know, however, that he had never attended college, and I was aware that many of our greatest lawyers had acquired their legal knowledge through the process of "reading" law with licensed members of the profession.

I only knew that Mr. Randolph appeared to possess a surer grasp of law than certain legislators, and my youthful sense of justice led me to see his exclusion from the profession as an act of injustice. I never heard him complain about the situation, but I felt that there was something shameful, even degrading, about such a state of affairs, and that there was something rotten in the lawyers, if not indeed in the law itself. Nor was it possible for me to ignore the obvious fact that race was a source of that rot, and that even within the mystery of the legal process, the law was colored and rigged against my people.

Later I became aware of the existence of a Negro lawyer, a Mr. Harrison, who was so skilled and eloquent that he got himself chased out of the state. Fortunately he landed in Chicago, where in time he became an Assistant Attorney General. Following this incident, however, there was much barbershop conversation centered on the Harrison affair, his legal skill, his way with words, and the inability of white lawyers and judges to stomach a Negro more knowledgeable in the law than themselves. Interestingly enough, the men who engaged in these conversations while I shined shoes or swept the floors directed their disapproval not so much against law in general, but against those persons and forces that imposed the law undemocratically.

This was a period during which the struggle to attain an antilynching bill was at its height, and Mr. Roscoe Dunjee, the editor and publisher of our local black newspaper, was writing eloquent editorials suggesting that the real ground for solving the racial predicament rested in the Constitution. I read his editorials, but I must confess that in my youthful cynicism I didn't quite believe them. Anyway, the men in the barbershop believed in the spirit of the law, if not in its application.

As for me, I saw no hope in the law. It was to be obeyed in everyday affairs, but in instances of extreme pressure it was to be defied, even at the cost of one's life. In our common usage, law was associated more with men than with statutes. Law-enforcement officers in our usage were "Laws," and many were men with reputations for being especially brutal toward Negroes.

If such men were the cutting edge of the racially biased law, those above them were seldom better. "Alfalfa Bill" Murray, who took great pride in his knowledge of Roman constitutions, was the governor of the state and a loudmouthed white supremacist. One occupant of the local bench, a certain Judge Estes, was famous for a quip made from the bench, to the effect that a Model T Ford full of Negroes ranging at large on the streets of the city was a more devastating piece of bad luck than having one's path crossed by a squad of thirteen howling jet-black tomcats. Well, we laughed, but we held it against him. With such opinions issuing from the bench, I felt little inspired to trust the fairness of judges.

During the Depression I noted something else about the relationship between the law and the attitudes of people—in this instance mostly white—who were suffering from the breakdown of economic order. This came in the form of their reaction to "Pretty Boy" Floyd, who at the time was in constant flight and on a rampage of lawbreaking, but was frequently given sanctuary in Oklahoma City by law-abiding citizens. This was true not only of the city itself, but of towns all around Oklahoma. It puzzled me.

During June of 1933, I found myself traveling by freight train in an effort to reach Tuskegee Institute in time to take advantage of a scholarship granted me. Having little money and no time left in which to earn the fare for a ticket, I grabbed an armful of freight car, a form of illegal travel quite common during the Great Depression. In fact so many young men and women, prostitutes, gamblers, and even some respectable but impoverished elderly and middle-aged couples were hoboing that it was difficult for the railroad to control such passengers. I justified this out of sheer desperation, college being my one hope of improving my condition. But I was young and adventurous and regarded hoboing as the next best thing to floating down the Mississippi on a raft. My head was full of readings of the *Rover Boys* and *Huckleberry Finn*. I converted hoboing into a lark until I found myself in the freight yards of Decatur, Alabama, where two white railroad detectives laying about them with the barrels of long nickel-plated .45 revolvers forced some forty or fifty of us, black and white alike, off the train and ordered us to line up along the tracks. For me, this was a frightening moment. Not only was I guilty of stealing passage on a freight train, but I realized that I had been caught in the act in the very town where, at that moment, the *Scotts-boro* case was being tried. The case and the incident leading to it had been widely reported in the black press, and what I had read of the atmosphere of the trial led me to believe that the young men in the case had absolutely no possibility of receiving a just decision. As I saw it, the trial was a macabre circus, a kangaroo proceeding that would be soon followed by an enactment of the gory rite of lynching, that ultimate form of racial victimage.

I had no idea of what the detectives intended to do with me, but given the atmosphere of the town, I feared that it would be unpleasant and brutal. I, too, might well be a sacrificial scapegoat simply because I was of the same race as the accused young men then being prepared for death. Therefore when a group of white boys broke and ran, I plunged into their midst, and running far closer to the ground than I had ever managed to do as a high school football running back, kept moving until I came to a shed with a railroad loading dock, under which I scooted; there I remained until dawn, when I grabbed the first thing that was smoking and headed south. A few days later I reached Tuskegee, but that scrape with the law—the fear, horror and sense of helplessness before legal injustice—was most vivid in my mind, and it has so remained.

Recently a television dramatization of the *Scottsboro* case presented one of the judges that sat on the case as its hero. I was made aware of the snarl of personal and public motives, political and private interests, which had become the focus of the case. I was aware of the many factors locked in contention in the name of the purity of white womanhood, and as a writer I came to ask myself just why was it that American fiction had given so little attention to the law. Why has the lawyer or the judge seldom appeared in our literature, serious or popular, in heroic roles?

One answer is that the presentation of the law in an unfavorable light allows for the formal expression and sharing of attitudes which are impious and irreverent, and that given such attitudes, they must be socially controlled, made visible and socialized; otherwise they might be a force for the destruction of social order.

When one recalls Mark Twain's drawing of the judge in *The Adventures of Huckleberry Finn*, he comes across as something of a self-serving hypocrite.

Or compare the following incident from *Pudd'nhead Wilson:* Mr. Wilson appears before a reception committee expecting to make a name for himself in the town, but the proceedings are interrupted by the barking of a dog, whereupon Wilson says, "I wish that I owned one half of that dog."

And someone said, "One half of the dog? What would you do with one *half* of the dog?"

He said, "I would kill my half."

Whereupon these legal-minded gentlemen looked at one another and said, "Could he be serious? Doesn't he realize that if he kills his half of the dog, the other owner, the owner of the other half will be upset, will bring litigation against him, and that he will end up in all kinds of trouble?"

Well, for being irreverent on the matter of ownership, poor Wilson was named "Pudd'nhead" and spent most of his life as an alien in the town.

When we recall Melville's *Benito Cereno*, and place it back in its historical perspective, we realize that it was influenced by the *Armistad* affair, a case in which a group of Africans were brought to trial at the insistence of Spain because they had revolted against the Spaniards who had sought to enslave them, killed several of the officers, and in attempting to sail the ship back to their homeland, found themselves off the coast of New England. Melville takes the incident and makes of it one of his finest works of fiction.

But what puzzles me a bit—and I know better than to be puzzled about such things—was why he made nothing of the fact that these Africans were freed by having been represented in court by John Quincy Adams. Remember, this was a time of slavery in our own country, and that it cost Mr. Adams something just to take that case. At any rate, Melville did not bother with the lawyer on that occasion.

But in *Bartleby the Scrivener*, we are introduced to the title character by his boss, a Wall Street lawyer who, for all of his goodwill, is as imperceptive in grasping the basic connotation as Captain Delano of *Benito Cereno* is unable to grasp the human complexity of the Africans who believed, like himself, so much in freedom that they were willing to kill for it.

I am not going to burden you with recounting the legal climate of 1894, when Mark Twain published *Pudd'nhead Wilson*. I will only remind you that it was a period of great theft, of much legal skulduggery, and no doubt this had something to do with the presentation. But if we think a little bit about Mark Twain as a humorist, and think about literary form as having a social function, perhaps Twain was being far more than irreverent when he presented men of the legal profession in a comic light, because by so presenting them he allowed people who were very upset by some of the legal goings-on in the society to reveal their feelings, to laugh at themselves, and most impious of all, to laugh at the courts and perhaps at the Constitution itself.

At some point people, especially American people, are pushed to recognize that behind the Constitution, which we say rests in principles that lie beyond the limits of death and dying, are really man-made legal fictions. This doesn't stop them from being precious or sacred, but we can only stand so much of the sacred or of piety. We must be able to express our dissent, especially when the members of the bench fail to do so for us.

In reading *Bartleby the Scrivener*, Melville's story, we encounter a contest of wills between the lawyer, a genteel, learned lawyer who is admired by Mr. John Jacob Astor, a representative of the law and thus of order, a man with what de Tocqueville termed certain aristocratic propensities, and poor Bartleby, who owns hardly anything but the clothing on his back. He has been hired to perform the job of copying legal documents. The lawyer, as boss, is in the habit of sending his other employees to do various errands, but Bartleby replies to each request with a simple phrase, "I prefer not to." It is so unusual, this obstinate negativism, that the lawyer doesn't throw him out, but becomes locked in a psychological struggle through which he tries to bend Bartleby to his will. In the process he reveals how little he understands of certain basic human attitudes which make the law and the order it imposes quite necessary. Bartleby is never forced or persuaded or cajoled to agree.

In reading the story, one has a sensation of watching a man walking backward past every boundary of human order and desire, saying, "I prefer not to, I prefer not to," until at last he fades from sight and we are left with only the faint sound of his voice hanging thinly upon the air, still saying no. Bartleby's last remaining force, the force which at the very last he is asked to give up, is the power of the negative, that capability of language which Kenneth Burke has identified as a symbolic agency through which man has separated himself from nature and gone on to establish this complex of human positives which we identify as civilization.

In this view language is a primary agency of order. Why? Because it is the identifying characteristic of a symbol-using, symbol-misusing animal. It is through language that man has separated himself from his natural biologic condition as an animal, but it is through the symbolic capabilities of language that we seek simultaneously to maintain and evade our commitments as social beings. Human society in this regard is fictitious, and it might well be that at this point the legal fictions through which we seek to impose order upon society meet and coincide with the fictions of literature. Perhaps law and literature operate or cooperate, if the term is suitable for an interaction which is far less than implicit; in their respective ways these two symbolic systems work in the interests of social order. The one strives for stability—that is, the law is the law—the other strives to socialize those emotions and interests held in check by manners, conventions and again by law.

"Does not law, like art," writes Professor Paul Freund, "seek change within the framework of continuity, to bring heresy and heritage into fruitful tension? They are not dissimilar, and in their resolution, the resolution of passion and pattern, of frenzy and form, of contention and revolt, of order and spontaneity lies the clue to the creativity that will endure." Given the bits of personal experience which I outlined at the start of this paper, I must both agree and disagree with the professor. He states the ideal as a writer; with my background, I must state something of the exception. By the way, I always found Justice Holmes and Justice Frankfurter a bit less attractive as human beings than I did as men of scholarly excellence. But then I was always a bit impatient, and something of the cat who was fated to stare at kings.

As one who somehow fits into the profession of Mark Twain, Emerson and Thoreau, I would also remind you that it is precisely the writer's function to yell "Fire" in crowded theaters. We do so, of course, through the form in which we work, and the forms of literature are social forms. We don't always take them seriously, but they are the start of seriousness, and an irreplaceable part of social order.

But if there is one Freund statement with which I could agree wholeheartedly, it is this: "I have likened the Constitution to a work of art in its capacity to respond through interpretation to changing needs, concerns and aspirations." I look upon the Constitution as the still-vital covenant by which Americans of diverse backgrounds, religions, races and interests are bound. They are bound by the principles with which it inspirits us, no less than by the legal apparatus that identifies us as a single American people. The Constitution is a script by which we seek to act out the drama of democracy, and the stage upon which we enact our roles.

Viewed "dramatistically," which is Kenneth Burke's term, we can even suggest that the Declaration of Independence marked the verbalization of our colonial forefathers' intentions of disposing of the king's authority. The Revolutionary War marked the agonistic contest of wills through which the opposing forces were overthrown. The Constitution marked the gloriously optimistic assertion and legitimization of a new form of authority and the proclaiming of a new set of purposes and promises. Upon these principles, which would be made manifest through the enactment of a new set of democratic hierarchal roles (or identities), the young nation would act. Through the dramatic conflict of democratic society, it would seek to fulfill its revolutionary assertions.

But then came a swift change of direction in which the young nation was forced to recognize that the mere assertion of revolutionary will was not enough to lead immediately to domestic tranquillity. It brought upon the stage a new alignment of political forces in which the collectivity that had made the Revolution became fragmented. Under the new dispensation the rights of individuals and minorities required protection from the will of the majority. As a new hierarchy began to function, those at its top were in better position to take advantage of these newfound benefits, while those at the bottom were hardly better off than they had been under the Crown.

Ironically, the nation's recognition of the new problems of its hierarchy was coeval with its increasing concern with its language and linguistic style, which reminds us of the paradox that the revolutionary documents which formed the constitutional grounds of our new system of justice and which set the stage for the enactment of a new democratic drama of human rights were written in the language of the very hierarchy which they had overthrown. Indeed, the new conflict of interest was foreshadowed in the very process of drawing up the new ground for action out of the English language. Even as the democratic documents of state announced a new corporate purpose, proclaimed a new identity, assigned new roles and aroused new expectations for a redistribution of material resources and authority, a conflict arose between the terms in which revolutionary action had been taken and those in which it would be fulfilled.

In drafting the Declaration of Independence, Thomas Jefferson had changed the old emotion-charged revolutionary slogan of equality, liberty and property to equality, liberty and the pursuit of happiness. His demands for eternal separation from England and its people were deleted. Also rejected was Jefferson's indictment of slavery, in which he overloaded the scapegoat, King George III, with a malignancy that was all too obviously shared by Americans. There was mystification here, if not blatant hypocrisy, because as Katherine Drinker Bowen observed of Jefferson's discarded first draft, "in Jefferson's indictment of the King he nowhere states that slavery is a disgrace to America, and should be abolished root and branch by Americans. Instead, he turns his anger on the wrong culprit, twists a shameful fact of American life into an instrument of propaganda against George III, condemns the slave trade, then draws the sting by putting the blame and responsibility on the King of England."

Ironically, by his extreme eloquence Jefferson provided his pro-slavery colleagues an escape from having to undergo the rigors of economic and perhaps spiritual mortification that would have given full credibility to their proclaimed principles of freedom and equality.

Thus the new edenic political scene incorporated a flaw similar to the crack that appeared in the Liberty Bell and embodied a serpent-like malignancy that would tempt government and individual alike to a constantly recurring fall from democratic innocence. With one of its cardinal principles violated, the drama of democratic equality began with its main actors revealing in their noblest gestures "mots vagues" that were at odds with their spoken lines. Indeed, more often than not they ignored the acting script, and being good Americans, they improvised. Portentously, the Founding Fathers' refusal to cleanse themselves was motivated by hierarchical status and economic interests. It was rationalized by the code of social manners that went with their inherited form and manner of speech, their linguistic style. Revolutionary fervor notwithstanding, they were gentlemen, and Jefferson's indictment provided these men with the convenient excuse for not violating their private interests and standards of good taste. Thus the glaring transparencies of Jefferson's rhetoric afforded them a purely formal escape from the immediate dilemma posed by the conflict between freedom and slavery, and allowed them to use social tact as a tactic of moral evasion.

One result of this evasion was to prove of far-reaching consequence, in that the principles of equality and freedom were splintered into warring entities, thus making for the unheralded emergence of a new principle or motive in the drama of American democracy. That motive or principle—and principles are motives, I will remind you—was race, a motive that would become a source of vast political power and authority, and a major theme in American literature. Though not committed to sacred print, it was to radiate a qualifying influence upon all of the nation's principles and become the source of a war of words that has continued to this day.

Men like John Adams fought against it, as did Jefferson, who himself owned slaves. But because this principle operated in the ethical sphere no less than in the material world—the principle of equality being a command that all men be treated as equals, while some were obviously being designated unequal on the basis of color and race—it made for a split in America's moral identity that would infuse all of its acts and institutions with a quality of hypocrisy. Worse, it would fog the American's perception of himself, distort his national image and blind him to the true nature of his cultural complexity.

Later, behind the guise of States' rights, it would explode the issue which led to the Civil War. Thus, even as the English support of the old hierarchical psychosis collapsed, it quickly reasserted itself in the immature and unfinished psyche of the new political order. That absentee authority and privilege once vested in kingship now reappeared as the all-too-present authoritarian privilege of those possessing property and high social position. Social order is arduous, and power filters down to the lower levels of society only under constant pressure. Thus new tensions arose, and while the Bill of Rights was enacted to relieve the new imbalance, the manifestations of those rights in the lives of those low in the order of social hierarchy would require time, contention, endless improvisation and many lawyers. As this process ensued, not even the most optimistic citizens found an adequate fulfillment of revolutionary expectations. Indeed, these expectations seemed for some to recede before the anguishing complexity of the new social reality. Instead of domestic tranquillity, Americans discovered that what their bloodshed and sacrifice had actually purchased them was not social perfection, but at best a firm new ground of hope. This was a great deal, but democratic equality remained the promise that would have to be achieved in the vividly imagined but illusory future.

At Philadelphia, the Founding Fathers were presented the fleeting opportunity of mounting to the very peak of social possibility afforded by democracy. But after ascending to within a few yards of the summit they paused, finding the view to be one combining splendor with terror. From this height of human aspiration the ethical implications of democratic equality were revealed as tragic, for if there was radiance and glory in the future that stretched so grandly before them, there was also mystery and turbulence and darkness astir in its depths. Therefore the final climb would require not only courage, but an acceptance of the tragic nature of their enterprise and the adoption of a tragic attitude that was rendered unacceptable by the optimism developed in revolutionary struggle, no less than by the tempting and virginal richness of the land which was now rendered accessible.

So having climbed so heroically, they descended and laid a foundation for democracy at a less breathtaking altitude, and in justification of their failure of nerve before the challenge of the summit, the Founding Fathers committed the sin of American racial pride. They designated one section of the American people to be the sacrificial victims for the benefit of the rest. In failing the test of what was later to be termed the American dilemma, they prepared the way for the evils that Jefferson had hoped to pile upon the royal head of England's king, and loaded them upon the black backs of anonymous American slaves. Worse, these Americans were designated as perfect victims for sacrifice, and were placed beyond any possibility of democratic redemption not because of any overt act of social guilt, but simply by virtue of their position in the social hierarchy. Indeed, they were thrust beneath the threshold of social hierarchy and expected to stay there.

To further justify this act of pride and failure of nerve, myths of racial superiority and inferiority were evoked, and endless sacrificial rites of moral evasion were set in motion. These appeared in folktales, jokes and then popular stories—indeed, in some unpopular but quite serious works. Ironically, however, this initial act of pride was to give the Afro-American an inadvertent and unrecognized but crucial role in the nation's drama of conscience. Racism took on the symbolic force of an American form of original sin, and as a man chosen to suffer to advance the nation's spiritual and material well-being, the black American was endowed linguistically with an ambivalent power, like that vested in Elizabethan clowns, Christian martyrs and tragic heroes. This is important if we are to understand the prevalence of black figures in our literature.

As a symbol of guilt and redemption, the Negro entered the deepest recesses of the American psyche and became crucially involved in its consciousness, subconsciousness and conscience. He became keeper of the nation's sense of democratic achievement, and the human scale by which would be measured its painfully slow advance toward true equality. Regardless of the white American's feelings about the economic, psychological and social conditions summed up in the term and symbol "Negro," that term and symbol was now firmly embedded in the operation of the American language. Despite their social powerlessness, Negro Americans were all unwittingly endowed with the vast powers of the linguistic negative, and would now be intricately involved in the use and misuse of a specific American form of symbolic action, the terminology of democracy. Not only in language, but through language into law and social arrangements, social ethics and manners, into sexuality and city planning or nonplanning, and into art, religion and literature.

In brief, race became a major cause, form and symbol of the American hierarchical psychosis. As the unwilling and unjust personification of that psychosis and its major victim, the Afro-American took on the complex symbolism of social health and social sickness. He became the raw labor force, the victim of social degradation, and symbolic of America's hope for future perfection. He was to be viewed, at least by many whites, as both cause and cure of our social malaise.

This development, of course, contained a lot of mystification, for if there was hope for a cure to our condition, it lay in the direction of both white and black men undergoing that agonistic effort necessary to the fulfillment of the nation's commitment to those ethical principles compromised by the Founding Fathers. Until the time that this should come about, race would assert a malignant effect in areas of national life that were far removed from that of civil rights for black Americans.

It would function as a motive in Melville's *Moby-Dick*, and far beneath the fine prose of Henry James it would goad the consciousness of his characters. It would form the moral core of Mark Twain's *Huckleberry Finn*, dominate the world of William Faulkner's fiction, and would influence the attitudes of individual "secessionism" displayed by the heroes of Ernest Hemingway. Further, the contentions it inspired would hinder the establishment of a national drama, a theater, and account for the dismal stereotypes of popular literature, plays, motion pictures and television dramas, and for their triviality and lack of moral seriousness. What is more, it would lead to the moral negations of the current crop of black films and to much of what we dislike in rock music.

But here we should pause. Here we will not recapitulate the Civil War. We know to what extent it was a war of words as well as of arms. We know to what extent the black American was involved. Often, however, the issues of the Civil War and even of blacks appear in novels and other works of literature by other names. For instance, Crane's *The Red Badge of Courage* is about the Civil War, but only one black person appears, and then very briefly. It is concerned with the invasion of the private life by warfare, by the army, and by large impersonal social processes, a fact of American democratic life which was becoming a matter of consciousness some thirty years after the Civil War.

We are in a period today when many of the men of my profession complain that American life has gotten out of hand, that it is too much for the methods and modes of fiction. They say that it is too dramatic, that it overwhelms the fictional imagination. I am not so sure about that. I think that the resources are there, and that we have only to seek to use them. But I think something else should be said, since much of the atmosphere of our time is created by major transformations in our way of looking at the law and at the racial aspects of the law, going back to 1954 and up to the measures passed during the sixties.

We went about that with a feeling of good intentions. We sacrificed. We did much to rectify past injustices. But then, with our usual American innocence, we failed to grasp that it was going to cost us something in terms of personal sacrifices and in the rearrangement of the cities and the suburbs. It would cost us something in terms of the sheer acceleration of turmoil and conflict. And so, we have become a bit tired of this old business.

As a writer, I would remind you, however, that when the Afro-American became symbolic of so many other issues in American life, his increase in freedom acted on the youth at least as a sort of sudden release for which they were unprepared. It was as though the word had gone out that the outsider, the unacceptable, was now acceptable, and young people translated it to mean that all of the repressed psychological drives, all of the discipline of the instincts, were now fair game. "Let it all hang out," they said. "We have all become black men and women."

This projection, this identification of the socially unacceptable with blacks, must be raised to consciousness. We must be aware of what is going on because only through this will we be able to reassume that optimism so necessary for living and dealing with the many problems of this diverse pluralistic society. Democracy is a collectivity of individuals.

The great writers of the nineteenth century and the best of the twentieth have always reminded us that the business of being an American is an arduous task, as Henry James said, and it requires constant attention to our consciousness and conscientiousness. The law ensures the conditions, the stage upon which we act; the rest of it is up to the individual.

"A COMPLETION OF PERSONALITY": A TALK WITH RALPH ELLISON

Over five decades Ellison collaborated on numerous interviews, perhaps because he considered the interview an art form. One of his fullest and richest was done with his friend, the writer John Hersey. Part I was published in 1974 as the Introduction to Hersey's Ralph Ellison: A Collection of Critical Essays. *Part II, in which Ellison comments at length about his novel-in-progress, was conducted in 1982 and published, along with Part I, in* Speaking For You: The Vision of Ralph Ellison, *ed. Kimberly W. Benston, Howard University Press, 1987.*

I

ONE *of the most significant views of the work of Ralph Ellison happens to be his own. He is, as he himself says, a slow worker, and over the course of the years, while he was writing away at his second novel—and while* Invisible Man *paradoxically refused to drop out of sight—Ellison granted a number of interviews, each of which offered some telling comments on the situation of a novelist who had been thrust into more gnawing fame than most writers would want in their own time. He reproduced three of the interviews in* Shadow and Act. *Two other valuable ones are noted in the bibliography of this book, and the vivid picture of Ellison by a younger writer, James Alan McPherson, also in this collection, originally included an exchange of letters between the two authors, in which Ellison further elaborated his predicament.*

For predicament it has been, and what is forced upon a reader of these interviews is a sense that the polemic-versus-artistic argument—the argument, as old as art itself, over the question: "What use has art?"—hounds Ellison perhaps more than any other first-rank novelist of our time, unless it be Alexander Solzhenitsyn. That argument dominates several of the essays in this book, and it hums in harmonic overtones over the rest of them.

It occurred to me as I assembled and read these various views that in the din of this argument we had never had a chance to hear much from Ellison about his attitude toward the actuality of his craft, about the processes of his creative ordeal, about what he thinks actually happens *when he writes, about the deep familial sources of his ways of being and doing, about how his mind works through problems of shape and dream and sound, and about the particular, idiosyncratic inner workings of his art which may have been molded by his existential past. Although it is entitled "The Art of Fiction," not even the* Paris Review *interview, reprinted in* Shadow and Act, *goes beneath the surface of his struggle to achieve an art worth arguing about as much as his has been.*

And so, on a weekend that Ellison and his wife spent in my home, we talked late into one night about all these matters, and in the cool light of the next morning we had a conversation in which Ellison, with extraordinary finish and economy, and yet with a fabulist's deceptive randomness, too, synthesized and compressed his views of his labor of choice. Here is what we said:

HERSEY: You were talking about your mother last night, and as you talked I wondered how much she had been a force in moving you toward your calling as a writer, and even in supplying materials that you have drawn on.

ELLISON: She certainly had something to do with encouraging my interest in reading. She had no idea that I was going to become a writer, or if she did, she had more insight into me than I had into myself, because I thought I was going to be a musician. My mother always encouraged me to do *something*, and to be good at it—she insisted upon that.

It was my father who wanted me to be a writer. I didn't discover that until many years later—he died when I was three—until after I had written *Invisible Man* and talked with an older cousin, who told me that my father had used to say, "I'm raising this boy to be a poet." Of course he had given me the name [Ralph Waldo].

But my mother did feed my passion for reading. She brought home books and magazines. My concern with the Picassos and Stravinskys of this world started at an earlier age than usual because she brought home *Vanity Fair*. Here was a world so far from Oklahoma City, in any expected sense, yet it was shaping my sense of what was possible. And she understood that that was what was going on.

And what I did get from my mother was an understanding of people. I was very quick-tempered and impatient, and things began to happen when I reached adolescence; and she would just talk about how people acted, what motives were, and why things were sometimes done. I remember being so outraged by something one of her friends had said that I didn't want to see her or her husband anymore. At thirteen I went to work as the husband's office boy, and this close friend of my father was so delighted with having me around that his childless wife was upset. Her reaction was to spread the word around that she suspected that I was actually her husband's child. Oh, boy! When the gossip reached me I was outraged—and not only over what it implied about my mother, but because of my love for my father. I had learned to walk at six months and had been his companion from that time until his death, and I was so far from accepting the reality of his death that I was still telling myself that any day he would reappear to take his place as the head of our family. Now I suspect that my fondness for my employer-friend and my vague awareness that he was, in fact, something of a father-figure added to my shock and outrage.

At any rate, when I went to my mother about this matter she proceeded to calm me down. "Well now," she said, "you should understand what's happening. You remember your daddy and you've been around and seen a few people and have some idea how they act. You've been working in drugstores and barbershops and at that office and since you've been around as much as you have, you must know that she's crazy. So use your head. She doesn't have to be put in an institution, but you have to understand and accept the fact that she isn't responsible."

It was a shocking notion for me and I didn't want to surrender my anger, but I realized that my mother was right. What's more, I realized that often I could save myself a lot of wear and tear with people if I just learned to understand them.

Beyond that, although she was religious, my mother had a great tolerance for the affairs of the world which had nothing to do with religion, and I think that this helped me to sort of balance things out, so to speak. The great emphasis in my school was upon classical music, but such great jazz musicians as Hot Lips Paige, Jimmy Rushing and Lester Young were living in Oklahoma City, and through her allowing me to attend public dances and to maintain a certain friendship with some of them, even though she watched what I was doing, she made it possible to approach the life of the Negro community there with some sense of its wholeness instead of trying to distort it into some hoped-for, religion-conceived perfection. As it turned out, the perfection, the artistic dedication which helped me as a writer, was not so much in the classical emphasis as within the jazz itself.

She also helped me to escape the limitations of trying to impose any ingroup class distinctions upon the people of my community. We were very poor, but my father had been a small businessman who sold ice and coal to both whites and blacks, and since he and my mother were pioneers in a young state, my mother knew some of the city's leaders; they were my father's friends and remained my mother's after his death. She didn't strive to be part of the social leadership of the black community; that was left to the wives of professional men, to teachers and preachers. Her background and attitudes were such that all kinds of people came to the house, or we visited their houses. That was one of the enriching parts of my experience, because I knew people who went right back to the farm and plantation, along with those who had gone to college and medical school. Thus my sense of their stories, lifestyles and so on was never far from my mind. My mother had grown up on a Georgia plantation and was a farm girl; then she left and went to live in Atlanta. This gave me a sense of a past which was far from narrow.

She liked to talk. She never allowed me to lose the vividness of my father, and she told me all kinds of things that he had done—that he had run away from his own father in South Carolina when he was quite young, had become a professional soldier, and had been in Cuba, the Philippines and China. He was with our troops that fought the Boxer Rebellion. Afterwards, he and his brother had operated a candy kitchen in Chattanooga. He had also operated a restaurant—always trying to get at something—and then had become a construction foreman; that was how they came West to Oklahoma.

There was also her overt and explicit concern with political conditions. There was never a time when I was not aware of what these were all about. When I was in college, my mother broke a segregated-housing ordinance in Oklahoma City; they were throwing her in jail, the NAACP would get her out, and they'd come back and throw her in jail again. This went on until my brother beat up one of the white inspectors; then she decided that it was about time to get out of that situation before he got himself shot. She had that kind of forthrightness, and I like to think that this was much more valuable than anything literary that she gave me.

HERSEY: The creative drive seems always to have been strong in you, ever since childhood. You said once that you couldn't remember a time when you hadn't wanted to make something—a one-tube radio, a crystal set, a toy. A little later you had an urge to compose music. Where do you think this drive came from?

ELLISON: I don't know where it comes from. Maybe it had something to do with my father's working as a construction foreman, building buildings. It certainly came from some of the boys that I grew up with as a child. They were always *doing* things. I always admired the guys who could make things, who could draw. This was something that gave me a great deal of pleasure.

But maybe the desire to write goes back to a Christmas gift. One Christmas my mother gave me—I must have been five—a little roll-top desk and a chair, not a swivel chair but a little straight chair, oak, and a little toy typewriter. I had forgotten that. We were living in the parsonage of the old A.M.E. Church, Avery Chapel, which the leaders of the congregation turned over to my mother after the new minister turned out to have his own home. "Why don't you be the janitress of the church and live in the parsonage?" they said. We did, and that's where I got the desk and the little typewriter. I was also given a chemistry set. This might have been unusual in such relatively uneducated families—I think my mother went to the eighth grade in school—but she felt that these were the kinds of things that her boys should have. She was also very explicit, as we grew older, about our economic condition. We knew why we could not have a bicycle, why we could not have this, that or the other. She explained that we could not have such things because she didn't have the money, and we had to accept that fact. So what did we do? We learned to do other things. Instead of playing with store-bought toys, you made your own. You fished and hunted, you listened to music, you danced and you spent a great amount of time reading and dreaming over books.

When Mr. Mead next door taught me the fundamentals of playing an old brass alto horn, my mother bought me a pawnshop cornet. She could afford that, and owning the instrument made it possible for me to acquire enough skill to get into the school band. She did what she could, and in addition to encouraging my interest in reading she encouraged my interest in music.

But the desire to make something out of my imagination and to experiment was constant. In one story of mine ["That I Had the Wings" (1943)] there is an incident taken from life, where my brother and I took baby chickens, made little parachutes and got up on top of the chicken house and dropped them down. The lady next door told my mother, and we caught hell for that. We didn't kill the chickens, understand; we just floated them down. We did this, you see, because we had learned to take iron taps, tie strings to them and then attach the strings to pieces of cloth. When we threw these into the air we'd get a parachute effect and imagine that the taps were parachutists. We simply took it a step further.

HERSEY: What would you say was the starting point for your new novel?

ELLISON: I guess it started with the idea of an old man being so outraged by his life that he goes poking around in the cellar to find a forgotten coffin, which he had bought years before as insurance against his possible ruin. He discovers that he has lived so long that the coffin is full of termites, and that even the things he had stored in the coffin have fallen apart. Somehow this said something to my imagination and got me started. You can see that it could go in *any* direction. But then it led to the other idea, which I wrote first, of a little boy being placed in a coffin in a ritual of death and transcendence, celebrated by a Negro evangelist who was unsure whether he was simply exploiting the circus-sideshow shock set off by the sight of a child rising up out of a coffin, or had hit upon an inspired way of presenting the sacred drama of the Resurrection. In my mind all of this is tied up in some way with the significance of being a Negro in America, and at the same time with the problem of our democratic faith as a whole. Anyway, as a product of the imagination it's like a big sponge, maybe, or a waterbed, with a lot of needles sticking in it at various points. You don't know what is being touched, where the needles are going to end up once you get them threaded and penetrated, but somehow I keep trying to tie those threads together and the needle points pressing home without letting whatever lies in the center leak out.

HERSEY: How soon after *Invisible Man* was published [1952] did you start working on the new novel?

ELLISON: I was pretty depleted by *Invisible Man*, so I didn't start on another book immediately. I played around with various ideas and spent some time trying to salvage material I had edited out of *Invisible Man*. It was in Rome, during 1956, that I began to think vaguely about this book and conceived the basic situation, which had to do with a political assassination; this was involved with the other patterns—the coffin business.

HERSEY: This was before the Kennedys and King were assassinated, of course.

ELLISON: Yes, this was before. Almost eight years before. One of the things which really chilled me—slowed down the writing—was that eruption of assassinations, especially the first. Because, you see, much of the mood of this book was conceived as comic. Not that the assassination was treated comically, but there is humor involved, and that was rather chilling for me because suddenly life was stepping in and imposing itself upon my fiction. Anyway, I managed to keep going with it, I guess because there was nothing else to do. I know that it led me to try to give the book a richer structuring, so that the tragic elements could contain the comic and the comic the tragic, without violating our national pieties—if there are any left. Americans have always been divided in their pieties, but today there is such a deliberate flaunting of the pieties and traditions—of others, anyway—that it's become difficult to distinguish what is admissible from that which is inadmissible. Even the flag and motherhood are under attack.

HERSEY: With such fast-moving reality so close at hand, how much in control of your fictional characters can you feel that you are?

ELLISON: Once a logic is set up for a character, once he begins to move, then that which is implicit within him tends to realize itself, and for you to discover the *form* of the fiction, you have to go where he takes you and follow him. In the process you change your ideas. You remember, Dostoevski wrote about eight versions of a certain scene in *The Brothers Karamazov*, and in some instances the original incidents were retained but the characters who performed them were changed. I find that happens with me. I get to the point where something has to be done, and discover that it isn't logical for the character who started out to do it, to act this way; then suddenly another character pops up. In this book there is an instance wherein McIntyre has to interview the man who burns his Cadillac. This man is being held in the observation cell of a hospital because the authorities believe that a Negro who burns his own Cadillac has to be crazy. For McIntyre to see the man there has to be an intermediary, so suddenly I found myself dealing with a new character, a Negro employed by the hospital, who gets McIntyre past the barriers to the car burner. This fellow wasn't foreseen; he simply appeared to help me get on with the form.

HERSEY: About motive—what gives you the psychic energy to take on a massive work and keep at it for a very long time?

ELLISON: I guess it is the writing itself. I am terribly stubborn, and once I get engaged in that kind of project, I just have to keep going until I finally make something out of it. I don't know what the something is going to be, but the process is one through which I make a good part of my own experience meaningful. I don't mean in any easy autobiographical sense, but in the matter of drawing actual experience, thought and emotion together in a way that creates an artifact through which I can reach other people. Maybe that's vanity; I don't know. Still, I believe that fiction does help create value, and I regard this as a very serious—I almost said "sacred"—function of the writer.

Psychic energy? I don't know; I think of myself as kind of lazy. Yet I do find that working slowly, which is the only way I seem able to work—although I write fast much of the time—the problem is one of being able to receive from my work that sense of tension and of high purpose being realized that keeps me going. This is a crazy area that I don't understand; none of the Freudian explanations seem adequate.

HERSEY: As to the short range, you used a phrase last night that interested me. You said you wanted to keep the early morning free "in case the night before had generated something that could be put to good use." What did you mean by that?

ELLISON: I never know quite what has gone on in my subconscious in the night. I dream vividly, and all kinds of things happen, but by morning they have fallen below the threshold again. But I like to feel that whatever takes place becomes active in some way in what I do at the typewriter. In other words, I believe that a human being's life is of a whole, and that he lives the full twenty-four hours. If he is a writer or an artist, what happens during the night feeds back in some way into what he does consciously during the day—that is, when he is doing that which is self-achieving, so to speak. Part of the pleasure of writing, as well as the pain, is involved in pouring into that thing which is being created all of what he cannot understand, cannot say, cannot deal with or cannot even admit in any other way. The artifact is a completion of personality.

HERSEY: Do you experience anything like daydreaming or dreaming when you are writing? Do you feel that the writing process may involve a somewhat altered state of consciousness in itself?

ELLISON: I think a writer learns to be as conscious about his craft as he can possibly be—not because this will make him absolutely lucid about what he does, but because it prepares the stage for structuring his daydreaming, and allows him to draw upon the various irrational elements involved in writing. You know that when you begin to structure literary forms you are going to have to play variations on your themes, and you are going to have to make everything vivid, so that the reader can see, hear, feel, smell and, if you're lucky, even taste. All that is on a conscious level and very important. But then, once you get going, strange things occur. There are things in *Invisible Man*, for instance, that I can't *imagine* my having consciously planned. They materialized as I worked consciously at other things. Take three of the speeches: the speech made at the eviction, the funeral address in Mount Morris Park, and the one that Barbee made in chapel. I realized consciously, or I *discovered* as I wrote, that I was playing variations on what Otto Rank identified as the myth of the birth and death of the hero. So in the rewriting, that conscious knowledge, that insight, made it possible to come back and add elements to the design which I had written myself into under the passion of telling a story.

What should also be said in this connection is that somewhere—it doesn't have to be right in the front of the mind, of the consciousness—writers, like other artists, are involved in a process of comparative culture. I looked at that copy of *The Lower Depths* on the table there this morning, and I remembered how much of Gorki I had read, and how I was always not putting his characters into blackface, but finding equivalents for the experience he depicted; the equivalents for turns of phrase, for parables and proverbs, which existed within the various backgrounds that I knew. I think that something like that goes on when a conscious writer goes about creating a fiction. It's part of his workshop, his possession of the culture of the form in which he works.

HERSEY: You once said that it took you a long time to learn how to adapt myth and ritual into your work. Faulkner speaks of a "lumber room in the subconscious," where old things are kept. How do you get at the sources of these things deep down in your mind?

ELLISON: I think I get at them through sheer work, converting incidents into patterns—and also by simply continuing at a thing when I don't seem to be getting anywhere. For instance, I wrote a scene in which Hickman is thinking about the difficulty of communicating with someone as constituting a "wall"; he thinks this as he is drifting off to sleep. Well, later in my work I suddenly realized that this damn wall had turned up again in another form. That's when that voice in my unconscious finally said, "Hey, *this* is what you've been getting at." Looking back, I saw that I had worked up a little pattern with these walls. What the unconscious mind does is to put all manner of things into juxtaposition. The conscious mind has to provide the logical structure of narrative and incident through which these unconscious patterns can be allowed to radiate by throwing them into artful juxtaposition on the page.

HERSEY: Do you, as some writers do, have a sense of standing in a magic circle when you write?

ELLISON: To the extent that unexpected things occur, that characters say or see things which, for all my attempts to be conscious and to work out of what I call a conceptual outline, are suddenly just *there*. That *is* magical, because such things seem to emerge out of the empty air. Yet you know that somehow the dreams, emotions, ironies and hidden implications of your material often find ways of making themselves manifest. You work to make them reveal themselves.

HERSEY: When you are writing, do you sometimes find yourself so totally engaged by a character that you are carried away outside yourself by *his* feelings—are literally beside yourself?

ELLISON: I find myself carried away and emotionally moved, sometimes quite unexpectedly, and my tendency is to distrust it, feeling that perhaps I'm being sentimental, being caught in a situation which I am not adequately transforming into art. So I put it aside and wait awhile, maybe months, and then go back, and if it still works after I've examined it as well as I can, as objectively as I can, then I perhaps read it to Fanny, and if she doesn't indicate that it's slobbering sentimentality, in bad taste or just poorly achieved, then I leave it in.

HERSEY: Would you say that by and large when you have had these surges of feeling the writing does hold up in the long run?

ELLISON: Sometimes it does, sometimes it doesn't. I won't be able to say about this book until it has been read by enough objective readers. I won't be able to judge until then because it has some crazy developments.

I found myself writing a scene in which Hickman and Wilhite, his deacon, go into a strange house in Washington, and find a bunch of people in the hallway who are upset because the police won't tell them what has happened in the apartment of one of their neighbors. Then one of the women gets hysterical, and pretty soon she's outraging the crowd by talking about the most personal matters as she addresses herself to a bewildered Wilhite and Hickman. Not only was I shocked to discover myself writing this unplanned scene, but I still have questions about how it functions. Yet for all its wild, tragicomic emotion—there it is! Now, when your material takes over like that, you are really being pushed. Thus, when this woman started confessing, she forced *me* to think about Hickman's role as minister on a different level; I mean on the theological level, which was something I hadn't planned, since I wasn't writing an essay but a novel. Finally Hickman came to my aid by recognizing that the woman had been unfolding a distorted and highly personalized dream-version of the immaculate birth. To me she sounded merely irrational and comic, but Hickman, being a minister, forced himself to look beneath her raving, even though she is without question a most unacceptable surrogate for the Virgin. After that, I was forced to realize that this crazy development was really tied in with the central situation of the novel: that of an old man searching throughout the years for a little boy who ran away. So I guess it sprang from that magic circle you referred to, from that amorphous level which lies somewhere between the emotions and the intellect, between the consciousness and the unconscious, which supports our creative powers but which we cannot control.

HERSEY: I have wondered about the ways in which your musical experience has fed into your writing.

ELLISON: My basic sense of artistic form is musical. As a boy I tried to write songs, marches, exercises in symphonic form, really before I received any training, and then I studied. I listened constantly to music, trying to learn the processes of developing a theme, of expanding and contracting and turning it inside out, of making bridges, working with techniques of musical continuity, and so on. I think that basically my instinctive approach to writing is through *sound*. A change of mood and mode comes to me in terms of sound. That's one part of it, in the sense of composing the architecture of a fiction.

On the other hand, one of the things I work for is to make a line of prose *sound* right, or for a bit of dialogue to fall on the page in the way I hear it, aurally, in my mind. The same goes for the sound and intonation of a character's voice. When I am writing of characters who speak in the Negro idiom, in the vernacular, it is still a real problem for me to make their accents fall in the proper place in the visual line.

HERSEY: Which comes first for you in writing, hearing or seeing?

ELLISON: I might conceive of a thing aurally, but to realize it you have to make it vivid. The two things must operate together. What is the old phrase—"the planned dislocation of the senses"? That *is* the condition of fiction, I think. Here is where sound becomes sight and sight becomes sound, and where sign becomes symbol and symbol becomes sign; where fact and idea must not just be hanging there but must become a functioning part of the total design, involving itself in the reader as idea as well as drama. You do this by providing the reader with as much detail as is possible in terms of the visual *and* the aural *and* the rhythmic—to allow him to involve himself, to attach himself, and then begin to collaborate in the creation of the fictional spell. Because you simply cannot put it all there on the page; you can only evoke it—or evoke what is already there implicitly in the reader's head, his sense of life.

HERSEY: You mentioned "making bridges" a minute ago. I remember that you once said that your anxiety about transitions greatly prolonged the writing of *Invisible Man*.

ELLISON: Yes, that has continued to be something of a problem. I try to tell myself that it is irrational, but it is what happens when you're making something and you know that you are *making* something rather than simply relating an anecdote that actually happened. But at the same time you have to strike a balance between that which you can imply and that which you must make explicit, so that the reader can follow you. One source of this anxiety comes, I think, from my sense of the variations in American backgrounds, especially as imposed by the racial situation. I can't always be certain that what I write is going to be understood. This doesn't mean that I am writing for whites, but that I realize that as an American writer I have a problem of communicating across our various social divisions, whether of race, class, education, region or religion—and much of this holds true even within my own racial group. It's dangerous to take things for granted.

This reminds me of something that happened out at a northwestern university. A young white professor said to me, "Mr. Ellison, how does it feel to be able to go to places where most Negroes can't go?" Before I could think to be polite I answered, "What you mean is: 'How does it feel to be able to go places where most *white* men can't go?" He was shocked and turned red, and I was embarrassed; nevertheless, it was a teaching situation, so I told him the truth. I wanted him to understand that individuality is still operative beyond the racial structuring of American society, and that, conversely, there are many areas of black society that are closed to *me* while open to certain whites. Friendship and shared interests make the difference.

When you are writing fiction out of your individual sense of American life, it's difficult to know what to take for granted. For instance, I don't know whether I can simply refer to an element of decor and communicate the social values it stands for, because so much depends upon the way a reader makes associations. I am more confident in such matters than I was when writing *Invisible Man*, but for such an allusion—say, to a certain type of chair or vase or painting—to function, the reader must not be allowed to limit his understanding of what is implied simply because the experience you are presenting is, in its immediate sense, that of a black person. The writer must be aware that the reality of race conceals a complex of manners and culture, because such matters influence the shaping of fictional form, to a large extent govern the writer's sense of proportion, and determine what he feels obligated to render as well as what he feels he can simply imply.

I had to learn, for instance, that in dramatic scenes, if you get the reader going along with your own rhythm, you can omit any number of explanations. You can leave great gaps because in his sense of urgency the reader will say, "Hell, don't waste time telling me how many steps he walked to get there, I want to know what he *did once he* got there!" An ellipsis is possible and the reader will fill in the gap.

Still, I have uncertainty about some of the things I'm doing, especially when I'm using more than one main voice, and with a time scheme that is much more fragmented than in *Invisible Man*. There I was using a more tidy dramatic form. This novel is dramatic within its incidents, but it moves back and forth in time. In such a case I guess an act of faith is necessary, a faith that if what you are writing is of social and artistic importance and its diverse parts are presented vividly in the light of its overall conception, and if you *render* the story rather than just tell it, then the reader will go along. That's a lot of "ifs," but if you can involve him in the process his reading becomes a pleasurable act of discovery.

HERSEY: Do you have in mind an image of some actualized reader to whom you are communicating as you write?

ELLISON: There is no *specific* person there, but there is a sort of ideal reader, or informed persona, who has some immediate sense of the material that I'm working with. Beyond that there is my sense of the rhetorical levers within American society, and these attach to all kinds of experiences and values. I don't want to be a behaviorist here, but I'm referring to the systems of values, beliefs, customs, sense of the past, and that hope for the future which have evolved through the history of the Republic. These do provide a medium of communication.

For instance, the old underdog pattern turns up in many guises, and it allows the writer to communicate with the public over and beyond whatever the immediate issues of his fiction happen to be. That is, deep down we believe in the underdog, even though we give him hell, and this provides a rhetoric through which the writer can communicate with a reader beyond any questions of their disagreements over class values, race or anything else. But the writer must be aware that this is what is there. At the same time, I do not think he can manipulate his readers too directly; it must be an oblique process, if for no other reason than that to do it too directly throws you into propaganda, as against that brooding, questioning stance that is necessary for fiction.

HERSEY: How do literary influences make themselves felt concretely in your work? You have spoken often of Joyce, Eliot, Dostoevski, Hemingway, Stein, Malraux and others as having influenced you early. How do the influences manifest themselves? How have you transformed them for your own ends?

ELLISON: It is best, of course, when they don't show themselves directly, but they are there in many ways. Joyce and Eliot, for instance, made me aware of the playful possibilities of language. You look at a page of *Finnegans Wake* and see references to all sorts of American popular music; yet the context gives it an extension from the popular back to the classical and beyond. This is just something that Joyce teaches you that you can do, and you can abstract the process and apply it to a frame of reference which is American and historical; it can refer to class, to the fractions and frictions of color, to popular and folk culture—it can do many things.

A writer makes himself present in your work through allowing you to focus upon certain aspects of experience. Malraux's concern with the individual caught up consciously in a historical, a revolutionary situation provided insights which allowed me to understand certain possibilities in the fictional material around me. From him I learned that the condition of that type of individual is essentially the same, regardless of his culture or the political climate in which he finds his existence.

Or again, some writers—say, Dostoevski, or even Tolstoy—will make you very much aware of what is possible in depicting a society in which class lines either are fluid or have broken down without the cultural style and values on either extreme of society being dissipated. From such writers you learn to explore the rich fictional possibilities to be achieved in juxtaposing the peasant's consciousness with that of the aristocrat and the aristocrat's with the peasant's.

This insight is useful when you are dealing with American society. For years white people went through Grand Central Station having their luggage carried by Ph.D.'s. They couldn't see the Ph.D.'s because their race and class attitudes had trained them to see only the uniforms and the dark faces, but the Ph.D.'s could see them and judge them on any number of levels. This makes for drama, and it is a drama which goes right to the core of the democratic faith. So you get your moral perception of the contradictions of American class and personality from such literature—even more, perhaps, than from psychiatry or sociology, because such novelists have always dealt with the drama of social living.

HERSEY: You once had some very interesting things to say about the similarities and differences of the stances of black and Jewish writers in this country. It seems clear that Russian novelists have had a special kind of access to the deeper resources we were talking about earlier, access to primary feelings. Do you think there are particular ways in which Negro writers have had a corresponding access to those deeper resources—different in kind or degree from that of the Jewish writer, or the white Protestant writer in America, say, or the Russian writer or the English writer?

ELLISON: You will have to be very careful about that, because writers are individuals, each unique in his own way. But I would think that the access to primary feelings that the great Russian novelists had grew out of the nature of their society and the extreme disruption of hierarchal relationships which occurred during the nineteenth century. Then you had a great declassed aristocracy, with the Tsar still at the top and an awakening peasantry at the bottom. On one hand, society was plunging headlong into chaos, and on the other there was a growing identification on the part of many declassed aristocrats with the peasantry, an identification across traditional hierarchal divisions which was sustained by the unifying force of Russian Greek Orthodox Christianity. The friction generated by these social unities and divisions in that chaotic scene made possible all kinds of intensities of emotion and aggravations of sensibility. The belief in the Tsar as a sacred "Little Father" remained a unifying force, but was no longer strong enough to rationalize and impose order upon the expression of primary emotions—class hate, greed, ambition, and so on. Such disruption of the traditional ordering of society, as in our own country since 1954, made for an atmosphere of irrationality, and this created a situation of unrestrained expressiveness. Eyeballs were peeled, nerves were laid bare, and private sensibilities were subjected to public laceration. In fact, life became so theatrical (not to say nightmarish) that even Dostoevski's smoking imagination was barely able to keep a step ahead of what was actually happening in the garrets and streets. Today, here in the United States, we have something similar, but there's no point in my trying to explain Russian extremism, or the genius of the great nineteenth-century Russian novelists. Not even Dostoevski was able to do that.

Anyway, for all its expressiveness and chaos, the Negro American situation is something else, both in degree and source. Except for the brief period of Reconstruction, when we helped create the new constitutions of the Southern states and attempted to restructure society so as to provide a more equal set of relationships between the classes and races, we were *below* the threshold of social hierarchy. Our social mobility was strictly and violently limited, and in a way that neither our Christianity nor belief in the principles of the Constitution could change. As the sociologists say, we were indeed disadvantaged, both by law and by custom. Yet our actual position was ambiguous, for although we were outside the social compact, we were existentially right in the middle of the social drama. I mean that as servants we were right in the bedroom, so to speak. Thus we saw things, and we understood the difference between ideal assertions and crude realities. Much of the rhetorical and political energy of white society went toward proving to itself that we were not human and that we had no sense of the refinement of human values. But this in itself pressured you, motivated you, to make even finer distinctions, both as to personality and value. You *had* to, because your life depended upon it and your sense of your own humanity demanded that you do so. You had to identify those values which were human and preserving of your life and interests, as against those which were inhuman and destructive. So we were thrown upon our own resources and sense of life. We were forced to define and act out our own idea of the heights and depths of the human condition. Human beings cannot live in a situation where violence can be visited upon them without any concern for justice—and in many instances without possibility of redress—without developing a very intense sense of the precariousness of all human life, not to mention the frailty and arbitrariness of human institutions. So you were forced to be existential in your outlook, and this gives a poignancy and added value to little things and you discover the value of modes and attitudes that are rejected by the larger society. It also makes you terribly brutal and thick-skinned toward some values, while ultrasensitive to others.

Now, this background provides the black writer with much to write about. As fictional material it rivals that of the nineteenth-century Russians. But to the extent that other American writers, writers of different backgrounds, understand this material, or can implicate it in their own experience, they too have a way into what is currently known as "the black experience"—which I prefer to call "the *Negro* American experience"—because for it to be worthy of fictional treatment, worthy of art, it has to be meaningful to others who do not share in its immediacy. I'll add that since it is both my own and an irrevocable part of the basic experience of the United States, *I* think that it is not only worthy, but indispensable to any profoundly *American* depiction of reality.

To repeat myself, this society has structured itself to be unaware of what it owes in both the positive and negative sense to the condition of inhumanity that it has imposed upon a great mass of its citizens. The fact that many whites refuse to recognize this is responsible for much of the anger erupting among young blacks today. It makes them furious when whites respond to their complaints with, "Yes, but *I* had nothing to do with any of that," or reply to their demands for equal opportunity in a racially rigged society,

"We're against a quota system because *we* made it on our individual merits"—because this not only sidesteps a pressing reality, but is only partially true. Perhaps they *did* make it on their own, but if that's true the way was made easier because their parents did not have to contend with *my* parents, who were ruled out of the competition. They had their troubles too, but the relative benevolence of democracy shared by their parents, and now by them, was paid for by *somebody* other than themselves, and was being paid long before many of them arrived on these shores. *We* know that as the nation's unwilling scapegoat we paid for much of it. Nor is this knowledge a matter of saying, "Pay us off," or saying, in the words of the old joke, "Your granddaddy kicked my granddaddy a hundred years ago, so now I've come to collect the debt—bend over." That's not the point. The point is one of moral perception, the perception of the wholeness of American life and the cost of its successes and its failures. What makes for a great deal of black fury is the refusal of many Americans to understand that somebody paid for the nation's peace and prosperity in terms of blood and frustrated dreams, that somebody now denied his proper share helped convert raw materials into sophisticated gadgetry. I don't mean to imply that only the blacks did this; the poor Southern whites, the Irish, numbers of peoples also did. They too underwent the crudities and inequities of democracy so that the high rhetoric could retain some resonance of possibility and truth.

HERSEY: How much is anger a motive force for novelists of all kinds? Does the artist start with anger more than with other emotions?

ELLISON: I don't think that he necessarily starts with anger. Indeed, anger can get in the way, as it does for a fighter. If the writer starts with anger, then if he is truly writing he immediately translates it through his craft into consciousness, and thus into understanding, insight and perception. Perhaps that's where the morality of fiction lies. You see a situation which outrages you, but as you write about the characters who embody that which outrages, your sense of craft and the moral role of your craft demands that you depict those characters in the breadth of their humanity. You try to give them the density of the human rather than the narrow intensity of the demonic. This means that you try to delineate them as men and women who possess feelings and ideals, no matter how much you reject their feelings and ideals. Anyway, I find this happening in my own work; it humanizes *me*. The main motive is not to express raw anger, but to present, as sentimental as it might sound, the wonder of life in the fullness of which all these outrageous things occur.

HERSEY: Have you felt some defiance of death as a writer, in the sense that what you are making may possibly circumvent death?

ELLISON: No, I dare not. *(He laughs)* No, you just write for your own time, while trying to write in terms of the density of experience, knowing perfectly well that life repeats itself. Even in this rapidly changing United States it repeats itself. The mystery is that while repeating itself it always manages slightly to change its mask. To be able to grasp a little of that change within continuity and to communicate it across all these divisions of background and individual experience seems enough for me. If you're lucky, of course, if you splice into one of the deeper currents of life, then you have a chance of having your work last a little bit longer.

II

Ellison and I resumed this conversation some time later in Key West, where he and I are off-and-on next-door neighbors in small "conch" houses. This time I began asking him to tell me about his formative years.

HERSEY: Could we talk a bit about your fledgling years in writing? Would you talk about how you got started?

ELLISON: Well, it was kind of play at first. I had begun to read Eliot, Pound, Hemingway and others—I think I read my first Hemingway in *Esquire* in barbershops in my home city, but it was Eliot's *Waste Land*, with its footnotes, that made me become fascinated with how writing was written. I always read a lot; I took a course in the nine-teenth-century English novel at Tuskegee.

HERSEY: Who put *The Waste Land* in your way?

ELLISON: It was in the library at Tuskegee—a good library, even though it wasn't enough used. In fact, you could find most of the anthropological and geological references in that library. I worked in the library one year, just prowling the stacks and reading. No one taught Eliot there. I think I got one professor interested in that area, a good man with a very good mind.

HERSEY: You've told me in the past about Richard Wright's taking you under his wing when you moved to New York. When did you meet him?

ELLISON: When I got to New York I happened to see a copy of the *New Masses*, which had a poem by Wright. I was interested because I did not see the techniques of modern poetry in the work of Afro-American poets. I happened to meet Langston Hughes the first morning that I was in New York. Staying at the Harlem Annex of the YMCA, I went across the street to get breakfast, and there he was talking with Alain Locke, who was a professor of philosophy at How-ard, one of the theorists of the Negro Renaissance. I had read Locke's work, and had met him a few weeks before, when he had been at Tuskegee to visit Hazel Harrison. So I re-introduced myself to him, and he introduced me to Hughes. Hughes put me to work immediately to return some books to the library. They happened to be Malraux's *Days of Wrath* and *Man's Fate*. He said, "You can read these before you return them if you like," and of course I read them. I had read some Marxism even at Tuskegee—that, too, was in the library! I was quite excited by these books of Malraux's, and I asked Hughes if he knew a Negro writer by the name of Wright. He said, "Yes, he'll be here next week," and he dropped Wright a card. When

Wright got to New York, he sent me a card telling me where I could meet him. We hit it off because I was, I guess, one of the few Afro-Americans at that point who could talk about writing. At that time I had no thought of becoming a writer myself; my world was music. I had tried to write some poetry at Tuskegee, but just for myself, just playing around with it. One poem was published; my first publication was a poem, which I wrote after a friend of mine died. He hadn't attended Tuskegee but had gone to some other university, and coming home he had had an attack of appendicitis; they wouldn't accept him at a white hospital, and peritonitis had set in.

One of Wright's reasons for coming to New York was to work in the Harlem bureau of *The Daily Worker* and to edit a magazine which they were trying to resuscitate. It had been called *Challenge* during the Harlem Renaissance; now they called it *New Challenge*. He was editing this with two women, and he wanted a book review, so I wrote my first book review—not a very good one. I later reviewed the same book for the *Times*, and I think I did a *little* better. Then as he planned his next issue, he didn't have any short fiction, and he asked me to write a story. I said, "I don't know anything about writing a story." He said, "You talk well about stories. Why don't you try? You've had some experiences." I had ridden freight trains, so I wrote a story about an incident occurring on a hobo trip and he accepted it. I still have the galleys somewhere. The magazine folded—the girls didn't get along—but by that time, I was hooked. I began to write little stories and the *New Masses* published them; then I began to write book reviews for them. In some of the issues I wrote most of the unsigned reviews. They encouraged me. Some of the people there didn't particularly care for Wright. I guess he was rising too fast. They told me, "Oh, you're going to be a better writer than he is." I said, "You're crazy," and let it go, but I kept writing.

There's something of a misunderstanding about Wright and my fiction. I met him in 1937 and I was writing a lot of fiction, but I approached writing as I approached music. I'd been playing since I was eight years old, and I knew you didn't reach a capable performance in any craft without *work*. I'd play one set of scales over and over again. In Tuskegee I'd get up early in the morning—this was required of brass instrument players—and blow sustained tones for an hour. I knew other students used to hate it, but this developed embouchure, breath control, and so on. I approached writing in the same way. I wrote a hell of a lot of stuff that I didn't submit to anybody. At first I showed some of my things to Wright, and then by 1940 I wrote a story which had to do with some fight that broke out between a chef and a hallboy in a club, basing it upon a club where I had worked in Oklahoma City—I'd worked there as a bread-and-butter boy and then as an extra waiter—and I showed this to Dick, and he kept it and kept it and didn't say anything. I let a few weeks go by and then finally said, "Well, what *about* it? What *about* it?" And he answered, "This is *my* stuff." And I said, "Okay, but what do you expect? I thought I was taking your advice." After that I never showed him another piece of fiction.

HERSEY: What kind of advice had he been giving you?

ELLISON: Well, he'd suggest how to tighten, that kind of thing. He did not have the kind of experience I'd had and was not familiar with it, but generally he gave me suggestions on structure. I was struggling with the problem of how to render Afro-American speech without resorting to misspellings—to give a *suggestion* of the idiom. Of course I had a musician's ear, and I kept working with that. Some of the first things were embarrassing. You go from something that you've read until you find out how *you* really feel about it. But after 1940 I'd show him some of my essays and book reviews, and often he felt that I had too many ideas in the pieces. I told myself, "Well, there may be too many ideas, but I guess the real problem is in articulating them," because by then I was reading a hell of a lot of Malraux, and I knew that I didn't have enough ideas to cause confusion; it was a matter of writing with clarity. So I kept working for that. I started to come in contact with writer-intellectuals in New York—on the [New York Federal] Writers Project, and because

Wright introduced me to people in the League of American Writers. I began to meet people. They were so available during those days! You know, you began to *measure* yourself. In trying to learn something I talked to well-known Afro-American writers, and I found that they did not know consciously what was going on in literature. I could not discuss technique with them, and even though we shared some points of ideology, because a number of them were leftists, they couldn't talk to me about technical matters.

HERSEY: Who might some of them have been?

ELLISON: Well, Hughes was one, Claude McKay was another, and there were lesser writers, some newspapermen. But they were all on the Project. Some of the stuff I worked on back then has recently been published.

HERSEY: What sorts of things did you do with the Project?

ELLISON: I did several things, but the main thing was a book to be titled *Negroes in New York*. When I got into the research, I realized I was dealing with American history. It was an education in itself. I also worked on a projected book of folklore—B. A. Botkin was at the top somewhere, though I didn't work directly under him; I collected kids' rhymes, game songs and so on, but I'd take the opportunity to question old people and get them to tell me stories. It was a rich harvest, just tremendous, and it fit right into some of the things I was reading. By this time I was rereading Mark Twain, and I'd started reading Henry James. It was in this kind of thing where Wright was important. He introduced me to the Henry James prefaces, which were edited by Dick Blackmur. I used to repunctuate James's prose so that I could get the most out of it. I had to teach myself to read him. I was also reading Conrad's essays, and any writer who wrote about the craft—the Goncourt brothers, the Russians. I was also reading essays on the cinema by Eisenstein and Pudovkin. I would collect old copies of *Hound and Horn* and of *International Literature*. I had a hell of a lot of Gorki's works, and the pamphlets on literature which were published by the Communists. I was reading *Partisan Review*, even though I disagreed with the politics. Hell, I could read Eliot in the *Partisan Review*; I used to say, "I wonder why these guys are publishing people whose politics disagree with theirs." But I was glad that they did, because what Eliot had to say was far more interesting than what Philip Rahv had to say.

HERSEY: There is one other thing about those early days I'd like to explore with you. In my previous interview with you, we talked about family influences, and you told me how your mother and your father had helped to shape what you have become. You've often talked about Fanny's role in your literary life. Would you talk about that a little? She must have come into your life at about that time.

ELLISON: As I said in the introduction to the thirtieth-anniversary edition of *Invisible Man*, when I met Fanny she had a steady job. I had been working on the *Negro Quarterly*, and sometimes you got paid and sometimes you didn't. Angelo Herndon had set up the *Negro Quarterly* and wanted someone who was familiar with literature to work with him. I was doing well on the Writers Project; it wasn't much money, but it *came* on payday. Finally I said, "All right, Angelo, if you'll pay me what I make on the Writers Project, I'll come there." I'd gone on the Project in 1938, and this was 1942, and of course the money was not always there. I guess I should say that I had been married once before.

HERSEY: Yes, I know.

ELLISON: By the time I met Fanny I was going to sea—in 1944. She worked for the Urban League. Of course I had money from my voyages; you got a bonus whenever you went into the war zone. That was fine, but by the time we were married in 1944, the war was still on and I was going to sea. In 1945, I started *Invisible Man*. I had come back from the sea and had no job. She was working. I began building high-fidelity amplifiers and installing sound systems with a friend of mine who knew more about such things than I did. I took photographs, sold a few pieces, and so on. But the main—and secure—financial support was Fanny. Beyond that, she would read the damn stuff, type it and correct the spelling! We laugh now, because I've become a much better speller just by giving my attention to it.

HERSEY: Does she still help in these ways?

ELLISON: She still types final drafts; I type my rough stuff. I read aloud to her over and over again.

HERSEY: Do her responses make a difference to you?

ELLISON: Yes, they do, very definitely. I don't always agree, because in an oral reading you don't always get the nuances or visual rhythm. But she knows quite a bit. Fanny studied drama and speech at the University of Iowa, so she's had her training. She directed a little in Chicago before she was married. I think one of the reasons we became attracted to each other was that we both liked books. We combined our libraries. One of the things which always struck me is that we both had the same copy of the magazine *Vanity Fair* which we'd kept; it had a cover with a Balinese woman by Covarrubias. I'd begun reading *Vanity Fair* when I was a kid; when I was able to I'd buy it. What you were exposed to in the magazine was the avant-garde. I was familiar with names that didn't turn up in college courses until many years later—even at Harvard! That's what I mean when I speak of "free-floating educational possibilities." If you're attuned, the stuff is there.

HERSEY: And then, of course, in 1952 you published *Invisible Man*, and everything must have changed in your life; all your relationships must have changed. What about your relationship with your former mentor, Wright, for instance?

ELLISON: Dick and I remained friends, although of course we had not been so close after he had gone to live in Paris. Fanny and I went over to Europe first in 1954, when I lectured at the Salzburg Seminars; then in 1955 when we went to Rome we stopped in Paris and saw him. Then I think I saw him again in 1956 when I went to Mexico for a conference and went to see him as we passed through. There was some correspondence; a lot of the letters are in the collection at Yale. Our relationship changed, of course. After all, I had read all kinds of books most of my life, and Wright was self-taught, without even any structured instruction.

HERSEY: More than thirty years have passed since *Invisible Man.* You've grown and changed. America has changed. How will the big book you've been working on all this time differ in tone and purpose and method from *Invisible Man?*

ELLISON: *Invisible Man* took on its own life, and has more or less gone its own way. I am identified with it, but I haven't read the book in years and years. I've read sections. It's out there, and I certainly appreciate the fact that it lives. But the main thing is to make a rounded form out of the material I'm dealing with *now.* The book uses comic effects; maybe ultimately what I write always turns out to be tragicomedy, which I think has proved to be the underlying mode of American experience. We don't remember enough; we don't allow ourselves to remember events, and I suppose this helps us to continue our belief in progress. But the undercurrents are always there. You and I were speaking the other day about how we turn our eyes away from the role that religion has continued to play in American life. It has re-emerged recently as a potent and in some ways dangerous force, and it has taken on danger because we were not paying attention to its significance in all those earlier years. This is not just to take a negative view of it. Negro religion has been a counterbalance to much of the inequality and imposed chaos which has been the American Negro experience. When Martin Luther King, Jr., emerged as an important American figure, it was an instance of the church making itself visible in the political and social life and fulfilling its role in the realm of morality. The kinds of things which are involved in this book seem to have grown out of what has been happening all along.

HERSEY: The religious element in these intervening years operates in the book, then?

ELLISON: Yes. I guess that in all my work there is an undergrounding of American history as it comes to focus in the racial situation. One of the characters is a Negro minister who was once a jazz trombonist, and he underwent an experience which turned him from his wild life as a musician into a serious minister, but one who also brought with him his experience as a showman. He isn't always sure when he's using religious methods, even though his motives are religious, or when he's allowing the devices of his old past to intrude.

HERSEY: Is this a metaphor for the tour of Ralph Ellison from jazz musician to another kind of performer in the moral realm?

ELLISON: No, I don't think of it that way. So much of American life evolves around the dedication toward a religious outlook, but religion always runs into the limitations of politics. Many of our politicians were ministers. We had a recent instance of a Catholic priest, Father Drinan, who had to be ordered out of Congress by Rome. This book was conceived before Martin Luther King became such a figure, but he too had to enter the realm of politics while trying to stay outside it. When he began to connect the struggle for racial justice with Vietnam, he made himself vulnerable; that might well have played a role in his being killed. This fellow Hickman developed, as I worked on the book, from a musician who adopted the more folkish ways of ministers into something fairly sophisticated. He was always capable with words. He was the son of a preacher, and thus inherited that kind of eloquence from his own family. The other part of it has to do with a little boy of indefinite race who looks white and who, through a series of circumstances, comes to be reared by the Negro minister. They used to go around and the little boy preached; there have been plenty of examples of pairings like this, too, in actual life. One of the devices used was to bring the little boy into a service in a white coffin, and, at a certain point, when the minister would preach of Christ's agony on the cross, saying "Lord! Lord! Why hast thou forsaken me?" the little boy would rise up from the coffin.

HERSEY: Can you recall a little of the history of the development of the book?

ELLISON: I started working on it in 1958. Some of what I just told you appeared in *Noble Savage*, for which Saul Bellow was one of the editors. It was the same period when, at Saul's urging, I started teaching at Bard College. That was an unsettled period for us. We had spent two years in Rome, and Fanny was working, having gone back to the job she'd had before we went to Rome—where incidentally she had also worked. The Catholic Church had set up something called La Lampada della Fraternita, which was a veterans organization; they needed someone to set up a clerical system, and she went in there with her Berlitz Italian. It was quite admirable the way she went about it. When I came back, I didn't have a job. I was trying to stay out of activities in New York, so Bellow suggested that I live in his house in Tivoli because he and his wife and baby were spending most of the year in Minnesota, at the university. I got started on the book and wrote quite a lot of it, but was never satisfied with how the parts connected. The sections I have published have gotten good responses, and I've given public readings of other sections, always with satisfaction. I'm finding myself having to try first-person narration, and then try it again as third-person in an effort to stay out of it as narrator myself. It's exasperating, but at the same time I've come to feel that one of the challenges for a writer who handles the kind of material I'm working with is to let people speak for themselves in whatever way you can. Then you draw upon more of the resources of American vernacular speech. One of the narrators is a newspaperman, a white, who had some radical experiences during the thirties and had an affair, which didn't end well, with a Negro girl.

HERSEY: What sort of time span do you cover?

ELLISON: Roughly from 1954 to 1956 or 1957. That is time present in the novel, but the story goes back into earlier experiences, too, even to some of the childhood experiences of Hickman, who is an elderly man in time present. It's just a matter of the past being active in the present—or of the characters becoming aware of the manner in which the past operates on their present lives. Of course this gets into the general history, because one of the characters is a senator. He, too, is a trickster.

HERSEY: In our earlier talk you said, "I believe that fiction does help create value, and I regard this as a very serious—I almost said 'sacred'—function of the writer." I know you have strong views about the moral fabric of the country. To what extent does fiction have a bearing on that fabric?

ELLISON: At its best, fiction allows for a summing up. The fiction writer abstracts from the flow of experience certain abiding patterns, and projects those patterns as they affect the lives and consciousnesses of the characters. So fiction allows for a summing up. It allows for contemplation of the moral significance of human events. We don't always live up to the broader implications of this aspect of fiction, I think, because sometimes, out of a sense of frustration or disgust, we don't consider what a powerful effect vividly projected images of symbolic actions can have upon readers. Think of the popularization of drugs and the let-it-all-hang-out syndrome; these are very suggestive, and I believe writers might think a little bit about the implications of what they project, and of the kinds of heroes or antiheroes they project. Of course I'm not offering formulas. Everyone has to work out his writing for himself, but the things he writes do have consequences. Sometimes you touch upon forces which are implicit, and you establish moods and give forms to attitudes. These are not always for the best. Someone asked me about all the burnings of tenements which occurred during the period after *Invisible Man* had been published; I had to point out that I had covered the Harlem Riot of 1943 for the *New York Post*, and I certainly wasn't recommending that people burn buildings but was suggesting that this was a negative alternative to more democratic political action. When it is impossible to be heard within the democratic forum, people inevitably go to other extremes. There is always somebody to suggest that we live in an era of revolutions. In any case, it is that aura of a summing up, that pause for contemplation of the moral significance of the history we've been through, that I have been reaching for in my work on this new book.

ON BEING THE TARGET OF DISCRIMINATION

Ellison wrote this reminiscence and reflection on two childhood experiences with "the strange ways of segregated democracy," and his complex, self-sustaining, comic responses, for "A World of Difference," a New York Times *supplement. It was published in* The New York Times Magazine, *April 16, 1989.*

IT isn't necessarily through acts of physical violence—lynching, mob attacks, or slaps in the face, whether experienced first-hand or by word of mouth—that a child is initiated into the contradictions of segregated democracy. Rather, it is through brief impersonal encounters, stares, vocal inflections, hostile laughter, or public reversals of private expectations that occur at the age when children are most receptive to the world and all its wonders. It is then begins the process of conscious questioning of self, family, and the social order which determines a child's attitudes, hopeful or cynical, as a citizen of this free-wheeling, self-improvised society. Thus for its victims segregation is far more than a negative social condition; it is also a perspective that fosters an endless exercise of irony, and often inspires a redeeming laughter.

It got to you first at the age of six, and through your own curiosity. With kindergarten completed and the first grade ahead, you were eagerly anticipating your first day of public school. For months you had been imagining your new experience and the children, known and unknown, with whom you would study and play. But the physical framework of your imagining, an elementary school in the process of construction, lay close at hand on the block-square site across the street from your home. For over a year you had watched it rise and spread in the air to become a handsome structure of brick and stone, then seen its broad encircling grounds arrayed with seesaws, swings, and baseball diamonds. You had imagined this picture-book setting as the scene of your new experience, and when enrollment day arrived, with its grounds astir with bright colors and voices of kids like yourself, it did indeed become the site of your very first lesson in public schooling—though not within its classrooms, as you had imagined, but well outside its walls. For while located within a fairly mixed neighborhood, this new public school was exclusively for whites.

It was then you learned that you would attend a school located far to the south of your neighborhood, and that reaching it involved a journey which took you over, either directly or by way of a viaduct which arched head-spinning high above, a broad expanse of railroad tracks along which a constant traffic of freight cars, switch engines, and passenger trains made it dangerous for a child to cross. And that once the tracks were safely negotiated you continued past warehouses, factories, and loading docks, and then through a notorious red-light district where black prostitutes in brightly colored housecoats and Mary Jane shoes supplied the fantasies and needs of a white clientele. Considering the fact that you couldn't attend school with white kids, this made for a confusion that was further confounded by the giggling jokes which older boys whispered about the district's peculiar form of integration. For you it was a grown-up's mystery, but streets being no less schools than routes to schools, the district would soon add a few forbidden words to your vocabulary.

It took a bit of time to forget the sense of incongruity aroused by your having to walk *past* a school to get *to* a school, but soon you came to like your school, your teachers and most of your schoolmates. Indeed, you soon enjoyed the long walks and anticipated the sights you might see, the adventures you might encounter, and the many things not taught in school that could be learned along the way. Your school was not nearly so fine as that which faced your home, but it had its attractions. Among them its nearness to a park, now abandoned by whites, in which you picnicked and played. And there were the two tall cylindrical fire escapes on either wing of its main building down which it was a joy to lie full-length and slide, spiraling down and around three stories to the ground—providing no outraged teacher was waiting to strap your legs once you sailed out of its chute like a shot off a fireman's shovel. Besides, in your childish way you were learning that it was better to take self-selected risks and pay the price than be denied the joy or pain of risk-taking by those who begrudged your existence.

Beginning when you were four or five you had known the joy of trips to the city's zoo, but one day you would ask your mother to take you there and have her sigh and explain that it was now against the law for Negro kids to view the animals. Had someone done something bad to the animals? No. Had someone tried to steal them or feed them poison? No. Could white kids still go? Yes. So why? Quit asking questions; it's the law, and only because some white folks are out to turn this state into a part of the South.

This sudden and puzzling denial of a Saturday's pleasure was disappointing, and so angered your mother that later, after the zoo was moved north of the city, she decided to do something about it. Thus one warm Saturday afternoon with you and your baby brother dressed in your best she took you on a long streetcar ride which ended at a strange lakeside park, in which you found a crowd of noisy white people. Having assumed that you were on your way to the integrated cemetery where at the age of three you had been horrified beyond all tears or forgetting when you saw your father's coffin placed in the ground, you were bewildered. But now as your mother herded you and your brother into the park you discovered that you'd come to the zoo, and were so delighted that soon you were laughing and babbling as excitedly as the kids around you.

Your mother was pleased, and as you moved through the crowd of white parents and children she held your brother's hand and allowed as much time for staring at the cages of rare animals as either of you desired. But once your brother began to tire she herded you out of the park and toward the streetcar line. And then it happened.

Just as you reached the gate through which crowds of whites were coming and going, you had a memorable lesson in the strange ways of segregated democracy as instructed by a guard in civilian clothes. He was a white man dressed in a black suit and a white straw hat, and when he looked at the fashion in which your mother was dressed, then down to you and your brother, he stiffened, turned red in the face, and stared as though at something dangerous.

"Girl," he shouted, "where are your *white* folks!"

"*White* folks," your mother said. "What white folks? I don't *have* any white folks. I'm a Negro!"

"Now, don't you get smart with me, colored gal," the white man said. "I mean where are the white folks you come *out* here with!"

"But I just told you that I didn't come here with any white people," your mother said. "I came here with my boys . . ."

"Then what are you doing in this park," the white man said.

And now when your mother answered you could hear the familiar sound of anger in her voice.

"I'm here," she said, "because I'm a *tax-payer*, and I thought it was about time that my boys have a look at those animals. And for that I didn't *need* any *white* folks to show me the way!"

"Well," the white man said, "*I'm* here to tell you that you're breaking the law! So now you'll have to leave. Both you and your chillun too. The rule says no niggers is allowed in the zoo. That's the law and I'm enforcing it!"

"Very well," your mother said, "we've seen the animals anyway and were on our way to the streetcar line when you stopped us."

"That's fine," the white man said, "and when that car comes you be sure that you get on it, you hear? You and your chillun too!"

So it was quite a day. You had enjoyed the animals with your baby brother and had another lesson in the sudden ways good times could be turned into bad when white people looked at your color instead of *you*. But better still, you had learned something of your mother's courage and were proud that she had broken an unfair law and stood up for her right to do so. For while the white man kept staring until the streetcar arrived she ignored him and answered your brother's questions about the various animals. Then the car came with its crowd of white parents and children, and when you were entrained and rumbling home past the fine lawns and houses, your mother gave way to a gale of laughter; in which, hesitantly at first, and then with assurance and pride, you joined. And from that day the incident became the source of a family joke that was sparked by accidents, faux pas, or obvious lies. Then one of you was sure to frown and say, "Well, I think you'll have to go now, both you and your chillun too!" And the family would laugh hilariously. Discrimination teaches one to discriminate between discriminators while countering absurdity with black (Negro? Afro-American? African-American?) comedy.

When you were eight you would move to one of the white sections through which you often passed on the way to your father's grave and your truly last trip to the zoo. For now your mother was the custodian of several apartments located in a building which housed on its street floor a drug store, a tailor shop, a Piggly Wiggly market, and a branch post office. Built on a downward slope, the building had at its rear a long driveway which led from the side street past an empty lot to a group of garages in which the apartments' tenants stored their cars. Built at an angle with wings facing north and east, the structure supported a servant's quarters which sat above its angle like a mock watchtower atop a battlement, and it was there that you now lived.

Reached by a flight of outside stairs, it consisted of four small rooms, a bath, and a kitchen. Windows on three of its sides provided a view across the empty frontage to the street, of the backyards behind it, and of the back wall and windows of the building in which your mother worked. It was quite comfortable but you secretly disliked the idea of your mother living in service and missed your friends who now lived far away. Nevertheless, the neighborhood was pleasant, served by a substation of the streetcar line, and marked by a variety of activities which challenged your curiosity. Even its affluent alleys were more exciting to explore than those of your old neighborhood, and the one white friend you were to acquire in the area lived nearby.

This friend was a brilliant but sickly boy who was tutored at home, and with him you shared your new interest in building radios, a hobby at which he was quite skilled. Your friendship eased your loneliness and helped dispel some of the mystery and resentment imposed by segregation. Through access to his family, headed by an important Episcopalian minister, you learned more about whites and thus about yourself. With him you could make comparisons that were not so distorted by the racial myths which obstructed your thrust toward self-perception; compare their differences in taste, discipline, and manners with those of Negro families of comparable status and income; observe variations between your friend's boyish lore and your own, and measure his intelligence, knowledge, and ambitions against your own. For you this was a most important experience and a rare privilege, because up to now the prevailing separation of the races had made it impossible to learn how you and your Negro friends compared with boys who lived on the white side of the color line. It was said by word of mouth, proclaimed in newsprint, and dramatized by acts of discriminatory law that you were inferior. You were barred from vying with them in sports games, competing in the classroom or the world of art. Yet what you saw, heard, and smelled of them left irrepressible doubts, so you ached for objective proof, for a fair field of testing.

Even your school's proud marching band was denied participation in the statewide music contests, so popular at the time, as though so airy and earth-transcending an art as music would be contaminated if performed by musicians of different races.

Which was especially disturbing because after the father of a friend who lived next door in your old neighborhood had taught you the beginner's techniques required to play valved instruments, you had decided to become a musician. Then shortly before moving among whites your mother had given you a brass cornet, which in the isolation of the servant's quarters you practiced hours on end. But you yearned to play with other musicians and found none available. Now you lived less than a block from a white school with a famous band, but there was no one in the neighborhood with whom to explore the mysteries of the horn. You could hear the school band's music and watch their marching, but joining in making the thrilling sounds was impossible. Nor did it help that you owned the scores to a few of their marches and could play with a certain facility and fairly good tone. So there, surrounded by sounds but unable to share a sound, you went it alone. You turned yourself into a one-man band.

You played along as best you could with the phonograph, read the score to *The Carnival of Venice* while listening to Del Steigers executing triple-tongue variations on its themes; played the trumpet parts of your bandbook's marches while humming in your head the supporting voices of horns and reeds. And since your city was a seedbed of Southwestern jazz you played Kansas City riffs, bugle calls, and wha-wha-muted imitations of blues singers' pleas. But none of this made up for your lack of fellow musicians. Then, late one Saturday afternoon when your mother and brother were away, and when you had dozed off while reading, you awoke to the nearby sound of live music. At first you thought you were dreaming, and then that you were listening to the high school band, but that couldn't be the source because instead of floating over building tops and bouncing off wall and windowpane, the sounds you heard rose up, somewhat muffled, from below.

With that you ran to a window which faced the driveway, and looking down through the high windowpane of the lighted post office you could see the metal glint of instruments. Then you were on your feet and down the stairs, keeping to the shadows as you drew close and peeped below. There you looked down upon a room full of men and women postal workers who were playing away at a familiar march. It was like the answer to a silent prayer because you could tell by the sound that they were beginners like yourself, and the covers of the thicket of bandbooks revealed that they were of the same set as yours. For a while you listened and hummed along, unseen but shaking with excitement in the dimming twilight. Then, hardly before the idea formed in your head, you were skipping up the stairs to grab your cornet, lyre, and bandbook and hurtling down again to the drive.

For a while you listened, hearing the music come to a pause and the sound of the conductor's voice. Then came a rap on a music stand and once again the music. Now turning to the march by the light from the window, you snapped score to lyre, raised horn to lip, and began to play, at first silently tonguing the notes through the mouthpiece and then, carried away with the thrill of stealing a part of the music, you tensed your diaphragm and blew. As you played, keeping time with your foot on the concrete drive, you realized that you were a better cornetist than some in the band, and grew bold in the pride of your sound. Now in your mind you were marching along a downtown street to the flying of flags, the tramping of feet, and the cheering of excited crowds. At last by an isolated act of brassy cunning you had become a member of the band.

Yes, but unfortunately you then let yourself become so carried away that you forgot to listen for the conductor's instructions which you were too high and hidden to see. Suddenly the music faded and you opened your ears to the fact that you were now rendering a lonely solo in the startled quietness. Before you could fully return to reality there came the sound of table legs across a floor and a rustle of movement, ending in the appearance of a white startled face in the opened window. Then you heard a man's voice exclaim, "I'll be damn, it's a little nigger!" Whereupon you took off like quail at the sound of sudden shotgun fire.

Next thing you knew, you were up the stairs and on your bed, crying away in the dark your guilt and embarrassment. You cried and cried, asking yourself how you could have been so lacking in pride as to shame yourself and your entire race by butting in where you weren't wanted. And this just to make some amateur music. To this you had no answers, but then and there you made a vow that it would never happen again. Then, slowly, slowly, as you lay in the dark, your earlier lessons in the absurd nature of racial relations came to your aid, and suddenly you found yourself laughing, both at the way you'd run away and the shock you'd caused by joining unasked in the music.

Then you could hear yourself intoning in your eight-year-old's imitation of a white Southern accent. "Well, boy, you broke the law, so you have to go, and that means you and your chillun too!"

BEARDEN

A friend of painter Romare Bearden for nearly five decades, Ellison delivered this eulogy in which he notes the aptness of collage as an American form, on April 6, 1988, at the Cathedral of St. John the Divine in New York City. It was published in Callaloo, Summer 1988.

LET me begin by saying that Romie frequently got me into trouble. Nothing physical, mind you, but difficulties arising out of our attempts to make some practical sense of the relationship between art and living, between ideas and the complex details of consciousness and experience. Of course there can be no final answers to such questions, and so today I find Romie challenging me from beyond the limits of death and dying.

It was my good fortune to know Romie from my early days in New York. I met him when I was a fledgling writer working (some would say "boondoggling") on the Federal Writers Project, and when he was an unknown painter who worked for the New York Department of Welfare. At the time I knew very little about painting as such, but thanks to having taken a class in sculpture at Tuskegee and to my exposure to avant-garde magazines, I had developed a more than casual interest in the visual arts. I became even more interested once I realized that I had found in Romie an artist who could talk knowledgeably about my own passion, which was literature.

At the time I was very much involved with the poetry and plays of Frederico García Lorca. I discovered that Romie knew a great deal about García Lorca. I was interested in the poetry of Eliot and the fiction of Hemingway, and I was delighted that they too had aroused his interest. Indeed, I soon discovered that Romie knew about many matters that I in my naïveté hadn't expected a painter to know, and when I accepted this fact my life was unexpectedly enriched.

Earlier today I tried to think back to the circumstance through which I was prepared for my relationship with Romie, and by what stroke of fate I had been made ready for his impact upon my sensibilities. (Incidentally, I have no concrete idea about how *Romie* was prepared for his contact with such an oddball as myself, but I suspect that reading played a part.) Nevertheless, as I thought back I realized that there had indeed been a forerunner of Romie in my life, and that my interest in drawing and painting went directly back to an older boy who lived next door.

This was in Oklahoma City, and that boy, that hero of my childhood, filled his notebooks with cartoon characters who acted out visual narratives that I found far more interesting than those provided by the newspaper comic sections. More interesting because they were about *us*, about Negro boys like ourselves. He filled his notebooks with drawings which told the stories of Negro cowboys and rodeo stars like Bill Pickett, of detectives and gangsters, athletes, clowns and heroes. Indeed, he created such a variety of characters and adventures that our entire neighborhood took on a dimension of wonder. But for me the most amazing part was the fact that all this was done by someone I knew, by the fellow living just next door who allowed me to look on as he gave form to figures, scenes and adventures on page after page of notebook paper. But then as my friend and I grew older, Fate, the old "good-bad," struck our lives in its ever ambiguous way.

There came a day when his father sat us down beneath their towering apricot tree and proceeded to teach him the trumpet and me the alto horn. For me this was a stroke of good fortune, but there's a question about whether that was true for my friend. While our community was highly enthusiastic in fostering music, it lacked adults who might have encouraged my friend's artistic talents. Thus it was that he went on to become a musician and barber like his father. So it was in Romie that I found the fulfillment of my earlier friend's promise and the continuation of that stimulating friendship. However, it was no mere duplication of past experience, for while Romie was more mature and intellectually curious, he was no less generous in sharing his talent and in discussing his struggle for mastery with me.

I can remember visits to Romie's 125th Street studio during which he stood at his easel sketching and explaining the perspectives of the Dutch and Italian masters. At other times he played with the rhythms of Mondrian and related them to the structure of jazz, and on still other occasions he explained some of the magic by which color became space, space became perspective, and color became form. He also had much to say about the nature of African sculpture.

It was his generosity in sharing such knowledge that made Romie Bearden such an affirmative figure in my own struggle to acquire writing skills. True, among my friends there was a world-famous writer, and another, with whom I held endless discussions of our mutual craft, who would soon be widely acclaimed, but Romie's approach to art and his line of development seemed closer to my own. Thus when it seemed impossible that I would ever get anywhere with my writing, I could talk with him, take heart from his progress and feel encouraged. Better, I could observe and discuss his search for more effective techniques with which to give artistic form to his conceptions of our general experience. Each of us was concerned with the relationship between artistic technique and individual vision, and we were especially concerned with the relationship between our racial identity, our identity as Americans, and our mission as writer and artist.

Romie's father was a teller of tales, and Romie, whose art even at its most abstract retains an element of narrative, enjoyed regaling his friends with folk tales. These arose out of a need to impose form upon experience, and Romie's delight in them led me to realize that here again we shared a stream of Afro-American culture which I had received from my Oklahoma background and Romie from living in North Carolina, Pennsylvania and New York. This shared ancestral lore made for a level of unspoken communication which connected the past to the present, and of course we shared many of the wide variety of experiences that were available during the thirties. New York was a center of opportunity in which the aspiring could form contacts with recognized artists and writers. Libraries, art galleries and museums were there to be used by those with the curiosity and interest to use them, and we did.

Those were also days of great excitement in Harlem, for in many ways it was still a place of glamour. Those were the days of the swinging big bands, days when the streets of Harlem were filled with celebration every time Joe Louis knocked somebody out in the ring, days when we danced the Lindy at the Savoy Ballroom, and nights when new stars were initiated on the stage of the Apollo Theater.

Yes, but those were also the days of the Depression, days of *dis*-possession and of protest marches. Harlem was growing edgy, and Romie observed its effects most intimately through his work with the Welfare Department. There was a great turbulence growing in American society, much of it racial, and it became a subject both of our discussions and our artistic efforts. The question was, how did one express it in art? How sharpen its impact and render it artisti-cally effective? How transform dismal sociological facts into art? Many attempts were being made, and certain ideological formulas were recommended as solutions, but I myself felt that they were re-ductive, that they overemphasized the negative aspects of our condi-tion while leaving unnoticed the tragic-comic transcendence through which we had survived and remained hopeful, both as in-dividuals and as a people. Most of all, such ideological formulas sought to reduce our complex American identity to the single aspect of race. I suspected, and Romie's work affirmed, that perhaps there were other ways of going about giving expression to the times. Per-haps the solution lay in other, more eclectic approaches. Art itself was a form of freedom, and there was a world of art complete with all the styles and complex techniques through which artists had con-fronted experience and given it artistic form. That world was ours to draw upon. Yes, and there were the rituals—religious, fraternal, so-cial—through which our people had imposed order upon the chaos of their lives. There were the interrelations between such rituals that were shared by Americans of various backgrounds to be drawn upon. Therefore the image of American society presented by the newspa-pers, magazines and radio often missed much of the sheer human complexity of the life we knew. That life was marked by a ceaseless resistance against all attempts to reduce its complex humanity, whether by force or ideology, and by example it pointed a direction for the writer and artist. Thus each of us decided in his own way to find the artistic means with which to express our complex sense of American and Afro-American variety and diversity, discord and unity, and we decided that to do this one had to draw upon one's own unique experience. One had to discover one's means and direction by going into the self, and by identifying one's self with all that claimed one's respect and aroused one's sense of wonder. In brief, we came to believe that it was the role of the artist to confront and impose his own artistic sense of order upon the world.

Since there are hundreds of you gathered here who knew those times and who shared their hopes and disappointments, there is no need for me to continue with this bit of background. You know very well how it worked out for Romie. Some of the results, the paintings, are here in this cathedral. Some are in magazines, in books and in many museums. They are in many places, and in all their settings they speak eloquently of a promise which goes far beyond the designs and figures displayed within their frames.

Over the years we have come to speak of Romie as "Bearden" and we recognize him as a great master of collage. Now perhaps we should remind ourselves that we are a *collage of a nation*, and a nation that is ever shifting about and grousing as we seek to achieve the promised design of democracy. Therefore one of the reasons that *we* revere Romie is for his discovery that one of the ways for getting at many of the complex matters which we experience, but seldom find recorded in official history, is through art. Art is the mystery which gets left out of history.

We are thankful to have known him, and to have shared some of his discoveries. Of this we are certain: we shall be discovering more and more about Bearden and his work as we discover more about— and accept the responsibility of confronting—the wonderful complexity of American life.

NOTES FOR
CLASS DAY TALK AT
COLUMBIA UNIVERSITY

*Ellison spoke at Columbia University's Class Day cere-
mony on May 15, 1990. Found in his papers, this fragment, dated May 24, 1990, exemplifies his characteristic
use of Kenneth Burke's "representative anecdote" to illustrate the incongruities and complexity of American life—
in this case an encounter with a young black man wearing
a Confederate Army cap.*

YESTERDAY while I was taking my after-lunch walk, a tall young brown-skinned man strode toward me carrying himself with a proud military bearing subtly combined with a subdued version of Harlem strut. In itself this was not unusual. Traditionally, Afro-Americans have made walking a form of art, as with "Walking the Dog" and "Strutting with some Barbecue," both of which began as playful vernacular struts through which such chores as walking pets and going on errands for food became steps in the stage routines of professional dancers. Symbolic communication through bodily movement is not only traditional but linked to modes of unspoken social commentary, satire, caricature, disavowal, intimidation and one-upmanship. You now see it in basketball, a sport which such young men as the one now approaching me have endowed with touches of ballet and aerial gymnastics.

Therefore as the young man drew closer it wasn't his artful walk that drew my attention. Nor was it the grim set of his features. But when we were face to face and I looked up to see that he was wearing a gray cap which bore the insignia of the Confederate Army, I was flabbergasted. It was as though the most tragic incident in American history had leaped from a New York sidewalk to confound me with a transformation of the color symbolism which had ignited the Civil War.

"So you've joined the Confederacy," I managed to sputter, to which tentative question there was only a grim look of reply.

The young man continued his march and I continued mine, but then I paused, looked back, and there he was, hands on hips, Confederate-capped head thrown back, bubbling with uncontrollable laughter.

I joined in his laughter as I continued my walk, but frankly my head was spinning. While I knew that such caps and insignia were available in novelty stores and had often seen Northern white boys driving cars adorned with the "Stars and Bars," this was the first time ever that I had seen a man of color so adorned. The question of what it all meant—what was comic put-on, what desperate threat—gave a somber note to my laughter. Then as I passed the homeless, the young drug hustlers and addicts who make use of the benches on Riverside Drive, and the lovable nursery school children playing nearby, I thought of the newspaper and television reports of recent developments in racial relations that are taking place in cities and on college campuses, and my mood became grim.

After all, I had been asked here to Columbia to participate in the celebration of this wonderful occasion, this rite of passage, through which you are moving up to find your places in our democratic social hierarchy, and I felt obligated to be as joyful as you yourselves have the right to be. You've earned it, and I hope that your next steps will move each of you always higher and higher toward your envisioned goal. Thus, as I thought of what I might say to you, my mind kept returning to that Confederate cap on the young man's head, and I was startled when my alter ego whispered, "Ellison, the Confederates were also *Americans*, and so, God help him, is he!" With that I recalled that comedy and gallows humor are traditional ways that hard-pressed Americans have used in dealing with the problems of social hierarchy.

Then I recalled Robert Penn Warren's stress upon the Declaration of Independence as the basic script from which the drama of American social hierarchy is enacted. The Declaration is the moral imperative to which all of us, black and white alike, are committed. Though our history is one long list of struggles to make the values of that document manifest in the structure of our society, our history has also been marked by endless attempts to evade our moral commitment to the ideal of social equality. To do violence to Francis Thompson's *The Hound of Heaven:* We've fled it, down the arches of the years; / We've fled it down the labyrinthine ways / Of our own minds; and in the midst of tears / We've hid from it, and under running laughter. / Up vistaed hopes we've sped; / And shot, precipitated, / Adown Titanic glooms of chasméd fears, / From those strong Feet that followed, followed after. / But with unhurrying chase, / And unperturbéd pace, / Deliberate speed, majestic instancy, / They beat—and a Voice beat / More instant than the Feet— / "All things betray thee, who betrayest Me."

FOREWORD TO
THE BEER CAN
BY THE HIGHWAY

*E*llison was long an admirer of John Kouwenhoven's work on the "interaction"—sometimes "in a complex process of antagonistic cooperation"—"between the cultivated and vernacular modes as they find expression in American culture." Written in 1987, this essay was published in 1988 as the foreword to the Johns Hopkins University Press edition of The Beer Can by the Highway.

THERE sits on a glass-topped stainless steel table in our living room a small goblet with slitted sides that swirl upward from its round, pinched shaft to form a bowl that is "bellied," to borrow a figure from T. S. Eliot, "like the fig's fruit." This surprising object was created on a busy downtown New York street by an Afro-American craftsman-vendor out of a Shasta Lemon Lime Soda can. My wife, who had watched its magical creation (during which the craftsman knelt on the sidewalk carrying on an open-ended, P. T. Barnum spiel), was so delighted that she bought it right out of his flickering fingers. When she arrived home all excited and began explaining the origin of her prize I took a look, felt a light bulb glow in my head, and thought to myself, "Well, now, John Kouwenhoven, it's not exactly a *beer* can, but it's more than ample proof that somebody out there is continuing to affirm your insights into the interaction between the cultivated and vernacular modes as they find expression in American culture!"

Of course they are, whether it be our street craftsman, the artists of Pop Art, architects responsible for the rash of skyscrapers that are darkening the streets of New York, the exponents of the latest variant of rock-and-roll, or the designers of automobiles who have found a more functional form for hoods, tops and fenders. And for all the reasons—geographical, political, economic, technological and aesthetic—that Kouwenhoven analyzes in *The Beer Can by the Highway*.

But for the moment let's keep an eye on our gobletized soda can and consider what must have happened before this marvelous product of vernacular prestidigitation became possible: a beverage can worth all of five cents (if returned to a supermarket) was emptied of its bubbly contents and discarded. It doesn't matter whether it was beside a highway or in the aisle of a subway car; the point here is that in the course of its transformation this sibling to a beer can escaped its expected, routine fate of recycling as scrap metal and became instead an *objet trouvé*. Then, as though to challenge our easy definitions of "waste" and "raw material," *high* style and *low*, and propel us back to Kouwenhoven's writings, our can lands in the hands of a "vernacular" craftsman who proceeds (and without attempting to erase any evidence of its past identity as mere container—neither paint, gleam, computerized bar-code, nor lettering) to transform it into a charming classical form.

Here we have a poker-faced American joke in which an object democratically available to even the commonest of common citizens ends up mocking both the elaborate technology and economic motive which gave it birth, while flaunting the impulses, vernacular and classical, that interacted in a complex process of antagonistic cooperation to give it its present shape and setting. In its metamorphosis toward its present form our can progressed, thanks to industrial technology, from a handful of common ore to a mass-produced utilitarian vessel, and then had been transformed by an anonymous craftsman of pluralistic American background and taste into a work of art.

"But wait!" you say. "A can is a can is a can, and as such a form is admirably fitted to an admirable function. But that gaudy, split-sided thing you're describing couldn't contain a bubble of ale or bail the spray from a boat!" Which, if you insist upon looking only for the *old* in the new, is quite true. But while it is evident that our gobletized can is no longer functional as in its old utilitarian state, it has assumed nevertheless a *new* and useful function indeed. For now, as it sits on its Miesian table, not only does it delight its viewers' eyes, but it challenges us to think with playful seriousness about the relationship between America's democratic ideals and its culture. Yes, and about the ways in which those ideals inspirit not only our diverse citizenry, but also even the humblest of products and processes, sports and games, nightmares and dreams. It challenges us to think about such matters as carefully as Kouwenhoven has thought about the *Americanness* of everything that binds us, from our technology-propelled search for national self-consciousness as it is affected by our pervasive self-doubt, to our volatile mixture of vernacular and cultivated taste, to the designs of our skyscrapers, the nature of jazz, comic strips and advertising, to our grids of beer-can-strewn streets and highways.

The Beer Can by the Highway was first published in 1961, and since that time it has been quietly teaching Americans to discern in things both great and small, dignified and pedestrian, that which is essentially "American" about American civilization. It is a work that springs from deep within that rich segment of the American grain which gave us the likes of Emerson, Whitman, Horatio Greenough and Constance Rourke—yes, and Mark Twain—and was written by a critic who has looked long and hard at American culture with that native mixture of comic and tragic vision which is so necessary if we are to make sense of our diverse, pluralistic society. Fortunately Kouwenhoven is a writer who possesses the irreverent eloquence to make us recognize the old in the new and the new that is emergent in old processes and objects, attitudes and customs.

Which is to say that he has an insightful knowledge of history, taste, and design. Thus he is able to make us see the negative in our vaunted positives, and the positives in our downplayed negatives. Best of all, during a period when we are once again evaluating the meaning of the Constitution and assessing the gains and losses of the past two hundred years, he makes us aware of the intricate ways in which our ways of life mesh and/or clash with our democratic ideals. A mixture of scholarly erudition and wry, vernacular perception, *The Beer Can by the Highway* arrives at its larger insights through a careful scrutiny of small facts and processes, thereby making its perceptions democratically available to all readers, whether learned or casual. Since I have long rated it one of the most provocatively American of books, I am not surprised, only delighted, that during these times of crisis, of abundance and famine, of controversy over who shall interpret the Constitution, of stock market dives, startling new technologies, atomic piles, industrial waste and garbage barges making futile trips through international seas in search of a noncontroversial burial site, the voluble *Beer Can* has taken on, like its Shasta cousin, a new and vibrant life.

ADDRESS AT THE
WHITING FOUNDATION

One of Ellison's last public addresses was given at the Whiting Foundation's Writers' Awards Ceremony at the Morgan Library in New York City on October 23, 1992. Once again his theme is the complexity and continuity of American experience, exemplified in this talk by his response to recent research on his grandfather, Big Alfred Ellison, a former slave who never learned to read or write but nevertheless was elected town marshal in Abbeville, South Carolina, during the Reconstruction.

I'м a bit unsure of why I'm up here on this dais, but now that I am we'll get on with it, catch-as-catch-can. Which is to say that finding myself participating in a ceremony during which so many gifted writers are to be presented the Whiting Foundation's prestigious awards is intimidating. For while most writers exercise their craft isolated in shadows, and do so out of their dedication to art, the efforts of tonight's winners are being recognized in public, and that alone endows this occasion with an aura of dreamlike fulfillment.

I'm reminded of something that Robert Penn Warren once wrote about the challenge which the Founding Fathers left future Americans to solve when they committed to paper the democratic ideals upon which this nation was founded. In a sense the Constitution and Bill of Rights made up the acting script which future Americans would follow in the process of improvising the futuristic drama of American democracy. The Founders' dream was a dream of felicity, but those who inherited the task of making it manifest in reality were, alas, only human. Not only do Americans spring from different geographical areas, but they possess—and are possessed by—a variety of conflicting attitudes, personal, social and regional. What's more, since the revolutionary days of its founding, this nation has grown so rapidly and transformed its landmass so chaotically that frequently we don't know where we are or where we're headed. In the course of our recent attempts to make the Founders' dream a reality, the media, especially television, that facile transmitter of composite images, has further increased our confusion—and this despite the fact that it also provides us with copious details from the past that charm, delight and instruct us.

Of such matters we're all aware, but tonight's occasion makes me realize once again how important it is that the United States continues to have writers, such as tonight's winners, who make the most of their personal experience. The Founding Fathers conceived this nation as a collectivity of *individuals* who, ideally, are united in their diversity. We are one and yet many, an ambiguity that involves our personal identities no less than it gives shape to our politics. Thus, given the zigs and zags of our country's development, it is imperative that we keep the responsibility of achieving our individuality always consciously in mind.

Under the pressure of our nation's unresolved issues from the past and the rapidity with which technology is changing the modes of our living, the conflict between our national ideals and everyday reality is constantly increasing in intensity. This combination of forces increases our American tendency toward historical forgetfulness as we move toward and away from our national ideals. Deny it or not, we live simultaneously in the past *and* the present, but all too often while looking to the future to correct our failures, we pretend that the past is no longer with us.

Our national tendency to ignore or forget important details of our past reminds me of the philosophical stance of certain adults with whom I hunted during my boyhood in Oklahoma. After bringing down a rabbit or quail, men would proclaim in voices that throbbed with true American optimism, "A hit, my boy, is history!"

But if they missed and the game got away, they'd stare at the sky or cover and say, "A miss, my boy, is a mystery."

Well, in this country there have been many hits that are now attributed to the success of our democratic ideals. On the other hand, there have been misses in our attempts to achieve our democratic commitments that are so embarrassing that we have a tendency to assign our failures to the world of mystery.

Actually such failures spring from our confusions of motive and misguided efforts, which too often we try to sweep under the rug instead of addressing their consequences forthrightly. This, I think, is one of the implicit functions of American writers. Whether they be poets or novelists, essayists or dramatists, they are challenged to take individual responsibility for the health of American democracy. It is their role to transform the misses of history into hits of imaginative symbolic action that aid their readers in reclaiming details of the past that find meaning in the experience of individuals.

At any rate, such ideas came to mind recently when I began reading a book which its author was kind enough to send me. This book, titled *Old Abbeville: Scenes of the Past of a Town Where "Old Time Things Are Not Forgotten,"* is a history of old Abbeville, South Carolina, which you might recall as the birthplace of the national conflict over slavery, the war which is known in the South as the War Between the States. It was also the home of John C. Calhoun and General Sam McGowan, one of General Robert E. Lee's lieutenants and later the chief justice of South Carolina. The author of *Old Abbeville* is Professor Lowry Ware, a historian emeritus of South Carolina's Erskine College.

Somehow in poking into the mysteries of his native state's history, Professor Ware discovered that I too sprang from South Carolina via my father, who was born and grew up in old Abbeville. In his scholarly research Professor Ware came across information about my grandfather that I found so unexpected that I erupted with laughter. While I had met my grandfather during the fourth year of my life, I had known him best as a mute patriarchal figure who stared from the wall in an old photograph. But now he had been brought so vividly to life in printed words on a page that I felt I'd been given a view of the mystery surrounding my roots.

Even more startling was the fact that the book had been written by a white South Carolinian. Thus I discovered a thread of my parental background snarled in the national tragedy which came close to destroying this nation but which left it drawn closer, if most contentiously, together. My reaction at finding my personal connection with slavery and emancipation stated in words was such a mixture of tragedy and comedy that it filled me with a blueslike laughter which caused my wife to ask what had come over me.

What had come over me was Professor Ware's research into my

grandfather's activities during the Reconstruction. My laughter was ignited by learning that the man I knew as Grandpa was known in the town and surroundings as "Big" Alfred Ellison. Professor Ware then revealed that my grandfather had been a slave of the Reverend M. A. Ellison, who was pastor of the First Presbyterian Church, and that my grandfather and his brother, William Ellison, "became freedmen in Abbeville in 1865." According to Professor Ware, "the latter was, or soon became, educated and he served as a school-teacher during the Reconstruction and later. Alfred never learned to read or write, but his strength of body and character led to his appointment as town marshal in the spring of 1871 and enabled him to keep that position for most of the next seven years."

The Press and Banner, a local newspaper, "often made favorable comments on [Big Alfred's] services to the town. For example, on January 3, 1872, it noted, 'The peace of the village and the harmony of Christmas week were broken by two shooting scrapes. . . . John McCord, who had been arrested by Alfred Ellison, the town marshal, resisted the officer and discharged his pistol without effect, however, upon the marshal, who knocked him down, giving him a serious blow.'

"On August 5, 1873, [*The Press and Banner*] reported on an altercation between Arthur Jefferson, a black county commissioner, and the marshal, when the former was 'using a few more expletives than the marshal thought proper. Ellison, who is a powerful man, immediately disarmed Jefferson and threw him down, without any particular regard as to which part struck the floor first. . . . Alfred is usually able to take care of himself.'

"*The Press and Banner* on September 20, 1876, following a town election in which the white Democrats regained control of the local government, declared 'the election of the town marshal takes place on next Monday. We think justice and our best interests as a town demand that a coloured man get the place.' A week later, it reported that Alfred Ellison was re-elected."

Ladies and gentlemen and my fellow followers of the writer's trade, I hope that what I've read from *Old Abbeville* has given you an idea of the living texture of human relationships that existed in the South during that turbulent phase of our history, and a better sense of the humanity of ex-slaves like my grandfather and his brother William. To that end I'll bring this closer to our own times by reading the following:

> In later years, Alfred Ellison took part in local Republican meetings, and in 1895 he testified before a Congressional Investigating Committee which was concerned with alleged irregularities in the election between Republican Robert Moorman and A. C. Latimer, Democrat. [Sounds like today!] Cross-examined by Coleman L. Blease, Latimer's attorney and later governor of South Carolina, Ellison's testimony in part was: "Abbeville is my precinct. Been here nearly all my life. I voted. I registered. I had trouble in registering. I applied on the first Monday in April, but got one in May by paying 25 cents for an affidavit. I got the registration ticket but had to wait, on account of the Supervisor of Registration not doing his duty. . . . He waited on ten white men and more, and I standing there holding my affidavit ready for him to register me. I was there between five and six hours, waiting. . . . No trouble for white men to get registration tickets. Colored men had trouble. . . . I voted for General Hampton in 1876, but I am not a Democrat."

The point that Big Alfred's grandson makes of all this is that the past still lives within each of us and repeats itself with variations. Looking back, you feel the pain we'd like to forget because of its tragedy, but if we're to survive and get on with the task of making sense of American experience, we'll view it through the wry perspective of sanity-saving comedy. Incidentally, Professor Ware's research reveals that there are still existing records of more socializing between the white slave owners, freemen and slaves than even Faulkner has told us about, and I don't mean merely in the dark.

There also were interracial parties that became the source of recriminations aired during political elections, which is another example of the mixture of past and present.

I'll close by reminding my fellow writers, as I frequently remind myself, that you're doing far more than creating interesting tales based on your individual view of the American experience. Underneath your efforts you're helping this country discover a fuller sense of itself as it goes about making its founders' dream a reality.

A NOTE ON THE TYPE

The principal text of this Modern Library edition
was set in a digitized version of Janson, a typeface that
dates from about 1690 and was cut by Nicholas Kis,
a Hungarian working in Amsterdam. The original matrices
have survived and are held by the Stempel foundry in Germany.
Hermann Zapf redesigned some of the weights and sizes for
Stempel, basing his revisions on the original design.

THE LIFE

OF

WILLIAM EWART GLADSTONE

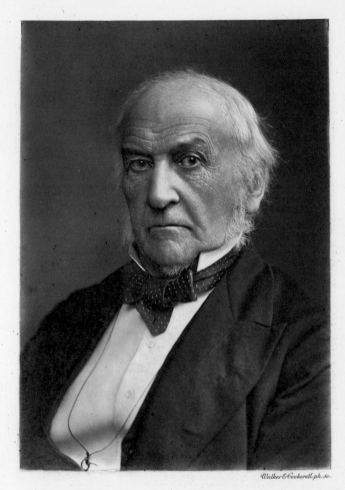

William Ewart Gladstone
from a photograph by The London Stereoscopic Company.

THE LIFE OF

WILLIAM EWART

GLADSTONE

BY

JOHN MORLEY

IN THREE VOLUMES — VOL. III

(1880–1898)

TORONTO

MORANG & CO., LIMITED

PUBLISHERS

CONTENTS

BOOK VIII

(1880-1885)

BOOK IX

(1885-1886)

BOOK X

(1886–1898)

LIST OF ILLUSTRATIONS

ERRATA

𝕭𝖔𝖔𝖐 𝖁𝕴𝕴𝕴

1880–1885

CHAPTER I

OPENING DAYS OF THE NEW PARLIAMENT

(1880)

IL y a bien du factice dans le classement politique des hommes.
— GUIZOT.

There is plenty of what is purely artificial in the political classification of men.

ON May 20, after eight-and-forty years of strenuous public life, Mr. Gladstone met his twelfth parliament, and the second in which he had been chief minister of the crown. 'At 4.15,' he records, 'I went down to the House with Herbert. There was a great and fervent crowd in Palace Yard, and much feeling in the House. It almost overpowered me, as I thought by what deep and hidden agencies I have been brought back into the midst of the vortex of political action and contention. It has not been in my power during these last six months to have made notes, as I would have wished, of my own thoughts and observations from time to time; of the new access of strength which in some important respects has been administered to me in my old age; and of the remarkable manner in which Holy Scripture has been applied to me for admonition and for comfort. Looking calmly on this course of experience, I do believe that the Almighty has employed me for His purposes in a manner larger or more special than before, and has strengthened me and led me on accordingly, though I must not forget the admirable saying of Hooker, that even ministers of good things are like torches, a light to others, waste and destruction to themselves.'

One who approached his task in such a spirit as this was at least impregnable to ordinary mortifications, and it was well; for before many days were over it became perceptible that the new parliament and the new majority would be no docile instrument of ministerial will.   An acute chill followed the discovery that there was to be no recall of Frere or Layard. Very early in its history Speaker Brand, surveying his flock from the august altitude of the Chair with an acute, experienced, and friendly eye, made up his mind that the liberal party were 'not only strong, but determined to have their own way in spite of Mr. Gladstone.   He has a difficult team to drive.'   Two men of striking character on the benches opposite quickly became formidable.   Lord Randolph Churchill headed a little group of four tories, and Mr. Parnell a resolute band of five and thirty Irishmen, with momentous results both for ministers and for the House of Commons.

No more capable set of ruling men were ever got together than the cabinet of 1880 ; no men who better represented the leading elements in the country, in all their variety and strength.   The great possessors of land were there, and the heirs of long governing tradition were there; the industrious and the sedate of the middle classes found their men seated at the council board, by the side of others whose keen-sighted ambition sought sources of power in the ranks of manual toil; the church saw one of the most ardent of her sons upon the woolsack, and the most illustrious of them in the highest place of all; the people of the chapel beheld with complacency the rising man of the future in one who publicly boasted an unbroken line of nonconformist descent.   They were all men well trained in the habits of business, of large affairs, and in experience of English life ; they were all in spite of difference of shade genuinely liberal; and they all professed a devoted loyalty to their chief.   The incident of the resolutions on the eastern question [1] was effaced from all

[1] Above, vol. ii. pp. 563-8.

memories, and men who in those days had assured themselves that there was no return from Elba, became faithful marshals of the conquering hero. Mediocrity in a long-lived cabinet in the earlier part of the century was the object of Disraeli's keenest mockery. Still a slight ballast of mediocrity in a government steadies the ship and makes for unity — a truth, by the way, that Mr. Disraeli himself, in forming governments, sometimes conspicuously put in practice.

In fact Mr. Gladstone found that the ministry of which he stood at the head was a coalition, and what was more, a coalition of that vexatious kind, where those who happened not to agree sometimes seemed to be almost as well pleased with contention as with harmony. The two sections were not always divided by differences of class or station, for some of the peers in the cabinet often showed as bold a liberalism as any of the commoners. This notwithstanding, it happened on more than one critical occasion, that all the peers *plus* Lord Hartington were on one side, and all the commoners on the other. Lord Hartington was in many respects the lineal successor of Palmerston in his coolness on parliamentary reform, in his inclination to stand in the old ways, in his extreme suspicion of what savoured of sentiment or idealism or high-flown profession. But he was a Palmerston who respected Mr. Gladstone, and desired to work faithfully under him, instead of being a Palmerston who always intended to keep the upper hand of him. Confronting Lord Hartington was Mr. Chamberlain, eager, intrepid, self-reliant, alert, daring, with notions about property, taxation, land, schools, popular rights, that he expressed with a plainness and pungency of speech that had never been heard from a privy councillor and cabinet minister before, that exasperated opponents, startled the whigs, and brought him hosts of adherents among radicals out of doors. It was at a very early stage in the existence of the government, that this important man said to an ally in the cabinet, 'I don't see how we are to get on, if Mr. Gladstone goes.' And here was the key to many leading incidents, both during the life of this administration and for the eventful year in Mr. Gladstone's career that followed its demise.

The Duke of Argyll, who resigned very early, wrote to Mr. Gladstone after the government was overthrown (Dec. 18, 1885), urging him in effect to side definitely with the whigs against the radicals : —

From the moment our government was fairly under way, I saw and felt that speeches *outside* were allowed to affect opinion, and politically to commit the cabinet in a direction which was not determined by you deliberately, or by the government as a whole, but by the audacity . . . of our new associates. Month by month I became more and more uncomfortable, feeling that there was no paramount direction — nothing but *slip* and *slide*, what the Scotch call ' slithering.' The outside world, knowing your great gifts and powers, assume that you are dictator in your own cabinet. And in one sense you are so, that is to say, that when you choose to put your foot down, others will give way. But your amiability to colleagues, your even extreme gentleness towards them, whilst it has always endeared you to them personally, has enabled men playing their own game . . . to take out of your hands the *formation* of opinion.

On a connected aspect of the same thing, Mr. Gladstone wrote to Lord Rosebery (Sept. 16, 1880) : —

. . . All this is too long to bore people with — and yet it is not so long, nor so interesting, as one at least of the subjects which we just touched in conversation at Mentmore ; the future of politics, and the food they offer to the mind. What is outside parliament seems to me to be fast mounting, nay to have already mounted, to an importance much exceeding what is inside. Parliament deals with laws, and branches of the social tree, not with the root. I always admired Mrs. Grote's saying that politics and theology were the only two really great subjects ; it was wonderful considering the atmosphere in which she had lived. I do not doubt which of the two she would have put in the first place ; and to theology I have no doubt she would have given a wide sense, as including everything that touches the relation between the seen and the unseen.

What is curious to note is that, though Mr. Gladstone in making his cabinet had thrown the main weight against the radicals, yet when they got to work, it was with them he found himself more often than not in energetic agreement. In common talk and in partisan speeches, the prime minister was regarded as dictatorial and imperious. The complaint of some at least among his colleagues in the cabinet of 1880 was rather that he was not imperious enough. Almost from the first he too frequently allowed himself to be over-ruled; often in secondary matters, it is true, but sometimes also in matters on the uncertain frontier between secondary and primary. Then he adopted a practice of taking votes and counting numbers, of which more than one old hand complained as an innovation. Lord Granville said to him in 1886, 'I think you too often counted noses in your last cabinet.'

What Mr. Gladstone described as the severest fight that he had ever known in any cabinet occurred in 1883, upon the removal of the Duke of Wellington's statue from Hyde Park Corner. A vote took place, and three times over he took down the names. He was against removal, but was unable to have his own way over the majority. Members of the government thought themselves curiously free to walk out from divisions. On a Transvaal division two members of the cabinet abstained, and so did two other ministers out of the cabinet. In other cases, the same thing happened, not only breaking discipline, but breeding much trouble with the Queen. Then an unusual number of men of ability and of a degree of self-esteem not below their ability, had been left out of the inner circle; and they and their backers were sometimes apt to bring their pretensions rather fretfully forward. These were the things that to Mr. Gladstone's temperament proved more harassing than graver concerns.

II

All through the first two months of its business, the House showed signs of independence that almost broke the spirit of the ministerial whips. A bill about hares and rabbits produced lively excitement, ministerialists moved amendments upon the measure of their own leaders, and the minister in charge boldly taxed the mutineers with insincerity. A motion for local option was carried by 229 to 203, both Mr. Gladstone and Lord Hartington in the minority. On a motion about clerical restrictions, only a strong and conciliatory appeal from the prime minister averted defeat. A more remarkable demonstration soon followed. The Prince Imperial, unfortunate son of unfortunate sire, who had undergone his famous baptism of fire in the first reverses among the Vosges in the Franco-German war of 1870, was killed in our war in Zululand. Parliament was asked to sanction a vote of money for a memorial of him in the Abbey. A radical member brought forward a motion against it. Both Mr. Gladstone and Sir Stafford Northcote resisted him, yet by a considerable majority the radical carried his point. The feeling was so strong among the ministerialists, that notwithstanding Mr. Gladstone's earnest exhortation, they voted almost to a man against him, and he only carried into the lobby ten official votes on the treasury bench.

The great case in which the government were taken to have missed the import of the election was the failure to recall Sir Bartle Frere from South Africa. Of this I shall have enough to say by and by. Meanwhile it gave an undoubted shock to the confidence of the party, and their energetic remonstrance on this head strained Mr. Gladstone's authority to the uttermost. The Queen complained of the tendency of the House of Commons to trench upon the business of the executive. Mr. Gladstone said in reply generally, that no doubt within the half century 'there had been considerable invasion by the House of Commons of the province assigned by the constitution to the executive,' but he perceived no increase in recent times or in the present House. Then he proceeded (June 8, 1880) : —

. . . Your Majesty may possibly have in view the pressure which has been exercised on the present government in the case of Sir Bartle Frere. But apart from the fact that this pressure represents a feeling which extends far beyond the walls of parliament, your Majesty may probably remember that, in the early part of 1835, the House of Commons addressed the crown against the appointment of Lord Londonderry to be ambassador at St. Petersburg, on

account, if Mr. Gladstone remembers rightly, of a general ante-
cedent disapproval. This was an exercise of power going far
beyond what has happened now; nor does it seem easy in
principle to place the conduct of Sir B. Frere beyond that general
right of challenge and censure which is unquestionably within the
function of parliament and especially of the House of Commons.

In the field where mastery had never failed him, Mr. Gladstone achieved an early success, and he lost no time in justifying his assumption of the exchequer. The budget (June
10) was marked by the boldness of former days, and was
explained and defended in one of those statements of which
he alone possessed the secret. Even unfriendly witnesses
agreed that it was many years since the House of Commons
had the opportunity of enjoying so extraordinary an intellectual treat, where 'novelties assumed the air of indisputable
truths, and complicated figures were woven into the thread
of intelligible and animated narrative.' He converted the
malt tax into a beer duty, reduced the duties on light
foreign wines, added a penny to the income tax, and adjusted
the licence duties for the sale of alcoholic liquors. Everybody said that 'none but a *cordon bleu* could have made
such a sauce with so few materials.' The dish was excellently received, and the ministerial party were in high
spirits. The conservatives stood angry and amazed that
their own leaders had found no device for the repeal of
the malt duty. The farmer's friends, they cried, had been
in office for six years and had done nothing ; no sooner
is Gladstone at the exchequer than with magic wand he
effects a transformation, and the long-suffering agriculturist
has justice and relief.

In the course of an effort that seemed to show full vigour
of body and mind, Mr. Gladstone incidentally mentioned that
when a new member he recollected hearing a speech upon the
malt tax in the old House of Commons in the year 1833. Yet
the lapse of nearly half a century of life in that great arena
had not relaxed his stringent sense of parliamentary duty.
During most of the course of this first session, he was always
early in his place and always left late. In every discussion

he came to the front, and though an under-secretary made
the official reply, it was the prime minister who wound up.
One night he made no fewer than six speeches, touching all
the questions raised in a miscellaneous night's sitting.

In the middle of the summer Mr. Gladstone fell ill.
Consternation reigned in London. It even exceeded the
dismay caused by the defeat at Maiwand. A friend went to
see him as he lay in bed. 'He talked most of the time, not
on politics, but on Shakespeare's Henry VIII., and the decay
of theological study at Oxford. He never intended his
reform measure to produce this result.' After his recovery,
he went for a cruise in the *Grantully Castle*, not returning
to parliament until September 4, three days before the
session ended, when he spoke with all his force on the
eastern question.

III

In the electoral campaign Mr. Gladstone had used expressions about Austria that gave some offence at Vienna. On
coming into power he volunteered an assurance to the
Austrian ambassador that he would willingly withdraw his
language if he understood that he had misapprehended the
circumstances. The ambassador said that Austria meant
strictly to observe the treaty of Berlin. Mr. Gladstone then
expressed his regret for the words 'of a painful and wounding
character' that had fallen from him. At the time, he explained, he was 'in a position of greater freedom and less
responsibility.'

At the close of the session of 1880, ministers went to work
upon the unfulfilled portions of the Berlin treaty relating to
Greece and Montenegro. Those stipulations were positive in
the case of Montenegro; as to Greece they were less definite,
but they absolutely implied a cession of more or less territory
by Turkey. They formed the basis of Lord Salisbury's correspondence, but his arguments and representations were
without effect.

Mr. Gladstone and his colleagues went further. They proposed and obtained a demonstration off the Albanian coast
on behalf of Montenegro. Each great Power sent a man-
of-war, but the concert of Europe instantly became what

Mr. Gladstone called a farce, for Austria and Germany made known that under no circumstances would they fire a shot. France rather less prominently took the same course. This defection, which was almost boastful on the part of Austria and Germany, convinced the British cabinet that Turkish obduracy would only be overcome by force, and the question was how to apply force effectually with the least risk to peace. As it happened, the port of Smyrna received an amount of customs' duties too considerable for the Porte to spare it. The idea was that the united fleet at Cattaro should straightway sail to Smyrna and lay hold upon it. The cabinet, with experts from the two fighting departments, weighed carefully all the military responsibilities, and considered the sequestration of the customs' dues at Smyrna to be practicable. Russia and Italy were friendly. France had in a certain way assumed special cognisance of the Greek case, but did nothing particular. From Austria and Germany nothing was to be hoped. On October 4, the Sultan refused the joint European request for the fulfilment of the engagements entered into at Berlin. This refusal was despatched in ignorance of the intention to coerce. The British government had only resolved upon coercion in concert with Europe. Full concert was now out of the question. But on the morning of Sunday, the 10th, Mr. Gladstone and Lord Granville learned with as much surprise as delight from Mr. Goschen, then ambassador extraordinary at Constantinople, that the Sultan had heard of the British proposal of force, and apparently had not heard of the two refusals. On learning how far England had gone, he determined to give way on both the territorial questions. As Mr. Gladstone enters in his diary, 'a faint tinge of doubt remained.' That is to say, the Sultan might find out the rift in the concert and retract. Russia, however, had actually agreed to force. On Tuesday, the 12th, Mr. Gladstone, meeting Lord Granville and another colleague, was 'under the circumstances prepared to proceed *en trois*.' The other two 'rather differed.' Of course it would have been for the whole cabinet to decide. But between eleven and twelve Lord Granville came in with the news that the note had arrived and all was well. 'The whole of this extraordinary volte-face,' as Mr. Gladstone said with some complacency, 'had been effected within six days; and it was entirely due not to a threat of coercion from Europe, but to the knowledge that Great Britain had asked Europe to coerce.' Dulcigno was ceded by the Porte to Montenegro. On the Greek side of the case, the minister for once was less ardent than for the complete triumph of his heroic Montenegrins, but after tedious negotiations Mr. Gladstone had the satisfaction of seeing an important rectification of the Greek frontier, almost restoring his Homeric Greece. The eastern question looked as if it might fall into one of its fitful slumbers once more, but we shall soon see that this was illusory. Mr. Goschen left Constantinople in May, and the prime minister said to him (June 3, 1881) : —

I write principally for the purpose of offering you my hearty congratulations on the place you have taken in diplomacy by force of mind and character, and on the services which, in thus far serving the most honourable aims a man can have, you have rendered to liberty and humanity.

Only in Afghanistan was there a direct reversal of the policy of the fallen government. The new cabinet were not long in deciding on a return to the older policy in respect of the north-west frontier of India. All that had happened since it had been abandoned, strengthened the case against the new departure. The policy that had been pursued amid so many lamentable and untoward circumstances, including the destruction of a very gallant agent of England at Cabul, had involved the incorporation of Candahar within the sphere of the Indian system. Mr. Gladstone and his cabinet determined on the evacuation of Candahar. The decision was made public in the royal speech of the following January (1881). Lord Hartington stated the case of the government with masterly and crushing force, in a speech,[1] which is no less than a strong text-book of the whole argument, if any reader should now desire to comprehend it. The evacuation was censured in the Lords by 165 against 79 ; in the Commons ministers carried the day by a majority of 120.

[1] March 25–6, 1881.

CHAPTER II

AN EPISODE IN TOLERATION

(*1880–1883*)

> THE state, in choosing men to serve it, takes no notice of their
> opinions; if they be willing faithfully to serve it, that satisfies.
> . . . Take heed of being sharp, or too easily sharpened by others,
> against those to whom you can object little but that they square
> not with you in every opinion concerning matters of religion.
>
> —OLIVER CROMWELL.

ONE discordant refrain rang hoarsely throughout the five
years of this administration, and its first notes were heard
even before Mr. Gladstone had taken his seat. It drew him
into a controversy that was probably more distasteful to him
than any other of the myriad contentions, small and great,
with which his life was encumbered. Whether or not he
threaded his way with his usual skill through a labyrinth
of parliamentary tactics incomparably intricate, experts may
dispute, but in an ordeal beyond the region of tactics he
never swerved from the path alike of liberty and common-
sense. It was a question of exacting the oath of allegiance
before a member could take his seat.

Mr. Bradlaugh, the new member for Northampton, who
now forced the question forward, as O'Connell had forced
forward the civil equality of catholics, and Rothschild and
others the civil equality of Jews, was a free-thinker of a
daring and defiant type. Blank negation could go no
further. He had abundant and genuine public spirit, and a
strong love of truth according to his own lights, and he
was both a brave and a disinterested man. This hard-grit
secularism of his was not the worst of his offences in the
view of the new majority and their constituents. He had
published an impeachment of the House of Brunswick,

11

which few members of parliament had ever heard of or looked at. But even abstract republicanism was not the worst. What placed him at extreme disadvantage in fighting the battle in which he was now engaged, was his republication of a pamphlet by an American doctor on that impracticable question of population, which though too rigorously excluded from public discussion, confessedly lies among the roots of most other social questions. For this he had some years before been indicted in the courts, and had only escaped conviction and punishment by a technicality. It was Mr. Bradlaugh's refusal to take the oath in a court of justice that led to the law of 1869, enabling a witness to affirm instead of swearing. He now carried the principle a step further.

When the time came, the Speaker (April 29) received a letter from the iconoclast, claiming to make an affirmation, instead of taking the oath of allegiance.[1] He consulted his legal advisers, and they gave an opinion strongly adverse to the claim. On this the Speaker wrote to Mr. Gladstone and to Sir Stafford Northcote, stating his concurrence in the opinion of the lawyers, and telling them that he should leave the question to the House. His practical suggestion was that on his statement being made, a motion should be proposed for a select committee. The committee was duly appointed, and it reported by a majority of one, against a minority that contained names so weighty as Sir Henry James, Herschell, Whitbread, and Bright, that the claim to affirm was not a good claim. So opened a series of incidents that went on as long as the parliament, clouded the radiance of the party triumph, threw the new government at once into a minority, dimmed the ascendency of the great minister, and what was more, showed human nature at its worst. The incidents themselves are in detail not worth recalling here, but they are a striking episode in the history of toleration, as well as a landmark in Mr. Gladstone's journey from the day five-and-forty years before when, in

[1] Bradlaugh, who was a little vain of his legal skill, founded this claim upon the Evidence Amendment Act, taken in connection with the Parliamentary Oaths and other Acts.

reference to Molesworth as candidate for Leeds, he had told
his friends at Newark that men who had no belief in divine
revelation were not the men to govern this nation whether
they be whigs or radicals.[1]

His claim to affirm having been rejected, Bradlaugh next
desired to swear. The ministerial whip reported that the
feeling against him in the House was uncontrollable. The
Speaker held a council in his library with Mr. Gladstone,
the law officers, the whip, and two or three other persons of
authority and sense. He told them that if Bradlaugh had
in the first instance come to take the oath, he should have
allowed no intervention, but that the case was altered by the
claimant's open declaration that an oath was not binding on
his conscience. A hostile motion was expected when Bradlaugh came to the table to be sworn, and the Speaker
suggested that it should be met by the previous question, to
be moved by Mr. Gladstone. Then the whip broke in with
the assurance that the usual supporters of the government
could not be relied upon. The Speaker went upstairs to
dress, and on his return found that they had agreed on
moving another select committee. He told them that he
thought this a weak course, but if the previous question
would be defeated, perhaps a committee could not be helped.
Bradlaugh came to the table, and the hostile motion was
made. Mr. Gladstone proposed his committee, and carried it
by a good majority against the motion that Bradlaugh, being
without religious belief, could not take an oath. The debate
was warm, and the attacks on Bradlaugh were often gross.
The Speaker honourably pointed out that such attacks on
an elected member whose absence was enforced by their own
order, were unfair and unbecoming, but the feelings of the
House were too strong for him and too strong for chivalry.
The opposition turned affairs to ignoble party account, and
were not ashamed in their prints and elsewhere to level the
charge of 'open patronage of unbelief and Malthusianism,
Bradlaugh and Blasphemy,' against a government that
contained Gladstone, Bright, and Selborne, three of the most
conspicuously devout men to be found in all England. One

[1] See vol. i. p. 138.

expression of faith used by a leader in the attack on Bradlaugh lived in Mr. Gladstone's memory to the end of his
days. 'You know, Mr. Speaker,' cried the champion of
orthodox creeds, 'we all of us believe in a God of some sort
or another.' That a man should consent to clothe the naked
human soul in this truly singular and scanty remnant of
spiritual apparel, was held to be the unalterable condition
of fitness for a seat in parliament and the company of
decent people. Well might Mr. Gladstone point out how
vast a disparagement of Christianity, and of orthodox theism
also, was here involved : —

They say this, that you may go any length you please in the
denial of religion, provided only you do not reject the name of the
Deity. They tear religion into shreds, so to speak, and say that
there is one particular shred with which nothing will ever induce
them to part. They divide religion into the dispensable and the
indispensable, and among that kind which can be dispensed with —
I am not now speaking of those who declare, or are admitted,
under a special law, I am not speaking of Jews or those who make
a declaration, I am speaking solely of those for whom no provision
is made except the provision of oath — they divide, I say, religion
into what can and what cannot be dispensed with. There is something, however, that cannot be dispensed with. I am not willing,
Sir, that Christianity, if the appeal is made to us as a Christian
legislature, shall stand in any rank lower than that which is indispensable. I may illustrate what I mean. Suppose a commander
has to despatch a small body of men on an expedition on which it
is necessary for them to carry on their backs all that they can take
with them ; the men will part with everything that is unnecessary,
and take only that which is essential. That is the course you
ask us to take in drawing us upon theological ground ; you require
us to distinguish between superfluities and necessaries, and you
tell us that Christianity is one of the superfluities, one of the
excrescences, and has nothing to do with the vital substance, the
name of the Deity, which is indispensable. I say that the adoption of such a proposition as that, which is in reality at the very
root of your contention, is disparaging in the very highest degree
to the Christian faith. . . .[1]

[1] Speech on second reading of Affirmation bill, 1883.

Even viewed as a theistic test, he contended, this oath embraced no acknowledgment of Providence, of divine government, of responsibility, or retribution ; it involved nothing but a bare and abstract admission, a form void of all practical meaning and concern.

The House, however, speedily showed how inaccessible were most of its members to reason and argument of this kind or any kind. On June 21, Mr. Gladstone thus described the proceedings to the Queen. 'With the renewal of the discussion,' he wrote, 'the temper of the House does not improve, both excitement and suspicion appearing to prevail in different quarters.' A motion made by Mr. Bradlaugh's colleague that he should be permitted to affirm, was met by a motion that he should not be allowed either to affirm or to swear.

To the Queen.

Many warm speeches were made by the opposition in the name of religion ; to those Mr. Bright has warmly replied in the name of religious liberty. The contention on the other side really is that as to a certain ill-defined fragment of truth the House is still, under the Oaths Act, the guardian of religion. The primary question, whether the House has jurisdiction under the statute, is almost hopelessly mixed with the question whether an atheist, who has declared himself an atheist, ought to sit in parliament. Mr. Gladstone's own view is that the House has no jurisdiction for the purpose of excluding any one willing to qualify when he has been duly elected ; but he is very uncertain how the House will vote or what will be the end of the business, if the House undertakes the business of exclusion.

June 22. — The House of Commons has been occupied from the commencement of the evening until a late hour with the adjourned debate on the case of Mr. Bradlaugh. The divided state of opinion in the House made itself manifest throughout the evening. Mr. Newdegate made a speech which turned almost wholly upon the respective merits of theism and atheism. Mr. Gladstone thought it his duty to advise the House to beware of entangling itself in difficulties possibly of a serious character, by assuming a jurisdiction in cases of this class.

At one o'clock in the morning, the first great division was taken, and the House resolved by 275 votes against 230 that Mr. Bradlaugh should neither affirm nor swear. The excitement at this result was tremendous. Some minutes elapsed before the Speaker could declare the numbers. 'Indeed,' wrote Mr. Gladstone to the Queen, 'it was an ecstatic transport, and exceeded anything which Mr. Gladstone remembers to have witnesed. He read in it only a witness to the dangers of the course on which the House has entered, and to its unfitness for the office which it has rashly chosen to assume.' He might also have read in it, if he had liked, the exquisite delight of the first stroke of revenge for Midlothian.

The next day (June 23) the matter entered on a more violent phase.

To the Queen.

This day, when the Speaker took the chair at a quarter past twelve, Mr. Bradlaugh came to the table and claimed to take the oath. The Speaker read to him the resolution of the House which forbids it. Mr. Bradlaugh asked to be heard, and no objection was taken. He then addressed the House from the bar. His address was that of a consummate speaker. But it was an address which could not have any effect unless the House had undergone a complete revolution of mind. He challenged the legality of the act of the House, expressing hereby an opinion in which Mr. Gladstone himself, going beyond some other members of the minority, has the misfortune to lean towards agreeing with him. . . . The Speaker now again announced to Mr. Bradlaugh the resolution of the House. Only a small minority voted against enforcing it. Mr. Bradlaugh declining to withdraw, was removed by the serjeant-at-arms. Having suffered this removal, he again came beyond the bar, and entered into what was almost a corporal struggle with the serjeant. Hereupon Sir S. Northcote moved that Mr. Bradlaugh be committed for his offence. Mr. Gladstone said that while he thought it did not belong to him, under the circumstances of the case, to advise the House, he could take no objection to the advice thus given.

The Speaker, it may be said, thought this view of

Mr. Gladstone's a mistake, and that when Bradlaugh refused to withdraw, the leader of the House ought, as a matter of policy, to have been the person to move first the order to withdraw, next the committal to the custody of the serjeant-at-arms. 'I was placed in a false position,' says the Speaker, 'and so was the House, in having to follow the lead of the leader of the opposition, while the leader of the House and the great majority were passive spectators.'[1] As Mr. Gladstone and other members of the government voted for Bradlaugh's committal, on the ground that his resistance to the serjeant had nothing to do with the establishment of his rights before either a court or his constituency, it would seem that the Speaker's complaint is not unjust. To this position, however, Mr. Gladstone adhered, in entire conformity apparently to the wishes of the keenest members of his cabinet and the leading men of his party.

The Speaker wrote to Sir Stafford Northcote urging on him the propriety of allowing Bradlaugh to take the oath without question. But Northcote was forced on against his better judgment by his more ardent supporters. It was a strange and painful situation, and the party system assuredly did not work at its best — one leading man forced on to mischief by the least responsible of his sections, the other held back from providing a cure by the narrowest of the other sections. In the April of 1881 Mr. Gladstone gave notice of a bill providing for affirmation, but it was immediately apparent that the opposition would make the most of every obstacle to a settlement, and the proposal fell through. In August of this year the Speaker notes, 'The difficulties in the way of settling this question satisfactorily are great, and in the present temper of the House almost insuperable.'

II

It is not necessary to recount all the stages of this protracted struggle : what devices and expedients and motions, how many odious scenes of physical violence, how many hard-fought actions in the lawcourts, how many conflicts

[1] *Lord Hampden's Diaries.*

between the House of Commons and the constituency, what glee and rubbing of hands in the camp of the opposition at having thrust their rivals deep into a quagmire so unpleasant. The scandal was intolerable, but ministers were helpless, as a marked incident now demonstrated. It was not until 1883 that a serious attempt was made to change the law. The Affirmation bill of that year has a biographic place, because it marks in a definite way how far Mr. Gladstone's mind — perhaps not, as I have said before, by nature or by instinct peculiarly tolerant — had travelled along one of the grand highroads of human progress. The occasion was for many reasons one of great anxiety. Here are one or two short entries, the reader remembering that by this time the question was two years old : —

April 24, *Tuesday.* — On Sunday night a gap of three hours in my sleep was rather ominous; but it was not repeated. . . . Saw the Archbishop of Canterbury, with whom I had a very long conversation on the Affirmation bill and on *Church and State.* Policy generally as well as on special subjects. . . . Globe Theatre in the evening; excellent acting. . . . 25. . . . Worked on Oaths question. . . . 26. . . . Made a long and *begeistert*[1] speech on the Affirmation bill, taking the bull by the horns.

His speech upon this measure was a noble effort. It was delivered under circumstances of unsurpassed difficulty, for there was revolt in the party, the client was repugnant, the opinions brought into issue were to Mr. Gladstone hateful. Yet the speech proved one of his greatest. Imposing, lofty, persuasive, sage it would have been, from whatever lips it might have fallen; it was signal indeed as coming from one so fervid, so definite, so unfaltering in a faith of his own, one who had started from the opposite pole to that great civil principle of which he now displayed a grasp invincible. If it be true of a writer that the best style is that which most directly flows from living qualities in the writer's own mind and is a pattern of their actual working, so is the same thing to be said of oratory. These high themes of Faith, on the one hand, and Freedom on the

---

[1] Perhaps the best equivalent for *begeistert* here is ' *daemonic.* '

other, exactly fitted the range of the thoughts in which Mr.
Gladstone habitually lived. ' I have no fear of Atheism in
this House,' he said ; ' Truth is the expression of the Divine
mind, and however little our feeble vision may be able to
discern the means by which God may provide for its preservation, we may leave the matter in His hands, and we may
be sure that a firm and courageous application of every
principle of equity and of justice is the best method we can
adopt for the preservation and influence of Truth.' This
was Mr. Gladstone at his sincerest and his highest. I
wonder, too, if there has been a leader in parliament
since the seventeenth century, who could venture to address it in the strain of the memorable passage now to be
transcribed : —

You draw your line at the point where the abstract denial of
God is severed from the abstract admission of the Deity. My proposition is that the line thus drawn is worthless, and that much on
your side of the line is as objectionable as the atheism on the other.
If you call upon us to make distinctions, let them at least be
rational ; I do not say let them be Christian distinctions, but let
them be rational. I can understand one rational distinction, that
you should frame the oath in such a way as to recognise not only the
existence of the Deity, but the providence of the Deity, and man's
responsibility to the Deity ; and in such a way as to indicate the
knowledge in a man's own mind that he must answer to the Deity for
what he does, and is able to do. But is that your present rule ?
No, Sir, you know very well that from ancient times there have been
sects and schools that have admitted in the abstract as freely as
Christians the existence of a Deity, but have held that of practical
relations between Him and man there can be none. Many of the
members of this House will recollect the majestic and noble lines —

Omnis enim per se divom natura necesse est
Immortali ævo summa cum pace fruatur,
Semota a nostris rebus sejunctaque longe.
Nam privata dolore omni, privata periclis,
Ipsa suis pollens opibus, nihil indiga nostri,
Nec bene promeritis capitur, nec tangitur ira.[1]

---

[1] Lucretius, ii. 646. ' For the
nature of the gods must ever of itself
enjoy repose supreme through endless
time, far withdrawn from all concerns
of ours ; free from all our pains, free
from all our perils, strong in resources
of its own, needing nought from us,
no favours win it, no anger moves.'

'Divinity exists' — according to these, I must say, magnificent
lines — 'in remote and inaccessible recesses; but with us it has
no dealing, of us it has no need, with us it has no relation.'
I do not hesitate to say that the specific evil, the specific form of
irreligion, with which in the educated society of this country you
have to contend, and with respect to which you ought to be on
your guard, is not blank atheism. That is a rare opinion very
seldom met with; but what is frequently met with is that form
of opinion which would teach us that, whatever may be beyond
the visible things of this world, whatever there may be beyond
this short span of life, you know and you can know nothing of it,
and that it is a bootless undertaking to attempt to establish relations
with it. That is the mischief of the age, and that mischief you do
not attempt to touch.

The House, though but few perhaps recollected their Lucretius or had ever even read him, sat, as I well remember, with
reverential stillness, hearkening from this born master of
moving cadence and high sustained modulation to 'the rise
and long roll of the hexameter,' — to the plangent lines that
have come down across the night of time to us from great
Rome. But all these impressions of sublime feeling and
strong reasoning were soon effaced by honest bigotry, by
narrow and selfish calculation, by flat cowardice. The relieving bill was cast out by a majority of three. The catholics in the main voted against it, and many nonconformists,
hereditary champions of all the rights of private judgment,
either voted against it or did not vote at all. So soon in these
affairs, as the world has long ago found out, do bodies of men
forget in a day of power the maxims that they held sacred and
inviolable in days when they were weak.

The drama did not end here. In that parliament Bradlaugh was never allowed to discharge his duty as a member,
but when after the general election of 1885, being once more
chosen by Northampton, he went to the table to take the oath,
as in former days Mill and others of like non-theologic complexion had taken it, the Speaker would suffer no intervention
against him. Then in 1888, though the majority was conservative, Bradlaugh himself secured the passing of an affirmation

law. Finally, in the beginning of 1891, upon the motion of a Scotch member, supported by Mr. Gladstone, the House formally struck out from its records the resolution of June 22, 1881, that had been passed, as we have seen, amid 'ecstatic transports.' Bradlaugh then lay upon his deathbed, and was unconscious of what had been done. Mr. Gladstone a few days later, in moving a bill of his own to discard a lingering case of civil disability attached to religious profession, made a last reference to Mr. Bradlaugh : —

A distinguished man, he said, and admirable member of this House, was laid yesterday in his mother-earth. He was the subject of a long controversy in this House — a controversy the beginning of which we recollect, and the ending of which we recollect. We remember with what zeal it was prosecuted; we remember how summarily it was dropped; we remember also what reparation has been done within the last few days to the distinguished man who was the immediate object of that controversy. But does anybody who hears me believe that that controversy, so prosecuted and so abandoned, was beneficial to the Christian religion ? [1]

[1] Religious Disabilities Removal bill, Feb. 4, 1891.

CHAPTER III

MAJUBA

(*1880–1881*)

εἰς ἀπέραντον δίκτυον ἄτης
ἐμπλεχθήσεσθ' ὑπ' ἀνοίας.
— *Æsch. Prom.* 1078.

In a boundless coil of mischief pure senselessness will entangle you.

BOOK
VIII.

1880.
It would almost need the pen of Tacitus or Dante to tell the
story of European power in South Africa. For forty years,
said Mr. Gladstone in 1881, 'I have always regarded the
South African question as the one great unsolved and perhaps
insoluble problem of our colonial system.' Among the other
legacies of the forward policy that the constituencies had
decisively condemned in 1880, this insoluble problem rapidly
became acute and formidable.

One of the great heads of impeachment in Midlothian had
been a war undertaken in 1878–9 against a fierce tribe on the
borders of the colony of Natal. The author and instrument
of the Zulu war was Sir Bartle Frere, a man of tenacious
character and grave and lofty if ill-calculated aims. The
conservative government, as I have already said,[1] without
enthusiasm assented, and at one stage they even formally
censured him. When Mr. Gladstone acceded to office, the
expectation was universal that Sir Bartle would be at once
recalled. At the first meeting of the new cabinet (May 3) it
was decided to retain him. The prime minister at first was
his marked protector. The substantial reason against recall
was that his presence was needed to carry out the policy
of confederation, and towards confederation it was hoped
that the Cape parliament was immediately about to take

[1] Vol. ii. p. 583.

22

a long preliminary step. 'Confederation,' Mr. Gladstone said, 'is the pole-star of the present action of our government.' In a few weeks, for a reason that will be mentioned in treating the second episode of this chapter, confederation broke down. A less substantial but still not wholly inoperative reason was the strong feeling of the Queen for the high commissioner. The royal prepossessions notwithstanding, and in spite of the former leanings of Mr. Gladstone, the cabinet determined, at the end of July, that Sir Bartle should be recalled. The whole state of the case is made sufficiently clear in the two following communications from the prime minister to the Queen: —

CHAP.
III.

Æt. 71.

To the Queen.

May 28, 1880. — Mr. Gladstone presents his humble duty, and has had the honour to receive your Majesty's telegram respecting Sir B. Frere. Mr. Gladstone used on Saturday his best efforts to avert a movement for his dismissal, which it was intended by a powerful body of members on the liberal side to promote by a memorial to Mr. Gladstone, and by a motion in the House. He hopes that he has in some degree succeeded, and he understands that it is to be decided on Monday whether they will at present desist or persevere. Of course no sign will be given by your Majesty's advisers which could tend to promote perseverance, at the same time Mr. Gladstone does not conceal from himself two things: the first, that the only chance of Sir B. Frere's remaining seems to depend upon his ability to make progress in the matter of confederation; the second, that if the agitation respecting him in the House, the press, and the country should continue, confidence in him may be so paralysed as to render his situation intolerable to a high-minded man and to weaken his hands fatally for any purpose of good.

July 29, 1880. — It was not without some differences of opinion among themselves that, upon their accession to office, the cabinet arrived at the conclusion that, if there was a prospect of progress in the great matter of confederation, this might afford a ground of co-operation between them and Sir B. Frere, notwithstanding the strong censures which many of them in opposition had pro-

nounced upon his policy. This conclusion gave the liveliest satisfaction to a large portion, perhaps to the majority, of the House
of Commons; but they embraced it with the more satisfaction
because of your Majesty's warm regard for Sir B. Frere, a
sentiment which some among them personally share.

It was evident, however, and it was perhaps in the nature of
the case, that a confidence thus restricted was far from agreeable
to Sir B. Frere, who, in the opinion of Mr. Gladstone, has only
been held back by a commendable self-restraint and sense of duty,
from declaring himself aggrieved. Thus, though the cabinet have
done the best they could, his standing ground was not firm, nor
could they make it so. But the total failure of the effort made to
induce the Cape parliament to move, has put confederation wholly
out of view, for a time quite indefinite, and almost certainly considerable. Mr. Gladstone has therefore the painful duty of submitting to your Majesty, on behalf of the Cabinet, the enclosed
copy of a ciphered telegram of recall.

II

The breaking of the military power of the Zulus was
destined to prove much less important than another proceeding closely related to it, though not drawing the same
attention at the moment. I advise the reader not to grudge
a rather strict regard to the main details of transactions that,
owing to unhappy events of later date, have to this day held
a conspicuous place in the general controversy as to the
great minister's statesmanship.

For some time past, powerful native tribes had been
slowly but steadily pushing the Boers of the Transvaal
back, and the inability to resist was now dangerously plain.
In 1876 the Boers had been worsted in one of their incessant struggles with the native races, and this time they had
barely been able to hold their own against an insignificant
tribe of one of the least warlike branches. It was thought
certain by English officials on the ground, that the example
would not be lost on fiercer warriors, and that a native conflagration might any day burst into blaze in other regions of
the immense territory. The British government despatched
an agent of great local experience; he found the Boer

government, which was loosely organised even at its best, now completely paralysed, without money, without internal authority, without defensive power against external foes. In alarm at the possible result of such a situation on the peace of the European domain in South Africa, he proclaimed the sovereignty of the Queen, and set up an administration. This he was empowered by secret instructions to do, if he should think fit. Here was the initial error. The secretary of state in Downing Street approved (June 21, 1877), on the express assumption that a sufficient number of the inhabitants desired to become the Queen's subjects. Some have thought that if he had waited the Boers would have sought annexation, but this seems to be highly improbable. In the annexation proclamation promises were made to the Boers of 'the fullest legislative privileges compatible with the circumstances of the country and the intelligence of the people.' An assembly was also promised.

The soundness of the assumption was immediately disputed. The Boer government protested against annexation. Two delegates — one of them Mr. Kruger — repaired to England, assured Lord Carnarvon that their fellow-Boers were vehemently opposed to annexation, and earnestly besought its reversal. The minister insisted that he was right and they were wrong. They went back, and in order to convince the government of the true strength of feeling for independence, petitions were prepared seeking the restoration of independence. The signatures were those of qualified electors of the old republic. The government were informed by Sir Garnet Wolseley that there were about 8000 persons of the age to be electors, of whom rather fewer than 7000 were Boers. To the petitions were appended almost exactly 7000 names. The colonial office recognised that the opposition of the Boers to annexation was practically unanimous. The comparatively insignificant addresses on the other side came from the town and digging population, which was as strong in favour of the suppression of the old republic, as the rural population was strong against it.

For many months the Boers persevered. They again sent Kruger and Joubert to England; they held huge mass meetings; they poured out prayers to the high commissioner to give back their independence; they sent memorial after memorial to the secretary of state. In the autumn of 1879 Sir Garnet Wolseley assumed the administration of the Transvaal, and issued a proclamation setting forth the will and determination of the government of the Queen that this Transvaal territory should be, and should continue to be for ever, an integral part of her dominions in South Africa. In the closing days of 1879 the secretary of state, Sir Michael Hicks Beach, who had succeeded Carnarvon (Jan. 1878), received from the same eminent soldier a comprehensive despatch, warning him that the meetings of protest against annexation, attended by thousands of armed men in angry mood, would be likely to end in a serious explosion. While putting all sides of the question before his government, Sir Garnet inserted one paragraph of momentous import. ' The Transvaal,' he said, 'is rich in minerals; gold has already been found in quantities, and there can be little doubt that larger and still more valuable goldfields will sooner or later be discovered. Any such discovery would soon bring a large British population here. The time must eventually arrive when the Boers will be in a small minority, as the country is very sparsely peopled, and would it not therefore be a very near-sighted policy to recede now from the position we have taken up here, simply because for some years to come, the retention of 2000 or 3000 troops may be necessary to reconsolidate our power?'[1] This pregnant and far-sighted warning seems to have been little considered by English statesmen of either party at this critical time or afterwards, though it proved a vital element in any far-sighted decision.

On March 9 — the day, as it happened, on which the intention to dissolve parliament was made public — Sir Garnet telegraphed for a renewed expression of the determination of the government to retain the country, and he received the assurance that he sought. The Vaal river, he told the Boers, would flow backwards through the Drakensberg sooner than the British would be withdrawn from the Transvaal. The picturesque figure did not soften the Boer heart.

[1] Sir Garnet Wolseley to Sir M. Hicks Beach, Nov. 13, 1879.

This was the final share of the conservative cabinet in the unfortunate enterprise on which they had allowed the country to be launched.

III

When the question of annexation had originally come before parliament, Mr. Gladstone was silent. He was averse to it; he believed that it would involve us in unmixed mischief; but he felt that to make this judgment known at that period would not have had any effect towards reversing what had been done, while it might impede the chances of a good issue, slender as these might be.[1] In the discussion at the opening of the final session of the old parliament, Lord Hartington as leader of the opposition, enforcing the general doctrine that it behoved us to concentrate our resources, and to limit instead of extending the empire, took the Transvaal for an illustration. It was now conclusively proved, he said, that a large majority of the Boers were bitterly against annexation. That being so, it ought not to be considered a settled question merely because annexation had taken place; and if we should find that the balance of advantage was in favour of the restoration of independence, no false sense of dignity should stand in the way. Mr. Gladstone in Midlothian had been more reserved. In that indictment, there are only two or three references, and those comparatively fugitive and secondary, to this article of charge. There is a sentence in one of the Midlothian speeches about bringing a territory inhabited by a free European Christian republic within the limits of a monarchy, though out of 8000 persons qualified to vote, 6500 voted against it. In another sentence he speaks of the Transvaal as a country 'where we have chosen most unwisely, I am tempted to say insanely, to place ourselves in the strange predicament of the free subjects of a monarchy going to coerce the free subjects of a republic, and to compel them to accept a citizenship which they decline and refuse; but if that is to be done, it must be done by force.'[2] A third sentence completes the tale: 'If Cyprus and the

---

[1] In H. of C., Jan. 21, 1881. [2] *Speeches in Scotland*, i. pp. 48, 63.

Transvaal were as valuable as they are valueless, I would repudiate them because they are obtained by means dishonourable to the character of the country.' These utterances of the mighty unofficial chief and the responsible official leader of the opposition were all. The Boer republicans thought that they were enough.

On coming into power, the Gladstone government found the official evidence all to the effect that the political aspect of the Transvaal was decidedly improving. The commissioners, the administrators, the agents, were unanimous. Even those among them who insisted on the rooted dislike of the main body of the Boers to British authority, still thought that they were acquiescing, exactly as the Boers in the Cape Colony had acquiesced. Could ministers justify abandonment, without far stronger evidence than they then possessed that they could not govern the Transvaal peaceably? Among other things, they were assured that abandonment would be fatal to the prospects of confederation, and might besides entail a civil war. On May 7, Sir Bartle Frere pressed the new ministers for an early announcement of their policy, in order to prevent the mischiefs of agitation. The cabinet decided the question on May 12, and agreed upon the terms of a telegram [1] by which Lord Kimberley was to inform Frere that the sovereignty of the Queen over the Transvaal could not be relinquished, but that he hoped the speedy accomplishment of confederation would enable free institutions to be conferred with promptitude. In other words, in spite of all that had been defiantly said by Lord Hartington, and more cautiously implied by Mr. Gladstone, the new government at once placed themselves exactly in the position of the old one.[2]

The case was stated in his usual nervous language by Mr. Chamberlain a few months later.[3] 'When we came into

[1] C, 2586, No. 3.

[2] Mr. Grant Duff, then colonial under-secretary, said in the House of Commons, May 21, 1880, 'Under the very difficult circumstances of the case, the plan which seemed likely best to conciliate the interests at once of the Boers, the natives and the English population, was that the Trans-vaal should receive, and receive with promptitude, as a portion of confederation, the largest possible measure of local liberties that could be granted, and that was the direction in which her Majesty's present advisers meant to move.'

[3] At Birmingham, June 1881.

office,' he said, 'we were all agreed that the original annexation was a mistake, that it ought never to have been made;
and there arose the question could it then be undone? We
were in possession of information to the effect that the great
majority of the people of the Transvaal were reconciled to
annexation; we were told that if we reversed the decision of
the late government, there would be a great probability
of civil war and anarchy; and acting upon these representations, we decided that we could not recommend the Queen
to relinquish her sovereignty. But we assured the Boers
that we would take the earliest opportunity of granting to
them the freest and most complete local institutions compatible with the welfare of South Africa. It is easy to be
wise after the event. It is easy to see now that we were
wrong in so deciding. I frankly admit we made a mistake.
Whatever the risk was, and I believe it was a great risk, of
civil war and anarchy in the Transvaal, it was not so great
a danger as that we actually incurred by maintaining the
wrong of our predecessors.' Such was the language used
by Mr. Chamberlain after special consultation with Lord
Kimberley. With characteristic tenacity and that aversion
ever to yield even the smallest point, which comes to a man
saturated with the habit of a lifetime of debate, Mr. Gladstone wrote to Mr. Chamberlain (June 8, 1881): 'I have read
with pleasure what you say of the Transvaal. Yet I am not
prepared, for myself, to concede that we made a mistake
in not advising a revocation of the annexation when we
came in.'

At this instant a letter reached Mr. Gladstone from Kruger
and Joubert (May 10, 1880), telling him that there was
a firm belief among their people that truth prevailed. 'They
were confident that one day or another, by the mercy of the
Lord, the reins of the imperial government would be
entrusted again to men who look out for the honour and glory
of England, not by acts of injustice and crushing force, but
by the way of justice and good faith. And, indeed, this belief
has proven to be a good belief.' It would have been well
for the Boers and well for us, if that had indeed been so.
Unluckily the reply sent in Mr. Gladstone's name (June 15),

informed them that obligations had now been contracted,
especially towards the natives, that could not be set aside,
but that consistently with the maintenance of the Queen's
sovereignty over the Transvaal, ministers desired that the
white inhabitants should enjoy the fullest liberty to manage
their local affairs. 'We believe that this liberty may be most
easily and promptly conceded to the Transvaal, as a member
of a South African confederation.' Solemn and deliberate
as this sounds, no step whatever was effectively taken
towards conferring this full liberty, or any liberty at all.

It is worth while, on this material point, to look back. The
original proclamation had promised the people the fullest
legislative privileges compatible with the circumstances of
the country and the intelligence of the people. Then, at a later
date (April 1877), Sir Bartle Frere met a great assemblage
of Boers, and told them that they should receive, as soon as
circumstances rendered it practicable, as large a measure
of self-government as was enjoyed by any colony in South
Africa.[1] The secretary of state had also spoken to the same
effect. During the short period in which Sir Bartle Frere
was connected with the administration of the Transvaal, he
earnestly pressed upon the government the necessity for
redeeming the promises made at the time of annexation, 'of
the same measure of perfect self-government now enjoyed
by Cape Colony,' always, of course, under the authority
of the crown.[2] As the months went on, no attempt was
made to fulfil all these solemn pledges, and the Boers naturally
began to look on them as so much mockery. Their anger
in turn increased the timidity of government, and it was
argued that the first use that the Boers would make of a free
constitution would be to stop the supplies. So a thing
called an Assembly was set up (November 9, 1879), composed
partly of British officers and partly of nominated members.
This was a complete falsification of a whole set of our national
promises. Still annexation might conceivably have been

[1] C, 2367, p. 55.
[2] *Afghanistan and S. Africa:* A
letter to Mr. Gladstone by Sir Bartle
Frere. Murray, 1891, pp. 24-6.
Frere, on his return to England, once
more impressed on the colonial office
the necessity of speedily granting the
Boers a constitution, otherwise there
would be serious trouble. (*Life*, ii.
p. 408.)

accepted, even the sting might have been partially taken out of the delay of the promised free institutions, if only the administration had been considerate, judicious, and adapted to the ways and habits of the people. Instead of being all these things it was stiff, headstrong, and intensely stupid.[1]

The value of the official assurances from agents on the spot that restoration of independence would destroy the chances of confederation, and would give fuel to the fires of agitation, was speedily tested. It was precisely these results that flowed from the denial of independence. The incensed Boer leaders worked so successfully on the Cape parliament against confederation, that this favourite panacea was indefinitely hung up. Here, again, it is puzzling to know why ministers did not retrace their steps. Here, again, their blind guides in the Transvaal persisted that they knew the road; persisted that with the exception of a turbulent handful, the Boers of the Transvaal only sighed for the enjoyment of the *pax britannica*, or, if even that should happen to be not quite true, at any rate they were incapable of united action, were mortal cowards, and could never make a stand in the field. While folly of this kind was finding its way by every mail to Downing Street, violent disturbances broke out in the collection of taxes. Still Sir Owen Lanyon — who had been placed in control in the Transvaal in March 1879 — assured Lord Kimberley that no serious trouble would arise (November 14). At the end of the month he still denies that there is much or any cause for anxiety. In December several thousands of Boers assembled at Paardekraal, declared for the restoration of their republic, and a general rising followed. Colley, who had succeeded General Wolseley as governor of Natal and high commissioner for south-east Africa, had been so little prepared for this, that at the end of August he had recommended a reduction of the Transvaal garrisons,[2] and even now he

[1] Sir George Colley pressed Lord Kimberley in his correspondence with the reality of this grievance, and the urgency of trying to remove it. This was after the Boers had taken to arms at the end of 1880.

[2] Before the Gladstone government came into office, between August 1879 and April 1880, whilst General Wolseley was in command, the force in Natal and the Transvaal had been reduced by six batteries of artillery,

BOOK
VIII.

1880.

thought the case so little serious that he contented himself (December 4) with ordering four companies to march for the Transvaal. Then he and Lanyon began to get alarmed, and with good reason. The whole country, except three or four beleaguered British posts, fell into the hands of the Boers.

The pleas for failure to take measures to conciliate the Boers in the interval between Frere's recall and the outbreak, were that Sir Hercules Robinson had not arrived;[1] that confederation was not yet wholly given up; that resistance to annexation was said to be abating; that time was in our favour; that the one thing indispensable to conciliate the Boers was a railway to Delagoa Bay; that this needed a treaty, and we hoped soon to get Portugal to ratify a treaty, and then we might tell the Boers that we should soon make a survey, with a view at some early date to proceed with the project, and thus all would in the end come right. So a fresh page was turned in the story of loitering unwisdom.

IV

On December 6, Mr. Brand, the sagacious president of the Orange Free State, sent a message of anxious warning to the acting governor at Cape Town, urging that means should be devised to avert an imminent collision. That message, which might possibly have wakened up the colonial office to the real state of the case, did not reach London until December 30. Excuses for this fatal delay were abundant: a wire was broken; the governor did not think himself concerned with Transvaal affairs; he sent the message on to the general, supposing that the general would send it on home; and so forth. For a whole string of the very best reasons in the world the message that

three companies of engineers, one cavalry regiment, eleven battalions of infantry, and five companies of army service corps. The force at the time of the outbreak was: in Natal 1772, and in the Transvaal 1759 — a total of 3531. As soon as the news of the insurrection reached London, large reinforcements were at once despatched to Colley, the first of

them leaving Gibraltar on Dec. 27, 1880.

[1] Sir B. Frere was recalled on August 1, 1880, and sailed for England September 15. Sir Hercules Robinson, his successor, did not reach the Cape until the end of January 1881. In the interval Sir George Strahan was acting governor.

might have prevented the outbreak, arrived through the slow post at Whitehall just eleven days after the outbreak had begun. Members of the legislature at the Cape urged the British government to send a special commissioner to inquire and report. The policy of giving consideration to the counsels of the Cape legislature had usually been pursued by the wiser heads concerned in South African affairs, and when the counsels of the chief of the Free State were urgent in the same direction, their weight should perhaps have been decisive. Lord Kimberley, however, did not think the moment opportune (Dec. 30).[1] Before many weeks, as it happened, a commission was indeed sent, but unfortunately not until after the mischief had been done. Meanwhile in the Queen's speech a week later an emphatic paragraph announced that the duty of vindicating her Majesty's authority had set aside for the time any plan for securing to European settlers in the Transvaal full control over their own local affairs. Seldom has the sovereign been made the mouthpiece of an utterance more shortsighted.

Again the curtain rose upon a new and memorable act. Four days after the Queen's speech, President Brand a second time appeared upon the scene (Jan. 10, 1881), with a message hoping that an effort would be made without the least delay to prevent further bloodshed. Lord Kimberley replied that provided the Boers would desist from their armed opposition, the government did not despair of making a satisfactory settlement. Two days later (Jan. 12) the president told the government that not a moment should be lost, and some one (say Chief Justice de Villiers) should be sent to the Transvaal burghers by the government, to stop further collision and with a clear and definite proposal

---

[1] Lord Kimberley justified this decision on the ground that it was impossible to send a commissioner to inquire and report, at a moment when our garrisons were besieged, and we had collected no troops to relieve them, and when we had just received the news that the detachment of the 94th had been cut off on the march from Lydenberg to Pretoria. 'Is it not practically certain,' he wrote, 'that the Boers would have refused at that time to listen to any reasonable terms, and would have simply insisted that we should withdraw our troops and quit the country?' Of course, the Boer overture, some six weeks after the rejection by Lord Kimberley of the Cape proposal, and after continued military success on the side of the Boers, showed that this supposed practical certainty was the exact reverse of certain.

for a settlement. 'Moments,' he said, 'are precious.' For twelve days these precious moments passed. On Jan. 26 the secretary of state informed the high commissioner at Cape Town, now Sir Hercules Robinson, that President Brand pressed for the offer of terms and conditions to the Boers through Robinson, 'provided they cease from armed opposition, making it clear to them how this is to be understood.' On this suggestion he instructed Robinson to inform Brand that if armed opposition should at once cease, the government 'would thereupon endeavour to frame such a scheme as in their belief would satisfy all friends of the Transvaal community.' Brand promptly advised that the Boers should be told of this forthwith, before the satisfactory arrangements proposed had been made more difficult by further collision. This was on Jan. 29. Unhappily on the very day before, the British force had been repulsed at Laing's Nek. Colley, on Jan. 23, had written to Joubert, calling on the Boer leaders to disperse, informing them that large forces were already arriving from England and India, and assuring them that if they would dismiss their followers, he would forward to London any statement of their grievances. It would have been a great deal more sensible to wait for an answer. Instead of waiting for an answer Colley attacked (Jan. 28) and was beaten back — the whole proceeding a rehearsal of a still more disastrous error a month later.

Brand was now more importunate than ever, earnestly urging on General Colley that the nature of the scheme should be made known to the Boers, and a guarantee undertaken that if they submitted they would not be treated as rebels. 'I have replied,' Colley tells Lord Kimberley, 'that I can give no such assurance, and can add nothing to your words.' In other correspondence he uses grim language about the deserts of some of the leaders. On this Mr. Gladstone, writing to Lord Kimberley (Feb. 5), says truly enough, ' Colley with a vengeance counts his chickens before they are hatched, and his curious letter throws some light backward on the proceedings in India. His line is singularly wide of ours.' The secretary of state, finding barrack-room rigidity out of place, directs Colley (Feb. 8) to inform Brand

that the government would be ready to give all reasonable guarantees as to treatment of Boers after submission,
if they ceased from armed opposition, and a scheme would
be framed for permanent friendly settlement. As it happened, on the day on which this was despatched from
Downing Street, Colley suffered a second check at the
Ingogo River (Feb. 8). Let us note that he was always eager
in his recognition of the readiness and promptitude of the
military support from the government at home.[1]

Then an important move took place from the other
quarter. The Boers made their first overture. It came
in a letter from Kruger to Colley (Feb. 12). Its purport was fairly summarised by Colley in a telegram to
the colonial secretary, and the pith of it was that Kruger
and his Boers were so certain of the English government
being on their side if the truth only reached them, that they
would not fear the result of inquiry by a royal commission,
and were ready, if troops were ordered to withdraw from the
Transvaal, to retire from their position, and give such a
commission a free passage. This telegram reached London
on Feb. 13th, and on the 15th it was brought before the
cabinet.

Mr. Gladstone immediately informed the Queen (Feb. 15)
that viewing the likelihood of early and sanguinary actions,
Lord Kimberley thought that the receipt of such an overture
at such a juncture, although its terms were inadmissible,
made it a duty to examine whether it afforded any hope of
settlement. The cabinet were still more strongly inclined
towards coming to terms. Any other decision would have
broken up the government, for on at least one division in the
House on Transvaal affairs Mr. Bright and Mr. Chamberlain,
along with three other ministers not in the cabinet, had
abstained from voting. Colley was directed (Feb. 16)
to inform the Boers that on their desisting from armed
opposition, the government would be ready to send com-

---

[1] 'I do not know whether I am
indebted to you or to Mr. Childers
or to both, for the continuance of
H.M.'s confidence, but I shall always
feel more deeply grateful than I can
express; and can never forget H.M.'s
gracious message of encouragement
at a time of great trouble.' — Colley
to Kimberley, Jan. 31, 1881.

missioners to develop a scheme of settlement, and that meanwhile if this proposal were accepted, the English general
was authorised to agree to the suspension of hostilities.
This was in substance a conditional acceptance of the Boer
overture.[1] On the same day the general was told from the
war office that, as respected the interval before receiving a
reply from Mr. Kruger, the government did not bind his
discretion, but 'we are anxious for your making arrangements to avoid effusion of blood.' The spirit of these instructions was clear. A week later (Feb. 23) the general showed
that he understood this, for he wrote to Mr. Childers that
'he would not without strong reason undertake any operation likely to bring on another engagement, until Kruger's
reply was received.'[2] If he had only stood firm to this, a
tragedy would have been averted.

On receiving the telegram of Feb. 16, Colley was puzzled
to know what was the meaning of suspending hostilities if
armed opposition were abandoned by the Boers, and he asked
the plain question (Feb. 19) whether he was to leave Laing's
Nek (which was in Natal territory) in Boer occupation, and
our garrisons isolated and short of provisions, or was he
to occupy Laing's Nek and relieve the garrisons. Colley's in-
quiries were instantly considered by the cabinet, and the reply
settled. The garrisons were to be free to provision themselves and peaceful intercourse allowed; 'but,' Kimberley
tells Colley, 'we do not mean that you should march to
the relief of garrisons or occupy Laing's Nek, if the arrangement proceeds. *Fix reasonable time within which answer
must be sent by Boers.*'

On Feb. 21 Colley despatched a letter to Kruger, stating
that on the Boers ceasing from armed opposition, the Queen
would appoint a commission. He added that 'upon this
proposal being accepted *within forty-eight hours from the
receipt of this letter*,' he was authorised to agree to a suspension of hostilities on the part of the British.

---

[1] 'The directions to Colley,' says
Mr. Bright in a cabinet minute, 'intended to convey the offer of a suspension of hostilities on both sides,
with a proposal that a commissioner
should be appointed to enter into
negotiations and arrangements with
a view to peace.'

[2] *Life of Childers,* ii. p. 24.

v

In this interval a calamity, destined to be historic, occurred, trivial in a military sense, but formidable for many years to come in the issues moral and political that it raised, and in the passions for which it became a burning watchword. On the night of Feb. 26, Colley with a force of 359 men all told, made up of three different corps, marched out of his camp and occupied Majuba Hill. The general's motives for this precipitancy are obscure. The best explanation seems to be that he observed the Boers to be pushing gradually forward on to advanced ground, and thought it well, without waiting for Kruger's reply, to seize a height lying between the Nek and his own little camp, the possession of which would make Laing's Nek untenable. He probably did not expect that his move would necessarily lead to fighting, and in fact when they saw the height occupied, the Boers did at first for a little time actually begin to retire from the Nek, though they soon changed their minds.[1] The British operation is held by military experts to have been rash; proper steps were not taken by the general to protect himself upon Majuba, the men were not well handled, and the Boers showed determined intrepidity as they climbed steadily up the hill from platform to platform, taking from seven in the morning (Feb. 27) up to half-past eleven to advance some three thousand yards and not losing a man, until at last they scaled the crest and poured a deadly fire upon the small British force, driving them headlong from the summit, seasoned soldiers though most of them were. The general who was responsible for the disaster paid the penalty with his life. Some ninety others fell and sixty were taken prisoners.

At home the sensation was profound. The hysterical complaints about our men and officers, General Wood wrote to Childers, 'are more like French character than English used to be.' Mr. Gladstone and his colleagues had a political question to consider. Colley could not be technically accused of want of good faith in moving forward on the 26th, as the

[1] Colley's letter to Childers, Feb. 23, *Life of Childers*, ii. p. 24.

time that he had appointed had expired. But though Majuba is just inside Natal—some four miles over the border —his advance was, under the circumstances of the moment, essentially an aggressive movement. Could his defeat justify us in withdrawing our previous proposals to the Boers? Was a military miscarriage, of no magnitude in itself, to be turned into a plea for abandoning a policy deliberately adopted for what were thought powerful and decisive reasons? 'Suppose, for argument's sake,' Mr. Gladstone wrote to Lord Kimberley when the sinister news arrived (Mar. 2), 'that at the moment when Colley made the unhappy attack on Majuba Hill, there shall turn out to have been decided on, and possibly on its way, a satisfactory or friendly reply from the Boer government to your telegram? I fear the chances may be against this; but if it prove to be the case, we could not because we had failed on Sunday last, insist on shedding more blood.' As it happened, the Boer answer was decided on before the attack at Majuba, and was sent to Colley by Kruger at Heidelberg in ignorance of the event, the day after the ill-fated general's death. The members of the Transvaal government set out their gratitude for the declaration that under certain conditions the government of the Queen was inclined to cease hostilities; and expressed their opinion that a meeting of representatives from both sides would probably lead with all speed to a satisfactory result. This reply was despatched by Kruger on the day on which Colley's letter of the 21st came into his hands (Feb. 28), and it reached Colley's successor on March 7.

Sir Evelyn Wood, now after the death of Colley in chief command, throughout recommended military action. Considering the disasters we had sustained, he thought the happiest result would be that after a successful battle, which he hoped to fight in about a fortnight, the Boers would disperse without any guarantee, and many now in the field against their will would readily settle down. He explained that by happy result, he did not mean that a series of actions fought by any six companies could affect our military prestige, but that a British victory would enable the Boer leaders to quench a fire that had got beyond their control. The next day after this recommendation to fight (March 6), he, of his own motion, accepted a proposal telegraphed from Joubert at the instigation of the indefatigable Brand, for a suspension of hostilities for eight days, for the purpose of receiving Kruger's reply. There was a military reason behind. General Wood knew that the garrison in Potchefstrom must surrender unless the place were revictualled, and three other beleaguered garrisons were in almost equal danger. The government at once told him that his armistice was approved. This armistice, though Wood's reasons were military rather than diplomatic, virtually put a stop to suggestions for further fighting, for it implied, and could in truth mean nothing else, that if Kruger's reply were promising, the next step would not be a fight, but the continuance of negotiation. Sir Evelyn Wood had not advised a fight for the sake of restoring military prestige, but to make it easier for the Boer leaders to break up bands that were getting beyond their control. There was also present in his mind the intention, if the government would sanction it, of driving the Boers out of Natal, as soon as ever he had got his men up across the swollen river. So far from sanctioning it, the government expressly forbade him to take offensive action. On March 8, General Wood telegraphed home: 'Do not imagine I wish to fight. I know the attending misery too well. But now you have so many troops coming, I recommend decisive though lenient action; and I can, humanly speaking, promise victory. Sir G. Colley never engaged more than six companies. I shall use twenty and two regiments of cavalry in direction known to myself only, and undertake to enforce dispersion.' This then was General Wood's view. On the day before he sent this telegram, the general already had received Kruger's reply to the effect that they were anxious to negotiate, and it would be best for commissioners from the two sides to meet. It is important to add that the government were at the same time receiving urgent warnings from President Brand that Dutch sympathy, both in the Cape Colony and in the Orange Free State, with the Dutch in the Transvaal was

CHAP.
III.

Æt. 72.

growing dangerous, and that the prolongation of hostilities would end in a formidable extension of their area.[1] Even in January Lanyon had told Colley that men from the Free State were in the field against him. Three days before Majuba, Lord Kimberley had written to Colley (February 24), ' My great fear has been lest the Free State should take part against us, or even some movement take place in the Cape Colony. If our willingness to come to terms has avoided such a calamity, I shall consider it will have been a most important point gained.' [2]

Two memoranda for the Queen show the views of the cabinet on the new position of affairs : —

To the Queen.

March 8, 1881. — The cabinet considered with much care the terms of the reply to Sir Evelyn Wood's telegram reporting (not textually) the answer of the Boer leaders to the proposals which Sir George Colley had sent to them. They felt justified in construing the Boer answer as leaving the way open to the appointment of commissioners, according to the telegram previously seen and approved by your Majesty. They were anxious to keep the question moving in this direction, and under the extreme urgency of the circumstances as to time, they have despatched a telegram to Sir Evelyn Wood accordingly. Mr. Gladstone has always urged, and still feels, that the proposal of the Boers for the appointment of commissioners was fortunate on this among other grounds, that it involved a recognition of your Majesty's *de facto* authority in the Transvaal.

March 12. — The cabinet determined, in order to obviate misapprehension or suspicion, to desire Sir E. Wood to inform the government from what quarter the suggestion of an armistice

[1] See Selborne's *Memorials*, ii. p. 3, and also a speech by Lord Kimberley at Newcastle, Nov. 14, 1899.

[2] In a speech at Edinburgh (Sept. 1, 1884), Mr. Gladstone put the same argument — ' The people of the Transvaal, few in number, were in close and strong sympathy with their brethren in race, language, and religion. Throughout South Africa these men, partly British subjects and partly not, were as one man associated in feeling with the people of the Transvaal ; and had we persisted in that dishonourable attempt, against all our own interests, to coerce the Transvaal as we attempted to coerce Afghanistan, we should have had the whole mass of the Dutch population at the Cape and throughout South Africa rising in arms against us.'

actually proceeded. They agreed that the proper persons to be appointed as commissioners were Sir H. Robinson, Sir E. Wood, and Mr. De Villiers, chief justice of the Cape; together with Mr. Brand of the Free State as *amicus curiæ*, should he be willing to lend his good offices in the spirit in which he has hitherto acted. The cabinet then considered fully the terms of the communication to be made to the Boers by Sir E. Wood. In this, which is matter of extreme urgency, they prescribe a time for the reply of the Boers not later than the 18th; renew the promise of amnesty; require the dispersion of the Boers to their own homes; and state the general outlines of the permanent arrangement which they would propose for the territory. . . . The cabinet believe that in requiring the dispersion of the Boers to their homes, they will have made the necessary provision for the vindication of your Majesty's authority, so as to open the way for considering terms of pacific settlement.

On March 22, under instructions from home, the general concluded an agreement for peace. The Boers made some preliminary requests to which the government declined to assent. Their proposal that the commission should be joint was rejected; its members were named exclusively by the crown. They agreed to withdraw from the Nek and disperse to their homes; we agreed not to occupy the Nek, and not to follow them up with troops, though General Roberts with a large force had sailed for the Cape on March 6. Then the political negotiation went forward. Would it have been wise, as the question was well put by the Duke of Argyll (not then a member of the government), 'to stop the negotiation for the sake of defeating a body of farmers who had succeeded under accidental circumstances and by great rashness on the part of our commanders, in gaining a victory over us?' This was the true point.

The parliamentary attack was severe. The galling argument was that government had conceded to three defeats what they had refused to ten times as many petitions, memorials, remonstrances; and we had given to men with arms in their hands what we refused to their peaceful prayers. A great lawyer in the House of Lords made the speech that is expected from a great lawyer who is also a conspicuous party leader; and ministers undoubtedly exposed an extent of surface that was not easy to defend, not because they had made a peace, but because they had failed to prevent the rising. High military authorities found a curious plea for going on, in the fact that this was our first contest with Europeans since the breech-loader came in, and it was desirable to give our troops confidence in the new-fashioned weapon. Reasons of a very different sort from this were needed to overthrow the case for peace. How could the miscarriage at Majuba, brought on by our own action, warrant us in drawing back from an engagement already deliberately proffered? Would not such a proceeding, asked Lord Kimberley, have been little short of an act of bad faith? Or were we, in Mr. Gladstone's language, to say to the Boers, 'Although we might have treated with you before these military miscarriages, we cannot do so now, until we offer up a certain number of victims in expiation of the blood that has been shed. Until that has been done, the very things which we believed before to be reasonable, which we were ready to discuss with you, we refuse to discuss now, and we must wait until Moloch has been appeased'? We had opened a door for negotiation; were we to close it again, because a handful of our forces had rashly seized a post they could not hold? The action of the Boers had been defensive of the *status quo*, for if we had established ourselves on Majuba, their camp at Laing's Nek would have been untenable. The minister protested in the face of the House of Commons that 'it would have been most unjust and cruel, it would have been cowardly and mean, if on account of these defensive operations we had refused to go forward with the negotiations which, before the first of these miscarriages had occurred, we had already declared that we were willing to promote and undertake.'[1]

The policy of the reversal of annexation is likely to remain a topic of endless dispute.[2] As Sir Hercules Robinson put

[1] July 25, 1881.

[2] One of the most determined enemies of the government in 1881, ten years later, in a visit to South Africa, changed his mind. 'The Dutch sentiment in the Cape Colony,' wrote Lord Randolph Churchill, ' had been so exasperated by what it con-

it in a letter to Lord Kimberley, written a week before Majuba (Feb. 21), no possible course was free from grave objection. If you determine, he said, to hold by the annexation of the Transvaal, the country would have to be conquered and held in subjection for many years by a large force. Free institutions and self-government under British rule would be an impossibility. The only palliative would be to dilute Dutch feeling by extensive English immigration, like that of 1820 to the Eastern Province. But that would take time, and need careful watching; and in the meantime the result of holding the Transvaal as a conquered colony would undoubtedly be to excite bitter hatred between the English and Dutch throughout the Free State and this colony, which would be a constant source of discomfort and danger. On the other hand, he believed that if they were, after a series of reverses and before any success, to yield all the Boers asked for, they would be so overbearing and quarrelsome that we should soon be at war with them again. On the whole, Sir Hercules was disposed to think — extraordinary as such a view must appear — that the best plan would be to re-establish the supremacy of our arms, and then let the malcontents go. He thought no middle course any longer practicable. Yet surely this course was open to all the objections. To hold on to annexation at any cost was intelligible. But to face all the cost and all the risks of a prolonged and a widely extended conflict, with the deliberate intention of allowing the enemy to have his own way after the conflict had been brought to an end, was not intelligible and was not defensible.

Some have argued that we ought to have brought up an overwhelming force, to demonstrate that we were able to beat them, before we made peace. Unfortunately demonstrations of this species easily turn into provocations, and talk of this kind mostly comes from those who believe, not

sidered the unjust, faithless, and arbitrary policy pursued towards the free Dutchmen of the Transvaal by Frere, Shepstone, and Lanyon, that the final triumph of the British arms, mainly by brute force, would have permanently and hopelessly alienated it from Great Britain. . . . On the whole, I find myself free to confess, and without reluctance to admit, that the English escaped from a wretched and discreditable muddle, not without harm and damage, but perhaps in the best possible manner.'

that peace was made in the wrong way, but that a peace
giving their country back to the Boers ought never to
have been made at all, on any terms or in any way.
This was not the point from which either cabinet or
parliament started. The government had decided that
annexation had been an error. The Boers had proposed
inquiry. The government assented on condition that the
Boers dispersed. Without waiting a reasonable time for a
reply, our general was worsted in a rash and trivial attack.
Did this cancel our proffered bargain? The point was simple
and unmistakable, though party heat at home, race passion
in the colony, and our everlasting human proneness to mix
up different questions, and to answer one point by arguments
that belong to another, all combined to produce a confusion
of mind that a certain school of partisans have traded upon
ever since. Strange in mighty nations is moral cowardice,
disguised as a Roman pride. All the more may we admire
the moral courage of the minister. For moral courage may
be needed even where aversion to bloodshed fortunately
happens to coincide with high prudence and sound policy
of state.

VI

The negotiations proceeded, if negotiation be the right
word. The Boers disbanded, a powerful British force was
encamped on the frontier, no Boer representative sat on the
commission, and the terms of final agreement were in fact,
as the Boers afterwards alleged, dictated and imposed. Mr.
Gladstone watched with a closeness that, considering the
tremendous load of Ireland, parliamentary procedure, and
the incessant general business of a prime minister, is
amazing. When the Boers were over-pressing, he warned
them that it was only 'the unshorn strength' of the
administration that enabled the English cabinet, rather to
the surprise of the world, to spare them the sufferings of
a war. 'We could not,' he said to Lord Kimberley, 'have
carried our Transvaal policy, unless we had here a strong
government, and we spent some, if not much, of our strength
in carrying it.' A convention was concluded at Pretoria in

August, recognising the quasi-independence of the Transvaal, subject to the suzerainty of the Queen, and with certain specified reservations. The Pretoria convention of 1881 did not work smoothly. Transvaal affairs were discussed from time to time in the cabinet, and Mr. Chamberlain became the spokesman of the government on a business where he was destined many years after to make so conspicuous and irreparable a mark. The Boers again sent Kruger to London, and he made out a good enough case in the opinion of Lord Derby, then secretary of state, to justify a fresh arrangement. By the London convention of 1884, the Transvaal state was restored to its old title of the South African Republic; the assertion of suzerainty in the preamble of the old convention did not appear in the new one;[1] and various other modifications were introduced — the most important of them, in the light of later events, being a provision for white men to have full liberty to reside in any part of the republic, to trade in it, and to be liable to the same taxes only as those exacted from citizens of the republic.

Whether we look at the Sand River Convention in 1852, which conferred independence; or at Shepstone's proclamation in 1877, which took independence away; or at the convention of Pretoria in 1881, which in a qualified shape gave it back; or at the convention of London in 1884, which qualified the qualification over again, till independence, subject to two or three specified conditions, was restored, — we can but recall the caustic apologue of sage Selden in his table-talk on

[1] 'I apprehend, whether you call it a Protectorate, or a Suzerainty, or the recognition of England as a Paramount Power, the fact is that a certain controlling power is retained when the state which exercises this suzerainty has a right to veto any negotiations into which the dependent state may enter with foreign powers. Whatever suzerainty meant in the Convention of Pretoria, the condition of things which it implied still remains; although the word is not actually employed, we have kept the substance. We have abstained from using the word because it was not capable of legal definition, and because it seemed to be a word which was likely to lead to misconception and misunderstanding.' — *Lord Derby in the House of Lords*, March 17, 1884. I do not desire to multiply points of controversy, but the ill-starred raising of the ghost of suzerainty in 1897–9 calls for the twofold remark that the preamble was struck out by Lord Derby's own hand, and that alike when Lord Knutsford and Lord Ripon were at the colonial office, answers were given in the House of Commons practically admitting that no claim of suzerainty could be put forward.

contracts. 'Lady Kent,' he says, 'articled with Sir Edward Herbert that he should come to her when she sent for him, and stay with her as long as she would have him; to which he set his hand. Then he articled with her that he should go away when he pleased, and stay away as long as he pleased; to which she set her hand. This is the epitome of all the contracts in the world, betwixt man and man, betwixt prince and subject.'

CHAPTER IV

NEW PHASES OF THE IRISH REVOLUTION

(1880–1882)

> THE agitation of the Irish land league strikes at the roots of all contract, and therefore at the very foundations of modern society; but if we would effectually withstand it, we must cease to insist on maintaining the forms of free contract where the reality is impossible. — T. H. GREEN.[1]

ON the day in 1880 when Lord Beaconsfield was finally quitting the official house in Downing Street, one who had been the ablest and most zealous supporter of his policy in the press, called to bid him good-bye. The visitor talked gloomily of the national prospect; of difficulties with Austria, with Russia, with the Turk; of the confusions to come upon Europe from the doctrines of Midlothian. The fallen minister listened. Then looking at his friend, he uttered in deep tones a single word. '*Ireland!*' he said.

In a speech made in 1882 Mr. Gladstone put the case to the House of Commons : —

The government had to deal with a state of things in Ireland entirely different from any that had been known there for fifty years. . . . With a political revolution we have ample strength to cope. There is no reason why our cheeks should grow pale, or why our hearts should sink, at the idea of grappling with a political revolution. The strength of this country is tenfold what is required for such a purpose. But a social revolution is a very different matter. . . . The seat and source of the movement was not to be found during the time the government was in power. It is to be looked for in the foundation of the land league.[2]

Two years later he said at Edinburgh : —

I frankly admit I had had much upon my hands connected with

---

[1] *Works of T. H. Green*, iii. 382. [2] House of Commons, April 4, 1882.

the doings of the Beaconsfield government in almost every quarter of the world, and I did not know, no one knew, the severity of the crisis that was already swelling upon the horizon, and that shortly after rushed upon us like a flood.[1]

So came upon them by degrees the predominance of Irish affairs and Irish activity in the parliament of 1880, which had been chosen without much reference to Ireland.

II

A social revolution with the land league for its organ in Ireland, and Mr. Parnell and his party for its organ in parliament, now, in Mr. Gladstone's words, rushed upon him and his government like a flood. The mind of the country was violently drawn from Dulcigno and Thessaly, from Batoum and Erzeroum, from the wild squalor of Macedonia and Armenia to squalor not less wild in Connaught and Munster, in Mayo, Galway, Sligo, Kerry. Agrarian agitation on the one hand, parliamentary violence on the other, were the two potent weapons by which the Irish revolutionary leader assailed the misrule of the British garrison as the agents of the British parliament in his country. This formidable movement slowly unmasked itself. The Irish government, represented by Mr. Forster in the cabinet, began by allowing the law conferring exceptional powers upon the executive to lapse. The main reason was want of time to pass a fresh Act. In view of the undoubted distress in some parts of Ireland, and of the harshness of certain evictions, the government further persuaded the House of Commons to pass a bill for compensating an evicted tenant on certain conditions, if the landlord turned him out of his holding. The bill was no easy dose either for the cabinet or its friends. Lord Lansdowne stirred much commotion by retiring from the government, and landowners and capitalists were full of consternation. At least one member of the cabinet was profoundly uneasy. It is impossible to read the letters of the Duke of Argyll to Mr. Gladstone on land, church establishment, the Zulu war, without wondering on what theory a cabinet was formed that included him, able and

[1] Edinburgh, Sept. 1, 1884.

upright as he was, along with radicals like Mr. Chamberlain. Before the cabinet was six months old the duke was plucking Mr. Gladstone's sleeve with some vivacity at the Birmingham language on Irish land. Mr. Parnell in the committee stage abstained from supporting the measure, sixteen liberals voted against the third reading, and the House of Lords, in which nationalist Ireland had not a single representative, threw out the bill by a majority of 282 against 51. It was said that if all the opposition peers had stayed away, still ministers would have been beaten by their own supporters.

Looking back upon these events, Mr. Gladstone set out in a memorandum of later years, that during the session of 1880 the details of the budget gave him a good deal to do, while the absorbing nature of foreign questions before and after his accession to office had withdrawn his attention from his own Land Act of 1870 : [1] —

Late in the session came the decisive and disastrous rejection by the House of Lords of the bill by means of which the government had hoped to arrest the progress of disorder, and avert the necessity for measures in the direction of coercion. The rapid and vast extension of agrarian disturbance followed, as was to be expected, this wild excess of landlordism, and the Irish government proceeded to warn the cabinet that coercive legislation would be necessary.

Forster allowed himself to be persuaded by the governmental agents in Ireland that the root of the evil lay within small compass; that there were in the several parishes a certain limited number of unreasonable and mischievous men, that these men were known to the police, and that if summary powers were confided to the Irish government, by the exercise of which these objectionable persons might be removed, the evil would die out of itself. I must say I never fell into this extraordinary illusion of Forster's about his 'village ruffian.' But he was a very impracticable man placed in a position of great responsibility. He was set upon a method of legislation adapted to the erroneous belief that the mischief lay only with a very limited number of well-known individuals, that is to say, the suspension of the Habeas Corpus

[1] See vol. ii. book vi. chap. ii.

Act. . . . Two points of difference arose : first, as to the nature of the coercion to be used; secondly, as to its time. I insisted that we were bound to try what we could do against Parnell under the existing law, before asking for extraordinary powers. Both Bright and Chamberlain, if I remember right, did very good service in protesting against haste, and resisting Forster's desire to anticipate the ordinary session for the purpose of obtaining coercive powers. When, however, the argument of time was exhausted by the Parnell trial [1] and otherwise, I obtained no support from them in regard to the kind of coercion we were to ask. I considered it should be done by giving stringency to the existing law, but not by abolishing the right to be tried before being imprisoned. I felt the pulse of various members of the cabinet, among whom I seem to recollect Kimberley and Carlingford, but I could obtain no sympathy, and to my dismay both Chamberlain and Bright arrived at the conclusion that if there was to be coercion at all, which they lamented, there was something simple and effective in the suspension of the Habeas Corpus Act which made such a method preferable to others.[2] I finally acquiesced. It may be asked why ? My resistance would have broken up the government or involved my own retirement. My reason for acquiescence was that I bore in mind the special commission under which the government had taken office. It related to the foreign policy of the country, the whole spirit and effect of which we were to reconstruct. This work had not yet been fully accomplished, and it seemed to me that the effective prosecution of it was our first and highest duty. I therefore submitted.

By the end of November Mr. Gladstone explained to the Queen that the state of Ireland was menacing ; its distinctive character was not so much that of general insecurity of life, as that of a widespread conspiracy against property. The worst of it was, he said, that the leaders, unlike O'Connell, failed to denounce crime. The outbreak was not comparable to that of 1832. In 1879 homicides were 64 against 242 for the earlier year of disturbance. But things were bad enough.

[1] Proceedings had been instituted in the Dublin courts against Parnell and others for seditious conspiracy. The jury were unable to agree on a verdict.

[2] Tried by Lord Spencer in Westmeath in 1871, it had been successful, but the area of disturbance was there comparatively insignificant.

In Galway they had a policeman for every forty-seven adult males, and a soldier for every ninety-seven. Yet dangerous terrorism was rampant. 'During more than thirty-seven years since I first entered a cabinet,' Mr. Gladstone told the Speaker (November 25), 'I have hardly known so difficult a question of administration, as that of the immediate duty of the government in the present state of Ireland. The multitude of circumstances to be taken into account must strike every observer. Among these stand the novelty of the suspension of Habeas Corpus in a case of agrarian crime stimulated by a public society, and the rather serious difficulty of obtaining it; but more important than these is the grave doubt whether it would really reach the great characteristic evil of the time, namely, the paralysis of most important civil and proprietary rights, and whether the immediate proposal of a remedy, probably ineffective and even in a coercive sense partial, would not seriously damage the prospects of that arduous and comprehensive task which without doubt we must undertake when parliament is summoned.' In view of considerations of this kind, the awkwardness of directing an Act of parliament virtually against leaders who were at the moment the object of indictment in the Irish law courts; difficulties of time; doubts as to the case being really made out; doubts as to the efficacy of the proposed remedy, Mr. Forster did not carry the cabinet, but agreed to continue the experiment of the ordinary law. The experiment was no success, and coercion accompanied by land reform became the urgent policy.

III

The opening of the session of 1881 at once brought obstruction into full view. The Irish took up their position as a party of action. They spoke incessantly; as Mr. Gladstone put it, 'sometimes rising to the level of mediocrity, and more often grovelling amidst mere trash in unbounded profusion.' Obstruction is obstruction all the world over. It was not quite new at Westminster, but it was new on this scale. Closure proposals sprang up like mushrooms. Liberal members with a historical bent ran privately to the Speaker with ancient precedents of dictatorial powers asserted by his official ancestors, and they exhorted him to revive them.

Mr. Forster brought in his bill. Its scope may be described in a sentence. It practically enabled the viceroy to lock up anybody he pleased, and to detain him as long as he pleased, while the Act remained in force.[1] The debate for leave to introduce the bill lasted several days, without any sign of coming to an end. Here is the Speaker's account of his own memorable act in forcing a close : —

Monday, Jan. 31. — The House was boiling over with indignation at the apparent triumph of obstruction, and Mr. G., yielding to the pressure of his friends, committed himself unwisely, as I thought, to a continuous sitting on this day in order to force the bill through its first stage.

On Tuesday, after a sitting of twenty-four hours, I saw plainly that this attempt to carry the bill by continuous sitting would fail, the Parnell party being strong in numbers, discipline, and organisation, and with great gifts of speech. I reflected on the situation, and came to the conclusion that it was my duty to extricate the House from the difficulty by closing the debate of my own authority, and so asserting the undoubted will of the House against a rebellious minority. I sent for Mr. G. on Tuesday (Feb. 1), about noon, and told him that I should be prepared to put the question in spite of obstruction on the following conditions : 1. That the debate should be carried on until the following morning, my object in this delay being to mark distinctly to the outside world the extreme gravity of the situation, and the necessity of the step which I was about to take. 2. That he should reconsider the regulation of business, either by giving more authority to the House, or by conferring authority on the Speaker.

He agreed to these conditions, and summoned a meeting of the cabinet, which assembled in my library at four P.M. on Tuesday while the House was sitting, and I was in the chair. At that meeting the resolution as to business assumed the shape in which it finally appeared on the following Thursday, it having been pre-

---

[1] For a plain and precise description of the Coercion Act of 1881, see Dicey's *Law of the Constitution*, pp. 243-8.

viously considered at former meetings of the cabinet. I arranged
with Playfair to take the chair on Tuesday night about midnight,
engaging to resume it on Wednesday morning at nine. Accordingly at nine I took the chair, Biggar being in possession of the
House. I rose, and he resumed his seat. I proceeded with my
address as concerted with May, and when I had concluded I put
the question. The scene was most dramatic; but all passed off
without disturbance, the Irish party on the second division retiring
under protest.

I had communicated, with Mr. G.'s approval, my intention to
close the debate to Northcote, but to no one else, except May,
from whom I received much assistance. Northcote was startled,
but expressed no disapproval of the course proposed.

So ended the memorable sitting of January 31. At noon,
on February 2, the House assembled in much excitement.
The question was put challenging the Speaker's conduct.
'I answered,' he says, 'on the spur of the moment that I had
acted on my own responsibility, and from a sense of duty to
the House. I never heard such loud and protracted cheering, none cheering more loudly than Gladstone.' 'The
Speaker's firmness in mind,' Mr. Gladstone reported to the
Queen, 'his suavity in manner, his unwearied patience, his
incomparable temper, under a thousand provocations, have
rendered possible a really important result.'

IV

After coercion came a land bill, and here Mr. Gladstone
once more displayed his unequalled mastery of legislative
skill and power. He had to explain and be ready to
explain again and again, what he told Lord Selborne was
'the most difficult measure he had ever known to come
under the detailed consideration of a cabinet.' It was
no affair this time of speeches out of a railway carriage,
or addressed to excited multitudes in vast halls. That
might be, if you so pleased, 'the empty verbosity of exuberant rhetoric'; but nobody could say that of the contest
over the complexities of Irish tenure, against the clever and
indomitable Irish experts who fought under the banner of
Mr. Parnell. Northcote was not far wrong when he said

that though the bill was carried by two to one, there was hardly a man in the House beyond the Irish ranks who cared a straw about it. Another critic said that if the prime minister had asked the House to pass the *Koran* or the *Nautical Almanac* as a land bill, he would have met no difficulty.

The history of the session was described as the carriage of a single measure by a single man. Few British members understood it, none mastered it. The whigs were disaffected about it, the radicals doubted it, the tories thought that property as a principle was ruined by it, the Irishmen, when the humour seized them, bade him send the bill to line trunks. Mr. Gladstone, as one observer truly says, 'faced difficulties such as no other bill of this country has ever encountered, difficulties of politics and difficulties of law, difficulties of principle and difficulties of detail, difficulties of party and difficulties of personnel, difficulties of race and difficulties of class, and he has never once failed, or even seemed to fail, in his clear command of the question, in his dignity and authority of demeanour, in his impartiality in accepting amending suggestions, in his firmness in resisting destructive suggestions, in his clear perception of his aim, and his strong grasp of the fitting means. And yet it is hardly possible to appreciate adequately the embarrassments of the situation.'

Enough has already been said of the legislation of 1870, and its establishment of the principle that Irish land is not the subject of an undivided ownership, but a partnership.[1] The act of 1870 failed because it had too many exceptions and limitations; because in administration the compensation to the tenant for disturbance was inadequate; and because it did not fix the cultivator in his holding. Things had now ripened. The Richmond Commission shortly before had pointed to a court for fixing rents; that is, for settling the terms of the partnership. A commission nominated by Mr. Gladstone and presided over by Lord Bessborough had reported early in 1881 in favour not only of fair rents to be settled by a tribunal, but of fixity of tenure or the right of

[1] See vol. ii. p. 284.

the tenant to remain in his holding if he paid his rent, and of free sale ; that is, his right to part with his interest. These ' three F's ' were the substance of the legislation of 1881.

Rents could not be paid, and landlords either would not or could not reduce them. In the deepest interests of social order, and in confirmation of the tenant's equitable and customary ownership, the only course open to the imperial legislature was to erect machinery for fixing fair rents. The alternative to what became matter of much objurgation as dual ownership, was a single ownership that was only a short name for allowing the landlord to deal as he liked with the equitable interest of the tenant. Without the machinery set up by Mr. Gladstone, there could be no security for the protection of the cultivator's interest. What is more, even in view of a wide and general extension of the policy of buying out the landlord and turning the tenant into single owner, still a process of valuation for purposes of fair price would have been just as indispensable, as under the existing system was the tiresome and costly process of valuation for purposes of fair rent. It is true that if the policy of purchase had been adopted, this process would have been performed once for all. But opinion was not nearly ready either in England or Ireland for general purchase. And as Mr. Gladstone had put it to Bright in 1870, to turn a little handful of occupiers into owners would not have touched the fringe of the case of the bulk of the Irish cultivators, then undergoing acute mischief and urgently crying for prompt relief. Mr. Bright's idea of purchase, moreover, assumed that the buyer would come with at least a quarter of the price in his hand, — an assumption not consistent with the practical possibilities of the case.

The legislation of 1881 no doubt encountered angry criticism from the English conservative, and little more than frigid approval from the Irish nationalist. It offended the fundamental principle of the landlords ; its administration and the construction of some of its leading provisions by the courts disappointed and irritated the tenant party. Nevertheless any attempt in later times to impair the authority of the Land Act of 1881 brought the fact instantly to light, that the tenant knew it to be the fundamental charter of his redemption from worse than Egyptian bondage. In measuring this great agrarian law, not only by parliamentary force and legislative skill and power, but by the vast and abiding depth of its social results, both direct and still more indirect, many will be disposed to give it the highest place among Mr. Gladstone's achievements as lawmaker.

Fault has sometimes been found with Mr. Gladstone for not introducing his bill in the session of 1880. If this had been done, it is argued, Ireland would have been appeased, no coercion would have been necessary, and we should have been spared disastrous parliamentary exasperations and all the other mischiefs and perils of the quarrel between England and Ireland that followed. Criticism of this kind overlooks three facts. Neither Mr. Gladstone nor Forster nor the new House of Commons was at all ready in 1880 to accept the Three F's. Second, the Bessborough commission had not taken its evidence, and made its momentous report. Third, this argument assumes motives in Mr. Parnell, that probably do not at all cover the whole ground of his policy. As it happened, I called on Mr. Gladstone one morning early in 1881. 'You have heard,' I asked, 'that the Bessborough commission are to report for the Three F's?' 'I have not heard,' he said; 'it is incredible!' As so often comes to pass in politics, it was only a step from the incredible to the indispensable. But in 1880 the indispensable was also the impossible. It was the cruel winter of 1880–1 that made much difference.

In point of endurance the session was one of the most remarkable on record. The House of Commons sat 154 days and for 1400 hours; some 240 of these hours were after midnight. Only three times since the Reform bill had the House sat for more days; only once, in 1847, had the total number of hours been exceeded and that only by seven, and never before had the House sat so many hours after midnight. On the Coercion bill the House sat continuously once for 22 hours, and once for 41. The debates on the Land bill took up 58 sittings, and the Coercion bill 22. No such length of discussion, Mr. Gladstone told the Queen, was recorded on any measure since the committee on the first Reform bill. The Reform bill of 1867 was the only measure since 1843 that took as many as 35 days of debate. The Irish Church bill took 21 days and the Land bill of 1870 took 25. Of the 14,836 speeches delivered, 6315 were made by Irish members. The Speaker and chairman of committees interposed on points of order nearly 2000 times during the session. Mr. Parnell, the Speaker notes, 'with his minority of 24 dominates the House. When will the House take courage and reform its procedure?' After all, the suspension of *habeas corpus* is a thing that men may well think it worth while to fight about, and a revolution in a country's land-system might be expected to take up a good deal of time.

V

It soon appeared that no miracle had been wrought by either Coercion Act or Land Act. Mr. Parnell drew up test cases for submission to the new land court. His advice to the army of tenants would depend, he said, on the fate of these cases. In September Mr. Forster visited Hawarden, and gave a bad account of the real meaning of Mr. Parnell's plausible propositions for sending test cases to the newly established land commission, as well as of other ugly circumstances. 'It is quite clear as you said,' wrote Mr. Gladstone to Forster in Ireland, 'that Parnell means to present cases which the commission must refuse, and then to treat their refusal as showing that they cannot be trusted, and that the bill has failed.' As he interpreted it afterwards, there was no doubt that in one sense the Land Act tended to accelerate a crisis in Ireland, for it brought to a head the affairs of the party connected with the land league. It made it almost a necessity for that party either to advance or to recede. They chose the desperate course. At the same date, he wrote in a letter to Lord Granville:—

With respect to Parnellism, I should not propose to do more than a severe and strong denunciation of it by severing him altogether from the Irish people and the mass of the Irish members, and by saying that home rule has for one of its aims local government — an excellent thing to which I would affix no limits except the supremacy of the imperial parliament, and the rights of all parts of the country to claim whatever might be accorded to Ireland. This is only a repetition of what I have often said before, and I have nothing to add or enlarge. But I have the fear that when the occasion for action comes, which will not be in my time, many liberals may perhaps hang back and may cause further trouble.

In view of what was to come four years later, one of his letters to Forster is interesting (April 12, 1882), among other reasons as illustrating the depth to which the essence of political liberalism had now penetrated Mr. Gladstone's mind : —

1. About local government for Ireland, the ideas which more and more establish themselves in my mind are such as these.

(1.) Until we have seriously responsible bodies to deal with us in Ireland, every plan we frame comes to Irishmen, say what we may, as an English plan. As such it is probably condemned. At best it is a one-sided bargain, which binds us, not them.

(2.) If your excellent plans for obtaining local aid towards the execution of the law break down, it will be on account of this miserable and almost total want of the sense of responsibility for the public good and public peace in Ireland; and this responsibility we cannot create except through local self-government.

(3.) If we say we must postpone the question till the state of the country is more fit for it, I should answer that the least danger is in going forward at once. It is liberty alone which fits men for liberty. This proposition, like every other in politics, has its bounds; but it is far safer than the counter doctrine, wait till they are fit.

(4.) In truth I should say (differing perhaps from many), that for the Ireland of to-day, the first question is the rectification of the relations between landlord and tenant, which happily is going on; the next is to relieve Great Britain from the enormous weight of the government of Ireland unaided by the people, and from the hopeless contradiction in which we stand while we give a parliamentary representation, hardly effective for anything but mischief without the local institutions of self-government which it presupposes, and on which alone it can have a sound and healthy basis.

We have before us in administration, he wrote to Forster in September —

a problem not less delicate and arduous than the problem of legislation with which we have lately had to deal in parliament. Of the leaders, the officials, the skeleton of the land league I have no hope whatever. The better the prospects of the Land Act with their adherents outside the circle of wire-pullers, and with the Irish people, the more bitter will be their hatred, and the more sure they will be to go as far as fear of the people will allow them in keeping up the agitation, which they cannot afford to part with on account of their ulterior ends. All we can do is to turn more and more the masses of their followers, to fine them down by good laws and good government, and it is in this view that the question of judicious releases from prison, should improving statistics of crime encourage it, may become one of early importance.

VI

It was in the autumn of 1881 that Mr. Gladstone visited Leeds, in payment of the debt of gratitude due for his triumphant return in the general election of the year before. This progress extended over four days, and almost surpassed in magnitude and fervour any of his experiences in other parts of the kingdom. We have an interesting glimpse of the physical effort of such experiences in a couple of his letters written to Mr. Kitson, who with immense labour and spirit had organized this severe if glorious enterprise : —

Hawarden Castle, Sept. 28, 1881. — I thank you for the very clear and careful account of the proposed proceedings at Leeds. It lacks as yet that *rough* statement of numbers at each meeting, which is requisite to enable me to understand what I shall have to do. This will be fixed by the scale of the meeting. I see no difficulty but one — a procession through the principal thoroughfares is one of the most exhausting processes I know as a *preliminary* to addressing a mass meeting. A mass meeting requires the physical powers to be in their best and freshest state, as far as anything can be fresh in a man near seventy-two; and I have on one or more former occasions felt them wofully contracted. In Midlothian I never had anything of the kind before a great physical effort in speaking; and the lapse even of a couple of years is something. It would certainly be most desirable to have the mass meeting first, and then I have not any fear at all of the procession through whatever thoroughfares you think fit.

Oct. 2, 1881. — I should be very sorry to put aside any of the opportunities of vision at Leeds which the public may care to use; but what I had hoped was that these might come *after* any speeches of considerable effort and not *before* them. To understand what a physical drain, and what a reaction from tension of the senses is caused by a 'progress' before addressing a great audience, a person must probably have gone through it, and gone through it at my time of life. When I went to Midlothian, I begged that this might never happen; and it was avoided throughout. Since that time I have myself been sensible for the first time of a diminished power of voice in the House of Commons, and others also for the first time have remarked it.

Vast torchlight processions, addresses from the corporation, four score addresses from political bodies, a giant banquet in the Cloth Hall Yard covered in for the purpose, on one day; on another, more addresses, a public luncheon followed by a mass meeting of over five-and-twenty thousand persons, then a long journey through dense throngs vociferous with an exultation that knew no limits, a large dinner party, and at the end of all a night train. The only concessions that the veteran asked to weakness of the flesh, were that at the banquet he should not appear until the eating and drinking were over, and that at the mass meeting some preliminary speakers should intervene to give him time to take breath after his long and serious exercises of the morning. When the time came his voice was heard like the note of a clear and deep-toned bell. So much had vital energy, hardly less rare than his mental power, to do with the varied exploits of this spacious career.

The topics of his Leeds speeches I need not travel over.

What attracted most attention and perhaps drew most applause was his warning to Mr. Parnell. 'He desires,' said
the minister, 'to arrest the operation of the Land Act; to
stand as Moses stood between the living and the dead; to
stand there not as Moses stood, to arrest, but to spread the
plague.' The menace that followed became a catchword of
the day: 'If it shall appear that there is still to be fought
a final conflict in Ireland between law on the one side and
sheer lawlessness upon the other, if the law purged from
defect and from any taint of injustice is still to be repelled
and refused, and the first conditions of political society to
remain unfulfilled, then I say, gentlemen, without hesitation,
the resources of civilisation against its enemies are not yet
exhausted.'[1]

Nor was the pageant all excitement. The long speech,
which by way of prelusion to the great mass meeting he
addressed to the chamber of commerce, was devoted to the
destruction of the economic sophisters who tried to persuade
us that 'the vampire of free-trade was insidiously sucking
the life-blood of the country.' In large survey of broad social
facts, exposition of diligently assorted figures, power of
scientific analysis, sustained chain of reasoning, he was never
better. The consummate mastery of this argumentative
performance did not slay a heresy that has nine lives, but
it drove the thing out of sight in Yorkshire for some time
to come.[2]

VII

On Wednesday October 12, the cabinet met, and after five
hours of deliberation decided that Mr. Parnell should be
sent to prison under the Coercion Act. The Irish leader
was arrested at his hotel the next morning, and carried
off to Kilmainham, where he remained for some six
months. The same day Mr. Gladstone was presented with
an address from the Common Council of London, and in his
speech at the Guildhall gave them the news: —

Our determination has been that to the best of our power, our
words should be carried into acts [referring to what he had said

---

[1] At the Cloth Hall banquet, Leeds, Oct. 8, 1881.
[2] Speech to the Leeds Chamber of Commerce, Oct. 8, 1881.

at Leeds], and even within these few moments I have been informed that towards the vindication of law and order, of the rights of property, of the freedom of the land, of the first elements of political life and civilisation, the first step has been taken in the arrest of the man who unhappily from motives which I do not challenge, which I cannot examine and with which I have nothing to do, has made himself beyond all others prominent in the attempt to destroy the authority of the law, and to substitute what would end in being nothing more or less than anarchical oppression exercised upon the people of Ireland.

The arrest of Mr. Parnell was no doubt a pretty considerable strain upon powers conferred by parliament to put down village ruffians; but times were revolutionary, and though the Act of parliament was not a wise one, but altogether the reverse of wise, it was no wonder that having got the instrument, ministers thought they might as well use it. Still executive violence did not seem to work, and Mr. Gladstone looked in a natural direction for help in the milder way of persuasion. He wrote (December 17th) to Cardinal Newman:—

I will begin with defining strictly the limits of this appeal. I ask you to read the inclosed papers; and to consider whether you will write anything to Rome upon them. I do not ask you to write, nor to tell me whether you write, nor to make any reply to this letter, beyond returning the inclosures in an envelope to me in Downing Street. I will state briefly the grounds of my request, thus limited. In 1844, when I was young as a cabinet minister, and the government of Sir R. Peel was troubled with the O'Connell manifestations, they made what I think was an appeal to Pope Gregory xvi. for his intervention to discourage agitation in Ireland. I should be very loath now to tender such a request at Rome. But now a different case arises. Some members of the Roman catholic priesthood in Ireland deliver certain sermons and otherwise express themselves in the way which my inclosures exhibit. I doubt whether if they were laymen we should not have settled their cases by putting them into gaol. I need not describe the sentiments uttered. Your eminence will feel them and judge them as strongly as I do. But now as to the Supreme

Pontiff.   You will hardly be surprised when I say that I regard him, if apprised of the facts, as responsible for the conduct of these priests.   For I know perfectly well that he has the means of silencing them; and that, if any one of them were in public to dispute the decrees of the council of 1870 as plainly as he has denounced law and order, he would be silenced.

Mr. Errington, who is at Rome, will I believe have seen these papers, and will I hope have brought the facts as far as he is able to the knowledge of his holiness.   But I do not know how far he is able; nor how he may use his discretion.   He is not our official servant, but an independent Roman catholic gentleman and a volunteer.

My wish is as regards Ireland, in this hour of her peril and her hope, to leave nothing undone by which to give heart and strength to the hope and to abate the peril.   But my wish as regards the Pope is that he should have the means of bringing those for whom he is responsible to fulfil the elementary duties of citizenship.   I say of citizenship; of Christianity, of priesthood, it is not for me to speak.

The cardinal replied that he would gladly find himself able to be of service, however slight it might be, in a political crisis which must be felt as of grave anxiety by all who understand the blessing of national unity and peace. He thought Mr. Gladstone overrated the pope's power in political and social matters.   Absolute in questions of theology, it was not so in political matters.   If the contest in Ireland were whether 'rebellion' or whether 'robbery' was a sin, we might expect him to anathematise its denial. But his action in concrete matters, as whether a political party is censurable or not, was not direct, and only in the long run effective.   Local power and influence was often a match for Roman right.   The pope's right keeps things together, it checks extravagances, and at length prevails, but not without a fight.   Its exercise is a matter of great prudence, and depends upon times and circumstances.   As for the intemperate dangerous words of priests and curates, surely such persons belonged to their respective bishops, and scarcely required the introduction of the Supreme Authority.

VIII

We have now arrived at April 1882. The reports brought to the cabinet by Mr. Forster were of the gloomiest. The Land Act had brought no improvement. In the south-west and many of the midland counties lawlessness and intimidation were worse than ever. Returns of agrarian crime were presented in every shape, and comparisons framed by weeks, by months, by quarters; do what the statisticians would, and in spite of fluctuations, murders and other serious outrages had increased. The policy of arbitrary arrest had completely failed, and the officials and crown lawyers at the Castle were at their wits' end.

While the cabinet was face to face with this ugly prospect, Mr. Gladstone received a communication volunteered by an Irish member, as to the new attitude of Mr. Parnell and the possibility of turning it to good account. Mr. Gladstone sent this letter on to Forster, replying meanwhile 'in the sense of not shutting the door.' When the thing came before the cabinet, Mr. Chamberlain — who had previously told Mr. Gladstone that he thought the time opportune for something like a reconciliation with the Irish party — with characteristic courage took his life in his hands, as he put it, and set to work to ascertain through the emissary what use for the public good could be made of Mr. Parnell's changed frame of mind. On April 25th, the cabinet heard what Mr. Chamberlain had to tell them, and it came to this, that Mr. Parnell was desirous to use his influence on behalf of peace, but his influence for good depended on the settlement of the question of arrears. Ministers decided that they could enter into no agreement and would give no pledge. They would act on their own responsibility in the light of the knowledge they had gained of Mr. Parnell's views. Mr. Gladstone was always impatient of any reference to 'reciprocal assurances' or 'tacit understanding' in respect of the dealings with the prisoner in Kilmainham. Still the nature of the proceedings was plain enough. The object of the communications to which the government were invited by Mr. Parnell through his emissary, was, supposing him to be anxious to do what he could for law and order, to find out what action on the part of the government would enable him to adopt this line.

Events then moved rapidly. Rumours that something was going on got abroad, and questions began to be put in parliament. A stout tory gave notice of a motion aiming at the release of the suspects. As Mr. Gladstone informed the Queen, there was no doubt that the general opinion of the public was moving in a direction adverse to arbitrary imprisonment, though the question was a nice one for consideration whether the recent surrender by the no-rent party of its extreme and most subversive contentions, amounted to anything like a guarantee for their future conduct in respect of peace and order. The rising excitement was swelled by the retirement of Lord Cowper from the viceroyalty, and the appointment as his successor of Lord Spencer, who had filled that post in Mr. Gladstone's first government. On May 2nd, Mr. Gladstone read a memorandum to the cabinet to which they agreed : —

The cabinet are of opinion that the time has now arrived when with a view to the interests of law and order in Ireland, the three members of parliament who have been imprisoned on suspicion since last October, should be immediately released ; and that the list of suspects should be examined with a view to the release of all persons not believed to be associated with crimes. They propose at once to announce to parliament their intention to propose, as soon as necessary business will permit, a bill to strengthen the ordinary law in Ireland for the security of life and property, while reserving their discretion with regard to the Life and Property Protection Act [of 1881], which however they do not at present think it will be possible to renew, if a favourable state of affairs shall prevail in Ireland.

From this proceeding Mr. Forster dissented, and he resigned his office. His point seems to have been that no suspect should be released until the new Coercion Act had been fashioned, whereas the rest of the cabinet held that there was no excuse for the continued detention under arbitrary warrant of men as to whom the ground for the 'reasonable suspicion' required by the law had now disappeared. He

CHAP.
IV.

_Æt._ 73.

probably felt that the appointment of a viceroy of cabinet rank and with successful Irish experience was in fact his own supersession. 'I have received your letter,' Mr. Gladstone wrote to him (May 2), 'with much grief, but on this it would be selfish to expatiate. I have no choice ; followed or not followed I must go on. There are portions of the subject which touch you personally, and which seem to me to deserve *much* attention. But I have such an interest in the main issue, that I could not be deemed impartial ; so I had better not enter on them. One thing, however, I wish to say. You wish to minimise in any further statement the cause of your retreat. In my opinion — *and I speak from experience* — viewing the nature of that course, you will find this hardly possible. For a justification you, I fear, will have to found upon the doctrine of "a new departure." We must protest against it, and deny it with heart and soul.'

The way in which Mr. Gladstone chose to put things was stated in a letter to the Queen (May 3) : 'In his judgment there had been two, and only two, vital powers of commanding efficacy in Ireland, the Land Act, and the land league ; they had been locked in a combat of life and death ; and the cardinal question was which of the two would win. From the serious effort to amend the Land Act by the Arrears bill of the nationalists,[1] from the speeches made in support of it, and from information voluntarily tendered to the government as to the views of the leaders of the league, the cabinet believed that those who governed the land league were now conscious of having been defeated by the Land Act on the main question, that of paying rent.'

For the office of Irish secretary Mr. Gladstone selected Lord Frederick Cavendish, who was the husband of a niece of Mrs. Gladstone's, and one of the most devoted of his friends and adherents. The special reason for the choice of this capable and high-minded man, was that Lord Frederick had framed a plan of finance at the treasury for a new scheme of land purchase. The two freshly appointed Irish ministers at once crossed over to a country seething in disorder. The

[1] Introduced by Mr. Redmond.

afternoon of the fatal sixth of May was passed by the
new viceroy and Lord Frederick in that grim apartment in
Dublin Castle, where successive secretaries spend unshining
hours in saying No to impossible demands, and hunting
for plausible answers to insoluble riddles. Never did so
dreadful a shadow overhang it as on that day. The task
on which the two ministers were engaged was the consideration of the new provisions for coping with disorder, which
had been prepared in London. The under-secretary, Mr.
Burke, and one of the lawyers, were present. Lord Spencer
rode out to the park about five o'clock, and Lord Frederick
followed him an hour later. He was overtaken by the
under-secretary walking homewards, and as the two strolled
on together, they were both brutally murdered in front
of the vice-regal residence. The assassins did not know who
Lord Frederick was. Well has it been said that Ireland
seems the sport of a destiny that is aimless.[1]

The official world of London was on that Saturday night
in the full round of its pleasures. The Gladstones were
dining at the Austrian embassy. So, too, was Sir William
Harcourt, and to him as home secretary the black tidings
were sent from Dublin late in the evening. Mr. and Mrs.
Gladstone had already left, she for a party at the admiralty,
he walking home to Downing Street. At the admiralty
they told her of bad news from Ireland and hurried her
away. Mr. Gladstone arrived at home a few minutes after
her. When his secretary in the hall told him of the
horrible thing that had been done, it was as if he had
been felled to the ground. Then they hastened to bear
what solace they could, to the anguish-stricken home where
solace would be so sorely needed.

The effect of this blind and hideous crime was at once to
arrest the spirit and the policy of conciliation. While the
Irish leaders were locked up, a secret murder club had
taken matters in hand in their own way, and ripened plots

[1] It had been Mr. Burke's practice
to drive from the Castle to the Park
gate, then to descend and walk home,
followed by two detectives. On this
occasion he found at the gate that
the chief secretary had passed, and
drove forward to overtake him. The
detectives did not follow him as usual.
If they had followed, he would have
been saved.

within a stone's throw of the Castle.   No worse blow could
have been struck at Mr. Parnell's policy.   It has been said
that the nineteenth century had seen the course of its history
twenty-five times diverted by actual or attempted crime.
In that sinister list the murders in the Phœnix Park have a
tragic place.

The voice of party was for the moment hushed.   Sir
Stafford Northcote wrote a letter of admirable feeling, saying
that if there was any way in which Mr. Gladstone thought
they could serve the government, he would of course let
them know.   The Prince of Wales wrote of his own horror
and indignation at the crime, and of his sympathy with
Mr. Gladstone in the loss of one who was not only a colleague
of many merits, but a near connection and devoted friend.
With one or two scandalous exceptions, the tone of the
English press was sober, sensible, and self-possessed.   'If a
nation,' said a leading journal in Paris, 'should be judged
by the way in which it acts on grave occasions, the spectacle
offered by England is calculated to produce a high opinion
of the political character and spirit of the British people.'
Things of the baser sort were not quite absent, but they did not
matter.   An appeal confronted the electors of the North-West
Riding as they went to the poll at a bye-election a few days
later, to 'Vote for——, and avenge the death of Lord
Frederick Cavendish!'   They responded by placing——'s
opponent at the head of the poll by a majority of two
thousand.

The scene in the House had all the air of tragedy, and
Mr. Gladstone summoned courage enough to do his part
with impressive composure.   A colleague was doing some
business with him in his room before the solemnity began.
When it was over, they resumed it, Mr. Gladstone making
no word of reference to the sombre interlude, before or after.
'Went reluctantly to the House,' he says in his diary, 'and
by the help of God forced out what was needful on the
question of the adjournment.'   His words were not many,
when after commemorating the marked qualities of Mr.
Burke, he went on in laboured tones and slow speech and
hardly repressed emotion : —

The hand of the assassin has come nearer home; and though
I feel it difficult to say a word, yet I must say that one of the very
noblest hearts in England has ceased to beat, and has ceased at the
very moment when it was just devoted to the service of Ireland,
full of love for that country, full of hope for her future, full of
capacity to render her service.

Writing to Lady Frederick on a later day, he mentions a
public reference to some pathetic words of hers (May 19) : —

Sexton just now returned to the subject, with much approval
from the House. You will find it near the middle of a long
speech. Nothing could be better either in feeling or in grace
(the man is little short of a master), and I think it will warm
your heart. You have made a mark deeper than any wound.

To Lord Ripon in India, he wrote (June 1) : —

The black act brought indeed a great personal grief to my wife
and me; but we are bound to merge our own sorrow in the larger
and deeper affliction of the widow and the father, in the sense of
the public loss of a life so valuable to the nation, and in the consideration of the great and varied effects it may have on immediate
and vital interests. Since the death of this dearly loved son, we
have heard much good of the Duke, whom indeed we saw at Chatsworth after the funeral, and we have seen much of Lady Frederick,
who has been good even beyond what we could have hoped. I
have no doubt you have heard in India the echo of words spoken
by Spencer from a letter of hers, in which she said she could give
up even him if his death were to work good to his fellow-men,
which indeed was the whole object of his life. These words have
had a tender effect, as remarkable as the horror excited by the
slaughter. Spencer wrote to me that a priest in Connemara read
them from the altar; when the whole congregation spontaneously
fell down upon their knees. In England, the national attitude has
been admirable. The general strain of language has been, 'Do not
let this terrible and flagitious crime deter you from persevering
with the work of justice.

Well did Dean Church say that no Roman or Florentine
lady ever uttered a more heroic thing than was said by this

English lady when on first seeing Mr. Gladstone that terrible midnight she said, 'You did right to send him to Ireland.'[1] 'The loss of F. Cavendish,' Mr. Gladstone wrote to his eldest son, 'will ever be to us all as an unhealed wound.'

On the day after the murders Mr. Gladstone received a note through the same channel by which Mr. Chamberlain had carried on his communications : 'I am authorised by Mr. Parnell to state that if Mr. Gladstone considers it necessary for the maintenance of his [Mr. G.'s] position and for carrying out his views, that Mr. Parnell should resign his seat, Mr. Parnell is prepared to do so immediately.' To this Mr. Gladstone replied (May 7) : —

My duty does not permit me for a moment to entertain Mr. Parnell's proposal, just conveyed to me by you, that he should if I think it needful resign his seat; but I am deeply sensible of the honourable motives by which it has been prompted.

'My opinion is,' said Mr. Gladstone to Lord Granville, 'that if Parnell goes, no restraining influence will remain ; the scale of outrages will be again enlarged ; and no repressive bill can avail to put it down.' Those of the cabinet who had the best chance of knowing, were convinced that Mr. Parnell was 'sincerely anxious for the pacification of Ireland.'

The reaction produced by the murders in the Park made perseverance in a milder policy impossible in face of English opinion, and parliament eagerly passed the Coercion Act of 1882. I once asked an Irishman of consummate experience and equitable mind, with no leanings that I know of to political nationalism, whether the task of any later ruler of Ireland was comparable to Lord Spencer's. 'Assuredly not,' he replied : 'in 1882 Ireland seemed to be literally a society on the eve of dissolution. The Invincibles still roved with knives about the streets of Dublin. Discontent had been stirred in the ranks of the Royal Irish Constabulary, and a dangerous mutiny broke out in the metropolitan force. Over half of the country the demoralisation of every class, the terror, the fierce hatred, the universal distrust, had grown to an incredible pitch. The moral cowardice of what ought

[1] *Life of Dean Church*, p. 299.

to have been the governing class was astounding. The landlords would hold meetings and agree not to go beyond a certain
abatement, and then they would go individually and privately
offer to the tenant a greater abatement. Even the agents
of the law and the courts were shaken in their duty. The
power of random arrest and detention under the Coercion
Act of 1881 had not improved the *moral* of magistrates and
police. The sheriff would let the word get out that he was
coming to make a seizure, and profess surprise that the
cattle had vanished. The whole country-side turned out in
thousands in half the counties in Ireland to attend flaming
meetings, and if a man did not attend, angry neighbours
trooped up to know the reason why. The clergy hardly
stirred a finger to restrain the wildness of the storm ; some
did their best to raise it. All that was what Lord Spencer
had to deal with ; the very foundations of the social fabric
rocking.'

The new viceroy attacked the formidable task before him
with resolution, minute assiduity, and an inexhaustible store
of that steady-eyed patience which is the sovereign requisite
of any man who, whether with coercion or without, takes in
hand the government of Ireland. He was seconded with high
ability and courage by Mr. Trevelyan, the new Irish secretary,
whose fortitude was subjected to a far severer trial than has
ever fallen to the lot of any Irish secretary before or since.
The coercion that Lord Spencer had to administer was at
least law. The coercion with which parliament entrusted
Mr. Forster the year before was the negation of the spirit of
law, and the substitution for it of naked and arbitrary
control over the liberty of the subject by executive power —
a system as unconstitutional in theory as it was infatuated
in policy and calamitous in result. Even before the end
of the parliament, Mr. Bright frankly told the House of
Commons of this Coercion Act : ' I think that the legislation of 1881 was unfortunately a great mistake, though I
was myself a member of the government concerned in it.'

CHAPTER V

EGYPT

(*1881–1882*)

> I FIND many very ready to say what I ought to have done when
> a battle is over; but I wish some of these persons would come
> and tell me what to do before the battle. — WELLINGTON.

IN 1877 Mr. Gladstone penned words to which later events
gave an only too striking verification. 'Territorial questions,'
he said, 'are not to be disposed of by arbitrary limits; we
cannot enjoy the luxury of taking Egyptian soil by pinches.
We may seize an Aden and a Perim, where is no already
formed community of inhabitants, and circumscribe a tract
at will. But our first site in Egypt, be it by larceny or be it
by emption, will be the almost certain egg of a North African
empire, that will grow and grow until another Victoria and
another Albert, titles of the lake-sources of the White Nile,
come within our borders; and till we finally join hands
across the equator with Natal and Cape Town, to say nothing
of the Transvaal and the Orange River on the south, or of
Abyssinia or Zanzibar to be swallowed by way of viaticum on
our journey.' [1] It was one of the ironies in which every
active statesman's life abounds, that the author of that forecast should have been fated to take his country over its first
marches towards this uncoveted destination.

I

For many months after Mr. Gladstone formed his second
ministry, there was no reason to suppose that the Egyptian
branch of the eastern question, which for ever casts its

[1] *Nineteenth Century*, August, 1877; *Gleanings*, iv. p. 357.

perplexing shadow over Europe, was likely to give trouble. CHAP.
The new Khedive held a regularly defined position, alike V.
towards his titular sovereign at Constantinople, towards Æт. 72.
reforming ministers at Cairo, towards the creditors of his
state, and towards the two strong European Powers who for
different reasons had the supervision of Egyptian affairs
in charge. The oppression common to oriental governments
seemed to be yielding before western standards. The load of
interest on a profligate debt was heavy, but it was not unskil-
fully adjusted. The rate of village usury was falling, and the
value of land was rising. Unluckily the Khedive and his
ministers neglected the grievances of the army, and in
January 1881 its leaders broke out in revolt. The Khedive,
without an armed force on whose fidelity he could rely, gave
way to the mutineers, and a situation was created, familiar
enough in all oriental states, and not unlike that in our own
country between Charles I., or in later days the parliament, and
the roundhead troopers: anger and revenge in the breast of
the affronted civil ruler, distrust and dread of punishment in
the mind of the soldiery. During the autumn (1881) the crisis
grew more alarming. The Khedive showed neither energy
nor tact; he neither calmed the terror of the mutineers nor
crushed them. Insubordination in the army began to affect
the civil population, and a national party came into open
existence in the chamber of notables. The soldiers found a
head in Arabi, a native Egyptian, sprung of fellah origin.
Want either of stern resolution or of politic vision in the
Khedive and his minister had transferred the reality of
power to the insurgents. The Sultan of Turkey here saw his
chance; he made a series of diplomatic endeavours to re-
establish a shattered sovereignty over his nominal feudatory
on the Nile. This pretension, and the spreading tide of
disorder, brought England and France actively upon the
scene. We can see now, what expert observers on the spot
saw then, that the two Powers mistook the nature of the
Arabist movement. They perceived in it no more than a
military rising. It was in truth national as well as military;
it was anti-European, and above all, it was in its objects
anti-Turk.

In 1879 the two governments had insisted on imposing over Egypt two controllers, with limited functions but irremovable. This, as Mr. Gladstone argued later, was to bring foreign intervention into the heart of the country, and to establish in the strictest sense a political control.[1] As a matter of fact, not then well known, in September 1879 Lord Salisbury had come to a definite understanding with the French ambassador in London, that the two governments would not tolerate the establishment in Egypt of political influence by any competing European Power ; and what was more important, that they were prepared to take action to any extent that might be found necessary to give effect to their views in this respect. The notable acquisition by Lord Beaconsfield of an interest in the Suez Canal, always regarded by Mr. Gladstone as a politically ill-advised and hazardous transaction, had tied the English knot in Egypt still tighter.

The policy of the Gladstone cabinet was defined in general words in a despatch from the foreign minister to the British agent at Cairo. Lord Granville (November 1881) disclaimed any self-aggrandising designs on the part of either England or France. He proclaimed the desire of the cabinet to uphold in Egypt the administrative independence secured to her by the decrees of the sovereign power on the Bosphorus. Finally he set forth that the only circumstances likely to force the government of the Queen to depart from this course of conduct, would be the occurrence in Egypt of a state of anarchy.[2]

Justly averse to a joint occupation of Egypt by England and France, as the most perilous of all possible courses, the London cabinet looked to the Sultan as the best instrument for restoring order. Here they were confronted by two insurmountable obstacles : first, the steadfast hostility of France to any form of Turkish intervention, and second, that strong current of antipathy to the Sultan which had been set flowing over British opinion in the days of Midlothian.[3]

---

[1] July 27, 1882.

[2] Granville and Malet, November 4, 1881.

[3] Before Midlothian, however, Mr.

Gladstone had in 1877 drawn an important distinction : 'If I find the Turk incapable of establishing a good, just, and well-proportioned govern-

In December (1881) the puissant genius of Gambetta
acquired supremacy for a season, and he without delay
pressed upon the British cabinet the necessity of preparing for joint and immediate action. Gambetta prevailed.
The Turk was ruled out, and the two Powers of the west
determined on action of their own. The particular mode
of common action, however, in case action should become
necessary, was left entirely open.

Meanwhile the British cabinet was induced to agree to
Gambetta's proposal to send instructions to Cairo, assuring
the Khedive that England and France were closely associated
in the resolve to guard by their united efforts against
all causes of complaint, internal or external, which might
menace the existing order of things in Egypt. This was a
memorable starting-point in what proved an amazing journey.
This Joint Note (January 6, 1881) was the first link in a
chain of proceedings that brought each of the two governments who were its authors, into the very position that they
were most strenuously bent on averting; France eventually ousted herself from Egypt, and England was eventually
landed in plenary and permanent occupation. So extraordinary a result only shows how impenetrable were the windings of the labyrinth. The foremost statesmen of England
and France were in their conning towers, and England at any
rate employed some of the ablest of her agents. Yet each
was driven out of an appointed course to an unforeseen
and an unwelcome termination. Circumstances like these
might teach moderation both to the French partisans who
curse the vacillations of M. de Freycinet, and to the English
partisans who, while rejoicing in the ultimate result, curse
the vacillations of the cabinet of Mr. Gladstone, in wisely
striving to unravel a knot instead of at all risks cutting it.

II

The present writer described the effect of the Joint Note
in the following words written at the time [1]: 'At Cairo the

ment over civilised and Christian
races, it does not follow that he is
under a similar incapacity when his
task shall only be to hold empire
over populations wholly or principally Orientals and Mahomedans.

On this head I do not know that any
verdict of guilty has yet been found
by a competent tribunal.' — *Gleanings*, iv. p. 364.

[1] *Fortnightly Review*, July 1882.

Note fell like a bombshell. Nobody there had expected any
such declaration, and nobody was aware of any reason why
it should have been launched. What was felt was that so
serious a step on such delicate ground could not have been
adopted without deliberate calculation, nor without some
grave intention. The Note was, therefore, taken to mean
that the Sultan was to be thrust still further in the background; that the Khedive was to become more plainly the
puppet of England and France; and that Egypt would sooner
or later in some shape or other be made to share the fate
of Tunis. The general effect was, therefore, mischievous in
the highest degree. The Khedive was encouraged in his
opposition to the sentiments of his Chamber. The military,
national, or popular party was alarmed. The Sultan was
irritated. The other European Powers were made uneasy.
Every element of disturbance was roused into activity.'

It is true that even if no Joint Note had ever been despatched, the prospects of order were unpromising. The
most careful analysis of the various elements of society in
Egypt by those best acquainted at first hand with all those
elements, whether internal or external, whether Egyptian or
European, and with all the roots of antagonism thriving
among them, exhibited no promise of stability. If Egypt
had been a simple case of an oriental government in revolutionary commotion, the ferment might have been left to
work itself out. Unfortunately Egypt, in spite of the maps,
lies in Europe. So far from being a simple case, it was
indescribably entangled, and even the desperate questions
that rise in our minds at the mention of the Balkan peninsula, of Armenia, of Constantinople, offer no such complex
of difficulties as the Egyptian riddle in 1881–2. The law of
liquidation [1] — whatever else we may think of it — at least
made the policy of Egypt for the Egyptians unworkable.
Yet the British cabinet were not wrong in thinking that
this was no reason for sliding into the competing policy of
Egypt for the English *and* the French, which would have
been more unworkable still.

England strove manfully to hold the ground that she

[1] Defining the claims of the European bondholder on revenue.

had taken in November. Lord Granville told the British CHAP.
ambassador in Paris that his government disliked interven- V.
tion either by themselves or anybody else as much as ever; Æt. 72.
that they looked upon the experiment of the Chamber with
favourable eyes; that they wished to keep the connection
of the Porte with Egypt so far as it was compatible with
Egyptian liberties; and that the object of the Joint Note was
to strengthen the existing government of Egypt. Gambetta,
on the other hand, was convinced that all explanations of this
sort would only serve further to inflate the enemies of France
and England in the Egyptian community, and would encourage their designs upon the law of liquidation. Lord Granville
was honourably and consistently anxious to confine himself
within the letter of international right, while Gambetta was
equally anxious to intervene in Egyptian administration,
within right or without it, and to force forward that Anglo-
French occupation in which Lord Granville so justly saw
nothing but danger and mischief. Once more Lord
Granville, at the end of the month which had opened with
the Joint Note, in a despatch to the ambassador at Paris
(January 30), defined the position of the British cabinet.
What measures should be taken to meet Egyptian dis-
orders? The Queen's government had 'a strong objection
to the occupation of Egypt by themselves.' Egypt and
Turkey would oppose; it would arouse the jealousy of other
Powers, who would, as there was even already good reason to
believe, make counter demonstrations; and, finally, such an
occupation would be as distasteful to the French nation as
the sole occupation of Egypt by the French would be to ourselves. Joint occupation by England and France, in short,
might lessen some difficulties, but it would seriously aggravate others. Turkish occupation would be a great evil, but it
would not entail political dangers as great as those attending
the other two courses. As for the French objections to the
farther admission of the other European Powers to intervene
in Egyptian affairs, the cabinet agreed that England and
France had an exceptional position in Egypt, but might it
not be desirable to enter into some communication with the
other Powers, as to the best way of dealing with a state of

things that appeared likely to interfere both with the Sultan's firmans and with Egypt's international engagements?

At this critical moment Gambetta fell from power. The mark that he had set upon western policy in Egypt remained. Good observers on the spot, trained in the great school of India, thought that even if there were no more than a chance of working with the national party, the chance was well worth trying. As the case was put at the time, 'It is impossible to conceive a situation that more imperatively called for caution, circumspection, and deference to the knowledge of observers on the scene, or one that was actually handled with greater rashness and hurry. Gambetta had made up his mind that the military movement was leading to the abyss, and that it must be peremptorily arrested. It may be that he was right in supposing that the army, which had first found its power in the time of Ismail, would go from bad to worse. But everything turned upon the possibility of pulling up the army, without arousing other elements more dangerous still. M. Gambetta's impatient policy was worked out in his own head without reference to the conditions on the scene, and the result was what might have been expected.' [1]

III

The dual control, the system of carrying on the Egyptian government under the advice of an English and a French agent, came to an end. The rude administration in the provinces fell to pieces. The Khedive was helplessly involved in struggle after struggle with the military insurgents. The army became as undisputed masters of the government, as the Cromwellian army at some moments in our civil war. Meanwhile the British government, true to Mr. Gladstone's constant principle, endeavoured to turn the question from being purely Anglo-French, into an international question. The Powers were not unfavourable, but nothing came of it. Both from Paris and from London somewhat bewildered suggestions proceeded by way of evading the central enigma, whether the intervention should be Turkish

[1] *Fortnightly Review*, July 1882.

or Anglo-French. It was decided at any rate to send powerful Anglo-French fleets to Alexandria, and Mr. Gladstone
only regretted that the other Powers (including Turkey)
had not been invited to have their flags represented. To
this the French objected, with the evil result that the other
Powers were displeased, and the good effect that the appearance of the Sultan in the field might have had upon the
revolutionary parties in Egypt was lost. On May 21, 1882,
M. de Freycinet went so far as to say that, though he
was still opposed to Turkish intervention, he would not
regard as intervention a case in which Turkish forces were
summoned by England and France to operate under Anglo-
French control, upon conditions specified by the two
Powers. If it became advisable to land troops, recourse
should be had on these terms to Turkish troops and them
only. Lord Granville acceded. He proposed (May 24) to
address the Powers, to procure international sanction for the
possible despatch of Turkish troops to Egypt. M. Freycinet
insisted that no such step was necessary. At the same
time (June 1), M. de Freycinet told the Chamber that there
were various courses to which they might be led, but he
excluded one, and this was a French military intervention.
That declaration narrowed the case to a choice between
English intervention, or Turkish, or Anglo-Turkish, all of
them known to be profoundly unpalatable to French sentiment. Such was the end of Lord Granville's prudent and
loyal endeavour to move in step with France.

The next proposal from M. de Freycinet was a European
conference, as Prince Bismarck presumed, to cover the admis-
sibility of Turkish intervention. A conference was too much
in accord with the ideas of the British cabinet, not to be
welcomed by them. The Turk, however, who now might
have had the game in his own hands, after a curious exhibition of duplicity and folly, declined to join, and the conference at first met without him (June 23). Then, pursuing
tactics well known at all times at Constantinople, the Sultan
made one of his attempts to divide the Powers, by sending a
telegram to London (June 25), conferring upon England
rights of exclusive control in the administration of Egypt.

This Mr. Gladstone and Lord Granville declined without even consulting the cabinet, as too violent an infraction, I suppose, of the cardinal principle of European concert. The Queen, anxious for an undivided English control at any price, complained that the question was settled without reference to the cabinet, and here the Queen was clearly not wrong, on doctrines of cabinet authority and cabinet responsibility that were usually held by nobody more strongly than by the prime minister himself.

Mr. Gladstone and his cabinet fought as hard as they could, and for good reasons, against single-handed intervention by Great Britain. When they saw that order could not be re-established without the exercise of force from without, they insisted that this force should be applied by the Sultan as sovereign of Egypt. They proposed this solution to the conference, and Lord Dufferin urged it upon the Sultan. With curious infatuation (repeated a few years later) the Sultan stood aside. When it became necessary to make immediate provision for the safety of the Suez Canal, England proposed to undertake this duty conjointly with France, and solicited the co-operation of any other Power. Italy was specially invited to join. Then when the progress of the rebellion had broken the Khedive's authority and brought Egypt to anarchy, England invited France and Italy to act with her in putting the rebellion down. France and Italy declined. England still urged the Porte to send troops, insisting only on such conditions as were indispensable to secure united action. The Porte again held back, and before it carried out an agreement to sign a military convention, events had moved too fast.[1] Thus, by the Sultan's perversities and the fluctuations of purpose and temper in France, single-handed intervention was inexorably forced upon the one Power that had most consistently striven to avoid it. Bismarck, it is true, judged that Arabi was now a power to be reckoned with; the Austrian representatives used language of like purport; and Freycinet also inclined to coming to terms with Arabi. The British cabinet had persuaded themselves that the overthrow of the military

[1] Lord Granville to Lord Dufferin.   Oct. 5, 1882.

arty was an indispensable precedent to any return of
ecently stable order.

The situation in Egypt can hardly be adequately under-
tood without a multiplicity of details for which this is no
lace, and in such cases details are everything. Diplomacy
1 which the Sultan of Turkey plays a part is always com-
licated, and at the Conference of Constantinople the cob-
vebs were spun and brushed away and spun again with
iligence unexampled. The proceedings were without any
ffect upon the course of events. The Egyptian revolution
an its course. The moral support of Turkish commissioners
ent by the Sultan to Cairo came to nothing, and the
1oral influence of the Anglo-French squadron at Alexandria
ame to nothing, and in truth it did more harm than good.
'he Khedive's throne and life were alike in danger. The
Christians flocked down from the interior. The residents
1 Alexandria were trembling for their lives. At the end
f May our agent at Cairo informed his government that a
ollision between Moslems and Christians might occur at
ny moment. On June 11 some fifty Europeans were
1assacred by a riotous mob at Alexandria. The British
onsul was severely wounded, and some sailors of the
'rench fleet were among the killed. Greeks and Jews were
1urdered in other places. At last a decisive blow was
truck. For several weeks the Egyptians had been at work
1pon the fortifications of Alexandria, and upon batteries
ommanding the British fleet. The British admiral was
1structed (July 3) that if this operation were continued,
.e should immediately destroy the earthworks and silence
he batteries. After due formalities he (July 11) opened
re at seven in the morning, and by half-past five in the
vening the Alexandria guns were silenced. Incendiaries
et the town on fire, the mob pillaged it, and some
1urders were committed. The French ships had sailed
way, their government having previously informed the
3ritish ambassador in Paris that the proposed operation
vould be an act of war against Egypt, and such an act
f war without the express consent of the Chamber would
iolate the constitution.

The new situation in which England now found hersel
was quickly described by the prime minister to the Hous
of Commons. On July 22, he said : ' We should not full
discharge our duty, if we did not endeavour to convert th
present interior state of Egypt from anarchy and conflic
to peace and order. We shall look during the time tha
remains to us to the co-operation of the Powers of civilise
Europe, if it be in any case open to us. But if every chanc
of obtaining co-operation is exhausted, the work will b
undertaken by the single power of England.' As for th
position of the Powers it may be described in this way
Germany and Austria were cordial and respectful; Franc
anxious to retain a completely friendly understanding, bu
wanting some equivalent for the inevitable decline of he
power in Egypt; Italy jealous of our renewing close rela
tions with France; Russia still sore, and on the lookou
for some plausible excuse for getting the Berlin arrange
ment of 1878 revised in her favour, without getting int
difficulties with Berlin itself.

France was not unwilling to take joint action wit
England for the defence of the canal, but would not joi
England in intervention beyond that object. At the sam
time Freycinet wished it to be understood that France ha
no objection to our advance, if we decided to make a
advance. This was more than once repeated. Gambett
in vehement wrath declared his dread lest the refusal t
co-operate with England should shake an alliance of price
less value; and lest besides that immense catastrophe, i
should hand over to the possession of England for ever
territories, rivers, and ports where the French right t
live and trade was as good as hers. The mighty orato
declaimed in vain. Suspicion of the craft of Bismarck was i
France more lively than suspicion of aggressive designs i
the cabinet of Mr. Gladstone, and the Chamber was reminde
how extremely well it would suit Germany that Franc
should lock up her military force in Tunis yesterday, i
Egypt to-day. Ingenious speakers, pointing to Europ
covered with camps of armed men; pointing to the artfu
statesmanship that had pushed Austria into Bosnia an

Herzegovina, and encouraged France herself to occupy Tunis; pointing to the expectant nations reserving their liberty for future occasions — all urgently exhorted France now to reserve her own liberty of action too. Under the influence of such ideas as these, and by the working of rival personalities and parties, the Chamber by an immense majority turned the Freycinet government out of office (July 29) rather than sanction even such a degree of intervention as concerned the protection of the Suez Canal.

CHAP.
V.

Æt. 73.

Nine days after the bombardment of Alexandria, the British cabinet decided on the despatch of what was mildly called an expeditionary force to the Mediterranean, under the command of Sir Garnet Wolseley. The general's alertness, energy, and prescient calculation brought him up to Arabi at Tel-el-Kebir (Sept. 13), and there at one rapid and decisive blow he crushed the military insurrection.[1]

IV

The bombardment of Alexandria cost Mr. Gladstone the British colleague who in fundamentals stood closest to him of them all. In the opening days of July, amid differences of opinion that revealed themselves in frequent and protracted meetings of the cabinet, it was thought probable that Mr. Gladstone and Bright would resign rather than be parties to despatching troops to the Mediterranean; and the two representative radicals were expected to join them. Then came the bombardment, but only Bright went — not until after earnest protestations from the prime minister. As Mr. Gladstone described things later to the Queen, Bright's letters and conversation consisted very much more of references to his past career and strong statements of feeling, than of attempts to reason on the existing facts of the case, with the obligations that they appeared to entail. Not satisfied with his own efforts, Mr. Gladstone turned to Lord Granville, who had been a stout friend in old days when Bright's was a name of reproach and obloquy : —

July 12. — Here is the apprehended letter from dear old John

[1] A share of the credit of success is due to the admirable efficiency of Mr. Childers at the War Office. See Sir Garnet's letter to him, *Life of Childers*, ii. p. 117.

Bright, which turns a white day into a black one. It would not be fair in me to beg an interview. His kindness would make him reluctant to decline; but he would come laden with an apprehension, that I by impetuosity and tenacity should endeavour to overbear him. But pray consider whether you could do it. He would not have the same fear of your dealings with him. I do not think you could get a *reversal*, but perhaps he would give you another short delay, and at the end of this the sky might be further settled.

Two days later Mr. Gladstone and Bright had a long, and we may be sure that it was an earnest, conversation. The former of them the same day put his remarks into the shape of a letter, which the reader may care to have, as a statement of the case for the first act of armed intervention, which led up by a direct line to the English occupation of Egypt, Soudan wars, and to some other events from which the veil is not even yet lifted: —

The act of Tuesday [the bombardment of Alexandria] was a solemn and painful one, for which I feel myself to be highly responsible, and it is my earnest desire that we should all view it now, as we shall wish at the last that we had viewed it. Subject to this testing rule, I address you as one whom I suppose not to believe all use whatever of military force to be unlawful; as one who detests war in general and believes most wars to have been sad errors (in which I greatly agree with you), but who in regard to any particular use of force would look upon it for a justifying cause, and after it would endeavour to appreciate its actual effect.

The general situation in Egypt had latterly become one in which everything was governed by sheer military violence. Every legitimate authority—the Khedive, the Sultan, the notables, and the best men of the country, such as Cherif and Sultan pashas—had been put down, and a situation of *force* had been created, which could only be met by force. This being so, we had laboured to the uttermost, almost alone but not without success, to secure that if force were employed against the violence of Arabi, it should be force armed with the highest sanction of law; that it should be the force of the sovereign, authorised and restrained by the united Powers of Europe, who in such a case represent the civilised world.

While this is going on, a by-question arises. The British fleet, lawfully present in the waters of Alexandria, had the right and duty of self-defence. It demanded the discontinuance of attempts made to strengthen the armament of the fortifications. . . . Met by fraud and falsehood in its demand, it required surrender with a view to immediate dismantling, and this being refused, it proceeded to destroy. . . . The conflagration which followed, the pillage and any other outrages effected by the released convicts, these are not due to us, but to the seemingly wanton wickedness of Arabi. . . .

Such being the amount of our act, what has been its reception and its effect? As to its reception, we have not received nor heard of a word of disapproval from any Power great or small, or from any source having the slightest authority. As to its effect, it has taught many lessons, struck a heavy, perhaps a deadly, blow at the reign of violence, brought again into light the beginnings of legitimate rule, shown the fanaticism of the East that massacre of Europeans is not likely to be perpetrated with impunity, and greatly advanced the Egyptian question towards a permanent and peaceable solution. I feel that in being party to this work I have been a labourer in the cause of peace. Your co-operation in that cause, with reference to preceding and collateral points, has been of the utmost value, and has enabled me to hold my ground, when without you it might have been difficult.

The correspondence closed with a wish from Mr. Gladstone: 'Believe in the sore sense of practical loss, and the (I trust) unalterable friendship and regard with which I remain, etc.' When Bright came to explain his resignation in parliament, he said something about the moral law, which led to a sharp retort from the prime minister, but still their friendship did appear to remain unalterable, as Mr. Gladstone trusted that it would.

When the question by and by arose whether Arabi should be put to death, Bright wrote to the prime minister on behalf of clemency. Mr. Gladstone in replying took a severe line: 'I am sorry to say the inquiry is too likely to show that Arabi is very much more than a rebel. Crimes of the gravest kind have been committed; and with most of them he stands, I fear, in *presumptive* (that is, unproved) connection. In truth I must say that, having begun with no prejudice against him, and with the strong desire that he should be saved, I am almost driven to the conclusion that he is a bad man, and that it will not be an injustice if he goes the road which thousands of his innocent countrymen through him have trodden.' It is a great mistake to suppose that Mr. Gladstone was all leniency, or that when he thought ill of men, he stayed either at palliating words or at half-measures.

CHAPTER VI

POLITICAL JUBILEE

(1882-1883)

ἀγωνίζεται γὰρ ὥσπερ ἀθλητὴς κατὰ τὸν βίον, ὅταν δὲ διαγωνίσηται, τότε
τυγχάνει τῶν προσηκόντων. — PLUTARCH, *Moralia*, c. 18.

He strives like an athlete all his life long, and then when he comes
to the end of his striving, he has what is meet.

ἐπάμεροι· τί δέ τις; τί δ᾽ οὔ τις; σκιᾶς ὄναρ
ἄνθρωπος. ἀλλ᾽ ὅταν αἴγλα διόσδοτος ἔλθῃ,
λαμπρὸν φέγγος ἔπεστιν ἀνδρῶν καὶ μείλιχος αἰών.
— PINDAR, *Pyth.* viii. 135.

Things of a day! What is a man? What, when he is not? A
dream of shadow is mankind. Yet when there comes down glory imparted from God, radiant light shines among men and genial days.

θανεῖν δ᾽ οἷσιν ἀνάγκα, τί κέ τις ἀνώνυμον
γῆρας ἐν σκότῳ καθήμενος ἕψοι μάταν; — *Ol.* i. 131.

Die since we must, wherefore should a man sit idle and nurse in
the gloom days of long life without aim, without name?

THE words from 'antique books' that I have just translated
and transcribed, were written out by Mr. Gladstone inside
the cover of the little diary for 1882-3. To what the old
world had to say, he added Dante's majestic commonplace:
'You were not to live like brutes, but to pursue virtue and
knowledge.'[1] These meditations on the human lot, on the
mingling of our great hopes with the implacable realities,
made the vital air in which all through his life he drew

[1] Considerate la vostra semenza :
Fatti non foste a viver come bruti,
Ma per seguir virtute e conoscenza.
— *Inferno*, xxvi. 118.

deep breath. Adjusted to his ever vivid religious creed, amid all the turbid business of the worldly elements, they were the sedative and the restorer. Yet here and always the last word was Effort. The moods that in less strenuous natures ended in melancholy, philosophic or poetic, to him were fresh incentives to redeem the time.

The middle of December 1882 marked his political jubilee. It was now half a century since he had entered public life, and the youthful graduate from Oxford had grown to be the foremost man in his country. Yet these fifty courses of the sun and all the pageant of the world had in some ways made but little difference in him. In some ways, it seemed as if time had rolled over him in vain. He had learned many lessons. He had changed his party, his horizons were far wider, new social truths had made their way into his impressionable mind, he recognised new social forces. His aims for the church, that he loved as ardently as he gloried in a powerful and beneficent state, had undergone a revolution. Since 1866 he had come into contact with democracy at close quarters; the Bulgarian campaign and Midlothian lighting up his early faith in liberty, had inflamed him with new feeling for the voice of the people. As much as in the early time when he had prayed to be allowed to go into orders, he was moved by a dominating sense of the common claims and interests of mankind. 'The contagion of the world's slow stain' had not infected him; the lustre and long continuity of his public performances still left all his innermost ideals constant and undimmed.

His fifty years of public life had wrought his early habits of severe toil, method, exactness, concentration, into cast-iron. Whether they had sharpened what is called knowledge of the world, or taught him insight into men and skill in discrimination among men, it is hard to say. He always talked as if he found the world pretty much what he had expected. Man, he used often to say, is the least comprehensible of creatures, and of men the most incomprehensible are the politicians. Yet nobody was less of the cynic. As for Weltschmerz, world-weariness, ennui, tedium

vitæ — that enervating family were no acquaintances of his,
now nor at any time.   None of the vicissitudes of long
experience ever tempted him either into the shallow satire
on life that is so often the solace of the little and the weak;
or on the other hand into the *saeva indignatio*, the sombre
brooding reprobation, that has haunted some strong souls
from Tacitus and Dante to Pascal, Butler, Swift, Turgot.
We may, indeed, be sure that neither of these two moods
can ever hold a place in the breast of a commanding orator.

II

I have spoken of his new feeling for democracy.   At the
point of time at which we have arrived, it was heartily
reciprocated.   The many difficulties in the course of public
affairs that confronted parliament and the nation for two
years or more after Mr. Gladstone's second accession to
power, did little to weaken either his personal popularity or
his hold upon the confidence of the constituencies.   For
many years he and Mr. Disraeli had stood out above the
level of their adherents; they were the centre of every
political storm.   Disraeli was gone (April 19, 1881), commemorated by Mr. Gladstone in a parliamentary tribute that
cost him much searching of heart beforehand, and was a
masterpiece of grace and good feeling.   Mr. Gladstone
stood alone, concentrating upon himself by his personal
ascendency and public history the bitter antagonism of his
opponents, only matched by the enthusiasm and devotion of
his followers.   The rage of faction had seldom been more
unbridled.   The Irish and the young fourth party were
rivals in malicious vituperation; of the two, the Irish on the
whole observed the better manners.   Once Mr. Gladstone
was wounded to the quick, as letters show, when a member
of the fourth party denounced as 'a government of infamy'
the ministry with whose head he had long been on terms
of more than friendship alike as host and guest.   He could
not fell his trees, he could not read the lessons in Hawarden
church, without finding these innocent habits turned into
material for platform mockery.   'In the eyes of the opposition, as indeed of the country,' said a great print that was

never much his friend, 'he is the government and he is the liberal party,' and the writer went on to scold Lord Salisbury for wasting his time in the concoction of angry epigrams and pungent phrases that were neither new nor instructive.[1] They pierced no joint in the mail of the warrior at whom they were levelled. The nation at large knew nothing of difficulties at Windsor, nothing of awkward passages in the cabinet, nothing of the trying egotisms of gentlemen out of the cabinet who insisted that they ought to be in. Nor would such things have made any difference except in his favour, if the public had known all about them. The Duke of Argyll and Lord Lansdowne had left him; his Irish policy had cost him his Irish secretary, and his Egyptian policy had cost him Mr. Bright. They had got into a war, they had been baffled in legislation, they had to raise the most unpopular of taxes, there had been the frightful tragedy in Ireland. Yet all seemed to have been completely overcome in the public mind by the power of Mr. Gladstone in uniting his friends and frustrating his foes, and the more bitterly he was hated by society, the more warmly attached were the mass of the people. Anybody who had foreseen all this would have concluded that the government must be in extremity, but he went to the Guildhall on the 9th of November 1882, and had the best possible reception on that famous stage. One tory newspaper felt bound to admit that Mr. Gladstone and his colleagues had rehabilitated themselves in the public judgment with astounding rapidity, and were now almost as strong in popular and parliamentary support as when they first took office.[2] Another tory print declared Mr. Gladstone to be stronger, more popular, more despotic, than at any time since the policy to carry out which he was placed in office was disclosed.[3] The session of 1882 had only been exceeded in duration by two sessions for fifty years.

The reader has had pictures enough from friendly hands, so here is one from a persistent foe, one of the most brilliant journalists of that time, who listened to him from

---

[1] *Times*, Dec. 8, 1882.   [3] *Morning Post*, Oct. 20, 1882.
[2] *Standard*, Nov. 16, 1882.

the gallery for years. The words are from an imaginary dialogue, and are put into the mouth of a well-known whig in parliament : —

Sir, I can only tell you that, profoundly as I distrusted him, and lightly as on the whole I valued the external qualities of his eloquence, I have never listened to him even for a few minutes without ceasing to marvel at his influence over men. That white-hot face, stern as a Covenanter's yet mobile as a comedian's; those restless, flashing eyes; that wondrous voice, whose richness its northern burr enriched as the tang of the wood brings out the mellowness of a rare old wine; the masterly cadence of his elocution; the vivid energy of his attitudes; the fine animation of his gestures; — sir, when I am assailed through eye and ear by this compacted phalanx of assailants, what wonder that the stormed outposts of the senses should spread the contagion of their own surrender through the main encampment of the mind, and that against my judgment, in contempt of my conscience, nay, in defiance of my very will, I should exclaim, 'This is indeed the voice of truth and wisdom. This man is honest and sagacious beyond his fellows. He must be believed, he must be obeyed!'[1]

On the day of his political jubilee (Dec. 13), the event was celebrated in many parts of the country, and he received congratulatory telegrams from all parts of the world ; for it was not only two hundred and forty liberal associations who sent him joyful addresses. The Roumelians poured out aloud their gratitude to him for the interest he constantly manifested in their cause, and for his powerful and persistent efforts for their emancipation. From Athens came the news that they had subscribed for the erection of his statue, and from the Greeks also came a splendid casket. In his letter of thanks,[2] after remonstrating against its too great material value, he said : —

I know not well how to accept it, yet I am still less able to decline it, when I read the touching lines of the accompanying address, in itself an ample token, in which you have so closely

[1] Traill's *New Lucian*, pp. 305-6, — in spite of politics, a book of admirable wit, scholarship, and ingenious play of mind.
[2] To Mr. Hazzopolo, Dec. 22, 1882.

associated my name with the history and destinies of your country. I am not vain enough to think that I have deserved any of the numerous acknowledgments which I have received, especially from Greeks, on completing half a century of parliamentary life. Your over-estimate of my deeds ought rather to humble than to inflate me. But to have laboured within the measure of justice for the Greece of the future, is one of my happiest political recollections, and to have been trained in a partial knowledge of the Greece of the past has largely contributed to whatever slender faculties I possess for serving my own country or my kind. I earnestly thank you for your indulgent judgment and for your too costly gifts, and I have the honour to remain, etc.

What was deeper to him than statues or caskets was found in letters from comparative newcomers into the political arena thanking him not only for his long roll of public service, but much more for the example and encouragement that his life gave to younger men endeavouring to do something for the public good. To one of these he wrote (Dec. 15) : —

I thank you most sincerely for your kind and friendly letter. As regards the prospective part of it, I can assure you that I should be slow to plead the mere title to retirement which long labour is supposed to earn. But I have always watched, and worked according to what I felt to be the measure of my own mental force. A monitor from within tells me that though I may still be equal to some portions of my duties, or as little unequal as heretofore, there are others which I cannot face. I fear therefore I must keep in view an issue which cannot be evaded.

III

As it happened, this volume of testimony to the affection, gratitude, and admiration thus ready to go out to him from so many quarters coincided in point of time with one or two extreme vexations in the conduct of his daily business as head of the government. Some of them were aggravated by the loss of a man whom he regarded as one of his two or three most important friends. In September 1882 the Dean of Windsor died, and in his death Mr. Gladstone suffered a heavy blow. To the end he always spoke of Dr. Wellesley's friendship, and the value of his sagacity and honest service, with a warmth by this time given to few.

Death of the Dean of Windsor.

To Lord Granville, Sept. 18, 1882. — My belief is that he has been cognizant of every crown appointment in the church for nearly a quarter of a century, and that the whole of his influence has been exercised with a deep insight and a large heart for the best interests of the crown and the church. If their character during this period has been in the main more satisfactory to the general mind of the country than at some former periods, it has been in no small degree owing to him.

It has been my duty to recommend I think for fully forty of the higher appointments, including twelve which were episcopal. I rejoice to say that every one of them has had his approval. But I do not scruple to own that he has been in no small degree a help and guide to me ; and as to the Queen, whose heart I am sure is at this moment bleeding, I do not believe she can possibly fill his place as a friendly adviser either in ecclesiastical or other matters.

To the Duchess of Wellington, Sept. 24. — He might, if he had chosen, have been on his way to the Archbishopric of Canterbury. Ten or eleven years ago, when the present primate was not expected to recover, the question of the succession was considered, and I had her Majesty's consent to the idea I have now mentioned. But, governed I think by his great modesty, he at once refused.

To Mrs. Wellesley, Nov. 19, 1882. — I have remained silent, at least to you, on a subject which for no day has been absent from my thoughts, because I felt that I could add nothing to your consolations and could take away nothing from your grief under your great calamity. But the time has perhaps come when I may record my sense of a loss of which even a small share is so large. The recollections of nearly sixty years are upon my mind, and through all that period I have felt more and more the force and value of your husband's simple and noble character. No less have I entertained an ever-growing sense of his great sagacity and the singularly true and just balance of his mind. We owe much indeed to you both for your constantly renewed kindness, but I have another debt to acknowledge in the invaluable assistance which he afforded me in the discharge of one among the most important and most delicate of my duties. This void never can be filled, and it helps me in some degree to feel what must be the void to you. Certainly he was happy in the enjoyment of love and honour from all who knew him; yet these were few in comparison with those whom he so wisely and so warmly served without their knowing it; and the love and honour paid him, great as they were, could not be as great as he deserved. His memory is blessed — may his rest be deep and sweet, and may the memory and example of him ever help you in your onward pilgrimage.

The same week Dr. Pusey died — a name that filled so large a space in the religious history of England for some thirty years of the century. Between Mr. Gladstone and him the old relations of affectionate friendship subsisted unbroken, notwithstanding the emancipation, as we may call it, of the statesman from maxims and principles, though not, so far as I know, from any of the leading dogmatic beliefs cherished by the divine. 'I hope,' he wrote to Phillimore (Sept. 20, 1882), 'to attend Dr. Pusey's funeral to-morrow at Oxford. . . . I shall have another mournful office to discharge in attending the funeral of the Dean of Windsor, more mournful than the first. Dr. Pusey's death is the ingathering of a ripe shock, and I go to his obsequies in token of deep respect and in memory of much kindness from him early in my life. But the death of Dean Wellesley is to my wife and me an unexpected and very heavy blow, also to me an irreparable loss. I had honoured and loved him from Eton days.'

The loss of Dean Wellesley's counsels was especially felt in ecclesiastical appointments, and the greatest of these was made necessary by the death of the Archbishop of Canterbury at the beginning of December. That the prime minister should regard so sage, conciliatory, and large-minded a steersman as Dr. Tait with esteem was certain, and their relations were easy and manly. Still, Tait had been an active liberal when Mr. Gladstone was a tory, and from the distant days of the *Tracts for the Times*, when Tait had stood amongst the foremost in open dislike of the new tenets, their paths in the region of theology lay wide apart. 'I well remember,' says Dean Lake, 'a conversation with Mr. Gladstone on Tait's appointment to London in 1856, when he was much annoyed at Tait's being preferred to Bishop Wilberforce, and of which he reminded me nearly thirty years afterwards, at the time of the archbishop's death, by saying, "Ah! I remember you maintaining to me at that time that his σεμνότης and his judgment would make him a great bishop."'[1] And so, from the point of ecclesiastical statesmanship, he unquestionably was.

The recommendation of a successor in the historic see of Canterbury, we may be very certain, was no common event to Mr. Gladstone. Tait on his deathbed had given his opinion that Dr. Harold Browne, the Bishop of Winchester, would do more than any other man to keep the peace of the church. The Queen was strong in the same sense, thinking that the bishop might resign in a year or two, if he could not do the work. He was now seventy-one years old, and Mr. Gladstone judged this to be too advanced an age for the metropolitan throne. He was himself now seventy-three, and though his sense of humour was not always of the protective kind, he felt the necessity of some explanatory reason, and with him to seek a plea was to find one. He wrote to the Bishop of Winchester : —

. . . It may seem strange that I, who in my own person exhibit so conspicuously the anomaly of a disparate conjunction between years and duties, should be thus forward in interpreting the circumstances of another case certainly more mitigated in many respects, yet differing from my own case in one vital point, the newness of the duties of the English, or rather anglican or British, primacy to a diocesan bishop, however able and experienced, and the newness of mental attitude and action, which they would require. Among the materials of judgment in such an instance, it seems right to reckon precedents for what they are worth; and I cannot find that from the time of Archbishop Sheldon any one has

[1] *Life of Tait*, i. p. 109.

assumed the primacy at so great an age as seventy. Juxon, the
predecessor of Sheldon, was much older; but his case was altogether
peculiar. I cannot say how pleasant it would have been to me
personally, but for the barrier I have named, to mark my respect
and affection for your lordship by making to you such a proposal.
What is more important is, that I am directly authorised by her
Majesty to state that this has been the single impediment to her
conferring the honour, and imposing the burden, upon you of such
an offer.[1]

The world made free with the honoured name of Church,
the Dean of Saint Paul's, and it has constantly been said
that he declined the august preferment to Canterbury on
this occasion.   In that story there is no truth.   'Formal
offer,' the Dean himself wrote to a friend, 'there was none,
and could not be, for I had already on another occasion
told my mind to Gladstone, and said that reasons of health,
apart from other reasons, made it impossible for me to
think of anything, except a retirement altogether from
office.'[2]

When it was rumoured that Mr. Gladstone intended to
recommend Dr. Benson, then Bishop of Truro, to the archbishopric, a political supporter came to remonstrate with
him. 'The Bishop of Truro is a strong tory,' he said, 'but
that is not all. He has joined Mr. Raikes's election committee at Cambridge ; and it was only last week that Raikes
made a violent personal attack on yourself.' 'Do you know,'
replied Mr. Gladstone, 'you have just supplied me with
a strong argument in Dr. Benson's favour ? For if he had
been a worldly man or self-seeker, he would not have done
anything so imprudent.' Perhaps we cannot wonder that
whips and wirepullers deemed this to be somewhat over-
ingenious, a Christianity out of season. Even liberals who
took another point of view, still asked themselves how it was

---

[1] Bishop Browne writes to a friend
(*Life*, p. 457): 'Gladstone, I learned
both from himself and others, searched
into all precedents from the Com-
monwealth to the present day for a
primate who began his work at
seventy, and found none but Juxon.
Curiously, I have been reading that

he himself, prompted by Bishop
Wilberforce, wanted Palmerston to
appoint Sumner (of Winchester)
when he was seventy-two. It was
when they feared they could not get
Longley (who was sixty-eight).'
[2] *Life and Letters of Dean Church*,
p. 307.

that when church preferment came his way, the prime minister CHAP.
so often found the best clergymen in the worst politicians. VI.
They should have remembered that he was of those who ÆT. 73.
believed 'no more glorious church in Christendom to
exist than the church of England'; and its official ordering
was in his eyes not any less, even if it was not infinitely
more, important in the highest interests of the nation
than the construction of a cabinet or the appointment
of permanent heads of departments. The church was at
this moment, moreover, in one of those angry and perilous
crises that came of the Elizabethan settlement and the
Act of Uniformity, and the anglican revival forty years
ago, and all the other things that mark the arrested progress of the Reformation in England. The anti-ritualist
hunt was up. Civil courts were busy with the conscience
and conduct of the clergy. Harmless but contumacious
priests were under lock and key. It seemed as if more
might follow them, or else as if the shock of the great trac-
tarian catastrophe of the forties might in some new shape
recur. To recommend an archbishop in times like these
could to a churchman be no light responsibility.

With such thoughts in his mind, however we may judge
them, it is not altogether surprising that in seeking an ecclesiastical governor for an institution to him the most sacred
and beloved of all forms of human association, Mr. Gladstone
should have cared very little whether the personage best
fitted in spirituals was quite of the right shade as to state
temporals. The labour that he now expended on finding the
best man is attested by voluminous correspondence. Dean
Church, who was perhaps the most freely consulted by the
prime minister, says, 'Of one thing I am quite certain, that
never for hundreds of years has so much honest disinterested
pains been taken to fill the primacy — such inquiry and
trouble resolutely followed out to find the really fittest man,
apart from every personal and political consideration, as in
this case.' [1]

Another ecclesiastical vacancy that led to volumes of
correspondence was the deanery of Westminster the year

_____
[1] *Life and Letters of Dean Church*, p. 307.

before. In the summer of 1881 Dean Stanley died, and it is interesting to note how easy Mr. Gladstone found it to do full justice to one for whom as erastian and latitudinarian he could in opinion have such moderate approval. In offering to the Queen his 'cordial sympathy' for the friend whom she had lost, he told her how early in his own life and earlier still in the dean's he had opportunities of watching the development of his powers, for they had both been educated at a small school near the home of Mr. Gladstone's boyhood.[1] He went on to speak of Stanley's boundless generosity and brilliant gifts, his genial and attaching disposition. 'There may be,' he said, 'and must be much diversity as to parts of the opinions of Dean Stanley, but he will be long remembered as one who was capable of the deepest and widest love, and who received it in return.'

Far away from these regions of what he irreverently called the shovel hat, about this time Carlyle died (Feb. 4, 1881), a firm sympathiser with Mr. Gladstone in his views of the unspeakable Turk, but in all else the rather boisterous preacher of a gospel directly antipathetic. 'Carlyle is at least a great fact in the literature of his time; and has contributed largely, in some respects too largely, towards forming its characteristic habits of thought.' So Mr. Gladstone wrote in 1876, in a highly interesting parallel between Carlyle and Macaulay — both of them honest, he said, both notwithstanding their honesty partisans; both of them, though variously, poets using the vehicle of prose; both having the power of painting portraits extraordinary for vividness and strength; each of them vastly though diversely powerful in expression, each more powerful in expression than in thought; neither of them to be resorted to for comprehensive disquisition, nor for balanced and impartial judgments.[2] Perhaps it was too early in 1876 to speak of Carlyle as forming the characteristic habits of thought of his time, but undoubtedly now when he died, his influence was beginning to tell heavily against the speculative liberalism that had reigned in England for two generations, with enormous advantage to the peace, prosperity and power of

[1] See vol. i. p. 47. [2] *Gleanings*, ii. p. 287.

the country and the two generations concerned. Half lights
and half truths are, as Mr. Gladstone implies, the utmost
that Carlyle's works were found to yield in philosophy and
history, but his half lights pointed in the direction in which
men for more material reasons thought that they desired
to go.

IV

A reconstruction of the ministry had become necessary by
his own abandonment of the exchequer. For one moment it
was thought that Lord Hartington might become chancellor,
leaving room for Lord Derby at the India office, but Lord
Derby was not yet ready to join. In inviting Mr. Childers to
take his place as chancellor of the exchequer, Mr. Gladstone
told him (Dec. 1, 1882): 'The basis of my action is not
so much a desire to be relieved from labour, as an anxiety
to give the country a much better finance minister than
myself, — one whose eyes will be always ranging freely and
vigilantly over the whole area of the great establishments,
the public service and the laws connected with his office,
for the purposes of improvement and of good husbandry.'

The claim of Sir Charles Dilke to a seat in the cabinet
had become irresistible alike by his good service as under-
secretary at the foreign office, and by his position out of
doors; and as the admission of a radical must be balanced
by a whig — so at least it was judged — Mr. Gladstone
succeeded in inducing Lord Derby to join, though he had
failed with him not long before.[1]

Apart from general objections at court, difficulties arose
about the distribution of office. Mr. Chamberlain, who has
always had his full share of the virtues of staunch friendship, agreed to give up to Sir C. Dilke his own office, which
he much liked, and take the duchy, which he did not like
at all. In acknowledging Mr. Chamberlain's letter (Dec. 14)
Mr. Gladstone wrote to him, 'I shall be glad, if I can, to
avoid acting upon it. But I cannot refrain from at once
writing a hearty line to acknowledge the self-sacrificing
spirit in which it is written; and which, I am sure, you
will never see cause to repent or change.' This, however,

---

[1] Lord Derby had refused office in the previous May.

was found to be no improvement, for Mr. Chamberlain's language about ransoms to be paid by possessors of property, the offence of not toiling and spinning, and the services rendered by courtiers to kings, was not much less repugnant than rash assertions about the monarch evading the income-tax. All contention on personal points was a severe trial to Mr. Gladstone, and any conflict with the wishes of the Queen tried him most of all. One of his audiences upon these affairs Mr. Gladstone mentions in his diary: 'Dec. 11. — Off at 12.45 to Windsor in the frost and fog. Audience of her Majesty at 3. Most difficult ground, but aided by her beautiful manners, we got over it better than might have been expected.' The dispute was stubborn, but like all else it came to an end; colleagues were obliging, holes and pegs were accommodated, and Lord Derby went to the colonial office, and Sir C. Dilke to the local government board. An officer of the court, who was in all the secrets and had foreseen all the difficulties, wrote that the actual result was due 'to the judicious manner in which Mr. Gladstone managed everything. He argued in a friendly way, urging his views with moderation, and appealed to the Queen's sense of courtesy.'

In the course of his correspondence with the Queen, the prime minister drew her attention (Dec. 18) to the fact that when the cabinet was formed it included three ministers reputed to belong to the radical section, Mr. Bright, Mr. Forster, and Mr. Chamberlain, and of these only the last remained. The addition of Lord Derby was an addition drawn from the other wing of the party. Another point presented itself. The cabinet originally contained eight commoners and six peers. There were now seven peers and six commoners. This made it requisite to add a commoner. As for Mr. Chamberlain, the minister assured the Queen that though he had not yet, like Mr. Bright, undergone the mollifying influence of age and experience, his leanings on foreign policy would be far more acceptable to her Majesty than those of Mr. Bright, while his views were not known to be any more democratic in principle. He further expressed his firm opinion (Dec. 22) that though Lord Derby might on questions of peace and war be some shades nearer to the views of Mr. Bright than the other members of the cabinet, yet he would never go anything like the length of Mr. Bright in such matters. In fact, said Mr. Gladstone, the cabinet must be deemed a little less pacific now than it was at its first formation. This at least was a consolatory reflection.

Ministerial reconstruction is a trying moment for the politician who thinks himself ' not a favourite with his stars,' and is in a hurry for a box seat before his time has come. Mr. Gladstone was now harassed with some importunities of this kind.[1] Personal collision with any who stood in the place of friends was always terrible to him. His gift of sleep deserted him. ' It is disagreeable to talk of oneself,' he wrote to Lord Granville (Jan. 2, 1883), ' when there is so much of more importance to think and speak about, but I am sorry to say that the incessant strain and pressure of work, and especially the multiplication of these personal questions, is overdoing me, and for the first time my power of sleep is seriously giving way. I dare say it would soon right itself if I could offer it any other medicine than the medicine in Hood's " Song of the Shirt." ' And the next day he wrote: ' Last night I improved, $3\frac{1}{2}$ hours to $4\frac{1}{2}$, but this is different from 7 and 8, my uniform standard through life.' And two days later: ' The matter of sleep is with me a very grave one. I am afraid I may have to go up and consult Clark. My habit has always been to reckon my hours rather exultingly, and say how little I am awake. It is not impossible that I may have to ask you to meet me in London, but I will not do this except in necessity. I think that, to convey a clear idea, I should say I attach no importance to the broken sleep itself; it is the state of the brain, tested by my own sensations, when I begin my work in the morning, which may

[1] The matter itself has no importance, but a point of principle or etiquette at one time connected with it is perhaps worth mentioning. To a colleague earlier in the year Mr. Gladstone wrote: 'I can affirm with confidence that the notion of a title in the cabinet to be consulted on the succession to a cabinet office is absurd. It is a title which cabinet ministers do not possess. During thirty-eight years since I first entered the cabinet, I have never known more than a friendly announcement before publicity, and very partial consultation perhaps with one or two, especially the leaders in the second House.'

make me need higher assurance.' Sir Andrew Clark, 'over-flowing with kindness, as always,' went down to Hawarden (Jan. 7), examined, and listened to the tale of heavy wakeful nights. While treating the case as one of temporary and accidental derangement, he instantly forbade a projected expedition to Midlothian, and urged change of air and scene.

This prohibition eased some of the difficulties at Windsor, where Midlothian was a name of dubious association, and in announcing to the Queen the abandonment by Dr. Clark's orders of the intended journey to the north, Mr. Gladstone wrote (Jan. 8, 1883): —

In your Majesty's very kind reference on the 5th to his former visits to Midlothian, and to his own observations on the 24th April 1880, your Majesty remarked that he had said he did not then think himself a responsible person. He prays leave to fill up the outline which these words convey by saying he at that time (to the best of his recollection) humbly submitted to your Majesty his admission that he must personally bear the consequences of all that he had said, and that he thought some things suitable to be said by a person out of office which could not suitably be said by a person in office; also that, as is intimated by your Majesty's words, the responsibilities of the two positions severally were different. With respect to the political changes named by your Majesty, Mr. Gladstone considers that the very safe measure of extending to the counties the franchise enjoyed by the boroughs stands in all likelihood for early consideration; but he doubts whether there can be any serious dealing of a general character with the land laws by the present parliament, and so far as Scottish disestablishment is concerned he does not conceive that that question has made progress during recent years; and he may state that in making arrangements recently for his expected visit to Midlothian, he had received various overtures for deputations on this subject, which he had been able to put aside.

V

On January 17, along with Mrs. Gladstone, at Charing Cross he said good-bye to many friends, and at Dover to Lord Granville, and the following afternoon he found himself at Cannes, the guest of the Wolvertons at the Château

Scott, 'nobly situated, admirably planned, and the kindness exceeded even the beauty and the comfort.' 'Here,' he says, 'we fell in with the foreign hours, the snack early, déjeuner at noon, dinner at seven, break-up at ten. . . . I am stunned by this wonderful place, and so vast a change at a moment's notice in the conditions of life.' He read steadily through the *Odyssey*, Dixon's *History of the Church of England*, Scherer's *Miscellanies*, and *The Life of Clerk-Maxwell*, and every day he had long talks and walks with Lord Acton on themes personal, political and religious — and we may believe what a restorative he found in communion with that deep and well-filled mind — that 'most satisfactory mind,' as Mr. Gladstone here one day calls it. He took drives to gardens that struck him as fairyland. The Prince of Wales paid him kindly attentions as always. He had long conversations with the Comte de Paris, and with M. Clémenceau, and with the Duke of Argyll, the oldest of his surviving friends. In the evening he played whist. Home affairs he kept at bay pretty successfully, though a speech of Lord Hartington's about local government in Ireland drew from him a longish letter to Lord Granville that the reader, if he likes, will find elsewhere.[1] His conversation with M. Clémenceau (whom he found 'decidedly pleasing') was thought indiscreet, but though the most circumspect of men, the buckram of a spurious discretion was no favourite wear with Mr. Gladstone. As for the report of his conversation with the French radical, he wrote to Lord Granville, 'It includes much which Clémenceau did not say to me, and omits much which he did, for our principal conversation was on Egypt, about which he spoke in a most temperate and reasonable manner.' He read the 'harrowing details' of the terrible scene in the court-house at Kilmainham, where the murderous Invincibles were found out. 'About Carey,' he said to Lord Granville, 'the spectacle is indeed loathsome, but I cannot doubt that the Irish government are distinctly *right*. In accepting an approver you do not incite him to do what is in itself wrong; only his own bad mind can make it wrong to him. The government looks for the truth. Approvers are, I suppose,

---

[1] See Appendix.

for the most part base, but I do not see how you could act on a distinction of degree between them. Still, one would have heard the hiss from the dock with sympathy.'

Lord Granville wrote to him (Jan. 31, 1883) that the Queen insisted much upon his diminishing the amount of labour thrown upon him, and expressed her opinion that his acceptance of a peerage would relieve him of the heavy strain. Lord Granville told her that personally he should be delighted to see him in the Lords, but that he had great doubts whether Mr. Gladstone would be willing. From Cannes Mr. Gladstone replied (Feb. 3): —

As to removal into the House of Lords, I think the reasons against it of general application are conclusive. At least I cannot see my way in regard to them. But at any rate it is obvious that such a step is quite inapplicable to the circumstances created by the present difficulty. It is really most kind of the Queen to testify such an interest, and the question is how to answer her. You would do this better and perhaps more easily than I.

Perhaps he remembered the case of Pulteney and of the Great Commoner.

He was not without remorse at the thought of his colleagues in harness while he was lotus-eating. On the day before the opening of the session he writes, 'I feel dual: I am at Cannes, and in Downing Street eating my parliamentary dinner.' By February 21 he was able to write to Lord Granville : —

As regards my health there is no excuse. It has got better and better as I have stayed on, and is now, I think, on a higher level than for a long time past. My sleep, for example, is now about as good as it can be, and far better than it was during the autumn sittings, *after* which it got so bad. The pleasure I have had in staying does not make an argument at all; it is a mere expression or anticipation of my desire to be turned out to grass for good. . . .

At last the end of the holiday came. 'I part from Cannes with a heavy heart,' he records on Feb. 26 : —

Read the *Iliad*, copiously. Off by the 12.30 train. We exchanged bright sun, splendid views, and a little dust at the beginning of our journey, for frost and fog, which however hid no scenery, at the end. *27th, Tuesday.* — Reached Paris at 8, and drove to the Embassy, where we had a most kind reception [from Lord Lyons]. Wrote to Lord Granville, Lord Spencer, Sir W. Harcourt. Went with Lord L. to see M. Grévy ; also Challemel-Lacour in his most palatial abode. Looked about among the shops ; and at the sad face of the Tuileries. An embassy party to dinner; excellent company.

To Lord Granville.

Feb. 27th. — I have been with Lord Lyons to see Grévy and Challemel-Lacour. Grévy's conversation consisted of civilities and a mournful lecture on the political history of France, with many compliments to the superiority of England. Challemel thought the burdens of public life intolerable and greater here than in England, which is rather strong. Neither made the smallest allusion to present questions, and it was none of my business to introduce them. . . .

After three days of bookstalls, ivory-hunting, and conversation, by the evening of March 2 the travellers were once more after a bright day and rapid passage safe in Downing Street.

Shortly after their return from the south of France the Gladstones paid a visit to the Prince and Princess of Wales : —

March 30, 1883. — Off at 11.30 to Sandringham. Reception kinder if possible even than heretofore. Wrote. . . . Read and worked on London municipality. 31, *Saturday.* — Wrote. Root-cut a small tree in the forenoon ; then measured oaks in the park ; one of 30 feet. In the afternoon we drove to Houghton, a stately house and place, but woe-begone. Conversation with Archbishop of Canterbury, Prince of Wales and others. Read . . . *Life of Hatherley,* Law's account of Craig. *April* 1. — Sandringham church, morning. West Newton, evening. Good services and sermons from the archbishop. The Prince bade me read the lessons. Much conversation with the archbishop, also Duke of Cambridge. Read *Nineteenth Century* on Revised Version ; Manning on Education; *Life of Hatherley;* Craig's *Catechism.* Wrote, etc. 2. — Off at 11.   D. Street 3.15.   Wrote to the Queen.   Long conversation with the archbishop in the train.

Here a short letter or two may find a place : —

To Lady Jessel on her husband's death.

March 30. — Though I am reluctant to intrude upon your sorrow still so fresh, and while I beg of you on no account to acknowledge this note, I cannot refrain from writing to assure you not only of my sympathy with your grief, but of my profound sense of the loss which the country and its judiciary have sustained by the death of your distinguished husband.   From the time of his first entrance into parliament I followed his legal expositions with an ignorant but fervid admiration, and could not help placing him in the first rank, a rank held by few, of the many able and powerful lawyers whom during half a century I have known and heard in parliament.   When I came to know him as a colleague, I found reason to admire no less sincerely his superiority to considerations of pecuniary interest, his strong and tenacious sense of the dignity of his office, and his thoroughly frank, resolute, and manly character.   These few words, if they be a feeble, yet I assure you are also a genuine, tribute to a memory which I trust will long be cherished.   Earnestly anxious that you may have every consolation in your heavy bereavement.

To Cardinal Manning.

April 19. — I thank you much for your kind note, though I am sorry to have given you the trouble of writing it.   Both of us have much to be thankful for in the way of health, but I should have hoped that your extremely spare living would have saved you from the action of anything like gouty tendencies.   As for myself, I can in no way understand how it is that for a full half century I have been permitted and enabled to resist a pressure of special liabilities attaching to my path of life, to which so many have given way.   I am left as a solitary, surviving all his compeers. But I trust it may not be long ere I escape into some position better suited to declining years.

To Sir W. V. Harcourt.

April 27. — A separate line to thank you for your more than kind words about my rather Alexandrine speech last night; as to

which I can only admit that it contained one fine passage — six
lines in length.[1] Your 'instincts' of kindliness in all personal
matters are known to all the world. I should be glad, on selfish
grounds, if I could feel sure that they had not a little warped your
judicial faculty for the moment. But this misgiving abates
nothing from my grateful acknowledgment.

An application was made to him on behalf of a member
of the opposite party for a political pension, and here is his
reply, to which it may be added that ten years later he had
come rather strongly to the view that political pensions
should be abolished, and he was only deterred from trying to carry out his view by the reminder from younger
ministers, not themselves applicants nor ever likely to be,
that it would hardly be a gracious thing to cut off benefac-
tions at a time when the bestowal of them was passing away
from him, though he had used them freely while that
bestowal was within his reach.

Political Pensions.

July 4, 1883. — You are probably aware that during the fifty
years which have passed since the system of political and civil
pensions was essentially remodelled, no political pension has been
granted by any minister except to one of those with whom he
stood on terms of general confidence and co-operation. It is
needless to refer to older practice.

This is not to be accounted for by the fact that after meeting
the just claims of political adherents, there has been nothing left
to bestow. For, although it has happened that the list of pensions
of the first class has usually been full, it has not been so with
political pensions of the other classes, which have, I think, rarely
if ever been granted to the fullest extent that the Acts have
allowed. At the present time, out of twelve pensions which may
legally be conferred, only seven have been actually given, if I
reckon rightly. I do not think that this state of facts can have
been due to the absence of cases entitled to consideration, and
I am quite certain that it is not to be accounted for by what
are commonly termed party motives. It was obvious to me that I

[1] The lines from Lucretius (in his speech on the Affirmation bill). See
above, p. 19.

could not create a precedent of deviation from a course undeviatingly pursued by my predecessors of all parties, without satisfying myself that a new form of proceeding would be reasonable and safe. The examination of private circumstances, such as I consider the Act to require, is from its own nature difficult and invidious: but the examination of competing cases in the ex-official corps is a function that could not, I think, be discharged with the necessary combination of free responsible action, and of exemption from offence and suspicion. Such cases plainly may occur.[1]

To H.R.H. the Prince of Wales.

August 14th. — I am much shocked at an omission which I made last night in failing to ask your royal Highness's leave to be the first to quit Lord Alcester's agreeable party, in order that I might attend to my duties in the House of Commons. In my early days not only did the whole company remain united, if a member of the royal family were present, until the exalted personage had departed ; but I well recollect the application of the same rule in the case of the Archbishop (Howley) of Canterbury. I am sorry to say that I reached the House of Commons in time to hear some outrageous speeches from the ultra Irish members. I will not say that they were meant to encourage crime, but they tended directly to teach the Irish people to withhold their confidence from the law and its administrators; and they seemed to exhibit Lord Spencer as the enemy to the mass of the community —a sad and disgraceful fact, though I need not qualify what I told your royal Highness, that they had for some time past not been guilty of obstruction.

Even in pieces that were in their nature more or less official, he touched the occasions of life by a note that was not merely official, or was official in its best form. To Mrs. Garfield he wrote (July 21, 1881) : —

You will, I am sure, excuse me, though a personal stranger, for addressing you by letter, to convey to you the assurance of my

[1] In a party sense, as he told the cabinet, it might be wise enough to grant it, as it would please the public, displease the tories, and widen the breach between the fourth party and their front bench. Mr. Gladstone had suffered an unpleasant experience in another case, of the relations brought about by the refusal of a political pension after inquiry as to the accuracy of the necessary statement as to the applicant's need for it.

own feelings and those of my countrymen on the occasion of the late horrible attempt to murder the President of the United States, in a form more palpable at least than that of messages conveyed by telegraph.   Those feelings have been feelings in the first instance of sympathy, and afterwards of joy and thankfulness, almost comparable, and I venture to say only second to the strong emotions of the great nation of which he is the appointed head. Individually I have, let me beg you to believe, had my full share in the sentiments which have possessed the British nation.   They have been prompted and quickened largely by what I venture to think is the ever-growing sense of harmony and mutual respect and affection between the two countries, and of a relationship which from year to year becomes more and more a practical bond of union between us.   But they have also drawn much of their strength from a cordial admiration of the simple heroism which has marked the personal conduct of the President, for we have not yet wholly lost the capacity of appreciating such an example of Christian faith and manly fortitude.   This exemplary picture has been made complete by your own contribution to its noble and touching features, on which I only forbear to dwell because I am directly addressing you.

Under all the conventional solemnities in Mr. Gladstone on such occasions, we are conscious of a sincere feeling that they were in real relation to human life and all its chances and changes.

CHAPTER VII

COLLEAGUES — NORTHERN CRUISE — EGYPT

(*1883*)

Parran faville della sua virtute
In non curar d'argento nè d'affanni.

— *Paradiso,* xvii. 83.

Sparks of his worth shall show in the little heed he gives either to
riches or to heavy toils.

THE session of 1883 was marked by one legislative performance of the first order, the bill devised against corrupt
practices at elections. This invaluable measure was worked
through the House of Commons mainly by Sir Henry James,
the attorney general, whose skill and temper in a business
that was made none the easier by the fact of every man in the
House supposing himself to understand the subject, excited
Mr. Gladstone's cordial admiration; it strengthened that
peculiarly warm regard in which he held Sir Henry, not
only now but even when the evil days of political severance
came. The prime minister, though assiduous, as he always
was, in the discharge of those routine and secondary duties
which can never be neglected without damage to the House,
had, for the first session in his career as head of a government, no burden in the shaping of a great bill. He insisted, in
spite of some opposition in the cabinet, on accepting a motion
pledging parliament to economy (April 3). In a debate on
the Congo, he was taken by some to have gone near to
giving up the treaty-making power of the crown. He had
to face more than one of those emergencies that were
naturally common for the leader of a party with a zealous
radical wing represented in his cabinet, and in some
measure these occasions beset Mr. Gladstone from 1869

onwards.   His loyalty and kindness to colleagues who got
themselves and him into scrapes by imprudent speeches,
and his activity and resource in inventing ways out of
scrapes, were always unfailing.   Often the difficulty was
with the Queen, sometimes with the House of Lords, occasionally with the Irish members.   Birmingham, for instance,
held 'a grand celebration (June 13) on the twenty-fifth
anniversary of Mr. Bright's connection as its representative.
Mr. Bright used strong language about 'Irish rebels,' and
then learned that he would be called to account.   He consulted Mr. Gladstone, and from him received a reply that
exhibits the use of logic as applied to inconvenient displays
of the sister art of rhetoric : —

CHAP.
VII.

Æt. 74.

To Mr. Bright.

June 15, 1883. — I have received your note, and I am extremely
sorry either that you should have personal trouble after your
great exertions, or that anything should occur to cloud the
brilliancy or mar the satisfaction of your recent celebration in
Birmingham.   I have looked at the extract from your speech,
which is to be alleged as the *corpus delicti*, with a jealous eye.
It seems well to be prepared for the worst.   The points are, I
think, *three :* — 1. 'Not a few' tories are guilty of determined
obstruction.   I cannot conceive it possible that this can be deemed
a breach of privilege.   2. These members are found 'in alliance'
with the Irish party.   Alliance is often predicated by those who
disapprove, upon the ground that certain persons have been voting
together.   This I think can hardly be a breach of privilege even in
cases where it may be disputable or untrue.

But then : 3. This Irish party are 'rebels' whose oath of allegiance is broken by association with the enemies of the country.
Whether these allegations are true or not, the following questions
arise : — (a) Can they be proved ; (b) Are they allegations which
would be allowed in debate ?   I suppose you would agree with me
that they cannot be proved ; and I doubt whether they would be
allowed in debate.   The question whether they are a breach of
privilege is for the House ; but the Speaker would have to say, if
called upon, whether they were allowable in debate.   My impres-

sion is that he would say no; and I think you would not wish to use elsewhere expressions that you could not repeat in the House of Commons.

The Speaker has a jotting in his diary which may end this case of a great man's excess: —

June 18. — Exciting sitting. Bright's language about Irish rebels. Certainly his language was very strong and quite inadmissible if spoken within the House. In conversation with Northcote I deprecated the taking notice of language outside the House, though I could not deny that the House, if it thought fit, might regard the words as a breach of privilege. But Northcote was no doubt urged by his friends.

Mr. Chamberlain's was a heavier business, and led to much correspondence and difficult conversation in high places. A little of it, containing general principles, will probably suffice here: —

To Sir Henry Ponsonby.

June 22. — *Re* Chamberlain's speech. I am sorry to say I had not read the report until I was warned by your letters to Granville and to Hamilton, for my sight does not allow me to read largely the small type of newspapers. I have now read it, and I must at once say with deep regret. We had done our best to keep the Bright celebration in harmony with the general tone of opinion by the mission which Granville kindly undertook. I am the more sorry about this speech, because Chamberlain has this year in parliament shown both tact and talent in the management of questions not polemical, such as the bankruptcy bill. The speech is open to exception from three points of view, as I think — first in relation to Bright, secondly in relation to the cabinet, thirdly and most especially in relation to the crown, to which the speech did not indicate the consciousness of his holding any special relation.

June 26. — It appeared to me in considering the case of Mr. Chamberlain's speech that by far the best correction would be found, if a natural opportunity should offer, in a speech differently coloured from himself. I found also that he was engaged to preside on Saturday next at the dinner of the Cobden Club. I addressed myself therefore to this point, and Mr. Chamberlain will revert, on that occasion, to the same line of thought. . . . But, like Granville, I consider that the offence does not consist in holding certain opinions, of which in my judgment the political force and effect are greatly exaggerated, but in the attitude assumed, and the tone and colour given to the speech.

CHAP.
VII.

Æт. 74.

To Lord Granville.

July 1, 1883. — I have read with care Chamberlain's speech of last night [at the Cobden Club dinner]. . . . Am I right or wrong in understanding the speech as follows? He admits without stint that in a cabinet concessions may be made as to action, but he seems to claim an unlimited liberty of speech. Now I should be as far as possible from asserting that under all circumstances speech must be confined within the exact limits to which action is tied down. But I think the dignity and authority, not to say the honour and integrity, of government require that the liberty of speaking beyond those limits should be exercised sparingly, reluctantly, and with much modesty and reserve. Whereas Chamberlain's Birmingham speech exceeded it largely, gratuitously, and with a total absence of recognition of the fact that he was not an individual but a member of a body. And the claim made last night to liberty of speech must be read with the practical illustration afforded by the Birmingham discourse, which evidently now stands as an instance, a sort of moral instance, of the mode in which liberty of speech is to be reconciled with limitation of action.[1]

In order to test the question, must we not bear in mind that the liberty claimed in one wing of a cabinet may also be claimed in another, and that while one minister says I support this measure, though it does not go far enough, another may just as lawfully say I support this measure, though it goes too far? For example, Argyll agreed to the Disturbance Compensation bill in 1880

[1] By an odd coincidence, on the day after my selection of this letter, I read that the French prime minister, M. Combes, laid down the doctrine that the government is never committed by a minister's individual declarations, but only by those of the head of the government. He alone has the power of making known the direction given to policy, and each minister individually has authority only for the administration of his department (September 25, 1902). Of course this is wholly incompatible with Mr. Gladstone's ideas of parliamentary responsibility and the cabinet system.

mainly out of regard to his colleagues and their authority. What if he had used in the House of Lords language like that I have just supposed ?   Every extravagance of this kind puts weapons into the hands of opponents, and weakens the authority of government, which is hardly ever too strong, and is often too weak already.

In a letter written some years before when he was leader of the House, Mr. Gladstone on the subject of the internal discipline of a ministerial corps told one, who was at that time and now his colleague, a little story : —

As the subject is one of interest, perhaps you will let me mention the incident which first obliged me to reflect upon it. . Nearly thirty years ago, my leader, Sir R. Peel, agreed in the Irish Tithes bills to give 25 per cent. of the tithe to the landlord in return for that 'Commutation.'   Thinking this too much (you see that twist was then already in me), I happened to say so in a private letter to an Irish clergyman.   Very shortly after I had a note from Peel, which inclosed one from Shaw, his head man in Ireland, complaining of my letter as making his work impossible if such things were allowed to go on.   Sir R. Peel indorsed the remonstrance, and I had to sing small.   The discipline was very tight in those days (and we were in opposition, not in government).   But it worked well on the whole, and I must say it was accompanied on Sir R. Peel's part with a most rigid regard to rights of all kinds within the official or quasi-official corps, which has somewhat declined in more recent times.

A minister had made some reference in a public speech to what happened in the cabinet of which he was a member. 'I am sure it cannot have occurred to you,' Mr. Gladstone wrote, 'that the cabinet is the operative part of the privy council, that the privy councillor's oath is applicable to its proceedings, that this is a very high obligation, and that no one can dispense with it except the Queen.   I may add that I believe no one is entitled even to make a note of the proceedings except the prime minister, who has to report its proceedings on every occasion of its meeting to the Queen, and who must by a few scraps assist his memory.'

By the end of the session, although its labours had not

been on the level of either 1881 or 1882, Mr. Gladstone was
somewhat strained. On Aug. 22 he writes to Mrs. Gladstone
at Hawarden: 'Yesterday at 4½ I entered the House hoping to get out soon and write you a letter, when the Speaker
told me Northcote was going to raise a debate on the Appropriation bill, and I had to wait, listen, and then to speak for
more than an hour, which tired me a good deal, finding me
weak after sitting till 2.30 the night before, and a long cabinet in the interval. Rough work for 73!'

II

In September he took a holiday in a shape that, though he
was no hearty sailor, was always a pleasure and a relief to
him. Three letters to the Queen tell the story, and give a
glimpse of court punctilio: —

On the North Sea, Sept. 15. Posted at Copenhagen, Sept. 16, 1883.
— Mr. Gladstone presents his humble duty to your Majesty, and
has to offer his humble apology for not having sought from your
Majesty the usual gracious permission before setting foot on
a foreign shore. He embarked on the 8th in a steamer of the
Castles Company under the auspices of Sir Donald Currie, with
no more ambitious expectation than that of a cruise among the
Western Isles. But the extraordinary solidity, so to call it, of a
very fine ship (the *Pembroke Castle*, 4000 tons, 410 feet long) on
the water, rendering her in no small degree independent of
weather, encouraged his fellow-voyagers, and even himself, though
a most indifferent sailor, to extend their views, and the vessel is
now on the North Sea running over to Christiansand in Norway,
from whence it is proposed to go to Copenhagen, with the expectation, however, of again touching British soil in the middle
of next week. Mr. Gladstone humbly trusts that, under these
circumstances, his omission may be excused.

Mr. Tennyson, who is one of the party, is an excellent sailor,
and seems to enjoy himself much in the floating castle, as it may
be termed in a wider sense than that of its appellation on the
register. The weather has been variable with a heavy roll from
the Atlantic at the points not sheltered; but the stormy North
Sea has on the whole behaved extremely well as regards its two
besetting liabilities to storm and fog.

Ship ' Pembroke Castle,' Mouth of the Thames. Sept. 20, 1883. — Mr. Gladstone with his humble duty reports to your Majesty his return this evening from Copenhagen to London. The passage was very rapid, and the weather favourable. He had the honour, with his wife and daughter and other companions of his voyage, to receive an invitation to dine at Fredensborg on Monday. He found there the entire circle of illustrious personages who have been gathered for some time in a family party, with a very few exceptions. The singularly domestic character of this remarkable assemblage, and the affectionate intimacy which appeared to pervade it, made an impression upon him not less deep than the demeanour of all its members, which was so kindly and so simple, that even the word condescending could hardly be applied to it. Nor must Mr. Gladstone allow himself to omit another striking feature of the remarkable picture, in the unrestrained and unbounded happiness of the royal children, nineteen in number, who appeared like a single family reared under a single roof.

[*The royal party, forty in number, visit the ship.*]

The Emperor of Russia proposed the health of your Majesty. Mr. Gladstone by arrangement with your Majesty's minister at this court, Mr. Vivian, proposed the health of the King and Queen of Denmark, and the Emperor and Empress of Russia, and the King and Queen of the Hellenes. The King of Denmark did Mr. Gladstone the honour to propose his health; and Mr. Gladstone in acknowledging this toast, thought he could not do otherwise, though no speeches had been made, than express the friendly feeling of Great Britain towards Denmark, and the satisfaction with which the British people recognised the tie of race which unites them with the inhabitants of the Scandinavian countries. Perhaps the most vigorous and remarkable portion of the British nation had, Mr. Gladstone said, been drawn from these countries. After luncheon, the senior imperial and royal personages crowded together into a small cabin on the deck to hear Mr. Tennyson read two of his poems, several of the younger branches clustering round the doors. Between 2 and 3, the illustrious party left the *Pembroke Castle*, and in the midst of an animated scene, went on board the King of Denmark's yacht, which steamed towards Elsinore.

Mr. Gladstone was much pleased to observe that the Emperor of Russia appeared to be entirely released from the immediate pressure of his anxieties supposed to weigh much upon his mind. The Empress of Russia has the genial and gracious manners which on this, and on every occasion, mark H.R.H. the Princess of Wales.

Sept. 22, 1883. — Mr. Gladstone presents his humble duty to your Majesty, and has to acknowledge your Majesty's letter of the 20th 'giving him full credit for not having reflected at the time' when he decided, as your Majesty believes, to extend his recent cruise to Norway and Denmark.

He may humbly state that he had no desire or idea beyond a glance, if only for a few hours, at a little of the fine and peculiar scenery of Norway. But he is also responsible for having acquiesced in the proposal (which originated with Mr. Tennyson) to spend a day at Copenhagen, where he happens to have some associations of literary interest; for having accepted an unexpected invitation to dine with the king some thirty miles off; and for having promoted the execution of a wish, again unexpectedly communicated to him, that a visit of the illustrious party to the *Pembroke Castle* should be arranged. Mr. Gladstone ought probably to have foreseen all these things. With respect to the construction put upon his act abroad, Mr. Gladstone ought again, perhaps, to have foreseen that, in countries habituated to more important personal meetings, which are uniformly declared to be held in the interests of general peace, his momentary and unpremeditated contact with the sovereigns at Fredensborg would be denounced, or suspected of a mischievous design. He has, however, some consolation in finding that, in England at least, such a suspicion appears to have been confined to two secondary journals, neither of which has ever found (so far as he is aware) in any act of his anything but guilt and folly.

Thus adopting, to a great extent, your Majesty's view, Mr. Gladstone can confirm your Majesty's belief that (with the exception of a sentence addressed by him to the King of the Hellenes singly respecting Bulgaria), there was on all hands an absolute silence in regard to public affairs. . . .

In proposing at Kirkwall the health of the poet who was

his fellow-guest on the cruise, Mr. Gladstone let fall a hint — a significant and perhaps a just one — on the comparative place of politics and letters, the difference between the statesman and orator and the poet. 'Mr. Tennyson's life and labour,' he said, 'correspond in point of time as nearly as possible to my own; but he has worked in a higher field, and his work will be more durable. We public men play a part which places us much in view of our countrymen, but the words which we speak have wings and fly away and disappear. . . . But the Poet Laureate has written his own song on the hearts of his countrymen that can never die.'

III

It was said in 1884 that the organisation of Egypt was a subject, whether regarded from the English or the European point of view, that was probably more complicated and more fraught with possible dangers in the future, than any question of foreign policy with which England had had to deal for the last fifty years or more.

The arguments against prolonged English occupation were tolerably clear. It would freeze all cordiality between ourselves and the French. It would make us a Mediterranean military power. In case of war, the necessity of holding Egypt would weaken us. In diplomacy it would expose fresh surface to new and hostile combinations. Yet, giving their full weight to every one of these considerations, a British statesman was confronted by one of those intractable dilemmas that make up the material of a good half of human history. The Khedive could not stand by himself. The Turk would not, and ought not to be endured for his protector. Some other European power would step in and block the English road. Would common prudence in such a case suffer England to acquiesce and stand aside? Did not subsisting obligations also confirm the precepts of policy and self-interest? In many minds this reasoning was clenched and clamped by the sacrifices that England had made when she took, and took alone, the initial military step.

Egyptian affairs were one of the heaviest loads that

weighed upon Mr. Gladstone during the whole of 1884.
One day in the autumn of this year, towards the end of the
business before the cabinet, a minister asked if there was
anything else. 'No,' said Mr. Gladstone with sombre irony
as he gathered up his papers, 'we have done our Egyptian
business, and we are an Egyptian government.' His general
position was sketched in a letter to Lord Granville (Mar. 22,
1884): 'In regard to the Egyptian question proper, I am
conscious of being moved by three powerful considerations.
(1) Respect for European law, and for the peace of eastern
Europe, essentially connected with its observance. (2) The
just claims of the Khedive, who has given us no case against
him, and his people as connected with him. (3) Indisposition to extend the responsibilities of this country. On the
first two I feel very stiff. On the third I should have due
regard to my personal condition as a vanishing quantity.'

The question of the continuance of the old dual control by
England and France was raised almost immediately after
the English occupation began, but English opinion supported or stimulated the cabinet in refusing to restore a
form of co-operation that had worked well originally in the
hands of Baring and de Blignières, but had subsequently
betrayed its inherent weakness. France resumed what is
diplomatically styled liberty of action in Egypt; and many
months were passed in negotiations, the most entangled in
which a British government was ever engaged. Why did
not England, impatient critics of Mr. Gladstone and his
cabinet inquire, at once formally proclaim a protectorate?
Because it would have been a direct breach of her moral
obligations of good faith to Europe. These were undisputed
and indisputable. It would have brought her within instant
reach of a possible war with France, for which the sinister
and interested approval of Germany would have been small
compensation.

The issue lay between annexation and withdrawal, —
annexation to be veiled and indirect, withdrawal to be
cautious and conditional. No member of the cabinet at
this time seems to have listened with any favour whatever to the mention of annexation. Apart from other

objections, it would undeniably have been a flagrant breach of solemn international engagements. The cabinet was pledged up to the lips to withdrawal, and when Lord Hartington talked to the House of Commons of the last British soldier quitting Egypt in a few months, nobody ever doubted then or since that he was declaring the sincere intention of the cabinet. Nor was any doubt possible that the intention of the cabinet entirely coincided at that time with the opinion and wishes of the general public. The operations in Egypt had not been popular,[1] and the national temper was still as hostile to all expansion as when it cast out Lord Beaconsfield. Withdrawal, however, was beset with inextricable difficulties. Either withdrawal or annexation would have simplified the position and brought its own advantages. Neither was possible. The British government after Tel-el-Kebir vainly strove to steer a course that would combine the advantages of both. Say what they would, military occupation was taken to make them responsible for everything that happened in Egypt. This encouraged the view that they should give orders to Egypt, and make Egypt obey. But then direct and continuous interference with the Egyptian administration was advance in a path that could only end in annexation. To govern Egypt from London through a native ministry, was in fact nothing but annexation, and annexation in its clumsiest and most troublesome shape. Such a policy was least of all to be reconciled with the avowed policy of withdrawal. To treat native ministers as mere ciphers and puppets, and then to hope to leave them at the end with authority enough to govern the country by themselves, was pure delusion.

So much for our relations with Egypt internally. Then came Europe and the Powers, and the regulation of a financial situation of indescribable complexity. 'I sometimes fear,' Mr. Gladstone wrote to Lord Granville (Dec. 8,

---

[1] Many indications of this could be cited, if there were room. A parade of the victors of Tel-el-Kebir through the streets of London stirred little excitement. Two ministers went to make speeches at Liverpool, and had to report on returning to town that references to Egypt fell altogether flat.

1884), 'that some of the foreign governments have the same notion of me that Nicholas was supposed to have of Lord Aberdeen. But there is no one in the cabinet less disposed than I am to knuckle down to them in this Egyptian matter, about which they, except Italy, behave so ill, some of them without excuse.' 'As to Bismarck,' he said, 'it is a case of sheer audacity, of which he has an unbounded stock.' Two months before he had complained to Lord Granville of the same powerful personage: 'Ought not some notice to be taken of Bismarck's impudent reference to the English exchequer? Ought you to have such a remark in your possession without protest? He coolly assumes in effect that we are responsible for all the financial wants and occasions of Egypt.'

The sensible reader would resist any attempt to drag him into the Serbonian bog of Egyptian finance. Nor need I describe either the protracted conference of the European Powers, or the mission of Lord Northbrook. To this able colleague, Mr. Gladstone wrote on the eve of his departure (Aug. 29, 1884) : —

I cannot let you quit our shores without a word of valediction. Your colleagues are too deeply interested to be impartial judges of your mission. But they certainly cannot be mistaken in their appreciation of the generosity and courage which could alone have induced you to undertake it. Our task in Egypt generally may not unfairly be called an impossible task, and with the impossible no man can successfully contend. But we are well satisfied that whatever is possible, you will achieve; whatever judgment, experience, firmness, gentleness can do, will be done. Our expectations from the nature of the case must be moderate; but be assured, they will not be the measure of our gratitude. All good go with you.

Lord Northbrook's report when in due time it came, engaged the prime minister's anxious consideration, but it could not be carried further. What the Powers might agree to, parliament would not look at. The situation was one of the utmost delicacy and danger, as anybody who is aware of the diplomatic embarrassments of it knows. An agreement with France about the Suez Canal came to nothing. A conference upon finance came to nothing. Bismarck was out of humour with England, partly from his dislike of certain exalted English personages and influences at his own court, partly because it suited him that France and England should be bad friends, partly because, as he complained, whenever he tried to found a colony, we closed in upon him. He preached a sermon on *do ut des*, and while scouting the idea of any real differences with this country, he hinted that if we could not accommodate him in colonial questions, he might not find it in his power to accommodate us in European questions. Mr. Gladstone declared for treating every German claim in an equitable spirit, but said we had our own colonial communities to consider.

In March 1885, after negotiations that threatened to be endless, the London Convention was signed and the riddle of the financial sphinx was solved. This made possible the coming years of beneficent reform. The wonder is, says a competent observer, how in view of the indifference of most of the Powers to the welfare of Egypt and the bitter annoyance of France at our position in that country, the English government ever succeeded in inducing all the parties concerned to agree to so reasonable an arrangement.[1]

Meanwhile, as we shall see all too soon, the question of Egypt proper, as it was then called, had brought up the question of the Soudan, and with it an incident that made what Mr. Gladstone called 'the blackest day since the Phœnix Park.' In 1884 the government still seemed prosperous. The ordinary human tendency to croak never dies, especially in the politics of party. Men talked of humiliation abroad, ruin at home, agricultural interests doomed, trade at a standstill — calamities all obviously due to a government without spirit, and a majority with no independence. But then humiliation, to be sure, only meant jealousy in other countries because we declined to put ourselves in the wrong, and to be hoodwinked into unwise alliances. Ruin only meant reform without revolution. Doom meant an inappreciable falling off in the vast volume of our trade.

[1] Milner's *England in Egypt*, p. 185.

CHAPTER VIII

REFORM

(*1884*)

DECISION by majorities is as much an expedient as lighting by gas. In adopting it as a rule, we are not realising perfection, but bowing to an imperfection. It has the great merit of avoiding, and that by a test perfectly definite, the last resort to violence ; and of making force itself the servant instead of the master of authority. But our country rejoices in the belief that she does not decide all things by majorities. — GLADSTONE (1858).

'THE word procedure,' said Mr. Gladstone to a club of young political missionaries in 1884, 'has in it something homely, and it is difficult for any one, except those who pass their lives within the walls of parliament, to understand how vital and urgent a truth it is, that there is no more urgent demand, there is no aim or purpose more absolutely essential to the future victories and the future efficiency of the House of Commons, than that it should effect, with the support of the nation — for it can be effected in no other way — some great reform in the matter of its procedure.' He spoke further of the 'absolute and daily-growing necessity of what I will describe as a great internal reform of the House of Commons, quite distinct from that reform beyond its doors on which our hearts are at present especially set.' Reform from within and reform from without were the two tasks, neither of them other than difficult in themselves and both made supremely difficult by the extraordinary spirit of faction at that time animating the minority. The internal reform had been made necessary, as Mr. Gladstone expressed it, by systematised obstruction, based upon the abuse of ancient and generous rules, under which system the House of Commons 'becomes more and more the slave of some of the poorest

123

and most insignificant among its members.' Forty years before he told the provost of Oriel, 'The forms of parliament are little more than a mature expression of the principles of justice in their application to the proceedings of deliberative bodies, having it for their object to secure freedom and reflection, and well fitted to attain that object.' These high ideals had been gradually lowered, for Mr. Parnell had found out that the rules which had for their object the security of freedom and reflection, could be still more effectually wrested to objects the very opposite.

In Mr. Gladstone's first session (1833) 395 members (the speaker excluded) spoke, and the total number of speeches was 5765. Fifty years later, in the session of 1883, the total number of speeches had risen to 21,160. The remedies proposed from time to time in this parliament by Mr. Gladstone were various, and were the occasion of many fierce and stubborn conflicts. But the subject is in the highest degree technical, and only intelligible to those who, as Mr. Gladstone said, 'pass their lives within the walls of parliament'— perhaps not by any means to all even of them. His papers contain nothing of interest or novelty upon the question either of devolution or of the compulsory stoppage of debate. We may as well, therefore, leave it alone, only observing that the necessity for the closure was probably the most unpalatable of all the changes forced on Mr. Gladstone by change in social and political circumstance. To leave the subject alone is not to ignore its extreme importance, either in the effect of revolution in procedure upon the character of the House, and its power of despatching and controlling national business ; or as an indication that the old order was yielding in the political sphere as everywhere else to the conditions of a new time.

II

The question of extending to householders in the country the franchise that in 1867 had been conferred on householders in boroughs, had been first pressed with eloquence and resolution by Mr. Trevelyan. In 1876 he introduced two resolutions, one for extended franchise, the other for a new arrangement of seats, made necessary by the creation of the new voters. In a tory parliament he had, of course, no chance. Mr. Gladstone, not naturally any more ardent for change in political machinery than Burke or Canning had been, was in no hurry about it, but was well aware that the triumphant parliament of 1880 could not be allowed to expire without the effective adoption by the government of proposals in principle such as those made by Mr. Trevelyan in 1876. One wing of the cabinet hung back. Mr. Gladstone himself, reading the signs in the political skies, felt that the hour had struck ; the cabinet followed, and the bill was framed. Never, said Mr. Gladstone, was a bill so large in respect of the numbers to have votes ; so innocent in point of principle, for it raised no new questions and sprang from no new principles. It went, he contended and most truly contended, to the extreme of consideration for opponents, and avoided several points that had especial attractions for friends. So likewise, the general principles on which redistribution of seats would be governed, were admittedly framed in a conservative spirit.

The comparative magnitude of the operation was thus described by Mr. Gladstone (Feb. 28, 1884) : —

In 1832 there was passed what was considered a Magna Charta of British liberties; but that Magna Charta of British liberties added, according to the previous estimate of Lord John Russell, 500,000, while according to the results considerably less than 500,000 were added to the entire constituency of the three countries. After 1832 we come to 1866. At that time the total constituency of the United Kingdom reached 1,364,000. By the bills which were passed between 1867 and 1869 that number was raised to 2,448,000. Under the action of the present law the constituency has reached in round numbers what I would call 3,000,000. This bill, if it passes as presented, will add to the English constituency over 1,300,000 persons. It will add to the Scotch constituency, Scotland being at present rather better provided in this respect than either of the other countries, over 200,000, and to the Irish constituency over 400,000; or in the main, to the present aggregate constituency of the United Kingdom taken at 3,000,000 it will add 2,000,000 more, nearly twice as much as was added since 1867, and more than four times as much as was added in 1832.

The bill was read a second time (April 7) by the overwhelming majority of 340 against 210. Even those who most disliked the measure admitted that a majority of this size could not be made light of, though they went on in charity to say that it did not represent the honest opinion of those who composed it. It was in fact, as such persons argued, the strongest proof of the degradation brought into our politics by the Act of 1867. 'All the bribes of Danby or of Walpole or of Pelham,' cried one excited critic, 'all the bullying of the Tudors, all the lobbying of George III., would have been powerless to secure it in the most corrupt or the most servile days of the ancient House of Commons.'[1]

On the third reading the opposition disappeared from the House, and on Mr. Gladstone's prompt initiative it was placed on record in the journals that the bill had been carried by a unanimous verdict. It went to the Lords, and by a majority, first of 59 and then of 50, they put what Mr. Gladstone mildly called 'an effectual stoppage on the bill, or in other words did practically reject it.' The plain issue, if we can call it plain, was this. What the tories, with different degrees of sincerity, professed to dread was that the election might take place on the new franchise, but with an unaltered disposition of parliamentary seats. At heart the bulk of them were as little friendly to a lowered franchise in the counties, as they had been in the case of the towns before Mr. Disraeli educated them. But this was a secret dangerous to let out, for the enfranchised workers in the towns would never understand why workers in the villages should not have a vote. Apart from this, the tory leaders believed that unless the allotment of seats went with the addition of a couple of million new voters, the prospect would be ruinously unfavourable to their party, and they offered determined resistance to the chance of a jockeying operation of this

[1] *Saturday Review*, April 12, 1884.

kind. At least one very eminent man among them had
privately made up his mind that the proceeding supposed to
be designed by their opponents — their distinct professions
notwithstanding — would efface the tory party for thirty years
to come. Mr. Gladstone and his government on the other
hand agreed, on grounds of their own and for reasons of
their own, that the two changes should come into operation
together. What they contended was, that to tack redistribution on to franchise, was to scotch or kill franchise. 'I do
not hesitate to say,' Mr. Gladstone told his electors, 'that
those who are opposing us, and making use of this topic of
redistribution of seats as a means for defeating the franchise
bill, know as well as we do that, had we been such idiots and
such dolts as to present to parliament a bill for the combined
purpose, or to bring in two bills for the two purposes as one
measure — I say, they know as well as we do, that a disgraceful failure would have been the result of our folly, and that
we should have been traitors to you, and to the cause we
had in hand.'[1] Disinterested onlookers thought there ought
to be no great difficulty in securing the result that both sides
desired. As the Duke of Argyll put it to Mr. Gladstone, if
in private business two men were to come to a breach, when
standing so near to one another in aim and profession, they
would be shut up in bedlam. This is just what the judicious
reader will think to-day.

The controversy was transported from parliament to the
platform, and a vigorous agitation marked the autumn
recess. It was a double agitation. What began as a campaign on behalf of the rural householder, threatened to end
as one against hereditary legislators. It is a well-known
advantage in movements of this sort to be not only for,
but also against, somebody or something ; against a minister,
by preference, or if not an individual, then against a body.
A hereditary legislature in a community that has reached the
self-governing stage is an anachronism that makes the easiest
of all marks for mockery and attack, so long as it lasts.
Nobody can doubt that if Mr. Gladstone had been the
frantic demagogue or fretful revolutionist that his opponents

[1] Edinburgh, August 30, 1884.

thought, he now had an excellent chance of bringing the question of the House of Lords irresistibly to the front. As it was, in the midst of the storm raised by his lieutenants and supporters all over the country, he was the moderating force, elaborately appealing, as he said, to the reason rather than the fears of his opponents.

One reproachful passage in his speeches this autumn acquires a rather peculiar significance in the light of the events that were in the coming years to follow. He is dealing with the argument that the hereditary House protects the nation against fleeting opinions : —

How is it with regard to the solid and permanent opinion of the nation ? We have had twelve parliaments since the Reform Act, — I have a right to say so, as I have sat in every one of them, — and the opinion, the national opinion, has been exhibited in the following manner. Ten of those parliaments have had a liberal majority. The eleventh parliament was the one that sat from 1841 to 1847. It was elected as a tory parliament; but in 1846 it put out the conservative government of Sir Robert Peel, and put in and supported till its dissolution, the liberal government of Lord John Russell. That is the eleventh parliament. But then there is the twelfth parliament, and that is one that you and I know a good deal about [Lord Beaconsfield's parliament], for we talked largely on the subject of its merits and demerits, whichever they may be, at the time of the last election. That parliament was, I admit, a tory parliament from the beginning to the end. But I want to know, looking back for a period of more than fifty years, which represented the solid permanent conviction of the nation ? — the ten parliaments that were elected upon ten out of the twelve dissolutions, or the one parliament that chanced to be elected from the disorganized state of the liberal party in the early part of the year 1874 ? Well, here are ten parliaments on the one side; here is one parliament on the other side. . . . The House of Lords was in sympathy with the one parliament, and was in opposition . . . to the ten parliaments. And yet you are told, when — we will say for forty-five years out of fifty — practically the nation has manifested its liberal tendencies by the election of liberal parliaments, and once only has chanced to elect a thoroughly tory parliament, you are told that it is the thoroughly tory parliament that represents the solid and permanent opinion of the country.[1]

In time a curious thing, not yet adequately explained, fell out, for the extension of the franchise in 1867 and now in 1884 resulted in a reversal of the apparent law of things that had ruled our political parties through the epoch that Mr. Gladstone has just sketched. The five parliaments since 1884 have not followed the line of the ten parliaments preceding, notwithstanding the enlargement of direct popular power.

III

In August Mr. Gladstone submitted to the Queen a memorandum on the political situation. It was much more elaborate than the ordinary official submissions. Lord Granville was the only colleague who had seen it, and Mr. Gladstone was alone responsible for laying it before the sovereign. It is a masterly statement of the case, starting from the assumption for the sake of argument that the tories were right and the liberals wrong as to the two bills ; then proceeding on the basis of a strongly expressed desire to keep back a movement for organic change ; next urging the signs that such a movement would go forward with irresistible force if the bill were again rejected ; and concluding thus : —

I may say in conclusion that there is no personal act if it be compatible with personal honour and likely to contribute to an end which I hold very dear, that I would not gladly do for the purpose of helping to close the present controversy, and in closing it to prevent the growth of one probably more complex and more formidable.

This document, tempered, unrhetorical, almost dispassionate, was the starting-point of proceedings that, after enormous difficulties had been surmounted by patience and perseverance, working through his power in parliament and his authority in the country, ended in final pacification and a sound political settlement. It was Mr. Gladstone's statesmanship that brought this pacification into sight and within reach.

[1] Corn Exchange, Edinburgh, August 30, 1884.

The Queen was deeply struck both by the force of his arguments and the earnest tone in which they were pressed. Though doubting whether there was any strong desire for a change in the position of the House of Lords, still she ' did not shut her eyes to the possible gravity of the situation ' (Aug. 31). She seemed inclined to take some steps for ascertaining the opinion of the leaders of opposition, with a view to inducing them to modify their programme. The Duke of Richmond visited Balmoral (Sept. 13), but when Mr. Gladstone, then himself on Deeside, heard what had passed in the direction of compromise, he could only say, ' Waste of breath ! ' To all suggestions of a dissolution on the case in issue, Mr. Gladstone said to a confidential emissary from Balmoral : —

Never will I be a party to dissolving in order to determine whether the Lords or the Commons were right upon the Franchise bill. If I have anything to do with dissolution, it will be a dissolution upon organic change in the House of Lords. Should this bill be again rejected in a definite manner, there will be only two courses open to me, one to cut out of public life, which I shall infinitely prefer ; the other to become a supporter of organic change in the House of Lords, which I hate and which I am making all this fuss in order to avoid. We have a few weeks before us to try and avert the mischief. After a second rejection it will be too late. There is perhaps the alternative of advising a large creation of peers; but to this there are great objections, even if the Queen were willing. I am not at present sure that I could bring myself to be a party to the adoption of a plan like that of 1832.

When people talked to him of dissolution as a means of bringing the Lords to account, he replied in scorn : ' A marvellous conception ! On such a dissolution, if the country disapproved of the conduct of its representatives, it would cashier them ; but, if it disapproved of the conduct of the peers, it would simply have to see them resume their place of power, to employ it to the best of their ability as opportunity might serve, in thwarting the desires of the country expressed through its representatives.'

It was reported to Mr. Gladstone that his speeches in

Scotland (though they were marked by much restraint) created some displeasure at Balmoral. He wrote to Lord Granville (Sept. 26) : —

The Queen does not know the facts. If she did, she would have known that while I have been compelled to deviate from the intention of speaking only to constituents which (with much difficulty) I kept until Aberdeen, I have thereby (and again with much difficulty in handling the audiences, every one of which would have wished a different course of proceeding) been enabled to do much in the way of keeping the question of organic change in the House of Lords out of the present stage of the controversy.

Sir Henry Ponsonby, of course at the Queen's instigation, was indefatigable and infinitely ingenious in inventing devices of possible compromise between Lords and Commons, or between Lords and ministers, such as might secure the passing of franchise and yet at the same time secure the creation of new electoral areas before the extended franchise should become operative. The Queen repeated to some members of the opposition — she did not at this stage communicate directly with Lord Salisbury — the essence of Mr. Gladstone's memorandum of August, and no doubt conveyed the impression that it had made upon her own mind. Later correspondence between her secretary and the Duke of Richmond set up a salutary ferment in what had not been at first a very promising quarter.

Meanwhile Mr. Gladstone was hard at work in other directions. He was urgent (Oct. 2) that Lord Granville should make every effort to bring more peers into the fold to save the bill when it reappeared in the autumn session. He had himself 'garnered in a rich harvest' of bishops in July. On previous occasions he had plied the episcopal bench with political appeals, and this time he wrote to the Archbishop of Canterbury : —

July 2, 1884. — I should have felt repugnance and scruple about addressing your Grace at any time on any subject of a political nature, if it were confined within the ordinary limits of such subjects. But it seems impossible to refuse credit to the accounts, which assure us that the peers of the opposition, under Lord

he will empower Lord Hartington to discuss the possibility of an agreement with Lord Salisbury.

In acknowledgment, Mr. Gladstone offered his thanks for all her Majesty's 'well-timed efforts to bring about an accommodation.' He could not, however, he proceeded, feel sanguine as to obtaining any concession from the leaders, but he is very glad that Lord Hartington should try.

Happily, and as might have been expected by anybody who remembered the action of the sensible peers who saved the Reform bill in 1832, the rash and headstrong men in high places in the tory party were not allowed to have their own way. Before the autumn was over, prudent members of the opposition became uneasy. They knew that in substance the conclusion was foregone, but they knew also that just as in their own body there was a division between hothead and moderate, so in the cabinet they could count upon a whig section, and probably upon the prime minister as well. They noted his words spoken in July, 'It is not our desire to see the bill carried by storm and tempest. It is our desire to see it win its way by persuasion and calm discussion to the rational minds of men.' [1]

Meanwhile Sir Michael Hicks Beach had already, with the knowledge and without the disapproval of other leading men on the tory side, suggested an exchange of views to Lord Hartington, who was warmly encouraged by the cabinet to carry on communications, as being a person peculiarly fitted for the task, 'enjoying full confidence on one side,' as Mr. Gladstone said to the Queen, 'and probably more on the other side than any other minister could enjoy.' These two cool and able men took the extension of county franchise for granted, and their conferences turned pretty exclusively on redistribution. Sir Michael pressed the separation of urban from rural areas, and what was more specifically important was his advocacy of single-member or one-horse constituencies. His own long experience of a scattered agricultural division had convinced him that such areas with household suffrage would be unworkable. Lord Hartington knew the advantage of two-member constituencies

[1] Dinner of the Eighty Club, July 11, 1884.

for his party, because they made an opening for one whig candidate and one radical.   But he did not make this a question of life or death, and the ground was thoroughly well hoed and raked.   Lord Salisbury, to whom the nature of these communications had been made known by the colleague concerned, told him of the suggestion from the Queen, and said that he and Sir Stafford Northcote had unreservedly accepted it.   So far the cabinet had found the several views in favour with their opponents as to electoral areas, rather more sweeping and radical than their own had been, and they hoped that on the basis thus informally laid, they might proceed to the more developed conversation with the two official leaders.   Then the tory ultras interposed.

IV

On the last day of October the Queen wrote to Mr. Gladstone from Balmoral : —

The Queen thinks that it would be a means of arriving at some understanding if the leaders of the parties in both Houses could exchange their views personally.   The Duke of Argyll or any other person unconnected for the present with the government or the opposition might be employed in bringing about a meeting, and in assisting to solve difficulties.   The Queen thinks the government should in any project forming the basis of resolutions on redistribution to be proposed to the House, distinctly define their plans at such a personal conference.   The Queen believes that were assurance given that the redistribution would not be wholly inimical to the prospects of the conservative party, their concurrence might be obtained.   The Queen feels most strongly that it is of the utmost importance that in this serious crisis such means, even if unusual, should be tried, and knowing how fully Mr. Gladstone recognises the great danger that might arise by prolonging the conflict, the Queen *earnestly* trusts that he will avail himself of such means to obviate it.

The Queen then wrote to Lord Salisbury in the same sense in which she had written to the prime minister.   Lord Salisbury replied that it would give him great pleasure to consult with anybody the Queen might desire, and that in

obedience to her commands he would do all that lay in him
to bring the controversy finally to a just and honourable
issue.   He went on however to say, in the caustic vein that
was one of his ruling traits, that while cheerfully com-
plying with the Queen's wishes, he thought it right to add
that, so far as his information went, no danger attached
to the prolongation of the controversy for a considerable
time, nor did he believe that there was any real excitement
in the country about it.   The Queen in replying (Nov. 5)
said that she would at once acquaint Mr. Gladstone with
what he had said.

The autumn session began, and the Franchise bill was
introduced again.   Three days later, in consequence of
a communication from the other camp, the debate on
the second reading was conciliatory, but the tories won a
bye-election, and the proceedings in committee became
menacing and clouded.   Discrepancies abounded in the
views of the opposition upon redistribution.   When the
third reading came (Nov. 11), important men on the tory
side insisted on the production of a Seats bill, and declared
there must be no communication with the enemy.   Mr.
Gladstone was elaborately pacific.   If he could not get
peace, he said, at least let it be recorded that he desired
peace.   The parleys of Lord Hartington and Sir Michael
Hicks Beach came to an end.

Mr. Gladstone, late one night soon after this (Nov. 14),
had a long conversation with Sir Stafford Northcote at the
house of a friend.   He had the authority of the cabinet (not
given for this special interview) to promise the introduction
of a Seats bill before the committee stage of the Franchise
bill in the Lords, provided he was assured that it could be
done without endangering or retarding franchise.   Northcote and Mr. Gladstone made good progress on the principles
of redistribution.   Then came an awkward message from
Lord Salisbury that the Lords could not let the Franchise
bill through, until they got the Seats bill from the Commons.
So negotiations were again broken off.

The only hope now was that a sufficient number of Lord
Salisbury's adherents would leave him in the lurch, if he

did not close with what was understood to be Mr. Gladstone's engagement, to procure and press a Seats bill as soon as ever franchise was out of danger. So it happened, and the door that had thus been shut, speedily opened. Indirect communication reached the treasury bench that seemed to show the leaders of opposition to be again alive. There were many surmises, everybody was excited, and two great tory leaders in the Lords called on Lord Granville one day, anxious for a *modus vivendi*. Mr. Gladstone in the Commons, in conformity with a previous decision of the cabinet, declared the willingness of the government to produce a bill or explain its provisions, on receiving a reasonable guarantee that the Franchise bill would be passed before the end of the sittings. The ultras of the opposition still insisted on making bets all round that the Franchise bill would not become law; besides betting, they declared they would die on the floor of the House in resisting an accommodation. A meeting of the party was summoned at the Carlton club for the purpose of declaring war to the knife, and Lord Salisbury was reported to hold to his determination. This resolve, however, proved to have been shaken by Mr. Gladstone's language on a previous day. The general principles of redistribution had been sufficiently sifted, tested, and compared to show that there was no insuperable discrepancy of view. It was made clear to Lord Salisbury circuitously, that though the government required adequate assurances of the safety of franchise before presenting their scheme upon seats, this did not preclude private and confidential illumination. So the bill was read a second time.

All went prosperously forward. On November 19, Lord Salisbury and Sir S. Northcote came to Downing Street in the afternoon, took tea with the prime minister, and had a friendly conversation for an hour in which much ground was covered. The heads of the government scheme were discussed and handed to the opposition leaders. Mr. Gladstone was well satisfied. He was much struck, he said after, with the quickness of the tory leader, and found it a pleasure to deal with so acute a man. Lord Salisbury, for his part, was interested in the novelty of the proceeding, for no precedent could be found in our political or party history for the discussion of a measure before its introduction between the leaders of the two sides. This novelty stirred his curiosity, while he also kept a sharp eye on the main party chance. He proved to be entirely devoid of respect for tradition, and Mr. Gladstone declared himself to be a strong conservative in comparison. The meetings went on for several days through the various parts of the questions, Lord Hartington, Lord Granville, and Sir Charles Dilke being also taken into council — the last of the three being unrivalled master of the intricate details.

The operation was watched with jealous eyes by the radicals, though they had their guardians in the cabinet. To Mr. Bright who, having been all his life denounced as a violent republican, was now in the view of the new school hardly even so much as a sound radical, Mr. Gladstone thought it well to write (Nov. 25) words of comfort, if comfort were needed : —

I wish to give you the assurance that in the private communications which are now going on, liberal principles such as we should conceive and term them, are in no danger. Those with whom we confer are thinking without doubt of party interests, as affected by this or that arrangement, but these are a distinct matter, and I am not so good at them as some others; but the general proposition which I have stated is I think one which I can pronounce with some confidence. . . . The whole operation is essentially delicate and slippery, and I can hardly conceive any other circumstance in which it would be justified, but in the present very peculiar case I think it is not only warranted, but called for.

On November 27 all was well over ; and Mr. Gladstone was able to inform the Queen that 'the delicate and novel communications' between the two sets of leaders had been brought to a happy termination. 'His first duty,' he said, 'was to tender his grateful thanks to your Majesty for the wise, gracious, and steady influence on your Majesty's part, which has so powerfully contributed to bring about this accommodation, and to avert a serious crisis of affairs.' He

adds that 'his cordial acknowledgments are due to Lord
Salisbury and Sir Stafford Northcote for the manner in
which they have conducted their difficult communications.'
The Queen promptly replied: 'I gladly and thankfully
return your telegrams. To be able to be of use is all I care
to live for now.' By way of winding up negotiations so
remarkable, Mr. Gladstone wrote to Lord Salisbury to thank
him for his kindness, and to say that he could have desired
nothing better in candour and equity. Their conversation
on the Seats bill would leave him none but the most agreeable recollections.

The Queen was in high good humour, as she had a right
to be. She gave Mr. Gladstone ample credit for his conciliatory spirit. The last two months had been very trying
to her, she said, but she confessed herself repaid by the
thought that she had assisted in a settlement. Mr. Gladstone's severest critics on the tory side confessed that 'they
did not think he had it in him.' Some friends of his
in high places even suggested that this would be a good
moment for giving him the garter. He wrote to Sir Arthur
Gordon (Dec. 5): 'The time of this government has been
on the whole the most stormy and difficult that I have known
in office, and the last six weeks have been perhaps the most
anxious and difficult of the government.'

V

One further episode deserves a section, if the reader will
turn back for a moment or two. The question whether
the extension of the parliamentary franchise to rural
householders should be limited to Great Britain or should
apply to the whole kingdom, had been finally discussed in
a couple of morning sittings in the month of May. Nobody
who heard it can forget the speech made against Irish
inclusion by Mr. Plunket, the eloquent grandson of the most
eloquent of all the orators whom Ireland has sent to the
imperial senate. He warned the House that to talk of
assimilating the franchise in Ireland to the franchise in
England, was to use language without meaning; that out of
seven hundred and sixty thousand inhabited houses in

Ireland, no fewer than four hundred and thirty-five thousand were rated at one pound and under; that those whom the bill would enfranchise would be taken from a class of whom more than forty per cent. could neither read nor write; that the measure would strengthen the hands of that disloyal party who boasted of their entire indifference to English opinion, and their undivided obligation to influences which Englishmen were wholly unable to realise. Then in a lofty strain Mr. Plunket foretold that the measure which they were asked to pass would lead up to, and would precipitate, the establishment of a separate Irish nationality. He reminded his hearers that the empire had been reared not more by the endurance of its soldiers and sailors than by the sagacity and firmness, the common sense and patriotism, of that ancient parliament; and he ended with a fervid prayer that the historian of the future might not have to tell that the union of these three kingdoms on which rested all its honour and all its power — a union that could never be broken by the force of domestic traitor or foreign foe — yielded at last under the pressure of the political ambitions and party exigencies of British statesmen.

The orator's stately diction, his solemn tone, the depth of his conviction, made a profound impression. Newer parliamentary hands below the government gangway, as he went on, asked one another by what arts of parliamentary defence the veteran minister could possibly deal with this searching appeal. Only a quarter of an hour remained. In two or three minutes Mr. Gladstone had swept the solemn impression entirely away. Contrary to his wont, he began at once upon the top note. With high passion in his voice, and mastering gesture in his uplifted arm, he dashed impetuously upon the foe. What weighs upon my mind is this, he said, that when the future historian speaks of the greatness of this empire, and traces the manner in which it has grown through successive generations, he will say that in that history there was one chapter of disgrace, and that chapter of disgrace was the treatment of Ireland. It is the scale of justice that will determine the issue of the conflict with Ireland, if conflict there is to be. There is nothing we can do, cried the orator, turning to the Irish members, except the imprudence of placing in your hands evidence that will show that we are not acting on principles of justice towards you, that can render you for a moment formidable in our eyes, should the day unfortunately arise when you endeavour to lay hands on this great structure of the British empire. Let us be as strong in right as we are in population, in wealth, and in historic traditions, and then we shall not fear to do justice to Ireland. There is but one mode of making England weak in the face of Ireland — that is by applying to her principles of inequality and principles of injustice.

As members sallied forth from the House to dine, they felt that this vehement improvisation had put the true answer. Mr. Plunket's fine appeal to those who had been comrades of the Irish loyalists in guarding the union was well enough, yet who but the Irish loyalists had held Ireland in the hollow of their hands for generation upon generation, and who but they were answerable for the odious and dishonouring failure, so patent before all the world, to effect a true incorporation of their country in a united realm? And if it should happen that Irish loyalists should suffer from extension of equal civil rights to Irishmen, what sort of reason was that why the principle of exclusion and ascendency which had worked such mischief in the past, should be persisted in for a long and indefinite future? These views, it is important to observe, were shared, not only by the minister's own party, but by a powerful body among his opponents. Some of the gentlemen who had been most furious against the government for not stopping Irish meetings in the autumn of 1883, were now most indignant at the bare idea of refusing or delaying a proposal for strengthening the hands of the very people who promoted and attended such meetings. It is true also that only two or three months before, Lord Hartington had declared that it would be most unwise to deal with the Irish franchise. Still more recently, Mr. W. H. Smith had declared that any extension of the suffrage in Ireland would draw after it 'confiscation of property, ruin of industry, withdrawal of capital, — misery, wretchedness, and war.' The valour of the platform, however, often expires in the

keener air of cabinet and parliament. It became Lord
Hartington's duty now to move the second reading of provisions which he had just described as most unwise provisions, and Mr. Smith found himself the object of brilliant
mockery from the daring leader below the gangway on his
own side.

Lord Randolph produced a more serious, though events
soon showed it to be not any more solid an argument, when
he said that the man who lives in a mud cabin very often
has a decent holding, and has money in the savings' bank
besides, and more than that, he is often more fit to take an
interest in politics, and to form a sound view about them,
than the English agricultural labourer. The same speaker
proceeded to argue that the Fenian proclivities of the towns
would be more than counterbalanced by the increased power
given to the peasantry. The incidents of agricultural life,
he observed, are unfavourable to revolutionary movements,
and the peasant is much more under the proper and legitimate influence of the Roman catholic priesthood than the
lower classes of the towns. On the whole, the extension of
the franchise to the peasantry of Ireland would not be unfavourable to the landlord interest. Yet Lord Randolph,
who regaled the House with these chimerical speculations,
had had far better opportunities than almost any other Englishman then in parliament of knowing something about
Ireland.

What is certain is that English and Scotch members acted
with their eyes open. Irish tories and Irish nationalists
agreed in menacing predictions. The vast masses of Irish
people, said the former, had no sense of loyalty and no love
of order to which a government could appeal. In many
districts the only person who was unsafe was the peace
officer or the relatives of a murdered man. The effect of
the change would be the utter annihilation of the political
power of the most orderly, the most loyal, the most educated
classes of Ireland, and the swamping of one-fourth of the
community, representing two-thirds of its property. A
representative of the great house of Hamilton in the
Commons, amid a little cloud of the dishevelled prophecies

too common in his class, assured the House that everybody knew that if the franchise in Ireland were extended, the days of home rule could not be far distant. The representative of the great house of Beresford in the Lords, the resident possessor of a noble domain, an able and determined man, with large knowledge of his country, so far as large knowledge can be acquired from a single point of view, expressed his strong conviction that after the passage of this bill the Irish outlook would be blacker than it had ever been before.[1]

Another person, far more powerful than any Hamilton or Beresford, was equally explicit. With characteristic frigidity, precision, and confidence, the Irish leader had defined his policy and his expectations. 'Beyond a shadow of doubt,' he had said to a meeting in the Rotunda at Dublin, 'it will be for the Irish people in England — separated, isolated as they are — and for your independent Irish members, to determine at the next general election whether a tory or a liberal English ministry shall rule England. This is a great force and a great power. If we cannot rule ourselves, we can at least cause them to be ruled as we choose. This force has already gained for Ireland inclusion in the coming Franchise bill. We have reason to be proud, hopeful, and energetic.'[2] In any case, he informed the House of Commons, even if Ireland were not included in the bill, the national party would come back seventy-five strong. If household suffrage were conceded to Ireland, they would come back ninety strong.[3] That was the only difference. Therefore, though he naturally supported inclusion,[4] it was not at all indispensable to the success of his policy, and he watched the proceedings in the committee as calmly as he might have watched a battle of frogs and mice.

[1] Lord Waterford, July 7, 1884.
[2] December 11, 1883.
[3] 'I am not at all sure,' Mr. Forster rashly said (March 31, 1884), 'that Mr. Parnell will increase his followers by means of this bill.'

[4] This was only the second occasion on which his party in cardinal divisions voted with the government.

CHAPTER IX

THE SOUDAN

(*1884-1885*)

You can only govern men by imagination: without imagination they are brutes. . . . 'Tis by speaking to the soul that you electrify men. — NAPOLEON.

IN the late summer of 1881 a certain native of Dongola, proclaiming himself a heaven-inspired Mahdi, began to rally to his banner the wild tribes of the southern Soudan. His mission was to confound the wicked, the hypocrite, the unbeliever, and to convert the world to the true faith in the one God and his prophet. The fame of the Mahdi's eloquence, his piety, his zeal, rapidly spread. At his ear he found a counsellor, so well known to us after as the khalifa, and this man soon taught the prophet politics. The misrule of the Soudan by Egypt had been atrocious, and the combination of a religious revival with the destruction of that hated yoke swelled a cry that was irresistible. The rising rapidly extended, for fanaticism in such regions soon takes fire, and the Egyptian pashas had been sore oppressors, even judged by the rude standards of oriental states. Never was insurrection more amply justified. From the first, Mr. Gladstone's curious instinct for liberty disclosed to him that here was a case of 'a people rightly struggling to be free.' The phrase was mocked and derided then and down to the end of the chapter. Yet it was the simple truth. 'During all my political life,' he said at a later stage of Soudanese affairs, 'I am thankful to say that I have never opened my lips in favour of a domination such as that which has been exercised upon certain countries by certain other countries, and

144

I am not going now to begin.' 'I look upon the possession of the Soudan,' he proceeded, 'as the calamity of Egypt. It has been a drain on her treasury, it has been a drain on her men. It is estimated that 100,000 Egyptians have laid down their lives in endeavouring to maintain that barren conquest.' Still stronger was the Soudanese side of the case. The rule of the Mahdi was itself a tyranny, and tribe fought with tribe, but that was deemed an easier yoke than the sway of the pashas from Cairo. Every vice of eastern rule flourished freely under Egyptian hands. At Khartoum whole families of Coptic clerks kept the accounts of plundering raids supported by Egyptian soldiers, and 'this was a government collecting its taxes.' The function of the Egyptian soldiers 'was that of honest countrymen sharing in the villainy of the brigands from the Levant and Asia Minor, who wrung money, women, and drink from a miserable population.'[1] Yet the railing against Mr. Gladstone for saying that the 'rebels' were rightly struggling to be free could not have been more furious if the Mahdi had been for dethroning Marcus Aurelius or Saint Louis of France.

The ministers at Cairo, however, naturally could not find in their hearts to withdraw from territory that had been theirs for over sixty years,[2] although in the winter of 1882-3 Colonel Stewart, an able British officer, had reported that the Egyptian government was wholly unfit to rule the Soudan; it had not money enough, nor fighting men enough, nor administrative skill enough, and abandonment at least of large portions of it was the only reasonable course. Such counsels found no favour with the khedive's advisers and agents, and General Hicks, an Indian officer, appointed on the staff of the Egyptian army in the spring of 1883, was now despatched by the government of the khedive from Khartoum, for the recovery of distant and formidable regions. If his operations had been limited to the original intention of clearing Sennaar

[1] Wingate, pp. 50, 51.
[2] The Soudan was conquered in 1819 by Ismail Pasha, the son of Mehemet Ali, and from that date Egypt had a more or less insecure hold over the country. In 1870 Sir Samuel Baker added the equatorial provinces to the Egyptian Soudan.

of rebels and protecting Khartoum, all might have been well. Unluckily some trivial successes over the Mahdi encouraged the Cairo government to design an advance into Kordofan, and the reconquest of all the vast wildernesses of the Soudan. Lord Dufferin, Sir E. Malet, Colonel Stewart, were all of them clear that to attempt any such task with an empty chest and a worthless army was madness, and they all argued for the abandonment of Kordofan and Darfur. The cabinet in London, fixed in their resolve not to accept responsibility for a Soudan war, and not to enter upon that responsibility by giving advice for or against the advance of Hicks, stood aloof.[1] In view of all that followed later, and of their subsequent adoption of the policy of abandoning the Soudan, British ministers would evidently have been wiser if they had now forbidden an advance so pregnant with disaster. Events showed this to have been the capital miscalculation whence all else of misfortune followed. The sounder the policy of abandonment, the stronger the reasons for insisting that the Egyptian government should not undertake operations inconsistent with that policy. The Soudan was not within the sphere of our responsibility, but Egypt was; and just because the separation of Egypt from the Soudan was wise and necessary, it might have been expected that England would peremptorily interpose to prevent a departure from the path of separation. What Hicks himself, a capable and dauntless man, thought of the chances we do not positively know, but he was certainly alive to the risks of such a march with such material. On November 5 (1883) the whole force was cut to pieces, the victorious dervishes were free to advance northwards, and the loose fabric of Egyptian authority was shattered to the ground.

---

[1] Mr. Gladstone said on Nov. 2, 1882: 'It is no part of the duty incumbent upon us to restore order in the Soudan. It is politically connected with Egypt in consequence of its very recent conquest; but it has not been included within the sphere of our operations, and we are by no means disposed to admit without qualification that it is within the sphere of our responsibility.' Lord Granville, May 7, 1883: 'H.M. government are in no way responsible for the operations in the Soudan, which have been undertaken under the authority of the Egyptian government, or for the appointment or actions of General Hicks.'

II

The three British military officers in Cairo all agreed that
the Egyptian government could not hold Khartoum if the
Mahdi should draw down upon it; and unless a British, an
Indian, or a Turkish force came to the rescue, abandonment
of the Soudan was the only possible alternative. The
London cabinet decided that they would not employ British
or Indian troops in the Soudan, and though they had no
objection to the resort to the Turks by Egypt, if the Turks
would pay their own expenses (a condition fatal to any such
resort), they strongly recommended the khedive to abandon
all territory south of Assouan or Wady-Halfa. Sir Evelyn
Baring, who had now assumed his post upon a theatre where
he was for long years to come to play the commanding part,
concurred in thinking that the policy of complete abandonment was the best admitted by the circumstances. It is the
way of the world to suppose that because a given course is
best, it must therefore be possible and ought to be simple.
Baring and his colleagues at Cairo were under no such
illusion, but it was the foundation of most of the criticism
that now broke forth in the English press.

The unparalleled difficulties that ultimately attended the
evacuation of the Soudan naturally led inconsiderate critics, —
and such must ever be the majority, — to condemn the policy
and the cabinet who ordered it. So apt are men in their
rough judgments on great disputable things, to mistake a
mere impression for a real opinion; and we must patiently
admit that the Result — success or failure in the Event — is
the most that they have time for, and all that they can go by.
Yet two remarks are to be made upon this facile censure.
The first is that those who knew the Soudan best, approved
most. On January 22, 1884, Gordon wrote to Lord Granville that the Soudan ever was and ever would be a useless
possession, and that he thought the Queen's ministers 'fully
justified in recommending evacuation, inasmuch as the sacrifices necessary towards securing good government would be
far too onerous to admit of such an attempt being made.'
Colonel Stewart quite agreed, and added the exclamation

that nobody who had ever visited the Soudan could escape the reflection, 'What a useless possession and what a huge encumbrance on Egypt!' As we shall see, the time soon came when Gordon accepted the policy of evacuation, even with an emphasis of his own. The second remark is that the reconquest of the Soudan and the holding of Khartoum were for the Egyptian government, if left to its own resources, neither more nor less than impossible; these objects, whether they were good objects or bad, not only meant recourse to British troops for the first immense operations, but the retention of them in a huge and most inhospitable region for an indefinite time. A third consideration will certainly not be overlooked by anybody who thinks on the course of the years of Egyptian reform that have since elapsed, and constitute so remarkable a chapter of British administration, — namely, that this beneficent achievement would have been fatally clogged, if those who conducted it had also had the Soudan on their hands. The renovation or reconstruction of what is called Egypt proper, its finances, its army, its civil rule, would have been absolutely out of reach, if at the same time its guiding statesmen had been charged with the responsibilities of recovering and holding that vaster tract which had been so rashly acquired and so mercilessly misgoverned. This is fully admitted by those who have had most to do with the result.

III

The policy of evacuation was taken as carrying with it the task of extricating the Egyptian garrisons. This aim induced Mr. Gladstone's cabinet once more to play an active military part, though Britain had no share in planting these garrisons where they were. Wise men in Egypt were of the same mind as General Gordon, that in the eastern Soudan it would have been better for the British government to keep quiet, and 'let events work themselves out.' Unfortunately the ready clamour of headlong philanthropists, political party men, and the men who think England humiliated if she ever lets slip an excuse for drawing her sword, drove the cabinet on to the rocks. When the decision of the cabinet was taken (Feb. 12, 1883) to send troops to Suakin, Mr. Gladstone stood alone in objecting. Many thousands of savages were slaughtered under humanitarian pressure, not a few English lives were sacrificed, much treasure flowed, and yet Sinkat fell, and Tokar fell, and our labours in the eastern Soudan were practically fruitless.[1] The operations had no effect upon the roll of the fierce mahdi wave over the Soudan.

In England, excitement of the unsound sort that is independent of knowledge, consideration, or deliberation; independent of any weighing of the actual facts and any forecast of latent possibilities, grew more and more vociferous. Ministers quailed. Twice they inquired of their agent in Egypt[2] whether General Gordon might not be of use, and twice they received an adverse reply, mainly on the ground that the presence in authority of a Christian officer was a dubious mode of confronting a sweeping outbreak of moslem fanaticism, and would inevitably alienate tribes that were still not caught by the Mahdi.[3] Unhappily a third application from London at last prevailed, and Sir E. Baring, supported by Nubar, by Sir Evelyn Wood, by Colonel Watson, who had served with Gordon and knew him well, all agreed that Gordon would be the best man if he would pledge himself to carry out the policy of withdrawing from the Soudan as quickly as possible. 'Whoever goes,' said Sir E. Baring in pregnant words to Lord Granville, will 'undertake a service of great difficulty and danger.' This was on January 16th. Two days later the die was cast. Mr. Gladstone was at Hawarden. Lord Granville submitted the question (Jan. 14, 1884) to him in this form : 'If Gordon says he

---

[1] It was a general mistake at that time to suppose that wherever a garrison fell into the hands of the Mahdi, they were massacred. At Tokar, for instance, the soldiers were incorporated by the victors. See Wingate, p. 553.

[2] Granville to Baring, Dec. 1, 1883 ; Jan. 10, 1884.

[3] Gordon had suppressed the Taiping rising in China in 1863. In 1874 he was appointed by the Egyptian government governor-general of the equatorial provinces of central Africa. In 1876 he resigned owing to trouble with the governor-general of the Soudan upon the suppression of the slave trade, but was appointed (1877) governor-general of the Soudan, Darfur, the equatorial provinces, and the Red Sea littoral. He held this position till the end of 1879, suppressing the slave trade with a strong hand and improving the means of communication throughout the Soudan. He succeeded in establishing comparative order. Then the new Egyptian government reversed Gordon's policy, and the result of his six years' work soon fell to pieces.

believes he could by his personal influence excite the tribes to escort the Khartoum garrison and inhabitants to Suakin, a little pressure on Baring might be advisable. The destruction of these poor people will be a great disaster.' Mr. Gladstone telegraphed that to this and other parts of the same letter, he agreed. Granville then sent him a copy of the telegram putting 'a little pressure on Baring.' To this Mr. Gladstone replied (Jan. 16) in words that, if they had only been taken to heart, would have made all the difference : —

I can find no fault with your telegram to Baring *re* Chinese Gordon, and the main point that strikes me is this: While his opinion on the Soudan may be of great value, must we not be very careful in any instruction we give, that he does not shift the centre of gravity as to political and military responsibility for that country? In brief, if he reports what should be done, he should not be the judge *who* should do it, nor ought he to commit us on that point by advice officially given. It would be extremely difficult after sending him to reject such advice, and it should therefore, I think, be made clear that he is not our agent for the purpose of advising on that point.

On January 18, Lord Hartington (then secretary of state for war), Lord Granville, Lord Northbrook, and Sir Charles Dilke met at the war office in Pall Mall. The summons was sudden. Lord Wolseley brought Gordon and left him in the ante-room. After a conversation with the ministers, he came out and said to Gordon, 'Government are determined to evacuate the Soudan, for they will not guarantee the future government. Will you go and do it?' '*I said*, "Yes." *He said*, "Go in." *I went in and saw them. They said*, "Did Wolseley tell you our orders?" *I said*, "Yes." *I said*, "You will not guarantee future government of the Soudan, and you wish me to go up and evacuate now." *They said*, "Yes," *and it was over, and I left at 8 p.m. for Calais.*'[1] This graphic story does not pretend to be a full version of all that passed, though it puts the essential point unmistakably enough. Lord Granville seems to have drawn Gordon's

[1] Gordon's Letters to Barnes, 1885. Lord Granville took his ticket, Lord Wolseley carried the General's bag, and the Duke of Cambridge held open the carriage door.

special attention to the measures to be taken for the security of the Egyptian garrisons (plural) still holding positions in the Soudan and to the best mode of evacuating the interior.[1] On the other hand, according to a very authentic account that I have seen, Gordon on this occasion stated that the danger at Khartoum was exaggerated, and that he would be able to bring away the garrisons without difficulty.

Thus in that conclave of sober statesmen a tragedy began. The next day one of the four ministers met another; 'We were proud of ourselves yesterday — are you sure we did not commit a gigantic folly?' The prime minister had agreed at once on receiving the news of what was done at the war office, and telegraphed assent the same night.[2] The whole cabinet met four days later, Mr. Gladstone among them, and the decision was approved. There was hardly a choice, for by that time Gordon was at Brindisi. Gordon, as Mr. Gladstone said, was a hero of heroes. He was a soldier of infinite personal courage and daring; of striking military energy, initiative, and resource; a high, pure, and single character, dwelling much in the region of the unseen. But as all who knew him admit, and as his own records testify, notwithstanding an under-current of shrewd common-sense, he was the creature, almost the sport, of impulse; his impressions and purposes changed with the speed of lightning; anger often mastered him; he went very often by intuitions and inspirations rather than by cool inference from carefully surveyed fact: with many variations of mood he mixed, as we often see in people less famous, an invincible faith in his own rapid prepossessions while they lasted. Everybody now discerns that to despatch a soldier of this temperament on a piece of business that was not only difficult and dangerous, as Sir E. Baring said, but profoundly obscure, and needing vigilant sanity and self-control, was little better than to call in a wizard with his magic. Mr. Gladstone always professed perplexity in understanding why the violent end of the gallant Cavagnari in Afghanistan,

[1] Baring's Instructions to Gordon (Jan. 25, 1884).
[2] Gladstone to Granville, Jan. 19, 1884. — 'I telegraphed last night my concurrence in your proceedings about Gordon: but Chester would not awake and the message only went on this morning.'

stirred the world so little in comparison with the fate of Gordon. The answer is that Gordon seized the imagination of England, and seized it on its higher side. His religion was eccentric, but it was religion; the Bible was the rock on which he founded himself, both old dispensation and new; he was known to hate forms, ceremonies, and all the 'solemn plausibilities'; his speech was sharp, pithy, rapid, and ironic; above all, he knew the ways of war and would not bear the sword for nought. All this was material enough to make a popular ideal, and this is what Gordon in an ever-increasing degree became, to the immense inconvenience of the statesmen, otherwise so sensible and wary, who had now improvidently let the genie forth from the jar.

IV

It has been sometimes contended that all the mischief that followed was caused by the diversion of Gordon from Suakin, his original destination. If he had gone to the Red Sea, as originally intended, there to report on the state and look of things in the Soudan, instead of being waylaid and brought to Cairo, and thence despatched to Khartoum, they say, no catastrophe would have happened. This is not certain, for the dervishes in the eastern Soudan were in the flush of open revolt, and Gordon might either have been killed or taken prisoner, or else he would have come back without performing any part of his mission. In fact, on his way from London to Port Said, Gordon had suggested that with a view to carrying out evacuation, the khedive should make him governor-general of the Soudan. Lord Granville authorised Baring to procure the nomination, and this Sir Evelyn did, 'for the time necessary to accomplish the evacuation.' The instructions were thus changed, in an important sense, but the change was suggested by Gordon and sanctioned by Lord Granville.[1]

[1] Dilke in House of Commons, Feb. 14, 1884. See also Lord Granville to Sir E. Baring, March 28, 1884. In recapitulating the instructions given to General Gordon, Lord Granville says: '*His* (Gordon's) *first proposal* was to proceed to Suakin with the object of reporting from thence on the best method of effecting the evacuation of the Soudan. . . . His instructions, *drawn up in accordance with his own views*, were to report to her Majesty's government on the military situation in the Soudan,' etc.

When Gordon left London his instructions, drafted in fact
by himself, were that he should 'consider and report upon
the best mode of effecting the evacuation of the interior of
the Soudan.' He was also to perform such duties as the
Egyptian government might wish to entrust to him, and
as might be communicated to him by Sir E. Baring.[1]
At Cairo, Baring and Nubar, after discussion with Gordon,
altered the mission from one of advice and report to an
executive mission — a change that was doubtless authorised
and covered by the original reference to duties to be
entrusted to him by Egypt. But there was no change in
the policy either at Downing Street or Cairo. Whether
advisory or executive, the only policy charged upon the
mission was abandonment. When the draft of the new
instructions was read to Gordon at Cairo, Sir E. Baring
expressly asked him whether he entirely concurred in 'the
policy of abandoning the Soudan,' and Gordon not only
concurred, but suggested the strengthening words, that he
thought 'it should on no account be changed.'[2] This
despatch, along with the instructions to Gordon making
this vast alteration, was not received in London until
Feb. 7. By this time Gordon was crossing the desert, and
out of reach of the English foreign office.

On his way from Brindisi, Gordon had prepared a memorandum for Sir E. Baring, in which he set out his opinion
that the Soudan had better be restored to the different petty
sultans in existence before the Egyptian conquest, and an
attempt should be made to form them into some sort of
confederation. These petty rulers might be left to accept the
Mahdi for their sovereign or not, just as they pleased. But
in the same document he emphasised the policy of abandonment. 'I understand,' he says, 'that H.M.'s government
have come to the irrevocable decision not to incur the very
onerous duty of granting to the peoples of the Soudan a just
future government.' Left to their independence, the sultans
'would doubtless fight among themselves.' As for future
good government, it was evident that 'this we could not

[1] For the full text of these instructions, see Appendix.

[2] Baring to Granville, January 28,
1884.

secure them without an inordinate expenditure of men and money. The Soudan is a useless possession; ever was so, and ever will be so. No one who has ever lived in the Soudan can escape the reflection, What a useless possession is this land.' Therefore — so he winds up — 'I think H.M.'s government are fully justified in recommending the evacuation, inasmuch as the sacrifices necessary towards securing a good government would be far too onerous to admit of any such attempt being made. Indeed, one may say it is impracticable at any cost. *H.M.'s government will now leave them as God has placed them.'* [1]

It was, therefore, and it is, pure sophistry to contend that Gordon's policy in undertaking his disastrous mission was evacuation but not abandonment. To say that the Soudanese should be left in the state in which God had placed them, to fight it out among themselves, if they were so minded, is as good a definition of abandonment as can be invented, and this was the whole spirit of the instructions imposed by the government of the Queen and accepted by Gordon.

Gordon took with him instruments from the khedive into which, along with definite and specific statements that evacuation was the object of his mission, two or three loose sentences are slipped about 'establishing organised government in the different provinces of the Soudan,' maintaining order, and the like. It is true also that the British cabinet sanctioned the extension of the area of evacuation from Khartoum to the whole Soudan.[2] Strictly construed, the whole body of instructions, including firmans and khedive's proclamations, is not technically compact nor coherent. But this is only another way of saying that Gordon was to have the widest discretionary powers as to the manner of carrying out the policy, and the best time and mode of announcing it. The policy itself, as well understood by Gordon as by everybody else, was untouched, and it was: to leave the Soudanese in the state in which God had placed them.

The hot controversy on this point is idle and without substance — the idlest controversies are always the hottest

---

[1] Dated, *Steamship 'Tanjore,' at Sea, Jan.* 22, 1884.
[2] Granville to Baring, March 28.

— for not only was Gordon the last man in all the world
to hold himself bound by official instructions, but the
actual conditions of the case were too little known, too
shifting, too unstable, to permit of hard and fast directions beforehand how to solve so desperate a problem. Two
things at any rate were clear — one, that Gordon should faithfully adhere to the policy of evacuation and abandonment
which he had formally accepted; the other, that the British
government should leave him a free hand. Unhappily
neither of these two clear things was accepted by either
of the parties.

V

Gordon's policies were many and very mutable. Viewing
the frightful embarrassments that enveloped him, we cannot wonder. Still the same considerateness that is always
so bounteously and so justly extended to the soldier in the
field, is no less due in its measure to the councillor in the
cabinet. This is a bit of equity often much neglected both
by contemporaries and by history.

He had undertaken his mission without any serious and
measured forecast, such as his comrade, Colonel Stewart,
was well fitted to supply. His first notion was that he could
restore the representatives of the old rulers, but when he got
into the country, he found that there were none; with one
by no means happy exception, they had all disappeared.
When he reached Berber, he learned more clearly how the
question of evacuation was interlaced with other questions.
Once at Khartoum, at first he thought himself welcome as
a deliverer, and then when new light as to the real feelings
of the Soudanese broke upon him, he flung the policy of his
mission overboard. Before the end of February, instead of the
suzerainty of Egypt, the British government should control
Soudanese administration, with Zobeir as their governor-
general. ' When Gordon left this country,' said Mr. Gladstone, 'and when he arrived in Egypt, he declared it to be,
and I have not the smallest doubt that it was — a fixed
portion of his policy, that no British force should be
employed in aid of his mission.' [1]   When March came, he

[1] Feb. 23, 1885.

flung himself with ardour into the policy of 'smashing up' the Mahdi, with resort to British and Indian troops. This was a violent reversal of all that had been either settled or dreamed of, whether in London or at Cairo. A still more vehement stride came next. He declared that to leave out-lying garrisons to their fate would be an 'indelible disgrace.' Yet, as Lord Hartington said, the government 'were under no moral obligation to use the military resources of this empire for the relief of those garrisons.' As for Gordon's opinion that 'indelible disgrace' would attach to the British government if they were not relieved, 'I do not admit,' said the minister very sensibly, 'that General Gordon is on this point a better authority than anybody else.'[1] All this illustrates the energy of Gordon's mental movements, and also, what is more important, the distracting difficulties of the case before him. In one view and one demand he strenuously persevered, as we shall now see.

Mr. Gladstone at first, when Gordon set all instructions at defiance, was for recalling him. A colleague also was for recalling him on the first instant when he changed his policy. Another important member of the cabinet was, on the contrary, for an expedition. 'I cannot admit,' wrote a fourth leading minister, 'that either generals or statesmen who have accepted the offer of a man to lead a forlorn hope, are in the least bound to risk the lives of thousands for the uncertain chance of saving the forlorn hope.' Some think that this was stern common sense, others call it ignoble. The nation, at any rate, was in one of its high idealising humours, though Gordon had roused some feeling against himself in this country (unjustly enough) by his decree formally sanctioning the holding of slaves.

The general had not been many hours in Khartoum (February 18) before he sent a telegram to Sir E. Baring, proposing that on his withdrawal from Khartoum, Zobeir Pasha should be named his successor as governor-general of the Soudan: he should be made a K.C.M.G., and have presents given to him. This request was strenuously pressed by Gordon. Zobeir had been a prime actor in the

[1] May 13, 1884.

devastations of the slave trade; it was he who had acquired
Darfur for Egypt; he was a first-rate fighting man, and
the ablest leader in the Soudan. He is described by the
English officer who knows the Soudan best, as a far-seeing,
thoughtful man of iron will — a born ruler of men.[1] The
Egyptian government had desired to send him down to aid
in the operations at Suakin in 1883, but the government in
London vetoed him, as they were now to veto him a second
time. The Egyptian government was to act on its own
responsibility, but not to do what it thought best. So now
with Gordon.

Gordon in other days had caused Zobeir's son to be shot,
and this was supposed to have set up an unquenchable blood-
feud between them. Before reaching Cairo, he had suggested
that Zobeir should be sent to Cyprus, and there kept out of
the way. This was not done. On Gordon's way through
Cairo, the two men met in what those present describe as
a highly dramatic interview. Zobeir bitterly upbraided
Gordon: 'You killed my son, whom I entrusted to you.
He was as your son. You brought my wives and women
and children in chains to Khartoum.' Still even after that
incident, Gordon declared that he had 'a mystical feeling'
that Zobeir and he were all right.[2] What inspired his
reiterated demand for the immediate despatch of Zobeir
is surmised to have been the conviction forced upon him
during his journey to Khartoum, that his first idea of
leaving the various petty sultans to fight it out with the
Mahdi, would not work; that the Mahdi had got so strong
a hold that he could only be met by a man of Zobeir's
political capacity, military skill, and old authority. Sir E.
Baring, after a brief interval of hesitation, now supported
Gordon's request. So did the shrewd and expert Colonel
Stewart. Nubar too favoured the idea. The cabinet could
not at once assent; they were startled by the change of front

CHAP.
IX.

Æt. 75.

[1] Wingate's *Mahdism*, p. 109.
[2] Baring to Granville, Jan. 28. —
'I had a good deal of conversation
with General Gordon as to the manner in which Zobeir Pasha should be
treated. Gen. Gordon entertains a
high opinion of Zobeir Pasha's energy and ability. He possesses great
influence in the Soudan, and General
Gordon is of opinion that *circumstances might arise which would render it desirable that he should be sent
back to the Soudan.*'

as to total withdrawal from the Soudan — the very object of
Gordon's mission, and accepted by him as such. On February 21 Mr. Gladstone reported to the Queen that the
cabinet were of opinion that there would be the gravest
objection to nominating by an assumption of British
authority a successor to General Gordon in the Soudan, nor
did they as yet see sufficient reasons for going beyond
Gordon's memorandum of January 25, by making special
provision for the government of that country. But at first
it looked as if ministers might yield, if Baring, Gordon, and
Nubar persisted.

As ill-fortune had it, the Zobeir plan leaked out at home by
Gordon's indiscretion before the government decided. The
omnipotent though not omniscient divinity called public
opinion intervened. The very men who had most loudly
clamoured for the extrication of the Egyptian garrisons, who
had pressed with most importunity for the despatch of
Gordon, who had been most urgent for the necessity of
giving him a free hand, now declared that it would be a
national degradation and a European scandal to listen to
Gordon's very first request. He had himself unluckily given
them a capital text, having once said that Zobeir was alone
responsible for the slave trade of the previous ten years.
Gordon's idea was, as he explained, to put Zobeir into
a position like that of the Ameer of Afghanistan, as a buffer
between Egypt and the Mahdi, with a subsidy, moral support, and all the rest of a buffer arrangement. The idea may
or may not have been a good one ; nobody else had a better.

It was not at all surprising that the cabinet should ask
what new reason had come to light why Zobeir should be
trusted ; why he should oppose the Mahdi whom at first he
was believed to have supported ; why he should turn the
friend of Egypt ; why he should be relied upon as the faithful
ally of England. To these and other doubts Gordon had
excellent answers (March 8). Zobeir would run straight,
because it was his interest. If he would be dangerous, was
not the Mahdi dangerous, and whom save Zobeir could you
set up against the Mahdi? You talked of slave-holding
and slave-hunting, but would slave-holding and slave-hunting

stop with your own policy of evacuation? Slave-holding you cannot interfere with, and as for slave-hunting, that depended on the equatorial provinces, where Zobeir could be prevented from going, and besides he would have his hands full in consolidating his power elsewhere. As for good faith towards Egypt, Zobeir's stay in Cairo had taught him our power, and being a great trader, he would rather seek Egypt's close alliance. Anyhow, said Gordon, 'if you do not send Zobeir, you have no chance of getting the garrisons away.'

The matter was considered at two meetings of the cabinet, but the prime minister was prevented by his physician from attending.[1] A difference of opinion showed itself upon the despatch of Zobeir; viewed as an abstract question, three of the Commons members inclined to favour it, but on the practical question, the Commons members were unanimous that no government from either side of the House could venture to sanction Zobeir. Mr. Gladstone had become a strong convert to the plan of sending Zobeir. 'I am better in chest and generally,' he wrote to Lord Granville, 'but unfortunately not in throat and voice, and Clark interdicts my appearance at cabinet; but I am available for any necessary communication, say with you, or you and Hartington.' One of the ministers went to see him in his bed, and they conversed for two hours. The minister, on his return, reported with some ironic amusement that Mr. Gladstone considered it very likely that they could not bring parliament to swallow Zobeir, but believed that he himself could. Whether his confidence in this was right or wrong, he was unable to turn his cabinet. The Queen telegraphed her agreement with the prime minister. But this made no difference. 'On Saturday 15,' Mr. Gladstone notes, 'it seemed as if by my casting vote Zobier was to be sent to Gordon. But

---

[1] (*From his diary.*) *March 9.* — . . . At night recognised the fact of a cold, and began to deal with it. 10th. Kept my bed all day. 11th. The cabinet sat, and Granville came to and fro with the communications, Clark having prohibited my attendance. Read *Sybil.* 12th. Bed as yesterday. 13th. Got to my sitting-room in the evening. It has, however, taken longer this time to clear the chest, and Clark reports the pulse still too high by ten. Saw Granville. Conclave, 7½ to 8½, on telegram to Baring for Gordon. I was not allowed to attend the cabinet.

on Sunday —— and —— receded from their ground, and I gave way. The nature of the evidence on which judgments are formed in this most strange of all cases, precludes (in reason) pressing all conclusions, which are but preferences, to extremes.' 'It is well known,' said Mr. Gladstone in the following year when the curtain had fallen on the catastrophe, 'that if, when the recommendation to send Zobeir was made, we had complied with it, an address from this House to the crown would have paralysed our action; and though it was perfectly true that the decision arrived at was the judgment of the cabinet, it was also no less the judgment of parliament and the people.' So Gordon's request was refused.

It is true that, as a minister put it at the time, to send Zobeir would have been a gambler's throw. But then what was it but a gambler's throw to send Gordon himself? The Soudanese chieftain might possibly have done all that Gordon and Stewart, who knew the ground and were watching the quick fluctuation of events with elastic minds, now positively declared that he would have the strongest motives not to do. Even then, could the issue have been worse? To run all the risks involved in the despatch of Gordon, and then immediately to refuse the request that he persistently represented as furnishing him his only chance, was an incoherence that the parliament and people of England have not often surpassed.[1] All through this critical month, from the 10th until the 30th, Mr. Gladstone was suffering more or less from indisposition which he found it difficult to throw off.

VI

The chance, whatever it may have been, passed like a flash. Just as the proposal inflamed many in England, so it did mischief in Cairo. Zobeir like other people got wind of it; enemies of England at Cairo set to work with him; Sir E. Baring might have found him hard to deal with. It was Gordon's rashness that had made the design public. Gordon, too, as it happened, had made a dire mistake on his way up. At Berber he had shown the khedive's secret firman,

[1] The case of the government was stated with all the force and reason of which it admitted, in Lord Granville's despatch of March 28, 1884.

announcing the intended abandonment of the Soudan. The news spread; it soon reached the Mahdi himself, and the Mahdi made politic use of it. He issued a proclamation of his own, asking all the sheikhs who stood aloof from him or against him, what they had to gain by supporting a pasha who was the next day going to give the Soudan up. Gordon's argument for this unhappy proceeding was that, the object of his mission being to get out of the country and leave them to their independence, he could have put no sharper spur into them to make them organise their own government. But he spoke of it after as the fatal proclamation, and so it was.[1]

What happened was that the tribes round Khartoum almost at once began to waver. From the middle of March, says a good observer, one searches in vain for a single circumstance hopeful for Gordon. 'When the eye wanders over the huge and hostile Soudan, notes the little pin-point garrisons, each smothered in a cloud of Arab spears, and remembers that Gordon and Stewart proceeded to rule this vast empire, already given away to others, one feels that the Soudanese view was marked by common sense.'[2] Gordon's too sanguine prediction that the men who had beaten Hicks, and the men who afterwards beat Baker, would never fight beyond their tribal limits, did not come true. Wild forces gathered round the Mahdi as he advanced northwards. The tribes that had wavered joined them. Berber fell on May 26. The pacific mission had failed, and Gordon and his comrade Stewart — a more careful and clear-sighted man than himself — were shut up in Khartoum.

[1] In the light of this proceeding, the following is curious : 'There is one subject which I cannot imagine any one differing about. That is the impolicy of announcing our intention to evacuate Khartoum. Even if we were bound to do so we should have said nothing about it. The moment it is known we have given up the game, every man will go over to the Mahdi. All men worship the rising sun. The difficulties of evacuation will be enormously increased, if, indeed, the withdrawal of our garrison is not rendered impossible.' — Interview with General Gordon, *Pall Mall*

Gazette, Jan. 8, 1884.

. . . 'In the afternoon of Feb. 13 Gordon assembled all the influential men of the province and showed them the secret firman. The reading of this document caused great excitement, but at the same time its purport was received evidently with much gratification. It is worthy of note that the whole of the notables present at this meeting subsequently threw in their cause with the Mahdi.' — Henry William Gordon's *Events in the Life of Charles George Gordon*, p. 340.

[2] Wingate, p. 110.

Distractions grew thicker upon the cabinet, and a just reader, now far away from the region of votes of censure, will bear them in mind. The Queen, like many of her subjects, grew impatient, but Mr. Gladstone was justified in reminding her of the imperfect knowledge, and he might have called it blank ignorance, with which the government was required on the shortest notice to form conclusions on a remote and more than half-barbarous region.

Gordon had told them that he wanted to take his steam vessels to Equatoria and serve the king of the Belgians. This Sir Evelyn Baring refused to allow, not believing Gordon to be in immediate danger (March 26). From Gordon himself came a telegram (March 28), 'I think we are now safe, and that, as the Nile rises, we shall account for the rebels.' Mr. Gladstone was still unwell and absent. Through Lord Granville he told the cabinet (March 15) that, with a view to speedy departure from Khartoum, he would not even refuse absolutely to send cavalry to Berber, much as he disliked it, provided the military authorities thought it could be done, and provided also that it was declared necessary for Gordon's safety, and was strictly confined to that object. The cabinet decided against an immediate expedition, one important member vowing that he would resign if an expedition were not sent in the autumn, another vowing that he would resign if it were. On April 7, the question of an autumn expedition again came up. Six were favourable, five the other way, including the prime minister.

Almost by the end of March it was too probable that no road of retreat was any longer open. If they could cut no way out, either by land or water, what form of relief was possible? A diversion from Suakin to Berber — one of Gordon's own suggestions? But the soldiers differed. Fierce summer heat and little water; an Indian force might stand it; even they would find it tough. A dash by a thousand cavalry across two hundred miles of desert — one hundred of them without water; without communication with its base, and with the certainty that whatever might befall, no reinforcements could reach it for months? What would be your feelings, and your language, asked Lord

Hartington, if besides having Gordon and Stewart beleaguered in Khartoum, we also knew that a small force of British cavalry unable to take the offensive was shut up in the town of Berber?[1] Then the government wondered whether a move on Dongola might not be advantageous. Here again the soldiers thought the torrid climate a fatal objection, and the benefits doubtful. Could not Gordon, some have asked, have made his retreat at an early date after reaching Khartoum, by way of Berber? Answer — the Nile was too low. All this it was that at a later day, when the time had come to call his government to its account, justified Mr. Gladstone in saying that in such enterprises as these in the Soudan, mistakes and miscarriages were inevitable, for they were the proper and certain consequences of undertakings that lie beyond the scope of human means and of rational and prudent human action, and are a war against nature.[2] If anybody now points to the victorious expedition to Khartoum thirteen years later, as falsifying such language as this, that experience so far from falsifying entirely justifies. A war against nature demands years of study, observation, preparation, and those who are best acquainted with the conditions at first hand all agree that neither the tribes nor the river nor the desert were well known enough in 1885, to guarantee that overthrow in the case of the Mahdi, which long afterwards destroyed his successor.

On April 14 Sir E. Baring, while as keenly averse as anybody in the world to an expedition for the relief of Khartoum if such an expedition could be avoided, still watching events with a clear and concentrated gaze, assured the government that it was very likely to be unavoidable; it would be well therefore, without loss of time, to prepare for a move as soon as ever the Nile should rise. Six days before, Lord Wolseley also had written to Lord Hartington at the war office, recommending immediate and active preparations for an exclusively British expedition to Khartoum. Time, he said, is the most important element in this

---

[1] Lord Hartington, House of Commons, May 13, 1884. An admirable speech, and the best defence of ministers up to this date.

[2] Address to the electors of Midlothian, September 17, 1885.

question; and in truth it was, for time was flying, and so were events. The cabinet were reported as feeling that Gordon, 'who was despatched on a mission essentially pacific, had found himself, from whatever cause, unable to prosecute it effectually, and now proposed the use of military means, which might fail, and which, even if they should succeed, might be found to mean a new subjugation of the Soudan — the very consummation which it was the object of Gordon's mission to avert.' On June 27 it was known in London that Berber had fallen a month before.

VII

Lord Hartington, as head of the war department, had a stronger leaning towards the despatch of troops than some of his colleagues, but, says Mr. Gladstone to Lord Granville in a letter of 1888, 'I don't think he ever came to any sharp issue (like mine about Zobeir) ; rather that in the main he got what he wanted.' Wherever the fault lay, the issue was unfortunate. The generals in London fought the battle of the routes with unabated tenacity for month after month. One was for the approach to Khartoum by the Nile; another by Suakin and Berber; a third by the Korosko desert. A departmental committee reported in favour of the Nile as the easiest, safest, and cheapest, but they did not report until July 29. It was not until the beginning of August that the House of Commons was asked for a vote of credit, and Lord Hartington authorised General Stephenson at Cairo to take measures for moving troops southward. In his despatch of August 8, Lord Hartington still only speaks of operations for the relief of Gordon, 'should they become necessary'; he says the government were still unconvinced that Gordon could not secure the withdrawal of the garrison from Khartoum; but 'they are of opinion that the time had arrived for obtaining accurate information as to his position,' and, 'if necessary, for rendering him assistance.'[1] As soon as the decision was taken, preparations were carried out with rapidity and skill. In the same month Lord Wolseley was

[1] See the official *History of the Soudan Campaign*, by Colonel Colvile, Part I. pp. 45-9.

appointed to command the expedition, and on September 9
he reached Cairo. The difficulties of a military decision had
been great, said Lord Hartington, and there was besides, he
added, a difference of opinion among the military authorities.[1]
It was October 5 before Lord Wolseley reached Wady-
Halfa, and the Nile campaign began.

Whatever decision military critics may ultimately form
upon the choice of the Nile route, or upon the question
whether the enterprise would have been any more successful if the route had been by Suakin or Korosko, it is at
least certain that no position, whether strategically false
or no, has ever evoked more splendid qualities in face of
almost preterhuman difficulties, hardship, and labour. The
treacherous and unknown river, for it was then unknown,
with its rapids, its shifting sandbanks and tortuous channels
and rocky barriers and heart-breaking cataracts; the
Bayuda desert, haunted by fierce and stealthy enemies; the
trying climate, the heat, the thirst, all the wearisome
embarrassments of transport on camels emaciated by lack
of food and water — such scenes exacted toil, patience, and
courage as worthy of remark and admiration as if the
advance had successfully achieved its object. Nobody lost
heart. 'Everything goes on swimmingly,' wrote Sir Herbert
Stewart to Lord Wolseley, '*except as to time*.' This was on
January 14, 1885. Five days later, he was mortally wounded.

The end of it all, in spite of the gallantry of Abu Klea and
Kirbekan, of desert column and river column, is only too
well known. Four of Gordon's small steamers coming down
from Khartoum met the British desert column at Gubat on
January 21. The general in command at once determined
to proceed to Khartoum, but delayed his start until the
morning of the 24th. The steamers needed repairs, and Sir
Charles Wilson deemed it necessary for the safety of his troops
to make a reconnaissance down the river towards Berber
before starting up to Khartoum. He took with him on two
of Gordon's steamers — described as of the dimensions of the
penny boats upon the Thames, but bullet proof — a force of
twenty-six British, and two hundred and forty Soudanese.

[1] February 27, 1885.

He had also in tow a nugger laden with dhura. This was what, when Khartoum came in sight (Jan. 28) the 'relief force' actually amounted to. As the two steamers ran slowly on, a solitary voice from the river-bank now and again called out to them that Khartoum was taken, and Gordon slain. Eagerly searching with their glasses, the officers perceived that the government-house was a wreck, and that no flag was flying. Gordon, in fact, had met his death two days before.

Mr. Gladstone afterwards always spoke of the betrayal of Khartoum. But Major Kitchener, who prepared the official report, says that the accusations of treachery were all vague, and to his mind, the outcome of mere supposition. 'In my opinion,' he says, 'Khartoum fell from sudden assault, when the garrison were too exhausted by privations to make proper resistance.'[1] The idea that the relieving force was only two days late is misleading. A nugger's load of dhura would not have put an end to the privations of the fourteen thousand people still in Khartoum; and even supposing that the handful of troops at Gubat could have effected their advance upon Khartoum many days earlier, it is hard to believe that they were strong enough either to drive off the Mahdi, or to hold him at bay until the river column had come up.

VIII

The prime minister was on a visit to the Duke of Devonshire at Holker, where he had many long conversations with Lord Hartington, and had to deal with heavy post-bags. On Thursday, Feb. 5, after writing to the Queen and others, he heard what had happened on the Nile ten days before. 'After 11 A.M.,' he records, 'I learned the sad news of the fall or betrayal of Khartoum. H[artington] and I, with C [his wife], went off by the first train, and reached Downing Street soon after 8.15. The circumstances are sad and trying. It is one of the least points about them that they may put an end to this government.'[2] The next day the cabinet met;

---

[1] Colvile, II., Appendix 47, p. 274. Apart from the authority of Kitchener, Gordon's own language shows that he knew himself to be *in extremis* by the end of December.

[2] The story that he went to the theatre the same night is untrue.

discussions 'difficult but harmonious.' The Queen sent to
him and to Lord Hartington at Holker an angry telegram
— blaming her ministers for what had happened — a telegram
not in cipher as usual, but open. Mr. Gladstone addressed
to the Queen in reply (Feb. 5, 1885) a vindication of the
course taken by the cabinet; and it may be left to close an
unedifying and a tragic chapter : —

To the Queen.

Mr. Gladstone has had the honour this day to receive your
Majesty's telegram *en clair*, relating to the deplorable intelligence
received this day from Lord Wolseley, and stating that it is too
fearful to consider that the fall of Khartoum might have been
prevented and many precious lives saved by earlier action. Mr.
Gladstone does not presume to estimate the means of judgment
possessed by your Majesty, but so far as his information and
recollection at the moment go, he is not altogether able to
follow the conclusion which your Majesty has been pleased
thus to announce. Mr. Gladstone is under the impression that
Lord Wolseley's force might have been sufficiently advanced to
save Khartoum, had not a large portion of it been detached by a
circuitous route along the river, upon the express application of
General Gordon, to occupy Berber on the way to the final destination. He speaks, however, with submission on a point of this
kind. There is indeed in some quarters a belief that the river
route ought to have been chosen at an earlier period, and had the
navigation of the Nile in its upper region been as well known as
that of the Thames, this might have been a just ground of reproach.
But when, on the first symptoms that the position of General
Gordon in Khartoum was not secure, your Majesty's advisers at
once sought from the most competent persons the best information
they could obtain respecting the Nile route, the balance of testimony and authority was decidedly against it, and the idea of the
Suakin and Berber route, with all its formidable difficulties, was
entertained in preference; nor was it until a much later period
that the weight of opinion and information warranted the definitive choice of the Nile route. Your Majesty's ministers were well
aware that climate and distance were far more formidable than the
sword of the enemy, and they deemed it right, while providing

adequate military means, never to lose from view what might have proved to be the destruction of the gallant army in the Soudan. It is probable that abundant wrath and indignation will on this occasion be poured out upon them. Nor will they complain if so it should be; but a partial consolation may be found on reflecting that neither aggressive policy, nor military disaster, nor any gross error in the application of means to ends, has marked this series of difficult proceedings, which, indeed, have greatly redounded to the honour of your Majesty's forces of all ranks and arms. In these remarks which Mr. Gladstone submits with his humble devotion, he has taken it for granted that Khartoum has fallen through the exhaustion of its means of defence. But your Majesty may observe from the telegram that this is uncertain. Both the correspondent's account and that of Major Wortley refer to the delivery of the town by treachery, a contingency which on some previous occasions General Gordon has treated as far from improbable; and which, if the notice existed, was likely to operate quite independently of the particular time at which a relieving force might arrive. The presence of the enemy in force would naturally suggest the occasion, or perhaps even the apprehension of the approach of the British army. In pointing to these considerations, Mr. Gladstone is far from assuming that they are conclusive upon the whole case; in dealing with which the government has hardly ever at any of its stages been furnished sufficiently with those means of judgment which rational men usually require. It may be that, on a retrospect, many errors will appear to have been committed. There are many reproaches, from the most opposite quarters, to which it might be difficult to supply a conclusive answer. Among them, and perhaps among the most difficult, as far as Mr. Gladstone can judge, would be the reproach of those who might argue that our proper business was the protection of Egypt, that it never was in military danger from the Mahdi, and that the most prudent course would have been to provide it with adequate frontier defences, and to assume no responsibility for the lands beyond the desert.

One word more. Writing to one of his former colleagues long after Mr. Gladstone says : —

Jan. 10, '90. — In the Gordon case we all, and I rather prominently, must continue to suffer in silence. Gordon was a hero, and a hero of heroes; but we ought to have known that a hero of heroes is not the proper person to give effect at a distant point, and in most difficult circumstances, to the views of ordinary men. It was unfortunate that he should claim the hero's privilege by turning upside down and inside out every idea and intention with which he had left England, and for which he had obtained our approval. Had my views about Zobeir prevailed, it would not have removed our difficulties, as Forster would certainly have moved, and with the tories and the Irish have carried, a condemnatory address. My own opinion is that it is harder to justify our doing so much to rescue him, than our not doing more. Had the party reached Khartoum in time, he would not have come away (as I suppose), and the dilemma would have arisen in another form.

In 1890 an application was made to Mr. Gladstone by a certain foreign writer who had undertaken an article on Gordon and his mission. Mr. Gladstone's reply (Jan. 11, '90) runs to this effect : —

I am much obliged by your kind letter and enclosure. I hope you will not think it belies this expression when I say that I feel myself precluded from supplying any material or entering upon any communications for the purpose of self-defence against the charges which are freely made and I believe widely accepted against myself and against the cabinet of 1880–5 in connection with General Gordon. It would be felt in this country, by friends I think in many cases as well as adversaries, that General Gordon's much-lamented death ought to secure him, so far as we are concerned, against the counter-argument which we should have to present on his language and proceedings. On this account you will, I hope, excuse me from entering into the matter. I do not doubt that a true and equitable judgment will eventually prevail.[1]

---

[1] *Belford's Magazine* (New York), Sept. 1890. A French translation of this letter will be found in *L'Égypte et ses Provinces Perdues*, by the recipient, Colonel C. Chaillé-Long Bey (1892), pp. 196–7. He was chief of the staff to Gordon in the Soudan, and consular-agent for the United States at Alexandria. Another book of his, published in 1884, is *The Three Prophets; Chinese Gordon, El Mahdi, and Arabi Pasha*. Burton reviewed Gordon's Khartoum Journals, *Academy*, June 11, 1885.

CHAPTER X

INTERIOR OF THE CABINET

(*1885*)

I AM aware that the age is not what we all wish, but I am sure that
the only means to check its degeneracy is heartily to concur in
whatever is best in our time. — BURKE.

THE year 1885 must be counted as in some respects the
severest epoch of Mr. Gladstone's life. The previous twelve
months had not ended cheerfully. Sleep, the indispensable
restorer, and usually his constant friend, was playing him
false. The last entry in his diary was this : —

The year closed with a bad night, only one hour and a half of
sleep, which will hardly do to work upon. There is much that I
should like to have recorded. . . . But the pressure on me is too
great for the requisite recollection. It is indeed a time of *Sturm
und Drang.* What with the confusion of affairs, and the disturbance of my daily life by the altered character of my nights, I
cannot think in calm, but can only trust and pray.

He was unable to be present at the dinner of the tenants,
and his eldest son in his absence dwelt once more on his
father's wish to retire, whenever occasion should come, from
the public service, or at least from that kind of service to the
public which imposed on him such arduous efforts.

One great element of confusion was the sphinx's riddle of
Egyptian finance. On his birthday, among a dozen occupations, he says : 'A little woodcraft for helping sleep ; wrote
mem. on Egyptian finance which I hope may help to clear
my brain and nerves.' And this was a characteristic way of
seeking a cure ; for now and at every time, any task that
demanded close thought and firm expression was his surest

sedative.   More perplexing even than the successive prob- CHAP.
lems of the hour, was the threatened disorganisation, not only   X.
of his cabinet, but of the party and its future.   On January 20 Æt. 76.
he was forced to London for two Egyptian cabinets, but he
speedily returned to Hawarden, whence he immediately wrote
a letter to Lord Granville : —

January 22, 1885. — Here I am after a journey of 5½ hours from
door to door, through the unsought and ill-deserved kindness of
the London and North-Western railway, which entirely spoils me
by special service.

There was one part of my conversation of to-day with Hartington which I should like not to leave in any case without record.
He referred to the difficulties he had had, and he 'gratefully'
acknowledged the considerateness of the cabinet.   He said the
point always urged upon him was, not to break up the liberal
party.   But, he said, can we avoid its breaking up, within a very
short time after you retire, and ought this consideration therefore
to be regarded as of such very great force?   I said, my reply is in
two sentences.   First, I admit that from various symptoms it is
not improbable there may be a plan or intention to break up the
party.   But if a rupture of that kind comes, — this is my second
sentence — it will come upon matters of principle, known and
understood by the whole country, and your duty will probably be
clear and your position unembarrassed.   But I entreat you to use
your utmost endeavour to avoid bringing about the rupture on
one of the points of this Egyptian question, which lies outside
the proper business of a government and is beyond its powers,
which does not turn upon clear principles of politics, and about
which the country understands almost nothing, and cares, for the
most part, very little.   All this he took without rejoinder.

P.S. — We are going to Holker next week, and Hartington said
he would try to come and see me there.

As we have already seen,[1] Mr. Gladstone paid his visit to
Holker (January 30), where he found the Duke of Devonshire
'wonderfully well, and kind as ever,' where he was joined by
Lord Hartington, and where they together spelled out the

[1] Above, p. 166.

cipher telegram (on February 5) bringing the evil news of the fall of Khartoum.

It is not uninteresting to see how the notion of Mr. Gladstone's retirement, now much talked of in his family, affected a friendly, philosophic, and most observant onlooker. Lord Acton wrote to him (February 2) : —

You mean that the new parliament, the first of our democratic constitution, shall begin its difficult and perilous course without the services of a leader who has greater experience and authority than any other man. You design to withdraw your assistance when most urgently needed, at the moment of most conservative apprehension and most popular excitement. By the choice of this particular moment for retirement you increase the danger of the critical transition, because nobody stands as you do between the old order of things and the new, or inspires general confidence; and the lieutenants of Alexander are not at their best. Next year's change will appear vast and formidable to the suspicious foreigner, who will be tempted to doubt our identity. It is in the national interest to reduce the outer signs of change, to bridge the apparent chasm, to maintain the traditional character of the state. The unavoidable elements of weakness will be largely and voluntarily aggravated by their untimely coincidence with an event which must, at any time, be a blow to the position of England among the Powers. Your absence just then must grievously diminish our credit. . . . You alone inspire confidence that what is done for the great masses shall be done with a full sense of economic responsibility. . . . A divided liberal party and a weak conservative party mean the supremacy of the revolutionary Irish. . . .'

To this Mr. Gladstone replied : —

10 *Downing Street, Feb.* 11, 1885. . . . Your argument against letting the outworn hack go to grass, depends wholly on a certain proposition, namely this, that there is about to be a crisis in the history of the constitution, growing out of the extension of the franchise, and that it is my duty to do what I can in aiding to steer the ship through the boiling waters of this crisis. My answer is simple. There is no crisis at all in view. There is a process of slow modification and development mainly in directions which

I view with misgiving. 'Tory democracy,' the favourite idea
on that side, is no more like the conservative party in which I was
bred, than it is like liberalism. In fact less. It is demagogism,
only a demagogism not ennobled by love and appreciation of
liberty, but applied in the worst way, to put down the pacific, law-
respecting, economic elements which ennobled the old conservatism,
living upon the fomentation of angry passions, and still in secret
as obstinately attached as ever to the evil principle of class
interests. The liberalism of to-day is better in what I have
described as ennobling the old conservatism; nay, much better, yet
far from being good. Its pet idea is what they call construction, — that is to say, taking into the hands of the state the business of the individual man. Both the one and the other have much
to estrange me, and have had for many, many years. But, with all
this, there is no crisis. I have even the hope that while the coming
change may give undue encouragement to ' construction,' it will be
favourable to the economic, pacific, law-regarding elements; and
the sense of justice which abides tenaciously in the masses will
never knowingly join hands with the fiend of Jingoism. On the
whole, I do not abandon the hope that it may mitigate the chronic
distemper, and have not the smallest fear of its bringing about an
acute or convulsive action. You leave me therefore rooted in my
evil mind. . . .

The activity of the left wing, acute, perhaps, but not convulsive, became much more embarrassing than the desire
of the right wing to be inactive. Mr. Chamberlain had been
rapidly advancing in public prominence, and he now showed
that the agitation against the House of Lords was to be only
the beginning and not the end. At Ipswich (January 14),
he said this country had been called the paradise of the rich,
and warned his audience no longer to allow it to remain
the purgatory of the poor. He told them that reform
of local government must be almost the first reform of the
next parliament, and spoke in favour of allotments, the
creation of small proprietors, the placing of a small tax on
the total property of the taxpayer, and of free education.
Mr. Gladstone's attention was drawn from Windsor to these
utterances, and he replied (January 22) that though he

thought some of them were 'on various grounds open to grave objection,' yet they seemed to raise no 'definite point on which, in his capacity of prime minister, he was entitled to interfere and lecture the speaker.' A few days later, more terrible things were said by Mr. Chamberlain at Birmingham. He pronounced for the abolition of plural voting, and in favour of payment of members, and manhood suffrage. He also advocated a bill for enabling local communities to acquire land, a graduated income-tax, and the breaking up of the great estates as the first step in land reform. This deliverance was described by not unfriendly critics as 'a little too much the speech of the agitator of the future, rather than of the minister of the present.' Mr. Gladstone made a lenient communication to the orator, to the effect that 'there had better be some explanations among them when they met.' To Lord Granville he wrote (January 31) : —

Upon the whole, weak-kneed liberals have caused us more trouble in the present parliament than radicals. But I think these declarations by Chamberlain upon matters which cannot, humanly speaking, become practical before the next parliament, can hardly be construed otherwise than as having a remote and (in that sense) far-sighted purpose which is ominous enough. The opposition can hardly fail in their opportunity, I must add in their duty, to make them matter of attack. Such things will happen casually from time to time, and always with inconvenience — but there is here a degree of method and system which seem to give the matter a new character.

It will be seen from his tone that Mr. Gladstone, in all the embarrassments arising from this source, showed complete freedom from personal irritation. Like the lofty-minded man he was, he imputed no low motives to a colleague because the colleague gave him trouble. He recognised by now that in his cabinet the battle was being fought between old time and new. He did not allow his dislike of some of the new methods of forming public opinion, to prevent him from doing full justice to the energetic and sincere public spirit behind them. He had, moreover, quite enough to do with the demands of the present, apart from signs that were ominous for the future. A year before, in a letter to Lord Granville (March 24, 1884), he had attempted a definition that will, perhaps, be of general interest to politicians of either party complexion. It is, at any rate, characteristic of his subtlety, if that be the right word, in drawing distinctions:—

CHAP.
X.

Æt. 76.

What are divisions in a cabinet? In my opinion, differences of views stated, and if need be argued, and then advisedly surrendered with a view to a common conclusion are not 'divisions in a cabinet.' By that phrase I understand unaccommodated differences on matters standing for immediate action.

It was unaccommodated differences of this kind that cost Mr. Disraeli secessions on the Reform bill, and secessions no less serious on his eastern policy, and it is one of the wonders of his history that Mr. Gladstone prevented secession on the matters now standing for immediate action before his own cabinet. During the four months between the meeting of parliament and the fall of the government, the two great difficulties of the government — Egypt and Ireland — reached their climax.

II

The news of the fall of Khartoum reached England on February 5. One of the least points, as Mr. Gladstone wrote on the day, was that the grievous news would put an end to the government, and so it very nearly did. As was to be expected, Sir Stafford Northcote moved a vote of censure. Mr. Gladstone informed the Queen, on the day before the division, that the aspect of the House was 'dubious and equivocal.' If there was a chance of overthrowing the ministry, he said, the nationalists were pretty sure to act and vote as a body with Sir Stafford. Mr. 'Forster, Mr. Goschen, and some members of the whig section of the liberal party, were likely either to do the same, or else to abstain. These circumstances looked towards an unfavour-able issue, if not in the shape of an adverse majority, yet in the form of a majority too small to enable the government to carry on with adequate authority and efficiency. In the debate, said Mr. Gladstone, Lord Hartington re-stated with measured force the position of the government, and overthrew the contention that had taken a very forward place in the indictment against ministers, that their great offence was the failure to send forward General Graham's force to relieve General Gordon. In the course of this debate Mr. Goschen warned the government that if they flinched from the policy of smashing the Mahdi at Khartoum, he should vote against them. A radical below the gangway upon this went to the party whip and declared, with equal resolution, that if the government insisted on the policy, then it would be for him and others to vote against them. Sir William Harcourt, in a speech of great power, satisfied the gentlemen below the gangway, and only a small handful of the party went into the lobby with the opposition and the Irish. The division was taken at four in the morning (February 28), and the result was that the government which had come in with morning radiance five years ago, was worn down to an attenuated majority of fourteen.[1]

When the numbers were declared, Mr. Gladstone said to a colleague on the bench, ' *That will do.*' Whether this delphic utterance meant that the size of the majority would justify resignation or retention, the colleague was not sure. When the cabinet met at a more mellowed hour in the day, the question between going out of office and staying in, was fully discussed. Mere considerations of ease all pointed one way, for, if they held on, they would seem to be dependent on tory support; trouble was brewing with Russia, and the Seats bill would not be through in a hurry. On the other hand, fourteen was majority enough to swear by, the party would be surprised by resignation and discouraged, and retirement would wear the look of a false position. In fact Mr. Gladstone, in spite of his incessant sighs for a hermit's calm, was always for fighting out every position to the last trench. I can think of no exception, and even when the time came ten years later, he thought his successors pusillanimous for

[1] For the censure, 288 ; against, 302.

retiring on a small scratch defeat on cordite.[1] So now he acted on the principle that with courage cabinets may weather almost any storm. No actual vote was taken, but the numbers for and against retirement were equal, until Mr. Gladstone spoke. He thought that they should try to go on, at least until the Seats bill was through. This was the final decision.

All this brought once more into his mind the general consideration that now naturally much haunted him. He wrote to the Queen (February 27) : —

Mr. Gladstone believes that circumstances independent of his own will enable him to estimate, with some impartiality, future political changes, and he is certainly under the impression that, partly from the present composition and temper of the liberal party, and still more, and even much more, from the changes which the conservative party has been undergoing during the last forty years (especially the last ten or fifteen of them), the next change of government may possibly form the introduction to a period presenting some new features, and may mean more than what is usually implied in the transfer of power from one party to another.

Mr. Bright has left a note of a meeting with him at this time : —

March 2, 1885. — Dined with Mrs. Gladstone. After dinner, sat for half an hour or more with Mr. Gladstone, who is ill with cold and hoarseness. Long talk on Egypt. He said he had suffered torment during the continuance of the difficulty in that country. The sending Gordon out a great mistake, — a man totally unsuited for the work he undertook. Mr. Gladstone never saw Gordon. He was appointed by ministers in town, and Gladstone concurred, but had never seen him.

At this moment clouds began to darken the remote horizon on the north-west boundary of our great Indian possessions. The entanglement in the deserts of the Soudan was an obvious temptation to any other Power with policies of its own, to disregard the susceptibilities or even the solid

---

[1] I often tried to persuade him that our retreat was to be explained apart   from pusillanimity, but he would not listen.

interests of Great Britain. As we shall see, Mr. Gladstone
was as little disposed as Chatham or Palmerston to shrink
from the defence of the legitimate rights or obligations of
his country. But the action of Russia in Afghanistan became an added and rather poignant anxiety.

As early as March 12 the cabinet found it necessary to
consider the menacing look of things on the Afghan frontier.
Military necessities in India, as Mr. Gladstone described to
the Queen what was in the mind of her ministers, 'might
conceivably at this juncture come to overrule the present
intentions as to the Soudan as part of them, and it would
consequently be imprudent to do anything which could
practically extend our obligations in that quarter; as it is the
entanglement of the British forces in Soudanese operations,
which would most powerfully tempt Russia to adopt aggressive measures.' Three or four weeks later these considerations
came to a head. The question put by Mr. Gladstone to his
colleagues was this: 'Apart from the defence of Egypt,
which no one would propose to abandon, does there appear
to be any obligation of honour or any inducement of policy
(for myself I should add, is there any moral warrant?) that
should lead us in the present state of the demands on the
empire, to waste a large portion of our army in fighting
against nature, and I fear also fighting against liberty (such
liberty as the case admits) in the Soudan?' The assumptions
on which the policy had been founded had all broken
down. Osman Digna, instead of being readily crushed, had
betaken himself to the mountains and could not be got at.
The railway from Suakin to Berber, instead of serving
the advance on Khartoum in the autumn, could not possibly be ready in time. Berber, instead of being taken before the hot season, could not be touched. Lord Wolseley,
instead of being able to proceed with his present forces
or a moderate addition, was already asking for twelve
more battalions of infantry, with a proportion of other
arms.

Mr. Gladstone's own view of this crisis is to be found in
a memorandum dated April 9, circulated to the cabinet three
or four days before the question came up for final settle-

ment. It is long, but then the case was intricate and the stages various. The reader may at least be satisfied to know that he will have little more of it.[1]

Three cabinets were held on three successive days (April 13-15). On the evening of the first day Mr. Gladstone sent a telegram to the Queen, then abroad, informing her that in the existing state of foreign affairs, her ministers felt bound to examine the question of the abandonment of offensive operations in the Soudan and the evacuation of the territory. The Queen, in reply, was rather vehement against withdrawal, partly on the ground that it would seriously affect our position in India. The Queen had throughout made a great point that the fullest powers should be granted to those on the spot, both Wolseley and Baring having been selected by the government for the offices they held. No question cuts deeper in the art of administering a vast system like that of Great Britain, than the influence of the agent at a distant place ; nowhere is the balance of peril between too slack a rein from home and a rein too tight, more delicate. Mr. Gladstone, perhaps taught by the experience of the Crimean war, always strongly inclined to the school of the tight rein, though I never heard of any representative abroad with a right to complain of insufficient support from a Gladstone cabinet.[2] On this aspect of matters, so raised by the Queen, Mr. Gladstone had (March 15) expressed his view to Sir Henry Ponsonby : —

Sir Evelyn Baring was appointed to carry onwards a declared and understood policy in Egypt, when all share in the management of the Soudan was beyond our province. To Lord Wolseley as general of the forces in Egypt, and on account of the arduous character of the work before him, we are bound to render in all military matters a firm and ungrudging support. We have accordingly not scrupled to counsel, on his recommendation, very heavy charges on the country, and military

[1] See Appendix.
[2] For instance when Mr. Gladstone fell from office in 1874, Lord Odo Russell wrote to him, 'how sorry I feel at your retirement, and how grateful I am to you for the great advantage and encouragement I have enjoyed while serving under your great administration, in Rome and Berlin.'

operations of the highest importance.   But we have no right to
cast on him any responsibility beyond what is strictly military.
It is not surely possible that he should decide policy, and that
we should adopt and answer for it, even where it is in conflict
with the announcements we have made in parliament.

By the time of these critical cabinets in April Sir Evelyn
Baring had spontaneously expressed his views, and with a
full discussion recommended abandonment of the expedition to Khartoum.

On the second day the matter was again probed and sifted
and weighed.

At the third cabinet the decision was taken to retire
from the Soudan, and to fix the southern frontier of Egypt
at the line where it was left for twelve years, until apprehension of designs of another European power on the
upper waters of the Nile was held to demand a new policy.
Meanwhile, the policy of Mr. Gladstone's cabinet was adopted
and followed by Lord Salisbury when he came into office.
He was sometimes pressed to reverse it, and to overthrow the
dervish power at Khartoum.   To any importunity of this
kind, Lord Salisbury's answer was until 1896 unwavering.[1]

It may be worth noting that, in the course of his correspondence with the Queen on the change of policy in the
Soudan, Mr. Gladstone casually indulged in the luxury of a
historical parallel.   'He must assure your Majesty,' he
wrote in a closing sentence (April 20), 'that at least he has
never in any cabinet known any question more laboriously
or more conscientiously discussed; and he is confident that
the basis of action has not been the mere change in the
public view (which, however, is in some cases imperative, as

[1] 'We do not depart in any degree
from the policy of leaving the Soudan.
As to the civilisation which the noble
and gallant earl [Lord Dundonald]
would impose upon us the duty of
restoring, it could only be carried
out by a large and costly expedition,
entailing enormous sacrifice of blood
and treasure, and for the present a
continuous expenditure, which I do
not think the people of this country
would sanction. . . .   The defence
of our retention of Suakin is that
it is a very serious obstacle to the
renewal and the conduct of that
slave trade which is always trying
to pass over from Africa into Asia.
I do not think that the retention
of Suakin is of any advantage to
the Egyptian government.   If I
were to speak purely from the
point of view of that government's
own interest, I should say, "Abandon
Suakin at once."' — Lord Salisbury,
in the House of Lords, March 16, 1888.

it was with King George III. in the case of the American
war), but a deep conviction of what the honour and interest
of the empire require them as faithful servants of your
Majesty to advise.' The most harmless parallel is apt to
be a challenge to discussion, and the parenthesis seems to
have provoked some rejoinder from the Queen, for on April
28 Mr. Gladstone wrote to her secretary a letter which takes
him away from Khartoum to a famous piece of the world's
history : —

To Sir Henry Ponsonby.

In further prosecution of my reply to your letter of the 25th,
I advert to your remarks upon Lord North. I made no reference
to his conduct, I believe, in writing to her Majesty. What I
endeavoured to show was that King George III., without changing his opinion of the justice of his war against the colonies, was
obliged to give it up on account of a change of public opinion,
and was not open to blame for so doing.

You state to me that Lord North never flinched from his task
till it became hopeless, that he then resigned office, but did not
change his opinions to suit the popular cry. The implied contrast
to be drawn with the present is obvious. I admit none of your
three propositions. Lord North did not, as I read history, require
to change his opinions to suit the popular cry. They were already
in accordance with the popular cry ; and it is a serious reproach
against him that without sharing his master's belief in the propriety of the war, he long persisted in carrying it on, through
subserviency to that master.

Lord North did not resign office for any reason but because
he could not help it, being driven from it by some adverse votes
of the House of Commons, to which he submitted with great
good humour, and probably with satisfaction.

Lord North did not, so far as I know, state the cause to be
hopeless. Nor did those who were opposed to him. The movers
of the resolution that drove him out of office did not proceed
upon that ground. General Conway in his speech advised the
retention of the ground we held in the colonies, and the resolution, which expressed the sense of the House as a body, bears a
singular resemblance to the announcement we have lately made,

as it declares, in its first clause, that the further prosecution of offensive war (on the continent of America) 'will be the means of weakening the efforts of this country against her European enemies,' February 27, 1782. This was followed, on March 4, by an address on the same basis ; and by a resolution declaring that any ministers who should advise or attempt to frustrate it should be considered 'as enemies to his Majesty and to this country.' I ought, perhaps, to add that I have never stated, and I do not conceive, that a change in the public opinion of the country is the ground on which the cabinet have founded the change in their advice concerning the Soudan.

III

The reader has by this time perhaps forgotten how Mr. Gladstone good-humouredly remonstrated with Lord Palmerston for associating him as one of the same school as Cobden and Bright.[1] The twenty intervening years had brought him more and more into sympathy with those two eminent comrades in good causes, but he was not any less alive to the inconvenience of the label. Speaking in Midlothian after the dissolution in 1880, he denied the cant allegation that to instal the liberals in power would be to hand over the destinies of the country to the Manchester school.[2] 'Abhorring all selfishness of policy,' he said, 'friendly to freedom in every country of the earth attached, to the modes of reason, detesting the ways of force, this Manchester school, this peace-party, has sprung prematurely to the conclusion that wars may be considered as having closed their melancholy and miserable history, and that the affairs of the world may henceforth be conducted by methods more adapted to the dignity of man, more suited both to his strength and to his weakness, less likely to lead him out of the ways of duty, to stimulate his evil passions, to make him guilty before God for inflicting misery on his fellow-creatures.' Such a view, he said, was a serious error, though it was not only a respectable, it was even a noble error. Then he went on, 'However much you may detest war — and you cannot detest it too much — there is

---

[1] Above, vol. ii. p. 49.   [2] Edinburgh, March 17, 1880.

no war — except one, the war for liberty — that does not contain in it elements of corruption, as well as of misery, that are deplorable to recollect and to consider; but however deplorable wars may be, they are among the necessities of our condition; and there are times when justice, when faith, when the welfare of mankind, require a man not to shrink from the responsibility of undertaking them. And if you undertake war, so also you are often obliged to undertake measures that may lead to war.'[1]

It is also, if not one of the necessities, at least one of the natural probabilities of our imperfect condition, that when a nation has its forces engaged in war, that is the moment when other nations may press inconvenient questions of their own. Accordingly, as I have already mentioned, when Egyptian distractions were at their height, a dangerous controversy arose with Russia in regard to the frontier of Afghanistan. The question had been first raised a dozen years before without effect, but it was now sharpened into actuality by recent advances of Russia in Central Asia, bringing her into close proximity to the territory of the Ameer. The British and Russian governments appointed a commission to lay down the precise line of division between the Turcoman territory recently annexed by Russia and Afghanistan. The question of instructions to the commission led to infinite discussion, of which no sane man not a biographer is now likely to read one word. While the diplomatists were thus teasing one another, Russian posts and Afghan pickets came closer together, and one day (March 30, 1885) the Russians broke in upon the Afghans at Penjdeh. The Afghans fought gallantly, their losses were heavy, and Penjdeh was occupied by the Russians. 'Whose was the provocation,' as Mr. Gladstone said later, 'is a matter of the utmost consequence. We only know that the attack was a Russian attack. We know that the Afghans suffered in life, in spirit, and in repute. We know that a blow was struck at

---

[1] In the letter to Mr. Bright (July 14, 1882) already given, Mr. Gladstone went somewhat nearer to the Manchester school, and expressed his agreement with Bright in believing most wars to have been sad errors.

the credit and the authority of a sovereign — our protected
ally — who had committed no offence.   All I say is, we
cannot in that state of things close this book and say, " We
will look into it no more."   We must do our best to have
right done in the matter.'

Here those who were most adverse to the Soudan policy
stood firmly with their leader, and when Mr. Gladstone
proposed a vote of credit for eleven millions, of which six
and a half were demanded to meet 'the case for preparation,' raised by the collision at Penjdeh, he was supported
with much more than a mechanical loyalty, alike by the
regular opposition and by independent adherents below his
own gangway.   The speech in which he moved this vote
of a war supply (April 27) was an admirable example both
of sustained force and lucidity in exposition, and of a combined firmness, dignity, reserve, and right human feeling,
worthy of a great minister dealing with an international
situation of extreme delicacy and peril.   Many anxious
moments followed; for the scene of quarrel was far off,
details were hard to clear up, diplomacy was sometimes
ambiguous, popular excitement was heated, and the language of faction was unmeasured in its violence.   The
preliminary resolution on the vote of credit had been received with acclamation, but a hostile motion was made
from the front opposition bench (May 11), though discord
on a high imperial matter was obviously inconvenient
enough for the public interest.   The mover declared the
government to have murdered so many thousand men and
to have arranged a sham arbitration, and this was the prelude to other speeches in the same key.   Sir S. Northcote
supported the motion — one to displace the ministers on a
bill that it was the declared intention not to oppose.   The
division was taken at half-past two in the morning, after
a vigorous speech from the prime minister, and the government only counted 290 against 260.   In the minority were
42 followers of Mr. Parnell.   This premature debate cleared
the air.   Worked with patience and with vigorous preparations at the back of conciliatory negotiation, the question was
prosecuted to a happy issue, and those who had done their

best to denounce Mr. Gladstone and Lord Granville for trampling the interests and honour of their country underfoot thought themselves very lucky, when the time came for them to take up the threads, in being able to complete the business by adopting and continuing the selfsame line. With justifiable triumph Mr. Gladstone asked how they would have confronted Russia if 'that insane policy — for so I still must call it' — of Afghan occupation which he had brought to an end in 1880, had been persevered in. In such a case, when Russia came to advance her claim so to adjust boundaries as to make her immediate neighbour to Afghanistan, she would have found the country full of friends and allies, ready to join her in opposing the foreigner and the invader; and she would have been recognised as the liberator.[1]

CHAP.
X.

Æt. 76.

IV

In some respects Mr. Gladstone was never more wonderful than in the few weeks that preceded the fall of his second administration. Between the middle of April and the middle of May, he jots down with half-rueful humour the names of no fewer than nine members of the cabinet who within that period, for one reason or another and at one moment or another, appeared to contemplate resignation; that is to say a majority. Of one meeting he said playfully to a colleague, 'A very fair cabinet to-day — only three resignations.' The large packets of copious letters of this date, written and received, show him a minister of unalterable patience, unruffled self-command; inexhaustible in resource, catching at every straw from the resource of others, indefatigable in bringing men of divergent opinions within friendly reach of one another; of tireless ingenuity in minimising differences and convincing recalcitrants that what they took for a yawning gulf was in fact no more than a narrow trench that any decent political gymnast ought to be ashamed not to be able to vault over. Though he takes it all as being in the day's work, in the confidence of the old jingle, that be the day short or never so long,

[1] West Calder, November 17, 1885.

at length it ringeth to evensong, he does not conceal the burden. To Mrs. Gladstone he writes from Downing Street on May-day: —

Rather oppressed and tired with the magnitude and the complication of subjects on my mind, I did not think of writing by the first post, but I will now supply the omission by making use of the second. As to all the later history of this ministry, which is now entering on its sixth year, it has been a wild romance of politics, with a continual succession of hairbreadth escapes and strange accidents pressing upon one another, and it is only from the number of dangers we have passed through already, that one can be bold enough to hope we may pass also through what yet remain. Some time ago I told you that dark as the sky was with many a thunder-cloud, there were the possibilities of an admirable situation and result, and *for me* a wind-up better than at any time I could have hoped. Russia and Ireland are the two *great* dangers remaining. The ' ray ' I mentioned yesterday for the first is by no means extinct to-day, but there is nothing new of a serious character ; what there is, is good. So also upon the Irish complications there is more hope than there was yesterday, although the odds may still be heavily against our getting forward unitedly in a satisfactory manner.

On May 2, as he was looking at the pictures in the Academy, Lord Granville brought him tidings of the Russian answer, which meant peace. His short entries tell a brave story: —

May 3, Sunday. — Dined at Marlborough House. They were most kind and pleasant. But it is so unsundaylike and unrestful. I am much fatigued in mind and body. Yet very happy. *May* 4. — Wrote to Lord Spencer, Mr. Chamberlain, Sir C. Dilke, Lord Granville. Conclave. H. of C., $4\frac{3}{4}$-$8\frac{1}{2}$ and $9\frac{1}{2}$-$2\frac{1}{2}$. Spoke on Russian question. A heavy day. Much knocked up. *May* 5. — ... Another anxious, very anxious day, and no clearing of the sky as yet. But after all that has come, what may not come ? *May* 14, *Ascension Day.* — Most of the day was spent in anxious interviews, and endeavours to bring and keep the members of the cabinet together. *May* 15. — Cabinet 2-$4\frac{1}{2}$. Again stiff. But I must not lose heart.

Difference of opinion upon the budget at one time wore
a threatening look, for the radicals disliked the proposed
increase of the duty on beer; but Mr. Gladstone pointed out
in compensation that on the other hand the equalisation of
the death duties struck at the very height of class preference. Mr. Childers was, as always, willing to accommodate difficulties; and in the cabinet the rising storm blew
over. Ireland never blows over.

The struggle had gone on for three years. Many murderers had been hanged, though more remained undetected;
conspirators had fled; confidence was restored to public
officers; society in all its various grades returned externally
to the paths of comparative order; and the dire emergency
of three years before had been brought to an apparent close.
The gratitude in this country to the viceroy who had
achieved this seeming triumph over the forces of disorder
was such as is felt to a military commander after a hazardous and successful campaign. The country was once more
half-conquered, but nothing was advanced, and the other
half of the conquest was not any nearer. The scene was not
hopeful. There lay Ireland, — squalid, dismal, sullen, dull,
expectant, sunk deep in hostile intent. A minority with
these misgivings and more felt that the minister's pregnant
phrase about the government 'having no moral force behind
them' too exactly described a fatal truth.

CHAPTER XI

DEFEAT OF MINISTERS

(May–June 1885)

Οὔπω
τὰν Διὸς ἁρμονίαν
θνατῶν παρεξίασι βουλαί.
— Æsch. *Prom.* v. 548.

Never do counsels of mortal men thwart the ordered purpose of Zeus.

BOOK VIII.

1885.

WHAT was to be the Irish policy? The Crimes Act would expire in August, and the state of parties in parliament and of sections within the cabinet, together with the approach of the general election, made the question whether that Act should be renewed, and if so on what terms, an issue of crucial importance. There were good grounds for suspecting that tories were even then intimating to the Irish that if Lord Salisbury should come into office, they would drop coercion, just as the liberals had dropped it when they came into office in 1880, and like them would rely upon the ordinary law. On May 15 Mr. Gladstone announced in terms necessarily vague, because the new bill was not settled, that they proposed to continue what he described as certain clauses of a valuable and equitable description in the existing Coercion Act.

No parliamentary situation could be more tempting to an astute opposition. The signs that the cabinet was not united were unmistakable. The leader of the little group of four clever men below the gangway on the tory side gave signs that he espied an opportunity. This was one of the occasions that disclosed the intrepidity of Lord Randolph Churchill. He made a speech after Mr. Gladstone's announcement of a renewal of portions of the Crimes Act, not in his place but at a tory club. He declared himself profoundly shocked that so grave an announcement should have been taken as a matter of course. It was really a terrible piece of news. Ireland must be in an awful state, or else the radical members of the cabinet would never have assented to such unanswerable evidence that the liberal party could not govern Ireland without resort to that arbitrary force which their greatest orators had so often declared to be no remedy. It did not much matter whether the demand was for large powers or for small. Why not put some kind thoughts towards England in Irish minds, by using the last days of this unlucky parliament to abrogate all that harsh legislation which is so odious to England, and which undoubtedly abridges the freedom and insults the dignity of a sensitive and imaginative race? The tory party should be careful beyond measure not to be committed to any act or policy which should unnecessarily wound or injure the feelings of our brothers on the other side of the channel of St. George.[1]

The key to an operation that should at once, with the aid of the disaffected liberals and the Irish, turn out Mr. Gladstone and secure the English elections, was an understanding with Mr. Parnell. The price of such an understanding was to drop coercion, and that price the tory leaders resolved to pay. The manœuvre was delicate. If too plainly disclosed, it might outrage some of the tory rank and file who would loathe an Irish alliance, and it was likely, moreover, to deter some of the disaffected liberals from joining in any motion for Mr. Gladstone's overthrow. Lord Salisbury and his friends considered the subject with 'immense deliberation some weeks before the fall of the government.' They came to the conclusion that in the absence of official information, they could see nothing to warrant a government in applying for a renewal of exceptional powers. That conclusion they profess to have kept sacredly in their own bosoms. Why they should give immense deliberation to a decision that in their view must be worthless without official information, and that was to remain for an indefinite time in mysterious

CHAP.
XI.

Æt. 76.

[1] May 20, 1885.

BOOK
VIII.

1885.

darkness, was never explained when this secret decision some months later was revealed to the public.[1]   If there was no intention of making the decision known to the Irishmen, the purpose of so unusual a proceeding would be inscrutable. Was it made known to them ?   Mr. McCarthy, at the time acting for his leader, has described circumstantially how the Irish were endeavouring to obtain a pledge against coercion ; how two members of the tory party, one of them its recognised whip, came to him in succession declaring that they came straight from Lord Salisbury with certain propositions ; how he found the assurance unsatisfactory, and asked each of these gentlemen in turn on different nights to go back to Lord Salisbury, and put further questions to him ; and how each of them professed to have gone back to Lord Salisbury, to have conferred with him, and to have brought back his personal assurance.[2]   On the other hand, it has been uniformly denied by the tory leaders that there was ever any compact whatever with the Irishmen at this moment.   We are not called upon here to decide in a conflict of testimony which turns, after all, upon words so notoriously slippery as pledge, compact, or understanding. It is enough to mark what is not denied, that Lord Salisbury and his confidential friends had resolved, subject to official information, to drop coercion, and that the only visible reason why they should form the resolution at that particular moment was its probable effect upon Mr. Parnell.

II

Let us now return to the ministerial camp.   There the whig wing of the cabinet, adhering to Lord Spencer, were for a modified renewal of the Coercion Act, with the balm of a land purchase bill and a limited extension of self-government in local areas.   The radical wing were averse to coercion, and averse to a purchase bill, but they were willing to yield a milder form of coercion, on condition that the cabinet would agree not merely to small measures of self-government in local areas, but to the erection of a

[1] The story was told by Lord R. Churchill in a speech at Sheffield, Sept 4, 1885.   [2] Mr. McCarthy's speech at Hull, Dec. 15, 1887.

central board clothed with important administrative functions for the whole of Ireland. In the House of Commons it was certain that a fairly strong radical contingent would resist coercion in any degree, and a liberal below the gangway, who had not been long in parliament but who had been in the press a strong opponent of the coercion policy of 1881, at once gave notice that if proposals were made for the renewal of exceptional law, he should move their rejection. Mr. Gladstone had also to inform the Queen that in what is considered the whig or moderate section of the House there had been recent indications of great dislike to special legislation, even of a mild character, for Ireland. These proceedings are all of capital importance in an eventful year, and bear pretty directly upon the better known crisis of the year following.

A memorandum by Mr. Gladstone of a conversation between himself and Lord Granville (May 6) will best show his own attitude at this opening of a momentous controversy : —

. . . I told him [Granville] I had given no pledge or indication of my future conduct to Mr. Chamberlain, who, however, knew my opinions to be strong in favour of some plan for a Central Board of Local Government in Ireland on something of an elective basis. . . . Under the circumstances, while the duty of the hour evidently was to study the means of possible accommodation, the present aspect of affairs was that of a probable split, *independently* of the question what course I might individually pursue. My opinions, I said, were very strong and inveterate. I did not calculate upon Parnell and his friends, nor upon Manning and his bishops. Nor was I under any obligation to follow or act with Chamberlain. But independently of all questions of party, of support, and of success, I looked upon the extension of a strong measure of local government like this to Ireland, now that the question is effectually revived by the Crimes Act, as invaluable itself, and as the only hopeful means of securing crown and state from an ignominious surrender in the next parliament after a mischievous and painful struggle. (I did not advert to the difficulties which will in this session be experienced in carrying on a great battle for the Crimes Act.)   My difficulty would lie not in my pledges or declarations (though these, of a public character, are serious), but in my opinions.

Under these circumstances, I said, I take into view the freedom of my own position. My engagements to my colleagues are fulfilled; the great Russian question is probably settled; if we stand firm on the Soudan, we are now released from that embarrassment; and the Egyptian question, if the financial convention be safe, no longer presents any very serious difficulties. I am entitled to lay down my office as having done my work.

Consequently the very last thing I should contemplate is opening the Irish difficulty in connection with my resignation, should I resign. It would come antecedently to any parliamentary treatment of that problem. If thereafter the secession of some members should break up the cabinet, it would leave behind it an excellent record at home and abroad. Lord Granville, while ready to resign his office, was not much consoled by this presentation of the case.

Late in the month (May 23) Mr. Gladstone wrote a long letter to the Queen, giving her 'some idea of the shades of opinion existing in the cabinet with reference to legislation for Ireland.' He thought it desirable to supply an outline of this kind, because the subject was sure to recur after a short time, and was 'likely to exercise a most important influence in the coming parliament on the course of affairs.' The two points on which there was considerable divergence of view were the expiry of the Crimes Act, and the concession of local government. The Irish viceroy was ready to drop a large portion of what Mr. Gladstone called coercive provisions, while retaining provisions special to Ireland, but favouring the efficiency of the law. Other ministers were doubtful whether any special legislation was needed for Irish criminal law. Then on the point whether the new bill should be for two years or one, some, including Mr. Gladstone and Lord Spencer, were for the longer term, others, including Mr. Chamberlain and Sir Charles Dilke, for the shorter. At last the whole cabinet agreed to two years. Next for local government, — some held that a liberal move in this region

would possibly obviate all need for special criminal legis- CHAP.
XI.
lation, and would at any rate take the sting out of it. To
this 'vastly important subject' the prime minister presumed Æт. 76.
to draw the Queen's special attention, as involving great
and far-reaching questions. He did not, he said, regard the
differences of leaning in the cabinet upon these matters
with either surprise or dismay. Such difficulties were due
to inherent difficulties in the matters themselves, and were
to be expected from the action of independent and energetic
minds in affairs so complex.

There were two main opinions. One favoured the erection
of a system of representative county government in Ireland.
The other view was that besides the county boards, there
should be in addition a central board for all Ireland,
essentially municipal and not political; in the main executive
and administrative, but also with a power to make bye-laws,
raise funds, and pledge public credit in such modes as
parliament should provide. The central board would take
over education, primary, in part intermediate, and perhaps
even higher; poor law and sanitary administration; and
public works. The whole charge of justice, police, and
prisons would remain with the executive. This board would
not be directly elective by the whole Irish people; it would
be chosen by the representative county boards. Property,
moreover, should have a representation upon it distinct from
numbers. This plan, 'first made known to Mr. Gladstone
by Mr. Chamberlain,' would, he believed, be supported by
six out of the eight Commons ministers. But a larger
number of ministers were not prepared to agree to any plan
involving the principle of an elective central board as the
policy of the cabinet. On account of this preliminary bar,
the particular provisions of the policy of a central board
were not discussed.

All this, however, was for the moment retrospective and
historic, because a fortnight before the letter was written,
the policy of the central board, of which Mr. Gladstone
so decisively approved, had been killed. A committee
of the cabinet was appointed to consider it; some remained stubbornly opposed; as the discussion went on,

some changed their minds and, having resisted, at last
inclined to acquiesce.   Ministers were aware from the correspondence of one of them with an eminent third person, that
Mr. Parnell approved the scheme, and in consideration of it
would even not oppose a very limited Crimes bill.   This,
however, was no temptation to all of them; perhaps it had
the contrary effect.   When it came to the full cabinet, it
could not be carried.   All the peers except Lord Granville
were against it.   All the Commoners except Lord Hartington
were for it.   As the cabinet broke up (May 9), the prime
minister said to one colleague, 'Ah, they will rue this
day'; and to another, 'Within six years, if it please God to
spare their lives, they will be repenting in sackcloth and
ashes.'   Later in the day he wrote to one of them, 'The
division of opinion in the cabinet on the subject of local
government with a central board for Ireland was so marked,
and if I may use the expression, so diametrical, that I
dismissed the subject from my mind, and sorrowfully
accepted the negative of what was either a majority, or
a moiety of the entire cabinet.'

This decision, more profoundly critical than anybody
excepting Mr. Gladstone and perhaps Mr. Chamberlain
seemed to be aware, left all existing difficulties as acute as
ever.   In the middle of May things looked very black.
The scheme for a central board was dead, though, wrote
Mr. Gladstone to the viceroy, 'for the present only.   *It will
quickly rise again, as I think, perhaps in larger dimensions.*'
Some members of the cabinet, he knew not how many, would
resign rather than demand from parliament, without a
Central Board bill, the new Coercion Act.   If such resignations took place, how was a Coercion bill to be fought
through the House, when some liberals had already declared
that they would resist it?

On May 15 drafts not only of a Coercion bill, but of a bill
for land purchase, came before the cabinet.   Much objection
was taken to land purchase, especially by the two radical leaders, and it was agreed to forego such a bill for the
present session.   The viceroy gravely lamented this decision,
and Mr. Gladstone entered into communication with Mr.

Chamberlain and Sir C. Dilke. From them he understood CHAP. that their main anxiety sprang from a fear lest the future XI. handling of local government should be prejudiced by pre- Æt. 76. mature disposal of the question of land purchase, but that in the main they thought the question of local government would not be prejudiced if the purchase bill only provided funds for a year. Under this impression and with a full belief that he was giving effect to the real desire of his colleagues in general to meet the views of Lord Spencer, and finding the prospects of such a bill favourable, Mr. Gladstone proceeded (May 20) to give notice of its introduction. Mr. Chamberlain and Sir C. Dilke took this to be a reversal of the position to which they had agreed, and would not assent to land purchase unless definitely coupled with assurances as to local government. They immediately resigned. The misapprehension was explained, and though the resignations were not formally withdrawn, they were suspended. But the two radical leaders did not conceal their view of the general state of the case, and in very direct terms told Mr. Gladstone that they differed so completely on the questions that were to occupy parliament for the rest of the session, as to feel the continuance of the government of doubtful advantage to the country. In Mr. Chamberlain's words, written to the prime minister at the time of the misunderstanding (May 21) —

I feel there has been a serious misapprehension on both sides with respect to the Land Purchase bill, and I take blame to myself if I did not express myself with sufficient clearness. . . . I doubt very much if it is wise or was right to cover over the serious differences of principle that have lately disclosed themselves in the cabinet. I think it is now certain that they will cause a split in the new parliament, and it seems hardly fair to the constituencies that this should only be admitted, after they have discharged their function and are unable to influence the result.

III

Still the prime minister altogether declined, in his own phrase, to lose heart, and new compromises were invented. Meanwhile he cheerfully went for the Whitsuntide recess to Hawarden, and dived into Lechler's *Wycliffe*, Walpole's *George III.*, Conrad on German Union, Cooper on the Atonement, and so forth. Among other guests at Hawarden came Lord Wolverton, 'with much conversation; we opened rather a new view as to my retirement.' What the new view was we do not know, but the conversation was resumed and again resumed, until the unwelcome day (June 4) for return to Downing Street. Before returning, however, Mr. Gladstone set forth his view of the internal crisis in a letter to Lord Hartington : —

To Lord Hartington.

May 30, 1885. — I am sorry but not surprised that your rather remarkable strength should have given way under the pressure of labour or anxiety or both. Almost the whole period of this ministry, particularly the year and a half since the defeat of Hicks, and most particularly of all, the four months since the morning when you deciphered the Khartoum telegram at Holker, have been without example in my experience, as to the gravity and diversity of difficulties which they have presented. What I hope is that they will not discourage you, or any of our colleagues, in your anticipations of the future. It appears to me that there is not one of them, viewed in the gross, which has been due to our own action. By viewing in the gross, I mean taking the Egyptian question as one. When we subdivide between Egypt proper and the Soudan, I find what seem to me two grave errors in our management of the Soudan business : the first our *landing* at Suakin, the second the mission of Gordon, or rather the choice of Gordon for that mission. But it sometimes happens that the errors gravest in their consequences are also the most pardonable. And these errors were surely pardonable enough in themselves, without relying on the fact that they were approved by the public opinion of the day and by the opposition. Plenty of other and worse errors have been urged upon us which we have refused or avoided. I do not remember a single good measure recommended by opponents, which we have declined to adopt (or indeed any good measure which they have recommended at all). We certainly have worked hard. I believe that according to the measure of human infirmity, we have done fairly well, but the duties we have

had to discharge have been duties, I mean in Egypt and the
Soudan, which it was impossible to discharge with the ordinary
measure of credit and satisfaction, which were beyond human
strength, and which it was very unwise of our predecessors to
saddle upon the country.

CHAP.
XI.

Æt. 76.

At this moment we have but two great *desiderata :* the Egyptian
Convention and the Afghan settlement (the evacuation of the Soudan
being in principle a thing done). Were these accomplished, we
should have attained for the empire at home and abroad a
position in most respects unusually satisfactory, and both of them
ought to be near accomplishment. With the Egyptian Convention
fairly at work, I should consider the Egyptian question as within
a few comparatively easy stages of satisfactory solution.

Now as regards the immediate subject. What if Chamberlain
and Dilke, as you seem to anticipate, raise the question of a prospective declaration about local government in Ireland as a
condition of their remaining in the cabinet? I consider that
question as disposed of for the present (much against my will),
and I do not see that any of us, having accepted the decision, can
attempt to disturb it. Moreover, their ground will be very weak
and narrow; for their actual reason of going, if they go, will be
the really small question arising upon the Land Purchase bill.

I think they will commit a great error if they take this course.
It will be straining at the gnat. No doubt it will weaken the
party at the election, but I entertain no fear of the immediate
effect. Their error will, however, in my view go beyond this.
Forgive me if I now speak with great frankness on a matter, one
of few, in which I agree with them, and not with you. I am
firmly convinced that on local government for Ireland they
hold a winning position; which by resignation now they will
greatly compromise. You will all, I am convinced, have to give
what they recommend; at the least what they recommend.

There are two differences between them and me on this subject.
First as to the matter; I go rather further than they do ; for I
would undoubtedly make a *beginning* with the Irish police.
Secondly as to the *ground ;* here I differ seriously. I do not reckon
with any confidence upon Manning or Parnell; I have never
looked much in Irish matters at negotiation or the conciliation of

leaders. I look at the question in itself, and I am deeply convinced that the measure in itself will (especially if accompanied
with similar measures elsewhere, *e.g.* in Scotland) be good for the
country and the empire; I do not say unmixedly good, but with
advantages enormously outweighing any drawbacks.

Apart from these differences, and taking their point of view, I
think they ought to endeavour to fight the election with you; and
in the *new state of affairs* which will be presented after the dissolution,
try and see what effect may be produced upon your mind, and on
other minds, when you have to look at the matter *cominus* and not
eminus, as actual, and not as hypothetical. I gave Chamberlain a
brief hint of these speculations when endeavouring to work upon
him; otherwise I have not mentioned them to any one.

IV

On the day of his return to London from Hawarden Mr.
Gladstone had an interview with the two ministers with
whom on the merits he was most disposed to agree, though
he differed strongly from them as to tactics. Resignations
were still only suspended, yet the prospects of compromise
were hopeful. At a cabinet held on the following day
(June 5) it was agreed that he should in the course of a
week give notice of a bill to take the place of the expiring
Crimes Act. The point left open was whether the operative
provisions of such an Act — agreed on some time before —
should not be brought into operation without some special
act of the executive government, by proclamation, order
in council, or otherwise. Local government was still left
open. Lord Spencer crossed over from Ireland on the night
of June 7, and the cabinet met next day. All differences
were narrowed down to the point whether the enactments
against intimidation should be inoperative unless and until
the lord lieutenant should waken them into life by proclamation. As it happened, intimidation had been for a
considerable time upon the increase — from which it might
be inferred either, on the one side, that coercion failed in
its object, or, on the other, that more coercion was still
indispensable. The precise state in which matters were left
at the eleventh hour before the crisis, now swiftly advancing,

was set out by Mr. Gladstone in a letter written by him to the Queen in the autumn (October 5), when he was no longer her Majesty's minister: —

To the Queen.

. . . He has perceived that in various quarters misapprehension prevails as to the point at which the deliberations of the late cabinet on the question of any renewal of, or substitution for, the Crimes Act in Ireland had arrived when their financial defeat on the 8th of June caused the tender of their resignation.

Mr. Gladstone prays your Majesty's gracious permission to remove this misapprehension by simply stating that which occurred in the cabinet at its latest meetings, with reference to this particular question. Substantially it would be a repetition, or little more (and without any mention of names), of his latest reports to your Majesty, to the effect —

1. That the cabinet had long before arrived at the conclusion that the coercion clauses of the Act, properly so called, might be safely abandoned.

2. With regard to the other clauses, which might be generally described as procedure clauses, they intended as a rule to advise, not their absolute re-enactment, but that the viceroy should be empowered to bring them into action, together or separately, as and when he might see cause.

3. But that, with respect to the intimidation or boycotting provisions, it still remained for consideration whether they should thus be left subject to executive discretion, or whether, as the offence had not ceased, they should, as an effective instrument of repression, remain in direct and full operation.

It is worth noticing here as a signal instance of Mr. Gladstone's tenacious and indomitable will after his defeat, that in a communication to the Queen four days later (June 12), he stated that the single outstanding point of difference on the Crimes bill was probably in a fair way of settlement, but that even if the dissent of the radical members of the cabinet had become operative, it was his firm intention to make new arrangements for filling the vacant offices and carrying on the government. The overthrow came in a different way. The deliberations thus summarised had been held under the shadow of a possibility, mentioned to the Queen in the report of this last cabinet, of a coalition between the tories and the Irish nationalists, in order to put an end to the existence of the government on their budget. This cloud at last burst, though Mr. Gladstone at any rate with his usual invincible adherence to the salutary rule never to bid good morrow to the devil until you meet him, did not strongly believe in the risk. The diary sheds no light on the state of his expectations : —

June 6. . . . Read Amiel's *Journal Intime.* Queen's birthday dinner, 39; went very well. Much conversation with the Prince of Wales, who was handy and pleasant even beyond his wont. Also had some speech of his son, who was on my left. *June 7, Trinity Sunday.* — Chapel Royal at noon and 5.30. Wrote. . . . Saw Lord Granville ; ditto *cum* Kimberley. Read Amiel. Edersheim on Old Testament. *June 8.* — Wrote, etc. . . . Pitiless rain. Cabinet, 2–3¾. . . . Spoke on budget. Beaten by 264 : 252. Adjourned the House. This is a considerable event.

The amendment that led to this 'considerable event' was moved by Sir Michael Hicks Beach. The two points raised by the fatal motion were, first, the increased duty on beer and spirits without a corresponding increase on wine ; and, second, the increase of the duty on real property while no relief was given to rates. The fiscal issue is not material. What was ominous was the alliance that brought about the result.

The defeat of the Gladstone government was the first success of a combination between tories and Irish, that proved of cardinal importance to policies and parties for several critical months to come. By a coincidence that cut too deep to be mere accident, divisions in the Gladstone cabinet found their counterpart in insurrection among the tory opposition. The same general forces of the hour, working through the energy, ambition, and initiative of individuals, produced the same effect in each of the two parties ; the radical programme of Mr. Chamberlain was matched by the

tory democracy of Lord Randolph Churchill; each saw that CHAP.
the final transfer of power from the ten-pound householder XI.
to artisans and labourers would rouse new social demands; ÆT. 76.
each was aware that Ireland was the electoral pivot of the
day, and while one of them was wrestling with those whom
he stigmatised as whigs, the other by dexterity and resolution
overthrew his leaders as 'the old gang.'

CHAPTER XII

ACCESSION OF LORD SALISBURY

(*1885*)

Politics are not a drama where scenes follow one another according to a methodical plan, where the actors exchange forms of speech, settled beforehand : politics are a conflict of which chance is incessantly modifying the whole course. — Sorel.

BOOK
VIII.

1885.

In tendering his resignation to the Queen on the day following his parliamentary defeat (June 9), and regretting that he had been unable to prepare her for the result, Mr. Gladstone explained that though the government had always been able to cope with the combined tory and nationalist oppositions, what had happened on this occasion was the silent withdrawal, under the pressure of powerful trades, from the government ranks of liberals who abstained from voting, while six or seven actually voted with the majority. ' There was no previous notice,' he said, ' and it was immediately before the division that Mr. Gladstone was apprised for the first time of the likelihood of a defeat.' The suspicious hinted that ministers, or at least some of them, unobtrusively contrived their own fall. Their supporters, it was afterwards remarked, received none of those imperative adjurations to return after dinner that are usual on solemn occasions ; else there could never have been seventy-six absentees. The majority was composed of members of the tory party, six liberals, and thirty-nine nationalists. Loud was the exultation of the latter contingent at the prostration of the coercion system. What was natural exultation in them, may have taken the form of modest satisfaction among many liberals, that they could go to the country without the obnoxious label of coercion tied round their necks. As for ministers, it was observed that if in the streets you saw a man coming along with a particularly elastic step and a joyful frame of countenance, ten to one on coming closer you would find that it was a member of the late cabinet.[1]

The ministerial crisis of 1885 was unusually prolonged, and it was curious. The victory had been won by a coalition with the Irish; its fruits could only be reaped with Irish support; and Irish support was to the tory victors both dangerous and compromising. The normal process of a dissolution was thought to be legally impossible, because by the redistribution bill the existing constituencies were for the most part radically changed; and a new parliament chosen on the old system of seats and franchise, even if it were legally possible, would still be empty of all semblance of moral authority. Under these circumstances, some in the tory party argued that instead of taking office, it would be far better for them to force Mr. Gladstone and his cabinet to come back, and leave them to get rid of their internal differences and their Irish embarrassments as they best could. Events were soon to demonstrate the prudence of these wary counsels. On the other hand, the bulk of the tory party like the bulk of any other party was keen for power, because power is the visible symbol of triumph over opponents, and to shrink from office would discourage their friends in the country in the electoral conflict now rapidly approaching.

The Queen meanwhile was surprised (June 10) that Mr. Gladstone should make his defeat a vital question, and asked whether, in case Lord Salisbury should be unwilling to form a government, the cabinet would remain. To this Mr. Gladstone replied that to treat otherwise an attack on the budget, made by an ex-cabinet minister with such breadth of front and after all the previous occurrences of the session, would be contrary to every precedent, — for instance, the notable case of December 1852, — and it would undoubtedly tend to weaken and lower parliamentary government.[2] If an opposition

[1] Duke of Argyll, July 10, 1885.

[2] As the reader will remember (vol. i. pp. 436–440), on Dec. 16, 1852, Mr. Disraeli's motion for imposing a house duty of a shilling in the pound was rejected by 305 to 286. Mr. Gladstone also referred to the case of the expulsion of the whigs by Peel. On May 13, 1841, after eight nights' debate, the government were defeated by a majority of 36 on their budget proposals in regard to sugar. Ministers not resigning, Sir Robert Peel moved a vote of want of confidence on May 27, which was carried by a majority of 1 (312–311), June 4, 1841. Parliament thereupon was dissolved.

defeated a government, they must be prepared to accept the responsibility of their action. As to the second question, he answered that a refusal by Lord Salisbury would obviously change the situation. On this, the Queen accepted the resignations (June 11), and summoned Lord Salisbury to Balmoral. The resignations were announced to parliament the next day. Remarks were made at the time, indeed by the Queen herself, at the failure of Mr. Gladstone to seek the royal presence. Mr. Gladstone's explanation was that, viewing 'the probably long reach of Lord Hartington's life into the future,' he thought that he would be more useful in conversation with her Majesty than ' one whose ideas might be unconsciously coloured by the limited range of the prospect before him,' and Lord Hartington prepared to comply with the request that he should repair to Balmoral. The visit was eventually not thought necessary by the Queen.

In his first audience Lord Salisbury stated that though he and his friends were not desirous of taking office, he was ready to form a government; but in view of the difficulties in which a government formed by him would stand, confronted by a hostile majority and unable to dissolve, he recommended that Mr. Gladstone should be invited to reconsider his resignation. Mr. Gladstone, however (June 13), regarded the situation and the chain of facts that had led up to it, as being so definite, when coupled with the readiness of Lord Salisbury to undertake an administration, that it would be a mere waste of valuable time for him to consult his colleagues as to the resumption of office. Then Lord Salisbury sought assurances of Mr. Gladstone's support, as to finance, parliamentary time, and other points in the working of executive government. These assurances neither Mr. Gladstone's own temperament, nor the humour of his friends and his party — for the embers of the quarrel with the Lords upon the franchise bill were still hot — allowed him to give, and he founded himself on the precedent of the communications of December 1845 between Peel and Russell. In this default of assurances, Lord Salisbury thought that he should render the Queen no useful service by taking office. So concluded the first stage.

Though declining specific pledges, Mr. Gladstone now wrote to the Queen (June 17) that in the conduct of the necessary business of the country, he believed there would be no disposition to embarrass her ministers. Lord Salisbury, however, and his colleagues were unanimous in thinking this general language insufficient. The interregnum continued. On the day following (June 18), Mr. Gladstone had an audience at Windsor, whither the Queen had now returned. It lasted over three-quarters of an hour. 'The Queen was most gracious and I thought most reasonable.' (*Diary.*) He put down in her presence some heads of a memorandum to assist her recollection, and the one to which she rightly attached most value was this: 'In my opinion,' Mr. Gladstone wrote, 'the whole value of any such declaration as at the present circumstances permit, really depends upon the spirit in which it is given and taken. For myself and any friend of mine, I can only say that the spirit in which we should endeavour to interpret and apply the declaration I have made, would be the same spirit in which we entered upon the recent conferences concerning the Seats bill.' To this declaration his colleagues on his return to London gave their entire and marked approval, but they would not compromise the liberty of the House of Commons by further and particular pledges.

It was sometimes charged against Mr. Gladstone that he neglected his duty to the crown, and abandoned the Queen in a difficulty. This is wholly untrue. On June 20, Sir Henry Ponsonby called and opened one or two aspects of the position, among them these : —

1. Can the Queen do anything more ?

I answered, As you ask me, it occurs to me that it might help Lord Salisbury's going on, were she to make reference to No. 2 of my memorandum [the paragraph just quoted], and to say that in her judgment he would be safe in receiving it in a spirit of trust.

2. If Lord Salisbury fails, may the Queen rely on you ?

I answered that on a previous day I had said that if S. failed, the situation would be altered. I hoped, and on the whole thought, he would go on. But if he did not ? I could not

CHAP.
XII.

Æt. 76.

promise or expect smooth water. The movement of questions such as the Crimes Act and Irish Local Government might be accelerated. But my desire would be to do my best to prevent the Queen being left without a government.[1]

Mr. Gladstone's view of the position is lucidly stated in the following memorandum, like the others, in his own hand, (June 21) : —

1. I have endeavoured in my letters (*a*) to avoid all controversial matter ; (*b*) to consider not what the incoming ministers had a right to ask, but what it was possible for us in a spirit of conciliation to give.

2. In our opinion there was no right to demand from us anything whatever. The declarations we have made represent an extreme of concession. The conditions required, *e.g.* the first of them [control of time], place in abeyance the liberties of parliament, by leaving it solely and absolutely in the power of the ministers to determine on what legislative or other questions (except supply) it shall be permitted to give a judgment. The House of Commons may and ought to be disposed to facilitate the progress of all necessary business by all reasonable means as to supply and otherwise, but would deeply resent any act of ours by which we agreed beforehand to the extinction of its discretion.

The difficulties pleaded by Lord Salisbury were all in view when his political friend, Sir M. H. Beach, made the motion which, as we apprised him, would if carried eject us from office, and are simply the direct consequences of their own action. If it be true that Lord Salisbury loses the legal power to advise and the crown to grant a dissolution, that cannot be a reason for leaving in the hands of the executive an absolute power to stop the action (except as to supply) of the legislative and corrective power of the House of Commons. At the same time these conditions do not appear to me to attain the end proposed by Lord Salisbury, for it would still be left in the power of the House to refuse supplies, and thereby to bring about in its worst form the difficulty which he apprehends.

It looked for a couple of days as if he would be compelled

[1] Memo. by Mr. Gladstone, on a sheet of notepaper, June 20, 1885.

to return, even though it would almost certainly lead to disruption of the liberal cabinet and party.[1] The Queen, acting apparently on Mr. Gladstone's suggestion of June 20, was ready to express her confidence in Mr. Gladstone's assurance that there would be no disposition on the part of himself or his friends to embarrass new ministers. By this expression of confidence, the Queen would thus make herself in some degree responsible as it were for the action of the members of the defeated Gladstone government in the two Houses. Still Lord Salisbury's difficulties — and some difficulties are believed to have arisen pretty acutely within the interior conclaves of his own party — remained for forty-eight hours insuperable. His retreat to Hatfield was taken to mark a second stage in the interregnum.

June 22 is set down in the diary as 'a day of much stir and vicissitude.' Mr. Gladstone received no fewer than six visits during the day from Sir Henry Ponsonby, whose activity, judgment, and tact in these duties of infinite delicacy were afterwards commemorated by Lord Granville in the House of Lords.[2] He brought up from Windsor the draft of a letter that might be written by the Queen to Lord Salisbury, testifying to her belief in the sincerity and loyalty of Mr. Gladstone's words. Sir Henry showed the draft to Mr. Gladstone, who said that he could not be party to certain passages in it, though willing to agree to the rest. The draft so altered was submitted to Lord Salisbury; he demanded modification, placing a more definite interpretation on the words of Mr. Gladstone's previous letters to the Queen. Mr. Gladstone was immovable throughout the day in declining to admit any modifications in the sense desired; nor would he consent to be privy to any construction or interpretation placed upon his words which Lord Salisbury, with no less tenacity than his own, desired to extend.

At 5.40 [June 22] Sir H. Ponsonby returned for a fifth interview, his infinite patience not yet exhausted. . . . He said the Queen believed the late government did not wish to come back.

[1] Mr. Gladstone was reminded by a colleague that when Sir Robert Peel resumed office in 1845, at the request of the Queen, he did so before and without consultation with his colleagues. In the end they all, excepting Lord Stanley, supported him.
[2] June 25, 1885.

I simply reminded him of my previous replies, which he remembered, nearly as follows: — That if Lord Salisbury failed, the situation would be altered. That I could not in such a case promise her Majesty smooth water. That, however, a great duty in such circumstances lay upon any one holding my situation, to use his best efforts so as, *quoad* what depended upon him, not to leave the Queen without a government. I think he will now go to Windsor. — *June 22, '85, 6 P.M.*

The next day (June 23), the Queen sent on to Lord Salisbury the letter written by Mr. Gladstone on June 21, containing his opinion that facilities of supply might reasonably be provided, without placing the liberties of the House of Commons in abeyance, and further, his declaration that he felt sure there was no idea of withholding ways and means, and that there was no danger to be apprehended on that score. In forwarding this letter, the Queen expressed to Lord Salisbury her earnest desire to bring to a close a crisis calculated to endanger the best interests of the state; and she felt no hesitation in further communicating to Lord Salisbury her opinion that he might reasonably accept Mr. Gladstone's assurances. In deference to these representations from the Queen, Lord Salisbury felt it his duty to take office, the crisis ended, and the tory party entered on the first portion of a term of power that was destined, with two rather brief interruptions, to be prolonged for many years.[1] In reviewing this interesting episode in the annals of the party system, it is impossible not to observe the dignity in form, the patriotism in substance, the common-sense in result, that marked the proceedings alike of the sovereign and of her two ministers.

II

After accepting Mr. Gladstone's resignation the Queen, on June 13, proffered him a peerage: —

[1] The correspondence with the Queen up to June 21 was read by Mr. Gladstone in the House of Commons on June 24, and Lord Salisbury made his statement in the House of Lords on the next day. Mr. Gladstone told the House of Commons that he omitted one or two sentences from one of his letters, as having hardly any bearing on the real points of the correspondence. The omitted sentences related to the Afghan frontier, and the state of the negotiations with Russia.

The Queen to Mr. Gladstone.

Mr. Gladstone mentioned in his last letter but one, his intention of proposing some honours. But before she considers these, she wishes to offer him an Earldom, as a mark of her recognition of his long and distinguished services, and she believes and thinks he will thereby be enabled still to render great service to his sovereign and country — which if he retired, as he has repeatedly told her of late he intended to do shortly, — he could not. The country would doubtless be pleased at any signal mark of recognition of Mr. Gladstone's long and eminent services, and the Queen believes that it would be beneficial to his health, — no longer exposing him to the pressure from without, for more active work than he ought to undertake. Only the other day — without reference to the present events — the Queen mentioned to Mrs. Gladstone at Windsor the advantage to Mr. Gladstone's health of a removal from one House to the other, in which she seemed to agree. The Queen trusts, therefore, that Mr. Gladstone will accept the offer of an earldom, which would be very gratifying to her.

The outgoing minister replied on the following day: —

Mr. Gladstone offers his humble apology to your Majesty. It would not be easy for him to describe the feelings with which he has read your Majesty's generous, most generous letter. He prizes every word of it, for he is fully alive to all the circumstances which give it value. It will be a precious possession to him and to his children after him. All that could recommend an earldom to him, it already has given him. He remains, however, of the belief that he ought not to avail himself of this most gracious offer. Any service that he can render, if small, will, however, be greater in the House of Commons than in the House of Lords; and it has never formed part of his views to enter that historic chamber, although he does not share the feeling which led Sir R. Peel to put upon record what seemed a perpetual or almost a perpetual self-denying ordinance for his family.

When the circumstances of the state cease, as he hopes they may ere long, to impose on him any special duty, he will greatly covet that interval between an active career and death, which the profession of politics has always appeared to him especially to require. There are circumstances connected with the position of his family, which he will not obtrude upon your Majesty, but which, as he conceives, recommend in point of prudence the personal intention from which he has never swerved. He might hesitate to act upon the motives to which he has last adverted, grave as they are, did he not feel rooted in the persuasion that the small good he may hope hereafter to effect, can best be prosecuted without the change in his position. He must beg your Majesty to supply all that is lacking in his expression from the heart of profound and lasting gratitude.

To Lord Granville, the nearest of his friends, he wrote on the same day : —

I send you herewith a letter from the Queen which moves and almost upsets me. It must have cost her much to write, and it is really a pearl of great price. Such a letter makes the subject of it secondary — but though it would take me long to set out my reasons, I remain firm in the intention to accept nothing for myself.

Lord Granville replied that he was not surprised at the decision. 'I should have greatly welcomed you,' he said, ' and under some circumstances it might be desirable, but I think you are right now.'

Here is Mr. Gladstone's letter to an invaluable occupant of the all-important office of private secretary : —

To Mr. E. W. Hamilton.

June 30, 1885. — Since you have in substance (and in form ?) received the appointment [at the Treasury], I am unmuzzled, and may now express the unbounded pleasure which it gives me, together with my strong sense (not disparaging any one else) of your desert. The modesty of your letter is as remarkable as its other qualities, and does you the highest honour. I can accept no tribute from you, or from any one, with regard to the office of private secretary under me except this, that it has always been made by me a strict and severe office, and that this is really the only favour I have ever done you, or any of your colleagues to whom in their several places and measures I am similarly obliged.

As to your services to me they have been simply indescribable. CHAP.
No one I think could dream, until by experience he knew, to XII.
what an extent in these close personal relations devolution can be Æt. 76.
carried, and how it strengthens the feeble knees and thus also
sustains the fainting heart.

III

The declaration of the Irish policy of the new government
was made to parliament by no less a personage than the lord-
lieutenant.[1] The prime minister had discoursed on frontiers
in Asia and frontiers in Africa, but on Ireland he was silent.
Lord Carnarvon, on the contrary, came forward voluntarily
with a statement of policy, and he opened it on the broadest
general lines. His speech deserves as close attention as any
deliverance of this memorable period. It laid down the principles of that alternative system of government, with which
the new ministers formally challenged their predecessors.
Ought the Crimes Act to be re-enacted as it stood; or in
part; or ought it to be allowed to lapse? These were the
three courses. Nobody, he thought, would be for the first,
because some provisions had never been put in force; others
had been put in force but found useless; and others again
did nothing that might not be done just as well under the
ordinary law. The re-enactment of the whole statute, therefore, was dismissed. But the powers for changing venue at
the discretion of the executive; for securing special juries at
the same discretion; for holding secret inquiry without an
accused person; for dealing summarily with charges of
intimidation — might they not be continued? They were
not unconstitutional, and they were not opposed to legal
instincts. No, all quite true; but then the Lords should
not conceal from themselves that their re-enactment would
be in the nature of special or exceptional legislation.
He had been looking through coercion Acts, he continued,
and had been astonished to find that ever since 1847, with
some very short intervals hardly worth mentioning, Ireland

[1] This proceeding was so unusual
as to be almost without a precedent.
Lord Mulgrave had addressed the
House of Lords in 1837, and Lord
Clarendon in 1850. But on each of these occasions the viceroy's administration had been the object of
vigorous attack, and no one but the
viceroy himself was capable of making
an effective parliamentary defence.

had lived under exceptional and coercive legislation. What sane man could admit this to be a satisfactory or a wholesome state of things? Why should not they try to extricate themselves from this miserable habit, and aim at some better solution? 'Just as I have seen in English colonies across the sea a combination of English, Irish, and Scotch settlers bound together in loyal obedience to the law and the crown, and contributing to the general prosperity of the country, so I cannot conceive that there is any irreconcilable bar here in their native home and in England to the unity and the amity of the two nations.' He went to his task individually with a perfectly free, open, and unprejudiced mind, to hear, to question, and, as far as might be, to understand. 'My Lords, I do not believe that with honesty and single-mindedness of purpose on the one side, and with the willingness of the Irish people on the other, it is hopeless to look for some satisfactory solution of this terrible question. My Lords, these I believe to be the opinions and the views of my colleagues.'[1]

This remarkable announcement, made in the presence of the prime minister, in the name of the cabinet as a whole, and by a man of known purity and sincerity of character, was taken to be an express renunciation, not merely of the policy of which notice had been given by the outgoing administration, but of coercion as a final instrument of imperial rule. It was an elaborate repudiation in advance of that panacea of firm and resolute government, which became so famous before twelve months were over. It was the suggestion, almost in terms, that a solution should be sought in that policy which had brought union both within our colonies, and between the colonies and the mother country, and men did not forget that this suggestion was being made by a statesman who had carried federation in Canada, and tried to carry it in South Africa. We cannot wonder that upon leading members of the late government, and especially upon the statesman who had been specially responsible for Ireland, the impression was startling and profound. Important members of the tory party hurried

[1] July 6, 1885. *Hans.* 298, p. 1659.

from Ireland to Arlington Street, and earnestly warned their leader that he would never be able to carry on with the ordinary law. They were coldly informed that Lord Salisbury had received quite different counsel from persons well acquainted with the country.

The new government were not content with renouncing coercion for the present. They cast off all responsibility for its practice in the past. Ostentatiously they threw overboard the viceroy with whom the only fault that they had hitherto found, was that his sword was not sharp enough. A motion was made by the Irish leader calling attention to the maladministration of the criminal law by Lord Spencer. Forty men had been condemned to death, and in twenty-one of these cases the capital sentence had been carried out. Of the twenty-one executions six were savagely impugned, and Mr. Parnell's motion called for a strict inquiry into these and some other convictions, with a view to the full discovery of truth and the relief of innocent persons. The debate soon became famous from the principal case adduced, as the Maamtrasna debate. The topic had been so copiously discussed as to occupy three full sittings of the House in the previous October. The lawyer who had just been made Irish chancellor, at that time pronounced against the demand. In substance the new government made no fresh concession. They said that if memorials or statements were laid before him, the viceroy would carefully attend to them. No minister could say less. But incidental remarks fell from the government that created lively alarm in tories and deep disgust in liberals. Sir Michael Hicks Beach, then leader of the House, told them that while believing Lord Spencer to be a man of perfect honour and sense of duty, 'he must say very frankly that there was much in the Irish policy of the late government which, though in the absence of complete information he did not condemn, he should be very sorry to make himself responsible for.'[1] An even more important minister emphasised the severance of the new policy from the old. 'I will tell you,' cried Lord Randolph Churchill, 'how the present government is foredoomed to failure.

[1] Sir M. H. Beach, July 17, 1885. *Hans.* 299, p. 1085.

They will be foredoomed to failure if they go out of their way unnecessarily to assume one jot or tittle of the responsibility for the acts of the late administration. It is only by divesting ourselves of all responsibility for the acts of the late government, that we can hope to arrive at a successful issue.'[1]

Tory members got up in angry fright, to denounce this practical acquiescence by the heads of their party in what was a violent Irish attack not only upon the late viceroy, but upon Irish judges, juries, and law officers. They remonstrated against 'the pusillanimous way' in which their two leaders had thrown over Lord Spencer. 'During the last three years,' said one of these protesting tories, 'Lord Spencer has upheld respect for law at the risk of his life from day to day, with the sanction, with the approval, and with the acknowledgment inside and outside of this House, of the country, and especially of the conservative party. Therefore I for one will not consent to be dragged into any implied, however slight, condemnation of Lord Spencer, because it happens to suit the exigencies of party warfare.'[2] This whole transaction disgusted plain men, tory and liberal alike; it puzzled calculating men; and it had much to do with the silent conversion of important and leading men.

The general sentiment about the outgoing viceroy took the form of a banquet in his honour (July 24), and some three hundred members of the two Houses attended, including Lord Hartington, who presided, and Mr. Bright. The two younger leaders of the radical wing who had been in the late cabinet neither signed the invitation nor were present. But on the same evening in another place, Mr. Chamberlain recognised the high qualities and great services of Lord Spencer, though they had not always agreed upon details. He expressed, however, his approval both of the policy and of the arguments which had led the new government to drop the Crimes Act. At the same time he denounced the 'astounding tergiversation' of ministers, and energetically declared that 'a strategic movement of that kind, executed in opposition to the notorious convictions of

[1] *Hans.* 299, p. 1098.   [2] *Ibid.* p. 1119.

the men who effected it, carried out for party purposes and
party purposes alone, is the most flagrant instance of political
dishonesty this country has ever known.' Lord Hartington
a few weeks later told his constituents that the conduct of
the government, in regard to Ireland, had dealt a heavy
blow 'both at political morality, and at the cause of order in
Ireland.' The severity of such judgments from these two
weighty statesmen testifies to the grave importance of the
new departure.

The enormous change arising from the line adopted by
the government was visible enough even to men of less keen
vision than Mr. Gladstone, and it was promptly indicated by
him in a few sentences in a letter to Lord Derby on the very
day of the Maamtrasna debate :—

Within the last two or three weeks, he wrote, the situation
has undergone important changes. I am not fully informed,
but what I know looks as if the Irish party so-called in
parliament, excited by the high biddings of Lord Randolph, had
changed what was undoubtedly Parnell's ground until within
a very short time back. It is now said that a central board
will not suffice, and that there must be a parliament. This I
suppose may mean the repeal of the Act of Union, or may
mean an Austro-Hungarian scheme, or may mean that Ireland
is to be like a great colony such as Canada. Of all or any
of these schemes I will now only say that, of course, they constitute an entirely new point of departure and raise questions of
an order totally different to any that are involved in a central
board appointed for local purposes.

Lord Derby recording his first impressions in reply (July
19) took the rather conventional objection made to most
schemes on all subjects, that it either went too far or did not
go far enough. Local government he understood, and home
rule he understood, but a quasi-parliament in Dublin, not
calling itself such though invested with most of the authority
of a parliament, seemed to him to lead to the demand for
fuller recognition. If we were forced, he said, to move beyond
local government as commonly understood, he would rather
have Ireland treated like Canada. 'But the difficulties every

way are enormous.' On this Mr. Gladstone wrote a little later to Lord Granville (Aug. 6) : —

As far as I can learn, both you and Derby are on the same lines as Parnell, in rejecting the smaller and repudiating the larger scheme. It would not surprise me if he were to formulate something on the subject. For my own part I have seen my way pretty well as to the particulars of the minor and rejected plan, but the idea of the wider one puzzles me much. At the same time, *if* the election gives a return of a decisive character, the sooner the subject is dealt with the better.

So little true is it to say that Mr. Gladstone only thought of the possibility of Irish autonomy after the election.

IV

Apart from public and party cares, the bodily machinery gave trouble, and the fine organ that had served him so nobly for so long showed serious signs of disorder.

To Lord Richard Grosvenor.

July 14. — After two partial examinations, a thorough examination of my throat (larynx *versus* pharynx) has been made to-day by Dr. Semon in the presence of Sir A. Clark, and the result is rather bigger than I had expected. It is, that I have a fair chance of real recovery provided I keep silent almost like a Trappist, but all treatment would be nugatory without this rest; that the other alternative is nothing dangerous, but merely the constant passage of the organ from bad to worse. He asked what demands the H. of C. would make on me. I answered about three speeches of about five minutes each, but he was not satisfied and wished me to get rid of it altogether, which I must do, perhaps saying instead a word by letter to some friend. Much time has almost of necessity been lost, but I must be rigid for the future, and even then I shall be well satisfied if I get back before winter to a natural use of the voice in conversation. This imports a considerable change in the course of my daily life. Here it is difficult to organise it afresh. At Hawarden I can easily do it, but there I am at a distance from the best aid. I am disposed to

' top up,' with a sea voyage, but this is No. 3 — Nos. 1 and 2 being rest and then treatment.

The sea voyage that was to ' top up ' the rest of the treatment began on August 8, when the Gladstones became the guests of Sir Thomas and Lady Brassey on the *Sunbeam*. They sailed from Greenhithe to Norway, and after a three weeks' cruise, were set ashore at Fort George on September 1. Mr. Gladstone made an excellent tourist; was full of interest in all he saw ; and, I dare say, drew some pleasure from the demonstrations of curiosity and admiration that attended his presence from the simple population wherever he moved. Long expeditions with much climbing and scrambling were his delight, and he let nothing beat him. One of these excursions, the ascent to the Vöringfos, seems to deserve a word of commemoration, in the interest either of physiology or of philosophic musings after Cicero's manner upon old age. ' I am not sure,' says Lady Brassey in her most agreeable diary of the cruise,[1] ' that the descent did not seem rougher and longer than our journey up had been, although, as a matter of fact, we got over the ground much more quickly. As we crossed the green pastures on the level ground near the village of Sæbö we met several people taking their evening stroll, and also a tourist apparently on his way up to spend the night near the Vöringfos. The wind had gone down since the morning, and we crossed the little lake with fair rapidity, admiring as we went the glorious effects of the setting sun upon the tops of the precipitous mountains, and the wonderful echo which was aroused for our benefit by the boatmen. An extremely jolty drive, in springless country carts, soon brought us to the little inn at Vik, and by half-past eight we were once more on board the *Sunbeam*, exactly ten hours after setting out upon our expedition, which had included a ride or walk, as the case might be, of eighteen miles, independently of the journey by boat and cart — a hardish day's work for any one, but really a wonderful undertaking for a man of seventy-five, who disdained all proffered help, and insisted on walking the whole distance. No one who saw Mr. Gladstone that evening

[1] In *The Contemporary Review*, October 1885, p. 491.

at dinner in the highest spirits, and discussing subjects both grave and gay with the greatest animation, could fail to admire his marvellous pluck and energy, or, knowing what he had shown himself capable of doing in the way of physical exertion, could feel much anxiety on the score of the failure of his strength.'

He was touched by a visit from the son of an old farmer, who brought him as an offering from his father to Mr. Gladstone a curiously carved Norwegian bowl three hundred years old, with two horse-head handles. Strolling about Aalesund, he was astonished to find in the bookshop of the place a Norse translation of Mill's *Logic*. He was closely observant of all religious services whenever he had the chance, and noticed that at Laurvig all the tombstones had prayers for the dead. He read perhaps a little less voraciously than usual, and on one or two days, being unable to read, he 'meditated and reviewed' — always, I think, from the same point of view — the point of view of Bunyan's *Grace Abounding*, or his own letters to his father half a century before. Not seldom a vision of the coming elections flitted before the mind's eye, and he made notes for what he calls an *abbozzo* or sketch of his address to Midlothian.

Book II

1885–1886

CHAPTER I

LEADERSHIP AND THE GENERAL ELECTION

(1885)

OUR understanding of history is spoiled by our knowledge of the event. — HELPS.

MR. GLADSTONE came back from his cruise in the *Sunbeam* at the beginning of September; leaving the yacht at Fort George and proceeding to Fasque to celebrate his elder brother's golden wedding. From Fasque he wrote to Lord Hartington (Sept. 3): 'I have returned to terra firma extremely well in general health, and with a better throat; in full expectation of having to consider anxious and doubtful matters, and now finding them rather more anxious and doubtful than I had anticipated. As yet I am free to take a share or not in the coming political issues, and I must weigh many things before finally surrendering this freedom.' His first business, he wrote to Sir W. Harcourt (Sept.12), was to throw his thoughts into order for an address to his constituents, framed only for the dissolution, and 'written with my best care to avoid treading on the toes of either the right or the left wing.' He had communicated, he said, with Granville, Hartington, and Chamberlain; by both of the two latter he had been a good deal buffeted; and having explained the general idea with which he proposed to write, he asked each of the pair whether upon the whole their wish was that he should go on or cut out. 'To this question I have not yet got a clear affirmative answer from either of them.'

'The subject of Ireland,' he told Lord Hartington, 'has perplexed me much even on the North Sea,' and he expressed some regret that in a recent speech his correspondent had felt it necessary at this early period to join issue in so pointed a manner with Mr. Parnell and his party. Parnell's speech was, no doubt, he said, 'as bad as bad could be, and admitted of only one answer. But the whole question of the position which Ireland will assume after the general election is so new, so difficult, and as yet, I think, so little understood, that it seems most important to reserve until the proper time all possible liberty of examining it.'

The address to his electors, of which he had begun to think on board the *Sunbeam*, was given to the public on September 17. It was, as he said, as long as a pamphlet, and a considerable number of politicians doubtless passed judgment upon it without reading it through. The whigs, we are told, found it vague, the radicals cautious, the tories crafty; but everybody admitted that it tended to heal feuds. Mr. Goschen praised it, and Mr. Chamberlain, though raising his own flag, was respectful to his leader's manifesto.[1]

The surface was thus stilled for the moment, yet the waters ran very deep. What were 'the anxious and doubtful matters,' what 'the coming political issues,' of which Mr. Gladstone had written to Lord Hartington? They were, in a word, twofold: to prevent the right wing from breaking with the left; and second, to make ready for an Irish crisis, which as he knew could not be averted. These were the two keys to all his thoughts, words, and deeds during the important autumn of 1885 — an Irish crisis, a solid party. He was not the first great parliamentary leader whose course lay between two impossibilities.

All his letters during the interval between his return from the cruise in the *Sunbeam* and the close of the general election disclose with perfect clearness the channels in which events and his judgment upon them were moving. Whigs and radicals alike looked to him, and across him fought their battle. The Duke of Argyll, for example,

[1] See *Spectator*, Sept. 26, 1885.

taking advantage of a lifelong friendship to deal faithfully
with him, warned him that the long fight with 'Beacons-
fieldism' had thrown him into antagonism with many
political conceptions and sympathies that once had a steady
hold upon him. Yet they had certainly no less value and
truth than they ever had, and perhaps were more needed
than ever in face of the present chaos of opinion. To this
Mr. Gladstone replied at length: —

To the Duke of Argyll.

Sept. 30, 1885. — I am very sensible of your kind and sympathetic
tone, and of your indulgent verdict upon my address. It was
written with a view to the election, and as a practical document,
aiming at the union of all, it propounds for immediate action what
all are supposed to be agreed on. This is necessarily somewhat
favourable to the moderate section of the liberal party. You will
feel that it would not have been quite fair to the advanced men
to add some special reproof to them. And reproof, if I had presumed upon it, would have been two-sided. Now as to your suggestion that I should say something in public to indicate that I am
not too sanguine as to the future. If I am unable to go in this
direction — and something I may do — it is not from want of
sympathy with much that you say. But my first and great cause
of anxiety is, believe me, the condition of the tory party. As at
present constituted, or at any rate moved, it is destitute of all the
effective qualities of a respectable conservatism. . . . For their
administrative spirit I point to the Beaconsfield finance. For their
foreign policy they have invented Jingoism, and at the same time
by their conduct *re* Lord Spencer and the Irish nationalists, they
have thrown over — and they formed their government only by
means of throwing over — those principles of executive order and
caution which have hitherto been common to all governments. . . .

There are other chapters which I have not time to open. I
deeply deplore the oblivion into which public economy has fallen;
the prevailing disposition to make a luxury of panics, which multitudes seem to enjoy as they would a sensational novel or a highly
seasoned cookery; and the leaning of both parties to socialism,
which I radically disapprove. I must lastly mention among my
causes of dissatisfaction the conduct of the timid or reactionary

whigs. They make it day by day more difficult to maintain that most valuable characteristic of our history, which has always exhibited a good proportion of our great houses at the head of the liberal movement. If you have ever noted of late years a too sanguine and high-coloured anticipation of our future, I should like to be reminded of it. I remain, and I hope always to be, your affectionate friend.

The correspondence with Lord Granville sets out more clearly than anything else could do Mr. Gladstone's general view of the situation of the party and his own relation to it, and the operative words in this correspondence, in view of the maelstrom to which they were all drawing nearer, will be accurately noted by any reader who cares to understand one of the most interesting situations in the history of party. To Lord Granville he says (September 9, 1885), 'The problem for me is to make if possible a statement which will hold through the election and not to go into conflict with either the right wing of the party for whom Hartington has spoken, or the left wing for whom Chamberlain, I suppose, spoke last night. I do not say they are to be treated as on a footing, but I must do no act disparaging to Chamberlain's wing.' And again to Lord Granville a month later (Oct. 5) : —

You hold a position of great impartiality in relation to any divergent opinions among members of the late cabinet. No other person occupies ground so thoroughly favourable. I turn to myself for one moment. I remain at present in the leadership of the party, first with a view to the election, and secondly with a view to being, by a bare possibility, of use afterwards in the Irish question if it should take a favourable turn; but as you know, with the intention of taking no part in any schism of the party should it arise, and of avoiding any and all official responsibility, should the question be merely one of liberal *v.* conservative and not one of commanding imperial necessity, such as that of Irish government may come to be after the dissolution.

He goes on to say that the ground had now been sufficiently laid for going to the election with a united front, that ground being the common profession of a limited creed

or programme in the liberal sense, with an entire freedom
for those so inclined, to travel beyond it, but not to impose
their own sense upon all other people. No one, he thought,
was bound to determine at that moment on what conditions
he would join a liberal government. If the party and its
leaders were agreed as to immediate measures on local
government, land, and registration, were not these enough
to find a liberal administration plenty of work, especially
with procedure, for several years? If so, did they not supply
a ground broad enough to start a government, that would
hold over, until the proper time should come, all the
questions on which its members might not be agreed, just
as the government of Lord Grey held over, from 1830 to
1834, the question whether Irish church property might
or might not be applied to secular uses?

As for himself, in the event of such a government
being formed (of which I suppose Lord Granville was to
be the head), ' My desire would be,' he says, ' to place myself in your hands for all purposes, except that of taking
office; to be present or absent from the House, and to be
absent for a time or for good, as you might on consultation
and reflection think best.' In other words Mr. Gladstone
would take office to try to settle the Irish question, but for
nothing else. Lord Granville held to the view that this
was fatal to the chances of a liberal government. No liberal
cabinet could be constructed unless Mr. Gladstone were
at its head. The indispensable chief, however, remained
obdurate.

An advance was made at this moment in the development
of a peculiar situation by important conversations with Mr.
Chamberlain. Two days later the redoubtable leader of the
left wing came to Hawarden for a couple of days, and
Mr. Gladstone wrote an extremely interesting account of
what passed to Lord Granville : [1]—

[1] Mr. Chamberlain has been good
enough to read these two letters, and he
assents to their substantial accuracy,
with a demurrer on two or three
points, justly observing that anybody
reporting a very long and varied conversation is almost certain, however
scrupulous in intention, to insert in
places what were thoughts much in
his own mind, rather than words
actually spoken. In inserting these
two letters, it may tend to prevent
controversy if we print such corrective hints as are desired.

To Lord Granville.

Hawarden, Oct. 8, 1885. — Chamberlain came here yesterday and I have had a great deal of conversation with him. He is a good man to talk to, not only from his force and clearness, but because he speaks with reflection, does not misapprehend or (I think) suspect, or make unnecessary difficulties, or endeavour to maintain pedantically the uniformity and consistency of his argument throughout.

As to the three points of which he was understood to say that they were indispensable to the starting of a liberal government, I gather that they stand as follows : —

1. As to the authority of local authorities for compulsory expropriation.[1] To this he adheres; though I have said I could not see the justification for withholding countenance from the formation of a government with considerable and intelligible plans in view, because it would not at the first moment bind all its members to this doctrine. He intimates, however, that the form would be simple, the application of the principle mild; that he does not expect wide results from it, and that Hartington, he conceives, is not disposed wholly to object to everything of the kind.

2. As regards readjustment of taxation, he is contented with the terms of my address, and indisposed to make any new terms.

3. As regards free education, he does not ask that its principle be adopted as part of the creed of a new cabinet. He said it would be necessary to reserve his right individually to vote for it. I urged that he and the new school of advanced liberals were not sufficiently alive to the necessity of refraining when in government from declaring by *vote* all their individual opinions; that a vote founded upon time, and the engagements of the House at the moment with other indispensable business, would imply no disparagement to the principle, which might even be expressly saved (' without prejudice ') by an amending resolution; that he could hardly carry this point to the rank of a *sine quâ non*. He said, — That the sense of the country might bind the liberal majority (presuming it to exist) to declare its opinion, even though unable

---

[1] In connection with a local government bill for small holdings and allotments, subsequently passed.

to give effect to it at the moment; that he looked to a single
declaration, not to the sustained support of a measure; and he
seemed to allow that if the liberal sense were so far divided as
not to show a unanimous front, in that case it might be a
question whether some plan other than, and short of, a direct
vote might be pursued.[1]

The question of the House of Lords and disestablishment he
regards as still lying in the remoter distance.

All these subjects I separated entirely from the question of
Ireland, on which I may add that he and I are pretty well agreed;
unless upon a secondary point, namely, whether Parnell would be
satisfied to acquiesce in a County Government bill, good so far as
it went, maintaining on other matters his present general attitude.[2] We agreed, I think, that a prolongation of the present
relations of the Irish party would be a national disgrace, and the
civilised world would scoff at the political genius of countries
which could not contrive so far to understand one another as to
bring their differences to an accommodation.

All through Chamberlain spoke of reducing to an absolute
minimum his idea of necessary conditions, and this conversation
so far left untouched the question of men, he apparently assuming (wrongly) that I was ready for another three or four years'
engagement.

Hawarden, Oct. 8, 1885. — In another 'private,' but less private
letter, I have touched on measures, and I have now to say what
passed in relation to men.

He said the outline he had given depended on the supposition
of my being at the head of the government. He did not say he
could adhere to it on no other terms, but appeared to stipulate for
a new point of departure.

I told him the question of my time of life had become such, that
in any case prudence bound him, and all who have a future, to
think of what is to follow me. That if a big Irish question should
arise, and arise in such a form as to promise a possibility of settle-

---

[1] He suggested, for instance, the
appointment of a committee.
[2] Mr. Chamberlain puts it that he
proposed to exclude home rule as impossible, and to offer a local government bill which he thought that

Parnell might accept. Mr. Gladstone's
statement that he and his visitor
were 'pretty well agreed' on Ireland,
cannot mean therefore that the visitor
was in favour of home rule.

ment, that would be a crisis with a beginning and an end, and perhaps one in which from age and circumstances I might be able to supply aid and service such as could not be exactly had without me.[1] Apart from an imperious demand of this kind the question would be that of dealing with land laws, with local government, and other matters, on which I could render *no* special service, and which would require me to enter into a new contest for several years, a demand that ought not to be made, and one to which I could not accede. I did not think the adjustment of personal relations, or the ordinary exigencies of party, constituted a call upon me to continue my long life in a course of constant pressure and constant contention with half my fellow-countrymen, until nothing remained but to step into the grave.

He agreed that the House of Lords was not an available resort. He thought I might continue at the head of the government, and leave the work of legislation to others.[2] I told him that all my life long I had had an essential and considerable share in the legislative work of government, and to abandon it would be an essential change, which the situation would not bear.

He spoke of the constant conflicts of opinion with Hartington in the late cabinet, but I reverted to the time when Hartington used to summon and lead meetings of the leading commoners, in which he was really the least antagonistic of men.

He said Hartington might lead a whig government aided by the tories, or might lead a radical government. . . . I recommended his considering carefully the personal composition of the group of leading men, apart from a single personality on which reliance could hardly be placed, except in the single contingency to which I have referred as one of a character probably brief.

He said it might be right for him to look as a friend on the formation of a liberal government, having (as I understood) moderate but intelligible plans, without forming part of it. I think this was the substance of what passed.

Interesting as was this interview, it did not materially alter Mr. Gladstone's disposition. After it had taken place he wrote to Lord Granville (Nov. 10) : —

---

[1] This is not remembered.   [2] " Some misunderstanding here."

To Lord Granville.

I quite understand how natural it is that at the present juncture pressure, and even the whole pressure, should from both quarters be brought to bear upon me. Well, if a special call of imperial interest, such as I have described, should arise, I am ready for the service it may entail, so far as my will is concerned. But a very different question is raised. Let us see how matters stand.

A course of action for the liberals, moderate but substantial, has been sketched. The party in general have accepted it. After the late conversations, there is no reason to anticipate a breach upon any of the conditions laid down anywhere for immediate adoption, between the less advanced and the more advanced among the leaders. It must occupy several years, and it may occupy the whole parliament. According to your view they will, unless on a single condition [*i.e.* Mr. Gladstone's leadership], refuse to combine in a cabinet, and to act, with a majority at their back; and will make over the business voluntarily to the tories in a minority, at the commencement of a parliament. Why? They agree on the subjects before them. Other subjects, unknown as yet, may arise to split them. But this is what may happen to any government, and *it* can form no reason.

But what *is* the condition demanded? It is that a man of seventy-five,[1] after fifty-three years' service, with *no* particular qualification for the questions in view should enter into a fresh contract of service in the House of Commons, reaching according to all likelihood over three, four, or five years, and without the smallest reasonable prospect of a break. And this is not to solve a political difficulty, but to soothe and conjure down personal misgivings and apprehensions. I have not said jealousies, because I do *not* believe them to be the operative cause; perhaps they do not exist at all.

I firmly say this is not a reasonable condition, or a tenable demand, in the circumstances supposed. Indeed no one has endeavoured to show that it is. Further, abated action in the House of Commons is out of the question. We cannot have, in these times, a figurehead prime minister. I have gone a very long way in what I have said, and I really cannot go further.

[1] That is, in his seventy-sixth year.

Lord Aberdeen, taking office at barely seventy in the House of
Lords, apologised in his opening speech for doing this at a time
when his mind ought rather to be given to 'other thoughts.'
Lord Palmerston in 1859 did not speak thus. But he was bound
to no plan of any kind; and he was seventy-four, *i.e.* in his
seventy-fifth year.

II

It is high time to turn to the other deciding issue in
the case. Though thus stubborn against resuming the
burden of leadership merely to compose discords between
Chatsworth and Birmingham, Mr. Gladstone was ready to
be of use in the Irish question, 'if it should take a favourable turn.' As if the Irish question ever took a favourable
turn. We have seen in the opening of the present chapter,
how he spoke to Lord Hartington of a certain speech
of Mr. Parnell's in September, 'as bad as bad could be.'
The secret of that speech was a certain fact that must be
counted a central hinge of these far-reaching transactions. In July, a singular incident had occurred, nothing
less strange than an interview between the new lord-
lieutenant and the leader of the Irish party. To realise
its full significance, we have to recall the profound odium
that at this time enveloped Mr. Parnell's name in the
minds of nearly all Englishmen. For several years and at
that moment he figured in the public imagination for all
that is sinister, treasonable, dark, mysterious, and unholy.
He had stood his trial for a criminal conspiracy, and was
supposed only to have been acquitted by the corrupt connivance of a Dublin jury. He had been flung into prison
and kept there for many months without trial, as a person
reasonably suspected of lawless practices. High treason was
the least dishonourable of the offences imputed to him and
commonly credited about him. He had been elaborately
accused before the House of Commons by one of the most
important men in it, of direct personal responsibility for
outrages and murders, and he left the accusation with scant
reply. He was constantly denounced as the apostle of
rapine and rebellion. That the viceroy of the Queen should

without duress enter into friendly communication with such a man, would have seemed to most people at that day incredible and abhorrent. Yet the incredible thing happened, and it was in its purpose one of the most sensible things that any viceroy ever did.[1]

The interview took place in a London drawing-room. Lord Carnarvon opened the conversation by informing Mr. Parnell, first, that he was acting of himself and by himself, on his own exclusive responsibility; second, that he sought information only, and that he had not come for the purpose of arriving at any agreement or understanding however shadowy; third, that he was there as the Queen's servant, and would neither hear nor say one word that was inconsistent with the union of the two countries. Exactly what Mr. Parnell said, and what was said in reply, the public were never authentically told. Mr. Parnell afterwards spoke[2] as if Lord Carnarvon had given him to understand that it was the intention of the government to offer Ireland a statutory legislature, with full control over taxation, and that a scheme of land purchase was to be coupled with it. On this, the viceroy denied that he had communicated any such intention. Mr. Parnell's story was this:—

Lord Carnarvon proceeded to say that he had sought the interview for the purpose of ascertaining my views regarding — should he call it? — a constitution for Ireland. But I soon found out that

[1] This episode was first mentioned in the House of Commons, June 7, 1886. Lord Carnarvon explained in the Lords, June 10. Mr. Parnell replied in a letter to the *Times*, June 12. He revived the subject in the House of Commons, Feb. 13, 1888, and Lord Carnarvon explained a second time in the Lords on May 3. On Lord Carnarvon's first explanation, the Duke of Argyll, while placing the utmost reliance on his personal honour and accuracy, 'felt bound to observe that the statement did not appear to be complete, for he had omitted to explain what the nature of the communication [with Mr. Parnell] absolutely was.' Neither then nor two years later was the omission made good. Curiously enough on the first occasion Lord Carnarvon did not even mention that Lord Salisbury in any way shared his responsibility for the interview, and in fact his language pointed the other way. What remains is his asseveration, supported by Lord Salisbury, that he had made no formal bargain with Mr. Parnell, and gave him no sort of promise, assurance, or pledge. This is not only entirely credible, it is certain; for the only body that could carry out such a promise had not been consulted. 'I may at least say this of what went on outside the cabinet — that I had no communication on the subject, *no authorisation*, and that I never communicated to them even that which I had done.' — *Hansard*, 306, p. 1258.

[2] *E.g. Hans.* 306, pp. 1181, 1199.

he had brought me there in order that he might communicate his own views upon the matter, as well as ascertain mine. . . . In reply to an inquiry as to a proposal which had been made to build up a central legislative body upon the foundation of county boards, I told him I thought this would be working in the wrong direction, and would not be accepted by Ireland; that the central legislative body should be a parliament in name and in fact. . . . Lord Carnarvon assured me that this was his own view also, and he strongly appreciated the importance of giving due weight to the sentiment of the Irish in this matter. . . . He had certain suggestions to this end, taking the colonial model as a basis, which struck me as being the result of much thought and knowledge of the subject. . . . At the conclusion of the conversation, which lasted for more than an hour, and to which Lord Carnarvon was very much the larger contributor, I left him, believing that I was in complete accord with him regarding the main outlines of a settlement conferring a legislature upon Ireland.[1]

It is certainly not for me to contend that Mr. Parnell was always an infallible reporter, but if closely scrutinised the discrepancy in the two stories as then told was less material than is commonly supposed. To the passage just quoted, Lord Carnarvon never at any time in public offered any real contradiction. What he contradicted was something different. He denied that he had ever stated to Mr. Parnell that it was the intention of the government, if they were successful at the polls, to establish the Irish legislature, with limited powers and not independent of imperial control, which he himself favoured. He did not deny, any more than he admitted, that he had told Mr. Parnell that on opinion and policy they were very much at one. How could he deny it, after his speech when he first took office? Though the cabinet was not cognisant of the nature of these proceedings, the prime minister was. To take so remarkable a step without the knowledge and assent of the head of the government, would have been against the whole practice and principles of our ministerial system. Lord Carnarvon informed Lord Salisbury of his intention of meeting Mr.

[1] Letter to the *Times*, June 12, 1886.

Parnell, and within twenty-four hours after the meeting, both in writing and orally, he gave Lord Salisbury as careful and accurate a statement as possible of what had passed. We can well imagine the close attention with which the prime minister followed so profoundly interesting a report, and at the end of it he told the viceroy that 'he had conducted the conversation with Mr. Parnell with perfect discretion.' The knowledge that the minister responsible for the government of Ireland was looking in the direction of home rule, and exchanging home rule views with the great home rule leader, did not shake Lord Salisbury's confidence in his fitness to be viceroy.

This is no mere case of barren wrangle and verbal recrimination. The transaction had consequences, and the Carnarvon episode was a pivot. The effect upon the mind of Mr. Parnell was easy to foresee. Was I not justified, he asked long afterwards, in supposing that Lord Carnarvon, holding the views that he now indicated, would not have been made viceroy unless there was a considerable feeling in the cabinet that his views were right?[1] Could he imagine that the viceroy would be allowed to talk home rule to him — however shadowy and vague the words — unless the prime minister considered such a solution to be at any rate well worth discussing? Why should he not believe that the alliance formed in June to turn Mr. Gladstone out of office and eject Lord Spencer from Ireland, had really blossomed from being a mere lobby manœuvre and election expedient, into a serious policy adopted by serious statesmen? Was it not certain that in such remarkable circumstances Mr. Parnell would throughout the election confidently state the national demand at its very highest?

In 1882 and onwards up to the Reform Act of 1885, Mr. Parnell had been ready to advocate the creation of a central council at Dublin for administrative purposes merely. This he thought would be a suitable achievement for a party that numbered only thirty-five members. But the assured increase of his strength at the coming election made all the difference. When semi-official soundings were

[1] *Hans.* 332, p. 336.

taken from more than one liberal quarter after the fall of
the Gladstone government, it was found that Mr. Parnell no
longer countenanced provisional reforms.   After the interview with Lord Carnarvon, the mercury rose rapidly to the
top of the tube.   Larger powers of administration were not
enough.   The claim for legislative power must now be
brought boldly to the front.   In unmistakable terms, the
Irish leader stated the Irish demand, and posed both
problem and solution.   He now declared his conviction
that the great and sole work of himself and his friends in
the new parliament would be the restoration of a national
parliament of their own, to do the things which they had
been vainly asking the imperial parliament to do for
them.[1]

III

When politicians ruminate upon the disastrous schism
that followed Mr. Gladstone's attempt to deal with the Irish
question in 1886, they ought closely to study the general
election of 1885.   In that election, though leading men foresaw the approach of a marked Irish crisis, and awaited the
outcome of events with an overshadowing sense of pregnant
issues, there was nothing like general concentration on the
Irish prospect.   The strife of programmes and the rivalries
of leaders were what engrossed the popular attention.
The main body of the British electors were thinking mainly
of promised agrarian booms, fair trade, the church in danger,
or some other of their own domestic affairs.

Few forms of literature or history are so dull as the narrative of political debates.   With a few exceptions, a political
speech like the manna in the wilderness loses its savour on
the second day.   Three or four marked utterances of this
critical autumn, following all that has been set forth already,
will enable the reader to understand the division of counsel
that prevailed immediately before the great change of
policy in 1886, and the various strategic evolutions, masked
movements, and play of mine, sap, and countermine, that
led to it.   As has just been described, and with good reason,

[1] August 24, 1885.

for he believed that he had the Irish viceroy on his side, Mr. Parnell stood inflexible.   In his speech of August 24 already mentioned, he had thrown down his gauntlet.

Much the most important answer to the challenge, if we regard the effect upon subsequent events, was that of Lord Salisbury two months later.   To this I shall have to return. The two liberal statesmen, Lord Hartington and Mr. Chamberlain, who were most active in this campaign, and whose activity was well spiced and salted by a lively political antagonism, agreed in a tolerably stiff negative to the Irish demand.   The whig leader with a slow mind, and the radical leader with a quick mind, on this single issue of the campaign spoke with one voice.   The whig leader [1] thought Mr. Parnell had made a mistake and ensured his own defeat: he overestimated his power in Ireland and his power in parliament ; the Irish would not for the sake of this impossible and impracticable undertaking, forego without duress all the other objects which parliament was ready to grant them ; and it remained to be seen whether he could enforce his iron discipline upon his eighty or ninety adherents, even if Ireland gave him so many.

The radical leader was hardly less emphatic, and his utterance was the more interesting of the two, because until this time Mr. Chamberlain had been generally taken throughout his parliamentary career as leaning strongly in the nationalist direction.   He had taken a bold and energetic part in the proceedings that ended in the release of Mr. Parnell from Kilmainham.   He had with much difficulty been persuaded to acquiesce in the renewal of any part of the Coercion Act, and had absented himself from the banquet in honour of Lord Spencer.   Together with his most intimate ally in the late government, he had projected a political tour in Ireland with Mr. Parnell's approval and under his auspices.   Above all, he had actually opened his electoral campaign with that famous declaration which was so long remembered: ' The pacification of Ireland at this moment depends, I believe, on the concession to Ireland of

[1] Lord Hartington at Waterfoot, August 29.

the right to govern itself in the matter of its purely domestic business. Is it not discreditable to us that even now it is only by unconstitutional means that we are able to secure peace and order in one portion of her Majesty's dominions? It is a system as completely centralised and bureaucratic as that with which Russia governs Poland, or as that which prevailed in Venice under the Austrian rule. An Irishman at this moment cannot move a step — he cannot lift a finger in any parochial, municipal, or educational work, without being confronted with, interfered with, controlled by, an English official, appointed by a foreign government, and without a shade or shadow of representative authority. I say the time has come to reform altogether the absurd and irritating anachronism which is known as Dublin Castle. That is the work to which the new parliament will be called.'[1] Masters of incisive speech must pay the price of their gifts, and the sentence about Poland and Venice was long a favourite in many a debate. But when the Irish leader now made his proposal for removing the Russian yoke and the Austrian yoke from Ireland, the English leader drew back. 'If these,' he said, 'are the terms on which Mr. Parnell's support is to be obtained, I will not enter into the compact.' This was Mr. Chamberlain's response.[2]

IV

The language used by Mr. Gladstone during this eventful time was that of a statesman conscious of the magnitude of the issue, impressed by the obscurity of the path along which parties and leaders were travelling, and keenly alive to the perils of a premature or unwary step. Nothing was easier for the moment either for quick minds or slow minds, than to face the Irish demand beforehand with a bare, blank, wooden *non possumus*. Mr. Gladstone had pondered the matter more deeply. His gift of political imagination, his wider experience, and his personal share in some chapters of the modern history of Europe and its changes, planted him on a height whence he commanded a view of possibili-

[1] June 17, 1885.   [2] Warrington, September 8.

ties and necessities, of hopes and of risks, that were unseen by politicians of the beaten track. Like a pilot amid wandering icebergs, or in waters where familiar buoys had been taken up and immemorial beacons put out, he scanned the scene with keen eyes and a glass sweeping the horizon in every direction. No wonder that his words seemed vague, and vague they undoubtedly were. Suppose that Cavour had been obliged to issue an election address on the eve of the interview at Plombières, or Bismarck while he was on his visit to Biarritz. Their language would hardly have been pellucid. This was no moment for ultimatums. There were too many unascertained elements. Yet some of those, for instance, who most ardently admired President Lincoln for the caution with which he advanced step by step to the abolition proclamation, have most freely censured the English statesman because he did not in the autumn of 1885 come out with either a downright Yes or a point-blank No. The point-blank is not for all occasions, and only a simpleton can think otherwise.

In September Mr. Childers — a most capable administrator, a zealous colleague, wise in what the world regards as the secondary sort of wisdom, and the last man to whom one would have looked for a plunge — wrote to Mr. Gladstone to seek his approval of a projected announcement to his constituents at Pontefract, which amounted to a tolerably full-fledged scheme of home rule.[1] In view of the charitable allegation that Mr. Gladstone picked up home rule after the elections had placed it in the power of the Irish either to put him into office or to keep him out of office, his reply to Mr. Childers deserves attention : —

To Mr. Childers.

Sept. 28, 1885. — I have a decided sympathy with the general scope and spirit of your proposed declaration about Ireland. If I offer any observations, they are meant to be simply in furtherance of your purpose.

1. I would disclaim giving any exhaustive list of Imperial subjects, and would not 'put my foot down' as to revenue, but

[1] *Life of Childers*, ii. p. 230.

would keep plenty of elbow-room to keep all customs and excise, which would probably be found necessary.

2. A general disclaimer of particulars as to the form of any local legislature might suffice, without giving the Irish expressly to know it might be decided mainly by their wish.

3. I think there is no doubt Ulster would be able to take care of itself in respect to education, but a question arises and forms, I think, the most difficult part of the whole subject, whether some defensive provisions for the owners of land and property should not be considered.

4. It is evident you have given the subject much thought, and my sympathy goes largely to your details as well as your principle. But considering the danger of placing confidence in the leaders of the national party at the present moment, and the decided disposition they have shown to raise their terms on any favourable indication, I would beg you to consider further whether you should *bind* yourself at present to any details, or go beyond general indications. If you say in terms (and this I do not dissuade) that you are ready to consider the question whether they can have a legislature for all questions not Imperial, this will be a great step in advance; and anything you may say beyond it, I should like to see veiled in language not such as to commit you.

The reader who is now acquainted with Mr. Gladstone's strong support of the Chamberlain plan in 1885, and with the bias already disclosed, knows in what direction the main current of his thought must have been setting. The position taken in 1885 was in entire harmony with all these premonitory notes. Subject, said Mr. Gladstone, to the supremacy of the crown, the unity of the empire, and all the authority of parliament necessary for the conservation of that unity, every grant to portions of the country of enlarged powers for the management of their own affairs, was not a source of danger, but a means of averting it. As to the legislative union, I believe history and posterity will consign to disgrace the name and memory of every man, be he who he may, and on whichever side of the Channel he may dwell, that having the power to aid in an equitable settlement between Ireland and Great Britain, shall use that power not to aid, but to prevent or retard it.'[1]   These and all the other large and profuse sentences of the Midlothian address were undoubtedly open to more than one construction, and they either admitted or excluded home rule, as might happen. The fact that, though it was running so freely in his own mind, he did not put Irish autonomy into the forefront of his address, has been made a common article of charge against him.   As if the view of Irish autonomy now running in his mind were not dependent on a string of hypotheses.   And who can imagine a party leader's election address that should have run thus ? — 'If Mr. Parnell returns with a great majority of members, and if the minority is not weighty enough, and if the demand is constitutionally framed, and if the Parnellites are unanimous, then we will try home rule.   And this possibility of a hypothetical experiment is to be the liberal cry with which to go into battle against Lord Salisbury, who, so far as I can see, is nursing the idea of the same experiment.'

Some weeks later, in speaking to his electors in Midlothian, Mr. Gladstone instead of minimising magnified the Irish case, pushed it into the very forefront, not in one speech, but in nearly all ; warned his hearers of the gravity of the questions soon to be raised by it, and assured them that it would probably throw into the shade the other measures that he had described as ripe for action.   He elaborated a declaration, of which much was heard for many months and years afterwards.   What Ireland, he said, may deliberately and constitutionally demand, unless it infringes the principles connected with the honourable maintenance of the unity of the empire, will be a demand that we are bound at any rate to treat with careful attention.   To stint Ireland in power which might be necessary or desirable for the management of matters purely Irish, would be a great error ; and if she was so stinted, the end that any such measure might contemplate could not be attained.   Then came the memorable appeal : 'Apart from the term of whig and tory, there is one thing I will say and will endeavour to impress upon you, and it is this. It will be a vital danger to the country and to the empire, if at a time when a demand from Ireland for larger powers

[1] Sept. 18, 1885.

of self-government is to be dealt with, there is not in parliament a party totally independent of the Irish vote.' [1] Loud and long sustained have been the reverberations of this clanging sentence. It was no mere passing dictum. Mr. Gladstone himself insisted upon the same position again and again, that 'for a government in a minority to deal with the Irish question would not be safe.' This view, propounded in his first speech, was expanded in his second. There he deliberately set out that the urgent expediency of a liberal majority independent of Ireland did not foreshadow the advent of a liberal government to power. He referred to the settlement of household suffrage in 1867. How was the tory government enabled to effect that settlement? Because there was in the House a liberal majority which did not care to eject the existing ministry.[2] He had already reminded his electors that tory governments were sometimes able to carry important measures, when once they had made up their minds to it, with greater facility than liberal governments could. For instance, if Peel had not been the person to propose the repeal of the corn laws, Lord John would not have had fair consideration from the tories ; and no liberal government could have carried the Maynooth Act.[3]

The plain English of the abundant references to Ireland in the Midlothian speeches of this election is, that Mr. Gladstone foresaw beyond all shadow of doubt that the Irish question in its largest extent would at once demand the instant attention of the new parliament ; that the best hope of settling it would be that the liberals should have a majority of their own ; that the second best hope lay in its settlement by the tory government with the aid of the liberals ; but that, in any case, the worst of all conditions under which a settlement could be attempted — an attempt that could not be avoided — would be a situation in which Mr. Parnell should hold the balance between parliamentary parties.

The precise state of Mr. Gladstone's mind at this moment is best shown in a very remarkable letter written by him to Lord Rosebery, under whose roof at Talmeny he was staying at the time : —

---

[1] Nov. 9, 1885.   [2] Midlothian Speeches, p. 49.   [3] *Ibid.* p. 39.

To Lord Rosebery.

Dalmeny Park, 13*th Nov.* 1885. — You have called my attention to the recent speech of Mr. Parnell, in which he expresses the desire that I should frame a plan for giving to Ireland, without prejudice to imperial unity and interests, the management of her own affairs. The subject is so important that, though we are together, I will put on paper my view of this proposal. For the moment I assume that such a plan can be framed. Indeed, if I had considered this to be hopeless, I should have been guilty of great rashness in speaking of it as a contingency that should be kept in view at the present election. I will first give reasons, which I deem to be of great weight, against my producing a scheme, reserving to the close one reason, which would be conclusive in the absence of every other reason.

1. It is not the province of the person leading the party in opposition, to frame and produce before the public detailed schemes of such a class.

2. There are reasons of great weight, which make it desirable that the party now in power should, if prepared to adopt the principle, and if supported by an adequate proportion of the coming House of Commons, undertake the construction and proposal of the measure.

3. The unfriendly relations between the party of nationalists and the late government in the expiring parliament, have of necessity left me and those with whom I act in great ignorance of the interior mind of the party, which has in parliament systematically confined itself to very general declarations.

4. That the principle and basis of an admissible measure have been clearly declared by myself, if not by others, before the country; more clearly, I think, than was done in the case of the Irish disestablishment; and that the particulars of such plans in all cases have been, and probably must be, left to the discretion of the legislature acting under the usual checks.

But my final and paramount reason is, that the production at this time of a plan by me would not only be injurious, but would destroy all reasonable hope of its adoption. Such a plan, proposed by the heads of the liberal party, is so certain to have the opposition of the tories *en bloc*, that every computation must be founded on this anticipation. This opposition, and the appeals with which it will be accompanied, will render the carrying of the measure difficult even by a united liberal party; hopeless or most difficult, should there be serious defection.

Mr. Parnell is apprehensive of the opposition of the House of Lords. That idea weighs little with me. I have to think of something nearer, and more formidable. The idea of constituting a legislature for Ireland, whenever seriously and responsibly proposed, will cause a mighty heave in the body politic. It will be as difficult to carry the liberal party and the two British nations in favour of a legislature for Ireland, as it was easy to carry them in the case of Irish disestablishment. I think that it may possibly be done; but only by the full use of a great leverage. That leverage can only be found in their equitable and mature consideration of what is due to the fixed desire of a nation, clearly and constitutionally expressed. Their prepossessions will not be altogether favourable; and they cannot in this matter be bullied.

I have therefore endeavoured to lay the ground by stating largely the possibility and the gravity, even the solemnity, of that demand. I am convinced that this is the only path which can lead to success. With such a weapon, one might go hopefully into action. But I well know, from a thousand indications past and present, that a new project of mine launched into the air, would have no *momentum* which could carry it to its aim. So, in my mind, stands the case. . . .

Three days before this letter, Mr. Gladstone had replied to one from Lord Hartington:—

To Lord Hartington.

Dalmeny, Nov. 10, 1885.—I made a beginning yesterday in one of my conversation speeches, so to call them, on the way, by laying it down that I was particularly bound to prevent, if I could, the domination of sectional opinion over the body and action of the party.

I wish to say something about the modern radicalism. But I must include this, that if it is rampant and ambitious, the two most prominent causes of its forwardness have been: 1. Tory democracy. 2. The gradual disintegration of the liberal aristocracy. On both these subjects my opinions are strong. I think the conduct of the Duke of Bedford and others has been as unjustifiable as it was foolish, especially after what we did to save the House of Lords from itself in the business of the franchise.

Nor can I deny that the question of the House of Lords, of the church, or both, will probably split the liberal party. But let it split decently, honourably, and for cause. That it should split now would, so far as I see, be ludicrous.

So far I have been writing in great sympathy with you, but now I touch a point where our lines have not been the same. You have, I think, courted the hostility of Parnell. Salisbury has carefully avoided doing this, and last night he simply confined himself to two conditions, which you and I both think vital; namely, the unity of the empire and an honourable regard to the position of the ' minority,' *i.e.* the landlords. You will see in the newspapers what Parnell, *making* for himself an opportunity, is reported to have said about the elections in Ulster now at hand. You have opened a vista which appears to terminate in a possible concession to Ireland of full power to manage her own local affairs. But I own my leaning to the opinion that, if that consummation is in any way to be contemplated, action at a stroke will be more honourable, less unsafe, less uneasy, than the jolting process of a series of partial measures. This is my opinion, but I have no intention, as at present advised, of signifying it. I have all along in public declarations avoided offering anything to the nationalists, beyond describing the limiting rule which must govern the question. It is for them to ask, and for us, as I think, to leave the space so defined as open and unencumbered as possible. I am much struck by the increased breadth of Salisbury's declaration last night; he dropped the ' I do not see how.'

We shall see how these great and difficult matters develop themselves. Meantime be assured that, with a good deal of misgiving as to the future, I shall do what little I can towards enabling all liberals at present to hold together with credit and good conscience.

V

Mr. Gladstone's cardinal deliverance in November had been preceded by an important event. On October 7, 1885, Lord Salisbury made that speech at Newport, which is one of the tallest and most striking landmarks in the shifting sands of this controversy. It must be taken in relation to Lord Carnarvon's declaration of policy on taking office, and to his exchange of views with Mr. Parnell at the end of July. Their first principle, said Lord Salisbury, was to extend to Ireland, so far as they could, all the institutions of this country. But one must remember that in Ireland the population is on several subjects deeply divided, and a government is bound 'on all matters of essential justice' to protect a minority against a majority. Then came remarkable sentences: 'Local authorities are more exposed to the temptation of enabling the majority to be unjust to the minority when they obtain jurisdiction over a small area, than is the case when the authority derives its sanction and extends its jurisdiction over a wider area. In a large central authority, the wisdom of several parts of the country will correct the folly and mistakes of one. In a local authority, that correction is to a much greater extent wanting, and it would be impossible to leave that out of sight, in any extension of any such local authority in Ireland.' This principle was often used in the later controversy as a recognition by Lord Salisbury that the creation of a great central body would be a safer policy than the mere extension of self-government in Irish counties. In another part of the speech, it is true, the finger-post or weather-vane pointed in the opposite direction. 'With respect to the larger organic questions connected with Ireland,' said Lord Salisbury, 'I cannot say much, though I can speak emphatically. I have nothing to say but that the traditions of the party to which we belong, are on this point clear and distinct, and you may rely upon it our party will not depart from them.' Yet this emphatic refusal to depart from the traditions of the tory party did not prevent Lord Salisbury from retaining at that moment in his cabinet an Irish viceroy, with whom he

was in close personal relations, and whose active Irish policy
he must have known to be as wide a breach in tory tradition
as the mind of man can imagine.   So hard is it in distracted
times, the reader may reflect, even for men of honourable
and lofty motive to be perfectly ingenuous.

The speaker next referred to the marked way in which
Mr. Parnell, a day or two before, had mentioned the position
of Austro-Hungary.   'I gathered that some notion of imperial federation was floating in his mind.   With respect to
Ireland, I am bound to say that I have never seen any plan
or any suggestion which gives me at present the slightest
ground for anticipating that it is in that direction that we
shall find any substantial solution of the difficulties of the
problem.'   In an electric state of the political atmosphere, a
statesman who said that at present he did not think federal
home rule possible, was taken to imply that he might think
it possible by-and-by.   No door was closed.

It was, however, Lord Salisbury's language upon social
order that gave most scandal to simple consciences in his
own ranks.   You ask us, he said, why we did not renew the
Crimes Act.   There are two answers: we could not, and
it would have done no good if we could.   To follow the
extension of the franchise by coercion, would have been a
gross inconsistency.   To show confidence by one act, and
the absence of confidence by a simultaneous act, would be
to stultify parliament.   Your inconsistency would have provoked such intense exasperation, that it would have led to
ten times more evil, ten times more resistance to the law,
than your Crimes Act could possibly have availed to check.
Then the audience was favoured with a philosophic view of
boycotting.   This, said the minister, is an offence which
legislation has very great difficulty in reaching.   The provisions of the Crimes Act against it had a very small effect.
It grew up under that Act.   And, after all, look at boycotting.   An unpopular man or his family go to mass.   The
congregation with one accord get up and walk out.   Are you
going to indict people for leaving church?   The plain fact
is that boycotting 'is more like the excommunication or
interdict of the middle ages, than anything that we know

now.'   ' The truth about boycotting is that it depends on the passing humour of the population.'

It is important to remember that in the month immediately preceding this polished apologetic, there were delivered some of the most violent boycotting speeches ever made in Ireland.[1]   These speeches must have been known to the Irish government, and their occurrence and the purport of them must presumably have been known therefore to the prime minister.   Here was indeed a removal of the ancient buoys and beacons that had hitherto guided English navigation in Irish waters.   There was even less of a solid ultimatum at Newport, than in those utterances in Midlothian which were at that time and long afterwards found so culpably vague, blind, and elusive.   Some of the more astute of the minister's own colleagues were delighted with his speech, as keeping the Irishmen steady to the tory party.   They began to hope that they might even come within five-and-twenty of the liberals when the polling began.

The question on which side the Irish vote in Great Britain should be thrown seems not to have been decided until after Mr. Gladstone's speech.   It was then speedily settled.   On Nov. 21 a manifesto was issued, handing over the Irish vote in Great Britain solid to the orator of the Newport speech.   The tactics were obvious.   It was Mr. Parnell's interest to bring the two contending British parties as near as might be to a level, and this he could only hope to do by throwing his strength upon the weaker side.   It was from the weaker side, if they could be retained in office, that he would get the best terms.[2]   The document was composed with vigour and astuteness.   But the phrases of the manifesto were the least important part of it.   It was enough that the hard word was passed.   Some estimated the loss to the liberal party in this island at twenty seats, others at forty.   Whether twenty or forty, these lost seats made a fatal difference in the division on the Irish bill a few months later, and when

---

[1] Some of them are set out in Special Commission *Report*, pp. 99, 100.
[2] See Mr. Gladstone upon these tactics in his fifth Midlothian speech, Nov. 24, 1885.   Also in the seventh, Nov. 28, pp. 159-60.

that day had come and gone, Mr. Parnell sometimes ruefully
asked himself whether the tactics of the electoral manifesto
were not on the whole a mistake.   But this was not all and
was not the worst of it.   The Irish manifesto became a fiery
element in a sharp electioneering war, and threw the liberals
in all constituencies where there was an Irish vote into a
direct and angry antagonism to the Irish cause and its
leaders ; passions were roused, and things were said about
Irishmen that could not at once be forgotten ; and the great
task of conversion in 1886, difficult in any case, was made
a thousand times more difficult still by the arguments and
antipathies of the electoral battle of 1885.   Meanwhile it
was for the moment, and for the purposes of the moment,
a striking success.

CHAPTER II

THE POLLS IN 1885

(1885)

I WOULD say that civil liberty can have no security without political power. — C. J. Fox.

BOOK
IX.

1885.
THE election ran a chequered course (Nov. 23–Dec. 19). It was the first trial of the whole body of male householders, and it was the first trial of the system of single-member districts. This is not the place for a discussion of the change of electoral area. As a scheme for securing representation of minorities it proved of little efficacy, and many believe that the substitution of a smaller constituency for a larger one has tended to slacken political interest, and to narrow political judgment. Meanwhile some of those who were most deeply concerned in establishing the new plan, were confident that an overwhelming liberal triumph would be the result. Many of their opponents took the same view, and were in despair. A liberal met a tory minister on the steps of a club in Pall Mall, as they were both going to the country for their elections. 'I suppose,' said the tory, 'we are out for twenty years to come.' *O pectora cœca!* He has been in office for nearly fifteen of the eighteen years since. In September one of the most authoritative liberal experts did not see how the tories were to have more than 210 out of the 670 seats, including the tory contingent from Ireland. Two months later the expert admitted that the tory chances were improving, mainly owing to what in electioneering slang was called the church scare. Fair trade, too, had made many converts in Lancashire. On the very eve of the polls the estimate at liberal headquarters was a majority of forty over tories and Irishmen combined.

246

II

As I should have told the reader on an earlier page, Mr. Gladstone had proceeded to his own constituency on November 9. The previous month had found, as usual, endless other interests to occupy him, quite apart from politics. These are the ordinary entries. 'Worked, say, five hours on books. Three more hours reduced my books and rooms to apparent order, but much detail remains. Worked mildly on books.' In this region he would have said of disorder and disarray what Carlyle said to dirt, 'Thou shalt not abide with me.' As to the insides of books, his reading was miscellaneous: Madame d'Arblay, Bodley's *Remains*, Bachaumont's *Anecdotes*, Cuvier's *Theory of the Earth*, Whewell on *Astronomy*, the *Life of B. Gilpin*, Hennell's *Inquiry*, Schmidt's *Social Effects of Christianity*, Miss Martineau's *Autobiography*, Anderson on *Glory of the Bible*, Barrow's *Towards the Truth*, and so on — many of the books now stone-dead. Besides such reading as this, he 'made a beginning of a paper on Hermes, and read for it,' and worked hard at a controversial article, in reply to M. Réville, upon the Dawn of Creation and Worship. When he corrected the proof, he found it ill-written, and in truth we may rather marvel at, than admire, the hardihood that handled such themes amid such distractions.[1] Much company arrived. 'Count Münster came to luncheon; long walk and talk with him. The Derby-Bedford party came and went. I had an hour's good conversation with Lord D. Tea in the open air. *Oct.* 7. — Mr. Chamberlain came. Well, and much conversation. *Oct.* 8. — Mr. Chamberlain. Three hours of conversation.

Before the end of the month the doctors reported excellently of the condition of his vocal cords, and when he started for Dalmeny and the scene of the exploits of 1880 once more, he was in spirits to enjoy 'an animated journey,' and the vast enthusiasm with which Edinburgh again received him. His speeches were marked by undiminished fire. He boldly challenged a verdict on policy in the Soudan, while freely admitting that in some points, not immaterial, his cabinet had fallen into error, though in every case the error was fostered by the party opposite; and he pointed to the vital

[1] *Nineteenth Century*, November 1885 ; reprinted in *Later Gleanings*.

fact that though the party opposite were in good time, they never dreamed of altering the policy. He asked triumphantly how they would have fared in the Afghan dispute, if the policy anterior to 1880 had not been repudiated. In his address he took the same valiant line about South Africa. 'In the Transvaal,' he said, 'we averted a war of European and Christian races throughout South African states, which would have been alike menacing to our power, and scandalous in the face of civilisation and of Christendom. As this has been with our opponents a favourite subject of unmeasured denunciation, so I for one hail and reciprocate their challenge, and I hope the nation will give a clear judgment on our refusal to put down liberty by force, and on the measures that have brought about the present tranquillity of South Africa.' His first speech was on Ireland, and Ireland figured, as we have seen, largely and emphatically to the last. Disestablishment was his thorniest topic, for the scare of the church in danger was working considerable havoc in England, and every word on Scottish establishment was sure to be translated to establishment elsewhere. On the day on which he was to handle it, his entry is: 'Much rumination, and made notes which in speaking I could not manage to see. Off to Edinburgh at 2.30. Back at 6. Spoke seventy minutes in Free Kirk Hall: a difficult subject. The present agitation does not strengthen in my mind the principle of establishment.' His leading text was a favourite and a salutary maxim of his, that 'it is a very serious responsibility to take political questions out of their proper time and their proper order,' and the summary of his speech was that the party was agreed upon certain large and complicated questions, such as were enough for one parliament to settle, and that it would be an error to attempt to thrust those questions aside, to cast them into the shade and the darkness, 'for the sake of a subject of which I will not undervalue the importance, but of which I utterly deny the maturity at the present moment.'[1]

On Nov. 27 the poll was taken; 11,241 electors out of 12,924, or 87 per cent., recorded their votes, and of these 7879 voted for Mr. Gladstone, and 3248 for Mr. Dalrymple, or a majority of 4631. So little impression had been made

[1] Speech in the Free Assembly Hall, Nov. 11, 1885.

in Midlothian by Kilmainham, Majuba, Khartoum, Penjdeh,
and the other party cries of a later period.

III

Let us turn to the general result, and the final composition of Mr. Gladstone's thirteenth parliament. The polls of the first three or four days were startling. It looked, in the phrases of the time, as if there were conservative reaction all round, as if the pendulum had swung back to the point of tory triumph in 1874, and as if early reverses would wind up in final rout. Where the tories did not capture the seat, their numbers rose and the liberal majorities fell. At the end of four days the liberals in England and Wales had scored 86 against 109 for their adversaries. When two-thirds of the House had been elected, the liberals counted 196, the tories 179, and the Irish nationalists 37. In spite of the early panic or exultation, it was found that in boroughs of over 100,000 the liberals had after all carried seventeen, against eight for their opponents. But the tories were victorious in a solid Liverpool, save one Irish seat; they won all the seats in Manchester save one; and in London, where liberals had been told by those who were believed to know, that they would make a clean sweep, there were thirty-six tories against twenty-six liberals. Two members of the late liberal cabinet and three subordinate ministers were thrown out. 'The verdict of the English borough constituencies,' cried the *Times*, 'will be recorded more emphatically than was even the case in 1874 in favour of the conservatives. The opposition have to thank Mr. Chamberlain not only for their defeat at the polls, but for the irremediable disruption and hopeless disorganisation of the liberal party with its high historic past and its high claims to national gratitude. His achievement may give him such immortality as was won by the man who burned down the temple of Diana at Ephesus.'[1] The same writers have ever since ascribed the irremediable disruption to Mr. Gladstone and the Irish question.

Now came the counties with their newly enfranchised

[1] November 26, 1885.

hosts.   Here the tide flowed strong and steady.   Squire and parson were amazed to see the labourer, of whose stagnant indifference to politics they had been so confident, trudging four or five miles to a political meeting, listening without asking for a glass of beer to political speeches, following point upon point, and then trudging back again dumbly chewing the cud.   Politicians with gifts of rhetoric began to talk of the grand revolt of the peasants, and declared that it was the most remarkable transformation since the conversion of the Franks.   Turned into prose, this meant that the liberals had extended their area into large rural provinces where hitherto tory supremacy had never been disputed. Whether or no Mr. Chamberlain had broken the party in the boroughs, his agrarian policy together with the natural uprising of the labourer against the party of squire and farmer, had saved it in the counties.   The nominees of such territorial magnates as the Northumberlands, the Pembrokes, the Baths, the Bradfords, the Watkin Wynns, were all routed, and the shock to territorial influence was felt to be profound.   An ardent agrarian reformer, who later became a conspicuous unionist, writing to Mr. Gladstone in July a description of a number of great rural gatherings, told him, ' One universal feature of these meetings is the joy, affection, and unbounded applause with which your name is received by these earnest men.   Never in all your history had you so strong a place in the hearts of the common people, as you have to-day.   It requires to be seen to be realised.'

All was at last over.   It then appeared that so far from there being a second version of the great tory reaction of 1874, the liberals had now in the new parliament a majority over tories of 82, or thirty under the corresponding majority in the year of marvel, 1880.   In great Britain they had a majority of 100, being 333 against 233.[1]   But

[1] *Result of General Election of* 1885 : —

	L.	C.	P.
English and Welsh boroughs and universities,	93	86	1
Metropolis,	26	36	0
English and Welsh counties,	152	101	0
Scottish boroughs,	30	3	0
" counties,	32	7	0
Ireland,	0	18	85
	333	251	86

they had no majority over tories and Irishmen combined.
That hopeful dream had glided away through the ivory gate.

Shots between right wing and left of the liberal party
were exchanged to the very last moment. When the
borough elections were over, the Birmingham leader cried
that so far from the loss in the boroughs being all the
fault of the extreme liberals, it was just because the election
had not been fought on their programme, but was fought
instead on a manifesto that did not include one of the points
to which the extreme liberals attached the greatest importance. For the sake of unity, they had put aside their
most cherished principles, disestablishment for instance, and
this, forsooth, was the result.[1] The retort came as quickly
as thunder after the flash. Lord Hartington promptly protested from Matlock, that the very crisis of the electoral
conflict was an ill-chosen moment for the public expression
of doubt by a prominent liberal as to the wisdom of a policy
accepted by the party, and announced by the acknowledged
leader of the whole party. When the party had found some
more tried, more trusted, more worthy leader, then might
perhaps be the time to impugn the policy. These reproachful ironies of Lord Hartington boded ill for any prospect of
the heroes of this fratricidal war of the platform smoothing
their wrinkled fronts in a liberal cabinet.

IV

In Ireland the result shed a strong light on the debating
prophecies that the extension of the county franchise would

The following figures may also be found interesting : —

Election of 1868 —

English and Welsh Liberals,	267
" " Tories,	225
Majority,	42

In 1880 —

English and Welsh Liberals,	284
" " Tories,	205
Majority,	79

In 1885 —

English and Welsh Liberals,	270
" " Tories,	223
Majority,	47

[1] Mr. Chamberlain at Leicester, December 3, 1885.

not be unfavourable to the landlord interest ; that it would enable the deep conservative interest of the peasantry to vindicate itself against the nationalism of the towns ; that it would prove beyond all doubt that the Irish leader did not really speak the mind of a decided majority of the people of Ireland. Relying on the accuracy of these abstract predictions, the Irish tories started candidates all over the country. Even some of them who passed for shrewd and candid actually persuaded themselves that they were making an impression on the constituencies. The effect of their ingenuous operations was to furnish such a measure of nationalist strength, as would otherwise have seemed incredible almost to the nationalists themselves. An instance or two will suffice. In two divisions of Cork, the tories polled 300 votes against nearly 10,000 for the nationalists. In two divisions of Mayo, the tories polled 200 votes against nearly 10,000 for the nationalists. In one division of Kilkenny there were 4000 nationalist votes against 170 for the tory, and in another division 4000 against 220. In a division of Kerry the nationalist had over 3000 votes against 30 for the tory, — a hundred to one. In prosperous counties with resident landlords and a good class of gentry such as Carlow and Kildare, in one case the popular vote was 4800 against 750, and in the other 3169 against 467. In some fifty constituencies the popular majorities ranged in round numbers from 6500 the highest, to 2400 the lowest. Besides these constituencies where a contest was so futile, were those others in which no contest was even attempted.

In Ulster a remarkable thing happened. This favoured province had in the last parliament returned nine liberals. Lord Hartington attended a banquet at Belfast (Nov. 5) just before the election. It was as unlucky an affair as the feast of Belshazzar. His mission was compared by Orange wits to that of the Greek hero who went forth to wrestle with Death for the body of an old woman. The whole of the liberal candidates in Ulster fell down as dead men. Orangemen and catholics, the men who cried damnation to King William and the men who cried 'To hell with the Pope,' joined hands against them. In Belfast itself, nationalists were

seen walking to the booths with orange cards in their hats
to vote for orangemen against liberals.[1] It is true that the
paradox did not last, and that the Pope and King William
were speedily on their old terms again.   Within six months,
the two parties atoned for this temporary backsliding into
brotherly love, by one of the most furious and protracted
conflagrations that ever raged even in the holy places of
Belfast.   Meanwhile nationalism had made its way in the
south of the province, partly by hopes of reduced rents,
partly by the energy of the catholic population, who had not
tasted political power for two centuries.   The adhesion of
their bishops to the national movement in the Monaghan
election had given them the signal three years before.
Fermanagh, hitherto invariably Orange, now sent two
nationalists.   Antrim was the single county out of the
thirty-two counties of Ireland that was solid against home
rule, and even in Antrim in one contest the nationalist was
beaten only by 35 votes.

Not a single liberal was returned in the whole of Ireland.
To the last parliament she had sent fourteen.   They were
all out bag and baggage.   Ulster now sent eighteen nationalists and seventeen tories.   Out of the eighty-nine contests
in Ireland, Mr. Parnell's men won no fewer than eighty-five,
and in most of them they won by such overwhelming
majorities as I have described.   It was noticed that twenty-
two of the persons elected, or more than one-fourth of the
triumphant party, had been put in prison under the Act of
1881.   A species of purge, moreover, had been performed.
All half-hearted nationalists, the doubters and the faithless,
were dismissed, and their places taken by men pledged
either to obey or else go.

The British public now found out on what illusions they
had for the last four years been fed.   Those of them who
had memories, could recollect how the Irish secretary of
the day, on the third reading of the first Coercion bill in
1881, had boldly appealed from the Irish members to the
people of Ireland. ' He was sure that he could appeal with
confidence from gentlemen sitting below the gangway
opposite to their constituents.'[2]   They remembered all the

---

[1] Macknight's *Ulster as it Is*, ii. p. 108.   [2] Mr. Forster, March 11, 1881.

talk about Mr. Parnell and his followers being a mere handful of men and not a political party at all, and the rest of it.
They had now a revelation what a fool's paradise it had been.

As a supreme electoral demonstration, the Irish elections
of 1885 have never been surpassed in any country. They
showed that neither remedial measures nor repressive measures had made even the fleeting shadow of an impression
on the tenacious sentiment of Ireland, or on the powerful
organisation that embodied and directed it. The Land Act
had made no impression. The two Coercion Acts had made
none. The imperial parliament had done its best for five
years. Some of the ablest of its ministers had set zealous
and intrepid hands to the task, and this was the end.
Whether you counted seats or counted votes, the result
could not be twisted into anything but what it was — the
vehement protest of one of the three kingdoms against the
whole system of its government, and a strenuous demand for
its reconstruction on new foundations.

Endeavours were made to discredit so startling and unwelcome a result. It was called 'the carefully prepared
verdict of a shamefully packed jury.' Much was made of
the number of voters who declared themselves illiterate,
said to be compelled so to do in order that the priest or
other intimidatory person might see that they voted right.
As a matter of fact the percentage of illiterate voters
answered closely to the percentage of males over twenty-one
in the census returns, who could neither read nor write.
Only two petitions followed the general election, one at
Belfast against a nationalist, and the other at Derry against
a tory, and in neither of the two was undue influence or
intimidation alleged. The routed candidates in Ireland, like
the same unlucky species elsewhere, raised the usual chorus
of dolorous explanation. The register, they cried, was in
a shameful condition; the polling stations were too few or
too remote; the loyalists were afraid, and the poll did not
represent their real numbers; people did not believe that
the ballot was really secret; the percentage of illiterates was
monstrous; promises and pledges went for nothing. Such
are ever the too familiar voices of mortified electioneering

There was also the best known of all the conclusive topics from tory Ireland. It was all done, vowed the tories, by the bishops and clergy; they were indefatigable; they canvassed at the houses and presided at meetings; they exhorted their flocks from the altar, and they drilled them at the polling-booths. The spiritual screw of the priest and the temporal screw of the league — there was the whole secret. Such was the story, and it was not wholly devoid of truth ; but then what balm, what comfort, had even the truth of it for British rulers ?

Some thousands of voters stayed away from the polls. It was ingeniously explained that their confidence in British rule had been destroyed by the Carnarvon surrender ; a shopkeeper would not offend his customers for the sake of a Union Jack that no longer waved triumphant in the breeze. They were like the Arab sheikhs at Berber, who, when they found that the Egyptian pashas were going to evacuate, went over to the Mahdi. The conventions appointed to select the candidates were denounced as the mere creatures of Mr. Parnell, the Grand Elector. As if anything could have shown a more politic appreciation of the circumstances. There are situations that require a dictator, not to impose an opinion, but to kindle an aspiration ; not to shape a demand, but to be the effective organ of opinion and demand. Now in the Irish view was one of those situations. In the last parliament twenty-six seats were held by persons designated nominal home rulers ; in the new parliament, not one. Every new nationalist member pledged himself to resign whenever the parliamentary party should call upon him. Such an instrument grasped in a hand of iron was indispensable, first to compel the British government to listen, and second, to satisfy any British government disposed to listen, that in dealing with Mr. Parnell they were dealing with nationalist Ireland, and with a statesman who had the power to make his engagements good. You need greater qualities, said Cardinal De Retz, to be a good party leader than to be emperor of the universe. Ireland is not that portion of the universe in which this is least true.

CHAPTER III

A CRITICAL MONTH

(*December 1885*)

WHOEVER has held the post of minister for any considerable time can never absolutely, unalterably maintain and carry out his original opinions. He finds himself in the presence of situations that are not always the same — of life and growth — in connection with which he must take one course one day, and then, perhaps, another on the next day. I could not always run straight ahead like a cannon ball. — BISMARCK.

BOOK
IX.

1885.

THE month of December was passed by Mr. Gladstone at Hawarden, in such depth of meditation as it is easy for us to conjecture. The composition of his party, the new situation in parliament, the mutual relations of important individuals, the Irish case, his own share in respect of the Irish case, the strange new departure in Irish policy announced and acted upon by the subsisting cabinet — from all these points of view it was now his business to survey the extraordinary scene. The knot to be unravelled in 1886 was hardly less entangled than that which engaged the powerful genius of Pitt at the opening of the century. Stripped of invidious innuendo, the words of Lord Salisbury a few weeks later state with strength and truth the problem that now confronted parliament and its chief men. 'Up to the time,' said the tory prime minister, 'when Mr. Gladstone took office, be it for good or evil, for many generations Ireland had been governed through the influence and the action of the landed gentry. I do not wish to defend that system. There is a good deal to be said for it, and a good deal to be said against it. What I wish to insist upon is, not that that system was good, but that the statesman who undertook to overthrow it, should have had something to put in its place.

256

He utterly destroyed it.   By the Land Act of 1870, by the
Ballot Act of 1872, by the Land Act of 1881, and last of all
by the Reform bill of 1884, the power of the landed gentry
in Ireland is absolutely shattered ; and he now stands before
the formidable problem of a country deprived of a system of
government under which it had existed for many generations, and absolutely without even a sketch of a substitute
by which the ordinary functions of law and order can be
maintained.   Those changes which he introduced into the
government of Ireland were changes that were admirable
from a parliamentary point of view.   They were suited to
the dominant humour of the moment.   But they were
barren of any institutions by which the country could be
governed and kept in prosperity for the future.'[1]   This is
a statement of the case that biographer and historian alike
should ponder.   Particularly should they remember that
both parties had renounced coercion.

Mr. Gladstone has publicly explained the working of his
mind, and both his private letters at the time, and many a
conversation later, attest the hold which the new aspect,
however chimerical it may now seem to those who do not
take long views, had gained upon him.   He could not be
blind to the fact that the action and the language of the
tory ministers during the last six months had shown an
unquestionable readiness to face the new necessities of a complex situation with new methods.   Why should not a solution
of the present difficulties be sought in the same co-operation
of parties, that had been as advantageous as it was indispensable in other critical occasions of the century ?   He
recalled other leading precedents of national crisis.   There
was the repeal of the Test Act in 1828; catholic emancipation in 1829 ; the repeal of the corn law in 1846 ; the
extension of the franchise in 1867.   In the history of these
memorable transactions, Mr. Gladstone perceived it to be
extremely doubtful whether any one of these measures, all
carried as they were by tory governments, could have become
law except under the peculiar conditions which secured for

[1] Lord Salisbury, at a dinner given   members for Hertfordshire, February
in London to the four conservative   17, 1886.

each of them both the aid of the liberal vote in the House of Commons, and the authority possessed by all tory governments in the House of Lords. What was the situation? The ministerial party just reached the figure of two hundred and fifty-one. Mr. Gladstone had said in the course of the election that for a government in a minority to deal with the Irish question would not be safe, such an operation could not but be attended by danger; but the tender of his support to Lord Salisbury was a demonstration that he thought the operation might still properly be undertaken.[1]

To Herbert Gladstone.

December 10, 1885. — 1. The nationalists have run in political alliance with the tories for years; more especially for six months; most of all at the close during the elections, when *they* have made us 335 (say) against 250 [conservatives] instead of 355 against 230. This alliance is therefore at its zenith. 2. The question of Irish government ought for the highest reasons to be settled at once, and settled by the allied forces, (1) because they have the government, (2) because their measure will have fair play from all, most, or many of us, which a measure of ours would not have from the tories. 3. As the allied forces are half the House, so that there is not a majority against them, no constitutional principle is violated by allowing the present cabinet to continue undisturbed for the purpose in view. 4. The plan for Ireland ought to be produced by the government of the day. Principles may be laid down by others, but not the detailed interpretation of them in a measure. I have publicly declared I produce no plan until the government has arrived at some issue with the Irish, as I hope they will. 5. If the moment ever came when a plan had to be considered with a view to production on behalf of the liberal party, I do not at present see how such a question could be dissociated from another vital question, namely, who are to be the government. For a government alone can carry a measure, though some outline of essentials might be put out in a motion or resolution.

Happening in these days to meet in the neighbouring

[1] *Special Aspects of the Irish Question*, p. 18.

palace of a whig magnate, Mr. Balfour, a young but even CHAP.
III.
then an important member of the government, with whom
as a veteran with a junior of high promise he had long Æt. 76.
been on terms of friendly intimacy, Mr. Gladstone began
an informal conversation with him upon the condition of
Ireland, on the stir that it was making in men's minds,
and on the urgency of the problem. The conversation he
followed up by a letter (Dec. 20). Every post, he said, bore
him testimony to the growing ferment. In urging how
great a calamity it would be if so vast a question should
fall into the lines of party conflict, he expressed his desire
to see it taken up by the government, and to be able, with
reserve of necessary freedom, to co-operate in their design.
Mr. Balfour replied with courteous scepticism, but promised
to inform Lord Salisbury. The tactical computation was
presumably this, that Lord Salisbury would lose the Orange
group from Ireland and the extreme tories in England, but
would keep the bulk of his party. On the other hand, Mr.
Gladstone in supporting a moderate home rule would drop
some of the old whigs and some of the extreme radicals, but
he too would keep the bulk of the liberal party. Therefore,
even if Mr. Parnell and his followers should find the scheme
too moderate to be endurable, still Lord Salisbury with Mr.
Gladstone's help would settle the Irish question as Peel
with the help of the whigs settled the question of corn.

Both at the time and afterwards Mr. Gladstone was wont
to lay great stress upon the fact that he had opened this suggestion and conveyed this proffer of support. For instance,
he writes to Lord Hartington (Dec. 20): 'On Tuesday I
had a conversation with Balfour at Eaton, which in conformity with my public statements, I think, conveyed informally
a hope that they would act, as the matter is so serious, and
as its becoming a party question would be a great national
calamity. I have written to him to say (without speaking
for others) that if they can make a proposal for the purpose
of settling definitely the question of Irish government, I
shall wish with proper reserves to treat it in the spirit in
which I have treated Afghanistan and the Balkan Peninsula.'

The language of Lord Carnarvon when he took office and

of Lord Salisbury at Newport, coupled with the more substantial fact of the alliance between tories and nationalists
before and during the election, no doubt warranted Mr.
Gladstone's assumption that the alliance might continue,
and that the talk of a new policy had been something more
than an electioneering manœuvre. Yet the importance that
he always attached to his offer of support for a definite
settlement, or in plainer English, some sort of home rule,
implies a certain simplicity. He forgot in his patriotic zeal
the party system. The tory leader, capable as his public
utterances show of piercing the exigencies of Irish government to the quick, might possibly, in the course of responsible consultations with opponents for a patriotic purpose,
have been drawn by argument and circumstance on to the
ground of Irish autonomy, which he had hitherto considered,
and considered with apparent favour, only in the dim distance of abstract meditation or through the eyes of Lord
Carnarvon. The abstract and intellectual temperament is
sometimes apt to be dogged and stubborn ; on the other
hand, it is often uncommonly elastic. Lord Salisbury's clear
and rationalising understanding might have been expected
to carry him to a thoroughgoing experiment to get rid of a
deep and inveterate disorder. If he thought it politic to
assent to communication with Mr. Parnell, why should he
not listen to overtures from Mr. Gladstone ? On the other
hand, Lord Salisbury's hesitation in facing the perils of
an Irish settlement in reliance upon the co-operation of
political opponents is far from being unintelligible. His
inferior parliamentary strength would leave him at the
mercy of an extremely formidable ally. He may have
anticipated that, apart from the ordinary temptations of
every majority to overthrow a minority, all the strong
natural impulses of the liberal leader, his vehement sympathy with the principle of nationality, the irresistible
attraction for him of all the grand and eternal commonplaces of liberty and self-government, would inevitably
carry him much further on the Irish road than either Lord
Salisbury himself may have been disposed to travel, or than
he could be sure of persuading his party to follow. He may

the *Times*. However, I repeated yesterday to R. Grosvenor all
that I have said to you about what seems to me the plain duty of
the *party*, in the event of a severance between nationalists and
tories. Meantime I care not who knows my anxiety to prevent that
severance, and for that reason among others to avoid all communications of ideas and intentions which could tend to bring it about.

On December 27, Lord Granville wrote to Mr. Gladstone
at Hawarden : —

I have been asked to request you to call a cabinet of your late
colleagues to discuss the present state of affairs. I have declined,
giving my reasons, which appear to me to be good. At the same
time, I think it would calm some fussiness that exists, if you let
it be known to a few that you will be in town and ready for consultation, before the actual meeting.

Mr. Gladstone answered, as those acquainted with his
modes of mind might have been sure that he would : —

December 28. — Thank you for stopping the request to which
your letter of yesterday refers. A cabinet does not exist out of
office, and no one in his senses could covenant to call *the late
cabinet* together, I think, even if there were something on which
it was ready to take counsel, which at this moment there is not.
On the other hand, you will have seen from my letter that the
idea before me has been that of going unusual lengths in the way
of consulting beforehand, not only leading men but the party, or
undertaking some special obligation to be assured of their concurrence generally, before undertaking new responsibilities.

The one great difficulty in proceeding to consult now, I think,
is that we cannot define the situation for ourselves, as an essential
element of it is the relation between nationalists and tories, which
they — not we — have to settle. If we meet on Tuesday 12th to
choose a Speaker, so far as I can learn, regular business will not
begin before the 19th. By the 12th we shall have given ourselves
a much better chance of knowing how the two parties stand together; and there will be plenty of time for our consultations.
Thus at least I map out the time; pray give me any comments
you think required.

I begged you to keep Derby informed; would you kindly do the same with Harcourt? Rosebery goes to London to-morrow.

Two days before this resistance to the request for a meeting, he had written to Lord Granville with an important enclosure : —

December 26, 1885.— I have put down on paper in a memorandum as well as I can, the possible forms of the question which may have to be decided at the opening of the session. I went over the ground in conversation with you, and afterwards with R. Grosvenor, and I requested R. Grosvenor, who was going to London, to speak to Hartington in that sense. After his recent act of publication, I should not like to challenge him by sending him the written paper. Please, however, to send it on to Spencer, who will send it back to me.

The memorandum itself must here be quoted, for it sets out in form, succinct, definite, and exhaustive, the situation as Mr. Gladstone at that time regarded it : —

Secret.   *Hawarden Castle, Chester, Dec.* 26, 1885.

1. Government should act.
2. Nationalists should support them in acting.
3. I have done what I can to bring about (1). I am confident the nationalists know my desire. They also publicly know there can be no plan from me in the present circumstances.
4. If (1) and (2) come about, we, who are half the House of Commons, may under the circumstances be justified in waiting for the production of a plan.
5. This would be in every sense the best situation.
6. But if ministers refuse to take up the question — or if from their not actually taking it up, or on any grounds, the nationalists publicly dissolve their alliance with them, the government then have a party of 250 in the face of 420, and in the face of 335 who were elected to oppose them.
7. The basis of our system is that the ministry shall have the confidence of the House of Commons. The exception is, when it is about to appeal to the people. The rule applies most strongly when an election has just taken place. Witness 1835, 1841, 1859,

and the *three* last elections, after each of which the rule has been acted upon, silent inference standing instead of a vote.

8. The present circumstances warrant, I think, an understanding as above, between ministers and the nationalists; but not one between us and the nationalists.

9. If from any cause the alliance of the tories and nationalists which did exist, and presumably does exist, should be known to be dissolved, I do not see how it is possible for what would then be the liberal majority to shrink from the duty appertaining to it as such, and to leave the business of government to the 250 men whom it was elected to oppose.

10. This looks towards an amendment to the Address, praying her Majesty to choose ministers possessed of the confidence of the House of Commons.

11. Which under the circumstances should, I think, have the sanction of a previous meeting of the party.

12. An attempt would probably be made to traverse the proceeding by drawing me on the Irish question.

13. It is impossible to justify the contention that *as a condition previous* to asserting the right and duty of a parliamentary majority, the party or the leaders should commit themselves on a measure about which they can form no final judgment, until by becoming the government they can hold all the necessary communications.

14. But in all likelihood jealousy will be stronger than logic; and to obviate such jealousy, it might be right for me [to go] to the very farthest allowable point.

15. The case supposed is, the motion made — carried — ministers resign — Queen sends for me.

Might I go so far as to say at the first meeting that in the case supposed, I should only accept the trust if assured of the adequate, that is of the general, support of the party to a plan of duly guarded home rule ?

16. If that support were withheld, it would be my duty to stand aside.

17. In that event it would, I consider, become the duty of that portion of the party, which was not prepared to support me in an effort to frame a plan of duly guarded home rule, to form a government itself if invited by the Queen to do so.

18. With me the Irish question would of course remain paramount; but preferring a liberal government without an adequate Irish measure to a tory government similarly lacking, such a liberal government would be entitled to the best general support I could give it.

The reference of this memorandum to Lords Granville and Spencer was regarded as one of the first informal steps towards a consultation of leaders. On receiving Lord Spencer's reply on the point of procedure Mr. Gladstone wrote to him (December 30) : —

To Lord Spencer.

I understand your idea to be that inasmuch as leaders of the party are likely to be divided on the subject of a bold Irish measure, and a divergence might be exhibited in a vote on the Address, it may be better to allow the tory government, with 250 supporters in a house of 670, to assume the direction of the session and continue the administration of imperial affairs. I do not undervalue the dangers of the other course. But let us look at this one —

1. It is an absolute novelty.

2. Is it not a novelty which strikes at the root of our parliamentary government ? under which the first duty of a majority freshly elected, according to a uniform course of precedent and a very clear principle, is to establish a government which has its confidence.

3. Will this abdication of primary duty avert or materially postpone the (apprehended) disruption of the party ? Who can guarantee us against an Irish or independent amendment to the Address ? The government must in any case produce at once their Irish plan. What will have been gained by waiting for it ? The Irish will know three things—(1) That I am conditionally in favour of at least examining their demand. (2) That from the nature of the case, I must hold this question paramount to every interest of party. (3) That a part, to speak within bounds, of the liberal party will follow me in this respect. Can it be supposed that in these circumstances they will long refrain, or possibly refrain at all ? With their knowledge of possibilities behind them,

dare they long refrain ?   An immense loss of dignity in a great
crisis of the empire would attend the forcing of our hands by
the Irish or otherwise.   There is no necessity for an instant
decision.   My desire is thoroughly to shake up all the materials
of the question.   The present leaning of my mind is to consider
the faults and dangers of abstention greater than those of a more
decided course.   Hence, in part, my great anxiety that the present
government should move.   Please send this on to Granville.

Finding Mr. Gladstone immovable at Hawarden, four of
the members of the last liberal cabinet of both wings met at
Devonshire House on New Year's day.   All, save one, found
themselves hopeless, especially after the Hawarden revela-
tions, as to the possibility of governing Ireland by mere
repression.   Lord Hartington at once communicated the
desires of the conclave for information of his views and
designs.   Mr. Gladstone replied (January 2, 1886) : —

On the 17th December I communicated to you *all* the opinions
I had formed on the Irish question.   But on the 21st you
published in the *Times* a re-affirmation of opposite opinions.

On the Irish question, I have not a word to add to that letter.
I am indeed doing what little the pressure of correspondence
permits, to prepare myself by study and reflection.   My object
was to facilitate study by you and others — I cannot say it was
wholly gained.   But I have done nothing, and shall do nothing,
to convert those opinions into intentions, for I have not the
material before me.   I do not know whether my 'postulate' is
satisfied. . . .   I have taken care by my letter of the 17th that
you should know my opinions *en bloc*.   You are quite welcome to
show it, if you think fit, to those whom you met.   But Harcourt
has, I believe, seen it, and the others, if I mistake not, know the
substance. . . .   There is no doubt that a very grave situation is
upon us, a little sooner or a little later.   All my desire and
thought was how to render it less grave, for next to the demands
of a question far higher than all or any party interests, is my duty
to labour for the consolidation of the party. . . .   Pray show this
letter, if you think fit, to those on whose behalf you write.   I
propose to be available in London about 4 P.M., for any who wish
to see me.

V

Signals and intimations were not wholly wanting from
the Irish camp. It was known among the subalterns in that
rather impenetrable region, partly by the light of nature,
partly by the indiscretions of dubiously accredited ambassadors, that Mr. Gladstone was not disposed on any terms to
meet the Irish demand by more coercion. For the liberal
party as a whole the Irish had a considerable aversion. The
violent scenes that attended the Coercion bill of 1881, the
interchange of hard words, the suspensions, the imprisonments — all mechanically acquiesced in by the ministerial
majority — had engendered both bitterness and contempt.
The Irishmen did not conceal the satisfaction with which
they saw the defeat of some of those liberals who had
openly gloated over their arrests and all the rest of their
humiliations. Mr. Gladstone, it is true, had laid a heavy
and chastening hand upon them. Yet, even when the
struggle had been fiercest, with the quick intuition of a
people long oppressed, they detected a note of half-sym-
pathetic passion which convinced them that he would be
their friend if he could, and would help them when he might.

Mr. Parnell was not open to impressions of this order. He
had a long memory for injuries, and he had by no means
satisfied himself that the same injuries might not recur.
As soon as the general election was over, he had at once
set to work upon the result. Whatever might be right for
others, his line of tactics was plain — to ascertain from which
of the two English parties he was most likely to obtain the
response that he desired to the Irish demand, and then to
concert the procedure best fitted to place that party in
power. He was at first not sure whether Lord Salisbury
would renounce the Irish alliance after it had served the
double purpose of ousting the liberals from office, and then
reducing their numbers at the election. He seems also to
have counted upon further communications with Lord
Carnarvon, and this expectation was made known to Mr.
Gladstone, who expressed his satisfaction at the news, though
it was also made known to him that Mr. Parnell doubted

Lord Carnarvon's power to carry out his unquestionably favourable dispositions. He at the same time very naturally did his best to get some light as to Mr. Gladstone's own frame of mind. If neither party would offer a solution of the problem of Irish government, Mr. Parnell would prefer to keep the tories in office, as they would at least work out gradually a solution of the problems of Irish land. To all these indirect communications Mr. Gladstone's consistent reply was that Mr. Parnell's immediate business was with the government of the day, first, because only the government could handle the matter; second, because a tory government with the aid that it would receive from liberals, might most certainly, safely, and quickly settle it. He declined to go beyond the ground already publicly taken by him, unless by way of a further public declaration. On to this new ground he would not go, until assured that the government had had a fair opportunity given them.

By the end of December Mr. Parnell decided that there was not the slightest possibility of any settlement being offered by the conservatives under the existing circumstances. 'Whatever chance there was,' he said, 'disappeared when the seemingly authoritative statements of Mr. Gladstone's intention to deal with the question were published.' He regarded it as quite probable that in spite of a direct refusal from the tories, the Irish members might prefer to pull along with them, rather than run the risk of fresh coercion from the liberals, should the latter return to power. 'Supposing,' he argued, 'that the liberals came into office, and that they offered a settlement of so incomplete a character that we could not accept it, or that owing to defections they could not carry it, should we not, if any long interval occurred before the proposal of a fresh settlement, incur considerable risk of further coercion?' At any rate, they had better keep the government in, rather than oust them in order to admit Lord Hartington or Mr. Chamberlain with a new coercion bill in their pockets.

Foreseeing these embarrassments, Mr. Gladstone wrote in a final memorandum (December 24) of this eventful year, 'I used every effort to obtain a clear majority at the election,

and failed. I am therefore at present a man in chains. Will
ministers bring in a measure? If "Aye," I see my way. If
"No": that I presume puts an end to all relations of confidence between nationalists and tories. If that is done, I
have then upon me, as is evident, the responsibilities of
the leader of a majority. But what if neither Aye nor No can
be had — will the nationalists then continue their support
and thus relieve me from responsibility, or withdraw their
support [from the government] and thus change essentially
my position? Nothing but a public or published dissolution
of a relation of amity publicly sealed could be of any avail.'

So the year ended.

CHAPTER IV

FALL OF THE FIRST SALISBURY GOVERNMENT

(January 1886)

HISTORIANS coolly dissect a man's thoughts as they please; and label them like specimens in a naturalist's cabinet. Such a thing, they argue, was done for mere personal aggrandizement; such a thing for national objects; such a thing from high religious motives. In real life we may be sure it was not so. — GARDINER.

MINISTERS meanwhile hesitated, balanced, doubted, and wavered. Their party was in a minority, and so they had a fair plea for resigning and not meeting the new parliament. On the other hand, they had a fair plea for continuing in office, for though they were in a minority, no other party had a majority. Nobody knew what the Hartington whigs would do, or what the Irish would do. There seemed to be many chances for expert angling. Then with what policy were they to meet the House of Commons? They might adhere to the conciliatory policy of the summer and autumn, keep clear of repressive legislation, and make a bold attempt in the direction of self-government. Taking the same courageous plunge as was taken by Wellington and Peel in 1829, by Peel in the winter of 1845, by Disraeli in 1867, they might carry the declarations made by Lord Carnarvon on behalf of the government in July to their only practical conclusion. But then they would have broken up their party, as Wellington and Peel broke it up; and Lord Salisbury may have asked himself whether the national emergency warranted the party risk.

Resistance then to the Irish demand being assumed, various tactics came under review. They might begin by asking for a vote of confidence, saying plainly that if they were turned out and Mr. Gladstone were put in, he would , propose home rule. In that case a majority was not wholly impossible, for the whig wing might come over, nor was it quite certain that the Irish would help to put the government out. At any rate the debate would force Mr. Gladstone into the open, and even if they did not have a majority, they would be in a position to advise immediate dissolution on the issue of home rule.

The only other course open to the .cabinet was to turn their backs upon the professions of the summer; to throw overboard the Carnarvon policy as a cargo for which there was no longer a market; to abandon a great experiment after a ludicrously short trial; and to pick up again the old instrument of coercion, which not six months before they had with such elaborate ostentation condemned and discarded. This grand manœuvre was kept carefully in the background, until there had been time for the whole chapter of accidents to exhaust itself, and it had become certain that no trump cards were falling to the ministerial hand. Not until this was quite clear, did ministers reveal their poignant uneasiness about the state of Ireland.

In the middle of October (1885) Lord Randolph Churchill visited the viceroy.in Dublin, and found him, as he afterwards said, extremely anxious and alarmed at the growing power of the National League. Yet the viceroy was not so anxious and alarmed as to prevent Lord Randolph from saying at Birmingham a month after, on November 20, that up to the present time their decision to preserve order by the same laws as in England had been abundantly justified, and that on the whole crime and outrage had greatly diminished. This was curious, and shows how tortuous was the crisis. Only a fortnight later the cabinet met (December 2), and heard of the extraordinary development and unlimited resources of the league. All the rest of the month of December, — so the public were by and by informed, — the condition of Ireland was the subject of the most anxious consideration. With great deliberation, a decision was at length reached. It was that ordinary law had broken down, and that exceptional means of repression were indispensable. Then a serious and embarrassing incident occurred. Lord Carnarvon 'threw up the government of Ireland,' and was followed by Sir William Hart Dyke, the chief secretary.[1] A measure of coercion was prepared, its provisions all drawn in statutory form, but who was to warrant the necessity for it to parliament?[2]

Though the viceroy's retirement was not publicly known until the middle of January, yet so early as December 17 the prime minister had applied to Mr. Smith, then secretary of state for war, to undertake the duties of Irish government.[3] This was one of the sacrifices that no man of public spirit can ever refuse, and Mr. Smith, who had plenty of public spirit, became Irish secretary. Still when parliament assembled more than a month after Lord Salisbury's letter to his new chief secretary, no policy was announced. Even on the second night of the session Mr. Smith answered questions for the war office. The parliamentary mystification was complete. Who, where, and what was the Irish government?

The parliamentary session was rapidly approaching, and Mr. Gladstone had good information of the various quarters whence the wind was blowing. Rumours reached him (January 9) from the purlieus of Parliament Street, that general words of confidence in the government would be found in the Queen's Speech. Next he was told of the report that an amendment would be moved by the ultras of law and order, — the same who had mutinied on the Maamtrasna debate, — censuring ministers for having failed to uphold the authority of the Queen. The same correspondent (January 15), who was well able to make his words good, wrote to Mr. Gladstone that even though home rule might perhaps not be in a parliamentary sense before the House, it was in a most distinct manner before the country, and no political party could avoid expressing an opinion upon it. On the same day another colleague of hardly less importance drew attention to an article in a

---

[1] Correspondence between Lord Salisbury and Lord Carnarvon, *Times*, Jan. 16, 1886.

[2] *Hans.* 302, pp. 1929-1993, March 4, 1886. See also Lord Randolph Churchill at Paddington, Feb. 13, 1886.

[3] Maxwell's *Life of W. H. Smith*, ii. p. 163.

journal supposed to be inspired by Lord Randolph, to the effect that conciliation in Ireland had totally failed, that Lord Carnarvon had retired because that policy was to be reversed and he was not the man for the rival policy of vigour, and finally, that the new policy would probably be announced in the Queen's Speech; in no circumstances would it be possible to avoid a general action on the Address.

II

The current of domestic life at Hawarden, in the midst of all these perplexities, flowed in its usual ordered channels. The engagement of his second daughter stirred Mr. Gladstone's deepest interest. He practised occasional woodcraft with his sons, though ending his seventy-sixth year. He spends a morning in reviewing his private money affairs, the first time for three years. He never misses church. He corrects the proofs of an article on Huxley; carries on tolerably profuse correspondence, coming to very little; he works among his books, and arranges his papers; reads Beaconsfield's *Home Letters*, Lord Stanhope's *Pitt*, Macaulay's *Warren Hastings*, which he counts the most brilliant of all that illustrious man's performances; Maine on *Popular Government*; *King Solomon's Mines*; something of Tolstoy; Dicey's *Law of the Constitution*, where a chapter on semi-sovereign assemblies made a deep impression on him in regard to the business that now absorbed his mind. Above all, he nearly every day reads Burke: '*December* 18. — Read Burke; what a magazine of wisdom on Ireland and America. *January* 9. — Made many extracts from Burke — *sometimes almost divine*.'[1] We may easily imagine how the heat from that profound and glowing furnace still further inflamed strong purposes and exalted resolution in Mr. Gladstone. The Duke of Argyll wrote to say that he was sorry to hear of the study of Burke: 'Your *perfervidum ingenium Scoti* does not need being touched with a live coal from that Irish altar. Of course your reference to Burke indicates a tendency to

[1] If this seems hyperbole, let the reader remember an entry in Macaulay's diary: 'I have now finished reading again most of Burke's works. Admirable! The greatest man since Milton.' Trevelyan's *Life*, ii. p. 377.

compare our position as regards Ireland to the position of
George III. towards the colonies. I deny that there is any
parallelism or even analogy.' It was during these months
that he renewed his friendly intercourse with Cardinal
Manning, which had been suspended since the controversy
upon the Vatican pamphlets. In November Mr. Gladstone
sent Manning his article on the ' Dawn of Creation.' The
cardinal thanked him for the paper — ' still more for your
words, which revive the memories of old days. Fifty-five
years are a long reach of life in which to remember each other.
We have twice been parted, but as the path declines, as you
say, it narrows, and I am glad that we are again nearing each
other as we near our end. . . . If we cannot unite in the
realm where " the morning stars sang together " we should be
indeed far off.' Much correspondence followed on the
articles against Huxley. Then his birthday came : —

Postal deliveries and other arrivals were seven hundred.
Immeasurable kindness almost overwhelmed us. There was also
the heavy and incessant weight of the Irish question, which
offers daily phases more or less new. It was a day for intense
thankfulness, but, alas, not for recollection and detachment.
When will that day come ? Until then, why string together the
commonplaces and generalities of great things, really unfelt ?
. . . I am certain there is one keen and deep desire to be extri-
cated from the life of contention in which a chain of incidents has
for the last four years detained me against all my will. Then,
indeed, I should reach an eminence from which I could look
before and after. But I know truly that I am not worthy of this
liberty with which Christ makes free his elect. In his own good
time, something, I trust, will for me too be mercifully devised.

III

At the end of this long travail, which anybody else would
have found all the sorer for the isolation and quietude that
it was ever Mr. Gladstone's fashion in moments of emergency
to seek, he reached London on January 11th; two days
later he took the oath in the new parliament, whose life was
destined to be so short; and then he found himself on the

edge of the whirlpool. Three days before formalities were over, and the House assembled for the despatch of business, he received a communication that much perturbed him, and shed an ominous light on the prospect of liberal unity. This communication he described to Lord Granville: —

21 *Carlton House Terrace, Jan.* 18, 1886. — Hartington writes to me a letter indicating the possibility that on Thursday, while I announce with reasons a policy of silence and reserve, he may feel it his duty to declare his determination 'to maintain the legislative union,' that is to proclaim a policy (so I understand the phrase) of absolute resistance without examination to the demand made by Ireland through five-sixths of her members. This is to play the tory game with a vengeance. They are now, most rashly not to say more, working the Irish question to split the liberal party.

It seems to me that if a gratuitous declaration of this kind is made, it must produce an explosion; and that in a week's time Hartington will have to consider whether he will lead the liberal party himself, or leave it to chaos. He will make my position impossible. When, in conformity with the wishes expressed to me, I changed my plans and became a candidate at the general election, my motives were two. The *first*, a hope that I might be able to contribute towards some pacific settlement of the Irish question. The *second*, a desire to prevent the splitting of the party, of which there appeared to be an immediate danger. The second object has thus far been attained. But it may at any moment be lost, and the most disastrous mode of losing it perhaps would be that now brought into view. It would be certainly opposed to my convictions and determination, to attempt to lead anything like a home rule opposition, and to make this subject — the strife of nations — the dividing line between parties. This being so, I do not see how I could as leader survive a gratuitous declaration of opposition to me such as Hartington appears to meditate. If he still meditates it, ought not the party to be previously informed?

Pray, consider whether you can bring this subject before him, less invidiously than I. I have explained to you and I believe to him, and I believe you approve, my general idea, that we ought not to join issue with the government on what is called home rule (which indeed the social state of Ireland may effectually thrust aside for the time); and that still less ought we to join issue among ourselves, if we have a choice, unless and until we are called upon to consider whether or not to take the government. I for one will have nothing to do with ruining the party if I can avoid it.

This letter discloses with precision the critical state of facts on the eve of action being taken. Issue was not directly joined with ministers on home rule; no choice was found to exist as to taking the government; and this brought deep and long-standing diversities among the liberal leaders to the issue that Mr. Gladstone had strenuously laboured to avoid from the beginning of 1885 to the end.

IV

The Irish paragraphs in the speech from the throne (January 21, 1886) were abstract, hypothetical, and vague. The sovereign was made to say that during the past year there had been no marked increase of serious crime, but there was in many places a concerted resistance to the enforcement of legal obligations, and the practice of intimidation continued to exist. 'If,' the speech went on, 'as my information leads me to apprehend, the existing provisions of the law should prove to be inadequate to cope with these growing evils, I look with confidence to your willingness to invest my government with all necessary powers.' There was also an abstract paragraph about the legislative union between the two islands.

In a fragment composed in the autumn of 1897, Mr. Gladstone has described the anxiety with which he watched the course of proceedings on the Address : —

I had no means of forming an estimate how far the bulk of the liberal party could be relied on to support a measure of home rule, which should constitute an Irish parliament subject to the supremacy of the parliament at Westminster. I was not sanguine on this head. Even in the month of December, when rumours of my intentions were afloat, I found how little I could reckon on a general support. Under the circumstances I certainly took upon myself a grave responsibility. I attached value to the acts and language of Lord Carnarvon, and the other favourable manifestations. Subsequently we had but too much evidence of a deliberate intention to deceive the Irish, with a view to their support at the election. But in the actual circumstances I thought it my duty to encourage the government of Lord Salisbury to settle the Irish question, so far as I could do this by promises of my personal support. Hence my communication with Mr. Balfour, which has long been in the hands of the public.

It has been unreasonably imputed to me, that the proposal of home rule was a bid for the Irish vote. But my desire for the adjustment of the question by the tories is surely a conclusive answer. The fact is that I could not rely upon the collective support of the liberals; but I could and did rely upon the support of so many of them as would make the success of the measure certain, in the event of its being proposed by the tory administration. It would have resembled in substance the liberal support given to Roman catholic emancipation in 1829, and the repeal of the corn laws in 1846. Before the meeting of parliament, I had to encounter uncomfortable symptoms among my principal friends, of which I think —— was the organ.

I was, therefore, by no means eager for the dismissal of the tory government, though it counted but 250 supporters out of 670, as long as there were hopes of its taking up the question, or at all events doing nothing to aggravate the situation.

When we came to the debate on the Address I had to face a night of extreme anxiety. The speech from the throne referred in a menacing way to Irish disturbances, and contained a distinct declaration in support of the legislative union. On referring to the clerks at the table to learn in what terms the Address in reply to the speech was couched, I found it was a 'thanking' address, which did not commit the House to an opinion. What I dreaded was lest some one should have gone back to the precedent of 1833, when the Address in reply to the speech was virtually made the vehicle of a solemn declaration in favour of the Act of Union.[1]

[1] In 1833 the King's Speech represented the state of Ireland in words that might be used at the present time, and expressed confidence that parliament would entrust the King with 'such additional powers

Home rule, rightly understood, altered indeed the terms of the Act of Union, but adhered to its principle, which was the supremacy of the imperial parliament.   Still [it] was pretty certain that any declaration of a substantive character, at the epoch we had now reached, would in its moral effect shut the doors of the existing parliament against home rule.

In a speech of pronounced clearness, Mr. Arthur Elliot endeavoured to obtain a movement in this direction.   I thought it would be morally fatal if this tone were extensively adopted on the liberal side; so I determined on an effort to secure reserve for the time, that our freedom might not be compromised.   I, therefore, ventured upon describing myself as an 'old parliamentary hand,' and in that capacity strongly advised the party to keep its own counsel, and await for a little the development of events.   Happily this counsel was taken; had it been otherwise, the early formation of a government favourable to home rule would in all likelihood have become an impossibility.   For although our Home Rule bill was eventually supported by more than 300 members, I doubt whether, if the question had been prematurely raised on the night of the Address, as many as 200 would have been disposed to act in that sense.

In the debate on the Address the draft Coercion bill reposing in the secret box was not mentioned.   Sir Michael Hicks Beach, the leader of the House, described the mischiefs then afoot, and went on to say that whether they could be dealt with by ordinary law, or would require exceptional powers, were questions that would receive the new chief secretary's immediate attention.[1]   Parliament was told that

as may be necessary for punishing the disturbers of the public peace and for preserving and strengthening the legislative union between the two countries, which with your support and under the blessing of divine Providence I am determined to maintain by all the means in my power.' The Address in answer assured his Majesty that his confidence should not be disappointed, and that 'we shall be ready to entrust to H.M. such additional measures, etc., for preserving and strengthening the legislative union which we have determined,' etc.   This was the address that Mr.

O'Connell denounced as a 'bloody and brutal address,' and he moved as an amendment that the House do resolve itself into a committee of the whole House to consider of an humble address to his Majesty.   Feb. 8. Amendment negatived, Ayes being 428, Noes 40. — *Memo.* by Sir T. E. May for Mr. Gladstone, Jan. 18, 1886.   O'Connell, that is to say, did not move an amendment in favour of repeal, but proposed the consideration of the Address in committee of the whole House.
[1] *Hans.* 302, p. 128.

the minister had actually gone to Ireland to make anxious inquiry into these questions. Mr. Smith arrived in Dublin at six o'clock on the morning of January 24, and he quitted it at six o'clock on the evening of the 26th. He was sworn in at the Castle in the forenoon of that day.[1] His views must have reached the cabinet in London not later than the morning of the 26th. Not often can conclusions on such a subject have been ripened with such electrifying precocity.

'I intend to reserve my own freedom of action,' Mr. Gladstone said; 'there are many who have taken their seats for the first time upon these benches, and I may avail myself of the privilege of old age to offer a recommendation. I would tell them of my own intention to keep my counsel and reserve my own freedom, until I see the moment and the occasion when there may be a prospect of public benefit in endeavouring to make a movement forward, and I will venture to recommend them, as an old parliamentary hand, to do the same.'[2] Something in this turn of phrase kindled lively irritation, and it drew bitter reproaches from more than one of the younger whigs. The angriest of these remonstrances was listened to from beginning to end without a solitary cheer from the liberal benches. The great bulk of the party took their leader's advice. Of course the reserve of his speech was as significant of Irish concession, as the most open declaration would have been. Yet there was no rebellion. This was felt by ministers to be a decisive omen of the general support likely to be given to Mr. Gladstone's supposed policy by his own party. Mr. Parnell offered some complimentary remarks on the language of Mr. Gladstone, but he made no move in the direction of an amendment. The public outside looked on with stupefaction. For two or three days all seemed to be in suspense. But the two ministerial leaders in the Commons knew how to read the signs. What Sir Michael

[1] Lord Carnarvon left Ireland on Jan. 28, and Lord Justices were then appointed. But the lawyers seem to hold that there cannot be Lord Justices without a viceroy, and Lord Carnarvon was therefore technically viceroy out of the kingdom (of Ireland), until Lord Aberdeen was sworn in upon Feb. 10, 1886. He must, accordingly, have signed the minute appointing Mr. Smith chief secretary, though of course Mr. Smith had gone over to reverse the Carnarvon policy.

[2] *Hans.* 302, p. 112.

Hicks Beach and Lord Randolph foresaw, for one thing was CHAP.
an understanding between Mr. Gladstone and the Irishmen, IV.
and for another, they foresaw the acquiescence of the mass of Æt. 77.
the liberals. This twofold discovery cleared the ground for
a decision. After the second night's debate ministers saw
that the only chance now was to propose coercion. Then it
was that the ephemeral chief secretary had started on his
voyage for the discovery of something that had already been
found.

V

On the afternoon of the 26th, the leader of the House
gave notice that two days later the new Irish secretary
would ask leave to introduce a bill dealing with the National
League, with intimidation, and with the protection of life,
property, and public order. This would be followed by a bill
dealing with land, pursuing in a more extensive sense the
policy of the Ashbourne Act of the year before. The great
issue was thus at last brought suddenly and ·nakedly into
view. When the Irish secretary reached Euston Square
on the morning of the 27th, he found that his government
was out.

The crucial announcement of the 26th of January compelled a prompt determination, and Mr. Gladstone did not
shrink. A protest against a return to coercion as the answer
of the British parliament to the extraordinary demonstration
from Ireland, carried with it the responsibility of office, and
this responsibility Mr. Gladstone had resolved to undertake.

The determining event of these transactions, — he says in the
fragment already cited, — was the declaration of the government
that they would propose coercion for Ireland. This declaration
put an end to all the hopes and expectations associated with the
mission of Lord Carnarvon. Not perhaps in mere logic, but
practically, it was now plain that Ireland had no hope from the
tories. This being so, my rule of action was changed at once, and
I determined on taking any and every legitimate opportunity to
remove the existing government from office. Immediately on
making up my mind about the rejection of the government, I went
to call upon Sir William Harcourt and informed him as to my

intentions and the grounds of them. He said, 'What! Are you prepared to go forward without either Hartington or Chamberlain?' I answered, 'Yes.' I believe it was in my mind to say, if I did not actually say it, that I was prepared to go forward without anybody. That is to say without any known and positive assurance of support. This was one of the great imperial occasions which call for such resolutions.

An amendment stood upon the notice-paper in the name of Mr. Collings, regretting the omission from the speech of measures for benefiting the rural labourer; and on this motion an immediate engagement was fought. Time was important. An exasperating debate on coercion with obstruction, disorder, suspensions, would have been a damning prologue to any policy of accommodation. The true significance of the motion was not concealed. On the agrarian aspect of it, the only important feature was the adhesion of Mr. Gladstone, now first formally declared, to the policy of Mr. Chamberlain. The author of the agrarian policy fought out once more on the floor of the House against Lord Hartington and Mr. Goschen the battle of the platform. It was left for Sir Michael Hicks Beach to remind the House that, whatever the honest mover might mean, the rural labourer had very little to do with the matter, and he implored the gentlemen in front of him to think twice and thrice before they committed the future of this country to the gravest dangers that ever awaited it.

The debate was not prolonged. The discussion opened shortly before dinner, and by one o'clock the division was taken. The government found itself in a minority of 79. The majority numbered 331, composed of 257 liberals and 74 Irish nationalists. The ministerialist minority was 252, made up of 234 tories and 18 liberals. Besides the fact that Lord Hartington, Mr. Goschen, and Sir Henry James voted with ministers, there was a still more ominous circumstance. No fewer than 76 liberals were absent, including among them the imposing personality of Mr. Bright. In a memorandum written for submission to the Queen a few days later, Mr. Gladstone said, 'I must express my personal con-

viction that had the late ministers remained in office and pro- CHAP.
ceeded with their proposed plan of repression, and even had IV.
that plan received my support, it would have ended in a dis- Æт. 77.
astrous parliamentary failure.'[1]

The next day (Jan. 28) ministers of course determined to resign. A liberal member of parliament was overtaken by Lord Randolph on the parade ground, walking away from the cabinet. ' You look a little pensive,' said the liberal. ' Yes; I was thinking. I have plenty to think of. Well, we are out, and you are in.' ' I suppose so,' the liberal replied, ' we are in for six months; we dissolve; you are in for six years.' ' Not at all sure,' said Lord Randolph; ' let me tell you one thing most solemnly and most surely : the conservative party are not going to be made the instrument of the Irish for turning out Mr. Gladstone, if he refuses repeal.' ' Nobody,' observed the sententious liberal, ' should so often as the politician say the prayer not to be led into temptation. Remember your doings last summer.'

[1] Mr. Gladstone was often taunted with having got in upon the question of allotments, and then throwing the agricultural labourer overboard. ' The proposition,' he said, ' is not only untrue but ridiculous. If true, it would prove that Lord Grey in 1830 came in upon the pension list, and Lord Derby in 1852 on the militia. . . . For myself, I may say personally that I made my public declaration on behalf of allotments in 1832, when Mr. Jesse Collings was just born.' — To Mr. C. A. Fyffe, May 6, 1890.

CHAPTER V

THE NEW POLICY

(*1886*)

> In reason all government without the consent of the governed is the very definition of slavery; but in fact eleven men well armed will certainly subdue one single man in his shirt. . . . Those who have used to cramp liberty have gone so far as to resent even the liberty of complaining; although a man upon the rack was never known to be refused the liberty of roaring as loud as he thought fit. — JONATHAN SWIFT.

THE tory government was defeated in the sitting of Tuesday (Jan. 26). On Friday, 'at a quarter after midnight, in came Sir H. Ponsonby, with verbal commission from her Majesty, which I at once accepted.'[1] The whole of Saturday was spent in consultations with colleagues. On Sunday, Mr. Gladstone records, 'except church, my day from one to eight was given to business. I got only fragmentary reading of the life of the admirable Mr. Suckling and other books. At night came a painful and harassing succession of letters, and my sleep for once gave way; yet for the soul it was profitable, driving me to the hope that the strength of God might be made manifest in my weakness.' On Monday, Feb. 1, he went to attend the Queen. 'Off at 9.10 to Osborne. Two audiences: an hour and half in all. Everything good in the main points. Large discourse upon Ireland in particular. Returned at 7¾. I kissed hands and am thereby prime minister for the third time. But, as I trust, for a brief time only. Slept well, *D. G.*'

The first question was, how many of his colleagues in the liberal cabinet that went out of office six months before, would now embark with him in the voyage into stormy and unexplored seas. I should suppose that no such difficulties

[1] *Diary.*

290

had ever confronted the attempt at making a cabinet since
Canning's in 1827.

Mr. Gladstone begins the fragment from which I have
already quoted with a sentence or two of retrospect, and then
proceeds : —

In 1885 (I think) Chamberlain had proposed a plan accepted
by Parnell (and supported by me) which, without establishing in
Ireland a national parliament, made very considerable advances
towards self-government. It was rejected by a small majority of
the cabinet — Granville said at the time he would rather take
home rule. Spencer thought it would introduce confusion into
executive duties.

On the present occasion a full half of the former ministers
declined to march with me. Spencer and Granville were my main
supports. Chamberlain and Trevelyan went with me, their basis
being that we were to seek for some method of dealing with the
Irish case other than coercion. What Chamberlain's motive was I
do not clearly understand. It was stated that he coveted the Irish
secretaryship. . . . To have given him the office would at that time
have been held to be a declaration of war against the Irish party.

Selborne nibbled at the offer, but I felt that it would not work,
and did not use great efforts to bring him in.[1] . . .

When I had accepted the commission, Ponsonby brought me a
message from the Queen that she hoped there would not be any
Separation in the cabinet. The word had not at that time acquired the offensive meaning in which it has since been stereotyped by the so-called unionists; and it was easy to frame a reply
in general but strong words. I am bound to say that at Osborne
in the course of a long conversation, the Queen was frank and free,
and showed none of the 'armed neutrality,' which as far as I know
has been the best definition of her attitude in the more recent
years towards a liberal minister. Upon the whole, when I look
back upon 1886, and consider the inveterate sentiment of hostility flavoured with contempt towards Ireland, which has from time

---

[1] ' When the matter was finally adjusted by Chamberlain's retirement,
we had against us — Derby, Northbrook, Carlingford, Selborne, Dodson,
Chamberlain, Hartington, Trevelyan,
Bright ; and for — Granville, Spencer,
Kimberley, Ripon, Rosebery, Harcourt, Childers, Lefevre, Dilke (unavailable).' Mr. Goschen was not in
the cabinet of 1880.

immemorial formed the basis of English tradition, I am much more disposed to be thankful for what we then and afterwards accomplished, than to murmur or to wonder at what we did not.

What Mr. Gladstone called the basis of his new government was set out in a short memorandum, which he read to each of those whom he hoped to include in his cabinet: 'I propose to examine whether it is or is not practicable to comply with the desire widely prevalent in Ireland, and testified by the return of eighty-five out of one hundred and three representatives, for the establishment by statute of a legislative body to sit in Dublin, and to deal with Irish as distinguished from imperial affairs; in such a manner as would be just to each of the three kingdoms, equitable with reference to every class of the people of Ireland, conducive to the social order and harmony of that country, and calculated to support and consolidate the unity of the empire on the continued basis of imperial authority and mutual attachment.'

No definite plan was propounded or foreshadowed, but only the proposition that it was a duty to seek a plan. The cynical version was that a cabinet was got together on the chance of being able to agree. To Lord Hartington, Mr. Gladstone applied as soon as he received the Queen's commission. The invitation was declined on reasoned grounds (January 30). Examination and inquiry, said Lord Hartington, must mean a proposal. If no proposal followed inquiry, the reaction of Irish disappointment would be severe, as it would be natural. His adherence, moreover, would be of little value. He had already, he observed, in the government of 1880 made concessions on other subjects that might be thought to have shaken public confidence in him; he could go no further without destroying that confidence altogether. However that might be, he could not depart from the traditions of British statesmen, and he was opposed to a separate Irish legislature. At the same time he concluded, in a sentence afterwards pressed by Mr. Gladstone on the notice of the Queen: 'I am fully convinced that the alternative policy of governing Ireland without large concessions

not a bit more radical than the government of last year; perhaps a little less. And we have got some good young hands, which please me very much. Yet short as the Salisbury government has been, it would not at all surprise me if this were to be shorter still, such are the difficulties that bristle round the Irish question. But the great thing is to be right; and as far as matters have yet advanced, I see no reason to be apprehensive in this capital respect. I have framed a plan for the land and for the finance of what must be a very large transaction. It is necessary to see our way a little on these at the outset, for, unless these portions of anything we attempt are sound and well constructed, we cannot hope to succeed. On the other hand, if we fail, as I believe the late ministers would have failed even to pass their plan of repressive legislation, the consequences will be deplorable in every way. There seems to be no doubt that some, and notably Lord R. Churchill, fully reckoned on my failing to form a government.[1]

II

The work pressed, and time was terribly short. The new ministers had barely gone through their re-elections before the opposition began to harry them for their policy, and went so far, before the government was five weeks old, as to make the extreme motion for refusing supply. Even if the opposition had been in more modest humour, no considerable delay could be defended. Social order in Ireland was in a profoundly unsatisfactory phase. That

[1] The cabinet was finally composed as follows: —

Mr. Gladstone, ...	*First lord of the treasury.*
Lord Herschell, . . .	*Lord chancellor.*
Lord Spencer, ...	*President of council.*
Sir W. Harcourt, . . .	*Chancellor of exchequer.*
Mr. Childers, ...	*Home secretary.*
Lord Rosebery, . . .	*Foreign* "
Lord Granville, . . .	*Colonial* "
Lord Kimberley, . . .	*Indian* "
Mr. Campbell-Bannerman, .	*War* "
Lord Ripon, ...	*Admiralty.*
Mr. Chamberlain, . . .	*Local government.*
Mr. Morley, ...	*Irish secretary.*
Mr. Trevelyan, ...	*Scotch secretary.*
Mr. Mundella, ...	*Board of trade.*

The Lord chancellor, Mr. C.-Bannerman, Mr. Mundella, and myself now sat in cabinet for the first time. After the two resignations at the end of March, Mr. Stansfeld came in as head of the Local government board, and we sat with the ominous number of thirteen at table.

fact was the starting-point of the reversal of policy which the government had come into existence to carry out. You cannot announce a grand revolution, and then beg the world to wait. The very reason that justified the policy commanded expedition. Anxiety and excitement were too intense out of doors for anything but a speedy date, and it was quite certain that if the new plan were not at once propounded, no other public business would have much chance.

The new administration did not meet parliament until after the middle of February, and the two Irish bills, in which their policy was contained, were ready by the end of the first week of April. Considering the enormous breadth and intricacy of the subjects, the pressure of parliamentary business all the time, the exigencies of administrative work in the case of at least one of the ministers principally concerned, and the distracting atmosphere of party perturbation and disquiet that daily and hourly harassed the work, the despatch of such a task within such limits of time was at least not discreditable to the industry and concentration of those who achieved it. I leave it still open to the hostile critic to say, as Molière's Alceste says of the sonnet composed in a quarter of an hour, that time has nothing to do with the business.

All through March Mr. Gladstone laboured in what he called ' stiff conclaves ' about finance and land, attended drawing rooms, and ' observed the variations of H.M.'s accueils'; had an audience of the Queen, 'very gracious, but avoided serious subjects'; was laid up with cold, and the weather made Sir Andrew Clark strict; then rose up to fresh grapples with finance and land and untoward colleagues, and all the 'inexorable demands of my political vocation.' His patience and self-control were as marvellous as his tireless industry. Sorely tried by something or another at a cabinet, he enters, — 'Angry with myself for not bearing it better. I ought to have been thankful for it all the time.' On a similar occasion, a junior colleague showed himself less thankful than he should have been for purposeless antagonism. 'Think of it as discipline,' said Mr.

Gladstone. 'But why,' said the unregenerate junior, 'should we grudge the blessings of discipline to some other people?'

Mr. Gladstone was often blamed even by Laodiceans among his supporters, not wise but foolish after the event, because he did not proceed by way of resolution, instead of by bill. Resolutions, it was argued, would have smoothed the way. General propositions would have found readier access to men's minds. Having accepted the general proposition, people would have found it harder to resist the particular application. Devices that startled in the precision of a clause, would in the vagueness of a broad and abstract principle have soothed and persuaded. Mr. Gladstone was perfectly alive to all this, but his answer to it was plain. Those who eventually threw out the bill would insist on unmasking the resolution. They would have exhausted all the stereotyped vituperation of abstract motions. They would have ridiculed any general proposition as mere platitude, and pertinaciously clamoured for working details. What would the resolution have affirmed? The expediency of setting up a legislative authority in Ireland to deal with exclusively Irish affairs. But such a resolution would be consistent equally with a narrow scheme on the one hand, such as a plan for national councils, and a broad scheme on the other, giving to Ireland a separate exchequer, separate control over customs and excise, and practically an independent and co-ordinate legislature.[1] How could the government meet the challenge to say outright whether they intended broad or narrow? Such a resolution could hardly have outlived an evening's debate, and would not have postponed the evil day of schism for a single week.

Precedents lent no support. It is true that the way was prepared for the Act of Union in the parliament of Great Britain, by the string of resolutions moved by Mr. Pitt in the beginning of 1799. But anybody who glances at them, will at once perceive that if resolutions on their model had been framed for the occasion of 1886, they would have covered the whole ground of the actual bill, and would instantly have

[1] See Mr. Chamberlain's speech, Also Lord Hartington at Bradford, June 1, 1886. *Hans.* 306, p. 677. May 18, 1886.

raised all the formidable objections and difficulties exactly as the bill itself raised them. The Bank Charter Act of 1833 was founded on eight resolutions, and they also set forth in detail the points of the ministerial plan.[1] The renewal of the East India Company's charter in the same year went on by way of resolutions, less abundant in particulars than the Bank Act, but preceded by correspondence and papers which had been exhaustively canvassed and discussed.[2] The question of Irish autonomy was in no position of that sort.

The most apt precedent in some respects is to be found on a glorious occasion, also in the year 1833. Mr. Stanley introduced the proposals of his government for the emancipation of the West Indian slaves in five resolutions. They furnished a key not only to policy and general principles, but also to the plan by which these were to be carried out.[3] Lord Howick followed the minister at once, raising directly the whole question of the plan. Who could doubt that Lord Hartington would now take precisely the same course towards Irish resolutions of similar scope ? The procedure on the India bill of 1858 was just as little to the point. The general disposition of the House was wholly friendly to a settlement of the question of Indian government by the existing ministry. No single section of the opposition wished to take it out of their hands, for neither Lord Russell nor the Peelites nor the Manchester men, and probably not even Lord Palmerston himself, were anxious for the immediate return of the last-named minister to power. Who will pretend that in the House of Commons in February 1886, anything at all like the same state of facts prevailed ? As for the resolutions in the case of the Irish church, they were moved by Mr. Gladstone in opposition, and he thought it obvious that a policy proposed in opposition stands on a totally different footing from a policy laid before parliament on the responsibility of a government, and a government bound by every necessity of the situation to prompt action.[4]

---

[1] June 1, 1833. *Hans.* 18, p. 186.
[2] June 13, 1833. *Ibid.* p. 700.
[3] May 14, 1833. *Hans.* 17, p. 1230.
[4] There is also the case of the

Reform bill of 1867. Disraeli laid thirteen resolutions on the table. Lowe and Bright both agreed in urging that the resolutions should be

At a later stage, as we shall see, it was actually proposed
that a vote for the second reading of the bill should be taken
to mean no more than a vote for its principle. Every one
of the objections that instantly sprang out of their ambush
against this proposal would have worked just as much
mischief against an initial resolution. In short, in opening
a policy of this difficulty and extent, the cabinet was bound
to produce to parliament not merely its policy but its plan
for carrying the policy out. By that course only could
parliament know what it was doing. Any other course
must have ended in a mystifying, irritating, and barren
confusion, alike in the House of Commons and in the
country.[1]

The same consideration that made procedure by resolution unadvisable told with equal force within the cabinet.
Examination into the feasibility of some sort of plan was
most rapidly brought to a head by the test of a particular
plan. It is a mere fable of faction that a cast iron policy
was arbitrarily imposed upon the cabinet ; as matter of
fact, the plan originally propounded did undergo large and
radical modifications.

The policy as a whole shaped itself in two measures.
First, a scheme for creating a legislative body, and defining
its powers ; second, a scheme for opening the way to a
settlement of the land question, in discharge of an obligation of honour and policy, imposed upon this country by its
active share in all the mischiefs that the Irish land system
had produced. The introduction of a plan for dealing with
the land was not very popular even among ministers, but it
was pressed by Lord Spencer and the Irish secretary, on the
double ground that the land was too burning a question to be
left where it then stood, and next that it was unfair to a new
and untried legislature in Ireland to find itself confronted
by such a question on the very threshold.

The plan was opened by Mr. Gladstone in cabinet on

dropped and the bill at once printed.
A meeting of liberal members at Mr.
Gladstone's house unanimously resolved to support an amendment setting aside the resolutions. Disraeli

at once abandoned them.
[1] Lord Hartington's argument on
the second reading shows how a resolution would have fared. *Hans.*
305, p. 610.

March 13th, and Mr. Chamberlain and Mr. Trevelyan at once wished to resign. He remonstrated in a vigorous correspondence. 'I have seen many and many a resignation,' he said, 'but never one based upon the intentions, nay the immature intentions, of the prime minister, and on a pure intuition of what may happen. Bricks and rafters are prepared for a house, but are not themselves a house.' The evil hour was postponed, but not for long. The Cabinet met again a few days later (March 26) and things came to a sharp issue. The question was raised in a sufficiently definite form by the proposition from the prime minister for the establishment of a statutory body sitting in Dublin with legislative powers. No difficulty was made about the bare proposition itself. Every one seemed to go as far as that. It needed to be tested, and tests were at once forthcoming. Mr. Trevelyan could not assent to the control of the immediate machinery of law and order being withdrawn from direct British authority, among other reasons because it was this proposal that created the necessity for buying out the Irish landlords, which he regarded as raising a problem absolutely insoluble.[1] Mr. Chamberlain raised four points. He objected to the cesser of Irish representation ; he could not consent to the grant of full rights of taxation to Ireland ; he resisted the surrender of the appointment of judges and magistrates ; and he argued strongly against proceeding by enumeration of the things that an Irish government might not do, instead of by a specific delegation of the things that it might do.[2] That these four objections were not in themselves incapable of accommodation was shown by subsequent events. The second was very speedily, and the first was ultimately allowed, while the fourth was held by good authority to be little more than a question of drafting. Even the third was not a point either way on which to break up a government, destroy a policy, and split a party. But everybody who is acquainted with either the great or the small conflicts of human history, knows how little the mere terms of a principle or of an objection are to be trusted as a clue either to its practical significance, or

[1] *Hans.* 304, p. 1116.   [2] *Hans.* 304, p. 1190.

to the design with which it is in reality advanced. The CHAP. design here under all the four heads of objection, was the <br> dwarfing of the legislative body, the cramping and con-
striction of its organs, its reduction to something which
the Irish could not have even pretended to accept, and
which they would have been no better than fools if they
had ever attempted to work.

Some supposed then, and Mr. Chamberlain has said since,
that when he entered the cabinet room on this memorable
occasion, he intended to be conciliatory. Witnesses of the
scene thought that the prime minister made little attempt
in that direction. Yet where two men of clear mind and
firm will mean two essentially different things under the
same name, whether autonomy or anything else, and each
intends to stand by his own interpretation, it is childish to
suppose that arts of deportment will smother or attenuate
fundamental divergence, or make people who are quite
aware how vitally they differ, pretend that they entirely
agree. Mr. Gladstone knew the giant burden that he had
taken up, and when he went to the cabinet of March 26, his
mind was no doubt fixed that success, so hazardous at best,
would be hopeless in face of personal antagonisms and
bitterly divided counsels. This, in his view, and in his
own phrase, was one of the 'great imperial occasions' that
call for imperial resolves. The two ministers accordingly
resigned.

Besides these two important secessions, some ministers
out of the cabinet resigned, but they were of the whig
complexion.[1] The new prospect of the whig schism extending into the camp of the extreme radicals created natural
alarm but hardly produced a panic. So deep were the roots
of party, so immense the authority of a veteran leader. It
used to be said of the administration of 1880, that the world
would never really know Mr. Gladstone's strength in parliament and the country, until every one of his colleagues

---

[1] Faint hopes were nourished that
Mr. Bright might be induced to
join, but there was unfortunately
no ground for them. Mr. Whitbread was invited, but preferred to
lend staunch and important support
outside. Lord Dalhousie, one of
the truest hearts that ever was
attracted to public life, too early
lost to his country, took the Scottish
secretaryship, not in the cabinet.

had in turn abandoned him to his own resources. Certainly the secessions of the end of March 1886 left him undaunted. Every consideration of duty and of policy bound him to persevere. He felt, justly enough, that a minister who had once deliberately invited his party and the people of the three kingdoms to follow him on so arduous and bold a march as this, had no right on any common plea to turn back until he had exhausted every available device to 'bring the army of the faithful through.'

III

From the first the Irish leader was in free and constant communication with the chief secretary. Proposals were once or twice made, not I think at Mr. Parnell's desire, for conversations to be held between Mr. Gladstone and himself, but they were always discouraged by Mr. Gladstone, who was never fond of direct personal contentions, or conversations when the purpose could be as well served otherwise, and he had a horror of what he called multiplying channels of communication. 'For the moment,' he replied, 'I think we may look to Mr. M. alone, and rely on all he says for accuracy as well as fidelity. I have been hard at work, and to-day I mean to have a further and full talk with Mr. M., who will probably soon after wish for some renewed conversation with Mr. Parnell.' Mr. Parnell showed himself acute, frank, patient, closely attentive, and possessed of striking though not rapid insight. He never slurred over difficulties, nor tried to pretend that rough was smooth. On the other hand, he had nothing in common with that desperate species of counsellor, who takes all the small points, and raises objections instead of helping to contrive expedients. He measured the ground with a slow and careful eye, and fixed tenaciously on the thing that was essential at the moment. Of constructive faculty he never showed a trace. He was a man of temperament, of will, of authority, of power; not of ideas or ideals, or knowledge, or political maxims, or even of the practical reason in any of its higher senses, as Hamilton, Madison, and Jefferson had practical reason. But he knew what he wanted.

He was always perfectly ready at this period to acquiesce CHAP. in Irish exclusion from Westminster, on the ground that V. they would want all the brains they had for their own Æt. 77. parliament. At the same time he would have liked a provision for sending a delegation to Westminster on occasion, with reference to some definite Irish questions such as might be expected to arise. As to the composition of the upper or protective order in the Irish parliament, he was wholly unfamiliar with the various utopian plans that have been advanced for the protection of minorities, and he declared himself tolerably indifferent whether the object should be sought in nomination by the crown, or through a special and narrower elective body, or by any other scheme. To such things he had given no thought. He was a party chief, not a maker of constitutions. He liked the idea of both orders sitting in one House. He made one significant suggestion : he wished the bill to impose the same disqualification upon the clergy as exists in our own parliament. But he would have liked to see certain ecclesiastical dignitaries included by virtue of their office in the upper or protective branch. All questions of this kind, however, interested him much less than finance. Into financial issues he threw himself with extraordinary energy, and he fought for better terms with a keenness and tenacity that almost baffled the mighty expert with whom he was matched. They only met once during the weeks of the preparation of the bill, though the indirect communication was constant. Here is my scanty note of the meeting : —

April 5. — Mr. Parnell came to my room at the House at 8.30, and we talked for two hours. At 10.30 I went to Mr. Gladstone next door, and told him how things stood. He asked me to open the points of discussion, and into my room we went. He shook hands cordially with Mr. Parnell, and sat down between him and me. We at once got to work. P. extraordinarily close, tenacious, and sharp. It was all finance. At midnight, Mr. Gladstone rose in his chair and said, 'I fear I must go; I cannot sit as late as I used to do.' 'Very clever, very clever,' he muttered to me as I held open the door of his room for him. I returned to Parnell, who went on repeating his points in his impenetrable way, until the policeman mercifully came to say the House was up.

Mr. Gladstone's own note must also be transcribed: —

April 5. — Wrote to Lord Spencer. The Queen and ministers. Four hours on the matter for my speech. 1½ hours with Welby and Hamilton on the figures. Saw Lord Spencer, Mr. Morley, Mr. A. M. H. of C., 5–8. Dined at Sir Thomas May's.

1½ hours with Morley and Parnell on the root of the matter; rather too late for me, 10½–12. A hard day. (*Diary.*)

On more than one financial point the conflict went perilously near to breaking down the whole operation. 'If we do not get a right budget,' said Mr. Parnell, 'all will go wrong from the very first hour.' To the last he held out that the just proportion of Irish contribution to the imperial fund was not one-fourteenth or one-fifteenth, but a twentieth or twenty-first part. He insisted all the more strongly on his own more liberal fraction, as a partial compensation for their surrender of fiscal liberty and the right to impose customs duties. Even an hour or two before the bill was actually to be unfolded to the House, he hurried to the Irish office in what was for him rather an excited state, to make one more appeal to me for his fraction. It is not at all improbable that if the bill had gone forward into committee, it would have been at the eleventh hour rejected by the Irish on this department of it, and then all would have been at an end. Mr. Parnell never concealed this danger ahead.

In the cabinet things went forward with such ups and downs as are usual when a difficult bill is on the anvil. In a project of this magnitude, it was inevitable that some minister should occasionally let fall the consecrated formula that if this or that were done or not done, he must reconsider his position. Financial arrangements, and the protection of the minority, were two of the knottiest points, — the first from the contention raised on the Irish side, the second from misgiving in some minds as to the possibility of satisfying protestant sentiment in England and Scotland. Some kept the colonial type more strongly in view than others, and the bill no doubt ultimately bore that cast.

The draft project of surrendering complete taxing-power to the Irish legislative body was eventually abandoned. It was soon felt that the bare possibility of Ireland putting duties on British goods — and it was not more than a bare possibility in view of Britain's position as practically Ireland's only market — would have destroyed the bill in every manufacturing and commercial centre in the land. Mr. Parnell agreed to give up the control of customs, and also to give up direct and continuous representation at Westminster. On this cardinal point of the cesser of Irish representation, Mr. Gladstone to the last professed to keep an open mind, though to most of the cabinet, including especially three of its oldest hands and coolest heads, exclusion was at this time almost vital. Exclusion was favoured not only on its merits. Mr. Bright was known to regard it as large compensation for what otherwise he viewed as pure mischief, and it was expected to win support in other quarters generally hostile. So in truth it did, but at the cost of support in quarters that were friendly. On April 30, Mr. Gladstone wrote to Lord Granville, 'I scarcely see how a cabinet could have been formed, if the inclusion of the Irish members had been insisted on; and now I do not see how the scheme and policy can be saved from shipwreck, if the exclusion is insisted on.'

The plan was bound to be extensive, as its objects were extensive, and it took for granted in the case of Ireland the fundamental probabilities of civil society. He who looks with 'indolent and kingly gaze' upon all projects of written constitutions need not turn to the Appendix unless he will. Two features of the plan were cardinal.

The foundation of the scheme was the establishment in Ireland of a domestic legislature to deal with Irish as distinguished from imperial affairs. It followed from this that if Irish members and representative peers remained at Westminster at all, though they might claim a share in the settlement of imperial affairs, they could not rightly control English or Scotch affairs. This was from the first, and has ever since remained, the Gordian knot. The cabinet on a review of all the courses open determined to propose the plan of total exclusion, save and unless for the purpose of revising this organic statute.

The next question was neither so hard nor so vital. Ought the powers of the Irish legislature to be specifically enumerated? Or was it better to enumerate the branches of legislation from which the statutory parliament was to be shut out? Should we enact the things that they might do, or the things that they might not do, leaving them the whole residue of law-making power outside of these exceptions and exclusions? The latter was the plan adopted in the bill. Disabilities were specified, and everything not so specified was left within the scope of the Irish authority. These disabilities comprehended all matters affecting the crown. All questions of defence and armed force were shut out; all foreign and colonial relations; the law of trade and navigation, of coinage and legal tender. The new legislature could not meddle with certain charters, nor with certain contracts, nor could it establish or endow any particular religion.[1]

IV

Among his five spurious types of courage, Aristotle names for one the man who seems to be brave, only because he does not see his danger. This, at least, was not Mr. Gladstone's case. No one knew better than the leader in the enterprise, how formidable were the difficulties that lay in his path. The giant mass of secular English prejudice against Ireland frowned like a mountain chain across the track. A strong and proud nation had trained itself for long courses of time in habits of dislike for the history, the political claims, the religion, the temperament, of a weaker nation. The violence of the Irish members in the last parliament, sporadic barbarities in some of the wilder portions of the island, the hideous murders in the Park, had all deepened and vivified the scowling impressions nursed by large bodies of Englishmen for many ages past about unfortunate Ireland. Then the practical operation of shaping an Irish constitution, whether on colonial, federal, or any

[1] See Appendix.

other lines, was in itself a task that, even if all external CHAP.
circumstance had been as smiling as it was in fact the V.
opposite, still abounded in every kind of knotty, intricate, and Æt. 77.
intractable matter.

It is true that elements could be discovered on the other
side. First, was Mr. Gladstone's own high place in the confidence of great masses of his countrymen, the result of a
lifetime of conspicuous service and achievement. Next, the
lacerating struggle with Ireland ever since 1880, and the
confusion into which it had brought our affairs, had bred
something like despair in many minds, and they were ready
to look in almost any direction for relief from an intolerable
burden. Third, the controversy had not gone very far before
opponents were astounded to find that the new policy, which
they angrily scouted as half insanity and half treason, gave
comparatively little shock to the new democracy. This was
at first imputed to mere ignorance and raw habits of political
judgment. Wider reflection might have warned them that
the plain people of this island, though quickly roused against
even the shadow of concession when the power or the greatness of their country is openly assailed, seem at the same
time ready to turn to moral claims of fair play, of conciliation, of pacific truce. With all these magnanimous sentiments the Irish case was only too easily made to associate
itself. The results of the Irish elections and the force of the
constitutional demand sank deep in the popular mind. The
grim spectre of Coercion as the other alternative wore its
most repulsive look in the eyes of men, themselves but
newly admitted to full citizenship. Rash experiment in
politics has been defined as raising grave issues without
grave cause. Nobody of any party denied in this crisis the
gravity of the cause.

CHAPTER VI

INTRODUCTION OF THE BILL

(*1886*)

MUCH have I seen and known ; cities of men
And manners, climates, councils, governments,
Myself not least, but honour'd of them all. . . .
There lies the port ; the vessel puffs her sail ;
There gloom the dark broad seas.
— TENNYSON, *Ulysses.*

BOOK
IX.

1886. IT was not within the compass either of human effort or
human endurance even for the most practised and skilful
of orators to unfold the whole plan, both government and
land, in a single speech. Nor was public interest at all
equally divided. Irish land had devoured an immense
amount of parliamentary time in late years ; it is one of the
most technical and repulsive of all political subjects ; and to
many of the warmest friends of Irish self-government, any
special consideration for the owners of Irish land was bitterly
unpalatable. Expectation was centred upon the plan for
general government. This was introduced on April 8. Here
is the entry in the little diary : —

The message came to me this morning: 'Hold thou up my
goings in thy path, that my footsteps slip not.' Settled finally my
figures with Welby and Hamilton; other points with Spencer and
Morley. Reflected much. Took a short drive. H. of C., $4\frac{1}{2}$–$8\frac{1}{4}$.
Extraordinary scenes outside the House and in. My speech, which
I have sometimes thought could never end, lasted nearly $3\frac{1}{2}$ hours.
Voice and strength and freedom were granted to me in a degree
beyond what I could have hoped. But many a prayer had gone
up for me, and not I believe in vain.

No such scene had ever been beheld in the House of
Commons. Members came down at break of day to secure
their places ; before noon every seat was marked, and

310

crowded benches were even arrayed on the floor of the CHAP. House from the mace to the bar. Princes, ambassadors, VI. great peers, high prelates, thronged the lobbies. The fame _Æт. 77._ of the orator, the boldness of his exploit, curiosity as to the plan, poignant anxiety as to the party result, wonder whether a wizard had at last actually arisen with a spell .for casting out the baleful spirits that had for so many ages made Ireland our torment and our dishonour, all these things brought together such an assemblage as no minister before had ever addressed within those world-renowned walls. The parliament was new. Many of its members had fought a hard battle for their seats, and trusted they were safe in the haven for half a dozen good years to come. Those who were moved by professional ambition, those whose object was social advancement, those who thought only of upright public service, the keen party men, the men who aspired to office, the men with a past and the men who looked for a future, all alike found themselves adrift on dark and troubled waters. The secrets of the bill had been well kept. To-day the disquieted host were first to learn what was the great project to which they would have to say that Aye or No on which for them and for the state so much would hang.

Of the chief comrades or rivals of the minister's own generation, the strong administrators, the eager and accomplished debaters, the sagacious leaders, the only survivor now comparable to him in eloquence or in influence was Mr. Bright. That illustrious man seldom came into the House in those distracted days ; and on this memorable occasion his stern and noble head was to be seen in dim obscurity. Various as were the emotions in other regions of the House, in one quarter rejoicing was unmixed. There, at least, was no doubt and no misgiving. There pallid and tranquil sat the Irish leader, whose hard insight, whose patience, energy, and spirit of command, had achieved this astounding result, and done that which he had vowed to his countrymen that he would assuredly be able to do. On the benches round him, genial excitement rose almost to tumult. Well it might. For the first time since the union, the Irish case was at last to be pressed in all its force and strength, in every aspect of policy and of conscience, by the most powerful Englishman then alive.

More striking than the audience was the man ; more striking than the multitude of eager onlookers from the shore was the rescuer with deliberate valour facing the floods ready to wash him down ; the veteran Ulysses, who after more than half a century of combat, service, toil, thought it not too late to try a further ' work of noble note.' In the hands of such a master of the instrument, the theme might easily have lent itself to one of those displays of exalted passion which the House had marvelled at in more than one of Mr. Gladstone's speeches on the Turkish question, or heard with religious reverence in his speech on the Affirmation bill in 1883. What the occasion now required was that passion should burn low, and reasoned persuasion hold up the guiding lamp. An elaborate scheme was to be unfolded, an unfamiliar policy to be explained and vindicated. Of that best kind of eloquence which dispenses with declamation, this was a fine and sustained example. There was a deep, rapid, steady, onflowing volume of argument, exposition, exhortation. Every hard or bitter stroke was avoided. Now and again a fervid note thrilled the ear and lifted all hearts. But political oratory is action, not words, — action, character, will, conviction, purpose, personality. As this eager muster of men underwent the enchantment of periods exquisite in their balance and modulation, the compulsion of his flashing glance and animated gesture, what stirred and commanded them was the recollection of national service, the thought of the speaker's mastering purpose, his unflagging resolution and strenuous will, his strength of thew and sinew well tried in long years of resounding war, his unquenched conviction that the just cause can never fail. Few are the heroic moments in our parliamentary politics, but this was one.

II

The first reading of the bill was allowed to pass without a division. To the second, Lord Hartington moved an amendment in the ordinary form of simple rejection.[1] His two speeches[2] present the case against the policy and the bill in its most massive form. The direct and unsophisticated nature of his antagonism, backed by a personal character of uprightness and plain dealing beyond all suspicion, gave a momentum to his attack that was beyond any effect of dialectics. It was noticed that he had never during his thirty years of parliamentary life spoken with anything like the same power before. The debates on the two stages occupied sixteen nights. They were not unworthy of the gravity of the issue, nor of the fame of the House of Commons. Only one speaker held the magic secret of Demosthenic oratory. Several others showed themselves masters of the higher arts of parliamentary discussion. One or two transient spurts of fire in the encounters of orange and green, served to reveal the intensity of the glow behind the closed doors of the furnace. But the general temper was good. The rule against irritating language was hardly ever broken. Swords crossed according to the strict rules of combat. The tone was rational and argumentative. There was plenty of strong, close, and acute reasoning ; there was some learning, a considerable acquaintance both with historic and contemporary, foreign and domestic fact, and when fact and reasoning broke down, their place was abundantly filled by eloquent prophecy of disaster on one side, or blessing on the other. Neither prophecy was demonstrable ; both could be made plausible.

Discussion was adorned by copious references to the mighty shades who had been the glory of the House in a great parliamentary age. We heard again the Virgilian hexameters in which Pitt had described the spirit of his policy at the union : —

> ' Paribus se legibus ambæ
> Invictæ gentes æterna in fœdera mittant.'

We heard once more how Grattan said that union of the legislatures was severance of the nations ; that the ocean

---

[1] First reading, April 13. Motion made for second reading and amendment, May 10. Land bill introduced and first reading, April 16.

[2] April 9, May 10.

forbade union, the channel forbade separation; that England in her government of Ireland had gone to hell for her principles and to bedlam for her discretion. There was, above all, a grand and copious anthology throughout the debate from Burke, the greatest of Irishmen and the largest master of civil wisdom in our tongue.

The appearance of a certain measure of the common form of all debates was inevitable. No bill is ever brought in of which its opponents do not say that it either goes too far, or else it does not go far enough ; no bill of which its defenders do not say as to some crucial flaw pounced upon and paraded by the enemy, that after all it is a mere question of drafting, or can be more appropriately discussed in committee. There was the usual evasion of the strong points of the adversary's case, the usual exaggeration of its weak ones. That is debating. Perorations ran in a monotonous mould ; integrity of the empire on one side, a real, happy, and indissoluble reconciliation between English and Irish on the other.

One side dwelt much on the recall of Lord Fitzwilliam in 1795, and the squalid corruption of the union ; the other, on the hopeless distraction left by the rebellion of 1798, and the impotent confusion of the Irish parliament. One speaker enumerated Mr. Pitt's arguments for the union — the argument about the regency and about the commercial treaty, the argument about foreign alliances and confederacies and the army, about free trade and catholic emancipation ; he showed that under all these six heads the new bill carefully respected and guarded the grounds taken by the minister of the union. He was bluntly answered by the exclamation that nobody cared a straw about what Mr. Pitt said, or what Sir Ralph Abercromby said ; what we had to deal with were the facts of the case in the year 1886. You show your mistrust of the Irish by inserting all these safeguards in the bill, said the opposition. No, replied ministers ; the safeguards are to meet no mistrusts of ours, but those entertained or feigned by other people. You had no mandate for home rule, said the opposition. Still less, ministers retorted, had you a mandate for coercion.

Such a scheme as this, exclaimed the critics, with all
its checks and counterchecks, its truncated functions, its
vetoes, exceptions, and reservations, is degrading to Ireland,
and every Irish patriot with a spark of spirit in his bosom
must feel it so.   As if, retorted the defenders, there were
no degradation to a free people in suffering twenty years of
your firm and resolute coercion.   One side argued that the
interests of Ireland and Great Britain were much too closely
intertwined to permit a double legislature.   The other
argued that this very interdependence was just what made
an Irish legislature safe, because it was incredible that they
should act as if they had no benefit to receive from us, and
no injury to suffer from injury inflicted upon us.   Do you,
asked some, blot out of your minds the bitter, incendiary,
and rebellious speech of Irish members ?   But do you then,
the rejoinder followed, suppose that the language that came
from men's hearts when a boon was refused, is a clue to the
sentiment in their hearts when the boon shall have been
granted ?   Ministers were bombarded with reproachful
quotations from their old speeches.   They answered the
fire by taunts about the dropping of coercion, and the
amazing manœuvres of the autumn of 1885.   The device of
the two orders was denounced as inconsistent with the
democratic tendencies of the age.   A very impressive argument forsooth from you, was the reply, who are either
stout defenders of the House of Lords as it is, or else stout
advocates for some of the multifarious schemes for mixing
hereditary peers with fossil officials, all of them equally
alien to the democratic tendencies whether of this age or
any other.   So, with stroke and counter-stroke, was the
ball kept flying.

Much was made of foreign and colonial analogies ; of the
union between Austria and Hungary, Norway and Sweden,
Denmark and Iceland ; how in forcing legislative union on
North America we lost the colonies ; how the union of legislatures ended in the severance of Holland from Belgium.
All this carried little conviction.   Most members of parliament like to think with pretty large blinkers on, and though
it may make for narrowness, this is consistent with much

practical wisdom.   Historical parallels in the actual politics of the day are usually rather decorative than substantial.

If people disbelieve premisses, nothing can be easier than to ridicule conclusions ; and what happened now was that critics argued against this or that contrivance in the machinery, because they insisted that no machinery was needed at all, and that no contrivance could ever be made to work, because the Irish mechanicians would infallibly devote all their infatuated energy and perverse skill, not to work it, but to break it in pieces.   The Irish, in Mr. Gladstone's ironical paraphrase of these singular opinions, had a double dose of original sin ; they belonged wholly to the kingdoms of darkness, and therefore the rules of that probability which wise men have made the guide of life can have no bearing in any case of theirs.   A more serious way of stating the fundamental objection with which Mr. Gladstone had to deal was this.   Popular government is at the best difficult to work.   It is supremely difficult to work in a statutory scheme with limits, reservations, and restrictions lurking round every corner.   Finally, owing to history and circumstance, no people in all the world is less fitted to try a supremely difficult experiment in government than the people who live in Ireland.   Your superstructure, they said, is enormously heavy, yet you are going to raise it on foundations that are a quaking bog of incapacity and discontent. This may have been a good answer to the policy of the bill. But to criticise its provisions from such a point of view was as inevitably unfruitful as it would be to set a hardened agnostic to revise the Thirty-nine articles or the mystic theses of the Athanasian creed.

On the first reading, Mr. Chamberlain astounded allies and opponents alike by suddenly revealing his view, that the true solution of the question was to be sought in some form of federation.   It was upon the line of federation, and not upon the pattern of the self-governing colonies, that we should find a way out of the difficulty.[1]   Men could hardly trust their ears.   On the second reading, he startled us once more by declaring that he was perfectly prepared, the very

[1] *Hans.* 304, pp. 1204-6.

next day if we pleased, to establish between this country and Ireland the relations subsisting between the provincial legislatures and the dominion parliament of Canada.[1] As to the first proposal, anybody could see that federation was a vastly more revolutionary operation than the delegation of certain legislative powers to a local parliament. Moreover before federating an Irish legislature, you must first create it. As to the second proposal, anybody could see on turning for a quarter of an hour to the Dominion Act of 1867, that in some of the particulars deemed by Mr. Chamberlain to be specially important, a provincial legislature in the Canadian system had more unfettered powers than the Irish legislature would have under the bill. Finally, he urged that inquiry into the possibility of satisfying the Irish demand should be carried on by a committee or commission representing all sections of the House.[2] In face of projects so strangely fashioned as this, Mr. Gladstone had a right to declare that just as the subject held the field in the public mind — for never before had been seen such signs of public absorption in the House and out of the House — so the ministerial plan held the field in parliament. It had many enemies, but it had not a single serious rival.

The debate on the second reading had hardly begun when Lord Salisbury placed in the hands of his adversaries a weapon with which they took care to do much execution. Ireland, he declared, is not one nation, but two nations. There were races like the Hottentots, and even the Hindoos, incapable of self-government. He would not place confidence in people who had acquired the habit of using knives and slugs. His policy was that parliament should enable the government of England to govern Ireland. 'Apply that recipe honestly, consistently, and resolutely for twenty years, and at the end of that time you will find that Ireland will be fit to accept any gifts in the way of local government or repeal of coercion laws that you may wish to give her.'[3] In the same genial vein, Lord Salisbury told his Hottentot fellow-citizens — one of the two *invictæ gentes* of Mr. Pitt's famous quotation — that if some great store of imperial

CHAP.
VI.

Æt. 77.

[1] *Hans.* 306, p. 697.   [2] *Hans.* 304, p. 1202.   [3] May 15, 1886.

treasure were going to be expended on Ireland, instead of buying out landlords, it would be far more usefully employed in providing for the emigration of a million Irishmen. Explanations followed this inconvenient candour, but explanations are apt to be clumsy, and the pungency of the indiscretion kept it long alive. A humdrum speaker, who was able to contribute nothing better to the animation of debate, could always by insinuating a reference to Hottentots, knives and slugs, the deportation of a million Irishmen, and twenty years of continuous coercion, make sure of a roar of angry protest from his opponents, followed by a lusty counter-volley from his friends.

V

The reception of the bill by the organs of Irish opinion was easy to foretell. The nationalists accepted it in sober and rational language, subject to amendments on the head of finance and the constabulary clauses. The tories said it was a bill for setting up an Irish republic. It is another selfish English plan, said the moderates. Some Irishmen who had played with home rule while it was a phrase, drew back when they saw it in a bill. Others, while holding to home rule, objected to being reduced to the status of colonists. The body of home rulers who were protestant was small, and even against them it was retorted that for every protestant nationalist there were ten catholic unionists. The Fenian organs across the Atlantic, while quarrelling with such provisions as the two orders, 'one of which would be Irish and the other English,' did justice to the bravery of the attempt, and to the new moral forces which it would call out. The florid violence which the Fenians abandoned was now with proper variations adopted by Orangemen in the north. The General Assembly of the presbyterian church in Ireland passed strong resolutions against a parliament, in favour of a peasant proprietary, in favour of loyalty, and of coercion. A few days later the general synod of the protestant episcopal church followed suit, and denounced a parliament. The Orange print in Belfast drew up a Solemn League and Covenant for Ulster,

to ignore and resist an Irish national government. Unionist
prints in Dublin declared and indignantly repelled 'the
selfish English design to get rid of the Irish nuisance from
Westminster, and reduce us to the position of a tributary
dependency.'[1]

The pivot of the whole policy was the acceptance of the
bill by the representatives of Ireland. On the evening when
the bill was produced, Mr. Parnell made certain complaints
as to the reservation of the control of the constabulary,
as to the power of the first order to effect a deadlock, and as
to finance. He explicitly and publicly warned the government from the first that, when the committee stage was
reached, he would claim a large decrease in the fraction
named for the imperial contribution. There was never any
dissembling as to this. In private discussion, he had always
held that the fair proportion of Irish contribution to imperial charges was not a fifteenth but a twentieth, and he
said no more in the House than he had persistently said in
the Irish secretary's room. There too he had urged what
he also declared in the House : that he had always insisted
that due representation should be given to the minority ;
that he should welcome any device for preventing ill-considered legislation, but that the provision in the bill, for the
veto of the first order, would lead to prolonged obstruction
and delay. Subject to modification on these three heads, he
accepted the bill. 'I am convinced,' he said in concluding,
'that if our views are fairly met in committee regarding the
defects to which I have briefly alluded, — the bill will be
cheerfully accepted by the Irish people, and by their representatives, as a solution of the long-standing dispute between
the two countries.'[2]

It transpired at a later date that just before the introduction of the bill, when Mr. Parnell had been made
acquainted with its main proposals, he called a meeting of
eight of his leading colleagues, told them what these proposals were, and asked them whether they would take the

[1] See for instance, *Irish Times*, May 8, and *Belfast Newsletter*, May 17, 18, 21, 1886.

[2] *Hans.* 304, p. 1134. Also 305, p. 1252.

bill or leave it.[1] Some began to object to the absence of
certain provisions, such as the immediate control of the
constabulary, and the right over duties of customs. Mr.
Parnell rose from the table, and clenched the discussion by
informing them that if they declined the bill, the government would go. They at once agreed 'to accept it *pro
tanto*, reserving for committee the right of enforcing and,
if necessary, reconsidering their position with regard to
these important questions.' This is neither more nor less
than the form in which Mr. Parnell made his declaration in
parliament. There was complete consistency between the
terms of this declaration, and the terms of acceptance
agreed to by his colleagues, as disclosed in the black days
of December four years later. The charge of bad faith and
hypocrisy so freely made against the Irishmen is wholly
unwarranted by a single word in these proceedings. If the
whole transaction had been known to the House of Commons, it could not have impaired by one jot or tittle the
value set by the supporters of the bill on the assurances of
the Irishmen that, in principle and subject to modification
on points named, they accepted the bill as a settlement of
the question, and would use their best endeavours to make
it work.[2]

[1] When the bill was practically
settled, he asked if he might have
a draft of the main provisions, for
communication to half a dozen of his
confidential colleagues. After some
demur, the Irish secretary consented, warning him of the damaging
consequences of any premature divul-
gation. The draft was duly returned,
and not a word leaked out. Some
time afterwards Mr. Parnell recalled
the incident to me. 'Three of the
men to whom I showed the draft
were newspaper men, and they were
poor men, and any newspaper would
have given them a thousand pounds
for it. No very wonderful virtue,
you may say. But how many of
your House of Commons would
believe it ? '

[2] For this point, see the *Times*
report of the famous proceedings in
Committee-room Fifteen, collected in
the volume entitled *The Parnellite
Split* (1891).

CHAPTER VII

THE POLITICAL ATMOSPHERE. DEFEAT OF THE BILL

(*1886*)

EVERYTHING on every side was full of traps and mines. . . . It was in the midst of this chaos of plots and counterplots . . . that the firmness of that noble person [Lord Rockingham] was put to the proof. He never stirred from his ground; no, not an inch. — BURKE (1766).

THE atmosphere in London became thick and hot with political passion. Veteran observers declared that our generation had not seen anything like it. Distinguished men of letters and, as it oddly happened, men who had won some distinction either by denouncing the legislative union, or by insisting on a decentralisation that should satisfy Irish national aspirations, now choked with anger because they were taken at their word. Just like irascible scholars of old time who settled controversies about corrupt texts by imputing to rival grammarians shameful crimes, so these writers could find no other explanation for an opinion that was not their own about Irish government, except moral turpitude and personal degradation. One professor of urbanity compared Mr. Gladstone to a desperate pirate burning his ship, or a gambler doubling and trebling his stake as luck goes against him. Such strange violence in calm natures, such pharisaic pretension in a world where we are all fallen, remains a riddle. Political differences were turned into social proscription. Whigs who could not accept the new policy were specially furious with whigs who could. Great ladies purified their lists of the names of old intimates. Amiable magnates excluded from their dinner-tables and their country houses once familiar friends who had fallen into the guilty heresy, and even harmless portraits of the heresiarch were sternly removed from the walls. At some of the political clubs it rained blackballs. It was a painful demonstration how thin after all is our social veneer, even when most highly polished.

When a royal birthday was drawing near, the prime minister wrote to Lord Granville, his unfailing counsellor in every difficulty political and social: 'I am becoming seriously perplexed about my birthday dinner. Hardly any peers of the higher ranks will be available, and not many of the lower. Will the seceding colleagues come if they are asked? (Argyll, to whom I applied privately on the score of old friendship, has already *refused* me.) I am for asking them; but I expect refusal. Lastly, it has become customary for the Prince of Wales to dine with me on that day, and he brings his eldest son now that the young Prince is of age. But his position would be very awkward, if he comes and witnesses a great nakedness of the land. What do you say to all this? If you cannot help me, who can?' Most of the seceding colleagues accepted, and the dinner came off well enough, though as the host wrote to a friend beforehand, 'If Hartington were to get up and move a vote of want of confidence after dinner, he would almost carry it.' The Prince was unable to be present, and so the great nakedness was by him unseen, but Prince Albert Victor, who was there instead, is described by Mr. Gladstone as 'most kind.'

The conversion of Peel to free trade forty years before had led to the same species of explosion, though Peel had the court strongly with him. Both then and now it was the case of a feud within the bosom of a party, and such feuds like civil wars have ever been the fiercest. In each case there was a sense of betrayal — at least as unreasonable in 1886 as it was in 1846. The provinces somehow took things more rationally than the metropolis. Those who were stunned by the fierce moans of London over the assured decline in national honour and credit, the imminence of civil war, and the ultimate destruction of British power, found their acquaintances in the country excited and interested, but still clothed and in their right minds. The gravity of the question was fully understood, but in taking sides ordinary men did not talk as if they were in for the battle of Armageddon. The attempt to kindle the torch of religious fear or hate was in Great Britain happily a failure. The mass of liberal presbyterians in Scotland, and of nonconformists in England and Wales, stood firm, though some of their most eminent and able divines resisted the new project, less on religious grounds than on what they took to be the balance of political arguments. Mr. Gladstone was able to point to the conclusive assurances he had received that the kindred peoples in the colonies and America regarded with warm and fraternal sympathy the present effort to settle the long-vexed and troubled relations between Great Britain and Ireland : —

We must not be discouraged if at home and particularly in the upper ranks of society, we hear a variety of discordant notes, notes alike discordant from our policy and from one another. You have before you a cabinet determined in its purpose and an intelligible plan. I own I see very little else in the political arena that is determined or that is intelligible.

Inside the House subterranean activity was at its height all through the month of May. This was the critical period. The regular opposition spoke little and did little ; with composed interest they watched others do their work. On the ministerial side men wavered and changed and changed again, from day to day and almost from hour to hour. Never were the motions of the pendulum so agitated and so irregular. So novel and complex a problem was a terrible burden for a new parliament. About half its members had not sat in any parliament before. The whips were new, some of the leaders on the front benches were new, and those of them who were most in earnest about the policy were too heavily engrossed in the business of the measure, to have much time for the exercises of explanation, argument, and persuasion with their adherents. One circumstance told powerfully for ministers. The great central organisation of the liberal party came decisively over to Mr. Gladstone (May 5), and was followed by nearly all the local associations in the country. Neither whig secession nor radical dubitation shook the strength inherent in such machinery, in a community where the principle of government by party has solidly established itself. This was almost the single consolidating and steadying element in that hour of dispersion. A serious move in the opposite direction had taken place three weeks earlier. A great meeting was held at the Opera House, in the Haymarket, presided over by the accomplished whig nobleman who had the misfortune to be Irish viceroy in the two dismal years from 1880, and it was attended both by Lord Salisbury on one side and Lord Hartington on the other. This was the first broad public mark of liberal secession, and of that practical fusion between whig and tory which the new Irish policy had actually precipitated, but to which all the signs in the political heavens had been for three or four years unmistakably pointing.

The strength of the friends of the bill was twofold : first, it lay in the dislike of coercion as the only visible alternative ; and second, it lay in the hope of at last touching the firm ground of a final settlement with Ireland. Their weakness was also twofold : first, misgivings about the exclusion of the Irish members; and second, repugnance to the scheme for land purchase. There were not a few, indeed, who pronounced the exclusion of Irish members to be the most sensible part of the plan. Mr. Gladstone retained his impartiality, but knew that if we proposed to keep the Irishmen, we should be run in upon quite as fiercely from the other side. Mr. Parnell stood to his original position. Any regular and compulsory attendance at Westminster, he said, would be highly objectionable to his friends. Further, the right of Irish members to take part in purely English as well as imperial business would be seized upon by English politicians, whenever it should answer their purpose, as a pretext for interfering in Irish affairs. In short, he foresaw, as all did, the difficulties that would inevitably arise from retention. But the tide ran more and more strongly the other way. Scotland grew rather restive at a proposal which, as she apprehended, would make a precedent for herself when her turn for extension of local powers should come, and Scotchmen had no intention of being shut out

from a voice in imperial affairs. In England, the catholics
professed alarm at the prospect of losing the only catholic
force in the House of Commons. 'We cannot spare one of
you,' cried Cardinal Manning. Some partisans of imperial
federation took it into their heads that the plan for Ireland
would be fatal to a plan for the whole empire, though others
more rationally conceived that if there was to be a scheme
for the empire, schemes for its several parts must come first.
Some sages, while pretending infinite friendship to home
rule, insisted that the parliament at Westminster should
retain a direct and active veto upon legislation at Dublin,
and that Irish members should remain as they were in
London. That is to say, every precaution should be taken
to ensure a stiff fight at Westminster over every Irish
measure of any importance that had already been fought on
College Green. Speaking generally, the feeling against this
provision was due less to the anomaly of taxation without
representation, than to fears for the unity of the empire and
the supremacy of parliament.

The Purchase bill proved from the first to be an almost
intolerable dose. Vivid pictures were drawn of a train of
railway trucks two miles long, loaded with millions of bright
sovereigns, all travelling from the pocket of the British son of
toil to the pocket of the idle Irish landlord. The nationalists
from the first urged that the scheme for home rule should
not be weighted with a land scheme, though they were willing
to accept it so long as it was not used to prejudice the larger
demand. On the other side the Irish landlords themselves
peremptorily rejected the plan that had been devised for
their protection.

The air was thick with suggestions, devices, contrivances,
expedients, possible or madly impossible. Proposals or
embryonic notions of proposals floated like motes in a sunbeam. Those to whom lobby diplomacy is as the breath of
their nostrils, were in their element. So were the worthy
persons who are always ready with ingenious schemes for
catching a vote or two here, at the cost of twenty votes elsewhere. Intrigue may be too dark a word, but coaxing, bullying, managing, and all the other arts of party emergency, went

on at an unprecedented rate. Of these arts, the supervising angels will hardly record that any section had a monopoly. The legerdemain that makes words pass for things, and liquefies things into words, achieved many flashes of success. But they were only momentary, and the solid obstacles remained. The foundations of human character are much the same in all historic ages, and every public crisis brings out the same types.

Much depended on Mr. Bright, the great citizen and noble orator, who had in the last five-and-forty years fought and helped to win more than one battle for wise and just government ; whose constancy had confronted storms of public obloquy without yielding an inch of his ground ; whose eye for the highest questions of state had proved itself singularly sure ; and whose simplicity, love of right, and unsophisticated purity of public and private conduct, commanded the trust and the reverence of nearly all the better part of his countrymen. To Mr. Bright the eyes of many thousands were turned in these weeks of anxiety and doubt. He had in public kept silence, though in private he made little secret of his disapproval of the new policy. Before the bill was produced he had a prolonged conversation (March 20) with Mr. Gladstone at Downing Street. 'Long and weighty' are the words in the diary. The minister sketched his general design. Mr. Bright stated his objections much in the form in which, as we shall see, he stated them later. Of the exclusion of the Irish members he approved. The Land bill he thought quite wrong, for why should so enormous an effort be made for one interest only ? He expressed his sympathy with Mr. Gladstone in his great difficulties, could not but admire his ardour, and came away with the expectation that the obstacles would be found invincible, and that the minister would retire and leave others to approach the task on other lines. Other important persons, it may be observed, derived at this time a similar impression from Mr. Gladstone's language to them : that he might discern the impossibility of his policy, that he would admit it, and would then hand the responsibility over to Lord Hartington, or whoever else might be willing to face it.

On the other hand, Mr. Bright left the minister himself CHAP. not without hopes that as things went forward he might VII. count on this potent auxiliary.   So late as the middle of Æt. 77. May, though he could not support, it was not certain that he would actively oppose.   The following letter to Mr. Gladstone best describes his attitude at this time : —

Mr. Bright to Mr. Gladstone.

Rochdale, May 13th, 1886.

MY DEAR GLADSTONE, — Your note just received has put me in a great difficulty.   To-day is the anniversary of the greatest sorrow of my life, and I feel pressed to spend it at home.   I sent a message to Mr. Arnold Morley last evening to say that I did not intend to return to town before Monday next — but I shall now arrange to go to-morrow — although I do not see how I can be of service in the great trouble which has arisen.

I feel outside all the contending sections of the liberal party — for I am not in favour of home rule, or the creation of a Dublin parliament — nor can I believe in any scheme of federation as shadowed forth by Mr. Chamberlain.

I do not believe that with regard to the Irish question 'the resources of civilisation are exhausted'; and I think the plan of your bill is full of complexity, and gives no hope of successful working in Ireland or of harmony between Westminster and Dublin.   I may say that my regard for you and my sympathy with you have made me silent in the discussion on the bills before the House.   I cannot consent to a measure which is so offensive to the whole protestant population of Ireland, and to the whole sentiment of the province of Ulster so far as its loyal and protestant people are concerned.   I cannot agree to exclude them from the protection of the imperial parliament.   I would do much to clear the rebel party from Westminster, and I do not sympathise with those who wish to retain them, but admit there is much force in the arguments on this point which are opposed to my views upon it.

Up to this time I have not been able to bring myself to the point of giving a vote in favour of your bills.   I am grieved to have to say this.   As to the Land bill, if it comes to a second reading, I fear I must vote against it.   It may be that my hostility to the rebel

party, looking at their conduct since your government was formed
six years ago, disables me from taking an impartial view of this
great question.   If I could believe them loyal, if they were
honourable and truthful men, I could yield them much; but I
suspect that your policy of surrender to them will only place more
power in their hands, to war with greater effect against the unity
of the three kingdoms with no increase of good to the Irish
people.

How then can I be of service to you or to the real interests of
Ireland if I come up to town ?   I cannot venture to advise you,
so superior to me in party tactics and in experienced statesmanship, and I am not so much in accord with Mr. Chamberlain as to
make it likely that I can say anything that will affect his course.
One thing I may remark, that it appears to me that measures of
the gravity of those now before parliament cannot and ought not
to be thrust through the House by force of a small majority.
The various reform bills, the Irish church bill, the two great land
bills, were passed by very large majorities.   In the present case,
not only the whole tory party oppose, but a very important section of the liberal party; and although numerous meetings of
clubs and associations have passed resolutions of confidence in
you, yet generally they have accepted your Irish government
bill as a 'basis' only, and have admitted the need of important
changes in the bill — changes which in reality would destroy the
bill.   Under these circumstances it seems to me that more time
should be given for the consideration of the Irish question.
Parliament is not ready for it, and the intelligence of the country
is not ready for it.   If it be possible, I should wish that no division should be taken upon the bill.   If the second reading should
be carried only by a *small* majority, it would not forward the bill ;
but it would strengthen the rebel party in their future agitation,
and make it more difficult for another session or another parliament to deal with the question with some sense of independence
of that party.   In any case of a division, it is I suppose certain
that a considerable majority of British members will oppose the
bill.   Thus, whilst it will have the support of the rebel members,
it will be opposed by a majority from Great Britain and by a most
hostile vote from all that is loyal in Ireland.   The result will

be, if a majority supports you it will be one composed in effect
of the men who for six years past have insulted the Queen, have
torn down the national flag, have declared your lord lieutenant
guilty of deliberate murder, and have made the imperial parliament an assembly totally unable to manage the legislative business for which it annually assembles at Westminster.

CHAP.
VII.
Æt. 77.

Pray forgive me for writing this long letter. I need not assure
you of my sympathy with you, or my sorrow at being unable to
support your present policy in the House or the country. The
more I consider the question, the more I am forced in a direction
contrary to my wishes.

For thirty years I have preached justice to Ireland. I am as
much in her favour now as in past times, but I do not think it
justice or wisdom for Great Britain to consign her population,
including Ulster and all her protestant families, to what there is
of justice and wisdom in the Irish party now sitting in the parliament in Westminster.

Still, if you think I can be of service, a note to the Reform
Club will, I hope, find me there to-morrow evening. — Ever most
sincerely yours,   JOHN BRIGHT.

An old parliamentary friend, of great weight and authority, went to Mr. Bright to urge him to support a proposal to read the bill a second time, and then to hang it
up for six months. Bright suffered sore travail of spirit.
At the end of an hour the peacemaker rose to depart.
Bright pressed him to continue the wrestle. After three-
quarters of an hour more of it, the same performance
took place. It was not until a third hour of discussion
that Mr. Bright would let it come to an end, and at the
end he was still uncertain. The next day the friend met
him, looking worn and gloomy. 'You may guess,' Mr.
Bright said, 'what sort of a night I have had.' He had
decided to vote against the second reading. The same person went to Lord Hartington. He took time to deliberate,
and then finally said, 'No ; Mr. Gladstone and I do not
mean the same thing.'

II

The centre of interest lay in the course that might be finally taken by those who declared that they accepted the principle of the bill, but demurred upon detail. It was upon the group led from Birmingham that the issue hung. 'There are two principles in the bill,' said Mr. Chamberlain at this time, 'which I regard as vital. The first is the principle of autonomy, to which I am able to give a hearty assent. The second is involved in the method of giving effect to this autonomy. In the bill the government have proceeded on the lines of separation or of colonial independence, whereas, in my humble judgment, they should have adopted the principle of federation as the only one in accordance with democratic aspirations and experience.'[1] He was even so strong for autonomy, that he was ready to face all the immense difficulties of federation, whether on the Canadian or some other pattern, rather than lose autonomy. Yet he was ready to slay the bill that made autonomy possible. To kill the bill was to kill autonomy. To say that they would go to the country on the plan, and not on the principle, was idle. If the election were to go against the government, that would destroy not only the plan which they disliked, but the principle of which they declared that they warmly approved. The new government that would in that case come into existence, would certainly have nothing to say either to plan or principle.

Two things, said Mr. Chamberlain on the ninth night of the debate, had become clear during the controversy. One was that the British democracy had a passionate devotion to the prime minister. The other was the display of a sentiment out of doors, 'the universality and completeness of which, I dare say, has taken many of us by surprise, in favour of some form of home rule to Ireland, which will give to the Irish people some greater control over their own affairs.'[2] It did not need so acute a strategist as Mr. Chamberlain to perceive that the only hope of rallying any

[1] Letter to Mr. T. H. Bolton, M.P. *Times*, May 8, 1886.
[2] *Hans.* 306, p. 698.

considerable portion of the left wing of the party to the dissentient flag, in face of this strong popular sentiment embodied in a supereminent minister, was to avoid as much as possible all irreconcilable language against either the minister or the sentiment, even while taking energetic steps to unhorse the one and to nullify the other.

The prime minister meanwhile fought the battle as a battle for a high public design once begun should be fought. He took few secondary arguments, but laboured only to hold up to men's imagination, and to burn into their understanding, the lines of central policy, the shame and dishonour from which it would relieve us, the new life with which it would inspire Ireland, the ease that it would bring to parliament in England. His tenacity, his force and resource, were inexhaustible. He was harassed on every side. The Irish leader pressed him hard upon finance. Old adherents urged concession about exclusion. The radicals disliked the two orders. Minor points for consideration in committee rained in upon him, as being good reasons for altering the bill before it came in sight of committee. Not a single constructive proposal made any way in the course of the debate. All was critical and negative. Mr. Gladstone's grasp was unshaken, and though he saw remote bearings and interdependent consequences where others supposed all to be plain sailing, yet if the principle were only saved he professed infinite pliancy. He protested that there ought to be no stereotyping of our minds against modifications, and that the widest possible variety of modes of action should be kept open; and he 'hammered hard at his head,' as he put it, to see what could be worked out in the way of admitting Irish members without danger, and without intolerable inconvenience. If anybody considered, he continued to repeat in endless forms, that there was another set of provisions by which better and fuller effect could be given to the principle of the bill, they were free to displace all the particulars that hindered this better and fuller effect being given to the principle.[1]

[1] *Hans.* 306, p. 1218.

III

At the beginning of May the unionist computation was that 119 on the ministerial side of the House had, with or without qualification, promised to vote against the second reading. Of these, 70 had publicly committed themselves, and 23 more were supposed to be absolutely certain. If the whole House voted, this estimate of 93 would give a majority of 17 against the bill.[1] The leader of the radical wing, however, reckoned that 55 out of the 119 would vote with him for the second reading, if he pronounced the ministerial amendments of the bill satisfactory. The amendments demanded were the retention of the Irish members, a definite declaration of the supremacy of the imperial parliament, a separate assembly for Ulster, and the abolition of the restrictive devices for the representation of minorities. Less than all this might have been taken in committee, provided that the government would expressly say before the second reading, that they would retain the Irish representation on its existing footing. The repeated offer by ministers to regard this as an open question was derided, because it was contended that if the bill were once safe through its second reading, Mr. Bright and the whigs would probably vote with ministers against Irish inclusion.

Even if this ultimatum had been accepted, there would still have remained the difficulty of the Land bill, of which Mr. Chamberlain had announced that he would move the rejection. In the face of ever-growing embarrassments and importunities, recourse was had to the usual device of a meeting of the party at the foreign office (May 27). The circular calling the meeting was addressed to those liberals who, while retaining full freedom on all particulars in the bill, were ‘in favour of the establishment of a legislative body in Dublin for the management of affairs specifically and exclusively Irish.’ This was henceforth to be the test of party membership. A man who was for an Irish legislative body was expected to come to the party meeting, and a man who was against it was expected to stay

[1] In the end exactly 93 liberals did vote against the bill.

away.   Many thought this discrimination a mistake.   Some   CHAP.
two hundred and twenty members attended.   The pith of   VII.
the prime minister's speech, which lasted for an hour, came   Æt. 77.
to this: that the government would not consent to emasculate the principle of the bill, or turn it into a mockery, a
delusion, and a snare; that members who did not wholly
agree with the bill, might still in accordance with the strict
spirit of parliamentary rules vote for the second reading
with a view to its amendment in committee; that such a
vote would not involve support of the Land bill; that he
was ready to consider any plan for the retention of the
Irish members, provided that it did not interfere with the
liberty of the Irish legislative body, and would not introduce
confusion into the imperial parliament.   Finally, as to procedure—and here his anxious audience fell almost breathless
—they could either after a second reading hang up the bill,
and defer committee until the autumn ; or they could wind
up the session, prorogue, and introduce the bill afresh with
the proper amendments in October.   The cabinet, he told
them, inclined to the later course.

Before the meeting Mr. Parnell had done his best to
impress upon ministers the mischievous effect that would
be produced on Irish members and in Ireland, by any
promise to withdraw the bill after the second reading.   On
the previous evening, I received from him a letter of unusual
length.   'You of course,' he said, 'are the best judges of what
the result may be in England, but if it be permitted me to
express an opinion, I should say that withdrawal could
scarcely fail to give great encouragement to those whom it
cannot conciliate, to depress and discourage those who are
now the strongest fighters for the measure, to produce doubt
and wonder in the country and to cool enthusiasm; and
finally, when the same bill is again produced in the autumn,
to disappoint and cause reaction among those who may
have been temporarily disarmed by withdrawal, and to
make them at once more hostile and less easy to appease.'
This letter I carried to Mr. Gladstone the next morning, and
read aloud to him a few minutes before he was to cross over
to the foreign office.   For a single instant—the only occasion

that I can recall during all these severe weeks — his patience broke. The recovery was as rapid as the flash, for he knew the duty of the lieutenant of the watch to report the signs of rock or shoal. He was quite as conscious of all that was urged in Mr. Parnell's letter as was its writer, but perception of risks on one side did not overcome risks on the other. The same evening they met for a second time : —

May 27. — . . . Mr. Gladstone and Parnell had a conversation in my room. Parnell courteous enough, but depressed and gloomy. Mr. Gladstone worn and fagged. . . . When he was gone, Parnell repeated moodily that he might not be able to vote for the second reading, if it were understood that after the second reading the bill was to be withdrawn. 'Very well,' said I, 'that will of course destroy the government and the policy; but be that as it may, the cabinet, I am positive, won't change their line.'

The proceedings at the foreign office brought to the supporters of government a lively sense of relief. In the course of the evening a score of the waverers were found to have been satisfied, and were struck off the dissentient lists. But the relief did not last for many hours. The opposition instantly challenged ministers (May 28) to say plainly which of the two courses they intended to adopt. Though short, this was the most vivacious debate of all. Was the bill to be withdrawn, or was it to be postponed? If it was to be withdrawn, then, argued the tory leader (Sir M. H. Beach) in angry tones, the vote on the second reading would be a farce. If it was to be postponed, what was that but to paralyse the forces of law and order in Ireland in the meantime? Such things were trifling with parliament, trifling with a vital constitutional question, and trifling with the social order which the government professed to be so anxious to restore. A bill read a second time on such terms as these would be neither more nor less than a Continuance-in-Office bill.

This biting sally raised the temper of the House on both sides, and Mr. Gladstone met it with that dignity which did not often fail to quell even the harshest of his adversaries. 'You pronounce that obviously the motive of the govern-

ment is to ensure their own continuance in office. They
prefer that to all the considerations connected with the
great issue before them, and their minds in fact are of such
a mean and degraded order, that they can only be acted
upon, not by motives of honour and duty, but simply by
those of selfishness and personal interest. Sir, I do not
condescend to discuss that imputation. The dart aimed at
our shield, being such a dart as that, is *telum imbelle sine
ictu.*' [1]

The speaker then got on to the more hazardous part of
the ground. He proceeded to criticise the observation of the
leader of the opposition that ministers had undertaken to
remodel the bill. 'That happy word,' he said, 'as applied
to the structure of the bill, is a pure invention.' Lord
Randolph interjected that the word used was not 'remodelled,' but 'reconstructed.' 'Does the noble lord dare
to say,' asked the minister, 'that it was used in respect of
the bill?' 'Yes,' said the noble lord. 'Never, never,' cried
the minister, with a vehemence that shook the hearts of
doubting followers; 'it was used with respect to one particular clause, and one particular point of the bill, namely
so much of it as touches the future relation of the representatives of Ireland to the imperial parliament.' Before
the exciting episode was over, it was stated definitely that if
the bill were read a second time, ministers would advise a
prorogation and re-introduce the bill with amendments.
The effect of this couple of hours was to convince the House
that the government had made up their minds that it was
easier and safer to go to the country with the plan as it
stood, than to agree to changes that would entangle them
in new embarrassments, and discredit their confidence in
their own handiwork. Ingenious negotiators perceived that
their toil had been fruitless. Every man now knew the
precise situation that he had to face, in respect alike of the
Irish bill and liberal unity.

On the day following this decisive scene (May 29), under
the direction of the radical leader an invitation to a conference was issued to those members 'who being in favour

[1] *Hans.* 306, p. 322.

of some sort of autonomy for Ireland, disapproved of the government bills in their present shape.' The form of the invitation is remarkable in view of its ultimate effect on Irish autonomy. The meeting was held on May 31, in the same committee room upstairs that four years later became associated with the most cruel of all phases of the Irish controversy. Mr. Chamberlain presided, and some fifty-five gentlemen attended. Not all of them had hitherto been understood to be in favour either of some sort, or of any sort, of autonomy for Ireland. The question was whether they should content themselves with abstention from the division, or should go into the lobby against the government. If they abstained, the bill would pass, and an extension of the party schism would be averted. The point was carried, as all great parliamentary issues are, by considerations apart from the nice and exact balance of argument on the merits. In anxious and distracting moments like this, when so many arguments tell in one way and so many tell in another, a casting vote often belongs to the moral weight of some particular person. The chairman opened in a neutral sense. It seems to have been mainly the moral weight of Mr. Bright that sent down the scale. He was not present, but he sent a letter. He hoped that every man would use his own mind, but for his part he must vote against the bill. This letter was afterwards described as the death-warrant of the bill and of the administration. The course of the men who had been summoned because they were favourable to some sort of home rule was decided by the illustrious statesman who opposed every sort of home rule. Their boat was driven straight upon the rocks of coercion by the influence of the great orator who had never in all his career been more eloquent than when he was denouncing the mischief and futility of Irish coercion, and protesting that force is no remedy.

One of the best speakers in the House, though not at that time in the cabinet, was making an admirably warm and convinced defence alike of the policy and the bill while these proceedings were going on. But Mr. Fowler was listened to by men of pre-occupied minds. All knew what momentous business was on foot in another part of the parliamentary precincts.   Many in the ranks were confident that abstention would carry the day.   Others knew that the meeting had been summoned for no such purpose, and they made sure that the conveners would have their way.   The quiet inside the House was intense and unnatural.   As at last the news of the determination upstairs to vote against the bill ran along the benches before the speaker sat down, men knew that the ministerial day was lost.   It was estimated by the heads of the ' Chamberlain group,' that if they abstained, the bill would pass by a majority of five.   Such a bill carried by such a majority could of course not have proceeded much further.   The principle of autonomy would have been saved, and time would have been secured for deliberation upon a new plan.   More than once Mr. Gladstone observed that no decision taken from the beginning of the crisis to the end was either more incomprehensible or more disastrous.

IV

The division was taken a little after one o'clock on the morning of the 8th of June.   The Irish leader made one of the most masterly speeches that ever fell from him. Whether agreeing with or differing from the policy, every un-prejudiced listener felt that this was not the mere dialectic of a party debater, dealing smartly with abstract or verbal or artificial arguments, but the utterance of a statesman with his eye firmly fixed upon the actual circumstances of the nation for whose government this bill would make him responsible.   As he dealt with Ulster, with finance, with the supremacy of parliament, with the loyal minority, with the settlement of education in an Irish legislature, — soberly, steadily, deliberately, with that full, familiar, deep insight into the facts of a country, which is only possible to a man who belongs to it and has passed his life in it, the effect of Mr. Parnell's speech was to make even able disputants on either side look little better than amateurs.

The debate was wound up for the regular opposition by Sir Michael Hicks Beach, who was justly regarded throughout the session as having led his party with remarkable skill and judgment. Like the Irish leader, he seemed to be inspired by the occasion to a performance beyond his usual range, and he delivered the final charge with strong effect. The bill, he said, was the concoction of the prime minister and the Irish secretary, and the cabinet had no voice in the matter. The government had delayed the progress of the bill for a whole long and weary month, in order to give party wirepullers plenty of time in which to frighten waverers. To treat a vote on the second reading as a mere vote on a principle, without reference to the possibility of applying it, was a mischievous farce. Could anybody dream that if he supported the second reading now, he would not compromise his action in the autumn, and would not be appealed to as having made a virtual promise to Ireland, of which it would be impossible to disappoint her? As for the bill itself, whatever lawyers might say of the theoretic maintenance of supremacy, in practice it would have gone. All this side of the case was put by the speaker with the straight and vigorous thrust that always works with strong effect in this great arena of contest.

Then came the unflagging veteran with the last of his five speeches. He was almost as white as the flower in his coat, but the splendid compass, the flexibility, the moving charm and power of his voice, were never more wonderful. The construction of the speech was a masterpiece, the temper of it unbroken, its freedom from taunt and bitterness and small personality incomparable. Even if Mr. Gladstone had been in the prime of his days, instead of a man of seventy-six years all struck; even if he had been at his ease for the last four months, instead of labouring with indomitable toil at the two bills, bearing all the multifarious burdens of the head of a government, and all the weight of the business of the leader of the House, undergoing all the hourly strain and contention of a political situation of unprecedented difficulty, — much of the contention being of that peculiarly trying and painful sort which means the parting of colleagues and friends, — his closing speech would still have been a surprising effort of free, argumentative, and fervid appeal. With the fervid

appeal was mingled more than one piece of piquant mockery.
Mr. Chamberlain had said that a dissolution had no terrors
for him. 'I do not wonder at it. I do not see how a dissolution can have any terrors for him. He has trimmed his
vessel, and he has touched his rudder in such a masterly
way, that in whichever direction the winds of heaven may
blow they must fill his sails. Supposing that at an election
public opinion should be very strong in favour of the bill,
my right hon. friend would then be perfectly prepared to
meet that public opinion, and tell it, "I declared strongly
that I adopted the principle of the bill." On the other
hand, if public opinion were very adverse to the bill, he
again is in complete armour, because he says, "Yes, I voted
against the bill." Supposing, again, public opinion is in
favour of a very large plan for Ireland, my right hon. friend
is perfectly provided for that case also. The government
plan was not large enough for him, and he proposed in his
speech on the introduction of the bill that we should have a
measure on the basis of federation, which goes beyond this
bill. Lastly — and now I have very nearly boxed the compass — supposing that public opinion should take quite a
different turn, and instead of wanting very large measures
for Ireland, should demand very small measures for Ireland,
still the resources of my right hon. friend are not exhausted,
because he is then able to point out that the last of his plans
was for four provincial circuits controlled from London.'
All these alternatives and provisions were visibly 'creations
of the vivid imagination, born of the hour and perishing
with the hour, totally unavailable for the solution of a great
and difficult problem.'

Now, said the orator, was one of the golden moments of
our history, one of those opportunities which may come and
may go, but which rarely return, or if they return, return at
long intervals, and under circumstances which no man can
forecast. There was such a golden moment in 1795, on the
mission of Lord Fitzwilliam. At that moment the parliament of Grattan was on the point of solving the Irish problem. The cup was at Ireland's lips, and she was ready to
drink it, when the hand of England rudely and ruthlessly

dashed it to the ground in obedience to the wild and dangerous intimations of an Irish faction.   There had been no great day of hope for Ireland since, no day when you might completely and definitely hope to end the controversy till now — more than ninety years.   The long periodic time had at last run out, and the star had again mounted into the heavens.

This strain of living passion was sustained with all its fire and speed to the very close.   'Ireland stands at your bar expectant, hopeful, almost suppliant.   Her words are the words of truth and soberness.   She asks a blessed oblivion of the past, and in that oblivion our interest is deeper even than hers.   You have been asked to-night to abide by the traditions of which we are the heirs.   What traditions?   By the Irish traditions?   Go into the length and breadth of the world, ransack the literature of all countries, find if you can a single voice, a single book, in which the conduct of England towards Ireland is anywhere treated except with profound and bitter condemnation.   Are these the traditions by which we are exhorted to stand?   No, they are a sad exception to the glory of our country.   They are a broad and black blot upon the pages of its history, and what we want to do is to stand by the traditions of which we are the heirs in all matters except our relations with Ireland, and to make our relation with Ireland to conform to the other traditions of our country.   So we treat our traditions, so we hail the demand of Ireland for what I call a blessed oblivion of the past.   She asks also a boon for the future ; and that boon for the future, unless we are much mistaken, will be a boon to us in respect of honour, no less than a boon to her in respect of happiness, prosperity and peace.   Such, sir, is her prayer.   Think, I beseech you ; think well, think wisely, think, not for the moment, but for the years that are to come, before you reject this bill.'

The question was put, the sand glass was turned upon the table, the division bells were set ringing.   Even at this moment, the ministerial whips believed that some were still wavering.   A reference made by Mr. Parnell to harmonious communications in the previous summer with a tory minister, inclined them to vote for the bill. On the other hand, the prospect of going to an election without a tory opponent was no weak temptation to a weak man. A common impression was that the bill would be beaten by ten or fifteen. Others were sure that it would be twice as much as either figure. Some on the treasury bench, perhaps including the prime minister himself, hoped against hope that the hostile majority might not be more than five or six. It proved to be thirty. The numbers were 343 against 313. Ninety-three liberals voted against the bill. These with the two tellers were between one-third and one-fourth of the full liberal strength from Great Britain. So ended the first engagement in this long campaign. As I passed into his room at the House with Mr. Gladstone that night, he seemed for the first time to bend under the crushing weight of the burden that he had taken up.

V

When ministers went into the cabinet on the following day, three of them inclined pretty strongly towards resignation as a better course than dissolution ; mainly on the ground that the incoming government would then have to go to the country with a policy of their own. Mr. Gladstone, however, entirely composed though pallid, at once opened the case with a list of twelve reasons for recommending dissolution, and the reasons were so cogent that his opening of the case was also its closing. They were entirely characteristic, for they began with precedent and the key was courage. He knew of no instance where a ministry defeated under circumstances like ours, upon a great policy or on a vote of confidence, failed to appeal to the country. Then with a view to the enthusiasm of our friends in this country, as well as to feeling in Ireland, it was essential that we should not let the flag go down. We had been constantly challenged to a dissolution, and not to take the challenge up would be a proof of mistrust, weakness, and a faint heart. 'My conclusion is,' he said, 'a dissolution is formidable, but resignation would mean for the present juncture abandonment of the cause.' His conclusion was accepted without comment. The experts outside the cabinet were convinced that a bold front was the best way of securing the full fighting power of the party. The white feather on such an issue, and with so many minds wavering, would be a sure provocative of defeat.

Mr. Gladstone enumerated to the Queen what he took to be the new elements in the case. There were on the side of the government, 1. The transfer of the Irish vote from the tories, 2. The popular enthusiasm in the liberal masses which he had never seen equalled. But what was the electoral value of enthusiasm against (*a*) anti-Irish prejudices, (*b*) the power of rank, station, and wealth, (*c*) the kind of influence exercised by the established clergy, 'perversely applied as of course Mr. Gladstone thinks in politics, but resting upon a very solid basis as founded on the generally excellent and devoted work which they do in their parishes'? This remained to be proved. On the other side there was the whig defection, with the strange and unnatural addition from Birmingham. 'Mr. Gladstone himself has no skill in these matters, and dare not lay an opinion before your Majesty on the probable general result.' He thought there was little chance, if any, of a tory majority in the new parliament. Opinion taken as a whole seemed to point to a majority not very large, whichever way it may be.

No election was ever fought more keenly, and never did so many powerful men fling themselves with livelier activity into a great struggle. The heaviest and most telling attack came from Mr. Bright, who had up to now in public been studiously silent. Every word, as they said of Daniel Webster, seemed to weigh a pound. His arguments were mainly those of his letter already given, but they were delivered with a gravity and force that told powerfully upon the large phalanx of doubters all over the kingdom. On the other side, Mr. Gladstone's plume waved in every part of the field. He unhorsed an opponent as he flew past on the road; his voice rang with calls as thrilling as were ever heard in England; he appealed to the individual, to his personal responsibility, to the best elements in him, to the sense of justice, to the powers of hope and of sympathy; he

displayed to the full that rare combination of qualities that CHAP.
had always enabled him to view affairs in all their range, VII.
at the same time from the high commanding eminence Æт. 77.
and on the near and sober level.

He left London on June 17 on his way to Edinburgh, and
found 'wonderful demonstrations all along the road; many
little speeches; could not be helped.' 'The feeling here,'
he wrote from Edinburgh (June 21), 'is truly wonderful,
especially when the detestable state of the press is considered.' Even Mr. Goschen, whom he described as
'supplying in the main, soul, brains, and movement to the
dissentient body,' was handsomely beaten in one of the
Edinburgh divisions, so fatal was the proximity of Achilles.
'*June* 22. Off to Glasgow, 12¾. Meeting at 3. Spoke an
hour and twenty minutes. Off at 5.50. Reached Hawarden
at 12.30 or 40. Some speeches by the way; others I declined.
The whole a scene of triumph. God help us, His poor
creatures.' At Hawarden, he found chaos in his room, and
he set to work upon it, but he did not linger. On June 25,
'off to Manchester; great meeting in the Free Trade Hall.
Strain excessive. Five miles through the streets to Mr.
Agnew's; a wonderful spectacle half the way.' From Manchester he wrote, 'I have found the display of enthusiasm
far beyond all former measure,' and the torrid heat of the
meeting almost broke him down, but friends around him
heard him murmur, 'I must do it,' and bracing himself with
tremendous effort he went on. Two days later (June 28) he
wound up the campaign in a speech at Liverpool, which
even old and practised political hands who were there, found
the most magnificent of them all. Staying at Courthey, the
residence of his nephews, in the morning he enters, 'Worked
up the Irish question once more for my last function. Seven
or eight hours of processional uproar, and a speech of an
hour and forty minutes to five or six thousand people in
Hengler's Circus. Few buildings give so noble a presentation of an audience. Once more my voice held out in a
marvellous manner. I went in bitterness, in the heat of my
spirit, but the hand of the Lord was strong upon me.'

He had no sooner returned to Hawarden, than he wrote to

tell Mrs. Gladstone (July 2) of a stroke which was thought
to have a curiously dæmonic air about it : —

The Leith business will show you I have not been inactive here.
—— former M.P. *attended my meeting in the Music Hall,* and was
greeted by me accordingly (he had voted against us after wobbling
about much).   Hearing by late post yesterday that waiting to the
last he had then declared against us, I telegraphed down to Edinburgh in much indignation, that they might if they liked put me
up against him, and I would go down again and speak if they
wished it.   They seem to have acted with admirable pluck and
promptitude.   Soon after mid-day to-day I received telegrams to
say I am elected for Midlothian,[1] and *also for Leith,* —— having
retired rather than wait to be beaten.   I told them instantly to
publish this, as it may do good.

The Queen, who had never relished these oratorical
crusades whether he was in opposition or in office, did
not approve of the first minister of the crown addressing
meetings outside of his own constituency.   In reply to a
gracious and frank letter from Balmoral, Mr. Gladstone
wrote : —

He must state frankly what it is that has induced him thus to
yield [to importunity for speeches].   It is that since the death
of Lord Beaconsfield, in fact since 1880, the leaders of the opposition, Lord Salisbury and Lord Iddesleigh (he has not observed the
same practice in the case of Sir M. H. Beach) have established
a rule of what may be called popular agitation, by addressing public
meetings from time to time at places with which they were not
connected.   This method was peculiarly marked in the case of
Lord Salisbury as a peer, and this change on the part of the
leaders of opposition has induced Mr. Gladstone to deviate on
this critical occasion from the rule which he had (he believes)
generally or uniformly observed in former years.   He is,
as he has previously apprised your Majesty, aware of the immense responsibility he has assumed, and of the severity of just
condemnation which will be pronounced upon him, if he should
eventually prove to have been wrong.   But your Majesty will be

---

[1] He was returned without opposition.

the first to perceive that, even if it had been possible for him to CHAP.
VII.
decline this great contest, it was not possible for him having
entered upon it, to conduct it in a half-hearted manner, or to omit Æt. 77.
the use of any means requisite in order to place (what he thinks)
the true issue before the country.

Nature, however, served the royal purpose. Before his
speech at Liverpool, he was pressed to speak in the
metropolis : —

As to my going to London, — he wrote in reply, — I have twice had
my chest rather seriously strained, and I have at this moment a sense
of internal fatigue within it which is quite new to me, from the
effects of a bad arrangement in the hall at Manchester. Should anything like it be repeated at Liverpool to-morrow I shall not be fit
physically to speak for a week, if then. Mentally I have never
undergone such an uninterrupted strain as since January 30 of
this year. The forming and reforming of the government, the
work of framing the bills, and *studying the subject* (which none of
the opponents would do), have left me almost stunned, and I have
the autumn in prospect with, perhaps, most of the work to do
over again if we succeed.

But this was not to be. The incomparable effort was in
vain. The sons of Zeruiah were too hard for him, and
England was unconvinced.

The final result was that the ministerialists or liberals of
the main body were reduced from 235 to 196, the tories rose
from 251 to 316, the dissentient liberals fell to 74, and Mr.
Parnell remained at his former strength. In other words,
the opponents of the Irish policy of the government were
390, as against 280 in its favour ; or a unionist majority of
110. Once more no single party possessed an independent
or absolute majority. An important member of the tory
party said to a liberal of his acquaintance (July 7), that he
was almost sorry the tories had not played the bold game
and fought independently of the dissentient liberals. 'But
then,' he added, 'we could not have beaten you on the bill,
without the compact to spare unionist seats.'

England had returned opponents of the liberal policy in

the proportion of two and a half to one against its friends;
but Scotland approved in the proportion of three to two,
Wales approved by five to one, and Ireland by four and a
half to one.   Another fact with a warning in it was that,
taking the total poll for Great Britain, the liberals had
1,344,000, the seceders 397,000, and the tories 1,041,000.
Therefore in contested constituencies the liberals of the
main body were only 76,000 behind the forces of tories
and seceders combined.   Considering the magnitude and
the surprise of the issue laid before the electors, and in
view of the confident prophecies of even some peculiar
friends of the policy, that both policy and its authors
would be swept out of existence by a universal explosion
of national anger and disgust, there was certainly no final
and irrevocable verdict in a hostile British majority of no
more than four per cent. of the votes polled.   Apart from
electoral figures, coercion loomed large and near at hand,
and coercion tried under the new political circumstances
that would for the first time attend it, might well be trusted
to do much more than wipe out the margin at the polls.
'There is nothing in the recent defeat,' said Mr. Gladstone,
'to abate the hopes or to modify the anticipations of those
who desire to meet the wants and wishes of Ireland.'

VI

The question now before Mr. Gladstone was whether to
meet the new parliament or at once to resign.   For a short
time he wavered, along with an important colleague, and
then he and all the rest came round to resignation.   The
considerations that guided him were these.   It is best for
Ireland that the party strongest in the new parliament
should be at once confronted with its responsibilities.   Again,
we were bound to consider what would most tend to reunite
the liberal party, and it was in opposition that the chances of
such reunion would be likely to stand highest, especially in
view of coercion which many of the dissidents had refused to
contemplate.   If he could remodel the bill or frame a new
one, that might be a possible ground for endeavouring to
make up a majority, but he could not see his way to any

such process, though he was ready for certain amendments.
Finally, if we remained, an amendment would be moved
definitely committing the new House against home rule.

The conclusion was for immediate resignation, and his
colleagues were unanimous in assent. The Irish view was
different and impossible. Returning from a visit to Ireland
I wrote to Mr. Gladstone (July 19): —

> You may perhaps care to see what —— [not a secular politician]
> thinks, so I enclose you a conversation between him and ——. He
> does not show much strength of political judgment, and one can
> understand why Parnell never takes him into counsel. Parnell,
> of course, is anxious for us to hold on to the last moment. Our
> fall will force him without delay to take up a new and difficult line.
> But his letters to me, especially the last, show a desperate
> willingness to blink the new parliamentary situation.

Mr. Parnell, in fact, pressed with some importunity that
we should meet the new parliament, on the strange view
that the result of the election was favourable on general
questions, and indecisive only on Irish policy. We were to
obtain the balance of supply in an autumn sitting, in
January to attack registration reform, and then to dissolve
upon that, without making any Irish proposition whatever.
This curious suggestion left altogether out of sight the certainty that an amendment referring to Ireland would be at
once moved on the Address, such as must beyond all doubt
command the whole of the tories and a large part, if not all,
of the liberal dissentients. Only one course was possible
for the defeated ministers, and they resigned.

On July 30, Mr. Gladstone had his final audience of the
Queen, of which he wrote the memorandum following: —

Conversation with the Queen, August 2, 1886.

The conversation at my closing audience on Friday was a
singular one; when regarded as the probable last word with the
sovereign after fifty-five years of political life, and a good quarter
of a century's service rendered to her in office.

The Queen was in good spirits; her manners altogether
pleasant. She made me sit at once. Asked after my wife as we

began, and sent a kind message to her as we ended. About me personally, I think, her single remark was that I should require some rest. I remember that on a closing audience in 1874 she said she felt sure I might be reckoned upon to support the throne. She did not say anything of the sort to-day. Her mind and opinions have since that day been seriously warped, and I respect her for the scrupulous avoidance of anything which could have seemed to indicate a desire on her part to claim anything in common with me.

Only at three points did the conversation touch upon anything even faintly related to public affairs. . . . The second point was the conclusion of some arrangement for appanages or incomes on behalf of the third generation of the royal house. I agreed that there ought at a suitable time to be a committee on this subject, as had been settled some time back, she observing that the recent circumstances had made the time unsuitable. I did not offer any suggestion as to the grounds of the affair, but said it seemed to me possible to try some plan under which intended marriages should be communicated without forcing a reply from the Houses. Also I agreed that the amounts were not excessive. I did not pretend to have a solution ready : but said it would, of course, be the duty of the government to submit a plan to the committee. The third matter was trivial : a question or two from her on the dates and proceedings connected with the meeting. The rest of the conversation, not a very long one, was filled up with nothings. It is rather melancholy. But on neither side, given the conditions, could it well be helped.

On the following day she wrote a letter, making it evident that, so far as Ireland was concerned, she could not trust herself to say what she wanted to say. . . .

Among the hundreds of letters that reached him every week was one from an evangelical lady of known piety, enclosing him a form of prayer that had been issued against home rule. His acknowledgment (July 27) shows none of the impatience of the baffled statesman : —

I thank you much for your note ; and though I greatly deplored the issue, and the ideas of the prayer in question, yet, from the moment when I heard it was your composition, I knew

perfectly well that it was written in entire good faith, and had no
relation to political controversy in the ordinary sense.   I cannot
but think that, in bringing the subject of Irish intolerance before
the Almighty Father, we ought to have some regard to the fact
that down to the present day, as between the two religions, the
offence has been in the proportion of perhaps a hundred to one
on the protestant side, and the suffering by it on the Roman side.
At the present hour, I am pained to express my belief that there
is far more of intolerance in action from so-called protestants
against Roman catholics, than from Roman catholics against
protestants.   It is a great satisfaction to agree with you, as I feel
confident that I must do, in the conviction that of prayers we
cannot possibly have too much in this great matter, and for my
own part I heartily desire that, unless the policy I am proposing
be for the honour of God and the good of His creatures, it may
be trampled under foot and broken into dust.   Of your most
charitable thoughts and feelings towards me I am deeply sensible,
and I remain with hearty regard.

As he wrote at this time to R. H. Hutton (July 2), one of
the choice spirits of our age, 'Rely upon it, I can never
quarrel with you or with Bright.   What vexes me is when
differences disclose baseness, which sometimes happens.'

Book X

1886–1892

CHAPTER I

THE MORROW OF DEFEAT

(1886–1887)

CHARITY rendereth a man truly great, enlarging his mind into a vast circumference, and to a capacity nearly infinite ; so that it by a general care doth reach all things, by an universal affection doth embrace and grace the world. . . . Even a spark of it in generosity of dealing breedeth admiration ; a glimpse of it in formal courtesy of behaviour procureth much esteem, being deemed to accomplish and adorn a man. — BARROW.

AFTER the rejection of his Irish policy in the summer of 1886, Mr. Gladstone had a period of six years before him, the life of the new parliament. Strangely dramatic years they were, in some respects unique in our later history. The party schism among liberals grew deeper and wider. The union between tories and seceders became consolidated and final. The alternative policy of coercion was passed through parliament in an extreme form and with violent strain on the legislative machinery, and it was carried out in Ireland in a fashion that pricked the consciences of many thousands of voters who had resisted the proposals of 1886. A fierce storm rent the Irish phalanx in two, and its leader vanished from the field where for sixteen years he had fought so bold and uncompromising a fight. During this period Mr. Gladstone stood in the most trying of all the varied positions of his life, and without flinching he confronted it in the strong faith that the national honour as well as the assuagement of the inveterate Irish wound in the flank of his country, were the issues at stake.

This intense pre-occupation in the political struggle did not for a single week impair his other interests, nor stay his ceaseless activity in controversies that were not touched by politics. Not even now, when the great cause to which he had so daringly committed himself was in decisive issue, could he allow it to dull or sever what had been the standing concerns of life and thought to him for so long a span of years. As from his youth up, so now behind the man of public action was the diligent, eager, watchful student, churchman, apologist, divine. And what is curious and delightful is that he never set a more admirable example of the tone and temper in which literary and religious controversy should be conducted, than in these years when in politics exasperation was at its worst. It was about this time that he wrote: 'Certainly one of the lessons life has taught me is that where there is known to be a common object, the pursuit of truth, there should also be a studious desire to interpret the adversary in the best sense his words will fairly bear; to avoid whatever widens the breach; and to make the most of whatever tends to narrow it. These I hold to be part of the laws of knightly tournament.' And to these laws he sedulously conformed. Perhaps at some happy time before the day of judgment they may be transferred from the tournament to the battle-fields of philosophy, criticism, and even politics.

II

After the defeat in which his tremendous labours had for the moment ended, he made his way to what was to him the most congenial atmosphere in the world, to the company of Döllinger and Acton, at Tegernsee in Bavaria. 'Tegernsee,' Lord Acton wrote to me (Sept. 7), 'is an out-of-the-way place, peaceful and silent, and as there is a good library in the house, I have taken some care of his mind, leading in the direction of little French comedies, and away from the tragedy of existence. It has done him good, and he has just started with Döllinger to climb a high mountain in the neighbourhood.'

To Mrs. Gladstone.

Tegernsee, Aug. 28, 1886. — We found Döllinger reading in the garden. The course of his life is quite unchanged. His constitution does not appear at all to have given way. He beats me utterly in standing, but that is not saying much, as it never was one of my gifts; and he is not conscious (eighty-seven last February) of any difficulty with the heart in going up hill. His deafness has increased materially, but not so that he cannot carry on very well conversation with a single person. We have talked much together even on disestablishment which he detests, and Ireland as to which he is very apprehensive, but he never seems to shut up his mind by prejudice. I had a good excuse for giving him my pamphlet,[1] but I do not know whether he will tell us what he thinks of it. He was reading it this morning. He rises at six and breakfasts alone. Makes a *good* dinner at two and has nothing more till the next morning. He does not appear after dark. On the whole one sees no reason why he should not last for several years yet.

'When Dr. Döllinger was eighty-seven,' Mr. Gladstone wrote later, 'he walked with me seven miles across the hill that separates the Tegernsee from the next valley to the eastward. At that time he began to find his sleep subject to occasional interruptions, and he had armed himself against them by committing to memory the first three books of the *Odyssey* for recital.'[2] Of Mr. Gladstone Döllinger had said in 1885, 'I have known Gladstone for thirty years, and would stand security for him any day; his character is a very fine one, and he possesses a rare capability for work. I differ from him in his political views on many points, and it is difficult to convince him, for he is clad in triple steel.'[3]

Another high personage in the Roman catholic world sent him letters through Acton, affectionately written and with signs of serious as well as sympathising study of his Irish policy. A little later (Sept. 21) Mr. Gladstone writes to his wife at Hawarden: —

Bishop Strossmayer may make a journey all the way to

[1] On the Irish Question — 'The History of an Idea and the Lesson of the Elections,' a fifty-page pamphlet prepared before leaving England.

[2] *Speaker,* Jan. 1, 1890.
[3] *Conversations of Döllinger.* By L. von Köbell, pp. 100, 102.

Hawarden, and it seems that Acton may even accompany him, CHAP.
which would make it much more manageable. His coming would I.
be a great compliment, and cannot be discouraged or refused. It ÆT. 77.
would, however, be a serious affair, for he speaks no language
with which as a spoken tongue we are familiar, his great cards
being Slavonic and Latin. Unfortunately I have a very great
increase of difficulty in *hearing* the words in foreign tongues, a
difficulty which I hope has hardly begun with you as yet.

Like a good host, Lord Acton kept politics out of his way
as well as he could, but some letter of mine ' set him on fire,
and he is full of ——'s blunder and of Parnell's bill.' Parliamentary duty was always a sting to him, and by September
20 he was back in the House of Commons, speaking on the
Tenants Relief (Ireland) bill. Then to the temple of peace
at Hawarden for the rest of the year, to read the *Iliad* ' for
the twenty-fifth or thirtieth time, and every time richer and
more glorious than before ' ; to write elaborately on Homeric
topics ; to receive a good many visitors ; and to compose the
admirable article on Tennyson's second *Locksley Hall*. On
this last let us pause for an instant. The moment was hardly
one in which, from a man of nature less great and powerful
than Mr. Gladstone, we should have counted on a buoyant
vindication of the spirit of his time. He had just been
roughly repulsed in the boldest enterprise of his career; his
name was a target for infinite obloquy; his motives were
largely denounced as of the basest; the conflict into which he
had plunged and from which he could not withdraw was hard ;
friends had turned away from him ; he was old ; the issue was
dubious and dark. Yet the personal, or even what to him
were the national discomfitures of the hour, were not allowed
to blot the sun out of the heavens. His whole soul rose in
challenge against the tragic tones of Tennyson's poem, as
he recalled the solid tale of the vast improvements, the
enormous mitigation of the sorrows and burdens of mankind,
that had been effected in the land by public opinion and
public authority, operative in the exhilarating sphere of self-
government during the sixty years between the first and
second *Locksley Hall*.

The sum of the matter seems to be that upon the whole, and in a degree, we who lived fifty, sixty, seventy years back, and are living now, have lived into a gentler time ; that the public conscience has grown more tender, as indeed was very needful; and that in matters of practice, at sight of evils formerly regarded with indifference or even connivance, it now not only winces but rebels ; that upon the whole the race has been reaping, and not scattering ; earning and not wasting ; and that without its being said that the old Prophet is wrong, it may be said that the young Prophet was unquestionably right.

Here is the way in which a man of noble heart and high vision as of a circling eagle, transcends his individual chagrins. All this optimism was the natural vein of a statesman who had lived a long life of effort in persuading opinion in so many regions, in overcoming difficulty upon difficulty, in content with a small reform where men would not let him achieve a great one, in patching where he could not build anew, in unquenchable faith, hope, patience, endeavour. Mr. Gladstone knew as well as Tennyson that ' every blessing has its drawbacks, and every age its dangers ' ; he was as sensitive as Tennyson or Ruskin or any of them, to the implacable tragedy of industrial civilisation — the city children ' blackening soul and sense in city slime,' progress halting on palsied feet ' among the glooming alleys,' crime and hunger casting maidens on the street, and all the other recesses of human life depicted by the poetic prophet in his sombre hours. But the triumphs of the past inspired confidence in victories for the future, and meanwhile he thought it well to remind Englishmen that ' their country is still young as well as old, and that in these latest days it has not been unworthy of itself.' [1]

On his birthday he enters in his diary : —

Dec. 29, 1886. — This day in its outer experience recalls the Scotch usage which would say, 'terrible pleasant.' In spite of the ruin of telegraph wires by snow, my letters and postal arrivals of to-day have much exceeded those of last year. Even my share of

[1] *Nineteenth Century*, January 1887. See also speech at Hawarden, on the Queen's Reign, August 30, 1887. The reader will remember Mr. Gladstone's contrast between poet and active statesman at Kirkwall in 1883.

the reading was very heavy. The day was gone before it seemed to have begun, all amidst stir and festivity. The estimate was nine hundred arrivals. O for a birthday of recollection. It is long since I have had one. There is so much to say on the soul's history, but bracing is necessary to say it, as it is for reading Dante. It has been a year of shock and strain. I think a year of some progress; but of greater absorption in interests which, though profoundly human, are quite off the line of an old man's direct preparation for passing the River of Death. I have not had a chance given me of creeping from this whirlpool, for I cannot abandon a cause which is so evidently that of my fellow-men, and in which a particular part seems to be assigned to me. Therefore am I not disturbed 'though the hills be carried into the middle of the sea.'

CHAP.
I.

Æт. 77.

III

To Lord Acton.

Hawarden, Jan. 13,1887. — It is with much pleasure that I read your estimate of Chamberlain. His character is remarkable, as are in a very high degree his talents. It is one of my common sayings that to me characters of the political class are the most mysterious of all I meet, so that I am obliged to travel the road of life surrounded by an immense number of judgments more or less in suspense, and getting on for practical purposes as well as I can.

I have with a clear mind and conscience not only assented to but promoted the present conferences, and I had laboured in that sense long before Mr. Chamberlain made his speech at Birmingham. It will surprise as well as grieve me if they do harm; if indeed they do not do some little good. Large and final arrangements, it would be rash I think to expect.

The tide is flowing, though perhaps not rapidly, in our favour. Without our lifting a finger, a crumbling process has begun in both the opposite parties. 'In quietness and in confidence shall be your strength' is a blessed maxim, often applicable to temporals as well as spirituals. I have indeed one temptation to haste, namely, that the hour may come for me to say farewell and claim my retirement; but inasmuch as I remain *in situ* for the Irish question only, I cannot be so foolish as to allow myself to ruin by precipitancy my own purpose. Though I am writing a paper

BOOK
X.
1888.

on the Irish question for Mr. Knowles, it is no trumpet-blast, but is meant to fill and turn to account a season of comparative quietude.

The death of Iddesleigh has shocked and saddened us all. He was full of excellent qualities, but had not the backbone and strength of fibre necessary to restore the tone of a party demoralised by his former leader. In gentleness, temper, sacrifice of himself to the common purpose of his friends, knowledge, quickness of perception, general integrity of intention, freedom from personal aims, he was admirable. . . . I have been constantly struggling to vindicate a portion of my time for the pursuits I want to follow, but with very little success indeed. Some rudiments of Olympian religion have partially taken shape. I have a paper ready for Knowles probably in his March number on the Poseidon of Homer, a most curious and exotic personage. . . . Williams and Norgate got me the books I wanted, but alack for the time to read them! In addition to want of time, I have to deplore my slowness in reading, declining sight, and declining memory; all very serious affairs for one who has such singular reason to be thankful as to general health and strength.

I wish I could acknowledge duly or pay even in part your unsparing, untiring kindness in the discharge of your engagements as 'Cook.' Come early to England — and stay long. We will try what we can to bind you.

A few months later, he added to his multifarious exercises in criticism and controversy, a performance that attracted especial attention.[1] 'Mamma and I,' he wrote to Mrs. Drew, ' are each of us still separately engaged in a death-grapple with *Robert Elsmere.* I complained of some of the novels you gave me to read as too stiff, but they are nothing to this. It is wholly out of the common order. At present I regard with doubt and dread the idea of doing anything on it, but cannot yet be sure whether your observations will be verified or not. In any case it is a tremendous book.' And on April 1 (1888), he wrote, ' By hard work I have finished and am correcting my article on *Robert Elsmere.*

[1] *Robert Elsmere: the Battle of Belief* (1888). Republished from the *Nineteenth Century* in *Later Gleanings*, 1898.

It is rather stiff work. I have had two letters from her. CHAP.
She is much to be liked personally, but is a fruit, I think, ⎱ I.
of what must be called Arnoldism.' Æt. 79.

To Lord Acton.

Aston Clinton, Tring, Easter Day, April 1, '88. — I do not like to
let too long a time elapse without some note of intercourse, even
though that season approaches which brings you back to the shores
of your country. Were you here I should have much to say on
many things; but I will now speak, or first speak, of what is
uppermost, and would, if a mind is like a portmanteau, be taken
or tumble out first.

You perhaps have not heard of *Robert Elsmere*, for I find without surprise, that it makes its way slowly into public notice. It is
not far from twice the length of an ordinary novel; and the labour
and effort of reading it all, I should say, sixfold; while one could
no more stop in it than in reading Thucydides. The idea of the
book, perhaps of the writer, appears to be a movement of retreat
from Christianity upon Theism : a Theism with a Christ glorified,
always in the human sense, but beyond the ordinary measure. It
is worked out through the medium of a being — one ought to say
a character, but I withhold the word, for there is no sufficient sub-
stratum of character to uphold the qualities — gifted with much
intellectual subtlety and readiness, and almost every conceivable
moral excellence. He finds vent in an energetic attempt to carry
his new gospel among the skilled artisans of London, whom the
writer apparently considers as supplying the *norm* for all right
human judgment. He has extraordinary success, establishes a new
church under the name of the new Christian brotherhood, kills
himself with overwork, but leaves his project flourishing in
a certain 'Elgood Street.' It is in fact (like the Salvation Army),
a new Kirche der Zukunft.

I am always inclined to consider this Theism as among the least
defensible of the positions alternative to Christianity. Robert
Elsmere, who has been a parish clergyman, is upset entirely, as it
appears, by the difficulty of accepting miracles, and by the suggestion that the existing Christianity grew up in an age specially
predisposed to them.

I want as usual to betray you into helping the lame dog over the stile; and I should like to know whether you would think me violently wrong in holding that the period of the Advent was a period when the appetite for, or disposition to, the supernatural was declining and decaying; that in the region of human thought, speculation was strong and scepticism advancing; that if our Lord were a mere man, armed only with human means, His whereabouts was in this and many other ways misplaced by Providence; that the gospels and the New Testament must have much else besides miracle torn out of them, in order to get us down to the *caput mortuum* of Elgood Street. This very remarkable work is in effect identical with the poor, thin, ineffectual production published with some arrogance by the Duke of Somerset, which found a quack remedy for difficulties in what he considered the impregnable citadel of belief in God.

Knowles has brought this book before me, and being as strong as it is strange, it cannot perish still-born. I am tossed about with doubt as to writing upon it.

To Lord Acton.

Oxford, April 8, '88. — I am grateful for your most interesting letter, which contains very valuable warnings. On the other side is copied what I have written on two of the points raised by the book. Have I said too much of the Academy? I have spoken only of the first century. You refer to (apparently) about 250 A.D. as a time of great progress? But I was astonished on first reading the census of Christian clergy in Rome *temp.* St. Cyprian, it was so slender. I am not certain, but does not Beugnot estimate the Christians, before Constantine's conversion, in the west at one-tenth of the population? Mrs. T. Arnold died yesterday here. Mrs. Ward had been summoned and she is coming to see me this evening. It is a very singular phase of the controversy which she has opened. When do you *repatriate?*

I am afraid that my kindness to the Positivists amounts only to a comparative approval of their not dropping the great human tradition out of view; *plus* a very high appreciation of the personal qualities of our friend ——.

To Lord Acton.

Dollis Hill, May 13, '88. — Your last letter was one of extreme
interest. It raised such a multitude of points, after your perusal
of my article on R. Elsmere, as to stimulate in the highest degree
my curiosity to know how far you would carry into propositions,
the ideas which you for the most part obliquely put forward.
I gave the letter to Mary, who paid us a flying visit in London,
that she might take it to Hawarden for full digestion. For myself I
feed upon the hope that when (when ?) you come back to England
we may go over the points, and I may reap further benefits from
your knowledge. I will not now attempt anything of the kind.
But I will say this generally, that I am not so much oppressed
as you appear to be, with the notion that great difficulties have
been imported by the researches of scientists into the religious
and theological argument. As respects cosmogony and *geogony,*
the Scripture has, I think, taken much benefit from them. Whatever be the date of the early books, Pentateuch or Hexateuch in
their present *edition,* the Assyriological investigations seem to me
to have fortified and accredited their substance by producing
similar traditions in variant forms inferior to the Mosaic forms,
and tending to throw them back to a higher antiquity, a fountainhead nearer the source. Then there is the great chapter
of the Dispersal: which Renan (I think) treats as exhibiting the
marvellous genius (!) of the Jews. As to unbroken sequences in
the physical order, they do not trouble me, because we have to
do not with the natural but the moral order, and over this science,
or as I call it natural science, does not wave her sceptre. It is
no small matter, again (if so it be, as I suppose), that, after
warring for a century against miracle as unsustained by experience, the assailants should now have to abandon that ground,
stand only upon sequence, and controvert the great facts of the
New Testament only by raising to an extravagant and unnatural
height the demands made under the law of testimony in order
to [justify] a rational belief. One admission has to be made,
that death did not come into the world by sin, namely the
sin of Adam, and this sits inconveniently by the declaration of
Saint Paul.

Mrs. Ward wrote to thank me for the tone of my article. Her

first intention was to make some reply in the *Nineteenth Century* itself. It appears that —— advised her not to do it. But Knowles told me that he was labouring to bring her up to the scratch again. There, I said, you show the cloven foot; you want to keep the *Nineteenth Century* pot boiling.

I own that your reasons for not being in England did not appear to me cogent, but it would be impertinent to make myself a judge of them. The worst of it was that you did not name *any* date. But I must assume that you are coming; and surely the time cannot now be far. Among other things, I want to speak with you about French novels, a subject on which there has for me been quite recently cast a most lurid light.

Acton's letters in reply may have convinced Mr. Gladstone that there were depths in this supreme controversy that he had hardly sounded; and adversaria that he might have mocked from a professor of the school or schools of unbelief, he could not in his inner mind make light of, when coming from the pen of a catholic believer. Before and after the article on *Robert Elsmere* appeared, Acton, the student with his vast historic knowledge and his deep penetrating gaze, warned the impassioned critic of some historic point over-stated or understated, some dangerous breach left all un-guarded, some lack of nicety in definition. Acton's letters will one day see the light, and the reader may then know how candidly Mr. Gladstone was admonished as to the excess of his description of the moral action of Christianity; as to the risk of sending modern questions to ancient answers, for the apologists of an age can only meet the difficulties of their age; that there are leaps and bounds in the history of thought; how well did Newman once say that in theology you have to meet questions that the Fathers could hardly have been made to understand; how if you go to St. Thomas or Leibnitz or Paley for rescue from Hegel or Haeckel your apologetics will be a record of disaster. You insist broadly, says Acton, on belief in the divine nature of Christ as the soul, substance, and creative force of Christian religion; you assign to it very much of the good the church has done; all this with little or no qualification or drawback from the other side : —

Enter Martineau or Stephen or —— (unattached), and loq. : —   CHAP.
Is this the final judgment of the chief of liberals ? the pontiff of   I.
a church whose fathers are the later Milton and the later Penn,   Æt. 79.
Locke, Bayle, Toland, Franklin, Turgot, Adam Smith, Washington,
Jefferson, Bentham, Dugald Stewart, Romilly, Tocqueville,
Channing, Macaulay, Mill ?   These men and others like them
disbelieved that doctrine established freedom, and they undid the
work of orthodox Christianity, they swept away that appalling
edifice of intolerance, tyranny, cruelty, which believers in Christ
built up to perpetuate their belief.

The philosophy of liberal history, Acton proceeds, which
has to acknowledge the invaluable services of early
Christianity, feels the anti-liberal and anti-social action of
later Christianity, before the rise of the sects that rejected,
some of them the divinity of Christ ; others, the institutions
of the church erected upon it.   Liberalism if it admits these
things as indifferent, surrenders its own *raison d'être*, and
ceases to strive for an ethical cause.   If the doctrine of
Torquemada make us condone his morality, there can be no
public right and no wrong, no political sin, no secular cause
to die for.   So it might be said that —

You do not work really from the principle of liberalism, but
from the cognate, though distinct principles of democracy,
nationality, progress, etc.   To some extent, I fear, you will
estrange valued friends, not assuredly by any expression of
theological belief, but by seeming to ignore the great central
problem of Christian politics.   If I had to put my own doubts,
instead of the average liberal's, I should state the case in other
words, but not altogether differently.[1]

[1] May 2, 1888.

CHAPTER II

THE ALTERNATIVE POLICY IN ACT

(*1886–1888*)

> THOSE who come over hither to us from England, and some weak
> people among ourselves, whenever in discourse we make mention of
> liberty and property, shake their heads, and tell us that 'Ireland is
> a depending kingdom,' as if they would seem by this phrase to
> intend, that the people of Ireland are in some state of slavery or
> dependence different from those of England. — JONATHAN SWIFT.

BOOK
X.

1886. IN the ministry that succeeded Mr. Gladstone in 1886,
Sir Michael Hicks Beach undertook for the second time the
office of Irish secretary, while Lord Randolph Churchill
filled his place at the exchequer and as leader of the House.
The new Irish policy was to open with the despatch of a
distinguished soldier to put down moonlighters in Kerry;
the creation of one royal commission under Lord Cowper,
to inquire into land rents and land purchase; and another
to inquire into the country's material resources. The two
commissions were well-established ways of marking time.
As for Irish industries and Irish resources, a committee of
the House of Commons had made a report in a blue book of
a thousand pages only a year before. On Irish land there
had been a grand commission in 1880, and a committee of
the House of Lords in 1882–3. The latest Purchase Act was
hardly yet a year old. Then to commission a general to hunt
down little handfuls of peasants who with blackened faces
and rude firearms crept stealthily in the dead of night
round lonely cabins in the remote hillsides and glens of
Kerry, was hardly more sensible than it would be to send
a squadron of life-guards to catch pickpockets in a London
slum.

A question that exercised Mr. Gladstone at least as
sharply as the proceedings of ministers, was the attitude

to be taken by those who had quitted him, ejected him in CHAP.
the short parliament of 1886, and fought the election against II.
him. We have seen how much controversy arose long years Æt. 77.
before as to the question whereabouts in the House of
Commons the Peelites should take their seats.[1] The same
perplexity now confronted the liberals who did not agree
with Mr. Gladstone upon Irish government. Lord Hartington
wrote to him, and here is his reply : —

August 2, 1886. — I fully appreciate the feeling which has
prompted your letter, and I admit the reality of the difficulties
you describe. It is also clear, I think, that so far as title to
places on the front opposition bench is concerned, your right to
them is identical with ours. I am afraid, however, that I cannot
materially contribute to relieve you from embarrassment. The
choice of a seat is more or less the choice of a symbol; and I have
no such acquaintance with your political views and intentions, as
could alone enable me to judge what materials I have before me
for making an answer to your inquiry. For my own part, I
earnestly desire, subject to the paramount exigencies of the Irish
question, to promote in every way the reunion of the liberal
party ; a desire in which I earnestly trust that you participate.
And I certainly could not directly or indirectly dissuade you
from any step which you may be inclined to take, and which
may appear to you to have a tendency in any measure to promote
that end.

A singular event occurred at the end of the year (1886),
that produced an important change in the relations of this
group of liberals to the government that they had placed and
maintained in power. Lord Randolph, the young minister
who with such extraordinary rapidity had risen to ascendency
in the councils of the government, suddenly in a fatal moment
of miscalculation or caprice resigned (Dec. 23). Political
suicide is not easy to a man with energy and resolution, but
this was one of the rare cases. In a situation so strangely
unstable and irregular, with an administration resting on
the support of a section sitting on benches opposite, and
still declaring every day that they adhered to old liberal

[1] See vol. i. p. 423.

BOOK
X.
1886.

principles and had no wish to sever old party ties, the withdrawal of Lord Randolph Churchill created boundless perturbation. It was one of those exquisite moments in which excited politicians enjoy the ineffable sensation that the end of the world has come. Everything seemed possible. Lord Hartington was summoned from the shores of the Mediterranean, but being by temperament incredulous of all vast elemental convulsions, he took his time. On his return he declined Lord Salisbury's offer to make way for him as head of the government. The glitter of the prize might have tempted a man of schoolboy ambition, but Lord Hartington was too experienced in affairs not to know that to be head of a group that held the balance was, under such equivocal circumstances, far the more substantial and commanding position of the two. Mr. Goschen's case was different, and by taking the vacant post at the exchequer he saved the prime minister from the necessity of going back under Lord Randolph's yoke. As it happened, all this gave a shake to both of the unionist wings. The ominous clouds of coercion were sailing slowly but discernibly along the horizon, and this made men in the unionist camp still more restless and uneasy. Mr. Chamberlain, on the very day of the announcement of the Churchill resignation, had made a speech that was taken to hold out an olive branch to his old friends. Sir William Harcourt, ever holding stoutly in fair weather and in foul to the party ship, thought the break-up of a great political combination to be so immense an evil, as to call for almost any sacrifices to prevent it. He instantly wrote to Birmingham to express his desire to co-operate in re-union, and in the course of a few days five members of the original liberal cabinet of 1886 met at his house in what was known as the Round Table Conference.[1]

A letter of Mr. Gladstone's to me puts some of his views on the situation created by the retirement of Lord Randolph : —

Hawarden, Christmas Day, 1886. — Between Christmas services, a flood of cards and congratulations for the season, and many

[1] Sir W. Harcourt, Mr. Chamberlain, Lord Herschell, Sir George Trevelyan, and myself.

interesting letters, I am drowned in work to-day, having just at
1¼ P.M. ascertained what my letters *are*. So forgive me if, first
thanking you very much for yours, I deal with some points
rather abruptly.

1. Churchill has committed an outrage as against the Queen, and
also the prime minister, in the method of resigning and making
known his resignation. This, of course, they will work against
him. 2. He is also entirely wrong in supposing that the finance
minister has any ruling authority on the great estimates of
defence. If he had, he would be the master of the country.
But although he has no right to demand the concurrence of his
colleagues in his view of the estimates, he has a rather special
right, because these do so much towards determining budget and
taxation, to indicate his own views by resignation. I have
repeatedly fought estimates to the extremity, with an intention
of resigning in *case*. But to send in a resignation makes it
impossible for his colleagues as men of honour to recede. 3. I
think one of his best points is that he had made before taking
office recent and formal declarations on behalf of economy, of
which his colleagues must be taken to have been cognisant, and
Salisbury in particular. He may plead that he could not reduce
these all at once to zero. 4. Cannot something be done, without
reference to the holes that may be picked, to give him some
support as a champion of economy ? This talk about the continental war, I for one regard as pure nonsense when aimed at
magnifying our estimates.

5. With regard to Hartington. What he will do I know not,
and our wishes could have no weight with him. . . . The position
is one of such difficulty for H. that I am very sorry for him,
though it was never more true that he who makes his own bed
in a certain way must lie in it. Chamberlain's speech hits him
very hard in case of acceptance. I take it for granted that he
will not accept to sit among thirteen tories, but will have to
demand an entry by force, *i.e.* with three or four friends. To
accept upon that footing would, I think, be the logical consequence of all he has said and done since April. In logic, he ought
to go forward, *or*, as Chamberlain has done, backward. The
Queen will, I have no doubt, be brought to bear upon him, and

the nine-tenths of his order. If the Irish question rules all others, all he has to consider is whether he (properly flanked) can serve his view of the Irish question. But with this logic we have nothing to do. The question for us also is (I think), what is best for our view of the Irish question? I am tempted to wish that he should accept; it would clear the ground. But I do not yet see my way with certainty.

6. With regard to Chamberlain. From what has already passed between us you know that, apart from the new situation and from his declaration, I was very desirous that everything honourable should be done to conciliate and soothe. Unquestionably his speech is a new fact of great weight. He is again a liberal, *quand même*, and will not on all points (as good old Joe Hume used to say) swear black is white for the sake of his views on Ireland. We ought not to waste this new fact, but take careful account of it. On the other hand, I think he will see that the moment for taking account of it has not come. Clearly the first thing is to see who are the government. When we see this, we shall also know something of its colour and intentions. I do not think Randolph can go back. He would go back at a heavy discount. If he wants to minimise, the only way I see is that he should isolate his vote on the estimates, form no *clique*, and proclaim strong support in Irish matters and general policy. Thus he might pave a roundabout road of return. . . . In *many* things Goschen is more of a liberal than Hartington, and he would carry with him next to nobody.

7. On the whole, I rejoice to think that, come what may, this affair will really effect progress in the Irish question.

A happy Christmas to you. It will be happier than that of the ministers.

Mr. Gladstone gave the Round Table his blessing, his 'general idea being that he had better meddle as little as possible with the conference, and retain a free hand.' Lord Hartington would neither join the conference, nor deny that he thought it premature. While negotiation was going on, he said, somebody must stay at home, guard the position, and keep a watch on the movements of the enemy, and this duty was his. In truth, after encouraging or pressing Mr.

Goschen to join the government, it was obviously impossible to do anything that would look like desertion either of him or of them. On the other side, both English liberals and Irish nationalists were equally uneasy lest the unity of the party should be bought by the sacrifice of fundamentals. The conference was denounced from this quarter as an attempt to find a compromise that would help a few men sitting on the fence to salve 'their consciences at the expense of a nation's rights.' Such remarks are worth quoting, to illustrate the temper of the rank and file. Mr. Parnell, though alive to the truth that when people go into a conference it usually means that they are ready to give up something, was thoroughly awake to the satisfactory significance of the Birmingham overtures.

Things at the round table for some time went smoothly enough. Mr. Chamberlain gradually advanced the whole length. He publicly committed himself to the expediency of establishing some kind of legislative authority in Dublin in accordance with Mr. Gladstone's principle, with a preference in his own mind for a plan on the lines of Canada. This he followed up, also in public, by the admission that of course the Irish legislature must be allowed to organise their own form of executive government, either by an imitation on a small scale of all that goes on at Westminster and Whitehall, or in whatever other shape they might think proper.[1] To assent to an Irish legislature for such affairs as parliament might determine to be distinctively Irish, with an executive responsible to it, was to accept the party credo on the subject. Then the surface became mysteriously ruffled. Language was used by some of the plenipotentiaries in public, of which each side in turn complained as inconsistent with conciliatory negotiation in private. At last on the very day on which the provisional result of the conference was laid before Mr. Gladstone, there appeared in a print called the *Baptist*[2] an article from Mr. Chamberlain, containing an ardent plea for the disestablishment of the Welsh church, but warning the Welshmen that they and the Scotch crofters and the English

---

[1] See speeches at Hawick, Jan. 22, and at Birmingham, Jan. 29, 1887. [2] *Baptist* article, in *Times*, Feb. 25, 1887.

labourers, thirty-two millions of people, must all go without much-needed legislation because three millions were disloyal, while nearly six hundred members of parliament would be reduced to forced inactivity, because some eighty delegates, representing the policy and receiving the pay of the Chicago convention, were determined to obstruct all business until their demands had been conceded. Men naturally asked what was the use of continuing a discussion, when one party to it was attacking in this peremptory fashion the very persons and the policy that in private he was supposed to accept. Mr. Gladstone showed no implacability. Viewing the actual character of the *Baptist* letter, he said to Sir W. Harcourt, 'I am inclined to think we can hardly do more now, than to say we fear it has interposed an unexpected obstacle in the way of any attempt at this moment to sum up the result of your communications, which we should otherwise hopefully have done; but on the other hand we are unwilling that so much ground apparently gained should be lost, that a little time may soften or remove the present ruffling of the surface, and that we are quite willing that the subject should stand over for resumption at a convenient season.'

The resumption never happened. Two or three weeks later, Mr. Chamberlain announced that he did not intend to return to the round table.[1] No other serious and formal attempt was ever made on either side to prevent the liberal unionists from hardening into a separate species. When they became accomplices in coercion, they cut off the chances of re-union. Coercion was the key to the new situation. Just as at the beginning of 1886, the announcement of it by the tory government marked the parting of the ways, so was it now.

II

We must now with reasonable cheerfulness turn our faces back towards Ireland. On the day of his return from

---

[1] If anybody should ever wish further to disinter the history of this fruitless episode, he will find all the details in a speech by Sir William Harcourt at Derby, Feb. 27, 1889. See also Sir G. O. Trevelyan, *Times*, July 26, 1887, Mr. Chamberlain's letter to Mr. Evelyn Ashley, *Times*, July 29, 1887, and a speech of my own at Wolverhampton, April 19, 1887.

Ireland (August 17, 1886) Mr. Parnell told me that he was quite sure that rents could not be paid in the coming winter, and if the country was to be kept quiet, the government would have to do something. He hoped that they would do something; otherwise there would be disturbance, and that he did not want. He had made up his mind that his interests would be best served by a quiet winter. For one thing he knew that disturbance would be followed by coercion, and he knew and often said that of course strong coercion must always in the long run win the day, little as the victory might be worth. For another thing he apprehended that disturbance might frighten away his new political allies in Great Britain, and destroy the combination which he had so dexterously built up. This was now a dominant element with him. He desired definitely that the next stage of his movement should be in the largest sense political and not agrarian. He brought two or three sets of proposals in this sense before the House, and finally produced a Tenants Relief bill. It was not brilliantly framed. For in truth it is not in human nature, either Irish or any other, to labour the framing of a bill which has no chance of being seriously considered.

The golden secret of Irish government was always to begin by trying to find all possible points for disagreement with anything that Mr. Parnell said or proposed, instead of seeking whether what he said or proposed might not furnish a basis for agreement. The conciliatory tone was soon over, and the Parnell bill was thrown out. The Irish secretary denounced it as permanently upsetting the settlement of 1881, as giving a death-blow to purchase, and as produced without the proof of any real grounds for a general reduction in judicial rents. Whatever else he did, said Sir Michael Hicks Beach, he would never agree to govern Ireland by a policy of blackmail.[1]

A serious movement followed the failure of the government to grapple with arrears of rent. The policy known as the plan of campaign was launched. The plan of campaign was this. The tenants of a given estate agreed with one another what abatement they thought just in the current half-year's

---

[1] *Hans.* 309, Sept. 21, 1886.

rent. This in a body they proffered to landlord or agent. If it was refused as payment in full, they handed the money to a managing committee, and the committee deposited it with some person in whom they had confidence, to be used for the purpose of the struggle.[1] That such proceeding constituted an unlawful conspiracy nobody doubts, any more than it can be doubted that before the Act of 1875 every trade combination of a like kind in this island was a conspiracy.

At an early stage the Irish leader gave his opinion to the present writer: —

Dec. 7, 1886. — Mr. Parnell called, looking very ill and worn. He wished to know what I thought of the effect of the plan of campaign upon public opinion. 'If you mean in Ireland,' I said, 'of course I have no view, and it would be worth nothing if I had. In England, the effect is wholly bad; it offends almost more even than outrages.' He said he had been very ill and had taken no part, so that he stands free and uncommitted. He was anxious to have it fully understood that the fixed point in his tactics is to maintain the alliance with the English liberals. He referred with much bitterness, and very justifiable too, to the fact that when Ireland seemed to be quiet some short time back, the government had at once begun to draw away from all their promises of remedial legislation. If now rents were paid, meetings abandoned, and newspapers moderated, the same thing would happen over again as usual. However, he would send for a certain one of his lieutenants, and would press for an immediate cessation of the violent speeches.

December 12. — Mr. Parnell came, and we had a prolonged conversation. The lieutenant had come over, and had defended the plan of campaign. Mr. Parnell persevered in his dissent and disapproval, and they parted with the understanding that the meetings should be dropped, and the movement calmed as much as could be. I told him that I had heard from Mr. Gladstone, and that he could not possibly show any tolerance for illegalities.

That his opponents should call upon Mr. Gladstone to denounce the plan of campaign and cut himself off from its authors, was to be expected. They made the most of it.

[1] See *United Ireland*, Oct. 23, 1886.

But he was the last man to be turned aside from the prosecution of a policy that he deemed of overwhelming
moment, by any minor currents. Immediately after the
election, Mr. Parnell had been informed of his view that it
would be a mistake for English and Irish to aim at uniform
action in parliament. Motives could not be at all points the
same. Liberals were bound to keep in view (next to what
the Irish question might require) the reunion of the liberal
party. The Irish were bound to have special regard to the
opinion and circumstances of Ireland. Common action up
to a certain degree would arise from the necessities of the
position. Such was Mr. Gladstone's view. He was bent on
bringing a revolutionary movement to what he confidently
anticipated would be a good end; to allow a passing phase
of that movement to divert him, would be to abandon his
own foundations. No reformer is fit for his task who suffers
himself to be frightened off by the excesses of an extreme
wing.

In reply to my account of the conversation with Mr.
Parnell, he wrote to me : —

Hawarden, December 8, 1886. — I have received your very clear
statement and reply in much haste for the post — making the same
request as yours for a return. I am glad to find the —— speech
is likely to be neutralised, I hope effectually. It was really very
bad. I am glad you write to ——. 2. As to the campaign in Ireland, I do not at present feel the force of Hartington's appeal to
me to speak out. I do not recollect that he ever spoke out about
Churchill, of whom he is for the time the enthusiastic follower.[1]
3. But all I say and do must be kept apart from the slightest
countenance direct or indirect to illegality. We too suffer under
the power of the landlord, but we cannot adopt this as a method
of breaking it. 4. I am glad you opened the question of intermediate measures. . . . 5. Upon the whole I suppose he sees he
cannot have countenance from us in the plan of campaign. The
question rather is how much disavowal. I have contradicted
a tory figment in Glasgow that I had approved.

At a later date (September 16, 1887) he wrote to me as to

---

[1] Lord Randolph had encouraged a plan of campaign in Ulster against
home rule.

an intended speech at Newcastle : 'You will, I have no
doubt, press even more earnestly than before on the Irish
people the duty and policy of maintaining order, and in
these instances I shall be very glad if you will associate me
with yourself.'

'The plan of campaign,' said Mr. Gladstone, 'was one of
those devices that cannot be reconciled with the principles
of law and order in a civilised country. Yet we all know
that such devices are the certain result of misgovernment.
With respect to this particular instance, if the plan be
blameable (I cannot deny that I feel it difficult to acquit any
such plan) I feel its authors are not one-tenth part so blameable as the government whose contemptuous refusal of what
they have now granted, was the parent and source of the
mischief.'[1] This is worth looking at.

The Cowper Commission, in February 1887, reported that
refusal by some landlords explained much that had occurred
in the way of combination, and that the growth of these
combinations had been facilitated by the fall in prices,
restriction of credit by the banks, and other circumstances
making the payment of rent impossible.[2] Remarkable
evidence was given by Sir Redvers Buller. He thought
there should be some means of modifying and redressing the
grievance of rents being still higher than the people can pay.
'You have got a very ignorant poor people, and the law
should look after them, instead of which it has only looked
after the rich.'[3] This was exactly what Mr. Parnell had said.
In the House the government did not believe him; in Ireland they admitted his case to be true. In one instance
General Buller wrote to the agents of the estate that he
believed it was impossible for the tenants to pay the rent
that was demanded; there might be five or six rogues
among them, but in his opinion the greater number of them
were nearer famine than paying rent.[4] In this very case
ruthless evictions followed. The same scenes were enacted
elsewhere. The landlords were within their rights, the courts
were bound by the law, the police had no choice but to back

[1] Speech at the Memorial Hall,
July 29, 1887.
[2] Report, p. 8, sect. 15.
[3] *Freeman*, Jan. 1887.
[4] Questions 16, 473–5.

the courts. The legal case was complete. The moral case remained, and it was through these barbarous scenes that in a rough and non-logical way the realities of the Irish land system for the first time gained access to the minds of the electors of Great Britain. Such devices as the plan of campaign came to be regarded in England and Scotland as what they were, incidents in a great social struggle. In a vast majority of cases the mutineers succeeded in extorting a reduction of rent, not any more immoderate than the reduction voluntarily made by good landlords, or decreed in the land-courts. No agrarian movement in Ireland was ever so unstained by crime.

Some who took part in these affairs made no secret of political motives. Unlike Mr. Parnell, they deliberately desired to make government difficult. Others feared that complete inaction would give an opening to the Fenian extremists. This section had already shown some signs both of their temper and their influence in certain proceedings of the Gaelic association at Thurles. But the main spring was undoubtedly agrarian, and the force of the spring came from mischiefs that ministers had refused to face in time. 'What they call a conspiracy now,' said one of the insurgent leaders, 'they will call an Act of parliament next year.' So it turned out.

The Commission felt themselves 'constrained to recommend an earlier revision of judicial rents, on account of the straitened circumstances of Irish farmers.' What the commissioners thus told ministers in the spring was exactly what the Irish leader had told them in the previous autumn. They found that there were 'real grounds' for some legislation of the kind that the chief secretary, unconscious of what his cabinet was so rapidly to come to, had stigmatised as the policy of blackmail.

On the last day of March 1887, the government felt the necessity of introducing a measure based on facts that they had disputed, and on principles that they had repudiated. Leaseholders were admitted, some hundred thousand of them. That is, the more solemn of the forms of agrarian contract were set aside. Other provisions we may pass over.

But this was not the bill to which the report of the Commission pointed. The pith of that report was the revision and abatement of judicial rents, and from the new bill this vital point was omitted. It could hardly have been otherwise after a curt declaration made by the prime minister in the previous August. 'We do not contemplate any revision of judicial rents,' he said — immediately, by the way, after appointing a commission to find out what it was that they ought to contemplate. 'We do not think it would be honest in the first place, and we think it would be exceedingly inexpedient.'[1] He now repeated that to interfere with judicial rents because prices had fallen, would be to 'lay your axe to the root of the fabric of civilised society.'[2] Before the bill was introduced, Mr. Balfour, who had gone to the Irish office on the retirement of Sir M. H. Beach in the month of March, proclaimed in language even more fervid, that it would be folly and madness to break these solemn contracts.[3]

For that matter, the bill even as it first stood was in direct contravention to all such high doctrine as this, inasmuch as it clothed a court with power to vary solemn contracts by fixing a composition for outstanding debt, and spreading the payment of it over such a time as the judge might think fit. That, however, was the least part of what finally overtook the haughty language of the month of April. In May the government accepted a proposal that the court should not only settle the sum due by an applicant for relief for outstanding debt, but should fix a reasonable rent for the rest of the term. This was the very power of variation that ministers had, as it were only the day before, so roundly denounced. But then the tenants in Ulster were beginning to growl. In June ministers withdrew the power of variation, for now it was the landlords who were growling. Then at last in July the prime minister called his party together, and told them that if the bill were not altered, Ulster would be lost to the unionist cause, and that after all he must put into the bill a general revision of judicial rents for three years. So finally, as it was put by a speaker of that time,

[1] *Hans.* August 19, 1886.   [3] *Ibid.* 312, April 22, 1887.
[2] *Ibid.* 313, March 22, 1887.

you have the prime minister rejecting in April the policy which in May he accepts; rejecting in June the policy which he had accepted in May; and then in July accepting the policy which he had rejected in June, and which had been within a few weeks declared by himself and his colleagues to be inexpedient and dishonest, to be madness and folly, and to be a laying of the axe to the very root of the fabric of civilised society. The simplest recapitulation made the bitterest satire.

The law that finally emerged from these singular operations dealt, it will be observed in passing, with nothing less than the chief object of Irish industry and the chief form of Irish property. No wonder that the landlords lifted up angry voices. True, the minister the year before had laid it down that if rectification of rents should be proved necessary, the landlords ought to be compensated by the state. Of this consolatory balm it is needless to say no more was ever heard; it was only a graceful sentence in a speech, and proved to have little relation to purpose or intention. At the Kildare Street club in Dublin members moodily asked one another whether they might not just as well have had the policy of Mr. Parnell's bill adopted on College Green, as adopted at Westminster.

III

The moment had by this time once more come for testing the proposition from which Mr. Gladstone's policy had first started. The tory government had been turned out at the beginning of 1886 upon coercion, and Mr. Gladstone's government had in the summer of that year been beaten upon conciliation. 'I ventured to state in 1886,' said Mr. Gladstone a year later,[1] 'that we had arrived at the point where two roads met, or rather where two roads parted; one of them the road that marked the endeavour to govern Ireland according to its constitutionally expressed wishes; the other the road principally marked by ultra-constitutional measures, growing more and more pronounced in character.' Others, he said, with whom we had

---

[1] Speech on Criminal Law Amendment (Ireland) bill, March 29, 1887.

BOOK
X.

1887.

been in close alliance down to that date, considered that a third course was open, namely liberal concession, stopping short of autonomy, but upon a careful avoidance of coercion. Now it became visible that this was a mistake, and that in default of effective conciliation, coercion was the inevitable alternative. So it happened.

The government again unlocked the ancient armoury, and brought out the well-worn engines. The new Crimes bill in most particulars followed the old Act, but it contained one or two serious extensions, including a clause afterwards dropped, that gave to the crown a choice in cases of murder or certain other aggravated offences of carrying the prisoner out of his own country over to England and trying him before a Middlesex jury at the Old Bailey — a puny imitation of the heroic expedient suggested in 1769, of bringing American rebels over for trial in England under a slumbering statute of King Henry VIII. The most startling innovation of all was that the new Act was henceforth to be the permanent law of Ireland, and all its drastic provisions were to be brought into force whenever the executive government pleased.[1] This Act was not restricted as every former law of the kind had been in point of time, to meet an emergency; it was made a standing instrument of government. Criminal law and procedure is one of the most important of all the branches of civil rule, and certainly is one of the most important of all its elements. This was now in Ireland to shift up and down, to be one thing to-day and another thing to-morrow at executive discretion. Acts would be innocent or would be crimes, just as it pleased the Irish minister. Parliament did not enact that given things were criminal, but only that they should be criminal when an Irish minister should choose to say so.[2] Persons charged with them would have the benefit of a jury or would be deprived of a jury, as the Irish minister might think proper.

[1] This vital feature of the bill was discussed in the report stage, on a motion limiting the operation of the Act to three years. June 27, 1887. *Hans.* 316, p. 1013. The clause was rejected by 180 to 119, or a majority of 61.

[2] See Palles, C. B., in Walsh's case. *Judgments of Superior Courts in cases under the Criminal Law and Procedure Amendment Act*, 1887, p. 110.

Mr. Parnell was in bad health and took little part, but he made more than one pulverising attack in that measured and frigid style which, in a man who knows his case at first hand, may be so much more awkward for a minister than more florid onslaughts. He discouraged obstruction, and advised his followers to select vital points and to leave others alone. This is said to have been the first Coercion bill that a majority of Irish members voting opposed.

It was at this point that the government suddenly introduced their historic proposal for closure by guillotine. They carried (June 10) a resolution that at ten o'clock on that day week the committee stage should be brought compulsorily to an end, and that any clauses remaining undisposed of should be put forthwith without amendment or debate. The most remarkable innovation upon parliamentary rule and practice since Cromwell and Colonel Pride, was introduced by Mr. Smith in a characteristic speech, well larded with phrases about duty, right, responsibility, business of the country, and efficiency of the House. These 'solemnising complacencies' did not hide the mortifying fact that if it had really been one of the objects of Irish members for ten years past to work a revolution in the parliament where they were forced against their will to sit, they had at least, be such a revolution good or bad, succeeded in their design.

Perhaps looking forward with prophetic eye to a day that actually arrived six years later, Mr. Gladstone, while objecting to the proposal as unjustified, threw the responsibility of it upon the government, and used none of the flaming colours of defiance. The bulk of the liberals abstained from the division. This practical accord between the two sets of leading men made the parliamentary revolution definite and finally clenched it. It was not without something of a funereal pang that members with a sense of the old traditions of the power, solemnity, and honour of the House of Commons came down on the evening of the seventeenth of June. Within a week they would be celebrating the fiftieth year of the reign of the Queen, and that night's business was the strange and unforeseen goal at which a journey of little more than the same period of time along the high democratic road had brought the commonalty of the realm since 1832. Among the provisions that went into the bill without any discussion in committee were those giving to the Irish executive the power of stamping an association as unlawful; those dealing with special juries and change of the place of trial; those specifying the various important conditions attaching to proclamations, which lay at the foundation of the Act; those dealing with rules, procedure, and the limits of penalty. The report next fell under what Burke calls the accursed slider. That stage had taken three sittings, when the government moved (June 30) that it must close in four days. So much grace, however, was not needed; for after the motion had been carried the liberals withdrew from the House, and the Irishmen betook themselves to the galleries, whence they looked down upon the mechanical proceedings below.

IV

In Ireland the battle now began in earnest. The Irish minister went into it with intrepid logic. Though very different men in the deeper parts of character, Macaulay's account of Halifax would not be an ill-natured account of Mr. Balfour. 'His understanding was keen, sceptical, inexhaustibly fertile in distinctions and objections, his taste refined, his sense of the ludicrous exquisite; his temper placid and forgiving, but fastidious, and by no means prone either to malevolence or to enthusiastic admiration.' His business was to show disaffected Ireland that parliament was her master. Parliament had put the weapon into his hands, and it was for him to smite his antagonists to the ground. He made no experiments in judicious mixture, hard blows and soft speech, but held steadily to force and fear. His apologists argued that after all substantial justice was done even in what seemed hard cases, and even if the spirit of law were sometimes a trifle strained. Unluckily the peasant with the blunderbuss, as he waits behind the hedge for the tyrant or the traitor, says just the same. The forces of disorder were infinitely less formidable than they had been a hundred times before. The contest was child's play compared with

the violence and confusion with which Mr. Forster or Lord
Spencer had to deal. On the other hand the alliance
between liberals and Irish gave to the struggle a parliamentary complexion, by which no coercion struggle had ever
been marked hitherto. In the dialectic of senate and platform, Mr. Balfour displayed a strength of wrist, a rapidity,
an instant readiness for combat, that took his foes by surprise, and roused in his friends a delight hardly surpassed in
the politics of our day.

There was another important novelty this time. To
England hitherto Irish coercion had been little more than
a word of common form, used without any thought what the
thing itself was like to the people coerced. Now it was
different. Coercion had for once become a flaming party
issue, and when that happens all the world awakes. Mr.
Gladstone had proclaimed that the choice lay between conciliation and coercion. The country would have liked
conciliation, but did not trust his plan. When coercion
came, the two British parties rushed to their swords, and
the deciding body of neutrals looked on with anxiety and
concern. There has never been a more strenuously sustained
contest in the history of political campaigns. No effort was
spared to bring the realities of repression vividly home to
the judgment and feelings of men and women of our own
island. English visitors trooped over to Ireland, and brought
back stories of rapacious landlords, violent police, and
famishing folk cast out homeless upon the wintry roadside.
Irishmen became the most welcome speakers on British
platforms, and for the first time in all our history they got
a hearing for their lamentable tale. To English audiences
it was as new and interesting as the narrative of an African
explorer or a navigator in the Pacific. Our Irish instructors
even came to the curious conclusion that ordinary international estimates must be revised, and that Englishmen
are in truth far more emotional than Irishmen. Ministerial
speakers, on the other hand, diligently exposed inaccuracy
here or over-colouring there. They appealed to the English
distaste for disorder, and to the English taste for mastery,
and they did not overlook the slumbering jealousy of popery

and priestcraft. But the course of affairs was too rapid for them, the strong harsh doses to the Irish patient were too incessant. The Irish convictions in cases where the land was concerned rose to 2805, and of these rather over one-half were in cases where in England the rights of the prisoner would have been guarded by a jury. The tide of common popular feeling in this island about the right to combine, the right of public meeting, the frequent barbarities of eviction, the jarring indignities of prison treatment, flowed stronger and stronger. The general impression spread more and more widely that the Irish did not have fair play, that they were not being treated about speeches and combination and meetings as Englishmen or Scotchmen would be treated. Even in breasts that had been most incensed by the sudden reversal of policy in 1886, the feeling slowly grew that it was perhaps a pity after all that Mr. Gladstone had not been allowed to persevere on the fair-shining path of conciliation.

v

The proceedings under exceptional law would make an instructive chapter in the history of the union. Mr. Gladstone followed them vigilantly, once or twice without his usual exercise of critical faculty, but always bringing into effective light the contrast between this squalid policy and his anticipations of his own. Here we are only concerned with what affected British opinion on the new policy. One set of distressing incidents, not connected with the Crimes Act, created disgust and even horror in the country and set Mr. Gladstone on fire. A meeting of some six thousand persons assembled in a large public square at Mitchelstown in the county of Cork.[1] It was a good illustration of Mr. Gladstone's habitual strategy in public movements, that he should have boldly and promptly seized on the doings at Mitchelstown as an incident well fitted to arrest the attention of the country. 'Remember Mitchelstown' became a watchword. The chairman, speaking from a carriage that did duty for a platform, opened the proceedings. Then a file of police endeavoured to force a way through the densest part of the

[1] On September 9, 1887.

crowd for a government note-taker. Why they did not choose an easier mode of approach from the rear, or by the side ; why they had not got their reporter on to the platform before the business began; and why they had not beforehand asked for accommodation as was the practice, were three points never explained. The police unable to make a way through the crowd retired to the outskirt. The meeting went on. In a few minutes a larger body of police pressed up through the thick of the throng to the platform. A violent struggle began, the police fighting their way through the crowd with batons and clubbed rifles. The crowd flung stones and struck out with sticks, and after three or four minutes the police fled to their barracks — some two hundred and fifty yards away. So far there is no material discrepancy in the various versions of this dismal story. What followed is matter of conflicting testimony. One side alleged that a furious throng rushed after the police, attacked the barrack, and half murdered a constable outside, and that the constables inside in order to save their comrade and to beat off the assailing force, opened fire from an upper window. The other side declared that no crowd followed the retreating police at all, that the assault on the barrack was a myth, and that the police fired without orders from any responsible officer, in mere blind panic and confusion. One old man was shot dead, two others were mortally wounded and died within a week.

Three days later the affray was brought before the House of Commons. Any one could see from the various reports that the conduct of the police, the resistance of the crowd, and the guilt or justification of the bloodshed, were all matters in the utmost doubt and demanding rigorous inquiry. Mr. Balfour pronounced instant and peremptory judgment. The thing had happened on the previous Friday. The official report, however rapidly prepared, could not have reached him until the morning of Sunday. His officers at the Castle had had no opportunity of testing their official report by cross-examination of the constables concerned, nor by inspection of the barrack, the line of fire, and other material elements of the case. Yet on the strength of this hastily drawn and unsifted report received by him from Ireland on Sunday, and without even waiting for any information that eye-witnesses in the House might have to lay before him in the course of the discussion, the Irish minister actually told parliament once for all, on the afternoon of Monday, that he was of opinion, 'looking at the matter in the most impartial spirit, that the police were in no way to blame, and that no responsibility rested upon any one except upon those who convened the meeting under circumstances which they knew would lead to excitement and might lead to outrage.'[1]   The country was astounded to see the most critical mind in all the House swallow an untested police report whole ; to hear one of the best judges in all the country of the fallibility of human testimony, give offhand, in what was really a charge of murder, a verdict of Not Guilty, after he had read the untested evidence on one side.

The rest was all of a piece.   The coroner's inquest was held in due course.   The proceedings were not more happily conducted than was to be expected where each side followed the counsels of ferocious exasperation.   The jury, after some seventeen days of it, returned a verdict of wilful murder against the chief police officer and five of his men.   This inquisition was afterwards quashed (February 10, 1888) in the Queen's bench, on the ground that the coroner had perpetrated certain irregularities of form.   Nobody has doubted that the Queen's bench was right ; it seemed as if there had been a conspiracy of all the demons of human stupidity in this tragic bungle, from the first forcing of the reporter through the crowd, down to the inquest on the three slain men and onwards.   The coroner's inquest having broken down, reasonable opinion demanded that some other public inquiry should be held.   Even supporters of the government demanded it.   If three men had been killed by the police in connection with a public meeting in England or Scotland, no home secretary would have dreamed for five minutes of resisting such a demand.   Instead of a public inquiry, what the chief secretary did was to appoint a

[1] Sept. 12, 1887.   *Hans.* 321, p. 327.

confidential departmental committee of policemen privately
to examine, not whether the firing was justified by the
circumstances, but how it came about that the police were
so handled by their officers that a large force was put to
flight by a disorderly mob. The three deaths were treated
as mere accident and irrelevance. The committee was appointed to correct the discipline of the force, said the Irish
minister, and in no sense to seek justification for actions
which, in his opinion, required no justification.[1] Endless
speeches were made in the House and out of it; members
went over to Mitchelstown to measure distances, calculate
angles, and fire imaginary rifles out of the barrack window;
all sorts of theories of ricochet shots were invented, photographs and diagrams were taken. Some held the police to
be justified, others held them to be wholly unjustified. But
without a judicial inquiry, such as had been set up in the
case of Belfast in 1886, all these doings were futile. The
government remained stubborn. The slaughter of the three
men was finally left just as if it had been the slaughter of
three dogs. No other incident of Irish administration stirred
deeper feelings of disgust in Ireland, or of misgiving and
indignation in England.

Here was, in a word, the key to the new policy. Every act
of Irish officials was to be defended. No constable could be
capable of excess. No magistrate could err. No prison rule
was over harsh. Every severity technically in order must be
politic.

VI

Among other remarkable incidents, the Pope came to the
rescue, and sent an emissary to inquire into Irish affairs.
The government had lively hopes of the emissary, and while
they beat the Orange drum in Ulster with one hand, with
the other they stealthily twitched the sleeve of Monsignor
Persico. It came to little. The Congregation at Rome were
directed by the Pope to examine whether it was lawful to
resort to the plan of campaign. They answered that it was
contrary both to natural justice and Christian charity. The
papal rescript, embodying this conclusion, was received in

[1] Dec. 3, 1888. *Hans.* 331, p. 916.

Ireland with little docility.   Unwisely the cardinals had given reasons, and the reasons, instead of springing in the mystic region of faith and morals, turned upon issues of fact as to fair rents. But then the Irish tenant thought himself a far better judge of a fair rent, than all the cardinals that ever wore red hats. If he had heard of such a thing as Jansenism, he would have known that he was in his own rude way taking up a position not unlike that of the famous teachers of Port Royal two hundred and thirty years before, that the authority of the Holy See is final as to doctrine, but may make a mistake as to fact.

Mr. Parnell spoke tranquilly of ' a document from a distant country,' and publicly left the matter to his catholic countrymen.[1] Forty catholic members of parliament met at the Mansion House in Dublin, and signed a document in which they flatly denied every one of the allegations and implications about fair rents, free contract, the land commission and all the rest, and roundly declared the Vatican circular to be an instrument of the unscrupulous foes both of the Holy See and of the people of Ireland.   They told the Pope, that while recognising unreservedly as catholics the spiritual jurisdiction of the Holy See, they were bound solemnly to affirm that Irish catholics recognise no rights in Rome to interfere in their political affairs.   A great meeting in the Phœnix Park ratified the same position by acclamation.   At Cork, under the presidency of the mayor, and jealously watched by forces of horse and foot, a great gathering in a scene of indescribable excitement protested that they would never allow the rack-renters of Ireland to grind them down at the instigation of intriguers at Rome.   Even in many cities in the United States the same voice was heard.   The bishops knew well that the voice was strongly marked by the harsh accent of their Fenian adversaries.   They issued a declaration of their own, protesting to their flocks that the rescript was confined within the spiritual sphere, and that his holiness was far from wishing to prejudice the nationalist movement.   In the closing week of the year, the Pope himself judged that the time had come for him to make known

[1] May 8, 1888.

that the action which had been 'so sadly misunderstood,' CHAP.
had been prompted by the desire to keep the cause in which $\underbrace{\qquad}$ II.
Ireland was struggling from being weakened by the intro-   ÆT. 78.
duction of anything that could justly be brought in reproach
against it.[1] The upshot of the intervention was that the
action condemned by the rescript was not materially affected
within the area already disturbed ; but the rescript may have
done something to prevent its extension elsewhere.

VII

Among the entries for 1887 there occur : —

Sandringham, Jan. 29. — A large party. We were received
with the usual delicacy and kindness. Much conversation with
the Prince of Wales. . . . Walk with ——, who charmed
me much. *Jan.* 31. — Off by 11 A.M. to Cambridge. . . . Dined
with the master of Trinity in hall. Went over the Newnham
buildings : greatly pleased. Saw Mr. Sidgwick. Evening service
at King's. . . . *Feb.* 2. — Hawarden at 5.30. Set to work on
papers. Finished Greville's Journals. *Feb.* 3.—Wrote on Greville.
Feb. 5. — Felled a chestnut. *Feb.* 27. — Read Lord Shaftesbury's
Memoirs — an excellent discipline for me. *March* 5. — Dollis Hill
[a house near Willesden often lent to him in these times by
Lord and Lady Aberdeen] a refuge from my timidity, unwilling
at 77 to begin a new London house. *March* 9. — Windsor
[to dine and sleep]. The Queen courteous as always ; somewhat embarrassed, as I thought. *March* 29. — Worked on
Homer, Apollo, etc. Then turned to the Irish business and
revolved much, with extreme difficulty in licking the question
into shape. Went to the House and spoke $1\frac{1}{2}$ hours as carefully and with as much measure as I could. Conclave on
coming course of business. *April* 5. — Conversation with Mr.
Chamberlain — ambiguous result, but some ground made. *April*
18. — H. of C. $4\frac{1}{2}$–$8\frac{1}{4}$ and 10–2. Spoke $1\frac{1}{4}$ h. My voice did its
duty but with great effort. *April* 25. — Spoke for an hour upon
the budget. R. Churchill excellent. Conclave on the forged
letters. *May* 4. — Read earlier speeches of yesterday with care,
and worked up the subject of Privilege. Spoke $1\frac{1}{4}$ h.

[1] *Tablet*, Jan. 5, 1889.

BOOK
X.

1887.

In June (1887) Mr. Gladstone started on a political campaign in South Wales, where his reception was one of the
most triumphant in all his career. Ninety-nine hundredths
of the vast crowds who gave up wages for the sake of seeing
him and doing him honour were strong protestants, yet he
said to a correspondent, 'they made this demonstration in
order to secure firstly and mainly justice to catholic Ireland.
It is not after all a bad country in which such things take
place.'

It was at Swansea that he said what he had to say about
the Irish members. He had never at any time from the
hour when he formed his government, set up their exclusion
as a necessary condition of home rule. All that he ever
bargained for was that no proposal for inclusion should be
made a ground for impairing real and effective self-government. Subject to this he was ready to adjourn the matter
and to leave things as they were, until experience should
show the extent of the difficulty and the best way of meeting
it. Provisional exclusion had been suggested by a member
of great weight in the party in 1886. The new formula was
provisional inclusion. This announcement restored one very
distinguished adherent to Mr. Gladstone, and it appeased the
clamour of the busy knot who called themselves imperial
federationists. Of course it opened just as many new difficulties as it closed old ones, but both old difficulties and new
fell into the background before the struggle in Ireland.

June 2, 1887. — Off at 11.40. A tumultuous but interesting
journey to Swansea and Singleton, where we were landed at 7.30.
Half a dozen speeches on the way. A small party to dinner. 3.—A
'quiet day.' Wrote draft to the associations on the road, as model.
Spent the forenoon in settling plans and discussing the lines
of my meditated statement to-morrow with Sir Hussey Vivian,
Lord Aberdare, and Mr. Stuart Rendel. In the afternoon we went
to the cliffs and the Mumbles, and I gave some hours to writing
preliminary notes on a business where all depends on the manner
of handling. Small party to dinner. Read Cardiff and Swansea
guides. 4. — More study and notes. 12–4½ the astonishing procession. Sixty thousand ! Then spoke for near an hour. Dinner at 8,

near an hundred, arrangements perfect. Spoke for nearly another hour; got through a most difficult business as well as I could expect. 5.— Church 11 A.M., notable sermon and H. C. (service long), again 6½ P.M., good sermon. Wrote to Sir W. Harcourt, Mr. Morley, etc. Walked in the garden. Considered the question of a non-political address 'in council'; we all decided against it. 6.— Surveys in the house, then 12–4 to Swansea for the freedom and opening the town library. I was rather jealous of a non-political affair at such a time, but could not do less than speak for thirty or thirty-five minutes for the two occasions. 4–8 to Park Farm, the beautiful vales, breezy common and the curious chambered cairn. Small dinner-party. 7.— Off at 8.15 and a hard day to London, the occasion of processions, hustles, and speeches; that at Newport in the worst atmosphere known since the Black Hole. Poor C. too was an invalid. Spoke near an hour to 3000 at Cardiff; about ¼ hour at Newport; more briefly at Gloucester and Swindon. Much enthusiasm even in the English part of the journey. Our party was reduced at Newport to the family, at Gloucester to our two selves. C. H. Terrace at 6.20. Wrote to get off the House of Commons. It has really been a 'progress,' and an extraordinary one.

In December 1887, under the pressing advice of his physician, though 'with a great lazy reluctance,' Mr. Gladstone set his face with a family party towards Florence. He found the weather more northern than at Hawarden, but it was healthy. He was favourably impressed by all he saw of Italian society (English being cultivated to a degree that surprised him), but he did his best to observe Sir Andrew Clark's injunction that he should practise the Trappist discipline of silence, and the condition of his voice improved in consequence. He read Scartazzini's book on Dante, and found it fervid, generally judicial, and most unsparing in labour ; and he was much interested in Beugnot's *Chute du Paganisme*. And as usual, he returned homeward as unwillingly as he had departed. During the session he fought his Irish battle with unsparing tenacity, and the most conspicuous piece of his activity out of parliament was a pilgrimage to Birmingham (November 1888). It was a great gathering of lieutenants and leading supporters from every part of the country.   Here is a note of mine : —

On the day of the great meeting in Bingley Hall, somebody came to say that Mr. Gladstone wanted to know if I could supply him with a certain passage from a speech of Lord Hartington's. I found him in his dressing-gown, conning his notes and as lively as youth.   He jumped up and pressed point after point on me, as if I had been a great public meeting.   I offered to go down to the public library and hunt for the passage; he deprecated this, but off I went, and after some search unearthed the passage, and copied it out.   In the evening I went to dine with him before the meeting.   He had been out for a short walk to the Oratory in the afternoon to call on Cardinal Newman.   He was not allowed, he told me, to see the cardinal, but he had had a long talk with Father Neville.   He found that Newman was in the habit of reading with a reflector candle, but had not a good one. ' So I said I had a good one, and I sent it round to him.'   He was entirely disengaged in mind during dinner, ate and drank his usual quantity, and talked at his best about all manner of things.   At the last moment he was telling us of John Hunter's confirmation, from his own medical observation, of Homer's re-mark about Dolon; a bad fellow, whose badness Homer explains by the fact that he was a brother brought up among sisters only : —

αὐτὰρ ὃ μοῦνος ἔην μετὰ πέντε κασιγνήτῃσιν.[1]

Oliver Cromwell, by the way, was an only surviving boy among seven sisters, so we cannot take either poet or surgeon for gospel. Time was up, and bore us away from Homer and Hunter.   He was perfectly silent in the carriage, as I remembered Bright had been when years before I drove with him to the same hall.   The sight of the vast meeting was almost appalling, from fifteen to seventeen thousand people.   He spoke with great vigour and freedom ; the fine passages probably heard all over; many other passages certainly not heard, but his gestures so strong and varied as to be almost as interesting as the words would have been.   The speech lasted an hour and fifty minutes ; and he was not at all

---

[1] *Iliad*, x. 317.   See *Homer and Homeric Age*, iii. 467 n.

exhausted when he sat down. The scene at the close was absolutely indescribable and incomparable, overwhelming like the sea.

He took part in parliamentary business at the beginning of December. On December 3rd he spoke on Ireland with immense fervour and passion. He was roused violently by the chairman's attempt to rule out strong language from debate, and made a vehement passage on that point. The substance of the speech was rather thin and not new, but the delivery magnificent. The Irish minister rose to reply at 7.50, and Mr. Gladstone reluctantly made up his mind to dine in the House. A friend by his side said No, and at 8.40 hurried him down the back-stairs to a hospitable board in Carlton Gardens. He was nearly voiceless, until it was time for the rest of us to go back. A speedy meal revived him, and he was soon discoursing on O'Connell and many other persons and things, with boundless force and vivacity.

A few days later he was carried off to Naples. Hereto, he told Lord Acton, ' we have been induced by three circumstances. First, a warm invitation from the Dufferins to Rome; as to which, however, there are *cons* as well as *pros* for a man who like me is neither Italian nor Curial in the view of present policies. Secondly, our kind friend Mr. Stuart Rendel has actually offered to be our conductor thither and back, to perform for us the great service which you rendered us in the trip to Munich and Saint Martin. Thirdly, I have the hope that the stimulating climate of Naples, together with an abstention from speech greater than any I have before enjoyed, may act upon my " vocal cord," and partially at least restore it.'

CHAPTER III

THE SPECIAL COMMISSION

(*1887–1890*)

> My Lords, it appears to me that the measure is unfortunate in its origin, unfortunate in its scope and object, and unfortunate in the circumstances which accompanied its passage through the other House. It appears to me to establish a precedent most novel, and fraught with the utmost danger. — Lord Herschell.[1]

Mr. Gladstone's ceaseless attention to the many phases of the struggle that was now the centre of his public life, was especially engaged on what remains the most amazing of them. I wish it were possible to pass it over, or throw it into a secondary place; but it is too closely connected with the progress of Mr. Gladstone's Irish policy in British opinion at a critical stage, and it is still the subject of too many perversions that affect his name. Transactions are to be found in our annals where wrong was done by government to individuals on a greater scale, where a powerful majority devised engines for the proscription of a weak minority with deadlier aim, and where the omnipotence of parliament was abused for the purpose of faction with more ruthless result. But whether we look at the squalid fraud in which the incident began, or at the tortuous parliamentary pretences by which it was worked out, or at the perversion of fundamental principles of legal administration involved in sending men to answer the gravest charges before a tribunal specially constituted at the absolute discretion of their bitterest political opponents — at the moment engaged in a fierce contest with them in another field — from whatever point of view we approach, the erection of the Special Commission of 1888 stands out as one of the ugliest things done in the name and under the forms of law in this island during the century.

[1] House of Lords, August 10, 1888.

In the spring of 1887 the conductors of *The Times*, intending to strengthen the hands of the government in their new
and doubtful struggle, published a series of articles, in
which old charges against the Irish leader and his men were
served up with fresh and fiery condiments. The allegations of crime were almost all indefinite; the method was
by allusion, suggestion, innuendo, and the combination of
ingeniously selected pieces, to form a crude and hideous
mosaic. Partly from its extravagance, partly because it was
in substance stale, the thing missed fire.

On the day on which the division was to be taken on the
second reading of the Coercion bill, a more formidable bolt
was shot. On that morning (April 18th, 1887), there appeared in the newspaper, with all the fascination of fac-
simile, a letter alleged to be written by Mr. Parnell. It was
dated nine days after the murders in the Phœnix Park,
and purported to be an apology, presumably to some violent
confederate, for having as a matter of expediency openly
condemned the murders, though in truth the writer thought
that one of the murdered men deserved his fate.[1] Special
point was given to the letter by a terrible charge, somewhat
obliquely but still unmistakably made, in an article five or
six weeks before, that Mr. Parnell closely consorted with
the leading Invincibles when he was released on parole in
April 1882; that he probably learned from them what they
were about; and that he recognised the murders in the
Phœnix Park as their handiwork.[2] The significance of the
letter therefore was that, knowing the bloody deed to be
theirs, he wrote for his own safety to qualify, recall, and
make a humble apology for the condemnation which he had
thought it politic publicly to pronounce. The town was

---

[1] Here is the text of this once
famous piece : —
'15/5/82.
'DEAR SIR, — I am not surprised at
your friend's anger, but he and you
should know that to denounce the
murders was the only course open to
us. To do that promptly was plainly
our best policy. But you can tell
him and all others concerned, that
though I regret the accident of Lord
F. Cavendish's death, I cannot refuse
to admit that Burke got no more than
his deserts. You are at liberty to
show him this, and others whom you
can trust also, but let not my address
be known. He can write to the House
of Commons. — Yours very truly,
'CHAS. S. PARNELL.'
[2] The three judges held this to be
a correct interpretation of the language used in the article of March
10th, 1887. Report, pp. 57–8.

thrown into a great ferment. At the political clubs and in the lobbies, all was complacent jubilation on the one side, and consternation on the other. Even people with whom politics were a minor interest were shocked by such an exposure of the grievous depravity of man.

Mr. Parnell did not speak until one o'clock in the morning, immediately before the division on the second reading of the bill. He began amid the deepest silence. His denial was scornful but explicit. The letter, he said, was an audacious fabrication. It is fair to admit that the ministerialists were not without some excuse of a sort for the incredulous laughter with which they received this repudiation. They put their trust in the most serious, the most powerful, the most responsible, newspaper in the world; greatest in resources, in authority, in universal renown. Neglect of any possible precaution against fraud and forgery in a document to be used for the purpose of blasting a great political opponent would be culpable in no common degree. Of this neglect people can hardly be blamed for thinking that the men of business, men of the world, and men of honour who were masters of the *Times*, must be held absolutely incapable.

Those who took this view were encouraged in it by the prime minister. Within four-and-twenty hours he publicly took the truth of the story, with all its worst innuendoes, entirely for granted. He went with rapid stride from possibility to probability, and from probability to certainty. In a speech, of which precipitate credulity was not the only fault, Lord Salisbury let fall the sentence: 'When men who knew gentlemen who intimately knew Mr. Parnell murdered Mr. Burke.' He denounced Mr. Gladstone for making a trusted friend of such a man — one who had 'mixed on terms of intimacy with those whose advocacy of assassination was well known.' Then he went further. 'You may go back,' he said, 'to the beginning of British government, you may go back from decade to decade, and from leader to leader, but you will never find a man who has accepted a position, in reference to an ally tainted with the strong presumption of conniving at assassination, which

has been accepted by Mr. Gladstone at the present time.'[1]
Seldom has party spirit led eminent personages to greater
lengths of dishonouring absurdity.

Now and afterwards people asked why Mr. Parnell did
not promptly bring his libellers before a court of law. The
answer was simple. The case would naturally have been
tried in London. In other words, not only the plaintiff's
own character, but the whole movement that he represented,
would have been submitted to a Middlesex jury, with all the
national and political prejudices inevitable in such a body,
and with all the twelve chances of a disagreement, that
would be almost as disastrous to Mr. Parnell as an actual
verdict for his assailants. The issues were too great to be
exposed to the hazards of a cast of the die. Then, why not
lay the venue in Ireland? It was true that a favourable
verdict might just as reasonably be expected from the prepossessions of Dublin, as an unfavourable one from the
prepossessions of London. But the moral effect of an Irish
verdict upon English opinion would be exactly as worthless,
as the effect of an English verdict in a political or international case would be upon the judgment and feeling of
Ireland. To procure a condemnation of the *Times* at the
Four Courts, as a means of affecting English opinion, would
not be worth a single guinea. Undoubtedly the subsequent
course of this strange history fully justified the advice that
Mr. Parnell received in this matter from the three persons
in the House of Commons with whom on this point he took
counsel.

II

The prudent decision against bringing a fierce political
controversy before an English judge and jury was in a few
months brought to nought, from motives that have remained
obscure, and with results that nobody could foresee. The
next act in the drama was the institution of proceedings
for libel against the *Times* in November 1887, by an Irishman who had formerly sat in parliament as a political
follower of Mr. Parnell. The newspaper met him by denying
that the articles on *Parnellism and Crime* related to him.

[1] April 20, 1887.

It went on to plead that the statements in the articles were true in substance and in fact. The action was tried before Lord Coleridge in July 1888, and the newspaper was represented by the advocate who happened to be the principal law officer of the crown. The plaintiff's counsel picked out certain passages, said that his client was one of the persons intended to be libelled, and claimed damages. He was held to have made an undoubted *prima facie* case on the two libels in which he had been specifically named. This gave the enemy his chance. The attorney general, speaking for three days, opened the whole case for the newspaper; repeated and enlarged upon the charges and allegations in its articles; stated the facts which he proposed to give in evidence; sought to establish that the fac-simile letter was really signed by Mr. Parnell; and finally put forward other letters, now produced for the first time, which carried complicity and connivance to a further point. These charges he said that he should prove. On the third day he entirely changed his tack. Having launched this mass of criminating imputation, he then suddenly bethought him, so he said, of the hardships which his course would entail upon the Irishmen, and asked that in that action he should not be called upon to prove anything at all. The Irishmen and their leader remained under a load of odium that the law officer of the crown had cast upon them, and declined to substantiate.

The production of this further batch of letters stirred Mr. Parnell from his usual impassiveness. His former determination to sit still was shaken. The day after the attorney general's speech, he came to the present writer to say that he thought of sending a paragraph to the newspapers that night, with an announcement of his intention to bring an action against the *Times*, narrowed to the issue of the letters. The old arguments against an action were again pressed upon him. He insisted, on the other side, that he was not afraid of cross-examination; that they might cross-examine as much as ever they pleased, either about the doings of the land league or the letters; that his hands would be found to be clean, and the letters to be gross forgeries. The question between us was adjourned; and meanwhile he fell in with my suggestion that he should the next day make a personal statement to the House. The personal statement was made in his most frigid manner, and it was as frigidly received. He went through the whole of the letters, one by one ; showed the palpable incredibility of some of them upon their very face, and in respect of those which purported to be written by himself, he declared, in words free from all trace of evasion, that he had never written them, never signed them, never directed nor author-ised them to be written.

So the matter was left on the evening of Friday (July 6, 1888). On Monday Mr. Parnell came to the House with the intention to ask for a select committee. The feeling of the English friend to whom he announced his intention in the lobby, still was that the matter might much better be left where it stood. The new batch of letters had strengthened his position, for the Kilmainham letter was a fraud upon the face of it, and a story that he had given a hundred pounds to a fugitive from justice after the murders, had been demolished. The press throughout the country had treated the subject very coolly. The government would pretty certainly refuse a select committee, and what would be the advantage to him in the minds of persons inclined to think him guilty, of making a demand which he knew beforehand would be declined? Such was the view now pressed upon Mr. Parnell. This time he was not moved. He took his own course, as he had a paramount right to do. He went into the House and asked the ministers to grant a select committee to inquire into the authenticity of the letters read at the recent trial. Mr. Smith replied, as before, that the House was absolutely incompetent to deal with the charges. Mr. Parnell then gave notice that he would that night put on the paper the motion for a committee, and on Thursday demand a day for its discussion.

When Thursday arrived, either because the hot passion of the majority was irresistible, or from a cool calcula-tion of policy, or simply because the situation was be-coming intolerable, a new decision had been taken, itself

CHAP.
III. *

Æt. 79.

far more intolerable than the scandal that it was to dis-sipate. The government met the Irish leader with a refusal and an offer. They would not give a committee, but they were willing to propose a commission to consist wholly or mainly of judges, with statutory power to inquire into 'the allegations and charges made against members of parliament by the defendants in the recent action.' If the gentlemen from Ireland were prepared to accept the offer, the government would at once put on the paper for the following Monday, notice of motion for leave to bring in a bill.[1]

When the words of the notice of motion appeared in print, it was found amid universal astonishment that the special commission was to inquire into the charges and allegations generally, not only against certain members of parliament, but also against 'other persons.' The enormity of this sudden extension of the operation was palpable. A certain member is charged with the authorship of incriminating letters. To clear his character as a member of parliament, he demands a select committee. We decline to give a committee, says the minister, but we offer you a commission of judges, and you may take our offer or refuse, as you please; only the judges must inquire not merely into your question of the letters, but into all the charges and allegations made against all of you, and not these only, but into the charges and allegations made against other people as well. This was extraordinary enough, but it was not all.

It is impossible to feel much surprise that Mr. Parnell was ready to assent to any course, however unconstitutional that course might be, if only it led to the exposure of an insufferable wrong. The credit of parliament and the sanctity of constitutional right were no supreme concern of his. He was burning to get at any expedient, committee or commission, which should enable him to unmask and smite his hidden foes. Much of his private language at this time was in some respects vague and ineffectual, but he was naturally averse to any course that might, in his own words, look like backing down. 'Of course,' he said, 'I am not

[1] *Hans.* July 12, 1888, p. 1102.

sure that we shall come off with flying colours. But I think we shall. I am never sure of anything.' He was still confident that he had the clue.

On the second stage of the transaction, Mr. Smith, in answer to various questions in the early part of the sitting, made a singular declaration. The bill, he said, of which he had given notice, was a bill to be introduced in accordance with the offer already made. 'I do not desire to debate the proposal; and I have put it in this position on the Order Book, in order that it may be rejected or accepted by the honourable member in the form in which it stands.' Then in the next sentence, he said, 'If the motion is received and accepted by the House, the bill will be printed and circulated, and I will then name a day for the second reading. But I may say frankly that I do not anticipate being able to make provision for a debate on the second reading of a measure of this kind. It was an offer made by the government to the honourable gentleman and his friends, to be either accepted or rejected.'[1] The minister treated his bill as lightly as if it were some small proposal of ordinary form and of even less than ordinary importance. It is not inconceivable that there was design in this, for Mr. Smith concealed under a surface of plain and homely worth a very full share of parliamentary craft, and he knew well enough that the more extraordinary the measure, the more politic it always is to open with an air of humdrum.

The bill came on at midnight July 16, in a House stirred with intense excitement, closely suppressed. The leader of the House made the motion for leave to introduce the most curious innovation of the century, in a speech of half-a-minute. It might have been a formal bill for a provisional order, to be taken as of course. Mr. Parnell, his ordinary pallor made deeper by anger, and with unusual though very natural vehemence of demeanour, at once hit the absurdity of asking him whether he accepted or rejected the bill, not only before it was printed but without explanation of its contents. He then pressed in two or three weighty sentences the deeper absurdity of leaving him any option at

[1] *Hans.* July 16, p. 1410.

all. The attorney general had said of the story of the fac-simile letter, that if it was not genuine, it was the worst libel ever launched on a public man. If the first lord believed his attorney, said Mr. Parnell, instead of talking about making a bargain with me, he ought to have come down and said, 'The government are determined to have this investigation, whether the honourable member, this alleged criminal, likes it or not.'[1]

That was in fact precisely what the government had determined. The profession that the bill was a benevolent device for enabling the alleged criminals to extricate themselves was very soon dropped. The offer of a boon to be accepted or declined at discretion was transformed into a grand compulsory investigation into the connection of the national and land leagues with agrarian crime, and the members of parliament were virtually put into the dock along with all sorts of other persons who chanced to be members of those associations. The effect was certain. Any facts showing criminality in this or that member of the league would be taken to show criminality in the organisation as a whole, and especially in the political leaders. And the proceeding could only be vindicated by the truly outrageous principle that where a counsel in a suit finds it his duty as advocate to make grave charges against members of parliament in court, then it becomes an obligation on the government to ask for an Act to appoint a judicial commission to examine those charges, if only they are grave enough.

The best chance of frustrating the device was lost when the bill was allowed to pass its first reading unopposed. Three of the leaders of the liberal opposition — two in the Commons, one in the Lords — were for making a bold stand against the bill from the first. Mr. Gladstone, on the contrary, with his lively instinct for popular feeling out of doors, disliked any action indicative of reluctance to face inquiry; and though holding a strong view that no case had been made out for putting aside the constitutional and convenient organ of a committee, yet he thought that an

[1] *Hans.* July 16, 1888, p. 1495.

inquiry under thoroughly competent and impartial judges, after the right and true method of proceeding had been refused, was still better than no proceeding at all. This much of assent, however, was qualified. 'I think,' he said, 'that an inquiry under thoroughly competent and impartial judges is better than none. But that inquiry must, I think, be put into such a shape as shall correspond with the general law and principles of justice.' As he believed, the first and most indispensable conditions of an effective inquiry were wanting, and without them he 'certainly would have no responsibility whatever.'[1]

For the first few days politicians were much adrift. They had moments of compunction. Whether friends or foes of the Irish, they were perplexed by the curious double aspect of the measure. Mr. Parnell himself began to feel misgivings, as he came to realise the magnitude of the inquiry, its vast expense, its interminable length, its unfathomable uncertainties. On the day appointed for the second reading of the bill appointing the commission (July 23), some other subject kept the business back until seven o'clock. Towards six, Mr. Parnell who was to open the debate on his own side, came to an English friend, to ask whether there would be time for him to go away for an hour; he wished to examine some new furnace for assaying purposes, the existence of gold in Wicklow being one of his fixed ideas. So steady was the composure of this extraordinary man. The English friend grimly remarked to him that it would perhaps be rather safer not to lose sight of the furnace in which at any moment his own assaying might begin. His speech on this critical occasion was not one of his best. Indifference to his audience often made him meagre, though he was scarcely ever other than clear, and in this debate there was only one effective point which it was necessary for him to press. The real issue was whether the reference to the judges should be limited or unlimited; should be a fishing inquiry at large into the history of an agrarian agitation ten years old, or an examination into definite and specified charges against named members of parliament. The minister, in moving

[1] *Hans.* 329, July 23, 1888, p. 263.

CHAP.
III.

Æt. 79.

the second reading, no longer left it to the Irish members to accept or reject; it now rested, he said, with the House to decide. It became evident that the acuter members of the majority, fully awakened to the opportunities for destroying the Irishmen which an unlimited inquisition might furnish, had made up their minds that no limit should be set to the scope of the inquisition. Boldly they tramped through a thick jungle of fallacy and inconsistency. They had never ceased to insist, and they insisted now, that Mr. Parnell ought to have gone into a court of law. Yet they fought as hard as they could against every proposal for making the procedure of the commission like the procedure of a law court. In a court there would have been a specific indictment. Here a specific indictment was what they most positively refused, and for it they substituted a roving inquiry, which is exactly what a court never undertakes. They first argued that nothing but a commission was available to test the charges against members of parliament. Then, when they had bethought themselves of further objects, they argued round that it was unheard of and inconceivable to institute a royal commission for members of parliament alone.

All arguments, however unanswerable, were at this stage idle, because Mr. Parnell had reverted to his original resolution to accept the bill, and at his request the radicals sitting below him abandoned their opposition. The bill passed the second reading without a division. This circumstance permitted the convenient assertion, made so freely afterwards, that the bill, irregular, unconstitutional, violent, as it might be, at any rate received the unanimous assent of the House of Commons.

Stormy scenes marked the progress of the bill through committee. Seeing the exasperation produced by their shifting of the ground, and the delay which it would naturally entail, ministers resolved on a bold step. It was now August. Government remembered the process by which they had carried the Coercion bill, and they improved upon it. After three days of committee, they moved that at one o'clock in the morning on the fourth sitting the chairman should break off discussion, put forthwith the question already proposed from the chair, then successively put forthwith all the remaining clauses, and so report the bill to the House. This process shut out all amendments not reached at the fatal hour, and is the most drastic and sweeping of all forms of closure. In the case of the Coercion bill, resort to the guillotine was declared to be warranted by the urgency of social order in Ireland. That plea was at least plausible. No such plea of urgency could be invoked for a measure, which only a few days before the government had considered to be of such secondary importance, that the simple rejection of it by Mr. Parnell was to be enough to induce them to withdraw it. The bill that had been proffered as a generous concession to Irish members, was now violently forced upon them without debate. Well might Mr. Gladstone speak of the most extraordinary series of proceedings that he had ever known.[1]

III

The three judges first met on September 17, 1888, to settle their procedure. They sat for one hundred and twenty-eight days, and rose for the last time on November 22, 1889. More than four hundred and fifty witnesses were examined. One counsel spoke for five days, another for seven, and a third for nearly twelve. The mammoth record of the proceedings fills eleven folio volumes, making between seven and eight thousand pages. The questions put to witnesses numbered ninety-eight thousand.

It was a strange and fantastic scene. Three judges were trying a social and political revolution. The leading actors in it were virtually in the dock. The tribunal had been specially set up by their political opponents, without giving them any effective voice either in its composition or upon the character and scope of its powers. For the first time in England since the Great Rebellion, men were practically put upon their trial on a political charge, without giving them the protection of a jury. For the first time in that period judges were to find a verdict upon the facts of crime. The

[1] *Hans.* Aug. 2, 1888, p. 1282.

charge placed in the forefront was a charge of conspiracy. But to call a combination a conspiracy does not make it a conspiracy or a guilty combination, unless the verdict of a jury pronounces it to be one. A jury would have taken all the large attendant circumstances into account. The three judges felt themselves bound expressly to shut out those circumstances. In words of vital importance, they said, 'We must leave it for politicians to discuss, and for statesmen to determine, in what respects the present laws affecting land in Ireland are capable of improvement. *We have no com-mission to consider whether the conduct of which they are accused can be palliated by the circumstances of the time, or whether it should be condoned in consideration of benefits alleged to have resulted from their action.*' [1] When the pro-ceedings were over, Lord Salisbury applauded the report as 'giving a very complete view of a very curious episode of our internal history.' [2] A very complete view of an agrarian rising — though it left out all palliating circumstances and the whole state of agrarian law!

Instead of opening with the letters, as the country ex-pected, the accusers began by rearing a prodigious accumula-tion of material, first for the Irish or agrarian branch of their case, and then for the American branch. The government helped them to find their witnesses, and so varied a host was never seen in London before. There was the peasant from Kerry in his frieze swallow-tail and knee-breeches, and the woman in her scarlet petticoat who runs barefoot over the bog in Galway. The convicted member of a murder club was brought up in custody from Mountjoy prison or Mary-borough. One of the most popular of the Irish representa-tives had been fetched from his dungeon, and was to be seen wandering through the lobbies in search of his warders. Men who had been shot by moonlighters limped into the box, and poor women in their blue-hooded cloaks told pitiful tales of midnight horror. The sharp spy was there, who dis-closed sinister secrets from cities across the Atlantic, and the uncouth informer who betrayed or invented the history of rude and ferocious plots hatched at the country cross-roads

[1] *Report*, p. 5.   [2] *Hans.* 342, p. 1357.

or over the peat fire in desolate cabins in western Ireland. CHAP.
Divisional commissioners with their ledgers of agrarian III.
offences, agents with bags full of figures and documents, Æt. 79.
landlords, priests, prelates, magistrates, detectives, smart
members of that famous constabulary force which is the
arm, eye, and ear of the Irish government — all the characters
of the Irish melodrama were crowded into the corridors, and
in their turn brought out upon the stage of this surprising
theatre.

The proceedings speedily settled down into the most
wearisome drone that was ever heard in a court of law. The
object of the accusers was to show the complicity of the
accused with crime by tracing crime to the league, and
making every member of the league constructively liable for
every act of which the league was constructively guilty.
Witnesses were produced in a series that seemed interminable, to tell the story of five-and-twenty outrages in Mayo,
of as many in Cork, of forty-two in Galway, of sixty-five
in Kerry, one after another, and all with immeasurable
detail. Some of the witnesses spoke no English, and the
English of others was hardly more intelligible than Erse.
Long extracts were read out from four hundred and forty
speeches. The counsel on one side produced a passage that
made against the speaker, and then the counsel on the other
side found and read some qualifying passage that made as
strongly for him. The three judges groaned. They had
already, they said plaintively, ploughed through the speeches
in the solitude of their own rooms. Could they not be taken
as read ? No, said the prosecuting counsel ; we are building
up an argument, and it cannot be built up in a silent
manner. In truth it was designed for the public outside
the court,[1] and not a touch could be spared that might
deepen the odium. Week after week the ugly tale went on
— a squalid ogre let loose among a population demoralised
by ages of wicked neglect, misery, and oppression. One side
strove to show that the ogre had been wantonly raised by
the land league for political objects of their own ; the
other, that it was the progeny of distress and wrong, that

1 *Evidence*, iv. p. 219.

the league had rather controlled than kindled its ferocity, and that crime and outrage were due to local animosities for which neither league nor parliamentary leaders were answerable.

On the forty-fourth day (February 5) came a lurid glimpse from across the Atlantic. The Irish emigration had carried with it to America the deadly passion for the secret society. A spy was produced, not an Irishman this time for a wonder, but an Englishman. He had been for eight-and-twenty years in the United States, and for more than twenty of them he had been in the pay of Scotland Yard, a military spy, as he put it, in the service of his country. There is no charge against him that he belonged to that foul species who provoke others to crime and then for a bribe betray them. He swore an oath of secrecy to his confederates in the camps of the Clan-na-Gael, and then he broke his oath by nearly every post that went from New York to London. It is not a nice trade, but then the dynamiter's is not a nice trade either.[1] The man had risen high in the secret brotherhood. Such an existence demanded nerves of steel; a moment of forgetfulness, an accident with a letter, the slip of a phrase in the two parts that he was playing, would have doomed him in the twinkling of an eye. He now stood a rigorous cross-examination like iron. There is no reason to think that he told lies. He was perhaps a good deal less trusted than he thought, for he does not appear on any occasion to have forewarned the police at home of any of the dynamite attempts that four or five years earlier had startled the English capital. The pith of his week's evidence was his account of an interview between himself and Mr. Parnell in the corridors of the House of Commons in April 1881. In this interview, Mr. Parnell, he said, expressed his desire to bring the Fenians in Ireland into line with his own constitutional movement, and to that end requested the spy to invite a notorious leader of the physical force party in America to come over to Ireland, to arrange a harmonious understanding. Mr. Parnell had no recollection of the inter-

[1] The common-sense view of the employment of such a man seems to be set out in the speech of Sir   Henry James (Cassell and Co.), pp 149–51, and 494–5.

view, though he thought it very possible that an interview might have taken place. It was undoubtedly odd that the spy having once got his line over so big a fish, should never afterwards have made any attempt to draw him on. The judges, however, found upon a review of 'the probabilities of the case,' that the conversation in the corridor really took place, that the spy's account was correct, and that it was not impossible that in conversation with a supposed revolutionist, Mr. Parnell may have used such language as to leave the impression that he agreed with his interlocutor. Perhaps a more exact way of putting it would be that the spy talked the Fenian doctrine of physical force, and that Mr. Parnell listened.

IV

At last, on the fiftieth day (February 14, 1889), and not before, the court reached the business that had led to its own creation. Three batches of letters had been produced by the newspaper. The manager of the newspaper told his story, and then the immediate purveyor of the letters told his. Marvellous stories they were.

The manager was convinced from the beginning, as he ingenuously said, quite independently of handwriting, that the letters were genuine. Why? he was asked. Because he felt they were the sort of letters that Mr. Parnell would be likely to write. He counted, not wholly without some reason, on the public sharing this inspiration of his own indwelling light. The day was approaching for the division on the Coercion bill. Every journalist, said the manager, must choose his moment. He now thought the moment suitable for making the public acquainted with the character of the Irishmen. So, with no better evidence of authority than his firm faith that it was the sort of letter that Mr. Parnell would be likely to write, on the morning of the second reading of the Coercion bill, he launched the fac-simile letter. In the early part of 1888 he received from the same hand a second batch of letters, and a third batch a few days later. His total payments amounted to over two thousand five hundred pounds. He still asked no questions as to the source of these expensive documents. On the contrary he particularly avoided the subject.   So much for the cautious and experienced man of business.

The natural course would have been now to carry the inquiry on to the source of the letters.   Instead of that, the prosecutors called an expert in handwriting.   The court expostulated.   Why should they not hear at once where the letters came from ; and then it might be proper enough to hear what an expert had to say ?   After a final struggle the prolonged tactics of deferring the evil day, and prejudicing the case up to the eleventh hour, were at last put to shame. The second of the two marvellous stories was now to be told.

The personage who had handed the three batches of letters to the newspaper, told the Court how he had in 1885 compiled a pamphlet called *Parnellism Unmasked*, partly from materials communicated to him by a certain broken-down Irish journalist.   To this unfortunate sinner, then in a state of penury little short of destitution, he betook himself one winter night in Dublin at the end of 1885.   Long after, when the game was up and the whole sordid tragi-comedy laid bare, the poor wretch wrote : ' I have been in difficulties and great distress for want of money for the last twenty years, and in order to find means of support for myself and my large family, I have been guilty of many acts which must for ever disgrace me.' [1]   He had now within reach a guinea a day, and much besides, if he would endeavour to find any documents that might be available to sustain the charges made in the pamphlet.   After some hesitation the bargain was struck, a guinea a day, hotel and travelling expenses, and a round price for documents.   Within a few months the needy man in clover pocketed many hundreds of pounds.   Only the author of the history of *Jonathan Wild the Great* could do justice to such a story of the Vagabond in Luck — a jaunt to Lausanne, a trip across the Atlantic, incessant journeys backward and forward to Paris, the jingling of guineas, the rustle of hundred-pound notes, and now and then perhaps a humorous thought of simple and solemn people in newspaper offices in London, or a moment's meditation on that perplexing law of human affairs by which the weak things

[1] Feb. 24, 1889. *Evidence,* vi. p. 20.

of the world are chosen to confound the things that are
mighty.

The moment came for delivering the documents in Paris,
and delivered they were with details more grotesque than
anything since the foolish baronet in Scott's novel was
taken by Dousterswivel to find the buried treasure in Saint
Ruth's. From first to last not a test or check was applied
by anybody to hinder the fabrication from running its course
without a hitch or a crease. When men have the demon of
a fixed idea in their cerebral convolutions, they easily fall
victims to a devastating credulity, and the victims were now
radiant as, with microscope and calligraphic expert by their
side, they fondly gazed upon their prize. About the time
when the judges were getting to work, clouds arose on
this smiling horizon. It is good, says the old Greek, that
men should carry a threatening shadow in their hearts
even under the full sunshine. Before this, the manager
learned for the first time, what was the source of the letters.
The blessed doctrine of intrinsic certainty, however, which
has before now done duty in far graver controversy, prevented him from inquiring as to the purity of the source.

The toils were rapidly enclosing both the impostor and the
dupes. He was put into the box at last (Feb. 21). By the
end of the second day, the torture had become more than
he could endure. Some miscalled the scene dramatic. That
is hardly the right name for the merciless hunt of an abject
fellow-creature through the doublings and windings of a
thousand lies. The breath of the hounds was on him, and
he could bear the chase no longer. After proceedings not
worth narrating, except that he made a confession and then
committed his last perjury, he disappeared. The police
traced him to Madrid. When they entered his room with
their warrant (March 1), he shot himself dead. They found
on his corpse the scapulary worn by devout catholics as a
visible badge and token of allegiance to the heavenly powers.
So in the ghastliest wreck of life, men still hope and seek for
some mysterious cleansing of the soul that shall repair all.

This damning experience was a sharp mortification to
the government, who had been throughout energetic con-

federates in the attack. Though it did not come at once formally into debate, it exhilarated the opposition, and Mr. Gladstone himself was in great spirits, mingled with intense indignation and genuine sympathy for Mr. Parnell as a man who had suffered an odious wrong.

VI

The report of the commission was made to the crown on February 13, 1890. It reached the House of Commons about ten o'clock the same evening. The scene was curious, — the various speakers droning away in a House otherwise profoundly silent, and every member on every bench, including high ministers of state, plunged deep and eager into the blue-book. The general impression was that the findings amounted to acquittal, and everybody went home in considerable excitement at this final explosion of the damaged blunderbuss. The next day Mr. Gladstone had a meeting with the lawyers in the case, and was keen for action in one form or another; but on the whole it was agreed that the government should be left to take the initiative.

The report was discussed in both Houses, and strong speeches were made on both sides. The government (Mar. 3) proposed a motion that the House adopted the report, thanked the judges for their just and impartial conduct, and ordered the report to be entered on the journals. Mr. Gladstone followed with an amendment, that the House deemed it to be a duty to record its reprobation of the false charges of the gravest and most odious description, based on calumny and on forgery, that had been brought against members of the House; and, while declaring its satisfaction at the exposure of these calumnies, the House expressed its regret at the wrong inflicted and the suffering and loss endured through a protracted period by reason of these acts of flagrant iniquity. After a handsome tribute to the honour and good faith of the judges, he took the point that some of the opinions in the report were in no sense and no degree judicial. How, for instance, could three judges, sitting ten years after the fact (1879–80), determine better than anybody else that distress and extravagant rents had nothing to do with crime? Why should the House of Commons declare its adoption of this finding without question or correction? Or of this, that the rejection of the Disturbance bill by the Lords in 1880 had nothing to do with the increase of crime? Mr. Forster had denounced the action of the Lords with indignation, and was not he, the responsible minister, a better witness than the three judges in no contact with contemporary fact? How were the judges authorised to affirm that the Land bill of 1881 had not been a great cause in mitigating the condition of Ireland? Another conclusive objection was that — on the declaration of the judges themselves, rightly made by them — what we know to be essential portions of the evidence were entirely excluded from their view.

He next turned to the findings, first of censure, then of acquittal. The findings of censure were in substance three. First, seven of the respondents had joined the league with a view of separating Ireland from England. The idea was dead, but Mr. Gladstone was compelled to say that in his opinion to deny the moral authority of the Act of Union was for an Irishman no moral offence whatever. Here the law-officer sitting opposite to him busily took down a note. 'Yes, yes,' Mr. Gladstone exclaimed, 'you may take my words down. I heard you examine your witness from a pedestal, as you felt, of the greatest elevation, endeavouring to press home the monstrous guilt of an Irishman who did not allow moral authority to the Act of Union. In my opinion the Englishman has far more cause to blush for the means by which that Act was obtained.' As it happened, on the only occasion on which Mr. Gladstone paid the Commission a visit, he had found the attorney general cross-examining a leading Irish member, and this passage of arms on the Act of Union between counsel and witness then occurred.

The second finding of censure was that the Irish members incited to intimidation by speeches, knowing that intimidation led to crime. The third was that they never placed themselves on the side of law and order; they did not assist the administration, and did not denounce the party of physical force. As if this, said Mr. Gladstone, had not been the subject of incessant discussion and denunciation in parliament at the time ten years ago, and yet no vote of condemnation was passed upon the Irish members then. On the contrary, the tory party, knowing all these charges, associated with them for purposes of votes and divisions; climbed into office on Mr. Parnell's shoulders; and through the viceroy with the concurrence of the prime minister, took Mr. Parnell into counsel upon the devising of a plan for Irish government. Was parliament now to affirm and record a finding that it had scrupulously abstained from ever making its own, and without regard to the counter-allegation that more crime and worse crime was prevented by agitation? It was the duty of parliament to look at the whole of the facts of the great crisis of 1880-1 — to the distress, to the rejection of the Compensation bill, to the growth of evictions, to the prevalence of excessive rents. The judges expressly shut out this comprehensive survey. But the House was not a body with a limited commission; it was a body of statesmen, legislators, politicians, bound to look at the whole range of circumstances, and guilty of misprision of justice if they failed so to do. 'Suppose I am told,' he said in notable and mournful words, ' that without the agitation Ireland would never have had the Land Act of 1881, are you prepared to deny that? I hear no challenges upon that statement, for I think it is generally and deeply felt that without the agitation the Land Act would not have been passed. As the man responsible more than any other for the Act of 1881 — as the man whose duty it was to consider that question day and night during nearly the whole of that session — I must record my firm opinion that it would not have become the law of the land, if it had not been for the agitation with which Irish society was convulsed.'[1]

This bare table of his leading points does nothing to convey the impression made by an extraordinarily fine performance. When the speaker came to the findings of acquittal, to the dismissal of the infamous charges of the forged letters, of intimacy with the Invincibles, of being

[1] See above, vol. iii. p. 56.

accessory to the assassinations in the Park, glowing passion
in voice and gesture reached its most powerful pitch, and
the moral appeal at its close was long remembered among
the most searching words that he had ever spoken. It was
not forensic argument, it was not literature; it had every
note of true oratory — a fervid, direct and pressing call to his
hearers as 'individuals, man by man, not with a responsibility diffused and severed until it became inoperative and
worthless, to place himself in the position of the victim of
this frightful outrage; to give such a judgment as would
bear the scrutiny of the heart and of the conscience of
every man when he betook himself to his chamber and was
still.'

The awe that impressed the House from this exhortation
to repair an enormous wrong soon passed away, and debate in
both Houses went on the regular lines of party. Everything
that was found not to be proved against the Irishmen, was
assumed against them. Not proven was treated as only an
evasive form of guilty. Though the three judges found that
there was no evidence that the accused had done this thing
or that, yet it was held legitimate to argue that evidence
must exist — if only it could be found. The public were to
nurse a sort of twilight conviction and keep their minds in
a limbo of beliefs that were substantial and alive — only the
light was bad.

In truth, the public did what the judges declined to do.
They took circumstances into account. The general effect
of this transaction was to promote the progress of the
great unsettled controversy in Mr. Gladstone's sense. The
abstract merits of home rule were no doubt untouched,
but it made a difference to the concrete argument, whether
the future leader of an Irish parliament was a proved
accomplice of the Park murderers or not. It presented
moreover the chameleon Irish case in a new and singular
colour. A squalid insurrection awoke parliament to the
mischiefs and wrongs of the Irish cultivators. Reluctantly
it provided a remedy. Then in the fulness of time, ten
years after, it dealt with the men who had roused it to its
duty. And how? It brought them to trial before a special

tribunal, invented for the purpose, and with no jury; it allowed them no voice in the constitution of the tribunal; it exposed them to long and harassing proceedings; and it thereby levied upon them a tremendous pecuniary fine. The report produced a strong recoil against the flagrant violence, passion, and calumny, that had given it birth; and it affected that margin of men, on the edge of either of the two great parties by whom electoral decisions are finally settled.

CHAPTER IV

THE nobler a soul is, the more objects of compassion it hath.
— BACON.

AT the end of 1888 Mr. Gladstone with his wife and others of his house was carried off by Mr. Rendel's friendly care to Naples. Hereto, he told Lord Acton, 'we have been induced by three circumstances. First, a warm invitation from the Dufferins to Rome; as to which, however, there are *cons* as well as *pros*, for a man who like me is neither Italian nor Curial in the view of present policies. Secondly, our kind friend Mr. Stuart Rendel has actually offered to be our conductor thither and back, to perform for us the great service which you rendered us in the trip to Munich and Saint-Martin. Thirdly, I have the hope that the stimulating climate of Naples, together with an abstention from speech greater than any I have before enjoyed, might act upon my " vocal cord," and partially at least restore it.'

At Naples he was much concerned with Italian policy.

To Lord Granville.

Jan. 13, 1889. — My stay here where the people really seem to regard me as not a foreigner, has brought Italian affairs and policy very much home to me, and given additional force and vividness to the belief I have always had, that it was sadly impolitic for Italy to make enemies for herself beyond the Alps. Though I might try and keep back this sentiment in Rome, even my silence might betray it and I could not promise to keep silence altogether. I think the impolicy amounts almost to madness especially for a

BOOK
X.

1889.

country which carries with her, nestling in her bosom, the 'standing menace' of the popedom. . . .

To J. Morley.

Jan. 10. — I hope you have had faith enough not to be troubled about my supposed utterances on the temporal power. . . . I will not trouble you with details, but you may rest assured I have never said the question of the temporal power was anything except an Italian question. I have a much greater anxiety than this about the Italian alliance with Germany. It is in my opinion an awful error and constitutes the great danger of the country. It may be asked, 'What have you to do with it?' More than people might suppose. I find myself hardly regarded here as a foreigner. They look upon me as having had a real though insignificant part in the Liberation. It will hardly be possible for me to get through the affair of this visit without making my mind known. On this account mainly I am verging towards the conclusion that it will be best for me not to visit Rome, and my wife as it happens is not anxious to go there. If you happen to see Granville or Rosebery please let them know this.

We have had on the whole a good season here thus far. Many of the days delicious. We have been subjected here as well as in London to a course of social kindnesses as abundant as the waters which the visitor has to drink at a watering place, and so enervating from the abstraction of cares that I am continually thinking of the historical Capuan writer. I am in fact totally demoralised, and cannot wish not to continue so. Under the circumstances Fortune has administered a slight, a very slight physical correction. A land-slip, or rather a Tufo rock-slip of 50,000 tons, has come down and blocked the proper road between us and Naples.

To Lord Acton.

Jan. 23, 1889. — Rome is I think definitely given up. I shall be curious to know your reasons for approving this *gran rifiuto*. Meantime I will just glance at mine. I am not so much afraid of the Pope as of the Italian government and court. My sentiments are so very strong about the present foreign policy. The foreign policy of the government but not I fear of the government only. If I went to Rome, and saw the King and the minister, as I must,

I should be treading upon eggs all the time with them. I could
not speak out uninvited; and it is not satisfactory to be silent
in the presence of those interested, when the feelings are very
strong. . . .

These feelings broke out in time in at least one anonymous article.[1] He told Lord Granville how anxious he was
that no acknowledgment of authorship, direct or indirect,
should come from any of his friends. 'Such an article of
necessity lectures the European states. As one of a public
of three hundred and more millions, I have a right to do
this, but not in my own person.' This strange simplicity
rather provoked his friends, for it ignored two things —
first, the certainty that the secret of authorship would get
out; second, if it did not get out, the certainty that the
European states would pay no attention to such a lecture
backed by no name of weight — perhaps even whether it
were so backed or not. Faith in lectures, sermons, articles,
even books, is one of the things most easily overdone.

Most of my reading, he went on to Acton, has been about the Jews
and the Old Testament. I have not looked at the books you kindly
sent me, except a little before leaving Hawarden ; but I want to get
a hold on the broader side of the Mosaic dispensation and the Jewish
history. The great historic features seem to me in a large degree
independent of the critical questions which have been raised about
the *redaction* of the Mosaic books. Setting aside Genesis, and the
Exodus proper, it seems difficult to understand how either Moses
or any one else could have advisedly published them in their
present form; and most of all difficult to believe that men going
to work deliberately after the captivity would not have managed
a more orderly execution. My thoughts are always running back
to the parallel question about Homer. In that case, those who
hold that Peisistratos or some one of his date was the compiler,
have at least this to say, that the poems in their present form are
such as a compiler, having liberty of action, might have aimed
at putting out from his workshop. Can that be said of the
Mosaic books ? Again, are we not to believe in the second and

---

[1] 'The Triple Alliance and Italy's Place in It.' By Outidanos. *Contemporary Review*, October 1889. See Appendix.

third Temples as centres of worship because there was a temple at Leontopolis, as we are told? Out of the frying-pan, into the fire.

When he left Amalfi (Feb. 14) for the north, he found himself, he says, in a public procession, with great crowds at the stations, including Crispi at Rome, who had once been his guest at Hawarden.

After his return home, he wrote again to Lord Acton : —

April 28, 1889. — I have long been wishing to write to you. But as a rule I never can write any letters that I wish to write. My volition of that kind is from day to day exhausted by the worrying demand of letters that I do not wish to write. Every year brings me, as I reckon, from three to five thousand new correspondents, of whom I could gladly dispense with 99 per cent. May you never be in a like plight.

Mary showed me a letter of recent date from you, which referred to the idea of my writing on the Old Testament. The matter stands thus : An appeal was made to me to write something on the general position and claims of the holy scriptures for the working men. I gave no pledge but read (what was for me) a good deal on the laws and history of the Jews with only two results: first, deepened impressions of the vast interest and importance attaching to them, and of their fitness to be made the subject of a telling popular account; secondly, a discovery of the necessity of reading much more. But I have never in this connection thought much about what is called the criticism of the Old Testament, only seeking to learn how far it impinged upon the matters that I really was thinking of. It seems to me that it does not impinge much. . . . It is the fact that among other things I wish to make some sort of record of my life. You say truly it has been very full. I add fearfully full. But it has been in a most remarkable degree the reverse of self-guided and self-suggested, with reference I mean to all its best known aims. Under this surface, and in its daily habit no doubt it has been selfish enough. Whether anything of this kind will ever come off is most doubtful. Until I am released from politics by the solution of the Irish problem, I cannot even survey the field.

I turn to the world of action. It has long been in my mind to found something of which a library would be the nucleus. I incline to begin with a temporary building here. Can you, who have built a library, give me any advice? On account of fire I have half a mind to corrugated iron, with felt sheets to regulate the temperature.

CHAP.
IV.

Æt. 80.

Have you read any of the works of Dr. Salmon? I have just finished his volume on Infallibility, which fills me with admiration of its easy movement, command of knowledge, singular faculty of disentanglement, and great skill and point in argument; though he does not quite make one love him. He touches much ground trodden by Dr. Döllinger; almost invariably agreeing with him.

II

July 25, 1889, was the fiftieth anniversary of his marriage. The Prince and Princess of Wales sent him what he calls a beautiful and splendid gift. The humblest were as ready as the highest with their tributes, and comparative strangers as ready as the nearest. Among countless others who wrote was Bishop Lightfoot, great master of so much learning : —

I hope you will receive this tribute from one who regards your private friendship as one of the great privileges of his life.

And Döllinger : —

If I were fifteen years younger than I am, how happy I would be to come over to my beloved England once more, and see you surrounded by your sons and daughters, loved, admired, I would almost say worshipped, by a whole grateful nation.

On the other side, a clever lady having suggested to Browning that he should write an inscription for her to some gift for Mr. Gladstone, received an answer that has interest, both by the genius and fame of its writer, and as a sign of widespread feeling in certain circles in those days : —

Surely your kindness, even your sympathy, will be extended to me when I say, with sorrow indeed, that I am unable now conscientiously to do what, but a few years ago, I would have at

least attempted with such pleasure and pride as might almos
promise success. I have received much kindness from that extra
ordinary personage, and what my admiration for his transcenden
abilities was and ever will be, there is no need to speak of. Bu
I am forced to altogether deplore his present attitude with respec
to the liberal party, of which I, the humblest unit, am still a
member, and as such grieved to the heart by every fresh utter
ance of his which comes to my knowledge. Were I in a position
to explain publicly how much the personal feeling is independen
of the political aversion, all would be easy; but I am a mere mar
of letters, and by the simple inscription which would truly testify
to what is enduring, unalterable in my esteem, I should lead
people — as well those who know me as those who do not — to
believe my approbation extended far beyond the bounds which
unfortunately circumscribe it now. All this — even more — was
on my mind as I sat, last evening, at the same table with the
brilliantly-gifted man whom once — but that 'once' is too sad to
remember.

At a gathering at Spencer House in the summer of 1888
when this year of felicitation opened, Lord Granville, on
behalf of a number of subscribers, presented Mr. and Mrs
Gladstone with two portraits, and in his address spoke of
the long span of years through which they had enjoyed
'the unclouded blessings of the home.' The expression was
a just one. The extraordinary splendour and exalted joys
of an outer life so illustrious were matched in the inner
circle of the hearth by a happy order, affectionate reciproca
attachments, a genial round of kindliness and duty, that
from year to year went on untarnished, unstrained, unbroken.
Visitors at Hawarden noticed that, though the two heads
of the house were now old, the whole atmosphere seemed
somehow to be alive with the freshness and vigour of youth ;
it was one of the youngest of households in its interests and
activities. The constant tension of his mind never impaired
his tenderness and wise solicitude for family and kinsfolk
and for all about him ; and no man ever had such observ
ance of decorum with such entire freedom from pharisaism.
Nor did the order and moral prosperity of his own home

leave him complacently forgetful of fellow-creatures to whom life's cup had been dealt in another measure. On his first entry upon the field of responsible life, he had formed a serious and solemn engagement with a friend — I suppose it was Hope-Scott — that each would devote himself to active service in some branch of religious work.[1] He could not, without treason to his gifts, go forth like Selwyn or Patteson to Melanesia to convert the savages. He sought a missionary field at home, and he found it among the unfortunate ministers to 'the great sin of great cities.' In these humane efforts at reclamation he persevered all through his life, fearless of misconstruction, fearless of the levity or baseness of men's tongues, regardless almost of the possible mischiefs to the public policies that depended on him. Greville[2] tells the story how in 1853 a man made an attempt one night to extort money from Mr. Gladstone, then in office as chancellor of the exchequer, by threats of exposure; and how he instantly gave the offender into custody, and met the case at the police office. Greville could not complete the story. The man was committed for trial. Mr. Gladstone directed his solicitors to see that the accused was properly defended. He was convicted and sent to prison. By and by Mr. Gladstone inquired from the governor of the prison how the delinquent was conducting himself. The report being satisfactory, he next wrote to Lord Palmerston, then at the home office, asking that the prisoner should be let out. There was no worldly wisdom in it, we all know. But then what are people Christians for?

We have already seen[3] his admonition to a son, and how much importance he attached to the dedication of a certain portion of our means to purposes of charity and religion. His example backed his precept. He kept detailed accounts under these heads from 1831 to 1897, and from these it appears that from 1831 to the end of 1890 he had devoted to objects of charity and religion upwards of seventy thousand pounds, and in the remaining years of his life the figure in this account stands at thirteen thousand five

---

[1] See above, vol. i. pp. 99, 568. [2] Third Part, vol. i. p. 62.
[3] Vol. i. p. 206.

hundred — this besides thirty thousand pounds for his cherished object of founding the hostel and library at Saint Deiniol's. His friend of early days, Henry Taylor, says in one of his notes on life that if you know how a man deals with money, how he gets it, spends it, keeps it, shares it, you know some of the most important things about him. His old chief at the colonial office in 1846 stands the test most nobly.

III

Near the end of 1889 among the visitors to Hawarden was Mr. Parnell. His air of good breeding and easy composure pleased everybody. Mr. Gladstone's own record is simple enough, and contains the substance of the affair as he told me of it later : —

Dec. 18, 1889. — Reviewed and threw into form all the points of possible amendment or change in the plan of Irish government, etc., for my meeting with Mr. Parnell. He arrived at 5.30, and we had two hours of satisfactory conversation ; but he put off the *gros* of it.   19. — Two hours more with Mr. P. on points in Irish government plans. He is certainly one of the very best people to deal with that I have ever known. Took him to the old castle. He seems to notice and appreciate everything.

Thinking of all that had gone before, and all that was so soon to come after, anybody with a turn for imaginary dialogue might easily upon this theme compose a striking piece.

In the spring of 1890 Mr. Gladstone spent a week at Oxford of which he spoke with immense enthusiasm. He was an honorary fellow of All Souls, and here he went into residence in his own right with all the zest of a virtuous freshman bent upon a first class. Though, I daresay, pretty nearly unanimous against his recent policies, they were all fascinated by his simplicity, his freedom from assumption or parade, his eagerness to know how leading branches of Oxford study fared, his naturalness and pleasant manners. He wrote to Mrs. Gladstone (Feb. 1) : —

Here I am safe and sound, and launched anew on my university career, all my days laid out and occupied until the morning of this day week, when I am to return to London. They press me to stay over the Sunday, but this cannot be thought of. I am received with infinite kindness, and the rooms they have given me are delightful. Weather dull, and light a medium between London and Hawarden. I have seen many already, including Liddon and Acland, who goes up to-morrow for a funeral early on Monday. Actually I have engaged to give a kind of Homeric lecture on Wednesday to the members of the union. The warden and his sisters are courteous and hospitable to the last degree. He is a unionist. The living here is very good, perhaps some put on for a guest, but I like the tone of the college; the fellows are men of a high class, and their conversation is that of men with work to do. I had a most special purpose in coming here which will be more than answered. It was to make myself safe so far as might be, in the articles [1] which eighteen months ago I undertook to write about the Old Testament. This, as you know perhaps, is now far more than the New, the battle-ground of belief. There are here most able and instructed men, and I am already deriving great benefit.

Something that fell from him one morning at breakfast in the common room led in due time to the election of Lord Acton to be also an honorary member of this distinguished society. 'If my suggestion,' Mr. Gladstone wrote to one of the fellows, 'really contributed to this election, then I feel that in the dregs of my life I have at least rendered one service to the college. My ambition is to visit it and Oxford in company with him.'

IV

In 1890 both Newman and Döllinger died.

I have been asked from many quarters, Mr. Gladstone said to Acton, to write about the Cardinal. But I dare not. First, I do not know enough. Secondly, I should be puzzled to use the little knowledge that I have. I was not a friend of his, but only an

[1] These articles appeared in *Good Words* (March–November 1900), and were subsequently published in volume form under the title of *The Impregnable Rock of Holy Scripture*.

acquaintance treated with extraordinary kindness whom it would ill become to note what he thinks defects, while the great powers and qualities have been and will be described far better by others. Ever since he published his University Sermons in 1843, I have thought him unsafe in philosophy, and no Butlerian though a warm admirer of Butler. No; it was before 1843, in 1841 when he published Tract XC. The *general* argument of that tract was unquestionable; but he put in sophistical matter without the smallest necessity. What I recollect is about General Councils: where in treating the declaration that they may err he virtually says, 'No doubt they may — unless the Holy Ghost prevents them.' But he was a wonderful man, a holy man, a very refined man, and (to me) a most kindly man.

Of Dr. Döllinger he contributed a charming account to a weekly print,[1] and to Acton he wrote : —

I have the fear that my Döllinger letters will disappoint you. When I was with him, he spoke to me with the utmost freedom; and so I think he wrote, but our correspondence was only occasional. I think nine-tenths of my intercourse with him was oral; with Cardinal Newman nothing like one-tenth. But with neither was the mere *corpus* of my intercourse great, though in D.'s case it was very precious, most of all the very first of it in 1845. . . . With my inferior faculty and means of observation, I have long adopted your main proposition. His attitude of mind was more historical than theological. When I first knew him in 1845, and he honoured me with very long and interesting conversations, they turned very much upon theology, and I derived from him what I thought very valuable and steadying knowledge. Again in 1874 during a long walk, when we spoke of the shocks and agitation of our time, he told me how the Vatican decrees had required him to reperuse and retry the whole circle of his thought. He did not make known to me any general result; but he had by that time found himself wholly detached from the Council of Trent, which was indeed a logical necessity from his preceding action. The Bonn Conference appeared to show him nearly at the standing point of anglican theology. I thought him more liberal as a

[1] *Speaker*, Aug. 30, 1890.

theologian than as a politician. On the point of church establishment he was as impenetrable as if he had been a Newdegate. He
would not see that there were two sides to the question. I long
earnestly to know what progress he had made at the last towards
redeeming the pledge given in one of his letters to me, that the
evening of his life was to be devoted to a great theological construction. . . . I should have called him an anti-Jesuit, but in
no other sense, that is in no sense, a Jansenist. I never saw the
least sign of leaning in that direction.

V

Here the reader may care to have a note or two of talk
with him in these days : —

At Dollis Hill, Sunday, Feb. 22, 1891. . . . A few minutes after
eight Mr. and Mrs. Gladstone came in from church, and we
three sat down to dinner. A delightful talk, he was in full
force, plenty of energy without vehemence. The range of topics
was pretty wide, yet marvellous to say, we had not a single
word about Ireland. Certainly no harm in that.

J. M. — A friend set me on a hunt this morning through
Wordsworth for the words about France standing on the top
of golden hours. I did not find them, but I came across a good
line of Hartley Coleridge's about the Thames : —

> ' And the thronged river toiling to the main.'

Mr. G. — Yes, a good line. Toiling to the main recalls
Dante : —

> ' Su la marina, dove 'l Po discende,
> Per aver pace co' seguaci sui.' [1]

J. M. — Have you seen Symonds's re-issued volume on Dante ?
'Tis very good. Shall I lend it to you ?

Mr. G. — Sure to be good, but not in the session. I never look
at Dante unless I can have a great continuous draught of him.
He's too big, he seizes and masters you.

J. M. — Oh, I like the picturesque bits, if it's only for half-an-
hour before dinner ; the bird looking out of its nest for the

---

[1] *Inf.* v. 98 : ' Where Po descends for rest with his tributary streams.'

dawn, the afternoon bell, the trembling of the water in the morning light, and the rest that everybody knows.

Mr. G. — No, I cannot do it. By the way, ladies nowadays keep question books, and among other things ask their friends for the finest line in poetry. I think I'm divided between three, perhaps the most glorious is Milton's — [*Somehow this line slipped from memory, but the reader might possibly do worse than turn over Milton in search for his finest line.*] Or else Wordsworth's — 'Or hear old Triton blow his wreathèd horn.' Yet what so splendid as Penelope's about not rejoicing the heart of anybody less than Odysseus?

μηδέ τι χείρονος ἀνδρὸς ἐϋφραίνοιμι νόημα.[1]

He talked a great deal to-night about Homer; very confident that he had done something to drive away the idea that Homer was an Asiatic Greek. Then we turned to Scott, whom he held to be by far the greatest of his countrymen. I suggested John Knox. 'No, the line must be drawn firm between the writer and the man of action; no comparisons there.'

J. M. — Well, then, though I love Scott so much that if any man chooses to put him first, I won't put him second, yet is there not a vein of pure gold in Burns that gives you pause?

Mr. G. — Burns very fine and true, no doubt; but to imagine a whole group of characters, to marshal them, to set them to work, to sustain the action — I must count that the test of highest and most diversified quality.

We spoke of the new Shakespeare coming out. I said I had been taking the opportunity of reading vol. i., and should go over it all in successive volumes. *Mr. G.* — 'Falstaff is wonderful — one of the most wonderful things in literature.'

Full of interest in *Hamlet*, and enthusiasm for it — comes closer than any other play to some of the strangest secrets of human nature — what *is* the key to the mysterious hold of this play on the world's mind? I produced my favourite proposition that *Measure for Measure* is one of the most modern of all the plays; the profound analysis of Angelo and his moral catastrophe, the strange figure of the duke, the deep irony of our modern time in it all. But I do not think he cared at all for this sort of criticism.

[1] *Od.* xx. 82.

He is too healthy, too objective, too simple, for all the complexities of modern morbid analysis.

Talked of historians; Lecky's two last volumes he had not yet read, but — had told him that, save for one or two blots due to contemporary passion, they were perfectly honourable to Lecky in every way. Lecky, said Mr. G., 'has real insight into the motives of statesmen. Now Carlyle, so mighty as he is in flash and penetration, has no eye for motives. Macaulay, too, is so caught by a picture, by colour, by surface, that he is seldom to be counted on for just account of motive.'

He had been reading with immense interest and satisfaction Sainte-Beuve's *History of Port Royal*, which for that matter deserves all his praise and more, though different parts of it are written from antagonistic points of view. Vastly struck by Saint-Cyran. When did the notion of the spiritual director make its appearance in Europe? Had asked both Döllinger and Acton on this curious point. For his own part, he doubted whether the office existed before the Reformation.

J. M. — Whom do you reckon the greatest Pope?

Mr. G. — I think on the whole, Innocent III. But his greatness was not for good. What did he do? He imposed the dogma of transubstantiation; he is responsible for the Albigensian persecutions; he is responsible for the crusade which ended in the conquest of Byzantium. Have you ever realised what a deadly blow was the ruin of Byzantium by the Latins, how wonderful a fabric the Eastern Empire was?

J. M. — Oh, yes, I used to know my Finlay better than most books. Mill used to say a page of Finlay was worth a chapter of Gibbon : he explains how decline and fall came about.

Mr. G. — Of course. Finlay has it all.

He tried then to make out that the eastern empire was more wonderful than anything done by the Romans; it stood out for eleven centuries, while Rome fell in three. I pointed out to him that the whole solid framework of the eastern empire was after all built up by the Romans. But he is philhellene all through past and present.

CHAPTER V

BREACH WITH MR. PARNELL

(*1890–1891*)

Fortuna vitrea est, — tum quum splendet frangitur. — PUBLIL. SYRUS.
Brittle like glass is fortune, — bright as light, and then the crash.

BOOK
X.

1890.

It would have been a miracle if the sight of all the methods of coercion, along with the ignominy of the forged letters, had not worked with strong effect upon the public mind. Distrust began to creep at a very rapid pace even into the ministerial ranks. The tory member for a large northern borough rose to resent 'the inexpedient treatment of the Irishmen from a party point of view,' to protest against the 'straining and stretching of the law' by the resident magistrates, to declare his opinion that these gentlemen were not qualified to exercise the jurisdiction entrusted to them, 'and to denounce the folly of making English law unpopular in Ireland, and provoking the leaders of the Irish people by illegal and unconstitutional acts.'[1] These sentiments were notoriously shared to the full by many who sat around him. Nobody in those days, discredited as he was with his party, had a keener scent for the drift of popular feeling than Lord Randolph Churchill, and he publicly proclaimed that this sending of Irish members of parliament to prison in such numbers was a feature which he did not like. Further, he said that the fact of the government not thinking it safe for public meetings of any sort to be held, excited painful feelings in English minds.[2] All this was after the system had been in operation for two years. Even strong unionist organs in the Irish press could not stand it.[3] They declared that if

[1] Mr. Hanbury, August 1, 1889. *Hans.* 339, p. 98.
[2] At Birmingham, July 30, 1889.
[3] *E.g. Northern Whig*, February 21, 1889.

the Irish government wished to make the coercive system appear as odious as possible, they would act just as they were acting. They could only explain all these doings, not by 'wrong-headedness or imbecility,' but by a strange theory that there must be deliberate treachery among the government agents.

Before the end of the year 1889 the electoral signs were unmistakable. Fifty-three bye-elections had been contested since the beginning of the parliament. The net result was the gain of one seat for ministers and of nine to the opposition. The Irish secretary with characteristic candour never denied the formidable extent of these victories, though he mourned over the evils that such temporary successes might entail, and was convinced that they would prove to be dearly bought.[1] A year later the tide still flowed on; the net gain of the opposition rose to eleven. In 1886 seventy-seven constituencies were represented by forty-seven unionists and thirty liberals. By the beginning of October in 1890 the unionist members in the same constituencies had sunk to thirty-six, and the liberals had risen to forty-one. Then came the most significant election of all.

There had been for some months a lull in Ireland. Government claimed the credit of it for coercion; their adversaries set it down partly to the operation of the Land Act, partly to the natural tendency in such agitations to fluctuate or to wear themselves out, and most of all to the strengthened reliance on the sincerity of the English liberals. Suddenly the country was amazed towards the middle of September by news that proceedings under the Coercion Act had been instituted against two nationalist leaders, and others. Even strong adherents of the government and their policy were deeply dismayed, when they saw that after three years of it, the dreary work was to begin over again. The proceedings seemed to be stamped in every aspect as impolitic. In a few days the two leaders would have been on their way to America, leaving a half-empty war chest behind them and the flame of agitation burning low. As

[1] Mr. Balfour at Manchester. *Times*, October 21, 1889.

the offences charged had been going on for six months, there was clearly no pressing emergency.

A critical bye-election was close at hand at the moment in the Eccles division of Lancashire. The polling took place four days after a vehement defence of his policy by Mr. Balfour at Newcastle. The liberal candidate at Eccles expressly declared from his election address onwards, that the great issue on which he fought was the alternative between conciliation and coercion. Each candidate increased the party vote, the tory by rather more than one hundred, the liberal by nearly six hundred. For the first time the seat was wrested from the tories, and the liberal triumphed by a substantial majority.[1] This was the latest gauge of the failure of the Irish policy to conquer public approval, the last indication of the direction in which the currents of public opinion were steadily moving.[2] Then all at once a blinding sandstorm swept the ground.

II

One of those events now occurred that with their stern irony so mock the statesman's foresight, and shatter political designs in their most prosperous hour. As a mightier figure than Mr. Parnell remorsefully said on a grander stage, a hundred years before, cases sometimes befall in the history of nations where private fault is public disaster.

At the end of 1889, the Irish leader had been made a party in a suit for divorce. He betrayed no trace in his demeanour, either to his friends or to the House, of embarrassment at the position. His earliest appearance after the evil news, was in the debate on the first night of the session (February 11, '90), upon a motion about the publication of the forged letter. Some twenty of

[1] October 22, 1890.

[2] See Mr. Roby's speech at the Manchester Reform Club, Oct. 24, and articles in *Manchester Guardian*, Oct. 16 and 25, 1890. The *Times* (Oct. 23), while denying the inference that the Irish question was the question most prominent in the minds of large numbers of the electors, admitted that this was the vital question really before the constituency, and says generally, 'The election, like so many other bye-elections, has been decided by the return to their party allegiance of numbers of Gladstonians who in 1886 absented themselves from the polling booths.'

his followers being absent, he wished the discussion to be prolonged into another sitting. Closely as it might be supposed to concern him, he listened to none of the debate. He had a sincere contempt for speeches in themselves, and was wont to set down most of them to vanity. A message was sent that he should come upstairs and speak. After some indolent remonstrance, he came. His speech was admirable ; firm without emphasis, penetrating, dignified, freezing, and unanswerable. Neither now nor on any later occasion did his air of composure in public or in private give way.

Mr. Gladstone was at Hawarden, wide awake to the possibility of peril. To Mr. Arnold Morley he wrote on November 4 : — 'I fear a thundercloud is about to burst over Parnell's head, and I suppose it will end the career of a man in many respects invaluable.' On the 13th he was told by the present writer that there were grounds for an impression that Mr. Parnell would emerge as triumphantly from the new charge, as he had emerged from the obloquy of the forged letters. The case was opened two days later, and enough came out upon the first day of the proceedings to point to an adverse result. A Sunday intervened, and Mr. Gladstone's self-command under storm-clouds may be seen in a letter written on that day to me : —

Nov. 16, 1890.— 1. It is, after all, a thunder-clap about Parnell. Will he ask for the Chiltern Hundreds ? He cannot continue to lead ? What could he mean by his language to you ? The Pope has now clearly got a commandment under which to pull him up. It surely cannot have been always thus; for he represented his diocese in the church synod. 2. I thank you for your kind scruple, but in the country my Sundays are habitually and largely invaded. 3. Query, whether if a bye-seat were open and chanced to have a large Irish vote W— might not be a good man there. 4. I do not think my Mem. is worth circulating but perhaps you would send it to Spencer. I sent a copy to Harcourt. 5. [A small parliamentary point, not related to the Parnell affair, nor otherwise significant.] 6. Most warmly do I agree with you about the Scott *Journal.* How one loves him. 7. Some day I hope to inflict on you a talk about Homer and Homerology (as I call it).

The court pronounced a condemnatory decree on Monday, November 17th. Parliament was appointed to meet on Tuesday, the 25th. There was only a week for Irish and English to resolve what effect this condemnation should have upon Mr. Parnell's position as leader of one and ally of the other. Mr. Parnell wrote the ordinary letter to his parliamentary followers. The first impulses of Mr. Gladstone are indicated in a letter to me on the day after the decree : —

Nov. 18, 1890. — Many thanks for your letter. I had noticed the Parnell circular, not without misgiving. I read in the *P. M. G.* this morning a noteworthy article in the *Daily Telegraph*,[1] or rather from it, with which I very much agree. But I think it plain that we have nothing to say and nothing to do in the matter. The party is as distinct from us as that of Smith or Hartington. I own to some surprise at the apparent facility with which the R. C. bishops and clergy appear to take the continued leadership, but they may have tried the ground and found it would not *bear.* It is the Irish parliamentary party, and that alone to which we have to look. . . .

Such were Mr. Gladstone's thoughts when the stroke first fell.

III

In England and Scotland loud voices were speedily lifted up. Some treated the offence itself as an inexpiable disqualification. Others argued that, even if the offence could be passed over as lying outside of politics, it

---

[1] 'That the effect of this trial will be to relegate Mr. Parnell for a time, at any rate, to private life, must we think be assumed. . . . Special exemptions from penalties which should apply to all public men alike cannot possibly be made in favour of exceptionally valuable politicians to suit the convenience of their parties. He must cease, for the present at any rate, to lead the nationalist party ; and conscious as we are of the loss our opponents will sustain by his resignation, we trust that they will believe us when we say that we are in no mood to exult in it. . . . It is no satisfaction to us to feel that a political adversary whose abilities and prowess it was impossible not to respect, has been overthrown by irrelevant accident, wholly unconnected with the struggle in which we are engaged.' — *Daily Telegraph,* Nov. 17, 1890.

had been surrounded by incidents of squalor and deceit CHAP.
that betrayed a character in which no trust could ever be V.
placed again. In some English quarters all this was expressed with a strident arrogance that set Irishmen on fire. Æt. 81.
It is ridiculous, if we remember what space Mr. Parnell
filled in Irish imagination and feeling, how popular, how
mysterious, how invincible he had been, to blame them
because in the first moment of shock and bewilderment
they did not instantly plant themselves in the judgment
seat, always so easily ascended by Englishmen with little
at stake. The politicians in Dublin did not hesitate. A
great meeting was held at Leinster Hall in Dublin on the
Thursday (November 20th). The result was easy to foresee.
Not a whisper of revolt was heard. The chief nationalist
newspaper stood firm for Mr. Parnell's continuance. At
least one ecclesiastic of commanding influence was supposed
to be among the journal's most ardent prompters. It has
since been stated that the bishops were in fact forging bolts
of commination. No lurid premonitory fork or sheet flashed
on the horizon, no rumble of the coming thunders reached
the public ear.

Three days after the decree in the court, the great English
liberal organization chanced to hold its annual meeting at
Sheffield (November 20–21). In reply to a request of mine
as to his views upon our position, Mr. Gladstone wrote to
me as follows : —

Nov. 19, 1890. — Your appeal as to your meeting of to-morrow
gives matter for thought. I feel (1) that the Irish have
abstractedly a right to decide the question; (2) that on account
of Parnell's enormous services — he has done for home rule
something like what Cobden did for free trade, set the argument
on its legs — they are in a position of immense difficulty; (3) that
we, the liberal party as a whole, and especially we its leaders,
have for the moment nothing to say to it, that we must be passive,
must wait and watch. But I again and again say to myself,
I say I mean in the interior and silent forum, 'It 'll na dee.'
I should not be surprised if there were to be rather painful manifestations in the House on Tuesday. It is yet to be seen what

our Nonconformist friends, such a man as ——, for example, or such a man as —— will say. . . . If I recollect right, Southey's *Life of Nelson* was in my early days published and circulated by the Society for Promoting Christian Knowledge. It would be curious to look back upon it and see how the biographer treats his narrative at the tender points. What I have said under figure 3 applies to me beyond all others, and notwithstanding my prognostications I shall maintain an extreme reserve in a position where I can do no good (in the present tense), and might by indiscretion do much harm. You will doubtless communicate with Harcourt and confidential friends only as to anything in this letter. The thing, one can see, is not a *res judicata*. It may ripen fast. Thus far, there is a total want of moral support from this side to the Irish judgment.

A fierce current was soon perceived to be running. All the elements so powerful for high enthusiasm, but hazardous where an occasion demands circumspection, were in full blast. The deep instinct for domestic order was awake. Many were even violently and irrationally impatient that Mr. Gladstone had not peremptorily renounced the alliance on the very morrow of the decree. As if, Mr. Gladstone himself used to say, it could be the duty of any party leader to take into his hands the intolerable burden of exercising the rigours of inquisition and private censorship over every man with whom what he judged the highest public expediency might draw him to co-operate. As if, moreover, it could be the duty of Mr. Gladstone to hurry headlong into action, without giving Mr. Parnell time or chance of taking such action of his own as might make intervention unnecessary. Why was it to be assumed that Mr. Parnell would not recognise the facts of the situation? 'I determined,' said Mr. Gladstone 'to watch the state of feeling in this country. I made no public declaration, but the country made up its mind. I was in some degree like the soothsayer Shakespeare introduces into one of his plays. He says, " I do not make the facts ; I only foresee them." I did not foresee the facts even ; they were present before me.'[1]

[1] Speech at Retford, Dec. 11, 1890. *Antony and Cleopatra*, Act i. Sc. 2.

The facts were plain, and Mr. Gladstone was keenly alive CHAP.
to the full purport of every one of them.   Men, in whose   V.
hearts religion and morals held the first place, were strongly   Æt. 81.
joined by men accustomed to settle political action by
political considerations.   Platform-men united with pulpit-
men in swelling the whirlwind.   Electoral calculation and
moral faithfulness were held for once to point the same way.
The report from every quarter, every letter to a member
from a constituent, all was in one sense.   Some, as I have
said, pressed the point that the misconduct itself made
co-operation impossible; others urged the impossibility of
relying upon political understandings with one to whom
habitual duplicity was believed to have been brought home.
We may set what value we choose upon such arguments.
Undoubtedly they would have proscribed some of the most
important and admired figures in the supreme doings of
modern Europe.   Undoubtedly some who have fallen into
shift and deceit in this particular relation, have yet been
true as steel in all else.   For a man's character is a strangely
fitted mosaic, and it is unsafe to assume that all his traits
are of one piece, or inseparable in fact because they ought
to be inseparable by logic.   But people were in no humour
for casuistry, and whether all this be sophistry or sense,
the volume of hostile judgment and obstinate intention
could neither be mistaken, nor be wisely breasted if home
rule was to be saved in Great Britain.

Mr. Gladstone remained at Hawarden during the week.
To Mr. Arnold Morley he wrote (Nov. 23): 'I have a
bundle of letters every morning on the Parnell business, and
the bundles increase.   My own opinion has been the same
from the first, and I conceive that the time for action has
now come.   All my correspondents are in unison.'   Every
post-bag was heavy with admonitions, of greater cogency
than such epistles sometimes possess; and a voluminous
bundle of letters still at Hawarden bears witness to the
emotions of the time.   Sir William Harcourt and I, who
had taken part in the proceedings at Sheffield, made our
reports.   The acute manager of the liberal party came to
announce that three of our candidates had bolted already,

that more were sure to follow, and that this indispensable commodity in elections would become scarcer than ever. Of the general party opinion, there could be no shadow of doubt. It was no application of special rigour because Mr. Parnell was an Irishman. Any English politician of his rank would have fared the same or worse, and retirement, temporary or for ever, would have been inevitable. Temporary withdrawal, said some; permanent withdrawal, said others; but for withdrawal of some sort, almost all were inexorable.

IV

Mr. Gladstone did not reach London until the afternoon of Monday, November 24. Parliament was to assemble on the next day. Three members of the cabinet of 1886, and the chief whip of the party,[1] met him in the library of Lord Rendel's house at Carlton Gardens. The issue before the liberal leaders was a plain one. It was no question of the right of the nationalists to choose their own chief. It was no question of inflicting political ostracism on a particular kind of moral delinquency. The question was whether the present continuance of the Irish leadership with the silent assent of the British leaders, did not involve decisive abstention at the polls on the day when Irish policy could once more be submitted to the electors of Great Britain? At the best the standing difficulties even to sanguine eyes, and under circumstances that had seemed so promising, were still formidable. What chance was there if this new burden were superadded? Only one conclusion was possible upon the state of facts, and even those among persons responsible for this decision who were most earnestly concerned in the success of the Irish policy, reviewing all the circumstances of the dilemma, deliberately hold to this day that though a catastrophe followed, a worse catastrophe was avoided. It is one of the commonest of all secrets of cheap misjudgment in human affairs, to start by assuming that there is always some good way out of a bad case. Alas for us all, this is not so. Situations arise alike

---

[1] Lord Granville, Sir W. Harcourt, Mr. Arnold Morley, and myself.

for individuals, for parties, and for states, from which no good way out exists, but only choice between bad way and worse. Here was one of those situations. The mischiefs that followed the course actually taken, we see ; then, as is the wont of human kind, we ignore the mischiefs that as surely awaited any other.

Mr. Gladstone always steadfastly resisted every call to express an opinion of his own that the delinquency itself had made Mr. Parnell unfit and impossible. It was vain to tell him that the party would expect such a declaration, or that his reputation required that he should found his action on moral censure all his own. 'What!' he cried, 'because a man is what is called leader of a party, does that constitute him a censor and a judge of faith and morals? I will not accept it. It would make life intolerable.' He adhered tenaciously to political ground. 'I have been for four years,' Mr. Gladstone justly argued, 'endeavouring to per-suade voters to support Irish autonomy. Now the voter says to me, "If a certain thing happens — namely, the reten-tion of the Irish leadership in its present hands — I will not support Irish autonomy." How can I go on with the work? We laboriously rolled the great stone up to the top of the hill, and now it topples down to the bottom again, unless Mr. Parnell sees fit to go.' From the point of view of Irish policy this was absolutely unanswerable. It would have been just as unanswerable, even if all the dire confusion that afterwards came to pass had then been actually in sight. Its force was wholly independent, and necessarily so, of any intention that might be formed by Mr. Parnell.

As for that intention, let us turn to him for a moment. Who could dream that a man so resolute in facing facts as Mr. Parnell, would expect all to go on as before? Sub-stantial people in Ireland who were preparing to come round to home rule at the prospect of a liberal victory in Great Britain, would assuredly be frightened back. Belfast would be more resolute than ever. A man might estimate as he pleased either the nonconformist conscience in England, or the catholic conscience in Ireland. But the most cynical of mere calculators, — and I should be slow to say that this was Mr. Parnell, — could not fall a prey to such a hallucination as to suppose that a scandal so frightfully public, so impossible for even the most mild-eyed charity to pretend not to see, and which political passion was so interested in keeping in full blaze, would instantly drop out of the mind of two of the most religious communities in the world ; or that either of these communities could tolerate without effective protest so impenitent an affront as the unruffled continuity of the stained leadership. All this was independent of anything that Mr. Gladstone might do or might not do. The liberal leaders had a right to assume that the case must be as obvious to Mr. Parnell as it was to everybody else, and unless loyalty and good faith have no place in political alliances, they had a right to look for his spontaneous action. Was unlimited consideration due from them to him and none from him to them ?

The result of the consultation was the decisive letter addressed to me by Mr. Gladstone, its purport to be by me communicated to Mr. Parnell. As any one may see, its language was courteous and considerate. Not an accent was left that could touch the pride of one who was known to be as proud a man as ever lived. It did no more than state an unquestionable fact, with an inevitable inference. It was not written in view of publication, for that it was hoped would be unnecessary. It was written with the expectation of finding the personage concerned in his usual rational frame of mind, and with the intention of informing him of what it was right that he should know. The same evening Mr. McCarthy was placed in possession of Mr. Gladstone's views, to be laid before Mr. Parnell at the earliest moment.

'1 *Carlton Gardens, Nov.* 24, 1890. — MY DEAR MORLEY. — Having arrived at a certain conclusion with regard to the continuance, at the present moment, of Mr. Parnell's leadership of the Irish party, I have seen Mr. McCarthy on my arrival in town, and have inquired from him whether I was likely to receive from Mr. Parnell himself any communication on the subject. Mr. McCarthy replied that he was unable to give me any information on the subject. I mentioned to him that in 1882, after the terrible murder in the Phœnix Park, Mr. Parnell, although totally removed from any idea of responsibility, had spontaneously written to me, and offered to take the Chiltern Hundreds, an offer much to his honour but one which I thought it my duty to decline.

While clinging to the hope of a communication from Mr. Parnell, to whomsoever addressed, I thought it necessary, viewing the arrangements for the commencement of the session to-morrow, to acquaint Mr. McCarthy with the conclusion at which, after using all the means of observation and reflection in my power, I had myself arrived. It was that notwithstanding the splendid services rendered by Mr. Parnell to his country, his continuance at the present moment in the leadership would be productive of consequences disastrous in the highest degree to the cause of Ireland. I think I may be warranted in asking you so far to expand the conclusion I have given above, as to add that the continuance I speak of would not only place many hearty and effective friends of the Irish cause in a position of great embarrassment, but would render my retention of the leadership of the liberal party, based as it has been mainly upon the prosecution of the Irish cause, almost a nullity. This explanation of my views I begged Mr. McCarthy to regard as confidential, and not intended for his colleagues generally, if he found that Mr. Parnell contemplated spontaneous action; but I also begged that he would make known to the Irish party, at their meeting to-morrow afternoon, that such was my conclusion, if he should find that Mr. Parnell had not in contemplation any step of the nature indicated. I now write to you, in case Mr. McCarthy should be unable to communicate with Mr. Parnell, as I understand you may possibly have an opening to-morrow through another channel. Should you have such an opening, I beg you to make known to Mr. Parnell the conclusion itself, which I have stated in the earlier part of this letter. I have thought it best to put it in terms simple and direct, much as I should have desired had it lain within my power, to alleviate the painful nature of the situation. As respects the manner of conveying what my public duty has made it an obligation to say, I rely entirely on your good feeling, tact, and judgment. — Believe me sincerely yours, W. E. GLADSTONE.

No direct communication had been possible, though every effort to open it was made. Indirect information had been received. Mr. Parnell's purpose was reported to have shifted during the week since the decree. On the Wednesday he had been at his stiffest, proudest, and coldest, bent on holding on at all cost. He thought he saw a way of getting something done for Ireland; the Irish people had given him a commission; he should stand to it, so long as ever they asked him. On the Friday, however (Nov. 21), he appeared, so I had been told, to be shaken in his resolution. He had bethought him that the government might possibly seize the moment for a dissolution; that if there were an immediate election, the government would under the circumstances be not unlikely to win; if so, Mr. Gladstone might be thrown for four or five years into opposition; in other words, that powerful man's part in the great international transaction would be at an end. In this mood he declared himself alive to the peril and the grave responsibility of taking any course that could lead to consequences so formidable. That was the last authentic news that reached us. His Irish colleagues had no news at all. After this glimpse the curtain had fallen, and all oracles fell dumb.

If Mr. Gladstone's decision was to have the anticipated effect, Mr. Parnell must be made aware of it before the meeting of the Irish party (Nov. 25). This according to custom was to be held at two o'clock in the afternoon, to choose their chairman for the session. Before the choice was made, both the leader and his political friends should know the view and the purpose that prevailed in the camp of their allies. Mr. Parnell kept himself invisible and inaccessible alike to English and Irish friends until a few minutes before the meeting. The Irish member who had seen Mr. Gladstone the previous evening, at the last moment was able to deliver the message that had been confided to him. Mr. Parnell replied that he should stand to his guns. The other members of the Irish party came together, and, wholly ignorant of the attitude taken by Mr. Gladstone, promptly and with hardly a word of discussion re-elected their leader to his usual post. The gravity of the unfortunate error

committed in the failure to communicate the private message
to the whole of the nationalist members, with or without
Mr. Parnell's leave, lay in the fact that it magnified and
distorted Mr. Gladstone's later intervention into a humiliating public ultimatum. The following note, made at the
time, describes the fortunes of Mr. Gladstone's letter : —

Nov. 25. — I had taken the usual means of sending a message to
Mr. Parnell, to the effect that Mr. Gladstone was coming to town
on the following day, and that I should almost certainly have
a communication to make to Mr. Parnell on Tuesday morning.
It was agreed at my interview with his emissary on Sunday
night (November 23) that I should be informed by eleven on
Tuesday forenoon where I should see him. I laid special stress
on my seeing him before the party met. At half-past eleven,
or a little later, on that day I received a telegram from the
emissary that he could not reach his friend.[1] I had no difficulty
in interpreting this. It meant that Mr. Parnell had made up
his mind to fight it out, whatever line we might adopt; that
he guessed that my wish to see him must from his point of
view mean mischief; and that he would secure his re-election as
chairman before the secret was out. Mr. McCarthy was at this
hour also entirely in the dark, and so were all the other members of the Irish party supposed to be much in Mr. Parnell's
confidence. When I reached the House a little after three, the
lobby was alive with the bustle and animation usual at the
opening of a session, and Mr. Parnell was in the thick of it,
talking to a group of his friends. He came forward with much
cordiality. 'I am very sorry,' he said, 'that I could not make
an appointment, but the truth is I did not get your message
until I came down to the House, and then it was too late.' I
asked him to come round with me to Mr. Gladstone's room. As
we went along the corridor he informed me in a casual way that
the party had again elected him chairman. When we reached
the sunless little room, I told him I was sorry to hear that the
election was over, for I had a communication to make to him
which might, as I hoped, still make a difference. I then read out

---

[1] If anybody cares to follow all
this up, he may read a speech of Mr.
Parnell's at Kells, Aug. 16, 1891,
and a full reply of mine sent to the
press, Aug. 17.

to him Mr. Gladstone's letter. As he listened, I knew the look on his face quite well enough to see that he was obdurate. The conversation did not last long. He said the feeling against him was a storm in a teacup, and would soon pass. I replied that he might know Ireland, but he did not half know England; that it was much more than a storm in a teacup; that if he set British feeling at defiance and brazened it out, it would be ruin to home rule at the election; that if he did not withdraw for a time, the storm would not pass; that if he withdrew from the actual leadership now as a concession due to public feeling in this country, this need not prevent him from again taking the helm when new circumstances might demand his presence; that he could very well treat his re-election as a public vote of confidence by his party; that, having secured this, he would suffer no loss of dignity or authority by a longer or shorter period of retirement. I reminded him that for two years he had been practically absent from active leadership. He answered, in his slow dry way, that he must look to the future; that he had made up his mind to stick to the House of Commons and to his present position in his party, until he was convinced, and he would not soon be convinced, that it was impossible to obtain home rule from a British parliament; that if he gave up the leadership for a time, he should never return to it; that if he once let go, it was all over. There was the usual iteration on both sides in a conversation of the kind, but this is the substance of what passed. His manner throughout was perfectly cool and quiet, and his unresonant voice was unshaken. He was paler than usual, and now and then a wintry smile passed over his face. I saw that nothing would be gained by further parley, so I rose and he somewhat slowly did the same. 'Of course,' he said, as I held the door open for him to leave, 'Mr. Gladstone will have to attack me. I shall expect that. He will have a right to do that.' So we parted.

I waited for Mr. Gladstone, who arrived in a few minutes. It was now four o'clock. 'Well?' he asked eagerly the moment the door was closed, and without taking off cape or hat. 'Have you seen him?' 'He is obdurate,' said I. I told him shortly what had passed. He stood at the table, dumb for some instants, looking at me as if he could not believe what I had said. Then he burst out that we must at once publish his letter to me; at once, that very afternoon. I said, "'Tis too late now.' 'Oh, no,' said he, 'the *Pall Mall* will bring it out in a special edition.' 'Well, but,' I persisted, 'we ought really to consider it a little.' Reluctantly he yielded, and we went into the House. Harcourt presently joined us on the bench, and we told him the news. It was by and by decided that the letter should be immediately published. Mr. Gladstone thought that I should at once inform Mr. Parnell of this. There he was at that moment, pleasant and smiling, in his usual place on the Irish bench. I went into our lobby, and sent somebody to bring him out. Out he came, and we took three or four turns in the lobby. I told him that it was thought right, under the new circumstances, to send the letter to the press. 'Yes,' he said amicably, as if it were no particular concern of his, 'I think Mr. Gladstone will be quite right to do that; it will put him straight with his party.'

The debate on the address had meanwhile been running its course. Mr. Gladstone had made his speech. One of the newspapers afterwards described the liberals as wearing pre-occupied countenances. 'We were pre-occupied with a vengeance,' said Mr. Gladstone, 'and even while I was speaking I could not help thinking to myself, Here am I talking about Portugal and about Armenia, while every single creature in the House is absorbed in one thing only, and that is an uncommonly long distance from either Armenia or Portugal.' News of the letter, which had been sent to the reporters about eight o'clock, swiftly spread. Members hurried to ex-ministers in the dining-room to ask if the story of the letter were true. The lobbies were seized by one of those strange and violent fevers to which on such occasions the House of Commons is liable. Unlike the clamour of the Stock Exchange or a continental Chamber, there is little noise, but the perturbation is profound. Men pace the corridors in couples and trios, or flit from one knot to another, listening to an oracle of the moment modestly retailing a rumour false on the face of it, or evolving monstrous hypotheses to explain incredible occurrences. This, however, was no common crisis of lobby or gallery.

One party quickly felt that, for them at least, it was an affair of life or death. It was no wonder that the Irish members were stirred to the very depths. For five years they had worked on English platforms, made active friendships with English and Scottish liberals in parliament and out of it, been taught to expect from their aid and alliance that deliverance which without allies must remain out of reach and out of sight; above all, for nearly five years they had been taught to count on the puissant voice and strong right arm of the leader of all the forces of British liberalism.

They suddenly learned that if they took a certain step in respect of the leadership of their own party, the alliance was broken off, the most powerful of Englishmen could help them no more, and that all the dreary and desperate marches since 1880 were to be faced once again in a blind and endless campaign, against the very party to whose friendship they had been taught to look for strength, encouragement, and victory. Well might they recoil. More astounded still, they learned at the same time that they had already taken the momentous step in the dark, and that the knowledge of what they were doing, the pregnant meanings and the tremendous consequences of it, had been carefully concealed from them. Never were consternation, panic, distraction, and resentment better justified.

The Irishmen were anxious to meet at once. Their leader sat moodily in the smoking-room downstairs. His faculty of concentrated vision had by this time revealed to him the certainty of a struggle, and its intensity. He knew in minute detail every element of peril both at Westminster and in Ireland. A few days before, he mentioned to the present writer his suspicion of designs on foot in ecclesiastical quarters, though he declared that he had no fear of them. He may have surmised that the demonstration at the Leinster Hall was superficial and impulsive. On the other hand, his confidence in the foundations of his dictatorship was unshaken. This being so, if deliberate calculation were the universal mainspring of every statesman's action — as it assuredly is not nor can ever be — he would have spontaneously withdrawn for a season, in the assurance that if signs of disorganisation were to appear among his followers, his prompt return from Elba would be instantly demanded in Ireland, whether or no it were acquiesced in by the leaders and main army of liberals in England. That would have been both politic and decent, even if we conceive his mind to have been working in another direction. He may, for instance, have believed that the scandal had destroyed the chances of a liberal victory at the election, whether he stayed or withdrew. Why should he surrender his position in Ireland and over contending factions in America, in reliance upon an English party to which, as he was well aware, he had just dealt a smashing blow? These speculations, however, upon the thoughts that may have been slowly moving through his mind, are hardly worth pursuing. Unluckily, the stubborn impulses of defiance that came naturally to his temperament were aroused to their most violent pitch and swept all calculations of policy aside. He now proceeded passionately to dash into the dust the whole fabric of policy which he had with such infinite sagacity, patience, skill, and energy devised and reared.

Two short private memoranda from his own hand on this transaction, I find among Mr. Gladstone's papers. He read them to me at the time, and they illustrate his habitual practice of shaping and clearing his thought and recollection by committal to black and white : —

Nov. 26, 1890. — Since the month of December 1885 my whole political life has been governed by a supreme regard to the Irish question. For every day, I may say, of these five, we have been engaged in laboriously rolling up hill the stone of Sisyphus. Mr. Parnell's decision of yesterday means that the stone is to break away from us and roll down again to the bottom of the hill. I cannot recall the years which have elapsed. It was daring, perhaps, to begin, at the age I had then attained, a process which it was obvious must be a prolonged one.

Simply to recommence it now, when I am within a very few weeks of the age at which Lord Palmerston, the marvel of parliamentary longevity, succumbed, and to contemplate my accompanying the cause of home rule to its probable triumph a rather long course of years hence, would be more than daring; it would be presumptuous. My views must be guided by rational probabilities, and they exclude any such anticipation. My statement, therefore, that my leadership would, under the contemplated decision of Mr. Parnell, be almost a nullity, is a moderate statement of the case. I have been endeavouring during all these years to reason with the voters of the kingdom, and when the voter now tells me that he cannot give a vote for making the Mr. Parnell of to-day the ruler of Irish affairs under British sanction, I do not know how to answer him, and I have yet to ask myself formally the question what under those circumstances is to be done. I must claim entire and absolute liberty to answer that question as I may think right.

Nov. 28, 1890. — The few following words afford a key to my proceedings in the painful business of the Irish leadership.

It was at first my expectation, and afterwards my desire, that Mr. Parnell would retire by a perfectly spontaneous act. As the likelihood of such a course became less and less, while time ran on, and the evidences of coming disaster were accumulated, I thought it would be best that he should be impelled to withdraw, but by an influence conveyed to him, at least, from within the limits of his own party. I therefore begged Mr. Justin McCarthy to acquaint Mr. Parnell of what I thought as to the consequences of his continuance; I also gave explanations of my meaning, including a reference to myself; and I begged that my message to Mr. Parnell might be made known to the Irish party, in the absence of a spontaneous retirement.

This was on Monday afternoon. But there was no certainty either of finding Mr. Parnell, or of an impression on him through one of his own followers. I therefore wrote the letter to Mr. Morley, as a more delicate form of proceeding than a direct communication from myself, but also as a stronger measure than that taken through Mr. McCarthy, because it was more full, and because, as it was in writing, it admitted of the ulterior step of immediate publication. Mr. Morley could not find Mr. Parnell until after the first meeting of the Irish party on Monday. When we found that Mr. McCarthy's representation had had no

effect, that the Irish party had not been informed, and that Mr.
Morley's making known the material parts of my letter was likewise without result, it at once was decided to publish the letter;
just too late for the *Pall Mall Gazette*, it was given for publication
to the morning papers, and during the evening it became known
in the lobbies of the House.

V

Mr. Parnell took up his new ground in a long manifesto
to the Irish people (November 29). It was free of rhetoric
and ornament, but the draught was skilfully brewed. He
charged Mr. Gladstone with having revealed to him during
his visit at Hawarden in the previous December, that in a
future scheme of home rule the Irish members would be
cut down from 103 to 32, land was to be withdrawn from
the competency of the Irish legislature, and the control
of the constabulary would be reserved to the Imperial
authority for an indefinite period, though Ireland would
have to find the money all the time. This perfidious trunca-
tion of self-government by Mr. Gladstone was matched by
an attempt on my part as his lieutenant only a few days
before, to seduce the Irish party into accepting places in a
liberal government, and this gross bribe of mine was accompanied by a despairing avowal that the hapless evicted
tenants must be flung overboard. In other words, the
English leaders intended to play Ireland false, and Mr.
Parnell stood between his country and betrayal. Such a
story was unluckily no new one in Irish history since the
union. On that theme Mr. Parnell played many adroit
variations during the eventful days that followed. Throw
me to the English wolves if you like, he said, but at any
rate make sure that real home rule and not its shadow is
to be your price, and that they mean to pay it. This was
to awaken the spectre of old suspicions, and to bring to life
again those forces of violence and desperation which it had
been the very crown of his policy to exorcise.

The reply on the Hawarden episode was prompt. Mr.
Gladstone asserted that the whole discussion was one of
those informal exchanges of view which go to all political

BOOK
X.
1890.

action, and in which men feel the ground and discover the leanings of one another's minds. No single proposal was made, no proposition was mentioned to which a binding assent was sought. Points of possible improvement in the bill of 1886 were named as having arisen in Mr. Gladstone's mind, or been suggested by others, but no positive conclusions were asked for or were expected or were possible. Mr. Parnell quite agreed that the real difficulty lay in finding the best form in which Irish representation should be retained at Westminster, but both saw the wisdom and necessity of leaving deliberation free until the time should come for taking practical steps. He offered no serious objection on any point; much less did he say that they augured any disappointment of Irish aspirations. Apart from this denial, men asked themselves how it was that if Mr. Parnell knew that the cause was already betrayed, he yet for a year kept the black secret to himself, and blew Mr. Gladstone's praise with as loud a trumpet as before?[1] As for my own guilty attempt at corruption in proposing an absorption of the Irish party in English politics by means of office and emolument, I denied it with reasonable emphasis at the time, and it does not concern us here, nor in fact anywhere else.

VI

We now come to what was in its day the famous story of Committee Room Fifteen, so called from the chamber in which the next act of this dismal play went on.[2] The proceedings between the leader and his party were watched with an eagerness that has never been surpassed in this kingdom or in America. They were protracted, intense, dramatic, and the issue for a time hung in poignant doubt. The party interest of the scene was supreme, for if the Irishmen should rally to their chief, then the English alliance was at an end, Mr. Gladstone would virtually close

[1] On the day after leaving Hawarden Mr. Parnell spoke at Liverpool, calling on Lancashire to rally to their 'grand old leader.' 'My countrymen rejoice,' he said, 'for we are on the safe path to our legitimate freedom and our future prosperity.' Decem-

ber 19, 1889.
[2] See *The Parnell Split*, reprinted from the *Times* in 1891. Especially also *The Story of Room 15*, by Donal Sullivan, M.P., the accuracy of which seems not to have been challenged.

his illustrious career, the rent in the liberal ranks might be repaired, and leading men and important sections would all group themselves afresh. 'Let us all keep quiet,' said one important unionist, 'we may now have to revise our positions.' Either way, the serpent of faction would raise its head in Ireland, and the strong life of organised and concentrated nationalism would perish in its coils. The personal interest was as vivid as the political, — the spectacle of a man of infinite boldness, determination, astuteness, and resource, with the will and pride of Lucifer, at bay with fortune and challenging a malignant star. Some talked of the famous Ninth Thermidor, when Robespierre fought inch by inch the fierce struggle that ended in his ruin. Others talked of the old mad discord of Zealot and Herodian in face of the Roman before the walls of Jerusalem. The great veteran of English politics looked on, wrathful and astounded at a preternatural perversity for which sixty years of public life could furnish him no parallel. The sage public looked on, some with the same interest that would in ancient days have made them relish a combat of gladiators ; others with glee at the mortification of political opponents ; others again with honest disgust at what threatened to be the ignoble rout of a beneficent policy.

It was the fashion for the moment in fastidious reactionary quarters to speak of the actors in this ordeal as 'a hustling group of yelling rowdies.' Seldom have terms so censorious been more misplaced. All depends upon the point of view. Men on a raft in a boiling sea have something to think of besides deportment and the graces of serenity. As a matter of fact, even hostile judges then and since agreed that no case was ever better opened within the walls of Westminster than in the three speeches made on the first day by Mr. Sexton and Mr. Healy on the one side, and Mr. Redmond on the other. In gravity, dignity, acute perception, and that good faith which is the soul of real as distinct from spurious debate, the parliamentary critic recognises them as all of the first order. So for the most part things continued. It was not until a protracted game had gone beyond limits of reason and patience, that words sometimes flamed high. Experience of national assemblies gives no reason to suppose that a body of French, German, Spanish, Italian, or even of English, Scotch, Welsh, or American politicians placed in circumstances of equal excitement, arising from an incident in itself at once so squalid and so provocative, would have borne the strain with any more self-control.

Mr. Parnell presided, frigid, severe, and lofty, 'as if,' said one present, 'it were we who had gone astray, and he were sitting there to judge us.' Six members were absent in America, including Mr. Dillon and Mr. O'Brien, two of the most important of all after Mr. Parnell himself. The attitude of this pair was felt to be a decisive element. At first, under the same impulse as moved the Leinster Hall meeting, they allowed their sense of past achievement to close their eyes ; they took for granted the impossible, that religious Britain and religious Ireland would blot what had happened out of their thoughts ; and so they stood for Mr. Parnell's leadership. The grim facts of the case were rapidly borne in upon them. The defiant manifesto convinced them that the leadership could not be continued. Travelling from Cincinnati to Chicago, they read it, made up their minds, and telegraphed to anxious colleagues in London. They spoke with warmth of Mr. Parnell's services, but protested against his unreasonable charges of servility to liberal wirepullers ; they described the 'endeavours to fasten the responsibility for what had happened upon Mr. Gladstone and Mr. Morley' as reckless and unjust ; and they foresaw in the position of isolation, discredit, and international ill-feeling which Mr. Parnell had now created, nothing but ruin for the cause. This deliverance from such a quarter (November 30) showed that either abdication or deposition was inevitable.

The day after Mr. Parnell's manifesto, the bishops came out of their shells. Cardinal Manning had more than once written most urgently to the Irish prelates the moment the decree was known, that Parnell could not be upheld in London, and that no political expediency could outweigh the moral sense. He knew well enough that the bishops in

Ireland were in a very difficult strait, but insisted 'that
plain and prompt speech was safest.' It was now a case, he
said to Mr. Gladstone (November 29), of *res ad triarios*, and
it was time for the Irish clergy to speak out from the house-
tops. He had also written to Rome. 'Did I not tell you,'
said Mr. Gladstone when he gave me this letter to read,
'that the Pope would now have one of the ten commandments on his side?' 'We have been slow to act,' Dr. Walsh
telegraphed to one of the Irish members (November 30),
'trusting that the party will act manfully. Our considerate
silence and reserve are being dishonestly misinterpreted.'
'All sorry for Parnell,' telegraphed Dr. Croke, the Archbishop of Cashel — a manly and patriotic Irishman if ever
one was — 'but still, in God's name, let him retire quietly
and with good grace from the leadership. If he does so, the
Irish party will be kept together, the honourable alliance
with Gladstonian liberals maintained, success at general
election secured, home rule certain. If he does not retire,
alliance will be dissolved, election lost, Irish party seriously
damaged if not wholly broken up, home rule indefinitely
postponed, coercion perpetuated, evicted tenants hopelessly
crushed, and the public conscience outraged. Manifesto flat
and otherwise discreditable.' This was emphatic enough,
but many of the flock had already committed themselves
before the pastors spoke. To Dr. Croke, Mr. Gladstone
wrote (Dec. 2): 'We in England seem to have done our
part within our lines, and what remains is for Ireland itself.
I am as unwilling as Mr. Parnell himself could be, to offer
an interference from without, for no one stands more stoutly
than I do for the independence of the Irish national party as
well as for its unity.'

A couple of days later (Dec. 2) a division was taken in
Room Fifteen upon a motion made in Mr. Parnell's interest,
to postpone the discussion until they could ascertain the
views of their constituents, and then meet in Dublin. It
was past midnight. The large room, dimly lighted by a few
lamps and candles placed upon the horse-shoe tables, was
more than half in shadow. Mr. Parnell, his features barely
discernible in the gloom, held a printed list of the party in

his hand, and he put the question in cold, unmoved tones. The numbers were 29 for the motion — that is to say, for him, and 44 against him. Of the majority, many had been put on their trial with him in 1880; had passed months in prison with him under the first Coercion Act and suffered many imprisonments besides ; they had faced storm, obloquy, and hatred with him in the House of Commons, a place where obloquy stings through tougher than Hibernian skins; they had undergone with him the long ordeal of the three judges; they had stood by his side with unswerving fidelity from the moment when his band was first founded for its mortal struggle down to to-day, when they saw the fruits of the struggle flung recklessly away, and the policy that had given to it all its reason and its only hope, wantonly brought to utter foolishness by a suicidal demonstration that no English party and no English leader could ever be trusted. If we think of even the least imaginative of them as haunted by such memories of the past, such distracting fears for the future, it was little wonder that when they saw Mr. Parnell slowly casting up the figures, and heard his voice through the sombre room announcing the ominous result, they all sat, both ayes and noes, in profound and painful stillness. Not a sound was heard, until the chairman rose and said without an accent of emotion that it would now be well for them to adjourn until the next day.

This was only the beginning. Though the ultimate decision of the party was quite certain, every device of strategy and tactics was meanwhile resolutely employed to avert it. His supple and trenchant blade was still in the hands of a consummate swordsman. It is not necessary to recapitulate all the moves in Mr. Parnell's grand manœuvre for turning the eyes of Ireland away from the question of leadership to the question of liberal good faith and the details of home rule. Mr. Gladstone finally announced that only after the question of leadership had been disposed of — one belonging entirely to the competence of the Irish party — could he renew former relations, and once more enter into confidential communications with any of them. There was only one guarantee, he said, that could be of any value to Ireland, namely the assured and unalterable fact that no English leader and no party could ever dream of either proposing or carrying any scheme of home rule which had not the full support of Irish representatives. This was obvious to all the world. Mr. Parnell knew it well enough, and the members knew it, but the members were bound to convince their countrymen that they had exhausted compliance with every hint from their falling leader, while Mr. Parnell's only object was to gain time, to confuse issues, and to carry the battle over from Westminster to the more buoyant and dangerously charged atmosphere of Ireland.

The majority resisted as long as they could the evidence that Mr. Parnell was audaciously trifling with them and openly abusing his position as chairman. On the evening of Friday (December 5) Mr. Sexton and Mr. Healy went to Mr. Parnell after the last communication from Mr. Gladstone. They urged him to bend to the plain necessities of the case. He replied that he would take the night to consider. The next morning (December 6) they returned to him. He informed them that his responsibility to Ireland would not allow him to retire. They warned him that the majority would not endure further obstruction beyond that day, and would withdraw. As they left, Mr. Parnell wished to shake hands, 'if it is to be the last time.' They all shook hands, and then went once more to the field of action.

It was not until after some twelve days of this excitement and stress that the scene approached such disorder as has often before and since been known in the House of Commons. The tension at last had begun to tell upon the impassive bronze of Mr. Parnell himself. He no longer made any pretence of the neutrality of the chair. He broke in upon one speaker more than forty times. In a flash of rage he snatched a paper from another speaker's hand. The hours wore away, confusion only became worse confounded, and the conclusion on both sides was foregone. Mr. McCarthy at last rose, and in a few moderate sentences expressed his opinion that there was no use in continuing a discussion that must be barren of anything but reproach, bitterness, and indignity, and he would therefore suggest that those who were of the same mind should withdraw. Then he moved from the table, and his forty-four colleagues stood up and silently followed him out of the room. In silence they were watched by the minority who remained, in number twenty-six.[1]

VII

A vacancy at Bassetlaw gave Mr. Gladstone an opportunity of describing the grounds on which he had acted. His speech was measured and weighty, but the result showed the effect of the disaster. The tide, that a few weeks before had been running so steadily, now turned. The unionist vote remained almost the same as in 1885; the liberal vote showed a falling off of over 400 and the unionist majority was increased from 295 to 728.

About this time having to go to Ireland, on my way back I stopped at Hawarden, and the following note gives a glimpse of Mr. Gladstone at this evil moment (Dec. 17) : —

I found him in his old corner in the 'temple of peace.' He was only half recovered from a bad cold, and looked in his worsted jacket, and dark tippet over his shoulders, and with his white, deep-furrowed face, like some strange Ancient of Days : so different from the man whom I had seen off at King's Cross less than a week before. He was cordial as always, but evidently in some perturbation. I sat down and told him what I had heard from different quarters about the approaching Kilkenny election. I mentioned X. as a Parnellite authority. 'What,' he flamed up with passionate vehemence, 'X. a Parnellite! Are they mad, then? Are they clean demented?' etc. etc.

I gave him my general impression as to the future. The bare idea that Parnell might find no inconsiderable following came upon him as if it had been a thunder-clap. He listened, and catechised, and knit his brow.

---

[1] The case for the change of mind which induced the majority who had elected Mr. Parnell to the chair less than a fortnight before, now to depose him, was clearly put by Mr. Sexton at a later date. To the considerations adduced by him nobody has ever made a serious political answer. The reader will find Mr. Sexton's argument in the reports of these proceedings already referred to.

Mr. G. — What do you think we should do in case (1) of a divided Ireland, (2) of a Parnellite Ireland?

J. M. — It is too soon to settle what to think. But, looking to Irish interests, I think a Parnellite Ireland infinitely better than a divided Ireland. Anything better than an Ireland divided, so far as she is concerned.

Mr. G. — Bassetlaw looks as if we were going back to 1886. For me that is notice to quit. Another five years' agitation at my age would be impossible — *ludicrous* (with much emphasis).

J. M. — I cannot profess to be surprised that in face of these precious dissensions men should have misgivings, or that even those who were with us, should now make up their minds to wait a little.

I said what there was to be said for Parnell's point of view; that, in his words to me of Nov. 25, he 'must look to the future'; that he was only five and forty; that he might well fear that factions would spring up in Ireland if he were to go; that he might have made up his mind, that whether he went or stayed, we should lose the general election when it came. The last notion seemed quite outrageous to Mr. G., and he could not suppose that it had ever entered Parnell's head.

Mr. G. — You have no regrets at the course we took?

J. M. — None — none. It was inevitable. I have never doubted. That does not prevent lamentation that it was inevitable. It is the old story. English interference is always at the root of mischief in Ireland. But how could we help what we did? We had a right to count on Parnell's sanity and his sincerity. . . .

Mr. G. then got up and fished out of a drawer the memorandum of his talk with Parnell at Hawarden on Dec. 18, 1889, and also a memorandum written for his own use on the general political position at the time of the divorce trial. The former contained not a word as to the constabulary, and in other matters only put a number of points, alternative courses, etc., without a single final or definite decision. While he was fishing in his drawer, he said, as if speaking to himself, 'It looks as if I should get my release even sooner than I had expected.'

'That,' I said, 'is a momentous matter which will need immense deliberation.' So it will, indeed.

CHAP.
V.

Æt. 81.

Mr. G. — Do you recall anything in history like the present distracted scenes in Ireland?

J. M. — Florence, Pisa, or some other Italian city, with the French or the Emperor at the gates?

Mr. G. — I'll tell you what is the only thing that I can think of as at all like it. Do you remember how it was at the siege of Jerusalem — the internecine fury of the Jewish factions, the Ζηλωταί, and the rest — while Titus and the legions were marching on the city!

We went in to luncheon. Something was said of our friend ——, and the new found malady, Renault's disease.

J. M. — Joseph de Maistre says that in the innocent primitive ages men died of diseases without names.

Mr. G. — Homer never mentions diseases at all.

J. M. — Not many of them die a natural death in Homer.

Mr. G. — Do you not recollect where Odysseus meets his mother among the shades, and she says: —

> Οὔτε τις οὖν μοι νοῦσος ἐπήλυθεν . . .
> ἀλλά με σός τε πόθος σά τε μήδεα, φαίδιμ' Ὀδυσσεῦ,
> σή τ' ἀγανοφροσύνη μελιηδέα θυμὸν ἀπηύρα.[1]

J. M. — Beautiful lines. Πόθος such a tender word, and it is untranslatable.

Mr. G. — Oh, *desiderium*.

> 'Quis desiderio sit pudor aut modus
> Tam cari capitis.'[2]

J. M. — The Scotch word '*wearying*' for somebody. And *Sehnsucht*.

Then Mr. G. went off to his library to hunt up the reference, and when I followed him, I found the worn old *Odyssey* open at the passage in the eleventh book. As he left the room, he looked at me and said, 'Ah, this is very different stuff for talking about, from all the wretched work we were speaking of just now. Homer's fellows would have cut a very different figure, and made short work in that committee room last week!' We had a few more words on politics. . . . So I bade him good-bye. . . .

---

[1] *Od.* xi. 200. 'It was not sickness that came upon me; it was wearying for thee and thy lost counsels, glorious Odysseus, and for all thy gentle kindness, this it was that broke the heart within me.'

[2] Hor. *Carm.* i. 24.

In view of the horrors of dissension in Ireland, well-
meaning attempts were made at the beginning of the year
to bring about an understanding. The Irish members,
returning from America where the schism at home had
quenched all enthusiasm and killed their operations, made
their way to Boulogne, for the two most important among
them were liable to instant arrest if they were found in the
United Kingdom.   They thought that Mr. Parnell was really
desirous to withdraw on such terms as would save his self-
respect, and if he could plead hereafter that before giving
way he had secured a genuine scheme of home rule.
Some suspicion may well have arisen in their minds when
a strange suggestion came from Mr. Parnell that the liberal
leaders should enter into a secret engagement about constabulary and the other points.   He had hardly given such
happy evidence of his measure of the sanctity of political
confidences, as to encourage further experiments.   The proposal was absurd on the face of it.   These suspicions soon
became certainties, and the Boulogne negotiations came
to an end.   I should conjecture that those days made the
severest ordeal through which Mr. Gladstone, with his extreme sensibility and his abhorrence of personal contention,
ever passed.   Yet his facility and versatility of mood was
unimpaired, as a casual note or two of mine may show : —

. . . Mr. G.'s confabulation [with an Irish member] proved to
have been sought for the purpose of warning him that Parnell was
about to issue a manifesto in which he would make all manner of
mischief.   Mr. G. and I had a few moments in the room at the
back of the chair; he seemed considerably perturbed, pale, and
concentrated.   We walked into the House together; he picked up
the points of the matter in hand (a motion for appropriating all
the time) and made one of the gayest, brightest, and most
delightful speeches in the world — the whole House enjoying it
consumedly.   Who else could perform these magic transitions ?

Mr. G. came into the House, looking rather anxious; gave us
an account of his interview with the Irish deputation; and in the
midst of it got up to say his few sentences of condolence with the
Speaker on the death of Mrs. Peel — the closing phrases admirably

chosen, and the tones of his voice grave, sincere, sonorous, and compassionate. When he sat down, he resumed his talk with H. and me. He was so touched, he said, by those 'poor wretches' on the deputation, that he would fain, if he could, make some announcement that would ease their unlucky position.

[A question of a letter in reply to some application prompted by Mr. Parnell. Mr. Gladstone asked two of us to try our hands at a draft.] At last we got it ready for him and presently we went to his room. It was now six o'clock. Mr. G. read aloud in full deep voice the letter he had prepared on the base of our short draft. We suggested this and that, and generally argued about phrases for an hour, winding up with a terrific battle on two prodigious points: (1) whether he ought to say, 'after this state-ment of my views,' or 'I have now fully stated my views on the points you raise'; (2) 'You will *doubtless* concur,' or '*probably* concur.' Most characteristic, most amazing. It was past seven before the veteran would let go — and then I must say that he looked his full years. Think what his day had been, in mere intellectual strain, apart from what strains him far more than that — his strife with persons and his compassion for the unlucky Irish-men. I heard afterwards that when he got home, he was for once in his life done up, and on the following morning he lay in bed. All the same, in the evening he went to see *Antony and Cleopatra*, and he had a little ovation. As he drove away the crowd cheered him with cries of 'Bravo, don't you mind Parnell!' Plenty of race feeling left, in spite of union of hearts!

No leader ever set a finer example under reverse than did Mr. Gladstone during these tedious and desperate pro-ceedings. He was steadfastly loyal, considerate, and sym-pathetic towards the Irishmen who had trusted him; his firm patience was not for a moment worn out; in vain a boisterous wave now and again beat upon him from one quarter or another. Not for a moment was he shaken; even under these starless skies his faith never drooped. 'The public mischief,' he wrote to Lord Acton (Dec. 27, 1890), 'ought to put out of view every private thought. But the blow to me is very heavy — the heaviest I ever

have received.   It is a great and high call to work by faith
and not by sight.'

Occasion had already offered for testing the feeling of
Ireland.   There was a vacancy in the representation of
Kilkenny, and the Parnellite candidate had been defeated.

To J. Morley.

Hawarden, Dec. 23, 1890. — Since your letter arrived this morning, the Kilkenny poll has brightened the sky.   It will have a
great effect in Ireland, although it is said not to be a representative constituency, but one too much for us.   It is a great gain;
and yet sad enough to think that even here one-third of the voters
should be either rogues or fools.   I suppose the ballot has largely
contributed to save Kilkenny.   It will be most interesting to
learn how the tories voted.

I return your enclosure. . . .   I have ventured, without asking
your leave, on keeping a copy of a part.   Only in one proposition
do I differ from you.   I would rather see Ireland disunited than
see it Parnellite.

I think that as the atmosphere is quiet for the moment we had
better give ourselves the benefit of a little further time for reflection.   Personally, I am hard hit.   My course of life was daring
enough as matters stood six weeks ago.   How it will shape in the
new situation I cannot tell.   But this is the selfish part.   Turning
for a moment to the larger outlook, I am extremely indisposed to
any harking back in the matter of home rule; we are now, I
think, freed from the enormous danger of seeing P. master in
Ireland; division and its consequences in diminishing force, are
the worst we have to fear.   What my mind leans to in a way still
vague is to rally ourselves by some affirmative legislation taken up
by and on behalf of the party.   Something of this kind would be
the best source to look to for reparative strength.

To Lord Acton.

Jan. 9, 1891. — To a greybeard in a hard winter the very name
of the south is musical, and the kind letters from you and Lord
Hampden make it harmony as well as melody.   But I have been
and am chained to the spot by this Parnell business, and every

day have to consider in one shape or other what ought to be said by myself or others. . . . I consider the Parnell chapter of politics finally closed for us, the British liberals, at least during my time. He has been even worse since the divorce court than he was in it. The most astounding revelation of my lifetime.

To J. Morley.

Hawarden, Dec. 30, 1890. — I must not longer delay thanking you for your most kind and much valued letter on my birthday — a birthday more formidable than usual, on account of the recent disasters, which, however, may all come to good. If I am able to effect in the world anything useful, be assured I know how much of it is owed to the counsel and consort of my friends.

It is not indeed the common lot of man to make serious additions to the friendships which so greatly help us in this pilgrimage, after seventy-six years old; but I rejoice to think that in your case it has been accomplished for me.

VIII

A few more sentences will end this chapter in Mr. Gladstone's life. As we have seen, an election took place in the closing days of December 1890. Mr. Parnell flung himself into the contest with frantic activity. A fierce conflict ended in the defeat of his candidate by nearly two to one.[1] Three months later a contest occurred in Sligo. Here again, though he had strained every nerve in the interval as well as in the immediate struggle, his candidate was beaten.[2] Another three months, then a third election at Carlow, — with the same result, the rejection of Mr. Parnell's man by a majority of much more than two to one.[3] It was in vain that his adherents denounced those who had left him as mutineers and helots, and exalted him as 'truer than Tone, abler than Grattan, greater than O'Connell, full of love for Ireland as Thomas Davis himself.' On the other side, he encountered antagonism in every key, from pathetic remonstrance or earnest reprobation, down to an unsparing fury that savoured

[1] December 23, 1890.   [2] April 3, 1891.   [3] July 8, 1891.

of the ruthless factions of the Seine. In America almost every name of consideration was hostile.

Yet undaunted by repulse upon repulse, he tore over from England to Ireland and back again, week after week and month after month, hoarse and haggard, seamed by sombre passions, waving the shreds of a tattered flag. Ireland must have been a hell on earth to him. To those Englishmen who could not forget that they had for so long been his fellow-workers, though they were now the mark of his attack, these were dark and desolating days. No more lamentable chapter is to be found in all the demented scroll of aimless and untoward things, that seem as if they made up the history of Ireland. It was not for very long. The last speech that Mr. Parnell ever made in England was at Newcastle-on-Tyne in July 1891, when he told the old story about the liberal leaders, of whom he said that there was but one whom he trusted. A few weeks later, not much more than ten months after the miserable act had opened, the Veiled Shadow stole upon the scene, and the world learned that Parnell was no more.[1]

[1] October 6. He was in his forty-sixth year (*b.* June 1846), and had been sixteen years in parliament.

CHAPTER VI

BIARRITZ

(*1891-1892*)

OMNIUM autem ineptiarum, quæ sunt innumerabiles, haud sciam
an nulla sit major, quam, ut illi solent, quocunque in loco,
quoscunque inter homines visum est, de rebus aut difficillimis
aut non necessariis argutissime disputare. — CICERO.

Of all the numberless sorts of bad taste and want of tact, perhaps
the worst is to insist, no matter where you are or with whom
you are, on arguing about the hardest subjects to the full pitch
of elaboration and detail.

BOOK
X.

1891.WE have seen how in 1889 Mr. and Mrs. Gladstone celebrated the fiftieth anniversary of one of the most devoted
and successful marriages that ever was made, and the
unbroken felicity of their home. In 1891, after the shadows
of approaching calamity had for many months hung doubt-
fully over them, a heavy blow fell, and their eldest son died.
Not deeply concerned in ordinary politics, he was a man of
many virtues and some admirable gifts ; he was an accomplished musician, and I have seen letters of his to his father,
marked by a rare delicacy of feeling and true power of
expression. 'I had known him for nearly thirty years,' one
friend wrote, 'and there was no man, until his long illness,
who had changed so little, or retained so long the best
qualities of youth, and my first thought was that the greater
the loss to you, the greater would be the consolation.'

To Archbishop Benson, Mr. Gladstone wrote (July 6) : —

It is now forty-six years since we lost a child,[1] and he who
has now passed away from our eyes, leaves to us only blessed
recollections. I suppose all feel that those deaths which reverse
the order of nature have a sharpness of their own. But setting

[1] Vol. i. p. 387.

460

this apart, there is nothing lacking to us in consolations human
or divine.   I can only wish that I may become less unworthy to
have been his father.

To me he wrote (July 10) : —

We feel deeply the kindness and tenderness of your letter.   It
supplies one more link in a long chain of recollection which I
deeply prize.   Yes, ours is a tribulation, and a sore one, but
yet we feel we ought to find ourselves carried out of ourselves
by sympathy with the wife whose noble and absorbing devotion
had become like an entire life of itself, and who is now face to face
with the void.   The grief of children too, which passes, is very
sharp while it remains.   The case has been very remarkable.
Though with abatement of some powers, my son has not been
without many among the signs and comforts of health during
a period of nearly two and a half years.   All this time the
terrible enemy was lodged in the royal seat, and only his healthy
and unyielding constitution kept it at defiance, and maintained
his mental and inward life intact. . . .   And most largely has
human, as well as divine compassion, flowed in upon us, from
none more conspicuously than from yourself, whom we hope
to count among near friends for the short remainder of our
lives.

To another correspondent who did not share his own
religious beliefs, he said (July 5) : —

When I received your last kind note, I fully intended to write to
you with freedom on the subject of *The Agnostic Island*.   But since
then I have been at close quarters, so to speak, with the dispensations of God, for yesterday morning my dearly beloved eldest son
was taken from the sight of our eyes.   At this moment of bleeding
hearts, I will only say what I hope you will in consideration of
the motives take without offence, namely this : I would from the
bottom of my heart that whenever the hour of bereavement shall
befall you or those whom you love, you and they may enjoy the
immeasurable consolation of believing, with all the mind and all
the heart, that the beloved one is gone into eternal rest, and that
those who remain behind may through the same mighty Deliverer
hope at their appointed time to rejoin him.

All this language on the great occasions of human life was not with him the tone of convention. Whatever the synthesis, as they call it, — whatever the form, whatever the creed and faith may be, he was one of that high and favoured household who, in Emerson's noble phrase, 'live from a great depth of being.'

Earlier in the year Lord Granville, who so long had been his best friend, died. The loss by his death was severe. As Acton, who knew of their relations well and from within, wrote to Mr. Gladstone (April 1) : —

There was an admirable fitness in your union, and I had been able to watch how it became closer and easier, in spite of so much to separate you, in mental habits, in early affinities, and even in the form of fundamental convictions, since he came home from your budget, overwhelmed, thirty-eight years ago. I saw all the connections which had their root in social habit fade before the one which took its rise from public life and proved more firm and more enduring than the rest.

II

In September he paid a visit to his relatives at Fasque, and thence he went to Glenalmond — spots that in his tenacious memory must have awakened hosts of old and dear associations. On October 1, he found himself after a long and busy day, at Newcastle-on-Tyne, where he had never stayed since his too memorable visit in 1862.[1] Since the defeat of the Irish policy in 1886, he had attended the annual meeting of the chief liberal organisation at Nottingham (1887), Birmingham (1888), and Manchester (1889). This year it was the turn of Newcastle. On October 2, he gave his blessing to various measures that afterwards came to be known as the Newcastle programme. After the shock caused by the Irish quarrel, every politician knew that it would be necessary to balance home rule by reforms expected in England and Scotland. No liberal, whatever his particular shade, thought that it would be either honourable or practical to throw the Irish policy overboard, and if there

[1] See above, vol. ii. p. 76.

were any who thought such a course honourable, they knew it would not be safe. The principle and expediency of home rule had taken a much deeper root in the party than it suited some of the trimming tribe later to admit. On the other hand, after five years of pretty exclusive devotion to the Irish case, to pass by the British case and its various demands for an indefinite time longer, would have been absurd.

III

In the eighties Mr. Gladstone grew into close friendship with one who had for many years been his faithful supporter in the House of Commons as member for Dundee. Nobody ever showed him devotion more considerate, loyal, and unselfish than did Mr. Armitstead, from about the close of the parliament of 1880 down to the end of this story.[1] In the middle of December 1891 Mr. Armitstead planned a foreign trip for his hero, and persuaded me to join. Biarritz was to be our destination, and the expedition proved a wonderful success. Some notes of mine, though intended only for domestic consumption, may help to bring Mr. Gladstone in his easiest moods before the reader's eye. No new ideas struck fire, no particular contribution was made to grand themes. But a great statesman on a holiday may be forgiven for not trying to discover bran-new keys to philosophy, history, and 'all the mythologies.' As a sketch from life of the veteran's buoyancy, vigour, genial freshness of heart and brain, after four-score strenuous years, these few pages may be found of interest.

We left Paris at nine in the morning (Dec. 16), and were listening to the swell of the mighty Bay resounding under our windows at Biarritz soon after midnight.

The long day's journey left no signs of fatigue on either Mr. or Mrs. Gladstone, and his only regret was that we had

---

[1] Once Mr. Gladstone presented him with a piece of plate, and set upon it one of those little Latin inscriptions to which he was so much addicted, and which must serve here instead of further commemoration of a remarkable friendship : Georgio Armitstead, Armigero, D.D. Gul. E. Gladstone. Amicitiæ Benevolentiæ Beneficiorum delatorum Valde memor Mense Augusti A.D., 1894.

not come straight through instead of staying a night in Paris. I'm always for going straight on, he said. For some odd reason in spite of the late hour he was full of stories of American humour, which he told with extraordinary verve and enjoyment. I contributed one that amused him much, of the Bostonian who, having read Shakespeare for the first time, observed, ' I call that a very clever book. Now, I don't suppose there are twenty men in Boston to-day who could have written that book! '

Thursday, Dec. 17. — Splendid morning for making acquaintance with a new place. Saw the western spur of the Pyrenees falling down to the Bidassoa and the first glimpse of the giant wall, beyond which, according to Michelet, Africa begins, and our first glimpse of Spain.

After breakfast we all sallied forth to look into the shops and to see the lie of the land. Mr. G. as interested as a child in all the objects in the shops — many of them showing that we are not far from Spain. The consul very polite, showed us about, and told us the hundred trifles that bring a place really into one's mind. Nothing is like a first morning's stroll in a foreign town. By afternoon the spell dissolves, and the mood comes of Dante's lines, ' *Era già l'ora,*' etc.[1]

Some mention was made of Charles Austin, the famous lawyer : it brought up the case of men who are suddenly torn from lives of great activity to complete idleness.

Mr. G. — I don't know how to reconcile it with what I've always regarded as the foundation of character — Bishop Butler's view of habit. How comes it that during the hundreds of years in which priests and fellows of Eton College have retired from hard work to college livings and leisure, not one of them has ever done anything whatever for either scholarship or divinity — not one?

Mr. G. did not know Mazzini, but Armellini, another of the Roman triumvirs, taught him Italian in 1832.

---

[1] Era già l'ora, che volge 'l disio
A' naviganti, e 'ntenerisce 'l cuore
Lo dì ch' han detto a' dolci amici addio, etc.
　　　　　　　　　　　　Purg. viii.

Byron's rendering is well enough known.

I spoke a word for Gambetta, but he would not have it. 'Gambetta was *autoritaire ;* I do not feel as if he were a true liberal in the old and best sense. I cannot forget how hostile he was to the movement for freedom in the Balkans.'

Said he only once saw Lord Liverpool. He went to call on Canning at Glos'ter House (close to our Glos'ter Road Station), and there through a glass door he saw Canning and Lord Liverpool talking together.

Peel. — Had a good deal of temper; not hot; but perhaps sulky. Not a farsighted man, but fairly clear-sighted. 'I called upon him after the election in 1847. The Janissaries, as Bentinck called us, that is the men who had stood by Peel, had been 110 before the election; we came back only 50. Peel said to me that what he looked forward to was a long and fierce struggle on behalf of protection. I must say I thought this foolish. If Bentinck had lived, with his strong will and dogged industry, there might have been a wide rally for protection, but everybody knew that Dizzy did not care a straw about it, and Derby had not constancy and force enough.'

Mr. G. said Disraeli's performances against Peel were quite as wonderful as report makes them. Peel altogether helpless in reply. Dealt with them with a kind of 'righteous dulness.' The Protectionist secession due to three men: Derby contributed prestige; Bentinck backbone; and Dizzy parliamentary brains.

The golden age of administrative reform was from 1832 to the Crimean War; Peel was always keenly interested in the progress of these reforms.

Northcote. — 'He was my private secretary; and one of the very best imaginable; pliant, ready, diligent, quick, acute, with plenty of humour, and a temper simply perfect. But as a leader, I think ill of him; you had a conversation; he saw the reason of your case; and when he left, you supposed all was right. But at the second interview, you always found that he had been unable to persuade his friends. What could be weaker than his conduct on the Bradlaugh affair ! You could not wonder that the rank and file of his men should be caught by the proposition that an atheist ought not to sit in parliament. But what is a leader good for, if he dare not tell his party that in a matter like this they are wrong, and of course nobody knew better than N. that they were wrong. A clever, quick man with fine temper. By the way, how is it that we have no word, no respectable word, for backbone?'

J. M. — Character?

Mr. G. — Well, character; yes; but that's vague. It means will, I suppose. (I ought to have thought of Novalis's well-known definition of character as 'a completely fashioned will.')

J. M. — Our inferiority to the Greeks in discriminations of language shown by our lack of precise equivalents for φρόνησις, σοφία, σωφροσύνη, etc., of which we used to hear so much when coached in the *Ethics.*

Mr. G. went on to argue that because the Greeks drew these fine distinctions in words, they were superior in conduct. 'You cannot beat the Greeks in noble qualities.'

Mr. G. — I admit there is no Greek word of good credit for the virtue of humility.

J. M. — ταπεινότης? But that has an association of meanness.

Mr. G. — Yes; a shabby sort of humility. Humility as a sovereign grace is the creation of Christianity.

Friday, December 18. — Brilliant sunshine, but bitterly cold; an east wind blowing straight from the Maritime Alps. Walking, reading, talking. Mr. G. after breakfast took me into his room, where he is reading Heine, Butcher on Greek genius, and Marbot. Thought Thiers's well-known remark on Heine's death capital, — 'To-day the wittiest Frenchman alive has died.'

Mr. G. — We have talked about the best line in poetry, etc. How do you answer this question—Which century of English history produced the greatest men?

J. M. — What do you say to the sixteenth?

Mr. G. — Yes, I think so. Gardiner was a great man. Henry VIII. was great. But bad. Poor Cranmer. Like Northcote, he'd no backbone. Do you remember Jeremy Collier's sentence about his bravery at the stake, which

I count one of the grandest in English prose — ' He seemed
to repel the force of the fire and to overlook the torture,
by strength of thought.'[1] Thucydides could not beat
that.

The old man twice declaimed the sentence with deep
sonorous voice, and his usual incomparable modulation.

Mr. G. talked of a certain General ——. He was thought
to be a first-rate man ; neglected nothing, looked to things
himself, conceived admirable plans, and at last got an
important command. Then to the universal surprise,
nothing came of it ; —— they said, 'could do everything that
a commander should do, except say, *Quick march.*' There
are plenty of politicians of that stamp, but Mr. G. decidedly
not one of them. I mentioned a farewell dinner given to
—— in the spring, by some rich man or other. It cost
£560 for forty-eight guests ! Flowers alone £150. Mr. G.
on this enormity, recalled a dinner to Talfourd about copyright at the old Clarendon Hotel in Bond Street, and the
price was £2, 17s. 6d. a head. The old East India Company
used to give dinners at a cost of seven guineas a head. He
has a wonderfully lively interest for these matters, and his
curiosity as to the prices of things in the shop-windows is
inexhaustible. We got round to Goethe. Goethe, he said,
never gave prominence to duty.

J. M. — Surely, surely in that fine psalm of life, *Das
Göttliche?*

Mr. G. — Döllinger used to confront me with the *Iphigenie*
as a great drama of duty.

He wished that I had known Döllinger — ' a man thoroughly
from beginning to end of his life *purged of self.*' Mistook
the nature of the Irish questions, from the erroneous view
that Irish catholicism is ultramontane, which it certainly
is not.

Saturday, Dec. 19. — *   *   *   *   *

What is extraordinary is that all Mr. G.'s versatility,
buoyancy, and the rest goes with the most profound accuracy
and intense concentration when any point of public business

---

[1] On some other occasion he set this against Macaulay's praise of a passage in Barrow mentioned above, ii. p. 536.

is raised.　Something was said of the salaries of bishops. He was ready in an instant with every figure and detail, and every circumstance of the history of the foundation of the Ecclesiastical Commission in 1835–6.　Then his *savoir faire* and wisdom of parliamentary conduct.　'I always made it a rule in the H. of C. to allow nobody to suppose that I did not like him, and to say as little as I could to prevent anybody from liking me.　Considering the intense friction and contention of public life, it is a saving of wear and tear that as many as possible even among opponents should think well of one.'

Sunday, Dec. 20. — At table, a little discussion as to the happiness and misery of animal creation.　Outside of man Mr. G. argued against Tennyson's description of Nature as red in tooth and claw.　Apart from man, he said, and the action of man, sentient beings are happy and not miserable. But Fear? we said.　No; they are unaware of impending doom; when hawk or kite pounces on its prey, the small bird has little or no apprehension; 'tis death, but death by appointed and unforeseen lot.

J. M. — There is Hunger.　Is not the probability that most creatures are always hungry, not excepting Man?

To this he rather assented.　Of course optimism like this is indispensable as the basis of natural theology.

Talked to Mr. G. about Michelet's Tableau de la France, which I had just finished in vol. 2 of the history.　A brilliant tour de force, but strains the relations of soil to character; compels words and facts to be the slaves of his phantasy; the modicum of reality overlaid with violent paradox and foregone conclusion.　Mr. G. not very much interested — seems only to care for political and church history.

Monday, Dec. 31. — Mr. G. did not appear at table to-day, suffering from a surfeit of wild strawberries the day before. But he dined in his dressing gown, and I had some chat with him in his room after lunch.

Mr. G. — ' 'Tis a hard law of political things that if a man shows special competence in a department, that is the very thing most likely to keep him there, and prevent his promotion.'

Mr. G. — I consider Burke a tripartite man : America, France, Ireland — right as to two, wrong in one.

J. M. — Must you not add home affairs and India? His *Thoughts on the Discontents* is a masterpiece of civil wisdom, and the right defence in a great constitutional struggle. Then he gave fourteen years of industry to Warren Hastings, and teaching England the rights of the natives, princes and people, and her own duties. So he was right in four out of five.

Mr. G. — Yes, yes — quite true. Those two ought to be added to my three. There is a saying of Burke's from which I must utterly dissent. 'Property is sluggish and inert.' Quite the contrary. Property is vigilant, active, sleepless ; if ever it seems to slumber, be sure that one eye is open.

Marie Antoinette. I once read the three volumes of letters from Mercy d'Argenteau to Maria Theresa. He seems to have performed the duty imposed upon him with fidelity.

J. M. — Don't you think the Empress comes out well in the correspondence?

Mr. G. — Yes, she shows always judgment and sagacity.

J. M. — Ah, but besides sagacity, worth and as much integrity as those slippery times allowed.

Mr. G. — Yes (but rather reluctantly, I thought). As for Marie Antoinette, she was not a striking character in any sense, she was horribly frivolous ; and, I suppose, we must say she was, what shall I call it — a very considerable flirt ?

J. M. — The only case with real foundation seems to be that of the *beau Fersen*, the Swedish secretary. He too came to as tragic an end as the Queen.

Tuesday, Dec. 22. — Mr. G. still somewhat indisposed — but reading away all day long. Full of Marbot. Delighted with the story of the battle of Castiglione: how when Napoleon held a council of war, and they all said they were hemmed in, and that their only chance was to back out, Augereau roughly cried that they might all do what they liked, but he would attack the enemy cost what it might. 'Exactly like a place in the *Iliad;* when Agamemnon and the rest sit sorrowful in the assembly arguing that it was useless to withstand the sovereign will of Zeus, and that they had better flee into their ships, Diomed bursts out that whatever others think, in any event he and Sthenelus, his squire, will hold firm, and never desist from the onslaught until they have laid waste the walls of Troy.'[1] A large dose of Diomed in Mr. G. himself.

Talk about the dangerous isolation in which the monarchy will find itself in England if the hereditary principle goes down in the House of Lords; 'it will stand bare, naked, with no shelter or shield, only endured as the better of two evils.' 'I once asked,' he said, 'who besides myself in the party cares for the hereditary principle? The answer was, That perhaps —— cared for it !!' — naming a member of the party supposed to be rather sapient than sage.

News in the paper that the Comte de Paris in his discouragement was about to renounce his claims, and break up his party. Somehow this brought us round to Tocqueville, of whom Mr. G. spoke as the nearest French approach to Burke.

J. M. — But pale and without passion. Who was it that said of him that he was an aristocrat who accepted his defeat? That is, he knew democracy to be the conqueror, but he doubted how far it would be an improvement, he saw its perils, etc.

Mr. G. — I have not much faith in these estimates, whether in favour of progress or against it. I don't believe in comparisons of age with age. How can a man strike a balance between one government and another? How can he place himself in such an attitude, and with such comprehensive sureness of vision, as to say that the thirteenth century was better or higher or worse or lower than the nineteenth?

Thursday, Dec. 24. — At lunch we had the news of the Parnellite victory at Waterford. A disagreeable reverse for us. Mr. G. did not say many words about it, only that it would give heart to the mischief makers — only too certain. But we said no more about it. He and I took a walk on the sands in the afternoon, and had a curious talk (considering), about the prospects of the church of England. He was

---

[1] *Iliad*, ix. 32.

anxious to know about my talk some time ago with the
Bishop of —— whom I had met at a feast at Lincoln's Inn.
I gave him as good an account as I could of what had
passed. Mr. G. doubted that this prelate was fundamentally
an Erastian, as Tait was. Mr. G. is eager to read the signs
of the times as to the prospects of Anglican Christianity, to
which his heart is given ; and he fears the peril of Eras-
tianism to the spiritual life of the church, which is naturally
the only thing worth caring about. Hence, he talked with
much interest of the question whether the clever fellows at
Oxford and Cambridge now take orders. He wants to know
what kind of defenders his church is likely to have in days
to come. Said that for the first time interest has moved
away both from politics and theology, towards the vague
something which they call social reform ; and he thinks
they won't make much out of that in the way of permanent
results. The establishment he considers safer than it has
been for a long time.

As to Welsh disestablishment, he said it was a pity that
where the national sentiment was so unanimous as it was in
Wales, the operation itself should not be as simple as
in Scotland. In Scotland sentiment is not unanimous, but
the operation is easy. In Wales sentiment is all one way,
but the operation difficult — a good deal more difficult than
people suppose, as they will find out when they come to
tackle it.

[Perhaps it may be mentioned here that, though we
always talked freely and abundantly together upon ecclesiastical affairs and persons, we never once exchanged a word
upon theology or religious creed, either at Biarritz or anywhere else.]

Pitt.—A strong denunciation of Pitt for the French war.
People don't realise what the French war meant. In 1812
wheat at Liverpool was 20s. (?) the imperial bushel of
65 pounds (?) ! Think of that, when you bring it into
figures of the cost of a loaf. And that was the time when
Eaton, Eastnor, and other great palaces were built by the
landlords out of the high rents which the war and war prices
enabled them to exact.

Wished we knew more of Melbourne. He was in many
ways a very fine fellow. ' In two of the most important of all
the relations of a prime minister, he was perfect ; I mean
first, his relations to the Queen, second to his colleagues.'

Somebody at dinner quoted a capital description of the
perverse fashion of talking that prevailed at Oxford soon
after my time, and prevails there now, I fancy — 'hunting
for epigrammatic ways of saying what you don't think.'
—— was the father of this pestilent mode.

Rather puzzled him by repeating a saying of mine that
used to amuse Fitzjames Stephen, that Love of Truth is more
often than we think only a fine name for Temper. I think
Mr. G. has a thorough dislike for anything that has a
cynical or sardonic flavour about it. I wish I had thought,
by the way, of asking him what he had to say of that piece of
Swift's, about all objects being insipid that do not come by
delusion, and everything being shrunken as it appears in the
glass of nature, so that if it were not for artificial mediums,
refracted angles, false lights, varnish and tinsel, there would
be pretty much of a level in the felicity of mortal man.

Am always feeling how strong is his aversion to seeing
more than he can help of what is sordid, mean, ignoble.
He has not been in public life all these years without rubbing
shoulders with plenty of baseness on every scale, and plenty
of pettiness in every hue, but he has always kept his eyes
well above it. Never was a man more wholly free of the
starch of the censor, more ready to make allowance, nor
more indulgent even ; he enters into human nature in all
its compass. But he won't linger a minute longer than he
must in the dingy places of life and character.

Christmas Day, 1891. — A divine day, brilliant sunshine,
and mild spring air. Mr. G. heard what he called an admirable sermon from an English preacher, ' with a great
command of his art.' A quietish day, Mr. G. no doubt
engaged in φρονεῖν τὰ ὅσια.

Saturday, Dec. 26. — Once more a noble day. We started
in a couple of carriages for the Négress station, a couple
of miles away or more, I with the G.'s. Occasion produced the Greek epitaph of the nameless drowned sailor

who wished for others kinder seas.[1] Mr. G. felt its pathos and its noble charm — so direct and simple, such benignity, such a good lesson to men to forget their own misdeeds and mischance, and to pray for the passer-by a happier star. He repaid me by two epigrams of a different vein, and one admirable translation into Greek, of Tennyson on Sir John Franklin, which I do not carry in my mind ; another on a boisterous Eton fellow —

> Didactic, dry, declamatory, dull,
> The bursar —— bellows like a bull.

Just in the tone of Greek epigram, a sort of point, but not too much point.

Parliamentary Wit. — Thought Disraeli had never been surpassed, nor even equalled, in this line. He had a contest with General Grey, who stood upon the general merits of the whig government, after both Lord Grey and Stanley had left it. D. drew a picture of a circus man who advertised his show with its incomparable team of six grey horses. One died, he replaced it by a mule. Another died, and he put in a donkey, still he went on advertising his team of greys all the same. Canning's wit not to be found conspicuously in his speeches, but highly agreeable pleasantries, though many of them in a vein which would jar horribly on modern taste.

Some English redcoats and a pack of hounds passed us as we neared the station. They saluted Mr. G. with a politeness that astonished him, but was pleasant. Took the train for Irun, the fields and mountain slopes delightful in the sun, and the sea on our right a superb blue such as we never see in English waters. At Irun we found carriages waiting to take us on to Fuentarabia. From the balcony of the church had a beautiful view over the scene of Wellington's operations when he crossed the Bidassoa, in the presence of the astonished Soult. A lovely picture, made none the worse by this excellent historic association. The

---

[1] ναυτίλε, μὴ πεύθου τίνος ἐνθάδε τύμβος ὅδ' εἰμί,
    ἀλλ αὐτὸς πόντου τύγχανε χρηστοτέρου.

'Ask not, mariner, whose tomb I am here, but be thine own fortune a kinder sea.' — MACKAIL.

alcalde was extremely polite and intelligent. The consul who was with us showed a board on the old tower, in which *v* in some words was *b*, and I noted that the alcalde spoke of Viarritz. I reminded Mr. G. of Scaliger's epigram—

> Haud temere antiquas mutat Vasconia voces,
> Cui nihil est aliud vivere quam bibere.

Pretty cold driving home, but Mr. G. seemed not to care. He found both the churches at St. Jean and at Fuentarabia very noteworthy, though the latter very popish, but both, he felt, 'had a certain association with grandeur.'

Sunday, Dec. 27. — After some quarter of an hour of travellers' topics, we plunged into one of the most interesting talks we have yet had. *Apropos* of I do not know what, Mr. G. said that he had not advised his son to enter public life. 'No doubt there are some men to whom station, wealth, and family traditions make it a duty. But I have never advised any individual, as to whom I have been consulted, to enter the H. of C.'

J. M. — But isn't that rather to encourage self-indulgence? Nobody who cares for ease or mental composure would seek public life?

Mr. G. — Ah, I don't know that. Surely politics open up a great field for the natural man. Self-seeking, pride, domination, power — all these passions are gratified in politics.

J. M. — You cannot be sure of achievement in politics, whether personal or public?

Mr. G. — No; to use Bacon's pregnant phrase, they are too immersed in matter. Then as new matter, that is, new details and particulars, come into view, men change their judgment.

J. M. — You have spoken just now of somebody as a thorough good tory. You know the saying that nobody is worth much who has not been a bit of a radical in his youth, and a bit of a tory in his fuller age.

Mr. G. (laughing) — Ah, I'm afraid that hits me rather hard. But for myself, I think I can truly put up all the change that has come into my politics into a sentence; I was brought up to distrust and dislike liberty, I learned to believe in it. That is the key to all my changes.

J. M. — According to my observation, the change in my own generation is different. They have ceased either to trust or to distrust liberty, and have come to the mind that it matters little either way. Men are disenchanted. They have got what they wanted in the days of their youth, yet what of it, they ask? France has thrown off the Empire, but the statesmen of the republic are not a great breed. Italy has gained her unity, yet unity has not been followed by thrift, wisdom, or large increase of public virtue or happiness. America has purged herself of slavery, yet life in America is material, prosaic, — so say some of her own rarest sons. Don't think that I say all these things. But I know able and high-minded men who suffer from this disenchantment.

Mr. G. — Italy would have been very different if Cavour had only lived — and even Ricasoli. Men ought not to suffer from disenchantment. They ought to know that *ideals in politics are never realised.* And don't let us forget in eastern Europe the rescue in our time of some ten millions of men from the harrowing domination of the Turk. (On this he expatiated, and very justly, with much energy.)

We turned to our own country. Here he insisted that democracy had certainly not saved us from a distinct decline in the standard of public men. . . . Look at the whole conduct of opposition from '80 to '85 — every principle was flung overboard, if they could manufacture a combination against the government. For all this deterioration one man and one man alone is responsible, Disraeli. He is the grand corrupter. He it was who sowed the seed.

J. M. — Ought not Palmerston to bear some share in this?

Mr. G. — No, no; Pam. had many strong and liberal convictions. On one subject Dizzy had them too — the Jews. There he was much more than rational, he was fanatical. He said once that Providence would deal good or ill fortune to nations, according as they dealt well or ill by the Jews. I remember once sitting next to John Russell when D. was making a speech on Jewish emancipation. 'Look at him,' said J. R., 'how manfully he sticks to it, tho' he knows that every word he says is gall and wormwood to every man who sits around him and behind him.' A curious irony, was it not, that it should have fallen to me to propose a motion for a memorial both to Pam. and Dizzy?

A superb scene upon the ocean, with a grand wind from the west. Mr. G. and I walked on the shore; he has a passion for tumultuous seas. I have never seen such huge masses of water shattering themselves among the rocks.

In the evening Mr. G. remarked on our debt to Macaulay, for guarding the purity of the English tongue. I recalled a favourite passage from Milton, that next to the man who gives wise and intrepid counsels of government, he places the man who cares for the purity of his mother tongue. Mr. G. liked this. Said he only knew Bright once slip into an error in this respect, when he used 'transpire' for 'happen.' Macaulay of good example also in rigorously abstaining from the inclusion of matter in footnotes. Hallam an offender in this respect. I pointed out that he offended in company with Gibbon.

Monday, Dec. 28. — We had an animated hour at breakfast.

Oxford and Cambridge. — Curious how, like two buckets, whenever one was up, the other was down. Cambridge has never produced four such men of action in successive ages as Wolsey, Laud, Wesley, and Newman.

J. M. — In the region of thought Cambridge has produced the greatest of all names, Newton.

Mr. G. — In the earlier times Oxford has it — with Wycliff, Occam, above all Roger Bacon. And then in the eighteenth century, Butler.

J. M. — But why not Locke, too, in the century before?

This brought on a tremendous tussle, for Mr. G. was of the same mind, and perhaps for the same sort of reason, as Joseph de Maistre, that contempt for Locke is the beginning of knowledge. All very well for De Maistre, but not for a man in line with European liberalism. I pressed the very obvious point that you must take into account not only a man's intellectual product or his general stature, but also his influence as a historic force. From the point of view of influence Locke was the origin of the emancipatory movement of the eighteenth century abroad, and laid the philosophic foundations of liberalism in civil government at home. Mr. G. insisted on a passage of Hume's which he believed to be in the history, disparaging Locke as a metaphysical thinker.[1] 'That may be,' said I, 'though Hume in his *Essays* is not above paying many compliments to "the great reasoner," etc., to whom, for that matter, I fancy that he stood in pretty direct relation. But far be it from me to deny that Hume saw deeper than Locke into the metaphysical millstone. That is not the point. I'm only thinking of his historic place, and, after all, the history of philosophy is itself a philosophy.' To minds nursed in dogmatic schools, all this is both unpalatable and incredible.

Somehow we slid into the freedom of the will and Jonathan Edwards. I told him that Mill had often told us how Edwards argued the necessarian or determinist case as keenly as any modern.

Tuesday, Dec. 29. — Mr. G. 82 to-day. I gave him Mackail's Greek Epigrams, and if it affords him half as much pleasure as it has given me, he will be very grateful. Various people brought Mr. G. bouquets and addresses. Mr. G. went to church in the morning, and in the afternoon took a walk with me. . . . *Land Question.* As you go through France you see the soil cultivated by the population. In our little dash into Spain the other day, we saw again the soil cultivated by the population. In England it is cultivated by the capitalist, for the farmer is capitalist. Some astonishing views recently propounded by D. of Argyll on this matter. Unearned increment — so terribly difficult to catch it. Perhaps best try to get at it through the death duties. Physical condition of our people — always a subject of great anxiety — their stature, colour, and so on. Feared the atmosphere of cotton factories, etc., very deleterious. As against bad air, I said, you must set good food ; the Lancashire operative in decent times lives uncommonly well, as he deserves to do. He agreed there might be something in this.

CHAP.
VI.

Æt. 82.

[1] I have not succeeded in hitting on the passage in the *History*.

The day was humid and muggy, but the tumult of the sea was most majestic. Mr. G. delighted in it. He has a passion for the sound of the sea; would like to have it in his ear all day and all night. Again and again he recurred to this.

After dinner, long talk about Mazzini, of whom Mr. G. thought poorly in comparison with Poerio and the others who for freedom sacrificed their lives. I stood up for Mazzini, as one of the most morally impressive men I had ever known, or that his age knew; he breathed a soul into democracy.

Then we fell into a discussion as to the eastern and western churches. He thought the western popes by their proffered alliance with the mahometans, etc., had betrayed Christianity in the east. I offered De Maistre's view.

Mr. G. strongly assented to old Chatham's dictum that vacancy is worse than even the most anxious work. He has less to reproach himself with than most men under that head.

He repeated an observation that I have heard him make before, that he thought politicians are more *rapid* than other people. I told him that Bowen once said to me on this that he did not agree; that he thought rapidity the mark of all successful men in the practical line of life, merchants and stockbrokers, etc.

Wednesday, Dec. 30. — A very muggy day. A divine sunset, with the loveliest pink and opal tints in the sky. Mr. G. reading Gleig's *Subaltern*. Not a very entertaining book in itself, but the incidents belong to Wellington's Pyrenean campaign, and, for my own part, I rather enjoyed it on the principle on which one likes reading *Romola* at Florence, *Transformation* at Rome, *Sylvia's Lovers* at Whitby, and *Hurrish* on the northern edge of Clare.

Thursday, Dec. 31. — Down to the pier, and found all the party watching the breakers, and superb they were. Mr. G. exulting in the huge force of the Atlantic swell and the beat of the rollers on the shore, like a Titanic pulse.

After dinner Mr. G. raised the question of payment of members. He had been asked by somebody whether he meant at Newcastle to indicate that everybody should be paid, or only those who chose to take it or to ask for it. He produced the same extraordinary plan as he had described to me on the morning of his Newcastle speech — *i.e.* that the Inland Revenue should ascertain from their own books the income of every M.P., and if they found any below the limit of exemption, should notify the same to the Speaker, and the Speaker should thereupon send to the said M.P. below the limit an annual cheque for, say, £300, the name to appear in an annual return to Parliament of all the M.P.'s in receipt of public money on any grounds whatever. I demurred to this altogether, as drawing an invidious distinction between paid and unpaid members; said it was idle to ignore the theory on which the demand for paid members is based, namely, that it is desirable in the public interest that poor men should have access to the H. of C.; and that the poor man should stand there on the same footing as anybody else.

Friday, Jan. 1, 1892. — After breakfast Mrs. Gladstone came to my room and said how glad she was that I had not scrupled to put unpleasant points; that Mr. G. must not be shielded and sheltered as some great people are, who hear all the pleasant things and none of the unpleasant; that the perturbation from what is disagreeable only lasts an hour. I said I hoped that I was faithful with him, but of course I could not be always putting myself in an attitude of perpetual controversy. She said, 'He is never made angry by what you say.' And so she went away, and —— and I had a good and most useful set-to about Irish finance.

At luncheon Mr. G. asked what we had made out of our morning's work. When we told him he showed a good deal of impatience and vehemence, and, to my dismay, he came upon union finance and the general subject of the treatment of Ireland by England. . . .

In the afternoon we took a walk, he and I, afterwards joined by the rest. He was as delighted as ever with the swell of the waves, as they bounded over one another, with every variety of grace and tumultuous power. He wondered if we had not more and better words for the sea than the French — 'breaker,' 'billow,' 'roller,' as against 'flot,' 'vague,' 'onde,' 'lame,' etc.

At dinner he asked me whether I had made up my mind on the burning question of compulsory Greek for a university degree. I said, No, that as then advised I was half inclined to be against compulsory Greek, but it is so important that I would not decide before I was obliged. 'So with me,' he said, 'the question is one with many subtle and deep-reaching consequences.' He dwelt on the folly of striking Italian out of the course of modern education, thus cutting European history in two, and setting an artificial gulf between the ancient and modern worlds.

Saturday, Jan. 2. — Superb morning, and all the better for being much cooler. At breakfast somebody started the idle topic of quill pens. When they came to the length of time that so-and-so made a quill serve, 'De Retz,' said I, 'made up his mind that Cardinal Chigi was a poor creature, *maximus in minimis*, because at their first interview Chigi boasted that he had used one pen for three years.' That recalled another saying of Retz's about Cromwell's famous dictum, that nobody goes so far as the man who does not know where he is going. Mr. G. gave his deep and eager Ah! to this. He could not recall that Cromwell had produced many dicta of such quality. 'I don't love him, but he was a mighty big fellow. But he was intolerant. He was intolerant of the episcopalians.'

Mr. G. — Do you know whom I find the most tolerant churchman of that time? *Laud!* Laud got Davenant made Bishop of Salisbury, and he zealously befriended Chillingworth and Hales. (There was some other case, which I forget.)

The execution of Charles. — I told him of Gardiner's new volume which I had just been reading. 'Charles,' he said, 'was no doubt a dreadful liar; Cromwell perhaps did not always tell the truth; Elizabeth was a tremendous liar.'

J. M. — Charles was not wholly inexcusable, being what he was, for thinking that he had a good game in his hands, by playing off the parliament against the army, etc.

Mr. G. — There was less excuse for cutting off his head than in the case of poor Louis XVI., for Louis was the excuse for foreign invasion.

J. M. — Could you call foreign invasion the intervention of the Scotch?

Mr. G. — Well, not quite. I suppose it is certain that it was Cromwell who cut off Charles's head? Not one in a hundred in the nation desired it.

J. M. — No, nor one in twenty in the parliament. But then, ninety-nine in a hundred in the army.

In the afternoon we all drove towards Bayonne to watch the ships struggle over the bar at high water. As it happened we only saw one pass out, a countryman for Cardiff. A string of others were waiting to go, but a little steamer from Nantes came first, and having secured her station, found she had not force enough to make the bar, and the others remained swearing impatiently behind her. The Nantes steamer was like Ireland. The scene was very fresh and fine, and the cold most exhilarating after the mugginess of the last two or three days. Mr. G., who has a dizzy head, did not venture on the jetty, but watched things from the sands. He and I drove home together, at a good pace. 'I am inclined,' he said laughingly, 'to agree with Dr. Johnson that there is no pleasure greater than sitting behind four fast-going horses."[1] Talking of Johnson generally, 'I suppose we may take him as the best product of the eighteenth century.' Perhaps so, but is he its most characteristic product?

Wellington. — Curious that there should be no general estimate of W.'s character; his character not merely as a general but as a man. No love of freedom. His sense of duty very strong, but military rather than civil.

Montalembert. — Had often come into contact with him. A very amiable and attractive man. But less remarkable than Rio.

Latin Poets. — Would you place Virgil first?

J. M. — Oh, no, Lucretius much the first for the greatest and sublimest of poetic qualities. Mr. G. seemed to assent to this, though disposed to make a fight for the second *Aeneid* as equal to anything. He expressed his admiration for

[1] Boswell, March 21, 1776. Repeated, with a very remarkable qualification, Sept. 19, 1777. Birkbeck Hill's edition, iii. p. 162.

Catullus, and then he was strong that Horace would run anybody else very hard, breaking out with the lines about Regulus —

> 'Atqui sciebat quæ sibi barbarus
> Tortor pararet; ' etc.[1]

Blunders in Government. — How right Napoleon was when he said, reflecting on all the vast complexities of government, that the best to be said of a statesman is that he has avoided the biggest blunders.

It is not easy to define the charm of these conversations. Is charm the right word? They are in the highest degree stimulating, bracing, widening. That is certain. I return to my room with the sensations of a man who has taken delightful exercise in fresh air. He is so wholly free from the *ergoteur*. There's all the difference between the *ergoteur* and the great debater. He fits his tone to the thing ; he can be as playful as anybody. In truth I have many a time seen him in London and at Hawarden not far from trivial. But here at Biarritz all is appropriate, and though, as I say, he can be playful and gay as youth, he cannot resist rising in an instant to the general point of view — to grasp the elemental considerations of character, history, belief, conduct, affairs. There he is at home, there he is most himself. I never knew anybody less guilty of the tiresome sin of arguing for victory. It is not his knowledge that attracts ; it is not his ethical tests and standards ; it is not that dialectical strength of arm which, as Mark Pattison said of him, could twist a bar of iron to its purpose. It is the combination of these with elevation, with true sincerity, with extraordinary mental force.

Sunday, Jan. 3. — Vauvenargues is right when he says that to carry through great undertakings, one must act as though one could never die. My wonderful companion is a wonderful illustration. He is like M. Angelo, who, just before he died on the very edge of ninety, made an allegorical figure, and inscribed upon it, *ancora impara*, ' still learning.'

At dinner he showed in full force.

---

[1] *Carm.* iii. 5.

Heroes of the Old Testament. — He could not honestly say that he thought there was any figure in the O. T. comparable to the heroes of Homer. Moses was a fine fellow. But the others were of secondary quality — not great high personages, of commanding nature.

Thinkers. — Rather an absurd word — to call a man a thinker (and he repeated the word with gay mockery in his tone). When did it come into use ? Not until quite our own times, eh ? I said, I believed both Hobbes and Locke spoke of thinkers, and was pretty sure that *penseur*, as in *libre penseur*, had established itself in the last century. [Quite true ; Voltaire used it, but it was not common.]

Dr. Arnold. — A high, large, impressive figure — perhaps more important by his character and personality than his actual work. I mentioned M. A.'s poem on his father, *Rugby Chapel*, with admiration. Rather to my surprise, Mr. G. knew the poem well, and shared my admiration to the full. This brought us on to poetry generally, and he expatiated with much eloquence and sincerity for the rest of the talk. The wonderful continuity of fine poetry in England for five whole centuries, stretching from Chaucer to Tennyson, always a proof to his mind of the soundness, the sap, and the vitality of our nation and its character. What people, beginning with such a poet as Chaucer 500 years ago, could have burst forth into such astonishing production of poetry as marked the first quarter of the century, Byron, Wordsworth, Shelley, etc.

J. M. — It is true that Germany has nothing, save Goethe, Schiller, Heine, that's her whole list. But I should say a word for the poetic movement in France : Hugo, Gautier, etc. Mr. G. evidently knew but little, or even nothing, of modern French poetry. He spoke up for Leopardi, on whom he had written an article first introducing him to the British public, ever so many years ago — in the *Quarterly*.

Mr. G. — Wordsworth used occasionally to dine with me when I lived in the Albany. A most agreeable man. I always found him amiable, polite, and sympathetic. Only once did he jar upon me, when he spoke slightingly of Tennyson's first performance.

J. M. — But he was not so wrong as he would be now. Tennyson's Juvenilia are terribly artificial.

Mr. G. — Yes, perhaps. Tennyson has himself withdrawn some of them. I remember W., when he dined with me, used on leaving to change his silk stockings in the ante-room and put on grey worsted.

J. M. — I once said to M. Arnold that I'd rather have been Wordsworth than anybody [not exactly a modest ambition] ; and Arnold, who knew him well in the Grasmere country, said, ' Oh no, you would not ; you would wish you were dining with me at the Athenæum. He was too much of the peasant for you.'

Mr. G. — No, I never felt that ; I always thought him a polite and an amiable man.

Mentioned Macaulay's strange judgment in a note in the *History*, that Dryden's famous lines,

> '. . . Fool'd with hope, men favour the deceit ;
> Trust on, and think to-morrow will repay.
> To-morrow's falser than the former day ;
> Lies worse, and while it says we shall be blest
> With some new joys, cuts off what we possest.
> Strange cozenage ! . . .'

are as fine as any eight lines in Lucretius. Told him of an excellent remark of —— on this, that Dryden's passage wholly lacks the mystery and great superhuman air of Lucretius. Mr. G. warmly agreed.

He regards it as a remarkable sign of the closeness of the church of England to the roots of life and feeling in the country, that so many clergymen should have written so much good poetry. Who, for instance ? I asked. He named Heber, Moultrie, Newman (*Dream of Gerontius*), and Faber in at least one good poem, ' The poor Labourer ' (or some such title), Charles Tennyson. I doubt if this thesis has much body in it. He was for Shelley as the most musical of all our poets. I told him that I had once asked M. to get Tennyson to write an autograph line for a friend of mine, and Tennyson had sent this : —

> ' Coldly on the dead volcano sleeps the gleam of dying day.'

So I suppose the poet must think well of it himself. 'Tis

from the second *Locksley Hall*, and describes a man after passions have gone cool.

Mr. G. — Yes, in melody, in the picturesque, and as apt simile, a fine line.

Had been trying his hand at a translation of his favourite lines of Penelope about Odysseus. Said that, of course, you could translate similes and set passages, but to translate Homer as a whole, impossible. He was inclined, when all is said, to think Scott the nearest approach to a model.

Monday, Jan. 4. — At luncheon, Mr. Gladstone recalled the well-known story of Talleyrand on the death of Napoleon. The news was brought when T. chanced to be dining with Wellington. 'Quel événement!' they all cried. 'Non, ce n'est pas un événement,' said Talleyrand, 'c'est une nouvelle' — 'Tis no event, 'tis a piece of news. 'Imagine such a way,' said Mr. G., 'of taking the disappearance of that colossal man! Compare it with the opening of Manzoni's ode, which makes the whole earth stand still. Yet both points of view are right. In one sense, the giant's death was only news; in another, when we think of his history, it was enough to shake the world.' At the moment, he could not recall Manzoni's words, but at dinner he told me that he had succeeded in piecing them together, and after dinner he went to his room and wrote them down for me on a piece of paper. Curiously enough, he could not recall the passage in his own splendid translation.[1]

Talk about handsome men of the past; Sidney Herbert one of the handsomest and most attractive. But the Duke of Hamilton bore away the palm, as glorious as a Greek god. 'One day in Rotten Row, I said this to the Duchess of C. She set up James Hope-Scott against my Duke. No doubt he had an intellectual element which the Duke lacked.' Then we discussed the best-looking man in the H. of C. to-day. . . .

Duke of Wellington. — Somebody was expatiating on the incomparable position of the Duke; his popularity with kings, with nobles, with common people. Mr. G. remem-

[1] *Translations by Lyttelton and Gladstone*, p. 166.

bered that immediately after the formation of Canning's government in 1827, when it was generally thought that he had been most unfairly and factiously treated (as Mr. G. still thinks, always saving Peel) by the Duke and his friends, the Duke made an expedition to the north of England, and had an overwhelming reception. Of course, he was then only twelve years from Waterloo, and yet only four or five years later he had to put up his iron shutters.

Approved a remark that a friend of ours was not simple enough, not ready enough to take things as they come.

Mr. G. — Unless a man has a considerable gift for taking things as they come, he may make up his mind that political life will be sheer torment to him. He must meet fortune in all its moods.

Tuesday, Jan. 5. — After dinner to-day, Mr. G. extraordinarily gay. He had bought a present of silver for his wife. She tried to guess the price, and after the manner of wives in such a case, put the figure provokingly low. Mr. G. then put on the deprecating air of the tradesman with wounded feelings — and it was as capital fun as we could desire. That over, he fell to his backgammon with our host.

Wednesday, Jan. 6. — Mrs. Gladstone eighty to-day! What a marvel. . . .

Léon Say called to see Mr. G. Long and most interesting conversation about all sorts of aspects of French politics, the concordat, the schools, and all the rest of it.

He illustrated the ignorance of French peasantry as to current affairs. Thiers, long after he had become famous, went on a visit to his native region ; and there met a friend of his youth. 'Eh bien,' said his friend, 'tu as fait ton chemin.' 'Mais oui, j'ai fait un peu mon chemin. J'ai été ministre même.' 'Ah, tiens ! je ne savais pas que tu étais protestant.'

I am constantly struck by his solicitude for the well-being and right doing of Oxford and Cambridge — 'the two eyes of the country.' This connection between the higher education and the general movement of the national mind engages his profound attention, and no doubt deserves such attention

in any statesman who looks beyond the mere surface problems of the day. To perceive the bearings of such matters
as these, makes Mr. G. a statesman of the highest class, as
distinguished from men of clever expedients.

Mr. G. had been reading the Greek epigrams on religion
in Mackail; quoted the last of them as illustrating the
description of the dead as the inhabitants of the more
populous world : —

τ ῶν ἀπο κὴν ζωοῖσιν ἀκηδέα, κεῦτ' ἀν ἵκηαι
ἐς πλεόνων, ἕξεις θυμὸν ἐλαφρότερον.[1]

A more impressive epigram contains the same thought,
where the old man, leaning on his staff, likens himself to the
withered vine on its dry pole, and goes on to ask himself what
advantage it would be to warm himself for three or four more
years in the sun; and on that reflection without heroics put
off his life, and changed his home to the greater company,

κῆς πλεόνων ἦλθε μετοικεσίην.

All the rest of the evening he kept us alive by a stock of
infinite drolleries. A scene of a dish of over-boiled tea at
West Calder after a meeting, would have made the fortune
of a comedian.

I said that in the all-important quality of co-operation,
―― was only good on condition of being in front. Mr. G.
read him in the same sense. Reminded of a mare he once
had — admirable, provided you kept off spur, curb, or whip;
show her one of these things, and she would do nothing.
Mr. G. more of a judge of men than is commonly thought.

Told us of a Chinese despatch which came under his notice
when he was at the board of trade, and gave him food for
reflection. A ship laden with grain came to Canton. The
administrator wrote to the central government at Pekin to
know whether the ship was to pay duty and land its cargo.
The answer was to the effect that the central government of
the Flowery Land was quite indifferent as a rule to the goings
and comings of the Barbarians; whether they brought a cargo
or brought no cargo was a thing of supreme unconcern. 'But
this cargo, you say, is food for the people. There ought to be

[1] Thou shalt possess thy soul with- when thou goest to the place where
out care among the living, and lighter most are.

no obstacle to the entry of food for the people.   So let it in.
Your Younger Brother commends himself to you, etc. etc.'

Friday, Jan. 8. — A quiet evening.   We were all rather
piano at the end of an episode which had been thoroughly
delightful.   When Mr. G. bade me good-night, he said with
real feeling, 'More sorry than I can say that this is our last
evening together at Biarritz.'   He is painfully grieved to
lose the sound of the sea in his ears.

Saturday, Jan. 9. — Strolled about all the forenoon.   'What
a time of blessed composure it has been,' said Mr. G. with a
heavy sigh.   The distant hills covered with snow, and the
voice of the storm gradually swelling.   Still the savage fury
of the sea was yet some hours off, so we had to leave Biarritz
without the spectacle of Atlantic rage at its fiercest.

Found comfortable saloon awaiting us at Bayonne, and so
under weeping skies we made our way to Pau.   The landscape must be pretty, weather permitting.   As it was, we
saw but little.   Mr. G. dozed and read Max Müller's book on
Anthropological Religions.

Arrived at Pau towards 5.30; drenching rain: nothing to
be seen.

At tea time, a good little discussion raised by a protest
against Dante being praised for a complete survey of human
nature and the many phases of human lot.   Intensity he
has, but insight over the whole field of character and life ?
Mr. G. did not make any stand against this, and made the
curious admission that Dante was too optimist to be placed
on a level with Shakespeare, or even with Homer.

Then we turned to lighter themes.   He had once said to
Henry Taylor, 'I should have thought he was the sort of
man to have a good strong grasp of a subject,' speaking of
Lord Grey, who had been one of Taylor's many chiefs at the
Colonial Office.   'I should have thought,' replied Taylor
slowly and with a dreamy look, 'he was the sort of man to
have a good strong *nip* of a subject.'   Witty, and very
applicable to many men.

Wordsworth once gave Mr. G. with much complacency,
as an example of his own readiness and resource, this story.
A man came up to him at Rydal and said, 'Do you happen

to have seen my wife.' 'Why,' replied the Sage, 'I did not know you had a wife!' This peculiarly modest attempt at pointed repartee much tickled Mr. G., as well it might.

Tuesday, Jan. 12. — Mr. G. completely recovered from two days of indisposition. We had about an hour's talk on things in general, including policy in the approaching session. He did not expect a dissolution, at the same time a dissolution would not surprise him.

At noon they started for Périgord and Carcassonne, Nismes, Arles, and so on to the Riviera full of kind things at our parting.

CHAPTER VII

THE FOURTH ADMINISTRATION

(1892–1894)

Τῷ δ' ἤδη δύο μὲν γενεαὶ μερόπων ἀνθρώπων
ἐφθίαθ, οἳ οἱ πρόσθεν ἄμα τράφεν ἠδὲ γένοντο
ἐν Πύλῳ ἠγαθέῃ, μετὰ δὲ τριτάτοισιν ἄνασσεν.

Iliad, i. 250.

Two generations of mortal men had he already seen pass away, who
with him of old had been born and bred in sacred Pylos, and among
the third generation he held rule.

IN 1892 the general election came, after a session that was
not very long nor at all remarkable. Everybody knew that
we should soon be dismissed, and everybody knew that the
liberals would have a majority, but the size of it was beyond
prognostication. Mr. Gladstone did not talk much about it,
but in fact he reckoned on winning by eighty or a hundred.
A leading liberal-unionist at whose table we met (May 24)
gave us forty. That afternoon by the way the House had
heard a speech of great power and splendour. An Irish tory
peer in the gallery said afterwards, 'That old hero of yours
is a miracle. When he set off in that high pitch, I said that
won't last. Yet he kept it up all through as grand as ever,
and came in fresher and stronger than when he began.' His
sight failed him in reading an extract, and he asked me to
read it for him, so he sat down amid sympathetic cheers
while it was read out from the box.

After listening to a strong and undaunted reply from Mr.
Balfour, he asked me to go with him into the tea-room;
he was fresh, unperturbed, and in high spirits. He told
me he had once sat at table with Lord Melbourne, but
regretted that he had never known him. Said that of the
sixty men or so who had been his colleagues in cabinet, the

490

very easiest and most attractive was Clarendon. Constantly regretted that he had never met nor known Sir Walter Scott, as of course he might have done. Thought the effect of diplomacy to be bad on the character; to train yourself to practise the airs of genial friendship towards men from whom you are doing your best to hide yourself, and out of whom you are striving to worm that which they wish to conceal. Said that he was often asked for advice by young men as to objects of study. He bade them study and ponder, first, the history and working of freedom in America; second, the history of absolutism in France from Louis XIV. to the Revolution. It was suggested that if the great thing with the young is to attract them to fine types of character, the Huguenots had some grave, free, heroic figures, and in the eighteenth century Turgot was the one inspiring example: when Mill was in low spirits, he restored himself by Condorcet's life of Turgot. This reminded him that Canning had once praised Turgot in the House of Commons, though most likely nobody but himself knew anything at all about Turgot. Talking of the great centuries, the thirteenth, and the sixteenth, and the seventeenth, Mr. Gladstone let drop what for him seems the remarkable judgment that 'Man as a type has not improved since those great times; he is not so big, so grand, so heroic as he has been.' This, the reader will agree, demands a good deal of consideration.

Then he began to talk about offices, in view of what were now pretty obvious possibilities. After discussing more important people, he asked whether, after a recent conversation, I had thought more of my own office, and I told him that I fancied like Regulus I had better go back to the Irish department. 'Yes,' he answered with a flash of his eye, 'I think so. The truth is that we're both chained to the oar; I am chained to the oar; you are chained.'

II

The electoral period, when it arrived, he passed once more at Dalmeny. In a conversation the morning after I was allowed to join him there, he seemed already to have a grand majority of three figures, to have kissed hands, and to be installed in Downing Street. This confidence was indispensable to him. At the end of his talk he went up to prepare some notes for the speech that he was to make in the afternoon at Glasgow. Just before the carriage came to take him to the train, I heard him calling from the library. In I went, and found him hurriedly thumbing the leaves of a Horace. 'Tell me,' he cried, 'can you put your finger on the passage about Castor and Pollux? I've just thought of something; Castor and Pollux will finish my speech at Glasgow.' 'Isn't it in the Third Book?' said I. 'No, no; I'm pretty sure it is in the First Book'—busily turning over the pages. 'Ah, here it is,' and then he read out the noble lines with animated modulation, shut the book with a bang, and rushed off exultant to the carriage. This became one of the finest of his perorations.[1] His delivery of it that afternoon, they said, was most majestic—the picture of the wreck, and then the calm that gradually brought down the towering billows to the surface of the deep, entrancing the audience like magic.

Then came a depressing week. The polls flowed in, all day long, day after day. The illusory hopes of many months faded into night. The three-figure majority by the end of the week had vanished so completely, that one wondered how it could ever have been thought of. On July 13 his own Midlothian poll was declared, and instead of his old majority of 4000, or the 3000 on which he counted, he was only in by 690. His chagrin was undoubtedly intense, for he had put forth every atom of his strength in the campaign. But with that splendid suppression of vexation which is one of the good lessons that men learn in public life, he put a brave face on it, was perfectly cheery all through the luncheon, and afterwards took me to the music-room, where instead of constructing a triumphant cabinet with a majority of a hundred, he had to try to adjust an Irish policy to a parliament with hardly a majority at all. These topics exhausted, with a curiously quiet gravity of tone he told me

[1] See Appendix, Hor. *Carm.* i. 12, 25.

that cataract had formed over one eye, that its sight was
gone, and that in the other eye he was infested with a white
speck. 'One white speck,' he said, almost laughing, 'I can
do with, but if the one becomes many, it will be a bad business. They tell me that perhaps the fresh air of Braemar
will do me good.' To Braemar the ever loyal Mr. Armitstead
piloted them, in company with Lord Acton of whose society
Mr. Gladstone could never have too much.

III

It has sometimes been made a matter of blame by friends
no less than foes, that he should have undertaken the task
of government, depending on a majority not large enough to
coerce the House of Lords. One or two short observations
on this would seem to be enough. How could he refuse to
try to work his Irish policy through parliament, after the
bulk of the Irish members had quitted their own leader four
years before in absolute reliance on the sincerity and good
faith of Mr. Gladstone and his party? After all the confidence that Ireland had shown in him at the end of 1890, how
could he in honour throw up the attempt that had been the
only object of his public life since 1886? To do this would
have been to justify indeed the embittered warnings of Mr.
Parnell in his most reckless hour. How could either refusal
of office or the postponement of an Irish bill after taking
office, be made intelligible in Ireland itself? Again, the path
of honour in Ireland was equally the path of honour and of
safety in Great Britain. Were British liberals, who had
given him a majority, partly from disgust at Irish coercion,
partly from faith that he could produce a working plan of
Irish government, and partly from hopes of reforms of their
own — were they to learn that their leaders could do nothing
for any of their special objects?

Mr. Gladstone found some consolation in a precedent. In
1835, he argued, 'the Melbourne government came in with a
British minority, swelled into a majority hardly touching
thirty by the O'Connell contingent of forty. And they staid

in for six years and a half, the longest lived government since Lord Liverpool's.[1] But the Irish were under the command of a master ; and Ireland, scarcely beginning her political life, had to be content with small mercies. Lastly, that government was rather slack, and on this ground perhaps could not well be taken as a pattern.' In the present case, the attitude of the Parnellite group who continued the schism that began in the events of the winter of 1890, was not likely to prove a grave difficulty in parliament, and in fact it did not. The mischief here was in the effect of Irish feuds upon public opinion in the country. As Mr. Gladstone put it in the course of a letter that he had occasion to write to me (November 26, 1892) : —

Until the schism arose, we had every prospect of a majority approaching those of 1868 and 1880. With the death of Mr. Parnell it was supposed that it must perforce close. But this expectation has been disappointed. The existence and working of it have to no small extent puzzled and bewildered the English people. They cannot comprehend how a quarrel, to them utterly unintelligible (some even think it discreditable), should be allowed to divide the host in the face of the enemy; and their unity and zeal have been deadened in proportion. Herein we see the main cause why our majority is not more than double what it actually numbers, and the difference between these two scales of majority represents, as I apprehend, the difference between power to carry the bill as the Church and Land bills were carried into law, and the default of such power. The main mischief has already been done; but it receives additional confirmation with the lapse of every week or month.

In forming his fourth administration Mr. Gladstone found one or two obstacles on which he had not reckoned, and perhaps could not have been expected to reckon. By that forbearance of which he was a master, they were in good time surmounted. New men, of a promise soon amply fulfilled, were taken in, including, to Mr. Gladstone's own particular satisfaction, the son of the oldest

[1] Lord Palmerston's government of 1859 was shorter by only a few days.

of all the surviving friends of his youth, Sir Thomas Acland.[1]

Mr. Gladstone remained as head of the government for a year and a few months (Aug. 1892 to March 3, 1894). In that time several decisions of pith and moment were taken, one measure of high importance became law, operations began against the Welsh establishment, but far the most conspicuous biographic element of this short period was his own incomparable display of power of every kind in carrying the new bill for the better government of Ireland through the House of Commons.

In foreign affairs it was impossible that he should forget the case of Egypt. Lord Salisbury in 1887 had pressed forward an arrangement by which the British occupation was under definite conditions and at a definite date to come to an end. If this convention had been accepted by the Sultan, the British troops would probably have been home by the time of the change of government in this country. French diplomacy, however, at Constantinople, working as it might seem against its own professed aims, hindered the ratification of the convention, and Lord Salisbury's policy was frustrated. Negotiations did not entirely drop, and they had not passed out of existence when Lord Salisbury resigned. In the autumn of 1892 the French ambassador addressed a friendly inquiry to the new government as to the reception likely to be given to overtures for re-opening the negotiations. The

---

[1] Here is the Fourth Cabinet : —

First lord of the treasury and privy seal,	W. E. Gladstone.
Lord chancellor,	Lord Herschell.
President of the council and Indian secretary,	Earl of Kimberley.
Chancellor of the exchequer,	Sir W. V. Harcourt.
Home secretary,	H. H. Asquith.
Foreign secretary,	Earl of Rosebery.
Colonial secretary,	Marquis of Ripon.
Secretary for war,	H. Campbell-Bannerman.
First lord of the admiralty,	Earl Spencer.
Chief secretary for Ireland,	John Morley.
Secretary for Scotland,	Sir G. O. Trevelyan.
President of the board of trade,	A. J. Mundella.
President of the local government board,	H. H. Fowler.
Chancellor of the duchy of Lancaster,	James Bryce.
Postmaster-general,	Arnold Morley.
First commissioner of works,	J. G. Shaw Lefevre.
Vice-president of the council,	A. H. D. Acland.

answer was that if France had suggestions to offer, they would be received in the same friendly spirit in which they were tendered. When any communications were received, Mr. Gladstone said in the House of Commons, there would be no indisposition on our part to extend to them our friendly consideration. Of all this nothing came. A rather serious ministerial crisis in Egypt in January 1893, followed by a ministerial crisis in Paris in April, arrested whatever projects of negotiation France may have entertained.[1]

IV

In December (1892), at Hawarden, Mr. Gladstone said to me one day after we had been working for five or six hours at the heads of the new Home Rule bill, that his general health was good and sound, but his sight and his hearing were so rapidly declining, that he thought he might almost any day have to retire from office. It was no moment for banal deprecation. He sat silently pondering this vision in his own mind, of coming fate. It seemed like Tennyson's famous simile —

> So dark a forethought rolled about his brain,
> As on a dull day in an ocean cave
> The blind wave feeling round his long sea-hall
> In silence.

It would have been preternatural if he had shown the same overwhelming interest that had animated him when the Irish policy was fresh in 1886. Yet the instinct of a strong mind and the lifelong habit of ardent industry carried him through his Sisyphean toil. The routine business of head of a government he attended to, with all his usual assiduity, and in cabinet he was clear, careful, methodical, as always.

The preparation of the bill was carefully and elaborately worked by Mr. Gladstone through an excellent committee

---

[1] See Mr. Gladstone's speeches and answers to questions in the House of Commons, Jan. 1, Feb. 3, and May 1, 1893. See also the French Yellow Book for 1893, for M. Waddington's despatches of Nov. 1, 1892, May 5, 1893, and Feb. 1, 1893.

of the cabinet.[1] Here he was acute, adroit, patient, full of device, expedient, and the art of construction; now and then vehement and bearing down like a three-decker upon craft of more modest tonnage. But the vehemence was rare, and here as everywhere else he was eager to do justice to all the points and arguments of other people. He sought opportunities of deliberation in order to deliberate, and not under that excellent name to cultivate the art of the harangue, or to overwork secondary points, least of all to treat the many as made for one. That is to say, he went into counsel for the sake of counsel, and not to cajole, or bully, or insist on his own way because it was his own way. In the high article of finance, he would wrestle like a tiger. It was an intricate and difficult business by the necessity of the case, and among the aggravations of it was the discovery at one point that a wrong figure had been furnished to him by some department. He declared this truly heinous crime to be without a precedent in his huge experience.

The crucial difficulty was the Irish representation at Westminster. In the first bill of 1886, the Irish members were to come no more to the imperial parliament, except for one or two special purposes. The two alternatives to the policy of exclusion were either inclusion of the Irish members for all purposes, or else their inclusion for imperial purposes only. In his speech at Swansea in 1887, Mr. Gladstone favoured provisional inclusion, without prejudice to a return to the earlier plan of exclusion if that should be recommended by subsequent experience.[2] In the bill now introduced (Feb. 13, 1893), eighty representatives from Ireland were to have seats at Westminster, but they were not to vote upon motions or bills expressly confined to England or Scotland, and there were other limitations. This plan was soon found to be wholly intolerable to the House of Commons. Exclusion having failed, and inclusion of reduced numbers for limited purposes having failed, the only

---

[1] I hope I am not betraying a cabinet secret if I mention that this committee was composed of Mr. Gladstone, Lord Spencer, Lord Herschell, Mr. Campbell-Bannermann, Mr. Bryce, and myself.

[2] See above, p. 386.

course left open was what was called *omnes omnia*, or rather the inclusion of eighty Irish members, with power of voting on all purposes.

Each of the three courses was open to at least one single, but very direct, objection. Exclusion, along with the exaction of revenue from Ireland by the parliament at Westminster, was taxation without representation. Inclusion for all purposes was to allow the Irish to meddle in our affairs, while we were no longer to meddle in theirs. Inclusion for limited purposes still left them invested with the power of turning out a British government by a vote against it on an imperial question. Each plan, therefore, ended in a paradox. There was a fourth paradox, namely, that whenever the British supporters of a government did not suffice to build up a decisive majority, then the Irish vote descending into one or other scale of the parliamentary balance might decide who should be our rulers. This paradox—the most glaring of them all—habit and custom have made familiar, and familiarity might almost seem to have actually endeared it to us. In 1893 Mr. Gladstone and his colleagues thought themselves compelled to change clause 9 of the new bill, just as they had thought themselves forced to drop clause 24 of the old bill.

V

It was Mr. Gladstone's performances in the days of committee on the bill, that stirred the wonder and admiration of the House. If he had been fifty they would have been astonishing; at eighty-four they were indeed a marvel. He made speeches of powerful argument, of high constitutional reasoning, of trenchant debating force. No emergency arose for which he was not ready, no demand that his versatility was not adequate to meet. His energy never flagged. When the bill came on, he would put on his glasses, pick up the paper of amendments, and running through them like lightning, would say, 'Of course, that's absurd—that will never do—we can never accept that—is there any harm in this?' Too many concessions made on the spur of the

moment to the unionists stirred resentment in the nationalists, and once or twice they exploded. These rapid
splendours of his had their perils. I pointed out to him the
pretty obvious drawbacks of settling delicate questions as
we went along with no chance of sounding the Irishmen,
and asked him to spare me quarter of an hour before
luncheon, when the draftsman and I, having threshed out
the amendments of the day, could put the bare points for
his consideration. He was horrified at the very thought.
'Out of the question. Do you want to kill me? I must
have the whole of the morning for general government
business. Don't ask me.'[1]

Obstruction was freely practised and without remorse.
The chief fighting debater against the government made
a long second-reading speech, on the motion that the clause
stand part of the bill. A little before eight o'clock when
the fighting debater was winding up, Mr. Gladstone was
undecided about speaking. 'What do you advise?' he asked
of a friend. 'I am afraid it will take too much out of you,'
the friend replied; 'but still, speak for twenty minutes and
no more.' Up he rose, and for half an hour a delighted
House was treated to one of the most remarkable performances that ever was known. 'I have never seen Mr.
Gladstone,' says one observer, 'so dramatic, so prolific of all
the resources of the actor's art. The courage, the audacity,
and the melodrama of it were irresistible' (May 11).

For ten minutes, writes another chronicler, Mr. Gladstone
spoke, holding his audience spell-bound by his force. Then came
a sudden change, and it seemed that he was about to collapse
from sheer physical exhaustion. His voice failed, huskiness and
indistinctness took the place of clearness and lucidity. Then
pulling himself together for a great effort, Mr. Gladstone pointing
the deprecatory finger at Mr. Chamberlain, warned the Irishmen
to beware of him; to watch the fowler who would inveigle
them in his snare. Loud and long rang the liberal cheers.

---

[1] One poor biographic item perhaps the tolerant reader will not grudge me leave to copy from Mr. Glad-stone's diary:—'*October* 6, 1892. Saw J. Morley and made him envoy to ——. He is on the whole . . . about the best stay I have.'

In plain words he told the unionists that Mr. Chamberlain's purpose was none other than obstruction, and he conveyed the intimation with a delicate expressiveness, a superabundant good feeling, a dramatic action and a marvellous music of voice that conspired in their various qualities to produce a *tour de force.* By sheer strength of enthusiasm and an overflowing wealth of eloquence, Mr. Gladstone literally conquered every physical weakness and secured an effect electric in its influence even on seasoned ' old hands.' Amidst high excitement and the sound of cheering that promised never to die away the House gradually melted into the lobbies. Mr. Gladstone, exhausted with his effort, chatted to Mr. Morley on the treasury bench. Except for these two the government side was deserted, and the conservatives had already disappeared. The nationalists sat shoulder to shoulder, a solid phalanx. They eyed the prime minister with eager intent, and as soon as the venerable statesman rose to walk out of the House, they sprang to their feet and rent the air with wild hurrahs.

No wonder if the talk downstairs at dinner among his colleagues that night, all turned upon their chief, his art and power, his union of the highest qualities of brain and heart with extraordinary practical penetration, and close watchfulness of incident and trait and personality, disclosed in many a racy aside and pungent sally. The orator was fatigued, but full of keen enjoyment. This was one of the three or four occasions when he was induced not to return to the House after dinner. It had always been his habit in taking charge of bills to work the ship himself. No wonder that he held to this habit in this case.

On another occasion ministers had taken ground that, as the debate went on, everybody saw they could not hold. An official spokesman for the bill had expressed an opinion, or intention, that, as very speedily appeared, Irish opposition would not allow to be maintained. There was no great substance in the point, but even a small dose of humiliation will make a parliamentary dish as bitter to one side as it is savoury to the other. The opposition grew more and more radiant, as it grew more certain that the official spokesman must be thrown over. The discomfiture of the ministerialists at the prospect of the public mortification of their leaders was extreme in the same degree. 'I suppose we must give it up,' said Mr. Gladstone. This was clear; and when he rose, he was greeted with mocking cheers from the enemy, though the enemy's chief men who had long experience of his Protean resources were less confident. Beginning in a tone of easy gravity and candour, he went on to points of pleasant banter, got his audience interested and amused and a little bewildered; carried men with him in graceful arguments on the merits; and finally, with bye-play of consummate sport, showed in triumph that the concession that we consented to make was so right and natural, that it must have been inevitable from the very first. Never were tables more effectively turned; the opposition watched first with amazement, then with excitement and delight as children watch a wizard; and he sat down victorious. Not another word was said or could be said. 'Never in all my parliamentary years,' said a powerful veteran on the front bench opposite, as he passed behind the Speaker's chair, 'never have I seen so wonderful a thing done as that.'

The state of the county of Clare was a godsend to the obstructive. Clare was not at that moment quite as innocent as the garden of Eden before the fall, but the condition was not serious; it had been twenty times worse before without occupying the House of Commons five minutes. Now an evening a week was not thought too much for a hollow debate on disorder in Clare. It was described as a definite matter of urgent importance, though it had slept for years, and though three times in succession the judge of assize (travelling entirely out of his proper business) had denounced the state of things. It was made to support five votes of censure in eight weeks.

On one of these votes of censure on Irish administration, moved by Mr. Balfour (March 27), Mr. Gladstone listened to the debate. At 8 we begged him not to stay and not to take the trouble to speak, so trumpery was the whole affair. He said he must, if only for five minutes, to show that he identified himself with his Irish minister. He left to dine,

and then before ten was on his feet, making what Lord
Randolph Churchill rightly called 'a most impressive and
entrancing speech.' He talked of Pat this and Michael that,
and Father the other, as if he had pondered their cases for a
month, clenching every point with extraordinary strength
as well as consummate ease and grace, and winding up with
some phrases of wonderful simplicity and concentration.

A distinguished member made a motion for the exclusion
of Irish cabinet ministers from their chamber. Mr. Gladstone
was reminded on the bench just before he rose, that the same
proposal had been inserted in the Act of Settlement, and
repealed in 1705. He wove this into his speech with a skill,
and amplified confidence, that must have made everybody
suppose that it was a historic fact present every day to his
mind. The attention of a law-officer sitting by was called to
this rapid amplification. 'I never saw anything like it in
all my whole life,' said the law-officer; and he was a man
who had been accustomed to deal with some of the strongest
and quickest minds of the day as judges and advocates.

One day when a tremendous afternoon of obstruction had
almost worn him down, the adjournment came at seven
o'clock. He was haggard and depressed. On returning at
ten we found him making a most lively and amusing speech
upon procedure. He sat down as blithe as dawn. 'To
make a speech of that sort,' he said in deprecation of compliment, 'a man does best to dine out; 'tis no use to lie
on a sofa and think about it.'

Undoubtedly Mr. Gladstone's method in this long committee carried with it some disadvantages. His discursive
treatment exposed an enormous surface. His abundance of
illustration multiplied points for debate. His fertility in
improvised arguments encouraged improvisation in disputants without the gift. Mr. Gladstone always supposed
that a great theme needs to be copiously handled, which is
perhaps doubtful, and indeed is often an exact inversion of
the true state of things. However that may be, copiousness
is a game at which two can play, as a patriotic opposition
now and at other times has effectually disclosed. Some
thought in these days that a man like Lord Althorp, for

those obligations, the result has been that he has found it his duty humbly to tender to your Majesty his resignation of the high offices which your Majesty has been pleased to intrust to him. His desire to make this surrender is accompanied with a grateful sense of the condescending kindnesses, which your Majesty has graciously shown him on so many occasions during the various periods for which he has had the honour to serve your Majesty. Mr. Gladstone will not needlessly burden your Majesty with a recital of particulars. He may, however, say that although at eighty-four years of age he is sensible of a diminished capacity for prolonged labour, this is not of itself such as would justify his praying to be relieved from the restraints and exigencies of official life. But his deafness has become in parliament, and even in the cabinet, a serious inconvenience, of which he must reckon on more progressive increase. More grave than this, and more rapid in its growth, is the obstruction of vision which arises from cataract in both his eyes. It has cut him off in substance from the newspapers, and from all except the best types in the best lights, while even as to these he cannot master them with that ordinary facility and despatch which he deems absolutely required for the due despatch of his public duties. In other respects than reading the operation of the complaint is not as yet so serious, but this one he deems to be vital. Accordingly he brings together these two facts, the condition of his sight and hearing, and the break in the course of public affairs brought about in the ordinary way by the close of the session. He has therefore felt that this is the fitting opportunity for the resignation which by this letter he humbly prays your Majesty to accept.

In the course of the day the Queen wrote what I take to be her last letter to him : —

Windsor Castle, March 3, 1894.—Though the Queen has already accepted Mr. Gladstone's resignation, and has taken leave of him, she does not like to leave his letter tendering his resignation unanswered. She therefore writes these few lines to say that she thinks that after so many years of arduous labour and responsibility he is right in wishing to be relieved at his age of these arduous duties. And she trusts he will be able to enjoy peace and quiet with his excellent and devoted wife in health and happiness, and that his eyesight may improve.

The Queen would gladly have conferred a peerage on Mr. Gladstone, but she knows he would not accept it.

His last act in relation to this closing scene of the great official drama was a letter to General Ponsonby (March 5): —

The first entrance of a man to Windsor Castle in a responsible character, is a great event in his life; and his last departure from it is not less moving. But in and during the process which led up to this transaction on Saturday, my action has been in the strictest sense sole, and it has required me in circumstances partly known to harden my heart into a flint. However, it is not even now so hard, but that I can feel what you have most kindly written; nor do I fail to observe with pleasure that you do not speak absolutely in the singular. If there were feelings that made the occasion sad, such feelings do not die with the occasion. But this letter must not be wholly one of egotism. I have known and have liked and admired all the men who have served the Queen in your delicate and responsible office; and have liked most, probably because I knew him most, the last of them, that most true-hearted man, General Grey. But forgive me for saying you are 'to the manner born'; and such a combination of tact and temper with loyalty, intelligence, and truth I cannot expect to see again. Pray remember these are words which can only pass from an old man to one much younger, though trained in a long experience.

It is hardly in human nature, in spite of Charles v., Sulla, and some other historic persons, to lay down power beyond recall, without a secret pang. In Prior's lines that came to the mind of brave Sir Walter Scott, as he saw the curtain falling on his days, —

> The man in graver tragic known,
> (Though his best part long since was done,)
> Still on the stage desires to tarry . . .
> Unwilling to retire, though weary.

Whether the departing minister had a lingering thought that in the dispensations of the world, purposes and services would still arise to which even yet he might one day be summoned, we do not know. Those who were nearest to him believe not, and assuredly he made no outer sign.

CHAPTER IX

THE CLOSE

(1894-1898)

NATURAL death is as it were a haven and a rest to us after long navigation. And the noble Soul is like a good mariner; for he, when he draws near the port, lowers his sails and enters it softly with gentle steerage. . . . And herein we have from our own nature a great lesson of suavity; for in such a death as this there is no grief nor any bitterness: but as a ripe apple is lightly and without violence loosened from its branch, so our soul without grieving departs from the body in which it hath been. — DANTE, *Convito*.[1]

AFTER the first wrench was over, and an end had come to the demands, pursuits, duties, glories, of powerful and active station held for a long lifetime, Mr. Gladstone soon settled to the new conditions of his existence, knowing that for him all that could be left was, in the figure of his great Italian poet, ' to lower sails and gather in his ropes.'[2] He was not much in London, and when he came he stayed in the pleasant retreat to which his affectionate and ever-attached friends, Lord and Lady Aberdeen, so often invited him at Dollis Hill. Much against his will, he did not resign his seat in the House, and he held it until the dissolution of 1895.[3] In June (1895) he took a final cruise in one of Sir Donald Currie's ships, visiting Hamburg, the new North Sea canal, and Copenhagen once more. His injured sight was a far deadlier breach in the habit of his days than withdrawal from office or from parliament. His own tranquil words written in the year in which he laid down his part in the shows of the world's huge stage, tell the story: —

July 25, 1894.—For the first time in my life there has been given

[1] Dr. Carlyle's translation.
[2] *Inferno*, xxvii. 81.
[3] On July 1, 1895, he announced his formal withdrawal in a letter to Sir John Cowan, so long the loyal chairman of his electoral committee.

to me by the providence of God a period of comparative leisure, reckoning at the present date to four and a half months. Such a period drives the mind in upon itself, and invites, almost constrains, to recollection, and the rendering at least internally an account of life; further it lays the basis of a habit of meditation, to the formation of which the course of my existence, packed and crammed with occupation outwards, never stagnant, oft-times overdriven, has been extremely hostile. As there is no life which in its detail does not seem to afford intervals of brief leisure, or what is termed ' waiting' for others engaged with us in some common action, these are commonly spent in murmurs and in petulant desire for their termination. But in reality they supply excellent opportunities for brief or ejaculatory prayer.

As this new period of my life has brought with it my retirement from active business in the world, it affords a good opportunity for breaking off the commonly dry daily journal, or ledger as it might almost be called, in which for seventy years I have recorded the chief details of my outward life. If life be continued I propose to note in it henceforward only principal events or occupations. This first breach since the latter part of May in this year has been involuntary. When the operation on my eye for cataract came, it was necessary for a time to suspend all use of vision. Before that, from the beginning of March, it was only my out-of-door activity or intercourse that had been paralysed. . . . For my own part, *suave mari magno* steals upon me; or at any rate, an inexpressible sense of relief from an exhausting life of incessant contention. A great revolution has been operated in my correspondence, which had for many years been a serious burden, and at times one almost intolerable. During the last months of partial incapacity I have not written with my own hand probably so much as one letter per day. Few people have had a smaller number of *otiose* conversations probably than I in the last fifty years; but I have of late seen more friends and more freely, though without practical objects in view. Many kind friends have read books to me; I must place Lady Sarah Spencer at the head of the proficients in that difficult art; in distinctness of articulation, with low clear voice, she is supreme. Dearest Catherine has been my chaplain from morning to morning. My church-going has been almost confined to mid-day communions, which have not required my abandonment of the reclining posture for long periods of time. Authorship has not been quite in abeyance; I have been able to write what I was not allowed to read, and have composed two theological articles for the *Nineteenth Century* of August and September respectively.[1]

Independently of the days of blindness after the operation, the visits of doctors have become a noticeable item of demand upon time. Of physic I incline to believe I have had as much in 1894 as in my whole previous life. I have learned for the first time the extraordinary comfort of the aid which the attendance of a nurse can give. My health will now be matter of little interest except to myself. But I have not yet abandoned the hope that I may be permitted to grapple with that considerable armful of work, which had been long marked out for my old age; the question of my recovering sight being for the present in abeyance.

Sept. 13. — I am not yet thoroughly accustomed to my new stage of existence, in part because the remains of my influenza have not yet allowed me wholly to resume the habits of health. But I am thoroughly content with my retirement; and I cast no longing, lingering look behind. I pass onward from it *oculo irretorto.* There is plenty of work before me, peaceful work and work directed to the supreme, *i.e.* the spiritual cultivation of mankind, if it pleases God to give me time and vision to perform it.

Oct. 1. — As far as I can at present judge, all the signs of the eye being favourable, the new form of vision will enable me to get through in a given time about half the amount of work which would have been practicable under the old. I speak of reading and writing work, which have been principal with me when I had the option. In conversation there is no difference, although there are various drawbacks in what we call society. On the 20th of last month when I had gone through my crises of trials, Mr. Nettleship, [the oculist], at once declared that any further operation would be superfluous.

I am unable to continue attendance at the daily morning service, not on account of the eyesight but because I may not rise before

---

[1] 'The Place of Heresy and Schism and 'The True and False Conception in the Modern Christian Church' of the Atonement.'

ten at the earliest. And so a Hawarden practice of over fifty
years is interrupted; not without some degree of hope that it
may be resumed. Two evening services, one at 5 P.M. and the
other at 7, afford me a limited consolation. I drive almost every
day, and thus grow to my dissatisfaction more burdensome. My
walking powers are limited; once I have exceeded two miles by
a little. A large part of the day remains available at my table;
daylight is especially precious; my correspondence is still a weary
weight, though I have admirable help from children. Upon the
whole the change is considerable. In early and mature life a man
walks to his daily work with a sense of the duty and capacity of
self-provision, a certain αὐτάρκεια [independence] (which the
Greeks carried into the moral world). Now that sense is reversed; it seems as if I must, God knows how reluctantly, lay
burdens upon others; and as if capacity were, so to speak, dealt
out to me mercifully — but by armfuls.

Old age until the very end brought no grave changes in
physical conditions. He missed sorely his devoted friend,
Sir Andrew Clark, to whose worth as man and skill as
healer he had borne public testimony in May 1894. But
for physician's service there was no special need. His
ordinary life, though of diminished power, suffered little
interruption. 'The attitude,' he wrote, 'in which I endeavoured to fix myself was that of a soldier on parade, in a
line of men drawn up ready to march and waiting for the
word of command. I sought to be in preparation for prompt
obedience, feeling no desire to go, but on the other hand
without reluctance because firmly convinced that whatever
He ordains for us is best, best both for us and for all.'

He worked with all his old zest at his edition of Bishop
Butler, and his volume of studies subsidiary to Butler. He
wrote to the Duke of Argyll (Dec. 5, 1895) : —

I find my Butler a weighty undertaking, but I hope it will be
useful at least for the important improvements of form which I
am making.

It is very difficult to keep one's temper in dealing with M.
Arnold when he touches on religious matters. His patronage of
a Christianity fashioned by himself is to me more offensive and

trying than rank unbelief. But I try, or seem to myself to try, to
shrink from controversy of which I have had so much. Organic
evolution sounds to me a Butlerish idea, but I doubt if he ever
employed either term, certainly he has not the phrase, and I
cannot as yet identify the passage to which you may refer.

Dec. 9. — Many thanks for your letter. The idea of evolution is
without doubt deeply ingrained in Butler. The case of the animal
creation had a charm for him, and in his first chapter he opens,
without committing himself, the idea of their possible elevation to
a much higher state. I have always been struck by the glee with
which negative writers strive to get rid of ' special creation,' as if
by that method they got the idea of God out of their way, whereas
I know not what right they have to say that the small increments
effected by the divine workman are not as truly special as the
large. It is remarkable that Butler has taken such hold both on
nonconformists in England and outside of England, especially on
those bodies in America which are descended from English nonconformists.

He made progress with his writings on the Olympian
Religion, without regard to Acton's warnings and exhorta-
tions to read a score of volumes by learned explorers with
uncouth names. He collected a new series of his *Gleanings.*
By 1896 he had got his cherished project of hostel and
library at St. Deiniol's in Hawarden village, near to its
launch. He was drawn into a discussion on the validity of
anglican orders, and even wrote a letter to Cardinal Ram-
polla, in his effort to realise the dream of Christian unity.
The Vatican replied in such language as might have been
expected by anybody with less than Mr. Gladstone's in-
extinguishable faith in the virtues of argumentative persuasion. Soon he saw the effects of Christian disunion
upon a bloodier stage. In the autumn of this year he was
roused to one more vehement protest like that twenty years
before against the abominations of Turkish rule, this time
in Armenia. He had been induced to address a meeting in
Chester in August 1895, and now a year later he travelled to
Liverpool (Sept. 24) to a non-party gathering at Hengler's
Circus. He always described this as the place most agreeable
to the speaker of all those with which he was acquainted.

'Had I the years of 1876 upon me,' he said to one of his sons, 'gladly would I start another campaign, even if as long as that.' To discuss, almost even to describe, the course of his policy and proceedings in the matter of Armenia, would bring us into a mixed controversy affecting statesmen now living, who played an unexpected part, and that controversy may well stand over for another, and let us hope a very distant, day. Whether we had a right to interfere single-handed; whether we were bound as a duty to interfere under the Cyprus Convention; whether our intervention would provoke hostilities on the part of other Powers and even kindle a general conflagration in Europe; whether our severance of diplomatic relations with the Sultan or our withdrawal from the concert of Europe would do any good; what possible form armed intervention could take — all these are questions on which both liberals and tories vehemently differed from one another then, and will vehemently differ again. Mr. Gladstone was bold and firm in his replies. As to the idea, he said, that all independent action on the part of this great country was to be made chargeable for producing war in Europe, 'that is in my opinion a mistake almost more deplorable than almost any committed in the history of diplomacy.' We had a right under the convention. We had a duty under the responsi-bilities incurred at Paris in 1856, at Berlin in 1878. The upshot of his arguments at Liverpool was that we should break off relations with the Sultan; that we should under-take not to turn hostilities to our private advantage; that we should limit our proceedings to the suppression of mischief in its aggravated form; and if Europe threatened us with war it might be necessary to recede, as France had receded under parallel circumstances from her individual policy on the eastern question in 1840, — receded without loss either of honour or power, believing that she had been right and wise and others wrong and unwise.

If Mr. Gladstone had still had, as he puts it, 'the years of 1876,' he might have made as deep a mark. As it was, his speech at Liverpool was his last great deliverance to a public audience. As the year ended this was his birthday entry: —

Dec. 29, 1896. — My long and tangled life this day concludes its CHAP. 87th year. My father died four days short of that term. I know IX. of no other life so long in the Gladstone family, and my profession Æt. 87. has been that of politician, or, more strictly, minister of state, an extremely short-lived race when their scene of action has been in the House of Commons, Lord Palmerston being the only complete exception. In the last twelve months eyes and ears may have declined, but not materially. The occasional contraction of the chest is the only inconvenience that can be called new. I am not without hope that Cannes may have a [illegible] to act upon it. The blessings of family life continue to be poured in the largest measure upon my unworthy head. Even my temporal affairs have thriven. Still old age is appointed for the gradual loosening and succeeding snapping of the threads. I visited Lord Stratford when he was, say, 90 or 91 or thereabouts. He said to me, ' It is not a blessing.' As to politics, I think the basis of my mind is laid principally in finance and philanthropy. The prospects of the first are darker than I have ever known them. Those of the second are black also, but with more hope of some early dawn. I do not enter on interior matters. It is so easy to write, but to write honestly nearly impossible. Lady Grosvenor gave me to-day a delightful present of a small crucifix. I am rather too independent of symbol.

This is the last entry in the diaries of seventy years.

At the end of January 1897, the Gladstones betook themselves once more to Lord Rendel's *palazzetto*, as they called it, at Cannes.

I had hoped during this excursion, he journalises, to make much way with my autobiographica. But this was in a large degree frustrated, first by invalidism, next by the eastern question, on which I was finally obliged to write something.[1] Lastly, and not least, by a growing sense of decline in my daily amount of brain force available for serious work. My power to read (but to read very slowly indeed since the cataract came) for a considerable number of hours daily, thank God, continues. This is a great mercy. While on my outing, I may have read, of one kind and another, twenty volumes. Novels enter into this list

---

[1] *Letter to the Duke of Westminster.*

rather considerably. I have begun seriously to ask myself whether I shall ever be able to face 'The Olympian Religion.'

The Queen happened to be resident at Cimiez at this time, and Mr. Gladstone wrote about their last meeting : —

> A message came down to us inviting us to go into the hotel and take tea with the Princess Louise. We repaired to the hotel, and had our tea with Miss Paget, who was in attendance. The Princess soon came in, and after a short delay we were summoned into the Queen's presence. No other English people were on the ground. We were shown into a room tolerably, but not brilliantly lighted, much of which was populated by a copious supply of Hanoverian royalties. The Queen was in the inner part of the room, and behind her stood the Prince of Wales and the Duke of Cambridge. Notwithstanding my enfeebled sight, my vision is not much impaired for practical purposes in cases such as this, where I am thoroughly familiar with the countenance and whole contour of any person to be seen. My wife preceded, and Mary followed me. The Queen's manner did not show the old and usual vitality. It was still, but at the same time very decidedly kind, such as I had not seen it for a good while before my final resignation. She gave me her hand, a thing which is, I apprehended, rather rare with men, and which had never happened with me during all my life, though that life, be it remembered, had included some periods of rather decided favour. Catherine sat down near her, and I at a little distance. For a good many years she had habitually asked me to sit. My wife spoke freely and a good deal to the Queen, but the answers appeared to me to be very slight. As to myself, I expressed satisfaction at the favourable accounts I had heard of the accommodation at Cimiez, and perhaps a few more words of routine. To speak frankly, it seemed to me that the Queen's peculiar faculty and habit of conversation had disappeared. It was a faculty, not so much the free offspring of a rich and powerful mind, as the fruit of assiduous care with long practice and much opportunity. After about ten minutes, it was signified to us that we had to be presented to all the other royalties, and so passed the remainder of this meeting.

In the early autumn of 1897 he found himself affected by

what was supposed to be a peculiar form of catarrh. He
went to stay with Mr. Armitstead at Butterstone in Perth-
shire. I saw him on several occasions afterwards, but this
was the last time when I found him with all the freedom,
full self-possession, and kind geniality of old days. He was
keenly interested at my telling him that I had seen James
Martineau a few days before, in his cottage further north in
Inverness-shire ; that Martineau, though he had now passed
his ninety-second milestone on life's road, was able to walk
five or six hundred feet up his hillside every day, was at his
desk at eight each morning, and read theology a good many
hours before he went to bed at night. Mr. Gladstone's conversation was varied, glowing, full of reminiscence. He had
written me in the previous May, hoping among other kind
things that 'we may live more and more in sympathy and
communion.' I never saw him more attractive than in the
short pleasant talks of these three or four days. He discussed
some of the sixty or seventy men with whom he had been
associated in cabinet life,[1] freely but charitably, though he
named two whom he thought to have behaved worse to him
than others. He repeated his expression of enormous admiration for Graham. Talked about his own voice. After he had
made his long budget speech in 1860, a certain member, supposed to be an operatic expert, came to him and said, 'You
must take great care, or else you will destroy the *colour* in
your voice.' He had kept a watch on general affairs. The
speech of a foreign ruler upon divine right much incensed him.
He thought that Lord Salisbury had managed to set the Turk
up higher than he had reached since the Crimean war ; and
his policy had weakened Greece, the most liberal of the
eastern communities. We fought over again some old
battles of 1886 and 1892-4. Mr. Armitstead had said to
him — ' Oh, sir, you'll live ten years to come.' 'I do trust,'
he answered as he told me this, 'that God in his mercy
will spare me that.'

II

Then came months of distress. The facial annoyance
grew into acute and continued pain, and to pain he proved

[1] For the list see Appendix.

to be exceedingly sensitive. It did not master him, but there were moments that seemed almost of collapse and defeat. At last the night was gathering

> About the burning crest
> Of the old, feeble, and day-wearied sun.[1]

They took him at the end of November (1897) to Cannes, to the house of Lord Rendel.

Sometimes at dinner he talked with his host, with Lord Welby, or Lord Acton, with his usual force, but most of the time he lay in extreme suffering and weariness, only glad when they soothed him with music. It was decided that he had better return, and in hope that change of air might even yet be some palliative, he went to Bournemouth, which he reached on February 22. For weeks past he had not written nor read, save one letter that he wrote in his journey home to Lady Salisbury upon a rather narrow escape of her husband's in a carriage accident. On March 18 his malady was pronounced incurable, and he learned that it was likely to end in a few weeks. He received the verdict with perfect serenity and with a sense of unutterable relief, for his sufferings had been cruel. Four days later he started home to die. On leaving Bournemouth before stepping into the train, he turned round, and to those who were waiting on the platform to see him off, he said with quiet gravity, 'God bless you and this place, and the land you love.' At Hawarden he bore the dreadful burden of his pain with fortitude, supported by the ritual ordinances of his church and faith. Music soothed him, the old composers being those he liked best to hear. Messages of sympathy were read to him, and he listened silently or with a word of thanks.

'The retinue of the whole world's good wishes' flowed to the 'large upper chamber looking to the sunrising, where the aged pilgrim lay.' Men and women of every communion offered up earnest prayers for him. Those who were of no communion thought with pity, sympathy, and sorrow of

> A Power passing from the earth
> To breathless Nature's dark abyss.

---

[1] *King John.*

From every rank in social life came outpourings in every CHAP.
key of reverence and admiration. People appeared — as   IX.
is the way when death comes — to see his life and char- Æt. 89.
acter as a whole, and to gather up in his personality,
thus transfigured by the descending shades, all the best
hopes and aspirations of their own best hours. A certain
grandeur overspread the moving scene. Nothing was there
for tears. It was 'no importunate and heavy load.' The
force was spent, but it had been nobly spent in devoted and
effective service for his country and his fellow-men.

From the Prince of the Black Mountain came a telegram:
'Many years ago, when Montenegro, my beloved country,
was in difficulties and in danger, your eloquent voice and
powerful pen successfully pleaded and worked on her behalf.
At this time vigorous and prosperous, with a bright future
before her, she turns with sympathetic eye to the great
English statesman to whom she owes so much, and for whose
present sufferings she feels so deeply.' And he answered by
a message that 'his interest in Montenegro had always been
profound, and he prayed that it might prosper and be blessed
in all its undertakings.'

Of the thousand salutations of pity and hope none went
so much to his heart as one from Oxford — an expression of
true feeling, in language worthy of her fame : —

At yesterday's meeting of the hebdomadal council, wrote the
vice-chancellor, an unanimous wish was expressed that I should
convey to you the message of our profound sorrow and affection at
the sore trouble and distress which you are called upon to endure.
While we join in the universal regret with which the nation
watches the dark cloud which has fallen upon the evening of a
great and impressive life, we believe that Oxford may lay claim to
a deeper and more intimate share in this sorrow. Your brilliant
career in our university, your long political connection with it,
and your fine scholarship, kindled in this place of ancient learning,
have linked you to Oxford by no ordinary bond, and we cannot
but hope that you will receive with satisfaction this expression of
deep-seated kindliness and sympathy from us.

We pray that the Almighty may support you and those near

and dear to you in this trial, and may lighten the load of suffering which you bear with such heroic resignation.

To this he listened more attentively and over it he brooded long, then he dictated to his youngest daughter sentence by sentence at intervals his reply: —

There is no expression of Christian sympathy that I value more than that of the ancient university of Oxford, the God-fearing and God-sustaining university of Oxford. I served her, perhaps mistakenly, but to the best of my ability. My most earnest prayers are hers to the uttermost and to the last.

When May opened, it was evident that the end was drawing near. On the 13th he was allowed to receive visits of farewell from Lord Rosebery and from myself, the last persons beyond his household to see him. He was hardly conscious. On the early morning of the 19th, his family all kneeling around the bed on which he lay in the stupor of coming death, without a struggle he ceased to breathe. Nature outside — wood and wide lawn and cloudless far-off sky — shone at her fairest.

III

On the day after his death, in each of the two Houses the leader made the motion, identical in language in both cases save the few final words about financial provision in the resolution of the Commons: —

That an humble Address be presented to her Majesty praying that her Majesty will be graciously pleased to give directions that the remains of the Right Hon. William Ewart Gladstone be interred at the public charge, and that a monument be erected in the Collegiate Church of St. Peter, Westminster, with an inscription expressive of the public admiration and attachment and of the high sense entertained of his rare and splendid gifts, and of his devoted labours to parliament and in great offices of state, and to assure her Majesty that this House will make good the expenses attending the same.

The language of the movers was worthy of the British parliament at its best, worthy of the station of those who

used it, and worthy of the figure commemorated. Lord
Salisbury was thought by most to go nearest to the core of
the solemnity : —

What is the cause of this unanimous feeling? Of course, he
had qualities that distinguished him from all other men; and
you may say that it was his transcendent intellect, his astonishing power of attaching men to him, and the great influence he
was able to exert upon the thought and convictions of his contemporaries. But these things, which explain the attachment, the
adoration of those whose ideas he represented, would not explain
why it is that sentiments almost as fervent are felt and expressed
by those whose ideas were not carried out by his policy. My
Lords, I do not think the reason is to be found in anything so
far removed from the common feelings of mankind as the abstruse
and controversial questions of the policy of the day. They had
nothing to do with it. Whether he was right, or whether he
was wrong, in all the measures, or in most of the measures
which he proposed — those are matters of which the discussion
has passed by, and would certainly be singularly inappropriate
here; they are really remitted to the judgment of future generations, who will securely judge from experience what we can only
decide by forecast. It was on account of considerations more
common to the masses of human beings, to the general working
of the human mind, than any controversial questions of policy
that men recognised in him a man guided — whether under mistaken impressions or not, it matters not — but guided in all the
steps he took, in all the efforts that he made, by a high moral
ideal. What he sought were the attainments of great ideals,
and, whether they were based on sound convictions or not, they
could have issued from nothing but the greatest and the purest
moral aspirations; and he is honoured by his countrymen, because through so many years, across so many vicissitudes and
conflicts, they had recognised this one characteristic of his action,
which has never ceased to be felt. He will leave behind him,
especially to those who have followed with deep interest the
history of the later years — I might almost say the later months
of his life — he will leave behind him the memory of a great
Christian statesman. Set up necessarily on high — the sight of

his character, his motives, and his intentions would strike all the world. They will have left a deep and most salutary influence on the political thought and the social thought of the generation in which he lived, and he will be long remembered not so much for the causes in which he was engaged or the political projects which he favoured, but as a great example, to which history hardly furnishes a parallel, of a great Christian man.

Mr. Balfour, the leader in the Commons, specially spoke of him as ' the greatest member of the greatest deliberative assembly that the world has seen,' and most aptly pointed to Mr. Gladstone's special service in respect of that assembly.

One service he did, in my opinion incalculable, which is altogether apart from the judgment that we may be disposed to pass upon particular opinions, or particular lines of policy which Mr. Gladstone may from time to time have advocated. Sir, he added a dignity, as he added a weight, to the deliberations of this House by his genius, which I think it is impossible adequately to replace. It is not enough for us to keep up simply a level, though it be a high level, of probity and of patriotism. The mere average of civic virtue is not sufficient to preserve this Assembly from the fate that has overcome so many other Assemblies, products of democratic forces. More than this is required; more than this was given to us by Mr. Gladstone. He brought to our debates a genius which compelled attention, he raised in the public estimation the whole level of our proceedings, and they will be most ready to admit the infinite value of his service who realise how much of public prosperity is involved in the maintenance of the worth of public life, and how perilously difficult most democracies apparently feel it to be to avoid the opposite dangers into which so many of them have fallen.

Sir William Harcourt spoke of him as friend and official colleague : —

I have heard men who knew him not at all, who have asserted that the supremacy of his genius and the weight of his authority oppressed and overbore those who lived with him and those who worked under him. Nothing could be more untrue. Of all chiefs he was the least exacting. He was the most kind, the most tolerant, he was the most placable. How seldom in this House was the voice of personal anger heard from his lips. These are the true marks of greatness.

Lord Rosebery described his gifts and powers, his concentration, the multiplicity of his interests, his labour of every day, and almost of every hour of every day, in fashioning an intellect that was mighty by nature. And besides this panegyric on the departed warrior, he touched with felicity and sincerity a note of true feeling in recalling to his hearers

the solitary and pathetic figure, who for sixty years, shared all the sorrows and all the joys of Mr. Gladstone's life, who received his confidence and every aspiration, who shared his triumphs with him and cheered him under his defeats; who by her tender vigilance, I firmly believe, sustained and prolonged his years.

When the memorial speeches were over the House of Commons adjourned. The Queen, when the day of the funeral came, telegraphed to Mrs. Gladstone from Balmoral : —

My thoughts are much with you to-day, when your dear husband is laid to rest. To-day's ceremony will be most trying and painful for you, but it will be at the same time gratifying to you to see the respect and regret evinced by the nation for the memory of one whose character and intellectual abilities marked him as one of the most distinguished statesmen of my reign. I shall ever gratefully remember his devotion and zeal in all that concerned my personal welfare and that of my family.

IV

It was not at Westminster only that his praise went forth. Famous men, in the immortal words of Pericles to his Athenians, have the whole world for their tomb; they are commemorated not only by columns and inscriptions in their own land ; in foreign lands too a memorial of them is graven in the hearts of men. So it was here. No other statesman on our famous roll has touched the imagination of so wide a world.

The colonies through their officers or more directly, sent
to Mrs. Gladstone their expression of trust that the world-
wide admiration and esteem of her honoured and illustrious
husband would help her to sustain her burden of sorrow. The
ambassador of the United States reverently congratulated
her and the English race everywhere, upon the glorious
completion of a life filled with splendid achievements and
consecrated to the noblest purposes. The President followed
in the same vein, and in Congress words were found to
celebrate a splendid life and character. The President of
the French republic wished to be among the first to associate
himself with Mrs. Gladstone's grief : ' By the high liberality
of his character,' he said, ' and by the nobility of his political
ideal, Mr. Gladstone had worthily served his country and
humanity.' The entire French government requested the
British ambassador in Paris to convey the expression of their
sympathy and assurance of their appreciation, admiration,
and respect for the character of the illustrious departed.
The Czar of Russia telegraphed to Mrs. Gladstone: ' I
have just received the painful news of Mr. Gladstone's
decease, and consider it my duty to express to you my feelings of sincere sympathy on the occasion of the cruel and
irreparable bereavement which has befallen you, as well as
the deep regret which this sad event has given me. The
whole of the civilised world will beweep the loss of a great
statesman, whose political views were so widely humane and
peaceable.'

In Italy the sensation was said to be as great as when
Victor Emmanuel or Garibaldi died. The Italian parliament
and the prime minister telegraphed to the effect that ' the
cruel loss which had just struck England, was a grief
sincerely shared by all who are devoted to liberty. Italy
has not forgotten, and will never forget, the interest and
sympathy of Mr. Gladstone in events that led to its independence.' In the same key, Greece : the King, the first
minister, the university, the chamber, declared that he was
entitled to the gratitude of the Greek people, and his name
would be by them for ever venerated. From Roumania,
Macedonia, Norway, Denmark, tributes came ' to the great

memory of Gladstone, one of the glories of mankind.' Never
has so wide and honourable a pomp all over the globe followed
an English statesman to the grave.

IV

On May 25, the remains were brought from Hawarden,
and in the middle of the night the sealed coffin was placed
in Westminster Hall, watched until the funeral by the piety
of relays of friends.   For long hours each day great multitudes filed past the bier.   It was a striking demonstration
of national feeling, for the procession contained every rank,
and contingents came from every part of the kingdom.   On
Saturday, May 28, the body was committed to the grave in
Westminster Abbey.   No sign of high honour was absent.
The heir to the throne and his son were among those who
bore the pall.   So were the prime minister and the two
leaders of the parties in both Houses.   The other pall-bearers
were Lord Rosebery who had succeeded him as prime
minister, the Duke of Rutland who had half a century
before been Mr. Gladstone's colleague at Newark, and Mr.
Armitstead and Lord Rendel, who were his private friends.
Foreign sovereigns sent their representatives, the Speaker of
the House of Commons was there in state, and those were
there who had done stout battle against him for long years;
those also who had sat with him in council and stood by
his side in frowning hours.   At the head of the grave was
'the solitary and pathetic figure' of his wife.   Even men
most averse to all pomps and shows on the occasions and
scenes that declare so audibly their nothingness, here were
only conscious of a deep and moving simplicity, befitting a
great citizen now laid among the kings and heroes.   Two
years later, the tomb was opened to receive the faithful and
devoted companion of his life.

CHAPTER X

FINAL

BOOK X. ANYBODY can see the host of general and speculative questions raised by a career so extraordinary. How would his fame have stood if his political life had ended in 1854, or 1874, or 1881, or 1885? What light does it shed upon the working of the parliamentary system; on the weakness and strength of popular government; on the good and bad of political party; on the superiority of rule by cabinet or by an elected president; on the relations of opinion to law? Here is material for a volume of disquisition, and nobody can ever discuss such speculations without reference to power as it was exercised by Mr. Gladstone. Those thronged halls, those vast progresses, those strenuous orations — what did they amount to? Did they mean a real moulding of opinion, an actual impression, whether by argument or temper or personality or all three, on the minds of hearers? Or was it no more than the same kind of interest that takes men to stage-plays with a favourite performer? This could hardly be, for his hearers gave him long spells of power and a practical authority that was unique and supreme. What thoughts does his career suggest on the relations of Christianity to patriotism, or to empire, or to what has been called neo-paganism? How many points arise as to the dependence of ethics on dogma? These are deep and living and perhaps burning issues, not to be discussed at the end of what the reader may well have found a long journey. They offer themselves for his independent consideration.

I

Mr. Gladstone's own summary of the period in which he

had been so conspicuous a figure was this, when for him the
drama was at an end : —

Of his own career, he says, it is a career certainly chargeable with many errors of judgment, but I hope on the whole, governed at least by uprightness of intention and by a desire to learn. The personal aspect may now readily be dismissed as it concerns the past. But the public aspect of the period which closes for me with the fourteen years (so I love to reckon them) of my formal connection with Midlothian is too important to pass without a word. I consider it as beginning with the Reform Act of Lord Grey's government. That great Act was for England improvement and extension, for Scotland it was political birth, the beginning of a duty and a power, neither of which had attached to the Scottish nation in the preceding period. I rejoice to think how the solemnity of that duty has been recognised, and how that power has been used. The three-score years offer us the pictures of what the historian will recognise as a great legislative and administrative period — perhaps, on the whole, the greatest in our annals. It has been predominantly a history of emancipation — that is of enabling man to do his work of emancipation, political, economical, social, moral, intellectual. Not numerous merely, but almost numberless, have been the causes brought to issue, and in every one of them I rejoice to think that, so far as my knowledge goes, Scotland has done battle for the right.

Another period has opened and is opening still — a period possibly of yet greater moral dangers, certainly a great ordeal for those classes which are now becoming largely conscious of power, and never heretofore subject to its deteriorating influences. These have been confined in their actions to the classes above them, because they were its sole possessors. Now is the time for the true friend of his country to remind the masses that their present political elevation is owing to no principles less broad and noble than these — the love of liberty, of liberty for all without distinction of class, creed or country, and the resolute preference of the interests of the whole to any interest, be it what it may, of a narrower scope.[1]

A year later, in bidding farewell to his constituents ' with

[1] Letter to Sir John Cowan, March 17, 1894.

sentiments of gratitude and attachment that can never be effaced,' he proceeds : —

Though in regard to public affairs many things are disputable, there are some which belong to history and which have passed out of the region of contention. It is, for example as I conceive, beyond question that the century now expiring has exhibited since the close of its first quarter a period of unexampled activity both in legislative and administrative changes; that these changes, taken in the mass, have been in the direction of true and most beneficial progress; that both the conditions and the franchises of the people have made in relation to the former state of things, an extraordinary advance; that of these reforms an overwhelming proportion have been effected by direct action of the liberal party, or of statesmen such as Peel and Canning, ready to meet odium or to forfeit power for the public good; and that in every one of the fifteen parliaments the people of Scotland have decisively expressed their convictions in favour of this wise, temperate, and in every way remarkable policy.[1]

To charge him with habitually rousing popular forces into dangerous excitement, is to ignore or misread his action in some of the most critical of his movements. 'Here is a man,' said Huxley, 'with the greatest intellect in Europe, and yet he debases it by simply following majorities and the crowd.' He was called a mere mirror of the passing humours and intellectual confusions of the popular mind. He had nothing, said his detractors, but a sort of clever pilot's eye for winds and currents, and the rising of the tide to the exact height that would float him and his cargo over the bar. All this is the exact opposite of the truth. What he thought was that the statesman's gift consisted in insight into the facts of a particular era, disclosing the existence of material for forming public opinion and directing public opinion to a given purpose. In every one of his achievements of high mark — even in his last marked failure of achievement — he expressly formed, or endeavoured to form and create, the public opinion upon which he knew that in the last resort he must depend.

[1] July 1, 1895.

We have seen the triumph of 1853.[1] Did he, in renewing the most hated of taxes, run about anxiously feeling the pulse of public opinion? On the contrary, he grappled with the facts with infinite labour — and half his genius was labour — he built up a great plan; he carried it to the cabinet; they warned him that the House of Commons would be against him; the officials of the treasury told him the Bank would be against him; that a strong press of commercial interests would be against him. Like the bold and sinewy athlete that he always was, he stood to his plan; he carried the cabinet; he persuaded the House of Commons; he vanquished the Bank and the hostile interests; and in the words of Sir Stafford Northcote, he changed and turned for many years to come, a current of public opinion that seemed far too powerful for any minister to resist. In the tempestuous discussions during the seventies on the policy of this country in respect of the Christian races of the Balkan Peninsula, he with his own voice created, moulded, inspired, and kindled with resistless flame the whole of the public opinion that eventually guided the policy of the nation with such admirable effect both for its own fame, and for the good of the world. Take again the Land Act of 1881, in some ways the most deep-reaching of all his legislative achievements. Here he had no flowing tide, every current was against him. He carried his scheme against the ignorance of the country, against the prejudice of the country, and against the standing prejudices of both branches of the legislature, who were steeped from the crown of the head to the sole of the foot in the strictest doctrines of contract.

Then his passion for economy, his ceaseless war against public profusion, his insistence upon rigorous keeping of the national accounts — in this great department of affairs he led and did not follow. In no sphere of his activities was he more strenuous, and in no sphere, as he must well have known, was he less likely to win popularity. For democracy is spendthrift; if, to be sure, we may not say that most forms of government are apt to be the same.

In a survey of Mr. Gladstone's performances, some would

[1] See vol. i. p. 457.

place this of which I have last spoken, as foremost among
his services to the country. Others would call him greatest
in the associated service of a skilful handling and adjustment of the burden of taxation ; or the strengthening of the
foundations of national prosperity and well-being by his
reformation of the tariff. Yet others again choose to remember him for his share in guiding the successive extensions of popular power, and simplifying and purifying
electoral machinery. Irishmen at least, and others so far
as they are able to comprehend the history and vile wrongs
and sharp needs of Ireland, will have no doubt what rank in
legislation they will assign to the establishment of religious
equality and agrarian justice in that portion of the realm.
Not a few will count first the vigour with which he repaired
what had been an erroneous judgment of his own and of vast
hosts of his countrymen, by his courage in carrying through
the submission of the Alabama claims to arbitration. Still
more, looking from west to east, in this comparison among
his achievements, will judge alike in its result and in the
effort that produced it, nothing equal to the valour and
insight with which he burst the chains of a mischievous and
degrading policy as to the Ottoman empire. When we look
at this exploit, how in face of an opponent of genius and
authority and a tenacity not inferior to his own, in face of
strongly rooted tradition on behalf of the Turk, and an easily
roused antipathy against the Russian, by his own energy
and strength of arm he wrested the rudder from the hand of
the helmsman and put about the course of the ship, and held
England back from the enormity of trying to keep several
millions of men and women under the yoke of barbaric
oppression and misrule, — we may say that this great feat
alone was fame enough for one statesman. Let us make
what choice we will of this or that particular achievement,
how splendid a list it is of benefits conferred and public
work effectually performed. Was he a good parliamentary
tactician, they ask ? Was his eye sure, his hand firm, his
measurement of forces, distances, and possibilities of change
in wind and tide accurate ? Did he usually hit the proper
moment for a magisterial intervention ? Experts did not

always agree on his quality as tactician. At least he was
pilot enough to bring many valuable cargoes safely home.

He was one of the three statesmen in the House of
Commons of his own generation who had the gift of large
and spacious conception of the place and power of England
in the world, and of the policies by which she could maintain
it. Cobden and Disraeli were the other two. Wide as the
poles asunder in genius, in character, and in the mark they
made upon the nation, yet each of these three was capable
of wide surveys from high eminence. But Mr. Gladstone's
performances in the sphere of active government were
beyond comparison.

Again he was often harshly judged by that tenacious class
who insist that if a general principle be sound, there can never
be a reason why it should not be applied forthwith, and that
a rule subject to exceptions is not worth calling a rule; and
the worst of it is that these people are mostly the salt of the
earth. In their impatient moments they dismissed him as
an opportunist, but whenever there was a chance of getting
anything done, they mostly found that he was the only man
with courage and resolution enough to attempt to do it. In
thinking about him we have constantly to remember, as Sir
George Lewis said, that government is a very rough affair
at best, a huge rough machine, not the delicate springs,
wheels, and balances of a chronometer, and those concerned
in working it have to be satisfied with what is far below the
best. 'Men have no business to talk of disenchantment,'
Mr. Gladstone said; 'ideals are never realised.' That is no
reason, he meant, why men should not persist and toil and
hope, and this is plainly the true temper for the politician.
Yet he did not feed upon illusions. 'The history of nations,'
he wrote in 1876, 'is a melancholy chapter; that is, the
history of governments is one of the most immoral parts of
human history.'

II

It might well be said that Mr. Gladstone took too little,
rather than too much trouble to be popular. His religious
conservatism puzzled and irritated those who admired and

shared his political liberalism, just as churchmen watched with uneasiness and suspicion his radical alliances. Neither those who were churchmen first, nor those whose interests were keenest in politics, could comprehend the union of what seemed incompatibles, and because they could not comprehend they sometimes in their shallower humours doubted his sincerity. Mr. Gladstone was never, after say 1850, really afraid of disestablishment; on the contrary he was much more afraid of the perils of establishment for the integrity of the faith. Yet political disestablishers often doubted him, because they had not logic enough to see that a man may be a fervent believer in anglican institutions and what he thinks catholic tradition, and yet be as ready as Cavour for the principle of free church in free state.

It is curious that some of the things that made men suspicious, were in fact the liveliest tokens of his sincerity and simplicity. With all his power of political imagination, yet his mind was an intensely literal mind. He did not look at an act or a decision from the point of view at which it might be regarded by other people. Ewelme, the mission to the Ionian Islands, the royal warrant, the affair of the judicial committee, vaticanism, and all the other things that gave offence, and stirred misgivings even in friends, showed that the very last question he ever asked himself was how his action would look; what construction might be put upon it, or even would pretty certainly be put upon it; whom it would encourage, whom it would estrange, whom it would perplex. Is the given end right, he seemed to ask; what are the surest means; are the means as right as the end, as right as they are sure? But right — on strict and literal construction. What he sometimes forgot was that in political action, construction is part of the act, nay, may even be its most important part.[1]

The more you make of his errors, the more is the need to explain his vast renown, the long reign of his authority, the substance and reality of his powers. We call men great for many reasons apart from service wrought or eminence of intellect or even from force and depth of character. To

[1] See *Guardian*, Feb. 25, 1874.

have taken a leading part in transactions of decisive moment; to have proved himself able to meet demands on which high issues hung; to combine intellectual qualities, though moderate yet adequate and sufficient, with the moral qualities needed for the given circumstance — with daring, circumspection, energy, intrepid initiative; to have fallen in with one of those occasions in the world that impart their own greatness even to a mediocre actor, and surround his name with a halo not radiating from within but shed upon him from without — in all these and many other ways men come to be counted great. Mr. Gladstone belongs to the rarer class who acquired authority and fame by transcendent qualities of genius within, in half independence of any occasions beyond those they create for themselves.

III

Of his attitude in respect of church parties, it is not for me to speak. He has himself described at least one aspect of it in a letter to an inquirer, which would be a very noble piece by whomsoever written, and in the name of whatsoever creed or no-creed, whether Christian or Rationalist or Nathan the Wise Jew's creed. It was addressed to a clergyman who seems to have asked of what section Mr. Gladstone considered himself an adherent : —

Feb. 4, 1865. — It is impossible to misinterpret either the intention or the terms of your letter; and I thank you for it sincerely. But I cannot answer the question which you put to me, and I think I can even satisfy you that with my convictions I should do wrong in replying to it in any manner. Whatever reason I may have for being painfully and daily conscious of every kind of unworthiness, yet I am sufficiently aware of the dignity of religious belief to have been throughout a political life, now in its thirty-third year, steadily resolved never by my own voluntary act to make it the subject of any compact or assurance with a view to a political object. You think (and pray do not suppose I make this matter of complaint) that I have been associated with one party in the church of England, and that I may now lean rather towards another. . . . There is no one about whom information can be more easily had than myself. I have had and have friends of many colours, churchmen high and low, presbyterians, Greeks, Roman catholics, dissenters, who can speak abundantly, though perhaps not very well of me. And further, as member for the university, I have honestly endeavoured at all times to put my constituents in possession of all I could convey to them that could be considered as in the nature of a fact, by answering as explicitly as I was able all questions relating to the matters, and they are numerous enough, on which I have had to act or speak. Perhaps I shall surprise you by what I have yet further to say. I have never by any conscious act yielded my allegiance to any person or party in matters of religion. You and others may have called me (without the least offence) a churchman of some particular kind, and I have more than once seen announced in print my own secession from the church of England. These things I have not commonly contradicted, for the atmosphere of religious controversy and contradiction is as odious as the atmosphere of mental freedom is precious, to me; and I have feared to lose the one and be drawn into the other, by heat and bitterness creeping into the mind. If another chooses to call himself, or to call me, a member of this or that party, I am not to complain. But I respectfully claim the right not to call myself so, and on this claim, I have I believe acted throughout my life, without a single exception; and I feel that were I to waive it, I should at once put in hazard that allegiance to Truth, which is at once the supreme duty and the supreme joy of life. I have only to add the expression of my hope that in what I have said there is nothing to hurt or to offend you; and, if there be, very heartily to wish it unsaid.

Yet there was never the shadow of mistake about his own fervent faith. As he said to another correspondent: —

Feb. 5, 1876. — I am in principle a strong denominationalist. 'One fold and one shepherd' was the note of early Christendom. The shepherd is still one and knows his sheep; but the folds are many; and, without condemning any others, I am of opinion that it is best for us all that we should all of us be jealous for the honour of whatever we have and hold as positive truth, appertaining to the Divine Word and the foundation and history of

the Christian community. I admit that this question becomes
one of circumstance and degree, but I take it as I find it defined for myself by and in my own position.

IV

Of Mr. Gladstone as orator and improvisatore, enough has been said and seen. Besides being orator and statesman he was scholar and critic. Perhaps scholar in his interests, not in abiding contribution. The most copious of his productions in this delightful but arduous field was the three large volumes on *Homer and the Homeric Age*, given to the world in 1858. Into what has been well called the whirlpool of Homeric controversies, the reader shall not here be dragged. Mr. Gladstone himself gave them the go-by, with an indifference and disdain such as might have been well enough in the economic field if exhibited towards a protectionist farmer, or a partisan of retaliatory duties on manufactured goods, but that were hardly to the point in dealing with profound and original critics. What he too contemptuously dismissed as Homeric 'bubble-schemes,' were in truth centres of scientific illumination. At the end of the eighteenth century Wolf's famous *Prolegomena* appeared, in which he advanced the theory that Homer was no single poet, nor a name for two poets, nor an individual at all; the *Iliad* and *Odyssey* were collections of independent lays, folk-lore and folk-songs connected by a common set of themes, and edited, redacted, or compacted about the middle of the sixth century before Christ. A learned man of our own day has said that F. A. Wolf ought to be counted one of the half dozen writers that within the last three centuries have most influenced thought. This would bring Wolf into line with Descartes, Newton, Locke, Kant, Rousseau, or whatever other five master-spirits of thought from then to now the judicious reader may select. The present writer has assuredly no competence to assign Wolf's place in the history of modern criticism, but straying aside for a season from the green pastures of Hansard, and turning over again the slim volume of a hundred and fifty pages in which Wolf discusses his theme, one may easily discern a fountain of broad streams of modern thought (apart from the particular thesis) that to Mr. Gladstone, by the force of all his education and his deepest prepossessions, were in the highest degree chimerical and dangerous.

He once wrote to Lord Acton (1889) about the Old Testament and Mosaic legislation: —

Now I think that the most important parts of the argument have in a great degree a solid standing ground apart from the destructive criticism on dates and on the text: and I am sufficiently aware of my own rawness and ignorance in the matter not to allow myself to judge definitely, or condemn. I feel also that I have a prepossession derived from the criticisms in the case of Homer. Of them I have a very bad opinion, not only in themselves, but as to the levity, precipitancy, and shallowness of mind which they display; and here I do venture to speak, because I believe myself to have done a great deal more than any of the destructives in the examination of the text, which is the true source of the materials of judgment. They are a soulless lot; but there was a time when they had possession of the public ear as much I suppose as the Old Testament destructives now have, within their own precinct. It is only the constructive part of their work on which I feel tempted to judge; and I must own that it seems to me sadly wanting in the elements of rational probability.

This unpromising method is sufficiently set out when he says: 'I find in the plot of the *Iliad* enough of beauty, order, and structure, not merely to sustain the supposition of its own unity, but to bear an independent testimony, should it be still needed, to the existence of a personal and individual Homer as its author.' [1] From such a method no permanent contribution could come.

Yet scholars allow that Mr. Gladstone in these three volumes, as well as in *Juventus Mundi* and his *Homeric Primer*, has added not a little to our scientific knowledge of the Homeric poems,[2] by his extraordinary mastery of the text, the result of unwearied and prolonged industry, aided

[1] iii. p. 396.
[2] For instance, Geddes, *Problem of the Homeric Poems*, 1878, p. 16.

by a memory both tenacious and ready. Taking his own point of view, moreover, anybody who wishes to have his feeling about the *Iliad* and *Odyssey* as delightful poetry refreshed and quickened, will find inspiring elements in the profusion, the eager array of Homer's own lines, the diligent exploration of aspects and bearings hitherto unthought of. The 'theo-mythology' is commonly judged fantastic, and has been compared by sage critics to Warburton's *Divine Legation* — the same comprehensive general reading, the same heroic industry in marshalling the particulars of proof, the same dialectical strength of arm, and all brought to prove an unsound proposition.[1] Yet the comprehensive reading and the particulars of proof are by no means without an interest of their own, whatever we may think of the proposition; and here, as in all his literary writing distinguished from polemics, he abounds in the ethical elements. Here perhaps more than anywhere else he impresses us by his love of beauty in all its aspects and relations, in the human form, in landscape, in the affections, in animals, including above all else that sense of beauty which made his Greeks take it as one of the names for nobility in conduct. Conington, one of the finest of scholars, then lecturing at Oxford on Latin poets and deep in his own Virgilian studies, which afterwards bore such admirable fruit, writes at length (Feb. 14, 1857) to say how grateful he is to Mr. Gladstone for the care with which he has pursued into details a view of Virgil that they hold substantially in common, and proceeds with care and point to analyse the quality of the Roman poet's art, as some years later he defended against Munro the questionable proposition of the superiority in poetic style of the graceful, melodious, and pathetic Virgil to Lucretius's mighty muse.

No field has been more industriously worked for the last forty years than this of the relations of paganism to the historic religion that followed it in Europe. The knowledge and the speculations into which Mr. Gladstone was thus initiated in the sixties may now seem crude enough; but he deserves some credit in English, though not in view of

[1] Pattison, ii. p. 166.

German, speculation for an early perception of an unfamiliar region of comparative science, whence many a product most unwelcome to him and alien to his own beliefs has been since extracted. When all is said, however, Mr. Gladstone's place is not in literary or critical history, but elsewhere.

His style is sometimes called Johnsonian, but surely without good ground. Johnson was not involved and he was clear, and neither of these things can always be said of Mr. Gladstone. Some critic charged him in 1840 with 'prolix clearness.' The old charge, says Mr. Gladstone upon this, was 'obscure compression. I do not doubt that both may be true, and the former may have been the result of a well-meant effort to escape from the latter.' He was fond of abstract words, or the nearer to abstract the better, and the more general the better. One effect of this was undoubtedly to give an indirect, almost a shifty, air that exasperated plain people. Why does he beat about the bush, they asked; why cannot he say what he means? A reader might have to think twice or thrice or twenty times before he could be sure that he interpreted correctly. But then people are so apt to think once, or half of once; to take the meaning that suits their own wish or purpose best, and then to treat that as the only meaning. Hence their perplexity and wrath when they found that other doors were open, and they thought a mistake due to their own hurry was the result of a juggler's trick. On the other hand a good writer takes all the pains he can to keep his reader out of such scrapes.

His critical essays on Tennyson and Macaulay are excellent. They are acute, discriminating, generous. His estimate of Macaulay, apart from a piece of polemical church history at the end, is perhaps the best we have. 'You make a very just remark,' said Acton to him, 'that Macaulay was afraid of contradicting his former self, and remembered all he had written since 1825. At that time his mind was formed, and so it remained. What literary influences acted on the formation of his political opinions, what were his religious sympathies, and what is his exact place among historians, you have rather avoided discussing. There is still something to say on these points.' To Tennyson Mr. Gladstone believed himself to have been unjust, especially in the passages of *Maud* devoted to the war-frenzy, and when he came to reprint the article he admitted that he had not sufficiently remembered that he was dealing with a dramatic and imaginative composition.[1] As he frankly said of himself, he was not strong in the faculties of the artist, but perhaps Tennyson himself in these passages was prompted much more by politics than by art. Of this piece of retractation the poet truly said, 'Nobody but a noble-minded man would have done that.'[2] Mr. Gladstone would most likely have chosen to call his words a qualification rather than a recantation. In either case, it does not affect passages that give the finest expression to one of the very deepest convictions of his life, — that war, whatever else we may choose to say of it, is no antidote for Mammon-worship and can never be a cure for moral evils : —

It is, indeed, true that peace has its moral perils and temptations for degenerate man, as has every other blessing, without exception, that he can receive from the hand of God. It is moreover not less true that, amidst the clash of arms, the noblest forms of character may be reared, and the highest acts of duty done; that these great and precious results may be due to war as their cause; and that one high form of sentiment in particular, the love of country, receives a powerful and general stimulus from the bloody strife. But this is as the furious cruelty of Pharaoh made place for the benign virtue of his daughter; as the butchering sentence of Herod raised without doubt many a mother's love into heroic sublimity; as plague, as famine, as fire, as flood, as every curse and every scourge that is wielded by an angry Providence for the chastisement of man, is an appointed instrument for tempering human souls in the seven-times heated furnace of affliction, up to the standard of angelic and archangelic virtue.

War, indeed, has the property of exciting much generous and noble feeling on a large scale; but with this special recommendation it has, in its modern forms especially, peculiar and unequalled evils. As it has a wider sweep of desolating power than the rest,

[1] *Gleanings*, ii. p. 147. [2] *Life*, i. p. 398.

BOOK
X.

so it has the peculiar quality that it is more susceptible of being decked in gaudy trappings, and of fascinating the imagination of those whose proud and angry passions it inflames. But it is, on this very account, a perilous delusion to teach that war is a cure for moral evil, in any other sense than as the sister tribulations are. The eulogies of the frantic hero in *Maud*, however, deviate into grosser folly. It is natural that such vagaries should overlook the fixed laws of Providence. Under these laws the mass of mankind is composed of men, women, and children who can but just ward off hunger, cold, and nakedness; whose whole ideas of Mammon-worship are comprised in the search for their daily food, clothing, shelter, fuel; whom any casualty reduces to positive want; and whose already low estate is yet further lowered and ground down, when 'the blood-red blossom of war flames with its heart of fire.' . . .

Still war had, in times now gone by, ennobling elements and tendencies of the less sordid kind. But one inevitable characteristic of modern war is, that it is associated throughout, in all particulars, with a vast and most irregular formation of commercial enterprise. There is no incentive to Mammon-worship so remarkable as that which it affords. The political economy of war is now one of its most commanding aspects. Every farthing, with the smallest exceptions conceivable, of the scores or hundreds of millions which a war may cost, goes directly, and very violently, to stimulate production, though it is intended ultimately for waste or for destruction. Even apart from the fact that war suspends, *ipso facto*, every rule of public thrift, and tends to sap honesty itself in the use of the public treasure for which it makes such unbounded calls, it therefore is the greatest feeder of that lust of gold which we are told is the essence of commerce, though we had hoped it was only its occasional besetting sin. It is, however, more than this; for the regular commerce of peace is tameness itself compared with the gambling spirit which war, through the rapid shiftings and high prices which it brings, always introduces into trade. In its moral operation it more resembles, perhaps the finding of a new gold-field, than anything else.

More remarkable than either of these two is his piece on Leopardi (1850), the Italian poet, whose philosophy and frame of mind, said Mr. Gladstone, 'present more than any other that we know, more even than that of Shelley, the character of unrelieved, unredeemed desolation — the very qualities in it which attract pitying sympathy, depriving it of all seductive power.' It is curious that he should have selected one whose life lay along a course like Leopardi's for commemoration, as a man who in almost every branch of mental exertion seems to have had the capacity for attaining, and generally at a single bound, the very highest excellence. 'There are many things,' he adds, 'in which Christians would do well to follow him : in the warmth of his attachments ; in the moderation of his wants ; in his noble freedom from the love of money ; in his all-conquering assiduity.' [1] Perhaps the most remarkable sentence of all is this : '. . . what is not needful, and is commonly wrong, namely, is to pass a judgment on our fellow-creatures. Never let it be forgotten that there is scarcely a single moral action of a single man of which other men can have such a knowledge, in its ultimate grounds, its surrounding incidents, and the real determining causes of its merits, as to warrant their pronouncing a conclusive judgment upon it.'

The translation of poetry into poetry, as Coleridge said, is difficult because the translator must give brilliancy without the warmth of original conception, from which such brilliancy would follow of its own accord. But we must not judge Mr. Gladstone's translation either of Horace's odes or of detached pieces from Greek or Italian, as we should judge the professed man of letters or poet like Coleridge himself. His pieces are the diversions of the man of affairs, with educated tastes and interest in good literature. Perhaps the best single piece is his really noble rendering of Manzoni's noble ode on the death of Napoleon ; for instance : —

> From Alp to farthest Pyramid,
>   From Rhine to Mansanar,
>   How sure his lightning's flash foretold
>   His thunderbolts of war !
> To Don from Scilla's height they roar,
> From North to Southern shore.

---

[1] *Gleanings*, ii. p. 129.

And this was glory? After-men,
 Judge the dark problem. Low
We to the Mighty Maker bend
 The while, Who planned to show
What vaster mould Creative Will
 With him could fill.

  . . . .

As on the shipwrecked mariner
 The weltering wave's descent —
The wave, o'er which, a moment since,
 For distant shores he bent
And bent in vain, his eager eye;
 So on that stricken head
Came whelming down the mighty Past.
 How often did his pen
Essay to tell the wondrous tale
 For after times and men,
And o'er the lines that could not die
 His hand lay dead.

How often, as the listless day
 In silence died away,
He stood with lightning eye deprest,
 And arms across his breast,
And bygone years, in rushing train,
Smote on his soul amain :
 The breezy tents he seemed to see,
 And the battering cannon's course,
 And the flashing of the infantry,
 And the torrent of the horse,
And, obeyed as soon as heard,
 Th' ecstatic word.

Always let us remember that his literary life was part
of the rest of his life, as literature ought to be. He was
no mere reader of many books, used to relieve the strain
of mental anxiety or to slake the thirst of literary or intellectual curiosity. Reading with him in the days of his
full vigour was a habitual communing with the master
spirits of mankind, as a vivifying and nourishing part of life.
As we have seen, he would not read Dante in the session,
nor unless he could have a large draught. Here as elsewhere in the ordering of his days he was methodical,
systematic, full.

V

Though man of action, yet Mr. Gladstone too has a place by character and influences among what we may call the abstract, moral, spiritual forces that stamped the realm of Britain in his age. In a new time, marked in an incomparable degree by the progress of science and invention, by vast mechanical, industrial, and commercial development, he accepted it all, he adjusted his statesmanship to it all, nay, he revelled in it all, as tending to ameliorate the lot of the 'mass of men, women, and children who can just ward off hunger, cold, and nakedness.' He did not rail at his age, he strove to help it. Following Walpole and Cobden and Peel in the policies of peace, he knew how to augment the material resources on which our people depend. When was Britain stronger, richer, more honoured among the nations — I do not say always among the diplomatic chanceries and governments — than in the years when Mr. Gladstone was at the zenith of his authority among us? When were her armed forces by sea and land more adequate for defence of every interest? When was her material resource sounder? When was her moral credit higher? Besides all this, he upheld a golden lamp.

The unending revolutions of the world are for ever bringing old phases uppermost again. Events from season to season are taken to teach sinister lessons, that the Real is the only Rational, force is the test of right and wrong, the state has nothing to do with restraints of morals, the ruler is emancipated. Speculations in physical science were distorted for alien purposes, and survival of the fittest was taken to give brutality a more decent name. Even new conceptions and systems of history may be twisted into release of statesmen from the conscience of Bishop Butler's plain man. This gospel it was Mr. Gladstone's felicity to hold at bay. Without bringing back the cosmopolitanism of the eighteenth century, without sharing all the idealisms of the middle of the nineteenth, he resisted with his whole might the odious contention that moral progress in the relations of nations and states to one another is an illusion and a dream.

This vein perhaps brings us too near to the regions of
dissertation. Let us rather leave off with thoughts and
memories of one who was a vivid example of public duty
and of private faithfulness; of a long career that with every
circumstance of splendour, amid all the mire and all the
poisons of the world, lighted up in practice even for those
who have none of his genius and none of his power his
own precept, 'Be inspired with the belief that life is a
great and noble calling ; not a mean and grovelling thing,
that we are to shuffle through as we can, but an elevated
and lofty destiny.'

APPENDIX

Page 103

Mr. Gladstone to Lord Granville

Cannes, Jan. 22, 1883. — To-day I have been a good deal distressed by a passage as reported in Hartington's very strong and able speech, for which I am at a loss to account, so far does it travel out into the open, and so awkward are the intimations it seems to convey. I felt that I could not do otherwise than telegraph to you in cipher on the subject. But I used words intended to show that, while I thought an immediate notification needful, I was far from wishing to hasten the reply, and desired to leave altogether in your hands the mode of touching a delicate matter. Pray use the widest discretion.

I console myself with thinking it is hardly possible that Hartington can have meant to say what nevertheless both *Times* and *Daily News* make him seem to say, namely, that we recede from, or throw into abeyance, the declarations we have constantly made about our desire to extend local government, properly so called, to Ireland on the first opportunity which the state of business in parliament would permit. We announced our intention to do this at the very moment when we were preparing to suspend the Habeas Corpus Act. Since that time we have seen our position in Ireland immensely strengthened, and the leader of the agitation has even thought it wise, and has dared, to pursue a somewhat conciliatory course. Many of his coadjutors are still as vicious, it may be, as ever, but how can we say (for instance) to the Ulster men, you shall remain with shortened liberties and without local government, because Biggar & Co. are hostile to British connection?

There has also come prominently into view a new and powerful set of motives which, in my deliberate judgment, require us, for the sake of the United Kingdom even more than for the sake of Ireland, to push forward this question. Under the present highly centralised system of government, every demand which can be started on behalf of a poor and ill-organised country, comes directly on the British government and treasury; if refused it becomes at once a head of grievance, if granted not only a new drain but a certain source of political complication and embarrass-

553

ment. The peasant proprietary, the winter's distress, the state of the labourers, the loans to farmers, the promotion of public works, the encouragement of fisheries, the promotion of emigration, each and every one of these questions has a sting, and the sting can only be taken out of it by our treating it in correspondence with a popular and responsible Irish body, competent to act for its own portion of the country.

Every consideration which prompted our pledges, prompts the recognition of them, and their extension, rather than curtailment. The Irish government have in preparation a Local Government bill. Such a bill may even be an economy of time. By no other means that I can see shall we be able to ward off most critical and questionable discussions on questions of the class I have mentioned. The argument that we cannot yet trust Irishmen with popular local institutions is the mischievous argument by which the conservative opposition to the Melbourne government resisted, and finally crippled, the reform of municipal corporations in Ireland. By acting on principles diametrically opposite, we have broken down to thirty-five or forty what would have been a party, in this parliament, of sixty-five home rulers, and have thus arrested (or at the very least postponed) the perilous crisis, which no man has as yet looked in the face; the crisis which will arise when a large and united majority of Irish members demand some fundamental change in the legislative relations of the two countries. I can ill convey to you how clear are my thoughts, or how earnest my convictions, on this important subject. . . .

GENERAL GORDON'S INSTRUCTIONS

Page 153

The following is the text of General Gordon's Instructions (Jan. 18, 1884): —

Her Majesty's government are desirous that you should proceed at once to Egypt, to report to them on the military situation in the Soudan, and on the measures it may be advisable to take for the security of the Egyptian garrisons still holding positions in that country, and for the safety of the European population in Khartoum. You are also desired to consider and report upon the best mode of effecting the evacuation of the interior of the Soudan, and upon the manner in which the safety and good administration by the Egyptian government of the ports on the sea coast can best be secured. In connection with this subject you should pay especial consideration to the question of the steps that may usefully be taken to counteract the stimulus which it is feared may possibly be given to the slave trade by the present insurrectionary movement, and by the withdrawal of the Egyptian authority from the interior. You will be under the instructions of Her Majesty's agent and consul-general at Cairo, through whom your reports to Her Majesty's government should be sent under flying seal. You will consider yourself authorised and instructed to perform such other duties as the Egyptian government may desire to entrust to you, and as may be communicated to you by Sir E. Baring. You will be accompanied by Colonel Stewart, who will assist you in the duties thus confided to you. On your arrival in Egypt you will at once communicate with Sir E. Baring, who will arrange to meet you and will settle with you whether you should proceed direct to Suakin or should go yourself or despatch Colonel Stewart *viâ* the Nile.

THE MILITARY POSITION IN THE SOUDAN, APRIL 1885

Page 179

This Memorandum, dated April 9, 1885, was prepared by Mr. Gladstone for the cabinet : —

The commencement of the hot season appears, with other circumstances, to mark the time for considering at large our position in the Soudan. Also a declaration of policy is now demanded from us in nearly all quarters. . . . . When the betrayal of Khartoum had been announced, the desire and intention of the cabinet were to reserve for a later decision the question of an eventual advance upon that place, should no immediate movement on it be found possible. The objects they had immediately in view were to ascertain the fate of Gordon, to make every effort on his behalf, and to prevent the extension of the area of disturbance.

But Lord Wolseley at once impressed upon the cabinet that he required, in order to determine his immediate military movements, to know whether they were to be based upon the plan of an eventual advance on Khartoum, or whether the intention of such an advance was to be abandoned altogether. If the first plan were adopted, Lord Wolseley declared his power and intention to take Berber, and even gave a possible date for it, in the middle of March. The cabinet, adopting the phrase which Lord Wolseley had used, decided upon the facts as they then stood before it: (*a*) Lord Wolseley was to calculate upon proceeding to Khartoum after the hot season, to overthrow the power of the Mahdi there; (*b*) and, consequently, on this decision, they were to commence the construction of a railway from Suakin to Berber, in aid of the contemplated expedition; (*c*) an expedition was also to be sent against Osman Digna, which would open the road to Berber; but Lord Wolseley's demand for this expedition applied alike to each of the two military alternatives which he had laid before the cabinet.

There was no absolute decision to proceed to Khartoum at any time; and the declarations of ministers in parliament have treated it as a matter to be further weighed; but all steps have thus far been taken to prepare for it, and it has been regarded as at least probable. In approaching the question whether we are still to proceed on the same lines, it is necessary to refer to the motives which under the directions of the cabinet were stated by Lord Granville and by me, on the 19th of February, as having contributed to the decision. I copy out a part of the note from which he and I spoke:—

Objects in the Soudan which we have always deemed fit for consideration as far as circumstances might allow:—
1. The case of those to whom Gordon held himself bound in honour.
2. The possibility of establishing an orderly government at Khartoum.
3. Check to the slave trade.
4. The case of the garrisons.

A negative decision would probably have involved the abandonment at a stroke of all these objects. And also (we had to consider) whatever dangers, proximate or remote, in Egypt or in the East might follow from the triumphant position of the Mahdi; hard to estimate, but they may be very serious.

Two months, which have passed since the decision of the government (Feb. 5), have thrown light, more or less, upon the several points brought into view on the 19th February. 1. We have now no sufficient reason to assume that any of the population of Khartoum felt themselves bound to Gordon, or to have suffered on his account; or even that any large numbers of men in arms perished in the betrayal of the town, or took his part after the enemy were admitted into it. 2. We have had no tidings of anarchy at Khartoum, and we do not know that it is governed worse, or that the population is suffering more, than it would be under a Turkish or Egyptian ruler. 3. It is not believed that the possession of Khartoum is of any great value as regards the slave trade. 4. Or, after the failure of Gordon with respect to the garrisons, that the possession of Khartoum would, without further and formidable extensions of plan, avail for the purpose of relieving them. But further, what knowledge have we that these garrisons are unable to relieve themselves? There seems some reason to believe that the army of Hicks, when the action ceased, fraternised with the Mahdi's army, and that the same thing happened at Khartoum. Is there ground to suppose that they are hateful unless as representatives of Egyptian power? and ought they not to be released from any obligation to present themselves in that capacity?

With regard to the larger question of eventual consequences in Egypt or the East from the Mahdi's success at Khartoum, it is open to many views, and cannot be completely disposed of. But it may be observed — 1. That the Mahdi made a trial of marching down the Nile and speedily abandoned it, even in the first flush of his success. 2. That cessation of operations in the Soudan does not at this moment mean our military inaction in the East. 3. That the question is one of conflict, not with the arms of an

enemy, but with Nature in respect of climate and supply.
4. There remains also a grave question of justice, to which I
shall revert.

Should the idea of proceeding to Khartoum be abandoned, the
railway from Suakin, as now projected, would fall with it, since
it was adopted as a military measure, subsidiary to the advance
on Khartoum. The prosecution of it as a civil or commercial
enterprise would be a new proposal, to be examined on its merits.

The military situation appears in some respects favourable to
the re-examination of the whole subject. The general has found
himself unable to execute his intention of taking Berber, and this
failure alters the basis on which the cabinet proceeded in February,
and greatly increases the difficulty of the autumn enterprise. On
the one hand Wolseley's and Graham's forces have had five or six
considerable actions, and have been uniformly victorious. On the
other hand, the Mahdi has voluntarily retired from Khartoum,
and Osman Digna has been driven from the field, but cannot, as
Graham says, be followed into the mountains.[1] While the present
situation may thus seem opportune, the future of more extended
operations is dark. In at least one of his telegrams, Wolseley has
expressed a very keen desire to get the British army out of the
Soudan.[2] He has now made very large demands for the autumn
expedition, which, judging from previous experience and from
general likelihood, are almost certain to grow larger, as he comes
more closely to confront the very formidable task before him;
while in his letter to Lord Hartington he describes this affair to
be *the greatest 'since* 1815,' and expresses his hope that all the
members of the cabinet clearly understand this to be the case. He
also names a period of between two or three years for the completion of the railway, while he expresses an absolute confidence in
the power and resources of this country with vast effort to insure
success. He means without doubt military success. Political
success appears much more problematical.

There remains, however, to be considered a question which I
take to be of extreme importance. I mean the moral basis of the
projected military operations. I have from the first regarded the
rising of the Soudanese against Egypt as a justifiable and honourable revolt. The cabinet have, I think, never taken an opposite
view. Mr. Power, in his letter from Khartoum before Gordon's
arrival, is decided and even fervent in the same sense.

We sent Gordon on a mission of peace and liberation. From
such information as alone we have possessed, we found this
missionary of peace menaced and besieged, finally betrayed by
some of his troops, and slaughtered by those whom he came to set
free. This information, however, was fragmentary, and was also
one-sided. We have now the advantage of reviewing it as a whole,
of reading it in the light of events, and of some auxiliary evidence
such as that of Mr. Power.

I never understood how it was that Gordon's mission of peace

---

[1] Telegram of April 4.   [2] Despatch, March 9.

became one of war. But we knew the nobleness of his philanthropy, and we trusted him to the uttermost, as it was our duty to do. He never informed us that he had himself changed the character of the mission. It seemed strange that one who bore in his hands a charter of liberation should be besieged and threatened; but we took everything for granted in his favour, and against his enemies; and we could hardly do otherwise. Our obligations in this respect were greatly enhanced by the long interruption of telegraphic communication. It was our duty to believe that, if we could only know what he was prevented from saying to us, contradictions would be reconciled, and language of excess accounted for. We now know from the letters of Mr. Power that when he was at Khartoum with Colonel de Coetlogon before Gordon's arrival, a retreat on Berber had been actually ordered; it was regarded no doubt as a serious work of time, because it involved the removal of an Egyptian population;[1] but it was deemed feasible, and Power expresses no doubt of its accomplishment.[2] As far as, amidst its inconsistencies, a construction can be put on Gordon's language, it is to the effect that there was a population and a force attached to him, which he could not remove and would not leave.[3] But De Coetlogon did not regard this removal as impracticable, and was actually setting about it. Why Gordon did not prosecute it, why we hear no more of it from Power after Gordon's arrival, is a mystery. Instructed by results we now perceive that Gordon's title as governor-general might naturally be interpreted by the tribes in the light of much of the language used by him, which did not savour of liberation and evacuation, but of powers of government over the Soudan; powers to be used benevolently, but still powers of government. Why the Mahdi did not accept him is not hard to understand, but why was he not accepted by those local sultans, whom it was the basis of his declared policy to re-invest with their ancient powers, in spite of Egypt and of the Mahdi alike ? Was he not in short interpreted as associated with the work of Hicks, and did he not himself give probable colour to this interpretation? It must be borne in mind that on other matters of the gravest importance — on the use of Turkish force — on the use of British force — on the employment of Zobeir — Gordon announced within a very short time contradictory views, and never seemed to feel that there was any need of explanation, in order to account for the contradictions. There is every presumption, as well as every sign, that like fluctuation and inconsistency crept into his words and acts as to the liberation of the country; and this, if it was so, could not but produce ruinous effects. Upon the whole, it seems probable that Gordon, perhaps insensibly to himself, and certainly without our concurrence, altered the character of his mission, and worked in a considerable degree against our intentions and instructions.

There does not appear to be any question now of the security

[1] Power, p. 73 A.   [2] *Ibid.* 75 B.
[3] Egypt, No. 18, p. 34, 1884 (April) ; Egypt, No. 35, p. 122 (July 30).

of the army, but a most grave question whether we can demonstrate a necessity (nothing less will suffice) for making war on a people who are struggling against a foreign and armed yoke, not for the rescue of our own countrymen, not for the rescue *so far as we know* of an Egyptian population, but with very heavy cost of British life as well as treasure, with a serious strain on our military resources at a most critical time, and with the most serious fear that if we persist, we shall find ourselves engaged in an odious work of subjugation. The discontinuance of these military operations would, I presume, take the form of a suspension *sine die*, leaving the future open; would require attention to be paid to defence on the recognised southern frontier of Egypt, and need not involve any precipitate abandonment of Suakin.

HOME RULE BILL, 1886

Page 308

The following summary of the provisions of the Home Rule bill of 1886 supplements the description of the bill given in Chapter V. Book X. : —

One of the cardinal difficulties of all free government is to make it hard for majorities to act unjustly to minorities. You cannot make this injustice impossible but you may set up obstacles. In this case, there was no novelty in the device adopted. The legislative body was to be composed of two orders. The first order was to consist of the twenty-eight representative peers, together with seventy-five members elected by certain scheduled constituencies on an occupation franchise of twenty-five pounds and upwards. To be eligible for the first order, a person must have a property qualification, either in realty of two hundred pounds a year, or in personalty of the same amount, or a capital value of four thousand pounds. The representative peers now existing would sit for life, and, as they dropped off, the crown would nominate persons to take their place up to a certain date, and on the exhaustion of the twenty-eight existing peers, then the whole of the first order would become elective under the same conditions as the seventy-five other members.

The second order would consist of 206 members, chosen by existing counties and towns under the machinery now operative. The two orders were to sit and deliberate together, but either order could demand a separate vote. This right would enable a majority of one order to veto the proposal of the other. But the veto was only to operate until a dissolution, or for three years, whichever might be the longer interval of the two.

The executive transition was to be gradual. The office of viceroy would remain, but he would not be the minister of a party, nor quit office with an outgoing government. He would have a privy council; within that council would be formed an executive body of ministers like the British cabinet. This executive would be responsible to the Irish legislature, just as the executive government here is responsible to the legislature of this country. If any clause of a bill seemed to the viceroy to be *ultra vires*, he could refer it to the judicial committee of the privy council in London. The same reference, in respect of a section of an Irish Act, lay open either to the English secretary of state, or to a suitor, defendant, or other person concerned.

Future judges were to hold the same place in the Irish system as English judges in the English system; their office was to be during good behaviour; they were to be appointed on the advice of the Irish government, removable only on the joint address of the two orders, and their salaries charged on the Irish consolidated fund. The burning question of the royal Irish constabulary was dealt with provisionally. Until a local force was created by the new government, they were to remain at the orders of the lord lieutenant. Ultimately the Irish police were to come under the control of the legislative body. For two years from the passing of the Act, the legislative body was to fix the charge for the whole constabulary of Ireland.

In national as in domestic housekeeping, the figure of available income is the vital question. The total receipts of the Irish exchequer would be £8,350,000, from customs, excise, stamps, income-tax, and non-tax revenue. On a general comparison of the taxable revenues of Ireland and Great Britain, as tested more especially by the property passing under the death duties, the fair proportion due as Ireland's share for imperial purposes, such as interest on the debt, defence, and civil charge, was fixed at one-fifteenth. This would bring the total charge properly imperial up to £3,242,000. Civil charges in Ireland were put at £2,510,000, and the constabulary charge on Ireland was not to exceed £1,000,000, any excess over that sum being debited to England. The Irish government would be left with a surplus of £404,000. This may seem a ludicrously meagre amount, but, compared with the total revenue, it is equivalent to a surplus on our own budget of that date of something like five millions.

The true payment to imperial charges was to be £1,842,000 because of the gross revenue above stated of £1,400,000 though paid in Ireland in the first instance was really paid by British consumers of whisky, porter, and tobacco. This sum, deducted from £3,342,000, leaves the real Irish contribution, namely £1,842,000.

A further sum of uncertain, but substantial amount, would go to the Irish exchequer from another source, to which we have now to turn. With the proposals for self-government were coupled proposals for a settlement of the land question. The ground-work was an option offered to the landlords of being bought out under the terms of the Act. The purchaser was to be an Irish state authority, as the organ representing the legislative body. The occupier was to become the proprietor except in the congested districts, where the state authority was to be the proprietor. The normal price was to be twenty years' purchase of the net rental. The most important provision, in one sense, was that which recognised the salutary principle that the public credit should not be resorted to on such a scale as this merely for the benefit of a limited number of existing cultivators of the soil, without any direct advantage to the government as representing the community at large. That was effected by making the tenant pay an annual instalment, calculated on the gross rental, while the state authority would repay to the imperial treasury a percentage calculated on the net rental, and the state authority would pocket the difference, estimated to be about 18 per cent. on the sum payable to the selling landlord. How was all this to be secured? Principally, on the annuities paid by the tenants who had purchased their holdings, and if the holdings did not satisfy the charge, then on the revenues of Ireland. All public revenues whatever were to be collected by persons appointed by the Irish government, but these collectors were to pay over all sums that came into their hands to an imperial officer, to be styled a receiver-general. Through him all rents and Irish revenues whatever were to pass, and not a shilling was to be let out for Irish purposes until their obligations to the imperial exchequer had been discharged.

ON THE PLACE OF ITALY

Page 415

By the provisions of nature, Italy was marked out for a conservative force in Europe. As England is cut off by the channel, so is Italy by the mountains, from the continental mass. . . . If England commits follies they are the follies of a strong man who can afford to waste a portion of his resources without greatly affecting the sum total. . . . She has a huge free margin, on which she might scrawl a long list of follies and even crimes without damaging the letterpress. But where and what is the free margin in the case of Italy, a country which has contrived in less than a quarter of a century of peace, from the date of her restored independence, to treble (or something near it) the taxation of her people, to raise the charge of her debt to a point higher than that of England, and to arrive within one or two short paces of national bankruptcy? . . .

Italy by nature stands in alliance neither with anarchy nor with Caesarism, but with the cause and advocates of national liberty and progress throughout Europe. Never had a nation greater advantages from soil and climate, from the talents and dispositions of the people, never was there a more smiling prospect (if we may fall back upon the graceful fiction) from the Alpine tops, even down to the Sicilian promontories, than that which for the moment has been darkly blurred. It is the heart's desire of those, who are not indeed her teachers, but her friends, that she may rouse herself to dispel once and for ever the evil dream of what is not so much ambition as affectation, may acknowledge the true conditions under which she lives, and it perhaps may not yet be too late for her to disappoint the malevolent hopes of the foes of freedom, and to fulfil every bright and glowing prediction which its votaries have ever uttered on her behalf. — ' *The Triple Alliance and Italy's Place in it* ' (*Contemporary Review*, Oct. 1889).

THE GLASGOW PERORATION

Page 492

After describing the past history of Ireland as being for more than five hundred years ' *one almost unbroken succession of political storm and swollen tempest, except when those tempests were for a time interrupted by a period of servitude and by the stillness of death,*' *Mr. Gladstone went on :* —

Those storms are in strong contrast with the future, with the present. The condition of the Irish mind justifies us in anticipating. It recalls to my mind a beautiful legend of ancient paganism—for that ancient paganism, amongst many legends false and many foul, had also some that were beautiful. There were two Lacedæmonian heroes known as Castor and Pollux, honoured in their life and more honoured in their death, when a star was called after them, and upon that star the fond imagination of the people fastened lively conceptions; for they thought that when a ship at sea was caught in a storm, when dread began to possess the minds of the crew, and peril thickened round them, and even alarm was giving place to despair, that if then in the high heavens this star appeared, gradually and gently but effectually the clouds disappeared, the winds abated, the towering billows fell down to the surface of the deep, calm came where there had been uproar, safety came where there had been danger, and under the beneficent influence of this heavenly body the terrified and despairing crew came safely to port. The proposal which the liberal party of this country made in 1886, which they still cherish in their mind and heart, and which we trust and believe, they are about now to carry forward, that proposal has been to Ireland and the political relations of the two countries what the happy star was believed to be to the seamen of antiquity. It has produced already anticipations of love and good will, which are the first fruits of what is to come. It has already changed the whole tone and temper of the relations, I cannot say yet between the laws, but between the peoples and inhabitants of these two great islands. It has filled our hearts with hope and with joy, and it promises to give us in lieu of the terrible disturbances of other times, with their increasing, intolerable burdens and insoluble problems, the promise of a brotherhood exhibiting harmony and strength at home, and a

brotherhood which before the world shall, instead of being as it
hitherto has been for the most part, a scandal, be a model and an
example, and shall show that we whose political wisdom is for so
many purposes recognised by the nations of civilised Europe and
America have at length found the means of meeting this oldest
and worst of all our difficulties, and of substituting for disorder,
for misery, for contention, the actual arrival and the yet riper
promise of a reign of peace. — *Theatre Royal, Glasgow, July* 2, 1892.

THE NAVAL ESTIMATES OF 1894

The first paragraph of this memorandum will be found on p. 508 : —

This might be taken for granted as to 1854, 1870, and 1884.
That it was equally true in my mind of 1859 may be seen by any
one who reads my budget speech of July 18, 1859. I defended
the provision as required by and for the time, and for the time
only. The occasion in that year was the state of the continent.
It was immediately followed by the China war (No. 3) and by the
French affair (1861–2), but when these had been disposed of
economy began ; and, by 1863–4, the bulk of the new charge had
been got rid of.

There is also the case of the fortifications in 1860, which would
take me too long to state fully. But I will state briefly (1) my
conduct in that matter was mainly or wholly governed by regard
to peace, for I believed, and believe now, that in 1860 there were
only two alternatives ; one of them, the French treaty, and the
other, war with France. And I also believed in July 1860 that
the French treaty must break down, unless I held my office. (2)
The demand was reduced from nine millions to about five (has
this been done now ?) (3) I acted in concert with my old friend
and colleague, Sir James Graham. We were entirely agreed.

Terse figures of new estimates

The 'approximate figure' of charge involved in the new plan of
the admiralty is £4,240,000, say 4½ millions. Being an increase
(subject probably to some further increase in becoming an act)

1. On the normal navy estimate 1888–9 (*i.e.* before the Naval
   Defence Act) of, in round numbers,   . 4¼ millions
2. On the first year's total charge under the
   Naval Defence Act of (1, 979,000),   . 2 millions
3. On the estimates of last year 1893–94 of   3 millions
4. On the total charge of 1893–4 of (1,571,000) 1½ million
5. On the highest amount ever defrayed from
   the year's revenue (1892–3),   .   . 1½ million
6. On the highest expenditure of any year
   under the Naval Defence Act which included 1,150,000 of borrowed money,   . 359,000

MR. GLADSTONE'S CABINET COLLEAGUES

Page 525

The following is the list of the seventy ministers who served in cabinets of which Mr. Gladstone was a member: —

1843–45. Peel.
Wellington.
Lyndhurst.
Wharncliffe.
Haddington.
Buccleuch.
Aberdeen.
Graham.
Stanley.
Ripon.
Hardinge.
Goulburn.
Knatchbull.

1846. Ellenborough.
S. Herbert.
Granville Somerset.
Lincoln.

1852–55. Cranworth.
Granville.
Argyll.
Palmerston.
Clarendon.
C. Wood.
Molesworth.
Lansdowne.
Russell.
G. Grey.

1855. Panmure.
Carlisle.

1859–65. Campbell.
G. C. Lewis.
Duke of Somerset.
Milner Gibson.
Elgin.
C. Villiers.

1859–65. Cardwell.
Westbury.
Ripon.
Stanley of Alderley.

1865–66. Hartington.
Goschen.

1868–74. Hatherley.
Kimberley.
Bruce.
Lowe.
Childers.
Bright.
C. Fortescue.
Stansfeld.
Selborne.
Forster.

1880–85. Spencer.
Harcourt.
Northbrook.
Chamberlain.
Dodson.
Dilke.
Derby.
Trevelyan.
Lefevre.
Rosebery.

1886. Herschell.
C. Bannerman.
Mundella.
John Morley.

1892. Asquith.
Fowler.
Acland.
Bryce.
A. Morley.

CHRONOLOGY [1]

1880.

Feb. 'Free trade, railways and the growth of commerce,' in *Nineteenth Century.*

„ 27. At St. Pancras on obstruction, liberal unity and errors of government.

„ 27. On rules dealing with obstruction.

March 'Russia and England,' in *Nineteenth Century.*

„ 5. On motion in favour of local option.

„ 11. Issues address to electors of Midlothian.

„ 15. Criticises budget.

„ 17. At Music Hall, Edinburgh, on government's eastern policy.

„ 18. At Corstorphine on Anglo-Turkish convention.

„ 18. At Ratho on neglect of domestic legislation.

„ 19. At Davidson's Mains on indictment of the government. At Dalkeith on the government and class interests.

„ 20. At Juniper Green, and at Balerno, replies to tory criticism of liberal party. At Midcalder on abridgment of rights of parliament.

„ 22. At Gilmerton on church disestablishment. At Loanhead on the eastern policy of liberal and tory parties.

„ 23. At Gorebridge and at Pathhead.

„ 25. At Penicuik on Cyprus.

„ 30. At Stow on finance.

April 'Religion, Achaian and Semitic,' in *Nineteenth Century.*

„ 2. At West Calder on liberal record and shortcomings of the government.

1880.

April 5. Elected for Midlothian : Mr. Gladstone, 1579 ; Lord Dalkeith, 1368.

„ 7. Returns to Hawarden.

„ 28. Second administration formed.

May Anonymous article, 'The Conservative Collapse,' in *Fortnightly Review.*

„ 8. Returned unopposed for Midlothian.

„ 11. Publication of correspondence with Count Karolyi, Austrian ambassador.

„ 16. Receives deputation of farmers on agricultural reform.

„ 20. On government's Turkish policy.

„ 21. Moves reference to committee of Mr. Bradlaugh's claim to take his seat in parliament.

„ 25. On South African federation.

June 1. On government's policy regarding Cyprus.

„ 10. Introduces supplementary budget.

„ 16. On reduction of European armaments.

„ 18. On resolution in favour of local option. Moves second reading of Savings Banks bill.

„ 22. On resolution that Mr. Bradlaugh be allowed to make a declaration.

July 1. On Mr. Bradlaugh's case.

„ 5, 26. On Compensation for Disturbances (Ireland) bill.

„ 23. Explains government's policy regarding Armenia.

„ 30–Aug. 9. Confined to room by serious illness.

[1] All speeches unless otherwise stated were made in the House of Commons.

1880.

Aug. 26–Sept. 4. Makes sea trip in the *Grantully Castle* round England and Scotland.

Sept. 4. On government's Turkish policy.

Nov. 9. At lord mayor's banquet on Ireland and foreign and colonial questions.

1881.

Jan. 6. On Ireland.

,, 21. On annexation of Transvaal.

,, 28. On Irish Protection of Person and Property bill.

Feb. 3. Brings in closure resolution.

,, 23. Falls in garden at Downing Street.

March 15. Moves vote of condolence on assassination of Alexander ii.

,, 16. On grant in aid of India for expenses of Afghan war.

,, 28. On county government and local taxation.

April 4. Introduces budget.

,, 7. Brings in Land Law (Ireland) bill.

,, 26 and 27. On Mr. Bradlaugh's case.

May 2. Resigns personal trusteeship of British Museum.

,, 4. Supports Welsh Sunday Closing bill.

,, 5. Supports vote of thanks on military operations in Afghanistan.

,, 9. Tribute to Lord Beaconsfield.

,, 16. On second reading of Irish Land bill.

June 10. On the law of entail.

,, 24. On Anglo-Turkish convention.

July 25. On vote of censure on Transvaal.

,, 29. On third reading of Irish Land bill.

Aug. 6. At Mansion House on fifteen months' administration.

,, 18. On Mr. Parnell's vote of censure on the Irish executive.

Oct. 7. Presented with an address by corporation of Leeds: on land and ' fair trade.'

1881.

At banquet in Old Cloth Hall on Ireland.

Oct. 8. Presented with address by Leeds Chamber of Commerce: on free trade. Mass meeting of 25,000 persons in Old Cloth Hall on foreign and colonial policy.

,, 13. Presented with address by city corporation at Guildhall: on Ireland and arrest of Mr. Parnell.

,, 27. At Knowsley on the aims of the Irish policy.

Nov. 9. At lord mayor's banquet on government's Irish policy and parliamentary procedure.

1882.

Jan. 12. At Hawarden on agriculture.

,, 31. On local taxation to deputation from chambers of agriculture.

Feb. 7. On Mr. Bradlaugh's claim.

,, 9. On home rule amendment to address.

,, 16. On the Irish demand for home rule.

,, 20. Moves first of new procedure rules.

,, 21. On local taxation.

,, 21 and 22. On Mr. Bradlaugh's case.

,, 27. Meeting of liberal party at Downing Street. On House of Lords' committee to inquire into Irish Land Act.

,, 27. Moves resolution declaring parliamentary inquiry into Land Act injurious to interests of good government.

March 3. On persecution of Jews in Russia.

,, 6. Supports resolution for legislation on parliamentary oaths.

,, 10. On proposed state acquisition of Irish railways.

,, 17. On British North Borneo Company's charter.

,, 21. On parliamentary reform.

,, 23. On grant to Duke of Albany.

,, 30. On closure resolution.

1882.

March 31. On inquiry into ecclesiastical commission.

April 17. Opposes motion for release of Cetewayo.

,, 18. On diplomatic communications with Vatican.

,, 24. Introduces budget.

,, 26. On the Irish Land Act Amendment bill.

May 2. Statement of Irish policy, announces release of 'suspects,' and resignation of Mr. Forster.

,, 4. On Mr. Forster's resignation.

,, 8. Moves adjournment of the House on assassination of Lord F. Cavendish and Mr. Burke.

,, 15. Brings in Arrears of Rent (Ireland) bill.

,, 19. On second reading of Prevention of Crime (Ireland) bill.

,, 22. On Arrears bill.

,, 24. On Prevention of Crime bill.

,, 26–June 1. On government's Egyptian policy.

June 14. On Egyptian crisis.

,, 17. On Mr. Bright's resignation.

July 12. On bombardment of Alexandria.

,, 21. On third reading of Arrears bill.

,, 24. Asks for vote of credit for £2,300,000.

,, 27. Concludes debate on vote of credit.

,, 28. On national expenditure.

Aug. 8. On Lords' amendments to Arrears bill.

,, 9. On suspension of Irish members, July 1.

,, 16. On events leading to Egyptian war.

Oct. 25–31, and Dec. 1. On twelve new rules of procedure.

,, 26. Moves vote of thanks to forces engaged in Egyptian campaign.

Nov. 24. Opposes demand for select committee on release of Mr. Parnell.

Dec. 13. Celebrates political jubilee.

1883.

Jan. 6–16. Suffers from sleeplessness at Hawarden.

1883.

Jan. 17. Leaves England for south of France.

March 2. Returns to London.

,, 14. On Irish Land Law (1881) Amendment bill.

,, 16. On Boer invasion of Bechuanaland.

April 3. On Channel tunnel.

,, 6. On increase in national expenditure.

,, 17. On local taxation.

,, 19. On Lords Alcester and Wolseley's annuity bills.

,, 26. On Parliamentary Oaths Act (1866) Amendment bill.

May 2. At National Liberal club on conservative legacy of 1880 and work of liberal administration, 1880–1883.

,, 7. On Contagious Diseases Acts.

,, 25. On reforms in Turkey.

,, 29. Meeting of liberal party at foreign office: on state of public business.

June 2. At Stafford House: tribute to Garibaldi.

,, 12. On revision of purchase clauses of Land Act.

,, 23. On withdrawal of provisional agreement for second Suez canal.

July 27. On India and payment for Egyptian campaign.

,, 30. On future negotiations with Suez canal company.

Aug. 6. On government's Transvaal and Zululand policies.

,, 6–7. On British occupation of Egypt.

,, 18. Protests against violent speeches of Irish members.

,, 21. On work of the session.

Sept. Italian translation of Cowper's hymn: 'Hark my soul! It is the Lord,' in *Nineteenth Century.*

,, 8–21. In *Pembroke Castle* round coast of Scotland to Norway and Copenhagen.

,, 13. At Kirkwall: on changes during half century of his political life.

1883.

Sept. 18. Entertains the Emperor and Empress of Russia, the King and Queen of Denmark, at dinner on board *Pembroke Castle* in Copenhagen harbour.

Dec. 22. At Hawarden, to deputation of liberal working men on reform of the franchise.

1884.

Jan. 5. At Hawarden on condition of agriculture.

,, 31. Receives deputations from Leeds conference, etc., on Franchise bill.

Feb. 11 and 21. On Mr. Bradlaugh's attempt to take the oath.

,, 12. On Egyptian and Soudan policy in reply to vote of censure.

,, 13. On re-establishment of grand committees.

,, 25. Moves resolution of thanks to Speaker Brand on his retirement.

,, 28. Explains provisions of Representation of the People (Franchise) bill.

March 3. In defence of retention of Suakin.

,, 6. On government's Egyptian policy.

,, 10–19. Confined to his room by a chill.

,, 19 to April 7. Recuperates at Coombe Warren.

,, 31. On death of Duke of Albany.

April 3. On General Gordon's mission in Soudan.

,, 7. On second reading of Franchise bill.

May 12. On vote of censure regarding General Gordon.

,, 27. On Egyptian financial affairs.

June 10. Opposes amendment to Franchise bill granting suffrage to women.

,, 23. On terms of agreement with France on Egypt.

,, 26. On third reading of Franchise bill.

July 8. On second reading of London Government bill.

,, 10. Meeting of the liberal party : on rejection of

1884.

Franchise bill by House of Lords.

July 11. On negotiations with Lord Cairns on Franchise bill.

,, 18. At Eighty club on relation of politics of the past to politics of the future.

Aug. 2. On failure of conference on Egyptian finance.

,, 11. On Lord Northbrook's mission to Egypt.

,, 30. At Corn Exchange, Edinburgh, on Lords and Franchise bill.

Sept. 1. At Corn Exchange, Edinburgh, in defence of his administration.

,, 2. In Waverley Market on demand of Lords for dissolution.

,, 26. Returns to Hawarden.

Oct. 16. Cuts first sod on Wirral railway : on railway enterprise.

,, 23. On Franchise bill.

,, 28. Defends Lord Spencer's Irish administration.

Nov. 4. Lays foundation stone of National Liberal club : on liberal administrations of past half century.

,, 6 and 10. On second reading of Franchise bill.

,, 21. On Mr. Labouchere's motion for reform of House of Lords.

Dec. 1. Brings in Redistribution bill.

,, 4. On second reading of Redistribution bill.

1885.

Feb. 23. On vote of censure on Soudan policy.

March 26. Moves ratification of Egyptian financial agreement.

April 9. Announces occupation of Penjdeh by Russians.

,, 16. In defence of Egyptian Loan bill.

,, 21. Asks for vote of credit for war preparations.

,, 27. On Soudan and Afghanistan.

May 4. Announces agreement with Russia on Afghan boundary dispute.

1885.

May 14. On Princess Beatrice's dowry.

June 8. Defends increase of duties on beer and spirits.

,, 9. Resignation of government.

,, 24. Reads correspondence on crisis.

July 6. On legislation on parliamentary oaths.

,, 7. On intentions of the new government.

Aug. 8–Sept. 1. In Norway.

Sept. 17. Issues address to Midlothian electors.

Nov. 'Dawn of Creation and of Worship,' in *Nineteenth Century.*

,, 9. At Albert Hall, Edinburgh, on proposals of Irish party.

,, 11. At Free Assembly Hall, Edinburgh, on disestablishment.

,, 17. At West Calder on Ireland, foreign policy, and free trade.

,, 21. At Dalkeith on finance and land reform.

,, 23. At inauguration of Market Cross, Edinburgh: on history of the cross.

,, 24. At Music Hall, Edinburgh, on tory tactics and Mr. Parnell's charges.

,, 27. Elected for Midlothian: Mr. Gladstone, 7879; Mr. Dalrymple, 3248.

1886.

Jan. 'Proem to Genesis: a Plea for a Fair Trial,' in *Nineteenth Century.*

,, 21. On government's policy in India, the Near East and Ireland.

,, 26. In support of amendment for allotments.

Feb. 3. Third administration formed.

,, 4. Issues address to electors of Midlothian.

,, 10. Returned unopposed for Midlothian.

,, 22. On comparative taxation of England and Ireland. On annexation of Burmah.

1886.

Feb. 23. On Ireland's contribution to imperial revenue.

March 4. On condition of Ireland.

,, 6–12. Confined to his room by a cold.

April 6. On death of Mr. W. E. Forster.

,, 8. Brings in Government of Ireland (Home Rule) bill.

,, 13. On first reading of Home Rule bill.

,, 16. Explains provisions of Irish Land Purchase bill.

May 1. Issues address to electors of Midlothian on Home Rule bill.

,, 10. Moves second reading of Home Rule bill.

,, 27. Meeting of liberal party at the foreign office: on the Home Rule bill.

,, 28. Explains intentions regarding the Home Rule bill.

June 7–8. Concludes debate on Home Rule bill.

,, 10. Announces dissolution of parliament.

,, 14. Issues address to electors of Midlothian.

,, 18. At Music Hall, Edinburgh, on home rule.

,, 21. At Music Hall, Edinburgh, on home rule.

,, 22. At Glasgow on home rule.

,, 25. At Free Trade Hall, Manchester, on home rule.

,, 28. At Liverpool on Ulster and home rule.

July 2. Returned unopposed for Midlothian and Leith.

,, 20. Resignation of third administration.

Aug. 19–24. On government's Irish policy.

,, 25. Leaves England for Bavaria.

,, 28. '*The Irish Question:* (1) *History of an Idea;* (2) *Lessons of the Election,*' published.

Sept. 19. Returns to London.

,, 20. On Tenants Relief (Ireland) bill.

Oct. 4. At Hawarden. Receives address signed by 400,000 women of Ireland: on home rule.

1887.

Jan.   '*Locksley Hall* and the Jubilee,' in *Nineteenth Century*.

,,   27.   Tribute to memory of Lord Iddesleigh.

,,   27.   On Lord Randolph Churchill's retirement and Ireland.

Feb.   'Notes and Queries on the Irish Demand,' in *Nineteenth Century*.

March   'The Greater Gods of Olympus: (1) Poseidon,' in *Nineteenth Century*.

,,   17.   To the liberal members for Yorkshire: on home rule.

,,   24.   On the exaction of excessive rents.

,,   29.   On Criminal Law Amendment (Ireland) bill.

April   'The History of 1852–60 and Greville's Latest Journals,' in *English Historical Review*.

,,   18.   On second reading of Criminal Law Amendment bill.

,,   19.   At Eighty club on liberal unionist grammar of dissent.

,,   25.   Criticise Mr. Goschen's budget.

May   'The Greater Gods of Olympus: (2) Apollo,' in *Nineteenth Century*.

,,   5.   Moves for select committee to inquire into the *Times* articles on 'Parnellism and Crime.'

,,   11.   At Dr. Parker's house on Ireland.

,,   31.   On Crimes bill at Hawarden.

June   Reviews Mr. Lecky's *History of England in the Eighteenth Century* in *Nineteenth Century*.

,,   'The Great Olympian Sedition,' in *Contemporary Review*.

,,   4.   At Swansea, on Welsh nationality, Welsh grievances, and the Irish Crimes bill.

,,   6.   At Singleton Abbey on home rule and retention of Irish members.

,,   7.   At Cardiff on home rule.

July   'The Greater Gods of

1887.

    Olympus: (3) Athene,' in *Nineteenth Century*.

,,   2.   To the liberal members for Durham on Lord Hartington's Irish record.

,,   7.   Moves rejection of Irish Criminal Law Amendment bill.

,,   9.   Presented at Dollis Hill with address signed by 10,689 citizens of New York.

,,   14.   On second reading of the Irish Land bill.

,,   16.   At National Liberal club: on Ireland and home rule movement in Scotland and Wales.

,,   29.   At Memorial Hall on the lessons of bye-elections.

Aug.   'Mr. Lecky and Political Morality,' in *Nineteenth Century*.

,,   16.   Lays first cylinder of railway bridge over the Dee: on railway enterprise and the Channel tunnel.

,,   25.   On proclamation of Irish land league.

,,   30.   At Hawarden on Queen Victoria's reign.

Sept.   'Electoral Facts of 1887,' in *Nineteenth Century*.

,,   12.   On riot at Mitchelstown, Ireland.

Oct.   'Ingram's History of the Irish Union,' in *Nineteenth Century*.

,,   4.   At Hawarden on the absolutist methods of government.

,,   18.   At National Liberal Federation, Nottingham, on conduct of Irish police.

,,   19.   At Skating Rink, Nottingham, on home rule.

,,   20.   At Drill Hall, Derby, on Ireland.

Nov.   'An Olive Branch from America,' in *Nineteenth Century*.

Dec.   27.   At Dover on free trade and Irish Crimes Act.

,,   28.   Leaves England for Italy.

1888.

    'A reply to Dr. Ingram,' in *Westminster Review*.

Jan.   'The Homeric Herê,' in *Contemporary Review*.

Feb.

1888.

Feb. 8. Returns to London.
,, 17. On coercion in Ireland.
March 'Further Notes and Queries on the Irish Demand,' in *Contemporary Review*.
,, 23. On perpetual pensions.
April 9. On the budget.
,, 11. At National Liberal club on the budget and Local Government bill.
,, 23. Moves an amendment in favour of equalising the death duties on real and personal property.
,, 25. On second reading of County Government (Ireland) bill.
May 'Robert Elsmere, and the Battle of Belief,' in *Nineteenth Century*.
,, A reply to Colonel Ingersoll on 'Christianity,' in *North American Review*.
,, 1. On government control of railways.
,, 2. Opens Gladstone library at National Liberal club: on books.
,, 9. At Memorial Hall on Irish question.
,, 26. At Hawarden condemns licensing clauses of Local Government bill.
,, 30. Receives deputation of 1500 Lancashire liberals at Hawarden.
June 18. On death of German Emperor.
,, 26. Condemns administration of Irish criminal law.
,, 27. On Channel Tunnel bill.
,, 30. At Hampstead on Ireland and the bye-elections.
July 'The Elizabethan Settlement of Religion,' in *Nineteenth Century*.
,, 6. On payment of members.
,, 18. To liberal members for Northumberland and Cumberland on Parnell commission and retention of Irish members.
,, 23. On second reading of Parnell Commission bill.
,, 25. Mr. and Mrs. Gladstone presented with their portraits on entering on fiftieth year of married life.

1888.

July 30. On composition of Parnell commission.
Aug. 20. Receives deputation of 1500 liberals at Hawarden: on conservative government of Ireland.
,, 23. At Hawarden on spade husbandry and the cultivation of fruit.
Sept. 'Mr. Forster and Ireland,' in *Nineteenth Century*.
,, 4. At Wrexham on Irish and Welsh home rule.
,, 4. At the Eisteddfod on English feeling towards Wales.
Nov. 'Queen Elizabeth and the Church of England,' in *Nineteenth Century*.
,, 5. At Town Hall, Birmingham, on liberal unionists and one man one vote.
,, 6. To deputation at Birmingham on labour representation and payment of members.
,, 7. At Bingley Hall, Birmingham, on Irish question.
,, 8. To deputation of Birmingham Irish National club on Irish grievances.
,, 19. On Irish Land Purchase bill.
Dec. 3. On Mr. Balfour's administration of Ireland.
,, 15. At Limehouse Town Hall on necessary English reforms and the Irish question.
,, 17. On English occupation of Suakin.
,, 19. Leaves England for Naples.

1889.

Jan. 'Daniel O'Connell,' in *Nineteenth Century*.
Feb. Reviews *Divorce* by Margaret Lee in *Nineteenth Century*.
,, 20. Returns to London.
March 1. On conciliatory measures in administration of Ireland.
,, 29. On death of John Bright.
April Reviews *For the Right* in *Nineteenth Century*.
,, 4. On £21,000,000 for naval defence.
,, 9. On Scotch home rule.

1889.

May	'Italy in 1888–89,' in *Nineteenth Century*.
,, 15.	On second reading of Welsh Education bill.
,, 16.	Moves amendment to Mr. Goschen's proposed death duties on estates above £10,000.
June 5.	At Southampton on lessons of the bye-elections.
,, 7.	At Romsey on Lord Palmerston.
,, 8.	At Weymouth on shorter parliaments and Ireland.
,, 10.	At Torquay on Ireland.
,, 11.	At Falmouth and Redruth on Ireland.
,, 12.	At Truro, St. Austell, and Bodmin on Ireland, one man one vote, the death duties, etc.
,, 14.	At Launceston on dissentient liberals.
,, 14.	At Drill Hall, Plymouth, on home rule.
,, 17.	At Shaftesbury and Gillingham on the agricultural labourer.
July	'Plain Speaking on the Irish Union,' in *Nineteenth Century*.
,, 6.	Presented with freedom of Cardiff; on free trade; on foreign opinion of English rule in Ireland.
,, 25.	Golden wedding celebrated in London.
,, 25.	Speech on royal grants.
Aug.	'Phœnician Affinities of Ithaca,' in *Nineteenth Century*.
,, 22.	At Hawarden on cottage gardens and fruit culture.
,, 26.	Celebration of golden wedding at Hawarden.
Sept. 7.	Entertained in Paris by Society of Political Economy.
,, 23.	At Hawarden on dock strike and bimetallism.
,,	'The Triple Alliance and Italy's Place in it,' by Outidanos, in *Contemporary Review*.
Oct.	Reviews *Journal de Marie Bashkirtseff* in *Nineteenth Century*.
,, 23.	At Southport on Ireland.
,, 26.	Opens literary institute at Saltney, Chester.

1889.

Nov.	'The English Church under Henry the Eighth,' in *Nineteenth Century*.
,,	'The Question of Divorce,' in *North American Review*.
Dec.	Reviews *Memorials of a Southern Planter* in *Nineteenth Century*.
,, 2.	At Free Trade Hall, Manchester, on liberal unionists and foreign policy.
,, 3.	In Free Trade Hall on government of Ireland.
,, 4.	At luncheon at Town Hall on city of Manchester.

1890.

Jan.	'A Defence of Free Trade,' in *North American Review*.
,,	'The Melbourne Government: its Acts and Persons,' in *Nineteenth Century*.
,, 9.	At Hawarden on the effect of free trade on agriculture.
,, 22.	At Chester on Ireland.
Feb. 5.	At Oxford Union on vestiges of Assyrian mythology in Homer.
,, 11.	On motion declaring publication by *Times* of forged Parnell letter to be breach of privilege.
March	'On Books and the Housing of Them,' in *Nineteenth Century*.
,, 3.	On report of Parnell commission.
,, 24.	At National Liberal club on report of Parnell commission.
,, 26.	At Guy's Hospital on the medical profession.
April 24.	On second reading of Purchase of Land (Ireland) bill.
May 2.	On disestablishment of church of Scotland.
,, 12.	On free trade at Prince's Hall, Piccadilly.
,, 15.	On Local Taxation Duties bill.
,, 16.	At Norwich on Parnell commission, land purchase and licensing question.
,, 17.	At Lowestoft on Siberian

1890.

atrocities and the agricultural labourer.

April 27. Receives 10,000 liberals at Hawarden : on Mitchelstown, Irish Land bill, and Licensing bill.

June 5. On Channel Tunnel bill.

,, 13. On Local Taxation Duties bill.

,, 18. To depositors in railways' savings banks : on thrift.

July 17. At Burlington School, London, on the education of women.

,, 24. On Anglo-German Agreement bill.

,, 30. To Wesleyans at National Liberal club on Maltese marriage question, and Ireland.

Aug. 21. At Hawarden on cottage gardening and fruit farming.

,, 30. 'Dr. Döllinger's Posthumous Remains,' in the *Speaker.*

Sept. 12. At Dee iron works on industrial progress.

Oct. 21. At Corn Exchange, Edinburgh, on government's Irish administration.

,, 23. At West Calder on condition of working classes and Ireland.

,, 25. At Dalkeith on home rule for Scotland and Ireland.

,, 27. At Music Hall, Edinburgh, on retention of Irish members, procedure and obstruction.

,, 29. At Dundee on free trade and the McKinley tariff. Opens Victorian Art Gallery: on appreciation of beauty.

Nov. 'Mr. Carnegie's Gospel of Wealth,' in *Nineteenth Century.*

,, 24. Letter to Mr. Morley on Mr. Parnell and leadership of Irish party.

Dec. 1. Publishes reply to Mr. Parnell's manifesto to Irish people.

,, 2. On Purchase of Land (Ireland) bill.

,, 11. At Retford on Mr. Parnell and the home rule cause.

1890.

Publishes *The Impregnable Rock of Holy Scripture,* a reprint of articles in *Good Words.* *Landmarks of Homeric Study, together with an Essay on the Points of Contact between the Assyrian Tablets and the Homeric Text.*

1891.

Jan. 27. Supports motion to expunge from journals of the House the Bradlaugh resolution (1881).

Feb. 'Professor Huxley and the Swine-Miracle,' in *Nineteenth Century.*

,, 4. Moves second reading of Religious Disabilities Removal bill.

,, 13. Opens free library in St. Martin's Lane : on free libraries.

,, 16. Condemns action of Irish executive in Tipperary trials.

,, 20. On disestablishment of church in Wales.

,, 27. On taxation of land.

March 3. On registration reform.

,, 14. At Eton College on Homeric Artemis.

,, 17. At Hastings on Mr. Goschen's finance, Irish policy, and the career of Mr. Parnell.

May 'A Memoir of John Murray,' in *Murray's Magazine.*

June 19. At St. James's Hall, at jubilee of Colonial Bishoprics Fund, on development of colonial church.

July 4. Death of W. H. Gladstone.

,, 15. At Hawarden on fifty years of progress.

Sept. 'Electoral Facts, No. III.,' in *Nineteenth Century.*

Oct. 'On the Ancient Beliefs in a Future State,' in *Nineteenth Century.*

,, 1. At jubilee of Glenalmond College on study of nature and the clerical profession.

,, 2. At Newcastle on the liberal programme.

1891.

Nov. 3. At Newcastle on local self-government and freedom of trade.

„ 28. At Wirral on home rule. At Sunlight Soap works on profit-sharing and co-operation.

Dec. 11. At Holborn Restaurant to conference of labourers on rural reforms.

„ 15. Leaves London for Biarritz.

1892.

Feb.-May 'On the Olympian Religion,' in *North American Review*.

„ 29. Returns to London.

March 3. Opposes grant of £20,000 for survey of Uganda railway.

„ 16. On Welsh Land Tenure bill.

„ 24. On Small Agricultural Holdings bill.

„ 28. On Indian Councils Act (1861) Amendment bill.

April Reviews *The Platform, its Rise and Progress*, in *Nineteenth Century*.

„ 28. On Church Discipline (Immorality) bill.

May 24. On Local Government (Ireland) bill.

„ 31. At Memorial Hall on London government.

June 'Did Dante Study in Oxford?' in *Nineteenth Century*.

„ 5. At Dalkeith on Scotch home rule and disestablishment.

„ 16. Receives deputation from London trades council on Eight Hours bill.

„ 18. To nonconformists at Clapham on Ulster and home rule.

„ 24. Issues address to electors of Midlothian.

„ 25. Struck in the eye by piece of gingerbread in Chester. At Liberal club on the general election, the appeal to religious bigotry, and disestablishment.

„ 30. At Edinburgh Music Hall on Lord Salisbury's manifesto, home rule,

1892.

and retention of Irish members.

July 2. At Glasgow on Orangeism and home rule.

„ 4. At Gorebridge on labour questions.

„ 6. At Corstorphine on government's record.

„ 7. At West Calder on protection, the hours of labour and home rule.

„ 11. At Penicuik on conservative responsibility for recent wars, finance, disestablishment, and Irish question.

„ 13. Elected for Midlothian: Mr. Gladstone, 5845; Colonel Wauchope, 5155.

Aug. 9. On vote of want of confidence.

„ 15. Fourth administration formed.

„ 24. Returned unopposed for Midlothian.

„ 29. Knocked down by heifer in Hawarden Park.

Sept. 5. A paper on Archaic Greece and the East read before Congress of Orientalists.

„ 12. At Carnarvon on case of Wales.

Oct. 'A Vindication of Home Rule: a Reply to the Duke of Argyll,' in *North American Review*.

„ 22. Cuts first sod of the new Cheshire railway: on migration of population and mineral produce of Wales.

„ 24. Delivers Romanes lecture at Oxford on history of universities.

Dec. 3. Presented with freedom of Liverpool: on history of Liverpool and Manchester ship canal.

„ 21. Leaves England for Biarritz.

1893.

Jan. 10. Returns to England.

„ 31. Replies to Mr. Balfour's criticisms on the address.

Feb. 3. On Mr. Labouchere's amendment in favour of evacuation of Uganda.

1893.

Feb. 8. On amendment praying for immediate legislation for agricultural labourers.

„ 11. On motion for restriction of alien immigration.

„ 13. Brings in Government of Ireland (Home Rule) bill.

„ 28. On motion for international monetary conference.

March 3. Receives deputation from the miners' federation on Eight Hours bill.

„ 20. On Sir Gerald Portal's mission to Uganda.

„ 27. Meeting of the liberal party at foreign office: on programme for session.

„ 27. On Mr. Balfour's motion censuring action of Irish executive.

„ 28. Receives deputations from Belfast manufacturers and city of London merchants protesting against home rule.

April 6. Moves second reading of Home Rule bill.

„ 19. Receives a deputation from the miners' National Union on Eight Hours bill.

„ 21. Replies to criticisms on Home Rule bill.

May 1. On the occupation of Egypt.

„ 2. Receives a deputation of the Mining Association in opposition to Eight Hours bill.

„ 3. On second reading of Miners' Eight Hours bill.

„ 11. Replies to Mr. Chamberlain's speech on first clause of Home Rule bill.

„ 23. Opens Hawarden institute: on the working classes.

„ 29. At Chester on Home Rule bill.

June 'Some Eton Translations,' in Contemporary Review.

„ 16. On arbitration between England and United States.

„ 22. Statement regarding the financial clauses of Home Rule bill.

1893.

June 28. Moves resolution for closing debate on committee stage of Home Rule bill.

July 12. Announces government's decision regarding the retention of Irish members at Westminster.

„ 14. Moves address of congratulation on marriage of Duke of York.

„ 21. Moves a new clause to Home Rule bill regulating financial relations.

Aug. 5. At Agricultural Hall, Islington, on industry and art.

„ 30. Moves third reading of Home Rule bill.

Sept. 27. At Edinburgh on House of Lords and the Home Rule bill.

Nov. 9. On Matabeleland and the chartered company.

Dec. 19. On naval policy of the government.

1894.

Jan. 13. Leaves England for Biarritz.

Feb. 10. Returns to England.

March 1. On the Lords' amendments to Parish Councils bill.

„ 3. Resigns the premiership.

„ 7. Confined to bed by severe cold.

„ 17. At Brighton. Letter to Sir John Cowan — his farewell to parliamentary life.

May 'The Love Odes of Horace — five specimens,' in Nineteenth Century.

„ 3. At Prince's Hall on life and work of Sir Andrew Clark.

„ 24. Right eye operated on for cataract.

July 7. Announces decision not to seek re-election to parliament.

Aug. 'The Place of Heresy and Schism in the Modern Christian Church,' in Nineteenth Century.

„ 14. On cottage gardening at Hawarden.

„ 16. Receives deputation of 1500 liberals from Torquay at Hawarden.

1894.

Sept. 'The True and False Conception of the Atonement,' in *Nineteenth Century*.

Dec. 29. Receives deputation from the Armenian national church at Hawarden.

1895.

Jan. 7. Presented with an album by Irish-Americans : in favour of Irish unity.

„ **8.** Leaves England for south of France.

March Publishes *The Psalter with a concordance*.

„ 'The Lord's Day,' in *Church Monthly;* concluded in April number.

„ **23.** Returns to England from France.

„ **15.** At Hawarden to a deputation of Leeds and Huddersfield liberal clubs : on English people and political power, and on advantages of libraries.

June 12-24. Cruise in *Tantallon Castle* to Hamburg, Copenhagen, and Kiel.

July 1. Farewell letter to Midlothian constituents.

Aug. 5. At Hawarden on small holdings and his old age.

„ **6.** At Chester on Armenian question.

Nov. 'Bishop Butler and his Censors,' in *Nineteenth Century;* concluded in December number.

Dec. 28. Leaves England for Biarritz and Cannes.

1896.

Feb. Publishes *The Works of Bishop Butler*.

March 10. Returns to England from Cannes.

„ **28.** At Liverpool on the development of the English railway system.

April 'The Future Life and the Condition of Man Therein,' in *North American Review*.

„ Contributes an article on 'The Scriptures and

1896.

Modern Criticism' to the *People's Bible*.

May *Soliloquium and Postscript* —a letter to the Archbishop of York, published.

June 'Sheridan,' in *Nineteenth Century*.

„ **1.** Letter on Anglican Orders published.

Aug. 3. At Hawarden horticultural show on rural life.

Sept. 1. At fête in aid of Hawarden Institute on progress of music.

„ **2.** At Hawarden fête on Welsh music.

„ **24.** At Hengler's circus, Liverpool, on Armenian question.

Oct. 'The Massacres in Turkey,' in *Nineteenth Century*.

„ **16.** At Penmaenmawr in praise of seaside resorts.

1897.

Jan. 29. Leaves England for Cannes.

March 19. Letter to the Duke of Westminster on the Cretan question published.

„ **30.** Returns to England from Cannes.

May 4. At Hawarden on the condition of the clergy.

June 2. Opens Victoria jubilee bridge over the Dee at Queensferry.

Aug. 2. At Hawarden horticultural show on small culture.

Nov. 26. Leaves England for Cannes.

1898.

Jan. 5. 'Personal Recollections of Arthur H. Hallam,' in *Daily Telegraph*.

Feb. 18. Returns to London from Cannes.

„ **22.** Goes to Bournemouth.

March 22. Returns to Hawarden.

May 19. Death of Mr. Gladstone.

„ **26, 27.** Lying in state in Westminster Hall.

„ **28.** Burial in Westminster Abbey.

INDEX

ABERDARE, Lord (Henry Austin Bruce), home secretary (1868), ii. 644 ; on Collier affair, ii. 385; on Ewelme case, ii. 387; Licensing bill of, ii. 389–390 ; on *Alabama* case, ii. 409 *note*; on Irish University bill, ii. 439; Gladstone's appreciation of, ii. 462; president of the council (1873), ii. 463 *note*, 645; describes last cabinet meeting (1874), ii. 497; otherwise mentioned, ii. 421, 504; iii. 386.
—— papers, extract from, on position in 1872, ii. 389.

Aberdeen, Gladstone presented with freedom of, ii. 378.

Aberdeen, 4th Earl of : —
Chronology — on Wellington's anti-reform speech, i. 69; Gladstone's visit to (1836), i. 137; at Canada meeting, i. 641; party meetings, i. 239; on Maynooth resignation, i. 273; Gladstone's relations with, i. 280; estimate of Peel, i. 283; on Peel's eulogium of Cobden, i. 292; on freedom in official position, i. 298; home and foreign policy of, contrasted, i. 367; learns Gladstone's views of Neapolitan tyranny, i. 390, 393–395; on Don Pacifico case, i. 395; Gladstone's Letters to, i. 392, 394 *and note*, 396, 398, 399 *note* ², 400, 401 *note* ³, 641, 642; views on papal aggression question, i. 405, 407; asked to form a government (1851), i. 405 *and note*; leader of Peelites, i. 408; Reform bill of (1852), ii. 238; attitude of, towards first Derby administration, i. 417, 419, 429; on Gladstone's attitude towards Disraeli, i. 432; on possible heads for Peelite government, i. 443; Irish attitude towards, i. 444; undertakes to form a government, i. 445; Gladstone's budget, i. 464–466; letter to Prince Albert on Gladstone's speech, i. 468; letter to Gladstone, i. 469; attitude towards Turkey in 1828, i. 480;

Crimean war, preliminary negotiations, i. 481–484, 487, 490; on Gladstone's Manchester speech, i. 483; on effect of Crimean war, i. 484; suggests retirement, i. 491–492; opposes postponement of Reform bill, i. 648; regrets of, regarding the war, i. 494, 536–537; defeat of, ii. 653; Gladstone's consultations with, in ministerial crisis (1855), i. 526, 530–535; on position of premier, ii. 416; Gladstone's projected letters to, on Sebastopol committee, i. 542 *note*; discourages Gladstone's communicating with Derby, i. 556; Lewis's budget, i. 560; Divorce bill, i. 570; Conspiracy bill, i. 575; approves Gladstone's refusals to join Derby, i. 578, 586; uneasiness regarding Gladstone's position, i. 581; Gladstone's visit to, i. 594; discourages Ionian project, i. 595; desires closer relations between Gladstone and government, i. 596; Arthur Gordon's letter to, i. 604; Bright's visit to, i. 626 *note* ²; death of, ii. 87.
Foreign influence of, i. 392, 529; foreign estimate of, ii. 351; iii. 321.
Gladstone's estimate of, i. 124, 393, 417; ii. 87, 639–644; his estimate of Gladstone, i. 613; ii. 170, 203; Gladstone's letters to, i. 425–426, 429, 463, 549; ii. 3.
Palmerston contrasted with, i. 530.
Patience of, with colleagues' quarrels, i. 520; loyalty to colleagues, ii. 639–640.
Sobriquet of, i. 177.
Trustfulness of, i. 197; ii. 113, 640, 642–643.
   Otherwise mentioned, i. 139, 142 *note*, 270, 293, 294, 367, 420, 437, 458, 460, 482 *note*, 520, 539, 543, 548, 584; ii. 184, 194; iii. 228.
Aberdeen, 7th Earl of, iii. 385, 517.
Abeken, H., ii. 332–333 *and note*.